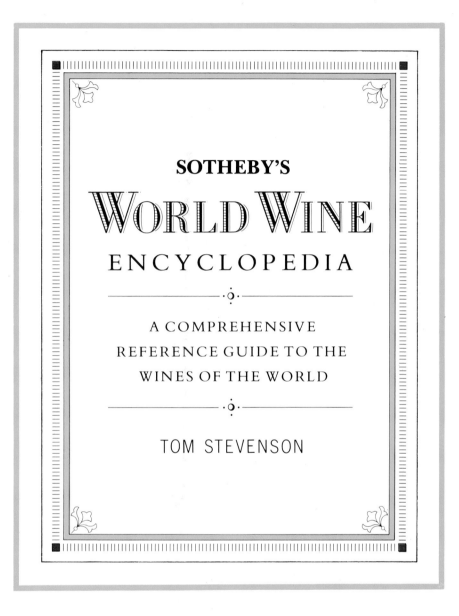

SOTHEBY'S
WORLD WINE
ENCYCLOPEDIA

·ọ·

A COMPREHENSIVE
REFERENCE GUIDE TO THE
WINES OF THE WORLD

·ọ·

TOM STEVENSON

DORLING KINDERSLEY
London • New York • Stuttgart

Contents

Author's Introduction & How to use this book 6

INTRODUCTION

The taste of wine 7
The factors affecting taste and quality 10
Annual life-cycle of the vine 16
How wine is made 18
Glossary of major grape varieties 24

· ○ ·

THE WINES OF FRANCE 33

Bordeaux 36
The Médoc 44
St.-Estèphe 51
Pauillac 54
St.-Julien 59
Margaux 63
Graves, Cérons, Sauternes and Barsac 69
The Libournais District 81
St.-Emilion 83
Pomerol 93
Bourg and Blaye 100
Entre-Deux-Mers 103

Burgundy 108
The Chablis District 114
Côte de Nuits and Hautes-Côtes de Nuits 116
Côte de Beaune and Hautes-Côtes de Beaune 121
The Région de Mercurey 128
The Mâconnais 130
The Beaujolais 133

Champagne 136
Alsace 149

The Loire Valley 156
Pays Nantais 161
Anjou-Saumur 163
Touraine 167
Central Vineyards 171

The Rhône Valley 173
The Northern Rhône 174
The Southern Rhône 176

The Jura and Savoie 181
Southwest France 184
Languedoc-Roussillon 189
Provence and Corsica 193
Vins de Pays 197

THE WINES OF GERMANY 201

The Ahr 214
The Mittelrhein 216
Mosel-Saar-Ruwer 218
The Nahe 222
The Rheingau 224
Rheinhessen 227
Rheinpfalz 230
The Hessische Bergstrasse 233
Franken 234
Württemberg 236
Baden 238

· ○ ·

THE WINES OF ITALY 241

Northwest Italy 245
Northeast Italy 250
Central Italy – West 255
Central Italy – East 260
Southern Italy and the Islands 263

· ○ ·

THE WINES OF SPAIN AND PORTUGAL 267

SPAIN 268
Rioja and Navarra 271
Catalonia 277
Southern Spain 282
Other Spanish wines 291

PORTUGAL 293
The Douro and the Minho 295
Bairrada and Dão 303
Madeira 305
Other Portuguese wines 307

· ○ ·

THE WINES OF THE REST OF EUROPE 309

GREAT BRITAIN 310
SWITZERLAND 316
AUSTRIA 319
BULGARIA 325
**CZECHOSLOVAKIA AND
HUNGARY** 327
ROMANIA 330
YUGOSLAVIA 332
USSR 334
GREECE 336
THE LEVANT 341

*I dedicate this book to Pat, my loving wife, best friend and
hard-working assistant, for her devotion beyond the call of
duty throughout the book's production and in humble apology for
all those occasions when I complained that I could not get any
constructive help from her after three o'clock in the morning!*

Editors Caroline Ollard, James Allen
Assistant Editor Linda Martin

Art Editor Derek Coombes
Designers Martyn Foote, Mustafa Sami

Managing Editor Victoria Davenport

Maps produced by Lovell Johns Limited, Oxford
Map Consultant Michael Schmidt

First published in Great Britain in 1988
by Dorling Kindersley Limited
9 Henrietta Street, London WC2E 8PS
Reprinted 1988, 1989. Revised edition 1991
First paperback edition published 1994. Reprinted 1995, 1996
Copyright © 1988, 1991 Dorling Kindersley Limited, London
Text copyright © 1988, 1991 Tom Stevenson

SOTHEBY'S
WORLD WINE
ENCYCLOPEDIA

THE WINES OF NORTH AND SOUTH AFRICA 343

NORTH AFRICA 344
SOUTH AFRICA 346

· ȯ ·

THE WINES OF NORTH AND SOUTH AMERICA 355

NORTH AMERICA 356

California 361
Mendocino County 368
Sonoma County 370
Napa County 374
The North-Central Coast 379
The South-Central Coast 383
The Central Valley 385
Other winemaking areas of California 387

The Pacific Northwest 389
The Atlantic Northeast 392
Other winemaking areas of the United States 398

Mexico 400
Canada 402

SOUTH AMERICA 406

Chile and Argentina 408

· ȯ ·

THE WINES OF AUSTRALIA AND NEW ZEALAND 413

AUSTRALIA 414
New South Wales 418
Victoria and Tasmania 423
South Australia 430
Western Australia 437
Queensland and Northern Territory 441

NEW ZEALAND 443

· ȯ ·

THE WINES OF THE FAR EAST 449

Storing and serving wine 452
Wine and food 453
Glossary of tasting and technical terms 456
Guide to good vintages 464
Index 466
Acknowledgments 480

British Library Cataloguing in Publication Data

Stevenson, Tom
   Sotheby's world wine encyclopedia.
   1. Wines – Encyclopaedias
   I. Title
   641.2'2'0321

ISBN 0-7513-0155-8

Typeset by Modern Text Typesetting
Reproduced by Colourscan, Singapore
Printed by Tien Wah Press, Singapore

Foreword

In this day and age when it seems that nearly everyone is cutting corners to remain competitive, it is perhaps something of a relief to know that at least one industry is not only producing better-quality and more varied products, but is producing them at a reduced price. In the last few years, a brief instant in time certainly in relation to the long history of the wine trade, there has been a veritable explosion of development in both quality and styles of wine on a truly international basis. It is as if the world of wine has suddenly discovered that there are no real frontiers and that all things are possible.

It is this, more than anything, that prompts the production of what is unquestionably the most comprehensive, up-to-date and seriously researched encyclopedia of the wines of the world. Although no work of this nature can ever be totally complete, and because of the speed of development within the industry there are bound to be certain things which at the time of writing no longer hold true at the time of publication, it nevertheless contains a cornucopia of fascinating information laid out in a most readable form. The greatest enjoyment of wine can only be achieved with a certain amount of knowledge of the subject matter and with the myriad wines to choose from, a helping hand will certainly not come amiss.

Tom Stevenson has had more opportunity than most to assess the plethora of wines available to the consumer. He was the originator of the Sunday Telegraph Good Wine Guide, which involved regular, substantial and well-organized tastings. Further research and, in particular, the six years it took him to develop and write his excellent book on Champagne, published in 1986, have only whetted his appetite for more knowledge, which in turn should whet yours.

Wine has made a major contribution to the quality of life in many societies of the world for centuries – even longer – millennia, and continues to do so. It has always had its critics, some misinformed, others genuinely concerned. Even more reason to look at the benefits that the product of the fermented grape has brought to the world and what enjoyment it can bring to future generations. Wine has always been part of our civilisation. Long may it remain so.

David Molyneux-Berry
Master of Wine

Author's Introduction

My aim in writing **The World Wine Encyclopedia** was twofold: to produce a highly illustrated guide to the wines of the world that could be dipped into and read with ease by an absolute novice, and secondly, to create a book so comprehensive that it could provide a depth of detailed information associated only with definitive single-subject works.

The Encyclopedia is arranged on a country-by-country basis, within which the wine-producing areas are, where appropriate, examined region-by-region and district-by-district. In some instances – Bordeaux and California, for example – this coverage extends to a further level to examine areas within each district. Each chapter has a specially commissioned wine map, and also includes a section on factors affecting taste and quality – location, climate, aspect, soil types, viticulture and vinification and grape varieties – pertinent to the area in question. The relevance of each of these factors is explained in the introduction to the book, which also includes an illustrated glossary to major grape varieties.

In each chapter I have endeavoured to answer the questions: What do the wines taste like? Where do they come from? Which ones can be recommended? Readers who have experienced the frustration of trying to locate a particular wine, only to find it mentioned merely in passing, will be pleased that over half the book is devoted to wine profiles and taste charts describing separately the red, white, rosé and sparkling styles of thousands of wines. In France, for example, every single AOC, VDQS and *Vin de Pays* is listed; in Bordeaux alone this includes fifty AOCs, with some 600 châteaux and their wines profiled. The North American section reveals the current extent of the relatively recent appellation scheme of the United States, describing almost 100 different AVAs (Approved Viticultural Areas), and profiling hundreds of wineries, from California to New York State. Finally, a comprehensive glossary and at-a-glance vintage charts of the top wines over the last twenty-eight years provides instant access to essential information.

How to use this book

Arranged by country, the main part of the Encyclopedia has pages of two types: general introductory text and taste guide (Appellation, Château or Winery listings).

INTRODUCTORY TEXT

Alongside general information, there are two regular features in the introduction to each area:

How to read ..... wine labels

Often illustrated with a sample label, these sections aim to supply all the information needed to understand the area's wine labels.

Factors affecting taste and quality

A quick-reference area guide featuring:

Location   Climate   Aspect   Soil

Viticulture and vinification   Grape varieties

HOW THE MAPS WORK

Alongside introductory text are **Country Maps,** which show all the main wine-producing areas of a country, including legally delimited zones, keyed in colour. Important wine-producing countries are covered in further detail by **Regional Maps,** and, in some cases, **District Maps.** These highlight intensive vine-growing zones and plot every major château or winery, as well as many others. These supplementary maps are cross-referenced in the keys attached to Country Maps. North is at the top on every map.

TASTE GUIDES

The wines of a country, region or district may be listed or described in one of several ways, depending on the structure of the country's wine trade and laws. You may be able to look up a wine under both its area of origin and its producer.

How the wines are described	Headings
1 By geographical area (regions, districts, sub-regions and wards)	Generic wines of .... The wines of .... The wine regions (or areas) of ....
2 By appellation (legally defined categories or areas)	
3 By grape variety	The grapes and wines of ....
4 By Producer listing	e.g. The best châteaux of :... etc. *See* Producer listings, below.

Producer listings

In major sections such as Bordeaux and Germany where there are many major generic wineries, these are listed first, before wines of any individual areas are described. In sections like North America, Australia and Spain, for example, winery listings fall in appropriate area sections and follow the descriptions of the main wine districts in the area.

The heading "The great châteaux of ..." is used for the classic appellations of Bordeaux; "The best châteaux of ..." for others. All "best", "greatest" and "major" categories are selected by the author on the basis of their quality and importance. Such listings are supplemented by "The best of the rest" and "Other wineries of ..." listings, depending on the importance of the country and its wines.

Information included in taste guides

All listings are alphabetical. Various levels of information are given, depending on the importance of the wine and/or its producer. In the most detailed entries, a profile of the wine area or establishment summarizes its history and main characteristics. Look for the **RED, WHITE, ROSÉ** or **SPARKLING** tasting notes, with symbols denoting other information as follows:

Grape varieties contained in the wine. Where certain percentages are stipulated by regulations, these are stated. Where a country, or part of it, uses a local synonym for a grape variety, this is used in the listing.

Best recent vintages since 1980.

When to drink the wine for optimum enjoyment.

☆ Recommended growers or producers of a particular wine. In Germany, this symbol is used to denote a recommended vineyard (Einzellage), and the recommended growers producing wine from it.

* An asterisk always denotes a recommendation unless otherwise stated.

EXPLANATIONS OF APPELLATION SYSTEMS

Where applicable, sections on major wine-producing countries include explanations of their official appellation systems as follows:
How French wine is classified p.34
Vins de Pays p.197
Germany's quality structure p.202
How to use the regional sections (Germany) p.208
Italy's wine laws p.242
Spain's Appellations p.270
Portugal, *see* **Note** to other Portuguese wines p.307
The appellation system of the United States p.358

The taste of wine

Tasting and drinking – what is the difference? It can be compared to test-driving a car you are about to buy and the relaxed enjoyment of driving it afterwards. For one, you concentrate on what is happening and attempt to zero-in on any faults, for the other the senses are relaxed and you simply enjoy the experience. Tasting is a matter of concentration, and the technique involved is something that anyone can acquire.

HOW TO TASTE

When tasting a wine it is important to eliminate all distractions, especially comments made by others; it is all too easy to be swayed. The wine should be tasted and an opinion registered before any ensuing discussions. Even at professionally led tastings, the expert's job is not to dictate but to educate, to lead from behind, putting into perspective other people's natural responses to smells or tastes through clear and concise explanation.

The three "basics" of wine tasting are sight, smell and taste, known as "eye", "nose" and "palate"

THE SIGHT OR "EYE" OF A WINE

The first step in evaluating the appearance of a wine is to assess its limpidity, as all wines should be perfectly clear. Many wines throw a deposit, but this is harmless if it settles to yield a bright and clear wine. A wine that is poured and allowed to settle, but remains cloudy or hazy, should be discarded. Tiny bubbles that appear on the bowl or cling persistently to the edge of the glass are perfectly acceptable in a few types of wines, such as Muscadet *sur lie* and Vinho Verde, but probably indicate a flaw in most other still wines.

The next step is to swirl the wine gently round the glass. So-called "legs" or "tears", thin sinewy threads that run down the side of the glass, may appear. Contrary to popular belief, they are not indicative of high glycerol content, but are simply the effect of alcohol on wine's viscosity, or the way the wine flows. The greater the alcohol content the *less* free-flowing, or *more* viscous, the wine actually becomes.

The colour of wine

Natural light is best for observing a wine's colour, the first clues to its identity once its condition has been assessed on first sight. Look at the wine against a white background, holding the glass at the bottom of the stem and tilting it away from you slightly. Red wines vary in colour from *clairet*, which is almost rosé, to tones so dark and opaque they seem black. White wines range from a colourless, water-white to deep gold, although the majority are a light straw-yellow colour. For some reason there are very few rosé wines that are truly pink in colour, the tonal range extending from blue-pink, through purple-pink to orange-pink. Disregard any impression about a wine's colour under artificial lighting because it will never be true – fluorescent light, for example, makes a red wine appear brown.

Factors affecting colour

The colour and tonal variation of any wine, whether red, white or rosé, is determined by the grape variety. Furthermore, it is influenced by the degree of ripeness of the actual grapes, the area of production, the method of vinification and the age of the wine. Dry, light-bodied wines from cooler climates are the lightest in colour, while fuller-bodied or sweeter-styled wines from hotter regions are the deepest. Youthful red wines usually have a purple tone, whereas young white wines may hint of green, particularly if they are from a cooler climate. The aging process involves a slow oxidation that has a browning effect similar to the discolouration of a peeled apple that has been exposed to the air.

THE SMELL OR "NOSE" OF A WINE

Whenever an experienced taster claims to be able to recognize in excess of 1,000 different smells, many wine-lovers give up all hope of acquiring the most basic tasting skills. Yet they should not. An experienced taster *can* detect and distinguish over 1,000 different smells, but so can everybody; the majority of these smells are ordinary everyday odours. Ask anyone to write down all the smells they can recognize and most will be able to list several hundred without really trying. Yet a far greater number of smells are locked away in our brains waiting to be triggered off by a similar odour. No smells are specific to wine as they can all be compared to something familiar.

The wine-smelling procedure is quite simple: give the glass a good swirl, put your nose into the glass and take a deep sniff. While it is essential to take a substantial sniff, it is not practicable to sniff the same wine again for at least two minutes. This is because each wine activates a unique pattern of nerve ends in the olfactory bulb, which is situated at the top of the nose; these nerve ends are like small candles that are snuffed out when activated and take a little time to reactivate. As a result, subsequent sniffs of the same smell can reveal less and less, yet it is perfectly feasible to smell different smells, therefore different wines, one after the other.

THE TASTE OR "PALATE" OF A WINE

As soon as one sniffs a wine the natural reaction is to taste it, but do this only after all questions concerning the nose have been addressed. The procedure is simple, although it may look and sound rather strange to the uninitiated. Take a good mouthful and draw air into the mouth through the wine. This makes a gurgling sound, but it is essential to do it in order to magnify the wine's volatile characteristics in the back of the throat.

The tongue itself reveals very little; sweetness is detected on its tip, sourness or acidity on the sides, bitterness at the back and top, and saltiness on the front and sides. Apart from these four basic taste perceptions, we smell tastes rather than taste tastes. Any food or drink emits odorous vapours in the mouth that are automatically conveyed to the roof of the nasal passages. Here the olfactory bulb examines, discerns and catalogues them – as they originate from the palate the natural inclination is to perceive them as tastes. For many of us it is difficult to believe that we taste with an organ located behind the eyes at the top of the nose, but when we eat ice-cream too quickly, we painfully experience precisely where the olfactory bulb is.

QUALITY AND TASTE: WHY OPINIONS DIFFER

Whether a novice or a Master of Wine, the final arbiter when judging wine will always be personal preference. The most experienced tasters argue endlessly over the relative merits and demerits of certain wines.

We all know that quality exists, and more often than not agree which wines have it, yet we are not able to define it. Lacking a solid definition, most experienced tasters would happily accept that a fine wine must have natural balance and finesse and show a definite, distinctive and individual character within its own type or style. If we occasionally differ on the question of quality of wine, should we disagree on what it tastes like? We may love or hate a wine, but surely the wine we taste is the same?

Conveying specific taste characteristics from the mind of one person to that of another is difficult enough, whether one is writing a book or simply discussing a wine at a tasting. Much of this difficulty lies in the words we choose, but the problem is not confined to semantics. In a world of perfect communication, conveying impressions of taste would still be an inexact art because of the different threshold levels at which we pick up elementary tastes and smells, and because of the various tolerance levels at which we enjoy them. If individuals require different quantities of acidity, tannin, alcohol, sugar, esters and aldehydes in a wine before actually detecting them, then the same wine has, literally, a different taste for each of us. In the unlikely event of people having the same threshold for every constituent and combination of constituents, disagreement would probably ensue because we also have different tolerance levels; therefore some of us would enjoy what others dislike *because* of what they dislike. The world is in fact populated by people with a vast range of thresholds and tolerance levels. Therefore it is surprising that we ever agree on anything!

Tasting wine — what to look for, what questions to ask

It would be impossible to answer many of the following questions without some sort of experience, however limited. Likewise, it would be difficult to identify a particular wine, or type of wine, having never tasted it. However, do not be discouraged: your whole range of questions and answers will increase with every tasting.

SIGHT: look at the colour: is it deep or pale, is there a positive quality about it, for example does it have a specific hue that reminds you of a particular grape variety, the growing climate or the area of production? Is the colour vivid and youthful, or is there any browning that could suggest its age? What does the rim, or meniscus, indicate? Does it retain the intensity of colour right to the rim of the glass and so imply a quality product, or does it fade to an unimpressive, watery finish?

SMELL: if the first impression is very heady, is the wine fortified? (Classic fortified wines, such as Port, Sherry and Madeira, do have easily recognizable characteristics, but it can still be difficult to distinguish between a robust wine with a naturally high alcohol level produced in a hot country and a fortified wine). Does the wine have any distinctive aromas, or are they obscure or bland or simply reticent? Does the wine smell as youthful or as mature as it appears to the eye? Is it smooth and harmonious, suggesting the wine is ready to drink? Is it ready should it be drunk up? If it is not ready, can you estimate when it will be? Is there a recognizable grape variety aroma? Are there any creamy or vanilla hints to suggest it has been fermented or aged in new oak? If so, which region ages such wine in oak? Is it a simple wine or is there a degree of complexity? Are there any hints as to the area of production? Is its quality obvious or do you need confirmation on the palate?

TASTE: this should reflect the wine's smell and therefore confirm any judgements already made. Should. But human organs are fallible, not least so the brain, therefore keep an open mind. Be

---

A SAMPLE TASTING
This chart provides a few examples from a whole range of possible options open in the complex business of wine tasting. It also demonstrates that it is possible to approach the task rationally. When tasting it is important to keep your options open until you have assessed sight, smell and taste. At

SIGHT: the clear, well-defined garnet colour of medium intensity suggests only moderately hot climatic origins. The tinge of purple on the meniscus could indicate youth.

SMELL: this is dominated by the distinctive pear-drop aroma of *macération carbonique*, the hallmark of all but the best *cru* Beaujolais. Often mistaken for the varietal aroma of the Gamay grape (from which Beaujolais *is* made), the aroma is in fact a characteristic of all wines fermented in this manner. If this is a Beaujolais, the colour would indicate something more serious than a lighter basic Beaujolais or a Nouveau.

TASTE: the balance between fruit, acidity and alcohol confirms that this is Beaujolais. The good depth of spicy-grapey fruit beneath the pervasive pear-drop character indicates that it is better-than-average.

CONCLUSION
Grape variety: Gamay
Region: Beaujolais
Age: 2-3 years old
Comment: Beaujolais Villages

SIGHT: water-white wine has obvious cool climatic origins, but the minuscule bubbles that collect on the glass suggest it could be a Vinho Verde, though the palest usually have a tell-tale hint of straw colour. Probably a modest Qualitätswein from the Mosel-Saar-Ruwer.

SMELL: this is not Vinho Verde. Its crisp, youthful, sherbety aroma is typical Mosel Riesling. Considering its water-white colour, the nose would confirm that this is probably a Qualitätswein, or a Kabinett at most, of a modest vintage, but from a very good grower who is possibly as high up as the Saar tributary.

TASTE: youthful, tangy fruit with the flower of the Riesling still evident. More flavour than expected, nice dry, piquant finish.

CONCLUSION
Grape variety: Riesling
Region: Mosel-Saar-Ruwer
Age: about 18-24 months
Comment: Kabinett, top grower

SIGHT: has an intense, almost black colour that is virtually opaque. Obviously from a thick-skinned grape variety like the Syrah, which has ripened under a very hot sun. Australia's Swan Valley or France's Rhône Valley? Maybe California?

SMELL: as intense on the nose as it is on the eye. It is definitely Syrah, and judging by its spicy aroma with hints of herbal scrub, it is almost certainly from the Northern Rhône. Australia and California can now be ruled out. More massive than complex, it must be from an exceptional vintage.

TASTE: powerful and tannic, the spicy fruit flavour is rich with plums, blackcurrants, blackberries and cinnamon. It has begun to develop, but has a long way to go. This is a high-quality Rhône Syrah, but has not quite got the class of Hermitage, nor the finesse of Côte Rôtie.

CONCLUSION
Grape variety: Syrah
Region: Cornas, Rhône Valley
Age: about 5 years old
Comment: top grower, great year

SIGHT: the brick-red colour and watery meniscus immediately suggest a young Bordeaux of petit-château quality. Although first impressions can deceive, more evidence is needed to confirm or discount the theory.

SMELL: an attractive violet aroma with a restrained hint of soft, spicy fruit. Nothing contradicts my first impressions here, although the lack of any indication of blackcurrants would suggest that the wine is a Bordeaux with a high proportion of Merlot rather than Cabernet sauvignon.

TASTE: the palate perfectly reflects the nose. This is a medium-bodied, modest claret of no great age. However, the fruit is well-rounded and the soft-tannin structure indicates that in little more than another two, possibly three years it will be at its peak.

CONCLUSION
Grape variety: Merlot-dominated blend
Region: Bordeaux
Age: 2 years old
Comment: petit château or good generic

prepared to accept contradiction as well as confirmation. Ask yourself all the questions you asked on the nose, but before you do, ask what your palate tells you about the acidity, sweetness, and alcoholic strength.

If you are tasting a red wine its tannin content can be revealing. Tannin is derived from the grape's skin, and the darker and thicker it is, and the longer the juice macerates with the skins, the more tannin there will be in the wine. A great red wine will contain so much tannin that it will literally pucker the mouth, while early drinking wines will contain little.

If you are tasting a sparkling wine, its *mousse*, or effervescence, will give extra clues. The strength of the *mousse* will determine the style – whether it is fully sparkling, semi-sparkling or merely *pétillant* – and the size of bubbles will indicate the quality; the smaller they are the better.

CONCLUSION: just try to name the grape variety and area of origin, and give some indication of age and quality.

each stage you should be seeking to confirm at least one of the possibilities that arose at the previous stage. Back your own judgement – it is the only way to learn.

THE SHAPE OF THE GLASS

Whether tasting or drinking, the shape of the glass is important. Any decent-sized tulip-shaped glass is the perfect vessel for any wine. Its bulbous base and inwardly-sloping sides concentrate the aromas in the top of the glass, allowing the drinker full benefit of the wine's bouquet. The glass must be large enough to ensure that a "good glassful" takes up barely more than half the glass, thus allowing the aromas to circulate.

The worst-possible glasses are those that are too small, have straight sides or sides that lean outwards, and the so-called Champagne *coupe* – its wide brim allows both the bubbles and the bouquet to escape.

SIGHT: this distinctive yellow-gold colour retains its intensity right to the rim. It could be so many things: a sweet wine, a full-bodied dry wine, a mature wine, or something obscure like Retsina. If none of these, it could be a Gewürztraminer.

SMELL: Gewürztraminer! Full, rich and spicy, the aroma of this grape hits you between the eyes and the first instinct is to think of Alsace. Nine times out of ten you will be right, but bear in mind the possibility of a top grower in the Rheinpfalz or Austria. If the aroma were muted, it might be Italian; if exotic it could be Californian or Australian. This, however, appears to be a classic example of a ripe Alsace vintage of maybe four years of age.

TASTE: a rich-flavoured wine; full, fat and fruity with well-developed spice and a soft, succulent finish. Evidently made from very ripe grapes.

CONCLUSION
Grape variety: Gewürztraminer
Region: Alsace
Age: about 4-5 years old
Comment: very good quality

SIGHT: stunning colour, even more distinctive than the Gewürztraminer, the old gold immediately suggests something full and rich, and probably very sweet. Sauternes first springs to mind, but it could also be from Austria, or even some unexpected oddity from Australia.

SMELL: this has the fabulously full, rich, and opulent nose of a botrytis wine. Anyone who dislikes sweet wine should smell the seductive complexity of a wine like this before giving up all hope. A touch of creamy-spicy oak rules out Austria and its maturity, probably between 10 and 15 years, realistically disposes of Australia.

TASTE: there is everything here from peaches, pineapple and cream, to the honeyed aromatics of a fairly mature wine. Only a classic Sauternes can have such intense flavours and yet possess such great finesse.

CONCLUSION
Grape variety: mostly Sémillon
Region: Sauternes
Age: about 15 years old
Comment: *Premier Cru*, great vintage

SIGHT: the orange-pink colour of this wine almost certainly pins it down to Provence or Tavel, although, if the orange hue is not indicative of the style and vinification of the wine, it could be almost any over-the-hill rosé.

SMELL: put the dunce's hat on and stand in the corner! The high-toned Pinot noir aroma dismisses the firm conviction of a Tavel or Provence rosé. But what is it? It is not oxidized, so it cannot be an otherwise obvious wine that has gone over. Is the orange hue a clue to its origin? More data is needed; must taste the wine.

TASTE: definitely Burgundian, but has a very distinctive piquant Pinot noir taste. At its peak now, but certainly not on the way down. By eliminating what it cannot be, only Rosé de Marsannay fits the bill.

CONCLUSION
Grape variety: Pinot noir
Region: Burgundy
Age: 4-5 years old
Comment: medium quality

SIGHT: this sparkling wine has an attractive, lively, lemon-yellow colour. Not young, but not old, its *mousse* is evident, but its power and the size of its bubbles cannot be assessed until the wine is tasted. Perhaps it is its star-bright limpidity, but for some reason this just looks like a fine wine.

SMELL: its quality is immediately evident. It has the autolytic characteristics of a wine with several years on its first cork (in contact with its lees prior to disgorgement), which eliminates every possibility other than a fine Champagne. It has the zippy tang of ripe Chardonnay grapes. This must be a Champagne *blanc de blancs* with a high proportion of wine from the Côte des Blancs.

TASTE: a gently persistent *mousse* of ultra-fine bubbles. The fresh, lively flavour has a long finish but requires another five years to reach perfection.

CONCLUSION
Grape variety: Chardonnay
Region: Champagne
Age: about 5 years old
Comment: top quality

Factors affecting taste and quality

The same grape grown in the same area can make two totally different wines, yet different grapes grown apart may produce two wines that are very similar. Whatever our personal perception of taste and quality might be, certain factors can and do affect the taste and quality of wine. These include: grape variety, which is always the single most important factor; location; climate, which determines the ability to grow grapes; aspect, which can either enhance or negate local conditions; soil (does it really have an influence?); viticulture, because the techniques used in the cultivation of a vine can stretch or concentrate the varietal character of its grapes; vinification, which is a bit like cooking and, as we are well aware, different methods of cooking produce totally different dishes from the same basic ingredient (*see* How Wine is Made, p.18); vintage, the vagaries of which can make or break a harvest; and the winemaker, the idiosyncratic joker in the pack.

Grape variety

The grape variety used to make a wine is the single most influential factor determining its taste.

THE FACTORS THAT DETERMINE the quintessential flavour of any grape variety are the same as those that determine the varietal taste of any fruit, and their importance to the taste of wine are outlined below. For information on specific grape varieties, *see* the Glossary of major grape varieties, p.24.

Size

The smaller the fruit, the more concentrated the flavour, therefore most classic grape varieties have small berries (for example, Cabernet sauvignon and Riesling), although some varieties that rely more on elegance than power of concentration may yield large berries, such as the Pinot noir. Numerous varieties are known as *petit*— something and *gros*— something, and it is normally the former that is the more famous quality variety (for example, Petit vidure = Cabernet sauvignon and Gros vidure = Cabernet franc; Petit rhin = Riesling and Gros rhin = Sylvaner).

Skin structure

The skin contains most of the aromatic characteristics with which we associate the varietal identity of any fruit. Its construction and thickness is therefore of paramount importance. For example, the thick-skinned Sauvignon blanc produces an aromatic wine that can vary in pungency from "gooseberry" through "elderflower" to "cat's pee", while the thin-skinned Sémillon produces a rather neutral wine, although its thin skin makes it susceptible to "noble rot" and thus is capable of producing one of the world's greatest botrytized sweet wines, with mind-blowing aromatics.

Skin colour and thickness

For example, the dark-coloured, thick-skinned Cabernet sauvignon produces very deep-coloured wines, while the lighter-coloured, thin-skinned Merlot produces less intensely coloured wines.

Acid/sugar ratio and presence of other constituents

The grape's sugar content dictates the alcohol level and whether any natural sweetness is possible, and this, together with the acidity level, determines the balance. The proportion of the grape's other constituents, or their products after fermentation, form the subtle nuances that differentiate the various varietal characters. Although soil, rootstock and climate have their effect on the ultimate flavour of the grape, the basic recipe for these ingredients is dictated by the vine's genetics.

Vitis vinifera (several thousand varieties)

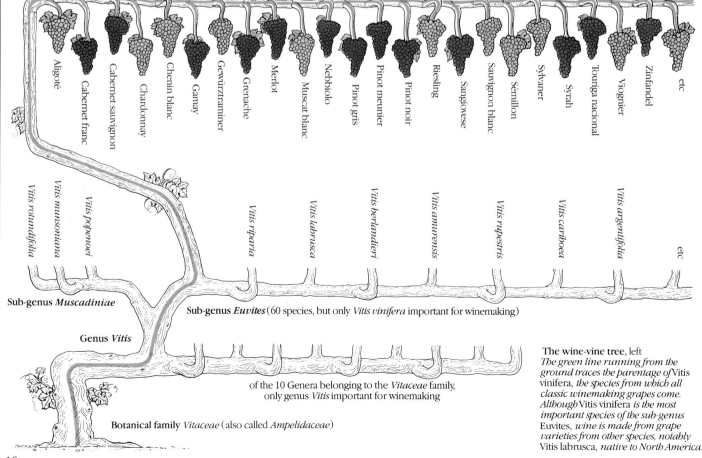

Aligoté | Cabernet franc | Cabernet sauvignon | Chardonnay | Chenin blanc | Gamay | Gewürztraminer | Grenache | Merlot | Muscat blanc | Nebbiolo | Pinot gris | Pinot meunier | Pinot noir | Riesling | Sangiovese | Sauvignon blanc | Sémillon | Sylvaner | Syrah | Touriga nacional | Viognier | Zinfandel | etc

Vitis rotundifolia | *Vitis munsoniana* | *Vitis popenoei* | *Vitis riparia* | *Vitis labrusca* | *Vitis berlandieri* | *Vitis amurensis* | *Vitis rupestris* | *Vitis cariboea* | *Vitis argentifolia* | etc

Sub-genus *Muscadiniae*

Sub-genus *Euvites* (60 species, but only *Vitis vinifera* important for winemaking)

Genus *Vitis*

of the 10 Genera belonging to the *Vitaceae* family, only genus *Vitis* important for winemaking

Botanical family *Vitaceae* (also called *Ampelidaceae*)

The wine-vine tree, left
The green line running from the ground traces the parentage of Vitis vinifera, *the species from which all classic winemaking grapes come. Although* Vitis vinifera *is the most important species of the sub-genus* Euvites, *wine is made from grape varieties from other species, notably* Vitis labrusca, *native to North America.*

THE *VITIS* FAMILY

Everyone knows that grapes are grown on a vine, but the vine is a large and diverse family of plants that encompasses everything from a miniature pot plant called the Kangaroo Vine to Virginia Creeper. Where do grape-bearing vines fit in? The Wine Vine Tree, (*see* opposite), clarifies the situation, making it easy to follow the botanical scheme of things by which *Vitis vinifera* emerges as the species that produces all the classic varieties of winemaking grapes such as the Pinot noir, Cabernet sauvignon and Chardonnay. The species *Vitis vinifera*, called *vinifera* for short, is one of many belonging to the sub-genus *Euvites*. Other species in this sub-genus are used for rootstock (*see* right).

PHYLLOXERA VASTATERIX — PEST OR BLESSING?

The vine louse that devastated the vineyards of Europe in the late nineteenth century — phylloxera vastaterix — still infests the soils of virtually all wine-growing regions of the world. Its advent is traditionally considered to be the greatest disaster in the history of wine, but with the benefit of hindsight it can be seen as the best thing that could have happened to the European wine industry.

Prior to phylloxera's arrival, many of Europe's greatest wine regions had undergone a gradual devaluation because of the increasing demand for their wines. This led to the planting of inferior bulk-producing grape varieties, and the extension of vineyards into unsuitable lands. With the disease's spread it became apparent that every vine in every vineyard would have to be grafted onto phylloxera-resistant American rootstock. This forced a much-needed rationalization, whereby only the best sites in the classic regions were replanted and only noble vines were cultivated, a costly and time-consuming operation that owners of vineyards in lesser areas could not afford. The grafting onto American rootstock took France fifty years to complete, and made possible the enormous task of establishing an *Appellation d'Origine Contrôlée* system. It would be hard to imagine what regional or varietal identities might exist today, if any, had phylloxera not happened.

Rootstock

Hundreds of rootstock varieties have been developed from various vine species, usually *berlandieri*, *riparia* or *rupestris*, because they are the most phylloxera-resistant. The choice of rootstock is dependent on its suitability to the vinestock on which it is to be grafted. It is also dependent on the rootstock's adaptability to the geographical location. But the choice can also increase or decrease the productivity of a vine, and therefore it has a profound effect upon the quality of wine produced. Generally speaking, the lower the quantity the higher the quality.

Location

The location of a vineyard basically determines whether or not its climate is suitable for viticulture.

VIRTUALLY ALL THE WINE-PRODUCING areas of the world are located between 30° and 50° latitude in both hemispheres. These are the temperate zones where the annual mean temperature is between 10°C (50°F) and 20°C (68°F). The most northerly vineyards of Germany are on the very limit, between 50° and 51° latitude, but survive because of the continental climatic influence, which assures the hotter summers and the shorter days that retard the cane growth in favour of fruit maturity. Interestingly, most of the world's finest wines are produced in west coast locations, which tend to be cooler and less humid than east coast areas. Forests and mountain ranges protect the vines from wind and rain. Relatively close proximity to forests and large masses of water can influence the climate through transpiration and evaporation, providing welcome humidity in times of drought, although they can encourage rot.

Young vines, Yugoslavia, above
A vineyard near Split in springtime, showing the typically twisting habit of the vines' stems as they develop.

The world of wine, right
The most important areas of cultivation in both the northern and southern hemispheres lie mainly between latitudes 30° and 50°. However, there are a number of smaller winemaking areas closer to the equator. Indeed, equatorial vinifera *wines are being produced in Kenya. In purely geographical terms the world of wine continues to expand.*

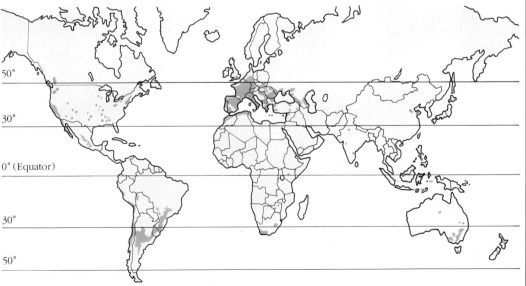

50°
30°
0° (Equator)
30°
50°

Climate

Climate is one of the most important factors influencing the growth of grapes for quality wines. We cannot change the climate, although nature can, and often does. A grower must select a region with an amenable climate and hope that nature does not inflict too many anomalies on it.

ALTHOUGH VARIOUS SPECIES OF VINE survive under extreme conditions, most winemaking vines and all classic winemaking vines are confined to two relatively narrow climatic bands that straddle the earth. Every vineyard needs the following:

Heat

Vines will not provide grapes suitable for winemaking if the annual mean temperature is less than 10°C (50°F). The ideal mean is 14-15°C (57-59°F), with an average of no less than 19°C (66°F) in summer and −1°C (30°F) in the winter.

In order to produce a good crop of ripe grapes the minimum heat-summation, measured in "degree-days" with an average temperature above 10°C (50°F) over the growing season, is 1,000 (using °C to calculate) or 1,800 (using °F to calculate). Below are degree-day totals over the growing season for a variety of vineyards from around the world.

Area/Region	Degree-days Celsius (Fahrenheit)
Trier, Mosel, Germany	945 (1,700)
Bordeaux, France	1,320 (2,375)
McLaren Vale, S.A., Australia	1,350 (2,425)
Russian River, California, USA	2,000 (3,600)

Sunshine

While light is required for photosynthesis, the most important biological process of green plants, there is sufficient light for this even in cloudy conditions. Sunshine is needed more for its heat than its light. Approximately 1,300 hours is the minimum sunshine required per growing season, but 1,500 hours is preferable.

Rainfall

A vine requires 675 millimetres (27 inches) of rain per year. Ideally, most of the rain should fall in the spring and the winter, but some is needed in the summer too. Vines can survive with less water if the temperature is higher, although rain in warm conditions is generally more harmful than rain in cool conditions. A little rain a few days before the harvest will wash the grapes of any sprays, and is therefore ideal if followed by sun and a gentle drying breeze. Torrential rain, however, can split berries and cause fungus.

Below are annual rainfall figures for a variety of vineyards from around the world.

Area/region	Rainfall
McLaren Vale, S.A., Australia	60 cm (24 inches)
Trier, Mosel, Germany	65 cm (26 inches)
Bordeaux, France	90 cm (36 inches)
Russian River, California, USA	135 cm (53 inches)

Preparing for rain, above
In southern Spain furrows are dug horizontally between rows of vines to provide channels for any rain.

Frost

Surprising as it may seem, some frost is desirable, providing it is in the winter. It hardens the wood and kills spores and pests, which the bark may be harbouring.

CLIMATIC CONDITIONS

Favourable

● Fine, long summers with warm, rather than hot, sunshine. This ensures that the grapes ripen slowly, resulting in a good acid-sugar balance.
● A dry, sunny autumn is essential for ripening grapes and avoiding rot, but, again, it must not be too hot.
● The winter months from November to February are climatically flexible, with the vine able to withstand temperatures as low as −20°C and anything other than absolute flood or drought.
● Within the above parameters, the climate must suit the viticultural requirements of specific grape varieties, for example a cooler climate for Riesling, hotter for Syrah, and so on.

Unfavourable

● The major dangers are frost, hail and strong winds, all of which can denude a vine and are particularly perilous when the vine is flowering or the grapes are ripening and at their most susceptible.
● Rain and/or cold temperatures during the flowering may cause imperfect fertilization, which results in a physiological disorder called *millerandage*. The affected grapes contain no seeds and will be small and partly developed when the rest of the cluster is fully matured.
● Persistent rain at, or immediately prior to the harvest can lead to rot or dilute the wine, both of which can cause vinification problems.
● Sun is not often thought of as a climatic danger, but, just as frost can be beneficial to the vine, so sun can be harmful. Too much sun encourages the sap to go straight past the embryo grape clusters to the leaves and shoots. This causes a physiological disorder called *coulure,* which is often confused with *millerandage,* but is totally different, although both disorders can appear together due to the vagaries of climate. Most seeds suffering from *coulure* drop to the ground, and those that remain never develop.
● Excessive heat during the harvest rapidly drops the acid level of grape juice and makes the grapes too hot, creating problems during fermentation. It is especially difficult to harvest grapes at an acceptable temperature in very hot areas, like South Africa, and some wine estates actually harvest the grapes at night when the grapes are at their coolest.

Aspect

The aspect of a vineyard refers to its general topography — which direction the vines face, the angle and height of slope, and so on — and how it interrelates with the climate.

THERE ARE VERY FEW PLACES in the world where winemaking grapes are successfully grown under the full effect of a prevailing climate. The basic climatic requirements of the vine are usually achieved by manipulating local conditions, with the following in mind:

Sunshine

South-facing slopes (north-facing in the southern hemisphere) attract more hours of sunshine. In hotter areas, however, the opposite facing slopes tend to be cultivated.

Sun strength and drainage

Because of its angle, a slope enables the vines to absorb the greater strength of the sun's rays. In temperate regions the sun is not directly overhead, even at noon, and therefore its rays are more or less perpendicular to a slope. Conversely, the sun's rays are dissipated across a wider area on flat ground, therefore their strength is diluted in a vineyard grown on the plains (which are, in any case, susceptible to flooding and have soils that are usually too fertile, yielding far larger crops of correspondingly inferior fruit). Lake- and river-valley slopes are particularly well suited for vines because the water reflects sunshine onto them.

Another intrinsically superior aspect of a sloping vineyard is that it affords natural drainage. Vines grown on hilltops, however, are too exposed to wind, rain and storms, and also deprive the vines below of their protective forested tops. Forested hilltops not only supply humidity in times of drought, but absorb the worst of any torrential rain that could wash away the topsoil below.

Temperature

While slopes are very desirable sites for vineyards, it must be remembered that for every 100 metres (330 feet) above sea level the vines are planted, the temperature falls 1°C (1.8°F). This can result in an extra 10-15 days needed to ripen grapes and, because of the extra time, their acidity will be relatively higher. Thus the altitude of a vineyard can be a very effective means of manipulating the quality and character of its crop. Riverside and lakeside slopes not only have the advantage of reflected sunlight, but also the benefit of the water masses acting as heat reservoirs, storing up heat in the day and releasing it at night. This not only reduces sudden drops in temperature that can be harmful to the vine, but lowers the risk of frost. However, depressions in the slopes and the very bottom of valleys collect cold air, are frost-prone and retard vine growth.

Soil

Just as various garden flowers, shrubs and vegetables perform better in one soil type as opposed to another, so do certain grape varieties.

WHEN CONSTANTLY CULTIVATED, topsoil eventually becomes man made. Topsoil is of primary importance to the vine because it supports most of its root system, including most of the feeding network. Subsoil always remains geologically true. Main roots penetrate several layers of subsoil, the structure of which influences drainage, the root system's depth, and its ability to collect minerals.

The metabolism of the vine is well known, and the interaction between it and the soil is generally understood. The ideal medium in which to grow vines for wine production is one that has a relatively thin topsoil and an easily penetrable (therefore well-drained) subsoil with good water-retention characteristics. The vine does not like "wet feet", so drainage is vital, yet it needs access to moisture, so access to a soil with good water-retention is also important. The temperature potential of a soil, its heat-retention capacity and heat-reflective characteristics affect the ripening period of grapes: warm soils (gravel, sand, loam) advance ripening, while cold soils (clay) retard it. Chalk comes in between these two extremes, and dark, dry soils are obviously warmer than light, wet soils. High pH (alkaline) soils (such as chalk) encourage the vine's metabolism to produce sap and grape juice with a relatively high acid content. The continual use of fertilizers has lowered the pH level of some viticultural areas in France, and these are now producing wines of higher pH (less acidity).

THE MINERAL REQUIREMENTS OF THE VINE

Certain minerals essential to plant growth are found in various soils. Apart from hydrogen and oxygen (supplied as water) the most important soil nutrients are: nitrogen, used in the production of a plant's green matter; phosphate, which directly encourages root development and indirectly promotes an earlier ripening of the grapes (an excess inhibits the uptake of magnesium); potassium, which improves the vine's metabolism, enriches the sap and is essential for the development of the next year's crop; iron, which is indispensable for photosynthesis (lack of iron will cause chlorosis); magnesium, which is the only mineral constituent of the chlorophyll molecule (lack of magnesium also causes chlorosis); and calcium, which feeds the root system, neutralizes acidity and helps create a friable soil structure (though an excess of calcium restricts the vine's ability to extract iron from the soil and thus causes chlorosis).

For information on specific soil types, refer to the Guide to vineyard soils, overleaf.

Terraced vineyards overlook the Rhine, above
Vines beside water masses benefit from the sun's rays reflecting off the water, an advantage in areas of cooler climate.

Hills near Sancerre, above
In the spring, vineyards give the rolling countryside in France's Loire Valley a speckled appearance. Most soils in the area are dominated by clay or limestone.

GUIDE TO VINEYARD SOILS

Aeolian soil Sediments deposited by wind.

Albariza White-surfaced soil formed by diatomaceous deposits, found in southern Spain.

Alluvial deposits Material that has been transported by river and deposited. Most alluvial soils contain silt, sand and gravel, and are highly fertile.

Argillaceous soils A group of sedimentary soils, commonly clays, shales, mudstones, siltstones and marls.

Basalt Material that accounts for 90 per cent of all lava-based volcanic rocks. It contains various minerals, is rich in lime and soda, but not quartz, the most abundant of all minerals, and it is poor in potash.

Bastard soil A Bordelais name for medium-heavy, sandy-clay soil of variable fertility.

Bentonite A fine clay containing a volcanic-ash derivative called montmorillonite, which activates a precipitation in wine when used as a fining agent.

Boulbènes A Bordelais name for a very fine siliceous soil that is easily compressed and hard to work. This "beaten" earth covers part of the Entre-Deux-Mers plateau.

Calcareous clay Argillaceous soil that has carbonate of lime content that neutralizes the clay's intrinsic acidity. The cold temperature of this type of soil also delays ripening, and so the wines produced on it tend to have more acidity.

Calcareous soil Any soil, or mixture of soils, with an accumulation of calcium and magnesium carbonates. Essentially alkaline, it promotes the production of acidity in grapes, although the pH of each soil will vary according to its level of "active" lime. Calcareous soils are cool, with good water-retention. With the exception of calcareous clays (see above), they allow the vine's root system to penetrate deeply and provide excellent drainage.

Carbonaceous soil Soil that is derived from rotting vegetation under anaerobic conditions. The most common carbonaceous soils are peat, lignite, coal and anthracite.

Chalk A specific type of limestone, chalk is a soft, cool and porous alkaline rock that encourages the production of grapes with a relatively high acidity level. It also allows the vine's roots to penetrate and provides excellent drainage, yet retains sufficient moisture for nourishment.

Clay A fine-grained argillaceous compound with malleable, plastic characteristics and excellent water-retention properties. It is, however, cold, acid, offers poor drainage and, because of its cohesive quality, is hard to work. An excess of clay can stifle the vine's root system, but a proportion of small clay particles mixed with other soils can be advantageous.

Clayey-loam A very fertile version of loam, but heavy to work under wet conditions with a tendency to become waterlogged.

Colluvial deposits Weathered material transported by gravity or hill-wash.

Crasse de fer Iron-rich hard-pan found in the Libournais area of France. Also called *machefer*.

Diatomaceous earth *See Kieselguhr*.

Ferruginous clay Iron-rich clay.

Flint A siliceous stone that stores and reflects heat, and is often associated with a certain "gun-flint" smell in wines, although this is not proven and may simply be the taster's auto-suggestion, unless it is picked up in a blind tasting.

Galestro A Tuscan name for the rocky, schistous soil found in most of the region's best vineyards.

Glacial moraine A gritty scree deposited by glacial action.

Granite A hard, mineral-rich rock that quickly warms up and retains its heat. It has a high pH that reduces wine acidity; thus, in Beaujolais, it is the best soil for the intrinsically acid Gamay grape.

Gravel A wide-ranging term that covers siliceous pebble of various sizes. This soil is loose, granular, airy and affords excellent drainage. It is also acid, infertile and encourages the vine to send its roots down deep in search of nutrients, so gravel beds located above limestone subsoils produce wines with markedly more acidity than those above clay subsoils.

Hard-pan A dense layer of clay that forms if the subsoil is more clayey than the topsoil at certain depths. As hard-pans are impermeable to both water and roots, they are not desirable too close to the surface, but may provide an easily reachable water-table if located deep down. A sandy, iron-rich hard-pan known as iron-pan is commonly found in parts of Bordeaux.

Humus Organic material that contains bacteria and other micro-organisms that are capable of converting complex chemicals into simple plant foods. Humus makes soil fertile; without it soil is nothing more than finely-ground rock.

Iron-pan A sandy, iron-rich hard-pan.

Kieselguhr A fine, powdered siliceous sediment commonly used for ultra-fine filtration in wine-making. It is also known as diatomaceous earth.

Kimmeridgian soil A greyish-coloured limestone originally identified in, and so named after, the village of Kimmeridge in Dorset, England. A sticky, calcareous clay containing this limestone is often called Kimmeridgian clay.

Lignite The "brown coal" of Germany and the "black gold" of Champagne, this is a brown carbonaceous material intermediate between coal and peat. Warm and very fertile, it is mined and used as a natural fertilizer in Champagne.

Limestone Any sedimentary rock consisting essentially of carbonates. Its hardness and water-retention varies, but as an alkaline rock it generally encourages the production of grapes with a relatively high acidity level.

Loam A warm, soft, crumbly soil with roughly equal proportions of clay, sand and silt. It is perfect for large-cropping mediocre-quality wines, but too fertile for fine wines.

Loess An accumulation of wind-borne material, mainly silty in nature, that is sometimes calcareous, but usually weathered and decalcified. It warms up quickly and has good water-retention properties.

Machefer Iron-rich hard-pan found in the Libournais area. Also called *crasse de fer*.

Marl A cold, calcareous clay that delays ripening and adds acidity to wine.

Marlstone Clayey limestone that has a similar effect to marl.

Mica A generic name encompassing various silicate minerals.

Mudstone A sedimentary soil similar to clay but without its plastic characteristics.

Palus A Bordelais name for a very fertile soil of modern alluvial origin that produces medium-quality, well-coloured, robust wines.

Perlite Fine, powdery light and lustrous substance of volcanic origin with similar properties to diatomaceous earth.

Porphyry A coloured igneous rock with high pH.

Quartz The most common and abundant mineral found in various sizes in many soils. It has a high pH that reduces wine acidity, but pebble-sized quartz, or larger, stores and reflects heat.

Red earth *See Terra rossa*.

Sand Tiny particles of weathered rocks and minerals that retain little water, but constitute a warm, airy soil that drains well and is supposedly phylloxera-free.

Sandstone Sedimentary rock composed of sand-sized particles that have either been formed by pressure or bound by various iron minerals.

Sandy-loam Warm, well-drained, sand-dominated loam that is easy to work and suitable for early-cropping grape varieties.

Schist Heat-retaining, coarse-grain, laminated, crystalline rock that is rich in potassium and magnesium, but poor in nitrogen and organic substances.

Scree Synonymous with colluvium deposits.

Shale Heat-retaining, fine-grain, laminated, moderately fertile sedimentary rock. Shale can turn into slate under pressure.

Siliceous soil A generic term for acid rock of a crystalline nature. It may be organic (flint and *kieselguhr*) or inorganic (quartz) and have good heat retention, but no water retention unless found in a finely-ground form in silt, clay and other sedimentary soils. Half of the Bordeaux region is covered with siliceous soils.

Silt A very fine deposit, with good water retention. Silt is more fertile than sand, but is cold and offers poor drainage.

Slate Hard, dark grey, fine-grain, plate-like rock formed under pressure from clay, siltstone, shale and other sediments. It warms up quickly, retains its heat well and is responsible for many fine wines, most notably from the Mosel.

Stone This word should be used in conjunction with rock types – limestone and sandstone, for example – but "stone" is often used synonymously with pebble.

Terra rossa A red, clay-like, sometimes flinty sedimentary soil that is deposited after carbonate has been leached out of limestone. It is often known as "Red earth".

Tufa Various vent-based volcanic rocks, the chalk-tufa of the Loire being the most important viticulturally speaking.

Volcanic soils Derived from two sources, volcanic soils are lava-based (the products of volcanic flow) and vent-based (material blown into the atmosphere). Some 90 per cent of lava-based rocks and soils are comprised of basalt, whilst others include andesite, pitchstone, rhyolite and trachyte. Vent-based matter has either been ejected as molten globules, cooled in the air, and dropped to earth as solid particles (pumice), or ejected as solid material and fractured through the explosive force with which it was flung (tufa).

Viticulture

While it is the variety of grape that determines the basic flavour of a wine, the way in which it is grown has the most profound effect on its quality.

VINE TRAINING

ONE ASPECT OF VINE TRAINING IS CRUCIAL: to ensure that no cane ever touches the ground. Should a cane find its way to the ground, its natural inclination is to send out suckers that would put down roots. Within two or three years the majority of the grafted vine's above-ground network would be dependent not upon grafted roots, but upon the regenerated root system of the producing vine. Not only would this put the vine at the mercy of phylloxera, but, ironically, that part of the vine still receiving its principal nourishment from the grafted rootstock would send out its own shoots and, unchecked by any sort of pruning, these would produce hybrid fruit. Therefore the fundamental reason for training and pruning a vine is to avoid phylloxera and to maintain the purity of its fruiting stock. But it is not the only reason.

The manner in which a vine is trained will guide the size, shape and height of the plant towards reaping maximum benefits from the local conditions of aspect and climate. Vines can be trained high to avoid ground frost, or low to hug any heat that may be reflected by stony soils at night. There may be a generous amount of space between rows to attract the sun and avoid humidity. On the other hand vines may be intensively cultivated to form a canopy of foliage to avoid too much sun.

REGIONAL STYLES OF VINE TRAINING

There are two basic systems of vine training; cane training and spur training on which there are many local variations. Cane trained vines have no permanent branch because all canes are pruned back each year to provide a vine consisting of entirely new growth. This system gives a good spread of fruit over a large area, and allows easier regulation of annual production, because the number of fruiting buds can be increased or decreased. With spur training there is no annual replacement of the main branch, thus a solid framework is formed.

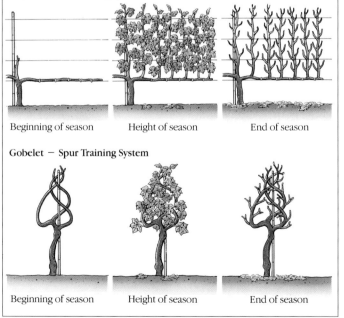

Guyot – Cane Training System

Beginning of season   Height of season   End of season

Gobelet – Spur Training System

Beginning of season   Height of season   End of season

VITICULTURAL SPRAYS

The use of sprays was once confined to protecting the vine against pests and diseases and controlling weeds, but they have additional uses today. There are foliar feeds that supply nutrients direct to the vine, while other sprays halt the growth of foliage, rendering summer pruning unnecessary. Some sprays deliberately induce two disorders called *millerandage* and *coulure* to reduce the yield and hopefully increase the quality.

PRUNING

Important for controlling quantity, pruning is equally important for producing quality fruit. As with any crop, be it grapes or prize roses, if the quantity is reduced, the quality is increased. Reducing the number of fruiting buds lowers the quantity of fruit.

FLOWERING

The most critical period of a vine's life is when it flowers – at this stage frost, hail, rain, wind and excessively high or low temperatures could wipe out a crop before the growing season begins in earnest. Even the quality-conscious growers usually leave a couple of extra buds on each vine just in case of poor weather during flowering. It follows, therefore, that if the weather permits a perfect flowering, even the best growers' vines end up with too many grape bunches. The weather is not often that kind in classic areas, but when it is, the perfect solution would be to remove some of the embryo bunches. Most growers wait until the beginning of *veraison*, when the grapes start to take on colour and begin to ripen, before cutting off unwanted bunches. At this point the vine has already wasted much of its energy on developing the clusters about to be discarded, but their removal will help the remaining bunches of grapes to ripen.

THE TIMING OF THE GRAPE HARVEST

When to pick is one of the most crucial decisions a grower has to make each year. As grapes ripen, there is a reduction in their acidity and an increase in sugar, colour, various minerals and essential aromatic compounds. The decision of when to pick will vary according to the variety of grape, the location of the vineyard and the style of wine to be made. White wine generally benefits from the extra acidity of early-harvested grapes, but they also need the varietal aroma and richness that can only be found in ripe grapes. It is essential to get the balance right. Red wine requires relatively low acidity and profits from the increased colour, sugar and tannin content of later-harvested grapes. The grower must also take the weather into account. Those who have the nerve to wait for perfectly ripe grapes every year can produce exceptional wines in even the poorest vintages, but run the risk of frost, rot or hail damage, which can totally destroy not only an entire crop, but also an entire year's income. Those who never take a chance may always harvest healthy grapes, but in poor years the crop will be unripe and wine mediocre.

MECHANICAL HARVESTING

Mechanical harvesting remains a contentious subject. The advantages of mechanization are obvious: dramatically reduced labour costs and a quick harvest of the entire crop at the optimum ripeness level, but investments must be made to adapt the vineyard to the machine chosen and for enlargement of the reception and fermentation facilities in order to cope with the larger amounts and quicker throughput. There are disadvantages, however, which relate to the efficiency of the machinery and the quality of the wine.

As giant machines move through the vineyards, beating the vine trunks with a battery of rubber sticks, the grapes drop from the vines onto a conveyor along with leaves and other ancillary matter, most of which is ejected as the fruit is sorted on its way to the hold. Apart from the rubbish that remains with the harvested grapes – which is getting less as more sophisticated machines are developed – the main disadvantage is the inability to distinguish between the ripe and unripe, the healthy and the diseased or the plain rotten (the first thing to drop from any plant when shaken.)

Despite these inadequacies many excellent-quality red wines have been made from mechanically harvested grapes. From a practical viewpoint it would seem that this method of harvesting is fine for red wine, but currently less useful for white wine because it splits grapes and so encourages oxidation and a loss of aromatics.

Annual life-cycle of the vine

The calendar of events by which any well-established vine seeks to reproduce, through the production of grapes, is outlined below, along with a commentary on man's cultivation of the vine in order to encourage it to produce the best possible grapes for wine-making. The vine's yearly routine generally starts and finishes with the end and approach of winter respectively, although man's activity is almost year-round, with vineyard maintenance continuing into winter.

WEEPING

Northern hemisphere:
February
Southern hemisphere:
August

Weeping is the vine's first external sign of its awakening after a winter of relative dormancy. When the soil temperature at a depth of 25 centimetres (10 inches) reaches 10.2°C (50°F), the roots begin to collect water and the vine pushes its sap up to the very limits of its branch system, oozing the sap out of the winter-pruned cane-ends in a manifestation called "weeping". This occurs suddenly, rapidly

As the soil warms up the vine awakes, pushing sap out of its cane ends.

increases in intensity and then decreases gradually. Each vine loses between one-half and five-and-a-half litres (ten pints) of sap, the variation depending on the location of the vineyard and the system of vine training. Weeping is the signal to prune for the spring growth, but this poses a problem for the grower because the vine, once pruned, is at its most vulnerable to frost. To wait for the danger of frost to subside, however, would be to waste the vine's preciously finite energy and retard its growth, delaying the ripening of its fruit by as much as ten days, thus risking exposure of the fruit to autumn frosts.

BUD-BREAK

Northern hemisphere:
March to April
Southern hemisphere:
September to October

In the spring, some 20 to 30 days after the vine starts weeping, the buds begin to open. This is known as the bud-break, and different varieties bud-break at different times; there are early bud-breakers (Chardonnay, for example), mid-season bud-breakers (Pinot noir) and late bud-breakers (Merlot). The same grape variety can bud-break at different times in some years due to climatic changes.

Buds begin to open at a time determined by variety and climate.

The type of soil can also affect the timing of bud-break: clay, which is cold, will retard the process, while sand, which is warm, will promote it. Early bud-break varieties are susceptible to frost in northerly vineyards (southerly in the southern hemisphere), just as late-ripeners are prone to autumn frosts. In the vineyard pruning continues into March (September in the southern hemisphere). The vines are secured to their training frames, and the protective mound of earth ploughed over the grafting wound to protect it in the winter is ploughed back, aerating the soil and levelling off the ground between the rows.

THE EMERGENCE OF SHOOTS, FOLIAGE AND EMBRYO BUNCHES

Northern hemisphere:
April to May
Southern hemisphere:
October to November

Following bud-break, foliage develops and shoots are sent out. In mid-April (mid-October in the southern hemisphere), after the fourth or fifth leaf has emerged, miniature green clusters are formed. These are the vine's flowers, but they have yet to bloom. When they do, each successful blossom develops into a grape, thus they are commonly called embryo

Embryo bunches, the vine's flowers, form.

bunches, and as such they are the first indication of the *potential* size of a crop. In the vineyard, spraying to ward off or cure various vine pests, diseases and other disorders commences in May (November in the southern hemisphere), and continues until the harvest. Many of these sprays are combined with systemic fertilizers to feed the vine directly through its foliage. These spraying operations are normally done by hand or tractor, but may be carried out by helicopter if the slopes are very steep or the vineyards too muddy to enter. At this time of year the vine can be affected by *coulure* or *millerandage* (*see* Climatic conditions, p.12)

FLOWERING OF THE VINE

Northern hemisphere:
May to June
Southern hemisphere:
November to December

The "embryo bunches" break into flower after the fifteenth or sixteenth leaf has emerged on the vine. This is normally some eight weeks after the bud-break and involves pollination and fertilization. The flowering lasts for about ten days. It is essential for the weather to be dry and frost-free, but temperature is the most critical requirement. A daily average of at least 15°C (59°F) is the minimum needed to enable a vine to flower and

For about ten days the vine flowers – a vulnerable period.

between 20-25°C (68-77°F) is considered ideal. Heat summation, however, is far more important than temperature levels, so the length of day has a great influence on the number of days the flowering will last. Soil temperature is more significant than air temperature, therefore the soil's heat-retention capacity is another contributory factor. Frost is the greatest hazard to the flowering vine, and many vineyards are equipped with stoves or sprinkling systems. Stoves can make the one-degree difference between survival and destruction and sprinklers force the frost to expend its energy freezing the water, not the vine.

FRUIT SET

Northern hemisphere:
June to July
Southern hemisphere:
December to January

After the flowering, the embryo bunches rapidly evolve into true clusters Each fertilized berry expands into a recognizable grape, the first visible sign of the actual fruit that will produce the wine. This is called fruit-set. The number of grapes per embryo bunch varies from variety to variety, as does the percentage that actually set into grapes. The following statistics of Alsace grapes illustrate this:

Clearly recognizable grapes begin to form.

Variety	Berries per embryo bunch	Grapes in a ripe cluster	Percentage of fruit-set
Chasselas	164	48	29%
Gewürztraminer	100	40	40%
Pinot gris	149	41	28%
Riesling	189	61	32%
Sylvaner	95	50	53%

In the vineyard, spraying continues and summer pruning, to concentrate the vine's energy on making fruit, commences. In some vineyards this is the time for weeding, but in others the weeds are allowed to grow as high as 50cm (20 in) before they are mowed and ploughed into the soil to break-up the soil and provide the vines with excellent green manure.

RIPENING OF THE GRAPES

Northern hemisphere:
August
Southern hemisphere:
January

As the grape develops its fleshy fruit very little chemical change takes place inside the berry until its skin begins to turn a different colour. Throughout the grape's green stage, the sugar and acid content remains the same, but during August (January in the southern hemisphere), the ripening process begins in earnest — the skin changes colour, the sugar content dramatically

The grapes begin to change colour, the sign of true ripening.

increases and the hard malic acid diminishes as the riper tartaric acid builds up. Although the tartaric acid content also begins to decline after about two weeks, it always remains the primary acid. It is at this stage that the grape's tannins are gradually hydrolyzed. This is a crucially important moment because only hydrolyzed tannins are capable of softening as a wine matures. In the vineyard spraying and weeding continue, and the vine's foliage is thinned to facilitate the circulation of air and thus reduce the risk of rot. Care has to be taken not to remove too much foliage as it is the effect of sunlight upon the leaves that ripens the grapes.

GRAPE HARVEST

Northern hemisphere:
August to October
Southern hemisphere:
February to March

The harvest usually begins mid- to late-September (mid-to late-February in the southern hemisphere) and may last for a month or more, but, as is the case with all vineyard operations, the timing is earlier nearer to the equator and is dependent on the weather. Picking may therefore start as early as August (February) and finish as late as November (April).

Grapes are picked at a time determined by the winemaker.

White grapes ripen before black grapes and must in any case be harvested relatively earlier to achieve a higher acidity balance.

GRAPES AFFECTED BY BOTRYTIS CINEREA

Northern hemisphere:
November to December
Southern hemisphere:
April to May

In November the sap retreats to the protection of the vine's root system. As a result of this, the year-old canes begin to harden and any remaining grapes, cut off from the vine's metabolic system, start dehydrating. The concentrated pulp that they become is subject to severe cold, which induces complex chemical changes in a process

Rotting grapes, soon to be harvested for sweet botrytized wines.

known as *passerillage*. In specialist sweet-wine areas the grapes are deliberately left on the vine to undergo this quality-enhancing experience and, in certain vineyards with suitable climatic conditions, growers pray for the appearance of botrytis cinerea or "noble rot".

EISWEIN

Northern hemisphere:
December to January
Southern hemisphere:
May to June

In Germany, it is possible to see grapes on the vine in December and even January. This is usually because the grower has hoped for botrytis cinerea, or *Edelfäule* as it is called in Germany, but it failed to occur. Should frost or snow freeze the grapes, they can be harvested to produce *Eiswein*, one of the world's most spectacular wines. As it is only the water that freezes, this

Grapes still on the vine may yet become wine.

can be skimmed off once the grapes are pressed in order to leave a super-concentrated unfrozen pulp that produces *Eiswein*.

Vintage

The anomalies of a vintage can bring disaster to reliable vineyards and produce miracles in unreliable ones.

A VINTAGE IS MADE BY WEATHER, which is not at all the same as climate. Climate is what it *should* be, while weather is what it *is*. The vintage's annual climatic adjustment can be very selective: on the edge of a summer hail storm, for example, some vineyards may be destroyed while others are unharmed. One produces good wine, while the other produces no wine at all. Vines situated between the two might be left with a partial crop of fruit that could result in wines of an exceptional quality, if given a further two to three months of warm sunshine prior to the harvest, as reduced yields per vine produce grapes with a greater concentration of flavour.

The winemaker

The winemaker, and that includes the winegrower, can maximize or minimize the fruits of nature by his or her skill.

TIME AND AGAIN I HAVE SEEN that neighbouring winemakers can make a different quality wine using the same raw product and technology. The analyses may be virtually indistinguishable, yet one wine will have all the definition, vitality and expression of character that the other lacks. Why? No doubt there are valid reasons that science may one day establish, but in our current state of ignorance I can only say that it is always the winemakers with passion who are able to produce the finer, more characterful wines. Of course many inferior wines are made by the misuse of up-to-date technology, but I have seen dedicated winemakers produce spell-binding wines using what I would consider to be totally inadequate or inferior equipment. From the grower who never hesitates to prune the vine for low yields, yet always agonizes over the optimum time to harvest, to the winemaker who literally nurses the wines through each and every stage of fermentation and maturation, who bottles at precisely the right time and at exactly the correct temperature, the human element is most seriously the joker in the pack when it comes to factors affecting taste and quality.

Inspecting maturing wine, *above*
Auguste Clape, one of the finest winemakers in France's Northern Rhône area, checks the progress of his oak-matured wine.

How wine is made

Methods of production vary not just from country to country, but also from region to region, and quite commonly from grower to grower within the same village. Much depends upon whether traditional values are upheld or innovations are sought, and in the case of the latter, if the technology is available. Whatever the winemaker decides, certain principles will, essentially, remain the same. These are described in detail below, before sections on different styles of wine and the processes common or unique to each one (p.21-23).

Principles of vinification

The quality of grapes when they arrive at the winery represents the maximum potential of any wine made from them, but a winemaker rarely manages to transfer 100 per cent of this quality from the grapes to the wine.

FERMENTATION

The biochemical process that transforms fresh grape juice into wine is called fermentation. Yeast cells excrete enzymes that convert natural fruit sugars into almost equal quantities of alcohol and carbonic gas. This process ceases when the supply of sugar is exhausted or when the alcoholic level reaches a point that is toxic for the yeast enzymes (15 to 16 per cent normally, although certain strains can survive 20 to 22 per cent). A winemaker traditionally racked (*see* p.20) his wine from cask to cask until he was sure that fermentation had stopped, but there are many other methods that halt fermentation artificially. These involve:

Heat

There are various forms of pasteurization (for table wines), flash-pasteurization (for finer wines) and chilling operations that are used to stabilize wine. These operate on the basis that yeast cells are incapacitated at temperatures above 36°C (97°F), or below −3°C (26°F), and that yeast enzymes are destroyed above 65°C (149°F). Flash-pasteurization subjects wines to a temperature of about 80°C (176°F) for between 30 seconds and one minute, whereas fully fledged pasteurization involves lower temperatures of 50-60°C (122-140°F) for a longer period.

Addition of sulphur dioxide or sorbic acid

Dosing with one or more aseptic substances will kill off the yeasts.

Centrifugal filtration or filtration

Modern equipment is now capable of physically removing all the yeasts from a wine, either by filtration, which is simply pouring the wine through a medium that prevents certain substances passing through, or by centrifugal filtration, which is a process that separates unwanted matter from wine (or grape juice, if used at an earlier stage) by so-called "centrifugal force".

Addition of alcohol

Fortification raises the alcohol content to a level toxic to yeast.

Pressure

Yeast cells are destroyed by pressure in excess of eight atmospheres (the pressure inside a Champagne bottle is around six atmospheres).

Carbonic gas (CO_2)

Yeast cells are destroyed in the presence of 15 grams per litre or more of carbonic gas.

MALOLACTIC FERMENTATION

Malolactic fermentation is sometimes known as the secondary fermentation, but it is an inappropriate description. The malolactic, or malo as it is simply called, is a biochemical process that converts the "hard" malic acid of unripe grapes into two-parts

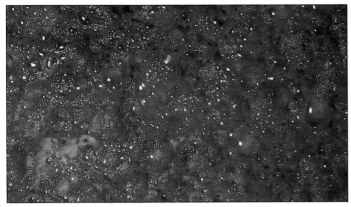

Furious fermentation, *above*
The wine yeasts on a single grape can split up to one billion sugar molecules every second.

"soft" lactic or "milk" acid (so-called because it is the acid that makes milk sour) and one-part carbonic gas. Malic acid is a very strong-tasting acid that is reduced during the fruit's ripening process, but a quantity persists in ripe grapes, and, although reduced by fermentation, in wine.

The quantity of malic acid present in a wine may be considered too much and the smoothing effect of replacing it with just two-thirds the quantity of the much weaker lactic acid is often desirable. The smoothing effect is considered vital for red wine, but optional only for white, rosé and sparkling wine. To ensure that the malo can take place, it is essential that specific bacteria be present. These are found naturally on grape skins among the yeasts and other micro-organisms. To undertake their task, they require a medium of a certain warmth, a low level of sulphur, a pH between 3 and 4 and a supply of various nutrients found naturally in the grapes.

STAINLESS STEEL OR OAK?

The reasons for using stainless-steel or oak containers for fermentation and maturation are totally opposite and are dependent not simply on cost (*see* below right), but on whether the winemaker wants to add character to a wine or to keep its purity.

A stainless-steel vat is a long-lasting, easy-to-clean vessel made from an impervious and inert material that is ideally suited to all forms of temperature control, and has the capacity to produce the freshest wines with the purest varietal character. An oak cask has a comparatively limited life, is not easy to clean (it can never be sterilized), makes temperature control very difficult, and is neither

YEAST – THE FERMENTER

The yeasts used for fermentation may be divided into two categories: cultured yeasts and natural yeasts.

Cultured yeasts are nothing more than thoroughbred strains of natural wine yeasts raised in a laboratory. They may be used because the juice has been cleansed of all organisms, including yeasts, prior to fermentation, or because the winemaker prefers their reliability, or for a specific purpose, such as withstanding higher alcohol levels or the increased osmotic pressure that affects bottle-fermented sparkling wines.

Natural yeasts are to be found adhering to the pruina, a waxy substance that covers the skin of ripe grapes and other fruits. By the time a grape has fully ripened, the coating of yeasts and other micro-organisms, commonly referred to as the "bloom", contains an average of ten million yeast cells, although only one per cent or just 100,000 cells are so-called "wine-yeasts". A yeast cell is only 1/5,000th of an inch, yet under favourable conditions it has the ability to split 10,000 sugar molecules every second during fermentation.

impervious nor inert. It allows access to the air, which encourages a faster rate of oxidation, but also causes evaporation, which concentrates the flavour. Vanillin, the essential aromatic of vanilla pods, is extracted from the oak by oxidation, and together with various wood lactones and unfermentable sugars, imparts a distinctive, sweet and creamy, vanilla nuance to wine. This oaky character takes on a smoky complexity if the wine is allowed to go through its malolactic fermentation in contact with the wood, and becomes even more complex, and certainly better integrated, if the wine has undergone all or most of its alcoholic fermentation in cask. Oak also imparts wood tannins to low tannin wine, absorbs tannins from very tannic wine, and can simply exchange tannins with some wines.

The choice of oak

Both American and European oaks are used for winemaking. The difference in preparation and barrel-manufacturing technique between the two are the most fundamental factors affecting the characteristics they impart. The aromatics of American oak, *Quercus alba*, are more pungent, while the tannin content of European oaks, *Quercus robur* and *Quercus sessilis*, is higher. Much of the coarser characteristics previously thought to be inherent in *Quercus alba* are now attributed to the American tendency to use sawn wood for barrel-making as opposed to the European preference for split wood. Sawing ruptures the wood cells and this imparts an aggressive character to the wine. Another important difference is that American oak is mostly kiln-dried, whereas European oak is traditionally air-dried. Air-dried oak is weathered outdoors for several years, and this process leaches out the wood's harsher characteristics.

The size of cask is critical to its influence because the smaller it is, the larger the oak-to-wine ratio. Square barrels have even been developed to increase this ratio and, although treated as a novelty, they are in fact more practical and economical than normal casks. More practical because they make more efficient use of storage space, and more economical because their straight sides are simply reversed to create a new oak barrel out of an old one. An

Oak aging, *above*
Hundreds of litres of wine maturing in Chianti, Italy. The wood, which is rarely new oak, has a profound effect on the wine's eventual flavour.

THE COST OF NEW OAK

Two-hundred 225-litre (49-gallon) oak casks with a total capacity of 450 hectolitres (9,900 gallons) cost between four and ten times the cost of a single 450 hectolitre (9,900 gallon) stainless-steel vat. After two years of substantially higher labour costs to operate and maintain the large number of small units, the volume of wine produced in the oak casks is 10 per cent less because of evaporation, and the winemaker faces the prospect of purchasing another two hundred casks.

Australian firm has gone one step further by constructing a square stainless-steel tank with two oak panels that are comprised of oak staves that can be replaced, reversed, and even adjusted in size to give different oak-to-wine ratios.

RACKING

Draining the clear wine off its lees, or sediment, into another vat or cask is known as "racking" because of the different levels, or racks, on which the wine is run from one container to another. In modern vinification, this operation is usually conducted several times throughout the maturation period in vat or cask. Gradually the wine throws off less and less of a deposit. Some wines, such as Muscadet *sur lie* for example, are never racked.

FINING

After fermentation, wine may or may not look hazy to the eye, yet still contain suspended matter that threatens cloudiness in the bottle. Fining usually assists the clarification of wine at this stage, although it is occasionally used on fresh grape juice prior to fermentation. In addition to this, special fining agents may be employed to remove unwanted characteristics. When a fining agent is added to wine, it adheres to cloudy matter by physical or electrolytic attraction, creating tiny clusters, known as colloids, which drop to the bottom of the vat in the form of sediment. The most commonly encountered fining agents are: egg white; tannin; gelatine; bentonite; isinglass; and casein. Winemakers have their preferences and fining agents also have their specific uses, thus positively charged egg white fines out negatively charged matter (for example, unwanted tannins or anthocyanins), while negatively charged bentonite fines out positively charged matter (for example, protein haze and other organic matter). Most common of the special finings is "blue fining" (illegal in some countries).

COLD STABILIZATION

When wines are subjected to low temperatures, a crystalline deposit of tartrates can form a deposit in the bottle. Should the wine be dropped to a very low temperature for a few days prior to bottling, this process can be precipitated, rendering the wine safe from the threat of a tartrate deposit in the bottle. For the past twenty years this operation has been almost obligatory for cheap commercial wines, but cold stabilization is now increasingly used for those of better quality. This recent trend is a pity because the crystals are harmless and their presence is a completely welcome indication of a considerably more natural, rather than heavily-processed, wine.

THE USE OF SULPHUR

Sulphur dioxide, or SO_2 as it is known, is used in winemaking from the time the grapes arrive at the winery until just before the wine is bottled. It has anti-oxidant, aseptic and other qualities that make it essential for commercial winemaking. All wines are oxidized to some extent, from the moment the grapes are pressed and the juice is exposed to the air, but the rate of oxidation must be controlled. Occasionally a winemaker claims that SO_2 is superfluous, but wines produced without it are either totally oxidized or downright filthy.

Wines can also be over-sulphured, though these are less common than they were in the past. Over-sulphured wines are easily recognizable by their smell, which ranges from the slight whiff of a recently ignited match to the pong of bad eggs. The methods for reducing the level of SO_2 are well-known, the most important of which is a very judicious initial dosage because a resistance to sulphur builds up and subsequent doses have to be proportionately larger.

FROM GRAPE TO GLASS

Virtually every ingredient of fresh grape juice can be found in the wine it makes. Although additional compounds are produced when wine is made and any sedimented matter is disposed of before wine is bottled, the most significant difference in the two lists below is the disappearance of fermentable sugar and the appearance of alcohol.

The "ingredients" of fresh grape juice

% BY VOLUME

73.5	**Water**	
25	**Carbohydrates**, of which:	
	5%	Cellulose
	20%	Sugar (plus pentoses, pectin, inositol)
0.8	**Organic acids**, of which:	
	0.54%	Tartaric acid
	0.25%	Malic acid
	0.01%	Citric acid (plus possible traces of succinic acid & lactic acid)
0.5	**Minerals**, of which:	
	0.025%	Calcium
	0.01%	Chloride
	0.025%	Magnesium
	0.25%	Potassium
	0.05%	Phosphate
	0.005%	Silicic acid
	0.035%	Sulphate
	0.1%	Others (aluminium, boron, copper, iron, molybdenum, rubidium, sodium, zinc)
0.13	**Tannin and colour pigments**	
0.07	**Nitrogenous matter**, of which:	
	0.05%	Amino acids (arginine, glutamic acid, proline, serine, threonine and others)
	0.005%	Protein
	0.015%	Other nitrogenous matter (humin, amide, ammonia and others)
Traces	**Mainly vitamins** (thiamine, riboflavin, pyridoxine, pantothenic acid, nicotinic acid and ascorbic acid)	

The "contents" of wine

% BY VOLUME

86	**Water**	
12	**Alcohol** (ethyl alcohol)	
1	**Glycerol**	
0.4	**Organic acids**, of which:	
	0.20%	Tartaric acid
	0.15%	Lactic acid
	0.05%	Succinic acid (plus traces of malic acid, citric acid)
0.2	**Carbohydrates** (unfermentable sugar)	
0.2	**Minerals**, of which:	
	0.02%	Calcium
	0.01%	Chloride
	0.02%	Magnesium
	0.075%	Potassium
	0.05%	Phosphate
	0.005%	Silicic acid
	0.02%	Sulphate
	Traces	Aluminium, boron, copper, iron, molybdenum, rubidium, sodium, zinc
0.1	**Tannin & colour pigments**	
0.045	**Volatile acids** (mostly acetic acid)	
0.025	**Nitrogenous matter**, of which:	
	0.01%	Amino acids (arginine, glutamic acid, proline, serine, threonine and others)
	0.015%	Protein and other nitrogenous matter (humin, amide, ammonia and others)
0.025	**Esters** (mostly ethyl acetate, but traces of numerous others)	
0.004	**Aldehydes** (mostly acetaldehyde, some vanillin and traces of others)	
0.001	**Higher alcohols** (minute quantities of amyl plus traces of isoamyl, butyl, isobutyl, hexyl, propyl and methyl may be present)	
Traces	**Vitamins** Includes thiamine, riboflavin, pyridoxine, pantothenic acid, nicotinic acid and ascorbic acids	

Red wines

On arrival at the winery the grapes nearly always go through a crusher and usually a de-stemmer, although in bygone days it was the accepted practice to leave the grapes on their stems in order to promote a more tannic wine. The tannins in the stems, however, were found to be too harsh and failed to soften as the wine matured. With this knowledge the modern winemaker is able to include a small percentage of stems if the grape variety he uses requires extra structure or if the vintage in question needs firming up.

Fermentation

After de-stemming and a light crushing, the grapes are pumped into a vat and fermentation can commence as soon as 12 hours later, or take several days to get going. Even wines that will be cask-fermented must start off in vats, whether they are old-fashioned oak *foudres* or modern stainless-steel tanks, because of the cap, or manta, of grapeskins with which they must ferment. To encourage fermentation the juice might be heated and selected yeast cultures or some partially fermented wine from another vat could be added. During fermentation the juice is pumped from the bottom of the vat to the top and sprayed over the manta to keep the juice in contact with the grapeskins. This ensures maximum extraction of colour pigments. Other methods entail the manual submerging of the manta by pushing it under the fermenting juice with poles. Some vats are equipped with crude but effective grids that prevent the cap rising, others rely on the carbonic gas given off during fermentation to form pressure that is periodically released to power the pushing of the manta beneath the surface, and one system has been developed that keeps the manta submerged in a sealed, rotating stainless-steel tank, called a "vinimatic", based on the cement-mixer principle.

The higher the temperature during fermentation, the greater the extraction of colour and tannin; the lower the temperature, the better the bouquet, freshness and fruit. The optimum temperature for the fermentation of red wine is 29.4°C (85°F). If too hot, certain substances (decanoic acid, octanoic acids and corresponding esters) are produced by yeasts that inhibit their own ability to feed on nutrients and so the yeasts die. It is, however, far better to ferment hot fresh juice than to wait two weeks (which is normal in many cases) to ferment cool but stale juice. The fuller, darker, more tannic and potentially longer-lived wines remain in contact with the skins for anything between ten and 30 days. Lighter wines are separated from the skins after merely a few days.

Vin de goutte and *vin de presse*

Whatever the style of wine, the moment the skins are separated from the juice the wine is divided into two: free-run, or *vin de goutte*, and press wine, or *vin de presse*. The free-run juice is, as its name implies, freely run out of the vat when the tap is opened. What remains, that is to say the manta of grapeskins, pips and other solids, is put into a press that extracts a very dark-coloured and extremely tannic juice called the press wine. The free-run wine and the press wine are pumped into separate containers, either vats or casks depending on the style of the wine to be produced. These wines then undergo their malolactic conversion separately and are then racked several times, fined, racked again, blended together then fined and racked once more before being bottled.

MACÉRATION CARBONIQUE

This is a generic term that covers many variants of a technique, used almost exclusively for red-winemaking, that involves an initial fermentation under pressure of carbonic gas. The traditional method, which dates back at least two hundred years, was to place the grapes, uncrushed, in a closed container and after a while a natural fermentation *inside* the grapes would take place. Eventually the grapes exploded, filling the container with carbonic gas, after which a normal fermentation continued under the building pressure and the grapes macerated in their own skins. Today the grapes are often placed in vats that are then filled with carbonic gas from a bottle. *Macération carbonique* produces light wines with good colour, soft fruit and a "pear-drop" aroma.

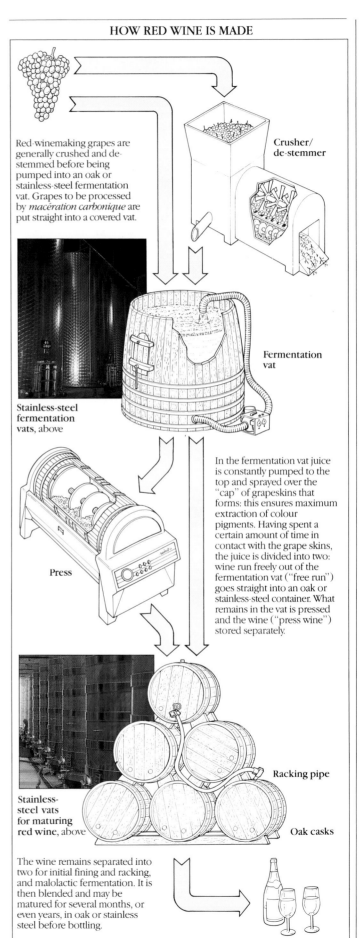

HOW RED WINE IS MADE

Red-winemaking grapes are generally crushed and de-stemmed before being pumped into an oak or stainless-steel fermentation vat. Grapes to be processed by *macération carbonique* are put straight into a covered vat.

Crusher/de-stemmer

Stainless-steel fermentation vats, above

Fermentation vat

In the fermentation vat juice is constantly pumped to the top and sprayed over the "cap" of grapeskins that forms: this ensures maximum extraction of colour pigments. Having spent a certain amount of time in contact with the grape skins, the juice is divided into two: wine run freely out of the fermentation vat ("free run") goes straight into an oak or stainless-steel container. What remains in the vat is pressed and the wine ("press wine") stored separately.

Press

Stainless-steel vats for maturing red wine, above

Racking pipe

Oak casks

The wine remains separated into two for initial fining and racking, and malolactic fermentation. It is then blended and may be matured for several months, or even years, in oak or stainless steel before bottling.

White wines

Until fairly recently it could be said that two initial operations distinguished the white-winemaking process from the red one: first, an immediate pressing to extract the juice and separate the skins, and, second, the purging or cleansing of this juice. But for wines of expressive varietal character the grapes are now often crushed and then macerated in a vinimatic for 12 to 48 hours to extract aromatics stored in the skins. The juice run out of the vinimatic, and the juice that is pressed out of the macerated pulp left inside it, then undergoes purging, cleansing and fermentation like any other white wine.

With the exception of wines macerated in a vinimatic, the grapes are pressed immediately on arrival at the winery or lightly crushed and then pressed. The juice from the last pressing is murky in colour, bitter and low in acidity and sugar, therefore only the first pressing, which is roughly equivalent to the free-run juice in red wine, together with the richest elements of the second pressing, should be used for white-wine production. Once pressed, the juice is pumped into a vat where it is purged, or cleansed, which in its simplest form merely entails leaving the juice to settle, during which time the particles of skin and other impurities fall to the bottom. This purging may be helped by chilling, adding sulphur dioxide and, possibly, a fining agent. Light filtration and centrifugation may also be applied.

After cleansing, the juice is pumped into the fermenting vat or directly into barrels if the wine is to be cask-fermented. The opportunity to add selected yeast cultures occurs more often in the production of white wine because of the wine's limited contact with the yeast-bearing skins and the additional cleansing that reduces the potential amount of wine yeasts available. The optimum temperature for fermenting white wine is 18°C (64°F), although many winemakers opt for between 10 and 17°C (50-63°F), and it is possible to ferment wine at temperatures as low as 4°C (39°F). At lower temperatures, more esters and other aromatics are created, less volatile acidity is produced, and a lower dose of sulphur dioxide is required, but the wines are lighter in body and contain less glycerol.

With acidity an essential factor in the balance of fruit and, where appropriate, sweetness in white wines, many products are not permitted to undergo malolactic conversion and are not bottled until some 12 months after the harvest. Oak-matured wines which, incidentally, always undergo malolactic conversion, may be bottled between nine and 18 months, but wines made for early drinking are racked, fined, filtered and bottled as quickly as the process will allow in order to retain as much freshness and fruitiness as possible.

Rosé wines

With the exception of pink Champagne, most of which is made by blending white wine with a little red, all quality rosés are produced by one of three basic methods: bleeding, pressing or limited maceration. A true-bled rosé is made from the tainted juice that issues from black grapes pressed under their own weight. This is a sort of *tête de cuvée* that, after fermentation, yields a very pale *vin gris* colour, but with a rich, fruity and exquisitely fresh flavour. Pressed rosé is made by pressing black grapes until the juice assumes sufficient colour. It too has a pale *vin gris* colour, but without the true richness of a *tête de cuvée* rosé. Limited maceration is the most common method, and during this process rosé is made in exactly the same way as red wine, but, as the name implies, the duration of skin-contact is limited to that which is sufficient to give the desired tint of pink. All shades of rosé exist, ranging from barely perceptible to *clairet* or almost red. Some superior rosé wines made by this last method are virtually by-products of red wine production. In certain areas that lack the climate to produce deep red wines, some free-run juice might be run off to produce rosé, in order to leave a greater ratio of colouring pigment in the juice that remains.

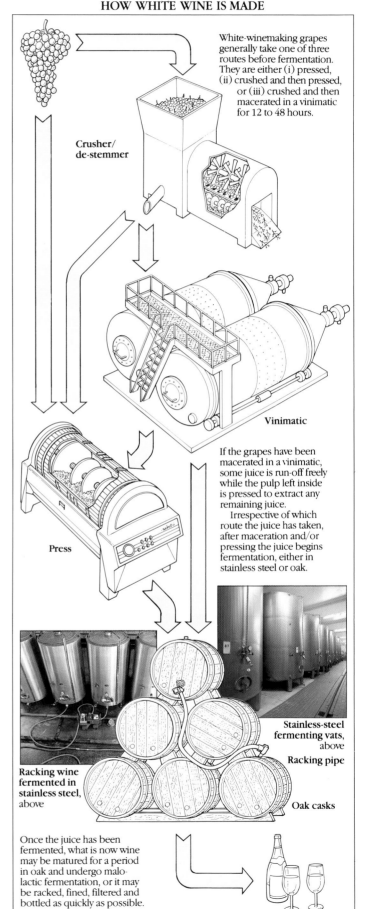

HOW WHITE WINE IS MADE

White-winemaking grapes generally take one of three routes before fermentation. They are either (i) pressed, (ii) crushed and then pressed, or (iii) crushed and then macerated in a vinimatic for 12 to 48 hours.

Crusher/de-stemmer

Vinimatic

If the grapes have been macerated in a vinimatic, some juice is run-off freely while the pulp left inside is pressed to extract any remaining juice.

Irrespective of which route the juice has taken, after maceration and/or pressing the juice begins fermentation, either in stainless steel or oak.

Press

Stainless-steel fermenting vats, above

Racking pipe

Racking wine fermented in stainless steel, above

Oak casks

Once the juice has been fermented, what is now wine may be matured for a period in oak and undergo malolactic fermentation, or it may be racked, fined, filtered and bottled as quickly as possible.

Sparkling wines

When grape juice is fermented, sugar is converted into alcohol and carbonic gas. In the production of still wines the gas is allowed to escape, but should it be prevented from so doing, by putting a lid on a vat or a cork in a bottle, it will remain dissolved in the wine itself until that lid or cork is removed. When the gas is released it rushes out of the wine in the form of bubbles. This is the basic principle upon which all natural sparkling wines are made, using one of the following methods:

Méthode champenoise

This refers to a sparkling wine that has undergone a second fermentation in the bottle in which it is sold. A label may refer to a wine being "Individually fermented in this bottle", which is the beautifully simple American equivalent of *méthode champenoise*.

Bottle fermented

This refers to a wine produced through a second fermentation in a bottle, but (and this is the catch) not the bottle in which it is sold. It is fermented in one bottle, transferred to a vat and, under pressure at –3°C (26°F), filtered and put into another bottle. This is also known as the "transfer method".

Méthode rurale

This refers to the precursor of *méthode champenoise* that is still used today, albeit for a few obscure wines. It involves no second fermentation, the wine being bottled prior to the termination of the first alcoholic fermentation.

Cuve close, Charmat or Tank method

This is used for the bulk production of inexpensive sparkling wines that have undergone second fermentation in large tanks prior to filtration and bottling under pressure at –3°C (26°F). Contrary to popular belief, there is no evidence to suggest that this is an intrinsically inferior method of sparkling-wine production. Only because it is a bulk production method does it tend to attract mediocre base wines and encourage a quick throughput. I genuinely suspect that a *cuve close* produced from the finest base wines of Champagne and given the autolytic benefit of at least three years on its lees before bottling might well be indistinguishable from the "real thing".

CARBONATION

This is the cheapest method of putting bubbles into wine and is, simply, injecting it with carbon dioxide. Because this is the method used to make lemonade, it is incorrectly assumed that the bubbles achieved through carbonation are large and short-lived. They can be, and fully sparkling wines made by this method will indeed be, cheapskates, but modern carbonation plants have the ability to induce the tiniest of bubbles, even to the point of imitating the "prickle" of wine bottled *sur lie*.

Fortified wines

Any wine, dry or sweet, red or white, to which alcohol has been added is classified as a fortified wine, whatever the inherent differences of vinification may be. Normal still wines have a strength of 8.5 to 18 per cent alcohol; fortified wines have a strength of 17 to 24 per cent. The spirit added is usually, but not always, brandy produced from local wines. It is absolutely neutral, with no hint of any sort of brandy flavour. The amount of alcohol added, and when and how it is added, is as critical to the character of a fortified wine as its grape variety or area of production. Any one of the following methods may be used:

Mutage

This is the addition of alcohol to fresh grape juice. This prevents fermentation and produces fortified wines, known as *vins de liqueurs* in France, such as Pineau des Charentes and Ratafia.

Manufacturing alcohol, *above*
At a government distillery in the Douro, Portugal, alcohol to fortify Port is made with mechanized efficiency.

Early fortification

This is the addition of alcohol after fermentation has commenced. This often happens not in one operation, but in several carefully measured and timed smaller additions spread out over several hours or even days. Exactly when during the fermentation this takes place will depend on the style of fortified wine being made, and this itself will be affected by the variable strength of the grapes harvested from year to year. On average, however, the alcohol added to Port is applied after fermentation has reached six to eight per cent, while that added to the *vins doux naturels* of France, such as Muscat de Beaumes de Venise, is applied at any stage of the fermentation after the alcohol level reaches five per cent but before ten per cent.

Late fortification

This is the addition of alcohol after fermentation has ceased. The classic drink produced by this method is Sherry, which is always vinified dry, with any sweetness being added afterwards.

Aromatized wines

With the exception of Retsina, the famous resinated Greek wine, aromatized wines are all of the fortified ilk. The one thing they have in common is, as the name suggests, the addition of various aromatic ingredients. The most important of these aromatized wines is Vermouth, which is made from neutral white wines of two to three years old that are blended with an extract of wormwood (Vermouth is a corruption of the German *wermut* or "wormwood"), vanilla and various other herbs and spices. Italian Vermouths are produced in Apulia and Sicily, and French Vermouths in Languedoc and Roussillon. "Chambéry" is a delicate generic Vermouth from the Savoie and "Chambéryzette", a red-pink version flavoured with alpine strawberries, but such precise geographical aromatized wines are rare. Most are in fact made and sold under internationally recognized brands such as "Cinzano" and "Martini". Other well-known aromatized wines include "Amer Picon", "Byrrh", "Dubonnet" (in both red and white styles), "Punt e Mes", "St.-Raphael", and "Suze".

Glossary of major grape varieties

Of the thousands of different grape varieties grown world-wide, the most significant − in one major area or across several continents − are profiled over the next nine pages.

CROSSES AND HYBRIDS

A CROSS BETWEEN GRAPE VARIETIES within one species is called simply, a cross, whereas a cross between varieties from different species is called a hybrid. Cross the same grape varieties more than once and the odds are that the new strains produced will not be the same. Thus *Sylvaner x Riesling* is not only the parentage of the Rieslaner, but also the Scheurebe, two totally different grapes. It is also possible to cross a variety with itself and produce a different grape. In this glossary, and throughout the book, the parentage of crosses and hybrids are always in italic.

CLONES AND CLONING

Intensive selection can, within varietal limitations, produce a vine to suit specific conditions: for example, to increase yield, or to resist certain diseases or to thrive in a particular climate. Identical clones of this vine can then be replicated an infinite number of times by micro-biogenetic techniques. Clones are named by number and initial. For instance, "Riesling clone 88Gm" is the 88th clone of the Riesling variety produced at Geisenheim (Gm), the German viticultural research station.

A "localized" clone is a vine that has evolved naturally under specific conditions within a particular environment. These may be named first by grape variety and then by locality and referred to as sub-varieties. However, the name of the original variety is often forgotten with the passing of time, so the variety acquires a new name altogether.

SYNONYMS

Many grape varieties are known by several different synonyms. The Malbec has at least 34; it is called the Pressac in St. Emilion and other names include the Auxerrois, Balouzet, Cahors, Cot, Estrangey, Grifforin and so on. This would not be too confusing if the synonyms applied, uniquely, to the same grape variety, but this is not so. To take the Malbec example; this grape is known as the Auxerrois in Cahors, yet the Auxerrois in Alsace and Chablis is a white grape similar to, but not the same as, the Pinot blanc, whereas the Malbec is of course a black grape. To add to the confusion, in parts of France the Malbec is known as the Cahors!

Synonyms relating to localized clones or sub-varieties are often regarded as singularly separate varieties in their own right. The Italian Trebbiano, itself a synonym for the French Ugni blanc, has many sub-varieties recognized by the Italian vine regulations. Also many synonyms revolve around the name of another grape variety, but they may not necessarily be related. Ampelographers distinguish between "erroneous" and "misleading" synonyms. The former refers to varieties given the name of another, totally different variety, while the latter refers to varieties whose names suggest, incorrectly, that they are related to another variety − for example, Pinot chardonnay.

GRAPE COLOUR

Most white wines are produced from so-called "white" grapes that can actually range in colour from green to amber-yellow. On the other hand, most red or rosé wines are made from so-called "black" grapes that in turn can be anything from red to blue-black. White wine can also be made from most of these black grapes because only the skin is coloured, not the juice (there are a very few exceptions, categorized as *teinturier* grapes, literally "dyer" grapes). Red wine, however, can only be made from black grapes, because it is pigments in the black skin, called anthocyanins, which give the wine its colour. The degree of acidity in the skin's sap affects the colour of its wine: high acid levels give wines of a ruddy colour, while the lower the acidity the more purple and eventually violet, wine becomes.

White grape varieties

Note: some pink-coloured varieties such as *Gewürztraminer* are included in this section because the wine they make is essentially white.

ALBALONGA

A *Rieslaner x Sylvaner* cross developed and grown in Germany for its naturally high sugar level and early-ripening qualities.

ALTESSE

The finest of Savoie's traditional varieties, this grape makes delightfully rich and fragrant wines.

Synonyms: *Mâconnais, Roussette*

ALIGOTÉ

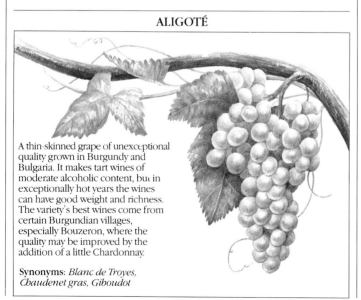

A thin-skinned grape of unexceptional quality grown in Burgundy and Bulgaria. It makes tart wines of moderate alcoholic content, but in exceptionally hot years the wines can have good weight and richness. The variety's best wines come from certain Burgundian villages, especially Bouzeron, where the quality may be improved by the addition of a little Chardonnay.

Synonyms: *Blanc de Troyes, Chaudenet gras, Giboudot*

ALVARINHO

The classic Vinho Verde grape, though it might not rank as a classic grape variety *per se.*

ARBOIS

An interesting but very localized variety cultivated in the Loire Valley, where it is sometimes blended with another obscure grape called the Romorantin.

Synonyms: *Menu pineau, Petit pineau, Verdet*

ARINTO

One of Portugal's potentially excellent white grapes. Its use in Bucelas is to make a crisp, lemony wine that ages well.

ASSYRTIKO

One of the better-quality indigenous varieties of Greece.

AUXERROIS

Often confused with the Pinot blanc, but in fact a totally separate variety, this grape is grown most successfully in Alsace and is up-and-coming in England. Its wine is fatter than that of the Pinot blanc and so suits cooler situations.

BACCHUS

A *(Sylvaner x Riesling)* x *Müller-Thurgau* cross that is one of Germany's more superior crosses. In recent years a considerable acreage has been grown in Germany's Rheinhessen region. It is also grown in England because of its inherently high sugar level and can produce vivacious, fruity wines in both countries.

BLANQUETTE

A synonym for the Colombard in the Tarn-et-Garonne *département* of France, the Clairette in the Aude *département,* and the Ondenc in Bordeaux.

BOUVIER

A modest-quality grape variety significantly cultivated in Austria and one which, under its Ranina synonym, produces the "Tiger's Milk" wine of Yugoslavia.

Synonyms: *Bouviertraube, Ranina*

BUAL

The richest and fattest of Madeira's four classic grape varieties. The Bual may also be grown in many parts of southern Portugal.

CHARDONNAY

The greatest dry white wine grape in the world, despite its proliferation in virtually every commercial wine-making area. Once erroneously thought to be a member of the Pinot family, this classic variety is responsible for producing the greatest white Burgundies and is one of the three major grape types used in the production of Champagne.

Synonyms: *Arnaison, Aubaine, Beaunois, Chasselas, Epinette blanche, Feiner weisser burgunder, Melon blanc, Melon d'arbois, Muscadet, Petite sainte-marie, Pinot blanc, Pinot blanc chardonnay, Pinot chardonnay, Weisser clevner*

CHASSELAS

A modest-quality variety that produces the best-forgotten Pouilly-sur-Loire wines (not to be confused with Pouilly-Blanc Fumé wines of the same area) and is probably at its modest best (and known as the Fendant) in the Valais, Switzerland.

The Chasselas is, by all accounts, the most popular table grape in France, but as strange as it might seem, good eating grapes rarely make good wine grapes.

Synonyms: *Chardonnay, Chasselas blanc, Chasselas doré, Dorin, Fendant, Fendant blanc, Frauentraube, Golden chasselas, Gutedel, Mosttraube, Royal muscadine, Süssling*

CLAIRETTE

A sugar-rich, intrinsically flabby grape best known for its many wines of southern France. It is the Muscat, though, not the Clairette, which is chiefly responsible for the "Clairette de Die" in the Rhône.

Synonyms: *Blanquette, Clairette blanc, Clairette blanche*

COLOMBARD

A grape that produces thin and acidic wine ideal for the distillation of Armagnac and Cognac, but that has adapted well to the hotter winelands of California and South Africa, where its high acidity is a positive attribute.

Synonyms: *Blanquette, Colombar, Colombier, French colombard, Guenille, Pied-tendre, Queue-tendre, Queue-verte*

CRUCHEN BLANC

A widely-cultivated variety that usually, but erroneously, has the tag of Riesling hung on it.

Synonyms: *Cape riesling* (in South Africa), *Clare riesling* (in Australia), *Paarl riesling* (in South Africa)

DELAWARE

An American hybrid of uncertain parentage that was developed in Frenchtown, New Jersey, and propagated in Delaware, Ohio, in the mid-nineteenth century. Although grown in New York State and Brazil, it is far more popular in Japan.

EHRENFELSER

A *Riesling* x *Sylvaner* cross; one of the best of Germany's new breed of crosses.

ELBLING

A variety once held in high esteem in both Germany and France. The major Mosel grape in the nineteenth century, it is now mostly confined to the Obermosel where its very acid, neutral flavour makes it useful for the German *Sekt* industry. In Alsace it was known as the Knipperlé and its former position was such that one of the *Grand Cru* Guebwiller slopes was named after it.

Synonyms: *Alben, Albig, Alva* (in Portugal), *Briesgaver, Briesgaver riesling, Burger elbling, Elben, Gelder ortlieber, Grossriesling, Kleinberger, Kleinergelber, Kleiner räuschling, Klein reuschling, Knipperlé, Kurztingel* (in Austria), *Ortlieber, Räuschling, Seretonina* (in Yugoslavia), *Weisser elbling*

EMERALD RIESLING

A *Muscadelle* x *Riesling* cross, developed for cultivation in California by a Professor Olmo as the sister to his Ruby cabernet cross, a combination of Cabernet sauvignon and Carignan.

FABER

A *Weissburgunder* x *Müller-Thurgau* cross grown in Germany, where it produces a fruity wine with a light Muscat aroma.

FOLLE BLANCHE

Traditionally used for the distillation of Armagnac and Cognac, this grape also produces the Gros plant wine of the Nantais district of the Loire Valley.

Synonyms: *Camobraque, Chalosse, Enragé, Enrageade, Folle enrageat, Gros plant, Gros plant du Nantais, Picpoul, Picpoule*

FORTA

A *Madeleine Angevine* x *Sylvaner* cross, a little of which is grown in Germany, where it produces good-quality grapes that are rich in sugar.

FREISAMER

A *Sylvaner* x *Pinot gris* cross that is grown in Germany and produces a full, neutral, Sylvaner-like wine.

FURMINT

A strong and distinctively flavoured grape that is the most important variety used to make Tokay in Hungary.

Synonym: *Sipon*

GARGANEGA BIANCO

An Italian variety that is the principal grape used in the production of Soave.

CHENIN BLANC

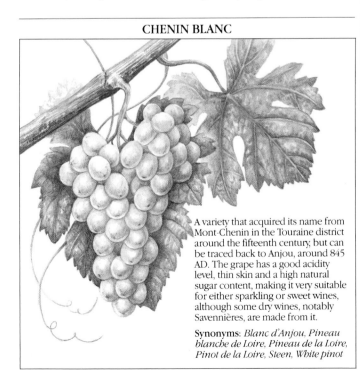

A variety that acquired its name from Mont-Chenin in the Touraine district around the fifteenth century, but can be traced back to Anjou, around 845 AD. The grape has a good acidity level, thin skin and a high natural sugar content, making it very suitable for either sparkling or sweet wines, although some dry wines, notably Savennières, are made from it.

Synonyms: *Blanc d'Anjou, Pineau blanche de Loire, Pineau de la Loire, Pinot de la Loire, Steen, White pinot*

GEWÜRZTRAMINER

At its most clear-cut and varietally distinctive in Alsace, this variety produces very aromatic wines, often described as spicy, but its complex bouquet can range from grapey-muskiness to pungent pepperyness. Originally from the Pfalz region in Germany, the Gewürztraminer was introduced into Alsace after 1871, since when it has been successfully transplanted as far afield as South Africa and California, where its characteristics are softer.

Synonyms: *Christkindltraube, Clevner, Dreimanner, Drumin, Edeltraube, Fermin rouge, Flaischweiner, Frankisch, Frenscher, Fromenteau rouge, Fuszeres, Gentil-duret rouge, Gris rouge, Haiden, Heida, Klavner, Kleinweiner, Mala dinka, Liwora, Pinat cervena, Ptinc cerveny, Ranfoliza, Rdeci traminac, Rotclevner, Rotedel, Roter nurnberger, Roter traminer, Rotfranke, Rousselet, Rusa, Savagnin rosé, Termeno aromatico, Traminac, Traminac creveni, Traminer, Traminer aromatico, Traminer aromatique, Traminer musqué, Traminer parfumé, Traminer rosé, Traminer rosso, Traminer roz, Traminer rozovy, Tramini, Tramini piros*

GLORIA

A *Sylvaner* x *Müller-Thurgau* cross grown in Germany, where it produces grapes that are rich in sugar, but wines of rather neutral character.

GRENACHE BLANC

The white Grenache variant that is widely planted in France and Spain. It is an ancient Spanish variety that has the potential to produce a good-quality, full-bodied wine.

Synonyms: *Garnacha blanca, Garnacho blanco, Garnaxta*

GRÜNER VELTLINER

The most important wine grape in Austria, where it produces fresh, well-balanced wines, with a light fruity, sometimes slightly spicy, flavour.

Synonyms: *Grüner, Grünmuskateller, Veltliner, Veltlini* (in Hungary), *Weissgipfler*

GUTENBORNER

A *Müller-Thurgau* x *Chasselas* cross grown in Germany and England. It produces grapes with intrinsically high sugar levels, but rather neutral wines.

HÁRSLEVELÜ

A Hungarian grape that is the second most important Tokay variety. It produces a full, rich and powerfully perfumed wine.

HUXELREBE

A *Chasselas* x *Muscat courtillier* cross grown in Germany and England, capable of producing good-quality wine.

JACQUÈRE

The work-horse grape of the Savoie.

Synonyms: *Buisserate, Cugnette*

JOHANNISBERG RIESLING

A synonym often used to distinguish a wine made from the true Riesling grape. Many people believe that the Riesling is at its classic best when grown in the Rheingau vineyards of Johannisberg, thus the synonym probably evolved as a way of indicating that a wine contained Riesling grapes "as grown in Johannisberg".

KANZLER

A *Müller-Thurgau* x *Sylvaner* cross that produces a good Sylvaner substitute in the Rheinhessen.

KERNER

A *Trollinger* x *Riesling* cross grown in Germany, South Africa and England. It produces Riesling-like wines with a high natural sugar content and good acidity, but a very light aroma.

LEN DE L'ELH

A flavoursome, naturally sugar-rich grape used in Gaillac, France.

Synonym: *Cavalier*

MACABÉO

A Spanish variety used to "lift" a sparkling Cava blend and give it freshness. Bearing the name of Viura, it is also responsible for the "new wave" of fresh, unoaked white Rioja.

Synonyms: *Alcañol, Alcañon, Ilegó, Lardot, Maccabéo, Maccabeu, Viura*

MADELEINE ANGEVINE

A *Précoce de Malingre* x *Madeleine royale* cross grown quite successfully in England, where it produces a light-bodied, aromatic wine.

MANSENG

The Gros manseng and Petit manseng are grown in southwest France, and are well known for producing the legendary Jurançon Moelleux.

Synonyms: *Manseng blanc, Petit mansenc*

MARIENSTEINER

A *Sylvaner* x *Rieslaner* cross grown in Germany and generally considered superior to the Sylvaner.

MARSANNE

A grape that makes fat, rich, full wines and one of the two major varieties used to produce the rare white wines of Hermitage and Châteauneuf-du-Pape.

Synonyms: *Grosse roussette, Ermitage blanc, Hermitage blanc*

MAUZAC

A late-ripening grape with good natural acidity, grown in southwest France. Flexible in the styles of wine it produces, it is particularly suitable for sparkling wine.

Synonyms: *Blanc-lafitte, Maussac, Mauzac blanc, Moisac*

MELON DE BOURGOGNE

A variety transplanted from Burgundy to the Nantais district to replace its less hardy vines after the terrible winter of 1709. It is most famous for its production of Muscadet. When fully ripe, it produces very flabby wines, lacking in acidity.

Synonyms: *Gamay blanc, Gamay blanc à feuille ronds, Gros auxerrois, Lyonnaise blanche, Melon, Muscadet, Pinot blanc* (in California), *Weisserburgunder* (in Germany)

MERLOT BLANC

A variety cultivated on a surprisingly large scale on the right-bank of the Gironde, yet according to ampelographer Pierre Galet it is not related to the more famous black Merlot variety.

MORIO-MUSKAT

A *Sylvaner* x *Pinot blanc* cross widely grown in the Rheinpfalz and Rheinhessen of Germany. Intriguingly, its powerfully aromatic character is the inverse of the neutral character displayed by both its parents.

MÜLLER-THURGAU

A variety bred at Geisenheim in 1882 by Professor Hermann Müller, who hailed from the canton of Thurgau in Switzerland, and named after him by August Dern in 1891. The variety was originally believed to be a *Riesling* x *Sylvaner* cross, but not one single plant has ever reverted to Sylvaner, and the closest resemblance to it is the Rabaner, a *Riesling* (clone 88Gm) x *Riesling* (clone 64Gm). This seems to confirm the theory that the Müller-Thurgau is in fact a self-pollinated Riesling seed. It is more prolific than the Riesling, has a typically flowery bouquet and good fruit, but lacks the Riesling's sharpness of definition. Although the variety has a justifiably important position in the production of German *tafelweins*, its cultivation in the classic Riesling vineyards of the Mosel devalues that great wine region. It is widely planted in English and New Zealand vineyards.

Synonyms: *Mueller-Thurgau, Rivaner, Riesling-sylvaner*

MULTANER

A *Riesling* x *Sylvaner* cross. A small amount is grown in Germany, but the area planted is declining because the grapes need to be very ripe to produce good-quality wine.

MUSCADELLE

A singular variety that has nothing to do with the Muscat family, although it does in fact have a distinctive musky aroma. There is, confusingly, a South African synonym for the Muscat – the Muskadel – though it is not related to the Muscadet or Melon de bourgogne, despite the inference of one of its synonyms. In Bordeaux, small quantities add a certain lingering "after-smell" to some of the sweet wines, but the Muscadelle is at its sublime best in Australia where it is called the Tokay and produces a fabulously rich and sweet "liqueur wine".

Synonyms: *Angélicant, Angélico, Auvernat blanc, Catape, Colle-musquette, Douzanelle, Guépie, Guépie-catape, Guillan, Guillan-musqué, Muscade, Muscadet, Muscadet doux, Muskadel, Musquette, Muscat fou, Raisinotte, Resinotte, Sauvignon vert* (in California), *Tokay* (in Australia)

MUSCAT

A family name for numerous related varieties, sub-varieties and localized clones of the same variety, all of which have a distinctive musky aroma and a pronounced grapey flavour. The wines produced range from dry to sweet, still to sparkling and fortified.

MUSCAT À PETITS GRAINS

There are two versions of this variety – the Muscat blanc à petits grains and the Muscat rosé à petits grains – and some vines that seem to produce a motley crop somewhere in between the two. Where one is cultivated it is common to find the other growing close by or intermingled. The two greatest products produced by petits grains are the dry wines of Alsace and the sweet and lightly fortified Muscat de Beaumes de Venise, although in the production of the former variety is giving way to the Muscat ottonel.

Synonyms for the *Muscat blanc à petits grains*: *Brown muscat, Frontignac, Gelber muscatel, Gelber muscateller, Gelber muskatel, Gelber muskateller, Moscata, Moscata bianca, Moscatel, Moscatel dorado, Moscatel de grano menudo, Moscatel menudo bianco, Moscatello, Moscatello bianco, Moscato, Moscato d'Asti, Moscato di Canelli, Muscatel, Muscatel branco, Muscateller, Muscat, Muscat Cknelli, Muscat doré, Muscat d'Alsace, Muscat Canelli, Muscat de Frontignan, Muscat doré de Frontignan, Muskat, Muskateller, Muskotaly, Muskuti, Sargamuskotaly, Tamyanka, Weisse muskateller, Weiss musketraube, Weissemuskateller, White Frontignan, Zuti muscat, Beli muscat*

Synonyms for the *Muscat rosé à petits grains*: *Moscatel rosé, Muscat d'Alsace, Muscat rosé à petits grains d'Alsace, Rotter muscateller, Rotter muskateller*

MUSCAT D'ALEXANDRIE

An extremely important grape in South Africa, where it makes mostly sweet, but some dry, wines. In France it is responsible for the fortified wine Muscat de Rivesaltes (a very tiny production of unfortified dry Muscat is also made in Rivesaltes), and the grape is also used for both wine and raisin production in California.

Synonyms: *Gordo blanco, Hanepoot, Iskendiriye misketi, Lexia, Moscatel, Moscatel de Alejandria, Moscatel gordo, Moscatel gordo blanco, Moscatel de Málaga, Moscatel romano, Moscatel samsó, Moscatel de Setúbal, Muscat gordo blanco, Muscat roumain, Muscatel, Panse musquée, Zibibbo*

MUSCAT OTTONEL

An east-European variety which, because of its relative hardiness, is replacing the Muscat à petits grains in Alsace.

Synonyms: *Muscadel ottonel, Muskotály*

NOBLESSA

A low-yielding *Madeleine Angevine* x *Sylvaner* cross grown in Germany that produces grapes with a high sugar level.

NOBLING

A *Sylvaner* x *Chasselas* cross grown in Baden, Germany. Its grapes have high sugar and acidity levels.

ONDENC

A grape that was once widely planted in southwest France and was particularly popular in Bergerac, but more is now grown in Australia than in all of France. Its intrinsically high acidity makes it useful for sparkling wines.

Synonyms: *Béquin* (in Bordeaux), *Blanc select, Blanquette, Sercial* (in Australia)

OPTIMA

A *(Sylvaner* x *Riesling)* x *Müller-Thurgau* cross developed relatively recently (1970), yet already widely grown in Germany because it is an even earlier, early-ripening variety than the Müller-Thurgau.

ORTEGA

A *Müller-Thurgau* x *Siegerrebe* cross that is grown in both Germany and England. Its aromatic grapes have a naturally high sugar content and make a pleasantly fragrant and spicy wine.

PALOMINO

The classic Sherry grape variety.

PARELLADA

The major white grape variety of Catalonia, used for still and sparkling Cava wines. In a Cava blend it imparts a distinctive aroma and is used to soften the firm Xarello grape.

Synonyms: *Montonec, Montonech*

PERLE

A *Gewürztraminer* x *Müller-Thurgau* cross grown in Franken, Germany, that can survive winter temperatures as low as $-30°C$ ($-22°F$), and produce a light, fragrant and fruity wine, but in low yields.

Synonyms: *Alzeyer perle*

PINOT BLANC

A variety perhaps at its best in Alsace where it is most successful, producing fruity, well-balanced wines with good grip and alcohol content. Plantings of the true Pinot blanc are gradually diminishing worldwide.

Synonyms: *Beaunois, Chardonnay, Clevner, Fehérburgundi, Grau clevner, Klevner, Pinot blanc vrai auxerrois, Weissburgunder, Weiss clevner*

POULSARD

The Jura's famous pink-skin and pink-juice grape that can produce a fine and aromatic *vin gris.*

Synonym: *Plousard*

PROSECCO

The grape responsible for producing a great deal of very ordinary Italian sparkling wine.

Synonyms: *Glera, Serprina*

RABANER

A *Riesling* (clone 88Gm) x *Riesling* (clone 64Gm) cross that has the dubious honour of being the variety that most resembles the Müller-Thurgau. It is grown in Germany on an experimental basis.

RABIGATO

This is the main white Port grape variety.

Synonyms: *Estreito, Moscatel bravo, Rabo de Ovelha*

RKATSITELI

A grape variety that is grown extensively in Russia, on a scale that would cover the vineyards of Champagne at least ten times over. The Soviets consider it to be a high-quality wine grape; it is also grown in Bulgaria, China, California and New York State.

Synonym: *Rcatzitelli*

REGNER

A *Luglienca bianca* x *Gamay* cross. The parents are a curious combination. Why anyone would consider crossing a table grape with the red wine grape of Beaujolais to create a German white wine variety is a mystery. It produces sugar-rich grapes and mild, Müller-Thurgau-like wines.

REICHENSTEINER

A *Müller-Thurgau* x *Madeleine angevine* x *Calabreser-fröhlich* cross grown in Germany and England. It produces sugar-rich grapes and a mild, delicate, somewhat neutral Sylvaner-like wine.

RHODITIS

A grape used as a supporting variety in the making of Retsina, a use only eclipsed by its suitability for the distilling pot!

RIESLANER

A *Sylvaner* x *Riesling* cross mainly grown in Franken, Germany, where it produces sugar-rich grapes and full-bodied, rather neutral wines.

RIESLING

See below.

ROBOLA

A good-quality Greek grape confined to the island of Cephalonia.

ROMORANTIN

An obscure variety confined to the Loire Valley. It can produce a delicate, attractive and flowery wine if it is not overcropped.

Synonyms: *Dannery, Petit Dannezy, Verneuil*

ROUSSANNE

One of two major varieties used to produce the rare white wines of Hermitage and Châteauneuf-du-Pape in France's Rhône Valley. This grape makes the finer, more delicate wines, while those made from the Marsanne are fatter and richer.

Synonyms: *Bergeron, Greffou, Picotin blanc*

PINOT GRIS

A variety undoubtedly at its best in Alsace, where it can produce succulent, rich and complex wines of great quality. It is also responsible for many sweet fortified wines throughout the world.

Synonyms: *Auvernat gris, Auxerrois gris, Auxois, Fauvet, Fromentot, Grauerburgunder, Grauklevner, Grauer mönch, Grey friar, Grey pinot, Gris cordelier, Malmsey, Malvagia, Malvasia, Malvoisie, Monemrasia, Pinot beurot, Pinot grigio, Ruländer, Rulonski Szürkebarát, Tokaier, Tokay, Tokay d'Alsace, Tokayer, Tokay-Pinot gris*

RIESLING

A classic German grape variety. Although other German grapes and crosses can make good commercial wines, the Riesling, if properly handled, produces a wine of such tremendous fruit-acidity ratio that it is in a different class. It is light in body and low in alcohol, yet intensely flavoured and very long-lived. With some bottle age, the finest Rieslings develop a vivid and zesty bouquet that may be referred to as "petrolly". The grape's susceptibility to botrytis also makes it one of the most scintillating producers of intensely sweet wines.

Synonyms: *Hocheimer, Johannisberger, Johannisberg riesling, Moselriesling, Mosel riesling, Petit rhin, Petit riesling, Rajinski rizling, Rajnai rizling, Reno, Rezlink, Rezlink rynsky, Rheingauer, Rheingau riesling, Rheinriesling, Rhein riesling, Rhine riesling, Riesler, Rieslinger, Riesling du rhin, Riesling renano, Rislig rejnski, Rizling rajinski bijeli, Rýnski rizling, Rössling, Weisser riesling, White riesling*

SACY

A minor grape variety that produces bland "stretching" wine and is grown in small quantities in the Chablis district. Its high acidity could make it very useful in the production of sparkling wines.

Synonyms: *Blanc vert, Farine, Gros blanc, Tresallier*

SAINT-EMILION

A synonym for the Ugni blanc in France and for the Sémillon in Romania.

SAVAGNIN

The grape responsible for the sherry-like "Vin Jaune" of the Jura, the best known of which is Château Chalon. The wine, in fact, takes the name of a commune, not a specific château. A Savagnin rosé grows in the village of Heiligenstein, Alsace, where it is known as the Klevener, as opposed to the Klevner, which is a synonym for the Pinot blanc. The Savagnin noir is merely a synonym for the Pinot noir.

Synonyms: *Formentin* (in Hungary), *Fromenté, Naturé, Salvagnin, Savagnin blanc, Sauvagnin*

SAVATIANO

The grape used by the Greeks to make their famous Retsina. A pure, unresinated Savatiano called Kanza is made in Attica, the heartland of Retsina.

SCHEUREBE

A *Sylvaner* x *Riesling* cross that is one of the best of Germany's new varieties. When ripe, it makes very good varietal wines, but, if harvested early, the bouquet can be quite unpleasant.

SCHÖNBERGER

A *Spatburgunder* x *(Chasselas rosé* x *Muscat Hamburg)* cross grown in Germany and England. It produces sugar-rich grapes that make wine with good aromatic qualities but low acidity.

SÉMILLON

See below left.

SEPTIMER

A *Gewürztraminer* x *Müller-Thurgau* cross grown in Germany, where it is early-ripening and produces sugar-rich grapes and aromatic wines.

SERCIAL

This classic grape of Madeira is reputed to be a distant relative of the Riesling. Judging by its totally different leaf shape, however, this seems unlikely.

SEYVAL BLANC

This *Seibel 5656* x *Seibel 4986* hybrid is the most successful of the many Seyve-Villard crosses. It is grown in France, New York State and England, where it produces attractive wines.

Synonyms: *Seyve-Villard, Seyve-Villard 5276*

SIEGERREBE

A *Madeleine-Angevine* x *Gewürztraminer* cross, widely grown in Germany.

STEEN

The usually accepted synonym for the Chenin blanc used in South Africa. The term "Stein" is also used in South Africa, but refers to a semi-sweet style of white wine. However, many "Stein" blends do contain a large percentage of Steen wine.

SYLVANER

See below.

TROUSSEAU GRIS

A grape now more widely grown in California and New Zealand than in its traditional home of the northern Jura, France. It is yet another grape that has been erroneously tagged with the Riesling name in the new world.

Synonyms: *Gray riesling, Grey riesling*

UGNI BLANC

A variety that usually makes light, even thin wines, which have to be distilled. Because of this, they are ideal for making Armagnac and Cognac. There are exceptions, but most are light, fresh, quaffing wines at their very best,.

Synonyms: *Clairette à grains ronds, Clairette ronde, Clairette de Vence, Graisse, Graisse blanc, Muscat aigre, Rossola, Roussan, Roussanne, Saint-Emilion, Trebbiano* (often with local place name appendaged), *White hermitage*

VERDELHO

A classic Madeira grape.

SAUVIGNON BLANC

A grape at its varietally best-defined in the central vineyards of the Loire, where it produces characteristically aromatic dry wines. In Bordeaux, the dry wines made from it take on a dusty quality, although this is changing due to earlier picking and improved vinification techniques. The grape also contributes to Sauternes and Barsac blends.

Synonyms: *Sauvignon jaune, Blanc fumé, Surin, Fié dans le Neuvillois, Punechon, Puiechou, Gentin à romorantin, Muskat-silvaner, Savagnin musqué, Fumé blanc*

SÉMILLON

The principal grape susceptible to botrytis, or "noble rot", in Sauternes and Barsac. Its aroma is supposed to be reminiscent of lanolin according to some experts, but as pure lanolin is virtually odourless, the comparison does little to convey the distinctive bouquet of this grape. Other, more helpful, suggestive odours are melon or fig, but quite often one is trying to describe the odour and character of botrytized grapes, rather than that of the Sémillon itself.

Synonyms: *Blanc doux, Chevier, Chevrier, Colombier, Crucillant, Hunter riesling* (in Australia), *Hunter River riesling* (in Australia), *Riesling* (in Australia), *Saint-Emilion* (in Romania), *Semijon, Sémillon muscat, Sémillon roux*

SYLVANER

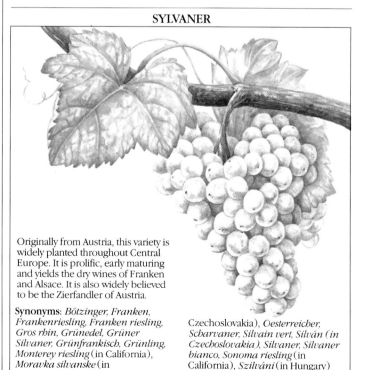

Originally from Austria, this variety is widely planted throughout Central Europe. It is prolific, early maturing and yields the dry wines of Franken and Alsace. It is also widely believed to be the Zierfandler of Austria.

Synonyms: *Bötzinger, Franken, Frankenriesling, Franken riesling, Gros rhin, Grünedel, Grüner Silvaner, Grünfrankisch, Grünling, Monterey riesling* (in California), *Moravka silvanske* (in Czechoslovakia), *Oesterreicher, Scharvaner, Silvain vert, Silván* (in Czechoslovakia), *Silvaner, Silvaner bianco, Sonoma riesling* (in California), *Szilváni* (in Hungary)

VERDICCHIO

Apart from making Verdicchio wine, this grape is also used for blending.

Synonyms: *Marchigiano, Verdone, Uva marana*

VILLARD BLANC

A *Seibel 6468* x *Seibel 6905* hybrid that is the widest-cultivated of the Seyve-Villard crosses in France. Its slightly bitter, iron-rich wine cannot be compared with the attractive wine of the Seyve-Villard 5276 or Seyval blanc grown in England.

VIOGNIER

See right.

WELSCHRIESLING

No relation whatsoever to the true Riesling, this variety is grown throughout Europe, producing ordinary medium-dry to medium-sweet white wines.

Synonyms: *Banatski rizling, Biela sladka grasica, Laskiriesling, Laski rizling, Grassevina, Grasica, Italianski rizling, Italiansky rizling, Olaszriesling, Olasz rizling, Riesling italico, Riesling italianski, Riesling italien, Rismi, Rizling vlassky, Talijanski rizling, Wälschriesling*

WÜRZER

A German variety with the same *Gewürztraminer* x *Müller-Thurgau* origins as the Perle.

XARELLO

A Spanish grape that is very important to the sparkling Cava industry. It makes firm, alcoholic wines that are softened by Parellada and Macabéo grapes.

Synonyms: *Pansa blanca, Xarel·lo*

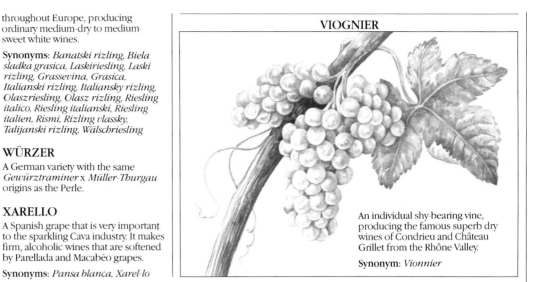

VIOGNIER

An individual shy-bearing vine, producing the famous superb dry wines of Condrieu and Château Grillet from the Rhône Valley.

Synonym: *Vionnier*

Black grape varieties

AGIORGITIKO

An excellent indigenous Greek variety responsible for the rich, and often oak-aged wines of Nemea.

ALICANTE BOUSCHET

A *Petit bouschet* x *Grenache* cross that is a *teinturier* grape, with its vividly-coloured red juice. It is surprisingly widely planted in France and Corsica, is an authorized variety for the production of Port, and is cultivated in Italy, Yugoslavia, North Africa, South Africa and California. In California, it is usually planted in the Central Valley and blended into cheap wine.

ARAMON

The fact that this is the Ugni noir of the wine world says it all. Its wines are usually thin and harsh, but its import-ance in terms of quantity has to be recognized.

Synonyms: *Pisse vin, Ugni noir*

BAGA

Based on the potential of the Bairrada region of Portugal, where this grape accounts for 80 per cent of all grapes grown, it must surely be a dependable variety. However, it has yet to establish truly fine varietal characteristics.

BARBERA

A prolific Italian variety grown in Piedmont, making light, fresh, fruity wines that are sometimes very good.

BASTARDO

The classic Port grape identified as the Trousseau, an ancient variety once widely cultivated in the Jura, France.

BLAUFRÄNKISCH

Some believe this Austrian variety to be the Gamay, and judging from its light and poor-quality wine they could be close to the truth.

Synonyms: *Blauer limberger, Crna moravka, Gamé, Kékfrankos, Lemberger, Schwarze frankishe*

CABERNET

An ambiguous name that refers to the *Cabernet sauvignon* or *Cabernet franc.*

CABERNET FRANC

See right.

CABERNET SAUVIGNON

See below right

CAMINA

A German *Portugieser* x *Pinot noir* cross that yields grapes with more sugar and acidity than either parent.

CAMPBELL'S EARLY

An American hybrid that is particularly popular in Japan.

Synonym: *Island belle*

CANAIOLO NERO

A secondary grape used to add softness to Chianti's principal variety, the Sangiovese.

CARIGNAN

A Spanish variety grown extensively in southern France and California, producing table wine. One of the Carignan's synonyms – Mataro – is the common name for the Mouvèdre. This is also widely planted in southern France and provides a similar well-coloured, harsh wine, though it is not the same variety. A Carignan blanc and a Carignan gris also exist.

Synonyms: *Carignane, Carignan noir, Carinena, Catalan, Crujillon, Bois dur, Mataro, Mazuelo, Roussillonen, Tinto mazuela*

CABERNET FRANC

A variety grown throughout Bordeaux, though it is only planted irregularly in the Médoc, and increasingly less so in Graves. It really fares best as Bouchet in St.-Emilion and Pomerol, across the Dordogne river, where the Cabernet sauvignon is less well represented. Grown under neutral conditions, it might not be easy to distinguish any significant varietal differences between the two Cabernets, but, suited as they are to different situations, the Cabernet franc tends to produce a slightly earthy style of wine that is very aromatic, but has less fine characteristics on the palate when compared to the Cabernet sauvignon.

Synonyms: *Bouchet, Bouschet sauvignon, Breton, Cabernet, Cabernet gris, Carmenet, Gros bouchet, Gros bouschet, Gros cabernet, Gros vidure, Petit-fer, Véron*

CABERNET SAUVIGNON

The noblest variety of Bordeaux, vitally important to the classic Médoc wines, rich in colour, aroma and depth. Many of its classical traits have been transplanted round the world, as far afield as California, Chile and Australia. The complexities that this grape can achieve transcend simplistic comparisons to cedar, blackcurrants or violets.

Synonyms: *Bouchet, Bouschet sauvignon, Petit bouschet, Petit cabernet, Petite-vidure, Vidure*

CARMENÈRE

A Bordeaux grape that is not very widely cultivated, yet produces deliciously rich, soft-textured wines of excellent colour.

Synonyms: *Cabarnelle, Carmenelle, Grande vidure*

CÉSAR

A minor grape variety of moderate quality that is still used in some areas of Burgundy, most notably for Bourgogne Irancy.

Synonyms: *Romain, Ronçain, Gros monsieur, Gros noir*

CINSAULT

A prolific grape found mainly in southern Rhône and Languedoc-Roussillon vineyards, where it makes robust, well-coloured wines. Best results are obtained when it is blended, as at Châteauneuf-du-Pape, for example.

Synonyms: *Black malvoisie, Bourdalès, Cinq-saou, Cinsaut, Cuviller, Espagna, Hermitage, Malaga, Morterille noire, Picardin noir, Plant d'arles*

CONCORD

The widest-cultivated variety in North America outside of California. It has an extremely pronounced "foxy" flavour.

CORVINA

A prolific Italian variety, found mainly in Veneto, where it is blended into the wines of Bardolino and Valpolicella, the grape's thick skins contributing colour and tannin.

Synonyms: *Corvina veronese, Cruina*

DECKROT

A *Pinot gris* x *Teinturier färbertraube* cross that produces a coloured juice that is welcomed by growers in the cool climate of Germany's vineyards, as they are unable to grow black grapes with a dark skin in order to produce red wines in the normal way.

DOMINA

A *Portugieser* x *Pinot noir* cross that is more suited to Germany's vineyards than either of its parents.

GAMAY

See below.

GRACIANO

An important variety used in the production of Rioja, where a small amount lends richness and fruit to a blend.

Synonyms: *Morrastel, Perpignanou*

GAMAY

The famous grape of Beaujolais, where the mass-produced basic product has a tell-tale "pear-drop" characteristic to its bouquet, a by-product of its *macération carbonique* style of vinification. These are wines that should be drunk very young and very fresh, although traditionally vinified wines from Beaujolais' nine classic *crus* can be aged like other red wines and, after 10 or 15 years, will develop Pinot noir varietal traits. This may just be a phenomenon or, as some believe, occur because the grape is possibly the result of an ancient, natural clone of the Pinot noir. In France, the synonym Gamay Beaujolais is used for the true Gamay, but in California it is the synonym of the Pinot noir. As Leon Adams notes in "The Wines of America", this erroneous American synonym arose out of genuine confusion when Paul Masson brought back to his winery several Burgundian grapes, one of which he honestly believed to be the Gamay of Beaujolais. It was positively identified as the Pinot noir in the mid-1960s, but by this time several

Californian wineries were selling their own brand of Gamay Beaujolais. Before its true identity was revealed, another grape – the Napa gamay – that had been cultivated in California for some time, was identified as the true Gamay.

Synonyms: *Blaufränkisch, Borgogna crna, Bourgvignon noir, Frankinja crna, Frankinja modra, Gaamez, Gamay Beaujolais, Gamay noir, Gamay noir à jus blanc, Gamay rond, Kékfrankos, Limberger, Napa gamay, Petit gamai*

Gamay teinturiers: *Gamay fréaux, Gamay de bouze, Gamay de chaudenay, Gamay Castille, Gamay teinturier mouro, Fréaux hatif*

GRENACHE

A variety grown in southern France where it is responsible, in part, for the wines of Châteauneuf-du-Pape, Tavel and many others. It is the mainstay of Rioja, makes port-style and light rosé types of wine in California and is also grown in South Africa. Its wines are rich, warm and alcoholic, sometimes too much so, and require blending with other varieties. The true Grenache has nothing to do with the Grenache de logroña of Spain that is, in fact, the Tempranillo or Tinto de rioja. Some sources give the Alicante (a synonym of the Grenache) as being the Alicante bouschet (or plain Bouschet in California), but this too is misleading. The Alicante viz Grenache has colourless juice, whereas the Alicante bouschet has bright red juice derived from the *teinturier* half of its parentage. The Petit bouschet (in its true form, and not as the synonym of the Cabernet sauvignon) is itself a cross of *Teinturier du cher x Aramon*.

Synonyms: *Alicante, Alicante grenache, Aragón, Garnacha, Garnache, Garnacho, Granaccia, Grenache nera, Roussillon tinto, Tinto aragonés, Uva di spagno*

GROLLEAU

A prolific grape that has a high natural sugar content, is important for the bulk production of Anjou rosé, but is rarely interesting in quality terms.

Synonyms: *Groslot, Gros lot, Plant Boisnard, Pineau de Saumur*

HEROLDREBE

A *Portugieser* x *Limberger* cross that produces light-coloured, neutral-flavoured wines in Germany.

KADARKA

Hungary's most widely-cultivated grape variety, grown throughout the Balkans. It was once thought to be the same as the Zinfandel, but this theory no longer persists. It makes pleasant, light and fruity wine.

Synonyms: *Balkan kadarka, Codarka, Gamza, Kadarska*

KOLOR

One of Gemany's *teinturier* varieties, a *Pinot noir* x *Teinturier färbertraube* cross developed to put colour into the blends of the country's northern red wines.

LAMBRUSCO

An Italian variety, famous for its production of the medium-sweet, red, frothy wine of the same name in the Emilia-Romagna area.

MALBEC

A grape traditionally used in Bordeaux blends to provide colour and tannin. It is also grown in the Loire, Cahors and Mediterranean regions, amongst many others, and was the grape responsible for the "black wine of Cahors" – a legendary name, if not wine, in the nineteenth century. However, Cahors is now made from a blend of grapes and is an infinitely superior wine to its predecessor.

Synonyms: *Auxerrois, Balouzet, Cahors, Cot, Estrangey, Etaulier, Etranger, Gourdoux, Grifforin, Gros noir, Guillan rouge, Jacobain, Luckens, Magret, Malbeck, Mausat, Mauzac, Mourane, Moustère, Negri, Noir doux, Noir de Pressac, Parde, Pied noir, Pied de perdrix, Pied rouge, Piperdy, Prèchat, Pressac, Prolongeau, Quercy, Séme, Teinturier, Terranis*

MAVROUD

A Bulgarian variety that produces dark, rich and plummy wines.

Synonym: *Mavrud*

MAZUELO

A variety grown in Rioja and believed to be the Carignan, though it bears little resemblance to it, producing wines of light, yet rich, fruit and low alcohol.

MERLOT

See p.31, top left.

MONASTRELL

An underrated Spanish variety that is usually hidden in blends. However, it does have a full and distinctive flavour and could make individual wines of some appeal.

MERLOT

A grape that produces not deep, but nicely-coloured, wines, soft in fruit but capable of great richness. It is invaluable in Bordeaux, bringing lusciousness of fruit and a velvet-like quality to the finish of wines that might otherwise be somewhat hard and austere. It is the chief grape in Château Pétrus, the top name in Pomerol.

Synonyms: *Bigney, Crabutet noir, Médoc noir, Petit merle, Vitraille*

MONDEUSE
A variety that may have originally hailed from Friuli in northeastern Italy, where it is known as the Refosco. It is now planted as far afield as the Savoie in France, California, USA, Switzerland, Yugoslavia, the Argentine and Australia, where it is often an important constituent of the fortified port-type wines.

Synonyms: *Grand picot, Gros rouge du pays, Grosse syrah, Molette noir, Refosco, Savoyanche, Terrano*

MOURVÈDRE
An excellent-quality grape variety that has been used more than other lesser varieties in Châteauneuf-du-Pape blends in recent years. It is grown extensively throughout the Rhône and the Midi of France, and, under the name of the Mataro, in Spain. The Mataro is Australia's fifth widest-cultivated black grape, but is a declining force in southern California.

Synonyms: *Balzac, Beni carlo, Catalan, Espar, Esparte, Mataro, Negron, Tinto*

PAMID
The widest-cultivated of Bulgaria's indigenous black grape varieties. It makes light and fruity quaffing wine.

PETIT VERDOT
A grape that has been used to good effect in Bordeaux because it is a late-ripener, bringing acidity to the overall balance of a wine. Certain modern techniques of viticulture and vinification have rendered it less valuable, which might prove to be a pity because it also produces a characterful, long-lived and tannic wine when ripe.

Synonyms: *Carmelin, Petit verdau, Verdot, Verdot rouge*

PINEAU D'AUNIS
A grape best known for its supporting role in the production of Rosé d'Anjou.

Synonyms: *Chenin noir, Cot à queue rouge, Pineau rouge, Plant d'Aunis*

PINOT MEUNIER

An important variety in Champagne, where, vinified white, it gives more up-front appeal of fruit than the Pinot noir when young, and is therefore essential for early-drinking Champagnes. Its characteristics are more immediate, but less fine and somewhat earthier than those of the Pinot noir. The Pinot meunier is extensively cultivated in the Marne Valley area of Champagne, where its resistance to frost makes it the most suitable vine.

Synonyms: *Auvernat gris, Blanche feuille, Dusty miller, Goujan, Gris meunier, Morillon taconé, Müllerrebe, Müller rebe, Müller schwarzriesling, Plant de brie, Schwarzriesling, Wrotham pinot*

PINOTAGE
A *Pinot noir* x *Cinsault* cross developed in 1925. It occupies an important position in South African viticulture where its rustic and high-toned wine is greatly appreciated.

PINOT MEUNIER
See above.

PINOT NOIR
See below.

PORTUGIESER
The widest-planted black grape variety in Germany, originating not from Portugal as its name suggests, but from the Danube district of Austria. As it makes very ordinary and extremely light red wine, it is often used in bad years to blend with the too acidic white wine.

Synonyms: *Oporto, Portugais bleu, Portugalka*

PRIMITIVO
An Italian variety, grown in Apulia where it produces rich wines, some-times sweet or fortified. Some think it is the same variety as Zinfandel.

Synonyms: *Primativo, Zingarello, Zinfandel*

RONDINELLA
An Italian variety, secondary to the Corvina grape in terms of area planted, used for the production of Bardolino and Valpolicella.

ROTBERGER
A *Trollinger* x *Riesling* cross. The parents seem an odd couple, but the offspring is surprisingly successful, producing some excellent rosé wines.

RUBY CABERNET
An American *Carignan* x *Cabernet sauvignon* cross that originated in 1936, first fruited in 1940 and made its first wine in 1946.

NEBBIOLO

Famous for its production of Barolo, this grape is also responsible, in part or whole, for the other splendid wines of Piemonte in Italy, such as Gattinara, Barbaresco, Carema and Donnaz. It often needs to be softened by the addition of Bonarda grapes, which have the same role as Merlot in Bordeaux. In fact, Merlot is used in Lombardy to soften Nebbiolo grapes for the production of Valtelina and Valtelina Superiore wines, of which Sassella can be the most velvety of all.

Synonyms: *Chiavennasca, Nebbiolo Lampia, Nebbiolo michet, Nebbiolo-spanna, Nebbiolo rosé, Picoutener, Picutener, Pugnet, Spanna, Spauna*

PINOT NOIR

One of the classic varieties of Champagne, though its claim to great fame lies immediately south in Burgundy. In the right place, under ideal climatic conditions, the Pinot noir can produce the richest, most velvet-smooth wines in the world.

Synonyms: *Auvernat, Blauburgunder, Blauer spätburgunder, Cortaillod, Klevner, Morillon, Nagi-burgundi, Nagyburgundi, Noiren, Pineau, Plant doré, Pinot vérot, Rotclevner, Savagnin noir, Savignin, Schwartz klevner, Spätburgunder, Vert doré*

SANGIOVESE

The principal variety used in Chianti. In a pure varietal form it can lack fruit and have a metallic finish.

Synonyms: *Brunello* (in Montalcino), *Calabrese, Sangiovese dolce, Sangiovese gentile, Sangiovese di lamole, Sangiovese Toscano, Morellino, Nerino, Sanvicetro, Prugnolo* (in Montepulciano)

SYRAH

A variety whose name is derived from Shiraz, the capital of Fars, a province of Iran; most people therefore believe the vine to have originated from Persia, possibly as far back as 600 BC. In Hermitage, in the northern Rhône, the grape makes big, rich, tannic wines, with a good deal of fruit.

Synonyms: *Chira, Entournerien, Hignin, Hignin noir, Petite syrah* (France), *Schiras, Serine, Serenne, Shiraz, Shyraz, Sirac, Sirah, Sirrah, Sirras, Syra, Syrac, Syras*

TANNAT

A grape that originated from the Basque region, with the potential to produce deeply-coloured, tannic wines of great longevity, though certain modern methods of vinification often change the traditional character of Tannat wines. The variety's best known wines are the attractive red Madiran and Irouléguy. A little Tannat wine is used for blending purposes in and around the town of Cahors.

Synonyms: *Bordeleza belcha, Harriague, Madiran, Moustrou, Moustroun, Tanat*

TEMPRANILLO

The most important variety in Rioja, where it is traditional to blend the grapes, although many pure Tempranillo wines of excellent quality are made. It is capable of producing long-lived wines of some finesse and complexity. It is also an important variety in Argentina.

Synonyms: *Aragonez, Cencibel, Grenache de Logrono, Ojo de liebre, Tempranilla, Tempranillo de la Rioja, Tinta roriz, Tinto fino, Tinto Madrid, Tinto de la Rioja, Tinto de Toro, Ull de llebre*

TINTA AMARELA

An important Port grape.

TINTA BARROCA

One of the Douro's up-and-coming varieties, this grape makes very full and well-coloured wines that can be somewhat rustic in character compared to the two Touriga varieties (*see* below).

TINTA CÃO

One of the best Port grapes.

TOURIGA FRANCESA

A classic Port grape that is no relation to the Touriga nacional. Its wine is less concentrated, but of fine quality.

TROLLINGER

A variety mainly restricted to the Württemberg region of Germany. It produces fresh and fruity red wine.

Synonyms: *Black Hamburg, Blauer malvasier, Frankenthaler, Gross-vernatsch, Red trollinger, Schiava-grossa*

VRANAC

A grape indigenous to Yugoslavia, where it makes dark-coloured, full-bodied, characterful wines.

XYNOMAVRO

An excellent Greek variety that produces the rich and smooth Naoussa.

ZINFANDEL

See below.

TOURIGA NACIONAL

The finest Port grape in the entire Douro. The wine is fantastically rich and tannic, with masses of fruit, and is capable of great longevity and complexity.

Synonym: *Touriga*

ZINFANDEL

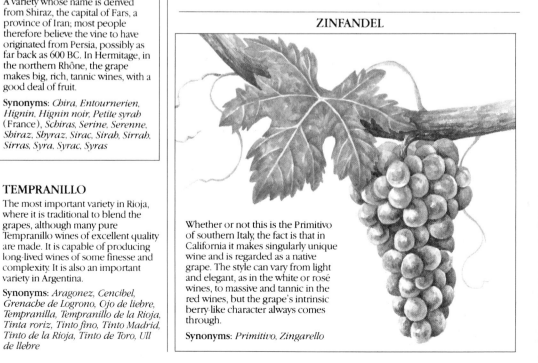

Whether or not this is the Primitivo of southern Italy, the fact is that in California it makes singularly unique wine and is regarded as a native grape. The style can vary from light and elegant, as in the white or rosé wines, to massive and tannic in the red wines, but the grape's intrinsic berry-like character always comes through.

Synonyms: *Primitivo, Zingarello*

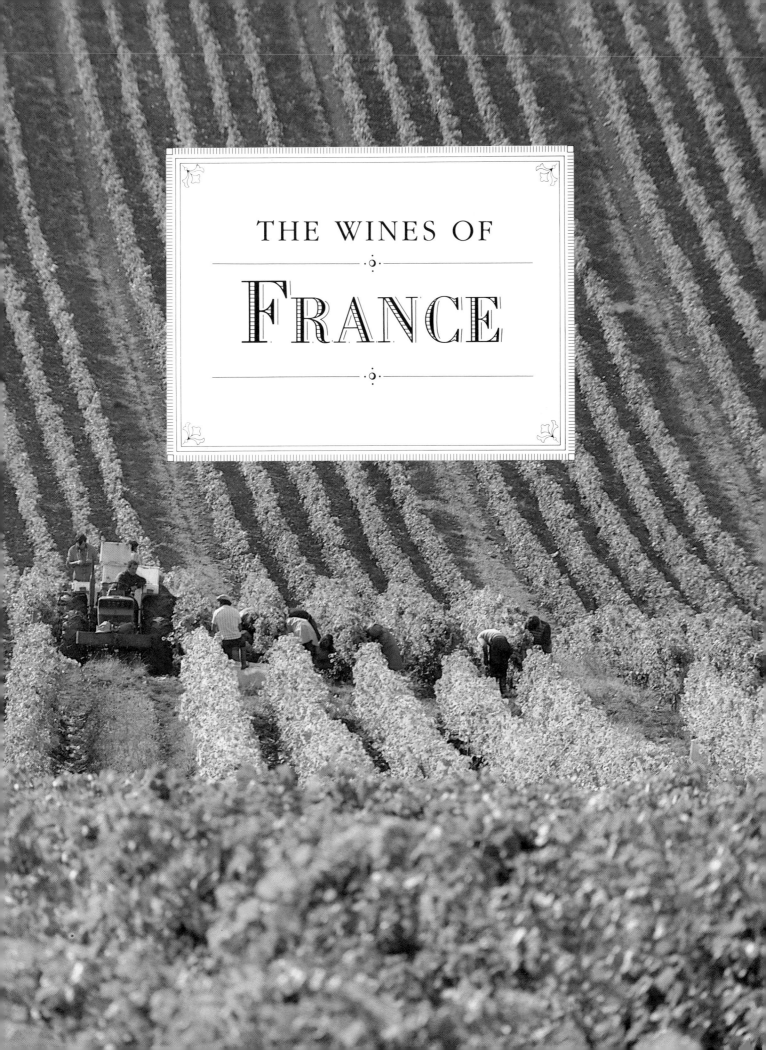

THE WINES OF
FRANCE

France

NO OTHER COUNTRY IN THE WORLD can rival France for the quality and diversity of its wine, and only Italy can be compared with it in terms of quantity. An average of 76 million hectolitres of wine is produced every year in France. However, it is a regrettable but unavoidable fact that quality wine can only be made in limited amounts. Thus, more than half of France's enormous annual yield is *vin de table* (officially designated as *vin de consommation courante*), a very ordinary wine without the right to any appellation of origin or quality. Even the wines that receive one of the higher classifications can be unpredictable: while some bearing illustrious appellations may disappoint, the very best produced in lesser known areas can often be outstanding.

HOW FRENCH WINE IS CLASSIFIED

Appellation d'Origine Contrôlée *28% of total production*

30% exported, 70% consumed within France

France was the first country to set up a system for controlling the origin and quality of its wines. In 1935 an Institut National des Appellations d'Origine (INAO) was established. Now there are some 400 separate AOCs, covering 380,000 hectares (939,000 acres) and producing an annual average of 21 million hectolitres.

The best French wines are almost all AOC. The label indicates where the wine comes from, and the appellation law regulates the grape varieties used, viticultural methods, harvest and yield restrictions, minimum alcoholic content, winemaking techniques and the quality of the product – approved by an official tasting panel.

Vin Délimité de Qualité Supérieure *1.3% of total production*

20% exported, 80% consumed within France

VDQS wines are subject to controls similar to those with AOC status, but the yields may be higher, the wine can be lower in strength, and the overall standard is not required to be as high – although it may be argued in certain cases that the quality is easily comparable. Many VDQS wines have been promoted to AOC status and this has reduced the average annual production in recent years.

Vin de Pays *13% of total production*

10% exported, 90% consumed within France

A recent category, introduced to help stem the large flow of inferior wines, the term *vins de pays* describes what are often known as "French country wines". Current production averages ten million hectolitres. There are three categories of *vin de pays*, each with its own controls. Although they must all have a specified origin on the label, a wide range of grape varieties can be used and high yields are allowed – with the result that the quality of the wine varies greatly. For a description of the categories and a detailed map showing the areas producing *vins de pays*, see p.197.

Vin de Table *44.7% of total production*

12% exported, 88% consumed within France

Also known as *vins ordinaires* or *vins de consommation courante*, these are inexpensive wines for everyday drinking and are not intended for keeping. With an output of 34 million hectolitres, this is by far the largest category in terms of volume produced, and nearly all is consumed by the French. The label must not specify the wine's origin, and both strength and quality may vary.

Observant readers will notice that the production percentages for each sector total only 87 per cent when added together, and that while I state that *vin de table* accounts for more than half of all French wine, its percentage of total production is just 44.7 per cent. This is explained by the fact that ten of France's 76 million hectolitres of wine are classified as *vins blancs de cognac*, and are distilled.

CURRENT BREAKDOWN OF FRENCH WINE PRODUCTION

	AOC	VDQS	Vin de Pays	Vin de Table
Red	55%	52%	70%	73%
White	25%	39%	10%	13%
Rosé	10%	9%	20%	7%
Sparkling	10%	negligible	none	7%

WORLD CONSUMPTION OF FRENCH WINE

France produces 76 million hectolitres of wine annually, of which 62 per cent is red. While home consumption is falling (83 litres per head compared with 120 in 1969) exports are increasing, in value terms and as a percentage of production.

France exports 13 million hectolitres of wine per year. □ AOC □ Other

1	2	3	4	5	6	7	8	9	10	11	12	13
29%				54%	55%	63%	65%	33%	93%	49%	–	
71%				46%	45%	37%	35%	67%	7%	51%	–	
A				B	C	D	E	F	G	H		I

A West Germany 29% B Great Britain 16% C Benelux 11% D USA 8%
E Netherlands 7.9% F Canada 5% G Switzerland 5% H Sweden 3%
I Other countries 14.1%

HOW TO READ FRENCH WINE LABELS

Wine labels give certain mandatory information, such as the name of the bottler who, in France, is legally responsible for the wine.

Other details include colour and style of wine, grape variety and vintage; these are not always obligatory but assist the consumer.

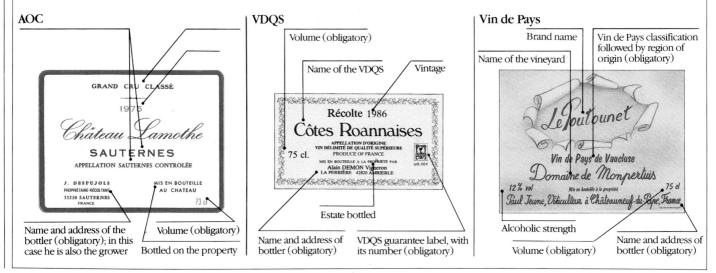

AOC

GRAND CRU CLASSÉ
1975
Château Lamothe
SAUTERNES
APPELLATION SAUTERNES CONTRÔLÉE
J. DESPUJOLS
PROPRIÉTAIRE-RÉCOLTANT
33210 SAUTERNES
FRANCE
MIS EN BOUTEILLE
AU CHÂTEAU
73 cl

Name and address of the bottler (obligatory); in this case he is also the grower
Volume (obligatory)
Bottled on the property

VDQS

Volume (obligatory)
Name of the VDQS
Vintage
Récolte 1986
Côtes Roannaises
APPELLATION D'ORIGINE
VIN DÉLIMITÉ DE QUALITÉ SUPÉRIEURE
PRODUCE OF FRANCE
75 cl.
MIS EN BOUTEILLE A LA PROPRIÉTÉ PAR
Alain DEMON Vigneron
LA PERRIÈRE 42820 AMBIERLE
VDQS
U0.701

Estate bottled
Name and address of bottler (obligatory)
VDQS guarantee label, with its number (obligatory)

Vin de Pays

Brand name
Vin de Pays classification followed by region of origin (obligatory)
Name of the vineyard
Le Poutounet
Vin de Pays de Vaucluse
Domaine de Monpertuis
12% vol
75 cl
Mis en bouteille à la propriété
Paul Jeune, Viticulteur à Châteauneuf-du-Pape, France

Alcoholic strength
Volume (obligatory)
Name and address of bottler (obligatory)

FRANCE

The coloured areas on this map identify the ten main wine-producing regions of France, where the areas of Appellation d'Origine Contrôlée are concentrated. However, the country has over one million hectares of vineyards, and many good, everyday-drinking wines are made in other parts of the country. See also the maps of Vin de Pays areas, p.198.

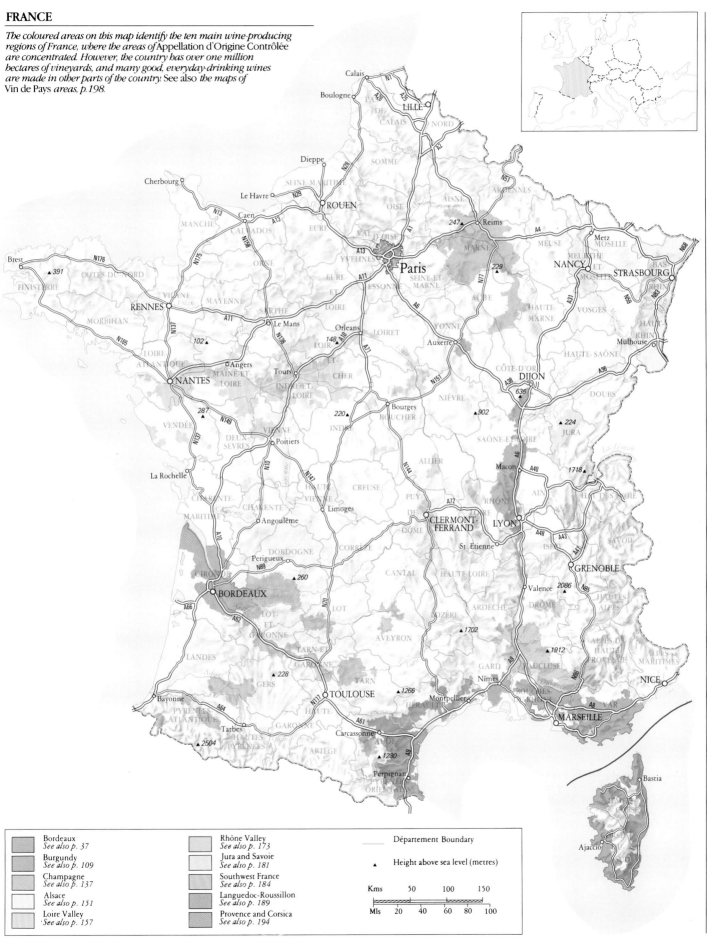

Bordeaux *See also p. 37*		Rhône Valley *See also p. 173*	Département Boundary
Burgundy *See also p. 109*		Jura and Savoie *See also p. 181*	▲ Height above sea level (metres)
Champagne *See also p. 137*		Southwest France *See also p. 184*	
Alsace *See also p. 151*		Languedoc-Roussillon *See also p. 189*	Kms 50 100 150
Loire Valley *See also p. 157*		Provence and Corsica *See also p. 194*	Mls 20 40 60 80 100

Bordeaux

From the classic reds of the Médoc, Graves, St.-Emilion and Pomerol to the great sweet whites of Sauternes and Barsac, Bordeaux is the largest source of quality wines in the world.

BORDEAUX OCCUPIES AN ALMOST-PERFECT viticultural situation. Its flat countryside is attractive, if not spectacular. However, without the lush vineyards and the illustrious names of the great châteaux, there would be little to thrill the traveller. The famous *crus classés* offer a remarkable range of architectural styles spanning over seven centuries, but although many *petits châteaux* can be equally grand, some may be no more than a bungalow or a tin shed.

THE APPELLATION

The borders of the Bordeaux appellation coincide with those of the Gironde *département*. It is the largest *département* in France and the Bordeaux wine it produces generates more revenue and more controversy than any other region in the world. Today there are more than 22,000 vineyard proprietors working 100,000 hectares (247,000 acres), producing 4 million hectolitres (over 44 million cases) of Bordeaux wine every year. Of these 22,000 properties, the current edition of Féret, the "Bordeaux Bible", identifies no less than 7,000 wine-producing châteaux and domaines. Yet the reputation of this great region has been built upon the quality of less than one per cent of this number, and just three per cent of the vast volume of wine produced is classified as *Grand Cru* – the highest-ranking status of AOC Bordeaux.

THE CHÂTEAU SYSTEM AND MERCHANT POWER

Prior to the concept of château wine estates, the land was worked on a crop-sharing basis. From the late seventeenth century this feudal system slowly changed. As the Bordelais brokers developed the habit of recording and classifying wines according to their *cru* or growth (which is to say their geographical origin) and the prices they fetched, thus the fame of individual properties developed.

The nineteenth century saw the rise of the merchant or *négociant* in Bordeaux. Many of these were of English origin, and some were established by Scottish, Irish, Dutch and German businessmen. The best château wines were not consumed by the French themselves; they were the preserve of the British, German and other north European populations. Thus foreign merchants had an obvious advantage over their French counterparts. In the spring these *négociants* took delivery of young wines in cask from the various châteaux and matured them in their cellars prior to shipping. They were thus responsible for their upbringing, or *élevage*, and became known as *négociants-éleveurs*.

The modern Bordeaux wine trade

Bordeaux's 400 *négociants* or *négociants-éleveurs* are the inevitable middlemen found in every aspect of trading. In many instances a foreign buyer finds it easier to deal through a *négociant*, and sometimes he has no alternative. A number of châteaux are owned by, or are exclusive to, certain *négociants*. In today's market, the *élevage* role of a *négociant* is primarily restricted to branded wines.

A *courtier* is a local expert with an intimate knowledge of the wines of his area and the needs of his customers. He does not possess stocks, but he has many roles, some straightforward, others not. He charges a fee for bringing buyers and sellers together; in fact he charges both parties – the buyer because he vouches that the wines delivered will be identical to the samples tasted, and the seller because he underwrites payment of the invoice. For my selection of Bordeaux *négociants, see* p.40.

THE CLASSIC GRAPE VARIETIES OF BORDEAUX

The worldwide imitation of the Bordeaux style has created a widespread cultivation of the region's Cabernet sauvignon vine, resulting in a cluster of international "clarets". However, Cabernet sauvignon actually represents only 18 per cent of the vines cultivated in Bordeaux, whereas the Merlot, generally considered the second variety, accounts for more than 32 per cent. On the

Médoc's hallowed ground, where it is blasphemy to mention the name of Merlot, 40 per cent of the vines grown *are* Merlot.

The Merlot, and not the Cabernet sauvignon, is the most important grape variety in Bordeaux. Although dependent upon quality and quantity of grapes used, it is nearer the truth to say that the Cabernet sauvignon gives backbone to the Merlot, than to suggest that the Merlot softens the Cabernet sauvignon. Château Mouton-Rothschild contains no less than 90 per cent Cabernet sauvignon, but Château Pétrus, one of the most expensive wines in the world, contains 95 per cent Merlot, without a drop of Cabernet sauvignon. Cabernet sauvignon is a classic grape, quite possibly the greatest red-wine grape in the world, but its importance in Bordeaux has been exaggerated.

Sémillon is Bordeaux's most important white grape variety, both in terms of its extent of cultivation and quality. Susceptible to "noble rot", the disease responsible for classic Sauternes and Barsac, it must be the world's greatest sweet wine grape. It also accounts for most of the finest dry white wines of Bordeaux, but these are relatively few in number and lack prestige. Sauvignon blanc plays the supporting role in the production of sweet wines, and is used to a greater or lesser degree for dry wines. Many of the less expensive dry white wines are pure Sauvignon blanc varietals.

The Garonne and Bordeaux, above
The broad sweep of the Garonne river takes in the city of Bordeaux, the commercial centre of the region's wine industry.

Mass production, left
Corking being carefully monitored at the bottling plant of the firm of Alexis Lichine and Company, who produce about 700,000 cases (63,000 hectolitres) of wine per year.

Quai des Chartrons, Bordeaux, below
The Garonne's depth and width allow ocean-going vessels to dock with ease, providing a convenient export outlet. Not surprisingly, the Quai is the centre of the négoce.

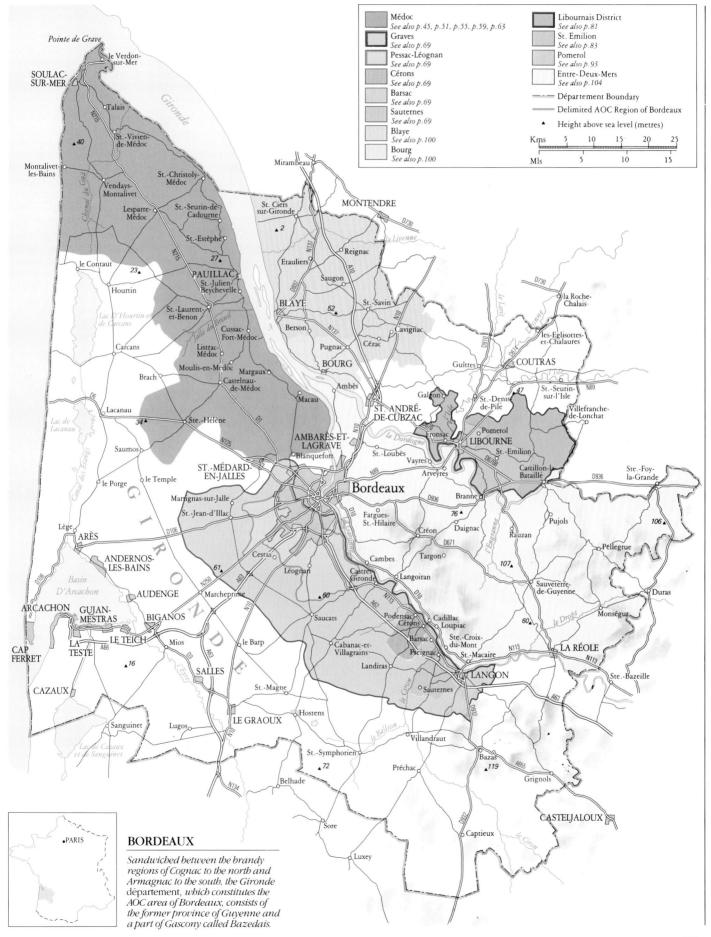

Legend:

Médoc
See also p.45, p.51, p.55, p.59, p.63

Graves
See also p.69

Pessac-Léognan
See also p.69

Cérons
See also p.69

Barsac
See also p.69

Sauternes
See also p.69

Blaye
See also p.100

Bourg
See also p.100

Libournais District
See also p.81

St. Emilion
See also p.83

Pomerol
See also p.93

Entre-Deux-Mers
See also p.104

- - - Département Boundary

——— Delimited AOC Region of Bordeaux

▲ Height above sea level (metres)

Kms 5 10 15 20 25

Mls 5 10 15

BORDEAUX

Sandwiched between the brandy regions of Cognac to the north and Armagnac to the south, the Gironde département, which constitutes the AOC area of Bordeaux, consists of the former province of Guyenne and a part of Gascony called Bazedais.

VARIETAL CONTRIBUTIONS TO A *CUVÉE*

Each grape variety makes its own contribution to a particular wine. The Cabernet sauvignon is the most complex and distinctive of all Bordeaux grapes. It has a firm tannic structure, yet with time reveals a powerful, rich and long-lasting flavour. Wines from this grape can have great finesse; their bouquets often possess a "blackcurrant" or "violets" character. The Cabernet franc has similar characteristics, but may also have a leafy, sappy or earthy taste depending on where it is cultivated. It does, however, shine through as the superior variety when grown in St.-Emilion and Pomerol, and can compete on even terms with its more famous cousin in parts of Graves. The Merlot is soft, silky and sometimes opulent. It is a grape that charms, and can make wines with lots of juicy-rich and spicy fruit. The Petit verdot is a late ripener with a naturally high acidity, while the Malbec has a thick skin that is rich in colour pigments. Small amounts of these last two varieties were traditionally used to correct the colour and acidity of a blend. Their cultivation has been on the decrease for the last twenty years due to various modern techniques of viticulture and vinification.

The Sémillon grape provides a wine naturally rich in flavour and high in alcohol. It makes succulent sweet wines capable of great longevity, but its intrinsically low acidity is unsuitable for dry wines. In exceptional circumstances the highest quality Sémillon does make a fine dry white wine – if matured in new oak. This enhances the aromatic character of the wine and gives it a firm structure without which it would be too "fat" and "flabby".

The Sauvignon blanc in Bordeaux is soft, delicate and easy to drink. It does not have the same bite as it does in the Loire vineyards of Sancerre or Pouilly-Fumé, but the varietal character is more pronounced now than it used to be a few years ago. Early harvesting, pre-fermentation maceration on the grape skins to draw out the aromatics, and longer, cooler fermentation in stainless steel, have all combined to produce a far more interesting, medium-quality, dry white wine.

FERMENTATION AND MATURATION

Although some *crus classés* retain their wooden vats for fermentation – more because they lack the funds to re-equip than for any idealistic reasons – hardly any of them actually invest in new oak vats, preferring those made of stainless steel. The one startling exception is Château Margaux, the property that has spent more money following the advice of Professor Peynaud than any other. This is puzzling because it was principally on the recommendations of this legendary oenologist (wine chemist) that virtually everyone else in Bordeaux invested in stainless steel.

Adding *vin de presse*

One vinification technique that is more characteristic of red winemaking in Bordeaux than in any other region is the addition of a certain amount of *vin de presse*. This is produced after the wine has completed its alcoholic fermentation and has undergone malolactic conversion. The wine is drawn off its lees into casks and the residue of skin and pips at the bottom of the vat is pressed.

HOW TO READ BORDEAUX LABELS

Vintage
Local variations in vintage quality must always be considered. The excellent 1970 vintage was not quite as excellent in St.-Emilion, yet the 1971 was far more successful there than in the Médoc. Do not be disillusioned by the complexity of it all: the experts are still arguing about the 1961 and 1945 vintages. Master of Wine Michael Broadbent freely admits it took him 40 years to finally opt for 1945; however, he would not turn down a 1961!

Appellation
As with all French wines, the first thing to do is to search out the appellation. All the famous châteaux have small, specific appellations. If the wine is from one of the catch-all generic Bordeaux appellations or from a lesser area like Bourg, Blaye or Entre-Deux-Mers, it might be good, but it won't be great.

Produce of France or *Produit de France*
It is a legal requirement that the country of production should be clearly indicated on the label of any wine due for export. There is one innocent reason why this might not, in fact, be the case: Bordeaux wines tend to pass through the hands of many owners in various countries before they are consumed, and can end up almost anywhere.

Name
Is it a brand name or does it purport to be a château? Branded wines will normally be from generic appellations and should be moderately priced. If it is a château, does it have a reputation you are prepared to pay for?

Grand Cru Classé
In the Médoc and in Graves, this term is used synonymously with *Cru Classé* (see below).

Proprietor
The name and address of the proprietor of the château.

Is it château bottled?
All the great wines of Bordeaux will clearly show the term *Mis en bouteille au château* on the cork and the label, but earlier vintages may be bottled by a *négociant* in Bordeaux or shipped in cask and bottled abroad and should be significantly cheaper. If the bottler is (or was) a reputable merchant, the wine could be a bargain way of enjoying an old vintage – this Château Batailley 1966 bottled by Peter Dominic was, in fact, quite superb. Buying old vintages is a bit of a risk anyway, but buying an English-, Scottish-, Belgian-, or Bordeaux-bottled old vintage is supposed to increase that risk, hence the lower price.

The following classifications may be found on Bordeaux labels. Some apply only to St.-Emilion:

Cru Bourgeois
A category of good-quality wines representing one-third of the production of the various appellations of the Médoc. These wines fall between the *petits châteaux* and the *crus classés* and some can be outstanding.

Cru Classé
In Bordeaux this can only be used if the property is an officially classified growth.

Premier Cru* or *Premier Grand Cru Classé
The First Growths of Bordeaux may boast their superior classification; the Second to Fifth rarely do.

Grand Cru
An annually awarded classification for certain St.-Emilion wines, up to and including the 1985 vintage (*see also* p.83).

Grand Cru Classé
This permanent classification of St.-Emilion is a higher category than wines bearing the *Grand Cru* without any indication of the word *classé*. The term is also used synonymously with *Cru Classé* in the Médoc and Graves regions.

Premier Grand Cru
Ranked above *Grand Cru Classé*, this is the highest quality category of permanently classified St.-Emilion.

Grand Vin
Although this term has no legal significance, it should refer to the "great wine" or principal label of a château. The so-called "Second Wines" (there may be more than one) are sold under other labels.

Normally this requires two pressings: the first *vin de presse* is the best and represents about ten per cent of the total wine produced, the second provides a further five per cent. The *vin de presse* is relatively low in alcohol and, because the residue mainly consists of grape skins, it is very dark and rich in tannic acid. In a wine made for early drinking, *vin de presse* would be harsh and unpleasant, but with the structure of a classic oak-matured Bordeaux, it gives extra body and increases longevity.

Oak cask maturation

After fermentation and prior to bottling, all the best red Bordeaux wines are matured in 225-litre (59-gallon) Bordeaux oak casks called *barriques*. The duration of this operation and the percentage of new oak casks employed should depend entirely on the quality and structure of the wine and this will vary according to the vintage. The bigger the wine, the more new oak it can take and the longer the maturation it will need. The greatest wines – most obviously all the First Growths – require at least 18-24 months in 100 per cent new oak. Other fine-quality Bordeaux require less time, maybe 12-18 months, and do not necessarily benefit from 100 per cent new oak; between 30-50 per cent may be sufficient.

If you get the chance to put your nose into a new oak cask before it has been used, do it. The wonderful creamy-smoky, vanilla and charcoal aroma is the very essence of what should come through when a fine wine has been properly matured in oak.

THE CLASSIFICATION OF BORDEAUX WINES

Of all the classifications that exist, it is the 1855 Classification which is meant whenever anyone refers to "The Classification". It was commissioned by the Bordeaux Chamber of Commerce, which was required by the government of the Second Empire to present a selection of its wines at the 1855 Exposition Universelle in Paris. For their own ends, the brokers of the Bordeaux Stock Exchange traditionally categorized the most famous Bordeaux properties on the basis of the prices they fetched, so they were charged by the Chamber of Commerce to submit a "complete list of classified red Bordeaux wines, as well as our great white wines".

The classifications below give the nineteenth-century names in their original order and form as listed by the brokers on April 18, 1855. The frequent absence of the word "château" has been followed, as has the circumflex in *Crûs*, and the use of *Seconds Crûs* for red wines and *Deuxièmes Crûs* for white wines.

THE 1855 CLASSIFICATION OF THE RED WINES OF THE GIRONDE

PREMIERS CRÛS (First Growths)
Château Lafite, Pauillac (now *Château Lafite-Rothschild*)
Château Margaux, Margaux
Château Latour, Pauillac
Haut-Brion (Graves)

SECONDS CRÛS (Second Growths)
Mouton, Pauillac (now *Château Mouton-Rothschild* and a First Growth since 1973)
Rauzan-Ségla, Margaux (now *Château Rauzan Ségla*)
Rauzan-Gassies, Margaux
Léoville, St.-Julien (now châteaux *Léoville-Las-Cases, Léoville-Poyferré* and *Léoville-Barton*)
Vivens Durfort, Margaux (now *Château Durfort-Vivens*)
Gruau-Laroze, St.-Julien (now *Château Gruaud-Larose*)
Lascombe, Margaux (now *Château Lascombes*)
Brane, Cantenac (now *Château Brane-Cantenac*)
Pichon Longueville, Pauillac (now châteaux *Pichon-Longueville-Baron* and *Pichon-Longueville-Comtesse-de-Lalande*)

Ducru Beau Caillou, St.-Julien (now *Château Ducru-Beaucaillou*)
Cos Destournel, St.-Estèphe (now *Château Cos d'Estournel*)
Montrose, St.-Estèphe

TROISIÈME CRÛS (Third Growths)
Kirwan, Cantenac
Château d'Issan, Cantenac
Lagrange, St.-Julien
Langoa, St.-Julien (now *Château Langoa-Barton*)
Giscours, Labarde
St.-Exupéray, Margaux (now *Château Malescot-St.-Exupéray*)
Boyd, Cantenac (now châteaux *Boyd-Cantenac* and *Cantenac-Brown*)
Palmer, Cantenac
Lalagune, Ludon (now *Château La Lagune*)
Desmirail, Margaux
Dubignon, Margaux (no longer in existence, but some of these original vineyards now belong to châteaux *Malescot-St.-Exupéray, Palmer* and *Margaux*)
Calon, St.-Estèphe (now *Château Calon-Ségur*)

Ferrière, Margaux
Becker, Margaux (now *Château Marquis d'Alseme-Becker*)

QUATRIÈMES CRÛS (Fourth Growths)
St-Pierre, St.-Julien (now *Château St-Pierre-Sevaistre*)
Talbot, St.-Julien
Du-Luc, St.-Julien (now *Château Branaire-Ducru*)
Duhart, Pauillac (now *Château Duhart-Milon-Rothschild*)
Pouget-Lassale, Cantenac (now *Château Pouget*)
Pouget, Cantenac (now *Château Pouget*)
Carnet, St.-Laurent (now *Château La Tour-Carnet*)
Rochet, St.-Estèphe (now *Chateau Lafon-Rochet*)
Château de Beychevele, St.-Julien (now *Château Beychevelle*)
Le Prieuré, Cantenac (now *Château Prieuré-Lichine*)
Marquis de Thermes, Margaux (now *Château Marquis-de-Terme*)

CINQUIÈMES CRÛS (Fifth Growths)
Canet, Pauillac (now *Château Pontet-Canet*)
Batailley, Pauillac (now châteaux *Batailley* and *Haut-Batailley*)
Grand Puy, Pauillac (now *Château Grand-Puy-Lacoste*)
Artigues Arnaud, Pauillac (now *Château Grand-Puy-Ducasse*)
Lynch, Pauillac (now *Château Lynch-Bages*)
Lynch Moussas, Pauillac
Dauzac, Labarde
Darmailhac, Pauillac (now *Château Mouton-Baronne-Philippe*)
Le Tertre, Arsac (now *Château du Tertre*)
Haut Bages, Pauillac (now *Château Haut-Bages-Libéral*)
Pedesclaux, Pauillac (now *Château Pédesclaux*)
Coutenceau, St.-Laurent (now *Château Belgrave*)
Camensac, St.-Laurent
Cos Labory, St.-Estèphe
Clerc Milon, Pauillac
Croizet-Bages, Pauillac
Cantemerle, Macau

THE 1855 CLASSIFICATION OF THE WHITE WINES OF THE GIRONDE

1er CRÛ SUPÉRIEUR (Superior First Growth)
Yquem, Sauternes

PREMIERS CRÛS (First Growths)
Latour Blanche, Bommes (now *Château La Tour Blanche*)
Peyraguey, Bommes (now châteaux *Lafaurie-Peyraguey* and *Clos Haut-Peyraguey*)
Vigneau, Bommes (now *Château Rayne-Vigneau*)

Suduiraut, Preignac
Coutet, Barsac
Climens, Barsac
Bayle, Sauternes (now *Château Guiraud*)
Rieusec, Sauternes (now *Château Rieussec, Fargues*)
Rabaud, Bommes (now châteaux *Rabaud-Promis* and *Sigalas-Rabaud*)

DEUXIÈMES CRÛS (Second Growths)
Mirat, Barsac (now *Château Myrat*)
Doisy, Barsac (now châteaux *Doisy-Daëne, Doisy-Dubroca* and *Doisy-Védrines*)
Pexoto, Bommes (now part of *Château Rabaud-Promis*)
D'arche, Sauternes (now *Château d'Arche*)
Filhot, Sauternes

Brousset Nérac, Barsac (now châteaux *Brousset* and *Nairac*)
Caillou, Barsac
Suau, Barsac
Malle, Preignac (now *Château de Malle*)
Romer, Preignac (now châteaux *Romer* and *Romer-du-Hayot, Fargues*)
Lamothe, Sauternes (now châteaux *Lamothe* and *Lamothe-Guignard*)

Major wine firms of Bordeaux

Sales figures (in cases) represent the average yearly sales of the *négociant*, both in bulk and bottle. The châteaux referred to are properties owned by, part-owned by, or exclusive to, the *négociant*. The Second Wines are those other than the *Grand Vin*.

KEY
(Bsc) = Barsac; (B) = Bordeaux; (BG) = Bourg; (BL) = Blaye; (BS) = Bordeaux Supérieur; (CC) = Côtes de Castillon; (CF) = Canon-Fronsac; (1er CdB) = Premières Côtes de Bordeaux; (EDM) = Entre-Deux-Mers; (F) = Fronsac; (G) = Graves; (GS) = Graves Supérieur; (L) = Listrac; (LP) = Lalande de Pomerol; (LSE) = Lussac-St.-Emilion; (Mgx) = Margaux; (HM) = Haut-Médoc; (M) = Médoc; (MSE) = Montagne-St.-Emilion; (MM) = Moulis (en Médoc); (P) = Pauillac; (Pom) = Pomerol; (PSE) = Puisseguin-St.-Emilion; (St.-Est) = St.-Estèphe; (St.-Em) = St.-Emilion; (SFB) = Ste.-Foy-Bordeaux; (SGSE) = St.-Georges-St.-Emilion; (St.-J) = St.-Julien; (S) = Sauternes

LA BARONNIE,
BP 117
33250 Pauillac

Sales: *2 million cases*
Bordeaux brands: *"Mouton-Cadet"*
Châteaux: *Clerc-Milon* (P), *Mouton-Baronne-Philippe* (P), *Mouton-Rothschild* (P)

The commercial arm of Baron Philippe de Rothschild's wine interests, its "Mouton-Cadet" is the largest-selling branded Bordeaux.

BARTON & GUESTIER
Château du Dehez,
33290 Blanquefort

Sales: *2.7 million cases*
Bordeaux brands: *"Fonset Lacour"*, *"Prince Noir Bordeaux Supérieur"*
Château: *de Mangol* (HM)

The largest shipper of Bordeaux wine, established in 1725 by Irishman Thomas Barton, later known as "French Tom". His grandson, Hugh Barton, purchased two châteaux, Langoa-Barton and Léoville-Barton.

BORIE-MANOUX
86-90 cours Balguerie-Stuttenberg,
33082 Bordeaux

Sales: *700,000 cases*
Bordeaux brands: *"Beau-Rivage"*, *"Chapelle de la Trinité"*, *"Pont-Royale"*
Châteaux: *Baret* (G), *Batailley* (P), *Beau-Site* (St.-Est), *Belair* (GS), *Bergat* (St.-Em), *Domaine de l'Eglise* (Pom), *Grand St.-Julien*, (St.-J), *Haut-Bages Montpelou* (P), *Trottevieille* (St.-Em)

Owner of some good châteaux that are well distributed in France.

CALVET
75 cours du Médoc,
33300 Bordeaux

Sales: *2.3 million cases*
Bordeaux brands: *"Calvet Réserve"*

Established in 1818 and now jointly owned by Allied-Lyons and Whitbread.

CASTEL FRÈRES
26 rue Georges Guynemer,
33290 Blanquefort

Sales: *2 million cases*
Bordeaux brands: *"de Lestiac"*

Bulk-wine specialist.

CHEVAL QUANCARD
Rue Barbère,
33440 la Grave d'Ambarès

Sales: *1 million cases*
Bordeaux brands: *"Canter"*, *"Chai de Bordes"*, *"Crin Rouge"*
Châteaux: *l'Annonciation* (St.-Em), *Cossieu Coutelin* (St.-Est), *Haut-Logat* (HM), *de Paillet* (1er CdB), *Ribeau Castenac* (M), *Rocher Belair* (St.-Em), *Sadran* (BS), *de Terrefort* (BS), *Tour St.-Joseph* (HM)

Founded in 1844 by Marcel Quancard.

CORDIER
7-13 quai de Paludate,
33800 Bordeaux

Sales: *850,000 cases*
Bordeaux brands: *"Labottière"*, *"Jean Cordier Sélection"*
Châteaux: *Cantemerle* (HM), *Le Gardera* (BS), *Gruaud-Larose* (St.-J), *Clos des Jacobins* (St.-Em), *Lafaurie-Peyraguey* (S), *Lauretan* (BS), *Meyney* (St.-Est), *Plagnac* (M), *Talbot* (St.-J), *Tanesse* (BS)
Second Wines: *"Connétable Talbot"*, *"Prieuré de Meyney"*, *"Sarget de Gruaud-Larose"*

Very reliable, with large *cru classé* holdings, excellent *petits châteaux* and outstanding "Labottière" brand.

EDMUND COSTE & FILS
6-10 rue de la Poste,
33210 Langon

Sales: *500,000 cases*
Châteaux: *Chicane* (G), *Domaine de Gaillat* (G)

Soft, fragrant wines for early drinking.

DOURTHE FRÈRES
35 rue de Bordeaux,
BP 70, Parempuyre,
33290 Blanquefort

Bordeaux brands: *"Beau Mayne"*
Châteaux: *la Croix Landon* (M), *Maucaillou* (MM), *la Providence* (B), *Piada-Clos du Roy* (B), *Teyssier* (St.-Em), *Tronquoy-Lalande* (St.-Est)

Belongs to CVBG (Consortium Vinicole de Bordeaux et de Gironde).

DUBOS FRÈRES
24 quai des Chartrons,
33000 Bordeaux

Bordeaux brands: *"Lafleur Chevalier"*
Châteaux: *Calon* (MSE), *Calon* (SGSE), *Corbin-Michotte* (SE), *Pouget* (Mgx)

This firm underwent a major expansion in the 1970s. Dubos makes a very respectable *vin de table* called "Chevalier Dubos", and good-quality generic Bordeaux wines. It also boasts a substantial list of top *cru classé* châteaux.

LOUIS DUBROCA
Domaine du Ribet,
33450 St.-Loubès

Sales: *750,000 cases*
Château: *Guerry* (BG)

The firm of de Rivoyre & Diprovin exports under the name "Louis Dubroca" and is a specialist in selling *petits châteaux* and *crus classés en primeur*.

DULONG FRÈRES & FILS
29 rue Jules Guesde,
33270 Floirac

Sales: *750,000 cases*
Bordeaux brands: *"Carayon la Rose"*, *"la Parisian"*, *"Michel Cravate"*

A firm that is well established in the UK and USA and produces some attractive supermarket clarets.

LOUIS ESCHENAUER
42 avenue Emile Counord,
33000 Bordeaux

Sales: *400,000 cases*
Bordeaux brands: *"Baron Ségla"*, *"Olivier de France"*
Châteaux: *la Garde* (G), *Rausan-Ségla* (Mgx), *Smith-Haut-Lafitte* (G)

Château la Garde can often rise above its status and Eschenauer's *crus classés*, which seldom used to, have had a resurgence in quality over recent years. Their generic wines are always sound and can be good value. This *négociant* is part of the Lonrho Group.

GALLAIRE & FILS
(May trade as Peter A. Sichel)
19 quai de Bacalan,
BP 12,
33028 Bordeaux

Sales: *400,000 cases*
Bordeaux brands: *"Le Prestige de Bordeaux"*
Châteaux: *d'Angludet* (Mgx), *Chaluimont* (G), *la Chartreuse* (S), *Durand Laplagne* (PSE), *Monlot Clapet* (St.-E), *Palmer* (Mgx), *Pierredon* (BS), *la Tulerie* (EDM)

This firm is run by Peter Sichel who lives at Château d'Angludet – close to Château Palmer, another property in which he has an interest. Soft, fruity styles of generic Bordeaux wines are produced at Verdelais and the introduction of "Le Bordeaux Prestige" is nothing short of revolutionary for the Bordeaux branded market.

VINS RENÉ GERMAIN
Château Perdoulle,
Berson,
33390 Blaye

Sales: *500,000 cases*
Châteaux: *Barrière* (B), *Le Peuy-Saincrit* (B), *Peychaud* (BG), *Peyredoulle* (BL), *Yon Figeac* (St.-Em)

Petits châteaux specialist producing some interesting, good-value wines.

GILBEY DE LOUDENNE
(May trade as IDV France)
14 rue Scandri,
93500 Pantin

Sales: *2.2 million cases*
Bordeaux brands: *"la Cour Pavillon"*
Châteaux: *Giscours* (Mgx), *Loudenne* (M), *de Pez* (St.-Est)

ROBERT GIRAUD
Domaine de Loiseau,
BP 31,
33240 St.-André-de-Cubzac

Sales: 250,000 cases
Bordeaux brands: *"Baron de Vassal"*, *"la Collection Robert Giraud"*, *"Pavillon Cardinal"*, *"Timerlay-Giraud"*
Châteaux: *Bertinat-Lartigue* (St.-Em), *le Bocage* (B), *la Bridane* (St.-J), *de Cadillac* (B), *du Canesse* (BG), *Domaine de Cheval Blanc* (B), *Decorde* (HM), *Flamand* (B), *la Fleur Fourcadet* (BS), *Galley* (BS), *Haut-Baillan* (G), *Haut-Bousquet* (EDM), *Haut-Fourtat* (B), *Moulin de Bel-Air* (M), *Puy-Lesplanques* (Mgx), *Sarabot* (HM), *Timerlay* (B), *la Vieille France* (G), *Vieux Duché* (LP), *Villemaurine* (St.-Em)

Reliable *petits châteaux* specialist.

AURELIEN GRENOUILEAU
5 avenue Foch Pineuilh,
33220 Ste.-Foy-la-Grande

Sales: *500,000 cases*
Bordeaux brands: *"Guy de Beauchamp"*, *"Louis Bert"*, *"Cevim"*, *"Chanceaulme de Ste.-Croix"*, *"Pierre Dantrac"*, *"Paul Davin"*, *"Henri Duroux"*, *"Entrepôts Agricoles Girondins"*, *"Henri Marsal"*, *"André Feraut"*, *"Jean Peytraut"*, *"Thomas Rival"*

Japanese-owned blender of supermarket and own-label claret.

ROGER JOANNE
Fargues Saint Hilaire,
BP 9,
33370 Tresses

Sales: *1 million cases*
Bordeaux brands: *"Chevalier de Vedrines"*, *"Cuvée Petit Hallet"*, *"Duc de Bordeaux"*
Châteaux: *Doisy-Vedrines* (Bsc); *Labat* (HM); *Domaine de l'Ile Margaux* (B); *Pindefleurs* (St.-Em); *Vieille Tour* (EDM)

Although this firm does deal in the *cru classé* market, it is very much a white wine *petits châteaux* specialist.

NATHANIEL JOHNSTON
93 bis quai des Chartrons,
33300 Bordeaux

This family-run business is active in the fine end of the Bordeaux market. The generic wines are sought out by British buyers looking for superior own-label clarets.

KRESSMANN
72 quai de Baclan,
BP 58,
33028 Bordeaux

Sales: *2.5 million cases*
Bordeaux brands: *"Cour Royale"*, *"Kressmann Monopole Dry"*, *"Kressmann Monopole Rouge"*,

"Kressmann Sélectionné"
Châteaux: *Belgrave* (HM), *Capbern* (St.-Est), *la Commanderie* (St.-Est), *Jean-Faure* (St.-Em), *Lafon* (S), *la Marzelle* (St.-Em), *de la Pierrière* (CC), *la Tour Martillac* (G)

This *négociant* belongs to CVBG.

ALEXIS LICHINE & CO
109 rue Archaud,
33028 Bordeaux

Sales: *700,000 cases*
Bordeaux brands: *"Le Bordeaux d'Alexis Lichine"*, *"Chevalier de Lascombes"*, *"Margaux de Lascombes"*, *"Le Reverdon"*, *"Le Saint Emilion d'Alexis Lichine"*, *"Vin Sec Chevalier de Lascombes"*
Châteaux: *Canteloup* (B), *les Cardinaux* (B), *Castéra* (M), *Coutet* (Bsc), *Ferrière* (Mgx), *du Juge* (1er CdB), *Lachesnaye* (HM), *Lamote* (B), *Lanette* (G), *Laroque* (St.-Em), *Lascombes* (Mgx), *Montgrand-Milon* (P), *Thomas* (LSE)
Second Wines: *"Vin Sec de Château Coutet"*, *"Rosé de Lascombes"*, *"Château Segonnes"*

ANDRÉ LURTON
Château Bonnet,
33420 Grézillac

Sales: *175,000 cases*
Châteaux: *Bonnet* (B), *Bonnet*

(EDM), *Coucheroy* (G), *Coubins-Lurton* (G), *Cruzeau* (G), *Goumin* (B/EDM), *Guibon* (B/EDM), *La Louvière* (G), *Rochemorin* (G)

DE LUZE
90 quai des Chartrons,
33300 Bordeaux

Sales: *110 million francs*
Bordeaux brands: *"Baron de Luze"*
Château: *de Malloret* (HM)

MÄHLER-BESSE
49 rue Camille Godard,
33000 Bordeaux

Bordeaux brands: *"la Barbanne"*, *"Bois Gentil"*, *"la Chapelle"*, *"les Cloches"*, *"la Coquille"*, *"la Cour"*, *"Fort Anvin"*, *"Fortin"*, *"Gasquet"*, *"Haut-Gravière"*, *"la Perle Blanche"*, *"Sant-Léon"*, *"le Vieux Moulin"*
Châteaux: *Cheval Noir* (St.-Em); *Palmer* (Mgx)

YVON MAU
Rue de la Gare,
33190 Gironde-sur-Dropt

Sales: *2.7 million cases*
Bordeaux brands: *"Prestige Vieux Cellier d'Yvecourt"*
Châteaux: *de Carles* (F), *la Chaume-Grillée* (EDM), *Coulonges* (B), *la Croix-du-Breuil* (M), *Ducla* (B),

Faugeras (EDM), *Fernon* (G), *la Fleur-Villate* (B), *Girême* (EDM), *la Gravette* (B), *Lavison* (EDM), *de Malbat* (SFB), *Terrefort* (EDM)

MESTREZAT
17 cours de la Martinique,
BP 90,
33027 Bordeaux

Sales: *400,000 cases*
Bordeaux brands: *"les Douelles Bordeaux"*
Châteaux: *Blaignan* (M), *Grand Puy-Ducasse* (P), *Lamothe Bergeron* (HM), *Marsac Seguineau* (M), *Reysson* (HM), *Romefort* (HM), *Tourteau Chollet* (G)
Second Wines: *"le Sec du Rayne Vigneau"*

ARMAND MOUEIX & FILS
Taillefer,
BP 137,
33500 Libourne

Sales: *500,000 cases*
Bordeaux brands: *"Bordeaux"*, *"les Grands Vins de Bordeaux"*, *"les Beaux Vins de Bordeaux"*
Châteaux: *Clos Beauregard* (Pom), *la Croix Bellevue* (LP), *la Fleur Figeac* (St.-Em), *Fonplégade* (St.-Em), *Moulinet* (Pom), *Taillifer* (Pom), *Tauzinat l'Hermitage* (St.-Em), *Toulifaut* (Pom), *la Tour du Pin Figeac* (St.-Em)

High-quality house specializing in single-property wines of the Libournais.

JEAN-PIERRE MOUEIX
54 quai du Priourat,
33500 Libourne

Châteaux: *Canon-de-Brem* (CF), *Canon-Moueix* (CF), *de la Dauphine* (F), *La Fleur Pétrus* (Pom), *Fonroque* (St.-Em), *Magdeleine* (Pom), *Pétrus* (Pom), *Trotanoy* (Pom)

One of the great success stories of the twentieth century.

SCHRÖDER & SCHŸLER
97 quai des Chartrons,
33900 Bordeaux

Sales: *350,000 cases*
Château: *Kirwan* (M)

Established in 1739, this old firm is associated with J-P Moueix.

SDVF
(Société des Vins de France)
Z.I. de la Mouline,
33560 Carbon-Blanc

Sales: *585,000 cases*
Châteaux: *1,200 different châteaux and vintages*.

Established in 1970, this firm expanded by promoting *cru classé* wines.

Important Bordeaux coopératives

CAVES ST-ROCH
"Le Sable",
Queyrac,
33340 Lesparre

Production: *50,000 cases*
Bordeaux brands: *"St-Roch"*
Châteaux: *Laubspin, Pessange, les Trois-Têtons*
Members: *165*
Vineyards: *125 ha (309 acres)*
Established: *1939*

This *coopérative* and the next belong to Uni-Médoc (see below).

CAVE COOPÉRATIVE BELLEVUE
"Plautignan",
Ordonnac,
33340 Lesparre

Production: *100,000 cases*
Members: *75*
Vineyards: *About 225 ha (556 acres)*
Established: *1936*
Bordeaux brands: *"Pavillon de Bellevue"*
Châteaux: *Belfort, de Brie, les Graves Lagorce, Moulin de Bouscateau, Moulin de la Rivière, l'Oume de Pey, la Rose Picot, and Domaine du Grand-Bois*

CAVE COOPÉRATIVE GRAND LISTRAC
33480 Castelnau-Médoc

Production: *65,000 cases*
Members: *About 70*

Vineyards: *160 ha (395 acres)*
Bordeaux brands: *"Grand Listrac"*, *"Clos du Fourcas"*
Châteaux: *Capdet, Vieux Moulin, Guitignan*

This *coopérative* specializes in older vintages and produces soft, early-drinking, Merlot-dominated wines.

CAVE COOPÉRATIVE LA PAROISSE
St.-Seurin-de-Cadourne,
33250 Pauillac

Production: *65,000 cases*
Bordeaux brands: *"La Paroisse"*
Châteaux: *Maurac, Quimper and la Tralle and domaines du Haut-et-de-Brion and de Villa*
Members: *60*
Vineyards: *120 ha (297 acres)*
Established: *1935*

This *coopérative* lies in the AOC Haut-Médoc area.

CAVE COOPÉRATIVE LA ROSE PAUILLAC
La Rose Pauillac,
33250 Pauillac

Production: *60,000 cases*
Bordeaux brands: *"La Rose Pauillac"*
Châteaux: *Haut-Milon and Haut-Saint-Lambert*
Members: *125 (originally 52)*
Established: *1933*

The wines of this, the oldest Médoc *coopérative*, have steadily carved out a fine reputation.

CAVE COOPÉRATIVE ST.-JEAN
Bégadan,
33340 Lesparre

Production: *300,000 cases*
Châteaux: *Begadanet, le Barrail, le Bernet, Breuil-Renaissance, Haut-Condissas, Labadie, Lassus, Meilhan, la Monge, Pey-de-By, Rose-du-Pont, Vimenay*
Members: *75*

A member of Uni-Médoc (see below).

CAVE COOPÉRATIVE DE SAINT-YZANS
Saint-Yzans-de-Médoc,
33340 Lesparre

Production: *100,000 cases*
Bordeaux brands: *"Saint-Brice"*
Châteaux: *Lestruelle, Taffard, Tour-St-Vincent*
Members: *120*
Vineyards: *200 ha (490 acres)*

SOVICOP PRODUCTA
Maison du Paysan,
13 rue Foy,
33082 Bordeaux

Sales: *6 million cases*
Bordeaux brands: *"Belle France"*, *"Bordeaux Mousseux"*, *"Cellier de Fontaurais"*, *"Monsieur de Cyrano"*, *"Marquis de St.-Estèphe"*, *"Médoc Prestige"*

Giant organization marketing the wines of numerous *coopératives*, including the Uni-Médoc combine.

UNI-MÉDOC
Gaillan-en-Médoc,
33340 Lesparre-Médoc

Sales: *150,000 cases*
Bordeaux brands: *"Prestige-Médoc"*

A union of five *coopératives* whose wines are marketed through Sovicop.

UNION DE PRODUCTEURS
BP 27,
33330 St.-Emilion

Production: *300,000 cases*
Bordeaux brands: *"Cuvée Galius"*, *"Haut Quercus" (oak-aged)*, *"Côtes Rocheuses"*, *"Royal St.-Emilion"*
Château: *Berliquet, plus 35 coop-bottled petits châteaux*
Members: *380 (originally 7)*
Established: *1937*
Vineyards: *1,000 ha (2,470 acres)*

This *coopérative* is now the largest in France for a single appellation and produces one-quarter of all the wines in St.-Emilion.

UNIVITIS
Les Lèves-et-Thoumeyragues,
33220 Ste.-Foy-la-Grande

Production: *320,000 cases*
Bordeaux brands: *"Comte de Sansac"*, *"Generique"*
Châteaux: *la Beauze, la Combe, la Mayne, Moulin des Gorins, la Tour les Vergnes and Domaine de Grangeneuve*

Generic wines of Bordeaux

BORDEAUX AOC

As with any large, and thus variable appellation, the generic Bordeaux AOC is responsible for the good, bad and ugly wines of the region. Its overall quality is, however, of a very decent standard, even though the best wines are hardly likely to fit the classic descriptions that have made this region famous. Wines carrying the basic Bordeaux appellation may come from any AOC vineyard in the entire Gironde *département*. Some of the most interesting wines are from classic areas where the more specific appellation is confined to a precise style of wine: for example, a red Bordeaux produced by a château in the Sauternes area. If the wine is a brand, it should be ready to drink. If it is a château wine, the address should reveal its probable area of origin, and the price will be an indication of its quality and thus a guide to when it should be drunk.

RED Most are simply dry, light- to medium-bodied luncheon claret styles, made for early drinking and usually softened by a high Merlot content.

Cabernet sauvignon, Cabernet franc, Carmenère, Merlot, Malbec, Petit verdot

1982, 1983, 1985, 1986

Within 1-5 years

WHITE All of these medium-dry, light- to medium-bodied, basic white Bordeaux contain at least four grams per litre of residual sugar, so they have a certain sweetness. However this is by far the most variable category of this appellation, and there is still a tendency to produce fat, flat and flabby, over-sulphured wines.
If the wine contains less than four grams per litre of residual sugar, it must be described as "Bordeaux Sec" or "Vin Sec de Bordeaux". These dry whites are almost as variable, but most of the best wines of the appellation are found amongst them.

Sémillon, Sauvignon, Muscadelle plus up to 30% in total of Merlot blanc, Colombard, Mauzac, Ondenc, Ugni blanc

1984, 1986, 1988, 1989, 1990

Within 1-2 years

ROSÉ When made by individual properties, this medium-dry, medium-bodied wine can be attractive.

Cabernet sauvignon, Cabernet franc, Carmenère, Merlot, Malbec, Petit verdot

1985, 1986, 1988, 1989, 1990

Immediately

BORDEAUX CLAIRET AOC

"Clairet" is a term that refers to a red wine that is light in body and colour. Vin *claret* in Old French was a term of respect; this suggests that Bordeaux achieved a reputation for limpidity before other wines.

ROSÉ Richer, darker rosé or failed, feeble red? The best examples of this medium-dry, medium-bodied wine come from the village of Quinsac in the Premières Côtes de Bordeaux.

Cabernet sauvignon, Cabernet franc, Carmenère, Merlot, Malbec, Petit verdot

1983, 1985, 1988, 1989, 1990

Within 1-2 years

BORDEAUX MOUSSEUX AOC

A reasonable quantity of modest quality, sparkling wine is made in Bordeaux, from Bordeaux grapes, by the *méthode champenoise*. Not as tart as Loire equivalents, yet there is a tendency to over-sweeten them.

SPARKLING WHITE This white Bordeaux bubbly varies from dry to sweet and is light- to medium-bodied. Strangely enough, very little is made compared to the production of rosé, yet most of the best wines are white.

Sémillon, Sauvignon, Muscadelle, Cabernet sauvignon, Cabernet franc, Carmenère, Merlot, Malbec, Petit verdot plus up to 30% in total of Ugni blanc, Merlot blanc, Colombard, Mauzac and Ondenc

Normally non-vintage

Within 1-2 years

SPARKLING ROSÉ The potential quality of this dry to sweet, light- to medium-bodied wine could be improved if the regulations allowed for the inclusion of white grapes.

Cabernet sauvignon, Cabernet franc, Carmenère, Merlot, Malbec, Petit verdot

Normally non-vintage

Between 2-3 years

BORDEAUX ROSÉ AOC

The theory is that this appellation is reserved for wine deliberately produced as rosé, while "Bordeaux Clairet" is for a light-coloured red wine. Both may simply be labelled "Bordeaux AOC". For technical details *see* Bordeaux AOC.

BORDEAUX SEC

White Bordeaux with less than four grams per litre of residual sugar. For technical details *see* Bordeaux AOC.

BORDEAUX SUPÉRIEUR AOC

Technically superior by only half a degree of alcohol, yet most of these wines do seem to have a greater consistency of quality, and therefore value. All generics are variable, but this one is less so than most.

RED Dry, light- or medium- to full-bodied wines with a lot of variation but generally fuller and richer than the basic Bordeaux appellation.

Cabernet sauvignon, Cabernet franc, Carmenère, Merlot, Malbec, Petit verdot

1983, 1985, 1988, 1989, 1990

Between 2-6 years

WHITE Dry and sometimes sweet, light- to medium-bodied white wines that are little seen.

Sémillon, Sauvignon, Muscadelle plus up to 30% in total of Merlot blanc, Colombard, Mauzac, Ondenc, Ugni blanc; the proportion of Merlot blanc must not exceed 15%

1985, 1986, 1988, 1989, 1990

Within 1-2 years

BORDEAUX SUPÉRIEUR CLAIRET AOC

Little-seen appellation: the wines are either sold as "Bordeaux Supérieur" or "Bordeaux Clairet".

ROSÉ Medium-dry and medium-bodied as Bordeaux Clairet, but with an extra half-degree of alcohol.

Cabernet sauvignon, Cabernet franc, Carmenère, Merlot, Malbec, Petit verdot

1984, 1985, 1988, 1989, 1990

Within 1-2 years

BORDEAUX SUPÉRIEUR ROSÉ AOC

This appellation has a small cast – and Château Lascombe's Rosé de Lascombes tops the bill.

ROSÉ As few examples of these medium-dry, medium-bodied wines exist, it is possible to generalize and describe them as fuller, richer and having more class than any other Bordeaux Rosé.

Cabernet sauvignon, Cabernet franc, Carmenère, Merlot, Malbec, Petit verdot

1984, 1985, 1988, 1989, 1990

Within 1-2 years

CRÉMANT DE BORDEAUX AOC

This new sparkling wine appellation was introduced in 1990 and will eventually replace Bordeaux Mousseux.

VIN SEC DE BORDEAUX AOC

White Bordeaux with less than four grams of residual sugar. For technical details, *see* Bordeaux AOC.

GENERIC BORDEAUX BRANDS

Bordeaux has the greatest reputation in the world, but as in all regions, ordinary wines do exist. In Bordeaux, such products can boast the same illustrious appellations as the greatest wines. Remember, however, that more than money separates a generic Margaux from Château Margaux. The former is the blended product of relatively inferior wines grown anywhere within the appellation, the latter a selection of only the finest wines grown on one estate — the premier growth of Margaux. As a branded generic Bordeaux wine can be the most disappointing introduction to the world's greatest wine region, the following brands — all modest wines — are suggested as consistently giving the best value:

BORIE-MANOUX
"Beau-Rivage"

CORDIER
"Labottière"

DOURTHE FRÈRES
"Beau Mayne"

DUBOS FRÈRES
"Lafleur Chevalier"

ESCHENAUER
"Eschenauer Claret"

IDV FRANCE
"la Cour Pavillon"

JOANNE, Roger
"Chevalier de Vedrines"

KRESSMANN
"Kressmann Sélectionné"

MOUEIX & FILS, Armand
"les Beaux Vins de Bordeaux"

SICHEL
"Le Prestige de Bordeaux"

The best châteaux of generic Bordeaux

RED WINES

CHÂTEAU DE BERTIN
Cantois,
33760 Targon

Powerful Cabernet sauvignon-dominated wines that age gracefully.

CHÂTEAU FAUGAS
33410 Cadillac

Well-balanced wines with attractive berry-fruit flavours.

CHÂTEAU LA LALNADE SAINT-JEAN
33450 St.-Loubès

Fresh, light and easy to drink.

CHÂTEAU LAPEYÈRE
33410 Cadillac

Well-structured wine, dominated by Cabernet sauvignon.

CHÂTEAU DE LUGAGNAC
33790 Pellegrue

Firm and fleshy wine that can show some finesse.

DOMAINE DE MALINEAU
33490 St.-Macaire

Sometimes light in body, but never lacking a certain depth of interest.

CHÂTEAU MORILLON
33580 Monségur

Rich, fat and juicy wines.

CLOS DE PELIGON
33450 St.-Loubès

Fine, full-bodied with a hint of oak.

CHÂTEAU POUCHAUD-LARQUEY
33190 La Réole

Full and rich with lots of fruit.

"LE PRESTIGE BORDEAUX"
(Peter A. Sichel brand)

A branded wine with nine months in new oak which deserves "best wine" status.

CHÂTEAU ROC-DE-CAYLA
33760 Targon

Easy-drinking, well-balanced wines with good fruit and some finesse.

CHÂTEAU THIEULEY
33580 Créon

These medium-bodied wines are definitely elegant and have more than a hint of cask-aging.

CHÂTEAU TIMBERLAY
33240 St.-André-de-Cubzac

Deep-coloured wines, full of flavour, but not without a certain elegance.

WHITE WINES

CHÂTEAU COURTEY
33490 St.-Macaire

Intensely flavoured old-style wines that have a remarkable bouquet.

CHÂTEAU GUIRAUD
Sauternes,
33210 Langon

When Hamilton Narby purchased this First Growth property in Sauternes, his prime objective was to elevate its sweet wine to the quality and reputation it once enjoyed. There was too little Sémillon, so he began planting more and created a dry white Bordeaux AOC called "G", to use up the excess Sauvignon blanc. It could be improved with a pre-fermentation maceration.

"LE PRESTIGE BORDEAUX"
(Peter A. Sichel brand)

A basic white Bordeaux wine, fermented in cask and wood-aged for a further seven months.

CHÂTEAU RENON
33550 Langoiran

Pleasantly fresh and floral Sauvignon-style wine.

CHÂTEAU REYNON
33410 Cadillac

Star-performing château producing two styles of dry white wine. Both are excellent, but the élite cuvée sold as "Sauvignon Vieilles Vignes du Château Reynon" is quite extraordinary.

CHÂTEAU THIEULEY
33580 Créon

Fine, fresh floral and fruity wines.

BORDEAUX SUPÉRIEUR WINES

CHÂTEAU DES ARRAS
33240 St.-André-de-Cubzac

Deep-coloured wines with good structure and lots of chunky fruit flavour.

MARQUIS DE BOIRAC
33350 Castillon-la-Bataille

Super value coopérative wine with a big, oaky bouquet and the fruit to match.

CHÂTEAU FONCHEREAU
33450 St.-Loubès

Well-structured, finely-balanced vins de garde of extremely good quality.

CHÂTEAU FOUCHÉ
33710 Bourg-sur-Gironde

This wine is firm yet has fat, juicy fruit and a smooth finish.

CHÂTEAU LACOMBE-CADIOT
Ludon-Médoc,
33290 Blanquefort

These well-coloured wines have a big bouquet, delicious fruit, oaky-vanilla undertones and a lengthy finish.

CHÂTEAU LAGRANGE-LES-TOURS
33240 St.-André-de-Cubzac

Well-made, full and flavourful wines.

CHÂTEAU LATOUR
St.-Martin-du-Puy,
33540 Sauveterre-de-Guyenne

Medium-bodied wines of consistent quality, good fruit and smooth flavour.

CHÂTEAU LAVILLE
St.-Sulpice-et-Cameyrac,
33450 St.-Loubès

Very rich, tannic and powerfully structured wines with spicy fruit undertones.

CHÂTEAU LA MICHELERIE
33240 St.-André-de-Cubzac

Another property producing a big, tannic style of wine.

CHÂTEAU LES MOINES-MARTIN
33133 Galgon

Well-made wine for reasonably early drinking, with an attractive bouquet, round fruit and fine balance.

CHÂTEAU PUYFROMAGE
St.-Cibbard,
33570 Lussac

Attractive, well-balanced, medium-bodied and easy to drink.

CHÂTEAU SARRAIL-LA-GUILLAMERIE
33450 St.-Loubès

Rich and fleshy wine that softens nicely with age.

CHÂTEAU TOUR-DE-L'ESPERANCE
33133 Galgon

Soft and smooth wines, full of fat, ripe and juicy fruit, yet not without finesse.

CHÂTEAU TOUR PETIT PUCH
33750 St.-Germain-du-Puch

Attractively-coloured, well-made, well-balanced wines, with a touch of spice.

CHÂTEAU VIEUX MOULIN
33141 Villegouge

These are well-rounded, long and supple wines of consistently fine quality.

BORDEAUX ROSÉ WINES

CHÂTEAU BERTINERIE
33620 Cavignac

Quite a serious rosé, pleasantly aromatic, with delicately rich, floral fruit on the palate and a smooth finish.

CHÂTEAU CHANET
33420 Branne

Aromatic wine with a floral palate.

CHÂTEAU LA MONGIE
33240 St.-André-de-Cubzac

Pleasant, floral and fruity wine.

LE ROSÉ DE CLARKE
Listrac,
33480 Castelnau-de-Médoc

This relatively recent introduction from Château Clarke has all the fragrance expected from a classic dry rosé.

BORDEAUX CLAIRET WINES

DOMAINE DU BRU
St.-Avit-St.-Nazaire,
33220 Ste.-Foy-la-Grande

Refreshing wines that are light in colour and body and easy to drink.

CAVE DE QUINSAC
Quinsac,
33360 La Tresne

Delicately-coloured, light-bodied, rosé-styled wines.

BORDEAUX MOUSSEUX WINES

CORDELIERS
33330 St.-Emilion

A range of decent-quality sparkling wines.

LAYTERON
Montagne,
33570 Lussac

More than 40,000 cases of unpretentious sparkling wine produced from grapes grown in the Entre-Deux-Mers.

CHÂTEAU LESCURE
Verdelais,
33490 St.-Macaire

An interesting property due to its small production of château-bottled bubbly.

BORDEAUX SUPÉRIEUR ROSÉ WINES

ROSÉ DE LASCOMBES

Refreshing, fruity rosé of excellent character, quality and finesse.

The Médoc

Travelling northwest from Bordeaux into the Médoc, the first vineyards encountered produce mild, unexceptional wines, but from Ludon onwards, the wines become progressively more characterful, acquire finesse and, after Margaux, gain considerable body. Beyond St.-Estèphe the wines are rustic, the firmness of body eventually turns to coarseness, and the finesse fades.

THE MÉDOC TAKES ITS NAME from the Latin *medio aquae* – "between the waters" – referring to the Gironde and the Atlantic. It is a long, thin strip of prized vines, extending northwest from the city limits of Bordeaux to the Pointe de Grave. At its centre is the classic area of Bordeaux where the vast majority of the most famous châteaux are located, and yet this was the last major district of the region to be cultivated.

While winemaking in St.-Emilion began as early as the Roman occupation, it was another thousand years before scattered plots of vines spread along the Médoc. Across the large, brown expanse of water called the Gironde, the Romans viewed Bourg and considered its hilly area far more suitable for growing vines. At that time the marshland of the Médoc was difficult to cross and impossible to cultivate. Now the Médoc is the envy of winemakers the world over and Bourg merely a source of inexpensive, if good-value, basic Bordeaux.

The Médoc style: variations on a theme

The four famous communes of Margaux, St.-Julien, Pauillac and St.-Estèphe, plus the two less well-known but developing communes of Listrac and Moulis, are to be found in the Haut-Médoc, where the wines are fine, firm and fleshy. The Haut-Médoc begins at Blanquefort and le Taillan, on the outskirts of the city, along the northern reaches of the Graves district. The wines here are fairly neutral and lack definition. The greatest wines of Haut-Médoc are found in the area beginning at Ludon with Château la Lagune – the first *cru classé* encountered north of the city. It is no coincidence that fine Bourgeois growths like Château

PROPORTION OF AOC AREA UNDER VINE REPRESENTED BY THE *CRUS CLASSÉS* OF THE MÉDOC

APPELLATION	Total ha (acres)	*Crus classés* ha (acres)	represents
Haut-Médoc	3,175 (7,846)	255 (630)	(8% of AOC, 9% of *crus classés*)
Margaux	1,165 (2,878)	854 (2,100)	(73% of AOC, 31% of *crus classés*)
Pauillac	950 (2,347)	842 (2,081)	(89% of AOC, 30% of *crus classés*)
St.-Estèphe	1,100 (2,718)	226 (558)	(21% of AOC, 8% of *crus classés*)
St.-Julien	750 (1,853)	628 (1,552)	(84% of AOC, 22% of *crus classés*)
Listrac	555 (1,371)		(no *crus classés*)
Moulis	605 (1,495)		(no *crus classés*)
Médoc	3,075 (7,598)		(no *crus classés*)
TOTAL	11,375 (28,106)	2,805 (6,921)	(25% of Médoc AOCs, 100% of *crus classés*)

DISTRIBUTION OF *CRUS CLASSÉS* OF THE MÉDOC THROUGHOUT THE APPELLATIONS

APPELLATION	GROWTHS					TOTAL
	1st	2nd	3rd	4th	5th	
Haut-Médoc	–	–	1	1	3	5
Margaux	1	5	10	3	2	21
Pauillac	3	2	–	1	12	18
St.-Estèphe	–	2	1	1	1	5
St.-Julien	–	5	2	4	–	11
TOTAL	4	14	14	10	18	60

Barrel making at Lafite-Rothschild, below
Wines are aged in new oak at Château Lafite-Rothschild, though for a shorter length of time than in the past. The barrels are made with great care in time-honoured, traditional manner.

Protecting the vines, right
At the end of the rows of vines the bright blue residue of copper sulphate is much in evidence. "Bordeaux mixture", as the copper sulphate is known, protects the vine against various forms of rot.

FACTORS AFFECTING TASTE AND QUALITY

Location
The left bank of the Gironde estuary, stretching northwest from Bordeaux to Soulac.

Climate
Two large masses of water either side of the Médoc – the ocean and the estuary – act as a heat-regulator and help provide a micro-climate ideal for viticulture. The Gulf Stream gives generally mild winters, warm summers and long, sunny autumns. The district is protected from westerly and north-westerly winds by the continuous coastal strip of pine forest which runs roughly parallel to the Médoc.

Aspect
Undulating hillsides with knolls and gentle slopes. The best vineyards can "see the river" and virtually all areas of the Haut-Médoc gradually slope from the watershed to the Gironde. Marshy areas, where vines cannot be grown, punctuate most communes.

Soil
A combination of similar topsoils over different subsoils. The topsoil is characterized by its outcrops of gravel, consisting of sand from the Landes region which has intermingled with siliceous gravel of varying particle size. Subsoils may contain gravel and reach a depth of several metres, or may consist of sand, often rich in humus. Limestone and clay are also present.

Viticulture and vinification
Only red wines have the right to the Médoc appellation. Mechanical harvesting is commonplace and all grapes must be de-stalked prior to fermentation, which takes place in tanks or vats. The use of stainless steel vats is increasing. The duration of skin-contact varies between one and two weeks, although some châteaux have reverted to four weeks, as was once fairly standard.

Primary grape varieties
Cabernet sauvignon, Cabernet franc, Merlot

Secondary grape varieties
Carmenère, Malbec, Petit verdot

d'Agassac are also to be found nearby.

The wines at Margaux are soft and velvety and full of feminine charm, although very much *vins de garde*. The wines of St.-Julien are elegant with a very pure flavour. They have the delicate touch of Margaux, yet lean closer to Pauillac in body. The wines of Pauillac are powerful, often having a rich blackcurrant flavour with intriguing hints of cedar and tobacco. These are wines of great finesse and, with no less than three of the four First Growths, Pauillac can be considered the greatest appellation of the Médoc. St.-Estèphe includes many minor growths of rustic charm and a few classic wines. Technology is changing the robustness of its spicy wines to richness.

Beyond St.-Estèphe lies the commune of St.-Seurin-de-Cadourne which is entitled to AOC Haut-Médoc, after which the appellation becomes simply Médoc. This area, formerly known as the Bas-Médoc, has a somewhat lesser reputation. However, many exceptional wines are made here: the triangle from St.-Yzans to Lesparre to Valeyrac includes such outstanding minor growths as

Loudenne, Potensac, la Cardonne, Blaignan, les Ormes-Sorbet, la Tour-St.-Bonnet, la Tour-de-By and Patache d'Aux. Some of these wines have a luxurious touch of new oak and some are simply stunning on their own, but it is true to say that the general style is more simplistic than in the Haut-Médoc.

THE FIGHT FOR GRAVEL

The best soils for vine-growing also happen to be the most suitable for gravel quarrying. After the war, in the absence of any legislation, gravel quarrying started in abandoned vineyards. Once the gravel was gone, the opportunity to reclaim the area as a vineyard was lost.

There is plenty of gravel in the Gironde estuary, but it is more profitable to take it from an open pit. Quarrying companies will continue to plunder the Médoc's finite resources until the government agrees to protect them.

THE MÉDOC, see also p. 37

A narrow strip of land between the Gironde and the Atlantic, the Médoc stretches northwards from the city of Bordeaux to the Pointe de Grave.

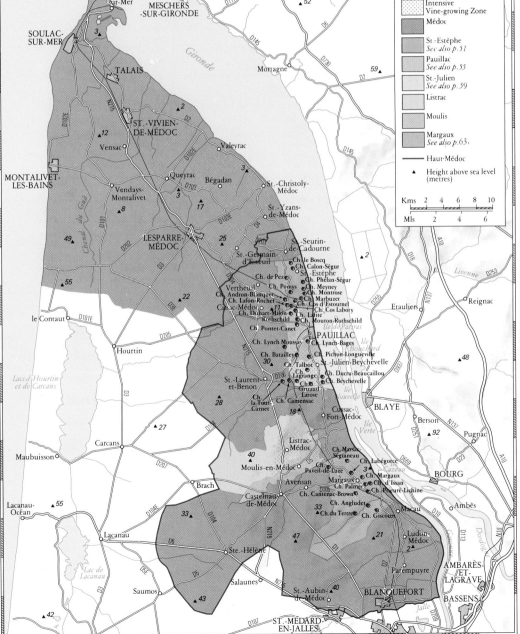

The wines of the Médoc

HAUT-MÉDOC AOC

This appellation is generally very reliable, with a few great value *crus classés* and many high-quality Bourgeois Growths.

RED These bone-dry or dry wines have a generosity of fruit tempered by a firm structure, and are medium- to full-bodied.

🍇 Cabernet sauvignon, Cabernet franc, Merlot, Malbec, Petit verdot, Carmenère

🍷 1985, 1986, 1988, 1989, 1990

🍾 Between 6-15 years (*crus classés*), between 5-8 years (others)

LISTRAC AOC

Significant funds have been invested here over the last ten years and this has produced a number of high-performance châteaux.

RED These dry, medium- to full-bodied wines have the fruit and finesse of St.-Julien combined with the firmness of St.-Estèphe.

🍇 Cabernet sauvignon, Cabernet franc, Carmenère, Merlot, Malbec, Petit verdot

🍷 1985, 1986, 1988, 1989, 1990

🍾 Between 5-10 years

MARGAUX AOC

This appellation covers five communes, Cantenac and Margaux itself being the most important. It is in the unique position of having a namesake château.

RED Exquisite, dry, medium- to full-bodied wines that can be deep-coloured and fabulously rich, yet they have great finesse and a silky finish.

🍇 Cabernet sauvignon, Cabernet franc, Carmenère, Merlot, Malbec, Petit verdot

🍷 1985, 1986, 1988, 1989, 1990

🍾 Between 5-20 years (*crus classés*), between 5-10 years (others)

MÉDOC AOC

Technically this appellation covers the entire Médoc, but most wines actually come from north of the Haut-Médoc in the area which was once called Bas-Médoc. Its vineyards have undergone a rapid and extensive expansion since the mid-1970s.

RED The best of these bone-dry to dry, medium-bodied wines are similar in style to good Haut-Médocs, although the style is less sophisticated.

🍇 Cabernet sauvignon, Cabernet franc, Carmenère, Merlot, Malbec, Petit verdot

🍷 1985, 1986, 1988, 1989, 1990

🍾 Between 4-8 years

MOULIS or MOULIS-EN-MÉDOC AOC

One of the two communal appellations located on the Atlantic side of the Médoc. It is immediately south of Listrac and, although it adjoins Margaux, the appellation with the highest number of *cru classé* châteaux, there are none here.

RED These dry, medium- to full-bodied wines have more power than those of Margaux, but far less finesse, although there is no lack of fruit or length or individual character.

🍇 Cabernet sauvignon, Cabernet franc, Carmenère, Merlot, Malbec, Petit verdot

🍷 1981, 1982, 1983, 1985, 1986

🍾 Between 5-12 years

PAUILLAC AOC

This commune vies with Margaux as the most famous appellation and its First Growths of Latour, Lafite and Mouton make it the most important.

RED Dark and virtually opaque, great Pauillac is a bone-dry or dry, powerfully constructed wine, typically redolent of blackcurrants and new oak. It might be unapproachable when young, but is always rich and warm when mature.

🍇 Cabernet sauvignon, Cabernet franc, Carmenère, Merlot, Malbec, Petit verdot

🍷 1985, 1986, 1988, 1989, 1990

🍾 Between 9-25 years (*crus classés*), 5-12 years (others)

ST.-ESTÈPHE AOC

Cos d'Estournel is one of the best Second Growths in the Médoc but the strength of this appellation lies in its range of *crus Bourgeois*. The area under vine is only slightly less than that of Margaux, which has the largest area, but St.-Estèphe has far more unclassified châteaux.

RED If Pauillac is the stallion of the four famous appellations, St.-Estèphe must be the shire-horse. These dry or bone-dry, medium- to very full-bodied wines are big and strong, yet majestic and not without dignity. St.-Estèphe demands affection and, with the rich fruit of a sunny year, deserves it. This is an immensely enjoyable, sweet-spice and cedary wine that can have lots of honest, chunky, fruit. Cos d'Estournel is the thoroughbred of the commune.

🍇 Cabernet sauvignon, Cabernet franc, Carmenère, Merlot, Malbec, Petit verdot

🍷 1982, 1983, 1985, 1989, 1990

🍾 Between 8-25 years (*crus classés*), between 5-12 years (others)

ST.-JULIEN AOC

This is the smallest of the four famous appellations, yet it is the most intensively cultivated, with almost 50 per cent of the commune under vine. There are no First Growths, but there are five Seconds and the standard and consistency of style is very high.

RED These are distinguished dry, medium- to full-bodied wines that have an intense purity of style and varietal flavour and can be long-lived. Well balanced and elegant, the wines fall between the lushness of Margaux and the firmer structure of Pauillac.

🍇 Cabernet sauvignon, Cabernet franc, Carmenère, Merlot, Malbec, Petit verdot

🍷 1985, 1986, 1988, 1989, 1990

🍾 Between 6-20 years (*crus classés*), 5-12 years (others)

The best châteaux of Haut-Médoc, Listrac and Moulis

CHÂTEAU BELGRAVE
St.-Laurent

AOC Haut-Médoc
5ème Cru Classé
Production: *18,000 cases*

Situated on a good gravel bank behind Château Lagrange, the wine, which is matured in wood for 24 months with up to 50 per cent new oak, seldom lives up to its *terroir*.

RED The 1983 shows a good balance of blackcurrant fruit and ripe acidity, with firm tannin structure and vanilla overtones of new oak.

🍇 Cabernet sauvignon 60%, Merlot 35%, Petit verdot 5%

🍷 1983, 1986

🍾 Between 8-16 years

CHÂTEAU CAMENSAC
St.-Laurent

AOC Haut-Médoc
5ème Cru Classé
Production: *20,000 cases*

Situated behind Château Belgrave, this property was renovated in the mid-1960s, and now makes wine equivalent to its classification. It is matured in wood for 14-18 months, with 40 per cent of the casks new oak.

RED Well-structured wine, with a medium weight of fruit and a certain amount of finesse.

🍇 Cabernet sauvignon 60%, Cabernet franc 20%, Merlot 20%

🍷 1982, 1983, 1985

🍾 Between 8-20 years

CHÂTEAU CANTEMERLE
Macau

AOC Haut-Médoc
5ème Cru Classé
Production: *20,000 cases*

In 1980 new stainless-steel fermentation vats replaced the old wooden ones that had been responsible for some stingy vintages. Also discarded were all the old casks, so the 1980 vintage was uniquely matured in 100 per cent new oak. The wine is normally matured in wood for 18-20 months, with one-third new oak.

RED Deliciously rich wines of fine colour, creamy-oaky fruit, beautiful balance and increasing finesse.

🍇 Cabernet sauvignon 45%, Cabernet franc 13%, Merlot 40%, Petit verdot 2%

🍷 1980, 1982, 1983, 1985

🍾 Between 8-20 years

Second Wine: "Baron Villeneuve de Cantemerle"

CHÂTEAU LA LAGUNE
Ludon

AOC Haut-Médoc
3ème Cru Classé
Production: *25,000 cases*

Owned by Jean-Michel Ducellier of Champagne Ayala, the immaculate vineyard of this fine château is situated on sand and gravel soil. It is the first *cru classé* encountered after leaving Bordeaux. The wine is consistently excellent.

RED Deep-coloured wines with complex *cassis* and stone-fruit flavours intermingled with rich, creamy-vanilla oak nuances. These wines are full-bodied but supple.

🍇 Cabernet sauvignon 55%, Cabernet franc 20%, Merlot 20%, Petit verdot 5%

🍷 1982, 1983, 1985, 1986, 1988

🍾 Between 10-30 years

Second Wine: "Ludon-Pomies-Agassac"

CHÂTEAU LA TOUR-CARNET
St.-Laurent

AOC Haut-Médoc
4ème Cru Classé
Production: *16,000 cases*

This charming, thirteenth-century, miniature moated castle has a well-kept vineyard. Unfortunately, the reputation of its wines is very lacklustre. Some critics believe it is improving.

RED Medium- to full-bodied wines of good colour, but light in fruit and lacking any real richness of flavour.

🍇 Cabernet sauvignon 53%, Cabernet franc 10%, Merlot 33%, Petit verdot 4%

🍷 1982, 1983, 1986

🍾 Between 6-12 years

Second Wine: "Le Sire de Camin"

The best of the rest

CHÂTEAU D'AGASSAC
Ludon

AOC Haut-Médoc
Cru Bourgeois
Production: *9,000 cases*

This property produces one of the best unclassified wines in Haut-Médoc.

RED Dark-coloured, plummy wine with masses of soft, ripe fruit.

- Cabernet sauvignon 60%, Merlot 40%
- 1982, 1983, 1985, 1988
- Between 4-10 years

CHÂTEAU D'ARSAC
Arsac

AOC Haut-Médoc
Production: *5,500 cases*

The only property in this commune not to benefit from the Margaux appellation. The wines are matured in wood for 12-18 months, with 20 per cent new oak.

RED Deep-coloured, full-bodied wines.

- Cabernet sauvignon 80%, Cabernet franc 5%, Merlot 15%
- 1982, 1985
- Between 7-15 years

Second Wine: Château Ségur-d'Arsac
Other wines: Château Le Monteil-d'Arsac

CHÂTEAU BEAUMONT
Cussac

AOC Haut-Médoc
Cru Bourgeois
Production: *30,000 cases*

This large property consistently produces wines of good quality.

RED Aromatically attractive wines with elegant fruit and supple tannin.

- Cabernet sauvignon 56%, Cabernet franc 7%, Merlot 36%, Petit verdot 1%
- 1981, 1982, 1983, 1985, 1988
- Between 4-8 years

Second Wine: Château Moulin-d'Arvigny

CHÂTEAU BÉCADE
Listrac

AOC Haut-Médoc
Cru Bourgeois
Production: *13,000 cases*

This well-situated vineyard produces wines that regularly win medals.

RED These well-coloured wines of good bouquet are medium- to full-bodied with generous fruit.

- Cabernet sauvignon 75%, Merlot 25%
- 1982, 1985
- Between 4-8 years

Second Wine: "La Fleur Bécade"

CHÂTEAU BEL-AIR-LAGRAVE

AOC Moulis
Production: *5,500 cases*

Classified *Cru Bourgeois* in 1932, but not included in the *Syndicat's* 1978 list, although it is superior to a few that were.

RED Vividly-coloured wines of fine bouquet and firm tannic structure.

- Cabernet sauvignon 60%, Merlot 35%, Petit verdot 5%
- 1982, 1983, 1985
- Between 8-20 years

CHÂTEAU BEL-ORME-TRONQUOY-DE-LALANDE
St.-Seurin-de-Cadourne

AOC Haut-Médoc
Cru Bourgeois
Production: *10,000 cases*

A confusingly similar name to Château Tronquoy-Lalande, St.-Estèphe.

RED Firm, fruity, four-square wines.

- Cabernet sauvignon 30%, Cabernet franc 30%, Merlot 30%, Malbec and Petit verdot 10%
- 1982, 1983, 1985, 1988
- Between 7-15 years

CHÂTEAU BISTON-BRILLETTE

AOC Moulis
Production: *7,000 cases*

Classified *Cru Bourgeois* in 1932, but not included in 1978, although it is superior to a few that were.

RED Wines that are rich in colour and fruit with a spicy-*cassis* character and a supple tannin structure.

- Cabernet sauvignon and Cabernet franc 50%, Merlot 50%
- 1981, 1982, 1983, 1985
- Between 5-15 years

CHÂTEAU LE BOURDIEU

AOC Haut-Médoc
Production: *25,000 cases*

Situated between Vertheuil and St.-Estèphe, this château was classified *Cru Bourgeois* in 1932, but not included in the *Syndicat's* 1978 list, although it is superior to a few that were.

RED Well-coloured, full-bodied wines of robust character, which are not lacking in charm.

- Cabernet sauvignon 50%, Cabernet franc 20%, Merlot 30%
- 1982, 1983, 1985, 1988
- Between 7-15 years

Second Wine: Château les Sablons
Other wines: Château la Croix des Sablons

CHÂTEAU BRANAS-GRAND-POUJEAUX

AOC Moulis
Production: *4,000 cases*

Excellent and rapidly improving wines aged in wood for 18-22 months, with one-third new oak.

RED Well-structured wine with plenty of accessible fruit, charming aromatic properties and increasing finesse.

- Cabernet sauvignon 60%, Merlot 35%, Petit verdot 5%
- 1981, 1983, 1985, 1988
- Between 5-12 years

CHÂTEAU BRILLETTE

AOC Moulis
Cru Bourgeois
Production: *11,000 cases*

This château's name is supposed to derive from its glinting pebbly soil.

RED Attractively coloured wines of full but supple body, with delightful summer fruit and vanilla aromas.

- Cabernet sauvignon 55%, Merlot 40%, Petit verdot 5%
- 1981, 1982, 1983, 1985
- Between 5-12 years

CHÂTEAU CAMBON-LA-PELOUSE
Macau

AOC Haut-Médoc
Production: *25,000 cases*

Under the same ownership as Château Grand Barrail-Lamarzelle-Figeac, this estate was classified *Cru Bourgeois* in 1932, but not included in the *Syndicat's* 1978 list.

RED Soft, medium- to full-bodied wines with fresh and juicy flavours.

- Cabernet sauvignon 30%, Cabernet franc 20%, Merlot 50%
- 1981, 1982, 1983, 1985, 1988
- Between 3-8 years

CHÂTEAU CAP-LÉON-VEYRIN

AOC Listrac
Cru Bourgeois
Production: *7,000 cases*

Simply called Château Cap-Léon originally, the vines of this property are planted in two plots of clay-gravel soil over marl.

RED Deep-coloured, full-bodied, richly flavoured wines with high extract levels and a good balance of tannin.

- Cabernet sauvignon 45%, Cabernet franc 2%, Merlot 50%, Petit verdot 3%
- 1980, 1981, 1982, 1983, 1985
- Between 8-20 years

CHÂTEAU LA CARDONNE
Blaignan

AOC Médoc
Cru Bourgeois
Production: *35,000 cases*

This property was purchased by the Rothschilds of Lafite in 1973 and has since been expanded and renovated.

RED Attractive, medium-bodied wines with a good, grapey perfume and silky texture, made in an elegant style.

- Cabernet sauvignon 34%, Cabernet franc 8%, Merlot 58%
- 1981, 1982, 1983, 1985, 1988
- Between 6-10 years

CHÂTEAU CARONNE-STE-GEMME
St.-Laurent

AOC Haut-Médoc
Cru Bourgeois
Production: *23,000 cases*

A superb island of vines on a gravel plateau south of Château Lagrange.

RED Full-bodied, classy wines rich in flavour with creamy-oaky undertones, supple tannin structure and finesse.

- Cabernet sauvignon 65%, Merlot 35%
- 1981, 1982, 1983, 1985
- Between 8-20 years

CHÂTEAU CASTÉRA
St.-Germain d'Esteuil

AOC Médoc
Production: *15,000 cases*

The original château was reduced to ruins by the Black Prince in the fourteenth century. Castéra was classified *Cru Bourgeois* in 1932, but not included in 1978.

RED Soft-textured, medium-bodied wines best drunk relatively young.

🍇 Cabernet sauvignon and Cabernet franc 60%, Merlot 40%

🍷 1981, 1983, 1985

🍶 Between 4-8 years

CHÂTEAU CHASSE-SPLEEN

AOC Moulis
Cru Bourgeois
Production: *25,000 cases*

The proprietor of this quality-conscious property also owns *cru classé* Château Haut-Bages-Libéral and the excellent unclassified growth of Château la Gurgue in Margaux.

RED Full-bodied wine of great finesse, vivid colour and a luxuriant, creamy-rich flavour of *cassis* and chocolate with warm, spicy-vanilla undertones.

🍇 Cabernet sauvignon 50%, Cabernet franc 2%, Merlot 45%, Petit verdot 3%

🍷 1980, 1981, 1982, 1983, 1985, 1986, 1988

🍶 Between 8-20 years

CHÂTEAU CISSAC
Cissac-Médoc

AOC Haut-Médoc
Cru Bourgeois
Production: *13,500 cases*

This wine is always good value, especially in hot years. It is fermented in wood and matured in cask with no *vin de presse*.

RED Well-coloured, full-bodied wines.

🍇 Cabernet sauvignon 75%, Merlot 20%, Petit verdot 5%

🍷 1982, 1983, 1985, 1986, 1988

🍶 Between 8-20 years

Second Wine: Château Abiet

CHÂTEAU CITRAN
Avensan

AOC Haut-Médoc
Cru Bourgeois
Production: *32,000 cases*

A substantial-sized property once run by Jean Miailhe of Château Coufran, until it passed into the hands of his brother-in-law, Jean Casseline. It is now Japanese owned.

RED A solid, if plodding, Médoc of robust character.

🍇 Cabernet sauvignon 50%, Cabernet franc 10%, Merlot 40%

🍷 1983, 1985

🍶 Between 8-15 years

CHÂTEAU CLARKE

AOC Listrac
Cru Bourgeois
Production: *30,000 cases*

This estate's vines were dug up and its château pulled down in 1950. All was abandoned until 1973, when it was purchased by Baron Edmund de Rothschild. He completely restored the vineyard and installed an ultra-modern winery. Since the 1981 vintage, it has become one of the Médoc's fastest-rising stars. The wine is fermented in stainless steel and matured in wood for 12 months, with up to 60 per cent new oak. A wine to watch.

RED These well-coloured, medium- to full-bodied wines have a good measure of creamy-smoky oak and soft fruit.

🍇 Cabernet sauvignon 48%, Cabernet franc 14%, Merlot 35%, Petit verdot 3%

🍷 1981, 1982, 1983, 1985, 1986

🍶 Between 7-25 years

Second Wine: Château Malmaison
Other wines: "Granges de Clarke", "Le Rosé de Clarke"

CHÂTEAU COUFRAN
St.-Seurin-de-Cadourne

AOC Haut-Médoc
Cru Bourgeois
Production: *33,600 cases*

These wines are matured in wood for 13-18 months, with 25 per cent new oak.

RED Frank and fruity, this medium- to full-bodied wine has a chunky, choco-latey flavour, dominated by Merlot.

🍇 Cabernet sauvignon 10%, Merlot 85%, Petit verdot 5%

🍷 1982, 1983, 1985

🍶 Between 4-12 years

Second Wine: "Domaine de la Rose-Maréchale"

CHÂTEAU DUTRUCH-GRAND-POUJEAUX

AOC Moulis
Cru Bourgeois
Production: *10,000 cases*

One of the best Grand-Poujeaux satellite properties. Dutruch also makes two other wines from the specific-named plots "La Bernède" and "La Gravière".

RED Fine, full-bodied wines of excellent colour, fruit and finesse.

🍇 Cabernet sauvignon and Cabernet franc 60%, Merlot 35%, Petit verdot 5%

🍷 1981, 1982, 1983, 1985

🍶 Between 7-15 years

Other wines: "La Bernède-Grand-Poujeaux", "La Gravière-Grand-Poujeaux"

CHÂTEAU FONRÉAUD

AOC Listrac
Cru Bourgeois
Production: *20,500 cases*

Splendid château with south-facing vineyards situated on and around a knoll called Puy-de-Menjon.

RED Attractive medium- to full-bodied wines of good fruit and some style.

🍇 Cabernet sauvignon 66%, Merlot 31%, Petit verdot 3%

🍷 1982, 1983, 1985

🍶 Between 6-12 years

Second Wine: Château Chemin-Royal-Moulis-en-Médoc
Other wines: "Fontaine-Royale"

CHÂTEAU FOURCAS-DUPRÉ

AOC Listrac
Cru Bourgeois
Production: *22,000 cases*

A charming house, with vineyards situated on gravel over iron-pan, which can excel in hotter vintages.

RED The good colour, bouquet and tannic structure of these wines is amply rewarded with rich fruit in good years.

🍇 Cabernet sauvignon 50%, Cabernet franc 10%, Merlot 38%, Petit verdot 2%

🍷 1982, 1983, 1985, 1986

🍶 Between 6-12 years

Second Wine: Château Bellevue-Laffont

CHÂTEAU FOURCAS-HOSTEN

AOC Listrac
Cru Bourgeois
Production: *15,000 cases*

Under multi-national ownership (French, Danish and American) since 1972, the winemaking facilities here have been renovated.

RED Deeply coloured and full-bodied wines, rich in fruit and supported by a firm tannic structure, although the style is becoming more supple, and can even be quite fat in ripe years like 1982.

🍇 Cabernet sauvignon 50%, Cabernet franc 10%, Merlot 40%

🍷 1981, 1982, 1983, 1985, 1986

🍶 Between 8-20 years

CHÂTEAU LE FOURNAS BERNADOTTE
St.-Sauveur

AOC Haut-Médoc
Production: *10,000 cases*

This château is situated on fine, gravelly ground that once had the right to the Pauillac appellation and formed part of a *cru classé* until certain changes of ownership.

RED These wines are very stylish with oodles of lush Cabernet fruit, backed up by the creamy richness of new oak.

🍇 Cabernet sauvignon 60%, Cabernet franc 10%, Merlot 30%

🍷 1980, 1981, 1982, 1983, 1985

🍶 Between 6-12 years

CHÂTEAU GRESSIER-GRAND-POUJEAUX

AOC Moulis
Production: *9,000 cases*

Classified *Cru Bourgeois* in 1932, but not in 1978, although it is superior to a few that were.

RED Full-bodied wines with plenty of fruit and flavour.

🍇 Cabernet sauvignon 50%, Cabernet franc 10%, Merlot 40%

🍷 1982, 1985

🍶 Between 6-12 years

CHÂTEAU GREYSAC
Bégadan

AOC Médoc
Cru Bourgeois
Production: *30,000 cases*

Since it was purchased by Baron de Gunzbourg in 1973, the facilities of this château have undergone extensive modernization. The quality is excellent and the future promising.

RED Stylish, medium-bodied wines with silky-textured, ripe fruit flavours.

🍇 Cabernet sauvignon 50%, Cabernet franc 10%, Merlot 38%, Petit verdot 2%

🍷 1982, 1983, 1985, 1986, 1988

🍴 Between 6-10 years

CHÂTEAU HANTEILLAN
Cissac-Médoc

AOC Haut-Médoc
Cru Bourgeois
Production: *35,000 cases*

This large property produces a consistently good standard of wine.

RED The wine has a fine colour, spicy bouquet with underlying vanilla-oak tones, ripe fruit and supple tannin.

🍇 Cabernet sauvignon 48%, Cabernet franc 6%, Merlot 42%, Malbec and Petit verdot 4%

🍷 1981, 1982, 1983

🍴 Between 6-12 years

Second Wine: Château Larrivaux-Hanteillan

CHÂTEAU LAMARQUE
Lamarque

AOC Haut-Médoc
Cru Bourgeois
Production: *25,000 cases*

A large and steadily-improving property.

RED This wine has the supple style of Médoc with plenty of real fruit flavour, and an enticingly perfumed bouquet.

🍇 Cabernet sauvignon 50%, Cabernet franc 20%, Merlot 25%, Petit verdot 5%

🍷 1981, 1982

🍴 Between 5-12 years

Second Wine: "Réserve du Marquis d'Evry"

CHÂTEAU LANESSAN
Cussac-Fort-Médoc

AOC Haut-Médoc
Production: *17,500 cases*

This château was classified *Cru Bourgeois* in 1932, but not included in 1978.

RED Big, intensely flavoured wines of deep, often opaque, colour and a quality that closely approaches that of a *cru classé*.

🍇 Cabernet sauvignon 75%, Cabernet franc and Petit verdot 5%, Merlot 20%

🍷 1981, 1983, 1985, 1986, 1988

🍴 Between 7-20 years

CHÂTEAU LAROSE-TRINTAUDON
St.-Laurent

AOC Haut-Médoc
Cru Bourgeois
Production: *80,000 cases*

This is the largest estate in the Médoc and was under the same ownership as Château Camensac until 1986, during which time vast sums were spent on renovation. While Camensac makes a respectable wine for its Fifth Growth status, Larose-Trintaudon excels as a *Bourgeois* Growth. The standard of these wines, which are matured in wood for 24 months with up to one-third new oak, is consistently high.

RED Medium- to full-bodied wines with an elegantly rich flavour of juicy summer fruits, vanilla and truffles backed up by supple tannins.

🍇 Cabernet sauvignon 60%, Cabernet franc 20%, Merlot 20%

🍷 1982, 1983, 1985, 1988, 1989

🍴 Between 6-15 years

CHÂTEAU LESTAGE-DARQUIER-GRAND-POUJEAUX

AOC Moulis
Production: *1,800 cases*

Classified *Cru Bourgeois* in 1932, but not included in the *Syndicat's* 1978 list, although the little-seen wines of this small property are superior to a few that were.

RED Densely coloured wines, rich in bouquet and fruit, with a powerful structure.

🍇 Cabernet sauvignon 50%, Cabernet franc 10%, Merlot 40%

🍷 1982 (only one vintage from the 1980s appears in my tasting notes, but I would strongly recommend trying this wine if you come across it)

🍴 Between 8-20 years

CHÂTEAU LIVERSAN
St.-Sauveur

AOC Haut-Médoc
Cru Bourgeois
Production: *20,000 cases*

This estate was purchased in 1984 by Prince Guy de Polignac, who is inexorably linked with Champagne Pommery. The vineyard is on fine, sandy gravel over a limestone subsoil, and the wine is fermented in stainless steel and matured in wood for 18-20 months, with up to 50 per cent new oak.

RED Rich and flavourful wines of full body and some style that are gaining in class with each vintage.

🍇 Cabernet sauvignon 49%, Cabernet franc 10%, Merlot 38%, Petit verdot 3%

🍷 1981, 1982, 1983, 1985, 1988

🍴 Between 7-20 years

CHÂTEAU LOUDENNE
St.-Yzans

AOC Médoc
Cru Bourgeois
Production: *15,000 cases*

This pink-washed, *chartreuse*-style château, with its lawns running down to the Gironde, belongs to W & A Gilbey, who run it in a style which harks back to the last days of the British Empire. Remarkably, it is an experience that anyone can enjoy. Gilbeys run residential courses at this château, in what is the best school of wine open to the public.
Production techniques are very modern, and only the British could employ a Burgundian as winemaker in a Bordeaux château – but then, why not? The wine is matured in wood for 15-18 months, with 25 per cent new oak. Loudenne also produces a dry white wine that is attractive when drunk one to two years after the harvest.

RED Full-bodied wines with a spicy-blackcurrant bouquet, sometimes silky and hinting of violets, with underlying vanilla oak, a big mouthful of rich and ripe fruit, excellent extract and length.

🍇 Cabernet sauvignon 55%, Cabernet franc 7%, Merlot 38%

🍷 1982, 1983, 1984, 1985

🍴 Between 5-15 years

CHÂTEAU DE MALLERET
Le Pian

AOC Haut-Médoc
Cru Bourgeois
Production: *25,000 cases*

This is a vast estate incorporating a stud farm with two training race-tracks and stables for both hunting and racing as well as a 60-hectare (148-acre) vineyard.

RED Delightful wines of good bouquet, medium body and juicy-rich fruit.

🍇 Cabernet sauvignon 70%, Cabernet franc 10%, Merlot 15%, Petit verdot 5%

🍷 1981, 1982, 1983, 1985

🍴 Between 5-12 years

Second Wine: Château Barthez
Other wines: Château Nexon, Domaine de l'Ermitage Lamourous

CHÂTEAU MAUCAILLOU

AOC Moulis
Production: *19,000 cases*

Classified *Cru Bourgeois* in 1932, but not included in the *Syndicat's* 1978 list. As a member of the current *Syndicat*, however, the 1982, 1983 and 1984 were tasted in July 1986 against the same vintages of 83 other *Bourgeois* Growths. Château Maucaillou was declared the winner.

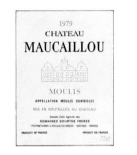

RED Deep-coloured, full-bodied wine with masses of velvety-textured fruit, stunning *cassis* and vanilla flavours and supple tannins.

🍇 Cabernet sauvignon 45%, Cabernet franc 15%, Merlot 35%, Petit verdot 5%

🍷 1983, 1984, 1985, 1986, 1988

🍴 Between 6-15 years

CHÂTEAU LE MEYNIEU
Vertheuil

AOC Haut-Médoc
Cru Bourgeois
Production: *5,000 cases*

Under the same ownership as Château Lavillotte in St.-Estèphe. The wine is not filtered before bottling.

RED The 1982 is a deep, dark, brooding wine of dense bouquet and solid fruit which promises well for the future.

🍇 Cabernet sauvignon 70%, Merlot 30%

🍷 1982

🍴 Between 7-15 years

CHÂTEAU MOULIN-À-VENT

AOC Moulis
Cru Bourgeois
Production: *10,000 cases*

One-third of this property overlaps the commune of Listrac, but its appellation is still Moulis.

RED Medium-bodied wines with an elegant bouquet and a full flavour.

🍇 Cabernet sauvignon 65%, Merlot 30%, Petit verdot 5%

🍷 1982, 1983

🍴 Between 7-15 years

Second Wine: "Moulin-de-St.-Vincent"

CHÂTEAU LES ORMES-SORBET
Couquèques

AOC Médoc
Cru Bourgeois
Production: *11,500 cases*

These wines are matured in wood for 18-24 months, with one-third new oak.

RED Characterful wines of substantial body, dense fruit and positive flavour.

🍇	Cabernet sauvignon 65%, Merlot 35%
🍷	1982, 1983, 1985
🥂	Between 7-15 years

CHÂTEAU PATACHE-D'AUX
Bégadan

AOC Médoc
Cru Bourgeois
Production: *25,000 cases*

This old property once belonged to the Aux family, descendants of the counts of Armagnac.

RED Stylish, highly perfumed, medium-bodied wine with very accessible fruit.

🍇	Cabernet sauvignon 70%, Cabernet franc 10%, Merlot 20%
🍷	1981, 1982, 1983, 1985, 1988
🥂	Between 4-8 years

CHÂTEAU PLAGNAC
Bégadan

AOC Médoc
Production: *15,000 cases*

Since this château's acquisition by Cordier in 1972 and since the late 1970s, it deserves more recognition. The wine is matured in wood for 18-20 months, with a little new oak.

RED Full-bodied and full-flavoured, with some breed, lots of upfront Merlot fruit, and a smooth finish.

🍇	Cabernet sauvignon 60%, Merlot 40%
🍷	1982, 1983, 1985, 1986, 1988
🥂	Between 4-10 years

CHÂTEAU POTENSAC
Potensac

AOC Médoc
Cru Bourgeois
Production: *25,000 cases*

This property is under the same ownership as Château Léoville-Las-Cases in St.-Julien. The wines often aspire to *cru classé* quality.

RED Full-bodied wines of a lovely brick-red colour, with heaps of fruit and underlying chocolate and spice.

🍇	Cabernet sauvignon 55%, Cabernet franc 20%, Merlot 25%
🍷	1980, 1981, 1982, 1983, 1985, 1986, 1988
🥂	Between 6-15 years

Second Wine: Château Lassalle
Other wines: Château Gallais-Bellevue

CHÂTEAU POUJEAUX

AOC Moulis
Cru Bourgeois
Production: *21,000 cases*

After Chasse-Spleen, this château produces the best wine in Moulis.

RED Full-bodied and deep-coloured wine with a very expensive bouquet and creamy-rich, spicy fruit.

🍇	Cabernet sauvignon 40%, Cabernet franc 12%, Merlot 36%, Petit verdot 12%
🍷	1981, 1982, 1983, 1984, 1985, 1986
🥂	Between 10-25 years

Second Wine: Château la Salle-de-Poujeaux

CHÂTEAU RAMAGE-LA-BATISSE
St.-Sauveur

AOC Haut-Médoc
Cru Bourgeois
Production: *25,000 cases*

This property has excelled itself in recent years and is making wines of remarkable quality-price ratio.

RED Rich, well-flavoured, oaky style wines with a classic Cabernet bouquet. These wines are immediately attractive in light years like 1980.

🍇	Cabernet sauvignon 60%, Cabernet franc 10%, Merlot 30%
🍷	1982, 1983, 1985, 1986, 1988
🥂	Between 7-15 years

Second Wine: "Le Terrey"
Other wines: Château Dutellier

CHÂTEAU ST.-BONNET
St.-Christoly

AOC Médoc
Cru Bourgeois
Production: *20,000 cases*

Some 35 of this important estate's 55 hectares (86 of its 134 acres) are planted with vines.

RED Full-flavoured wines of promising quality and immediate aromatic appeal.

🍇	Cabernet sauvignon 28%, Cabernet franc 22%, Merlot 50%
🍷	1982, 1983, 1985
🥂	Between 5-10 years

CHÂTEAU SOCIANDO-MALLET
St.-Seurin-de-Cadourne

AOC Haut-Médoc
Cru Bourgeois
Production: *16,000 cases*

This property has been making a name for itself since 1970, after it was purchased by Jean Gautreau.

RED Powerfully built wines that are rich in colour and extract. Often totally dominated by vanilla oak in their youth, they are backed up with plenty of concentrated *cassis* fruit.

🍇	Cabernet sauvignon 60%, Cabernet franc 10%. Merlot 30%
🍷	1980, 1981, 1982, 1983, 1985, 1986, 1988
🥂	Between 10-25 years

Second Wine: Château Lartigue-de-Brochon

CHÂTEAU LA TOUR-DE-BY
Bégadan

AOC Médoc
Cru Bourgeois
Production: *39,000 cases*

The turreted tower of Tour-de-By was once a lighthouse. The wine is consistently of very good *Bourgeois* quality.

RED These deeply coloured, full-bodied, richly flavoured wines have good spicy fruit, backed up by a firm tannic structure.

🍇	Cabernet sauvignon 70%, Cabernet franc 5%, Merlot 25%
🍷	1982, 1983, 1985, 1986, 1988
🥂	Between 6-12 years

Second Wine: "La Roque-de-By"
Other wines: "Moulin de Roque"

CHÂTEAU TOUR-DU-HAUT-MOULIN
Cussac-Fort-Médoc

AOC Haut-Médoc
Cru Bourgeois
Production: *12,000 cases*

Well-made wines from good gravelly slopes, matured in wood for 18 months, with 25 per cent new oak.

RED Rich and concentrated wines in a similar style to Château Sociando-Mallet, but not as tannic, nor in the same class.

🍇	Cabernet sauvignon and Cabernet franc 50%, Merlot 45%, Petit verdot 5%
🍷	1981, 1982, 1983, 1985, 1988
🥂	Between 7-15 years

CHÂTEAU LA TOUR SAINT-BONNET
St.-Christoly

AOC Médoc
Cru Bourgeois
Production: *20,000 cases*

Situated on fine gravelly ridges, this property was known as Château la Tour Saint-Bonnet-Cazenave in the nineteenth century.

RED Firm, full-flavoured, well-coloured wines of consistent quality.

🍇	Cabernet sauvignon 28%, Cabernet franc 22%, Merlot 50%
🍷	1982, 1983, 1985, 1986, 1988
🥂	Between 7-15 years

Second Wine: Château la Fuie-Saint-Bonnet

CHÂTEAU VERDIGNAN
St.-Seurin-de-Cadourne

AOC Haut-Médoc
Cru Bourgeois
Production: *30,000 cases*

This property has belonged to the Miailhe family since 1972. The wine is fermented in stainless steel and matured in wood for 18-20 months.

RED Medium-bodied wines that have easily accessible fruit, made in a soft and silky style.

🍇	Cabernet sauvignon 60%, Cabernet franc 5%, Merlot 35%
🍷	1981, 1982, 1983, 1985, 1988
🥂	Between 5-10 years

Other wines: Château Plantey-de-la-Croix

CHÂTEAU VILLEGORGE
Avensan

AOC Haut-Médoc
Production: *2,700 cases*

This château was classified *Cru Bourgeois* in 1932. It was purchased by Lucien Lurton in 1973, but he then resigned from the *Syndicat* and the château was not therefore included in its 1978 list, although it is superior to a few that were.

RED Well-coloured, full-bodied wines with a good, spicy Merlot flavour.

🍇	Cabernet sauvignon 30%, Cabernet franc 10%, Merlot 60%
🍷	1983, 1985, 1988
🥂	Between 6-12 years

St.-Estèphe

AN ABUNDANCE OF HIGH-QUALITY Bourgeois Growths such as the Châteaux of Andron-Blanquet, Beau-Site, le Bosq, Domeyne, la Haye, Lavilotte, Meyney and de Pez, to name but a few, makes St.-Estèphe the "bargain basement" of Bordeaux. And with just five *crus classés* covering a mere six per cent of the commune, it is a rich source of undervalued clarets where the prices paid by wine-drinkers are unlikely to be "gazumped" by wine-investors.

CHÂTEAU COS D'ESTOURNEL

While the commune might lack classed growths, it does not lack class. If it had just one *cru classé*– the stunning, stylish Château Cos d'Estournel, St.-Estèphe would still be famous. The reputation of this château soared after perfectionist Bruno Prats took over in 1971. Essentially, this success can be put down to his maximizing the true potential of Cos d'Estournel's exceptional *terroir*, a superb south-facing ridge of gravel with perfect drainage. Those vineyards on heavier soil with less gravel and more clay tend to produce wines of a more rustic style.

THE NEW WAVE

Most St.-Estèphe wines are well structured and have great longevity, but they have more fruit than they used to, and this fruit is now accessible at a relatively young age. It was once essential to buy only the greatest vintages and wait twenty years or more before drinking them. These wines are still capable of great longevity, but an increasing use of the Merlot and vinification techniques that extract the colour and fruit in preference to the harsher tannins, makes them richer, fruitier and drinkable in most vintages.

ST.-ESTÈPHE *CRU CLASSÉ* STATISTICS

Crus classés in AOC St.-Estèphe
5 châteaux (8% of all *crus classés*) with 226 ha (558 acres) of vineyards (8% of all *crus classés*)

1st Growths:	None
2nd Growths:	2 châteaux (14% of all 2nd Growths) with 121 ha (299 acres) of vineyards (15% of all 2nd Growths)
3rd Growths	1 château (7% of all 3rd Growths) with 48 ha (119 acres) of vineyards (11% of all 3rd Growths)
4th Growths	1 château (10% of all 4th Growths) with 45 ha (111 acres) of vineyards (10% of all 4th Growths)
5th Growths	1 château (6% of all 5th Growths) with 12 ha (30 acres) of vineyards (2% of all 5th Growths)

FACTORS AFFECTING TASTE AND QUALITY

Location
St.-Estèphe, the most northerly of the classic communes, is situated 18 kilometres (11 miles) south of Lesparre, bordering the Gironde.

Climate
As for the Médoc, *see* p.44.

Aspect
Well-drained, well-sited, softly sloping vineyards. The south-east-facing crest of gravel overlooks Château Lafite-Rothschild in Pauillac and is relatively steep for the Médoc.

Soil
Gravelly topsoil, more fertile than in communes further south, with clay subsoil exposed in parts, consisting of clay beds, stony-clay and limestone over iron-pan.

Viticulture and vinification
Only red wines have the right to the appellation. With increasing emphasis placed on the Merlot grape, which can now account for up to 50 per cent of the vines cultivated in some châteaux, less use of *vin de presse* and improved vinification techniques, these wines are becoming far more accessible in less sunny years. All grapes must be de-stalked, duration of skin-contact averages three weeks and maturation in cask currently varies between 15 and 24 months.

Primary grape varieties
Cabernet sauvignon, Cabernet franc, Merlot

Secondary grape varieties
Carmenère, Malbec, Petit verdot

ST.-ESTÈPHE PROFILE

Appellation area
Covers parts of the commune of St.-Estèphe only.

Size of commune
3,757 ha (9,284 acres).

AOC Area under vine
1,100 ha (2,718 acres), (29% of commune).

Surface area of *crus classés*
226 ha (558 acres), (6% of commune, 21% of AOC).

Special comments
Approximately 5 ha (12.3 acres) of vineyards within St.-Estèphe are classified as AOC Pauillac.

Harvest, Château Cos d'Estournel, above
Grapes are collected as the bizarre eastern façade of the purpose-built winery oversees the army of pickers. The château is owned by Bruno Prats, and under his management has realized its potential.

ST.-ESTÈPHE, see also p.45
Of the Haut-Médoc's four best-known communes, St.-Estèphe is the most northerly, though the actual AOC area covers only part of the commune.

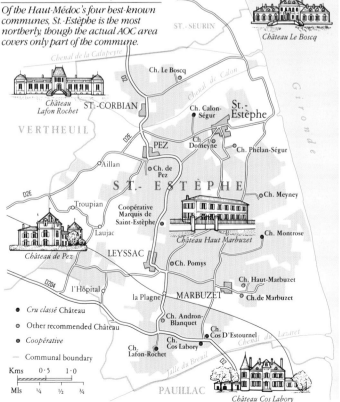

The great châteaux of St.-Estèphe

CHÂTEAU CALON-SÉGUR

3ème Cru Classé
Production: *20,000 cases*

From the Gallo-Roman origins of this château grew the community of St.-Estèphe. The first wine estate in the commune, it used to boast "Premier Cru de St.-Estèphe" on its label–until other producers objected.

RED This full, fruity, well-structured wine has a creamy, rich flavour. It is of consistently good quality and improves well in bottle.

🍇 Cabernet sauvignon 60%, Cabernet franc 20%, Merlot 20%

🍷 1981, 1982, 1983, 1985, 1988

🍸 Between 3-20 years

Second Wine: "Marquis de Ségur"

CHÂTEAU COS D'ESTOURNEL

2ème Cru Classé
Production: *25,000 cases*

The château of Cos d'Estournel is not a residence but a purpose-built working winery. Its bizarre façade has huge, elaborately carved oak doors that once adorned the palace of the Sultan of Zanzibar! Some of the wine is fermented in stainless steel and all of it is matured in cask for 18-24 months: 100 per cent new oak for big years, up to 70 per cent for lighter vintages.

RED A rich, flavourful and attractive wine of full body, great class and distinction; without doubt the finest wine in St.-Estèphe. It is uniquely generous for the appellation and capable of amazing longevity, even in the poorest years. A complex wine with silky fruit and great finesse.

🍇 Cabernet sauvignon 60%, Merlot 40%

🍷 1980, 1981, 1982, 1983, 1984, 1986, 1987, 1988

🍸 Between 8-20 years

Second Wine: blended with Château Marbuzet

CHÂTEAU COS LABORY

5ème Cru Classé
Production: *6,500 cases*

Until the late nineteenth century this property formed part of Château Cos d'Estournel. In the 1920s it was purchased by an Argentinian family who were distant cousins of Madame Audoy, the current owner. The wine is matured in wood for 15-18 months; one-third of the casks are new oak.

RED At best these wines used to be merely light and elegant with a certain degree of finesse. Recent vintages have displayed a welcome change to a distinctly fuller, fruitier and fatter style.

🍇 Cabernet sauvignon 40%, Cabernet franc 20%, Merlot 35%, Petit verdot 5%

🍷 1980, 1981, 1982, 1985, 1986

🍸 Between 5-15 years

CHÂTEAU LAFON-ROCHET

4ème Cru Classé
Production: *15,000 cases*

In 1959 Guy Tesseron purchased this vineyard bordering Pauillac and set about increasing the proportion of Cabernet sauvignon. The wine is matured in wood for 18-24 months; one-third of the casks are new oak.

RED This is not typical St.-Estèphe, either of the traditional school or the fruitier new wave. The heavy influence of Cabernet sauvignon makes it very difficult to describe. Some vintages can taste green and astringent while good years can produce wines that become velvety with bottle maturity.

🍇 Cabernet sauvignon 70%, Merlot 20%, Cabernet franc 8%, Malbec 2%

🍷 1982, 1985, 1986, 1988

🍸 Between 8-15 years

CHÂTEAU MONTROSE

2ème Cru Classé
Production: *27,000 cases*

Until the beginning of the nineteenth century, this youngest of *cru classé* vineyards was uncultivated scrubland belonging to Third Growth Calon-Ségur. The wine is matured in wood for 24 months, with up to one-third new oak.

RED A long-maturing wine that has been inconsistent in style over the last ten years, although 1982 and 1986 are probably its best vintages since 1962.

🍇 Cabernet sauvignon 65%, Cabernet franc 10%, Merlot 25%

🍷 1982, 1986, 1988

🍸 Between 5-25 years

Second Wine: "La Dame de Montrose"

The best of the rest

CHÂTEAU ANDRON-BLANQUET

Cru Bourgeois
Production: *6,000 cases*

Under the same ownership as Château Cos Labory, the vineyards of this property are situated above the gravel crest of *cru classé* châteaux that overlook Château Lafite-Rothschild in the neighbouring commune of Pauillac.

RED An exceptionally well-made wine that consistently rises above its *petit château* status. Fermented and matured in cask, it has good fruit and a distinctive style.

🍇 Cabernet sauvignon 30%, Cabernet franc 30%, Merlot 35%, Petit verdot 5%

🍷 1982, 1983, 1985, 1986, 1988

🍸 Between 4-10 years

CHÂTEAU BEAU-SITE

Cru Bourgeois
Production: *15,000 cases*

This property should not be confused with Château Beau-Site Haut-Vignoble, a lesser St.-Estèphe.

RED A stylish, medium- to full-bodied wine that often has an elegant finish reminiscent of violets.

🍇 Cabernet sauvignon and Cabernet franc 65%, Merlot 35%

🍷 1980, 1981, 1982, 1983, 1985, 1986

🍸 Between 3-10 years

CHÂTEAU LE BOSCQ

Production: *7,500 cases*

This property has always produced a good wine and, since the 1982 vintage, the increase in quality has been quite dramatic.

RED Superbly aromatic, almost exotic, full-bodied wine that is elegant and rich with the flavour of summer fruits, and is nicely backed up with new oak.

🍇 Cabernet sauvignon 60%, Merlot 40%

🍷 1982, 1983, 1985, 1986, 1988

🍸 Between 5-12 years

CHÂTEAU CAPBERN GASQUETON

Cru Bourgeois
Production: *10,000 cases*

Under the same ownership as Château Calon-Ségur. The vineyards are found both north and south of the village of St.-Estèphe.

RED Medium-weight, ripe and fruity wine of consistent quality, which is mellowed by 24 months in wood.

🍇 Cabernet sauvignon 60%, Cabernet franc 15%, Merlot 25%

🍷 1980, 1981, 1982, 1983, 1984, 1985, 1986, 1988

🍸 Between 4-12 years

CHÂTEAU CHAMBERT-MARBUZET

Cru Bourgeois
Production: *3,800 cases*

RED This technically faultless wine is produced year-in and year-out. Aromatically attractive, medium- to full-bodied, rich, ripe and fruity with sufficient tannin to last.

🍇 Cabernet sauvignon 70%, Merlot 30%

🍷 1980, 1981, 1982, 1983, 1985, 1986

🍸 Between 3-10 years

CHÂTEAU LE CROCK

Cru Bourgeois
Production: *15,500 cases*

This property is under the same ownership as Château Léoville-Poyferré of St.-Julien.

RED These are dark-coloured, substantial wines that are rich in tannin and require time to mellow.

🍇 Cabernet sauvignon 65%, Merlot 35%

🍷 1981, 1982, 1983, 1985

🍸 Between 6-15 years

CHÂTEAU DOMEYNE

Production: *1,700 cases*

Not classified as a *Cru Bourgeois* in 1932, nor listed by the *Syndicat* in 1978, but it certainly should have been.

RED Typically deep-coloured, rich-flavoured wine with an excellent marriage of fruit and oak. A smooth and well-rounded wine that can be drunk fairly young.

🍇 Cabernet sauvignon 75%, Merlot 25%

🍷 1982, 1983, 1985, 1986

🍸 Between 3-8 years

CHÂTEAU FAGET

Production: *2,000 cases*

Classified *Cru Bourgeois* in 1932, but not included in the *Syndicat's* 1978 list, although this *coopérative*-produced wine is now superior to a few that were.

RED This well-made wine has a solid mouthful of flavour, and ages well.

🍇 Cabernet sauvignon 60%, Cabernet franc 10%, Merlot 30%

🍷 1982, 1983, 1985

🍷 Between 6-10 years

CHÂTEAU LA HAYE

Production: *3,000 cases*

New equipment, 25 per cent new oak casks every year, and a fair proportion of old vines, combine to produce some exciting vintages.

RED Always limpid, this medium- to full-bodied wine is rich in colour and flavour, well balanced and lengthy with vanilla-oak quite evident on the finish.

🍇 Cabernet sauvignon 65%, Merlot 30%, Petit verdot 5%

🍷 1982, 1983, 1985

🍷 Between 5-8 years

CHÂTEAU HAUT-MARBUZET

Cru Bourgeois
Production: *18,500 cases*

This is one of several properties belonging to Henri Duboscq. Extremely rare for *cru classé* châteaux, totally unprecedented for Bourgeois Growths, these wines receive 18 months in 100 per cent new oak.

RED These full-bodied, deep-coloured wines are packed with juicy fruit, backed up by supple tannin. They are marked by a generous buttered-toast and creamy-vanilla character.

🍇 Cabernet sauvignon 40%, Cabernet franc 10%, Merlot 50%

🍷 1980, 1981, 1982, 1983, 1985, 1986, 1988

🍷 Between 4-12 years

CHÂTEAU HOUISSANT

Production: *10,000 cases*

Classified *Cru Bourgeois* in 1932, but not included in the 1978 list, but it is superior to a few that were.

RED Well-produced, full-flavoured, medium- to full-bodied wines.

🍇 Cabernet sauvignon 70%, Merlot 30%

🍷 1980, 1981, 1982, 1983, 1985

🍷 Between 3-8 years

CHÂTEAU LAVILOTTE

Cru Bourgeois
Production: *5,500 cases*

A star-performing château.

RED Dark-coloured wines of deep and distinctive bouquet. Smoky, full-bodied, intense and complex.

🍇 Cabernet sauvignon 75%, Merlot 25%

🍷 1982, 1983, 1985, 1986, 1988

🍷 Between 5-12 years

CHÂTEAU DE MARBUZET

Cru Bourgeois
Production: *10,000 cases*

This elegant château is the home of Bruno Prats of Cos d'Estournel.

RED These elegant, medium- to full-bodied wines are well-balanced and have good fruit and a supple finish.

🍇 Cabernet sauvignon 44%, Merlot 56%

🍷 1982, 1983, 1985, 1986, 1988

🍷 Between 4-10 years

LE MARQUIS DE SAINT-ESTÈPHE

Production: *varies*

Produced by Cave Coopérative Marquis de Saint-Estèphe.

RED Consistently well-made, good-value, medium- to full-bodied wine.

🍇 Cabernet sauvignon and Cabernet franc 60%, Merlot 35%, Malbec and Petit verdot 5%

🍷 1982, 1983, 1985, 1988

🍷 Between 3-6 years

CHÂTEAU MEYNEY

Cru Bourgeois
Production: *25,000 cases*

This property belongs to Domaines Cordier. The one-storey buildings are unoccupied and used solely for the production of wine. The château manages to produce fine wines in virtually every vintage.

RED These wines used to be big, beefy, chunky and chewy and required at least ten years in bottle. They have changed, and for the better. They have acquired a silky-textured finesse and no longer require many years in bottle, but age gracefully.

🍇 Cabernet sauvignon 70%, Cabernet franc 4%, Merlot 24%, Petit verdot 2%

🍷 1980, 1981, 1982, 1983, 1984, 1985, 1986, 1988

🍷 Between 5-25 years

Second Wine: "Prieuré de Meyney"

CHÂTEAU LES ORMES DE PEZ

Cru Bourgeois
Production: *14,000 cases*

Owned by Jean-Michel Cazes of Château Lynch-Bages in Pauillac, who installed new stainless-steel vats in 1981. The wine is matured in wood for 12 to 15 months.

RED A fine, fruity, medium-bodied wine that can have minty-herbal undertones.

🍇 Cabernet sauvignon 55%, Cabernet franc 10%, Merlot 35%

🍷 1982, 1983, 1985, 1986, 1988

🍷 Between 3-15 years

CHÂTEAU DE PEZ

Production: *14,500 cases*

This wine is matured in wood for between 20 and 22 months and 25 per cent of the casks are new oak. Owner Robert Dousson makes a feature of bottling in magnums and various larger-sized bottles.

RED Consistently one of the best Bourgeois growths in the entire Médoc. A medium- to full-bodied wine, it has a deep flavour of rich fruit, plus a good tannic structure, and can mature into a sublime wine of multi-faceted cedary-spiciness.

🍇 Cabernet sauvignon 70%, Cabernet franc 15%, Merlot 15%

🍷 1980, 1981, 1982, 1983, 1984, 1985, 1986, 1988

🍷 Between 6-20 years

CHÂTEAU PHÉLAN-SÉGUR

Cru Bourgeois
Production: *20,000 cases*

This property changed ownership recently, but has not improved.

RED The 1982 was good, but the last vintage to really excite me before that was the 1955!

🍇 Cabernet sauvignon 50%, Cabernet franc 10%, Merlot 40%

🍷 1982

🍷 Between 4-6 years

CHÂTEAU POMYS

Production: *3,000 cases*

Classified *Cru Bourgeois* in 1932, but not included in the 1978 list, although it is superior to a few that were. The wines are aged in wood for 24 months; 25 per cent new oak.

RED Serious and substantial wines with good fruit and tannin balance.

🍇 Cabernet sauvignon 50%, Cabernet franc 20%, Merlot 25%, Petit verdot 5%

🍷 1981, 1982, 1983, 1985

🍷 Between 3-10 years

CHÂTEAU LES PRADINES

Production: *3,500 cases*

This *coopérative*-produced, château-bottled wine was not classified as a *Cru Bourgeois* in 1932, nor listed in 1978, but it certainly should have been.

RED A positive wine, full of fruit and character, with a very satisfying finish.

🍇 Cabernet sauvignon 60%, Cabernet franc 5%, Merlot 35%

🍷 1982, 1983, 1985

🍷 Between 2-7 years

CHÂTEAU LA TOUR DE PEZ

Production: *4,500 cases*

This wine proves the technical expertise of the local *coopérative*.

RED An elegant, medium- to full-bodied wine with good, assertive fruit.

🍇 Cabernet sauvignon 70%, Cabernet franc 15%, Merlot 15%

🍷 1982, 1983, 1985, 1988

🍷 Between 3-7 years

CHÂTEAU TRONQUOY-LALANDE

Cru Bourgeois
Production: *7,000 cases*

In 1973, Jean-Philippe Castéja tragically died and his widow, Arlette, was left to run a business she knew nothing about. She has succeeded admirably.

RED These wines range from being pleasantly fruity to big, dark and tannic.

🍇 Cabernet sauvignon and Cabernet franc 50%, Merlot 45%, Petit verdot 5%

🍷 1981, 1982, 1983, 1985, 1988

🍷 Between 3-7 years

Pauillac

IF ANY BORDEAUX APPELLATION CAN be described as "big, black and beautiful", it is Pauillac – the commune most famous for the three First Growths of Latour, Lafite and Mouton. But Pauillac is an appellation of contrasts. Although it does boast three-quarters of the Médoc's First Growths, it also contains two-thirds of its Fifth Growths. Very little lies between these two extremes, and Bourgeois Growths are the exception rather than the rule. It would be wrong to generalize about wines of such varying quality, but it is right to say that the Cabernet sauvignon is at its most majestic in Pauillac. While the much-vaunted blackcurrant character of this king of grapes may be elusive in many clarets, it is certainly evident in great Pauillacs. This full-blown, sometimes opulent, *cassis* character, is never blowsy, but always beautifully balanced by an incomparable tannic structure.

Only Margaux has more *cru classé* châteaux, but Pauillac's estates are larger and thus its concentration of *cru classé* vineyards higher. Nine out of every ten Pauillac vines are *crus classés*, compared to seven out of ten in Margaux.

PAUILLAC *CRU CLASSÉ* STATISTICS

Crus classés in AOC Pauillac

18 châteaux (30% of all *crus classés*) with 842 ha (2,080 acres) of vineyards (30% of all *crus classés*)

1st Growths:	3 châteaux (75% of all 1st Growths) with 230 ha (568 acres) of vineyards (75% of all 1st Growths)
2nd Growths:	2 châteaux (14% of all 2nd Growths) with 90 ha (222 acres) of vineyards (11% of all 2nd Growths)
3rd Growths:	None
4th Growths:	1 château (10% of all 4th Growths) with 45 ha (111 acres) of vineyards (10% of all 4th Growths)
5th Growths:	12 châteaux (67% of all 5th Growths) with 477 ha (1,179 acres) of vineyards (63% of all 5th Growths)

PAUILLAC PROFILE

Appellation area
Covers parts of the commune of Pauillac, plus 34 ha (84 acres) in St.-Sauveur, 16 ha (40 acres) in St.-Julien, 5 ha (12.4 acres) in St.-Estèphe and 1 ha (2.5 acres) in Cissac.

Size of commune:
2,539 ha (6,274 acres)

AOC Area under vine:
950 ha (2,347 acres) (37% of commune)

Surface area of *crus classés*:
842 ha (2,080 acres) (33% of commune, 89% of AOC)

FACTORS AFFECTING TASTE AND QUALITY

Location
Sandwiched between St.-Estèphe to the north and St.-Julien to the south.

Climate
As for the Médoc, *see* p.44.

Aspect
Two large, low-lying plateaux, one to the northwest of the town of Pauillac, the other to the southwest. Exposure is excellent, and both drain down gentle slopes, eastwards to the Gironde, westwards to the forest or north and south to canals and streams.

Soil
The two plateaux are massive gravel beds, reaching a greater depth than any found elsewhere in the Médoc. The water drains away before the iron-pan subsoil is reached. St.-Sauveur consists of shallow sand over a stony subsoil to the west, and gravel over iron-pan (or more gravel) in the centre and south.

Viticulture and vinification
Only red wines have the right to the appellation. Some *vin de presse* is traditionally used by most châteaux. Skin-contact duration averages three to four weeks and maturation in cask currently varies between 18 and 24 months.

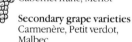 **Primary grape varieties**
Cabernet sauvignon, Cabernet franc, Merlot

Secondary grape varieties
Carmenère, Petit verdot, Malbec

Château Pichon-Lalande, below
The exact symmetry of the building is bathed in nature's less formal, but no less impressive, autumnal colours. Archive material has it that Louis XIV stayed here and was charmed by both woods and vineyards.

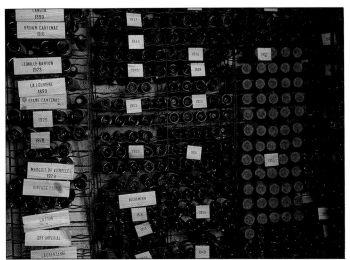

Caveau privé, Château Pichon-Longueville-Comtesse-de-Lalande, above
One wall of the château's private cellars encapsulates a wine-making history, particularly of Bordeaux, stretching back nearly two hundred years.

PAUILLAC, see also p.45

Blessed with three first growths, Lafite-Rothschild and Mouton-Rothschild in the north, and Latour to the south, Pauillac is sandwiched between St.-Estèphe and St.-Julien.

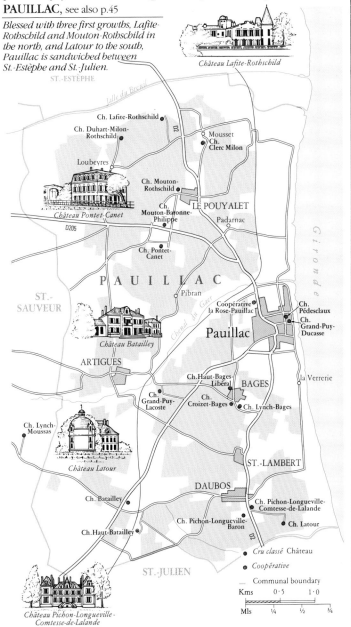

Château Pichon-Longueville-Comtesse-de-Lalande

Pauillac, above
The town of Pauillac, the largest of the Médoc, sits on the west bank of the Gironde. Despite its size and position, it still retains a quiet, rural character.

Cave Coopérative La Rose, above
The headquarters are in Pauillac, where the grapes are delivered. It is the oldest coopérative in the Médoc, and has a well-deserved reputation.

The great châteaux of Pauillac

CHÂTEAU BATAILLEY

5ème Cru Classé
Production: *22,000 cases*

A château that responds well to sunny years and produces underrated and undervalued wine. The 1985 was possibly the best bargain in Bordeaux, and the 1986 is probably even better. The wine is matured in wood (one-third new oak) for 16-18 months.

RED This wine has sometimes been rustic and too assertive in the past, but now shows its class with fine, succulent fruit supported by a ripe tannic structure and a complex creamy-oak aftertaste.

🍇 Cabernet sauvignon 73%, Cabernet franc 5%, Merlot 20%, Petit verdot 2%

🍷 1981, 1982, 1985, 1986, 1988

🍶 Between 10-25 years

CHÂTEAU CLERC MILON

5ème Cru Classé
Production: *8,700 cases*

This property was purchased by Baron Philippe de Rothschild in 1970. After more than a decade of investment and quite a few disappointing vintages along the way, it came good in 1981 and achieved sensational quality in 1982. This is another wine to watch, matured in wood for 22-24 months with 20-30 per cent new oak.

RED Deep-coloured, *cassis*-cum-spicy-oak aroma, medium- to full-bodied, rich berry flavours well balanced with ripe acidity.

🍇 Cabernet sauvignon 70%, Cabernet franc 10%, Merlot 20%

🍷 1981, 1982, 1983, 1985, 1986

🍶 Between 10-20 years

CHÂTEAU CROIZET-BAGES

5ème Cru Classé
Production: *8,500 cases*

Under the same ownership as Château Rauzan-Gassies of Margaux, and situated on the Bages plateau, Croizet-Bages is a classic example of a "château with no château". Its wine is matured in wood for 18 months and although not unattractive, lacks class and rarely excites. Improvements are slowly taking place, however.

RED Not one of the most deeply coloured Pauillacs, this medium-bodied wine has a clean, easy-to-drink fruity flavour.

🍇 Cabernet sauvignon 37%, Cabernet franc 30%, Merlot 30%, Malbec and Petit verdot 3%

🍷 1983

🍶 Between 6-12 years

CHÂTEAU D'ARMAILHAC

5ème Cru Classé
Production: *15,000 cases*

Baron Philippe de Rothschild purchased Château Mouton d'Armailhac in 1933. In 1956 he renamed it Château Mouton Baron-Philippe. In 1975 it was changed to Mouton-Baronne-Philippe in honour of the baron's late wife. In 1991 it reverted to d'Armailhac, but without the Mouton tag because the baron believed the wine to be in danger of assuming second-wine status due to the overwhelming prestige of Mouton-Rothschild. This property borders that of Mouton and one of Baron Philippe's reasons for acquiring it was to provide an easier, more impressive access to the famous First Growth. The wines, which are matured in wood for 22-24 months, with 20 per cent new oak, are produced with the same care and consideration.

RED Austere in youth, the light and attenuated style of this wine proves that even money cannot buy *terroir*.

🍇 Cabernet sauvignon 65%, Cabernet franc 5%, Merlot 30%

🍷 1981, 1982, 1986, 1988

🍶 Between 10-20 years

CHÂTEAU DUHART-MILON-ROTHSCHILD

4ème Cru Classé
Production: *12,500 cases*

Another "château with no château", Duhart-Milon was purchased by the Lafite branch of the Rothschild family in 1962. Wines prior to this date were almost entirely Petit verdot varietals and so only in abnormally hot years did it excel with this late-ripening grape, traditionally cultivated for its acidity. Interestingly, in the near-tropical heat of 1947, Duhart-Milon managed

to produce a wine that many considered to be the best of the vintage. The Rothschilds expanded these vineyards bordering those of Lafite, and replanted them with the correct combination of varieties to suit the *terroir*. The wine is matured for 18-24 months in wood with one-third new oak.

RED Much closer in style to St.-Julien, these wines do not have the Pauillac opaqueness, but they are vividly coloured. They are elegantly perfumed, deliciously rich in creamy-oaky fruit and have exceptional balance and finesse.

🍇 Cabernet sauvignon 70%, Cabernet franc 5%, Merlot 20%, Petit verdot 5%

🍷 1982, 1983, 1985, 1986, 1988

🍶 Between 8-16 years

Second Wine: "Moulin de Duhart"

CHÂTEAU GRAND-PUY-DUCASSE

5ème Cru Classé
Production: *17,500 cases*

Under the same ownership as Château Rayne-Vigneau in Sauternes, this property produces an undervalued wine from various plots that are scattered across half the commune and matured in wood for 15-18 months.

RED A well-balanced, relatively early-drinking, medium- to full-bodied wine of classic Pauillac *cassis* character and more suppleness than is usual for this commune.

🍇 Cabernet sauvignon 70%, Merlot 25%, Petit verdot 5%

🍷 1982, 1983, 1985

🍶 Between 5-10 years

Second Wine: Château Artigues-Arnaud

CHÂTEAU GRAND-PUY-LACOSTE

5ème Cru Classé
Production: *14,000 cases*

Under the same ownership as Château Ducru-Beaucaillou, Grand-Puy-Lacoste is going from strength to strength under the skilful guidance of François-Xavier Borie. The wine is matured in wood for 18-20 months, with one-third new oak.

RED A deep-coloured wine with a complex *cassis*, spice and vanilla bouquet, heaps of fruit, great length and finesse.

🍇 Cabernet sauvignon 70%, Cabernet franc 5%, Merlot 25%

🍷 1982, 1983, 1985, 1986, 1988

🍶 Between 10-20 years

Second Wine: Lacoste-Borie

CHÂTEAU HAUT-BAGES-LIBÉRAL

5ème Cru Classé
Production: *10,000 cases*

Under the same ownership as the Bourgeois growth of Château Chasse-Spleen in Moulis and the excellent unclassified Château la Gurgue in Margaux, this dynamic property is currently producing sensational wines. They are matured for 18-20 months in wood, with up to 40 per cent new oak. The 1986 has to be tasted to be believed.

RED Dark, full-bodied wines with masses of concentrated spicy-*cassis* fruit, great tannic structure and ripe, vanilla oak. In a word – complete.

🍇 Cabernet sauvignon 75%, Merlot 20%, Petit verdot 5%

🍷 1982, 1983, 1985, 1986, 1988

🍶 Between 10-20 years

CHÂTEAU HAUT-BATAILLEY

5ème Cru Classé
Production: *11,000 cases*

This property is under the same ownership as châteaux Grand-Puy-Lacoste, and in St.-Julien, Ducru-Beaucaillou. When the Borie family purchased Château Batailley in 1942, this part of the vineyard was hived off and given to one son, while the bulk of the property, including the château itself, was given to the other. The wine is matured in wood for 20 months, with one-third new oak.

RED The wine of Haut-Batailley is well-coloured, medium-bodied and shows more elegance and finesse than that of Batailley, although it can lack the latter's fullness of fruit.

🍇 Cabernet sauvignon 65%, Cabernet franc 10%, Merlot 25%

🗓 1981, 1983, 1985, 1986, 1988

🍷 Between 7-15 years

Second Wine: Château La Tour l'Aspic

CHÂTEAU LAFITE-ROTHSCHILD

1er Cru Classé
Production: *25,000 cases*

This famous château, the vineyard of which includes a small plot in St.-Estèphe, is run along traditional lines and with fastidious care, by Baron Eric of the French branch of the Rothschilds. The St.-Estèphe portion of the Lafite vineyard is allowed to bear the Pauillac appellation, having been part of the Lafite-Rothschild estate for several hundred years.

A change of style can be traced back to the mid-1970s, when the decision was taken to give the wines less time in cask. They now receive 18-24 months in wood, with 100 per cent new oak. The Second Wine, "Moulin des Carruades", has been produced since the 1974 vintage.

RED Not the biggest of the First Growths, but Lafite is nevertheless textbook stuff: a magnificent delicacy of spicy fruit flavours, continuously unfolding and supported by an array of creamy-oak and ripe tannins; incomparable finesse.

🍇 Cabernet sauvignon 70%, Cabernet franc 13%, Merlot 15%, Petit verdot 2%

🗓 1983, 1985, 1986, 1988, 1989

🍷 Between 25-50 years

Second Wine: "Moulin des Carruades"

CHÂTEAU LATOUR

1er Cru Classé
Production: *16,000 cases*

The Pearson Group of London was accused by the French of turning this First Growth into a dairy when temperature-controlled stainless-steel vats were installed in 1964 (this conveniently ignored the fact that Château Haut-Brion had done the same three years earlier). The change did nothing to detract from the wine; Latour is the most consistent of all the First Growths, excelling even in off-years. The wine is matured in wood for 20-24 months, with 100 per cent new oak.

RED Despite its close proximity to St.-Julien, Latour is the archetypal Pauillac. Its ink-black colour accurately reflects the immense structure and hugely concentrated flavour of this wine. If Lafite is the ultimate example of finesse, then Latour is the ideal illustration of how massive a wine can be, and still retain great finesse.

🍇 Cabernet sauvignon 80%, Cabernet franc 10%, Merlot 10%

🗓 1980, 1981, 1982, 1983, 1984, 1985, 1986, 1987, 1988, 1989

🍷 Between 30-60 years

Second Wine: "Les Forts de Latour"
Other wines: Pauillac AOC

CHÂTEAU LYNCH-BAGES

5ème Cru Classé
Production: *28,000 cases*

This château is situated on the edge of the Bages plateau, a little way out of Pauillac. Jean-Michel Cazes produces wines that some people describe as "poor man's Latour (or Mouton)". Well, that cannot be such a bad thing, but if I were rich, I would drink as much Lynch-Bages as First Growths. No expense was spared in building the new vinification and storage facilities at this château, and since 1980 the successes in off-vintages have been quite extraordinary. The wine is matured in wood for 12-15 months, with 50 per cent new oak. A little white wine is also produced, and an interesting experimental batch of white Lynch-Bages wines was made by Peter Vinding-Diers of Château Rahoul (*see* p.77).

RED An intensely deep purple-coloured wine of seductive character that is packed with fruit and has obvious class. There is a degree of complexity on the nose, a rich, plummy flavour, supple tannin structure and a spicy, blackcurrant and vanilla aftertaste.

🍇 Cabernet sauvignon 73%, Cabernet franc 10%, Merlot 15%, Petit verdot 2%

🗓 1980, 1981, 1982, 1983, 1984, 1985, 1986, 1988, 1989

🍷 Between 8-30 years

Second Wine: Château Haut-Bages-Avérous

CHÂTEAU LYNCH MOUSSAS

5ème Cru Classé
Production: *12,500 cases*

Owned by Emile Castéja of Borie-Manoux, this property has been renovated and the wines could well improve. The wine is matured in wood for 18-20 months, with 25 per cent new oak.

RED Not unpleasant; merely light, rather insubstantial wines of no specific character or quality, although the 1985 was exceptionally stylish.

🍇 Cabernet sauvignon 70%, Merlot 30%

🗓 1981, 1983, 1985

🍷 Between 4-8 years

CHÂTEAU MOUTON-ROTHSCHILD

1er Cru Classé
Production: *20,000 cases*

The famous case of the only wine ever to be officially reclassified since 1855, Baron Philippe de Rothschild's plight ended with Mouton's status being justly raised to First Growth in 1973. Through promotion of Mouton's unique character, he was probably responsible for elevating the Cabernet sauvignon grape to its present high profile. Part of his campaign to keep this château in the headlines was the introduction of a specially commissioned painting for the label of each new vintage. The wine is matured in wood for 22-24 months, with 100 per cent new oak.

RED It is difficult to describe this wine without using the same descriptive terms as those used for Latour, but perhaps the colour of Mouton reminds one more of damsons and the underlying character is more herbal, sometimes even minty. And although it ages just as well, it becomes accessible slightly earlier.

🍇 Cabernet sauvignon 85%, Cabernet franc 10%, Merlot 5%

🗓 1980, 1981, 1982, 1983, 1985, 1986, 1987, 1988, 1989

🍷 Between 20-60 years

CHÂTEAU PICHON-LONGUEVILLE-BARON

2ème Cru Classé
Production: *14,000 cases*

The smaller of the two Pichon vineyards, and the less inspiring wine, although many experts believe the *terroir* of Pichon-Baron is intrinsically superior to that of the star-performing Pichon-Comtesse. One day it might live up to its

potential. The wine is matured in wood for 24 months, with one-third new oak.

RED A deep-coloured, full-bodied wine with true Pauillac *cassis* character, but somewhat austere and requiring time to soften.

🍇 Cabernet sauvignon 75%, Merlot 23%, Malbec 2%

🗓 1980, 1982, 1983, 1986, 1988

🍷 Between 10-20 years

Second Wine: "Le Baronet de Pichot"

CHÂTEAU PICHON-LONGUEVILLE-COMTESSE-DE-LALANDE

2ème Cru Classé
Production: *28,000 cases*

There is a limit to the quality of any wine that is determined by the potential quality of its grapes. But at Pichon-Comtesse (as it is known), the formidable Madame de Lencquesaing demands the maximum from her *terroir* — and consistently gets it. If, as they say, Pichon-Baron has an even greater potential, perhaps she should try to buy it, and reunite the properties. The wine is matured in wood for 18-20 months, with 50 per cent new oak.

RED This temptress is the Château Margaux of Pauillac. It is silky-textured, beautifully balanced and seductive. A wine of great finesse, even in humble years.

🍇 Cabernet sauvignon 58%, Merlot 34%, Petit verdot 8%

🗓 1980, 1981, 1982, 1983, 1985, 1986, 1987, 1988, 1989

🍷 Between 10-30 years

Second Wine: "Réserve de la Comtesse"

CHÂTEAU PÉDESCLAUX

5ème Cru Classé
Production: *8,300 cases*

Little-seen *cru classé* produced from two very well-situated plots of vines, one bordering Lynch Bages, the other between Mouton-Rothschild and Pontet-Canet. Most of its exported production goes to Belgium. It is matured in wood for 20-22 months, with 50 per cent new oak. Wine rejected for the *grand vin* is blended into the wine of Château

Belle Rose, a *Cru Bourgeois* under the same ownership.

🍷 RED Full, firm, traditional style of Pauillac that is slow-maturing and long-lasting.

🍇 Cabernet sauvignon 70%, Cabernet franc 5%, Merlot 20%, Petit verdot 5%

🍾 1981, 1985, 1988

🍷 Between 15-40 years

CHÂTEAU PONTET-CANET

5ème Cru Classé
Production: *30,000 cases*

The reputation of this château has suffered in recent decades, but many thought the situation would be reversed when Guy Tesseron purchased the property in 1975. There has been a long wait, but the 1985 vintage revealed the first glimmers of hope. A wine to watch? It is matured in wood for 18-24 months, with one-third new oak.

🍷 RED Typically it is too austere, shows a lack of charm and has a rustic feel that should not be present in a wine of this class. However, the 1985 is fruity and graceful with a rich, oaky touch.

🍇 Cabernet sauvignon 68%, Cabernet franc 10%, Merlot 20%, Malbec 2%

🍾 1985, 1986, 1988

🍷 Between 6-12 years

Second Wine: "Les Hauts de Pontet"

The best of the rest

CHÂTEAU BELLE ROSE

Cru Bourgeois
Production: *2,000 cases*

This property belongs to Monsieur Jugla, the owner of the *cru classé* Château Pédesclaux.

🍷 RED Solid, medium- to full-bodied, well-made wine, of good longevity and with a hint of oak.

🍇 Cabernet sauvignon 55%, Cabernet franc 20%, Merlot 20%, Petit verdot 5%

🍾 1981, 1982, 1983, 1985

🍷 Between 5-12 years

CHÂTEAU LA BÉCASSE

Production: *2,000 cases*

A rapidly rising star that was not classified as a *Cru Bourgeois* in 1932 nor listed in 1978, but certainly deserves the status now.

🍷 RED A consistently deep-coloured, well-structured wine that is rich in fruit, hinting of blackcurrants, and obviously matured in a certain percentage of new oak.

🍇 Cabernet sauvignon 70%, Cabernet franc 10%, Merlot 20%

🍾 1982, 1983, 1985

🍷 Between 5-12 years

CHÂTEAU COLOMBIER-MONPELOU

Cru Bourgeois
Production: *7,000 cases*

In the third edition of *Bordeaux and its Wines,* published in 1874, this property was described as a Fourth Growth. Of course it was never classified as such, but its use of 30 per cent new oak gives this château a touch of *cru classé* luxury.

🍷 RED Rich, spicy fruit with fine Cabernet characteristics, backed up by good, ripe, tannic structure and vanilla-oaky undertones.

🍇 Cabernet sauvignon 70%, Cabernet franc 5%, Merlot 20%, Petit verdot 5%

🍾 1982, 1985, 1986, 1988

🍷 Between 5-12 years

CHÂTEAU DE CORDEILLAN

Jean-Michel Cazes of Château Lynch-Bages was the driving force behind the group of Médoc growers who renovated Château de Cordeillan, turning it into an hotel, restaurant and wine school complex. Formerly a wine-producing estate, this property will once again market its own wines and, as a showpiece for the commune, they could be worth keeping an eye on.

CHÂTEAU LA COURONNE

Production: *1,750 cases*

Classified *Cru Bourgeois* in 1932, but not included in the *Syndicat's* 1978 list, although it is certainly one of the best non-classified growths in Pauillac. Owned by Madame de Brest-Borie and managed by her brother, Jean-Eugène Borie of Château Ducru-Beaucaillou in St.-Julien. Wine from Château Batailley is vinified in the *cuverie* at La Couronne.

🍷 RED The best vintages of this medium- to full-bodied, damson-coloured wine are spicy, blackcurranty and supple.

🍇 Cabernet sauvignon 70%, Merlot 30%

🍾 1982, 1983, 1985

🍷 Between 5-12 years

CHÂTEAU LA FLEUR-MILON

Cru Bourgeois
Production: *5,000 cases*

A "château with no château", La Fleur-Milon produces a wine accumulated from various parcels of vines bordering such prestigious properties as Lafite, Mouton and Duhart-Milon.

🍷 RED A consistently firm, solid and decent sort of wine, which somehow fails to live up to the favoured origins of its vines.

🍇 Cabernet sauvignon 45%, Cabernet franc 20%, Merlot 35%

🍾 1982, 1985

🍷 Between 4-10 years

CHÂTEAU FONBADET

Production: *6,500 cases*

Classified *Cru Bourgeois* in 1932, but not included in the *Syndicat's* 1978 list, although it is superior to a few that were. Many of the vines are very old, up to 80 years and 15 per cent new oak is used.

🍷 RED This typical Pauillac has a deep, almost opaque colour, an intense *cassis*, cigar-box and cedarwood bouquet, a concentrated spicy-fruit flavour with creamy-oak undertones, and a long finish.

🍇 Cabernet sauvignon 60%, Cabernet franc 15%, Merlot 19%, Malbec 4%, Petit verdot 2%

🍾 1982, 1983, 1985, 1986, 1988

🍷 Between 6-15 years

Second Wine: Château Tour du Roc Moulin

CHÂTEAU HAUT-BAGES AVÉROUS

Production: *2,500 cases*

Classified *Cru Bourgeois* in 1932, but not included in the *Syndicat's* 1978 list, although this property, owned by Jean-Michel Cazes of Château Lynch-Bages, is superior to a few that were. The Second Wines of Château Lynch-Bages are blended with this wine.

🍷 RED Spice, balance and fine acidity are the hallmarks of this wine. This is a medium- to full-bodied wine of very good quality. In some rich years, like 1983, there is an additional, attractive, minty-herbal touch.

🍇 Cabernet sauvignon 75%, Cabernet franc 10%, Merlot 15%

🍾 1982, 1983, 1984, 1985, 1986

🍷 Between 5-12 years

LA ROSE PAUILLAC

Production: *52,000 cases*

This is the local *coopérative's* wine – and pretty good it is, too.

🍷 RED This medium-bodied wine has good fruit and is a typical, if lesser, version of true Pauillac without seeming attenuated or disappointing.

🍇 Cabernet sauvignon and Cabernet franc 45%, Merlot 40%, Petit verdot 15%

🍾 1982, 1983, 1985

🍷 Between 5-10 years

CHÂTEAU LA TOUR-PIBRAN

Production: *3,500 cases*

Classified *Cru Bourgeois* in 1932, but not included in the *Syndicat's* 1978 list, although it is superior to a few that were.

🍷 RED This wine has bags of blackcurranty fruit, yet retains the characteristic Pauillac structure and firm finish. The superb 1985 is not unlike a "mini-Mouton".

🍇 Cabernet sauvignon 75%, Cabernet franc 10%, Merlot 15%

🍾 1982, 1983, 1985

🍷 Between 6-16 years

St.-Julien

THE FAME OF ST.-JULIEN IS DISPROPORTIONATE to its size: of all the Médoc's classic appellations, St.-Julien has the smallest area under vine. It also, however, boasts the highest concentration of AOC vineyards, and its châteaux have discernibly larger estates. They are, for example, 40 per cent larger that those of Margaux.

Significantly, St.-Julien has no First Growths, nor Fifth Growths, although there are years when some of its châteaux produce wines that are undeniably First Growth quality. This is not a commune of extremes, however; the concentration of its eleven *crus classés* in the middle of the Classification is its real strength, enabling St.-Julien to justly claim that it is the most consistent of Médoc appellations. These quintessential clarets have a vivid colour, elegant fruit, superb balance and great finesse.

It is perhaps surprising that wine from 16 hectares (39.5 acres) within this commune is classified as AOC Pauillac, particularly in view of the perceived difference in style. This illustrates the "grey area" that exists when communal boundaries overlap the historical borders of great wine estates, and highlights the existence and importance of blending, even in a region reputed for its single-vineyard wines. Although time has allowed us to discern the communal differences of style, we should not be too pedantic about them, and a little history might serve to make us more humble in this respect. The village of St.-Lambert was once under the auspices of St.-Julien, and both villages were suffixed with the name "Reignac". When the barge was the major means of communication, a substantial traffic existed between St.-Lambert-de-Reignac, St.-Julien-de-Reignac and the actual village of Reignac – located in Blaye, on the opposite bank of the Gironde. If the communal borders followed local history, Château Latour would today be in St.-Julien – and that makes me wonder how we might describe the wines of this commune in such circumstances?

ST.-JULIEN PROFILE

Appellation area
Covers part of the commune of St.-Julien only.

Size of commune
1,554 ha (3,840 acres)

AOC Area under vine
750 ha (1,853 acres) (48% of commune)

Surface area of *crus classés*
628 ha (1,552 acres) (40% of commune, 84% of AOC)

Special comment
Some 16 hectares (40 acres) of St.-Julien are classified as AOC Pauillac.

FACTORS AFFECTING TASTE AND QUALITY

Location
In the centre of the Haut-Médoc, 4 kilometres (two-and-a-half miles) south of Pauillac.

Climate
As for the Médoc, *see* p.44.

Aspect
The gravel crest of St.-Julien slopes almost imperceptibly eastwards towards the village and drains into the Gironde.

Soil
Fine gravel topsoil of good-sized pebbles in vineyards within sight of the Gironde. Further inland, the particle size gradually decreases and the soil begins to mix with sandy loess. The subsoil consists of iron-pan, marl and gravel.

Viticulture and vinification
Only red wines have the right to the appellation. All grapes must be de-stalked. Some *vin de presse* may be used according to the needs of the vintage. Skin-contact duration averages two to three weeks and most châteaux allow 18-22 months maturation in cask.

Primary grape varieties
Cabernet sauvignon, Cabernet franc, Merlot

Secondary grape varieties
Carmenère, Malbec, Petit verdot

ST.-JULIEN *CRU CLASSÉ* STATISTICS

Crus classés in AOC St.-Julien
11 châteaux (18% of all *crus classés*) with 628 ha (1,552 acres) of vineyards (22% of all *crus classés*)
1st Growths: None
2nd Growths: 5 châteaux (36% of all 2nd Growths) with 318 ha (786 acres) of vineyards (40% of all 2nd Growths)
3rd Growths: 2 châteaux (14% of all 3rd Growths) with 69 ha (170 acres) of vineyards (16% of all 3rd Growths)
4th Growths: 4 châteaux (40% of all 4th Growths) with 241 ha (596 acres) of vineyards (51% of all 4th Growths)
5th Growths: None

St.-Julien-Beychevelle, above
The Médoc's most consistent appellation has two small villages as its major centres, St.-Julien-Beychevelle itself and, to the south, Beychevelle.

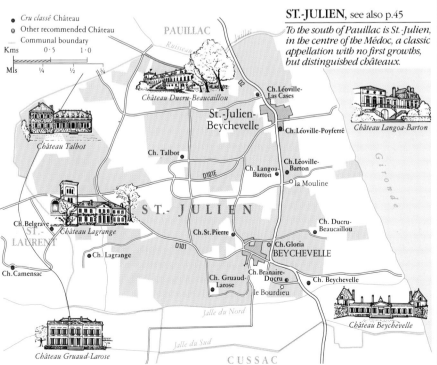

ST.-JULIEN, see also p.45

To the south of Pauillac is St.-Julien, in the centre of the Médoc, a classic appellation with no first growths, but distinguished châteaux.

THE IMPORTANCE OF *TERROIR*

The château or *cru* system is based on the ultimate importance of the *terroir*. This term has often been mistranslated as "soil", which more accurately is *sol*. The concept of *terroir* is an agricultural one that involves the complete growing environment of a specific area. In St.-Julien, two particular châteaux demonstrate the dramatic effect the *terroir* can have on wines produced barely a stone's throw away from each other. Château Talbot and Château Gruaud-Larose produce totally different wines in peculiarly similar situations. The unique aspect of this comparison is that man is not the Joker in this pack. Both properties are owned by Cordier and run according to the same philosophy.

CHÂTEAU TALBOT

Classification: Fourth Growth

Area under vine: 100 ha (247 acres)

Location: Plateau, west of St.-Julien.

Aspect: Southwest-facing.

Soil: Sand and medium-sized siliceous gravel over chalky-marl, and some iron-pan. The geological nature of these layers is different from that of Gruaud-Larose.

Vin de Presse: 6-8%

New oak: one-third

Cask maturation: 18-20 months

Fining agent: Egg white

Filtering: Light plate

Oenologist: Georges Pauli

Grape varieties cultivated:
71% Cabernet sauvignon
20% Merlot
5% Cabernet franc
5% Petit verdot

Density of vines:
7,500-10,000 per ha
(3,000-4,000 per acre)

Age of vines: 25-30 years

Average yield:
42-45 hectolitres/hectare
(189-202 cases/acre)

Average production after rejection of any unsuitable wines:
40,000 cases

Second Wine:
"Connétable Talbot"
(15-20% of production)

Fermentation:
In glass-lined steel vats, water cooled, maximum of 30°C (86°F), natural yeasts.

CHÂTEAU GRUAUD-LAROSE

Classification: Second Growth

Area under vine: 84 ha (207.5 acres)

Location: Plateau, west of Beychevelle. Slightly higher than Talbot and nearer the river.

Aspect: South-facing, undulating.

Soil: Deep bed of large, pebbly, siliceous gravel over chalky-marl, and more iron-pan than Talbot. Because of the higher clay and iron-pan content, pipes are installed when replanting to improve drainage.

Vin de Presse: 8-10%

New oak: one-third

Cask maturation: 18-20 months

Fining agent: Egg white

Filtering: Light plate

Oenologist: Georges Pauli

Grape varieties cultivated:
63% Cabernet sauvignon
23% Merlot
8% Cabernet franc
4% Petit verdot

Density of vines:
7,500-10,000 per ha
(3,000-4,000 per acre)

Age of vines: 25-30 years

Average yield:
40-42 hectolitres/hectare
(180-189 cases/acre)

Average production after rejection of any unsuitable wines:
35,000 cases

Second Wine:
"Sarget de Gruaud-Larose"
(15-20% of production)

Fermentation:
In glass-lined cement vats, water cooled, maximum of 30°C (86°F), natural yeasts.

Difference in the wine:
The small difference in grape varieties grown is hardly likely to make a discernible difference. If any difference could be detected, it should, in theory, mean a slightly fuller wine at Talbot because of its greater proportion of Cabernet sauvignon. Yet Talbot consistently produces the lighter style of wine, whereas Gruaud-Larose is well known for making a rich, full-bodied wine that can be almost fat with fruit, yet always has balance and class. Despite the same plant density, method of training and pruning, the average yield of Talbot (with its higher proportion of intrinsically lower-yielding Cabernet franc) is, in fact, slightly higher than that of Gruaud-Larose. It helps to explain some, although not all, of the difference in concentration, but the reason why the yields differ is a matter of *terroir*, not the design of man. Because it crops higher and the weight of the wine is lighter, the amount of *vin de presse* that can be added to Talbot is necessarily less, but the maturation in new oak is, surprisingly, the same.

The great châteaux of St.-Julien

CHÂTEAU BEYCHEVELLE

4ème Cru Classé
Production: *25,000 cases*

The immaculate and colourful gardens of this château never fail to catch the breath of passers-by. Beychevelle also boasts one of the most famous legends of Bordeaux. Apparently its name is a corruption of *basse-voile*, the command to "lower sail". The Duc d'Épernon, a former owner who was also an admiral of France, required the ships that passed through the Gironde to lower their sails in respect. His wife would then wave her kerchief in reply. This, however, is not true. Épernon actually held the title of Baron de Beychevelle prior to being made the Amiral de Valette, and did not actually live at Beychevelle. I prefer the story of the sailors who lowered their trousers and revealed their sterns, which shocked the duchess, but made her children laugh. The wines are matured in wood for 20 months with 40 per cent new oak.

RED Medium- to full-bodied wines of good colour, ripe fruit and an elegant oak and tannin structure. They can be quite fat in big years.

🍇 Cabernet sauvignon 60%, Cabernet franc 8%, Merlot 28%, Petit verdot 4%

🍷 1982, 1983, 1985, 1986, 1988

🥂 Between 12-20 years

Second Wine: "Réserve de l'Amiral"
Other wines: "Les Brulières de Beychevelle"

CHÂTEAU BRANAIRE-DUCRU

4ème Cru Classé
Production: *23,000 cases*

The vineyards of this château are situated further inland than those of Beychevelle and Ducru-Beaucaillou. The soil has more clay and iron-pan, thus the wine is fuller and can be assertive, although never austere. It is matured in wood for 18 months, with up to 50 per cent new oak, and is remarkably consistent.

RED This wine has a distinctive bouquet that sets it apart from other Pauillacs. It is quite full-bodied, richly flavoured and can show a certain chocolate character in big years.

🍇 Cabernet sauvignon 75%, Cabernet franc 5%, Merlot 20%

🍷 1980, 1981, 1982, 1983, 1985

🥂 Between 12-25 years

CHÂTEAU DUCRU-BEAUCAILLOU

2ème Cru Classé
Production: *20,000 cases*

The quality of this classic St.-Julien château, the flagship property of the Borie Empire, is both legendary and inimitable. In good years and bad it remains remarkably consistent and, although relatively expensive, the price fetched falls short of those demanded by First Growths, making it a relative bargain. The wine is matured in wood for 20 months, with 50 per cent new oak.

RED This wine has a fine, deep colour that can belie its deft elegance of style. There is richness of fruit, complex spiciness of oak, great finesse and exquisite balance.

🍇 Cabernet sauvignon 65%, Cabernet franc 5%, Merlot 25%, Petit verdot 5%

🍷 1980, 1981, 1982, 1983, 1985, 1986, 1988, 1989

🥂 Between 15-30 years

Second Wine: "La Croix"

CHÂTEAU GRUAUD-LAROSE

2ème Cru Classé
Production: *35,000 cases*

A large property that consistently produces great wines of a far more solid structure than one expects from St.-Julien. Neither man nor nature seems capable of interfering with the quality of wines produced at this half of Cordier's twin flagship châteaux. Anyone who has tasted the supposedly mediocre 1980 vintage of "Sarget de Gruaud-Larose" (made from the wines rejected from the *grand vin*), will realize the true potential of Château Gruaud-Larose in any year. The wine is matured in wood for 18-20 months, with one-third new oak.

RED Full-bodied, rich and plummy with masses of fruit. Its concentrated, spicy blackcurrant flavour is well supported by a powerful structure of ripe tannins.

🍇 Cabernet sauvignon 65%, Cabernet franc 8%, Merlot 23%, Petit verdot 4%

🍷 1980, 1981, 1982, 1983, 1985, 1986, 1988

🥂 Between 10-40 years

Second Wine: "Sarget de Gruaud-Larose"

CHÂTEAU LAGRANGE

3ème Cru Classé
Production: *20,000 cases*

When the *Ban de Vendanges* was held at this Japanese-owned château in 1986, everyone realized that the Japanese were not simply content to apply state-of-the-art technology; they seriously intended to make Lagrange the best quality wine in St.-Julien. They could well succeed. The formidable Professor Peynaud has dubbed Lagrange a "dream estate", and describes its vinification centre as "unlike any other in the whole of Bordeaux". Each vat is, according to Peynaud, a "wine-making laboratory". The wine spends 20 months in wood with from 30 per cent new oak in light years to 50 per cent in big years.

RED A deeply-coloured wine with intense spicy-fruit aromas. It is full-bodied, silky-textured, extremely rich and long, with an exquisite balance and finish.

🍇 Cabernet sauvignon 65%, Merlot 25%, Cabernet franc and Petit verdot 10%

🍷 1983, 1985, 1986, 1988

🥂 Between 8-25 years

Second Wine: "Fiefs de Lagrange"

CHÂTEAU LANGOA-BARTON

3ème Cru Classé
Production: *8,000 cases*

This beautiful château was known as Pontet-Langlois until 1821, when it was purchased by Hugh Barton, the grandson of "French Tom" Barton, the founder of Bordeaux *négociant* Barton & Guestier. Now run by Anthony Barton, both Langoa-Barton and Léoville-Barton are made on this property, utilizing very traditional techniques. The wine is matured in wood for 24 months, with a minimum of one-third new oak.

RED Attractive, easy-drinking wine with good fruit and acidity. Lighter than the Léoville and can sometimes taste a little rustic – but then that is its charm.

🍇 Cabernet sauvignon 70%, Cabernet franc 7%, Merlot 15%, Petit verdot 8%

🍷 1980, 1981, 1982, 1983, 1985, 1986, 1988

🥂 Between 10-25 years

Second Wine: "St.-Julien" (a blend of Langoa-Barton and Léoville Barton)

CHÂTEAU LÉOVILLE-BARTON

2ème Cru Classé
Production: *16,000 cases*

A quarter of the original Léoville estate was sold to Hugh Barton in 1826, consequently there is no château here. The wine is made by Anthony Barton at Langoa-Barton (see above), where it is matured in wood for 24 months, with a minimum of one-third new oak.

RED Excellent wines of great finesse and breeding; they are darker, deeper and richer than the, albeit very good quality, Langoa-Barton. With maturity, a certain cedarwood complexity develops that gradually overwhelms its youthful *cassis* and vanilla character.

🍇 Cabernet sauvignon 70%, Cabernet franc 7%, Merlot 15%, Petit verdot 8%

🍷 1981, 1982, 1983, 1984, 1985, 1986, 1988

🥂 Between 15-30 years

Second Wine: "St.-Julien" (a blend of Langoa-Barton and Léoville Barton)

CHÂTEAU LÉOVILLE-LAS CASES

2ème Cru Classé
Production: *30,000 cases*

The label reads "Grand Vin de Léoville du Marquis de Las Cases", although it is commonly referred to as Château Léoville-Las Cases. This estate represents the largest portion of the original Léoville estate. Not only do its vineyards come close to Château Latour, the size and quality of the wines approach it too. This is a great wine – many consider it the greatest of all St.-Juliens. The wine spends 18 months in wood, with 50 per cent new oak.

RED This is a dark damson-coloured, full-bodied and intensely flavoured wine that is complex, classy and aromatically stunning. A skilful amalgam of power and finesse.

🍇 Cabernet sauvignon 65%, Cabernet franc 14%, Merlot 18%, Petit verdot 3%

🍷 1980, 1981, 1982, 1983, 1985, 1986, 1987, 1988

🥂 Between 15-35 years

Second Wine: "Clos du Marquis"

CHÂTEAU LÉOVILLE-POYFERRÉ

2ème Cru Classé
Production: *23,000 cases*

This is the other quarter of the original Léoville estate, and probably suffers from being compared to the other two châteaux – Léoville-Barton and Léoville-las-Cases. Yet taking this wine in the context of St.-Julien as a whole, it fares very well, and since 1982 it has had some extraordinary successes. The wine is matured in wood for 18 months, with one-third new oak.

RED Always a tannic wine, but it is now much fuller in fruit, richer in flavour and darker in colour, with attractive oaky nuances.

Cabernet sauvignon 65%, Merlot 30%, Cabernet franc 5%

1981, 1982, 1983, 1985, 1986

Between 12-25 years

Second Wine: Château Moulin-Riche

CHÂTEAU ST.-PIERRE

4ème Cru Classé
Production: *9,000 cases*

Purchased in 1982 by Henri Martin, who now makes this wine at his *Bourgeois* Growth, Château Gloria. Once a lacklustre *cru classé*, the quality picked up in the mid-1970s and this is likely to continue under Martin's guidance. The wine is matured in wood for 18-20 months with 50 per cent new oak.

GRAND CRU CLASSÉ EN 1855

CHATEAU SAINT-PIERRE
1982
MIS EN BOUTEILLES   NEC PLURIBUS
AU CHATEAU   SAINT-JULIEN   IMPAR
APPELLATION SAINT-JULIEN CONTROLEE
DOMAINES HENRI MARTIN
PROPRIETAIRE A SAINT-JULIEN BEYCHEVELLE, GIRONDE 75cl

RED This wine used to be astringent, even coarse, but it is now ripe and fat and full of complex cedarwood, spice and fruit.

Cabernet sauvignon 70%, Cabernet franc and Petit verdot 5%, Merlot 25%

1980, 1981, 1982, 1983, 1985, 1986

Between 8-25 years

Second Wine: Château Saint-Louis-le-Bosq

CHÂTEAU TALBOT

4ème Cru Classé
Production: *40,000 cases*

Named after the English Commander who fell at the Battle of Castillon in 1453, this is the second of Cordier's twin flagship châteaux. To contrast the style of these two St.-Juliens is totally justifiable, but to compare their quality is not. Talbot is a great wine and closer to one's perceived idea of a St.-Julien, but intrinsically it has not the quality nor the consistency of Gruaud-Larose (*see also* p.60). The wine is matured in wood for 18-20 months, with one-third new oak.

RED A graceful wine, medium-bodied, with elegant fruit, gently structured by ripe oak tannins and capable of considerable finesse.

Cabernet sauvignon 71%, Cabernet franc 5%, Merlot 20%, Petit verdot 4%

1982, 1983, 1985, 1986, 1988

Between 8-30 years

Second Wine: "Connétable Talbot"

The best of the rest

CHÂTEAU LA BRIDANE

Cru Bourgeois
Production: *8,000 cases*

The owners of this property have maintained a vineyard here since the fourteenth century.

RED Attractive, fruity, medium-bodied wine that is supple and easy to drink.

Cabernet sauvignon 55%, Merlot 45%

1982, 1985

Between 3-6 years

CHÂTEAU DU GLANA

Cru Bourgeois
Production: *20,000 cases*

This property is under the same ownership as Château Plantey in Pauillac and Château la Commanderie in St.-Estèphe.

RED Normally an unpretentious, medium-weight wine, Du Glana excels in really hot years, when it can be deliciously ripe and juicy.

Cabernet sauvignon 68%, Cabernet franc 2%, Merlot 25%, Petit verdot 5%

1982

Between 3-6 years

CHÂTEAU GLORIA

Production: *16,000 cases*

Gloria excites opposite passions in wine drinkers: some consider it the equal of several *cru classé* wines – even superior in some cases – while others believe it earns an exaggerated price based on the reputation of merely a handful of vintages.

Certainly the 1970 would not appear out of place in a blind tasting with some of the best *crus classés*. The wine is matured in wood for 16 months, with one-third new oak.

RED A deep plum-coloured, full-bodied wine with masses of fruit and a rich, almost exuberant character.

Cabernet sauvignon 65%, Cabernet franc 5%, Merlot 25%, Petit verdot 5%

1982, 1983, 1985, 1986, 1989

Between 12-30 years

Second Wine: Château Peymartin
Other wines: Château Haut-Beychevelle-Gloria

CHÂTEAU HORTEVIE

Production: *1,500 cases*

No château exists as such and the wine is made at Château Terrey-Gros-Caillou by Henri Pradère.

RED A silky-soft, rich and succulent wine of excellent quality.

Cabernet sauvignon and Cabernet franc 70%, Merlot 25%, Petit verdot 5%

1981, 1982, 1983, 1985

Between 7-15 years

CHÂTEAU DE LACOUFOURQUE

Production: *600 cases*

This tiny one-and-a-quarter-hectare (3-acre) vineyard is mentioned not because of its past performance, but because its unique character, as a 100 per cent Cabernet franc varietal, should be preserved.

RED Sold in bulk as generic St.-Julien, so it is impossible to generalize.

Cabernet franc 100%

CHÂTEAU LALANDE-BORIE

Production: *8,000 cases*

Under the same ownership as the illustrious Château Ducru-Beaucaillou, Lalande-Borie is an inexpensive introduction to the wines of St.-Julien.

RED Well-coloured wines, dominated by rich, blackcurranty Cabernet sauvignon flavours. Some are fat and juicy, others more ethereal and tannic.

Cabernet sauvignon 65%, Cabernet franc 10%, Merlot 25%

1981, 1982, 1983, 1985

Between 5-10 years

CHÂTEAU MOULIN-DE-LA-ROSE

Production: *2,000 cases*

The vineyard is well situated, being surrounded by *crus classés* on virtually all sides. Its wine is fermented in stainless steel and aged in cask for 18 months, with 25 per cent new oak.

RED An attractively aromatic wine that is unusually concentrated and firm for a minor St.-Julien, but rounds out nicely after a few years in bottle.

Cabernet sauvignon 55%, Cabernet franc 10%, Merlot 30%, Petit verdot 5%

1982, 1983, 1985

Between 6-12 years

CHÂTEAU TERREY-GROS-CAILLOU

Production: *8,000 cases*

Under the same ownership as Château Hortevie, this is a top-performing property.

RED This beautifully coloured, medium- to full-bodied wine is always well endowed with rich fruit.

Cabernet sauvignon 65%, Merlot 30%, Petit verdot 5%

1982, 1983, 1985

Between 5-12 years

TERROIR DE LA CABANE

Production: *220 cases*

Tiny production from barely more than one-third of a hectare (three-quarters of an acre) of old vines, mostly sold in bulk but 50 or 60 cases are available from the château.

RED Tasted only once, but it was pure delight, rich and fat with ripe fruit, supple tannins and a silky texture.

CHÂTEAU TEYNAC

Production: *2,500 cases*

This fine gravel vineyard once formed part of *cru classé* Château Saint-Pierre.

RED Well-balanced, medium- to full-bodied wine with good Cabernet spice and a firm tannin structure.

Cabernet sauvignon 65%, Merlot 35%

1982, 1983, 1985, 1988

Between 6-10 years

Margaux

THE MOST FAMOUS OF ALL BORDEAUX appellations, Margaux bathes in the reflected glory of its namesake First Growth. It is also the largest of the four classic Médoc appellations. While the other three are connected in one unbroken chain of vineyards, Margaux stands alone to the south, with its vines spread across five communes – Labarde, Arsac and Cantenac to the south, Margaux in the centre and Soussans to the north. Margaux and Cantenac are the most important communes and, of course, Margaux contains the First Growth of Château Margaux itself. Cantenac has a slightly larger area under vine and no less than eight classified growths, including the star-performing Château Palmer.

Margaux and Pauillac are the only appellations in the Médoc with First Growth vineyards, but only Margaux can boast vineyards in all five categories of the Classification. It also has more *cru classé* châteaux than any other Médoc appellation, including an impressive total of ten Third Growths.

MARGAUX *CRU CLASSÉ* STATISTICS

Crus classés in AOC Margaux: 21 châteaux (35% of all *crus classés*) with 854 ha (2,110 acres) of vineyards (35% of all *crus classés*)

1st Growths: 1 château (25% of all 1st Growths) with 75 ha (185 acres) of vineyards (25% of all 1st Growths)

2nd Growths: 5 châteaux (36% of all 2nd Growths) with 271 ha (670 acres) of vineyards (34% of all 2nd Growths)

3rd Growths: 10 châteaux (72% of all 3rd Growths) with 305 ha (754 acres) of vineyards (72% of all 3rd Growths)

4th Growths: 3 châteaux (30% of all 4th Growths) with 105 ha (259 acres) of vineyards (22% of all 4th Growths)

5th Growths: 2 châteaux (11% of all 5th Growths) with 98 ha (242 acres) of vineyards (13% of all 5th Growths)

MARGAUX PROFILE

Appellation covers: parts of the communes of Arsac, Cantenac, Labarde, Margaux and Soussans as follows.

	Size of commune	AOC Area under vine	Vine area as proportion of Commune	Appellation
Arsac	3,219 ha (7,954 acres)	95 ha (235 acres)	3%	8%
Cantenac	1,417 ha (3,502 acres)	400 ha (988 acres)	28%	34%
Labarde	475 ha (1,174 acres)	130 ha (321 acres)	27%	11%
Margaux	843 ha (2,083 acres)	390 ha (964 acres)	46%	34%
Soussans	1,558 ha (3,850 acres)	150 ha (370 acres)	10%	13%
TOTAL	7,512 ha (18,562 acres)	1,165 ha (2,878 acres)	16%	100%

Total size of all five communes: 7,512 ha (18,562 acres)

Total AOC area under vine: 1,165 ha (2,878 acres) (16% of communes)

Surface area of *crus classés*: 854 ha (2,110 acres) (11% of communes, 73% of AOC)

MARGAUX, see also p.45

Of the classic Médoc appellations, Margaux– the most famous– stands alone to the south, and can boast more cru classé *châteaux than any of the others.*

Château Margaux, above
Margaux's celebrated First Growth vineyards are matched by the grandeur of the building itself. Both the building and the wine are justifiably famous.

An outstanding wine

As Bernard Ginestet says in his book *Margaux,* "While other areas produce wines with pronounced characteristics which are readily identifiable – like a man with a beard or a big nose – Margaux is the epitome of refinement and subtlety". If the massive wines of Latour and Mouton are an object lesson in how it is possible to bombard the senses with power and flavour, and yet retain remarkable finesse, then the exquisite wines of Margaux are proof that complexity does not necessarily issue from an intense concentration of flavour. This is not to suggest that Margaux wines do not possess some concentration; for Château Margaux has remarkable concentration, yet remains the quintessential wine of this appellation.

Nouveaux chais, **Margaux,** above
Evidence of the investment made in Château Margaux since the late 1970s is the refurbished wine store and its full complement of new oak barrels.

FACTORS AFFECTING TASTE AND QUALITY

Location
In the centre of the Haut-Médoc, some 28 kilometres (17 miles) northwest of Bordeaux, encompassing the communes of Cantenac, Soussans, Arsac and Labarde in addition to Margaux itself.

Climate
As for the Médoc, *see* p.44.

Aspect
One large, low-lying plateau centring on Margaux plus several modest outcrops that slope west towards the forest.

Soil
Shallow, pebbly, siliceous gravel over a gravel subsoil interbedded with limestone.

Viticulture and vinification
Only red wines have the right to the appellation. All grapes must be de-stalked. On average, between five and ten per cent *vin de presse* may be used in the wine, according to the needs of the vintage. Skin-contact duration averages 15-25 days, with the period of maturation in cask currently varying between 18 and 24 months.

Primary grape varieties
Cabernet sauvignon, Cabernet franc, Merlot

Secondary grape varieties
Carmenère, Malbec, Petit verdot

Soutirage, **Château Margaux,** above
As the wine matures in the barrel, its clarity is checked regularly. It spends 18-24 months in new oak.

Peter Sichel, above
A leading Bordeaux négociant, Peter Sichel owns Château Angludet and has a share in Château Palmer.

Château Giscours, left
Purchased and then restored by the Tari family in 1952, the property also boasts a magnificent natural wood.

The great châteaux of Margaux

CHÂTEAU BOYD-CANTENAC

3ème Cru Classé
Production: *9,000 cases*

A property producing traditional-style wines from old vines. The wine is made at Monsieur Guillemet's other property, Château Pouget, under the supervision of Professor Peynaud. It is matured in wood for 24 months, with 30 per cent new oak and, in my opinion, would benefit from more Merlot and no Petit verdot.

RED Full-bodied, firm wine of good colour that needs a long time in bottle to soften. The 1980 was particularly successful.

🍇 Cabernet sauvignon 70%, Cabernet franc 5%, Merlot 20%, Petit verdot 5%

🍷 1980, 1982, 1983, 1985

🍶 Between 12-20 years

CHÂTEAU BRANE-CANTENAC

2ème Cru Classé
Production: *26,000 cases*

A superb plateau of immaculately kept vines on gravel over limestone. The wine is matured in wood for 18 months, with 25-30 per cent new oak.

RED Stylish wines with a smoky-cream, new oak bouquet and deliciously rich fruit and finesse on the palate. These are top-quality wines, velvety and beautifully balanced.

🍇 Cabernet sauvignon 70%, Cabernet franc 15%, Merlot 13%, Petit verdot 2%

🍷 1982, 1983, 1985, 1986, 1989

🍶 Between 8-25 years

Second Wine: Château Notton

CHÂTEAU CANTENAC-BROWN

3ème Cru Classé
Production: *15,000 cases*

Ever since I drank a fifty-year-old half-bottle of 1926 Cantenac-Brown in splendid condition, I have had a soft spot for this château that is frankly disproportionate to the quality of its wines. However, I enjoy them immensely. They are matured in wood for 18 months, with one-third of the casks new oak.

RED A similar weight and style to Brane-Cantenac, but less velvety and generally more rustic. The vintages of the 1980s have more finesse than those of the 1970s.

🍇 Cabernet sauvignon 75%, Cabernet franc 8%, Merlot 15%, Petit verdot 2%

🍷 1982, 1983, 1985, 1988, 1989

🍶 Between 10-25 years

CHÂTEAU DAUZAC

5ème Cru Classé
Production: *15,000 cases*

Since 1978 this property has belonged to Félix Chatellier, whose other interests include the Goulet-Lepitre-de-Saint-Marceaux trio of Champagne houses. He has renovated the *cuverie* and started to replant the vineyard. The wine, which is matured in wood for 16-18 months with one-third new oak, is steadily improving.

RED Ruby-coloured, medium-bodied, round and attractively fruity wines that are easy to drink.

🍇 Cabernet sauvignon 65%, Cabernet franc 5%, Merlot 25%, Petit verdot 5%

🍷 1980, 1981, 1983, 1985

🍶 Between 6-12 years

Second Wine: Château Labarde

CHÂTEAU DESMIRAIL

3ème Cru Classé
Production: *4,000 cases*

A "château with no château" (it was purchased by Paul Zuger and is now the château of Château Marquis d'Alesme-Becker), Desmirail has been on the ascent since its purchase by Lucien Lurton of Brane-Cantenac and Durfort-Vivens in 1981. The wine is matured in wood for 20 months, with 25-50 per cent new oak; Professor Peynaud advises.

RED A medium-bodied wine that is nicely balanced with gentle fruit flavours and supple tannins. It is well made and gradually gaining in finesse.

🍇 Cabernet sauvignon 80%, Cabernet franc 9%, Merlot 10%, Petit verdot 1%

🍷 1982, 1983

🍶 Between 7-15 years

Second Wine: Château Baudry
Other wines: Domaine de Fontarney

CHÂTEAU DURFORT-VIVENS

2ème Cru Classé
Production: *6,000 cases*

Under the same ownership as Brane-Cantenac, this property matures its wine in wood for 18-20 months, with up to one-third new oak.

RED Higher tannic structure than Brane-Cantenac, but without the luxurious new-oak character, and with less fruit and charm. The 1985 was particularly rich and impressive.

🍇 Cabernet sauvignon 82%, Cabernet franc 10%, Merlot 8%

🍷 1981, 1983, 1985

🍶 Between 10-25 years

Second Wine: Domaine de Cure-Bourse

CHÂTEAU FERRIÈRE

3ème Cru Classé
Production: *2,500 cases*

Little-seen wine from barely five hectares (12 acres) of vines owned by Madame Durand-Feuillerat, but managed by Château Lascombes. It has frankly little more than second-label status, which is a pity for a Third Growth.

RED Quick-maturing wine of medium weight and accessible fruit.

🍇 Cabernet sauvignon 46%, Cabernet franc 8%, Merlot 33%, Petit verdot 12%, Malbec 1%

🍷 1981

🍶 Between 4-8 years

CHÂTEAU GISCOURS

3ème Cru Classé
Production: *25,000 cases*

Situated in the commune of Labarde, this property was purchased in 1952 by the Tari family, who have restored the château, its vineyard and, more importantly, the quality of its wines to its former glory. The wine is matured in wood for 20-34 months, with 50 per cent new oak.

RED Vividly coloured wine, rich in fruit and finesse. Its vibrant style keeps it remarkably fresh for many years.

🍇 Cabernet sauvignon 75%, Cabernet franc 3%, Merlot 20%, Petit verdot 2%

🍷 1980, 1981, 1982, 1983, 1984, 1985

🍶 Between 8-30 years

CHÂTEAU D'ISSAN

3ème Cru Classé
Production: *11,000 cases*

This beautiful seventeenth-century château is often cited as the most impressive in the entire Médoc, and its remarkable wines, matured in wood for 18 months, with up to one-third new oak, are consistently just as spectacular.

RED This wine really is glorious! Its luxuriant bouquet is immediately seductive, its fruit is unbelievably rich and sumptuous. A great wine of great finesse.

🍇 Cabernet sauvignon 85%, Merlot 15%

🍷 1980, 1981, 1982, 1983, 1984, 1985, 1986, 1989

🍶 Between 10-40 years

CHÂTEAU KIRWAN

3ème Cru Classé
Production: *14,000 cases*

A well-run and improving property owned by the Bordeaux *négociant* Schröder & Schÿler. The wine is matured in wood for 18-24 months, with up to 50 per cent new oak.

RED Deep-coloured, full-bodied, rich and concentrated wines that are well made and gaining in generosity and new oak influence with each passing vintage.

🍇 Cabernet sauvignon 40%, Cabernet franc 20%, Merlot 30%, Petit verdot 10%

🍷 1981, 1982, 1983, 1984, 1985

🍷 Between 10-35 years

CHÂTEAU LASCOMBES

2ème Cru Classé
Production: *20,000 cases*

Owned by Bass Charrington, the wines of this large property have always been good, yet they have improved dramatically since 1982; some are stunning. The wine is matured in wood for 14-20 months, with one-third new oak.

RED Full-bodied, rich and concentrated wine with ripe fruit, a lovely cedarwood complexity, and supple tannin.

🍇 Cabernet sauvignon 52%, Cabernet franc 11%, Merlot 33%, Petit verdot and Malbec 4%

🍷 1980, 1981, 1982, 1983, 1984, 1985, 1988

🍷 Between 8-30 years

Second Wine: Château Segonnes
Other wines: "Chevalier Lascombes", Margaux AOC, "Rosé de Lascombes", "Vin Sec Chevalier Lascombes"

CHÂTEAU MALESCOT ST.-EXUPÉRY

3ème Cru Classé
Production: *15,000 cases*

English-owned until 1955 when it was purchased by Roger Zuger, who

also owns Château Marquis-d'Alesme-Becker. The wine is matured in wood for 18 months, with 20 per cent new oak.

RED Supposed to be of the elegant, light style, but I have found too many vintages that lack fruit and charm – 1982, 1983 and 1985 making a welcome trio of exceptions.

🍇 Cabernet sauvignon 50%, Cabernet franc 10%, Merlot 35%, Petit verdot 5%

🍷 1982, 1983, 1985, 1988, 1989

🍷 Between 8-25 years

Second Wine: Château de Loyac

CHÂTEAU MARGAUX

1er Cru Classé
Production: *25,000 cases*

This is the most famous wine in the world and, since its glorious rebirth in 1978, the greatest. Its quality may occasionally be matched, but it is never surpassed. Purchased in 1977 for 72 million francs by the late André Mentzelopoulos, who spent an equal sum renovating it, this fabulous jewel in the crown of the Médoc is now run by his daughter, Corinne Mentzelopoulos-Petit and her husband.

It has been rumoured that the Mentzelopoulos family had invested too heavily in Margaux and were seeking buyers, but this is ridiculous. Quite apart from the vast family fortune (which in 1977 included the Félix Potin grocery shop chain with an annual turnover of 3.5 billion francs), the Mentzelopoulos family made Château Margaux profitable within just three years. In 1985 it turned over 94 million francs of which 62.1 million was declared as pre-tax profit, and it is therefore recouping the equivalent of its purchase price every year. Both Château Margaux and its Second Wine, "Pavillon Rouge", are vinified in oak vats and matured for 18-24 months in 100 per cent new oak.

RED If finesse can be picked up on the nose, then the stunning and complex bouquet of Château Margaux is the yardstick. The softness, finesse and velvety texture of this wine belies its depth. Amazingly rich and concentrated, with an elegant, long and complex finish supported by ripe tannins and wonderful smoky-creamy oak aromas. Perfection!

🍇 Cabernet sauvignon 75%, Cabernet franc and Petit verdot 5%, Merlot 20%

🍷 1981, 1982, 1983, 1984, 1985, 1986, 1988, 1989

🍷 Between 15-50 years

Second Wine: "Pavillon Rouge du Château Margaux"
Other wines: "Pavillon Blanc du Château Margaux"

CHÂTEAU MARQUIS D'ALESME-BECKER

3ème Cru Classé
Production: *4,150 cases*

Like Château Malescot-St.-Exupéry, this was English-owned until purchased by Roger Zuger, who also purchased the maison of neighbouring Desmirail to act as its château. The wine is matured in wood for 12 months, with one-sixth new oak.

RED Austere and charmless wines from my point of view, although they have their admirers. They are well made, but lack sufficient selection, although the *terroir* has potential. The disappointing wines cannot be the style Zuger intends if he can make such a splendid 1985 and can even excel in a poor vintage like 1984.

🍇 Cabernet sauvignon 40%, Cabernet franc 20%, Merlot 30%, Petit verdot 10%

🍷 1984, 1985

🍷 Between 8-20 years

CHÂTEAU MARQUIS-DE-TERME

4ème Cru Classé
Production: *11,000 cases*

Situated next to Château Margaux, this once majestic estate developed the reputation for producing tight, tannic one-dimensional wines, but its quality has picked up since the late 1970s and has been performing extremely well since 1983. The wine is matured in wood for 24 months, with one-third new oak.

RED Appears to be developing a style that is ripe and rich, with definite and delightful signs of new oak. The 1984 was quite a revelation.

🍇 Cabernet sauvignon 45%, Cabernet franc 15%, Merlot 35%, Petit verdot 5%

🍷 1983, 1984, 1985, 1988

🍷 Between 10-25 years

Second Wine: Domaine des Goudat

CHÂTEAU PALMER

3ème Cru Classé
Production: *12,500 cases*

Only Château Margaux outshines this property which is jointly owned by the Belgian and British Bordeaux *négociants* Mähler-Besse and Peter Sichel. Château Palmer 1961 and 1966 regularly fetch prices at auction that equal those fetched by the First Growths. Judged at the very highest level, it could be more consistent. It is usually excellent, but not always astonishing. The wine is matured in wood for 18-24 months, with one-third new oak.

RED Deep-, almost opaque-coloured wine with masses of *cassis* fruit and an exceedingly rich, intense and complex construction of creamy, spicy, cedarwood and vanilla flavours, supported by a fine tannic structure.

🍇 Cabernet sauvignon 55%, Cabernet franc 3%, Merlot 40%, Petit verdot 2%

🍷 1981, 1982, 1986, 1988, 1989

🍷 Between 12-35 years

CHÂTEAU POUGET

4ème Cru Classé
Production: *3,500 cases*

Under the same ownership as Boyd-Cantenac, this property houses the winemaking and storage facilities for both châteaux. The wine is matured in wood for 22-24 months, with 30 per cent new oak.

RED Well-coloured, full-bodied wine with good depth of flavour. Good, but not great, and could be more consistent.

🍇 Cabernet sauvignon 70%, Cabernet franc 8%, Merlot 17%, Petit verdot 5%

🍷 1983, 1985, 1988

🍷 Between 10-25 years

CHÂTEAU PRIEURÉ-LICHINE

4ème Cru Classé
Production: *19,000 cases*

Alexis Lichine purchased Château Prieuré in 1951 and added his name to it. To develop the small run-down vineyard he bought various prized plots of vines from Palmer, Kirwan, Giscours, Boyd-Cantenac, Brane-Cantenac and Durfort-Vivens – some 60 hectares (148 acres). The composite classification must be higher than its official status – the wines certainly are. They are matured in wood for 19 months, with one-third new oak.

RED Well-coloured, full-bodied wines, plummy and rich, with good blackcurrant fruit supported by supple tannins and a touch of vanilla-oak.

Cabernet sauvignon 55%, Cabernet franc 5%, Merlot 35%, Petit verdot 5%

1981, 1982, 1983, 1986, 1988

Between 7-20 years

Second Wine: Château de Clairefont

CHÂTEAU RAUSAN-SÉGLA

2ème Cru Classé
Production: *16,000 cases*

Owned by Bordeaux *négociant* Eschenauer, the quality of this once-disappointing château is improving due to significant investment in the property and far stricter selection of the *grand vin*. The wine is matured in wood for 20 months, with 50 per cent new oak.

RED Now, thankfully, deep, dark and intensely flavoured with a powerful tannic construction.

Cabernet sauvignon 60%, Cabernet franc 10%, Merlot 30%

1982, 1983, 1984, 1985, 1986

Between 15-30 years

CHÂTEAU RAUZAN-GASSIES

2ème Cru Classé
Production: *8,300 cases*

Until the Revolution of 1789, this property and Château Rausan-Ségla were one large estate. Rauzan with a "z" was the original spelling for both properties in the 1855 Classification.

The globe-trotting Professor Peynaud was brought in to steer this wine back on course in the early 1980s. It is matured in wood for 17-20 months, with 20 per cent new oak, although there is little evidence of it on the palate.

RED Full-bodied, coarse, rustic, tannic and ungenerous: the 1982 had some ripe fruit, but the last vintage I really enjoyed was 1961 – and it was difficult not to make a good wine in that year. This is a great shame for a Second Growth, but it seems that not even Peynaud can work miracles!

Cabernet sauvignon 40%, Cabernet franc 20%, Merlot 39%, Petit verdot 1%

1982

Between 7-15 years

Second Wine: "Enclos de Moncabon"

CHÂTEAU DU TERTRE

5ème Cru Classé
Production: *14,000 cases*

A little-seen, underrated *cru classé* with particularly well-situated vineyards. The wine is matured in wood for 24 months, with 25 per cent new oak.

RED This is one of the few Margaux in which I pick up the real impression of violets on the nose, although other experts suggest that the scent of violets is a common characteristic of this commune. The wine is medium- to full-bodied, lightly rich in very fragrant and delightful fruit, and has excellent balance and length, with obvious class.

Cabernet sauvignon 80%, Cabernet franc 10%, Merlot 10%

1982, 1983, 1985, 1986, 1988

Between 8-25 years

The best of the rest

CHÂTEAU ANGLUDET

Production: *12,000 cases*

Owned by Peter Sichel, Bordeaux *négociant* and part-owner of Château Palmer, this property was classified *Cru Bourgeois* in 1932, but not included in the *Syndicat's* 1978 list, although it is superior to a few that were. Only the relative youth of this vineyard stops it competing with the very best Margaux. The wine is matured in wood for 12 months, with up to one-third new oak.

RED Vividly coloured, medium- to full-bodied wines with excellent fruit, finesse and finish – classic Margaux.

Cabernet sauvignon 50%, Cabernet franc 15%, Merlot 30%, Petit verdot 5%

1980, 1982, 1983, 1984, 1985, 1986, 1987, 1988

Between 10-20 years

Second Wine: Château Bory

CHÂTEAU BEL-AIR MARQUIS D'ALIGRE

Production: *4,500 cases*

Classified *Cru Bourgeois* in 1932, but not included in the *Syndicat's* 1978 list, although it is superior to a few that were. The vineyard has limestone subsoil and only organic fertilizers are used.

RED Well-made wines of fine colour, elegant fruit and distinctive style.

Cabernet sauvignon 30%, Cabernet franc 20%, Merlot 35%, Petit verdot 15%

1983, 1985

Between 6-12 years

CHATEAU CANUET

Cru Bourgeois
Production: *5,000 cases*

Owned by Jean and Sabine Rooryck, who have roots in Champagne and Flanders. The vineyard is relatively young and it already produces wine of a very high standard.

RED Wine of an attractive style that is rich in colour and flavour and backed up by a good tannic structure.

Cabernet sauvignon 45%, Merlot 50%, Petit verdot 5%

1980, 1981, 1982, 1985

Between 4-10 years

CHÂTEAU CHARMANT

Production: *2,500 cases*

Not classified as a *Cru Bourgeois* in 1932 nor listed by the *Syndicat* in 1978, but it certainly deserves recognition now.

RED An elegant wine with plenty of fruit and a soft finish. It makes delightful drinking when young.

Cabernet sauvignon 60%, Cabernet franc 5%, Merlot 35%

1982, 1983, 1985

Between 3-8 years

CHÂTEAU DEYREM-VALENTIN

Production: *5,000 cases*

Classified *Cru Bourgeois* in 1932, but not included in the *Syndicat's* 1978 list, although it is superior to a few that were. Its vineyards adjoin those of Château Lascombes.

RED Honest, medium-bodied, fruity wine of some elegance.

Cabernet sauvignon 45%, Cabernet franc 5%, Merlot 45%, Petit verdot 5%

1982, 1983

Between 4-10 years

CHÂTEAU LA GURGUE

Production: *5,000 cases*

Classified *Cru Bourgeois* in 1932, but not included in the *Syndicat's* 1978 list, although it is superior to a few that were. The proprietor of this quality-conscious property close to Château Margaux, also owns the *cru classé* Haut-Bages-Libéral and the *Cru Bourgeois* Chasse-Spleen.

RED Soft, elegant, medium-bodied wine of attractive flavour and some finesse.

Cabernet sauvignon 70%, Merlot 25%, Petit verdot 5%

1983, 1985, 1988

Between 4-12 years

CHÂTEAU LABÉGORCE

Production: *13,500 cases*

Classified *Cru Bourgeois* in 1932, but not included in the *Syndicat's* 1978 list. The wine is matured in wood for 18 months, with up to one-third new oak.

RED Well-coloured wine with good balance of concentration and finesse.

🍇 Cabernet sauvignon 60%, Cabernet franc 5%, Merlot 35%

🍷 1982, 1985

🍾 Between 5-15 years

CHÂTEAU LABÉGORCE-ZÉDÉ

Production: *9,500 cases*

Classified *Cru Bourgeois* in 1932, but not included in the 1978 list, although it is one of the best non-*cru classé* wines of the commune.

RED Fine flavour and great length, combined with a certain complexity, give the wines of this château a slight edge over those of Château Labégorce.

🍇 Cabernet sauvignon 50%, Cabernet franc 10%, Merlot 35%, Petit verdot 5%

🍷 1980, 1983, 1985, 1989

🍾 Between 5-15 years

CHÂTEAU MARSAC-SÉGUINEAU

Production: *5,000 cases*

Classified *Cru Bourgeois* in 1932, but not included in the *Syndicat's* 1978 list, although it is superior to a few that were. The vineyards of this château include some plots that originally belonged to a *cru classé*.

RED Medium- to full-bodied wines of good bouquet and a soft style.

🍇 Cabernet sauvignon 65%, Merlot 35%

🍷 1981, 1982, 1983

🍾 Between 5-12 years

CHÂTEAU MARTINENS

Cru Bourgeois
Production: *9,000 cases*

This château's 30-hectare (74-acre) vineyard occupies one uninterrupted block of land, and its wine is matured in wood for 12 months, with 25 per cent new oak.

RED Well-made wines with good Margaux aromas and elegant fruit.

🍇 Cabernet sauvignon 30%, Cabernet franc 10%, Merlot 40%, Petit verdot 20%

🍷 1983, 1985

🍾 Between 5-10 years

CHÂTEAU MONBRISON

Production: *5,500 cases*

Classified *Cru Bourgeois* in 1932, but not included in the *Syndicat's* 1978 list, although it is superior to a few that were. Used to be part of *cru classé* Château Desmirail.

RED A second label allows a good selection of well-coloured wines that have spicy oak and super-rich, juicy fruit with a fine structure of supple tannin.

🍇 Cabernet sauvignon 30%, Cabernet franc 30%, Merlot 35%, Petit verdot 5%

🍷 1980, 1981, 1983, 1985, 1986

🍾 Between 8-15 years

Second Wine: "Clos Cordat"

CHÂTEAU MONTBRUN

Production: *3,500 cases*

Classified *Cru Bourgeois* in 1932, but not included in the *Syndicat's* 1978 list, although it is superior to a few that were. This used to be part of *cru classé* Château Palmer.

RED Beautifully made, ripe and juicy, medium- to full-bodied, Merlot-dominated wine.

🍇 Cabernet sauvignon and Cabernet franc 25%, Merlot 75%

🍷 1982, 1983, 1985, 1988

🍾 Between 5-12 years

CHÂTEAU PAVEIL-DE-LUZE

Cru Bourgeois
Production: *7,000 cases*

Fine, well-drained, gravelly soil with good-sized pebbles. The vineyard was replanted in the early 1970s; the vines are young and so the wines will continue to improve.

RED Soft, easy-drinking, medium-bodied wines of some elegance that would benefit from a little finesse.

🍇 Cabernet sauvignon and Cabernet franc 70%, Merlot 30%

🍷 1980, 1981, 1982, 1983, 1985

🍾 Between 4-8 years

Second Wine: Château de la Coste

CHÂTEAU PONTAC-LYNCH

Production: *3,000 cases*

Classified *Cru Bourgeois* in 1932, but not included in the *Syndicat's*

1978 list, although it is superior to a few that were. Well-situated vineyards, surrounded by *crus classés* on all sides.

RED Richly perfumed, deeply coloured, full-bodied wines of good structure.

🍇 Cabernet sauvignon and Cabernet franc 45%, Merlot 47%, Petit verdot 8%

🍷 1982, 1983, 1984, 1985, 1986

🍾 Between 6-15 years

CHÂTEAU SIRAN

Production: *12,500 cases*

Classified *Cru Bourgeois* in 1932, but not included in the *Syndicat's* 1978 list, although it is superior to a few that were. Well situated vineyard of immaculately manicured vines, bordering those of châteaux Giscours and Dauzac. The wine is matured in wood for 24 months, with one-third new oak, in air-conditioned cellars. Monsieur Miailhe, the owner, also likes to provide his guests with every facility, including a nuclear bunker with a well-stocked cellar.

RED Stylish wines of aromatic charm, good body, creamy-spicy fruit, great length and obvious class.

🍇 Cabernet sauvignon 50%, Cabernet franc 10%, Merlot 25%, Petit verdot 15%

🍷 1980, 1981, 1982, 1983, 1985

🍾 Between 8-20 years

Second Wine: Château Bellegarde

CHÂTEAU TAYAC

Cru Bourgeois
Production: *15,000 cases*

As Bernard Ginestet once wrote, "this is one of the largest of the smaller properties, and one of the smallest of the larger". The wines are aged in wood for 18 months, with one-third new oak.

RED Firm, medium- to full-bodied wines of good character, although somewhat rustic; they tend to be coarse in lesser years.

🍇 Cabernet sauvignon 65%, Cabernet franc 5%, Merlot 25%, Petit verdot 5%

🍷 1981, 1982, 1983, 1985

🍾 Between 6-12 years

CHÂTEAU LA TOUR DE BESSAN

Production: *8,000 cases*

Owned by Lucien Lurton, the proprietor of Château Brane Cantenac and the largest owner of vineyards in the Médoc. The building here is not so much a château as the remains of a thirteenth-century tower, which was given to the Duke of Gloucester by Henry V of England.

RED Soft and easy-to-drink style of medium-bodied wine with light but attractive fruit.

🍇 Cabernet sauvignon 90%, Merlot 10%

🍷 1982, 1983, 1985

🍾 Between 3-8 years

CHÂTEAU LA TOUR DE MONS

Production: *10,000 cases*

Classified *Cru Bourgeois* in 1932, but not included in the *Syndicat's* 1978 list, although it is potentially superior to a few that were. The wines are aged in wood for 22 months, with 20 per cent new oak.

RED Richly flavoured, rather muscular wines, the delights of which are all too often hidden by harsh tannins and strong acidity. They have great aging capacity, but often lack fruit by the time they have rounded out. A wine that could definitely be better.

🍇 Cabernet sauvignon 45%, Cabernet franc 10%, Merlot 40%, Petit verdot 5%

🍷 1981, 1982, 1983

🍾 Between 10-30 years

CHÂTEAU DES TROIS-CHARDONS

Production: *800 cases*

A tiny production of very high-quality wine from a château named after the current owner, a Monsieur Chardon, and his two sons.

RED Ultra-clean, soft, fruity but serious wines of some finesse and well defined Margaux character.

🍇 Cabernet sauvignon 50%, Cabernet franc 10%, Merlot 40%

🍷 1981, 1982, 1983, 1985

🍾 Between 6-15 years

Graves, Cérons, Sauternes and Barsac

The finest red wines are produced in the north of Graves, very good red and improving dry white in the centre, and the great sweet white wines of Sauternes and Barsac in the south.

GRAVES

THE GRAVES DISTRICT PRODUCES both classic red and variable dry white wines, the emphasis being, quite rightly, on the former. The area under vine where black grapes are cultivated is about 1,900 hectares (4,695 acres), compared with 1,430 hectares (3,534 acres) for white grapes. On the map, Graves looks about the same size as the Médoc, but this is deceptive for its vineyards cover less than one-third of the 10,950 hectares (27,050 acres) under vine in its northern neighbour.

The silky-smooth red wines of the Graves district have been famous since the Middle Ages, when they were protected by local laws that punished those who dared to blend them with other Bordeaux wines. Château Haut-Brion was the only red wine outside the Médoc to be classified in 1855, and such was its reputation that it was placed alongside the First Growths of Latour, Lafite, Mouton and Margaux. Beneath Haut-Brion, there are a few great wines equivalent in quality to Second or Third Growth but only a few. The relative lack of superstars in Graves is offset by a higher base quality and greater consistency of performance. Of the 43 communes in this appellation, Léognan, Talence and Pessac are much the best, after which Martillac and Portet are the most

outstanding, followed by Illats and Podensac. All the greatest wines are thus in the north of Graves, amid the urban sprawl of Bordeaux, and this presents something of a problem. The once-peaceful left bank of the river Garonne is slowly and inexorably disappearing. As the city bursts outwards, more and more rural vineyards are encircled by the concrete jungle, and many quite simply vanish. I wonder how many Bordeaux aficionados who fly directly to the airport in Mérignac stop to consider the cost of such progress? In 1908 there were 30 active winemaking properties in this commune; today there is just one—Château Picque-Caillou. The conurbated communes of Gradignan, Mérignac, Pessac, Talence, Léognan, Martillac, Cadaujac and Villenave d'Ornan have lost no less than 214 wine châteaux over the same period.

The problems of Graves

The white wine of Graves faces a difficult future. While the quality and reputation of the red wines are well established, white Graves has a serious identity problem. This is puzzling in a district that has a climate and soil envied by wine-growers from California to China, and where there is nothing wrong with the variety and quality of the grapes grown, or the technology of winemaking available.

Graves is a classic appellation and the quality of its wines should be equally classic. White Graves is not cheap, but for Graves prices, the consumer rightly expects something special. Yet, apart from a few notable exceptions, most examples of white Graves have long been extremely disappointing. Even the lowest quality white Graves should be fine and distinctive—like Domaine de la Grave, Domaine Benoit, Château Constantin and Château La Garance. This stunning new generation of wines is produced by wine-wizard Peter Vinding-Diers, the Australian-trained, Anglo-Danish winemaker of Château Rahoul. His wines have the cleanest rendition of essentially Sémillon fruit flavours, mixed with a tiny, but intriguing hint of new oak. His more expensive Château Rahoul is, in its idiosyncratic way, worthy to rub shoulders with the very best wines of this district, but until the other Graves proprietors follow Vinding-Diers' lead and pay as much attention to their white wines as their reds, there will be precious little worth buying if you lack the resources to buy a vintage of Château Haut-Brion blanc or Château Laville-Haut-Brion.

Fermentation vats, Haut-Brion, *above*
This illustrious château was one of the first to install stainless-steel vats.

Haut-Brion vineyards, *below*
Rose bushes at the end of each row act as a pest early-warning system.

GRAVES, CÉRONS, SAUTERNES AND BARSAC, *see also p.37*

The winemaking area that includes Graves, Cérons, Sauternes and Barsac forms a swathe that sweeps down from Bordeaux, parallel with the Garonne.

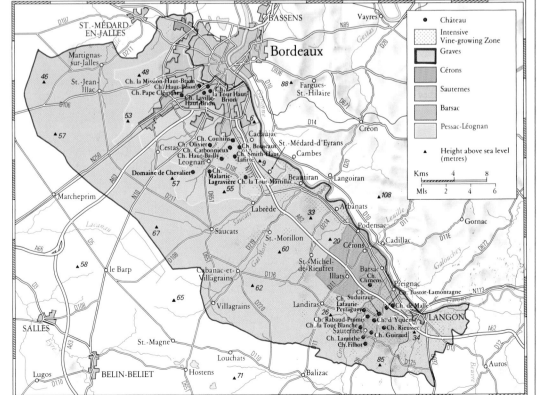

THE CLASSIFICATION OF GRAVES

The only Graves property to be classified in 1855 was Château Haut-Brion. The *Syndicat* for the defence of the Graves appellation wanted to create its own classification, but was prevented from doing so until the 1921 law was changed in 1949. The first classification was not made until 1953, and this itself was modified in 1959. Distinction is made between red wines and white wines, but no attempt at ranking between the various growths is made—they all have the right to use the term *cru classé*. It can be seen from the current size of the properties listed below that less than 19 per cent of the 1,900 hectares (4,695 acres) growing black grapes and less than five per cent of the 1,430 hectares (3,534 acres) growing white grapes are of *cru classé* status. However, there is a definite élite of châteaux that are vastly superior to the rest. These are marked with an asterisk* and may be compared to the very best classified growths of the Médoc.

Red wines	Commune	Area currently under vine
Château Bouscaut	Cadaujac	50 ha (124 acres)
Château Carbonnieux	Léognan	35 ha (86 acres)
Domaine de Chevalier*	Léognan	15 ha (37 acres)
Château de Fieuzal*	Léognan	20 ha (49 acres)
Château Haut-Bailly*	Léognan	23 ha (57 acres)
Château Haut-Brion*	Pessac	40 ha (99 acres)
Château La Mission-Haut-Brion*	Pessac	18.5 ha (46 acres)
Château Latour-Haut-Brion	Talence	4.5 ha (11 acres)
Château La Tour-Martillac	Martillac	20 ha (49 acres)
Château Malartic-Lagravière	Léognan	14 ha (35 acres)
Château Olivier	Léognan	18 ha (44 acres)
Château Pape-Clément	Pessac	27 ha (67 acres)
Château Smith-Haut-Lafite	Martillac	45 ha (111 acres)
Total area under vine		330 ha (815 acres)

White wines	Commune	Area currently under vine
Château Bouscaut	Cadaujac	20 ha (49 acres)
Château Carbonnieux	Léognan	35 ha (86 acres)
Domaine de Chevalier*	Léognan	3 ha (7 acres)
Château Couhins*	Villenave d'Ornan	6 ha (15 acres)
Château Haut-Brion*	Pessac	4 ha (10 acres)
Château La Tour-Martillac	Martillac	5 ha (12 acres)
Château Laville-Haut-Brion*	Talence	4 ha (10 acres)
Château Malartic-Lagravière	Léognan	2 ha (5 acres)
Château Olivier	Léognan	17 ha (42 acres)
Total area under vine		96 ha (236 acres)

CÉRONS

Situated within the boundaries of Graves, Cérons is the stepping stone between the dry white Graves, and the sweet white Sauternes and Barsac wines. Its châteaux have the right to make both the red and white Graves, Graves Supérieur (which may be dry but is usually sweet) and, of course, the sweet wine of Cérons. In fact, only 20 per cent of the production in this area is sold as Cérons–a wine that has enjoyed a modest reputation for nearly 200 years. The appellation covers three communes, those of Illats, Podensac and Cérons itself. Many of the vineyards are comprised of scattered plots, some of which are partially planted with acacias.

SAUTERNES AND BARSAC

The gap between ordinary sweet wines and the great wines of Sauternes and Barsac is as wide as that between sweet and dry wines. What creates this gap is something called "complexity"–to find out what that is, sample the aroma of a glass of mature Sauternes. These are not only the world's most luscious wines, but also its most complex. I have seen hardened men who resolutely refuse to drink anything sweeter than lemon juice go weak at the knees after one sniff of Château Suduiraut, and I defy the most stubborn and bigoted anti-sweet wine drinker not to drool over a glass of Château d'Yquem 1967! Astonishingly there are dissenters, but for me Yquem is by far the best wine of these two appellations. The battle for second place is always between the soft, luscious style of Suduiraut, and the rich, powerful character of Rieussec, with Climens, Nairac and the non-classified growths of Gilette and de Fargues in close pursuit. Guiraud has the potential to go right to the top of this pack, and with so many châteaux suddenly and seriously improving, they could all end up chasing each other for the number two spot.

The glowing tints of Château d'Yquem, above
Château d'Yquem vintages, stretching back from a bottle of the 1980. The younger wines are a rich gold with a greenish tinge, deepening to old gold and amber with the older vintages.

Vineyards at Château d'Yquem, left
The vineyard in winter showing the characteristic pebbly topsoil and the system of wires and stakes that supports the vines.

Yquem: the Inner Courtyard, right
A huge stone well dominates the square central courtyard of this beautiful château, which is comprised of disparate elements dating from the fifteenth, sixteenth and seventeenth centuries.

The "noble rot"

Yquem might be the ultimate, but many other great wines are made in these two small areas tucked away in the Bordeaux backwaters. What gives all of these wines their hallmark of complexity is, literally, a lot of rot – namely "noble rot", or the fungal growth botrytis cinerea. The low-lying, undulating hills of Sauternes and, to a lesser extent, of Barsac, together with a naturally warm but humid climate, provide a natural breeding ground for botrytis, the spores of which are indigenous to the area. These spores remain dormant in the vineyard soil and on vine bark until they are activated by suitable atmospheric conditions. These conditions are alternate moisture and heat – the early-morning mist being followed, day after day, by hot mid-morning autumn sunshine. The spores latch on to the skin of each grape, replacing its structure with a fungal growth and feeding on moisture from within the grape. They also devour five-sixths of the grape's acidity and one-third of its sugar, but as the amount of water consumed is between one-half and two-thirds, the effect is to concentrate the juice into a sticky, sugar-rich pulp. A healthy, ripe grape with a potential of 13 per cent alcohol is thus converted into a mangy-looking mess with a potential of between 17.5 per cent and 26 per cent. The spread of botrytis through a vineyard is neither orderly nor regular, and the harvest may take as long as ten weeks to complete, with the pickers making various sorties, or *tries*, through the vineyard. On each *trie*, only the affected grapes should be picked, but care must be taken to leave some rot on each bunch to facilitate its spread.

The longer the growers await the miraculous "noble rot", which only comes in sufficient and unhindered strength about three years in ten, the more the vines are prone to the ravages of frost, snow, hail and rain, any or all of which could destroy an entire crop. The viticultural methods of Sauternes and Barsac are the most labour-intensive of any region. The yield is very low, officially a maximum of 25 hectolitres per hectare (112 cases per acre), about half that in the Médoc–and the levels achieved in the best châteaux are much lower, around 15-20 hectolitres per hectare (67-90 cases per acre). At Yquem it is even less, the equivalent of one glass per vine. On top of all this, the vinification is, at the very least, difficult to handle and maturation of a fine sweet wine demands a good proportion of very expensive new oak.

FACTORS AFFECTING TASTE AND QUALITY

Location
The left bank of the Garonne river, stretching southeast from just north of Bordeaux to 10 kilometres (6 miles) east of Langon. Cérons, Sauternes and Barsac are tucked into the southern section of the Graves district.

Climate
Very similar to the Médoc, but fractionally hotter and with slightly more rainfall. Mild and humid in Sauternes and Barsac, with an all-important autumnal alternation of misty mornings and sunshine, the ideal recipe for "noble rot".

Aspect
The suburbs of Bordeaux sprawl across the northern section of this district, becoming more rural beyond Cadaujac. Graves has a much hillier terrain than the Médoc, with little valleys cut out by a myriad of streams that drain into the Garonne. Some of the vineyards here are quite steep. The communes of Sauternes, Bommes and Fargues are hilly, but Preignac and Barsac, on either side of the Ciron, a small tributary of the Garonne, possess gentler slopes.

Soil
Travelling south through the district, the gravelly topsoil of Graves gradually becomes mixed with sand, then with weathered limestone and eventually with clay. The subsoil also varies, but basically it is iron-pan, limestone and clay—either pure or mixed. Cérons has a stony soil, mostly flint and gravel, over marl. Reddish clay-gravel over clay or gravelly iron-pan in Sauternes and clay-limestone over clay-gravel in Fargues. The gravel slopes of Bommes are sometimes mixed with heavy clay soils, while the plain is sandy clay with a reddish clay or limestone subsoil. Preignac is sand, gravel and clay over clay-gravel in the south, becoming more alluvial over sand, clay and limestone closer to Barsac. Where the classified growths of Barsac are situated, the soil is clay-limestone over limestone, elsewhere the topsoil mingles with sandy gravel.

Viticulture and vinification
It is common practice in Graves for châteaux that produce some white wine as well as red to use 100 per cent new oak for the white for two months or so. This is not an extravagance – the black grapes ripen after the white and it makes sense to utilize the new casks. However, classic white Graves frankly deserve more than two or three months in new oak.

Some châteaux add a certain amount of *vin de presse* to the red wine. The *cuvaison* varies between eight and 15 days, although some Graves châteaux permit 15-25 days. Maturation in cask is generally 15-18 months. The sweet white wines of Sauternes and Barsac are made from several *tries* of late-harvested, overripe grapes which, ideally, have "noble rot". De-stalking is usually unnecessary. The fermentation of grape juice so high in sugar content is difficult to start and awkward to control, but it is usually over within two to eight weeks. The exact period of fermentation depends upon the style desired. Many of the best wines are matured in cask for one and a half to three and a half years.

Primary grape varieties
Cabernet sauvignon, Cabernet franc, Merlot, Sémillon, Sauvignon blanc

Secondary grape varieties
Malbec, Petit verdot, Muscadelle

Traditional horse-drawn plough, above
At Château d'Yquem work-horses are used to help plough the topsoil between the rows, both after the harvest and again in March.

Château de Fargues, right
The original family home of the Lur-Saluces family is now a ghostly ruin. The family moved to Yquem in 1785 upon its union with the De Sauvage family.

Variations in character

Not all the sugar is used up during fermentation, and a wine of perhaps 14-15 per cent alcohol is made. The remaining unfermented sugar, often between 50 and 120 grams per litre, gives the wine its natural sweetness. However, unlike its great German Beerenauslese and Trockenbeerenauslese counterparts, the alcohol level of Sauternes is crucial to its character. Its strength, in harmony with the wine's sweetness, acidity and fruit give it a lusciousness of concentration that simply cannot be matched anywhere else in the world. But this complexity is not the effect of concentration, although increased mineral levels no doubt influence it. Sauternes's complexity is created by certain new elements that are introduced into the grape's fresh juice during the metabolic activities of its botrytis – glycerol, gluconic acid, saccharic acid, dextrin, various oxidizing enzymes and an elusive antibiotic substance called "botrycine". It is impossible to explain how all these components of a botrytized wine form its inimitably complex character, but they do.

When tasting the wine from different *tries* at the same château, it can be noticed that the intensity of botrytized character varies according to the "age" of the fungus when the grapes bearing it are harvested. Wines made from the same percentage of botrytized grapes collected at the beginning and the end of the harvest are noticeably mute compared to those in the middle when the rot is at its most rampant. If it is of little surprise that youthful botrytis cinerea has an undeveloped character, the same cannot be said of late-harvested. Many people believe that the longer botrytis establishes itself, the more potent its effect, but this is not true.

The "pourriture noble", or noble rot, above
A bunch of Sémillon grapes ready for the first trie. *Some of the grapes are still unaffected by the fungus, some are affected and discoloured but not shrivelled, others are dried, withered and covered with the fungus bloom.*

Crop spraying at Château Carbonnieux, Graves, right
Sulphur and fungicide are sprayed on to the vines from late Spring onwards, to protect them against oidium, mildew and other fungi and pests.

The rewards, the reality and the future

Good Sauternes is the most arduous, expensive and frustrating wine in the world to produce – and what is the winemaker's reward? Very little, I am afraid. Apart from the enormous sums paid for Château d'Yquem, not only the greatest Sauternes but the greatest wine *per se*, the wines of this region miserably fail to realize their true value. This is perhaps predictable in a world where the trend is towards lighter and drier styles of wine, and may have a positive effect for Sauternes aficionados, for it means a cheap and adequate supply of their favourite wine. In the long term, however, this is not a positive way to operate, and some proprietors simply cannot afford to continue. The Comte de Pontac uprooted all the vines at his Second Growth Château de Myrat in Barsac, and even Tom Heeter, the fanatically optimistic former owner of Château Nairac (another Second Growth of Barsac), admits: "You have to be at least half-crazy to make a living out of these wines". Certainly we do not deserve the luscious wines of Sauternes and Barsac if we continue to ignore them, but if the authorities had more sense, and the proprietors more business acumen, these wines could literally be "liquid gold".

The way ahead

The vineyards of Sauternes and Barsac should also be allowed to sell red and dry white wines under the Graves appellation. If this is a right accorded to modest Cérons, why not to its illustrious neighbours? Many châteaux already make red and dry white wines, but they are sold under the cheaper "Bordeaux" appellation. And Tom Heeter is right, the proprietors must be half-crazy, because the driving force behind these alternative products is to subsidize the cost of producing their botrytized wine, when it should really be to supplement their income.

Given the incentive and higher price level of a superior appellation, the châteaux should concentrate on making the finest red and dry white wines every year. Only when conditions appear favourable should a proportion of the white grape crop be left on the vine, with fingers crossed for an abundance of botrytis cinerea. Instead of these châteaux investing in new oak for modest vintages that can never be improved, they should utilize the casks for the red and the dry white. By cutting yields and resolving to compete with the best of Graves, many top Sauternes and Barsacs could really excel in this direction. The result would be a tiny production of the world's most luscious wine, maybe three or four years in ten. It would no longer be necessary to attempt the impossible task of selling an old-fashioned image to a new generation of wine drinkers; the limited supply would outstrip the current demand, forcing the converted to pay a realistic price. After watching thirty years of this area's vain attempts to win over popular support for its wines, I have come to accept the view of Comte Alexandre de Lur Saluces. When asked how he could justify the price of Château d'Yquem, he simply said his wines are not made for everyone; they are made for those who can afford them. I, for one, would be willing to pay more for the best Sauternes and Barsacs if due respect was restored to these great wines.

Generic wines of Graves, Cérons, Sauternes and Barsac

BARSAC AOC

The commune of Barsac is one of five that have the right to the Sauternes appellation. (The others are Preignac, Fargues, Bommes and Sauternes itself.) Some generic wines sold in bulk may take advantage of this, but all individual properties are sold as Barsac. The wine must include overripe botrytized grapes harvested in *tries*.

WHITE Luscious, intensely sweet wines similar in style to Sauternes, but perhaps lighter in weight, slightly drier and less rich. As in Sauternes, 1983 is one of the best vintages of the century.

🍇 Sémillon, Sauvignon blanc, Muscadelle

🗓 1985, 1986, 1988, 1989, 1990

🛢 Between 6-25 years for most wines; between 15-60 years for the greatest

CÉRONS AOC

These inexpensive wines from an area adjacent to Barsac are the best value-for-money sweet wines in Bordeaux. They must include overripe botrytized grapes harvested in *tries*.

WHITE Lighter than Barsac, but often just as luscious, the best of these wines can show true botrytis complexity.

🍇 Sémillon, Sauvignon blanc, Muscadelle

🗓 1985, 1986, 1988, 1989, 1990

🛢 Between 6-15 years for most wines

GRAVES AOC

This appellation begins at the Jalle de Blanquefort, where the Médoc finishes and runs for 60 kilometres (37 miles) along the left bank of the Garonne. Almost two-thirds of the wine is red, and is consistently high in quality and value.

RED I was brought up on the notion that with full maturity a Graves reveals itself through a certain earthiness of character. Experience has taught me the opposite. The biggest Graves from hot years can have a denseness that may combine with the smoky character of new oak to give the wine a roasted or tobacco-like complexity, but Graves is intrinsically clean. Its hallmark is its vivid fruit, clarity of style and silky texture, and hints of violets.

🍇 Cabernet sauvignon, Cabernet franc, Merlot
Secondary grape varieties: Malbec, Petit verdot

🗓 1985, 1987, 1988, 1989, 1990

🛢 Between 6-15 years

WHITE This is the disappointing half of the appellation. Light-to full-bodied, from pure Sauvignon to pure Sémillon (with all proportions of blends inbetween), flabby to zingy and unoaked to heavily-oaked. Pay strict attention to the château profiles.

🍇 Sémillon, Sauvignon blanc, Muscadelle

🗓 1985, 1986, 1988, 1989, 1990

🛢 Within 1-2 years for modest wines; between 8-20 years for the best

GRAVES SUPÉRIEUR AOC

Some surprisingly good would-be Barsacs lurk beneath this appellation that is rarely seen, yet accounts for more than one-fifth of all white Graves produced.

WHITE This wine can be dry, but most is a sweet style, similar to Barsac.

🍇 Sémillon, Sauvignon blanc, Muscadelle

🗓 1985, 1986, 1988, 1989, 1990

🛢 Between 6-15 years

PESSAC-LÉOGNAN AOC

A new appellation introduced in September 1987, it covers the ten best communes that have the right to the Graves appellation. The technical requirements are similar to Graves, except that the Carmenère may be used for red wines and white wines must contain at least 25 per cent Sauvignon blanc.

The smaller growers have longed for a more specific appellation than Graves, but whether that of Pessac-Léognan will ever achieve the same degree of public recognition as, say, that of Margaux, remains to be seen.

SAUTERNES AOC

The much hillier communes of Bommes, Fargues and Sauternes produce the richest of all Bordeaux's dessert wines, while the châteaux in the lower-lying, flatter Preignac make wines very close in style to Barsac. The wine must include overripe botrytized grapes harvested in *tries*.

WHITE Golden, intense, powerful and complex wines that defy the senses and boggle the mind. They are rich in texture, with masses of rich, ripe and fat fruit. Pineapple, peach, apricot and strawberry are some of the lush flavours that can be found, and the creamy-vanilla character of fruit and new oak matures into a splendid honeyed sumptuousness that is spicy and complex.

Above all, these wines are marked by the distinctive botrytis character. The 1983 is one of the best vintages of the century.

🍇 Sémillon, Sauvignon blanc, Muscadelle

🗓 1985, 1986, 1988, 1989, 1990

🛢 Between 10-30 years for most wines; between 20-70 for the greatest

---

The best châteaux of Graves

CHÂTEAU BOUSCAUT
Cadaujac,
33140 Pont-de-la-Maye

Cru Classé (red and white)
Red wine production: *14,000 cases*
White wine production: *3,000 cases*

This château belongs to Lucien Lurton. The red wine is matured in wood for 18 months, with 25 per cent new oak. The white wine is fermented and matured for up to six months in 100 per cent new oak.

RED Until the 1980s this wine was big, tough and tannic with little charm. Recent vintages have shown increasing suppleness, but it still struggles to find form, while its Second Wine, Château Valoux, really excels for its class.

🍇 Cabernet sauvignon 35%, Cabernet franc 5%, Merlot 55%, Malbec 5%

🗓 1981, 1983, 1985

🛢 Between 8-20 years

Second Wine: Château Valoux

WHITE This dry, medium-bodied white wine has exotic fruit flavours supported by gentle oak.

🍇 Sémillon 70%, Sauvignon 30%

🗓 1983, 1985, 1986

🛢 Between 5-10 years

CHÂTEAU CARBONNIEUX
33850 Léognan

Cru Classé (red and white)
Red wine production: *15,000 cases*
White wine production: *15,000 cases*

The largest wine estate in Graves. The white wine, the better known of the two styles, is cool-fermented in stainless steel and matured in 100 per cent new oak for three months.

RED I frankly did not care for this wine until the splendid 1985 vintage, which seduced me with its creamy-oak nose, silky-textured fruit and supple tannin.

🍇 Cabernet sauvignon 55%, Cabernet franc 10%, Merlot 30%, Malbec and Petit verdot 5%

🗓 1985, 1988

🛢 Between 6-18 years

WHITE A solid and clean wine, but variable, and all too often uninspiring.

The 1982 is surprisingly good in a citrussy, *vin de garde* style, the 1984 fresh and crisp – for early drinking, and the 1985 interesting in a round, vegetal style.

🍇 Sémillon 40%, Sauvignon 60%

🗓 1982, 1984, 1985

🛢 Between 2-5 years

Second Wine: Château La Tour Léognan

DOMAINE DE CHEVALIER
33850 Léognan

Cru Classé (red and white)
Red wine production: *5,000 cases*
White wine production: *800 cases*

This extraordinary property gives me more pleasure than any other in Graves. It utilizes the most traditional of methods to produce outstanding red and dry white wine. Fermenting red wine at a temperature as high as 32°C (89°F) might encourage problems elsewhere, but under the meticulous care of those at the Domaine de Chevalier, this practice, designed to extract the maximum of tannins and colouring material, is a positive advantage. The red wine is matured in wood for up to 24 months, with 50 per cent new oak. The white wine is fermented and matured in wood for 18 months, with up to 25 per cent new oak.

RED Deep-coloured, medium- to full or full-bodied wines, stunningly rich in fruit and oak, with intense cedarwood and tobacco overtones, yet subtle, seductive and full of finesse. These are wines of great quality, longevity and complexity.

🍇 Cabernet sauvignon 65%, Cabernet franc 5%, Merlot 30%

🗓 1980, 1981, 1982, 1983, 1984, 1985, 1986, 1987, 1988, 1989

🛢 Between 15-40 years

WHITE Very small production of high-quality, intensely flavoured, dry wines. Almost fat, these wines are simply brimming with exotic flavours, and epitomize finesse.

🍇 Sémillon 30%, Sauvignon 70%

🗓 1980, 1981, 1982, 1983, 1984, 1985, 1986, 1987, 1988

🛢 Between 8-20 years

CHÂTEAU COUHINS
Villenave-d'Ornon,
33140 Pont-de-la-Maye

Cru Classé (white only)
Production: *1,500 cases*

The Institut National de La Récherche Agronomique (INRA) and Lucien Lurton share this estate. INRA produces a separate wine, which is cool fermented with no maturation in wood.

WHITE Clean, crisp and fruity dry white wines that are well made.

🍇	Sémillon 50%, Sauvignon 50%
🍷	1983
🕰	Between 2-4 years

Note: This château also produces a red Graves, but it is not a *cru classé*.

CHÂTEAU COUHINS-LURTON
Villenave d'Ornon,
33140 Pont-de-La-Maye

Cru Classé (white only)
Production: *800 cases*

The highest-performing half of the Couhins estate owned by André Lurton. The wine is fermented and matured in 100 per cent new oak.

WHITE Delicious dry wines that have all the advantages of freshness and fruitiness, plus the complexity of oak. Surprisingly fat for pure Sauvignon.

🍇	Sauvignon 100%
🍷	1982, 1983, 1985, 1986, 1987
🕰	Between 3-8 years

CHÂTEAU DE FIEUZAL
33850 Léognan

Cru Classé (red only)
Production: *7,500 cases*

This property occupies the highest and best exposed gravel crest in the commune. The vineyard and the château are immaculate, which is reflected in the style of its wines.

RED A deeply coloured, full-bodied, rich, stylish wine with typical Graves silky texture and ample finesse.

🍇	Cabernet sauvignon 60%, Merlot 30%, Malbec 5%, Petit verdot 5%
🍷	1984, 1985, 1986, 1988, 1989
🕰	Between 12-30 years

Second Wine: "l'Abeille de Fieuzal"
Note: De Fieuzal also produces a rich, exotic and oaky dry white wine that is not *cru classé*, yet is one of the finest white Graves produced.

CHÂTEAU HAUT-BAILLY
33850 Léognan

Cru Classé (red only)
Production: *11,000 cases*

This château's well-kept vineyard is located on an excellent gravel crest bordering the eastern suburbs of Léognan. This red Graves is matured in wood for up to 20 months, with 50 per cent new oak.

RED The class of fruit and quality of new oak is immediately discernible on the creamy-ripe nose of this medium-bodied wine. Never blockbusting stuff, but always elegant and stylish.

🍇	Cabernet sauvignon 60%, Cabernet franc 10%, Merlot 30%
🍷	1983, 1984, 1985, 1986, 1989
🕰	Between 12-25 years

Second Wine: "Le Pardre de Haut-Bailly"
Note: This château also produces a white Graves, but it is not a *cru classé*.

CHÂTEAU HAUT-BRION
33600 Pessac

Cru Classé (red and white)
Red wine production: *12,000 cases*
White wine production: *800 cases*

In 1663 this famous château was mentioned in Pepys' Diary as "Ho Bryan". It has been under American ownership since 1935, when it was purchased by Clarence Dillon, the banker. Since 1962 this First Growth has been run by his son Clarence Dillon, former American Ambassador in Paris and US Treasury Secretary.
    The red wine is fermented in stainless steel and matured in wood for 24-27 months, with 100 per cent new oak. The white wine is fermented and matured in 100 per cent new oak.

RED This supple, stylish, medium- to full-bodied wine has a surprisingly dense flavour for the weight, and a chocolatey-violet character. The ideal commercial product, it develops quickly and ages gracefully.

🍇	Cabernet sauvignon 55%, Cabernet franc 20%, Merlot 25%
🍷	1980, 1981, 1982, 1983, 1985, 1986, 1987, 1988, 1989
🕰	Between 10-40 years

Second Wine: "Bahans-Haut-Brion"

WHITE This is not one of the biggest white Graves, but it is built to last. It is sumptuous, oaky and teeming with citrus and more exotic fruit flavours.

🍇	Sémillon 50%, Sauvignon 50%
🍷	1981, 1982, 1983, 1988, 1989
🕰	Between 5-20 years

CHÂTEAU LAVILLE-HAUT-BRION
33400 Talence

Cru Classé (white only)
Production: *2,000 cases*

Since 1983, this small vineyard has been owned by Clarence Dillon, the American proprietor of Château Haut-Brion. This "château with no château" is commonly thought of as the white wine of La Mission. The wine is fermented and matured in cask.

WHITE Until 1982, the style was full, rich, oaky and exuberant, tending to be more honeyed and spicy with a floral finesse since 1983. Both styles are stunning and complex.

🍇	Sémillon 40%, Sauvignon 60%
🍷	1984, 1985, 1987, 1988, 1989
🕰	Between 6-20 years

CHÂTEAU MALARTIC-LAGRAVIÈRE
33850 Léognan

Cru Classé (red and white)
Red wine production: *8,000 cases*
White wine production: *900 cases*

This 20-hectare (50-acre) vineyard forms a single block around the château. An underrated property, which has consistently produced much higher quality wines in the 1980s. The red wine is fermented in stainless steel at a low temperature (16°C/61°F), and matured in wood for 20-22 months, with one-third new oak. The white wine is now matured in 100 per cent new oak for seven to eight months.

RED Rich, garnet-coloured wines with an opulent sweet-oak nose, penetrating flavour and supple tannin structure.

🍇	Cabernet sauvignon 50%, Cabernet franc 25%, Merlot 25%
🍷	1983, 1985, 1986, 1987
🕰	Between 7-25 years

WHITE Recent vintages of this once lacklustre white Graves prove the worth of new oak. It is not difficult to mistake this honey-rich, ripe and succulent wine for pure Sémillon.

🍇	Sauvignon 100%
🍷	1983, 1985, 1986, 1987
🕰	Between 5-12 years

CHÂTEAU LA MISSION-HAUT-BRION
33600 Pessac

Cru Classé (red only)
Production: *8,000 cases*

Under the ownership of Henri Woltner, this was the pretender to the throne of Graves. Little wonder, then, that Clarence Dillon of Haut-Brion snapped it up when the opportunity arose in 1983. The red wine is matured in wood for 24 months, with 50 per cent new oak.

RED Despite different winemaking techniques, Dillon's La Mission is no less stunning than Woltner's. Both styles are deeper, darker and denser than any other wine Graves can manage. They are essentially powerful wines that require great bottle-age, but they do lack a certain finesse.

🍇	Cabernet sauvignon 60%, Cabernet franc 10%, Merlot 30%
🍷	1980, 1981, 1982, 1983, 1984, 1986, 1987, 1988, 1989
🕰	Between 15-45 years

CHÂTEAU OLIVIER
33850 Léognan

Cru Classé (red and white)
Red wine production: *10,000 cases*
White wine production: *11,000 cases*

The red wine is matured in wood for 18 months; the white wine for one to three months, with 100 per cent new oak.

RED I have searched and searched for a favourable tasting note on this wine, but cannot find one – my most common remark is "drab and lacklustre"

| 🍇 | Cabernet sauvignon 70%, Merlot 30% |

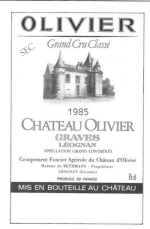

WHITE Since 1985 this wine has begun to sparkle; there seems to be added freshness, real fruit flavour and some character developing. This is, I hope, a wine to watch.

Sémillon 65%, Sauvignon 30%, Muscadelle 5%

1985, 1986

Between 3-7 years

CHÂTEAU PAPE-CLÉMENT
33600 Pessac

Cru Classé (red only)
Production: *13,000 cases*

This vineyard has the potential to produce some of the finest wines in Graves, but the sad fact is that it has long disappointed. There have been too many excuses made for these wines; it is about time somebody admitted that the peculiar Pape-Clément nose is simply "musty". Why this should be so, it is difficult to say. At first I thought I was experiencing a disproportionate number of corked wines, but there were simply too many of them. Curiously, I occasionally come across bottles of beautifully clean Pape-Clément that do not show the barest hint of this musty character. Whatever the cause, I hope the château can recognize that a problem does exist, and can put its wines back at the very top of this appellation where they belong. The red wine is matured in wood for 24 months, with 50 per cent new oak.

RED These medium-bodied wines have excellent deep colour, a distinctive style and considerable finesse (sufficient, at any rate, to shine through the "musty" character).

Cabernet sauvignon 67%, Merlot 33%

Note: This château also produces a little non-*cru classé* white Graves, made from equal proportions of Sémillon, Sauvignon and Muscadelle.

CHÂTEAU SMITH-HAUT-LAFITTE
Martillac,
33650 La Brède

Cru Classé (red only)
Production: *22,500 cases*

This château is run by Eschenauer, the Lonrho-owned Bordeaux *négociant*. It has 50 hectares (124 acres) of fine vineyards and since the mid-1970s, new underground cellars and excellent up-to-date winemaking facilities. After such extensive renovations, the wines remained disappointing until 1983 when the investment began to pay off and a marked improvement in quality could be detected. The red wine is matured in wood for 18 months, with 50 per cent new oak.

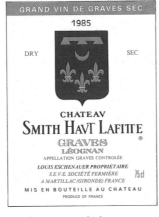

GRAND VIN DE GRAVES SEC
1985
DRY SEC
CHÂTEAV
SMITH HAVT LAFITE
GRAVES
LÉOGNAN
APPELLATION GRAVES CONTRÔLÉE
LOUIS ESCHENAUER PROPRIÉTAIRE
S.E.V.E. SOCIÉTÉ FERMIÈRE
À MARTILLAC (GIRONDE) FRANCE   75 cl
MIS EN BOUTEILLE AU CHATEAU
PRODUCE OF FRANCE

RED These wines, which were once characterless, are now made in a richer style with creamy-oak under-tones, up-front fruit and a soft finish.

Cabernet sauvignon 69%, Cabernet franc 11%, Merlot 20%

1983, 1984, 1985

Second Wine: Château Hauts-de-Smith-Haut-Lafitte
Note: This château also produces a white Graves, but it is not a *cru classé*.

CHÂTEAU LA TOUR-HAUT-BRION
33400 Talence

Cru Classé (red only)
Production: *2,500 cases*

This château is situated close to Château La Mission-Haut-Brion. The two are separated by a railway. By 1980 the production of wine sold under the label of this château was merely regarded as the Second Wine of Château La Mission-Haut-Brion. All the grapes from both vineyards were vinified together, and the two wines made by a method of selection. However, after its acquisition by Clarence Dillon in 1983, some 4.5 hectares (11 acres) of vines were delimited as Château La Tour-Haut-Brion, and from the 1984 all its wines can be said to be from one specific site. I have every confidence that under Dillon this château will be at least as successful as before. This wine has always been difficult to taste when young, and I am unprepared to predict how its style will develop under new management. The only wine I describe and refer to in the best vintages is 1982, but this is a classy wine and all vintages should be observed and followed with interest. The wine is matured in wood for 24 months, with 50 per cent new oak.

RED The 1982 is an extremely dark and tannic, full-bodied wine that is bulging with chunky, chocolatey, tannic fruit and an underlying earthy-smoky bitterness of undeveloped extract. Because of its awesome attack of flavour it would be too easy to say it lacks both balance and finesse, but wise wine-drinkers will wait for its maturity from the year 2000 before making judgement.

Cabernet sauvignon 60%, Cabernet franc 10%, Merlot 30%

1982

Between 20-40 years

CHÂTEAU LA TOUR-MARTILLAC
Martillac,
33650 La Brède

Cru Classé (red and white)
Red wine production: *8,500 cases*
White wine production: *2,500 cases*

This property, which belongs to Bordeaux Kressmann, has its own herd of cattle that supplies manure for the château's strictly "organically grown" wine. Its red wine is not as consistent as some of the very best Graves and has a tendency to lack charm in cask. These two characteristics make it an underrated wine. It is matured in wood for 18-22 months with one-third new oak. The white wine is fermented in stainless steel, and matured for nine months in 100 per cent new oak.

RED These are not big or bold wines that appeal immediately; they are elegant wines of some finesse. The fruit in recent vintages has tended to be a bit more plump, but it is in bottle that these wines take on their richness, developing a creamy-oak flavour.

Cabernet sauvignon 60%, Cabernet franc 6%, Merlot 25%, Malbec 5%, Petit verdot 4%

1981, 1982, 1983, 1985

Between 8-20 years

Second Wine: Château La Grave-Martillac

WHITE The stunning 1986 vintage heralds a new era of exciting dry white wines from this château. It has very fresh, elegant and stylish fruit, gently balanced by complex nuances of oak.

Sémillon 55%, Sauvignon 35%, Muscadelle 3%, old diverse varieties 7%

1986, 1987, 1988

Between 4-8 years

The best of the rest (including Cérons)

CHÂTEAU D'ARCHAMBEAU
Illats,
33720 Podensac

Located in one of the three communes of Cérons, this excellent property is owned by Dr. Jean Dubourdieu, nephew of Pierre Dubourdieu of Château Doisy-Daëne, a Second Growth in Barsac. He produces a fine-quality, fragrant and attractively aromatic red wine, which is matured in cask for six months and has the typical silky Graves texture. Dubordieu's deliciously fresh, crisp and fruity dry white Graves is better than some efforts by certain *cru classé* châteaux, and his soft, fruity Cérons is *moelleux* with the emphasis more on perfume than richness.

Second Wine: Château Mourlet

DOMAINE BENOIT
33640 Portets

The name of this small property originates from its current owner, Michel Benoit. The wines are made by Peter Vinding-Diers of nearby Château Rahoul. Benoit produces 1,300 cases of a red Graves. It is a sophisticated, soft and fruity wine of good colour, medium body and supple tannin structure (Merlot 70%, Cabernet franc 10%, Malbec 20%). It peaks within three to four years, but ages gracefully. The dry white Graves (100% Sémillon), of which 1,000 cases are produced on two hectares (five acres), is a benchmark that all the smaller properties of this district should strive to follow. Made in classic Vinding-Diers style, it is light in body with fragrant fruit and underlying sweet-oak.

CHÂTEAU LA BLANCHERIE
33650 La Brède

This fresh and lively dry white Graves is cool fermented, and has plenty of juicy fruit flavour balanced with ripe acidity.

CHÂTEAU LA BLANCHERIE-PEYRAT
33650 La Brède

The red wine of La Blancherie is sold under this label. It is a medium- to full-bodied wine that is matured in casks and has an engaging, spicy bouquet and a rich, fruity flavour.

CHÂTEAU DE CALVIMONT
Cérons,
33720 Podensac

This red wine of Château de Cérons is an interesting pure Cabernet sauvignon Graves. Its proprietor, Jean Perromat, also owns châteaux Mayne-Binet, De Bessanes, Ferbos and Ferbos-Lalanette in Cérons, and Prost in Barsac.

CHÂTEAU DE CARDAILLAN
Toulenne,
33210 Langon

Under the same ownership as its neighbour, Château de Malle, this is a Second Growth Sauternes in the commune of Preignac. This excellent property produces a technically brilliant red Graves with a voluptuous blackcurrant flavour, which develops quickly, yet ages well (Cabernet sauvignon 80%, Merlot 20%).

CHÂTEAU LES CARMES-HAUT-BRION
33600 Pessac

From 1584 until the Revolution this property belonged to the white friars *Carmes,* hence the name. Its wine is a reliable, soft, Merlot-dominated shadow of its more famous neighbour, Haut-Brion.

CHÂTEAU DE CÉRONS
Cérons,
33720 Podensac

This seventeenth-century château, which produces an attractively light, sweet, white Cérons, is owned by Jean Perromat, the proprietor of châteaux Mayne-Binet, de Bessanes, Ferbos and Ferbos-Lalanette in Cérons and Prost in Barsac.

GRAND ENCLOS DU CHÂTEAU DE CÉRONS
Cérons,
33720 Podensac

This property, entirely enclosed by a wall, once formed the largest part of the estate of Château de Cérons. The wines produced here – far superior to those of Château de Cérons, and possibly the best of the appellation – are fat, rich and viscous, with good aging potential and some complexity. The proprietor also makes dry white wines at nearby Château Lamouroux.

CHÂTEAU DE CHANTEGRIVE
33720 Podensac

This château produces a substantial quantity of an excellent, soft and fruity red Graves (Cabernet sauvignon 50%, Merlot 40%, Cabernet franc 10%) that is matured in wooden vats for six months and then transferred to casks for a further 12 months with 20 per cent new oak. It also produces an elegant, aromatic, cool-fermented dry white Graves that is produced entirely from the first pressing (Sémillon 60%, Sauvignon 30%, Muscadelle 10%). The proprietor also owns Château d'Anice.

Second Wine: Château Mayne-Lévêque
Other wines: Château Bon-Dieu-des-Vignes

CHÂTEAU CHICANE
Toulenne,
33210 Langon

This red-wine-only château is typical of the large number of properties that consistently produce an excellent style of basic Graves. Here is an elegant, medium-bodied wine, with a bouquet of violets, and heaps of clean, silky-smooth fruit.

CHÂTEAU CONSTANTIN
33640 Portets

Another of master-winemaker Peter Vinding-Diers' protegés, this small property is owned by Robert Constantin. His red Graves, grown on three hectares (seven-and-a-half acres) is a clean and characterful wine of medium body and elegant fruit. Constantin makes 1,300 cases from Merlot 60%, Cabernet franc 20%, Malbec 20%. He also makes a tiny amount of red wine under the generic Bordeaux appellation. The dry white pure Sémillon Graves (1,000 cases) is in the classic Vinding-Diers style with his tell-tale underlying sweet-oak character.

CHÂTEAU DE CRUZEAU
St-Médard-d'Eyrans,
33650 La Brède

Situated on a high, south-facing crest of deep gravel soil, this property belongs to André Lurton, owner of Château Couhins-Lurton, the high-performance white Graves *cru classé.* De Cruzeau makes 18,000 cases of full-bodied red Graves (Cabernet sauvignon 60%, Merlot 40%) that is ripe and velvety with a spicy-cedarwood complexity. It also produces around 5,000 cases of a fine-quality white Graves (Sémillon 10%, Sauvignon 90%) that after some five years of maturation, develops an intense citrussy bouquet and flavour.

CHÂTEAU FERRANDE
Castres,
33640 Portets

A large property which, like so many, produces better red wine than white. The red wine (Cabernet sauvignon 35%, Cabernet franc 30%, Merlot 35%) is a consistently good-quality, chocolatey Graves that is matured in wood for 15-18 months, with 10-15 per cent new oak. The dry white Graves (Sémillon 60%, Sauvignon 35%, Muscadelle 5%) is less inspiring.

CLOS FLORIDÈNE
Pujols-sur-Ciron
33210 Langon

The dry white Graves produced by this small estate is revolutionary. Made from Sémillon 70%, Sauvignon 30%, it is an extraordinary combination of rich fruit and elegant new oak, that shows what can be done with white wines in this area. I have only met the owner, Denis Dubourdieu, once, but after tasting so many of his stunning

wines – not just from here, but also from his principal estate, Château Reynon in Béguey on the Premiers Côtes de Bordeaux – I am determined to go back and see him sometime. He told me he even grows a little Chardonnay on an experimental basis, and why not? Given the same climate anywhere else in the world, it would be the first grape cultivated by anyone other than a Bordelais.

CHÂTEAU LA GARENCE
33640 Portets

I have no experience of this property, but as the owner, Monsieur Thienot, has the sense to utilize the skills of Peter Vinding-Diers, its wines must be worth looking out for on the basis of that man's track record alone. 1,800 cases of red Graves are made from Merlot 60%, Cabernet franc 40%, grown on four hectares (9.8 acres) and 1,000 cases of a dry white, pure Sémillon Graves from two hectares (five acres).

DOMAINE DE LA GRAVE
33640 Portets

This property is owned by Peter Vinding-Diers, the winemaker of Château Rahoul. The red Graves (Cabernet sauvignon 50%, Merlot 50%) is the most successful of Vinding-Diers' red wines; (1,800 cases are produced on three-and-a-half hectares/eight-and-a-half acres). It is very soft, fruity and easy to drink, but still has style and class. The Château also produces another red wine, made entirely from Merlot grapes and sold under the Bordeaux appellation. The dry white, pure Sémillon Graves (500 cases are made from one hectare/two-and-a-half acres of vines) has a lovely light richness of fruit, an elegant style and the inevitable underlying sweet-oak character which is Vinding-Diers' hallmark.

CHÂTEAU HAURA
Illats,
33720 Podensac

Haura produces wines under the Cérons appellation. Although not as consistent as it should be, it can sometimes produce a fine, honey-sweet wine with some distinction and concentration. The residence on this property is known as Château Hillot and red and dry white Graves are sold under this name that come from vines contiguous with those of Haura. The proprietor also owns Château Tucau in Barsac.

CHÂTEAU LARRIVET-HAUT-BRION
33850 Léognan

Originally called Château Canolle, the name was at one point changed to Château Haut-Brion-Larrivet. Larrivet is a small stream that flows through the property, and Haut-Brion means "high gravel", referring to the gravel plateau west of Léognan on which the vineyard is situated. A not-very-amused Château Haut-Brion took legal action over

the re-naming, and since 1941 the property and its wines have been known as Château Larrivet-Haut-Brion. The red wine (Cabernet sauvignon 60%, Merlot 40%), which is matured in wood for 18 months, with 25 per cent new oak, is certainly *cru classé* standard, being a well-coloured and full-bodied Graves with good flavour, spicy-cedarwood undertones and a firm tannic structure. A little white Graves of reliable quality is also made. This property was purchased in 1987 by a French jam company which, it is hoped, will preserve the quality.

CHÂTEAU LA LOUVIÈRE
33850 Léognan

Part of André Lurton's Graves empire, this château has made a smart about-turn since 1985 as far as the quality of its red wine goes. A string of dull, lifeless vintages has come to an end with the beautiful, deep and vividly coloured wines of 1985 and 1986. These are truly splendid, full-bodied Graves that are rich in spicy-blackcurranty fruit and new oak (Cabernet sauvignon 70%, Cabernet franc 10%, Merlot 20%). The white wines of La Louvière have always been excellent, but even here there has been a gigantic leap in quality. These are exciting and complex wines that deserve to be among the very best *crus classés.*

Second Wine: Château Coucheroy
Other wines: Château Les Agunelles, Château Cantebau, Château Clos-du-Roy, Château Le Vieux-Moulin

CHÂTEAU MAGENCE
St.-Pierre-de-Mons,
33210 Langon

A good property producing 5,000 cases of a supple, well-perfumed, red Graves (Cabernet sauvignon 40%, Cabernet franc 30%, Merlot 30%) and 10,000 cases of an attractive, aromatic, cool-fermented dry white Graves (Sémillon 36%, Sauvignon 64%).

CHÂTEAU MAYNE-BINET

Proprietor Jean Perromat also owns the châteaux of De Cérons, De Bessanes, Ferbos and Ferbos-Lalanette in Cérons and Château Prost in Barsac. At Mayne-Binet he produces a fine, sweet white Cérons.

CHÂTEAU MILLET
33640 Portets

Monsieur Henri de la Mette, the owner of this property, is not a modest man, but then he does not produce a modest wine. He makes about 12,000 cases of red Graves (Cabernet sauvignon and Cabernet franc 20%, Merlot 80%), but only in the finest years. (If the vintage is not good enough, as in 1980, it is not sold under the Château Millet label). It is a deep, dark-coloured wine made in a traditional style with a dense flavour of concentrated spicy-fruit. Although it has a firm tannin structure, this quickly rounds out with a few years in bottle. There is a similar-sized production of dry white Graves, but it lacks the boldness and character of the red.

Other wines: Château du Clos Renon

CHÂTEAU RAHOUL
33640 Portets

The home of the maestro! Peter Vinding-Diers produces some 6,000 cases of red Graves (Cabernet sauvignon 30%, Merlot 70%), an elegantly balanced wine that is matured in wood for 18 months, with one-third new oak, but his real love is white wine. While he is no lover of the many artificial ways in which science can assist wine production, he is also not an "organic" wine devotee, preferring to find natural solutions or to give fundamental processes a gentle nudge. His pure Sémillon white Graves undergoes prefermentation maceration to extract the maximum of aromatics from the grape skins before fermentation with a special yeast strain, which Vinding-Diers believes to be critical to the character and quality of Château Rahoul. The wines are almost, but not quite, completely fermented out before maturation in 100 per cent new oak for six months. Vinding-Diers is currently experimenting with introducing the malolactic process just long enough to contribute aromatic and flavour-enhancing compounds, but without actually allowing the conversion to take place. The result of all this is a stunning, if idiosyncratic, dry white wine that initially is lightly rich and fragrant with an underlying sweet, ripe-oak flavour, reminiscent of a delicately oaked Australian Chardonnay. With time in bottle it develops greater richness and blossoms into a myriad of new, wild and exotic flavours. Frankly, I am not sure how half of Vinding-Diers' wines are going to develop; as he constantly strives to improve the quality, he inevitably alters the style. One thing I am sure of: we will not grow bored of these exciting wines.

CHÂTEAU RESPIDE-MÉDEVILLE
Toulenne,
33210 Langon

Christian Médeville, the man responsible for Château Gilette, the rising star of Sauternes, produces excellent wines here using a totally different wine philosophy. Both the red and the white are fine examples of the best of modern vinification combined with new oak. The red is a well-coloured wine with rich, ripe fruit, some spice and a creamy new-oak aftertaste. The white is a rich, creamy-vanilla concoction with soft, succulent fruit and a fat finish.

CHÂTEAU DE ROCHEMORIN
Martillac,
33650 La Brède

Originally called "La Roche Morine", the history of this estate extends at least as far back as the eighth-century defence of Bordeaux by the Moors from attacking Saracens. Another André Lurton château, Rochemorin produces a fine, elegant, fruity red Graves that is well balanced and has a good spicy finish (Cabernet sauvignon 60%, Merlot 40%) and a very clean and correct dry white Graves.

CHÂTEAU DE ROQUETAILLADE-LA-GRANGE
Mazères,
33210 Langon

A very old property that produces some 12,000 cases of an attractive, well-coloured red Graves that has an aromatic bouquet and a delicious spicy-cassis flavour. Made from Cabernet sauvignon 25%, Cabernet franc 25%, Merlot 40%, Malbec 5%, Petit verdot 5%, its firm tannic structure means it matures gracefully over 15 or more years. The white (Sémillon 80%, Sauvignon 20%) is less successful.

Other wines: Château de Roquetaillade-le-Bernet

CLOS SAINT-GEORGES
Illats,
33720 Podensac

This property produces a small amount of red Graves, but is most famous for its scintillating sweet Graves Supérieur. A stunningly rich and flavoursome wine, full of botrytis complexity. We can thank the efforts of Sainsbury's, the UK supermarket chain, for its current reputation.

The great châteaux of Sauternes and Barsac

CHÂTEAU D'ARCHE
Sauternes

2ème Cru Classé
Production: *4,500 cases*

This old property, which dates from the year 1530, was known as Cru de Bran-Eyre until it was purchased by the Comte d'Arche in the eighteenth century. It has suffered from inconsistency in the past, but a change of ownership in 1981 might redress the situation in time. The wine is now matured in up to 50 per cent new oak.

WHITE The successful d'Arche is an elegantly balanced wine that is more in the style of Barsac than Sauternes. It is sweet, rich and has complex botrytis flavours, but its lusciousness is less plump than most Sauternes.

🍇	Sémillon 80%, Sauvignon 15%, Muscadelle 5%
🍷	1983, 1986, 1988
🥂	Between 8-25 years

Other wines: Château d'Arche "Crème de Tête"

CHÂTEAU BROUSTET
Barsac

2ème Cru Classé
Production: *2,000 cases*

The wine is matured in wood for 20 months with what was until recently just 10 per cent new oak, but this has increased to 40 per cent with the 1986 vintage.

WHITE This can be a delightful wine, with a fruit-salad and cream taste, a very elegant balance and some spicy-botrytis complexity.

🍇	Sémillon 63%, Sauvignon 25%, Muscadelle 12%
🍷	1985, 1986, 1988
🥂	Between 8-25 years

Second Wine: Château Ségur

CHÂTEAU CAILLOU
Barsac

2ème Cru Classé
Production: *4,000 cases*

This château derives its name from the *cailloux* the boulders that surface during ploughing. While *cailloux* have been used to enclose the entire 15-hectare (37-acre) vineyard and to provide hardcore for the tennis courts, Monsieur Bravo, the owner, has run out of uses but he is still churning them up. This is not one of the better-known Second Growths, but it consistently produces wines of a very high standard, and so deserves to be.

WHITE A rich, ripe and spicy-sweet Barsac with concentrated botrytis flavours underscored by refined oak. Not the fattest of Barsacs, but made in the richer, rather than lighter style.

🍇	Sémillon 90%, Sauvignon 10%
🍷	1981, 1981 Private Cuvée, 1983, 1985, 1986, 1988
🥂	Between 8-30 years

Other wines: "Cru du Clocher" (red), Château Caillou Sec (dry white), "Rosé St.-Vincent" (dry rosé)

CHÂTEAU CLIMENS
Barsac

1er Cru Classé
Production: *5,000 cases*

Under the same ownership as *cru classé* châteaux Brane-Cantenac and Durfort-Vivens in Margaux, this has long been considered one of the very top wines of both appellations. The wine is matured in wood for 24 months with up to one-third new oak.

WHITE The fattest of Barsacs, yet its superb acidity and characteristic citrussy style give it an amazingly fresh and zippy balance. This wine has masses of creamy-ripe botrytis fruit supported by good cinnamon and vanilla-oak flavours.

🍇	Sémillon 98%, Sauvignon 2%
🍷	1983, 1985, 1986, 1988, 1989
🥂	Between 10-40 years

CHÂTEAU CLOS HAUT-PEYRAGUEY
Bommes

1er Cru Classé
Production: *3,000 cases*

Originally part of Château Lafaurie-Peyraguey, this property has been owned by the Pauly family since 1934. A good dose of sulphur dioxide used to be the method of stopping fermentation at Clos Haut-Peyraguey and the bouquet was often marred by an excess of sulphur. Thankfully this has not been evident since the 1985 vintage, when coincidentally, the wines began to benefit from some new oak. The wine is now matured in wood for 18 months, with up to 25 per cent new oak.

WHITE This wine now flaunts a positively eloquent bouquet, and has a rich flavour with complex botrytis creamy-oak nuances – very stylish.

🍇	Sémillon 83%, Sauvignon 15%, Muscadelle 2%
🍷	1985, 1986
🥂	Between 8-25 years

CHÂTEAU COUTET
Barsac

1er Cru Classé
Production: *8,000 cases*

This château is usually rated a close second to Climens, but in fact it is capable of matching it in some vintages and its occasional production of tiny quantities of a *tête de cuvée* called "Cuvée Madame" often surpasses it. It is fermented and matured for 24 months in cask with 30-50 per cent new oak. The dry white "Vin Sec" is disappointing.

WHITE This wine has a creamy vanilla and spice bouquet, an initially delicate richness that builds on the palate, good botrytis character and oaky fruit.

🍇	Sémillon 75%, Sauvignon 23%, Muscadelle 2%
🍷	1981, 1983, 1985, 1988, 1989
🕰	Between 8-25 years (15-40 years for "Cuvée Madame")

Other wines: "Vin Sec du Château Coutet"

CHÂTEAU DOISY-DAËNE
Barsac

2ème Cru Classé
Production: *4,000 cases*

Owner Pierre Dubourdieu cool-ferments this wine in stainless steel until the desired balance of alcohol and sweetness is achieved, and then matures it in 100 per cent new oak for a short while. The wine also undergoes various low-sulphur techniques. The result is a wine equal to a Barsac First Growth.

WHITE This is a wine of great floral freshness and elegance, with a delightful honeyed fragrance of deliciously sweet fruit, delicate botrytis character, hints of creamy oak and perfect balance.

🍇	Sémillon 100%
🍷	1982, 1983, 1985, 1986, 1988
🕰	Between 8-20 years

Second Wine: Château Cantegril
Other wines: "Vin Sec de Doisy-Daëne"

CHÂTEAU DOISY-DUBROCA
Barsac

2ème Cru Classé
Production: *600 cases*

This is the smallest part of the original Doisy estate. The wine, which is consistent but not in the same class as Doisy-Daëne, is matured in cask for 24-30 months with 25 per cent new oak.

WHITE A soft, light and fragrant wine with some spice and oak, but lacking a certain lusciousness.

🍇	Sémillon 90%, Sauvignon 10%
🍷	1980, 1981, 1983
🕰	Between 6-15 years

CHÂTEAU DOISY-VÉDRINES
Barsac

2ème Cru Classé
Production: *2,200 cases*

This is the original of the three Doisy châteaux – and the largest. The château is owned by Pierre Castéja, the head of Bordeaux *négociant* Roger Joanne. The wine is matured in wood for 18 months with one-third new oak.

WHITE Somewhat lacklustre until 1983, since when it has exploded with character. Rich, ripe and oaky with a concentrated botrytis complexity.

🍇	Sémillon 80%, Sauvignon 20%
🍷	1983, 1985, 1986, 1988
🕰	Between 8-25 years

CHÂTEAU FILHOT
Sauternes

2ème Cru Classé
Production: *9,500 cases*

The beautiful Château Filhot was built between 1780 and 1850. This splendid château has a potentially great vineyard that consistently produces boring wine. Investment is required on a large scale in nearly every department: the proportion of Sémillon should be increased, the number of *tries* should be increased, the wine should contain more botrytized grapes and should be matured in cask, with some new oak.

WHITE At best these are well-made wines that are simply fruity and sweet.

🍇	Sémillon 60%, Sauvignon 37%, Muscadelle 3%

CHÂTEAU GUIRAUD
Sauternes

1er Cru Classé
Production: *7,000 cases*

In 1981 Canadian millionaire Hamilton Narby purchased this property in a very run-down state. Because there was as much as 65 per cent Sauvignon blanc, he dug some up and planted Sémillon, then totally re-equipped the winery and renovated the château. Only Yquem is on as high ground as Guiraud and the potential for this property is very exciting indeed. The wine is now matured in wood for 30 months with at least 50 per cent new oak. The first vintages of the dry white Vin Blanc Sec "G" were dull, but subsequent efforts have improved.
The red wine, sold as a Bordeaux Supérieur under the "Le Dauphin" label, was at its best in 1982 when its Merlot content was higher. It is

planned to drop the Merlot from its original 55 per cent to just 30 per cent in favour of Cabernet sauvignon, but despite the name "Le Dauphin" is not a pretentious wine and does not require so much Cabernet sauvignon.

WHITE After two dismal decades, great Sauternes arrived at this château with the classic 1983 vintage. Guiraud is now plump with Sémillon fruit and fat with botrytis character. A deliciously sweet wine with luxuriant new oak, complexity and considerable finesse.

🍇	Sémillon 55%, Sauvignon 45%
🍷	1983, 1985, 1986
🕰	Between 12-35 years

Other wines: Vin Blanc Sec "G" and "Le Dauphin", Château Guiraud

CHÂTEAU LAFAURIE-PEYRAGUEY
Bommes

1er Cru Classé
Production: *3,500 cases*

Like all Cordier properties, Lafaurie-Peyraguey shows a remarkable consistency. The wine is matured in wood for 18-20 months with up to 50 per cent new oak.

WHITE The combination of botrytis and oak turns out like pineapples, peaches and cream in this elegant wine that keeps fresh and retains an incredibly light colour in old age.

🍇	Sémillon 98%, Sauvignon 2%
🍷	1980, 1981, 1982, 1983, 1985, 1986, 1988, 1989
🕰	Between 8-30 years

CHÂTEAU LAMOTHE
Sauternes

2ème Cru Classé
Production: *2,000 cases*

In 1961 the Lamothe vineyard was split in two. This section, belonging to Jean Despujols, has been the most disappointing half up until the 1985 vintage (1986 not tasted).

WHITE Sound, medium-bodied, medium-sweet white wine of little individual character.

🍇	Sémillon 70%, Sauvignon 20%, Muscadelle 10%

CHÂTEAU LAMOTHE-GUIGNARD
Sauternes

2ème Cru Classé
Production: *2,000 cases*

The Guignards are really trying to achieve something with their section of the Lamothe vineyard, which was called Lamothe-Bergey until 1981. The wine is matured in wood for 24 months with 20 per cent new oak.

WHITE These are rich, spicy and concentrated wines of full body and good botrytis character.

🍇	Sémillon 85%, Sauvignon 5%, Muscadelle 10%
🍷	1983, 1985, 1986, 1988
🕰	Between 7-20 years

CHÂTEAU DE MALLE
Preignac

2ème Cru Classé
Production: *2,700 cases*

Dry white wine is produced under the "Chevalier de Malle" label, and red Graves from contiguous vineyards under the Château du Cardaillan label. While this vineyard does not shine every year, when it does, it can be superb value.

WHITE At their best these are firm, well-concentrated wines often influenced more by *passerillage* than botrytis. Delicious, rich and luscious.

🍇	Sémillon 75%, Sauvignon 22%, Muscadelle 3%
🍷	1983, 1986, 1988
🕰	Between 7-20 years

CHÂTEAU NAIRAC
Barsac

2ème Cru Classé
Production: *2,000 cases*

Tom Heeter (now in America), established the practice of fermenting and maturing his wine in up to 100 per cent new oak: *Nevers* for vanilla and *Limousin* for backbone.

WHITE These are rich and oaky wines that require ample aging to show true finesse. With enough bottle maturity the tannin and vanilla harmonize with the fruit, and the rich botrytis complexity emerges.

🍇	Sémillon 90%, Sauvignon 6%, Muscadelle 4%
🍷	1980, 1981, 1982, 1983, 1985, 1986, 1988
🕰	Between 8-25 years

CHÂTEAU RABAUD-PROMIS
Bommes

1er Cru Classé
Production: *3,750 cases*

The wines of this once-grand property used to be awful. The neglect of vineyard, château and wine was a sad sight to see. What a joy to see such a dramatic change. It began with the 1983, the 1985 was better; the 1986 is something special

WHITE A lovely gold-coloured wine with full, fat and ripe botrytis character on the bouquet and palate.

🍇	Sémillon 80%, Sauvignon 18%, Muscadelle 2%
🗓	1983, 1985, 1986, 1988
🍷	Between 8-25 years

CHÂTEAU RAYNE-VIGNEAU
Bommes

1er Cru Classé
Production: *16,500 cases*

The quality of Rayne-Vigneau had plummeted to dismal depths until as recently as 1985. The wine, which is now matured in wood for 24 months with 50 per cent new oak, has a higher Sémillon content than the statistics suggest, due to the 5,000 cases of dry Sauvignon blanc that are sold as "Rayne Sec".

WHITE This is now a very high-quality wine that has an elegant peachy ripeness to its botrytis character.

🍇	Sémillon 65%, Sauvignon 35%
🗓	1985, 1986, 1988
🍷	Between 8-25 years

Second Wine: "Clos l'Abeilley"
Other wines: "Rayne Sec"

CHÂTEAU RIEUSSEC
Fargues

1er Cru Classé
Production: *6,000 cases*

This fine property threatens to make even better wine since its acquisition by Domaines Rothschild in 1984. It is matured in wood for 18-30 months with currently 50 per cent new oak.

WHITE These are rich and opulent Sauternes of a heavily botrytized character.

The concentrated 1982 ties with the soft Suduiraut 1982 as the best wine, bar Château d'Yquem, of that awkward vintage.

🍇	Sémillon 80%, Sauvignon 18%, Muscadelle 2%
🗓	1980, 1981, 1982, 1983, 1985, 1986, 1988, 1989
🍷	Between 12-35 years

Second Wine: Clos Labère
Other wines: "R" de Château Rieussec

CHÂTEAU ROMER
Fargues

2ème Cru Classé
Production: *1,500 cases*

The original Romer estate was divided in 1881, and at just five hectares (12.5 acres) this is the smallest part. I have never come across the wine.

🍇	Sémillon 50%, Sauvignon 40%, Muscadelle 10%

CHÂTEAU ROMER-DU-HAYOT
Fargues

2ème Cru Classé
Production: *4,000 cases*

Monsieur André du Hayot owns this 10 hectares (25 acres) of vines on a fine clayey-gravel crest that was once part of the original Romer estate. The wines are little seen, but represent very good value.

WHITE The 1980 and 1983 are in the fresh, not oversweet, fruit-salad and cream style, with light botrytis character and an elegant balance. More recent vintages have not been tasted.

🍇	Sémillon 70%, Sauvignon 25%, Muscadelle 5%
🗓	1980, 1983, 1988
🍷	Between 5-12 years

CHÂTEAU SIGALAS-RABAUD
Bommes

1er Cru Classé
Production: *3,000 cases*

This is the largest part of the original Rabaud estate. The wine, which is fermented and matured in vat, deserves its classification.

WHITE A stylish early-drinking wine with an elegant botrytis bouquet and deliciously fresh fruit on the palate.

🍇	Sémillon 85%, Sauvignon 15%
🗓	1981, 1983, 1988
🍷	Between 6-15 years

CHÂTEAU SUAU
Barsac

2ème Cru Classé
Production: *1,500 cases*

The vineyard belongs to Roger Biarnès, who makes the wine at his Château Navarro in Cérons because the château is under different ownership. These wines do not have a particularly high reputation, but if the attractive wine produced in the very modest 1980 vintage is anything to go by it is worth the benefit of the doubt.

WHITE The 1980 is an attractive, fresh and fragrantly fruity wine with a gentle citrussy-spicy botrytis complexity.

🍇	Sémillon 80%, Sauvignon 10%, Muscadelle 10%
🗓	1980
🍷	Between 6-12 years

CHÂTEAU SUDUIRAUT
Preignac

1er Cru Classé
Production: *8,500 cases*

This splendid seventeenth-century château, with its picturesque parkland, effectively evokes the graceful beauty found in its luscious wines. Suduiraut's superb 100-hectare (245-acre) vineyard enjoys a good susceptibility to "noble rot", and adjoins that of Yquem. The wines are fermented and matured in cask for 24 months, with at least one-third new oak.

WHITE Soft, succulent and sublime, this is an intensely sweet wine of classic stature. It is rich, ripe and viscous, with great botrytis complexity that benefits from good bottle-age.

🍇	Sémillon 80%, Sauvignon 20%
🗓	1983, 1985, 1986, 1988, 1989
🍷	Between 8-35 years

CHÂTEAU LA TOUR BLANCHE
Sauternes

1er Cru Classé
Production: *6,000 cases*

In recent years only the 1985 vintage has lived up to the quality expected from a First Growth Sauternes, and I hope it heralds the start of a new era.

WHITE The 1985 is rich and juicy with bags of botrytis character.

🍇	Sémillon 72%, Sauvignon 25%, Muscadelle 3%
🗓	1985
🍷	Between 8-20 years

CHÂTEAU D'YQUEM
Sauternes

1er Cru Supérieur
Production: *5,500 cases*

This most famous of all wine châteaux belonged to the English crown from 1152-1453. It then passed into the hands of Charles VII, King of France. In 1593 Jacques de Sauvage acquired tenant's rights to the royal property and in 1711 his descendants purchased the fiefdom of Yquem. It passed into the hands of the Lur-Saluces family in 1785. The property has been run with passionate care by succeeding generations of Lur-Saluces ever since. It was here that the tradition of *tries* was kept alive when it was long forgotten at other noble châteaux; Sauternes has suffered from a depressed market for many decades, and probably would not have survived without the glory of world-famous Yquem. The famous quote that one vine at Yquem produces just one glass of wine might be overworked, but it is true. Like Pétrus, one of Yquem's "secrets" is its pickers. Most importantly, they are all skilled; they know what to pick and, just as important, what to leave. The gap between *tries* can vary from three days to several weeks. Housing and feeding 120 pickers for several weeks of inactivity is not cheap. In 1972 the harvest consisted of 11 *tries* spread over 71 days. As it turned out no wine was sold as Château d'Yquem. This is not to say that Yquem's fastidious attention to selection and quality does not pay off in some poor vintages. But in good years, because of the strict selection in the vineyard, the amount of wine that is finally used is as high as 80-90 per cent. These wines are matured in wood for up to 42 months with 100 per cent new oak, which would be excessive for any wine other than Yquem. Other *terroirs* in Sauternes and Barsac are potentially comparable in quality, but no matter how conscientious their proprietors, none makes the same sacrifices as Yquem.

WHITE This wine represents the ultimate in richness, complexity and class. No other botrytis wine of equal body and concentration has a comparable finesse, breeding and balance. Some of the characteristic aromas and flavours include peach, pineapple, apricot, almond, coconut, caramel, melon, lemon, nutmeg and cinnamon, with toasty-creamy, vanilla and caramel flavours of new oak.

🍇	Sémillon 80%, Sauvignon 20%
🗓	1980, 1981, 1982, 1983, 1985, 1986, 1988
🍷	Between 20-60 years

Other wines: "Y" de Château d'Yquem

The best of the rest

CHÂTEAU BASTOR-LAMONTAGNE
Preignac

Production: *7,500 cases*

A large property bordering Château Suduiraut that deserves Second Growth status. The wine is matured in wood for up to 36 months, with 10-15 per cent new oak.

Lighter years such as 1980, 1982 and 1985 lack botrytis but are successful in an attractive mellow, citrus style. Big years like 1983 lack nothing: the wines are full, rich and stylish with concentrated botrytis flavour and ample class.

CHÂTEAU BOUYOT
Barsac

Production: *3,500 cases*

Jammy Fonbeney, the young winemaker at this little-known property, is producing some stunning wines that deserve recognition. They have classic Barsac elegance, light in body, but not in flavour, with rich pineapple and cream botrytis fruit, some spice and fine length.

CHÂTEAU DE FARGUES
Fargues

Production: *1,000 cases*

The eerie ruin of Château de Fargues is the ancestral home of the Lur-Saluces family. The small production of ultra-high-quality wine is produced by essentially the same fastidious methods as Yquem, including fermentation and maturation in 100 per cent new oak. It is powerful and viscous, very rich, succulent and complex with a fat, toasty character (Sémillon 80%, Sauvignon 20%).

CHÂTEAU GILETTE
Preignac

Production: *400-900 cases*

Christian Médeville rejects modern marketing methods, preferring instead to keep his precious nectar in vats under anaerobic conditions for an amazing 20 years before bottling and selling it. The wine (made from Sémillon 83%,

Sauvignon 15%, Muscadelle 2%) is of First Growth quality. It has a powerful bouquet and intense botrytis flavour of liquorice, peaches and cream, followed by a long barley-sugar aftertaste. The superb 1983 will not be released until well into the twenty-first century, but the extraordinary vintages of 1950, 1953 and 1955 are amazingly fresh.

CHÂTEAU HAUT-BOMMES
Bommes

Production: *2,000 cases*

The owner, Jacques Pauly, prefers to live here rather than at his First Growth Château Clos Haut-Peyraguey. Occasionally the wine used to excel for an unclassified growth; the recent improvements at Château Clos Haut-Peyraguey augur well for the future.

CHÂTEAU LES JUSTICES
Preignac

Production: *3,000 cases*

Under the same ownership as the star-performing Château Gilette, but here Christian Médeville gives his wines only four years aging in vats. Les Justices is a consistent wine of excellent quality that is riper and fruitier than Gilette and the equivalent of a Second Growth.

CHÂTEAU LIOT
Barsac

Production: *6,500 cases*

This wine is elegant, with light but fine botrytis character and the creamy vanilla of new oak – excellent value for money. The owner, Madame Nicole David, and her son also produce Château Saint-Jean, a dry white Graves, and Château Pinsas, a fruity red Graves.

CHÂTEAU DU MAYNE
Barsac

Production: *2,200 cases*

A good proportion of old vines adds concentration and weight to these wines, which are fatter than the norm for Barsac. Owned by the Sanders family of the splendid Château Haut-Bailly of Graves.

CHÂTEAU DE MÉNOTA
Barsac

Production: *4,000 cases*

With its historic towers and ramparts, this quaint old property has exported its wines to England since the sixteenth century. It produces some very good Barsac, despite its unusually high proportion of Sauvignon blanc (Sémillon 40%, Sauvignon 60%).

CHÂTEAU PADOUËN
Barsac

Production: *2,000 cases*

Until relatively recently these wines were made by Peter Vinding-Diers. He implemented a system of sorting the grapes on tables in the winery, using only botrytized grapes for the Barsac, and making the remainder into a dry white AOC Bordeaux. The wine is fermented at a very low temperature and matured in wood with a high percentage of new oak.

Other wines: Château Padouën (dry white)

CHÂTEAU PERNAUD
Barsac

Production: *4,500 cases*

This property was once part of the Sauvage d'Yquem estate. It was then in the hands of the Lur-Saluces family, but was abandoned after the oidium fungus devastated Bordeaux in the late eighteenth century. It has been completely replanted and renovated, and is now building up something of a reputation. This slightly richer style of Barsac (Sémillon 70%, Sauvignon 25%, Muscadelle 5%) has a typically elegant balance and is certainly a wine to watch.

CHÂTEAU RAYMOND-LAFON
Sauternes

Production: *1,000 cases*

It is quite easy to understand how people can get carried away by the thought of a vineyard so close to Yquem as Raymond-Lafon. This is, however, an overrated and overpriced wine. It has potential, as the much-improved 1983 (and even 1984) vintages demonstrate. The yield is, quite rightly, very small, but too many vintages have had the characteristics of *passerillage*, not botrytis. Another of Raymond-Lafon's failures is that the wine is often spoiled by too much fixed sulphur. It also spends 42 months in cask, which is far too long for any Sauternes other than Yquem itself. I think this property could make an exciting quality of Sauternes if it could find more botrytis as it did in the 1983 vintage, and if it used sulphur-reducing techniques allied with less time in wood. The current 25 per cent new oak might then be raised to 40-50 per cent, although I fear the 100 per cent Monsieur Meslier is aiming for, when he can afford it, would be too much (Sémillon 80%, Sauvignon 20%).

CHÂTEAU DE ROLLAND
Barsac

Production: *4,000 cases*

The château, which has been turned into a hotel with a good restaurant, is under separate ownership. The vineyard belongs to Jean and Pierre Guignard, who also own the excellent Château de Roquetaillade-la-Grange at Mazères in Graves. The wines (Sémillon 60%, Sauvignon 20%, Muscadelle 20%) are fresh and elegant with an emphasis on fruit.

CHÂTEAU ROUMIEU
Barsac

Production: *3,000 cases*

This property, which borders the classified growths of Climens and Doisy-Vedrines, has produced luscious sweet wines of a richer than normal style in some vintages (Sémillon 90%, Sauvignon 10%).

CHÂTEAU ROUMIEU-LACOSTE
Barsac

Production: *2,500 cases*

A Dubourdieu property producing consistently fine Barsac (Sémillon 80%, Sauvignon 20%) with good botrytis concentration.

CHÂTEAU SAINT-AMANDE
Preignac

Production: *4,000 cases*

Part of the production of this property is sold exclusively by Sichel under the Château de la Chartreuse label. An elegant and stylish wine (Sémillon 67%, Sauvignon 33%) that is very attractive when young, yet some vintages have potentially excellent longevity.

CHÂTEAU SIMON
Barsac

Production: *1,800 cases*

A combination of modern and traditional methods produces a gently sweet wine (Sémillon 70%, Sauvignon 30%). Most Sauternes and Barsacs are aged in *Nevers* or *Limousin* oak. Sometimes *Allier* is used, but at Simon they mature the wine in *Merrain* oak for two years.

Other wines: Château Simon (dry white and red AOC Bordeaux)

The Libournais district

The right-bank of the Dordogne river, known as the Libournais district, is red-wine country. Dominated by the Merlot grape, this district produces deep-coloured, silky- or velvety-rich wines of classic quality in Pomerol and St.-Emilion and wines of modest quality but excellent value and character in the surrounding, so-called "satellite" appellations.

TO ENCOMPASS ALL THE GREAT WINES of this district, one need only draw a boundary north from Libourne to Les Billaux, then southeast to St.-Christophe, southwest to St.-Laurent, and back again to Libourne—for this tiny area contains all of Pomerol and the very best of St.-Emilion. This is where the Merlot grape reigns supreme; seven out of every ten vines are of that variety and its succulent fruit is essential to the local style.

In the mid-1950s many Libournais wines were harsh, and even the best appellations generally did not enjoy the reputation they do today. Most growers slowly developed the opinion that they were cultivating too much Cabernet sauvignon and Malbec for their particular *terroir* and decided that they should plant more Cabernet franc. A few growers argued for the introduction of Merlot, which was allowed by the regulations, because it would give their wines the suppleness they desired. Even if the growers could have agreed on united action, however, changing the *encépagement* of an entire district would have been a very long-term task, as well as being fantastically expensive. However, in 1956 frost devastated the vineyards, forcing the Libournais growers into action. With short crops inevitable for some years to come, prices soared, enabling them to carry out the massive replanting programme which, ironically, they could not have afforded prior to the crisis. Just as there was a positive side to phylloxera, so there was to the frost of 1956: it led to the wholesale cultivation of Merlot and Cabernet franc, which established a totally different style of wines, providing the catalyst for the spectacular post-war success of St.-Emilion and Pomerol.

THE LIBOURNAIS DISTRICT
See also p.37

This great red-wine area includes St.-Emilion, Pomerol and their "satellites".

Château Figeac, right
Late in the year, when the vendange *is past, Thierry de Manoncourt, the distinguished owner of this château, strolls through his vineyard.*

THE SATELLITES OF ST.-EMILION AND POMEROL

The wines of Lussac, Montagne, Parsac, Puisseguin, Sables and St.-Georges were once sold as St.-Emilion, but in 1936 these outer areas were given their own appellations. In essence, this was done to protect the image of the greatest St.-Emilion châteaux, but through the established historical use of this famous name the areas won the right to attach the name of St.-Emilion to their appellations. The tiny Sables area was later reclaimed by the St.-Emilion appellation, and Parsac and St.-Georges were merged with the Montagne-St.-Emilion appellation. The reduction in the number of these confusingly similar wine names made sense, but the executive order that created the larger Montagne-St.-Emilion appellation did not disband Parsac-St.-Emilion and St.-Georges-St.-Emilion, and so a situation arose where the growers could choose between two very similar appellations.

All the wines of Parsac utilize the Montagne-St.-Emilion appellation, but many growers in St.-Georges still sell their wines as St.-Georges-St.-Emilion. All five of the "St.-Emilion-hyphenated" appellations should be merged. They all produce wines of essentially similar nature and with identical regulations.

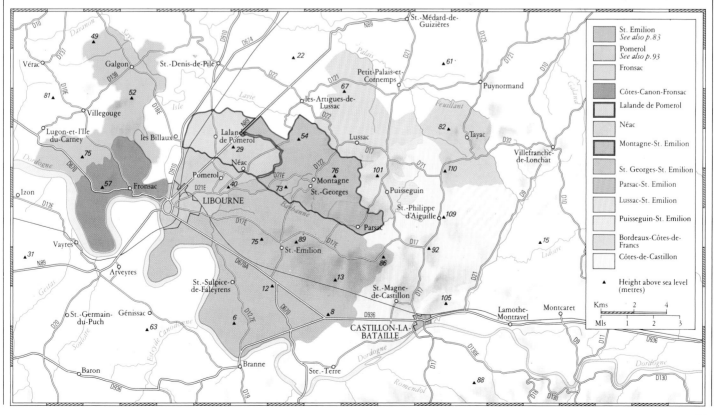

The wines of the Libournais district

BORDEAUX-CÔTES-DE-FRANCS AOC

This forgotten area's vineyards are contiguous with those of Puisseguin-St.-Emilion and Lussac-St.-Emilion, and have a very similar clay-limestone over limestone and iron-pan soil. The Bordeaux Supérieur version differs only in its higher alcohol level.

RED Essentially robust and rustic, full-bodied wines that are softened by their high Merlot content.

🍇 Cabernet sauvignon, Cabernet franc, Merlot, Malbec

🍷 1982, 1983, 1985, 1986

🍶 Between 5-10 years

WHITE Little-seen dry, semi-sweet and sweet wines of clean, fruity character.

🍇 Sémillon, Sauvignon blanc, Muscadelle

🍷 1985, 1986, 1988, 1989, 1990

🍶 Between 5-10 years

BORDEAUX-CÔTES-DE-FRANCS LIQUOREUX AOC

This style of Bordeaux-Côtes-de-Francs must by law be a naturally sweet wine made from overripe grapes that possess at least 223 grams per litre of sugar. The wines must have a minimum of 11.5 per cent alcohol and 27 grams per litre of residual sugar.

WHITE Rich, rare and genuinely *liquoreux* wines; only tiny amounts are made.

🍇 Sémillon, Sauvignon blanc, Muscadelle

🍷 1982, 1983, 1985, 1986

🍶 Between 5-15 years

BORDEAUX SUPÉRIEUR CÔTES-DE-FRANCS AOC
See Bordeaux-Côtes-de-Francs AOC.

CANON-FRONSAC AOC
See Côtes-Canon-Fronsac AOC.

CÔTES-CANON-FRONSAC AOC

I have no doubt that Fronsac will be the next wine to be "discovered" by budget-minded Bordeaux drinkers. The best Fronsac is Côtes-Canon-Fronsac, or Canon-Fronsac as it is sometimes called. With low yields and strict selection, there is no reason why these wines could not equal all but the best St.-Emilion and Pomerol.

RED Full-bodied, deep-coloured, rich and vigorous wines with dense fruit, fine spicy character, plenty of finesse and good length.

🍇 Cabernet sauvignon, Cabernet franc, Merlot, Malbec

🍷 1985, 1986, 1988, 1989, 1990

🍶 Between 7-20 years

CÔTES-DE-CASTILLON AOC

An attractive hilly area squeezed between St.-Emilion, the Dordogne river and the Dordogne *département*. Its wine has long been appreciated for quality, consistency and value. There used to be a Bordeaux and, at a slightly higher alcoholic level, Bordeaux Supérieur version of this wine until the 1989 vintage, when the appellation was awarded its own full AOC status.

RED Firm, full-bodied, fine-coloured wines with dense fruit and finesse.

🍇 Cabernet sauvignon, Cabernet franc, Carmenère, Merlot, Malbec, Petit verdot

🍷 1985, 1986, 1988, 1989, 1990

🍶 Between 5-15 years

FRONSAC AOC

This generic appellation covers the communes of La Rivière, St.-Germain-la-Rivière, St.-Aignan, Saillans, St.-Michel-de-Fronsac, Galgon and Fronsac, but it is nevertheless compact in Bordeaux terms.

RED These full-bodied, well-coloured wines have splendid chunky fruit and a fulsome, chocolatey character. Not quite the spice or finesse of Côtes-Canon-Fronsac, but splendid value.

🍇 Cabernet sauvignon, Cabernet franc, Merlot, Malbec

🍷 1985, 1986, 1988, 1989, 1990

🍶 Between 6-15 years

LALANDE-DE-POMEROL AOC

This good-value appellation covers the communes of Lalande-de-Pomerol and Néac, an area that caps Pomerol like the head of a mushroom sprouting out of its northeastern border. No matter how good they seem, even the best are but pale reflections of classic Pomerol.

RED Firm, meaty versions of Merlot with lots of character but without the texture and richness of Pomerol.

🍇 Cabernet sauvignon, Cabernet franc, Merlot, Malbec

🍷 1985, 1986, 1988, 1989, 1990

🍶 Between 7-20 years

LUSSAC-ST.-EMILION AOC

A single-commune appellation nine kilometres (five-and-a-half miles) northeast of St.-Emilion.

RED The wines produced on the small gravelly plateau to the west of this commune are the lightest, but have the most finesse. Those produced on the cold, clayey lands to the north are robust and earthy, while those from the clay-limestone in the southeast have the best balance of colour, richness and finesse.

🍇 Cabernet sauvignon, Cabernet franc, Merlot, Malbec

🍷 1985, 1986, 1988, 1989, 1990

🍶 Between 5-12 years

MONTAGNE-ST.-EMILION AOC

This appellation includes Parsac-St.-Emilion and St.-Georges-St.-Emilion, both former communes that are today part of Montagne-St.-Emilion. St.-Georges and Montagne are the best of all these appellations.

RED Full, rich and intensely flavoured wines that mature well.

🍇 Cabernet sauvignon, Cabernet franc, Merlot, Malbec

🍷 1985, 1986, 1988, 1989, 1990

🍶 Between 5-15 years

NÉAC AOC

This appellation has not been used since the proprietors have been allowed to use the Lalande-de-Pomerol appellation and should be scrapped. (*See* Lalande-de-Pomerol AOC.)

PARSAC-ST.-EMILION AOC

This former commune is now part of the Montagne-St.-Emilion appellation. Wines may be sold as Parsac-St.-Emilion, but none are at present. (*See* Montagne-St.-Emilion AOC.)

POMEROL AOC

The basic wines of Pomerol fetch higher prices than those of any other Bordeaux appellation. The average Merlot content of a typical Pomerol is around 80 per cent.

RED It is often said that these are the most velvety-rich of the world's classic wines and indeed they are, but they also have the firm tannin structure that is necessary for successful long-term maturation. The finest also have surprisingly deep colour, masses of spicy-oak complexity, and great finesse.

🍇 Merlot, Cabernet franc, Cabernet sauvignon, Malbec

🍷 1985, 1986, 1988, 1989, 1990

🍶 Between 5-10 years (modest growths); 10-30 years (great growths)

PUISSEGUIN-ST.-EMILION AOC

This commune has a clay-limestone topsoil over a stony subsoil and the wines it produces tend to be more rustic than those of the Montagne-St.-Emilion AOC.

RED Rich and robust wines with a deep flavour and lots of fruit and colour, but usually lacking in finesse.

🍇 Cabernet sauvignon, Cabernet franc, Merlot, Malbec

🍷 1985, 1986, 1988, 1989, 1990

🍶 Between 5-10 years

ST.-EMILION AOC

Like Pomerol these wines must have a minimum of 10.5 per cent alcohol, but in years when chaptalization is allowed there is also a maximum level of 13 per cent.

RED Even in the most basic St.-Emilions the ripe, spicy-juiciness of the Merlot grape should be supported by the firmness and finesse of the Cabernet franc. The great châteaux achieve this superbly: they are full, rich and concentrated, chocolatey and fruit-cakey.

🍇 Cabernet sauvignon, Cabernet franc, Merlot, Malbec, Carmenère

🍷 1985, 1986, 1988, 1989, 1990

🍶 Between 6-12 years (modest growths); 12-35 years (great growths)

ST.-GEORGES-ST.-EMILION AOC

Along with the Montagne part of Montagne-St.-Emilion, this is the best parish of the outer areas.

RED Deep-coloured, plummy wines with juicy, spicy fruit and good supporting tannic structure.

🍇 Cabernet sauvignon, Cabernet franc, Merlot, Malbec

🍷 1985, 1986, 1988, 1989, 1990

🍶 Between 5-15 years

St.-Emilion

THE ROMANS WERE THE FIRST TO CULTIVATE the vine in St.-Emilion, a small area that has exported its wines to various parts of the world for well over 800 years. In the first half of this century it lapsed into obscurity, but over the last 30 years St.-Emilion has risen like a phoenix to recapture its former fame.

There are many reminders of the wine's ancient past, from the famous Château Ausone, which is named after the Roman poet Ausonius, to the walled hilltop village of St.-Emilion itself, which has survived almost untouched from the Middle Ages. In contrast, the Union de Producteurs, which is the largest single-appellation *coopérative* in France, is a graphic illustration of the best in modern, technologically sophisticated wine production. Today there are no less than 1,000 *crus* within 10 kilometres (six miles) of the village of St.-Emilion that may use this appellation.

THE STYLE OF ST.-EMILION

For those who find red wines too harsh or too bitter, St.-Emilion is one of the easiest with which to make the transition from white to red. Its elegance and finesse make it particularly appealing.

The difference between St.-Emilion and its satellites is comparable to the difference between silk and satin, whereas the difference between St.-Emilion and Pomerol is like the difference between silk and velvet. The quality is similar, but the texture is not – although, of course, we must be humble about categorizing such complex entities as wine areas. It could justifiably be argued that the *graves* area that produces two of the very best St.-Emilions – châteaux Cheval-Blanc and Figeac – has more in common with Pomerol than with the rest of the appellation.

A LARGE PRODUCTION

It is a surprising but regular occurrence that an appellation as small as St.-Emilion produces more wine than Listrac, Moulis, St.-Estèphe, Pauillac, St.-Julien and Margaux put together. In 1986, for example, those six Médoc appellations produced 291,000 hectolitres (3.2 million cases), while St.-Emilion produced 305,000 hectolitres (3.4 million cases).

Making *marc* at Figeac, above
The mass of skins and stalks that collects in the base of the wine-press is made into the eau-de-vie known as marc.

Charming medieval St.-Emilion, left
Wine growers belonging to the association of the Jurade de St.-Emilion assemble at the top of an ancient tower.

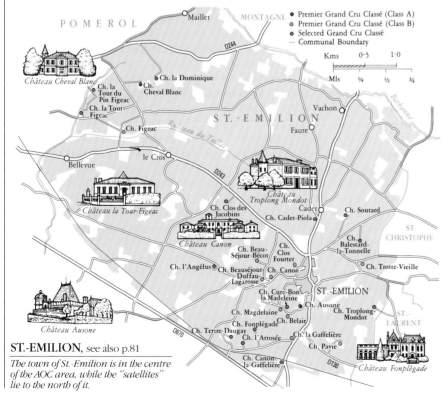

ST.-EMILION, see also p.81
The town of St.-Emilion is in the centre of the AOC area, while the "satellites" lie to the north of it.

Château Ausone, above
From its hilltop perch, this ancient château commands a spectacular view of the sweeping vineyards below.

THE CLASSIFICATION OF ST.-EMILION

An executive order dated October 7, 1954 called for the first-ever classification of St.-Emilion. It called for a revision of the classification every ten years, when it would be possible to promote or demote properties according to their performance during the intervening decade. After several attempts and rectifications, the first classification was passed in 1958. Three basic categories were established: *Premier Grand Cru Classé*, *Grand Cru Classé* and *Grand Cru*. Of the 12 châteaux that were classified *Premiers Grands Crus Classés*, Ausone and Cheval-Blanc were placed in a clearly superior subsection. The remainder were listed alphabetically, not qualitatively, as were the 64 *Grands Crus Classés*.

Although the original classification was revised in 1969, it was not revised again until 1985. When it was eventually published, one *Premier Grand Cru Classé* was demoted to *Grand Cru Classé* and no less than six *Grands Crus Classés* were denied any classification at all. If this did not ruffle enough feathers, one unclassified growth, a *coopérative*-produced wine, was elevated into the *Grand Cru Classé* aristocracy. The one promotion was certainly correct, as were perhaps four of the demotions, but of those that were downgraded, I cannot help but think: if these, why not others?

St.-Emilion Classification of 1958, 1969 and 1985 (Incorporating vineyard soil classification)

Premier Grand Cru Classé
(Class A)

1 Château Ausone
(Soil: *Côte and St.-Emilion plateau*)

2 Château Cheval Blanc
(Soil: *Graves and ancient sand*)

Premier Grand Cru Classé
(Class B)

3 Château Beau-Séjour-Bécot [1]
(Soil: *St.-Emilion plateau and côte*)

4 Château Beauséjour (Duffau Lagarosse)
(Soil: *Côte*)

5 Château Canon
(Soil: *St.-Emilion plateau and côte*)

6 Château Belair
(Soil: *St.-Emilion plateau and côte*)

7 Clos Fourtet
(Soil: *St.-Emilion plateau and ancient sand*)

8 Château-Figeac
(Soil: *Graves and ancient sand*)

9 Château la Gaffelière
(Soil: *Côte, pied de côte*)

10 Château Magdelaine
(Soil: *St.-Emilion plateau, côte and pied de côte*)

11 Château Pavie
(Soil: *Côte and St.-Emilion plateau*)

12 Château Trottevieille
(Soil: *St.-Emilion plateau*)

Grand Cru Classé

13 Château l'Angélus
(Soil: *Pied de côte, ancient sand*)

14 Château l'Arrosée
(Soil: *Côte*)

15 Château Baleau (now Château Côtes Baleau) [1,3]
(Soil: *Côte and ancient sand*)

16 Château Balestard la Tonnelle
(Soil: *St.-Emilion plateau*)

17 Château Bellevue
(Soil: *Côte and St.-Emilion plateau*)

18 Château Bergat
(Soil: *Côte and St.-Emilion plateau*)

19 Château Berliquet [2]
(Soil: *Côte and pied de côte*)

20 Château Cadet-Bon [1]
(Soil: *St.-Emilion plateau and côte*)

21 Château Cadet-Piola
(Soil: *St.-Emilion plateau and côte*)

22 Château Canon-la-Gaffelière
(Soil: *Pied de côte, sandy-gravel*)

23 Château Cap de Mourlin
(Soil: *Côte and ancient sand*)

Château la Carte [4]
(Soil: *St.-Emilion plateau and ancient sand*)

Château Chapelle-Madeleine [5]
(Soil: *Côte and St.-Emilion plateau*)

24 Château le Châtelet
(Soil: *Côte and ancient sand*)

25 Château Chauvin
(Soil: *Ancient sand*)

26 Château la Clotte
(Soil: *Côte*)

27 Château la Clusière
(Soil: *Côte*)

28 Château Corbin
(Soil: *Ancient sand*)

29 Château Corbin Michotte
(Soil: *Ancient sand*)

30 Château la Couspaude [1]
(Soil: *St.-Emilion plateau*)

31 Château Coutet [1]
(Soil: *Côte*)

Château le Couvent [6]
(Soil: *St.-Emilion plateau*)

32 Couvent des Jacobins [3]
(Soil: *Ancient sand and pied de côte*)

33 Château Croque Michotte
(Soil: *Ancient sand and graves*)

34 Château Curé Bon la Madeleine
(Soil: *St.-Emilion plateau and côte*)

35 Château Dassault [3]
(Soil: *Ancient sand*)

36 Château la Dominique
(Soil: *Ancient sand and graves*)

37 Château Faurie de Souchard
(Soil: *Pied de côte*)

38 Château Fonplégade
(Soil: *Côte*)

39 Château Fonroque
(Soil: *Côte and ancient sand*)

40 Château Franc-Mayne
(Soil: *Côte*)

41 Château Grand Barrail Lamarzelle Figeac
(Soil: *Ancient sand*)

42 Château Grand-Corbin-Despagne
(Soil: *Ancient sand*)

43 Château Grand Corbin
(Soil: *Ancient sand*)

44 Château Grand Mayne
(Soil: *Côte and ancient sand*)

45 Château Grandes Murailles [1]
(Soil: *Côte and ancient sand*)

46 Grand Pontet
(Soil: *Côte and ancient sand*)

47 Château Guadet-St.-Julien
(Soil: *St.-Emilion plateau*)

48 Château Haut-Corbin
(Soil: *Ancient sand*)

49 Château Haut-Sarpe [3]
(Soil: *St.-Emilion and St.-Christophe plateaux and côtes*)

50 Château Jean Faure [1]
(Soil: *Ancient sand*)

51 Château Clos des Jacobins
(Soil: *Côte and ancient sand*)

52 Château Laniote [3]
(Soil: *Ancient sand and pied de côte*)

53 Château Larcis Ducasse
(Soil: *Côte and pied de côte*)

54 Château Larmande
(Soil: *Ancient sand*)

55 Château Laroze
(Soil: *Ancient sand*)

56 Clos la Madeleine
(Soil: *St.-Emilion plateau and côte*)

57 Clos St.-Martin
(Soil: *Côte and ancient sand*)

58 Château la Marzelle (now Château Lamarzelle)
(Soil: *Ancient sand and graves*)

59 Château Matras [3]
(Soil: *Pied de côte*)

60 Château Mauvezin
(Soil: *St.-Emilion plateau and côte*)

61 Château Moulin du Cadet
(Soil: *Côte and ancient sand*)

62 Château Pavie Decesse
(Soil: *St.-Emilion plateau and côte*)

63 Château Pavie Macquin
(Soil: *St.-Emilion plateau, côte and sandy-gravel*)

64 Château Pavillon-Cadet
(Soil: *Côte and ancient sand*)

65 Château Petit-Faurie-de-Soutard
(Soil: *Ancient sand and côte*)

66 Château le Prieuré
(Soil: *St.-Emilion plateau and côte*)

67 Château Ripeau
(Soil: *Ancient sand*)

68 Château St.-Georges (Côtes Pavie)
(Soil: *Côte and pied de côte*)

69 Château Sansonnet
(Soil: *St.-Emilion plateau*)

70 Château la Serre
(Soil: *St.-Emilion plateau*)

71 Château Soutard
(Soil: *St.-Emilion plateau and côte*)

72 Château Tertre Daugay [3]
(Soil: *St.-Emilion plateau and côte*)

73 Château la Tour Figeac
(Soil: *Ancient sand and graves*)

74 Château la Tour du Pin Figeac (Giraud-Belivier)
(Soil: *Ancient sand and graves*)

75 Château la Tour du Pin Figeac (Moueix)
(Soil: *Ancient sand and graves*)

76 Château Trimoulet
(Soil: *Ancient sand and graves*)

Château Trois-Moulins [4]
(Soil: *St.-Emilion plateau and côte*)

77 Château Troplong Mondot
(Soil: *St.-Emilion plateau*)

78 Château Villemaurine
(Soil: *St.-Emilion plateau*)

79 Château Yon-Figeac
(Soil: *Ancient sand*)

80 Clos de l'Oratoire [3]
(Soil: *Pied de côte*)

See opposite for an explanation of soil types.

Notes

[1] One *Premier Grand Cru Classé* and six *Grands Crus Classés* demoted in the 1985 revision.

[2] This property was not in the original 1958 classification, nor was it included in the 1969 revision, but was awarded *Grand Cru Classé* status in 1985.

[3] These properties were not in the original 1958 classification, but were awarded *Grand Cru Classé* status in the 1969 revision.

[4] These two properties were merged with *Premier Grand Cru Classé* Château Beau-Séjour-Bécot in 1979. Wines bearing both labels can be found up to the 1978 vintage, and it is possible that they might reappear sometime in the future, particularly as the expansion of Château Beau-Séjour-Bécot vineyard was primarily responsible for its demotion in the 1985 classification.

[5] This property was merged with *Premier Grand Cru Classé* Château Ausone in 1970. Wines with this label can be found up to the 1969 vintage.

[6] This property changed hands prior to the recent revision and did not apply to be considered; it was not demoted, but simply ignored.

THE QUESTION OF QUALITY

The diverse nature of St.-Emilion's soil has led to many generalizations that attempt to relate the quality and character of the wines produced to the soils from which they come. Initially the wines were lumped into two crude categories, *côtes* and *graves*. The *côtes* were supposed to be fairly full-bodied wines that develop quickly; the *graves*, fuller, firmer and richer wines, taking longer to mature.

The simplicity was appealing, but it ignored the many wines produced on the stretch of deep sand between St.-Emilion and Pomerol, and those of the plateau, which has a heavier topsoil than the *côtes*. It also failed to distinguish between the eroded *côtes* and the deep-soiled bottom slopes. But most importantly, it ignored the fact that many châteaux are spread across more than one soil type (*see* the list of classified growths p.84) and that they have various other factors of *terroir*, such as aspect and drainage, which affect the character and quality of a wine, *see* Soil Survey of St.-Emilion, below.

The map below shows the positions of the 80 classified châteaux of St.-Emilion that are listed with their soil types on p.84. Châteaux la Carte and Chapelle-Madeleine are listed but do not appear on the map (*see* **Notes** on p.84).

FACTORS AFFECTING TASTE AND QUALITY

Location
The right bank of the Dordogne, 50 kilometres (80 miles) east of Bordeaux.

Climate
Less maritime and more continental than the Médoc, with a greater variation in daily temperatures. Slightly more rainfall in the spring, and substantially less in the summer and winter.

Aspect
St.-Emilion itself is situated on a plateau where vines grow at a height of 25-100 metres (80-330 ft). These vineyards are quite steep, particularly south of the village where two slopes face each other across the D122 approach road. The plateau continues eastwards in the form of hilly knolls. North and west of the village the vineyards are on flatter ground.

Soil
Extremely complex soil (*see* A question of quality). Part of the area known as "Pomerol-Figeac" *graves* that encompasses châteaux Cheval Blanc and Figeac.

Viticulture and vinification
Some of the *vin de presse*, usually the first pressing only, is considered necessary by many châteaux. Skin-contact usually lasts for 15-21 days, but up to four weeks in some cases. Quite a few wines spend as little as 12 months in cask, but the average is nearer to between 15 and 22 months.

Primary grape varieties
Cabernet franc, Cabernet sauvignon, Merlot

Secondary grape varieties
Malbec, Carmenère

SOIL SURVEY OF ST.-EMILION

The map shows the area covered by *Premier Grand Cru Classé* and *Grand Cru Classé* châteaux, illustrating how the major soil types overlap. Château numbers are as listed on p.84.

St.-Emilion soil map, below
Each soil type is described (right) and colour keyed on the map (see below, left).

1 St.-Christophe plateau: Clay-limestone and clay-sand topsoil over limestone and *terra rossa* subsoil. *Terra rossa* is a red, clay-like soil.

2 *Graves:* Deep gravel topsoil with a subsoil of large-grain sand over a very deep, hard and impermeable sedimentary rock called *molasse*. The gravel is similar to that found in the Médoc.

3 Ancient sand: Thick blanket of large-grain sand over a subsoil of *molasse*. The bulk of this sand extends northeast from the village of St.-Emilion towards Pomerol. Although this area appears to have a gentle slope all round and the sand is very permeable, the *molasse* underneath is flat and impermeable. The water collects, saturating root systems and increasing soil acidity. Some châteaux benefit greatly from underground drainage pipes.

4 Sandy-gravel: Sandy and sandy-gravel topsoil over sandy-gravel, ferruginous gravel and iron-pan.

5 St.-Emilion plateau: Shallow clay-limestone and clay sand, shell debris and silt topsoil over eroded limestone subsoil.

6 Bottom slopes: The gentler bottom slopes of the *côtes* have a deep, reddish-brown, sandy-loam topsoil over yellow sand subsoil.

7 *Côtes:* The lower-middle to upper slopes of the *côtes* have a shallow, calcareous, clay-silty-loam topsoil that has a high active lime content. It becomes quite sandy on the middle slopes and the topsoil thins out on the upper slopes. The subsoil is mostly *molasse*, but it is not the impermeable type found under the ancient sand and *graves*. This is a weathered *molasse* of either a limestone or sandstone construction, and highly absorbent.

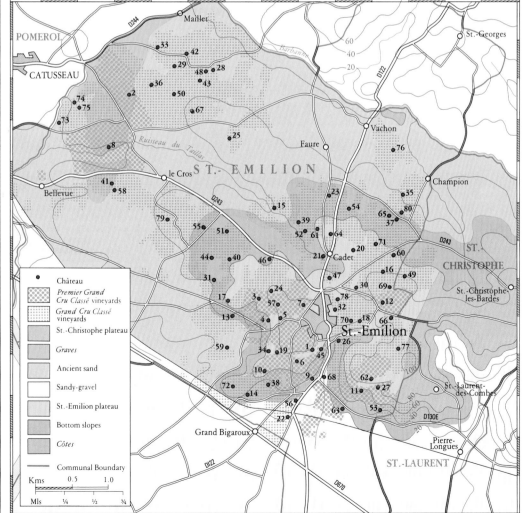

Château
Premier Grand Cru Classé vineyards
Grand Cru Classé vineyards
St.-Christophe plateau
Graves
Ancient sand
Sandy-gravel
St.-Emilion plateau
Bottom slopes
Côtes
Communal Boundary

The great châteaux of St.-Emilion

CHÂTEAU L'ANGÉLUS

Grand Cru Classé
Production: *12,000 cases*

A large property with a single plot of vines on the south-facing *côtes*. The château used to produce wines in the old "farmyard" style, but that disappeared with the 1980 vintage. Two-thirds of the wine is matured for 14-16 months in wood with 100 per cent new oak. This wine now shows great promise for the future.

RED Soft, silky and seductive. The luxury of new oak is having a positive effect on the quality, character and aging potential.

🍇 Cabernet sauvignon 5%, Cabernet franc 50%, Merlot 45%

🍷 1983, 1985, 1988, 1989

🍶 Between 7-20 years

Second Wine: "Jean du Nayne"

CHÂTEAU L'ARROSÉE

Grand Cru Classé
Production: *5,000 cases*

This property is situated on the *côtes* above the *coopérative*. Through excellent selection of only its finest wines, L'Arrosée has consistently produced wines that out-perform many of its peers.

RED This medium- to full-bodied wine has a lovely ruby colour, a voluptuous bouquet, and soft, creamy-rich fruit backed up by supple oak tannin.

🍇 Cabernet sauvignon 35%, Cabernet franc 15%, Merlot 50%

🍷 1981, 1982, 1983, 1985

🍶 Between 5-15 years

CHÂTEAU AUSONE

Premier Grand Cru Classé (A)
Production: *2,500 cases*

Since gifted winemaker Pascal Delbeck took control in 1975, this prestigious property has produced wines of stunning quality, and now deserves its superstar status. The vineyard has a privileged southeast exposure and its vines are quite old, between 40 and 45 years of age. They are capable of yielding very concentrated wines that are matured in wood for 16-22 months, with 100 per cent new oak.

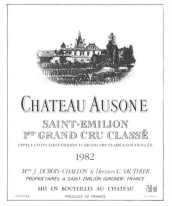

RED These rich, well-coloured wines have opulent aromas and scintillating flavours. They are full in body, compact in structure and refined in character, with masses of spicy-*cassis* fruit and creamy-oak undertones. The quintessence of class, complexity and finesse.

🍇 Cabernet franc 50%, Merlot 50%

🍷 1982, 1983, 1985, 1986, 1988

🍶 Between 15-45 years

CHÂTEAU BALESTARD LA TONNELLE

Grand Cru Classé
Production: *5,000 cases*

The label of this wine bears a fifteenth-century poem by François Villon that cites the name of the château. One-third of the wine is matured in 100 per cent new oak for up to 24 months, one-third is aged in two-year-old barrels, and the remainder rests in stainless-steel vats until bottling, when it is all blended together.

RED The gentle, ripe aromas of this wine belie its staunchly traditional style. It is a full-bodied wine of great extract, tannin and acidity that requires time to soften, but has masses of fruit, and so matures gracefully.

🍇 Cabernet sauvignon 10%, Cabernet franc 20%, Merlot 65%, Malbec 5%

🍷 1982, 1983, 1985

🍶 Between 10-30 years

CHÂTEAU BEAU-SÉJOUR-BÉCOT

Premier Grand Cru Classé until 1985
Production: *7,000 cases*

Since 1979 this property has almost doubled in size because of its merger with the vineyards of two *Grands Crus Classés*, Château la Carte and Château Trois Moulins. In 1985 this was the only *Premier Grand Cru Classé* to be demoted by the revision of the 1954 classification. Based on its performance between 1969 and 1985 as a whole, this demotion was justified. However 1982 and 1983, the two latest quality vintages available for tasting at the time, clearly showed the improvements that have begun to emerge as a result of the major capital investment made at this property on the advice of the famous Professor Peynaud. But two questions remain and the first concerns all seven of the demoted wines – why just these seven? There were other châteaux equally qualified for demotion if, as the original executive order intended, the reclassification was based on past performance.
The second question concerns the expansion of Beau-Séjour-Bécot that was the real reason for its demotion. In 1979 Château Ausone was allowed to add the *Grand Cru Classé* Château Chapelle-Madeleine to its own vineyard. Admittedly this

was a tiny expansion, just 0.2 hectares (0.5 acre), but surely the principle is the same? Whether it is the magnitude or the principle that is at stake, its general application would mean demoting nearly all the châteaux classified in 1855!
The wine is fermented in stainless steel and matured in wood for 18 months, with 90 per cent new oak.

RED Once lightweight and high-tone, these wines are now full, rich and truly characterful. The silky Merlot fruit develops quickly, but it is adequately backed up with creamy new oak.

🍇 Cabernet sauvignon 15%, Cabernet franc 15%, Merlot 70%

🍷 1982, 1983, 1986, 1988

🍶 Between 7-25 years

Second Wine: "La Tournelle des Moines"

CHÂTEAU BEAUSÉJOUR
(Owner: Duffau Lagarosse)

Premier Grand Cru Classé
Production: *3,000 cases*

The little-seen wines from this château have consistently under-whelmed critics until the 1980s, since when it has begun to produce darker, fuller wines with more class.

RED Not huge, but at its best this is a full-flavoured and deeply coloured wine made in an attractive plummy style

🍇 Cabernet sauvignon 25%, Cabernet franc 25%, Merlot 50%

🍷 1981, 1983, 1985, 1986

🍶 Between 7-15 years

Second Wine: "La Croix de Mazerat"

CHÂTEAU BELAIR

Premier Grand Cru Classé (B)
Production: *4,500 cases*

Pascal Delbeck, the gifted winemaker of Château Ausone, lives here and makes the wine with the same care and attention. The wine is matured in wood for 16-20 months. Up to half is aged in new oak, the balance in casks that have been used for one wine at Ausone. This is one of the very best *Premiers Grands Crus*.

RED This is a deep-coloured, full-bodied wine with a rich flavour of plums, chocolate, black cherries and

cassis. It has great finesse, an alluring style and a scintillating, spicy-cedarwood complexity.

🍇 Cabernet franc 40%, Merlot 60%

🍷 1982, 1983, 1986

🍶 Between 10-35 years

Second Wine: Château Roc Blanquet

CHÂTEAU BELLEVUE

Grand Cru Classé
Production: *3,000 cases*

This small property was originally called "Fief-de-Bellevue" and belonged to the Lacaze family from 1642 to 1938. It is situated on the *côtes* and produces a wine that is seldom seen outside France.

RED Only the 1982 vintage tasted: an attractive and fruity wine of medium body and elegant bouquet, but no better than many unclassified St.-Emilions.

🍇 Cabernet sauvignon 16.5%, Cabernet franc 16.5%, Merlot 67%

🍷 1982

🍶 Between 5-10 years

CHÂTEAU BERGAT

Grand Cru Classé
Production: *2,000 cases*

This small vineyard is managed by Philippe Castéja of Château Trottevielle. Its wine is rarely seen and I have never tasted.

🍇 Cabernet sauvignon 10%, Cabernet franc 40%, Merlot 50%

CHÂTEAU BERLIQUET

Grand Cru Classé
Production: *4,000 cases*

The only property to be upgraded to *Grand Cru Classé* in the 1985 reclassification – and if the current upward trend in quality continues, it would be difficult to deny Berliquet *Premier Grand Cru Classé* status during a future revision. The wine is made under the supervision of the local *coopérative*. It is fermented in stainless steel and matured in wood for 18 months, with one-third new oak.

RED Deep, dark and dense wines with spicy-*cassis* fruit and good vanilla oak.

🍇 Cabernet sauvignon and Cabernet franc 30%, Merlot 70%

🍷 1981, 1982, 1983, 1985, 1986

🍶 Between 10-30 years

CHÂTEAU CADET-BON

Grand Cru Classé until 1985
Production: *2,000 cases*

Demoted from *Grand Cru Classé* in the 1985 reclassification, this property has produced nothing outstanding since 1966.

🍇 Cabernet franc 40%, Merlot 60%

CHÂTEAU CADET-PIOLA

Grand Cru Classé
Production: *3,000 cases*

With the exception of two very light vintages 1980 and 1981, this property usually shows great consistency and, exquisite style. Up to 50 per cent of the wine is matured in new oak.

RED Full-bodied, intensely flavoured wines with powerful, new oak character and great tannic strength.

Cabernet sauvignon 28%, Cabernet franc 18%, Merlot 51%, Malbec 3%

1981, 1983, 1985, 1986, 1988

Between 12-25 years

CHÂTEAU CANON

Premier Grand Cru Classé (B)
Production: *7,500 cases*

Many years ago this château used to produce a Second Wine called "St.-Martin-de-Mazerat", which was the old Parish name before it was absorbed by the commune of St.-Emilion. The wine, which is fermented in oak vats and matured in wood for 20 months with 50 per cent new oak, is one of the best *Premiers Grands Crus Classés*.

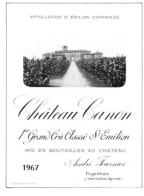

RED Deep purple colour, opulent *cassis* bouquet, very rich and voluptuous on the palate with masses of juicy Merlot fruit and spicy-complexity.

Cabernet sauvignon 3%, Cabernet franc 40%, Merlot 55%, Malbec 2%

1980, 1981, 1982, 1983, 1985, 1986, 1988, 1989

Between 8-30 years

CHÂTEAU CANON-LA-GAFFELIÈRE

Grand Cru Classé
Production: *10,000 cases*

This is one of the oldest properties in St.-Emilion. Its wine is fermented in stainless steel at 28-32°C (82-90°F) and matured in wood for 18 months, with up to 50 per cent new oak.

RED In years like those below when this château excels itself, and invests in 50 per cent new oak, the wine can be really plump, full of vivid fruit and creamy oak.

Cabernet sauvignon 5%, Cabernet franc 30%, Merlot 65%

1981, 1985, 1986

Between 8-20 years

Other wines: Château la Mondotte

CHÂTEAU CAP DE MOURLIN

Grand Cru Classé
Production: *6,000 cases*

Up to 1982 there were two versions – bearing the names of Jacques and Jean Capdemourlin. The property is run by Jacques. The wine is matured in wood for up to 24 months, with one-third new oak.

RED Attractive and well-made wines of medium body, an exquisite freshness of fruit and a smooth finish.

Cabernet sauvignon 12%, Cabernet franc 25%, Merlot 60%, Malbec 3%

1981 (Jacques), 1982 (Jacques), 1983, 1985

Between 6-15 years

Second Wine: Château Mayne d'Artagnon

CHÂTEAU LA CARTE

Grand Cru Classé

Since 1980, the vineyards of this property have been merged with those of *Premier Grand Cru Classé* Château Beau-Séjour-Bécot.

CHÂTEAU CHAPELLE-MADELEINE

Grand Cru Classé

Since 1971, these vineyards have been merged with those of *Premier Grand Cru Classé* Château Ausone.

CHÂTEAU LE CHÂTELET

Grand Cru Classé
Production: *3,000 cases*

This estate is very favourably situated among *Premier Grand Cru Classé* vineyards, yet often disappoints.

RED Usually this medium-bodied wine is attenuated in flavour and lacks the quality of a true *Grand Cru Classé*, but 1985 was exceptionally fine and fruity – a good omen for the future?

Cabernet sauvignon 33%, Cabernet franc 33%, Merlot 34%

1985

Between 4-10 years

CHÂTEAU CHAUVIN

Grand Cru Classé
Production: *6,500 cases*

The wine is matured in wood for 18 months, with one-third new oak. Little seen, but it is a wine which should be better distributed.

RED The two vintages below have excellent colour, aromatic bouquet, full body and chunky, plummy fruit.

Cabernet sauvignon 10%, Cabernet franc 30%, Merlot 60%

1982, 1983

Between 4-10 years

CHÂTEAU CHEVAL BLANC

Premier Grand Cru Classé (A)
Production: *12,500 cases*

The unusual aspect of this great château is its high proportion of Cabernet franc, which harks back to the pre-1956 era. Switching to a majority of Merlot vines was right for most Libournais properties but keeping 60 per cent Cabernet franc was even better for Cheval Blanc. The wine is matured in wood for 20 months, with 100 per cent new oak.

RED These wines have all the sweet, spicy richness one expects from a classic *graves* St.-Emilion.

Cabernet sauvignon 1%, Cabernet franc 60%, Merlot 34%, Malbec 5%

1980, 1981, 1982, 1983, 1985, 1986, 1988, 1989

Between 12-40 years

CLOS FOURTET

Premier Grand Cru Classé (B)
Production: *7,500 cases*

This property has an inconsistent record and its best wines are not quite of the same quality as the best *Premiers Grands Crus Classés*. The wines are matured in wood for 12-18 months, with 70 per cent new oak.

RED The best are opulent, medium-bodied wines with silky Merlot fruit.

Cabernet sauvignon 20%, Cabernet franc 20%, Merlot 60%

1982, 1985, 1986, 1988

Between 6-12 years

CHÂTEAU CLOS DES JACOBINS

Grand Cru Classé
Production: *4,500 cases*

This château, which is kept in the impeccable style to which all Cordier properties are accustomed, is impressive in "off-vintages".

RED This is a rich and fat wine, full of chocolatey and black-cherry flavours.

Cabernet sauvignon 5%, Cabernet franc 10%, Merlot 85%

1980, 1981, 1982, 1983, 1985, 1986, 1988, 1989

Between 8-25 years

CLOS LA MADELEINE

Grand Cru Classé
Production: *1,000 cases*

Tiny two-hectare (five-acre) vineyard in an excellent situation. So far, it has not lived up to its potential.

RED An honest and well-made wine – attractive, supple and fruity.

Cabernet franc 50%, Merlot 50%

1980, 1981

Between 5-10 years

Other wines: Château Magnan la Gaffelière

CLOS ST.-MARTIN

Grand Cru Classé
Production: *1,600 cases*

These wines are made and matured at Château Côte Baleau alongside those of that property and those of Château Grandes Murailles. Of these three wines, only Clos St.-Martin retained *Grand Cru Classé* status after the reclassification of 1985. It is aged in wood with 25 per cent new barrels every four years.

RED The 1981 and 1982 vintages are vividly coloured with ripe Merlot fruit, a silky texture and elegant style.

Cabernet sauvignon 10%, Cabernet franc 20%, Merlot 70%

1981, 1982

Between 6-15 years

CLOS DE L'ORATOIRE

Grand Cru Classé
Production: *4,000 cases*

This property belongs to Michel Boutet who also owns Château Peyreau, an unclassified St.-Emilion growth that included the vines of Clos de l'Oratoire until 1860. The wine is matured in wood for 18 months, with 25 per cent new oak.

RED Fine, full-flavoured wines that tend to have more concentration than style in the hottest years.

Cabernet franc 25%, Merlot 75%

1980, 1983

Between 7-15 years

CHÂTEAU LA CLOTTE

Grand Cru Classé
Production: *1,500 cases*

Under the same ownership as the Logis de la Cadène restaurant in St.-Emilion, where much of the wine is sold. The Libournais *négociant* Jean-Pierre Moueix takes three-quarters of the crop.

RED Not as consistent as some *Grands Crus Classés*, but when successful it can make attractive and elegant wines with lots of soft, silky fruit that are a match for its peers.

🍇 Cabernet franc 30%, Merlot 70%

🔟 1982, 1983, 1985

🍷 Between 5-12 years

CHÂTEAU LA CLUSIÈRE

Grand Cru Classé
Production: *900 cases*

A small enclave within the property of Château Pavie and under the same ownership as this and Château Pavie-Décesse. This wine is fermented in stainless steel and matured in wood (two-year-old barrels from Château Pavie) for up to 24 months.

RED This wine has a certain elegance, but lacks finesse and has a high-tone style that does not appeal to me. To be fair, I must point out that those who appreciate this style often find la Clusière solid and characterful.

🍇 Cabernet sauvignon 10%, Cabernet franc 20%, Merlot 70%

🔟 1981, 1982, 1983

🍷 Between 5-10 years

CHÂTEAU CORBIN

Grand Cru Classé
Production: *6,500 cases*

Under the same ownership as Château Grand Corbin, the original Corbin estate, now divided into five separate properties bordering the Pomerol district, once belonged to the Black Prince. The wine is fermented in stainless steel and one-third of the production is matured in 100 per cent new oak.

RED Deep-coloured, full-bodied and deliciously rich, but rather rustic for a classified growth.

🍇 Cabernet sauvignon and Cabernet franc 33%, Merlot 67%

🔟 1982, 1983

🍷 Between 6-12 years

Other wines: Château Latour Corbin, Château Corbin-Vieille-Tour

CHÂTEAU CORBIN MICHOTTE

Grand Cru Classé
Production: *3,000 cases*

One of five Corbins and two Michottes! This wine is fermented in stainless steel and some is matured in wood, with one-third new oak.

RED A dark, deeply flavoured, full-bodied wine that has rich, juicy-Merlot fruit and some finesse.

🍇 Cabernet sauvignon 5%, Cabernet franc 30%, Merlot 65%

🔟 1982, 1983

🍷 Between 6-15 years

CHÂTEAU CÔTE BALEAU

Grand Cru Classé until 1985
Production: *4,500 cases*

This property was unjustly demoted from its *Grand Cru Classé* status in 1985. It deserves its classification and is under the same ownership as Château Grandes Murailles and Clos St.-Martin, the former of which was also unfairly demoted. This wine is aged in wood and 25 per cent of the barrels are renewed every four years.

RED Full, rich and well-balanced wines that have good fruit, some fat and an attractive underlying vanilla character.

🍇 Cabernet sauvignon 20%, Cabernet franc 10%, Merlot 70%

🔟 1980, 1981, 1983, 1984, 1985, 1986

🍷 Between 4-12 years

Second Wine: Château des Roches Blanches

CHÂTEAU LA COUSPAUDE

Grand Cru Classé until 1985
Production: *3,500 cases*

Under the same ownership as Domaine-Roudier in Montagne-St.-Emilion and Domaine de Musset in the Lalande de Pomerol. This property was demoted from its *Grand Cru Classé* status in 1985. The wine is matured in wood, with some of the casks new oak.

RED Light, lean and lacklustre wines that badly need more fruit and character and better balance. The 1982 was reasonable and even hinted of vanilla-oak, but essentially a light wine.

🍇 Cabernet sauvignon and Cabernet franc 50%, Merlot 50%

🔟 1982

🍷 Between 3-7 years

Second Wine: Château Hubert

CHÂTEAU COUTET

Grand Cru Classé until 1985
Production: *4,500 cases*

This property was demoted from its *Grand Cru Classé* status in 1985. It has a record of producing finer wines than la Couspaude, but unfortunately has the same lack of consistency.

RED The 1983 has a light but elegant style, with a firm tannin structure.

🍇 Cabernet sauvignon 5%, Cabernet franc 45%, Merlot 45%, Malbec 5%

🔟 1983

🍷 Between 4-8 years

CHÂTEAU LE COUVENT

Grand Cru Classé until 1985
Production: *500 cases*

This property was purchased by Marne & Champagne in 1982. They did not apply for reclassification in 1985 and were consequently ignored, rather than demoted. The wine is matured in wood for 24 months with 100 per cent new oak.

RED I have not tasted this wine as often as I would like, but the 1982 and 1983 vintages are very successful, well-coloured, medium- to full-bodied wines with rich Merlot fruit and some creamy-spicy oak complexity.

🍇 Cabernet sauvignon 20%, Cabernet franc 25%, Merlot 55%

🔟 1983, 1985

🍷 Between 6-15 years

COUVENT DES JACOBINS

Grand Cru Classé
Production: *3,500 cases*

The wine from the young vines of this property is not included in its *Grand Vin*, but is used to make a Second Wine called "Château Beau Mayne". One-third of the production is matured in wood, with 100 per cent new oak.

RED The delicious, silky-seductive fruit in this consistently well-made wine is very stylish and harmonious.

🍇 Cabernet sauvignon and Cabernet franc 33%, Merlot 66%, Malbec 1%

🔟 1982, 1983, 1985, 1986, 1988

🍷 Between 5-15 years

Second Wine: Château Beau Mayne

CHÂTEAU CROQUE MICHOTTE

Grand Cru Classé
Production: *7,500 cases*

This property certainly deserves its *Grand Cru Classé* status. The wine is fermented in stainless steel and matured in wood for 18-24 months, with up to one-third new oak. I have not tasted the most recent vintages, but I have heard no suggestion of any downward trend in quality.

RED A delightful and elegant style of wine, brimming with juicy, soft and silky Merlot fruit.

🍇 Cabernet sauvignon and Cabernet franc 20%, Merlot 80%

🔟 1980, 1981, 1982

🍷 Between 5-12 years

CHÂTEAU CURÉ BON LA MADELEINE

Grand Cru Classé
Production: *2,500 cases*

Surrounded by *Premiers Grands Crus Classés* like Ausone, Belair and Canon, this property has an excellent record, yet could be even better with a little more selection and new oak. The wine is matured in wood for 18-24 months, with a small proportion of new oak.

RED Elegant, well-defined wine with fine fruit, supple structure and some finesse.

🍇 Merlot 90%, Cabernet franc 5%, Malbec 5%

🔟 1981, 1982, 1983, 1985, 1988

🍷 Between 7-20 years

CHÂTEAU DASSAULT

Grand Cru Classé
Production: *8,500 cases*

This property was promoted to *Grand Cru Classé* in 1969. It has an excellent record and more than deserves its classification. The wine is fermented in stainless steel and matured in wood for 12 months with one-third of the casks new oak, and undergoes as many as six rackings. With its beautifully under-stated Lafite-like label, Dassault's presentation is perfect.

RED Supremely elegant wines that always display a fine marriage of fruit and oak in perfect balance, with fine acidity and supple tannin.

🍇 Cabernet sauvignon 15%, Cabernet franc 20%, Merlot 65%

🔟 1980, 1981, 1982, 1983, 1985, 1986, 1988

🍷 Between 8-25 years

Second Wine: Château Merissac

CHÂTEAU LA DOMINIQUE

Grand Cru Classé
Production: *6,000 cases*

One of the best of the *Grands Crus Classés*, this property is situated close to Château Cheval Blanc on the *graves* in the extreme west of St.-Emilion. The wine is fermented in stainless-steel vats that are equipped with grilles to keep the *marc* submerged during the *cuvaison*. It is matured in wood for 24 months, with 50 per cent new oak.

RED Very open and expressive wines that are plump and attractive, full of ripe, creamy fruit with elegant underlying oak.

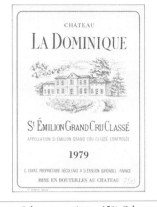

Cabernet sauvignon 15%, Cabernet franc 15%, Merlot 60%, Malbec 10%

1981, 1983, 1985, 1988, 1989

Between 8-25 years

CHÂTEAU FAURIE DE SOUCHARD

Grand Cru Classé
Production: *4,000 cases*

The most positive thing I can say about this château is that it could not be accused of producing a last-minute string of good vintages in preparation for the 1985 reclassification, as could others. I hope the modest but attractive 1986 heralds the beginning of a better reputation for Faurie de Souchard.

RED Most vintages are light-coloured, medium-bodied and either attenuated or tight and acidic, but the 1986 is easy to drink and has immediate charm.

Cabernet sauvignon 9%, Cabernet franc 26%, Merlot 65%

1986

Between 4-7 years

Other wines: Château Cadet-Peychez

CHÂTEAU-FIGEAC

Premier Grand Cru Classé (B)
Production: *12,500 cases*

Some critics suggest that the unusually high proportion of Cabernet sauvignon in the *encépagement* of this great château is wrong, but owner Thierry de Manoncourt refutes this. He has bottles of pure varietal wines produced at Figeac over several vintages, going back thirty years. As far as I am concerned, his blended *Grand Vin* says it all every year. This château belongs with the élite of Ausone and its *graves* neighbour, Cheval Blanc. The wine is matured in wood for 18-20 months, with 100 per cent new oak.

RED Impressively ripe, rich and concentrated wines that have fine colour, beautiful bouquet, stunning creamy-ripe fruit, great finesse and a wonderful spicy complexity.

Cabernet sauvignon 35%, Cabernet franc 35%, Merlot 30%

1982, 1983, 1985, 1986, 1988

Between 12-30 years

Second Wine: La Grange Neuve

CHÂTEAU FONPLÉGADE

Grand Cru Classé
Production: *7,500 cases*

Under the same ownership as Château la Tour du Pin Figeac, this property belongs to Armand Moueix, cousin of Jean-Pierre Moueix of Château Pétrus et al. The wine is matured in wood for 12 to 15 months, with one-third new oak.

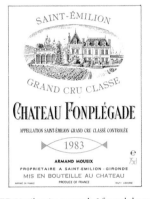

RED Until quite recently I found these wines astringent and vegetal, but this has changed — they are now delightfully clean and attractive, literally bursting with the soft, ripe, juicy fruit flavours of raspberries and strawberries.

Cabernet sauvignon 5%, Cabernet franc 35%, Merlot 60%

1983, 1985, 1989

Between 5-12 years

CHÂTEAU FONROQUE

Grand Cru Classé
Production: *8,000 cases*

Located just northwest of St.-Emilion itself, this secluded property has belonged to the *négociant* J.-P. Moueix since 1931. The wine is matured in wood for 24 months.

RED A deep-coloured, well-made wine with a fine plummy character that shows better on the bouquet and the initial and middle palate than on the finish.

Cabernet franc 30%, Merlot 70%

1982, 1983, 1985

Between 6-15 years

CHÂTEAU FRANC-MAYNE

Grand Cru Classé
Production: *3,500 cases*

This property has a modest reputation that I find difficult to

---

comment on, having only tasted the 1982 on a couple of occasions.

RED The 1982 has a deep colour and a solid, rather foursquare, character.

Cabernet sauvignon and Cabernet franc 30%, Merlot 70%

1982

Between 6-12 years

CHÂTEAU LA GAFFELIÈRE

Premier Grand Cru Classé
Production: *9,000 cases*

This property belongs to Comte Léo de Malet-Roquefort, who also owns the very old estate of Château Tertre Daugay, a *Grand Cru Classé*. After a string of aggressive, ungenerous vintages, Gaffelière produced a good 1983, an excellent 1985 and an outstanding 1986. The wine is matured in wood for 18 months, with 100 per cent new oak.

RED These wines are concentrated and tannic, but they now have much more finesse, fat and mouth-tingling richness.

Cabernet sauvignon 15%, Cabernet franc 20%, Merlot 65%

1983, 1985, 1986, 1988, 1989

Between 12-35 years

Second Wine: "Clos la Gaffelière"

CHÂTEAU GRAND BARRAIL LAMARZELLE-FIGEAC

Grand Cru Classé
Production: *15,000 cases*

This is a very large vineyard in Libournais terms, some 36 hectares (89 acres) in one continuous block created by the fusion of two properties. It is situated on predominantly sandy soil, but as the Figeac part of its name suggests, there is some gravel, albeit a mere two hectares (five acres). The wine is matured in wood for 18-24 months.

RED In good vintages these wines are deep in colour, full in body and rich in fruit — wholesome and flavourful, but lacking somewhat in finesse.

Cabernet sauvignon and Cabernet franc 30%, Merlot 70%

1982, 1985

Between 7-15 years

Second Wine: Château Lamarzelle-Figeac.

CHÂTEAU GRAND CORBIN

Grand Cru Classé
Production: *6,500 cases*

This property shares the same history and ownership as Château Corbin — it once belonged to the Black Prince, but is now owned by Alain Giraud. Production techniques differ, however, as the wine is fermented not in stainless steel, but in concrete, and matured in wood, with 25 per cent new oak.

RED These wines are somewhat lighter in colour than Château Corbin wines and have less richness and body, but they are well made and not without their own appeal.

Cabernet sauvignon 20%, Cabernet franc 20%, Merlot 60%

1981, 1982

Between 4-10 years

CHÂTEAU GRAND-CORBIN-DESPAGNE

Grand Cru Classé
Production: *13,000 cases*

This part of the original Corbin estate, which once belonged to the Black Prince, was purchased by the Despagne family — hence the name. The wine is fermented in stainless steel and matured in wood for up to 18 months, with some new oak.

RED I have not tasted vintages of this wine beyond that of 1983. It has always been a well-coloured wine of full and rich body with plenty of creamy fruit and oak, supported by supple tannin.

Cabernet franc 10%, Merlot 90%

1981, 1982, 1983

Between 7-25 years

Second Wine: Château Reine-Blanche

CHÂTEAU GRANDES MURAILLES

Grand Cru Classé until 1985
Production: *4,500 cases*

This property was demoted from its *Grand Cru Classé* status in 1985, unjustly I think. It is better and more consistent than many which were not demoted. It is under the same ownership as Château Côte Baleau and Clos St.-Martin, the former of which was also unfairly demoted. The wine is fermented in stainless steel and matured in wood for 20 months, with up to 25 per cent new oak.

RED These extremely elegant, harmonious wines have good extract and a supple tannin structure that quickly softens. They are a delight to drink when relatively young, yet age gracefully.

Cabernet sauvignon 20%, Cabernet franc 20%, Merlot 60%

1982, 1983, 1985, 1988

Between 5-20 years

CHÂTEAU GRAND MAYNE

Grand Cru Classé
Production: *10,000 cases*

This old château ferments its wine in stainless steel and ages it in wood with a variable amount of new oak.

RED This is a firm, fresh and fruity style of wine that has a rather inconsistent reputation, although I cannot comment beyond the 1982 − the last vintage tasted.

🍇 Cabernet sauvignon 10%, Cabernet franc 40%, Merlot 50%

🍷 1981, 1982, 1988, 1989

🍴 Between 4-10 years

Second Wine: Château Beau Mazerat
Other wines: Château Cassevert

CHÂTEAU GRAND-PONTET

Grand Cru Classé
Production: *7,000 cases*

Since 1980 this has been under the same ownership as Château Beau-Ségur-Bécot.

RED After a string of dull vintages, this property is now producing full-bodied wines of fine quality and character. They are fat and ripe, rich in fruit and tannin with delightful underlying creamy-oak.

🍇 Cabernet sauvignon and Cabernet franc 40%, Merlot 60%

🍷 1985, 1986

🍴 Between 6-15 years

CHÂTEAU GUADET ST.-JULIEN

Grand Cru Classé
Production: *2,000 cases*

This property consistently produces wines that well deserve their status. They are matured in wood for 18-20 months, with up to one-third new oak.

RED These are wines that show the silky charms of Merlot very early, then tighten up for a few years before blossoming into finer and fuller wines.

🍇 Cabernet sauvignon and Cabernet franc 25%, Merlot 75%

🍷 1980, 1981, 1983, 1985, 1986

🍴 Between 7-20 years

CHÂTEAU HAUT-CORBIN

Grand Cru Classé
Production: *3,500 cases*

This property belongs to Edouard Guinaudie, who also owns another St.-Emilion estate, Château le Jurat. The wine is matured in wood for 24 months, with up to 20 per cent new oak. Too infrequently tasted for a firm opinion.

🍇 Cabernet sauvignon and Cabernet franc 30%, Merlot 70%

Second Wine: Vin d'Edouard

CHÂTEAU HAUT-SARPE

Grand Cru Classé
Production: *6,000 cases*

If not one of the top-performers, this château certainly deserves its status. The wine is matured in wood for 20-22 months, with 25 per cent new oak.

RED Elegant, silky and stylish medium-bodied wines best appreciated young.

🍇 Cabernet franc 30%, Merlot 70%

🍷 1982, 1983, 1985, 1986

🍴 Between 4-8 years

CHÂTEAU JEAN FAURE

Grand Cru Classé until 1985
Production: *8,000 cases*

This property was demoted from its *Grand Cru Classé* status in 1985. I have not tasted vintages beyond 1983. The wine is matured in wood for 24 months, with 25 per cent new oak.

RED These wines have good colour and easy, attractive, supple fruit.

🍇 Cabernet franc 60%, Merlot 30%, Malbec 10%

🍷 1980, 1981, 1983

🍴 Between 3-8 years

CHÂTEAU LANIOTE

Grand Cru Classé
Production: *2,500 cases*

An old property that incorporates the "Holy Grotto" where St.-Emilion lived in the eighth century. The wine is fermented and matured in wood with 25 per cent new oak.

RED Infrequently tasted, but the 1982 and 1983 vintages are light- to medium-bodied wines of some elegance.

🍇 Cabernet sauvignon 10%, Cabernet franc 20%, Merlot 70%

🍷 1982, 1983

🍴 Between 6-12 years

CHÂTEAU LARCIS DUCASSE

Grand Cru Classé
Production: *5,000 cases*

A vineyard situated beneath Château Pavie. The wine is matured in vat and wood for 24 months.

RED This property has a certain reputation, but with the exception of an attractive if lightweight 1980, I usually find its wine thin and dried-out.

🍇 Cabernet sauvignon and Cabernet franc 35%, Merlot 65%

🍷 1980, 1988

🍴 Between 4-8 years

CHÂTEAU LARMANDE

Grand Cru Classé
Production: *7,000 cases*

This is consistently one of the best *Grands Crus Classés* in St.-Emilion. The wine is fermented in stainless steel and matured in wood for 12-18 months, with 35-50 per cent new oak.

RED These superb wines are typified by their great concentration of colour and fruit. They are rich and ripe with an abundance of creamy *cassis* and vanilla flavours that develop into a cedarwood complexity.

🍇 Cabernet sauvignon 5%, Cabernet franc 30%, Merlot 65%

🍷 1980, 1981, 1982, 1983, 1985, 1986, 1988, 1989

🍴 Between 8-25 years

Second Wine: Château des Templiers

CHÂTEAU LAROZE

Grand Cru Classé
Production: *12,000 cases*

This charming nieteenth-century château was named Laroze after a "characteristic scent of roses" found in its wines. The wine is matured in wood for one to three years.

RED The wine does have a soft and seductive bouquet, although I have yet to find "roses" in it. It is an immediately appealing wine of some finesse that is always a delight to drink early.

🍇 Cabernet sauvignon 5%, Cabernet franc 45%, Merlot 50%

🍷 1980, 1981, 1982, 1983, 1985

🍴 Between 4-10 years

CHÂTEAU MAGDELAINE

Premier Grand Cru Classé (B)
Production: *4,500 cases*

The Pétrus of St.-Emilion? This is the grandest St.-Emilion estate in the Jean-Pierre Moueix Libournais empire, but as fine as the *terroir* is, and as much as Moueix does to extract the maximum quality from it, it inevitably falls short of Pétrus. The wine is matured in wood for 18 months, with one-third new oak.

CHÂTEAU MATRAS

Grand Cru Classé
Production: *6,500 cases*

RED These well-coloured wines have excellent concentration, yet great finesse and a certain delicacy of style. They have a multi-layered flavour and a long, elegant and complex finish.

🍇 Cabernet franc 20%, Merlot 80%

🍷 1982, 1983, 1985, 1986, 1989

🍴 Between 10-35 years

The wine is matured in tank for 12 months, followed by 12 months in 100 per cent new oak. Not tasted.

🍇 Cabernet franc 60%, Merlot 30%, Malbec 10%

CHÂTEAU MAUVEZIN

Grand Cru Classé
Production: *1,500 cases*

This property is worthy of its *Grand Cru Classé* status. The wine is fermented and matured in new oak.

RED I have not tasted these wines for a while, but up to the 1982 vintages the style has been aromatic and supple with some oaky finesse.

🍇 Cabernet sauvignon 10%, Cabernet franc 50%, Merlot 40%

🍷 1980, 1982

🍴 Between 7-15 years

CHÂTEAU MOULIN DU CADET

Grand Cru Classé
Production: *1,800 cases*

This property, which is farmed by the Libournais *négociant* J.-P. Moueix, is consistently one of the best *Grands Crus Classés*. The wine is matured in wood for 18 months, with a small proportion of new oak.

RED These wines have good colour, a fine bouquet, delightfully perfumed Merlot fruit, excellent finesse and some complexity. They are not full or powerful, but what they lack in size, they more than make up for in style.

🍇 Cabernet franc 15%, Merlot 85%

🍷 1980, 1981, 1982, 1983, 1985

🍴 Between 6-15 years

CHÂTEAU PAVIE

Premier Grand Cru Classé (B)
Production: *15,000 cases*

Potentially one of the best *Premiers Grands Crus Classés*, Pavie can rank with Ausone, Cheval Blanc and Figeac. It is matured in wood for 18-20 months; one-third new oak.

RED Great and stylish wines packed with creamy fruit and lifted by exquisite new oak that may be sweet and spicy, or rich and toasty, but always gives the flavour a silky-smooth texture.

🍇 Cabernet sauvignon 20%, Cabernet franc 25%, Merlot 55%

📅 1983, 1985, 1986, 1988, 1989

🍷 Between 8-30 years

CHÂTEAU PAVIE DÉCESSE

Grand Cru Classé
Production: *4,500 cases*

This property is under the same ownership as Château Pavie. Although it is not one of the top *Grands Crus Classés*, it is consistent and certainly worthy of its status. The pleasant, early-drinking wine is matured in wood for 18-20 months, with one-third of the casks new oak.

RED These wines are much lighter than Pavie in weight and fruit, but they have an elegant, fruity style.

🍇 Cabernet sauvignon 15%, Cabernet franc 25%, Merlot 60%

📅 1983, 1985, 1986, 1988, 1989

🍷 Between 6-12 years

CHÂTEAU PAVIE MACQUIN

Grand Cru Classé
Production: *4,000 cases*

This property was named after Albert Macquin, a local grower who pioneered work to graft European vines onto American rootstock. Two-thirds of the production is matured in wood (half new oak), one-third is aged in vat.

RED Light and supple in body and fruit, with a certain spicy elegance.

🍇 Cabernet sauvignon and Cabernet franc 25%, Merlot 75%

📅 1982

🍷 Between 4-8 years

CHÂTEAU PAVILLON-CADET

Grand Cru Classé
Production: *1,500 cases*

This small vineyard produces a wine that is rarely seen on export markets. It is matured in wood for up to 24 months. My knowledge is limited to just one vintage.

RED The 1982 is a well-coloured wine with a generous bouquet and chunky, chocolatey fruit – enjoyable, but not really *Grand Cru Classé* quality.

🍇 Cabernet franc 50%, Merlot 50%

📅 1982

🍷 Between 4-8 years

CHÂTEAU PETIT-FAURIE-DE-SOUTARD

Grand Cru Classé
Production: *3,500 cases*

This excellent property used to be part of neighbouring Château Soutard, but is now run by Jacques Capdemourlin of Château Cap de Mourlin and Château Balestard la Tonnelle. Half the production is matured in wood for up to a year.

RED This wine has soft, creamy aromas on the bouquet, some concentration of smooth Merlot fruit on the palate, a silky texture and a dry, tannic finish. Absolutely delicious when young.

🍇 Cabernet sauvignon 10%, Cabernet franc 30%, Merlot 60%

📅 1980, 1981, 1983, 1985

🍷 Between 3-8 years

CHÂTEAU LE PRIEURÉ

Grand Cru Classé
Production: *2,300 cases*

This property is under the same ownership as Château Vray Croix de Gay in Pomerol and Château Siaurac in Lalande de Pomerol. This wine is matured in wood for 18-24 months, with 25 per cent new oak.

RED Light but lengthy wines of some elegance that are best enjoyed when young and fresh.

🍇 Cabernet sauvignon 10%, Cabernet franc 30%, Merlot 60%

📅 1980, 1982, 1985

🍷 Between 4-8 years

CHÂTEAU RIPEAU

Grand Cru Classé
Production: *7,500 cases*

Situated close to Château Cheval Blanc and the Pomerol district but on sandy, not gravelly, soil, this property changed hands in 1976, since when it has undergone considerable expansion and renovation. Although this is an inconsistent performer, one gets the feeling that it will all come together in the not too distant future. Part of the production is matured in wood, with an increasing proportion of new oak.

RED When successful this wine has fine aromatic character and plenty of oaky fruit.

🍇 Cabernet sauvignon 20%, Cabernet franc 30%, Merlot 50%

📅 1982, 1983

🍷 Between 4-10 years

CHÂTEAU ST.-GEORGES (CÔTE PAVIE)

Grand Cru Classé
Production: *2,000 cases*

Owned by Jacques Masson, the vineyard of this small property is well situated, close to those of châteaux Pavie and la Gaffelière. The wine is fermented in stainless steel and matured in wooden casks for 24 months.

RED This is a delicious medium-bodied wine with plump, spicy-juicy Merlot fruit, made in an attractive early-drinking style.

🍇 Cabernet sauvignon 25%, Cabernet franc 25%, Merlot 50%

📅 1980, 1981, 1982, 1983

🍷 Between 4-8 years

CHÂTEAU SANSONNET

Grand Cru Classé
Production: *4,000 cases*

Proprietor Francis Robin also owns Château Doumayne, an unclassified St.-Emilion growth and Château Gontet in Puisseguin-St.-Emilion. The wine at Sansonnet is matured in wood for 18 months.

RED This is an inconsistent wine and many vintages lack concentration, but the 1982, which is very light for the year, is supple and attractive.

🍇 Cabernet sauvignon 20%, Cabernet franc 30%, Merlot 50%

📅 1982

🍷 Between 3-7 years

CHÂTEAU LA SERRE

Grand Cru Classé
Production: *3,000 cases*

This is another property that is improving tremendously in quality, although it still lacks consistency. The wine is fermented in lined concrete tanks and matured in wood for 16 months with a small proportion of new oak.

RED The way this wine initially charms, then goes through a tight and sullen period is somewhat reminiscent of Château Guadet-St.-Julien. The style, however, is very different. When young this is quite a ripe and plump wine, but totally dominated by new oak. In time, the fruit emerges to form a luscious, stylish St.-Emilion of some finesse and complexity.

🍇 Cabernet franc 20%, Merlot 80%

📅 1980, 1982, 1983, 1986

🍷 Between 8-25 years

CHÂTEAU SOUTARD

Grand Cru Classé
Production: *7,500 cases*

The large and very fine château on this estate was built in 1740 for the use of the Soutard family in summer. Vines have grown here since Roman times. The wine of Soutard is matured in wood for 18 months, with up to one-third new oak casks.

RED This dark, muscular and full-bodied wine is made in true *vin de garde* style, with great concentrations of colour, fruit, tannin and extract. With time it can also achieve great finesse and complexity.

🍇 Cabernet sauvignon 5%, Cabernet franc 30%, Merlot 65%

📅 1981, 1982, 1983, 1985

🍷 Between 12-35 years

CHÂTEAU TERTRE DAUGAY

Grand Cru Classé
Production: *6,500 cases*

Purchased in 1978 by Comte Léo de Malet-Roquefort, the owner of *Premier Grand Cru Classé* Château la Gaffelière. The wine, which is matured in wood with one-third new oak, is already excellent and it is getting better by the vintage.

RED These wines are rich, plump and fruity with a fine bouquet, ripe underlying oak and great finesse.

- Cabernet sauvignon 10%, Cabernet franc 30%, Merlot 60%
- 1980, 1981, 1982, 1983, 1985, 1986, 1988, 1989
- Between 7-20 years

Second Wine: Château de Roquefort
Other wines: Château "Moulin du Biguey"

CHÂTEAU LA TOUR FIGEAC

Grand Cru Classé
Production: *6,000 cases*

This property was attached to Château Figeac in 1879 and today it is one of the best of the *Grands Crus Classés*. The wine is matured in wood for 18 months, with one-third new oak.

RED These are fat and supple wines with a very alluring bouquet and masses of rich, ripe *cassis* fruit.

- Cabernet franc 40%, Merlot 60%
- 1983, 1985, 1986, 1988, 1989
- Between 4-8 years

CHÂTEAU LA TOUR DU PIN FIGEAC
(Owner: Giraud-Bélivier)

Grand Cru Classé
Production: *4,000 cases*

This property is run by André Giraud, who also owns Château le Caillou in Pomerol. Unfortunately these wines have never impressed me and so I am unable to recommend any vintages.

- Cabernet franc 25%, Merlot 75%

CHÂTEAU LA TOUR DU PIN FIGEAC
(Owner: Moueix)

Grand Cru Classé
Production: *4,000 cases*

This property is one of the best of the *Grands Crus Classés*. It is now part of the Armand Moueix stable of châteaux. The wine is matured in wood for 12-15 months, with one-third new oak.

RED These consistently well-made wines always show a beautiful balance of spicy-juicy Merlot fruit, creamy-oak and supple tannin.

- Cabernet sauvignon and Malbec 10%, Cabernet franc 30%, Merlot 60%
- 1982, 1983, 1985, 1988, 1989
- Between 6-15 years

CHÂTEAU TRIMOULET

Grand Cru Classé
Production: *7,500 cases*

An old property overlooking St.-Georges-St.-Emilion. The wine is matured in wood for 12 months, with 100 per cent new oak.

RED This well-coloured wine has an overtly ripe and fruity aroma, lots of creamy-oaky character, an elegant fruit flavour and supple tannin.

- Cabernet sauvignon 20%, Cabernet franc 20%, Merlot 60%
- 1980, 1981, 1982, 1983, 1985
- Between 7-20 years

CHÂTEAU TROIS-MOULINS

Grand Cru Classé

These vineyards have been incorporated with those of Château Beau-Séjour-Bécot since 1979.

CHÂTEAU TROPLONG MONDOT

Grand Cru Classé
Production: *11,000 cases*

This property is run by Claude Valette, the brother of Jean-Paul Valette of châteaux Pavie, Pavie-Décesse and La Clusière. Half the production is matured in wood for 18 months with 100 per cent new oak.

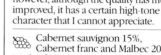

RED Since the 1985 vintage, some critics have believed the quality of this wine to be on a par with that of a *Premier Grand Cru Classé*. For me, however, although the quality has much improved, it has a certain high-tone character that I cannot appreciate.

- Cabernet sauvignon 15%, Cabernet franc and Malbec 20%, Merlot 65%
- 1985, 1986, 1988, 1989
- Between 4-8 years

CHÂTEAU TROTTEVIEILLE

Premier Grand Cru Classé (B)
Production: *4,000 cases*

This property has the reputation of producing a star wine every five years or so, interspersed by very mediocre wines indeed, but I hope two fine vintages in a row are a sign of more to come. The wine is matured in wood for 18 months, with up to 100 per cent new oak.

RED The 1985 shows promise, but the 1986 is in a different class. It has fabulous Merlot-fruit richness with new oak and the power of a true *Premier Grand Cru Classé*.

- Cabernet sauvignon 10%, Cabernet franc 40%, Merlot 50%
- 1985, 1986
- Between 8-25 years (successful years only)

CHÂTEAU VILLEMAURINE

Grand Cru Classé
Production: *4,000 cases*

This property belongs to Robert Giraud, the *négociant* which also owns some twenty *petits châteaux* in various Bordeaux districts. The wine is matured in wood for 18-24 months, with 50 per cent new oak.

RED These are full-bodied wines of excellent spicy Merlot fruit, good underlying oak and firm structure.

- Cabernet sauvignon 30%, Merlot 70%
- 1982, 1983, 1985
- Between 8-25 years

Other wines: "Maurinus" and "Beausoleil"

CHÂTEAU YON-FIGEAC

Grand Cru Classé
Production: *10,000 cases*

An important vineyard near Pomerol. The wine is matured for 18 months with 100 per cent new oak.

RED This wine is attractive and easy-to-drink with a rich bouquet, perfumed fruit and a silky texture.

- Cabernet sauvignon and Cabernet franc 70%, Merlot 30%
- 1982, 1983, 1985
- Between 5-15 years

The best of the rest

The following châteaux consistently make the finest wines in this category and those marked with an asterisk are often better than many *Grands Crus Classés*.

Château du Barry
Château Cheval Noir
Château la Commanderie*
Château Destieux*
Château de Ferrand
Château la Fleur*

Château Fleur Cardinale*
Château la Fleur Pourret
Château Fombrauge*
Château Franc Bigoroux
Château Grand Champs
Château la Grave Figeac*
Château Haut Brisson*
Château Haut Plantey*
Château Haut-Pontet
Haut-Quercus* (brand)

Clos Labarde
Château Lapelletrie
Château Laroque*
Château Magnan la Gaffelière
Château Martinet
Clos des Menuts
Château Monbousquet*
Château Patris
Château Pavillon Figeac*
Château Petit-Figeac*

Château Petit-Gravet
Château Petit Val*
Château Peyreau
Château Pindefleurs*
Château Puy Razac
Château Roc Blanquant
Château Rolland-Maillet*
Château Tour St.-Christophe

Pomerol

PASSING THROUGH POMEROL, WHICH IS SMALL and rural, with dilapidated farmhouses at every turn, few true châteaux and no really splendid ones, the traveller cannot fail to wonder how this tiny and uninspiring area can produce these magnificent wines whose softness makes them popular all over the world.

The prosperity of recent years has enabled these properties to indulge in a bit more than just an extra lick of paint, but renovation can only restore, not create, and it essentially remains an area with an air of obscurity. Even Château Pétrus, the greatest growth of Pomerol and probably the most expensive wine in the world, is nothing more than a simple farmhouse. It is interesting to reflect that, if this revered wine had achieved its current reputation and phenomenal price under the *nouveau* aristocracy of the First Empire, the finest architect in France would have been summoned to the backwoods of Libourne to construct a magnificent château as an eternal monument to its glorious success.

MY SELECTION OF POMEROL CHÂTEAUX

There has been no attempt to publish an official classification of Pomerol wines, but Château Pétrus is universally accepted as the leading growth and, as it commands prices that dwarf those of wines like Mouton and Margaux, it could not be denied a status equivalent to that of a First Growth. As for the other great growths, opinions may differ on the complete list, but few would disagree that, on the basis of recent performances, it would include the following properties:

Château Certan de May	Château la Grave-Trigant-de-Boisset
Château Certan-Giraud	Château Latour à Pomerol
Château la Conseillante	Château Petit-Village
Clos l'Eglise (Moreau)	Château le Pin
Château l'Eglise-Clinet	Château Trotanoy
Château l'Evangile	Vieux Château Certan
Château la Fleur Pétrus	

FACTORS AFFECTING TASTE AND QUALITY

Location
Small area on the western extremity of the St.-Emilion district, just northeast of Libourne.

Climate
As for St.-Emilion, *see* p.84.

Aspect
The modest mound that has châteaux Pétrus and Vieux Certan at its centre is the eastern extension of the Pomerol-Figeac *graves*. The vines grow at a height of 35 to 40 metres (115 to 130ft) on slightly undulating slopes that take a good two kilometres (1.2 miles) to descend to 10 metres (33ft) on the outskirts of Libourne.

Soil
Sandy to the west of the national highway and to the east, where the best properties are situated on the sandy-gravel soil of the Pomerol-Figeac *graves*. The subsoil consists of an iron-pan known as *crasse de fer* or *machefer*, with gravel in the east and clay in the north and centre. In the very centre of the Pomerol-Figeac *graves*, is situated the château of Pétrus on what is called the "buttonhole" of Pétrus – a unique geological formation of sandy-clay over *molasse*.

Viticulture and vinification
Some of the châteaux use a proportion of *vin de presse* according to the requirement of the vintage. At Pétrus this is added earlier than is normal practice because they believe the result is less harsh if the *vin de presse* is allowed to mature with the rest of the wine. Skin-contact usually lasts for 15-21 days, but can vary from ten days to four weeks in some cases. The wines stay in cask for between 18 and 20 months.

Primary grape varieties
Cabernet franc, Cabernet sauvignon, Merlot

Secondary grape varieties
Malbec

Château Trotanoy

Ch. de Sales
Ch. Moulinet
Vieux Château Certan
MARCHESSEAU
Château Clos l'Eglise
NÉAC
Barbanne
Néac
Ch. l'Enclos
Ch. la Grave Trigant de Boisset
Ch. Rouget
Pont de Cloquet
Ch. Latour-à-Pomerol
Ch. le Gay
Clos René
Ch. Clos l'Eglise
Ch. la-Croix-de-Gay
P O M E R O L
l'Eglise Clinet
Ch. Lafleur
Ch. Lafleur-Gazin
Ch. Pétrus
Ch. Gazin
Pomerol
Ch. Lagrange
Ch. la Fleur Pétrus
Maillet
Ch. Bourgneuf-Vayron
Ch. Trotanoy
Ch. la Violette
Ch. Certan Giraud
BEAUSÉJOUR
Clos du Clocher
Ch. Certan-de-May
Vieux Château Certan
BONALGUE
Ch. le Pin
Ch. la Pointe
Ch. Nénin
Ch. Petit Village
Ch. l'Evangile
Mauvais Temps
D244
Ch. la Conseillante
CATUSSEAU
la Brandaude
Ch. la Fleur du Roy
Libourne
Château Petit Village
la Bordette
Château la Pointe
ST.-EMILION
D243
Château Petrus

Kms 0·5 1·0
Mls ¼ ½

• Best château
⊙ Outstanding château
● Selected great château
— Communal Boundary

The vineyards of Vieux Château Certan, above
After Château Pétrus, this is one of the best wine-producing properties in Pomerol. A quaint signpost marks the boundary of the vineyard.

POMEROL, see also p.81

The sleepy country area of Pomerol and Lalande-de-Pomerol fans out above the riverside town of Libourne. None of the so-called "châteaux" is particularly imposing: among the most attractive are Château Nénin and Vieux Château Certan.

WHAT MAKES PÉTRUS THE WORLD'S MOST EXPENSIVE WINE?

Pétrus is the most expensive wine in the world. At the time of writing, a case of the 1961 vintage of Margaux, Mouton, Latour or Lafite fetches between £1,700 and £2,300 at auction, the 1967 vintage of Yquem £1,600 (the "lesser quality" 1961 £1,250) and the 1961 Romanée Conti a mere £900. The 1961 vintage of Krug Champagne must be considered a snip at just £900. Pétrus 1961 actually fetches £8,100. Why is it so special? The answer is nothing to do with the weather – there is no unique microclimate at Pétrus to conveniently explain its anomalous character and the neighbouring vineyards enjoy precisely the same climatic conditions. But there are other outstanding factors that influence the quality of the wine.

The Merlot grape
Of the 11.5 hectares (28 acres), barely four per cent is Cabernet franc; most of this is not used in the *Grand Vin* unless it is exceptionally ripe. Most Pétrus is virtually 100 per cent Merlot.

Frost
Pomerol is susceptible to frost and this quite often cuts the potential yield of its vineyards, producing wines of greater concentration.

Pruning
The famous firm that runs Château Pétrus, J.-P. Moueix, never relies on the frost for pruning and always restricts the number of buds to eight per vine. Ten buds would increase the yield by 25 per cent, but the wine would lose its essential Pétrus character.

Crop thinning
The cutting of healthy bunches of grapes in July is considered madness by most growers, but they are not making a wine as concentrated or as expensive as Pétrus.

Harvesting
Moueix has a highly-skilled force of 180 pickers for its empire of Libournais châteaux and they are all kept on alert for Château Pétrus. The day grapes reach perfect maturation

Château Pétrus, the greatest growth of Pomerol.

and there is no threat of rain, the entire force descends on Pétrus. They pick only in the afternoon, by which time the sun has evaporated all the dew that would otherwise dilute the wine. This also yields grapes at a temperature favourable to fermentation.

Vin de presse
This is not added during the *assemblage* of the *Grand Vin*, but is immediately mixed with the free-run juice. Christian Moueix believes that it

can take on a bitter taste if kept separately, but softens if allowed to age and develop with the *Grand Vin*.

Malolactic conversion
The process is encouraged to coincide with the alcoholic fermentation by adding lactic bacteria.

New oak
The wine is matured in wood for 18-22 months, with 100 per cent new oak.

The unique soil
As all the above factors affecting quality could be replicated by any of the neighbouring châteaux, the crucial remaining factor must be the soil. At last we find a unique situation – the so-called "buttonhole" of Pétrus, a geological anomaly that sets it apart from the rest. The "buttonhole" is situated in the centre of the gravelly area that overlaps St.-Emilion, the "Pomerol-Figeac" *graves* that is responsible for the outstanding quality of Cheval Blanc, Figeac and the best wines of Pomerol. Extraordinarily, it is the sandy-clay anomaly within it that is responsible for the even more outstanding quality of Pétrus. *See also* Soil description, p.93.

The "buttonhole" is no ordinary soil and the clay has no resemblance to the clay found close to the river, which produces rather coarse wine. Pétrus is positioned on a rise of *molasse* bedrock that was left bare when the bank of ancient gravel was laid down. Exposed to wind and water, the *molasse* was eroded and chemically altered, creating a sandy-clay. Subsequent decomposition and various climatic changes eventually formed three basic soil types: sandy-loam, sandy-clay-loam and clay. One aspect of these soils is that they are essentially acid and so produce wines that are inversely lower in acidity.

Pomerol country, above
Pomerol is flat and unprepossessing, divided into smallholdings and dotted with unpromising-looking properties that actually produce some fine wines.

Team of pickers in a Pomerol vineyard, left
The Moueix family, who own Château Pétrus and other good properties in the area, take the vendange *seriously, especially the decision of when to harvest. Christian Moueix says, "Things have to be done the day they have to be done".*

The great châteaux of Pomerol

CHÂTEAU BEAUREGARD

Production: *5,500 cases*

An American architect who visited Pomerol after the First World War built a replica called "Mille Fleurs" on Long Island, New York. The wine is matured in wood for 24 months with 30 per cent new oak.

RED A firm, elegant and lightly rich wine with floral-cedarwood fruit.

🍇 Cabernet sauvignon 6%, Cabernet franc 44%, Merlot 48%, Malbec 2%

🍷 1981, 1982, 1985

⌛ Between 5-10 years

Second Wine: "Domaine des Douves"

CHÂTEAU BONALGUE

Production: *2,000 cases*

This small property is on gravel and sand northwest of Libourne. The wine is matured in wood.

RED This medium-to full-bodied wine has always been of respectable quality with a frank attack of refreshing fruit flavours, a supple tannin structure and a crisp finish.

🍇 Cabernet franc and Cabernet sauvignon 30%, Merlot 65%, Malbec 5%

🍷 1981, 1982, 1983, 1985

⌛ Between 5-10 years

CHÂTEAU LE BON PASTEUR

Production: *3,500 cases*

This good and steadily improving wine is matured in wood for 24 months, with 35 per cent new oak.

RED These intensely coloured, full-bodied, complex wines are packed with *cassis*, plum and black-cherry flavours.

🍇 Cabernet franc 25%, Merlot 75%

🍷 1983, 1984, 1985, 1986, 1988

⌛ Between 8-25 years

CHÂTEAU BOURGNEUF-VAYRON

Production: *5,000 cases*

This property is situated close to Château Trotanoy. It has an honourable, if not exciting, record and a 25-hectare (10-acre) vineyard.

RED These wines are fresh and light, made in a quick-maturing style with soft fruit and a light herbal finish.

🍇 Cabernet franc 15%, Merlot 85%

🍷 1981, 1982, 1983, 1985

⌛ Between 4-8 years

CHÂTEAU LA CABANNE

Production: *5,000 cases*

A fine estate that is producing better and better wine. The wine is matured in wood for 18 months, with one-third new oak.

RED These are medium- to full-bodied wines with fine, rich, chocolatey-fruit.

🍇 Cabernet franc 30%, Merlot 60%, Malbec 10%

🍷 1982, 1983, 1985

⌛ Between 7-20 years

Second Wine: Château de Compostelle

CHÂTEAU CERTAN DE MAY DE CERTAN

Production: *2,000 cases*

This can be a confusing wine to identify as the "De May de Certan" part of its name is in much smaller type on the label and it is usually referred to as "Château Certan de May". It is matured in wood for 24 months, with 50 per cent new oak.

RED This firm and tannic wine has a powerful bouquet bursting with concentrated fruit, spice and vanilla.

🍇 Cabernet sauvignon and Malbec 10%, Cabernet franc 25%, Merlot 65%

🍷 1980, 1981, 1982, 1983, 1985, 1986, 1987, 1988, 1989

⌛ Between 15-35 years

CHÂTEAU CERTAN-GIRAUD

Production: *3,500 cases*

This property was once called Château Certan-Marzelle, but the name was changed in 1956. The wine is matured in wood for 24 months, with 15 per cent new oak.

RED These are ripe, voluptuous wines that improve with every vintage.

🍇 Cabernet franc and Cabernet sauvignon 33%, Merlot 67%

🍷 1982, 1985, 1986, 1988

⌛ Between 8-20 years

Other wines: Château Certan-Marzelle, "Clos du Roy"

CHÂTEAU CLINET

Production: *3,000 cases*

This wine, matured in wood with one-third new oak, will be a disappointment if you are looking for a typically fat, gushy-juicy Pomerol. Critics often blame this on the high proportion of Cabernet sauvignon, but the 1985 is promising.

RED The 1985 is plumper than previous years, with more juicy character.

🍇 Cabernet sauvignon 20%, Cabernet franc 20%, Merlot 60%

🍷 1985, 1988, 1989

⌛ Between 5-10 years

CLOS DU CLOCHER

Production: *3,000 cases*

This property has belonged to the Libournais *négociant* Audy since 1924. The wine is rotated in thirds between new oak, one-year-old casks and vat. It is probably one of the most undervalued Pomerols.

RED Deliciously deep-coloured, medium- to full-bodied wines that have plenty of plump, ripe fruit, a supple structure, intriguing vanilla undertones and plenty of finesse.

🍇 Cabernet 20%, Merlot 80%

🍷 1982, 1985, 1986, 1988, 1989

⌛ Between 8-20 years

Second Wine: Château Monregard-Lacroix

CHÂTEAU LA CONSEILLANTE

Production: *5,000 cases*

After the "megastar" status of Pétrus, this property must be rated at least a "superstar". The wine is matured in wood for 20-24 months, with 50 per cent new oak.

RED This wine has all the power and concentration of the greatest Pomerols, but its priorities are finesse and complexity; the result is mind-blowing.

🍇 Cabernet franc 45%, Merlot 45%, Malbec 10%

🍷 1980, 1981, 1982, 1983, 1985, 1986, 1988, 1989

⌛ Between 10-30 years

CHÂTEAU LA CROIX

Production: *4,500 cases*

This property is owned by the Société Civile J. Janoueix. The wine is matured in wood for 20-24 months.

RED These attractive wines are quite full-bodied, yet elegant and quick-maturing with fine spicy Merlot fruit.

🍇 Cabernet sauvignon 20%, Cabernet franc 20%, Merlot 60%

🍷 1981, 1982, 1983, 1985

⌛ Between 5-10 years

Second Wine: "Le Gabachot"

CHÂTEAU LA CROIX DE GAY

Production: *6,000 cases*

Situated in the north of Pomerol on sandy-gravel soil, this wine is matured in wood for 18 months, with up to 30 per cent new oak.

RED Somewhat lightweight, but honest, attractive and easy-to-drink.

🍇 Cabernet sauvignon 10%, Cabernet franc 10%, Merlot 80%

🍷 1983, 1985

⌛ Between 4-8 years

Other wines: Château le Commandeur, Vieux-Château-Groupey

CHÂTEAU DU DOMAINE DE L'EGLISE

Production: *3,000 cases*

This is the oldest estate in Pomerol. The wine is matured in wood for 18-24 months, with one-third new oak.

RED Another essentially elegant wine that is light in weight and fruit.

🍇 Cabernet franc 10%, Merlot 90%

🍷 1985, 1986

⌛ Between 4-8 years

CLOS L'EGLISE

Production: *2,500 cases*

Confusingly, there are several "Eglise" properties in Pomerol. The wine from this one is matured in wood for 24 months, with some new oak.

RED Consistently attractive wines with elegant, spicy Merlot fruit and a firm structure, eventually dominated by violet Cabernet perfumes.

- Cabernet sauvignon 25%, Cabernet franc 20%, Merlot 55%
- 1981, 1982, 1985, 1986
- Between 6-15 years

CHÂTEAU L'EGLISE-CLINET

Production: *2,500 cases*

This wine, matured in wood for up to 24 months with as much as 50 per cent new oak, is fast becoming one of the most exciting Pomerols.

RED Deeply coloured wines with a rich and seductive bouquet and a big, fat flavour bursting with spicy-blackcurrant fruit and creamy-vanilla oak.

- Cabernet franc 20%, Merlot 80%
- 1982, 1983, 1985, 1986, 1988
- Between 8-30 years

CHÂTEAU L'ENCLOS

Production: *5,000 cases*

The vineyard is situated on an extension of the sandy-gravel soil from the better side of the N89. The wine is matured in wood for 20 months, with a small proportion of new oak.

RED These are deliciously soft, rich and voluptuous wines, full of plump, juicy Merlot fruit and spice.

- Cabernet franc 19%, Merlot 80%, Malbec 1%
- 1982, 1983, 1985, 1986, 1988
- Between 7-15 years

CHÂTEAU L'EVANGILE

Production: *4,500 cases*

Run by the Ducasse family and situated close to two superstars of Pomerol, Vieux-Château-Certan and Conseillante, it is little wonder that the wines of this château, which are matured in wood for 15 months with one-third new oak, are excellent.

RED Dark but never brooding, these fruity wines are rich, packed with summer fruits and cedarwood.

- Cabernet franc and Cabernet sauvignon 29%, Merlot 71%
- 1983, 1985, 1986, 1988, 1989
- Between 8-20 years

CHÂTEAU FEYTIT-CLINET

Production: *2,800 cases*

Although not owned by J.-P. Moueix, he produces the wine and sells it on an exclusivity basis. Some vines are over 70 years old. The wine is matured in wood for 18-22 months.

RED Consistently well-coloured and stylish wines that are full of juicy plum and black-cherry flavours.

- Cabernet franc 20%, Merlot 80%
- 1982, 1983, 1985, 1986
- Between 7-15 years

CHÂTEAU LA FLEUR-PÉTRUS

Production: *3,000 cases*

One of the best Pomerols, situated close to Château Pétrus, but on more gravelly soil. The wine is matured in wood for 18-22 months.

RED Although recent vintages are relatively big and fat, these are essentially elegant wines that rely more on exquisiteness than richness. They are silky, soft and supple.

- Cabernet franc 20%, Merlot 80%
- 1985, 1986, 1987, 1988, 1989
- Between 6-20 years

CHÂTEAU LE GAY

Production: *2,800 cases*

This château is another that is exclusive to the Libournais *négociant* J.-P. Moueix. The wine is matured in wood for 18-22 months.

RED Firm and ripe, this big wine has dense fruit and coffee-toffee oak.

- Cabernet franc 30%, Merlot 70%
- 1982, 1983, 1985, 1986, 1988
- Between 10-25 years

CHÂTEAU GAZIN

Production: *10,000 cases*

The record has been disappointing until the stunning 1985. The wine is matured in wood for 18 months with up to one-third new oak.

RED The 1985 is a marvellously ripe and rich wine with a great future. The other vintages recommended are far less plump, but still of acceptable quality.

- Cabernet sauvignon 5%, Cabernet franc 15%, Merlot 80%
- 1981, 1982, 1985, 1986, 1988
- Between 8-20 years

CHÂTEAU LA GRAVE TRIGANT DE BOISSET

Production: *3,500 cases*

The gravelly vineyard of this property has an excellent location and the wines are improving as the vines begin to age. It is owned by Christian Moueix and farmed by J.-P. Moueix. The wine is matured in wood with 25 per cent new oak.

RED Not quite in the voluptuous and velvety mould, but this supple, rich and fruity, medium-bodied wine will get there. The 1986 is the best to date.

- Cabernet franc 5%, Merlot 95%
- 1982, 1985, 1986, 1988
- Between 7-15 years

CHÂTEAU LAFLEUR

Production: *1,500 cases*

This property has a potential for quality second only to Château Pétrus itself, but it has a very inconsistent record. Since 1981 it has been administered by the *négociant* J.-P. Moueix and the quality and concentration of the wines has soared.

RED This is a well-coloured wine with a rich, plummy-porty bouquet, masses of *cassis* fruit and a toasty-coffee oak complexity. The 1985 was stunning.

- Cabernet franc 50%, Merlot 50%
- 1982, 1983, 1985, 1986, 1988
- Between 10-25 years

CHÂTEAU LAFLEUR-GAZIN

Production: *3,500 cases*

This property has been run by the J.-P. Moueix team on behalf of its owners since 1976, and the wine is matured in wood for 18-22 months.

RED Well-made wines of good colour and bouquet, supple structure and some richness and concentration.

- Cabernet franc 30%, Merlot 70%
- 1982, 1983, 1985, 1986, 1988
- Between 6-15 years

CHÂTEAU LAGRANGE

Production: *3,500 cases*

Not to be confused with its namesake in St.-Julien, this property belongs to the firm J.-P. Moueix. The wine is aged in wood for 18-22 months, with some new oak.

RED Recent vintages of this full-bodied wine have been impressive, of an attractive and accessible style.

- Cabernet franc 10%, Merlot 90%
- 1982, 1985, 1986
- Between 8-20 years

CHÂTEAU LATOUR À POMEROL

Production: *2,500 cases*

This château belongs to the last surviving sister of Madame Labate, Madame Lily Lacoste (owner of one-third of Château Pétrus). The wine is matured in wood with 25 per cent new oak.

RED These deep, dark wines are luscious, voluptuous and velvety. They have a great concentration of fruit and a sensational complexity of flavours.

- Cabernet franc 10%, Merlot 90%
- 1980, 1981, 1982, 1983, 1985, 1986, 1988
- Between 12-35 years

CHÂTEAU MAZEYRES

Production: *4,500 cases*

Two-thirds of this wine is matured in wood with 25 per cent new oak, and one-third is aged in vat.

RED Not of top quality, but excellent nevertheless, these elegant wines are rich, ripe and juicy, and have silky Merlot fruit and some oaky finesse.

- Cabernet franc 30%, Merlot 70%
- 1980, 1982, 1983, 1985
- Between 5-12 years

CHÂTEAU MOULINET

Production: *7,500 cases*

This large estate belongs to Armand Moueix and its wine is matured in wood for 18 months, with one-third new oak.

RED Attractively supple wines with a light, creamy-ripe fruit and oak flavour.

- Cabernet sauvignon 30%, Cabernet franc 10%, Merlot 60%
- 1980, 1982, 1983, 1985
- Between 5-10 years

CHÂTEAU NÉNIN

Production: *12,000 cases*

A sizeable and well-known property situated between Catussau and the outskirts of Libourne. The wine has had a disappointing record.

RED The vintage recommended has little indication of the oak that is supposed to be used here. It is pleasant in a simple and fruity way.

- Cabernet sauvignon 20%, Cabernet franc 30%, Merlot 50%
- 1985
- Between 4-8 years

Second Wine: Château St. Roche

CHÂTEAU PETIT-VILLAGE

Production: *4,000 cases*

Owned by Bruno Prats, who also owns Château Cos d'Estournel in St.-Estèphe, this property borders Vieux-Château-Certan and Château La Conseillante. It therefore has the advantage of a superb *terroir* and a meticulous owner. The result is a wine of superstar quality, even in poor years. Petit-Village is matured in wood for 18 months with at least 50 per cent of the casks new oak.

RED These wines seem to have everything. Full and rich with lots of colour and unctuous fruit, they have a firm structure of ripe and supple tannins and a luscious, velvety texture. Classic, complex and complete.

- Cabernet sauvignon 10%, Cabernet franc 10%, Merlot 80%
- 1980, 1981, 1982, 1983, 1984, 1985
- Between 8-30 years

CHÂTEAU PÉTRUS

Production: *4,000 cases*

The Libournais *négociant* J.-P. Moueix has been in technical control of this estate since 1947. Before the previous owner, Madame Loubat, died in 1961, she gave one-third of Pétrus to Monsieur Moueix. She had no children, just two sisters who were not on the best of terms, so Madame Loubat wisely gave Moueix the means of ensuring that family disagreements would not harm the day-to-day running of Pétrus. In 1964 Moueix purchased one of the other two shares and has controlled the destiny of this château ever since.

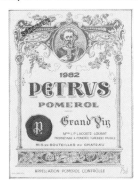

RED The low acidity of Château Pétrus makes it an intrinsically soft wine which, combined with the inherent lusciousness of the Merlot, enables Pétrus to produce intensely coloured, super-concentrated wines that would otherwise be too harsh to drink.

- Cabernet franc 5%, Merlot 95%
- 1983, 1985, 1986, 1988, 1989
- Between 20-50 years

CHÂTEAU LE PIN

Production: *350 cases*

This tiny one-hectare (2.5-acre) property was purchased in 1979 by the Thienpont family, the owners of neighbouring Vieux-Château-Certan. Since the 1981 vintage there has been a deliberate attempt to produce a wine of Pétrus-like dimensions, quality and, as you may have guessed, price. The yield is very low, the wine is fermented in stainless steel and matured in wood for 18 months with 100 per cent new oak. The Thienponts have taken a gamble. So far, however, the venture has worked perfectly – the vintages started well and have simply got better and better.

RED These oaky wines are very full-bodied, powerfully aromatic with a sensational spicy-*cassis* flavour dominated by decadently rich, creamy-toffee, toasty-coffee oak. Those who are not convinced by le Pin keep asking whether there is enough concentration in these wines to match the oak. My guess is that there is, but it will be a long time before we really know the answer.

- Cabernet franc 12%, Merlot 88%
- 1982, 1983, 1985, 1986, 1988
- Between 15-40 years

CHÂTEAU PLINCE

Production: *3,500 cases*

This property is owned by the Moreau family, but the wine is sold by J.-P. Moueix. It is matured in vat for six months and in wood for 18 months, with 15 per cent new oak.

RED These well-made wines are fat, ripe and ooze with juicy Merlot flavour. Not aristocratic but simply delicious.

- Cabernet sauvignon 5%, Cabernet franc 20%, Merlot 75%
- 1981, 1982, 1983, 1985, 1986
- Between 4-8 years

CHÂTEAU LA POINTE

Production: *10,000 cases*

Until recently, these light and lack-lustre wines have given me the impression of an overcropped vineyard. I hope 1985 will prove to be a turning point in the reputation of this important château. The wine is matured in wood for 18-20 months with 35 per cent new oak.

RED The vintages recommended have an elegant, stylish, ripe and oaky character missing from earlier vintages.

- Cabernet franc 15%, Merlot 80%, Malbec 5%
- 1985, 1986
- Between 5-12 years

CLOS RENÉ

Production: *5,500 cases*

This property is situated just south of l'Enclos on the western side of the N89. The wine is matured in wood for 24 months with up to 15 per cent new oak. An underrated wine, it represents good value.

RED These wines have a splendid spicy-blackcurrant bouquet, fine plummy fruit on the palate and a great deal of finesse. They can be complex and are always excellent quality.

- Cabernet franc 30%, Merlot 60%, Malbec 10%
- 1981, 1982, 1983, 1985, 1986
- Between 6-12 years

Other wines: Château Moulinet-Lasserre

CHÂTEAU ROUGET

Production: *6,000 cases*

One of the oldest properties in Pomerol, this château was listed as its fifth-best growth in the 1868 edition of *Cocks et Féret*. The current proprietor also owns the neighbouring estate of Vieux Château des Templiers. The wine is matured in wood for 24 months.

RED This is an excellent wine of fine bouquet and elegant flavour. A fat and rich wine that has lots of ripe fruit and good structure. It is at its most impressive when mature.

- Cabernet franc 10%, Merlot 90%
- 1982, 1983, 1985, 1986
- Between 10-25 years

CHÂTEAU DE SALES

Production: *20,000 cases*

At 48 hectares (119 acres), this is easily the largest property in the Pomerol appellation. It is situated in the very northwest of the district. Despite an uneven record, it has demonstrated its inherent qualities on many occasions and the wine, which is matured in wood for 18 months with 35 per cent new oak, is one to watch for the future.

RED When successful, these wines have a penetrating bouquet and a palate jam-packed with deliciously juicy flavours of succulent stone-fruits like plums, black cherries and apricots.

- Cabernet sauvignon 15%, Cabernet franc 15%, Merlot 70%
- 1982, 1985, 1986
- Between 7-20 years

Second Wine: Château Chantalouette
Other wines: Château de Délias

CHÂTEAU DU TAILHAS

Production: *5,000 cases*

The wines of this château are matured in wood for 18 months with 50 per cent new oak.

RED Consistently attractive wine with silky Merlot fruit and creamy oak.

- Cabernet sauvignon 10%, Cabernet franc 10%, Merlot 80%
- 1980, 1982, 1983, 1985
- Between 5-12 years

CHÂTEAU TAILLEFER

Production: *7,500 cases*

This excellent property has been in the hands of Armand Moueix since 1926. The wines are matured in wood for 18-22 months, with some new oak.

RED Of the 1980 vintages, I have tasted only the two recommended below. Both are very attractive, fruity wines.

- Cabernet sauvignon 15%, Cabernet franc 30%, Merlot 55%
- 1982, 1983
- Between 4-8 years

Second Wine: Clos Toulifaut

CHÂTEAU TROTANOY

Production: *3,000 cases*

This great growth is considered second only to Pétrus. The wine is matured in wood for up to 24 months, with 50 per cent new oak.

RED This inky-black, brooding wine has a powerful bouquet and a rich flavour of plums, black cherries and chocolate, supported by a firm tannin structure and a complex, creamy-toffee, spicy-coffee oak character. The 1985 is of extraordinary quality.

- Cabernet franc 10%, Merlot 90%
- 1982, 1983, 1985, 1986, 1988
- Between 15-35 years

VIEUX CHÂTEAU CERTAN

Production: *6,000 cases*

This was once regarded as the finest quality growth in Pomerol. It has not so much dropped its standards as witnessed the rapid rise of a new star – Pétrus. This wine is matured in wood for 18-24 months with up to 60 per cent new oak.

RED This garnet-coloured, full-bodied wine has a smouldering, smooth and mellow flavour that displays great finesse and complexity.

🍇 Cabernet sauvignon 20%, Cabernet franc 25%, Merlot 50%, Malbec 5%

🍷 1982, 1983, 1985, 1986, 1988

🍾 Between 12-35 years

Second Wine: "La Gravette de Certan"

CHÂTEAU LA VIOLETTE

Production: *1,800 cases*

As Château Laroze in St.-Emilion is supposed to be named after its aroma of roses, so this château is named after its aroma of violets – or so the story goes. It is located in Catussau and its vineyards are scattered about the commune. The wine, matured in wood for up to 24 months, can be inconsistent, but I think it has great potential.

RED Unfortunately I have not tasted this wine as frequently as I would wish, but I can enthusiastically recommend the two vintages below. They have a rich and jubilant flavour of Merlot fruit, which is ripe and fat.

🍇 Cabernet franc 5%, Merlot 95%

🍷 1982, 1985

🍾 Between 5-15 years

CHÂTEAU VRAY CROIX DE GAY

Production: *2,000 cases*

A small property on good gravelly soil next to Château le Gay and under the same ownership as Château le Prieuré. The wine is matured in wood for 18 months.

RED The 1982 is a full, rich, chocolate- and black-cherry-flavoured wine, the 1985 shows more fat and oak.

🍇 Cabernet sauvignon 5%, Cabernet franc 15%, Merlot 80%

🍷 1982, 1985, 1988

🍾 Between 5-10 years

The best châteaux of the Pomerol and St.-Emilion satellites

CHÂTEAU DES ANNEREAUX

AOC Lalande-de-Pomerol and Néac

Attractive, fruity, medium-bodied wines of some elegance.

CHÂTEAU BEL-AIR

AOC Puisseguin-St.-Emilion

This property makes generous, fruity, early-drinking wines.

CHÂTEAU DE BEL-AIR

AOC Lalande-de-Pomerol and Néac

One of the best of the appellation, this property has fine sandy gravel.

CHÂTEAU BELAIR-MONTAIGUILLON

AOC St.-Georges-St.-Emilion

Consistently rich, deliciously fruity.

CHÂTEAU DE BELCIER

AOC Bordeaux-Côtes-de-Francs and Bordeaux Supérieur Côtes-de-Francs

This property produces fruity wines that can claim the Côtes de Castillon or Côtes de Francs appellations.

CHÂTEAU CALON

AOC Montagne-St.-Emilion

Under the same ownership as *Grand Cru Classé* Château Corbin-Michotte. Good quality, juicy style, very Merlot in character.

CHÂTEAU CALON

AOC St.-Georges-St.-Emilion

A small portion of this Montagne-St.-Emilion vineyard falls within the St.-Georges-St.-Emilion area and is thus sold under this appellation.

CHÂTEAU CANON

AOC Côtes Canon-Fronsac

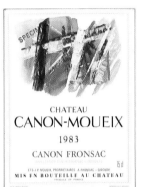

Tiny 1.5 hectare (3.7 acre) property owned by Christian Moueix of Château Pétrus, producing the best wine in this appellation.

CHÂTEAU CANON DE BREM

AOC Côtes Canon-Fronsac

Much larger than Château Canon, but this property still receives the full Moueix treatment and produces fine, firm and flavoursome *vins de garde* that are deep coloured and powerful, yet complex and spicy.

Second Wine: Château Pichelèbre

CHÂTEAU CAP DE MERLE

AOC Lussac-St.-Emilion

Wine guru Robert Parker's best Lussac performer for 1981-3 vintages.

CHÂTEAU CASSAGNE-HAUT-CANON

AOC Côtes Canon-Fronsac

Full, fat, fruit-cake flavoured wines that are attractive when young.

CHÂTEAU CASTEGENS

AOC Bordeaux-Côtes-de-Castillon and Bordeaux Supérieur Côtes-de-Castillon

Good quality, medium-bodied, red.

Other wines: Château de Fontenay

CHÂTEAU DE CLOTTE

AOC Bordeaux-Côtes-de-Castillon and Bordeaux Supérieur Côtes-de-Castillon

This property, with an average annual red wine production of 6,000 cases, has the right to Côtes de Castillon or Côtes de Francs appellations, but uses only the former.

CHÂTEAU DU COURLAT

AOC Lussac-St.-Emilion

Spicy-tannic wine with good fruit.

CHÂTEAU COUSTOLLE VINCENT

AOC Côtes Canon-Fronsac

Well-flavoured wines matured in up to 20 per cent new oak.

CHÂTEAU DALEM

AOC Fronsac

Soft, velvety wines that develop quickly yet retain their freshness.

CHÂTEAU DE LA DAUPHINE

AOC Fronsac

Fresh and fruity wines matured in oak, 20 per cent of which is new.

CHÂTEAU DURAND LAPLAIGNE

AOC Puisseguin-St.-Emilion

Clay-limestone soil, strict selection of grapes and modern vinification produce excellent quality wine.

CHÂTEAU DU GABY

AOC Côtes Canon-Fronsac

Intensely flavoured, well-structured wines designed for long life.

CHÂTEAU GRAND-BARIL

AOC Montagne-St.-Emilion

Attractive, fruity wine made by the agricultural school in Libourne.

CHÂTEAU HAUT-CHAIGNEAU

AOC Lalande-de-Pomerol and Néac

An excellent Néac property making plump, plummy, high-quality wines.

CHÂTEAU HAUT-CHATAIN

AOC Lalande-de-Pomerol and Néac

Fat, rich and juicy wines with definite hints of new-oak vanilla.

CHÂTEAU HAUT-TUQUET

AOC Bordeaux-Côtes-de-Castillon and Bordeaux Supérieur Côtes-de-Castillon. Consistently good red.

CHÂTEAU LES HAUTS-CONSEILLANTS

AOC Lalande-de-Pomerol and Néac

Another fine Néac property.

Other wines: Château les Hauts-Tuileries (export label)

CHÂTEAU JUNAYME

AOC Côtes Canon-Fronsac

Well-known wines of finesse.

CHÂTEAU JEANDEMAN

AOC Fronsac

Fresh, fruity wines with good aroma.

CHÂTEAU DES LAURETS

AOC Puisseguin-St.-Emilion

The largest in the appellation.

Other wines: Château la Rochette, Château Maison Rose

CHÂTEAU DE LUSSAC

AOC Lussac-St.-Emilion

Well-balanced, early-drinking wine.

CHÂTEAU DU LYONNAT

AOC Lussac-St.-Emilion

The largest in the appellation.

Other wines: "la Rose Peruchon"

CHÂTEAU MAISON BLANCHE

AOC Montagne-St.-Emilion

Attractive, fruity, easy-drinking wine.

CHÂTEAU MAQUIN-ST.-GEORGES

AOC St.-Georges-St.-Emilion

Attractive 70 per cent Merlot wine.

Other wines: Château Bellonne-St.-Georges

CHÂTEAU MAUSSE

AOC Côtes Canon-Fronsac

Flavoursome wines with good aroma.

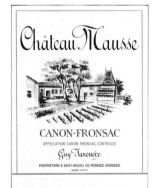

CHÂTEAU MAYNE-VIEIL

AOC Fronsac

Easy to drink wines with good Merlot spice and fruit.

CHÂTEAU MAZERIS

AOC Côtes Canon-Fronsac

There is an unusually high proportion of Cabernet sauvignon in these wines.

CHÂTEAU MILON

AOC Lussac-St.-Emilion

A château that produces a fine-quality, full yet fragrant wine.

CHÂTEAU MONCETS

AOC Lalande-de-Pomerol and Néac

This Néac property makes a fine, rich and elegant, Pomerol lookalike.

CHÂTEAU MOULIN HAUT-LAROQUE

AOC Fronsac

Well-perfumed, quite fat wines with lots of fruit and good tannin.

CHÂTEAU MOULIN NEUF

AOC Bordeaux-Côtes-de-Castillon and Bordeaux Supérieur Côtes-de-Castillon

These wines regularly win medals.

CHÂTEAU MOULIN ROUGE

AOC Bordeaux-Côtes-de-Castillon and Bordeaux Supérieur Côtes-de-Castillon

Easy-drinking, medium-bodied red.

CHÂTEAU LA PAPETERIE

AOC Montagne-St.-Emilion

Rich nose and big fruit-filled palate.

CHÂTEAU DU PONT DE GUESTRES

AOC Lalande-de-Pomerol and Néac

Full, ripe, fat wines of quality.

CHÂTEAU DU PUY

AOC Bordeaux-Côtes-de-Francs and Bordeaux Supérieur Côtes-de-Francs

Overtly fruity, rustic red wines.

CHÂTEAU PUYCARPIN

AOC Bordeaux-Côtes-de-Castillon and Bordeaux Supérieur Côtes-de-Castillon

Well-made red, plus a little dry white.

CHÂTEAU PUYGUERAUD

AOC Bordeaux-Côtes-de-Francs and Bordeaux Supérieur Côtes-de-Francs

Aromatically attractive wines with good colour and supple fruit.

CHÂTEAU LA RIVIÈRE

AOC Fronsac

Magnificent wines matured in up to 40 per cent new oak and built to last.

CHÂTEAU ROBIN

AOC Bordeaux Côtes-de-Castillon and Bordeaux Supérieur Côtes-de-Castillon

Award-winning red wines.

CHÂTEAU ROCHER-BELLEVUE

AOC Bordeaux-Côtes-de-Castillon and Bordeaux Supérieur Côtes-de-Castillon

Good St.-Emilion lookalike that regularly wins medals.

Other wines: "la Palène", "Coutet-St.-Magne"

CHÂTEAU ROUDIER

AOC Montagne-St.-Emilion

Quality wines that are well coloured, full of rich flavours, finely balanced, long and supple.

CHÂTEAU SIAURAC

AOC Lalande-de-Pomerol and Néac

Fine, firm and fruity wines.

CHÂTEAU ST.-GEORGES

AOC St.-Georges-St.-Emilion

Super quality wine of great finesse.

CHÂTEAU TARREYO

AOC Bordeaux-Côtes-de-Castillon and Bordeaux Supérieur Côtes-de-Castillon

This vineyard is sited on a limestone mound, as its name, which is Gascon for "knoll of stones", suggests.

CHÂTEAU THIBAUD-BELLEVUE

AOC Bordeaux-Côtes-de-Castillon and Bordeaux Supérieur Côtes-de-Castillon

Medium-bodied, fruity red wine.

CHÂTEAU TOUMALIN

AOC Côtes Canon-Fronsac

Fresh, fruity wine from a property under the same ownership as Château La Pointe in Pomerol.

CHÂTEAU TOUR-DU-PAS-ST.-GEORGES

AOC St.-Georges-St.-Emilion

An excellent and relatively inexpensive *entrée* into the world of *Premier Cru* claret.

CHÂTEAU DES TOURELLES

AOC Lalande-de-Pomerol and Néac

Fine, firm, attractive wines with soft fruit and vanilla undertones.

CHÂTEAU TOURNEFEUILLE

AOC Lalande-de-Pomerol and Néac

The best wine of the appellation, this is big, rich and long-lived.

CHÂTEAU DES TOURS

AOC Montagne-St.-Emilion

Owned by Marne & Champagne, this is the largest property in the appellation. The wine is big, full and fleshy, yet soft and easy to drink.

CHÂTEAU LA VALADE

AOC Fronsac

Elegant, aromatic and silky-textured wines made from Merlot grapes only.

CHÂTEAU LA VIEILLE CURE

AOC Fronsac

Clean, well made wines, showing good fruit, that are easy to drink after three or four years.

CHÂTEAU VILLARS

AOC Fronsac

Soft, fat and juicy wines of excellent quality, one-third of which spend time in new oak.

VIEUX-CHÂTEAU-ST.-ANDRÉ

AOC Montagne-St.-Emilion

Soft, exciting wine, full of cherries, vanilla and spice flavours. Owned and made by Jean-Claude Berrouet, the resident oenologist at Pétrus.

CHÂTEAU VRAI-CANON-BOYER

AOC Côtes Canon-Fronsac

Fruity, medium-bodied wine that is attractive for early drinking.

Bourg and Blaye

Ninety-five per cent of the wine produced here is good-value red. Tiny Bourg makes more wine than its five-times-larger neighbour, Blaye, and most of the vines grown in Blaye come from a cluster of châteaux close to the borders of Bourg.

AS ONE WOULD EXPECT OF AN AREA that has supported a settlement for 400,000 years, Bourg has a close-knit community. Comparatively recently, the Romans used neighbouring Blaye as a *castrum*, a fortified area in the defence system that shielded Bordeaux. According to some sources, the vine was cultivated in Bourg and Blaye as soon as the Romans arrived. Vineyards were certainly flourishing here long before those of the Médoc just the other side of the Gironde.

Bourg is a compact, heavily cultivated area with pretty hillside vineyards at every turn. The vine is less important in Blaye, which has other interests, including a caviare industry based at its ancient fishing port where sturgeon is still a major catch. The vineyards of Blaye are mostly clustered in the countryside immediately bordering Bourg, and, despite the similarity of the countryside, traditionally produce the slightly inferior wine. The D18 appears to be a barrier beyond which the less intensely cultivated hinterland takes on a totally different topography, where the more expansive scenery is dotted with lonely forests.

THE POTENTIAL OF BOURG AND BLAYE

To the Romans, these south-facing vineyards overlooking the Gironde seemed the ideal place to plant vines. Because they failed, understandably, to realize the possibilities that the Médoc concealed beyond its virtually impenetrable marshes, it does not necessarily follow that they were wrong about Bourg and Blaye. Indeed, the quality achieved today in these vineyards would have surpassed the most optimistic hopes of those past masters of the vine. Since their time, new and different concepts of classic wine have relegated this district to a viticultural backwater, but its potential remains the same. In twenty years time, when we have at long last discovered Fronsac and elevated Canon-Fronsac to a level equivalent to that of Pomerol, I am convinced that we will wake up to the potential of these wines. When we pay higher prices, this will enable the proprietors to restrict yields, improve vinification techniques and indulge in a percentage of new oak.

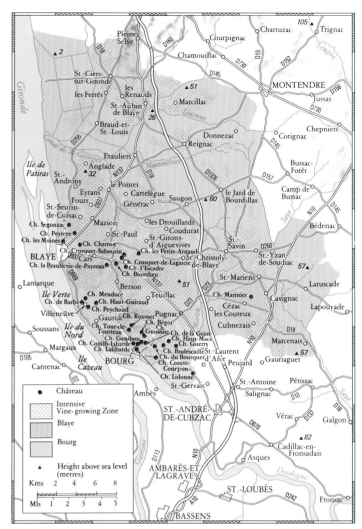

BOURG AND BLAYE, see also p.37

Most of the best growths of Bourg and Blaye are clustered behind the respective ports that give this wine-producing area its name. Bourg, the smaller area, has a higher concentration of vineyards and generally produces the better wines.

FACTORS AFFECTING TASTE AND QUALITY

 Location
The vineyards fan out behind the town of Bourg, situated on the right bank of the confluence of the Dordogne and the Garonne, some 20 kilometres (12.5 miles) north of Bordeaux. Blaye is a larger district that unfolds beyond Bourg.

Climate
These two areas are less protected than the Médoc from westerly and northwesterly winds, and have a higher rainfall.

Aspect
Bourg is very hilly with vines cultivated on steep limestone hills and knolls up to a height of 80 metres (260 ft). In the southern section of Blaye the country is rich and hilly, with steep slopes overlooking the Gironde that are really just a continuation of those in Bourg. The northern areas are gentle and the hills lower, with marshes bordering the viticultural areas.

 Soil
In Bourg the topsoil is clay-limestone or clay-gravel over a hard limestone subsoil, although in the east the subsoil sometimes gives way to gravel and clay. The soil in the Blaye is clay or clay-limestone over hard limestone on the hills overlooking the Gironde, getting progressively sandier going east.

Viticulture and vinification
There are many grape varieties here, some of which are far too inferior or unreliable to contribute to the quality of these wines, particularly the whites. Bourg produces the best reds, Blaye the best whites, but there is relatively little white wine made in both appellations – even Blaye is 90 per cent red and Bourg is in excess of 99 per cent red. Very few *petits châteaux* in both areas can afford the use of casks, let alone new ones, and much of the wine in Bourg is made by one of its five *coopératives*.

Primary grape varieties
Cabernet franc, Cabernet sauvignon, Merlot, Sauvignon blanc, Sémillon

Secondary grape varieties
Malbec, Prolongeau, Cahors, Béguignol (Fer), Petit verdot, Merlot blanc, Folle blanche, Colombard, Chenin blanc, Muscadelle, Ugni blanc

The town of Blaye, above
The attractive fishing port of Blaye with, in the foreground, the ruins of its ancient citadel guarding the approach of marauders from the sea.

The wines of Bourg and Blaye

The number of appellations in this area, and their various differences, are very confusing for the consumer. It is time the system was tidied up and there is no reason why just two AOCs – Côtes de Blaye and Côtes de Bourg – could not be used for all the wines produced in this district.

BLAYE AOC

A large and diverse appellation of variable quality.

RED This is almost a theoretical possibility, for few properties cultivate the more obscure varieties it allows and thus prefer to use the superior-sounding Premières Côtes de Blaye appellation.

🍇 Cabernet sauvignon, Cabernet franc, Merlot, Malbec, Prolongeau, Béguignol, Petit verdot

🍷 1985, 1986, 1988, 1989, 1990

🌡 Between 3-7 years

WHITE The best are predominantly Sauvignon blanc wines, but even these are simply fresh, dry, light and pleasant. This was once a catchment area for distillation wines for Cognac, hence the range of high-yielding, low-alcohol, high-acidity grapes and the intrinsically poor drinking wines they produce.

🍇 Merlot blanc, Folle blanche, Colombard, Chenin blanc, Sémillon, Sauvignon blanc, Muscadelle, Ugni blanc

🍷 1984, 1985, 1986, 1989, 1990

🌡 Within 1-2 years

BLAYAIS AOC
See Blaye AOC.

BOURG AOC

This appellation, which covers both red and white wines, has fallen into disuse because the growers prefer to use the Côtes de Bourg AOC, which is easier to market but conforms to the same regulations (*see* Côtes de Bourg AOC).

BOURGEAIS AOC
See Bourg AOC.

CÔTES DE BLAYE AOC

Unlike the Bourg and Côtes de Bourg appellations, which cover red and white wines, Côtes de Blaye is white only. Blaye, however, may be red or white.

WHITE As much white Côtes de Blaye is produced as basic Blaye. The wines are similar in style and quality.

🍇 Merlot blanc, Folle blanche, Colombard, Chenin blanc, Sémillon, Sauvignon blanc, Muscadelle

🍷 1983, 1985, 1986, 1989, 1990

🌡 Within 1-2 years

CÔTES DE BOURG AOC

Bourg is one-fifth of the size of Blaye, yet it traditionally produces a greater quantity and, more importantly, a much finer quality of wine than Blaye.

RED Excellent value wines of good colour, which are full of solid, fruity flavour. Many are very stylish indeed.

🍇 Cabernet sauvignon, Cabernet franc, Merlot, Malbec

🍷 1985, 1986, 1988, 1989, 1990

🌡 Between 3-10 years

WHITE A very small quantity of this light, dry wine is produced and sold each year.

🍇 Sémillon, Sauvignon blanc, Muscadelle, Merlot blanc, Colombard, plus a maximum of 10% Chenin blanc

🍷 1983, 1985, 1986, 1989, 1990

🌡 Within 1-2 years

PREMIÈRES CÔTES DE BLAYE AOC

This covers the same area as Blaye and Côtes de Blaye, but only classic grapes are used and the minimum alcoholic strength is higher. The area has very good potential for quality.

RED There are one or two excellent properties that use a little new oak.

🍇 Cabernet sauvignon, Cabernet franc, Merlot, Malbec

🍷 1985, 1986, 1988, 1989, 1990

🌡 Between 4-10 years

WHITE Dry, light-bodied wines that may have a fresh, lively, grapey flavour.

🍇 Sémillon, Sauvignon blanc, Muscadelle

🍷 1984, 1985, 1986, 1989, 1990

🌡 Within 1-2 years

The best châteaux of Bourg

CHÂTEAU DE BARBE
Villeneuve,
33710 Bourg-sur-Gironde

Substantial production of easy-drinking, light-styled, Merlot-dominated, gently fruity red wine.

CHÂTEAU BÉGOT
Lansac,
33710 Bourg-sur-Gironde

Some 5,000 cases of agreeably fruity red wine, best drunk young.

CHÂTEAU BRULESCAILLE
Tauriac,
33710 Bourg-sur-Gironde

Well-sited vineyards producing agreeable wines for early drinking.

CHÂTEAU DU BOUSQUET
33710 Bourg-sur-Gironde

Large, well-known château producing some 40,000 cases of red wine of excellent value for money. Fermented in stainless steel and aged in oak, it has a big bouquet and a smooth feel.

CHÂTEAU CONILH-LIBARDE
33710 Bourg-sur-Gironde

Soft, fruity red wine from a small vineyard overlooking Bourg-sur-Gironde and the river.

CHÂTEAU CROUTE-COURPON
33710 Bourg-sur-Gironde

A small but recently enlarged estate producing honest, fruity red wines.

CHÂTEAU EYQUEM
Bayon-sur-Gironde,
33710 Bourg-sur-Gironde

Owned by the serious winemaking Bayle-Carreau family which also owns several other properties. This wine is not normally, however, purchased for its quality. It is enjoyable as a light luncheon claret, but the real joy is in the spoof of serving a red Eyquem.

CHÂTEAU GÉNIBON
33710 Bourg-sur-Gironde

Small vineyard producing attractive wines that have all the enjoyment upfront and are easy to drink.

CHÂTEAU GRAND-LAUNAY
Teuillac,
33710 Bourg-sur-Gironde

This property has been developed from the vineyards of three estates: Domaine Haut-Launay, Château Launay and Domaine les Hermats. It produces mainly red wine, although a very tiny amount of white is also made. The star-performing wine at this château is a superb, special reserve *cuvée* of red that is sold under the Château Lion Noir label.

CHÂTEAU DE LA GRAVE
33710 Bourg-sur-Gironde

Important property situated on one of the highest points of Bourg-sur-Gironde, producing a large quantity of light, fruity red wine and a very tiny amount of white.

CHÂTEAU GUERRY
Tauriac,
33710 Bourg-sur-Gironde

Some 10,000 cases of really fine wood-aged red wines that have good structure, bags of fruit and a smooth, elegant flavour.

CHÂTEAU GUIONNE
Lansac,
33710 Bourg-sur-Gironde

Easy-drinking wines, full of attractive Merlot fruit, giving a good juicy flavour and some finesse. A little white wine of some interest and depth is also made.

CHÂTEAU HAUT-GUIRAUD
St.-Ciers-de-Canesse,
33710 Bourg-sur-Gironde

Red-only château producing medium- to full-bodied, well-structured red wine teeming with ripe fruit flavours. Under the same ownership as châteaux Castaing and Guiraud-Grimard in the same commune.

CHÂTEAU HAUT-MACÔ
Tauriac,
33710 Bourg-sur-Gironde

Deceptively light-looking, rustic red wine, full of rich, fruity flavours, and good acidity. The proprietors also own a property called Domaine de Lilotte in Bourg-sur-Gironde producing attractive, early drinking red wines under the Bordeaux Supérieur appellation.

Other wines: "Les Bascauds"

CHÂTEAU HAUT-ROUSSET
33710 Bourg-sur-Gironde

A fairly large property producing some 12,000 cases of decent, everyday drinking red wine and 1,000 cases of white. The red wines from a small vineyard close by are sold under the Château la Renardière label.

CHÂTEAU DE LIDONNE
33710 Bourg-sur-Gironde

This very old property produces an excellent quality red wine, powerfully aromatic and full of Cabernet character. Its name comes from the fifteenth-century monks who looked after the estate and offered lodgings to passing pilgrims: "Lit-Donne" or "Give Bed".

CHÂTEAU MENDOCE
Villeneuve,
33710 Bourg-sur-Gironde

The reputation of this turreted château is well deserved; it produces a rich red wine, which is full, smooth and lingers on the palate.

CHÂTEAU PEYCHAUD
Teuillac,
33710 Bourg-sur-Gironde

This fine property produces attractive, elegant and fruity red wines that are easy to drink when young, and a small amount of white. The proprietors also own Château Peyredoulle in the Blayais commune of Berson and the Bordeaux AOC of Château le Peuy-Saincrit.

CHÂTEAU ROUSSET
Samonac,
33710 Bourg-sur-Gironde

Fine estate of gravel vineyards producing lightly rich, juicy, Merlot-dominated wines of some finesse; they are perfect to drink when two or three years old.

CHÂTEAU SAUMAN
Villeneuve,
33710 Bourg-sur-Gironde

Immaculate vineyards producing a good-quality red wine for medium-term maturity. The proprietor also owns the red-wine producing Domaine du Moulin de Mendoce in the same commune.

CHÂTEAU TOUR-DE-TOURTEAU
Samonsac,
33710 Bourg-sur-Gironde

This property was once part of Château Rousset. These wines are, however, definitely bigger and richer than those of Rousset.

The best châteaux of Blaye

CHÂTEAU BARBÉ
Cars,
33390 Blaye

Well-made, overtly fruity red and white wines. One of several properties owned by the Bayle-Carreau family.

CHÂTEAU BOURDIEU
Berson,
33390 Blaye

An old and well known property producing Cabernet-dominated red wines of a very firm structure that receive time in oak. Seven hundred years ago this estate was accorded the privilege of selling "clairet", a tradition it maintains today by aging the blended production of various vineyards in oak. White wines of an improving quality are also made.

CHÂTEAU LA CARELLE
St.-Paul,
33390 Blaye

More than 11,000 cases of agreeable red wines and just 1,500 cases of white are made. Under the same ownership as châteaux Barbé and Pardaillan in Cars.

CHÂTEAU DE CASTETS
Plassac,
33390 Blaye

Promising property producing attractive red and white wines for early drinking.

CHÂTEAU CHARRON
St.-Martin-Lacaussade,
33390 Blaye

Very attractive, well-made, juicy-rich, Merlot-dominated red wine matured in oak, some of which is new. A small amount of white wine is also made.

CHÂTEAU CRUSQUET-DE-LAGARCIE
Cars,
33390 Blaye

Red wine of a tremendously exciting quality: deep coloured, bright, big and richly styled, full of fruit, vanilla and spice. A small amount of dry white wine is sold under the name "Clos-des-Rudel" and an even smaller quantity of sweet white wine as "Clos-Blanc de Lagarcie". The châteaux Les-Princesses-de-Lagarcie and Touzignan, also in Cars, are under the same ownership.

CHÂTEAU L'ESCADRE
Cars,
33390 Blaye

Well-coloured, full, fruity and elegant red wines that can be enjoyed young, but also improve with age. A small amount of fruity white wine is also produced.

DOMAINE DU GRAND BARRAIL
Plassac,
33390 Blaye

Fine-quality red wine that attracts by its purity of fruit, and a small production of white wine. The proprietor also owns Château Gardut-Haut-Cluzeau and Domaine du Cavalier in Cars.

CHÂTEAU DU GRAND PIERRE
Berson,
33390 Blaye

If the 1982 vintage is anything to go by, this property can produce tremendous value medium- to full-bodied red wine with sweet ripe fruit. Some white wine is also made.

CHÂTEAU DE HAUT SOCIONDO
Cars,
33390 Blaye

Agreeably light and fruity red and white wines.

CHÂTEAU LAMANCEAU
St.-Androny,
33390 Blaye

Production at this property is entirely red and of an excellent standard: richly coloured wine full of the juicy spice of Merlot.

CHÂTEAU MARINIER
Cézac,
33620 Cavignac

Twice as much red wine as white is produced. The red is agreeably fruity, but the white is much the better wine: smooth, well balanced, lightly rich and elegant. Red and rosé wines are also produced under the Bordeaux appellation.

CHÂTEAU MENAUDAT
St.-Androny,
33390 Blaye

Extremely attractive, full and fruity red wines.

CHÂTEAU LES MOINES
33390 Blaye

A red-only château, producing a light- to medium-bodied, fresh and fruity wine for easy drinking.

CHÂTEAU PARDAILLAN
Cars,
33390 Blaye

Well made, enjoyable, fruity red wines that are best drunk young.

CHÂTEAU LES PETITS ARNAUDS
Cars,
33390 Blaye

Attractively aromatic red wines, pleasingly round and fruity. Dry white Blaye and a *moelleux* white Bordeaux are also produced.

CHÂTEAU PEYREDOULLE
Berson,
33390 Blaye

Medium sized property producing a good quality of mainly red wine, although some white is also made. The proprietors also own Château Peychaud in the Bourgais commune of Teuillac and the Bordeaux AOC of Château le Peuy-Saincrit.

CHÂTEAU PEYREYRE
St.-Martin-Lacaussade,
33390 Blaye

Well-structured, rich-flavoured red wines of some finesse. Bordeaux Rosé is also made.

CHÂTEAU SEGONZAC
St.-Genès-de-Blaye,
33390 Blaye

Easy-drinking red wines that are light, well made, fresh, firm and agreeably fruity.

Entre-Deux-Mers

Entre-Deux-Mers ("between two seas") is situated between the Dordogne and Garonne rivers. It is Bordeaux's largest district, and produces dry white wines of modest but rapidly improving quality, plus an increasing volume of red wines entitled to the Bordeaux or Bordeaux Supérieur appellations.

IT IS A LONG TIME SINCE THIS DISTRICT was infamous for its over-sulphured, tired and flabby, semi-sweet white wine that used to catch the back of the throat and cause the eyes to water. Indeed, that sort of unforgiveable product persisted in the more respectable Graves district far longer than it did in Entre-Deux-Mers. Although the regulations were changed in 1977 to prohibit anything other than dry white wines for this appellation, this did not mean that the consumer was protected from unpalatable wines; the bureaucrats merely acknowledged what was happening in this large winemaking district and tailored the law to fit.

As early as the 1950s and 1960s there was a grass-roots viticultural movement to drop the traditional vine-training systems and adopt the revolutionary "high-culture" system. This was followed by a widespread adoption of cool-fermentation techniques in the 1970s. With fresh, light and attractively dry white wines being made at many châteaux, the major export markets suddenly realized it would be easier to sell Entre-Deux-Mers than what had become boring Bordeaux blanc, particularly if the wine could boast some sort of individual *petit château* personality.

Château Mouchac, right
This exceedingly pretty château, situated in Grézillac and owned by the ancient family of Du Serech de St.-Avit, produces AOC Bordeaux Supérieur wines.

Château Bonnet, below
In 1898 this vineyard was acquired by Léonce Recapet, one of the first to carry out replanting after the devastation of the Gironde vineyard by phylloxera at the turn of the century. His son-in-law, François Lurton, succeeded him, and in 1956 his grandson, André Lurton, became the owner.

THE "HIGH-CULTURE" SYSTEM

Entre-Deux-Mers in the late 1940s and early 1950s was a sorry place. The wines were sold in bulk, ending up as anonymous Bordeaux blanc, and much of the decline in the Bordeaux region was centred on the district. But the new post-war generation of winegrowers were not content with this state of affairs. Although times were difficult and the economy was deteriorating, the young, technically-minded *vignerons* realized that the district's compressed *boulbènes* soil, which was choking the vines, could not be worked by their fathers' old methods and they therefore took a considerable financial risk to rectify the situation. They grubbed up every other row of vines, thus increasing the spacing between the rows, and trained the plants on a "high-culture" system similar to that practised in Madiran and Jurançon further south (also in Austria where it was originally conceived and called the Lenz Möser system). This allowed machinery to work the land and break up the soil. It also increased the canopy of foliage, intensifying chlorophyll assimilation and improving ripening.

COOL FERMENTATION

In the 1970s university-trained personnel at the well-funded Entre-Deux-Mers *coopératives* invested in temperature-controlled stainless-steel vats and led the way in cool-fermentation

Harvesting near Le Puch, above
Since the 1950s, Entre-Deux-Mers has been one of the more technically up-to-date areas in the Bordeaux region.

Château du Grand Puch, below
Owned by the Société Viticole du Château de Grand Puch, this château is a well-preserved example of thirteenth-century architecture.

ENTRE-DEUX-MERS,

See also p.37

The varied countryside of this district spreads out between the rivers Dordogne and Garonne as their paths diverge. The Premières Côtes form a narrow strip along the south side.

techniques. Prior to this, fermentation temperatures were often in excess of 28°C (83°F), but it was soon discovered that the lower the temperature, the more aromatic compounds were released. They found out that fermentation can take place at temperatures as low as 4°C (39°F), but the risk of stuck-fermentation was high. It soon became clear that the ideal fermentation temperature, reckoned to be somewhere between 10°C (50°F) and 18°C (64°F) (only recently has it been confirmed that 18°C (64°F) is the optimum), increased the yield of alcohol and important aromatic and flavour compounds. It also reduced both the loss of carbonic gas and the presence of volatile acidity and required less sulphur dioxide.

FACTORS AFFECTING TASTE AND QUALITY

Location
A large area east of Bordeaux between the Garonne and Dordogne rivers.

Climate
More blustery and wetter than the Médoc; liable to flood near the rivers.

Aspect
Quiet and very attractive countryside of vine-covered hillsides, orchards and meadows.

Soil
Very varied topsoils, ranging from alluvium by the river to gravel on some hillsides and crests, and clay-gravel or clay-limestone on various plateaux. At the western end of the district a soil called *boulbènes* dominates. This is extremely fine and sandy and has a tendency to compress into an impermeable barrier. Vines have to be grafted onto special root-stock in order to be productive in such soil. Much of the subsoil is limestone or limestone-based, but others include sandy-clay, clay/limestone rubble, a quarry stone called *aslar* and a sandstone containing gravel and iron deposits called *ribot*.

Viticulture and vinification
This area is famed for its "high and wide" method of vine training, which was developed in the early 1950s and is similar to the Lenz Möser system used in Austria. Greater emphasis is now placed on the Sauvignon grape and cool-fermentation in stainless-steel vats.

Primary grape varieties
Sémillon, Sauvignon blanc, Muscadelle

Secondary grape varieties
Merlot blanc, Colombard, Mauzac, Ugni blanc

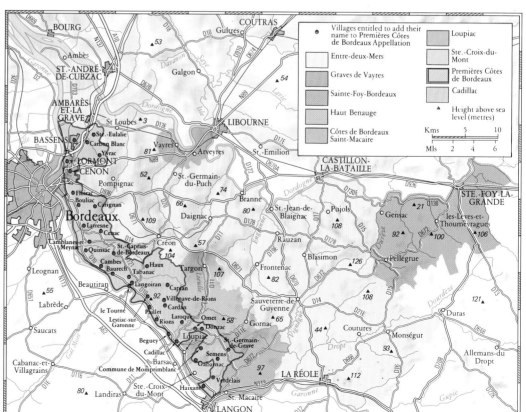

The wines of the Entre-Deux-Mers

BORDEAUX HAUT-BENAUGE AOC

Situated above the Premières Côtes, opposite Cérons, this area corresponds to the ancient and tiny county of Benauge. To claim this appellation, as opposed to Entre-Deux-Mers-Haut-Benauge, the grapes are restricted to the three classic varieties and must be riper, containing a minimum of 195 grams per litre of sugar instead of 170 grams per litre. The yield is 10 per cent lower and the minimum alcoholic level 1.5 per cent higher.

WHITE Dry, medium-sweet and sweet versions of this light-bodied, fruity wine may be made.

🍇 Sémillon, Sauvignon blanc, Muscadelle

🗓 1985 (dry and medium-sweet), 1986, 1989, 1990

🍷 Within 1-3 years for dry and medium-sweet wines; between 3-6 years for sweet wines

CADILLAC AOC

Of the trio of sweet-wine areas on the right bank of the Garonne, Cadillac is the least known. It encompasses 21 communes, 16 of which form the canton of Cadillac, yet very little wine is produced under its appellation. On average about 2,000 hectolitres (22,222 cases) are produced, the equivalent of one-fifth of that made in Loupiac, and one-tenth that made in St.-Croix-du-Mont. The regulations state that the wine must be made from botrytized grapes harvested in successive *tries,* but there is little evidence of this in the wines, which at best have the character of *passerillage.* The *terroir* could produce wines of a much superior quality, but it would be costly to do so, and sadly, this appellation does not fetch a high enough price to justify the investment.

WHITE Attractive honey-gold wines with fresh, floral aromas and a semi-sweet or sweet, fruity flavour.

🍇 Sémillon, Sauvignon blanc, Muscadelle

🗓 1983, 1986, 1988, 1989, 1990

🍷 Between 3-8 years

CÔTES-DE-BORDEAUX-ST.-MACAIRE AOC

This little-seen wine comes from an area at the eastern extremity of the Premières-Côtes-de-Bordeaux. Of the 2,300 hectares (6,000 acres) that may use this appellation, barely 30 hectares (75 acres) bother to do so.

WHITE Medium-bodied, medium-sweet or sweet wines that are attractive in a fruity way, but unpretentious.

🍇 Sémillon, Sauvignon blanc, Muscadelle

🗓 1985, 1986, 1988, 1989, 1990

🍷 Within 1-3 years

ENTRE-DEUX-MERS AOC

This is the largest district in the region, and after the generic Bordeaux blanc, it is its greatest volume white wine appellation. Entre-Deux-Mers has a growing reputation for exceptional-value wines of a high technical standard.

WHITE Crisp, dry, light-bodied wines that are fragrant, aromatic and usually predominantly Sauvignon blanc. These are clean, cool-fermented wines.

🍇 At least 70% Sémillon, Sauvignon blanc and Muscadelle, plus a maximum of 30% Merlot blanc and up to 10% in total of Colombard, Mauzac and Ugni blanc

🗓 1984, 1985, 1986, 1989, 1990

🍷 Within 1-2 years

ENTRE-DEUX-MERS-HAUT-BENAUGE AOC

This wine comes from the same nine communes that comprise the Bordeaux-Haut-Benauge appellation, but it must be dry and its blend may include various other grape varieties. The wines comply with the less rigorous regulations of Entre-Deux-Mers and, consequently, the volume produced under this dry-wine-only AOC is four times the amount of Bordeaux-Haut-Benauge. The only exception was 1983, a luscious vintage that arrived when it was easy to make sweet wines.

WHITE These dry wines are very similar to Entre-Deux-Mers.

🍇 At least 70% Sémillon, Sauvignon blanc and Muscadelle, plus a maximum of 30% Merlot blanc and up to 10% in total of Colombard, Mauzac and Ugni blanc

🗓 1984, 1985, 1986, 1989, 1990

🍷 Within 1-3 years

GRAVES DE VAYRES AOC

An enclave of gravelly soil on the left bank of the Dordogne that produces a substantial quantity (30,000 hectolitres, 333,000 cases) of excellent-value red and white wine.

RED Well-coloured, aromatic, medium-bodied wines with fragrant, juicy-spicy, predominantly Merlot fruit. These wines are richer than those found elsewhere in the Entre-Deux-Mers.

🍇 Cabernet sauvignon, Cabernet franc, Carmenère, Merlot, Malbec, Petit verdot

🗓 1983, 1985, 1988, 1989, 1990

🍷 Between 4-10 years

WHITE Mostly dry and off-dry styles of fresh, fragrant and fruity wines made for early drinking. Occasionally, sweeter styles are made.

🍇 Sémillon, Sauvignon blanc and Muscadelle plus a maximum of 30% Merlot blanc

🗓 1984, 1985, 1986, 1989, 1990

🍷 Within 1-3 years

LOUPIAC AOC

This appellation is located on the right bank of the Garonne, opposite Barsac. It is by far the best sweet-wine appellation in the Entre-Deux-Mers and its wines are always excellent value. According to the regulations, Loupiac must be made with the "assistance" of overripe botrytis grapes and, unlike Cadillac, these wines often have the honeyed complexity of "noble rot". The best wines come from vineyards with clay-limestone soil.

WHITE Luscious medium- to full-bodied wines that are sweet or intensely sweet, honey-rich and flavourful. They can be quite complex, and in suitable years have evident botrytis character.

🍇 Sémillon, Sauvignon blanc, Muscadelle

🗓 1983, 1986, 1988, 1989, 1990

🍷 Between 5-15 years (25 in exceptional cases)

PREMIÈRES-CÔTES-DE-BORDEAUX AOC

A 60-kilometre (37-mile) strip of southwest-facing slopes covering 37 communes, each of which has the right to add its name to this appellation. They are: Bassens, Carbon Blanc, Lormont, Cenon, Floirac, Bouliac, Carignan, La Tresne, Cenac, Camblanes, Quinsac, Cambes, St.-Caprais-de-Bordeaux, Haux, Tabanac, Baurech, Le Tourne, Lang-oiran, Capian, Lestiac, Paillet, Ville-nave de Rions, Cardan, Rions, Laroque, Béguey, Omet, Donzac, Cadillac, Monprimblanc, Gabarnac, Semens, Verdelais, St.-Maixant, Ste.-Eulalie, St.-Germain-de-Graves, Yvrac.

RED The best red wines come from the northern communes. These well-coloured, soft and fruity wines are a cut above basic Bordeaux AOC.

🍇 Cabernet sauvignon, Cabernet franc, Carmenère, Merlot, Malbec, Petit verdot

🗓 1981, 1982, 1983, 1985, 1986

🍷 Between 4-8 years

WHITE

WHITE Since the 1981 harvest no dry wines have been allowed under this generally unexciting appellation. They must have at least some sweetness, and most are in fact semi-sweet. Simple, fruity wines, well made for the most part, but lacking character.

🍇 Sémillon, Sauvignon blanc, Muscadelle

🗓 1983, 1986, 1988, 1989, 1990

🍷 Between 3-7 years

STE.-CROIX-DU-MONT AOC

This is the second-best sweet white appellation on the right bank of the Garonne, and it regularly produces more wine than Barsac. Like Loupiac, it must be made with the "assistance" of overripe botrytis grapes. The wines have less honeyed complexity of "noble rot" than Loupiac, but often more finesse.

WHITE Fine, viscous, honey-sweet wines that are lighter in body and colour than Loupiac. Excellent value when they have rich botrytis character.

🍇 Sémillon, Sauvignon blanc, Muscadelle

🗓 1983, 1986, 1988, 1989, 1990

🍷 Between 5-15 years (25 in exceptional cases)

STE.-FOY-BORDEAUX AOC

Until relatively recently Ste.-Foy-Bordeaux was known primarily for its white wines, but it now produces as much red as white. There appears to be an unusually high proportion of "organic" winemakers in this area.

RED Ruby-coloured, medium-bodied wine made in a soft, easy drinking style.

🍇 Cabernet Sauvignon, Cabernet franc, Merlot, Malbec, Petit verdot

🗓 1982, 1983, 1985

🍷 Between 3-7 years

WHITE Mellow, semi-sweet wines of uninspiring quality, and fresh, crisp, dry white wines that have good aroma and make attractive early drinking.

🍇 Sémillon, Sauvignon blanc and Muscadelle, plus a combined maximum of 10% Merlot blanc, Colombard, Mauzac and Ugni blanc

🗓 1982, 1983, 1985, 1986

🍷 Within 1-3 years

The best châteaux of the Entre-Deux-Mers

CHATEAU LA BLANQUERIE
Mérignas,
33350 Castillon-la-Bataille

Dry white wine with a Sauvignon character and a fine finish.

CHATEAU BONNET
Grézillac,
33420 Branne

André Lurton's top-performing Entre-Deux-Mers château. Crisp and characterful white wines and extremely successful, soft and fruity red wines (Bordeaux Supérieur).

Other wines: Château Tour-de-Bonnet, Château Gourmin, Château Peyraud

CHATEAU CANET
Guillac,
33420 Branne

Excellent white wines that are clean and crisp with good fruit and an elegant balance.

CHATEAU FONGRAVE
Gornac,
33420 Branne

Fresh and tangy dry white wines.

CHATEAU GOUMIN
Dardenac,
33420 Branne

Another successful André Lurton château. Goumin produces up to 10,000 cases of pleasant, soft and fruity red wine and 5,000 cases of white wine that is slightly fuller than other similar Lurton products.

CHATEAU GRAND MONTEIL
Salleboeuf,
33370 Tresses

Annual production reaches barely more than a thousand cases of white, but 35,000 cases of excellent-quality, soft and quaffing red.

CHATEAU LATOUR
St.-Martin-du-Puy,
33540 Sauveterre-de-Guyenne

From this ancient château, parts of which date back to the fourteenth century, 10,000 cases of attractive, well-balanced, smooth red Bordeaux Supérieur are produced every year. This château's technically sound wines often win prizes.

CHATEAU LAUNAY
Soussac,
33790 Pellegrue

This large property produces 40,000 cases of a fresh, dry white wine and 15,000 cases of a red wine sold under the "Haut-Castanet" label.

Other wines; Château Bradoire, Château Dubory, Château Haut-Courgeaux, Château La Vaillante

CHATEAU MOULIN DE LAUNAY
Soussac,
33790 Pellegrue

Despite the vast quantity of dry white wine produced it is crisp, fruity and of a very fine standard. A little red is also produced.

Other wines; Château Plessis, Château Tertre-de-Launay, Château de Tuilerie, Château la Vigerie

CHATEAU PEYREBON
Grézillac,
33420 Branne

This château produces red and white wine in almost equal quantities. The dry white is a fine, flavoursome wine.

CHATEAU THIEULEY
La Sauve,
33670 Créon

Run by Professor Courselle, a former Médoc professor of viticulture and oenology, the dry white combines good fruit with a fine Sauvignon style. His silky red is also very good.

The best châteaux of the Entre-Deux-Mers satellites

CHATEAU ARNAUD-JOUAN
33410 Cadillac

AOC Premières-Côtes-de-Bordeaux and Cadillac

Large, well-situated vineyard, making interesting and attractive wines.

DOMAINE DU BARRAIL
Monprimblanc,
33410 Cadillac,

AOC Premières-Côtes-de-Bordeaux and Cadillac

The red Premières Côtes and sweet white Cadillac produced at this property are worth watching.

CHATEAU BALLUE-MONDON
AOC Ste.-Foy-de-Bordeaux

This château produces 4,000 cases of "organic" red Bordeaux AOC.

CHATEAU DE BEAUREGARD
AOC Entre-Deux-Mers and Bordeaux-Haut-Benauge

Well-made red and white wines. The red has good structure, but is softened by the spice of the Merlot.

CHATEAU BEL-AIR
Vayres

AOC Graves de Vayres

Most of the well-coloured wines made here are red. They are aromatic wines of a Cabernet character.

CHATEAU BIROT
Béguey,
33410 Cadillac

AOC Premières-Côtes-de-Bordeaux and Cadillac

Popular for its easy-drinking whites, this property also produces well-balanced red wines of some finesse.

CHATEAU LA BOURGETTE
AOC Ste.-Foy-de-Bordeaux

A very old estate producing some of the most successful wines of the area. Two-thirds of the production is red, one-third white. Both are sold under the Bordeaux appellation.

CHATEAU BRÉTHOUS
Camblannes-et-Meynac,
33360 Latresne

AOC Premières-Côtes-de-Bordeaux and Cadillac

Red wines that are forward and overtly attractive, yet well-structured and succulent sweet white wines.

DOMAINE DE CHASTELET
Quinsac,
33360 Latresne

AOC Premières-Côtes-de-Bordeaux and Cadillac

A red wine that is complex, hinting of vanilla, well balanced and extraordinarily long.

CHATEAU LA CLYDE
Tabanac,
33550 Langoiran

AOC Premières-Côtes-de-Bordeaux and Cadillac

Aromatic, deep-coloured, ruby-red wines, showing good spice and fruit. The white has finesse and balance.

CHATEAU COURSOU
AOC Ste.-Foy-de-Bordeaux

"Organic" red and white wines claiming Bordeaux Supérieur and Bordeaux appellations, respectively.

CHATEAU DU CROS
AOC Loupiac

The fine, fat and succulent sweet wines of this château are among the best of the appellation.

CHATEAU DINTRANS
Ste.-Eulalie,
33560 Carbon-Blanc

AOC Premières-Côtes-de-Bordeaux and Cadillac

Nicely coloured, fruity red wines.

CHATEAU FAYAU
33410 Cadillac

AOC Premières-Côtes-de-Bordeaux and Cadillac

Succulent sweet wines in addition to red, clairet and dry white.

Other wines: Clos des Capucins

CHATEAU LE GARDERA
33550 Langoiran

AOC Premières-Côtes-de-Bordeaux and Cadillac

A soft red, produced by Cordier.

CHATEAU DE GORCE
Haux,
33550 Langoiran

AOC Premières-Côtes-de-Bordeaux and Cadillac

Fruity red and fresh, floral white.

CHATEAU GOUDICHAUD
Vayres

AOC Graves de Vayres

This property also extends into St.-Germain-du-Puch in the Entre-Deux-Mers, where it produces some very respectable wines.

CHATEAU GRAVELINES
Sémens,
33490 Cadillac

AOC Premières-Côtes-de-Bordeaux and Cadillac

This large property produces equal quantities of excellent red and white.

CHATEAU DU GUA
33440 Ambarès-et-Lagrave

AOC Premières-Côtes-de-Bordeaux and Cadillac

An attractive, well-structured red wine is produced from this eight-hectare (20-acre) vineyard of fine gravel.

CHÂTEAU HAUT-BRIGNON
Cénac,
33360 Latresne

AOC Premières-Côtes-de-Bordeaux and Cadillac

An improving château producing 150,000 cases of red and 10,000 cases of white.

CLOS JEAN
AOC Loupiac

Similar quality to Château du Cros, but more ethereal in character.

CHÂTEAU DU JUGE
33410 Cadillac

AOC Premières-Côtes-de-Bordeaux and Cadillac

Respectable red and dry white wines and, in some years, a little sweet white of high quality and extraordinarily good value.

CHÂTEAU DU JUGE
Haux,
33550 Langoiran

AOC Premières-Côtes-de-Bordeaux and Cadillac

Promising red wines that are full of easy-drinking, juicy fruit flavours and decent, if unexciting, whites.

CHÂTEAU LABATUT
St.-Maixant,
33490 Cadillac

AOC Premières-Côtes-de-Bordeaux and Cadillac

Well-coloured, aromatic, flavoursome red wines plus decent dry and exceptionally well-balanced sweet white wines. Red wines are also made at Château Fayon.

CHÂTEAU LAFITTE
Camblannes-et-Meynac,
33360 Latresne

AOC Premières-Côtes-de-Bordeaux and Cadillac

Nothing like the real thing, of course, but the wine is decent, well structured and capable of improving with age – a cheap way to get a Château Lafitte on the table, even if it is not *the* Château Lafite.

CHÂTEAU LAFUE
AOC Ste.-Croix-du-Mont

Attractive, sweet white wines that have a more fruity character than botrytis. Nearly one-quarter of the production is red wine.

CHÂTEAU LAMOTHE
Haux,
33550 Langoiran

AOC Premières-Côtes-de-Bordeaux and Cadillac

Some exceptionally good wines have been produced in recent years at this château, which derives its name from "La Motte", a rocky spur that protects the vineyard.

CHÂTEAU LATOUR
Camblannes-et-Meynac,
33360 Latresne

AOC Premières-Côtes-de-Bordeaux and Cadillac

An everyday drinking claret with a prestigious name.

CHÂTEAU LAURETTE
AOC Ste.-Croix-du-Mont

Under the same ownership as Château Lafue, and run along similar lines.

CHÂTEAU LOUBENS
AOC Ste.-Croix-du-Mont

This château produces rich, liquorous, superbly balanced sweet white wines. Dry wines are sold as "Fleur Blanc" and a little red is made.

Other wines: "Fleur Blanc de Château Loubens"

CHÂTEAU LOUPIAC-GAUDIET
AOC Loupiac

Fine, honey-rich sweet wines hinting of crystallized fruit.

CHÂTEAU LOUSTEAU-VIEIL
AOC Ste.-Croix-du-Mont

This property produces richly flavoured high-quality sweet wines.

CHÂTEAU DE LUGUGNAC
AOC Ste.-Foy-de-Bordeaux

This romantic fifteenth-century château produces a substantial quantity of attractive red wine.

CHÂTEAU MACHORRE
AOC Côtes-de-Bordeaux-St.-Macaire

The sweet white wine of this château has an attractive, fresh, fruit-salad flavour and is one of the best examples of the appellation. Very respectable red and dry Sauvignon wines are also produced, which are sold under the Bordeaux appellations.

CHÂTEAU DES MAILLES
AOC Ste.-Croix-du-Mont

Capable of producing some truly outstanding sweet wines, but can sometimes be disappointing.

CHÂTEAU LA MAUBASTIT
AOC Ste.-Foy-de-Bordeaux

Some 5,000 cases of white and 2,000 of red, both "organic" wines, are sold under the Bordeaux appellation.

CHÂTEAU MAZARIN
AOC Loupiac

Excellent sweet white wines.

CHÂTEAU MORLAN-TUILIÈRE
AOC Entre-Deux-Mers-Haut-Benauge and Bordeaux Haut-Benauge

One of the best properties of the area, producing a vibrant, crystal-clear Entre-Deux-Mers-Haut-Benauge, a Bordeaux Supérieur in the *moelleux* style, and a fairly full-bodied red AOC Bordeaux.

CHÂTEAU MOULIN DE ROMAGE
AOC Ste.-Foy-de-Bordeaux

The château produces equal quantities of "organic" red and white.

CHÂTEAU PETIT-PEY
AOC Côtes-de-Bordeaux-St.-Macaire

Good, sweet, white St.-Macaire and agreeably soft red Bordeaux.

CHÂTEAU PEYRINES
AOC Entre-Deux-Mers-Haut-Benauge and Bordeaux Haut-Benauge

The vineyard of this château has an excellent southern exposure and produces fruity red and white wines.

CHÂTEAU PICHON-BELLEVUE
Vayres

AOC Graves de Vayres

The red wines are variable but the dry whites are delicate and refined.

CHÂTEAU PONTETTE-BELLEGRAVE
Vayres

AOC Graves de Vayres

This property has a reputation for fine, subtly flavoured, dry white wines.

CHÂTEAU LA RAME
AOC Ste.-Croix-du-Mont

One of the top wines of the appellation, La Rame can have marvellous fruit, cream and honey flavours.

CHÂTEAU REYNON-PEYRAT
Béguey,
33410 Cadillac

AOC Premières-Côtes-de-Bordeaux

This property produces a superb, oak-aged Premières Côtes red wine and, under the Château Reynon label, two dry white wines.

CHÂTEAU RICAUD
AOC Loupiac

The wines of this property were once the best in the appellation, but suffered a decline and are now recovering under new ownership.

CHÂTEAU ROC DE CAYLA
AOC Entre-Deux-Mers-Haut-Benauge and Bordeaux Haut-Benauge

Twice as much red wine as white is produced on this little property.

CHÂTEAU LE RONDAILH
AOC Côtes-de-Bordeaux-St.-Macaire

Attractive, deeply coloured wines.

CHÂTEAU DE LA SABLIÈRE-FONGRAVE
AOC Entre-Deux-Mers-Haut-Benauge and Bordeaux Haut-Benauge

Sold as a Bordeaux Supérieur, the red wine is fairly robust and requires time in bottle to soften. A much better-quality dry white is produced and sold under the Entre-Deux-Mers appellation.

CHÂTEAU TANESSE
33550 Langoiran

AOC Premières-Côtes-de-Bordeaux and Cadillac

A Cordier property producing decent Cabernet-dominated red and fine-quality Sauvignon-styled, dry white.

CHÂTEAU DES TASTES
AOC Ste.-Croix-du-Mont

A truly exciting sweet white wine: luxurious in texture, with creamy-rich flavours and showing the classic complex character of botrytis.

CHÂTEAU TERFORT
AOC Ste.-Croix-du-Mont

Small production of excellent sweet white wine.

CHÂTEAU DE TOUTIGEAC
AOC Entre-Deux-Mers-Haut-Benauge and Bordeaux Haut-Benauge

This well-known property's full, rich, red wine made for early drinking, is the best.

Burgundy

The Burgundy region, which stretches from Champagne to the Rhône, produces the greatest Chardonnay and Pinot noir wines in the world, and the only Gamay wines ever to achieve classic status.

BURGUNDY IS AN AREA RICH IN HISTORY, gastronomy and wine; unlike the great estates of Bordeaux, the finest Burgundian vineyards are owned by a proliferation of smallholders, a direct result of the Revolution. Prior to 1789 the church owned most of the vineyards in Burgundy, but these were seized and broken up, the new order being as much anti-church as anti-aristocracy. While some of the large Bordeaux estates were owned by the aristocracy, many were owned by the bourgeois, who, because of their long association with the English, were anti-papist, and so escaped the full wrath of the Revolution. Burgundy's great vineyards were further fragmented by inheritance laws, which divided the plots into smaller and smaller parcels. Consequently, many are now owned by as many as 85 individual growers.

The initial effect of this proprietorial carve-up was to encourage the supremacy of the *négoce*. Few commercial houses had been established prior to the mid-eighteenth century because of the difficulty of exporting from a land-locked area, but with better transport and no opposition from land-owning aristocracy, merchant power grew rapidly. A network of brokers evolved in which dealers became experts on very small, localized areas. As ownership diversified even further, it became a very specialized, and therefore rewarding, job to keep an up-to-date and comprehensive knowledge of a very complex situation. The brokers were vital to the success of a *négociant*, and the *négoce* itself was essential to the success of international trade – and therefore responsible for establishing the reputation of Burgundy.

The role of the *négociant*

In Burgundy, more than anywhere else in France, it has become fashionable to decry the value of the merchant, to condemn the quality of his wines and to infer that every wine he produces is blended into an anonymous, expressionless product inferior to those produced by the growers. Much of this is unfair.

The merchant not only established the reputation of Burgundy (based on the wines produced from its greatest vineyards), but he is as crucial today as he has ever been to its continuance. Remove the merchant and the numerous growers would have no ready-made markets to sell their wines to, nor could they maintain their international image which, like it or not, is vital in selling to the world's increasingly sophisticated consumer markets. To say that a merchant's wines are poor *per se* is nonsense; there are good and bad merchants, just as there are good and bad growers. That many merchants are also growers who own superbly run estates is often overlooked. While it is logical that their greatest and most expressive wines will be those from their own domaine, this is not a justification to decry the fine, although admittedly not great, quality of a good merchant's blended wine. A blended wine may not be expressive of a single *terroir*, but blending does not necessarily result in anonymity; it can in fact build character (Champagne is a case in point). It is true that many of Burgundy's vineyards do not make individually complete and satisfying wines – some are even notorious for producing very inferior wines – but mixed together and blended with, perhaps, a judicious amount of wine not included in the merchant's *cuvée* of certain *Premiers* and *Grands Crus*, the result can be a large quantity of honest Burgundy that is enjoyable and affordable. And, by using the lesser wines of the greatest of Burgundy's vineyards to bolster those from the most modest, it enables a stricter selection of wines for famous *crus*.

As long as there is a demand for Burgundian wines there will always be an important role for the merchant to play. I am an enthusiastic supporter of the great number of growers who consistently and conspicuously produce many of the region's most fabulous wines, but, unlike those who would like to see the merchants' power diminish further, I think there are circumstances where it would be healthy to have it increased. Both consumers and Burgundians would benefit, for example, if one of the top firms purchased some of the most fragmented, such as Clos de Vougeot (owned by 85 growers who produce wines ranging from nectar to cabbage-water), and blended wines together from the component parts after a rigorous selection.

HOW TO READ BURGUNDY LABELS

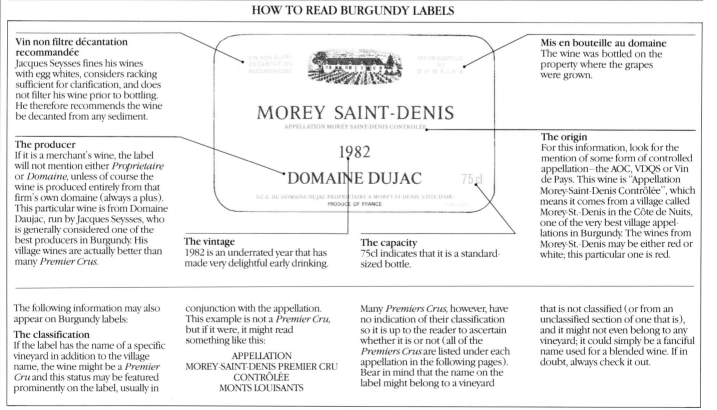

Vin non filtre décantation recommandée
Jacques Seysses fines his wines with egg whites, considers racking sufficient for clarification, and does not filter his wine prior to bottling. He therefore recommends the wine be decanted from any sediment.

The producer
If it is a merchant's wine, the label will not mention either *Proprietaire* or *Domaine*, unless of course the wine is produced entirely from that firm's own domaine (always a plus). This particular wine is from Domaine Daujac, run by Jacques Seysses, who is generally considered one of the best producers in Burgundy. His village wines are actually better than many *Premier Crus*.

Mis en bouteille au domaine
The wine was bottled on the property where the grapes were grown.

The origin
For this information, look for the mention of some form of controlled appellation – the AOC, VDQS or Vin de Pays. This wine is "Appellation Morey-Saint-Denis Contrôlée", which means it comes from a village called Morey-St.-Denis in the Côte de Nuits, one of the very best village appellations in Burgundy. The wines from Morey-St.-Denis may be either red or white; this particular one is red.

The vintage
1982 is an underrated year that has made very delightful early drinking.

The capacity
75cl indicates that it is a standard-sized bottle.

MOREY SAINT-DENIS
APPELLATION MOREY SAINT-DENIS CONTRÔLÉE

1982

DOMAINE DUJAC   75cl

S.C.E. DU DOMAINE DUJAC PROPRIETAIRE A MOREY ST-DENIS (CÔTE-D'OR)
PRODUCE OF FRANCE

The following information may also appear on Burgundy labels:

The classification
If the label has the name of a specific vineyard in addition to the village name, the wine might be a *Premier Cru* and this status may be featured prominently on the label, usually in

conjunction with the appellation. This example is not a *Premier Cru*, but if it were, it might read something like this:

APPELLATION
MOREY-SAINT-DENIS PREMIER CRU
CONTRÔLÉE
MONTS LOUISANTS

Many *Premiers Crus*, however, have no indication of their classification so it is up to the reader to ascertain whether it is or not (all of the *Premiers Crus* are listed under each appellation in the following pages). Bear in mind that the name on the label might belong to a vineyard

that is not classified (or from an unclassified section of one that is), and it might not even belong to any vineyard; it could simply be a fanciful name used for a blended wine. If in doubt, always check it out.

BURGUNDY

The route between Dijon and Lyon is studded with the illustrious names of the great growths of Burgundy. Above this north-south band are the Yonne appellations that include Chablis.

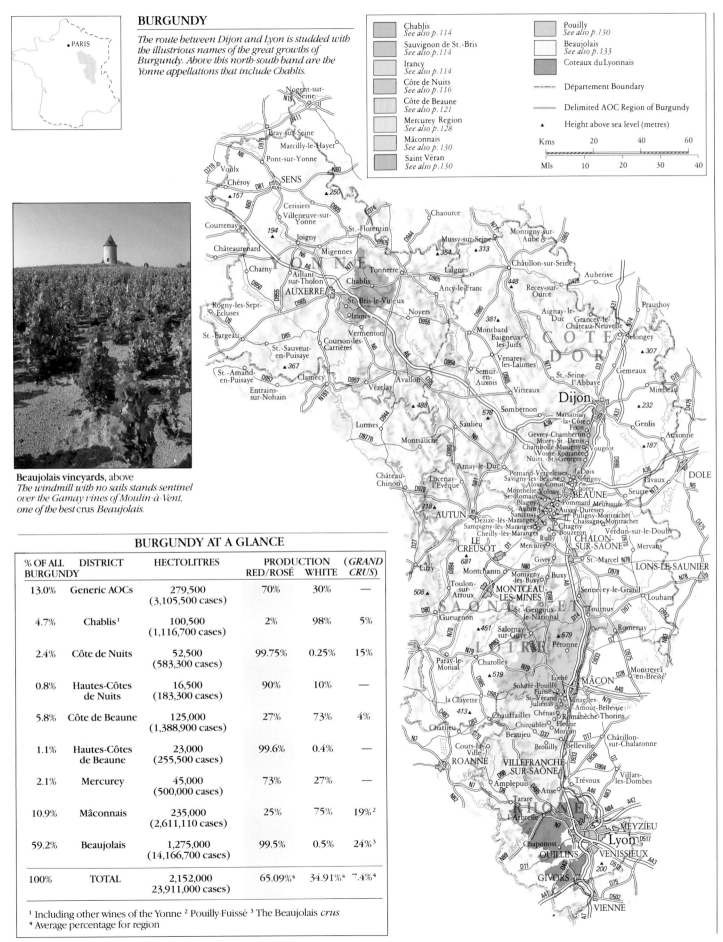

Legend:

- Chablis *See also p.114*
- Sauvignon de St.-Bris *See also p.114*
- Irancy *See also p.114*
- Côte de Nuits *See also p.116*
- Côte de Beaune *See also p.121*
- Mercurey Region *See also p.128*
- Mâconnais *See also p.130*
- Saint Véran *See also p.130*
- Pouilly *See also p.130*
- Beaujolais *See also p.133*
- Coteaux du Lyonnais
- –·–·– Département Boundary
- —— Delimited AOC Region of Burgundy
- ▲ Height above sea level (metres)

Kms 20 40 60
Mls 10 20 30 40

Beaujolais vineyards, above
The windmill with no sails stands sentinel over the Gamay vines of Moulin-à-Vent, one of the best crus *Beaujolais.*

BURGUNDY AT A GLANCE

% OF ALL BURGUNDY	DISTRICT	HECTOLITRES	PRODUCTION RED/ROSÉ	WHITE	(GRAND CRUS)
13.0%	Generic AOCs	279,500 (3,105,500 cases)	70%	30%	—
4.7%	Chablis[1]	100,500 (1,116,700 cases)	2%	98%	5%
2.4%	Côte de Nuits	52,500 (583,300 cases)	99.75%	0.25%	15%
0.8%	Hautes-Côtes de Nuits	16,500 (183,300 cases)	90%	10%	—
5.8%	Côte de Beaune	125,000 (1,388,900 cases)	27%	73%	4%
1.1%	Hautes-Côtes de Beaune	23,000 (255,500 cases)	99.6%	0.4%	—
2.1%	Mercurey	45,000 (500,000 cases)	73%	27%	—
10.9%	Mâconnais	235,000 (2,611,110 cases)	25%	75%	19%[2]
59.2%	Beaujolais	1,275,000 (14,166,700 cases)	99.5%	0.5%	24%[3]
100%	TOTAL	2,152,000 23,911,000 cases)	65.09%[4]	34.91%[4]	7.4%[4]

[1] Including other wines of the Yonne [2] Pouilly-Fuissé [3] The Beaujolais *crus*
[4] Average percentage for region

Major wine firms of Burgundy

PIERRE ANDRÉ
Château de Corton-André,
Aloxe Corton,
21420 Savigny-lès-Beaune

Sales: *95,000 cases*

Founded in 1923 by Pierre André, who also owns the firm of La Reine Pédauque, which he established in 1950. A large viticultural holding of some 60 hectares (148 acres) includes the domaines of Clos des Guettes, Juvinière and Les Terres Vineuses in the Côte d'Or and Viticole des Carmes. While most of the wines from this firm are merely of acceptable quality, he does excel with wines from Aloxe-Corton; his village wines often outshine the *crus*.

☆ Aloxe-Corton

BACHEROY-JOSSELIN
Rue Auxerroise,
89800 Chablis

Sales: *100,000 cases*

It is under the "Bacheroy-Josselin" brand that the wines of Laroche, the well-known Chablis family, are most often seen on export markets. Its major interests are of course in Chablis where its two domaines, Laroche and La Jouchère, have contrasting styles. The Laroche wines are firm and potentially long-lived, while La Jouchère Chablis are soft, often buttery, and made for early drinking. *Sous-marques* include "Ferdinand Bacheroy", "Jean Baulat", "Alain Combard", "Roland Foucard", "Henri Josset", "Jacques Millar".

☆ Wines from Domaine Laroche

A. BICHOT
Boulevard Jacques Copeau,
21200 Beaune

Sales: *1 million cases*

One of the largest *négociants* in Burgundy and, with more than 90 hectares (222 acres) of vineyards, one of the most important. In the *sous-marques* league, Bichot is to Burgundy what Marne et Champagne is to Champagne, with some 50 different labels, including "Jean Bouchard", "Paul Bouchard", "Buchot-Ludot", "Maurice Dard", "Charles Drapier", "Fortier-Picard", "Rémy Gauthier" and "Léon Rigault". Like Marne et Champagne, the quality of the wine very much depends upon how much the buyer is prepared to pay, therefore Bichot has a very inconsistent image, yet I have tasted some extraordinarily good wines.

☆ Chablis "La Mouton", Chablis from Domaine Long-Depaquit and Vosne-Romanée Malconsorts and Echézeaux from Domaine Clos Frantin

JEAN-CLAUDE BOISSET
2 rue des Frères Montgolfier,
21700 Nuits-St.-Georges

In 1982 Boisset acquired the firm of Charles Vienot, including its *sous-marques* of "L. J. Bruck" and "Thomas Bassot", and in 1986 took over "Pierre Ponnelle". Although in the past many of the wines have been little more than soundly made, Boisset remains one of the few *négociants* to produce excellent red Bourgogne Grand Ordinaire with true Pinot character. Its Hautes-Côtes de Nuits wines are very good and, generally, this company is beginning to put more character into all of its wines.

☆ Bourgogne Grand Ordinaire, Bourgogne Hautes-Côtes de Nuits, Gevrey-Chambertin, Nuits-St.-Georges

BOUCHARD AÎNÉ & FILS
36 rue Ste Marguerite,
21203 Beaune

Sales: *300,000 cases*

Established in 1750 by the same family as Bouchard Père, but now a totally separate company, Bouchard Aîné has a 22-hectare (57-acre) vineyard in the Region of Mercurey, the wines of which are consistently of fine quality.

☆ Clos de Bèze, Fixin "La Mazière", Mercurey blanc, Mercurey Clos la Marche, Mercurey Clos du Chapitre

BOUCHARD PÈRE & FILS
Au Château,
21200 Beaune

A great Burgundy house with the largest vineyard holding in the Côte d'Or. Some 90 per cent of the 95 hectares (235 acres) of its Domaines du Château de Beaune is classified as *Grand Cru*.

☆ Wines sold under Domaines du Château de Beaune, particularly Beaune "Grèves Vigne de l'Enfant Jésus"

EMILE CHANDESAIS
BP1-Fontaines,
71150 Chagny

Sales: *210,000 cases*

This fine, family-owned firm, which was established by Emile Chandesais in 1933, is located in the Mercurey region. Its rich, clean, fruity wines have a distinctive new-oak character, and always represent excellent value for money.

☆ Wines from Domaine de la Folie and Domaine de l'Hermitage, Gevrey Chambertin

CHANSON PÈRE & FILS
10 rue Paul Chanson,
21200 Beaune

Sales: *250,000 cases*

This firm has a substantial estate of some 45 hectares (111 acres), mostly in the Beaune appellations, which produces light, but elegant wines.

☆ Beaune "Bressandes", Beaune Clos des Fèves, Beaune "Teurons" and Savigny "La Dominode"

CHANUT FRÈRES
Romanèche-Thorins,
71570 La Chapelle de Ginchay

Sales: *180,000 cases*

Masters of the art of Beaujolais in all categories, from delicious *Nouveau* to truly exceptional Beaujolais *crus*.

☆ All Beaujolais

F. CHAUVENET
6 route de Chaux,
21700 Nuits-St.-Georges

A large firm that has 45 hectares (111 acres) of vineyards and claims to be the third-largest in Burgundy. Its range of wines is generally lacklustre, although I have tasted some fine single-vineyard Burgundies from Puligny-Montrachet.

☆ Puligny-Montrachet

CORON PÈRE & FILS
21200 Beaune

Founded in 1864 by Claude Coron, a schoolmaster, this is a small, fine and fastidious firm that produces classic Burgundy of great elegance, especially those from its own domaine, which consists of vineyards in five of Beaune's *Premiers Crus*.

☆ Beaune Les Cent Vignes, Beaune Clos du Roi, Beaune Les Grèves

DAVID & FOILLARD
69830 St.-Georges-de-Reneins

Sales: *200,000 cases*

A large range of wines from both southern Burgundy and the Rhône.

ANDRÉ DELORME
Rully,
71150 Chagny

This firm is very important in the Mercurey region where it controls a 60-hectare (148-acre) estate that is owned by various members of the Delorme family. It has a consistent standard in both *négociant* and own-vineyard wines, and a fine reputation for its Crémant de Bourgogne.

☆ Crémant de Bourgogne Brut, Crémant de Bourgogne Blanc de Blancs Brut, wines from Domaine de la Renarde

MAISON DOUDET-NAUDIN
1 rue Henri Cyrot,
21420 Savigny-lès-Beaune

This small house is proud of its *"méthode ancienne"* which, it considers, produces a richer, fuller style of wine. The wines rarely bear any resemblance to either Pinot noir or Burgundy. For my taste they are too thick and soupy, with a raw pepperyness when young that evolves into a stewed, hot taste when mature. They do, however, have a loyal following.

JOSEPH DROUHIN
7 rue d'Enfer,
21200 Beaune

This great firm has some 60 hectares (148 acres) of vineyards, more than half of which are in Chablis. The wines are always meticulously made, and the whites have a delicious oaky touch with lots of finesse.

☆ All Chablis, Montrachet; Beaune Clos des Mouches is its single best wine

GEORGES DUBOEUF
71570 Romanèche-Thorins

Sales: *1 million cases*

Georges Duboeuf is the self-proclaimed king of Beaujolais. He excels in purchasing, blending and perfecting the fruity Gamay wines loved and considered so typical of Beaujolais by aficionados of the *macération carbonique* style. These are his generics, which I consider to be over-priced. His *cru* Beaujolais wines, however, have great character, strength and finesse, and his vinification techniques result in extraordinarily elegant styles of *vins de table* that are worth the premium.

☆ Most *crus* Beaujolais

MAISON FAIVELEY
8 rue du Tribourg,
21700 Nuits-St.-Georges

With more than 100 hectares

(247 acres), Faiveley is the largest owner of vineyards in Burgundy. It makes aromatic wines that maintain freshness over a long life.

☆ Most Mercureys, particularly Mercurey Clos de Myglands

PIERRE FERRAUD & FILS
31 rue Maréchal Foch,
69823 Belleville

Sales: *110,000 cases*

A medium-sized Beaujolais merchant with a small domaine of eight hectares (20 acres) and exclusive rights on various properties. Its wines are made by modern techniques in a style that is expressive of its *terroir*.

☆ Most *crus* Beaujolais

GEISWEILER
1 rue de la Berchère,
21700 Nuits-St.-Georges

Sales: *500,000 cases*

With a total of 90 hectares (222 acres), Geisweiler is the second-largest owner of vineyards in Burgundy. Its Domaine des Dames Hautes in Nuits-St.-Georges produces full, rich and sound wines, but the Domaine de Bévy in the Hautes-Côtes de Nuits is its most famous. Although its wines are of a more modest quality, they represent much better value for money.

☆ Domaine de Bévy in the Hautes-Côtes de Nuits

JABOULET-VERCHERRE
5 rue Colbert,
21200 Beaune

Sales: *200,000 cases*

The Burgundies produced by this house are good commercial wines for those wanting something rich and full, but not wishing to pay too much.

LOUIS JADOT
5 rue Samuel Legay,
21200 Beaune

The wines of this great Burgundy house consistently prove their un-mistakable class. Nothing has changed on the quality front since its acquisi-tion by its American importer Kobrand, which gave Jadot the financial capacity to purchase Domaines Clair-Daü in 1986. This increased its vineyard holding from 24 to 40 hectares (59 to 99 acres). In 1987, Jadot signed a 20-year contract to make and sell the wines of Domaine de Magenta.

☆ Consistent high quality across the entire range

JAFFELIN
2 rue Paradis,
21200 Beaune

Sales: *70,000 cases*

An old family firm purchased by Joseph Drouhin in 1969 that still produces its own style of fine wines.

☆ Clos de Vougeot

LABOURÉ-ROI
21700 Nuits-St.-Georges

This small, quality-conscious firm owns two-and-a-half hectares (six acres) in Nuits-St.-Georges, and markets the Meursault wines of René Manuel.

☆ Chablis, Pommard

LAMBLIN & FILS
Maligny,
89800 Chablis

Sales: *60,000 cases*

A nice little firm producing very fresh, elegant Chablis, and an excellent "Chablis-style" Bourgogne Aligoté. Its *sous-marques* include "Jacques Arnouls", "Jacques de la Ferté", "Paul Javry" and "Bernard Miele".

☆ Bourgogne Aligoté, Chablis

MAISON LOUIS LATOUR
18 rue des Tonneliers,
21204 Beaune

Sales: *300,000 cases*

Louis Latour has a large domaine of 50 hectares (124 acres) that includes many prime sites, and produces very good red wines and exceptionally fine white wines. It was revealed in 1982 that this firm had flash-pasteurized its red wines at 70°C (158°F) since the beginning of this century. Despite this, the wines had often been rated very highly at blind tastings. Most rational-thinking wine-lovers should re-evaluate their feelings about pasteurization.

☆ Château Corton Grancey, basic Santenay and Gevrey-Chambertin, and virtually all the white wines

LEROY
Auxey Duresses,
21190 Meursault

Sales: *37,158 cases*

This important *négociant* business belongs to Madame Bize-Leroy, co-owner of Domaine de la Romanée-Conti. The domaine here, however, is barely more than four hectares (10 acres), but it does contain prime sites in Auxey-Duresses, Meursault and Pommard, plus parcels of *Grands Crus* Chambertin, Musigny and Clos-de-Vougeot.

☆ All qualities

LORON & FILS
"Pontanevaux",
71570 La Chapelle-de-Guinchay

Sales: *1.4 million cases*

This firm is best known for its success-ful blends of supermarket Beaujolais and *vins de table*, but also produces very good, top-quality *crus* Beaujolais.

☆ Some *crus* Beaujolais

LUPÉ-CHOLET
217 Nuits-St.-Georges

This firm has suffered from various changes of ownership. The wines used to be very good indeed when it was in charge of buying its own wines, espec-ially those from Chambolle-Musigny, but performance noticeably declined after its takeover by Chauvenet. The quality perked up between 1975 and 1978 under the ownership of Moillard, but it now belongs to Bichot.

P. DE MARCILLY FRÈRES
21200 Beaune

Marcilly's various generic wines are supposed to be based on Chambertin and other fine vineyards, hence their relatively expensive price. No guaran-tees, but some of the mysterious names can apparently be translated as: "Bourgogne Première" (Côte de Nuits, mainly Gevrey Chambertin), "Bourgogne Réserve" (Beaune area) "Bourgogne Spécial" (Côte de Beaune-Villages). These are generally rich, soupy and concentrated wines.

PROSPER MAUFOUX
21590 Santenay

One of the great houses of Burgundy that uses a high percentage of new oak. The quality and consistency of these wines cannot be disputed. They have a vivid colour, stunning richness and great finesse.

☆ Most wines across the range

MOILLARD
2 rue François Mignotte,
21701 Nuits-St.-Georges

Sales: *650,000 cases*

Established in 1850 by Symphorien Moillard, it is now owned by the Thomas family, the descendants of the founder's son-in-law. This firm pro-duces good-quality and good-value wine throughout most of its range, but truly excels with own-domaine wines sold under its "Moillard-Grivot" label.

☆ Bourgogne Rouge, Bourgogne Blanc and most "Moillard-Grivot" wines, especially Meursault Cromin, Bâtard Montrachet and Echézeaux

MOMMESSIN
La Grange Saint-Pierre,
71009 Mâcon

Sales: *1.5 million cases*

Although essentially a Beaujolais and Mâconnais *négociant*, Mommessin's pride and joy is its sole ownership of the Morey-St.-Denis *Grand Cru* Clos de Tart. The style is one of richness combined with finesse, and the overall standard of quality is excellent.

☆ Clos de Tart is impeccable and all wines from Mâcon and Beaujolais recommendable

J. MOREAU & FILS
Route d'Auxerre,
89800 Chablis

Half-owned by Hiram Walker, the whisky distillers, this is the most important *négociant* in Chablis. Its 75 hectares (185 acres) of vineyards, however, are entirely family-owned, and the whole enterprise is firmly managed by Jean Moreau, who is very much a working boss. The best of its own-domaine Chablis are truly superb, but the general range of *négociant* wines lacks character.

☆ *Grand* and *Premier Cru* Chablis

PASQUIER-DESVIGNES
St.-Lager,
69220 Belleville

The Desvignes have the longest unbroken record as winemakers in Burgundy, but the pity is that after more than 560 years they cannot produce more expressive wines. Most Beaujolais and Mâconnais sell more on brand than anything else.

PATRIARCHE PÈRE & FILS
7 rue du Collège,
21201 Beaune

Mainly humble wines, possibly because Patriarche produce more than any other Burgundy house and it all gets blended into a common denominator. Watch out for the Clos du Château, an inexpensive Meursault of fabulous quality rivalling Château de Meursault itself. It cannot claim the appellation it deserves because the land was part of the château's garden when Meursault was delimited.

☆ Virtually all Château de Meursault wines and Clos du Château

PIAT PÈRE ET FILS
71570 la Chapelle-de-Guichay

Famous for the use of its special "Piat" bottle, which is based on the traditional Beaujolais *pot*. Its wines are mostly sound but unexciting, although Le Piat de Mâcon Viré is usually fresh and attractive. It is perhaps best known for its table wines, the fantastically popular red and white Piat d'Or. This firm was the first to discover that a red wine made sweet but labelled "smooth", would sell like hot-cakes, which explains Piat d'Or's success as the world's largest-selling red wine.

☆ Le Piat de Mâcon Viré

MAISON PIERRE PONNELLE
**Abbaye St.-Martin,
53 avenue de l'Aigue,
21200 Beaune**

A small-sized, quality-conscious *négociant* with a tiny four-hectare (nine-acre) domaine but a large range of wines. The Ponnelle style is a fine balance between elegance and longevity.

☆ Most wines across the range

F. PROTHEAU & FILS
**Château d'Etroyes,
Mercurey,
71640 Givry**

Sales: *200,000 cases*

This important firm, based in the Mercurey region, has a 45-hectare (111-acre) domaine and produces a very competent quality of wine that usually shows both firmness and finesse. It is often very good value for money.

CAVES DE LA REINE PÉDAUQUE
**Aloxe-Corton,
21420 Savigny-lès-Beaune**

Sales: *966,000 cases*

This started out as a range launched by the firm of Pierre André in 1950 and its sales soon dwarfed its parent company. It now out-sells the other wines of Pierre André ten to one.

REMOISSENET PÈRE & FILS
21200 Beaune

An important *négociant* with a small domaine of barely three hectares (seven acres) of *Premier Cru* Beaune.

☆ Most wines, particularly whites

ANTONIN RODET
71640 Mercurey

Sales: *675,000 cases*

This very important *négociant* is based in the Mercurey region where it owns some 25 hectares (62 acres) and produces a stylish, silky-rich wine.

☆ Mercurey appellations

ROPITEAU FRÈRES
**Les Chanterelles,
21190 Meursault**

Sales: *230,000 cases*

Established in 1848 and taken over by Chantovent in 1974. Its reputation has very firmly rested on single-vineyard Meursaults ever since, particularly those of Charmes, Genevrières, Goutte d'Or and Poruzots. These and other fine vineyards are owned by members of the Ropiteau family, not the Ropiteau firm. The bulk of these holdings (Domaine Ropiteau-Mignon) passed to Chauvenet in 1987.

☆ Anything from Meursault is unreservedly recommended up until 1987.

SARRAU
**St.-Jean-d'Ardières,
69822 Belleville-sur-Saône**

Sales: *650,000 cases*

A large and progressive firm that specializes in producing a fine-quality fresh and fruity Beaujolais.

☆ Most *crus* Beaujolais

SIMONNET-FEBVRE
**9 avenue d'Oberwesel,
89800 Chablis**

With Chablis much closer to southern Champagne than it is to the rest of Burgundy, and with its good limey-marl soil, it is not surprising that Simonnet-Febvre produces truly superb sparkling wines. Simonnet-Febvre also makes classic *Premier Cru* Chablis from its ten-hectare (25-acre) estate.

☆ Crémant de Bourgogne and *Grand* and *Premier Cru* Chablis

THORIN S.A.
**Pontanevaux
71570 la-Chapelle-de-Guinchay**

This firm excelled in the legitimate supply of declassified Burgundies to the UK before membership of the EEC forbade it. Many of those wines were, however, better than most of the wines sold by Thorin today. It concentrates its efforts on Beaujolais, and owns the Château des Jacques in Moulin-à-Vent.

☆ Château des Jacques

CHARLES VIÉNOT
**5 quai Dumorey,
21700 Nuits-St.-Georges**

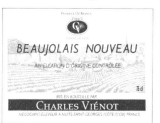

Part of Jean-Claude Boisset since 1982, this 250-year-old house has a fine domaine of ten hectares (25 acres). It has fine vineyards in Richebourg and Corton, but the style of wines produced, for which it uses an average of 25 per cent new oak, is somewhat old-fashioned.

HENRI DE VILLAMONT
**Rue du Docteur Guyot,
21420 Savigny-lès-Beaune**
Owned by the Swiss company Schenk, this firm produces some good-value wines, but they are often intermingled with more ordinary products, and can be hidden under one of many *sous-marques* that include "Arthur Barolet", "Mesnard", "Paul Rolland", "Louis Serrignon" and "Caves de Valclair".

☆ Savigny-lès-Beaune, Hautes-Côtes de Beaune

Important Burgundy coopératives

There are very few important *coopératives* in Burgundy outside of Mâconnais and Beaujolais. Within these two districts there are at least 36 *coopératives* of varying size and performance. Among these it is impossible to distinguish which belongs to what district because the appellations overlap. The *coopératives* of Mâconnais and Beaujolais are located at Aze, Bissey-sous-Cruchaud, Le Bois d'Oingt, Bully, Buxy, Chaintre, Chardonnay, Charnay-lès-Mâcon, Chassagne, Chénas, Chirroubles, Clessé ("La Vigne Blanche"), Corcelles, Fleurie, Genouilly, Gleizé, Igé, Juliénas, Létra, Liergues, Lugny, Mancey, Le Perréon, Prissé, Quincié, Sain-Bel, St.-Jean d'Ardières, St.-Laurent, St.-Vérand, St.-Etienne-des-Oullières, Sennece-lès-Mâcon, Sologny, Theizé, Verzy, Vinzelles and Viré. The most important of all Burgundy's *coopératives* are as follows:

CAVE COOPÉRATIVE LA CHABLISIENNE
**8 boulevard Pasteur,
89800 Chablis**

**Production: *350,000 cases*
Members: *190*
Vineyards: *472 ha (1,166 acres)*
Established: *1932***

La Chablisienne accounts for one-third of the total production of Chablis, with all but one of the *Grands Crus*

represented. Its generic Chablis has been known to beat certain *Premier Cru* Chablis in blind tastings.

CAVE COOPÉRATIVE DES HAUTES CÔTES DE BEAUNE ET NUITS
**Route de Pommard,
21200 Beaune**

**Production: *125,000 cases*
Established: *1961***

This dynamic organization evolved from the small *coopérative* of Orches, which was established after the creation of the Hautes-Côtes appellations in 1961. Its specialization in producing the less-expensive wines of the Hautes-Côtes has been successful.

CELLIER DES SAMSONS
**Le Pont de Samsons,
Quincie-en-Beaujolais,
69430 Beaujeu**

Production: *425,000 cases*

Cellier des Samsons consists of ten of the most important Beaujolais *coopératives*. It has a reputation for distributing wines of an excellent quality-price ratio.

CAVE DES VIGNERONS DE BUXY
**Les Vignes-de-la-Croix,
71390 Buxy**

**Production: *300,000 cases*
Members: *200 plus*
Vineyards: *550 ha (1,359 acres)*
Established: *1931***

This innovative *coopérative* produces an excellent-quality-and-super-value Bourgogne rouge, either with or without a touch of new oak. This *coopérative*, which has for a long time specialized in the use of oak, has recently begun to cask-ferment a selection of white wines; the Montagny is stunning.

CAVE DE VIRÉ
**En Vacheron, Viré,
71260 Lugny**

**Production: *175,000 cases*
Members: *235*
Vineyards: *250 ha (618 acres)***

Cave de Viré is a modern establishment equipped to vinify a multitude of wines

on a single-village basis. The results are usually of a very high standard. It also makes an excellent Crémant de Bourgogne from selected grapes.

GROUPEMENT DE PRODUCTEURS DE LUGNY-ST.-GENGOUX-DE-SCISSÉ
71260 Lugny

**Production: *800,000 cases*
Members: *490*
Vineyards: *850 ha (2,100 acres)***

This very large *coopérative* currently produces an excellent range of wines, many of which regularly win medals at the Mâcon and Paris Wine Fairs.

UNION DES COOPÉRATIVES VINICOLES DE BOURGOGNE DE SAÔNE-ET-LOIRE
**Charnay-les-Mâcons,
71008 Mâcon**

**Production: *750,000 cases*
Members: *1,400*
Vineyards: *1,250 ha (3,089 acres)***

This organization distributes and markets the wines of its ten member *coopératives*.

Generic wines of Burgundy

BOURGOGNE AOC

Many writers consider Bourgogne too basic and boring to warrant serious attention, but for me it is the most instructive of all Burgundy's appellations. If a producer cares about the quality of his Bourgogne, how much more effort goes into his other higher-quality wines? I delight in finding a scrummy, easy-to-drink Bourgogne, and I often get more of a kick discovering one that will improve for several years than I do from a superior appellation that *should* age well, considering its famous name and expensive price.

RED Despite the varieties that *may* be included in this wine, the only Bourgognes worth seeking out are those with the pure Pinot noir flavour and aroma. Many producers indicate the grape variety on the label, and this is worth watching out for.

🍇	Pinot noir, Pinot gris, Pinot liébault plus, in the Yonne district, César, Tressot
📅	1983, 1985, 1988, 1989, 1990
🍷	Between 2-5 years

WHITE A lot of boring white wines are made under the appellation, and it is probably safer to buy an inexpensive Mâcon. Clos du Château from Château du Meursault is consistently the finest of these wines (*see* Patriarche, p.111).

🍇	Chardonnay, Pinot blanc
📅	1984, 1985, 1986, 1989, 1990
🍷	Within 1-4 years

ROSÉ Michel Goubard is a quality-conscious grower who makes a tremendous Bourgogne rouge, Cuvée Mont-Avril, but his Bourgogne rosé, while acceptable, is nothing special.

🍇	Pinot noir, Pinot gris, Pinot liébault plus, in the Yonne district, César, Tressot
📅	1983, 1985, 1986, 1989, 1990
🍷	Within 1-4 years

☆ Paul Beaudet, Pierre Bernollin, Alain Berthault, Michel Colin-Deléger, Jean Deligny, Jean-Claude Desrayaud, Domaine Fougeray, Michel Goubard, Henri Jayer, Michel Lafarge, André Lhéritier, René Martin, Domaine Parent, Domaine Pitoiset-Uréna, Philippe Rossignol, Simon Fils, Gérard Thomas, Domaine de la Tour Bajole, Vallet Frères, A. & P. de Villaine

BOURGOGNE-ALIGOTÉ AOC

The finest Bourgogne-Aligoté comes from the village of Bouzeron in the Mercurey region, which has its own appellation (*see* Bourgogne Aligoté Bouzeron AOC, page 129). With the exception of those recommended below, the remaining Aligoté is improved by the addition of Cassis, a local blackcurrant liqueur, to create what is known as a "Kir".

WHITE Dry wines that are usually thin, acid and not very pleasant.

🍇	Aligoté and a maximum of 15% Chardonnay
📅	1984, 1985, 1986, 1989, 1990
🍷	Within 1-4 years

☆ N. & J.-M. Capron-Manieux, Coche-Dury, Michel Colbois, Claude Cornu, Gabriel Fournier, Guillemard-Dupont, Hubert Lamy, Laeure-Piot, Henri Naudin-Ferrand, Parigot Père & Fils, Domaine de Prieuré, Henri Prudhon, Daniel Rion, Maurice Rollin & Fils, Thévenot-le-Brun

BOURGOGNE CLAIRET AOC

Clairet is an unfashionable name for wine that is neither red nor rosé. It is rarely encountered.

🍇	Pinot noir, Pinot gris, Pinot liébault plus, in the Yonne district, César, Tressot

BOURGOGNE GRAND-ORDINAIRE AOC

In English-speaking markets the "Grand" sounds very grand indeed, and the fact that it qualifies "Ordinaire", not "Bourgogne" seems to get lost in the translation.

RED Mostly inferior Gamay wines, but there are some interesting Pinot noir-dominated versions.

🍇	Pinot noir, Gamay, plus, in the Yonne district, César, Tressot
📅	1983, 1985, 1988, 1989, 1990
🍷	Between 2-6 years

WHITE These dry wines are even more dismal than standard issue Bourgogne blanc. Buy Mâcon blanc!

🍇	Chardonnay, Pinot blanc, Aligoté, Melon de Bourgogne plus, in the Yonne district, Sacy

📅	1984, 1985, 1986, 1989, 1990
🍷	Within 1-4 years

ROSÉ The Hautes-Côtes *coopérative* produces a dry, light but elegant wine under this appellation, "Rosé d'Orches".

🍇	Pinot noir, Gamay, plus, in the Yonne district, César, Tressot
📅	1983, 1985, 1986, 1989, 1990
🍷	Within 1-3 years

☆ Gérard Borgnat, d'Heilly-Huberdeau

BOURGOGNE GRAND-ORDINAIRE CLAIRET AOC

This is another unfashionable, betwixt-and-between wine, which has all but disappeared from retailers' shelves.

🍇	Pinot noir, Gamay, plus, in the Yonne district, César, Tressot

BOURGOGNE MOUSSEUX AOC

Since December 1985 this appellation has been limited to, and remains the only outlet for, sparkling red Burgundy.

SPARKLING RED A favourite fizzy tipple in the pubs of pre-war Britain. This wine's sweet flavour is very much out of step with today's sophisticated consumers.

🍇	Pinot noir, Gamay, plus, in the Yonne district, César, Tressot
📅	Usually non-vintage
🍷	Immediately

BOURGOGNE ORDINAIRE AOC

See Bourgogne Grand-Ordinaire AOC.

BOURGOGNE ORDINAIRE CLAIRET AOC

See Bourgogne Grand-Ordinaire Clairet AOC.

BOURGOGNE PASSETOUTGRAINS AOC

Made from a melange of Pinot noir and Gamay grapes, this is the descendant of an authentic peasant wine. A grower would fill his vat with anything growing in his vineyard and ferment it all together. Thus *passetoutgrains* once contained numerous grape varieties. The Pinot noir and Gamay varieties were, however, the widest planted, and the wine naturally evolved as a two-grape product. Up until 1943 a minimum of one-fifth Pinot noir was enforced by law; now this appellation must contain at least one-third.

RED This is a dry, medium-bodied wine with a pleasant garnet colour. Many *passetoutgrains* are drunk too early; a good quality *passetoutgrains* will eventually show the aristocratic influence of its Pinot noir content.

🍇	A maximum of one-third Gamay plus Pinot noir, Pinot liébault
📅	1983, 1985, 1988, 1989, 1990
🍷	Between 2-6 years

ROSÉ This little-seen, dry, pink version is worth trying.

🍇	A maximum of one-third Gamay plus Pinot noir, Pinot liébault
📅	1983, 1985, 1986, 1989, 1990
🍷	Within 1-3 years

☆ Jean Laboureau, Pascal Laboureau, Robert Landré, Mazilly Père & Fils

CRÉMANT DE BOURGOGNE AOC

This appellation was created in 1975 to supersede the Bourgogne Mousseux AOC, which failed to inspire a quality image because the term *"mousseux"* also applied to the cheapest and nastiest of bulk-produced sparkling wines. Bourgogne Mousseux is now for red wines only. The three major production centres for Crémant de Bourgogne are the Yonne, Region de Mercurey and the Mâconnais. There are already many very exciting wines, and the quality is certain to improve as more producers specialize in cultivating grapes specifically for sparkling wines, rather than relying on excess or inferior grapes, as was traditionally the case in Burgundy.

SPARKLING WHITE Dry but round, the styles range from fresh and light to rich and toasty.

🍇	Pinot noir, Pinot gris, Pinot blanc, Chardonnay, Sacy, Aligoté, Melon de Bourgogne and a maximum of 20% Gamay
📅	1982, 1985, 1986, 1987, 1988
🍷	Between 3-7 years

SPARKLING ROSÉ Up until now the best pink *Crémant* produced outside of Champagne has come from Alsace. Good examples are made in Burgundy, but they have not realized their true potential.

🍇	Pinot noir, Pinot gris, Pinot blanc, Chardonnay, Sacy, Aligoté, Melon de Bourgogne and a maximum of 20% Gamay
📅	1982, 1985, 1986, 1987, 1988
🍷	Between 2-5 years

☆ Caves de Bailly, Pierre Bernollin, André Bonhomme, Dom Marly, François Laugerotte, Meurgis, Armand Monassier, Roux Père & Fils

The Chablis district

This classic white wine area is dominated by the Chardonnay grape, which is grown on soils and under climatic conditions similar to those of nearby Champagne.

CHABLIS IS AN ISLAND OF VINEYARDS closer to Champagne than to the rest of Burgundy. Known as the "Porte d'Or" or "Golden Gate", it has the advantage of being the inevitable first stop for anyone visiting the region by car, whether directly from Paris or via Champagne. Situated in the Yonne *département*, much of which once formed part of the ancient province of Champagne, Chablis gives the traveller the distinct impression of an area cut off not simply from the remainder of Burgundy but from the rest of France. Great *négociants* seldom visit the area and have never made significant penetration into what appears to be Chablis's closed-shop—although young growers from the Côte d'Or have recently begun to show a healthy interest in methods *à la chablis*. It is not wise to buy Chablis from a Beaune shipper, just as one should not buy Rhône wines from a Chablis shipper.

The varying styles of Chablis

The traditional description of Chablis is of a wine of clear, pale colour with a green hue around the rim. It is very straight and positive, with an aggressive, steely character, very direct attack and a high level of acidity that needs a few years to round out. This description, however, no longer applies, for much has changed in the way these wines are made at both ends of the quality spectrum.

Twenty or thirty years ago most Chablis did not undergo malolactic fermentation. The wines that resulted had a naturally high acidity, and were hard, green and ungenerous in their youth, although they often matured into wines of incomparable finesse. Now most Chablis are put through their malolactic and undergo cold stabilization to precipitate tartrates (although some wines fermented or matured in small oak casks are not) so that today's wines are fuller, softer and rounder. There is a tendency by some producers to over-chaptalize and this gives the wines an alcohol-extract balance that is contrary to the norm for Chablis.

At the top end of the market there are two distinctly different schools. Some wines are fermented in stainless steel and bottled early to produce the most direct and attacking style, while others are fermented in wood and matured in casks with some new oak to give a much fatter, richer, almost Côte d'Or style.

OTHER WINES OF THE YONNE

The two best-known other wines of the Yonne are the red wines of Irancy and the white of Sauvignon de St.-Bris. The former is an AOC and sells under the Bourgogne-Irancy appellation, the latter a VDQS made from the Sauvignon grape. Irancy is simple and fruity at its best (and that is not often), while the Sauvignon produces a finer wine in St.-Bris than it does in parts of Bordeaux and the Loire, where the wines receive full AOC status.

THE CHABLIS DISTRICT,
see also p. 109

Chablis lies at the centre of its namesake wine-producing area.

Chablis vineyards, right
Vines cover the southeast- and southwest-facing slopes of hills along the banks of the Serein, a small tributary of the Yonne.

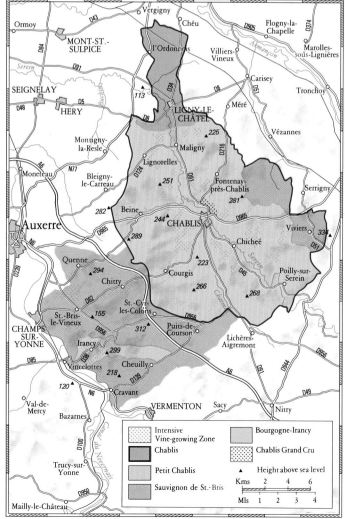

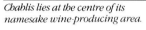

▒	Intensive Vine-growing Zone	
▒	Chablis	
▒	Petit Chablis	
▒	Sauvignon de St.-Bris	
▒	Bourgogne-Irancy	
▒	Chablis Grand Cru	
▲	Height above sea level	

Kms 2 4 6
Mls 1 2 3 4

FACTORS AFFECTING TASTE AND QUALITY

Location
Isolated halfway between Beaune and Paris, barely 30 kilometres (19 miles) from the southernmost vineyards of Champagne, but 100 kilometres (62 miles) from the rest of Burgundy.

Climate
This area has a semi-continental climate with minimal Atlantic influence, which results in a long, cold winter, a humid spring and a fairly hot, very sunny summer. Hail storms and spring frosts are the greatest hazards.

Aspect
All the *Grands Crus* are located on one stretch of southwest-facing slopes just north of Chablis itself, where the vineyards are at a height of between 150-200 metres (490-660 ft). Apart from the southwest-facing slopes of "Fourchaume" and "Montée de Tonnerre", the *Premier Cru* slopes face southeast.

Soil
This area is predominantly covered with calcareous clay, and the traditional view is that of the two major types, Kimmeridgian and Portlandian, only Kimmeridgian is suitable for classic Chablis, but this is neither proven nor likely. Geologically they have the same Upper Jurassic origin. Any intrinsic geographical differences should be put down to aspect, microclimate, and the varied nature of sedimentary beds that underlie and interbed with the Kimmeridgian and Portlandian soils.

Viticulture and vinification
The vineyards have undergone rapid expansion, most particularly in the generic appellation and the *Premiers Crus*, both of which have doubled in size since the early 1970s. Mechanical harvesting has now found its way to the *Grand Cru* slopes of Chablis, and most producers ferment in stainless steel.

Primary grape varieties
Chardonnay

Secondary grape varieties
Pinot noir, Pinot blanc, Pinot gris, Pinot liébault, Sauvignon blanc, Gamay, César, Tressot, Sacy, Aligoté, Melon de Bourgogne

The wines of the Chablis district

BOURGOGNE COULANGES-LA-VINEUSE AOC and BOURGOGNE EPINEUIL AOC

Two AOC oddities! While there are no separate appellations for either the red wines of Coulanges-la-Vineuse or the red, white or rosé wines of Epineuil, any wine produced entirely from these villages is allowed to indicate the village name on the label. I have not had the opportunity to taste these wines, but I am told that Epineuil makes a fine *vin gris,* and reliably informed that the following are well worth seeking out:

☆ Bourgogne Coulanges-la-Vineuse: Sergé Hugot, André Martin, Simmonet-Febvre

☆ Bourgogne Epineuil: André Durand, Jean-Claude Michaut

BOURGOGNE IRANCY AOC

The "famous" red wine of Chablis is not really that well-known, although it has had its own appellation for more than a decade.

RED Most of these are frank and fruity wines that are primarily Pinot noir with a small dash of César. Wines made from the authentic local grapes, César and Tressot, taste like thin and coarse Beaujolais.

🍇 Pinot noir, Pinot liébault, Pinot gris plus César and Tressot

🍷 1982, 1985, 1988, 1989, 1990

🍷 Between 2-5 years

☆ Léon Bienvenu, Bernard Cantin, Robert Meslin, Jean Renaud, Luc Sorin

CHABLIS AOC

With careful selection basic Chablis can be a source of tremendous value, classic 100 per cent Chardonnay wine, particularly in the best vintages, but the appellation covers a relatively large area with many vineyards that do not perform well under less-than-ideal conditions and there are too many mediocre winemakers producing it. *See also* Chablis Premier Cru AOC and Petit Chablis AOC.

WHITE When successful these wines are the quintessential character of true Chablis – dry, clean, green and expressive, with just enough fruit to balance the "steel".

🍇 Chardonnay

🍷 1985, 1986, 1988, 1989, 1990

🍷 Between 3-8 years

☆ Christian Adine, Jean-Marc Brocard, Jean Durup, Etienne Defaix, Alain Geoffroy, Albert Pic, Thomas-Bassot, A. Régnard & Fils, Michel Rémon

CHABLIS GRAND CRU AOC

The seven *Grands Crus* are all located on one hill that overlooks Chablis itself: Blanchot has a floral aroma and is the most delicate of the *Grands Crus;* the others are Bougros, Les Clos, Grenouilles, Les Preuses, Valmur and Vaudésir. One vineyard called "La Moutonne" is not classified in the appellation as a *Grand Cru,* but the authorities permit the use of the coveted status on the label because it is physically part of other *Grands Crus.* In the eighteenth century "La Moutonne" was a one-hectare (two-and-a-half acre) *climat* of Vaudésir, but under the ownership of Louis Long-Depaquit its wines were blended with those of three other *Grands Crus,* Les Preuses, Les Clos and Valmur. This practice came to a halt in 1950 when, in a bid to get "La Moutonne" classified as a separate *Grand Cru,* Long-Depaquit agreed to limit its production to its current location, a single plot of two-and-one-third hectares (five-and-a-half acres) that cuts across parts of Vaudésir and Les Preuses. Its classification as a *Grand Cru* never took place, but the two it overlaps are probably the finest of all the *Grands Crus,* and the wine it produces is consistently superb.

WHITE Always totally dry, the *Grands Crus* are the biggest, richest and most complex of all the wines of Chablis. Their individual styles depend very much on how the winemaker vinifies and matures his wine, but, essentially, "Blanchot" has a floral aroma and is the most delicate of the *Grands Crus;* "Bougros" has a vibrant and penetrating flavour; "Les Clos" is rich, luscious and complex; "Grenouilles" can be elegant and aromatic; "Les Preuses" is vivid, expressive and complex, with great finesse; "Valmur"

has a fine bouquet and a rich flavour; "Vaudésir" has complex, intense flavours that display great finesse and complexity; and "La Moutonne" is fine, long-flavoured and expressive.

🍇 Chardonnay

🍷 1985, 1986, 1988, 1989, 1990

🍷 Between 8-20 years

☆ René Dauvissat, Jean-Paul Droin, Maurice Duplessis, William Fèvre, Domaine de la Maladière, Louis Michel, Louis Pinson, J.-M. Raveneau, A. Regnard, Marcel Servin, Philippe Testut, Robert Vocoret

CHABLIS PREMIER CRU AOC

Premiers Crus: Beauroy, Côte de Léchet, Fourchaume, Les Fourneaux, Mélinots, Montée de Tonnerre, Montmains, Monts de Milieus, Vaillons, Vaucoupin, Vaudevey and Vosgros. Unlike the *Grands Crus,* the *Premiers Crus* of Chablis are not confined to the town of Chablis itself, but are scattered among the vineyards of 15 surrounding communes – and the quality and style is equally patchy. Montée de Tonnerre is without doubt consistently the finest *Premier Cru* throughout the different producers and across the many vintages, with Côte de Léchet, les Forêts (which is a *climat* within Montmains), Fourchaume and Mont de Milieu forming a tight bunch for second place.

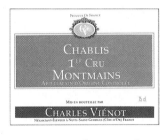

WHITE Dry wines that can vary from light- to fairly full-bodied, but should always be finer and longer-lasting than wines of the basic Chablis appellation, although without the concentration of flavour expected from a *Grand Cru.*

🍇 Chardonnay

🍷 1985, 1986, 1988, 1989, 1990

🍷 Between 5-15 years

☆ Jean Dauvissat, Jean-Paul Droin, Jean Durup, William Fèvre, Domaine de la Meulière, Louis Michel, Louis Pinson, J.-M. Raveneau, A. Regnard, Domaine Servin, Philippe Testut

PETIT CHABLIS AOC

A depreciatory appellation that covers the same area as generic Chablis, with the exception of the communes of Ligny-le-Châtel, Viviers and Collan. This appellation should either be downgraded to VDQS, or redesignated Coteaux du Chablis or something similar. Chablis-Villages has frequently been mooted as a possible alternative but "Villages" clearly indicates a superior wine in the rest of Burgundy and would therefore be somewhat misleading. Perhaps Chablis Grand Ordinaire might fit the bill?

WHITE These are mostly mean and meagre dry wines of light-to-medium body. In my experience the only producer that makes a decent Petit Chablis is the Cave Coopérative "La Chablisienne".

🍇 Chardonnay

🍷 1985, 1986, 1988, 1989, 1990

🍷 Between 2-3 years

SAUVIGNON DE ST.-BRIS VDQS

This single-village wine is as good as most Sauvignon blancs that have full AOC status, and considerably better than many other white AOCs made from lesser grape varieties. But I will eat my *tastevin* if Sauvignon de St.-Bris ever rises to the ranks of Appellation Contrôlée. Surely the chauvinistic Burgundians would never allow this upstart grape to rival their noble Chardonnay?

WHITE Fine wet-grass aromas, full smoky-Sauvignon flavours and a correct, crisp, dry finish.

🍇 Sauvignon blanc

🍷 1984, 1985, 1986, 1989, 1990

🍷 Between 2-5 years

☆ Bersan & Fils, Philippe Defrance, Jean-Hugues Goisot, Luc Sorin, Philippe Sorin

Côte de Nuits and Hautes-Côtes de Nuits

Firmness and weight are the key words here, and these characteristics generally intensify as the vineyards progress north. Production is essentially red, and with 22 of Burgundy's 23 red *Grands Crus,* the Côte de Nuits is the place par excellence for the Pinot noir.

THE CÔTE DE NUITS IS THE NORTHERN section of the Côte d'Or, the departmental name that has been coined by the *côtes* of Nuits and Beaune. With a string of villages owning some of the richest names in Burgundy – Gevrey-Chambertin, Chambolle-Musigny, Vosne-Romanée and Nuits-St.-Georges, these slopes ring up dollar signs in the minds of merchants throughout the world.

CONFRÉRIE DES CHEVALIERS DU TASTEVIN

After the three terrible vintages of 1930, 1931 and 1932, and four years of world slump, Camille Rodier and Georges Faiveley formed the Confrérie des Chevaliers du Tastevin in a bid to revive Burgundy's fortunes. They fashioned their initiative on the Ordre de la Boisson, a fraternity that had flourished, and died, during the reign of Louis XIV. Adopting colourful medieval robes and various dramatic rituals, they created four ranks: *Chevalier, Commandeur, Commandeur-Major* and *Grand Officier* and named the brotherhood after the traditional Burgundian *tastevin,* a shallow, dimpled, silver tasting cup with a fluted edge. This object dates from the sixteenth century and is worn around the neck, supported by a scarlet and gold ribbon, as part of the *Chevaliers'* attire.

The first investiture took place on 16 November 1934 in a cellar in Nuits-St.-Georges; the Confrérie now boasts thousands of members in numerous foreign chapters and averages 20 banquets a year at Château du Clos de Vougeot. Up to 600 members and their guests are subjected to five hours of feast and festivity.

CÔTE DE NUITS AND HAUTES-CÔTES DE NUITS, see also p. 109

The best vineyards of the Côte de Nuits form a tighter, more compact strip than those of the Côte de Beaune, (see p.121), and the wines produced are, coincidentally, tighter, with more compact fruit.

FACTORS AFFECTING TASTE AND QUALITY

 Location
The Côte de Nuits is a narrow, continuous strip of vines stretching from Dijon to just north of Beaune, with the Hautes-Côtes de Nuits in the south-western hinterland.

Climate
Semi-continental climate with minimal Atlantic influence, which results in a long, cold winter, a humid spring and a fairly hot, very sunny summer. Hail is its greatest natural hazard and heavy rain is often responsible for diluting the wines and causing rampant rot.

Aspect
A series of east-facing slopes which curve in and out to give some vineyards northeastern, some southeastern aspects. The vines grow at a height of between 225-350 metres (740-1,150 ft) and, apart from at Gevrey-Chambertin and Prémeaux-Prissey, those that have the right to the village and higher appellations rarely extend eastwards beyond the RN 74.

 Soil
A subsoil of sandy-limestone, which is exposed in places, but usually covered by a chalky scree mixed with marl and clay particles on higher slopes and richer alluvial deposits on lower ones. Higher slopes sometimes have red clay.

Viticulture and vinification
The vines are trained low to benefit from heat reflected from the soil at night. For red wines, the grapes are almost always destemmed and the juice is kept in contact with the skins for between eight and ten days. Less than three per cent of the wine produced is white, but this is mostly high quality and traditionally cask-fermented. The best wines are matured in oak.

 **Primary grape varieties**
Pinot noir, Chardonnay

Secondary grape varieties
Pinot gris, Pinot liébault, Pinot blanc, Aligoté, Melon de Bourgogne, Gamay

---

THE *TASTEVINAGE* LABEL

Twice a year wines are submitted to the Confrérie in the hope of obtaining the prestigious *Tastevinage* label. All the wines of Burgundy may be entered: red appellations other than Beaujolais in the spring and Beaujolais and white appellations in September. Producers naturally put some of their best wines forward, yet an average of 50 per cent of those submitted are rejected. Where the *Tastevinage* system is most useful is in identifying wines within basic appellations that rise above their station, for how else can a producer obtain a reasonable price for a truly fine wine that must bear a modest appellation?

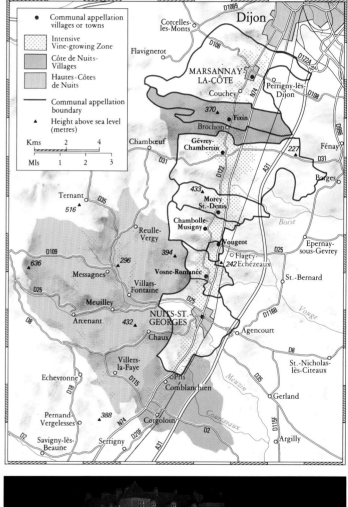

Château du Clos de Vougeot at night, above
Purchased by the Confrérie des Chevaliers du Tastevin in 1944 from Etienne Canazet, the château is the setting for the Society's splendid banquets.

The wines of the Côte de Nuits and Hautes-Côtes de Nuits

Note: All the *Grands Crus* of the Côte de Nuits have their own separate appellations and are therefore individually listed below. The *Premiers Crus*, however, do not have their own appellations and are therefore listed under the appellation of the village in which the vineyards are situated. Those *Premiers Crus* that are virtually contiguous with *Grand Cru* vineyards of the same appellation are italicized.

BONNES MARES AOC

Grand Cru

Largest of the two *Grands Crus* of Chambolle-Musigny, Bonnes Mares covers 13.5 hectares (33.5 acres) in the north of the village, the opposite side to that of Musigny, the village's other *Grand Cru* and extending a further one-and-a-half hectares (three-and-a-half acres) into Morey-St.-Denis.

RED This wine combines a fabulous femininity of style with sheer depth of flavour to give something rich and luscious, yet complex and complete.

🍇 Pinot noir, Pinot gris, Pinot liébault

🍷 1983, 1985, 1988, 1989, 1990

🍴 Between 12-25 years

☆ Domaine Bertheau, Domaine Dujac, Robert Groffier, Georges Lignier, Georges Roumier & Fils, Domaine des Varoilles, Comte Georges de Vogüé

BOURGOGNE CLAIRET HAUTES-CÔTES DE NUITS AOC

An appellation for a half-red/half-rosé wine that is outmoded, rare and conforms to Bourgogne AOC regulations. *See* Bourgogne AOC.

BOURGOGNE HAUTES-CÔTES DE NUITS AOC

A source of good-value wines, the vineyards of which have been expanded since the 1970s. The quality is improving noticeably.

RED Medium- and medium- to full-bodied wines with good fruit and some true Côte de Nuits character. The wines from some growers have fine oak nuances.

🍇 Pinot noir, Pinot liébault, Pinot gris

🍷 1983, 1985, 1988, 1989, 1990

🍴 Between 4-10 years

WHITE Just five per cent of the production is dry white. Most have a good weight of fruit, but little finesse.

🍇 Chardonnay, Pinot blanc

🍷 1984, 1985, 1986, 1989, 1990

🍴 Within 1-4 years

ROSÉ Little-seen, but those that have cropped up have been dry, fruity and delicious wines of some richness.

🍇 Pinot noir, Pinot liébault, Pinot gris

🍷 1983, 1985, 1986, 1989, 1990

🍴 Within 1-3 years

☆ Guy Dufouleur, Fribourg, Maurice Gavignet, Henri Hudelot, Patrick Hudelot, Robert Jayer-Gilles, Domaine Montmain, Thévenot-le-Brun & Fils

CHAMBERTIN AOC

Grand Cru

This is one of the nine *Grands Crus* of Gevrey-Chambertin. Chambertin's fame has been such that all the *Grands Crus* of Gevrey-Chambertin legally, but cheekily, add its name to their own and one, Clos de Bèze, actually has the right to sell its wines as Chambertin.

RED Always full in body and rich in extract, Chambertin is not, however, powerful like Corton, but graceful and feminine with a vivid colour, stunning flavour, impeccable balance and lush, velvety texture.

🍇 Pinot noir, Pinot gris, Pinot liébault

🍷 1983, 1985, 1988, 1989, 1990

🍴 Between 12-30 years

☆ Hubert Camus, Pierre Damoy, Domaine Leflaive, Domaine Ponsot, Henri Rebourseau, Domaine Tortochot, Louis Trapet

CHAMBERTIN-CLOS DE BÈZE AOC

Grand Cru

This is one of the nine *Grands Crus* of Gevrey-Chambertin. The wine of Clos de Bèze may be sold simply as Chambertin, the name of a neighbouring *Grand Cru*, but Chambertin may not call itself Clos de Bèze.

RED This wine is reputed to have a greater finesse than Chambertin but slightly less body. It is just as sublime.

🍇 Pinot noir, Pinot gris, Pinot liébault

🍷 1983, 1985, 1988, 1989, 1990

🍴 Between 12-30 years

☆ Pierre Damoy, Drouhin-Laroze, Domaine Gelin, Armand Rousseau

CHAMBOLLE-MUSIGNY AOC

A very favourably positioned village with a solid block of vines nestled in the shelter of a geological fold.

RED Many of these medium- to fairly full-bodied wines have surprising finesse and fragrance for mere village wines.

🍇 Pinot noir, Pinot gris, Pinot liébault

🍷 1983, 1985, 1988, 1989, 1990

🍴 Between 8-15 years

☆ Bernard Amiot, Gaston Barthod-Noëllat, Daniel Funès, Alain Hudelot-Noëllat, Jacques-Frédéric Mugnier, Domaine Pernot-Fourrier, Georges Roumier & Fils, Bernard Serveau, Domaine des Varoilles, Comte Georges de Vogüé

CHAMBOLLE-MUSIGNY PREMIER CRU AOC

Premier Crus: Les Sentiers, *Les Baudes,* Les Noirots, *Les Lavrottes, Les Fuées,* Aux Beaux Bruns, Aux Echanges, Les Charmes, Les Plantes, Aux Combottes, Les Combottes, Derrière la Grange, Les Gruenchers, Les Groseilles, Les Châtelots, Les Grands Murs, Les Feusselottes, Les Cras, Les Carrières, Les Chabiots, *Les Borniques, Les Amoureuses,* Les Hauts Doix, *La Combe d'Orveau.* The outstanding *Premier Cru* is Les Amoureuses, with Les Charmes a very respectable second.

RED The best have a seductive bouquet and deliciously fragrant flavour.

🍇 Pinot noir, Pinot gris, Pinot liébault

🍷 1983, 1985, 1988, 1989, 1990

🍴 Between 10-20 years

☆ G. Barthod-Noëllat, Alain Hudelot-Noëllat, Daniel Rion, Georges Roumier & Fils, Bernard Serveau

CHAPELLE-CHAMBERTIN AOC

Grand Cru

This is one of the nine *Grands Crus* of Gevrey-Chambertin, comprised of two *climats* called "En la Chapelle" and "Les Gémeaux", situated beneath the Clos de Bèze.

RED Although the lightest of all the *Grands Crus*, Chapelle-Chambertin has a delightful bouquet and flavour.

🍇 Pinot noir, Pinot gris, Pinot liébault

🍷 1983, 1985, 1988, 1989, 1990

🍴 Between 8-20 years

☆ Pierre Damoy, Drouhin-Laroze, Louis Trapet

CHARMES-CHAMBERTIN AOC

Grand Cru

The largest of the nine *Grands Crus* of Gevrey-Chambertin. Part of the vineyard is known as "Mazoyères", from which Mazoyères-Chambertin has evolved as an alternative name.

RED Soft, sumptuous wines with ripe fruit flavours and pure Pinot character, although some slightly lack finesse.

🍇 Pinot noir, Pinot gris, Pinot liébault

🍷 1983, 1985, 1988, 1989, 1990

🍴 Between 10-20 years

☆ Hubert Camus, Jean Raphet, Henri Rebourseau, Joseph Roty, Armand Rousseau, Domaine Tortochot

CLOS DE BÈZE AOC

An alternative appellation for Chambertin-Clos de Bèze. *See* Chambertin-Clos de Bèze AOC.

CLOS DES LAMBRAYS AOC

Grand Cru

This vineyard was classified as one of the four *Grands Crus* of Morey-St.-Denis only as recently as 1981, although the previous owner used to proclaim "*Grand Cru Classé*" (illegally) on the label.

RED The vineyard was replanted under new ownership and is still too youthful to assess. Its situation is, however, excellent and the new owners will probably be determined to make a mark.

🍇 Pinot noir, Pinot gris, Pinot liébault

🍷 1983, 1985, 1988, 1989, 1990

🍴 Between 10-20 years

☆ Domaine des Lambrays

CLOS DE LA ROCHE AOC

Grand Cru

Covering an area of almost 17 hectares (42 acres), this is twice the size of the other *Grands Crus* of Morey-St.-Denis.

RED A deep-coloured, rich and powerfully flavoured *vin de garde* with a silky texture. Many consider it the greatest *Grand Cru* of Morey-St.-Denis.

🍇 Pinot noir, Pinot gris, Pinot liébault

🍷 1983, 1985, 1988, 1989, 1990

🍴 Between 10-20 years

☆ Pierre Amiot, Domaine Dujac, George Lignier, Armand Rousseau

CLOS ST.-DENIS AOC

Grand Cru

This is the *Grand Cru* that the village of Morey attached to its name when it was the best growth in the village, a position now contested by Clos de la Roche and Clos de Tart.

RED Strong, fine and firm wines with rich liquorice and berry flavours that require time to come together.

🍇 Pinot noir, Pinot gris, Pinot liébault

🍷 1983, 1985, 1988, 1989, 1990

🍷 Between 10-25 years

☆ Domaine Bertagna, Domaine Dujac, Georges Lignier, Domaine Ponsot

CLOS DE TART AOC

Grand Cru

This is one of the four *Grands Crus* of Morey-St.-Denis. It is entirely owned by the *négociant* Mommessin. In addition to Clos de Tart itself, a tiny part of the Bonnes Mares *Grand Cru* also has the right to this appellation.

RED This monopoly yields wines with a penetrating Pinot flavour, to which Mommessin add such a spicy-vanilla character from 100 per cent new oak that great bottle-maturity is required for a completely harmonious flavour.

🍇 Pinot noir, Pinot gris, Pinot liébault

🍷 1983, 1985, 1988, 1989, 1990

🍷 Between 15-30 years

☆ Mommessin

CLOS DE VOUGEOT AOC

Grand Cru

The only *Grand Cru* of Vougeot, it is a massive 50-hectare (123.5-acre) block of vines with no less than 85 registered owners. It has been described as "an impressive sight, but a not very impressive site". This mass ownership situation has often been used to illustrate the classic difference between Burgundy and Bordeaux, where an entire vineyard belongs to one château and so can be blended to a standard quality and style every year.

RED With individual plots ranging in quality from truly great to very ordinary, operated by growers of varying skills, it is virtually impossible to unravel the intrinsic characteristics of a *cru*. The very best, however, have lots of silky Pinot fruit, an elegant balance and a tendency towards finesse rather than fullness.

🍇 Pinot noir, Pinot gris, Pinot liébault

🍷 1983, 1985, 1988, 1989, 1990

🍷 Between 10-25 years

☆ Robert Arnoux, Christian Confuron, Drouhin-Laroze, Engel, Jean Grivot, Jean Gros, Jacqueline Jayer, Mongeard-Mugneret, Charles Noëlat, Henri Rebourseau, Daniel Rion, Domaine des Varoilles, Noémie Vernaux

CLOS VOUGEOT AOC

See Clos de Vougeot AOC.

CÔTE DE NUITS-VILLAGES AOC

This appellation covers the wines produced in one or more of five communes: Fixin and Brochon in the north of the district and Comblanchien, Corgoloin and Prissy in the south.

RED Firm, fruity and distinctive wines made in true, well-structured, Côte de Nuits style.

🍇 Pinot noir, Pinot gris, Pinot liébault

🍷 1983, 1985, 1988, 1989, 1990

🍷 Between 6-10 years

WHITE Very little is made – just four hectolitres (44 cases) in 1985 – and I have never encountered it.

🍇 Chardonnay, Pinot blanc

☆ Bertrand Ambroise, Gachot-Monot, Robert Jayer-Gilles, Jean Jourdan-Guillemier, Domaine Gérard Julien, Daniel Rion

ECHÉZEAUX AOC

Grand Cru

This 30-hectare (74-acre) vineyard is the larger of the two *Grands Crus* of Flagey-Echézeaux and is comprised of 11 *climats* owned by no less than 84 smallholders.

RED The best have a fine and fragrant flavour that relies more on delicacy than power, but too many deserve no more than a village appellation.

🍇 Pinot noir, Pinot gris, Pinot liébault

🍷 1983, 1985, 1988, 1989, 1990

🍷 Between 10-20 years

☆ Jacques & Patrice Cacheux, Desvignes Aîné & Fils, Domaine Engel, Robert Jayer-Gilles, Henri Jayer, Jacqueline Jayer, Mongeard-Mugneret, Domaine de la Romanée-Conti

FIXIN AOC

Fixin was at one time the summer residence of the Dukes of Burgundy.

RED Well-coloured wines that can be firm, tannic *vins de garde* of excellent quality and even better value.

🍇 Pinot noir, Pinot gris, Pinot liébault

🍷 1983, 1985, 1988, 1989, 1990

🍷 Between 6-12 years

WHITE Rich, dry and concentrated wines that are rare, but exciting and well worth seeking out. Bruno Clair shows what Pinot blanc can produce when not allowed to over-crop.

🍇 Chardonnay, Pinot blanc

🍷 1984, 1985, 1986, 1989, 1990

🍷 Between 3-8 years

☆ Domaine Berthaut, Bruno Clair, Gelin & Molin, Pierre Gelin, Alain Guyard, Jean-Pierre Guyard, Philippe Joliet

FIXIN PREMIER CRU AOC

Premiers Crus: Le Meix Bas, Le Village, Aux Cheusots, Clos du Chapitre, La Perrière, En Suchot, Queue de Hareng (located in neighbouring Brochon), Les Arvelets, Les Hervelets, Meix Bas. The best *Premiers Crus* are La Perrière and Clos du Chapitre. *Clos de* la Perrière is a monopoly owned by Philippe Joliet that encompasses En Souchot and Queue de Hareng as well as La Perrière itself.

RED Splendidly deep in colour and full in body with masses of blackcurrant and redcurrant fruit, supported by a good tannic structure.

🍇 Pinot noir, Pinot gris, Pinot liébault

🍷 1983, 1985, 1988, 1989, 1990

🍷 Between 10-20 years

WHITE I have not encountered any but it would not be unreasonable to assume that it might be at least as good as a straight Fixin blanc.

☆ Domaine Berthaut, Gelin & Molin, Pierre Gelin, Philippe Joliet, Cie des Vins d'Autrefois

GEVREY-CHAMBERTIN AOC

Famous for its *Grand Cru* of Chambertin, the best growers also produce superb wines under this appellation. Some vineyards overlap the village of Brochon.

RED Well-coloured wines that are full, rich and elegant with a silky texture and a perfumed aftertaste reminiscent of the pure fruit of Pinot noir.

🍇 Pinot noir, Pinot gris, Pinot liébault

🍷 1983, 1985, 1988, 1989, 1990

🍷 Between 7-15 years

☆ Bernard Bachelet, Alain Burguet, Pierre Damoy, Drouhin-Laroze, Domaine Dujac, Philippe Leclerc, Henri Magnien, Mortet & Fils, Domaine Pernot-Fourrier, Domaine des Perrières, Ponsot, Henri Richard, Philippe Rossignol, Joseph Roty, Georges Roumier & Fils, Armand Rousseau, Louis Trapet, Domaine des Varoilles

GEVREY-CHAMBERTIN PREMIER CRU AOC

Premiers Crus: La Bossière, La Romanée Poissenot, Etournelles, Les Varoilles, Lavaut, Clos du Chapitre, Clos St.-Jacques, Les Cazetiers, Petits Cazetiers, Champeaux, Combe au Moine, Les Goulots, *Aux Combottes, Bel Air, Cherbandes, Champitennois* (or *Petite Chapelle*), En Ergot, *Clos Prieur-Haut, La Perrière, Au Closeau, Plantigone* (or *Issarts*), *Les Corbeaux,* Fonteny, Champonnet.

RED These wines generally have more colour, concentration and finesse than the village wines, but, with the possible exception of Clos St.-Jacques, do not quite match the *Grands Crus*.

🍇 Pinot noir, Pinot gris, Pinot liébault

🍷 1983, 1985, 1988, 1989, 1990

🍷 Between 10-20 years

☆ Bernard Bachelet, Alain Burguet, Pierre Damoy, Claudine Deschamps, Drouhin-Laroze, Domaine Dujac, Henri Magnien, Marchand-Grillot & Fils, Philippe Leclerc, Pernot-Fourrier, Domaine des Perrières, Domaine Ponsot, Henri Rebourseau, Philippe Rossignol, Joseph Roty, Georges Roumier & Fils, Armand Rousseau, Gabriel Tortochot, Domaine des Varoilles

GRANDS ECHÉZEAUX AOC

Grand Cru

The smaller and superior of the two *Grands Crus* of Flagey-Echézeaux, this area is separated from the upper slopes of the Clos de Vougeot by a village boundary.

RED Fine and complex wines that should have a silky bouquet, often reminiscent of violets. The flavour can be very round and rich, but is balanced by a certain delicacy of fruit.

🍇 Pinot noir, Pinot gris, Pinot liébault

🍷 1983, 1985, 1988, 1989, 1990

🍷 Between 10-20 years

☆ Mongeard-Mugneret, Domaine Engel, Domaine de la Romanée-Conti, Robert Sirugue

GRIOTTES-CHAMBERTIN AOC

Grand Cru

The smallest of the nine *Grands Crus* of Gevrey-Chambertin.

RED The best growers produce deep-coloured, delicious wines with masses of soft-fruit flavours and all the velvety texture that could be expected of Chambertin itself.

🍇 Pinot noir, Pinot gris, Pinot liébault

🍷 1983, 1985, 1988, 1989, 1990

🍷 Between 10-20 years

☆ Pernot-Fourrier, Domaine Gouroux, Domaine Ponsot, Joseph Roty

LATRICIÈRES-CHAMBERTIN AOC

Grand Cru

One of the nine *Grands Crus* of Gevrey-Chambertin, situated above the Mazoyères *climat* of Charmes-Chambertin. A tiny part of the adjoining *Premier Cru*, Aux Combottes, also has the right to use this AOC.

RED Solid structure and a certain austerity connect the two different styles of this wine (early-drinking and long-maturing). They sometimes lack fruit and generosity, but wines from the top growers recommended below are always the finest to be found.

🍇 Pinot noir, Pinot gris, Pinot liébault

🍷 1983, 1985, 1988, 1989, 1990

🍷 Between 10-20 years

☆ Hubert Camus, Drouhin-Laroze, Domaine Ponsot, Louis Trapet

MARSANNAY AOC

This village, situated in the very north of the Côte de Nuits, has long been famous for its rosé and has recently developed a reputation for its red wines. In May 1987 it was upgraded to full village AOC status from its previous appellation of Bourgogne-Marsannay.

RED Firm and fruity wines with juicy redcurrant flavours, hints of liquorice, cinnamon and, if new oak has been used, vanilla.

🍇 Pinot noir, Pinot gris, Pinot liébault

🍷 1983, 1985, 1988, 1989, 1990

🍷 Between 4-8 years

WHITE Until May 1987 any white wine made in Marsannay could only be sold under the generic Bourgogne appellation. It will be interesting to see the growers' response to this chance to create a new market for their wines.

🍇 Chardonnay

ROSÉ These dry wines are rich, rather than light and fragrant. Packed with ripe fruit flavours that can include blackberry, blackcurrant, raspberry

and cherry, they are best consumed young, although people do enjoy them when the wine has an orange tinge and the fruit is over-mature.

🍇 Pinot noir, Pinot gris, Pinot liébault

🍷 1982, 1985, 1986, 1989, 1990

🍷 Within 1-3 years

☆ André Bart, René Bouvier, Bruno Clair, Fougeray, Jean Fournier, Huguenot Père et Fils

MARSANNAY LA CÔTE AOC

See Marsannay AOC.

MAZIS-CHAMBERTIN AOC

Grand Cru

Sometimes known as Mazy-Chambertin. This is one of the nine *Grands Crus* of Gevrey-Chambertin.

RED These complex wines have a stature second only to Chambertin and Clos de Bèze. They have a fine, bright colour, super-silky finesse and a delicate flavour that lasts in the mouth.

🍇 Pinot noir, Pinot gris, Pinot liébault

🍷 1983, 1985, 1988, 1989, 1990

🍷 Between 10-20 years

☆ Henri Rebourseau, Joseph Roty, Armand Rousseau, Gabriel Tortochot

MAZOYÈRES-CHAMBERTIN AOC

An alternative appellation for Charmes-Chambertin. *See* Charmes-Chambertin AOC.

MOREY-ST.-DENIS AOC

This excellent little wine village tends to be overlooked. The fact that it is situated between two world-famous places, Gevrey-Chambertin and Chambolle-Musigny, coupled with the fact that Clos St.-Denis is no longer considered to be its top *Grand Cru* (unlike Gevrey's Chambertin and Chambolle's Musigny) does little to promote the name of this village.

RED The best of these village wines have a vivid colour, a very expressive bouquet and a smooth flavour with lots of finesse. A Morey-St.-Denis from a domaine such as Dujac can have the quality of a top *Premier Cru*.

🍇 Pinot noir, Pinot gris, Pinot liébault

🍷 1983, 1985, 1988, 1989, 1990

🍷 Between 8-15 years

WHITE Domaine Ponsot produces a superbly fresh, dry, buttery-rich Morey-St.-Denis blanc that most writers compare to Meursault.

🍇 Chardonnay, Pinot blanc

🍷 1984, 1985, 1986, 1989, 1990

🍷 Between 3-8 years

☆ Pierre Amiot, Georges Bryczek & Fils, Domaine Dujac, Georges Lignier, Ets Nicolas, Domaine Ponsot, Armand Rousseau, Taupenot-Merme, Gabriel Tortochot

MOREY-ST.-DENIS PREMIER CRU AOC

Premiers Crus: Les Genevrières, Monts Luisants, Les Chaffots, Clos Baulet, Les Blanchards, Les Gruenchers, *Les Millandes, Les Faconnières, Les Charrières, Clos des Ormes, Aux Charmes,* Aux Cheseaux, Les Chénevery, Les Sorbès, Clos Sorbè, La Bussière, *Les Ruchots,* Le Village, Côte Rôtie, La Riotte.

RED These wines should have all the colour, bouquet, flavour and finesse of the excellent village wines plus an added expression of *terroir*. The best *Premiers Crus* are: Clos des Ormes, Clos Sorbè and Les Sorbès.

🍇 Pinot noir, Pinot gris, Pinot liébault

🍷 1983, 1985, 1988, 1989, 1990

🍷 Between 10-20 years

WHITE The only white Morey-St.-Denis I know of is from the upper section of Monts Louisants, which is classified as a village appellation. To my knowledge, no white Morey-St.-Denis *Premier Cru* is made.

☆ Pierre Amiot, Georges Bryczek & Fils, Domaine Dujac, Georges Lignier, Louis Rémy, Bernard Sereau, Taupenot-Merme, Gabriel Tortochot

MUSIGNY AOC

Grand Cru

The smaller of Chambolle-Musigny's two *Grand Crus,* it covers some ten hectares (25 acres) on the opposite side of the village to Bonnes Mares.

RED These most stylish of wines have a fabulous colour and a smooth, seductive and spicy bouquet. The velvet-rich fruit flavour constantly unfolds to reveal a succession of taste experiences.

🍇 Pinot noir, Pinot gris, Pinot liébault

🍷 1980, 1982, 1983, 1985

🍷 Between 10-30 years

WHITE Musigny blanc is a rare and expensive dry wine produced solely at Domaine Comte Georges de Vogüé. It combines the steel of a Chablis with the richness of a Montrachet, although it never quite achieves the same quality.

🍇 Chardonnay

🍷 1983, 1984, 1985, 1986

🍷 Between 8-20 years

☆ Georges Roumier & Fils, Comte Georges de Vogüé

NUITS AOC

See Nuits-St.-Georges AOC.

NUITS PREMIER CRU AOC

See Nuits-St.-Georges *Premier Cru AOC.*

NUITS-ST.-GEORGES AOC

More than any other, the name of this town graphically projects the image of full flavour and sturdy structure for which the wines of the Côte de Nuits are justly famous.

RED These are deep-coloured, full and firm wines, but they can lack the style and character of wines such as Gevrey, Chambolle and Morey.

🍇 Pinot noir, Pinot gris, Pinot liébault

🍷 1985, 1988, 1989, 1990

🍷 Between 7-15 years

WHITE A wine that I have not encountered (*see* the *Premier Cru* white Nuits below).

☆ Michel Dupasquier, Roger Dupasquier & Fils, Michel Gavignet, Henri Jayer, Jacqueline Jayer, Henri Remoriquet, Daniel Rion

NUITS-ST.-GEORGES PREMIER CRU AOC

Premiers Crus: Aux Champs Perdrix, En la Perrière Noblet, Les Damodes, Aux Boudots, Aux Cras, La Richemone, Aux Murgers, Aux Vignerondes, Aux Chaignots, Aux Thorey, Les Argillats, Aux Bousselots, Les Crots, Rue de Chaux, Les Hauts Pruliers, Les Procès, Les Pruliers, La Roncière, Les St.-Georges, Les Cailles, Les Porets, Les Vallerots, Les Poulettes, Les Perrières, Les Chaboeufs, Les Vaucrains, Chaine-Carteau, Les Grandes Vignes*, Clos de La Maréchale*, Clos Arlot*, Les Didiers*, Les Forêts* Aux Perdrix*, Clos des Corvées*, Les Argillières* * In the village of Prémeaux-Prissey.

RED These wines have a splendid colour, a spicy-rich bouquet and a vibrant fruit flavour which can be nicely underpinned with vanilla.

🍇 Pinot noir, Pinot gris, Pinot liébault

🍷 1983, 1985, 1988, 1989, 1990

🍷 Between 10-20 years

continued overleaf

WHITE Henri Gouge's "La Perrière" is dry, powerful, almost fat, with a spicy-rich aftertaste. The vines used for this wine have been propagated from a mutant Pinot noir that produced bunches of both black and white grapes. Gouge cut a shoot from a white-grape-producing branch in the mid-1930s. There is now just less than half a hectare (just over one acre) of these vines, none of which have ever reverted to producing black grapes.

🍇 Chardonnay, Pinot blanc

🍷 1984, 1985, 1986, 1989, 1990

🥂 Between 5-10 years

☆ Robert Chevillon, J.-J. Confuron, Claudine Deschamps, Robert Dubois & Fils, Michel Gavignet, Henri Gouges, Jean Grivot, Machard de Gramont, Jacqueline Jayer, Alain Michelot, Gérard Mugneret, Domaine de la Poulette, Henri Remoriquet, Daniel Rion

RICHEBOURG AOC

Grand Cru

One of the five *Grands Crus* at the heart of Vosne-Romanée's vineyards.

RED This is a gloriously rich wine that has a heavenly bouquet and is full of velvety and voluptuous fruit flavours.

🍇 Pinot noir, Pinot gris, Pinot liébault

🍷 1983, 1985, 1988, 1989, 1990

🥂 Between 12-30 years

☆ Jean Grivot, Jean Gros, Domaine de la Romanée-Conti

LA ROMANÉE AOC

Grand Cru

This vineyard is owned by the Domaine du Château de Vosne-Romanée and the wine is matured, bottled and sold by Bouchard Père & Fils. Less than one hectare (two-and-a-half acres), it is the smallest *Grand Cru* of Vosne-Romanée.

RED This is a full, fine and complex wine that might not have the voluptuous appeal of a Richebourg, but has class.

🍇 Pinot noir, Pinot gris, Pinot liébault

🍷 1983, 1985, 1988, 1989, 1990

🥂 Between 12-30 years

☆ Domaine du Château de Vosne-Romanée

ROMANÉE-CONTI AOC

Grand Cru

This Vosne-Romanée *Grand Cru* is under two hectares (five acres) in size and belongs solely to the famous Domaine de la Romanée-Conti.

RED As the most expensive Burgundy in the world, this wine must always be judged by higher standards than all the rest. Yet I must admit that I never fail to be amazed by the stunning array of flavours that continuously unfold in this fabulously concentrated and utterly complex wine.

🍇 Pinot noir, Pinot gris, Pinot liébault

🍷 1983, 1985, 1988, 1989, 1990

🥂 Between 15-35 years

☆ Domaine de la Romanée-Conti

ROMANÉE-ST.-VIVANT AOC

Grand Cru

The largest of the five *Grands Crus* on the lowest slopes and closest to the village.

RED This is the lightest of the fabulous *Grands Crus* of Vosne-Romanée, but what it lacks in power and weight it makes up for in finesse and balance.

🍇 Pinot noir, Pinot gris, Pinot liébault

🍷 1983, 1985, 1988, 1989, 1990

🥂 Between 10-25 years

☆ Robert Arnoux, Alain Hudelot-Noëllat, Domaine de la Romanée-Conti (Marey-Monge)

RUCHOTTES-CHAMBERTIN AOC

Grand Cru

This is the second-smallest of the nine *Grands Crus* of Gevrey-Chambertin. It is situated above Mazis-Chambertin and is the last *Grand Cru* before the slope turns to face north.

RED Normally one of the lighter Chambertin lookalikes, but top growers Roumier and Rousseau seem to achieve a bag-full of added ingredients in their splendidly rich wines.

🍇 Pinot noir, Pinot gris, Pinot liébault

🍷 1983, 1985, 1988, 1989, 1990

🥂 Between 8-20 years

☆ Georges Roumier & Fils, Armand Rousseau

LA TÂCHE AOC

Grand Cru

One of Vosne-Romanée's five *Grands Crus,* this fabulous vineyard belongs to the world-famous Domaine de la Romanée-Conti (DRC), which also owns the *Grand Cru* Romanée-Conti.

RED While this wine is indeed extremely rich and very complex, it does not in comparative terms quite have the richness of Richebourg, nor the complexity of Romanée-Conti. It does, however, have all the silky texture anyone could expect from the finest of Burgundies, and no other wine surpasses La Tâche for finesse.

🍇 Pinot noir, Pinot gris, Pinot liébault

🍷 1983, 1985, 1988, 1989, 1990

🥂 Between 12-30 years

☆ Domaine de la Romanée-Conti

VOSNE-ROMANÉE AOC

The most southerly of the great villages of the Côte de Nuits, some Vosne-Romanée vineyards are in neighbouring Flagey-Echezeaux. This village encompasses the Romanée-Conti vineyard.

RED Sleek, stylish, medium-bodied wines of the purest Pinot noir character and with the silky texture so typical of the wines of this village.

🍇 Pinot noir, Pinot gris, Pinot liébault

🍷 1983, 1985, 1988, 1989, 1990

🥂 Between 10-15 years

☆ Robert Arnoux, Daniel Bissey, Jacques Cacheux, Jean Grivot, Jean Gros, Alain Hudelot-Noëllat, Henri Jayer, Jacqueline Jayer, René Mugneret, Marcel Niquet-Jayer, Daniel Rion

VOSNE-ROMANÉE PREMIER CRU AOC

Premiers Crus: Les Hauts Beaux Monts, Les Beaux Monts, *Les Beaux Monts Bas**, Les Beaux Monts Hauts*, *Les Rouges du Dessus**, En Orveaux*, *Les Brûlées,* La Combe Brûlées, *Les Suchots, La Croix Rameau,* Clos des Réas, *La Grande Rue, Les Gaudichots,* Les Chaumes, *Aux Malconsorts, Cros-Parantoux, Aux Reignots, Les Petits Monts.*
* These *Premier Cru* vineyards of Vosne-Romanée are in Flagey-Echézeaux.

RED Well-coloured wines with fine aromatic qualities that are often reminiscent of violets and blackberries. They have a silky texture and a stylish flavour that is pure Pinot noir. The best *Premiers Crus* to look out for are: La Grande Rue, Les Brûlées, Cros-Parantoux, Les Petits-Monts, Les Suchots and Les Beaumonts (an umbrella name for the various "Beaux Monts", high and low).

🍇 Pinot noir, Pinot gris, Pinot liébault

🍷 1980, 1982, 1983, 1985

🥂 Between 10-20 years

☆ Robert Arnoux, Daniel Bissey, Jacques Cacheux, François Gerbet, Jean Grivot, Jean Gros, Alain Hudelot-Noëllat, Henri Jayer, Jacqueline Jayer, Mongeard-Mugneret, Gerard Mugneret, René Mugneret, Marcel Niquet-Jayer, Michel Noëllat, Daniel Rion

VOUGEOT AOC

With the *Grand Cru* Clos de Vougeot covering 50.6 hectares (124 acres) and the four *Premiers Crus* 11.7 hectares (28.5 acres) of Vougeot's 67.1 hectares (165.5 acres), this appellation of just 4.7 hectares (12 acres) is a real rarity!

RED Little-seen, fine-flavoured, well-balanced wines that are overpriced due to their scarcity. Buy a *Premier Cru* or a well-selected Clos de Vougeot.

🍇 Pinot noir, Pinot gris, Pinot liébault

🍷 1983, 1985, 1988, 1989, 1990

🥂 Between 8-20 years

WHITE A theoretical possibility only, as far as I know.

☆ Robert Arnoux, Domaine Bertagna, Jean Grivot, Jean Gros, Mongeard-Mugneret

VOUGEOT PREMIER CRU AOC

Premiers Crus: Les Crâs, La Vigne Blanche, Les Petits Vougeots, Clos de la Perrière.

The *Premiers Crus* are located between Clos de Vougeot and Musigny and from a *terroir* point of view, should produce much better wines than they do.

RED The wines recommended below are nicely coloured, medium-bodied and have an attractive flavour with a good balance and a certain finesse.

🍇 Pinot noir, Pinot gris, Pinot liébault

🍷 1983, 1985, 1988, 1989, 1990

🥂 Between 10-20 years

WHITE A clean, rich and crisp wine of variable quality, called Clos Blanc de Vougeot, is produced by L'Héritier Guyot from the *Premier Cru* of La Vigne Blanche.

🍇 Chardonnay, Pinot blanc

🍷 1984, 1985, 1986, 1989, 1990

🥂 Between 4-10 years

☆ Domaine Bertagna, L'Héritier Guyot, Henry Lamarche

Côte de Beaune and Hautes-Côtes de Beaune

Softness and finesse are the main characteristics of these wines; they become more evident as the traveller progresses south across the region. Although the Côte de Beaune has some fine red wines, its production is predominantly white and with seven of Burgundy's eight white *Grands Crus,* it is the place par excellence for the Chardonnay grape.

ENTERING THE CÔTE DE BEAUNE from the Nuits-St.-Georges end, the most immediate viticultural differences are its more expansive look and the much greater contrast between the deep, dark and so obviously rich soil found on the inferior eastern side of the RN 74, and the scanty patches of pebble-strewn thick-drift that cover the classic slopes west of the road.

It is often said that the slopes of the Côte de Beaune are gentler than those of the Côte de Nuits, but there are many parts that are just as sheer, although the best vineyards of the Côte de Beaune are located on the middle slopes, which have a gentler incline. The steeper, upper slopes produce good but generally lesser wines in all cases, bar the vineyards of Aloxe-Corton—which is, anyway, more logically part of the Côte de Nuits than the Côte de Beaune. In fact, the Côte de Beaune begins with vineyards that are essentially Côte de Nuits and ends with those that are outside the Côte d'Or and are really part of the Région de Mercurey. The famous Hôtel-Dieu of Beaune, with its distinctive roof, gave rise to the charitable institution of the Hospices de Beaune wines.

Côte de Beaune vineyards, above
The slopes of the Côte de Beaune vineyards are generally a little gentler than those of the Côte de Nuits. In both areas, it is Pinot noir and Chardonnay vines that are the most widely planted.

Claude Bouchard, above
The great Burgundy house of Bouchard Père & Fils, not to be confused with Bouchard Aîné & Fils, produces excellent Grand Cru wines from its Côte d'Or vineyards.

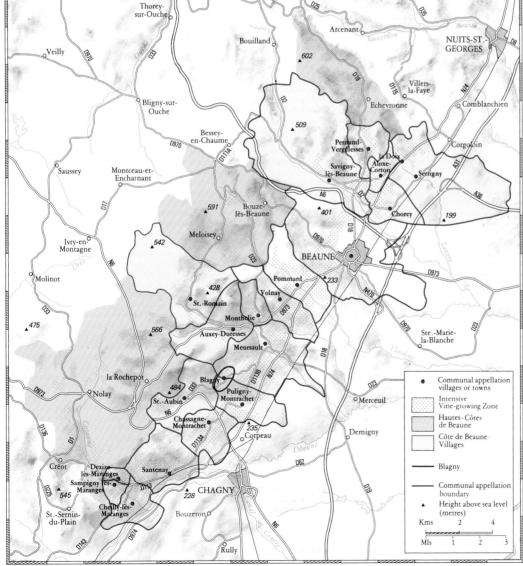

CÔTE DE BEAUNE AND HAUTES-CÔTES DE BEAUNE, see also p. 109

The Côte d'Or is essentially a hilly ridge that follows the trajectory of the Autoroute du Soleil. Most of the village and Hautes-Côtes appellations are clustered in the area between Nuits-St.-Georges in the north, and Chagny in the south.

FACTORS AFFECTING TASTE AND QUALITY

Location
The Côte de Beaune abuts the Côte de Nuits on its southern tip and stretches almost 30 kilometres (18.5 miles) past the town of Beaune to Cheilly-lès-Maranges. Its vines are unbroken, although those of the Hautes-Côtes de Beaune in the western hinterland are divided into two by the Côte de Beaune vineyards of St.-Romain.

Climate
This area has a slightly wetter, more temperate, climate than the Côte de Nuits and the grapes tend to ripen a little earlier. Hail is still a hazard, but less so, with wet winds and heavy rain being a greater nuisance.

Aspect
A series of east-facing slopes, up to two kilometres (one-and-a-quarter miles) wide, which curve in and out to give some vineyards northeastern, some southeastern aspects. Here the vines grow at a height of between 225–380 metres (740–1,250 ft) on slightly less steep slopes than those of the Côte de Nuits. South of Beaune, no vines with the right to the village (and higher) appellations extend past the RN 74 onto the flat and fertile ground beyond.

Soil
A limestone subsoil with sporadic beds of oolitic ironstones with flinty, clay and calcareous topsoils. Light-coloured marl topsoil is found in the vineyards of Chassagne and Puligny.

Viticulture and vinification
The vines are trained low to benefit from heat reflected from the soil at night. In the south of the district, the system employed is similar to that used in parts of Champagne and slightly different from elsewhere on the Côte de Beaune. For red wines, the grapes are almost always destemmed and the juice kept in contact with the skins for between eight and ten days. Classic white wines are cask-fermented and the best wines, both red and white, matured in oak. The flavour of the Pinot noir grape can easily be overwhelmed by oak so it always receives less new oak maturation than Chardonnay.

Primary grape varieties
Pinot noir, Chardonnay

Secondary grape varieties
Pinot gris, Pinot liébault, Pinot blanc, Aligoté, Melon de Bourgogne, Gamay

THE HOSPICES DE BEAUNE LABEL

This distinctive label indicates that the wine comes from vineyards belonging to the Hospices de Beaune, a charitable institution that has cared for the sick and poor of Beaune since 1443. Half a millennium of gifts and legacies has seen the accumulation of vineyards that now total some 55 hectares (136 acres) of *Premiers* and *Grands Crus*.

Since 1859 these wines have been sold by auction and, because of the publicity gained by this annual event, the prices fetched are now generally much higher than the going rate. We must be prepared to pay a relatively higher price for these wines and help the cause.

After some criticism of the unreliability of certain of these wines, a new *cuverie* was built at the rear of the famous Hôtel-Dieu, known for its magnificent Dutch-crafted roof. All the wines are now matured in new oak casks. There remain, however, the variations which result from the different *élevages* of the various casks of the same *cuvée*, for after they have been auctioned they become the responsibility of the purchaser. At the most innocent level, these variations may result from one *négociant* giving his wine more or less cask-maturation than another, and temperature and humidity levels can radically change the wine's alcohol and extract content. But there is also the question of cellar management – many less reputable practices have been known to take place in the dark depths of less scrupulous firms' cellars. These are the same problems that face the consumer when purchasing any Burgundy, so in the final analysis, it must be the consumer's confidence in the *négociant* (whose name appears on the label) that is the deciding factor.

Hospices de Beaune

MAZIS-CHAMBERTIN
Appellation Mazis-Chambertin Contrôlée

Cuvée Madeleine-Collignon

de la

Réserve Particulière des Hospices de Beaune

THE HOSPICES DE BEAUNE *CUVÉES*

RED WINES

Cuvée Clos des Avaux
AOC Beaune
Unblended Les Avaux

Cuvée Billardet
AOC Pommard
A blend of Petits-Epenots, Les Noizons, Les Arvelets, Les Rugiens

Cuvée Blondeau
AOC Volnay
A blend of Champans, Taille Pieds, Roceret, En l'Ormeau

Cuvée Boillot
AOC Auxey-Duresses
Unblended Les Duresses

Cuvée Brunet
AOC Beaune
A blend of Les Teurons, La Mignotte, Les Bressandes, Les Cents Vignes

Cuvée Madeleine Collignon
AOC Mazis-Chambertin
Unblended Mazis-Chambertin

Cuvée Cyrot Chaudron
AOC Beaune
Unblended Beaune

Cuvée Cyrot Chaudron
AOC Pommard
Unblended Pommard

Cuvée Dames de la Charité
AOC Pommard
A blend of Les Épenots, Les Rugiens, Les Noizons, La Refène, Les Combes Dessus

Cuvée Dames Hospitalières
AOC Beaune
A blend of Les Bressandes, La Mignotte, Les Teurons, Les Grèves

Cuvée Maurice Drouhin
AOC Beaune
A blend of Les Avaux, Les Grèves, Les Bourcherottes, Champs Pimont

Cuvée Charlotte Dummay
AOC Corton
A blend of Renardes, Les Bressandes, Clos du Roi

Cuvée Forneret
AOC Savigny-lès-Beaune
A blend of Les Vergelesses, Aux Gravains

Cuvée Fouquerand
AOC Savigny-lès-Beaune
A blend of Basses Vergelesses, Les Talmettes, Aux Gravains, Aux Serpentières

Cuvée Gauvain
AOC Volnay
A blend of Les Santenots, Les Pitures

Cuvée Arthur Girard
AOC Savigny-lès-Beaune
A blend of Les Peuillets, Les Marconnets

Cuvée Guigone de Salins
AOC Beaune
A blend of Les Bressandes, En Sebrey, Champs Pimont

Cuvée Hugues et Louis Bétault
AOC Beaune
A blend of Les Grèves, La Mignotte, Les Aigrots, Les Sizies, Les Vignes Franches

Cuvée Lebelin
AOC Monthélie
Unblended Les Duresses

Cuvée Jehan de Massol
AOC Volnay-Santenots
Unblended Les Santenots

Cuvée Muteau
AOC Volnay
A blend of Volnay-le-Village, Carelle sous la Chapelle, Cailleret Dessus, Fremiet, Taille-Pieds

Cuvée Docteur Peste
AOC Corton
A blend of Bressandes, Chaumes, Voirosses, Clos du Roi, Fiètre, Les Grèves

Cuvée Rameau-Lamarosse
AOC Pernaud-Vergelesses
Unblended Les Basses Vergelesses

Cuvée Nicolas Rolin
AOC Beaune
A blend of Les Cents Vignes, Les Grèves, En Genêt

Cuvée Rousseau-Deslandes
AOC Beaune
A blend of Les Cent Vignes, Les Montrevenots, La Mignotte, Les Avaux

WHITE WINES

Cuvée de Bahèzre de Lanlay
AOC Meursault-Charmes
A blend of Les Charmes Dessus, Les Charmes Dessous

Cuvée Baudot
AOC Meursault-Genevrières
A blend of Genevrières Dessus, Genevrières Dessous

Cuvée Philippe le Bon
AOC Meursault-Genevrières
A blend of Genevrières Dessus, Les Genevrières Dessous

Cuvée Paul Chanson
AOC Corton-Vergennes
Unblended Corton-Vergennes

Cuvée Goureau
AOC Meursault
A blend of Le Poruzot, Les Pitures, Les Cras

Cuvée Albert-Grivault
AOC Meursault-Charmes
Unblended Les Charmes Dessus

Cuvée Jehan Humblot
AOC Meursault
A blend of Le Poruzot, Grands Charrons

Cuvée Loppin
AOC Meursault
Unblended Les Criots

Cuvée Françoise-de-Salins
AOC Corton-Charlemagne
Unblended Corton-Charlemagne

The wines of the Côte de Beaune and Hautes-Côtes de Beaune

Note: All the *Grands Crus* of Côte de Beaune have their own separate appellations and are therefore listed individually below. The *Premiers Crus,* however, do not have their own appellations and so are listed under the appellation of the village in which the vineyards are situated. Those *Premiers Crus* that are virtually contiguous with *Grand Cru* vineyards of the same appellation are italicized.

ALOXE-CORTON AOC

This village is more Côte de Nuits than Côte de Beaune, as its 99 per cent red-wine production suggests.

RED These deeply coloured, firm-structured wines with compact fruit are excellent value and reminiscent of reds from northern Côte de Nuits.

🍇	Pinot noir, Pinot gris, Pinot liébault
🍷	1982, 1983, 1985
⌛	Between 10-20 years

WHITE Very little Aloxe-Corton blanc is made, but Daniel Senard makes a lovely buttery-rich, concentrated pure Pinot gris wine (which makes it a red wine according to the regulations).

🍇	Chardonnay
🍷	1985, 1986, 1988, 1989, 1990
⌛	Between 4-8 years

☆ Adrien Belland, Bonneau du Martray, Hubert Bouzereau-Gruère, Chandon de Briailles, Louis Chapuis, Dubreuil-Fontaine, Michel Gaunoux, Antonin Guyon, Guyot Père & Fils, Didier Meunevaux, Domaine Parent, Rapet Père & Fils, Rollin Père & Fils, Daniel Senard, Tollot-Beaut

ALOXE-CORTON PREMIER CRU AOC

Premiers Crus: Les Chaillots, Les Fournières, Les Meix, Les Guérets, Les Vercots, *Les Valozières, Les Paulands, Les Maréchaudes, La Maréchaude*, La Toppe au Vert*, Les Petites Lolières*, Les Moutottes*, La Coutière**
* Premier Cru vineyards of Aloxe-Corton in Ladoix-Serrigny.

RED These wines can have an intense bouquet and a firm, spicy fruit flavour. The best *Premiers Crus* are Les Fournières, Les Valozières, Les Paulands and Les Maréchaudes.

🍇	Pinot noir, Pinot gris, Pinot liébault
🍷	1983, 1985, 1988, 1989, 1990
⌛	Between 10-20 years

WHITE I have never encountered any.

☆ Capitain-Cagnerot, Louis Chapuis, Antonin Guyon, Didier Meunevaux, André Nudant & Fils

AUXEY-DURESSES AOC

A beautiful village, set in an idyllic valley behind Monthélie and Meursault.

RED Attractive wines that are not very deep in colour, but have a softness of fruit and a little finesse.

🍇	Pinot noir, Pinot gris, Pinot liébault
🍷	1983, 1985, 1988, 1989, 1990
⌛	Between 6-12 years

WHITE Medium-bodied wines that have a full, spicy-nutty flavour, not dissimilar to a modest Meursault.

🍇	Chardonnay, Pinot blanc
🍷	1981, 1983, 1984, 1985, 1986
⌛	Between 3-7 years

☆ Robert Ampeau, Julien Coche-Débord & Fils, Jean-Pierre Diconne, Olivier Leflaive, Claude Marechal-Jacquet, Naudin-Varrault, Michel Prunier, Guy Roulot, Bernard Roy, Cie des Vins d'Autrefois

AUXEY-DURESSES-CÔTES DE BEAUNE AOC

Alternative appellation for red wines only. *See* Auxey-Duresses AOC.

AUXEY-DURESSES PREMIER CRU AOC

Premiers Crus: Climat du Val, Les Bretterins, Reugne, Les Duresses, Bas des Duresses, Les Grands-Champs, Les Ecusseaux

RED The *Premiers Crus* provide nicely coloured soft wines with good finesse. The best have fine redcurrant Pinot character with the creamy-oak of cask maturity.

🍇	Pinot noir, Pinot gris, Pinot liébault
🍷	1983, 1985, 1988, 1989, 1990
⌛	Between 7-15 years

WHITE Excellent value, smooth and stylish wines in the Meursault mould.

🍇	Chardonnay, Pinot blanc
🍷	1984, 1985, 1986, 1989, 1990
⌛	Between 4-10 years

☆ Gérard Creusfond, Jean-Pierre Diconne, Charles Jobard, Bernard Roy, Jean Prunier

BÂTARD-MONTRACHET AOC

Grand Cru

This *Grand Cru* is situated on the slope beneath Le Montrachet and overlaps both Chassagne-Montrachet and Puligny-Montrachet.

WHITE This full-bodied, intensely rich wine has masses of nutty, honey and toast flavours and is one of the greatest dry white wines in the world.

🍇	Pinot chardonnay
🍷	1983, 1984, 1985, 1989, 1990
⌛	Between 8-20 years

☆ Blain-Gagnard, Gagnard-Delagrange, Lequin-Roussot, Pierre Morey, Michel Niellon, Etienne Sauzet

BEAUNE AOC

The famous town of Beaune gives its name to village wines and *Premiers Crus,* but not to any *Grands Crus.*

RED These soft-scented, gently fruity, wines are consistent and good value.

🍇	Pinot noir, Pinot gris, Pinot liébault
🍷	1983, 1985, 1988, 1989, 1990
⌛	Between 6-14 years

WHITE White Beaune is an uncomplicated dry Chardonnay wine with a characteristic soft finish.

🍇	Chardonnay, Pinot blanc
🍷	1985, 1988, 1989, 1990
⌛	Between 3-7 years

☆ Chantal-Lescure, Bertrand Darviot, Bernard Delagrange, Michel Gaunoux, Machard de Gramont, Albert Morey, Château St.-Nicolas, Thévenin-Monthélie, Tollot-Beaut, Domaine Voiret

BEAUNE PREMIER CRU AOC

Beaune's vineyards have an ideal southeast aspect, thus most are classified as *Premiers Crus.*
Premiers Crus: Les Boucherottes, Les Chouacheux, Les Beaux Fougets, Les Epenottes, Le Clos des Mouches, Les Montrevenots, Les Vignes Franches, Pertuisots, Les Aigrots, Les Sizies, Clos Landry, Les Tuvilains, Belissand, Les Avaux, Champ Pimont, Les Seurey, Le Clos de la Mousse, Les Reversées, Les Blanches Fleurs, Clos du Roi, Les Fèves, Les Cents Vignes, A l'Ecu, Les Bressandes, Les Toussaints, Les Marconnets, En Genêt, En l'Orme, Les Perrières, Les Grèves, Aux Coucherias, Sur les Grèves, Aux Cras, Le Bas des Teurons, Les Teurons, Montée Rouge, La Mignotte, Les Longes

RED The best *crus* are medium-bodied with a delightfully soft rendition of Pinot fruit and lots of finesse.

🍇	Pinot noir, Pinot gris, Pinot liébault
🍷	1983, 1985, 1988, 1989, 1990
⌛	Between 10-20 years

WHITE These wines have lovely finesse and can display a toasty flavour more common to richer growths.

🍇	Chardonnay, Pinot blanc
🍷	1983, 1984, 1985, 1989, 1990
⌛	Between 5-12 years

☆ Robert Ampeau, Arnoux Père & Fils, Besancenot-Mathouillet, Jacques Germain, Michel Lafarge, Chantal Lescure, Lycée Agricole et Viticole de Beaune, Machard de Gramont, Albert Morey, Domaine Mussy, Domaine Parent, Prieur-Brunet, Jacques Prieur, Tollot-Beaut, Cie des Vins d'Autrefois, Louis Violland, Domaine Voiret

BIENVENUES-BÂTARD-MONTRACHET AOC

Grand Cru

This is one of Puligny-Montrachet's four *Grands Crus.*

WHITE Not the fattest dry wines from this village, but they have great finesse, an immaculate balance and some of the nuttiness, honey and toast expected in all Montrachets.

🍇	Chardonnay
🍷	1984, 1985, 1986, 1989, 1990
⌛	Between 8-20 years

☆ Carillon Louis & Fils, Domaine Leflaive

BLAGNY AOC

A red-only appellation from Blagny, a tiny hamlet shared by the communes of Meursault and Puligny-Montrachet.

RED These rich, full-flavoured, Meursault-like red wines are underrated.

🍇	Pinot noir, Pinot gris, Pinot liébault
🍷	1983, 1985, 1988, 1989, 1990
⌛	Between 8-15 years

☆ Robert Ampeau, Domaine Matrot

BLAGNY-CÔTE DE BEAUNE AOC

Alternative appellation for Blagny.
See Blagny AOC.

BLAGNY PREMIER CRU AOC

Premiers Crus: La Jeunelotte, La Pièce sous le Bois, Sous le Dos d'Âne, Sous Blagny (in Meursault) and Sous le Puits, La Garenne or Sur la Garenne, Hameau de Blagny (in Puligny-Montrachet).

RED These rich wines have even more grip and attack than basic Blagny.

🍇	Pinot noir, Pinot gris, Pinot liébault
🍷	1983, 1985, 1988, 1989, 1990
⌛	Between 10-20 years

☆ Robert Ampeau, Domaine Matrot

BOURGOGNE CLAIRET HAUTES-CÔTES DE BEAUNE AOC

Another appellation that is outmoded and rarely seen. Its wines conform to Bourgogne AOC regulations. *See* Bourgogne AOC.

BOURGOGNE HAUTES-CÔTES DE BEAUNE AOC

This appellation is larger and more varied than Hautes-Côtes de Nuits.

RED Ruby-coloured, medium-bodied wines with an attractive Pinot perfume and a soft, creamy-fruit finish.

🍇 Pinot noir, Pinot gris, Pinot liébault

🍷 1983, 1985, 1988, 1989, 1990

🍾 Between 4-10 years

WHITE Not very frequently encountered, but Guillemard-Dupont's pure Pinot Buerot (Pinot gris) is rich, dry and expressive. Its grape variety makes it a very pale white, red or rosé according to the regulations!

🍇 Chardonnay, Pinot blanc

🍷 1984, 1985, 1986, 1989, 1990

🍾 Within 1-4 years

ROSÉ Pleasantly dry and fruity wines with some richness and a soft finish.

🍇 Pinot noir, Pinot gris, Pinot liébault

🍷 1983, 1985, 1986, 1989, 1990

🍾 Within 1-3 years

☆ François Charles, Guillemard-Dupont, Stéphane Demangeot, Lucien Jacob, Jean Joliot & fils, Domaine Mazilly, Claude Nouveau, Michel Serveau, Domaine des Vignes des Demoiselles

CHARLEMAGNE AOC

Grand Cru

This white-only *Grand Cru* of Aloxe-Corton overlaps Pernand-Vergelesses and is almost, but not quite identical to the *Grand Cru* of Corton-Charlemagne.

CHASSAGNE-MONTRACHET AOC

Village wines with less reputation than those of Puligny-Montrachet.

RED Firm, dry wines with more colour and less softness than most Côte de Beaune reds.

🍇 Pinot noir, Pinot gris, Pinot liébault

🍷 1983, 1985, 1988, 1989, 1990

🍾 Between 10-20 years

WHITE An affordable introduction to the great wines of Montrachet.

🍇 Chardonnay, Pinot blanc

🍷 1984, 1985, 1986, 1989, 1990

🍾 Between 5-10 years

☆ Adrien Belland, Blain-Gagnard, Madame François Colin, Marc Colin, Michel Colin-Deléger, Jean-Noël Gagnard, Gagnard-Delagrange, Fontaine-Gagnard, Château Génot-Boulanger, l'Héritier-Guyot, Bernard Morey, Jean-Marc Morey, Michel Niellon, Jean & Fernand Pillot, André Ramonet

CHASSAGNE-MONTRACHET-CÔTE DE BEAUNE AOC

Alternative appellation for red wines only. *See* Chassagne Montrachet AOC.

CHASSAGNE-MONTRACHET PREMIER CRU AOC

Premiers Crus: Clos St.-Jean, Les Rebichets, Les Murées, Chassagne du Clos St.-Jean, Chassagne, Les Combards, En Cailleret, Vigne Derrière, Les Chaumées, Petingeret, Les Pasquelles, Les Vergers, Les Commes, Les Chenevottes, Les Bondues, Les Macherelles, En Remilly, *Dent de Chien, Vide Bourse, Blanchot Dessus, Les Places, La Maltroie,* Ez Crets, La Grande Borne, La Cardeuse, Les Brussonnes, Les Boirettes, Clos Chareau, Francemont, Clos Pitois, Les Morgeots, La Chapelle, Vigne Blanche, Ez Crottes, Guerchère, Tête du Clos, Les Petits Clos, Les Grands Clos, La Roquemaure, Champ Jendreau, Les Chaumes, La Boudriotte, Les Fairendes, Les Petites Fairendes, Les Baudines, La Romanée, En Virondot, Les Grandes Ruchottes, Les Champs Gain, La Grande Montagne

RED The weight of a Côte de Nuits and the softness of a Côte de Beaune.

🍇 Pinot noir, Pinot gris, Pinot liébault

🍷 1983, 1985, 1988, 1989, 1990

🍾 Between 10-25 years

WHITE Flavoursome dry wines.

🍇 Chardonnay, Pinot blanc

🍷 1984, 1985, 1986, 1989, 1990

🍾 Between 6-15 years

☆ Bernard Bachelet & ses Fils, Adrien Belland, Madame François Colin, Marc Colin, Michel Colin-Deléger, Georges Deléger, Jean-Noël Gagnard, Gagnard-Delagrange, Château Génot-Boulanger, René Lamy, Jean-Marc Morey, Paul Pillot, Prieur-Brunet, André Ramonet, Roux Père & Fils

CHEILLY-LÈS-MARANGES AOC

One of a trio of villages sharing the once-famous *cru* of Marange.

RED Light wines in colour and body.

🍇 Pinot noir, Pinot gris, Pinot liébault

🍷 1983, 1985, 1988, 1989, 1990

🍾 Between 2-7 years

WHITE I have always assumed this wine to be a figment of regulatory imagination, but official statistics for the past twenty years reveal that 45 cases were produced in 1985 and 75 cases in 1983!

CHEILLY-LÈS-MARANGES CÔTE DE BEAUNE AOC

Alternative appellation for red wines only. *See* Cheilly-lès-Maranges AOC.

CHEILLY-LÈS-MARANGES PREMIER CRU AOC

Premiers Crus: En Marange, La Boutière, Les Plantes de Marange. Wines from one-quarter of the vineyards have *Premier Cru* status.

CHEVALIER-MONTRACHET AOC

Grand Cru

This is one of Puligny-Montrachet's four *Grands Crus*.

WHITE Fatter and richer than Bienvenues-Bâtard-Montrachet, this wine has more explosive flavour than Bâtard-Montrachet.

🍇 Chardonnay •

🍷 1984, 1985, 1986, 1989, 1990

🍾 Between 10-20 years

☆ Domaine Leflaive, Michel Niellon

CHOREY-LÈS-BEAUNE AOC

This satellite appellation of Beaune produces exciting, underrated wines.

RED Although next to Aloxe-Corton, Chorey has all the soft and sensuous charms that are quintessentially Beaune.

🍇 Pinot noir, Pinot gris, Pinot liébault

🍷 1983, 1985, 1988, 1989, 1990

🍾 Between 7-15 years

WHITE Less than one per cent of the wines produced in this village are white.

☆ Gay Père & Fils, Jacques Germain, Tollot-Beaut & Fils, Tollot-Voarick

CHOREY-LÈS-BEAUNE CÔTE DE BEAUNE AOC

Alternative appellation for red wines only. *See* Chorey-lès-Beaune AOC.

CORTON AOC

Grand Cru

One of the *Grands Crus* of Aloxe-Corton (part extends into Ladoix-Serrigny and Pernand-Vergelesses), it is the only *Grand Cru* in the Côte de Beaune that includes red and white wines and thus parallels the Côte de Nuits *Grand Cru* Musigny. Where applicable, the names of specific *climats* within the Corton vineyard itself are traditionally indicated on the label.

RED These wines may sometimes appear intense and brooding in their youth, but, when fully mature, a great Corton has such finesse and complexity that it can stun the senses.

🍇 Pinot noir, Pinot gris, Pinot liébault

🍷 1983, 1985, 1988, 1989, 1990

🍾 Between 12-30 years

WHITE A medium- to full-bodied wine with a fine and rich flavour.

🍇 Chardonnay

🍷 1984, 1985, 1986, 1989, 1990

🍾 Between 10-25 years

☆ Adrien Belland, Bonneau-du-Martray, Hubert Bouzereau-Gruère, Cachat-Occuidant, Capitain-Gagnerot, Chandon de Briailles, Dubreuil-Fontaine, Michel Gaunoux, Domaine Parent, Rapet Père & Fils, Daniel Senard

CORTON-CHARLEMAGNE AOC

Grand Cru

This famous *Grand Cru* of Aloxe-Corton extends into Ladoix-Serrigny and Pernand-Vergelesses.

WHITE This is the most sumptuous of all white Burgundies. It has a fabulous concentration of rich, buttery fruit flavours, a dazzling balance of acidity and delicious overtones of vanilla, honey and cinnamon.

🍇 Chardonnay

🍷 1984, 1985, 1986, 1989, 1990

🍾 Between 10-25 years

☆ Bonneau du Martray, Capitain-Gagnerot, Laleure-Piot, Domaine Leflaive, Rollin Père & Fils, André Thiély

CÔTE DE BEAUNE AOC

Wines that are entitled to the actual Côte de Beaune appellation are restricted to a few plots on the Montagne de Beaune around Beaune.

RED Fine, stylish wines that reveal the purest of Pinot noir fruit produced in the soft Beaune style.

🍇 Pinot noir, Pinot gris, Pinot liébault

🍷 1983, 1985, 1988, 1989, 1990

🍾 Between 10-20 years

WHITE Little-seen, dry basic Beaune.

🍇 Chardonnay, Pinot blanc

🍷 1984, 1985, 1986, 1989, 1990

🍷 Between 3-8 years

☆ Lycée Agricole & Viticole de Beaune, Marchard de Gramont, Maurice Joliette, Rossignol Frères, Domaine Voiret

CÔTE DE BEAUNE-VILLAGES AOC

While AOC Côte de Nuits-Villages covers red and white wines in a predominantly red-wine district, AOC Côte de Beaune-Villages applies only to red wines in a district that produces the greatest white Burgundies!

RED Excellent value fruity wines, made in true soft Beaune style.

🍇 Pinot noir, Pinot gris, Pinot liébault

🍷 1983, 1985, 1988, 1989, 1990

🍷 Between 7-15 years

☆ Bernard Bachelet & Fils, Lequin Roussot

CRIOTS-BÂTARD-MONTRACHET AOC

Grand Cru

The smallest of Chassagne-Montrachet's three *Grands Crus.*

WHITE This wine has some of the weight of its great neighbours and a lovely hint of honey-and-toast richness, but it is essentially the palest and most fragrant of all the Montrachets.

🍇 Pinot chardonnay

🍷 1984, 1985, 1986, 1989, 1990

🍷 Between 8-20 years

☆ Joseph Belland, Blain-Gagnard

DEZIZE-LÈS-MARANGES AOC

One of the trio of villages sharing the once-famous *cru* of Marange.

RED Production is erratic, with most of the wine sold to *négociants* for blending into Côte de Beaune-Villages.

🍇 Pinot noir, Pinot gris, Pinot liébault

WHITE Apart from 22 cases produced in 1984, the little white wine produced in this village usually ends up as Bourgogne blanc.

🍇 Chardonnay, Pinot blanc

DEZIZE-LÈS-MARANGES-CÔTE DE BEAUNE AOC

Alternative appellation for red wines only. *See* Dezize-lès-Maranges AOC.

DEZIZE-LÈS-MARANGES PREMIER CRU AOC

Premier Cru: Marange

Red and white wines from half of the vineyards of this village have the right to *Premier Cru* status.

LADOIX AOC

Parts of Ladoix-Serrigny have the right to the Aloxe-Corton *Premier Cru* appellation or the *Grands Crus* of Corton and Corton-Charlemagne. This appellation covers the rest of the wine produced.

RED Many wines are merely rustic versions of Aloxe-Corton, but there are some fine grower wines that combine the compact fruit and structure of a Nuits with the softness of a Beaune.

🍇 Pinot noir, Pinot gris, Pinot liébault

🍷 1982, 1983, 1985

🍷 Between 7-20 years

WHITE Just five per cent of the production is white and it is not very well distributed.

🍇 Chardonnay, Pinot blanc

🍷 1984, 1985, 1986, 1989, 1990

🍷 Between 4-8 years

☆ Pierre André, Capitain-Gagnerot, Christian Gros, Maillard Père & Fils, Michel Mallard, Domaine Rougeot

LADOIX-CÔTE DE BEAUNE AOC

Alternative appellation for red wines only. *See* Ladoix AOC.

LADOIX PREMIER CRU AOC

Premiers Crus: La Micaude, La Corvée, Le Clou d'Orge, Les Joyeuses, Bois Roussot, Basses Mourottes, Hautes Mourottes.
The *Premiers Crus* with the Ladoix appellation are separate from those with the Aloxe-Corton appellation.

RED These wines are decidedly finer in quality and deeper in colour than those with the basic village appellation.

🍇 Pinot noir, Pinot gris, Pinot liébault

🍷 1983, 1985, 1988, 1989, 1990

🍷 Between 7-20 years

WHITE I have never encountered any.

☆ Capitain-Gagnerot, André Nudant & Fils, Domaine G. & P. Ravaut

MEURSAULT AOC

While the greatest white Côte de Beaune is either Montrachet or Corton-Charlemagne, Meursault is probably better known and is certainly more popular.

RED Red Meursault is often treated as a novelty, but it is a fine wine in its own right, with a firm edge.

🍇 Pinot noir, Pinot gris, Pinot liébault

🍷 1983, 1985, 1988, 1989, 1990

🍷 Between 8-20 years

WHITE Even a basic Meursault should be deliciously dry with a nutty-buttery-spice to its typically rich flavour.

🍇 Chardonnay, Pinot blanc

🍷 1984, 1985, 1986, 1989, 1990

🍷 Between 5-12 years

☆ Robert Ampeau, Hubert Bouzereau-Gruère, Jean-François Coche Dury, Bernard Delagrange, Sélection Jean Germain, François Jobard, Domaine des Comtes Lafon, Domaine du Duc de Magenta, Domaine Matrot, Michelot-Buisson, Jean Monnier & Fils, Pierre Morey, Guy Roulot

MEURSAULT-BLAGNY AOC

Alternative appellation for Meursault wines from vineyards in the neighbouring village of Blagny. *See* Meursault AOC.

MEURSAULT-CÔTE DE BEAUNE AOC

Alternative red-wine-only appellation for Meursault. *See* Meursault AOC.

MEURSAULT PREMIER CRU AOC

Premiers Crus: Les Cras, Les Caillerets, Les Plures, Les Santenots Blancs, Les Santenots du Milieu, Les Charmes-Dessus, Les Charmes-Dessous, Aux Perrières, Les Perrières-Dessus, Les Perrières-Dessous, Les Chaumes des Perrières, Les Genevrières-Dessus, Les Chaumes de Narvaux, Les Genevrières-Dessous, Le Porusot-Dessus, Les Porusot-Dessous, Le Porusot, Les Bouchères, Les Gouttes d'Or, La Jeunelotte, La Pièce sous le Bois, Sous le Dos d'Âne, Sous Blagny.

RED Finer and firmer than the basic village wines, these reds need plenty of time to soften.

🍇 Pinot noir, Pinot gris, Pinot liébault

🍷 1983, 1985, 1988, 1989, 1990

🍷 Between 10-20 years

WHITE Great Meursaults should always be rich and some may even be fat. Their various permutations of nutty, buttery and spicy Chardonnay flavours may often be submerged by

the honey, cinnamon and vanilla of new oak until considerably mature.

🍇 Chardonnay, Pinot blanc

🍷 1984, 1985, 1986, 1989, 1990

🍷 Between 6-15 years

☆ Robert Ampeau, François Jobard, Michelot Buisson, Jean-François Coche Dury, Henri Germain, Sélection Jean Germain, Domaine des Comtes Lafon, Domaine du Duc de Magenta, Jean Monnier, Pierre Morey, Domaine Pitoiset-Uréna, Domaine Prieur-Brunet, Domaine Rougeot, Guy Roulot

MEURSAULT-SANTENOTS AOC

An alternative appellation for Meursault *Premier Cru* coming from a part of the Volnay-Santenots appellation. *See* Volnay-Santenots AOC.

MONTHÉLIE AOC

Monthélie's wines, especially the *Premiers Crus,* are probably the most underrated in Burgundy.

RED These excellent wines have a vivid colour, expressive fruit, a firm structure and a lingering, silky finish.

🍇 Pinot noir, Pinot gris, Pinot liébault

🍷 1982, 1983, 1985

🍷 Between 7-15 years

WHITE Relatively little white wine is produced, but Thomas-Bassot and Charles Vienot produce fine examples.

🍇 Chardonnay, Pinot blanc

🍷 1984, 1985, 1986, 1989, 1990

🍷 Between 3-7 years

☆ Thomas-Bassot, Jacques-Biogelot, Denis Boussey, Eric Boussey, Xavier Bouzerand, M. Deschamps, Paul Garaudet, Château de Monthélie, Monthélie-Douhairet, Charles Vienot

MONTHÉLIE-CÔTE DE BEAUNE AOC

Alternative appellation for red wines only. *See* Monthélie AOC.

MONTHÉLIE PREMIER CRU AOC

Premiers Crus: Les Riottes, Sur la Velle, Le Meix Bataille, Le Clos Gauthey, Les Vignes Rondes, Le Cas Rougeot, La Taupine, Les Champs Fulliot, Les Village de Monthélie, La Château Gaillard, Les Duresses

RED Monthélie's *Premiers Crus* are hard to find, but worth seeking out.

🍇 Pinot noir, Pinot gris, Pinot liébault

🍷 1983, 1985, 1988, 1989, 1990

🍷 Between 8-20 years

WHITE I have never encountered any.

☆ Jacques Boigelot, Denis Boussey, Paul Garaudet, Maison Pierre Porrot

MONTRACHET AOC

Grand Cru

Many consider this the greatest dry white wine in the world.

WHITE When fully mature, Montrachet has the most glorious and expressive character of all dry white wines. Its honeyed, toasty, floral, nutty, creamy and spicy aromas are stunning.

- Pinot chardonnay
- 1984, 1985, 1986, 1989, 1990
- Between 10-30 years

☆ Domaine de la Romanée-Conti, Delagrange-Bachelet, Gagnard-Delagrange, René Fleurot, Jacques Prieur, Ramonet-Prudhon, Domaine Baron Thénard

LE MONTRACHET AOC

See Montrachet AOC.

PERNAND-VERGELESSES AOC

This village, located just above Aloxe-Corton, is the most northerly appellation of the Côte de Beaune.

RED With the exception of the silky-wines recommended below, too many of these are rustic and overrated and would be better off in a *négociant* Côte de Beaune-Villages blend.

- Pinot noir, Pinot gris, Pinot liébault
- 1983, 1985, 1988, 1989, 1990
- Between 7-15 years

WHITE Although this village is famous for its Aligoté, some growers produce smooth and deliciously balanced wines that deserve more recognition.

- Chardonnay, Pinot blanc
- 1984, 1985, 1986, 1989, 1990
- Betweeh 4-8 years

☆ Denis Père & Fils, Dubreuil-Fontaine, Jacques Germain, Domaine de la Guyonnière, Laleure-Piot, Olivier Leflaive, Rollin Père & Fils, André Thiely, Michel Voarick

PERNAND-VERGELESSES-CÔTE DE BEAUNE AOC

Alternative appellation for red wines only. *See* Pernand-Vergelesses AOC.

PERNAND-VERGELESSES PREMIER CRU AOC

Premiers Crus: Creux de la Net, En Caradeux, Les Fichots, Ile des Vergelesses, Les Vergelesses.

RED These wines repay keeping until the fruit develops a silkiness that hangs gracefully on the wine's structure and gives Pernand's *Premiers Crus* the class its village wines lack.

- Pinot noir, Pinot gris, Pinot liébault
- 1983, 1985, 1988, 1989, 1990
- Between 10-20 years

WHITE The Beaune firm of Chanson Père & Fils produces a consistent wine of medium body, dry but mellow.

- Chardonnay, Pinot blanc
- 1984, 1985, 1986, 1989, 1990
- Between 4-8 years

☆ Dubreuil-Fontaine, Laleure-Piot, Rapet Père & Fils

POMMARD AOC

A very famous village with a "reborn" image built up by a group of dedicated and skilful winemakers.

RED The "famous" dark, alcoholic and soupy wines of Pommard are now mostly a thing of the past, having been replaced by exciting fine wines.

- Pinot noir, Pinot gris, Pinot liébault
- 1983, 1985, 1988, 1989, 1990
- Between 8-16 years

☆ Billard-Gonnet, Henri Boillot, Domaine de Coucel, Michel Gaunoux, Louis Glantenay, Guillemard-Dupont & ses Fils, Olivier Leflaive, Domaine Lejeune, Machard de Gramont, Domaine de Montille, Domaine Mussy, Domaine Parent, Pothier-Rieusset

POMMARD PREMIER CRU AOC

Premiers Crus: La Chanière, Les Charmots, La Platière, Les Arvelets, Les Saussilles, Les Pézerolles, En Largillière, Les Grands Epenots, Les Petits Epenots, Les Boucherottes, Clos Micot, Les Combes-Dessus, Clos de Verger, Clos de la Commaraine, La Refène, Clos Blanc, Village, Derrière St.-Jean, Les Chaponnières, Les Croix Noires, Les Poutures, Les Bertins, Les Fremiers, Les Jarolières, Les Rugiens-Bas, Les Rugiens-Hauts, Les Chanlins-Bas

RED The best *crus* are the various *climats* of Les Rugiens (deep and voluptuous) and Les Epenots (soft, fragrant and rich).

- Pinot noir, Pinot gris, Pinot liébault
- 1983, 1985, 1988, 1989, 1990
- Between 10-20 years

☆ Domaine Comte Armand, Billard-Gonnet, Henri Boillot, Domaine de Courcel, Michel Gaunoux, Jules Guillemard, Louis Glantenay, Domaine Lejeune, Machard de Gramont, Mazilly Père & Fils, Jean Monnier, Monthélie-Douhairet, Hubert de Montille, Domaine Parent, Pothier-Rieusset

PULIGNY-MONTRACHET AOC

One of two Montrachet villages responsible for producing some of the greatest dry whites in the world.

RED Although some fine wines are made, Puligny-Montrachet *rouge* demands a premium for its scarcity.

- Pinot noir, Pinot gris, Pinot liébault
- 1983, 1985, 1988, 1989, 1990
- Between 10-20 years

WHITE Basic Puligny-Montrachet from a top grower is a very high quality wine: full-bodied, fine and steely, requiring a few years to develop a nutty honey-and-toast flavour.

- Chardonnay, Pinot blanc
- 1984, 1985, 1986, 1989, 1990
- Between 5-12 years

☆ Robert Ampeau, Philippe Bouzereau, Gérard Chavy, Henri Clerc, Madame François Colin, Domaine Leflaive, Etienne Sauzet

PULIGNY-MONTRACHET-CÔTE DE BEAUNE AOC

Alternative appellation for red wines only. *See* Puligny-Montrachet AOC.

PULIGNY-MONTRACHET PREMIER CRU AOC

Premiers Crus: Sous le Courthil, Les Chalumeaux, Champ Canet, La Jaquelotte (or Champ Canet), Clos de la Garenne (or Champ Canet), La Garenne (or Sur la Garenne), Sous le Puits, Hameau de Blagny, La Truffière, Champ Gain, Ez Folatières, En la Richarde, Peux Bois, Au Chaniot, *Le Cailleret, Les Pucelles,* Clos des Meix, Clavaillon, Les Perrières, Les Referts, Les Combettes

RED I have never encountered any.

- Pinot noir, Pinot gris, Pinot liébault

WHITE A *Premier Cru* Puligny made by a top grower such as Etienne Sauzet is one of the most flavour-packed taste experiences you are likely to encounter.

- Chardonnay, Pinot blanc
- 1984, 1985, 1986, 1989, 1990
- Between 7-15 years

☆ Robert Ampeau, Philippe Bouzereau, Madame François Colin, Domaine Leflaive, Olivier Leflaive, Domaine Matrot, Domaine Monnot, Etienne Sauzet

ST.-AUBIN AOC

This underrated village has many talented winemakers and is an excellent source for good-value wines.

RED Delicious, ripe but light, fragrant and fruity red wines that quickly develop a taste of wild strawberries.

- Pinot noir, Pinot gris, Pinot liébault
- 1983, 1985, 1988, 1989, 1990
- Between 4-8 years

WHITE Super-value white wines – a sort of "Hautes-Côtes Montrachet!"

- Chardonnay, Pinot blanc
- 1984, 1985, 1986, 1989, 1990
- Between 3-8 years

☆ Domaine Bachelet, Raoul Clerget, Aimé Langoureau, André Moingeon, Henri Prudhon & Fils

ST.-AUBIN-CÔTE DE BEAUNE AOC

Alternative appellation for red wines only. *See* St.-Aubin AOC.

ST.-AUBIN PREMIER CRU AOC

Premiers Crus: Derrière la Tour, En Créot, Bas de Vermarain à l'Est, Les Champlots, En Montceau, Sous Roche Dumay, Sur Gamay, La Chatenière, Le Bas de Gamay à l'Est, Les Cortons, En Remilly, Les Murgers des Dents de Chien, Les Combes au Sud, Pitangeret, Le Charmois, En Vollon à l'Est, Le Village, Les Castets, Derrière chez Edouard, Le Puits, Les Travers de Marinot, Vignes Moingeon, En la Ranché, Sur le Sentier du Clou, Marinot, Echaille, Les Perrières, Les Frionnes, Es Champs.

The best are Les Frionnes and Les Murgers des Dents de Chien, followed by La Chatenière, Les Castets, En Remilly and Le Charmois.

RED Very appealing strawberry and oaky-vanilla wines that are delicious young, yet improve further with age.

- Pinot noir, Pinot gris, Pinot liébault
- 1983, 1985, 1988, 1989, 1990
- Between 5-15 years

WHITE These dry wines are often superior to the village wines of Puligny-Montrachet and always much cheaper.

- Chardonnay, Pinot blanc
- 1984, 1985, 1986, 1989, 1990
- Between 4-10 years

☆ Giles Bouton, Raoul Clerget, Marc Colin, Hubert Lamy, Aimé Langoureau, Henri Prudhon et Fils, Roux Père & Fils, Gérard Thomas

ST.-ROMAIN AOC

A little village amid picturesque surroundings in the hills above Auxey-Duresses.

RED Good-value, medium-bodied, rustic reds that have a good, characterful flavour and plenty of attack.

- Pinot noir, Pinot gris, Pinot liébault
- 1983, 1985, 1988, 1989, 1990
- Between 4-8 years

WHITE Fresh and lively, light- to medium-bodied dry white wines of an honest Chardonnay style.

- Chardonnay, Pinot blanc
- 1984, 1985, 1986, 1989, 1990
- Between 3-7 years

☆ Fernand Bazenet, Henri Buisson, Alain Gras, René Gras-Boisson, Domaine du Château de Puligny-Montrachet, Thévenin-Monthélie

ST.-ROMAIN-CÔTE DE BEAUNE AOC
Alternative appellation for red wines only. *See* St.-Romain AOC.

SAMPIGNY-LÈS-MARANGES AOC
One of the trio of villages sharing the once-famous *cru* of Marange. Before 1980, production was sporadic and it has not yet established any sort of reputation. White wines are allowed, but none have been produced.

SAMPIGNY-LÈS-MARANGES-CÔTE DE BEAUNE AOC
Alternative appellation for red wines. *See* Sampigny-lès-Maranges AOC.

SAMPIGNY-LÈS-MARANGES PREMIER CRU AOC
Premiers Crus: Le Clos des Rois, Maranges
See Sampigny-lès-Maranges AOC.

SANTENAY AOC
This most southerly village appellation of the Côte d'Or (but not of the Côte de Beaune) is a source of Burgundy that is good value.

RED These wines are fresh and frank, with a clean rendition of Pinot noir fruit supported by a firm structure.

- Pinot noir, Pinot gris, Pinot liébault
- 1983, 1985, 1988, 1989, 1990
- Between 7-15 years

WHITE Just two per cent of Santenay is white, but some good buys can be found amongst the top growers.

- Chardonnay, Pinot blanc
- 1984, 1985, 1986, 1989, 1990
- Between 4-8 years

☆ Domaine de l'Abbaye de Santenay, Adrien Belland, Hubert Bouzereau, Jean Giradin, Hervé Olivier, Lequin-Roussot, Bernard Morey, Domaine de la Pousse d'Or

SANTENAY-CÔTE DE BEAUNE AOC
Alternative appellation for red wines only. *See* Santenay AOC.

SANTENAY PREMIER CRU AOC
Premiers Crus: La Comme, Clos de Tavannes, Les Gravières, Beauregard, Comme Dessus, Clos Faubard, Clos des Mouches, Passetemps, La Maladière, Grand Clos Rousseau, Le Chainey, Petit Clos Rousseau, Les Fourneaux.
The best are Clos de Tavannes, Les Gravières, La Maladière and La Comme Dessus.

RED In the pure and frank mould of Pinot noir wines, but with an added expression of *terroir.*

- Pinot noir, Pinot gris, Pinot liébault
- 1983, 1985, 1988, 1989, 1990
- Between 6-15 years

WHITE Rarely encountered.

- Chardonnay, Pinot blanc
- 1984, 1985, 1986, 1989, 1990
- Between 5-10 years

☆ Domaine de l'Abbaye de Santenay, Adrien Belland, Roger Belland, Michel et Denis Clair, Jean Giradin, Jessiaume Père & Fils, Lequin-Roussot, Mestre Père & Fils, Bernard Morey, Lucien Muzard, Hervé Oliver, Domaine de la Pousse d'Or, Roux

SAVIGNY AOC
See Savigny-lès-Beaune AOC.

SAVIGNY-CÔTE DE BEAUNE AOC
Alternative appellation for red wine only. *See* Savigny-lès-Beaune AOC.

SAVIGNY-LÈS-BEAUNE AOC
This village has a number of gifted winemakers who produce very underrated and undervalued wines.

RED Delicious, easy-to-drink, medium-bodied wines that are very soft and Beaune-like in style.

- Pinot noir, Pinot gris, Pinot liébault
- 1983, 1985, 1988, 1989, 1990
- Between 7-15 years

WHITE Some excellent dry wines with good concentration of flavour, a smooth texture and some finesse are made but they are difficult to find.

- Chardonnay, Pinot blanc
- 1984, 1985, 1986, 1989, 1990
- Between 4-10 years

☆ Robert Ampeau, Simon Bize & Fils, Maurice Giboulot, Girard-Vollot, Pierre Guillemot, Lucien Jacob, Domaine Parent, Jean-Marc Pavelot, Domaine du Prieuré, Rollin Père & Fils, Tollot-Beaut

SAVIGNY-LÈS-BEAUNE-CÔTE DE BEAUNE AOC
Alternative appellation for red wines only. *See* Savigny-lès-Beaune AOC.

SAVIGNY PREMIER CRU AOC
See Savigny-lès-Beaune *Premier Cru* AOC.

SAVIGNY-LÈS-BEAUNE PREMIER CRU AOC
Premiers Crus: Les Charnières, Les Talmettes, Aux Vergelesses, Basses Vergelesses, Aux Fournaux, Les Lavières, Aux Gravains, Petits Godeaux, Aux Serpentières, Aux Clous, Aux Guettes, Les Rouvrettes, Les Narbantons, Les Jarrons (or La Dominodes), Hauts Jarrons, Redrescut, Les Peuillets, Bas Marconnets, Les Hauts Marconnets.

RED These wines have a very elegant, soft and stylish Pinot flavour that hints of strawberries, cherries and violets. They are of a far higher standard than the basic village wine and the best are: Les Lavières, La Dominodes, Aux Vergelesses, Les Marconnets and Aux Guettes.

- Pinot noir, Pinot gris, Pinot liébault
- 1983, 1985, 1988, 1989, 1990
- Between 7-20 years

WHITE Little produced and seldom seen, but Domaine des Terregelesses produces a splendidly rich, dry wine.

- Chardonnay, Pinot blanc
- 1984, 1985, 1986, 1989, 1990
- Between 5-15 years

☆ Pierre Bitouzet, Simon Bize & Fils, Valentin Bouchotte, N. & J.-M. Capron-Manieux, Domaine Chandon de Brailles, Maurice Ecard, Girard-Vollot, Pierre Guillemot, Guyot Père & Fils, Lucien Jacob, Domaine Parent, Jean-Marc Pavelot, Domaine des Terregelesses, Tollot-Beaut

VOLNAY AOC
This quaint village ranks in quality and performance with such great growths as Gevrey-Chambertin and Chambolle-Musigny.

RED These wines are not cheap, but they are firm and well coloured with more silky finesse than should be expected from a village appellation.

- Pinot noir, Pinot gris, Pinot liébault
- 1983, 1985, 1988, 1989, 1990
- Between 6-15 years

☆ Marquis d'Angerville, Bernard Delagrange, Louis Glantenay, Michel Lafarge, Olivier Leflaive, Domaine de Montille, Domaine de la Pousse d'Or

VOLNAY PREMIER CRU AOC
Premiers Crus: Chanlin, Pitures Dessus, Lassolle, Clos de Ducs, Le Village, La Barre, Bousse d'Or, Les Brouillards, Les Mitans, En l'Ormeau, Les Angles, Pointes d'Angles, Frémiets, La Gigotte, Les Grands Champs, Les Lurets, Robardelle, Carelle sous la Chapelle, Carelles Dessous, Le Ronceret, Les Aussy, En Champans, Cailleret Dessus (part of which may be called Clos des 60 Ouvrées), En Cailleret, En Chevret, Taille Pieds, En Verseuil, Clos des Chênes.

RED No *Grands Crus,* but its silky-smooth and fragrant *Premiers Crus* are great wines. The best are: Clos des Chêne, Taille Pieds, Bousse d'Or, Clos de Ducs, the various *climats* of Cailleret, Clos des 60 Ouvrées, En Champans.

- Pinot noir, Pinot liébault
- 1983, 1985, 1988, 1989, 1990
- Between 8-20 years

☆ Marquis d'Angerville, Henri Boillot, Félix Clerget, Bernard Delagrange, Bitouzet Prieur, Michel Lafarge, Monthélie-Douhairet, Hubert de Montille, Domaine de la Pousse d'Or, Domaine Prieur-Brunet

VOLNAY-SANTENOTS AOC
This confusing appellation is in Meursault, not Volnay, although it does run up to the boundary of that village. White wines cannot be called Volnay-Santenots and must be sold as Meursault or, if produced from the two-thirds of this vineyard furthest from the Volnay border, they may be sold as Meursault Premier Cru or Meursault-Santenots.

RED These wines, which are not often encountered, are similar to Volnay but can lack its silky elegance.

- Pinot noir, Pinot gris, Pinot liébault
- 1983, 1985, 1988, 1989, 1990
- Between 8-20 years

☆ Robert Ampeau, Domaine des Comtes de Lafon, Jacques Prieur, Prieur-Brunet

The Région de Mercurey

A simple district in winemaking terms, with just five appellations, two white-only and three red and white. The quality is very good and the value for money even better.

THE RÉGION DE MERCUREY, or Côte Chalonnaise as it is sometimes called, was once the forgotten area of Burgundy. While Chablis and the Côte d'Or have always been rightly perceived as producing the greatest of all Burgundy's wines, the Mâconnais and the Beaujolais succeeded because they were inexpensive producers of unpretentious, fresh, light and quaffing wines. The Côte Chalonnaise was, however, a bit too serious for its own good because its flavoursome and buttery style has more in common with the wines of the Côte de Beaune than anywhere else, so most merchants considered it inferior and pretentious.

Perhaps the Côte Chalonnaise need not have been forgotten had the merchants perceived it more as a superior Mâconnais than an inferior Côte de Beaune. Now it is no longer forgotten. Over the last ten years, as merchants across the world have become more willing to seek out lesser-known wines, it has built up a reputation as one of Burgundy's best sources of quality wines.

EXCELLENT *NÉGOCIANTS*

The Burgundy drinker is blessed with a fine choice of *négociants* in the Région de Mercurey, including Chandesais, Delorme and Faiveley. There is an excellent *coopérative* at Buxy and an increasing number of highly talented growers. This district produces a large amount of fine Crémant de Bourgogne and the only single-village appellation of Aligoté wine.

THE CHANTE FLÛTÉ LABEL OF MERCUREY

Since 1972 the Confrérie St.-Vincent et des Disciples de la Chante Flûté de Mercurey has held regular annual tastings in a similar fashion to those of the *Tastevinage* in the Côte de Nuits (*see* The *Tastevinage* label, p. 116), but restricted in this case to the wines of Mercurey.

Although the Mercurey appellation as a whole has a very consistent reputation for fine wines, these Chante Flûté wines are always amongst the very best produced in the Région de Mercurey.

FACTORS AFFECTING TASTE AND QUALITY

Location
Three islands of vines situated to the west of Chalon-sur-Saône, 350 kilometres (217 miles) southeast of Paris, between the Côte de Beaune in the north and the Mâconnais in the south.

Climate
Slightly dryer than that of the Côte d'Or, with many of the best slopes protected from the worst ravages of frost and hail.

Aspect
A disjointed district where the great plâteau of the Côte d'Or peters out into a complex chain of small hills with vines clinging to the most favourable slopes, at a height of between 230-320 metres (750-1,050 ft), in a far more sporadic fashion than those in the Côte d'Or.

Soil
Limestone subsoil with clay-sand topsoils that are sometimes enriched with iron deposits. At Mercurey there are limestone ooliths mixed with iron-enriched marl.

Viticulture and vinification
The wines are produced in an identical way to those of the Côte de Beaune, with no exceptional viticultural or vinification techniques involved, *see* p.122.

Primary grape varieties
Pinot noir, Chardonnay

Secondary grape varieties
Pinot gris, Pinot liébault, Pinot blanc, Aligoté, Melon de Bourgogne, Gamay

---

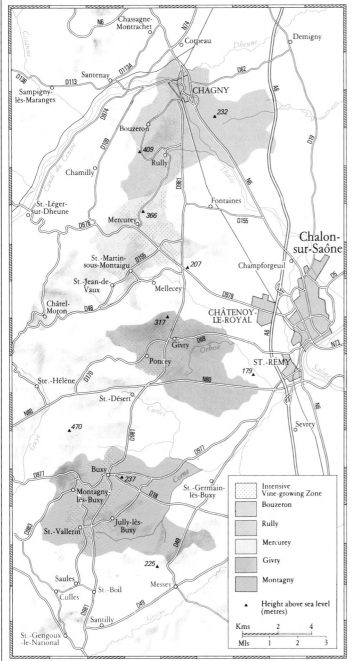

THE RÉGION DE MERCUREY, see also p. 109

The vine-growing zones form three separate "islands" west of Chalon.

Legend:
- Intensive Vine-growing Zone
- Bouzeron
- Rully
- Mercurey
- Givry
- Montagny
- ▲ Height above sea level (metres)

Vineyard and château of Rully, right
The most northerly AOC vineyards of the Côte Chalonnaise, Rully produces excellent dry Chardonnay wines and some pleasant red wines as well.

The wines of the Région de Mercurey

BOURGOGNE ALIGOTÉ BOUZERON AOC

In 1979 Bouzeron became the only *cru* to have its own appellation specifically for the Aligoté grape.

WHITE This excellent and interesting dry wine is much the fullest version of Aligoté available. In weight, fruit and spice its style is nearer to Pinot gris than Chardonnay.

🍇 Aligoté with up to 15% Chardonnay

📅 1984, 1985, 1986, 1989, 1990

⏳ Between 2-6 years

☆ Ancien Domaine Carnot, Chanzy Frères, A. & P. de Villaine

BOURGOGNE CÔTE CHALONNAISE AOC

As from the 1990 vintage, basic Bourgogne wines produced exclusively from grapes harvested within the region may be sold under this more specific appellation.

GIVRY AOC

Underrated wines from a village just south of Mercurey. There are no *Premiers Crus,* but the best wines are certainly of that standard.

RED Light- to medium-bodied, soft and fruity wine with delightful nuances of cherry and redcurrant.

🍇 Pinot noir, Pinot gris, Pinot liébault

📅 1983, 1985, 1988, 1989, 1990

⏳ Between 5-12 years

WHITE Just ten per cent of Givry is white – a deliciously clean, dry Chardonnay that can have an attractive spicy-buttery hint on the aftertaste.

🍇 Chardonnay, Pinot blanc

📅 1984, 1985, 1986, 1989, 1990

⏳ Between 3-8 years

☆ Jean Chofflet, Jean Cléau, Propriété Desvignes, Domaine Joblot, Domaine Ragot, Clos St.-Pierre, Domaine du Gardin, Bernard Tatraux, Domaine Baron Thénard

MERCUREY AOC

The wines of Mercurey, including the *Premiers Crus,* account for two-thirds of the production of the entire Région de Mercurey. Just five per cent of these two Mercurey appellations' wine is white.

RED Medium-bodied wines with excellent colour and fine varietal character that have an exceptional quality-for-price ratio.

🍇 Pinot noir, Pinot gris, Pinot liébault

📅 1983, 1985, 1988, 1989, 1990

⏳ Between 5-12 years

WHITE Dry wines that combine the lightness and freshness of the Mâconnais with some of the fat and butteryness of the Côte de Beaune.

🍇 Pinot chardonnay

📅 1984, 1985, 1986, 1989, 1990

⏳ Between 3-8 years

☆ Domaine Brintet, Michel Juillot, Paul de Launay, Jean Maréchal, Jean-Pierre Muelien, Domaine Saier, Yves de Suremain

MERCUREY PREMIER CRU AOC

Premiers Crus: Le Clos, Clos Voyens (or Les Voyens), Clos du Roi, Les Fourneaux (or Clos des Fourneaux), Les Grands Voyens, Le Marcilly (or Clos Marcilly), Les Montaigus (or Clos des Montaigus), Les Petits Voyens

RED These wines should have all the pure Pinot characteristics of basic Mercurey, but with added depth and more finesse.

🍇 Pinot noir, Pinot gris, Pinot liébault

📅 1983, 1985, 1988, 1989, 1990

⏳ Between 5-15 years

WHITE I have only encountered white Mercurey at the basic village level.

☆ Chanzy Frères, Yves de Suremain

MONTAGNY AOC

White wines only, from the southernmost area of the Région de Mercurey. As all the vineyards in Montagny are *Premiers Crus,* the only wines you will encounter under the basic village appellation are those that fail to meet the technical requirement of 11.5 per cent alcohol before chaptalization.

WHITE These light- to medium-bodied, dry white wines are good-value, fuller versions of the white Mâcon type.

🍇 Chardonnay

📅 1984, 1985, 1986, 1989, 1990

⏳ Between 3-10 years

☆ Arnoux Père & Fils, Producteurs de Buxy, Bernard Michel, Jean Vachet

MONTAGNY PREMIER CRU AOC

Premiers Crus: Les Bassets, Les Beaux Champs, Les Bonnevaux, Les Bordes, Les Bouchots, Le Breuil, Les Burnins, Les Carlins, Les Champs-Toiseau, Les Charmelottes, Les Chandits, Les Chazelles, Clos Chaudron, Le Choux, Les Clouzeaux, Les Coères, Les Combes, La Condemine, Cornevent, La Corvée, Les Coudrettes, Les Craboulettes, Les Crets, Creux des Beaux Champs, l'Epaule, Les Garchères, Les Gouresses, La Grand Pièce, Les Jardins, Les Las, Les Males, Les Marais, Les Marocs, Les Monts Cuchots, Le Mont Laurent, La Mouillère, Moulin l'Echenaud, Les Pandars, Les Pasquiers, Les Pidans, Les Platières, Les Resses, Les St.-Mortille, Les St.-Ytages, Sous les Roches, Les Thilles, La Tillonne, Les Treuffères, Les Varignys, Le Vieux Château, Vignes Blanches, Vignes sur le Clou, Les Vignes Couland, Les Vignes Derrière, Les Vignes Dessous, La Vigne Devant, Vignes Longues, Vignes du Puits, Les Vignes St-Pierre, Les Vignes du Soleil.

With every one of its 60 vineyards classified as *Premier Cru,* Montagny is unique amongst the villages of Burgundy.

WHITE These delicious dry wines have a buttery-rich Chardonnay flavour that is more akin to that of the Côte de Beaune than it is to neighbouring Mâconnais. The best of the cask-matured wines are firm in body with attractive nuances of creamy-ripe vanilla.

🍇 Chardonnay

📅 1984, 1985, 1986, 1989, 1990

⏳ Between 4-12 years

☆ Arnoux Père & Fils, Producteurs de Buxy, Château de la Saule, Jean Vachet

RULLY AOC

The Région de Mercurey's northernmost appellation produces wines that are closest in character to those from the southern Côte de Beaune. More than half the production is Rully blanc.

RED Delightfully fresh and fruity wines of light-to-medium body and some finesse, which are uncomplicated when young but develop well.

🍇 Pinot noir, Pinot gris, Pinot liébault

📅 1983, 1985, 1988, 1989, 1990

⏳ Between 5-12 years

WHITE These are serious dry wines that tend to have a crisper balance than wines produced further south in Montagny, although a few can be quite fat.

🍇 Chardonnay

📅 1984, 1985, 1986, 1989, 1990

⏳ Between 3-8 years

☆ Belleville, Raymond Betes, H. & P. Jacqueson, Noël-Bouton, Château de Rully

RULLY PREMIER CRU AOC

Premiers Crus: Bas de Vauvry, La Bressaude, Champ-Clou, Chapitre, Les Cloux, La Fosse, Grésigny, Margotey, Marrissou, Meix Caillet, Mont Palais, Moulesne, Phillot, Préau, Raboursay, Raclot, La Renarde.

RED Fine-quality, medium-bodied wines with a silky texture added to the summer-fruit flavour found in the basic village examples.

🍇 Pinot noir, Pinot gris, Pinot liébault

📅 1983, 1985, 1988, 1989, 1990

⏳ Between 5-15 years

WHITE Generally finer, fuller and richer dry wines, many with excellent finesse and even some complexity.

🍇 Chardonnay

📅 1984, 1985, 1986, 1989, 1990

⏳ Between 4-12 years

☆ Domaine Belleville, René Brelière, H. & P. Jacqueson, Domaine du Prieuré, Château de Rully, Robert de Suremain

The Mâconnais

The Mâconnais produces three times more white wine than the rest of Burgundy put together and, although it never quite matches the heights of quality achieved in the Côte d'Or, it is easily the best-value pure Chardonnay wine in the world.

THE MÂCONNAIS IS AN ANCIENT viticultural area that was renowned as long as 1,600 years ago when Ausonius, the Roman poet of St.-Emilion, mentioned its wines. Today it makes sense to couple it with the Beaujolais because, while Chardonnay is the dominant white grape in both districts (as it is in the rest of Burgundy), the Gamay is the dominant black grape, which it is not elsewhere; this forms a natural link between the two. Conceived as one large district, the Mâconnais can be seen as its essentially white-wine area and the Beaujolais as its almost entirely red-wine area.

MÂCON ROUGE – A RELIC OF THE PAST?

Essentially a white-wine district, some 25 per cent of the vines planted are in fact Gamay; a further seven-and-a-half per cent are Pinot noir. The Gamay does not, however, perform very well on the limestone soils of the Mâconnais and despite the smoothing effect of modern vinification techniques, these wines will always be of rustic quality with a characteristic hard edge. I well remember a particular blind tasting I once organized. All that the tasters knew about the wines was that they were produced from the Gamay grape and were mostly Beaujolais. British Master of Wine Christopher Tatham simply wrote "Limestone's the trouble!" against one wine. It turned out to be the only Mâcon Rouge.

It is possible to make a pure Pinot noir Mâcon Rouge, but because the market assumes that this appellation is pure Gamay, there is little incentive for producers to plant the more noble grape. It is, however, far more suitable and capable of producing wines of some finesse in the limestone vineyards of the Mâconnais. Perhaps it is time to introduce a Mâcon Rouge Pinot Noir appellation, or maybe producers should print the grape variety boldly on the label of the existing appellation.

FACTORS AFFECTING TASTE AND QUALITY

Location
Situated halfway between Lyon and Beaune, its vineyards adjoin those of the Mercurey region to the north and overlap with those of Beaujolais in the south.

Climate
The climate is similar to that of the Mercurey region, but with a Mediterranean influence gradually creeping in towards the south, so occasional storms are more likely.

Aspect
The soft, rolling hills in the north of the Mâconnais, which are a continuation of those in the Mercurey region, give way to a more closely-knit topography with steeper slopes and sharper contours becoming increasingly prominent as one travels further south.

Soil
A topsoil of scree and alluvium or clay and clay-sand, covering a limestone subsoil.

Viticulture and vinification
Some exceptional wines (like the "Vieilles Vignes" Château de Fuissé made in Pouilly Fuisse) can stand a very heavy oak influence, but most of the white wines are fermented in stainless steel and bottled very early,to retain as much freshness as possible. The red wines are vinified by *macération carbonique*, either fully or in part.

Primary grape varieties
Chardonnay, Gamay

Secondary grape varieties
Pinot noir, Pinot gris, Pinot liébault, Pinot blanc, Aligoté, Melon de Bourgogne

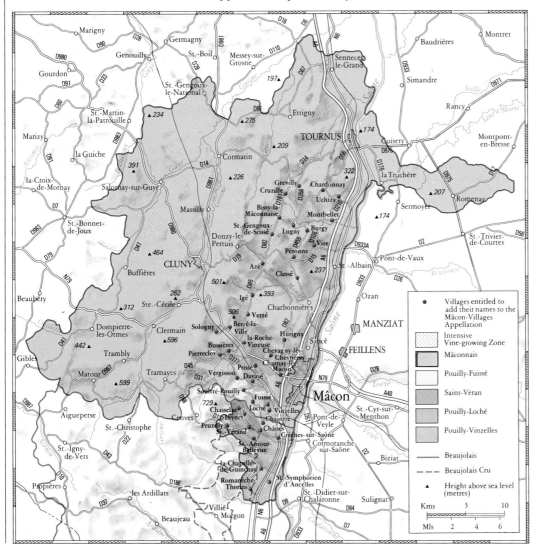

Villages entitled to add their names to the Mâcon-Villages Appellation

Intensive Vine-growing Zone

Mâconnais

Pouilly-Fuissé

Saint-Véran

Pouilly-Loché

Pouilly-Vinzelles

Beaujolais

Beaujolais Cru

▲ Height above sea level (metres)

Kms   5   10

Mls   2   4   6

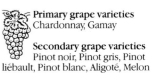

The rock of Solutré, above
The dramatic shape of the rock of Solutré, one of the 42 villages of the Mâcon-Villages appellation, and a commune of Pouilly-Fuissé, towers over its vineyard.

THE MÂCONNAIS,
see also p. 109

Concentrated to the west of the river Saône, the famous appellations of Mâconnais interlace with those of Beaujolais to the south and spread out over the area northwest of Mâcon itself.

The wines of the Mâconnais

MÂCON AOC

Most wines from this district-wide appellation are produced in the area north of the Mâcon-Villages area.

RED Better vinification techniques have improved the quality of these essentially Gamay wines, but it is still a grape that does not like limestone.

🔖 Gamay, Pinot noir, Pinot gris

🏷 1985, 1986, 1988, 1989, 1990

⌛ Between 2-6 years

WHITE Basic Chardonnay quality, but fresh, frank and tasty dry wines that are easy to quaff and superb value.

🔖 Chardonnay, Pinot blanc

🏷 1984, 1985, 1986, 1989, 1990

⌛ Within 1-4 years

ROSÉ Lightweight wines with an attractive pale raspberry colour and light fruit flavour that are more successful than their counterparts.

🔖 Gamay, Pinot noir, Pinot gris

🏷 1983, 1985, 1986, 1989, 1990

⌛ Within 1-3 years

MÂCON-VILLAGES AOC

This white-only appellation covers 42 villages, eight of which also fall within the Beaujolais-Villages appellation (see p.134); four of these have the additional right to the St.-Véran AOC (see p.132). If the wine comes from a single village, it may replace the "Villages" part of this appellation with the name of that specific village (see the list below for details of all 42 villages).

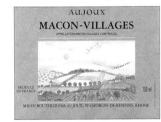

WHITE These are some of the world's most delicious, thirst-quenching and easy-to-drink, dry Chardonnay wines. They represent tremendous value.

🔖 Chardonnay, Pinot blanc

🏷 1984, 1985, 1986, 1989, 1990

⌛ Within 1-4 years

☆ Arcelin, André Bonhomme, Cave Coopérative de Chaintré, Cave des Crus Blancs, Jean Thévenet, Jean Signoret, Pierre Mahuet, René Michel & Fils, Gilbert Mornand, Henri Goyard

The 42 villages of Mâcon-Villages
The single-village version of the above appellation covers the white wines from the following 42 villages:

MÂCON-AZE AOC

This village has a good coopérative and a certain reputation for its wines, but I have had no experience of them.

MÂCON-BERZÉ-LE-VILLE AOC

I have not encountered any single-village wines from these steep vineyards.

MÂCON-BISSY-LA-MÂCONNAISE AOC

This village, located in the extreme north of the village appellations, has a good coopérative.

MÂCON-BURGY AOC

I have very little experience of single-village wines from this hamlet, but some elegant examples from Domaine de Chervin demonstrate its potential.

☆ Domaine de Chervin

MÂCON-BUSIÈRES AOC

I have not encountered this wine.

MÂCON-CHAINTRE AOC

One of five communes that form the appellation of Pouilly-Fuissé. The wines from this village are entitled to both appellations.

☆ Cave Coopérative de Chaintre

MÂCON-CHÂNES AOC

Also part of the Beaujolais-Villages and St.-Véran areas, the wines of this village have a choice of three appellations.

MÂCON-LA CHAPELLE-DE-GUINCHAY AOC

This village is also part of the Beaujolais-Villages area and its wines therefore have the right to both appellations.

MÂCON-CHARDONNAY AOC

The wines from this village have a certain following due in part, no doubt, to the novelty of its name. Its coopérative, however, produces fine wines.

☆ Cave Coopérative de Chardonnay

MÂCON-CHARNAY-LÈS-MÂCON AOC

These excellent wines are produced just east of Pouilly-Fuissé.

☆ Chevalier & Fils, Domaine Manciat

MÂCON-CHASSELAS AOC

Unfortunately, Chasselas is also the name of a table grape known for producing inferior wines. The growers here usually sell their wines as basic Mâcon or as St.-Véran.

MÂCON-CHEVAGNY-LÈS-CHEVRIÈRES AOC

I have not encountered this wine.

MÂCON-CLESSÉ AOC

One of the best Mâcon villages, the wines of Clessé are well perfumed and show great finesse.

☆ René Michel, Gilbert Mornand, Jean Signoret, Jean Thévenet

MÂCON-CRÈCHES-SUR-SAÔNE AOC

I have not encountered this wine.

MÂCON-CRUZILLE AOC

Little-seen wines from a tiny hamlet in the extreme north of the village appellations area.

☆ Guillot-Broux

MÂCON-DAVAYE AOC

Some excellent wines are made here, but they are usually sold under the St.-Véran appellation.

MÂCON-FUISSÉ AOC

This village is one of five communes that form the appellation of Pouilly-Fuissé. Who would be silly enough to sell Mâcon-Fuissé rather than Pouilly-Fuissé?

☆ Jean-Paul Thibert

MÂCON-GRÉVILLY AOC

A village with a good reputation located in the extreme north of the village appellations area.

☆ Guillot-Broux

MÂCON-HURIGNY AOC

I have not encountered this wine.

MÂCON-IGÉ AOC

The wines from this village are not very often seen, but have a good reputation.

☆ Cave Coopérative de d'Igé

MÂCON-LEYNES AOC

This village is in an area that is also part of the Beaujolais-Villages and St.-Véran AOCs and its wines therefore have a choice of all three appellations.

☆ André Depardon

MÂCON-LOCHÉ AOC

This village also has the right to the Pouilly-Loché and Pouilly-Vinzelles AOCs and its wines therefore have a choice of three appellations.

☆ Caves des Crus Blancs, Château de Loché

MÂCON-LUGNY AOC

Louis Latour has done much to promote the wines of this village.

☆ Louis Latour, Producteurs de Lugny-St.-Gengoux-de-Scissé, Domaine de Prieuré

MÂCON-MILLY-LAMARTINE AOC

I have not encountered this wine.

MÂCON-MONTBELLET AOC

I have not encountered this wine.

MÂCON-PÉRONNE AOC

I have seldom encountered these wines but some of them show promise.

☆ Maurice Josserand, Domaine du Mortier, Daniel Rousset

MÂCON-PIERRECLOS AOC

I have not encountered this wine.

MÂCON-PRISSÉ AOC

This village is also part of the St.-Véran area and its wines therefore have a choice of both appellations.

☆ Groupement Producteurs de Prissé

MÂCON-PRUZILLY AOC

This village is situated in the Beaujolais-Villages area and its wines therefore have a choice of both appellations.

MÂCON-LA ROCHE VINEUSE AOC

Underrated wines produced on west- and south-facing slopes north of Pouilly-Fuissé.

☆ Arcelin, René Gaillard, Pierre Mahuet, Pierre Santé

MÂCON-ROMANÈCHE-THORINS AOC

This village is also part of the Beaujolais-Villages area and its wines therefore have a choice of both appellations. Most of its production is red.

MÂCON-ST.-AMOUR-BELLEVUE AOC

This village is famous for its *cru* Beaujolais St.-Amour and also forms part of the Beaujolais-Villages and St.-Véran areas. Its wines therefore have a choice of four appellations, with this one the least appealing to its growers.

MÂCON-ST.-GENGOUX-DE-SCISSÉ AOC

The excellent *coopérative* in this village is part of the Producteurs de Lugny-St.-Genoux-de-Scissé.

MÂCON-ST.-SYMPHORIEN-D'ANCELLES AOC

This village is also part of the Beaujolais-Villages area and its wines therefore have a choice of both appellations.

MÂCON-ST.-VÉRAND AOC

This village is in an area that is also part of the Beaujolais-Villages and the similarly spelt St.-Véran areas and its wines therefore have a choice of all three appellations.

MÂCON-SOLOGNY AOC

This village is situated just north of the Pouilly-Fuissé appellation and has a good *coopérative*.

☆ Ets Bertrand

MÂCON-SOLUTRÉ AOC

This village is one of the five communes of Pouilly-Fuissé and also forms part of the St.-Véran area. Its wines therefore have a choice of three appellations.

MÂCON-VERGISSON AOC

This village is one of five communes that form the appellation of Pouilly-Fuissé.

MÂCON-VERZÉ AOC

I have not encountered this wine.

MÂCON-VINZELLES AOC

This village also has the right to the Pouilly-Vinzelles appellation and its wines therefore have a choice of two.

☆ Caves des Crus Blancs

MÂCON-VIRÉ AOC

This is perhaps the most popular of these village appellations. Its consistent quality makes it a fine ambassador, while its most outstanding examples, such as those from André Bonhomme or Henri Goyard, demonstrate that Viré can produce some of the finest wines in the Mâconnais.

☆ André Bonhomme, Jean-Noël Chaland, Domaine des Chazelles, Jacques Depagneux, Henri Goyard, Guillemot-Michel, Château de Viré

MÂCON-UCHIZY AOC

Occasionally seen, good-quality wines from a village adjacent to Chardonnay.

☆ Paul & Philebert Talmard

MÂCON (VILLAGE NAME) AOC

This differs from the Mâcon-Villages appellation above (which may attach a village name and has to be white) in that it covers a slightly different range of villages, the names of which must (rather than may) be indicated on the label, and applies only to red and rosé wines. Fewer villages use this appellation, but Mâcon-Bissy, Mâcon-Braye, Mâcon-Davaye and Mâcon-Pierreclos are most common.

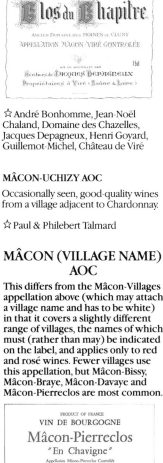

RED There is some indication that a few villages (or more accurately, individual growers with isolated plots of vines growing on favourable soils within a few villages) are capable of making better-balanced wines than the Gamay has hitherto been expected to produce in Mâcon.

🍇 Gamay, Pinot noir, Pinot gris
🍷 1985, 1986, 1988, 1989, 1990
🕰 Between 2-6 years

ROSÉ I have not encountered these.

☆ Pierre Mahuet, Domaine de Prieuré, Jean-Claude Thevenet

MÂCON SUPÉRIEUR AOC

All of France's so-called "Supérieur" appellations merely demand extra alcohol (usually one degree more), which does not necessarily make a superior wine.

RED Apart from the few recommended below, these well-coloured, medium-bodied wines are nothing special.

🍇 Gamay, Pinot noir, Pinot gris
🍷 1985, 1986, 1988, 1989, 1990
🕰 Between 3-8 years

WHITE It is curious why as much as 23 per cent of Mâcon-Supérieur should be white. The wines could just as easily sell as Mâcon plain and simple.

🍇 Chardonnay, Pinot blanc
🍷 1984, 1985, 1986, 1989, 1990
🕰 Within 1-4 years

ROSÉ Attractively coloured wines with a fresh and tasty fruit flavour.

🍇 Gamay, Pinot noir, Pinot gris
🍷 1981, 1982, 1983, 1984, 1985, 1986, 1989, 1990
🕰 Within 1-2 years

☆ Collin & Bourisset, Henri Lafarge, Pierre Santé, Jean Signoret, Jean-Claude Thévenet

MÂCON SUPÉRIEUR (VILLAGE NAME) AOC
See Mâcon (village name) AOC.

PINOT CHARDONNAY-MÂCON AOC
An alternative appellation for white Mâcon. *See* Mâcon AOC.

POUILLY-FUISSÉ AOC

This pure Chardonnay wine should not be confused with Pouilly-Fumé, the Sauvignon blanc wine from the Loire. This appellation covers a wide area of prime vineyards, but there is considerable variation.

WHITE These dry wines range from typical Mâcon blanc style, through slightly firmer versions to the power-packed, rich oaky-flavoured Château Fuissé "Vieilles Vignes", widely acclaimed as the finest Pouilly-Fuissé.

🍇 Chardonnay
🍷 1981, 1983, 1984, 1985, 1986
🕰 Between 3-8 years

☆ Daniel Balvay, André Besson, Roger Cordier, J.-J. Vincent & Fils, Jean Goyon, Charles Gruber, Jean-Paul Paquet, Bernard Léger-Plumet

POUILLY-LOCHÉ AOC

One of Pouilly-Fuissé's two satellite appellations.

WHITE This village may produce Mâcon-Loché, Pouilly-Loché or Pouilly-Vinzelles. Suffice it to say that the dry wines of this village are more of the Mâcon style, whatever the AOC.

🍇 Chardonnay
🍷 1984, 1985, 1986, 1989, 1990
🕰 Within 1-4 years

☆ Caves des Crus Blancs

POUILLY-VINZELLES AOC

One of Pouilly-Fuissé's two satellite appellations.

WHITE More the Mâcon-type of Pouilly-Fuissé, for similar reasons to those expressed for Pouilly-Loché.

🍇 Chardonnay
🍷 1981, 1983, 1984, 1985, 1986
🕰 Within 1-4 years

☆ René Boulay, Collin & Bourisset, Jean Mathias, Thomas-Bassot, Château de Vinzelles

ST.-VÉRAN AOC

This appellation, which overlaps the Mâconnais and Beaujolais districts, was introduced in 1971. The aim was to provide a more suitable outlet for white wines produced in Beaujolais than the Beaujolais blanc appellation. Producers rightly perceived that all the wines from an area that extended into the Mâconnais might be accepted as Mâcon in character.

WHITE Excellent value, deliciously fresh, dry and fruity Chardonnay wines that are very much in the Mâcon-Villages style. Vincent, the proprietor of Château Fuissé, produces an amazingly rich wine that is far closer to Pouilly-Fuissé, with hints of oak and honey.

🍇 Chardonnay
🍷 1984, 1985, 1986, 1989, 1990
🕰 Within 1-4 years

☆ Caves des Crus Blancs, Domaine des Deux Roches, Roger Luquet, Roger Tissier, M. Vincent & Fils

The Beaujolais

This huge district is famous for producing the only Gamay wine to gain classic status – a purple-coloured, fresh, light and quaffing wine that accounts for no less than six out of every ten bottles of Burgundy produced each year.

THE FACTORS THAT MAKE MOST BEAUJOLAIS the wine that it is are the grape variety, the method of vinification and the sheer volume of production. A massive amount of Beaujolais is produced each year – two-and-a-half times the entire red and white wine production of the rest of Burgundy put together – and more than half is sold as Beaujolais *Primeur* (Beaujolais *Nouveau*).

The profit generated by Beaujolais *Primeur* is considerable, but the wine itself ought not to be taken too seriously. To be fair, no Beaujolais winemaker claims that his *Primeur* is a fine wine; if somebody did he would not be thanked by the rest of the producers. It would destroy the carefully marketed image of a young wine to be consumed in copious quantities. Beaujolais *Primeur* is an honest, fun wine that promotes a greater awareness of wine *per se*. I acknowledge its role, just as I accept the contribution made by Liebfraumilch in attracting new wine-drinkers, but readers should be aware that the peardrop smell of ethyl-acetate is a far cry from the aroma of classic *cru* Beaujolais.

FACTORS AFFECTING TASTE AND QUALITY

Location
Beaujolais, the most southerly of Burgundy's districts, is located in the Rhône *département*, 400 kilometres (250 miles) southeast of Paris.

Climate
Essentially a sunny climate tempered by the Atlantic and Mediterranean, as well as continental influences. Although the annual rainfall and temperature means are ideal for winegrowing, they are subject to sudden stormy changes due to the influence of the Mediterranean.

Aspect
A hilly district where vines grow at between 150-550 metres (500-2,000 ft) on slopes facing all points of the compass.

Soil
The northern Beaujolais, which encompasses the famous *cru* and those communes entitled to the Beaujolais-Villages AOC, is an area renowned for its granite-based soil, the only type on which the Gamay has so far excelled. The topsoils are often schistous or comprised of decomposed granite mixed with sand and clay. The southern section is essentially limestone-based – a problem for the Gamay grape, which accordingly produces much lighter wines.

Viticulture and vinification
The vines are trained and pruned to the "gobelet" system. They look totally different from those in the rest of Burgundy. The usual method of vinification is *macération carbonique*, although *cru* Beaujolais wines are more traditionally produced, and may even be matured with some new oak.

Primary grape varieties
Gamay

Secondary grape varieties
Chardonnay, Pinot noir, Pinot gris, Pinot liébault, Pinot blanc, Aligoté, Melon de Bourgogne

THE LEGEND OF "PISSE VIEILLE"

The vineyard of "Pisse Vieille" in Brouilly amuses English-speaking consumers, who are dismayed by those writers who dare only to print it in French. The story goes like this:

One day, an old woman called Mariette went to confession. The priest was new to the village and unaware of its dialect. He also did not know that Mariette was hard of hearing. When he heard her confession, he merely said "Allez! Et ne péchez plus!" ("Go! And do not sin again!"). Mariette misheard this as "Allez! Et ne piché plus", which in the dialect meant "Go! And do not piss again", *piché* being the local form of *pisser*. Being a devout Catholic, Mariette did exactly as she was told. When her husband asked what terrible sin she had committed she refused to tell and, after several days, he went to ask the new priest. When he found out the truth he hurried home, and as soon as he was within shouting distance, began yelling "Pisse, vieille!" ("Piss, old woman!").

BROUILLY
Pisse-Vieille
APPELLATION BROUILLY CONTRÔLÉE
MIS EN BOUTEILLES À LA PROPRIÉTÉ
75 cl
JOEL ROCHETTE, viticulteur, «LE CHALET» 69430 RÉGNIÉ-DURETTE
Produce of France

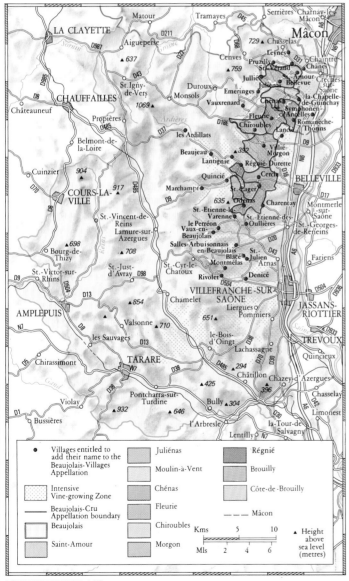

THE BEAUJOLAIS, see also p. 109

Forming the southernmost part of the Burgundy region, the Beaujolais area is approximately 50 kilometres (30 miles) long and an average of 15 kilometres (nine miles) across.

Legend:
- Villages entitled to add their name to the Beaujolais-Villages Appellation
- Intensive Vine-growing Zone
- Beaujolais-Cru Appellation boundary
- Beaujolais
- Saint-Amour
- Juliénas
- Moulin-à-Vent
- Chénas
- Fleurie
- Chiroubles
- Morgon
- Régnié
- Brouilly
- Côte-de-Brouilly
- Mâcon

Kms 5 10
Mls 2 4 6
▲ Height above sea level (metres)

Harvesting in Fleurie, above
To encourage macération carbonique, the Gamay grapes must arrive at the cuverie in whole bunches, on their stalks and as uncrushed as possible.

The wines of the Beaujolais

BEAUJOLAIS AOC

The generic Beaujolais appellation accounts for half the wine produced in the district and more than half of this is sold as Beaujolais "Primeur". These are not wines to buy from the great négociants of the Côte d'Or (although cru Beaujolais can be).

RED Due to their method of vinification, all these wines have a "peardrop" character to their fruitiness. The best also have a delightful freshness and frankness that beg for the wine to be consumed in large draughts.

🍇 Gamay, Pinot noir, Pinot gris

🗓 1985, 1986, 1988, 1989, 1990

🍷 Within 1-3 years

WHITE Less than 0.5 per cent of the basic appellation is dry white wine. Specialist producers usually make very fine wines. Pierre Charmet's Beaujolais blanc is aromatic and peachy.

🍇 Chardonnay, Aligoté

🗓 1984, 1985, 1986, 1989, 1990

🍷 Within 1-3 years

ROSÉ Fresh, "pretty" and fruity.

🍇 Gamay, Pinot noir, Pinot gris,

🗓 1983, 1985, 1986, 1989, 1990

🍷 Within 1-3 years

☆ Charles Bréchard, Jean-Paul Brun, Blaise Carron, Chanut Frères, Pierre Charmet, Jean Garlon, Philippe Jambon, René Marchand, René Riottot, Château de Tanay, Louis Tête, Trenel

BEAUJOLAIS (VILLAGE NAME) AOC

Of the 38 villages that may add their names to the appellation of Beaujolais, very few take advantage of it. One reason is that all or part of 15 of these villages (asterisked below) qualify for one of the superior cru Beaujolais appellations and it makes no sense to use a less famous name to market the wines. Another is that eight of the villages are entitled to the Mâcon-Villages AOC (marked M) and four of these are also within the St.-Véran AOC (marked S-V) which overlaps Mâconnais and Beaujolais; the

production in some of these villages is, of course, devoted more to white wine than red. Of those that use the appellation, only St.-Vérand has sometimes impressed me. It has been announced that the village of Régnié will become the tenth cru Beaujolais as from the harvest of 1988.

The following is a complete list of villages that may use the appellation: Arbuisonnas; Les Ardillats; Beaujeu; Blacé; Cercié*; Chânes M; S-V; La Chapelle-de-Guinchay M;*; Denicé; Durette; Emeringes*; Fleurie*; Juliénas*; Jullié*; Lancié; Lantignié; Leynes M-S-V; Marchampt; Montmelas; Odenas; Le Perréon; Pruzilly M;*; Quincié*; Rivolet; Romanèche-Thorins M;*; St.-Amour-Bellevue M;S-V;*; St.-Etienne-des-Ouillères; St.-Etienne-la-Varenne*; St.-Julien; St-Lager; St.-Symphorien-d'Ancelles M; St.-Vérand M; S-V; Salles; Vaux; Vauxrenard; Villié Morgon *

☆ **St.-Vérand:** Norbert Pauget
Régnié AOC: Paul Cinquin, Paul Collogne, René Desplace, Jean Durand, Roland Magrin, Patrick Péchard, Claude et Bernard Roux.

BEAUJOLAIS NOUVEAU AOC
See Beaujolais Primeur AOC.

BEAUJOLAIS PRIMEUR AOC

More than half of all the Beaujolais produced is sold as a *vin de primeur*, a wine made by intensive *macération-carbonique* methods that enable it to be consumed in export markets from the third Thursday of each November. "Beaujolais Nouveau" is synonymous with "Beaujolais Primeur" and more often seen on export market labels. Expect nothing exceptional – the wine is fun-loving, peardrop-smelling pop with a kick. *See Beaujolais AOC.*

BEAUJOLAIS SUPÉRIEUR AOC

Just one per cent of all Beaujolais wines carry this appellation, which merely means they contain one per cent extra alcohol.

RED By no means superior to Beaujolais AOC – buy basic Beaujolais for fun or cru Beaujolais for more serious drinking.

🍇 Gamay, Pinot noir, Pinot gris,

🗓 1985, 1986, 1988, 1989, 1990

🍷 Between 3-8 years

WHITE Barely five per cent of this tiny appellation is white. Fine as it may be, it has no intrinsic superiority over the quaffing quality of basic Beaujolais blanc.

🍇 Chardonnay, Aligoté

🗓 1984, 1985, 1986, 1989, 1990

🍷 Within 1-3 years

ROSÉ I have not encountered any pink versions of this appellation.

☆ Cave Beaujolais du Bois-d'Oingt

BEAUJOLAIS-VILLAGES AOC

The 38 villages that may add their names to the Beaujolais AOC (see "Beaujolais (village name) AOC") also have the right to this appellation and must use it if the wine is a blend of wines from two or more villages.

RED These well-coloured, richly-flavoured Gamay wines have all the superiority that Beaujolais Supérieur wines mysteriously lack.

🍇 Gamay, Pinot noir, Pinot gris,

🗓 1985, 1986, 1988, 1989, 1990

🍷 Between 3-8 years

WHITE Very little encountered, but more Villages *blanc* is produced than basic *blanc* in Beaujolais.

🍇 Chardonnay, Aligoté

🗓 1984, 1985, 1986, 1989, 1990

🍷 Within 1-3 years

ROSÉ Seldom encountered, but the Cave Beaujolais du Bois-d'Oingt makes an attractive wine.

☆ Cave Beaujolais du Bois-d'Oingt, Geny de Flammerécourt, Paul Gauthier, Château du Grand Vernay, Jean-Charles Pivot, George Roux, Jean Verger, Patrick Vermorel

BROUILLY AOC
Cru Beaujolais

This is both the largest and most southerly of the ten cru villages and, with Côte de Brouilly, the only one that permits grapes other than Gamay in its wine.

RED Most Brouillys are serious wines, even if they do not rank amongst the best crus Beaujolais. They are not quite as intense as Côte de Brouilly wines, but they are full, fruity and supple, if a little earthy. They should be rich and can be quite tannic.

🍇 Gamay, Chardonnay, Aligoté, Melon de Bourgogne

🗓 1985, 1986, 1988, 1989, 1990

🍷 Between 2-7 years (4-12 years for 1985)

☆ Château de la Chaize, Crêt des Garanches, Jean Lathuilière, Vignoble de l'Ecluse, Domaine Rolland, Jean-Paul Rouet, Château Thivin, Patrick Vermorel

CHÉNAS AOC
Cru Beaujolais

Chénas is the smallest of the crus Beaujolais and is situated on the slopes above Moulin-à-Vent that used to be occupied by oak trees, hence the name.

RED Although most Chénas cannot match the power of the wines from neighbouring Moulin-à-Vent, they are nevertheless in the full and generous mould, and good growers like Jean Benon can make seductively rich and oaky wines.

🍇 Gamay

🗓 1985, 1986, 1988, 1989, 1990

🍷 Between 3-8 years (5-15 years for 1985)

☆ Jean Benon, Louis Champagnon, Château de Chénas, Michel Crozet,

Gérard Lapierre, Hubert Lapierre, Henri Lespinasse, Pierre Perrachon, Domaine des Pins, Domaine Robin

CHIROUBLES AOC

Cru Beaujolais

Situated high in the hills above the Beaujolais plain, this is the most fragrant of all the *crus* Beaujolais.

RED These light-bodied wines have a perfumed bouquet and a deliciously delicate, crushed-grape flavour. They are charming to drink when young, but exceptional examples can improve with age.

🍇 Gamay

🍷 1985, 1986, 1988, 1989, 1990

🥂 Within 1-8 years (5-15 years for 1985)

☆ Domaine de la Combe au Loup, Domaine Cheysson-les-Farges, Gérard-Roger Méziat, Domaine du Moulin, Georges Passot, Trenel

CÔTE DE BROUILLY AOC

Cru Beaujolais

If there were such things as *Grands Crus* in Beaujolais, Côte de Brouilly would be classified as the *Grand Cru* of Brouilly (the vineyards of which practically surround those of this appellation).

RED A fine Côte de Brouilly is full, rich and flavoursome. Its fruit should be vivid and intense, with none of the earthiness that may be found in a Brouilly.

🍇 Gamay, Pinot noir, Pinot gris,

🍷 1985, 1986, 1988, 1989, 1990

🥂 Between 3-8 years (5-15 years for 1985)

☆ Domaine de Chavanne, Jacques Dépagneux, Domaine des Fournelles, Château du Grand Vernay, André Large, Robert Verger, Château Thivin

COTEAUX DU LYONNAIS AOC

This is not part of the true Beaujolais district, but it falls within its sphere of influence and certainly utilizes classic Beaujolais grapes. In May 1984 this wine was upgraded from VDQS to full AOC status.

RED Light-bodied wines with fresh Gamay fruit and a soft balance.

🍇 Gamay

🍷 1985, 1986, 1988, 1989, 1990

🥂 Between 2-5 years

WHITE Fresh and dry Chardonnay wine that is softer than a Mâcon and lacks the definition of a Beaujolais blanc.

🍇 Chardonnay, Aligoté

🍷 1984, 1985, 1986, 1989, 1990

🥂 Within 1-3 years

ROSÉ I have not encountered any.

☆ Bolieu Père & Fils, François Descotes, Gilbert Mazille, Cave Coopérative des Coteaux du Lyonnais

FLEURIE AOC

Cru Beaujolais

The evocatively-named Fleurie is the most expensive of the *crus* and its finest wines are the quintessence of classic Beaujolais.

RED The wines of Fleurie very quickly develop a fresh, floral and fragrant style. Not as light and delicate as some writers suggest, their initial charm belies a positive structure and a depth of fruit that can sustain the wines for many years.

🍇 Gamay

🍷 1985, 1986, 1988, 1989, 1990

🥂 Between 2-8 years (4-16 years for 1985)

☆ Michel Chignard, Château de Labourons, Domaine de Montgenas, Domaine de Quatre Vents, Fernand Verpoix

JULIÉNAS AOC

Cru Beaujolais

Situated in the hills above St.-Amour, Juliénas is probably the most underrated of the ten *crus* Beaujolais.

RED The spicy-rich, chunky-textured fruit of a youthful Juliénas will develop a classy, satin-smooth appeal if given sufficient bottle-age.

🍇 Gamay

🍷 1985, 1986, 1988, 1989, 1990

🥂 Between 3-8 years (5-15 years for 1985)

☆ Ernest Aujas, Jean Benon, François Condemine, Coopérative des Grands Vins, Henri Lespinasse, André Pelletier

MORGON AOC

Cru Beaujolais

Just as the Côte de Brouilly is a finer and more concentrated form of Brouilly, so the wines of Mont du Py in the centre of Morgon are far more powerful that those of the surrounding vineyards in this commune.

RED Although variable in character and quality, the best rank with those of Moulin-à-Vent as the most sturdy of all Beaujolais. They have a singularly penetrating bouquet and very compact fruit.

🍇 Gamay

🍷 1985, 1986, 1988, 1989, 1990

🥂 Between 4-9 years (6-20 years for 1985)

☆ Georges Brun, Paul Collonge, Roger Condemine-Pillet, Louis-Claude Desvignes, Château Gaillard, Marcel Lapierre, Aucouer Noël, Pierre Savoye, Domaine de Versauds, Syndicat Viticole de Villié-Morgon

MOULIN-A-VENT AOC

Cru Beaujolais

Because of its sheer size, power and reputation for longevity, Moulin-à-Vent is known as the "King of Beaujolais". The exceptionally powerful character of Moulin-à-Vent has been attributed to the high manganese content of its soil, Does this make sense? The availability of manganese to the vine's metabolic system depends on the pH of the soil in which it grows and in the acid, granite soil of Beaujolais, manganese is all too readily available. For a healthy metabolism, however, the vine requires only the tiniest trace of manganese, so its abundance at Moulin-à-Vent can be considered toxic (to the vine that is, not the consumer!), may well cause chlorosis and would certainly affect the vine's metabolism. This could alter the composition of the grapes produced.

RED These well-coloured wines have intense fruit, excellent tannic structure and, in many cases, spicy-rich oak.

🍇 Gamay

🍷 1985, 1986, 1988, 1989, 1990

🥂 Between 4-9 years (6-20 years for 1985)

☆ Louis Champagnon, Robert Diochon, Jacky Janodet, Domaine Lemonon, Château du Moulin-à-Vent, Jean Picolet

RÉGNIÉ AOC

Cru Beaujolais

See Beaujolais (Village name) AOC.

ST.-AMOUR AOC

Cru Beaujolais

The most northerly of the ten *crus*, more famous for its Mâcon.

RED Charming wines of fine colour, seductive bouquet and fragrant flavour. They quickly reveal a soft and fruity flavour, but also repay a little aging.

🍇 Gamay

🍷 1985, 1986, 1988, 1989, 1990

🥂 Between 2-8 years (4-12 years for 1985)

☆ Domaine des Ducs, Raymond Durand, Elie Mongénie, Guy Patissier, Jean Patissier, André Poitevin, Château de St.-Amour

Champagne

In other wine regions blending is frowned upon, and the best wines are made on one estate and from a single vintage. In Champagne the traditional view could not be more contrasting— classic non-vintage Champagnes are a blend of different grapes, from different areas and different harvests.

NOT EVEN HELEN OF TROY launched more ships than Champagne. Whether for cracking on the bow of a ship, toasting the bride and bridegroom or celebrating the winner of a Grand Prix, Champagne is the first choice.

Indispensable it might be, yet many people feel curiously disappointed when they drink it. Perhaps they have drunk a cheap bubbly which may be all fizz and no flavour, or have been given a glass to wash down a slice of wedding cake? The intense sweetness of the cake abuses the dry flavour of the wine and makes even the best Champagne taste sharp and unpleasant. No one should feel they have to like Champagne, but it is, however, one of the most remarkable drinks man has managed to produce with the fruits of the vine—a pale-coloured, richly flavoured, yet delicate wine, made vivacious by a constant stream of ultra-fine bubbles. Champagne's limited production, relatively high price and superb promotion do help to create the image of an inimitable product, but good Champagnes have a quality and finesse that no other sparkling wine has yet been able to match.

What is Champagne?

Champagne is a specific appellation reserved for the product of three grape varieties, the Chardonnay, Pinot noir and Pinot meunier, grown in a legally delimited region of northern France. Within the EEC no other sparkling wine may be called Champagne; other countries, which have in the past sold wines labelled Champagne without a blush, are now beginning to take pride in the origin and individuality of their home products and are voluntarily phasing out the term.

THE HISTORY OF CHAMPAGNE

The vine has been cultivated in Champagne since the Roman occupation of the first century AD, but the wines produced were originally still wines. Nobody knows exactly when Champagne became sparkling, although it evidently appeared in England before legend would have us believe it was "invented" at the Benedictine Abbey of Hautvillers by one of the monks – Dom Pérignon. In 1676, before Dom Pérignon had made his name as a great winemaker, the playwright Sir George Etherege wrote of "sparkling Champaign" in his comedy *The Man of Mode*.

Why should sparkling Champagne be found at this time in England, rather than France? Perhaps the answer lies in a combination of circumstances. During Champagne's chilly winters, winemakers would interpret the wine's inactivity as proof that the fermentation had finished. However, the wine probably still contained unfermented sugars and almost certainly had not undergone malolactic fermentation (*see* p.19). It was in this slumbering state that casks of still wine were originally shipped to England. Bottles were not used by the French for either shipping or aging the wine at this date, but English innkeepers would bottle wine from cask and store it until it was consumed at the table. During this temporary storage, the warmth of an inn might reactivate the fermentation in the bottle. At this time, English glass was stronger than French glass; it could withstand the internal pressure generated by carbonic gas. In addition, the cork stopper was in common use in England at the time (unlike most of France). Being airtight, it prevented the escape of carbonic gas.

Dom Pérignon

If Dom Pérignon did not invent sparkling Champagne, then what did he specifically achieve? We know that he was the first to develop the concept of blending wines from various grapes grown in different villages to effect a better-balanced wine; he used a shallow-based press to produce clear, untainted juice from black grapes; he reintroduced the cork (which was lost to most of

THE FIVE MAJOR DISTRICTS

There are five major districts in Champagne producing distinctly different base wines which, when blended in various proportions, can result in many contrasting styles. The best way to appreciate these regional influences is to seek out grower-producer *mono-cru* Champagnes.

Montagne de Reims
These vineyards, which generally face north and northeast, are planted with a high proportion of Pinot noir vines and produce well-structured, deeply flavoured wines. More aromatic qualities, combined with the same impressive body, are found in wines produced around Bouzy and Ambonnay.

Best villages Bouzy, Verzenay, Verzy

Côte des Blancs
The name of this area is derived from its almost exclusive cultivation of white Chardonnay grapes. The wines produced from these grapes have become the most sought after in all Champagne. They contribute finesse and delicacy yet mature to an unequalled intensity of flavour. The best vineyards are between Cramant and le Mesnil-sur-Oger, where the Chardonnay possesses a very special perfume, and even small quantities can dominate a *cuvée*.

Best villages Cramant, Avize, Oger, le Mesnil-sur-Oger

Vallée de la Marne
Essentially easy-drinking, fruity and forward wines produced from an extremely high proportion of Pinot meunier. This wine is cultivated in the frost-prone valley vineyards because of its late bud-break and early ripening.

Best villages Aÿ-Champagne, Mareuil-sur-Aÿ

Aube vineyards
Honest, ripe, rich and fruity wines are produced in this southern part of Champagne which is closer to Chablis than to the classic vineyards of the Marne. The wines are cleaner in style and better in quality than the outer areas of the Vallée de la Marne around Château-Thierry. Many *grandes marques* look down on the Aube, yet regularly buy its wines, but many grower-producers now produce Champagnes of some merit.

Best village les Riceys

Côte de Sézanne
A rapidly developing area south of the Côte des Blancs which favours the Chardonnay grape. For many years the great Champagne houses have treated these wines as useful blending fodder, but they deserve better recognition.

Best villages Bethon, Villenauxe-la-Grande

CHAMPAGNE

Within the EEC, only those wines produced within the delimited AOC region may be called Champagne. It is the most northerly wine producing region of France.

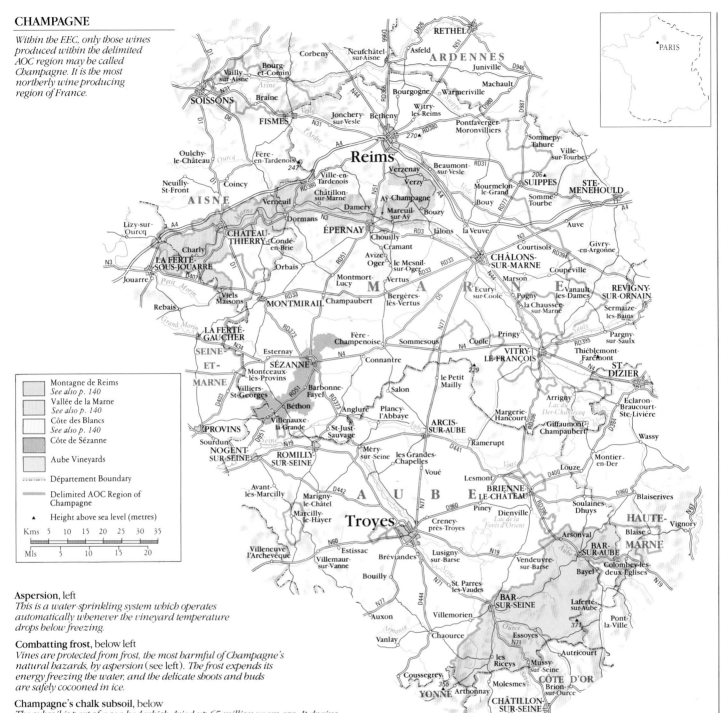

Montagne de Reims
See also p. 140

Vallée de la Marne
See also p. 140

Côte des Blancs
See also p. 140

Côte de Sézanne

Aube Vineyards

Département Boundary

Delimited AOC Region of Champagne

▲ Height above sea level (metres)

Kms 5 10 15 20 25 30 35

Mls 5 10 15 20

Aspersion, left
This is a water-sprinkling system which operates automatically whenever the vineyard temperature drops below freezing.

Combatting frost, below left
Vines are protected from frost, the most harmful of Champagne's natural hazards, by aspersion (see left). The frost expends its energy freezing the water, and the delicate shoots and buds are safely cocooned in ice.

Champagne's chalk subsoil, below
The subsoil is part of a sea-bed which dried up 65 million years ago. It drains well, yet retains enough water for the wines to survive a drought. Its high active lime content encourages grapes with a high acid content.

France after Roman withdrawal) to northern France, and we know he experimented with coal-fired furnaces to replicate the stronger English glass. His wines were known as *vins de Pérignon*.

The *méthode champenoise*

Although Dom Pérignon was responsible for much of the early development of the process we call the *méthode champenoise*, it is essentially a two-hundred-year accumulation of practices; the most important being the wine's secondary fermentation in the bottle in which it is sold. Many other sparkling wines are made by the *méthode champenoise*, but the EEC is proposing to ban the use of this term for all wines other than Champagne (whose producers never use it anyway), thus losing the information required to separate good sparkling wine made outside Champagne from inferior wines made by other methods.

HOW CHAMPAGNE IS MADE

The harvest in Champagne usually takes place in mid-October, although in exceptional years it has commenced as early as August and as late as November.

Although modern horizontal presses, both hydraulic and pneumatic, are used, the most popular press is a small, vertical one with a capacity of 4,000 kilograms (8,818 pounds) and a shallow base which allows the lid of the press to squeeze a thin mass of grapes. The grapes are not destalked and, when they are pressed, their fibrous material forms a network of canals through which the grape juice drains. It is essential that the pressing is carried out quickly, particularly with the black Pinot varieties, where the colouring matter in the grape skins give the juice an undesirable taint. Each 4,000 kilograms (8,818 pounds) of grapes is called a *marc* and one *marc* must yield no more than 2,666 litres (704 gallons) of juice. The first pressing extracts 2,050 litres (541 gallons) called the *cuvée,* which is the highest quality juice, the next 410 litres (108 gallons) is called the *première taille* and the remaining 205 litres (54 gallons) the *deuxième taille.*

Because the *taille* is of inferior quality to the *cuvée,* it is common practice for many houses to declare they never use *vins de taille* in their Champagnes, preferring to sell them on to houses that specialize in BOB (Buyer's Own Brand) Champagnes.

The first alcoholic fermentation

There is nothing mysterious about the initial fermentation of Champagne, which results in a dry still wine, very acid to taste with a quite unremarkable character. Like Port, the base wine must be intrinsically out of balance if the final product is to achieve a correct balance. Historically, the first fermentation took place in oak casks, but now stainless-steel vats have largely replaced them, although a few of the most traditional houses, and many thousands of grower-producers, still ferment some or all of their wines in cask.

Malolactic fermentation

Champagne normally undergoes what is called malolactic "fermentation"; this is not strictly speaking a fermentation, but another biochemical process which converts the hard malic acid to soft lactic acid. Those who cask-ferment their wines usually bottle without this conversion having taken place, because it is difficult to achieve in wood and is generally believed not to occur in bottle during or after the second fermentation. A Champagne which has not undergone malolactic conversion is quite often austere in character and hard to appreciate until properly matured, but once it has developed it will have the capacity to remain at its peak for far longer than other Champagnes.

Blending the wine

The critical operation of *assemblage,* or blending, is highly skilled and painstaking. To consistently blend together a non-vintage Champagne of a specific house style from as many as 70 different base wines each of which changes in character from year to year, is a remarkable feat. Even a vintage Champagne has to be blended, albeit from one year's wines, so as to convey both the quality and character of the year, and also the style of the house.

The second alcoholic fermentation

After the blended wine has undergone its final racking, what is known as the *liqueur de tirage* is added; this is a mixture of still Champagne, sugar and selected yeasts. The amount of sugar added depends on the degree of effervescence required and the amount of natural sugar in the wine. Dosed with a suitable amount of *liqueur,* the wines are bottled and capped with a temporary closure. This used to be a cork secured by a metal clip called an *agrafe,* but a crown-cap (which is the same as a beer-bottle cap) is now in common use and this holds in place a small plastic pot to catch the sediment produced by the second fermentation.

The wines are then stacked in the deepest cellars, often in the famous *crayères,* or chalk pits, dug by the Romans to provide

Sorting grapes, above
Both harvesting and sorting into shallow trays called osiers, *are carried out by hand in Champagne.*

Paniers de Mannequin, left
Once sorted, the grapes are packed into baskets or plastic trays.

Champagne press, below
The basic design of the pressoir coquart *is the same as it was in Dom Pérignon's day.*

Traditional fermentation, left
Some producers still favour fermentation in wooden casks or vats because of the oxidative complexity achieved by this method.

Modern fermentation methods, below left
The use of stainless steel is now widespread, and has resulted in fresher, cleaner styles of Champagne.

Blending, below
It is the highly skilful art of blending which makes a fine Champagne.

Sediment, above
The Champagne's second fermentation creates a sediment which falls in separate sticky layers; this must be worked down the bottle by an operation called remuage.

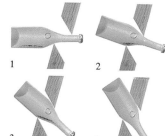

***Remuage* by hand**, below
Horizontal, through 90°, to vertical (as in the illustration, right) takes about eight weeks. Some firms are adopting alternative, quicker methods.

Champagne corks, right
From left to right: a crown-cap and plastic pot; a cork before insertion; a cork from a youthful Champagne; and the cork of a more mature Champagne.

Dégorgement à la volée, below
The removal of sediment is still carried out by hand at a few houses.

building materials. In the cool depths of these cellars the fermentation is very slow and this creates wines with great aromatic properties, complex flavours and minuscule bubbles. The carbon dioxide remains imprisoned in the wine and only when the bottle is opened will it be able to escape, rushing to the surface in the form of a stream of bubbles. The French use the term *prise de mousse,* or "capturing the sparkle", for this second fermentaion.

Remuage

When the second fermentation is over, which can take between ten days and three months, the bottles are transferred to *pupitres,* two-hinged, heavy, rectangular boards containing 60 holes, each allowing a bottle to be held by the neck in any position from horizontal, through 90°, to vertical. *Remuage,* a method of shaking and twisting the bottles to loosen the sediment and encourage it to move to the neck of the bottle, then takes place. By hand this takes about eight weeks, but a number of companies have installed computerized equipment which operates 500-bottle pallets, and performs the task in eight days.

Remuage versus yeast capsules

Experiments have been taking place with a new technique which obviates the need for *remuage.* Yeast capsules are inserted into the bottles to induce a secondary fermentation and the sediment produced is imprisoned inside the porous capsules. If these pills gain official approval, they may supersede the very expensive computerized *gyropalettes* in the 1990s. A rival to the yeast capsule, an agglomerating yeast which requires no special dispensing system, is also under development.

Aging the wine

After *remuage* many bottles will undergo a period of aging before the sediment is removed. The minimum period for non-vintage Champagnes is one year (from the January following the harvest) and this is extended to three years for vintage Champagnes. The longer the Champagne is aged the better, because the sediment contains dead yeast cells and the gradual breakdown of these cells gives Champagne its special flavour and bouquet. This process, known as autolysis, is largely responsible for the superior quality of prestige *cuvées.*

Dégorgement

This is the removal of the sediment which has collected in the plastic pot held in place by the crown-cap. The method used today is known as *dégorgement à la glace.* It involves the immersion of the bottle neck in a shallow bath of freezing brine. This causes the sediment to adhere to the base of the plastic pot attached to the crown-cap, enabling the bottle to be turned upright without disturbing the sediment. Then, the crown-cap is removed and the sediment is ejected by the internal pressure of the bottle. Only a little wine is lost, as the pressure is reduced by the freezing brine.

Adding the *liqueur d'expédition*

Before corking, the bottles are topped up with the *liqueur d'expédition* which may include a small amount of sugar – the addition of brandy is now virtually non-existent. The younger the wine, the greater the *dosage* of sugar required to balance the youthful acidity. High acidity is crucial to a fine Champagne; it carries the flavour to the palate through the tactile effect caused by thousands of bursting bubbles. But this acidity rounds out with age; the older the Champagne the less sugar needed.

Corking

The next stage is the insertion of a cork by machine. A protective metal cap is placed on the cork with a pulverizing blow, giving the cork its special mushroom-like appearance. A wire muzzle secures the cork to the bottle, which is then automatically shaken to homogenize the wine and *liqueur.* The best *cuvées* are often kept for a while to help marry the *liqueur.* It is always worth giving any good Champagne a year or two of extra aging before drinking it.

THE CLASSIFICATION OF CHAMPAGNE VINEYARDS

All the vineyards of Champagne are quality-rated on a percentage system ranging from 100 down to 80 per cent. This is known as the *échelle des crus*. Before each harvest, the price a grower gets for his grapes is fixed by a committee made up of officials, growers and producers. Villages with 100 per cent rating have *grand cru* status and must receive the full price for their grapes, while the *premiers crus*, rated between 99 and 90 per cent, and other lesser villages, receive a pro-rata price for their grapes.

The map below shows the positions of all the *grand cru* and *premier cru* villages in the Champagne region. It includes the three all-important districts of the Montagne de Reims, the Vallée de la Marne and the Côte des Blancs. There are 17 villages possessing official *grand cru* status. Until 1985 there were only 12; the five villages elevated to *grand cru* in 1985 were Chouilly, le Mesnil-sur-Oger, Oger, Oiry and Verzy. This upgrading has meant changes in the proportions of grape varieties grown. In particular, the cultivation of the Chardonnay has risen from nearly one-third to over one-half of the vines cultivated in *grand cru* villages, while it has dropped around ten per cent in the *premier cru* sector.

THE *GRAND CRU* AND *PREMIER CRU* VILLAGES

Within the three important districts surrounding Épernay, 17 villages have grand cru *status and 40 the status of* premier cru.

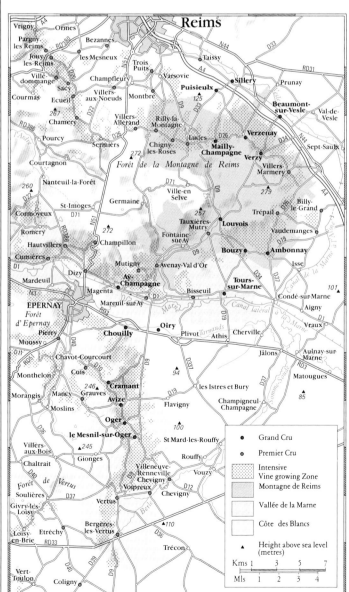

FACTORS AFFECTING TASTE AND QUALITY

Location
This most northerly of the AOC wine regions of France lies some 145 kilometres (90 miles) northeast of Paris, and is separated from Belgium by the forested hills of the Ardennes. Four-fifths of the region is in the Marne, the balance being spread over the Aube, Aisne, Seine-et-Marne and the Haute-Marne.

Climate
A cold and wet northern climate greatly influenced by the Atlantic which has a cooling effect on its summer and makes the seasons generally more variable. Its position at the northern edge of the winemaking belt stretches the duration of the vine's growth cycle to the limit, making frost a major problem in spring and autumn.

Aspect
Vineyards are planted on the gently rolling east- and southeast-facing slopes of the Côte des Blancs at a height of 120-200 metres (380-640ft). On the slopes of the Montagne de Reims (a plateau) the vines grow at altitudes similar to those on the Côte. The best valley vineyards lie in sheltered situations on the right bank of the Marne.

Soil
The Côte des Blancs, Montagne de Reims, Marne valley and Côte de Sézanne vineyards are all situated on a porous chalk subsoil up to 300 metres (960ft) thick. This chalk, which encourages the vine to produce grapes with a relatively high acidity, is covered by a thin layer of drift derived in various proportions from sand, lignite, marl, loam, clay and chalk rubble.

Viticulture and vinification
No mechanical harvesting is allowed and most grapes are still pressed using the traditional, vertical Champagne press. Increasing use is being made of stainless-steel vats with temperature-controlled conditions for the first fermentation, but a few houses and many growers still ferment part or all of their wines in cask. A second fermentation gives the wine its sparkle and always takes place in the bottle in which it is sold.

Primary grape varieties
Chardonnay, Pinot noir and Pinot meunier

Secondary grape varieties
Arbanne, Petit meslier and Pinot blanc vrai

Champagne vineyards in winter, above
In the coldest part of winter, the rows of vines which have been protected from frost by aspersion are hung with icicles.

Champagne vineyards in summer, above
In summer the landscape changes, with row upon row of lush green vines stretching into the distance. These vineyards, situated above the village of Aÿ-Champagne, belong to the house of Bollinger.

STYLES OF CHAMPAGNE

Non-vintage

Non-vintage Champagne accounts for three-quarters of the region's production. The bulk of a blend will be from the current harvest but between 10 and 20 per cent reserve wine from as few as two, or as many as seven, older vintages may be added. By law, a non-vintge Champagne must be aged for a minimum of one year (from January 1 following the harvest), but the best houses will give their wines at least three years in bottle. Non-vintage Champagnes are not usually the finest Champagnes, yet they are capable of being so, and in years when either the character of the wine is not to an individual's taste (for instance, the 1976 could be too heavy for lovers of elegant Champagne), or in poor harvests, the non-vintage is a better buy than the more expensive vintage.

Vintage

The only reason vintage Champagne is superior to non-vintage is that its relatively small production allows a far stricter control over the quality of base wines selected, and because it is sold when it is approximately twice as mature. No more than 80 per cent of the harvest may be sold as vintage Champagne; this conserves at least 20 per cent of the best years for future blending of non-vintage wines. Some houses stick rigidly to declaring a vintage only in years of exceptional quality; others sadly do not.

Blanc de blancs (non-vintage and vintage)

Literally "white of whites", these wines, which are water-white in colour, are produced entirely from white Chardonnay grapes and have the greatest aging potential of all Champagnes. *Blanc de blancs* may be made in any district of Champagne, but the best come from a small part of the Côte des Blancs between Cramant and le Mesnil-sur-Oger. If consumed too early, a *blanc de blancs* can appear austere and lacking in fruit, yet with proper maturity this style of Champagne develops a toasty, lemony bouquet and fills the mouth with an intensity of ripe-fruit flavours.

Blanc de noirs (non-vintage and vintage)

Literally "white of blacks", these are Champagnes made entirely of black grapes: either Pinot noir or Pinot meunier, or a blend of the two. A pure Pinot noir *blanc de noirs* is golden-yellow in colour and has a rich and fruity taste. Only a few producers make these Champagnes: Bollinger produce tiny amounts of the expensive Vieilles Vignes Françaises made entirely from ungrafted Pinot noir grapes; while the small house of Collery in Aÿ-Champagne produce two fine examples of *blanc de noirs*.

Rosé (non-vintage and vintage)

The first record of a commercially produced pink sparkling Champagne is that of Clicquot's in 1777 and this Champagne has enjoyed ephemeral bursts of popularity ever since. It is the only European rosé which may be made by blending white wine with a little red; all other rosés, whether still or sparkling, must be produced by macerating the skins and juice to extract pigments. More pink Champagne is produced by blending than through skin contact and in blind tasting it has been impossible to tell the difference. Most pink Champagnes have a higher proportion of black grapes than white, and some are pure Pinot noir, but many houses simply add a little red wine to their basic non-vintage or vintage *cuvées*. A good pink Champagne will have an attractive colour, perfect limpidity and a snow-white *mousse*. Many taste no different from white Champagne: their particular appeal is visual.

Crémant (non-vintage and vintage)

Most Champagnes are fully sparkling or *mousseux;* that is they have an internal pressure of 5 to 6 atmospheres. A *crémant* or "creaming" Champagne has a noticeably softer sparkle, traditionally 3.6 atmospheres and the *mousse* should possess minuscule bubbles which unfold very slowly. These qualities are difficult to achieve and true *crémant* Champagnes are hard to find, but

Besserat de Bellefon, Alfred Gratien, Abel Lepitre and Mumm all make fine examples of this style. As the Chardonnay grape is thought to give tinier bubbles than the Pinot, the best *crémant* Champagnes often contain a high proportion of this grape variety.

Non-dosage (non-vintage and vintage)

Non-dosage or unsweetened Champagne is not new. Laurent-Perrier sold a "Grand Vin Sans Sucre" as long ago as 1889, but under various names—from *Brut Zero* to *Brut Sauvage, Ultra Brut* and *Sans Sucre*—a wave of these Champagnes emerged in unison with the fashion for lighter, drier wines in the early 1980s. "Too tart", "ungenerous" and even "unpleasant to drink" are criticisms which have been levelled at this style, but a good Champagne needs either a little sugar or eight to ten years aging, thus these Champagnes only attain depth and complexity with age. They are now officially designated as *Extra Brut.*

Cuvées de prestige (non-vintage and vintage)

These Champagnes are the flagships of the Champagne houses offering what should be—and sometimes is—the ultimate in Champagne. A typical prestige *cuvée* may be made entirely of wines from *grands crus* vineyards and, if not a vintage Champagne made only in the greatest years, it will claim not to be non-vintage but a "blend of only the finest vintage years"—fine distinction indeed. Many of these wines are produced by the most traditional methods, aged for longer than normal and sold in special bottles at very high prices. Some are over-refined and have too much mellowness for a wine which should have dash and flair. Others, such as Bollinger's "Grande Année Rare" and Philipponat's "Clos des Goisses", are truly exciting Champagnes of the highest quality.

HOW TO READ CHAMPAGNE LABELS

The *marque*
The *marque* is usually the name of the house or grower who produced the wine, but it may be a brand name such as René Florancy, used by Union Champagne in Avize. Firms holding the status of *grande marque* are usually the most reliable source of good wines, but these are more expensive and not infallible. A *sous-marque* is a secondary brand.

The village
Village names in large type, such as Barancourt's Bouzy, indicate that the Champagne is made from grapes grown in that commune. Otherwise the place name will give the location of the producer. For example, René Florancy is made at Avize but the wine is unlikely to be pure Avize because that is a *grand cru* and this claims only *premier cru* status.

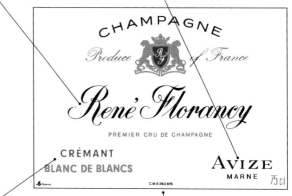

CHAMPAGNE
Produce of *France*
René Florancy
PREMIER CRU DE CHAMPAGNE
CRÉMANT
BLANC DE BLANCS
AVIZE
MARNE
75 cl
C.M 6 263.676

The style
The style of Champagne will indicate whether it is gently sparkling (*crémant*), pure Chardonnay (*blanc de blancs*), pure Pinot (*blanc de noirs*), pink (*rosé*), bone dry (*extra brut*), very dry (*brut*), dry to medium-dry (*extra sec*), medium-sweet (*sec*), sweet (*demi-sec*), intensely sweet (*doux*), and, if the label specifies a year, that it is vintage. These terms are optional and, if none are on the label, assume it is a non-vintage *brut* Champagne blended from both Pinot and Chardonnay grapes.

Matriculation number
Each producer has a matriculation number which is preceded by two letters that indicate his status: NM stands for *négociant-manipulant,* a commercial house which makes Champagne, but buys grapes from growers all over the region; CM is the product of a *coopérative-manipulant;* RM is a *recoltant-manipulant,* a grower-producer who grows and sells the produce of his own grapes; MA is a *marque-auxiliare,* a brand name owned by the producer or the purchaser.

Champagne houses

GM *Grande marque*
     see p.141

NV Non-vintage

V Vintage

PC Prestige *Cuvée*
     see p.141

CC Coteaux Champenois
     see p.148

House Style Profiles
One non-vintage Champagne which
typifies the house style is described
following each house profile.
Recommendations amongst the other
wines of a house are asterisked.

AYALA & CO GM
Château d' Aÿ,
51160 Aÿ-Champagne

Production: *75,000 cases*

The firm is named after Edmond d'Ayala,
the son of a Colombian diplomat who
married into the local aristocracy,
acquired vineyards and founded the
house in 1860. Since 1937 it has belonged
to Jean-Michel Ducellier, who also owns
Château La Lagune in the Médoc. Ayala
Champagnes are always honest, fruity
and generous wines of *grand mousseux*
and exceptional value.

Non-vintage Extra Quality Brut*
An elegant dry, light- to medium-bodied,
Champagne with a good acid balance
and pleasant yeasty aftertaste.

Chardonnay 25%, Pinot noir 50%, Pinot meunier 25%	
Within 2-4 years	

Other wines
NV Carte Blanche Demi-Sec*, Rosé
     Brut
V Brut*, Blanc de Blancs Brut*

BARANCOURT
Place André Tritant,
Bouzy,
51150 Tours-sur-Marne

Production: *30,000 cases*

The name of Barancourt was one of
the oldest and most respected in
Bouzy, so it is not surprising that
when three young growers formed this
house in 1969, they decided to sell their
Champagne under the label of
"Barancourt". With significant vineyard
holdings in prime sites, Barancourt is
able to produce a good commercial
standard of NV Réserve Brut and some
excellent *mono-cru* Champagnes. Both
the NV and Vintage Bouzy Brut benefit
from extra time in bottle, but whereas
the NV can be enjoyed when fairly
young, the vintage should not be drunk
until at least seven or eight years of age.
Barancourt's graceful Cramant Brut
has the fine, intense and highly
perfumed style expected from the
greatest wines of that village.

Non-vintage Bouzy Brut*
A bone-dry Champagne which is very
full bodied. Both the non-vintage and
vintage versions of Bouzy Brut are strong
flavoured wines with a persistent and
fine *mousse*.

Chardonnay 20%, Pinot noir 80%	
Between 2-5 years	

Other wines
NV Réserve Brut, Bouzy Brut Rosé*,
     Cramant Brut*
V Bouzy Brut*
CC Vintage Bouzy Rouge

BESSERAT DE BELLEFON
Allée du vignoble,
RN51, Murigny,
51001 Reims.

Production: *167,000 cases*

Established in Aÿ in 1843 by Edmond
Besserat, this was the first house to
specialize in *crémant* Champagnes.
Currently it is owned by the Pernod-
Ricard group, and still has the reputation
of being one of the very best *crémant*
producers. The Crémant Blanc is a full,
fine and strong Champagne which can
improve for up to one year in bottle.
The B de B prestige *cuvée* is an old-
fashioned style of Champagne utilizing
reserve wines of between six and seven
years of age to effect a blend with a
biscuity flavour. The Vintage Rosé is the
only disappointing wine in the range.

Non-vintage Réserve Brut*
An off-dry, medium-bodied Champagne
with good fruit and acidity and a
persistent *mousse*.

Chardonnay 33%, Pinot noir 50%, Pinot meunier 17%	
Within 1 year	

Other wines
NV Crémant Blanc Brut*, Crémant des
     Moines Brut*, Crémant des Moines
     Rosé Brut; **PC** B de B Brut*
V Réserve Brut*, Brut Intégral, Rosé
     Brut

BILLECART-SALMON GM
40 rue Carnot,
Mareuil-sur-Aÿ

Production: *42,000 cases*

This low-profile family house was
established in 1818 by Nicolas-François
Billecart. It produces high-quality
Champagnes but has no vineyards of its
own. Billecart-Salmon believe in a very
slow first fermentation, which results in
reduced volatile acidity and sulphur
giving their Champagne a light, very
refined character. The speciality of the
house is its pink Champagne, which it
has been producing since 1830.

Non-vintage Brut*
An off-dry, light-bodied, elegant
Champagne which is well-made, if not
as dry as other NV *bruts*.

Chardonnay 25%, Pinot noir 25%, Pinot meunier 50%	
Can be kept for up to 3 years	

Other wines
NV Sec, Demi-Sec, Rosé Brut*
V Blanc de Blancs Brut*; **PC** Brut
     Cuvée N.F. Billecart*

J. BOLLINGER GM
Rue Jules Lobet,
Aÿ-Champagne

Production: *125,000 cases*

Joseph Bollinger from Württemburg in
Germany began his career in the
Champagne trade in 1822. In 1829 he
and Paul Renaudin were asked to form a
company to sell wines from the vineyards
of the Comte de Villermont. As the
Comte did not want his family name to
be connected with commerce, it was
named Renaudin, Bollinger & Co.
     Bollinger's strength lies in its huge
viticultural holdings – an estate of some
140ha (345 acres) of the best sites,
which supplies 70 per cent of their
needs. Two-thirds of the wines undergo
first fermentation in cask, they are not
filtered and malolactic conversion
probably does not occur. The reserve

wines for Bollinger's NV Champagnes
are stored not in bulk, but in magnums.
All their vintage Champagnes are cask
fermented, and do not begin to develop
the classic style of Bollinger until at least
eight years old. Bollinger's RD
Champagne (RD meaning "recently
disgorged") has longer maturation on its
lees than normal vintage Champagne.
The new RD Année Rare Champagnes
spend even longer on their lees. A
curiosity is Bollinger's Vieilles Vignes
Francaises, made entirely from ungrafted
Pinot noir grapes.

Non-vintage Special Cuvée Brut*
A bone-dry, full-bodied Champagne that
is crisp and fresh and traditionally has a
good mature flavour and a long-lasting
mousse.

Chardonnay 20-25%, Pinot noir 65-70%, Pinot meunier 5%	
Improves for up to 10 years after purchase	

Other wines
V Grande Année Brut*, "RD"*,
     Année Rare*, Vieilles Vignes
     Françaises Blanc de Noirs,
     Grande Année Rosé*
CC La Côte aux Enfants*

CANARD DUCHÊNE GM
1 rue Edmond Canard,
51500 Ludes,
Rilly-la-Montagne

Production: *192,000 cases*

Founded in 1868, this firm has been
owned by Veuve Cliquot since 1978.
Despite the modern equipment and
knowledgeable management, their
Champagnes are seldom impressive.
The best Champagne is the prestige
cuvée Charles VII Brut.

Non-vintage Extra Quality Brut*
Light- to medium-bodied Champagne
which is rather coarse with an earthy
flavour.

Chardonnay 25%, Pinot noir 67.5%, Pinot meunier 7.5%	

Other wines
NV Demi-Sec,
V Brut, Imperial Star Brut, Blanc de
     Blancs Brut; **PC** Charles VII Brut*

DE CASTELLANE
57 rue Verdun,
51200 Epernay

Production: *125,000 cases*

Laurent-Perrier recently took a 20 per cent share in this house, which was established in 1890. The house style used to be characterized by ripeness of fruit and good bottle-age, but recently Champagnes in a lighter, fresher style have been made. However, little by little the lusciousness is creeping back as the firm gradually replenishes its stocks.

Non Vintage Brut*
A dry, medium-bodied Champagne which is well-made with a fine *mousse*. It is excellent value.

- Chardonnay 15%, Pinot noir 30%, Pinot meunier 55%
- Within 1-3 years

Other wines
NV   Blanc de Blancs*
V   Brut*, Blanc de Blancs Brut*, Rosé Brut*; **PC** Cuvée Commodore*

A. CHARBAUT & FILS
17 avenue de Champagne, Epernay

Production: *67,000 cases*

A family firm established in 1948 by André Charbaut and now run by his sons René and Guy. With 56ha (138 acres) of vineyards primarily at Mareuil-sur-Aÿ, there is opportunity for their Champagnes to excel. However, the quality has been very uneven, particularly in the early 1980s when demand outstripped supply.

Non-vintage Sélection Brut*
Medium-dry, light- to medium-bodied Champagne which is a clean, fresh commercial blend.

- Chardonnay 20%, Pinot noir 60%, Pinot meunier 20%
- Within 1-2 years

Other wines
NV   Sélection Sec, Sélection Demi-Sec, Brut Extra, Cuvée de Réserve, Blanc de Blancs Brut*, Rosé Brut*
V   Brut; **PC** Certificate Blanc de Blancs*, Certificate Rosé*

COLLERY
4 rue Anatole France, 51160 Aÿ-Champagne

Production: *5,000 cases*

The Collery family have resided in Aÿ for many centuries, and supplied grapes to the Abbey of Hautvillers before the time of Dom Pérignon. The firm own 7ha (7 acres) in Aÿ and 2ha (5 acres) in Mareuil-sur-Aÿ. The elegance and fruitiness of their Champagnes belie the fact that, apart from the NV Cuvée Réserve, they are 100 per cent Pinot.

Non-vintage Cuvée Réserve Brut
A dry, medium-bodied Champagne which is well-balanced and full of flavour.

- Chardonnay 10%, Pinot noir 70%, Pinot meunier 20%
- Within 1-2 years

Other wines
NV   Cuvée Réserve Extra Dry, Rosé Brut*
V   Cuvée Herbillon Brut*, Cuvée Special Club Brut*

DEUTZ AND GELDERMAN GM
16 rue Jeanson, Aÿ-Champagne

Production: *63,000 cases*

The firm was founded in 1838 by Pierre Gelderman and William Deutz. Today it holds 40ha (99 acres) of vineyards which include some prime sites. The wines are not fined or filtered prior to the second fermentation, and they are given an extra six months aging after *dégorgement*. These Champagnes are top class, displaying grace, delicacy and breeding.

Non-vintage Brut*
A dry, medium-bodied Champagne with a lively *mousse*, fragrant nose and elegant finish.

- Chardonnay 25%, Pinot noir 60%, Pinot meunier 15%
- Between 1-4 years

Other wines
NV   Extra Dry, Demi-Sec, Crémant Brut Brut, Blanc de Blancs Brut*, Rosé
V   Brut, Cuvée William Deutz*, Cuvée Georges Mathieu*

DUVAL-LEROY
Rue du Mont Cheril, Vertus

Production: *200,000 cases*

This house was formed in 1859 when Jules Duval & Fils merged with Edouard Leroy, and has been run by the Duval family ever since. It produces well-made wines with good flavour and aging potential which are excellent value. As much as 70 per cent of the production is sold under other labels, including various Buyer's Own Brands which are superior to most other examples of this type of wine.

Non-vintage Fleur de Champagne Brut*
A bone-dry to dry, medium-bodied, rich and fruity wine which is certainly better value than some of the more famous names.

- Chardonnay 70%, Pinot noir 30%
- Between 1-5 years

Other wines
NV   Crémant Blanc de Blancs Brut*, Rosé Brut, Cuvée du Roys Brut
V   Fleur de Champagne Brut*
CC   Vertus Rouge, Blanc de Blancs de Chardonnay

GOSSET
Rue Blondeau, Aÿ-Champagne

Production: *32,500 cases*

Established in 1584, Gosset is the oldest house in Champagne. Like Bollinger, Gosset ferments its fullest wines in cask. The malolactic conversion is avoided to produce fresher Champagnes of greater longevity. There is a luxurious texture to the *mousse* in these wines, and apart from the basic NV Resérve Brut they are all finely balanced, rich, soft Champagnes. The Grand Millésime is one of the greatest vintage Champagnes produced, and the Cuvée 4ème is a superb, ripe, round Champagne.

Non-vintage Spéciale Réserve Brut*
It is well worth buying this dry, medium-bodied, delicate and softly fruity Champagne rather than the disappointing NV Réserve Brut.

- Chardonnay 35%, Pinot noir 65%
- Between 1-5 years

Other wines
NV   Réserve Brut, Grande Réserve*, Rosé Brut*
V   Brut*, Grand Millésime*, **PC** Cuvée 4ème Centenaire*, Brut Intégral
CC   Bouzy Rouge, Blanc de Blancs

GEORGES GOULET
2 & 4 avenue du Général-Giraud, 51100 Reims

Production: *30,000 cases*

This house was established in 1834 and acquired by Abel Lepitre in 1960. The house style is one of smooth, full, rich wines heavily influenced by Pinot noir. They are high-quality Champagnes which represent exceptionally good value.

Non-vintage Extra Quality Brut
A dry, medium-bodied Champagne with plenty of fruit and balancing acidity but sometimes let down by a coarse *mousse*.

- Chardonnay 40%, Pinot noir 50%, Pinot meunier 10%

- Between 1-5 years

Other wines
NV   Goulet "G" Blanc de Blancs Brut
V   Extra Quality Brut*, Crémant Blanc de Blancs Brut, Extra Quality Rosé Brut*, Cuvée du Centenaire*

ALFRED GRATIEN
Gratien, Meyer, Sedoux & Cie, 30 rue Maurice-Cerveaux 51201 Epernay

Production: *17,000 cases*

This house is part of Gratien, Meyer, Seydoux & Cie who also market a range of Loire *méthode champenoise* wines under the Gratien and Meyer mark. Alfred Gratien Champagnes are the most traditionally produced of all *négociant-manipulant* Champagnes. They are cask-fermented, and reserve wines are stored in wooden vats. Their Vintage Crémant Brut is a classic Champagne which develops a rich and complex biscuity flavour after at least ten years aging.

Non-vintage Cuvée Réserve Brut
A bone-dry, very full-bodied Champagne. The non-vintage wines can be too oxidized for many people but, given a minimum of five years aging on top of the three or four Gratien give, they can turn into graceful Champagnes.

- Chardonnay 33%, Pinot noir and Pinot meunier 67%
- After at least 6 years

Other wines
NV   Rosé Brut
V   Crémant Brut*

CHARLES HEIDSIECK GM
3 place des Droits-de-l'Homme, Reims

Production: *292,000 cases*

The firm of Heidsieck was founded in 1785 by the German-born Florens-Louis Heidsieck. Charles Heidsieck was established in 1851 by Florens-Louis' great-nephew, Charles-Camille Heidsieck, who later acquired the nickname "Champagne Charlie" in the United States. Of the three Heidsieck firms, it is only one still to be run by the family, although it is now owned by Rémy-Martin, the Cognac house that *Continued overleaf*

also controls Krug. With significant sales and no vineyards, the quality of Charles Heidsieck has slipped once or twice in the past, but generally the Champagnes are extremely well made and good value.

Non-vintage Brut
A medium-dry Champagne that is medium-bodied with good fruit and length and a fine *mousse*.

- Chardonnay 20%, Pinot noir 40%, Pinot meunier 40%
- Within 1-2 years

Other wines
NV Blanc de Blancs Brut
V   Brut, Cuvée Royal Brut, Rosé Brut*; PC Cuvée "Champagne Charlie"*

HEIDSIECK & CO MONOPOLE GM
83 rue Coquebert,
51054 Reims

Production: *134,000 cases*

Another of Florens-Louis Heidsieck's relatives formed this business in 1834. The famous "Monopole" brand was first registered in 1860, and has been part of the firm's title since 1923. In 1972 Heidsieck & Co Monopole was sold to Mumm, which also owns Perrier-Jouët, and is itself part of the multi-national Seagram group.

With fine vineyards totalling 110ha (270 acres), the quality of Heidsieck's base wines is high. Although they possess a fine *mousse*, they often lack sparkle. The exception is the prestige *cuvée* Diamant Bleu, an immaculately balanced fifty-fifty blend of Pinot noir and Chardonnay.

Non-vintage Dry Monopole Brut
A dry, quite full-bodied, extremely well-made, commercial *brut* with good fruit.

- Chardonnay 33%, Pinot noir and Pinot meunier 67%
- Within 1-2 years

Other wines
NV Red Top Sec, Green Top Demi-Sec
V   Dry Monopole Brut, Rosé Brut; PC Cuvée Diamant Bleu Brut*

HENRIOT GM
3 place des Droits-de-l'Homme,
51066 Reims

Production: *125,000 cases*

This house was established in 1808 by Appoline Henriot to sell the wines produced from her father's vineyards. Since then Henriot has increased its viticultural estate and was taken over by Veuve Cliquot in 1985 in return for an 11 per cent holding in that house.

Henriot's temperature-controlled, stainless-steel vats are some of the newest in the region, and the house creates mild, gently rich Champagnes that deserve better recognition.

Non-vintage Souvrain Brut*
An old-fashioned style of Champagne that is off-dry and medium-bodied, with good fruit and length.

- Chardonnay 50-60%, Pinot noir and Pinot meunier 40-50%
- Within 2-3 years

Other wines
NV Crémant Blanc de Blancs Brut*
V   Souvrain Brut, Blanc de Blancs Brut*, Rosé Brut, Le Premier Brut; PC Réserve Baron Philippe de Rothschild*, PC Cuvée Baccarat*

IRROY GM
44 boulevard Lundy,
Reims

Production: *Figures not available*

The name of Irroy can be traced back as far as the fifteenth century in Mareuil-sur-Aÿ and Avenay, although the Champagne house of Irroy was not formed until 1820. In the late nineteenth century this was one of the great houses of Champagne, but today it is little more than a *sous marque* of Taittinger.

Vintage Cuvée Marie Antoinette
A dry to medium-dry, light- to medium-bodied Champagne.

- Unknown
- Within 1-2 years

Other wines
NV Brut

JACQUESSON & FILS
68 rue du Colonel Fabien,
Dizy,
51318 Epernay

Production: *30,000 cases*

Founded in 1798, this house currently has 11ha (27 acres) at Aÿ-Champagne,

Dizy and Hautvillers and a further 11ha (27 acres) of vineyards at Avize.

The Champagnes are essentially light and delicate in style. But the house's reputation does not rest upon its basic blended NV, but on its exceptional Blanc de Blancs.

Non-vintage Perfection Brut
A dry, light-bodied Champagne which, when properly matured, shows great finesse.

- Chardonnay 10-20%, Pinot noir and Pinot meunier 80-90%
- After 2-3 years

Other wines
NV Perfection Brut*, Blanc de Blancs Brut*, Rosé Brut
V   Perfection Brut*; PC Signature Brut*, PC Brut Zero Blanc de Blancs*
CC Avize Blanc de Blancs, Dizy Rouge

KRUG & CO GM
5 rue Coquebert,
51051 Reims

Production: *37,000 cases*

Johan-Josef Krug of Mainz established the firm of Krug in 1843 after working for nine years for Jacquesson. Today, Henri and Rémi Krug run the company, advised by their father Paul, although Rémy-Martin own a controlling interest.

Krug methods are traditional: wines are fermented in cask, there is no filtration, and the wine does not undergo malolactic conversion. All Krug Champagnes are said to have at least six years aging prior to sale, yet they benefit enormously from a further four years cellarage. They can be hard to appreciate but, given the appropriate amount of maturation, all Krug wines achieve unsurpassable depth and complexity.

Non-vintage Grande Cuvée Brut*
This bone-dry, very full-bodied Champagne is a blend of 40 to 50 different wines from seven or eight vintages. It has a complex nose and palate, and a deep, classically oxidative flavour.

- Chardonnay 35%, Pinot noir 50%, Pinot meunier 15%
- After at least 4 years

Other wines
NV Rosé Brut*
V   Brut*, Krug Collection*; PC Clos du Mesnil Blanc de Blancs*

LANSON PÈRE & FILS GM
12 boulevard Lundy,
51056 Reims

Production: *417,000 cases*

Founded in 1760 by François Delamotte under the name Delamotte Père & Fils. In 1828, Jean-Baptiste Lanson became associated with the firm, which is still run by the family. Lanson is now part of the giant French food group BSN, who also own Pommery & Greno. Although Lanson's production is huge, their 210ha (519 acres) of vineyards supply 40 per cent of their needs. Fermentation is in temperature-controlled, stainless-steel vats. The house style is soft and flowery, which is unusual for wines that have not undergone malolactic conversion. The vintage Champagnes are excellent and more consistent in quality than the non-vintage wines.

Non-vintage Black Label Brut
A medium-dry, light-bodied Champagne with a mild, fruity finish.

- Chardonnay 45%, Pinot noir 45%, Pinot meunier 10%

Other wines
NV Sec, Demi-Sec, Rosé Brut
V   Brut*; PC Spécial Cuvée 225
CC Blanc, Rouge

LAURENT-PERRIER GM
Avenue de Champagne,
51150 Tours-sur-Marne

Production: *580,000 cases*

Emile Laurent founded this house in 1812 and on his death in 1887 his widow, Mathilde Perrier, added her name to the company. Today, Laurent-Perrier is one of the biggest Champagne houses, and although they produce some superb Champagnes their rapidly expanding sales have caused great variations in quality. Their rich, complex, soft-fruit flavoured NV Rosé Brut is consistently good; the distinguished Vintage "LP" Brut is a fine, fleshy wine that rarely requires more bottle age, and the Cuvée Grand Siècle is exquisite.

Non-vintage "LP" Brut*
A dry, light-bodied Champagne with a crisp, fruity flavour and a fine *mousse*.

- Chardonnay 35%, Pinot noir 50%, Pinot meunier 15%
- Within 1-2 years

Other wines
NV Crémant Brut, Ultra Brut, Rosé Brut*; PC Grand Siècle*
V   "LP" Brut*; PC Millésimé Rare Brut, PC Grand Siècle Alexandra*
CC Bouzy Rouge, Pinot Franc, Blanc de Blancs de Chardonnay, Vintage Bouzy Rouge*

ABEL LEPITRE
2 & 4 avenue du Général-Giraud,
51055 Reims

Production: *42,000 cases*

Founded in 1924 by Abel Lepitre in the village of Ludes, this house is now part of Les Grands Champagnes de Reims, owned by Felix Chatellier, who also owns Château Dauzac, a *5 ème Grand Cru Classé* in Margaux. The vintage Rosé Brut is a fine wine by any standards, and the vintage Prince A. de Bourbon-Parme is very soft and full for a Chardonnay-dominated blend.

Non-vintage Carte Blanche Brut
A dry to medium-dry, light- to medium-bodied Champagne that is disappointing as it is not as good as the NV Idéal Cuvée, which it replaced.

🍇 Chardonnay 40%, Pinot noir 50%, Pinot meunier 10%

🥂 After 2-3 years

Other wines
NV Blanc de Blancs Cuvée No. 134
V Crémant Blanc de Blancs Brut*, Idéal Cuvée Brut, Rosé Brut*; PC Prince A. de Bourbon-Parme Brut*

MARNE & CHAMPAGNE
2 rue Maurice-Cerveaux,
Epernay

Production: *34,000 cases*

Few people have heard of Marne & Champagne, but it is the second largest stockholder in Champagne. It is the biggest supplier in the Buyer's Own Brand (BOB) business, and sells Champagne under no less than 300 different brand names. As much as 40 per cent of its base wine is *vin de taille*, and although many great Champagne houses that claim to use only *vins de cuvée* sell their *vins de taille* to Marne & Champagne, it is not known how many of the same houses buy back their *vins de taille*, in the form of Champagne sold *sur lattes*, in times of shortage.

The cheapest Buyer's Own Brand produced by Marne & Champagne can be very poor indeed, but there are several price levels, and some of its Champagnes are surprisingly good.

Non-vintage A. Rothschild Brut Réserve
An off-dry, medium-bodied Champagne marketed under Marne & Champagne's flagship label, "A. Rothschild", which offers consistently good quality and value.

🍇 Chardonnay 20%, Pinot noir 80%

Other wines
V A. Rothschild Brut Réserve*, A. Rothschild Rosé Brut Réserve; PC A. Rothschild Grand Trianon Brut*

MASSÉ GM
48 rue de Courlancy,
Reims

Production: *58,000 cases*

Established at Rilly-la-Montagne in 1853, this house was purchased by Lanson in 1976 and is now little more than a *sous marque* of its larger parent house (*see* p.144).

Non-vintage Brut
A medium-dry, light-bodied wine.

🍇 Chardonnay 35%, Pinot noir 45%, Pinot meunier 20%

🥂 Not recommended.

Other wines
NV Cuvée Henry Massé
V Brut

MERCIER GM
75 avenue de Champagne,
Epernay

Production: *500,000 cases*

This house, formed in 1858 by Eugène Mercier, when he combined five Champagne houses into one, was the original owner of the Dom Pérignon *marque*, which it sold to Moët & Chandon in 1930. At about this time also, the firm moved from Paris to its present premises in Epernay. In 1970 the entire company was bought by Moët & Chandon.

Mercier is the best-selling brand on the French market, but for some reason the wines, which are blended by Moët's *chef de caves*, appear to be much better in export markets than in France.

Non-vintage Brut Réserve
An off-dry, medium-bodied Champagne that lacks finesse. Export versions are fuller and have more fruit than those sold in their country of origin.

🍇 Chardonnay 35%, Pinot noir 45%, Pinot meunier 20%

🥂 Not recommended

Other wines
NV Demi-Sec Réserve, Crémant Brut
V Réserve Brut*, Rosé Brut; PC Réserve de l'Empereur Brut

MOËT & CHANDON GM
20 avenue de Champagne,
54120 Epernay

Production: *1,500,000 cases*

The house of Moët was established in 1743 by Claude Moët, a *courtier en vin* and owner of several well-known vineyards in the Vallée de la Marne. His grandson Jean-Rémy's friendship with Napoleon helped to make Moët the most famous Champagne of its time. By 1880 the house employed 350 cellarmen and 800 vineyard workers, owned 350ha (890 acres) of prime sites, had stocks in excess of 12 million bottles, and annual sales of 2.5 million bottles. Their extensive vineyards enabled Moët to dominate the Champagne trade in the twentieth century, and today Moët Champagne is shipped to 150 countries and is the best-selling brand in many of them. In 1971 Moët & Chandon and the Cognac house of Hennessy merged to form the powerful Moët-Hennessy group.

The house style of Moët is difficult to assess: its NV Première Cuvée Brut is usually a decent, commercial wine, but it can vary considerably in character; in Switzerland and other prestige markets it can be so outstanding that it might well be taken for vintage Champagne. Moët's vintage Champagnes are invariably fine, and Dom Pérignon is consistently one of the finest Champagnes produced.

Non-vintage Première Cuvée Brut
An off-dry, medium-bodied Champagne with a good strong *mousse*.

🍇 Chardonnay 30%, Pinot noir 50%, Pinot meunier 20%

Other wines
NV Crémant Demi-Sec
V Brut Imperial*, Brut Imperial Rosé; PC Dom Pérignon*, Dom Pérignon Rosé*
CC "Saran" Blanc de Blancs*

MONTEBELLO GM
Château du Mareuil-sur-Aÿ,
Mareuil-sur-Aÿ

Production: *20,000 cases*

Established in 1834 by the Duc de Montebello, eldest son of Maréchal Lannes. The Duc's daughter married Edouard Werlé, Veuve Clicquot's principal partner. In 1936 the firm was sold to Réné Chayoux, who bought Ayala shortly afterwards; this house is now owned by Ayala & Co. Like Irroy and Massé, this Champagne is treated like a *sous marque*, but its quality is somewhat better, and it is possible that the once fine reputation of this historically rich house might one day be restored. For the present, however, these Champagnes are light in body and *mousse*, with a mild, fruity flavour.

Non-vintage Brut
A dry, light-bodied Champagne that is best drunk when young and fresh.

🍇 Chardonnay 25%, Pinot noir 50%, Pinot meunier 25%

🥂 When young

Other wines
NV Sec, Demi-Sec
V Brut

G.H. MUMM & CO GM
29 & 34 rue du Champ-de-Mars,
51053 Reims

Production: *790,000 cases*

Mumm was founded by two Germans in 1827. In 1873 it launched its now famous Cordon Rouge brand, and this formed the basis of great expansion and success. After the First World War, the company was run by René Lalou, who built up Mumm into one of the largest Champagne houses. Mumm acquired Perrier-Jouët in 1959 and in 1969 Mumm was purchased by the Seagram group, the huge Canadian-based multi-national, who was one of its shareholders.

The style of the house is for light, elegant and fragrant Champagnes; its *bruts* tend to be relatively sweet. The exception is its justifiably famous Crémant de Cramant, which is a fine and delicate dry wine.

Non-vintage Cordon Rouge Brut
A medium-dry, light-bodied Champagne with a clean and fragrant finish.

🍇 Chardonnay 25%, Pinot noir and Pinot meunier 75%

Other wines
NV Cordon Vert Demi-Sec; PC Crémant de Cramant Blanc de Blancs Brut*
V Cordon Rouge Brut; PC René Lalou Brut, Rosé Brut*, PC Mumm de Mumm*

NAPOLEON GM
2 rue de Villiers-aux-Bois,
Vertus

Production: *12,500 cases*

Founded in 1825 under the name of Prieur-Pageot, this firm has sole right to use the name of Napoleon on its bottles. It owns no vineyards and purchases freshly pressed juice rather than grapes. About a third of the wines are cask-fermented, and the Champagnes produced are rich, honest and generous. The Carte Orange Brut is always a creamy-rich quality product with a fine *mousse*, while vintage Napoleon out-performs many of the more famous *grandes marques*.

Non-vintage Carte Verte Blanche Brut*
A dry, medium-bodied Champagne that is deceptively earthy when young, but develops extremely well for a three-parts Pinot meunier Champagne.

🍇 Chardonnay 25%, Pinot meunier 75%

🥂 Within 1-2 years

Other wines
NV Carte Orange Brut*, Rosé Brut
V Brut*

OUDINOT
**12 rue Roger Godart,
51207 Epernay**

Production: *50,000 cases*

This house was acquired by Michel Trouillard in 1981. Trouillard already owned 62ha (153 acres) of fine vineyards, and this estate gives Oudinot much future potential. The basic quality of Oudinot and Jeanmaire, a *marque* purchased by Oudinot in 1979, is showing well at present.

Non-vintage Brut*
A dry, medium-bodied, well-made Champagne that is clean, full and fruity.

🍇 Chardonnay 33%, Pinot noir 77%

🥂 Within 1-2 years

Other wines
NV Demi-Sec, Blanc de Blancs Brut*
V Brut*, Rosé*, Blanc de Blancs Brut, Blanc de Noirs; **PC** Cuvée Particulière*

BRUNO PAILLARD
**Rue Jacques Maritian,
51100 Reims**

Production: *20,000 cases*

Bruno Paillard first appeared on the market in 1981 as a *marque-auxiliaire* but was granted *négociant-manipulant* status in 1984. Some of these Champagnes have been quite outstanding, and now that Bruno Paillard produces most of his wines at new temperature-controlled *cuverie* and cellars at Murigny, he has attained a high degree of consistency.

Non-vintage Brut*
An off-dry, medium-bodied Champagne that is elegant and fruity, balancing freshness with a certain roundness.

🍇 Chardonnay 25%, Pinot noir 35%, Pinot meunier 40%

🥂 Within 2-3 years

Other wines
NV Crémant Blanc de Blancs Brut*, Rosé Brut*
V Brut*

JOSEPH PERRIER GM
**69 avenue de Paris,
51005 Châlons-sur-Marne**

Production: *50,000 cases*

When Joseph Perrier established this firm in 1825, Châlons-sur-Marne occupied a more important position in the Champagne trade than it does today, with as many as 15 houses situated there. Today it is very much a backwater, but this suits the relaxed style of the house. It produces mellow and fruity wines that are heavily influenced by Pinot grapes. While they

are definitely easy to drink when young, the freshness experienced in the occasional release of an old, classic vintage vividly demonstrates their potential longevity.

Non-vintage Cuvée Royale Brut*
A dry, full-bodied, elegant Champagne with plenty of fruit and depth.

🍇 Chardonnay 30%, Pinot noir 25%, Pinot meunier 45%

🥂 Good young, but better after 3-4 years

Other wines
NV Cuvée Royale Sec, Cuvée Royale Demi-Sec, Cuvée Royale Blanc de Blancs Brut*, Cuvée Royale Rosé Brut; **PC** Cuvée Cinquantenaire Brut*
V Cuvée Royale Brut*
CC Cumières Rouge, Blanc de Blancs de Chardonnay

PERRIER-JOUËT GM
**28 avenue de Champagne,
51200 Epernay**

Production: *235,000 cases*

This firm was established in 1811 by the uncle of Joseph Perrier, who combined his name with his wife's maiden name. Perrier-Jouët was purchased by Mumm in 1959 and has been part of Seagram since 1969.

Perrier-Jouët own a 108ha (267 acre) estate of fine vineyards and, although the basic non-vintage Grand Brut can be a bit young and appley, the other wines always display great elegance and breeding. This house is best known for its superb "Belle-Epoque" Champagne, which is sold in the famous "flower bottle".

Non-vintage Grand Brut
A dry, light-bodied Champagne with good acidity and fragrant fruit, which will develop if laid down.

🍇 Chardonnay 30%, Pinot noir and Pinot meunier 70%

🥂 Allow at least 2-3 years

Other wines
NV Grand Sec, Grand Demi-Sec, Blason de France Brut*, Blason de France Rosé Brut
V Extra Brut, Rosé Brut; **PC** Belle-Epoque Brut*, **PC** Belle-Epoque Rosé Brut*

PHILIPPONNAT
**13 rue du Pont,
Mareuil-sur-Aÿ,
51160 Aÿ-Champagne**

Production: *42,000 cases*

This house was established in 1912 by the Philipponnat family, who have lived in Champagne since the sixteenth century. In 1935 the firm purchased the steep, south-facing vineyard of Clos des Goisses. The Champagne produced from this vineyard is only matched in quality, but not in style, by the wines of Salon and Krug's single-vineyard Champagne – Clos du Mesnil. The rest of Philipponnat's range is delicately rich in flavour due to the firm's large stocks of reserve wines.

Non-vintage Royal Réserve Brut
A dry, light to medium-bodied Champagne that has rich fruit balanced by good acidity and a soft *mousse*.

🍇 Chardonnay 25%, Pinot noir 35%, Pinot meunier 40%

🥂 Within 1-2 years

Other wines
NV Royal Réserve Rosé Brut*
V Royal Réserve Rosé Brut* Première Blanc de Blancs Brut*; **PC** Clos des Goisses*

PIPER-HEIDSIECK GM
**51 boulevard Henri Vasnier,
51100 Reims**

Production: *400,000 cases*

Another nephew of Florens-Louis Heidsieck's founded this firm in 1834. In 1845 it started selling Champagne under the Piper-Heidsieck label in deference to its American customers, who insisted on calling the wine "Piper's Heidsieck". After first fermentation Piper-Heidsieck centrifuges its wines, which then do not go through the malolactic conversion. This results in wines that appear tightly closed in youth but, given sufficient aging, can gain considerable depth and finesse.

Non-vintage Brut Extra*
A bone-dry to dry, full-bodied Champagne with a fragrant flavour that lengthens and deepens with age.

🍇 Chardonnay 30%, Pinot noir 40%, Pinot meunier 30%

🥂 After 3-5 years

Other wines
V Brut Extra*, Rosé Brut, Brut Sauvage; **PC** Florens-Louis Brut, **PC** Rare

POL ROGER & CO GM
**1 rue Henri Lelarge,
51206 Epernay**

Production: *142,000 cases*

This house was founded in 1849 by Pol Roger. Sir Winston Churchill was a great admirer of Pol Roger Champagnes; he had his Champagne bottled in Imperial Pints. All the *cuvées* that were available at the time of his death bear a black border. Pol Roger owns 70ha (173 acres) of vineyards and consistently produces high-quality Champagnes in a classic style. The Réserve Spécial PR Brut has quite extraordinary depth and length, and the Cuvée Sir Winston Churchill is the finest prestige *cuvée* to be launched in recent times.

Non-vintage Brut*
A medium- to full-bodied Champagne that is not as dry as some *bruts*. This is a classic Pinot-dominated blend. It has a persistent *mousse* of tiny bubbles.

🍇 Chardonnay 30%, Pinot noir 25%, Pinot meunier 45%

🥂 After 2-3 years

Other wines
NV Sec, Demi-Sec
V Brut*, Rosé Brut*, Chardonnay Brut*; **PC** Spéciale Réserve PR Brut*, **PC** Cuvée Sir Winston Churchill*

POMMERY & GRENO GM
**5 place Général-Gouraud,
51053 Reims**

Production: *417,000 cases*

This firm was founded in 1836 and in 1856, on the death of Louis Pommery, it was left in the hands of his widow Louise. She purchased a site containing extensive chalk pits, which she turned into 18km (11 miles) of cellars, and built a bizarre house that is said to have been inspired by the stately homes of her five most important British customers. Today Pommery & Greno is owned by the giant BSN Group, which also controls Lanson and Massé.

With a superb estate of 307ha (759 acres), this firm produces totally dry full-bodied Champagnes. Pommery is probably the most underrated of the *grandes marques*.

Non-vintage Brut Royale*
An attractively bone-dry, full-bodied Champagne, which is very light in colour with a persistent *mousse* of tiny bubbles. It attains good depth of flavour with at least five years in bottle.

Chardonnay 25-30%, Pinot noir and Pinot meunier 70-75%

Will improve for up to 10 years

Other wines
NV   Extra Dry, Drapeau Sec, Demi-Sec
V   Brut*; **PC** Louise Pommery*, **PC** Louise Pommery Rose*

LOUIS ROEDERER GM
21 boulevard Lundy,
51100 Reims

Production: *142,000 cases*

The origins of this house go back to 1760, but it was not until 1827 that Louis Roederer entered the business. In 1876 at the request of Tsar Alexander II Louis Roederer produced the now famous Cristal Champagnes exclusively for the Russian Imperial family. Today Roederer have the most balanced estate of vineyards in the Champagne business. Approximately 185ha (457 acres) of prime sites in Avize, Aÿ-Champagne, Chouilly, Vertus, Verzenay and Verzy provide 80 per cent of their needs. The quality of Roederer's Champagne is high, and its style is extremely traditional: malolactic conversion is only allowed in years of high acidity, reserve wines are kept in cask, and the non-vintage Champagnes receive up to twice the average aging time. Roederer Champagnes have a high *dosage*: the vintage Blanc de Blancs is the driest *brut* in the range, and both the Cristal Champagnes have such a wealth of refined flavours that the sugar is only a small distraction, but the other *bruts* are relatively sweet.

Non-vintage Premier Brut*
A medium-dry Champagne that would benefit from less sweetness, but it has enough body, richness and flavour to prevent it from cloying.

Chardonnay 34%, Pinot noir 66%

Up to 5 years

Other wines
NV   Grand Vin Sec, Demi-Sec, Carte Blanche, Rosé Brut*
V   Brut, Blanc de Blancs Brut*, Vintage Cristal Brut*, Vintage Cristal Rosé Brut*, Ratafia

RUINART PÈRE & FILS GM
4 rue de Crayère,
51053 Reims

Production: *109,000 cases*

This house was established in 1727 by Nicolas Ruinart. In 1963 it was taken over by Moët et Chandon and, in spite of doubling production, Ruinart has managed to keep an independent, sophisticated image. Its reputation is firmly based on its prestige *cuvée* Dom Ruinart, not on its sometimes disappointing NV. The Blanc de Blancs version of Dom Ruinart is a blend of wines from Avize, Cramant and le Mesnil-sur-Oger, with wines from Verzy and Sillery to add strength and weight.

Non-vintage Brut Tradition
A medium-dry, medium-bodied Champagne that is crisp and fruity but rather short on the finish.

Chardonnay 25-30%, Pinot noir 30-40%, Pinot meunier 30-40%

Within 2-3 years

Other wines
V   Brut; **PC** Dom Ruinart Blanc de Blancs Brut*, **PC** Dom Ruinart Rosé Brut*
CC   Ruinart Chardonnay

DE SAINT-MARCEAUX
4 avenue du Général Giraud,
Reims

Production: *14,000 cases*

Established 1837 by Jean Alexandre de Saint-Marceaux, the Champagnes produced by this house soon gained a high reputation throughout Europe, particularly in Russia. De Saint-Marceaux passed through many hands and finally landed up with Jacques Lepitre in 1947. Under the umbrella company of the Société des Grandes Champagnes de Reims, this house now belongs to Félix Chatellier. It produces Champagnes of reliable, if rarely exciting quality.

Non-vintage Brut
A dry to medium-dry, light- to medium-bodied wine that can always be recommended for its good value.

Chardonnay 40%, Pinot noir 50%, Pinot Meunier 10%

Within 2-3 years

Other wines
NV   Sec, Demi-Sec
V   Brut

SALON GM
le Mesnil-sur-Oger,
51190 Avize

Production: *5,000 cases*

Salon was established in 1914 by Eugène-Aimé Salon, a Parisian furrier who had nursed an ambition to create

the first commercial *blanc de blancs*. He was convinced that something special about the Chardonnay grown in le Mesnil-sur-Oger would enable him to produce a perfectly balanced wine without Pinot grapes. He accordingly purchased 5ha (12 acres) of vineyards in the village, and his Champagne was so successful that it was listed at Maxim's in the 1920s as the house wine. Salon was purchased in 1963 by Besserat de Belefon, and they are now both owned by Pernod-Ricard.

Salon's methods are traditional: the wines never undergo malolactic conversion, reserve wines are stored in large wooden casks, and *dégorgement* is carried out manually. There is but one Salon *cuvée*, a vintage Champagne, which is restricted to the *vins de cuvée* of the very best vintage years. The result is a very special wine.

Vintage Cuvée S
A bone-dry Champagne that is deceptively light in flavour when young, but develops a creamy richness with age, eventually achieving a complex range of refined flavours that include hints of walnuts, hazelnuts and macaroons. Typically it has a fine, smooth but persistent *mousse*.

Chardonnay 100%

Within 10-50 years

TAITTINGER GM
9 place Saint-Niçaise,
51061 Reims

Production: *333,000 cases*

One of the oldest houses in Champagne, this firm was founded in 1734, but was not acquired by the Taittinger family until after the First World War. With 250ha (618 acres) of vineyards that look after half their needs, Taittinger produce Champagnes hallmarked by their length, style and elegance. They are classic Champagnes heavily influenced by the Chardonnay grape. Given sufficient maturity, six or seven years aging for the vintage Brut, and at least ten for the superb Comtes de Champagne, they attain an immaculate balance and a great intensity of flavour.

Taittinger owns the once famous *marque* of Irroy and the Loire *méthode champenoise* houses of Monmousseau and Bouvet.

Non-vintage Brut Réserve
A dry, medium-bodied Champagne that is very inconsistent in quality: it is sometimes good enough to be mistaken for a vintage *brut*, yet at other times too young, coarse and malic.

Chardonnay 40%, Pinot noir and Pinot meunier 60%

Within 2-5 years

Other wines
V   Brut*, Collection*; **PC** Comtes de Champagne Blanc de Blancs Brut*, **PC** Comtes de Champagne Rosé Brut*

VEUVE CLICQUOT-PONSARDIN GM
12 rue du Temple,
51054 Reims

Production: *542,000 cases*

In 1772 Philippe Clicquot Muiron opened a trading house in Reims dealing in fabrics, banking and very modest transactions in Champagne. The history of this great house really began in 1805 when his son, François Clicquot, died unexpectedly leaving a young widow. Nicole-Barbe Clicquot, née Ponsardin, took over the firm against her father-in-law's wishes, and was so successful that she became a legend in her own lifetime.

This house owns 280ha (692 acres) of vineyards in all the best areas. Its Champagnes are unusually well matured, although like every Champagne house the average quality of its basic NV wines suffered in the shortages of the early 1980s. The *brut* style is full and rich but rather sweet.

Non-vintage Brut*
A medium-dry, full-bodied Champagne that is rich in fruit with good body and length.

Chardonnay 30%, Pinot noir 50%, Pinot meunier 20%

Within 1-5 years

Other wines
NV   Demi-Sec
V   Brut*, Rosé Brut*; **PC** Grande Dame Brut*

Reliable Champagnes from other houses

Henri Abelé NV Sourire de Reims Brut

Beaumet Chaurey Vintage Cuvée Malakoff Brut

Boizel NV Brut, Vintage Brut

Bonnet Blanc de Blancs Brut

Bricout NV Brut, NV Rosé Brut, Vintage Brut

Albert le Brun NV Blanc de Blancs Brut

René Brun Vintage Brut

A Chauvet Cachet Vert Blanc de Blancs Brut

Cheurlin Spécial Réserve, Prestige

A Desmoulins NV Cuvée Prestige

André Drappier NV Brut, Vintage Brut, Grande Sendreé Brut

H Germain & Fils NV Carte Blanche Brut, Vintage Blanc de Blancs Brut, Vintage Grande Cuvée Venus Brut

Lang-Biémont Vintage Blanc de Blancs, Cuvée III*

R & L Legras Vintage Cuvée Saint-Vincent

Médot & Cie Vintage Clos des Chaulins

de Meric NV Blanc de Blancs Brut, Rosé Brut

Montaudon Vintage Brut

Ployez-Jacquemart Vintage Brut

J de Telmont NV Grande Réserve Brut, NV Crémant Blanc de Blancs Brut

Good coopérative Champagnes

Champagne Richard de Ayala Union des Propriétaires Récoltants at le Mesnil-sur-Oger.

Champagne Bur Centre Vinicole de la Champagne at Chouilly.

Champagne Raoul Collet Coopérative Générale des Vignerons at Aÿ-Champagne.

Champagne A. Deveaux Union Auboise.

Champagne René Florancy, Champagne Saint Gall and **Champagne Orpale** Union Champagne at Avize.

Champagne Gruet & Fils Coopérative des Coteaux de Bethon.

Champagne Jacquart Coopérative des Regionale des Vins de Champagne in Reims.

Champagne Lancelot Coopérative Vinicole de Mancy.

Champagne Mailly-Champagne Société de Producteurs Mailly-Champagne.

Champagne Palmer Société Coopérative de Producteurs des Grands Terroirs de Champagne in Reims.

Champagne Saint Reol ou Nectar de Noirs Sélection des Producteurs Associés at Ambonnay.

Champagne Saint Simon Coopérative la Crayère at Bethon.

Recommended grower Champagnes

It is possible to encounter more than 4,000 different labels purporting to be *Récoltants-Manipulants*. Many are merely "co-op clones", that is to say many growers who sell the same *coopérative*-produced Champagne under different labels. In some cases these may well be better than many genuinely individual Champagnes. To cut through the confusing mass of labels and the variable quality, the names listed, although in no way a definitive selection, represent a number of growers who can normally be relied upon to sell good Champagne.

Jean-Paul Arvois, Chavot-Courcourt

G E Autreau Père & Fils, Champillon

Paul Bara, Bouzy

H Beaufort & Fils, Bouzy

Yves Beautrait, Louvois

Gilbert Bertrand, Chamery

Bonnaire-Boquemont, Cramant

Alexandre Bonnet, les Riceys

M Brugnon, Ecueil

Lucien Carré, Vertus

Cattier, Chigny-les-Roses

Jacques Copinet, Montgenost

Pierre Delabarre, Vandières

Denois Père & Fils, Cumières

Paul Déthune, Ambonnay

Raymond Devilliers, Villedommange

Gallimard Père & Fils, les Riceys

Pierre Gimmonet & Fils, Cramant

Bertrand Godmé, Verzenay

Michel Gonnet, Avize

P Guiborat, Cramant

Bernard Hatté, Verzenay

Horiot Père & Fils, les Riceys

André Jacquart, le Mesnil-sur-Oger

Jeeper, Damery

Michel Laroche, Vauciennes

J Lassalle, Chigny-les-Roses

Launois Père & Fils, le Mesnil-sur-Oger

Lilbert Fils, Cramant

Henri Loriot, Festigny

Yves Mignon, Cumières

Pierre Paillard, Bouzy

Pierre Peters, le Mesnil-sur-Oger

Ricciuti-Révolte, Avenay

Camille Savès, Bouzy

Jacques Selosse, Avize

Christian Senez, Fontette

Séverin-Doublet, Vertus

Sugot-Feneuil, Cramant

Vazart-Cocquart, Chouilly

Jean Vesselle, Bouzy

Maurice Vesselle, Bouzy

Vilmart & Co, Rilly-la-Montagne

Still wines of Champagne

COTEAUX CHAMPENOIS AOC

The still wines, both red and white, produced in Champagne are low in quality and high in price. With a few exceptions, the white wines of this *appellation* have been treated as an unofficial source of base wines for turning into Champagne, if and when they are reclassified in times of shortage as happened with the crops of 1975, 1976 and 1977. There is a rosé, but it has little to recommend it.

RED Most examples are dry, light-to-medium-bodied wines that barely hint at the flush of fruit found in good Burgundies. The all-too-rare exceptions can be very impressive in their deep colour, rich fruit and often slightly smoky style of Pinot noir. Bouzy is the most famous wine boasted by this appellation, but a good vintage rarely

occurs in the same village more than once in ten years, therefore it is worthwhile trying other good growths, such as Ambonnay, Aÿ and Mareuil.

🍇 Mostly Pinot noir but also Pinot meunier

🍷 1982, 1985, 1989, 1990

🍺 Sometimes immediately, sometimes between 6-7 years

WHITE A restrained practice of *süssreserve* (see p.204) would enable the Champenois to make a drinkable, fruity wine every year. As it is, with the exception of Saran and Ruinart, most of these wines are thin, dry and acid, yet Bollinger's reserve wines emphatically demonstrate that classic Chardonnay wines could be made in Champagne. Fermented in oak and stored in magnums, they remain remarkably fresh for as long as 25 years, and achieve great richness.

ROSÉ DES RICEYS AOC

This is not part of the Coteaux Champenois AOC, but a totally separate appellation. The pure Pinot noir still, pink wine is made in the commune of Les Riceys in the Aube *département*. It should be dark pink in colour.

Production is tiny and erratic because producers know that the special character of Rosé des Riceys only emerges in the very best years.

ROSÉ Dry, medium-bodied wines; good examples are aromatic, reminiscent of chocolate and herbs, and can possess a penetrating, fruity flavour with a long, smooth finish.

🍇 Pinot noir

🍷 1981, 1982, 1989, 1990

🍺 Between 3-5 years

Alsace

Alsace is the only classic region in France that has built a reputation on pure varietal wines. Some 95 per cent are dry white wines produced from a collection of essentially French or German grape varieties.

THE VINEYARDS OF ALSACE ARE DOTTED with medieval towns of cobbled streets and timbered buildings. A fascinating mixture of French and German characteristics pervade this fragment of France that is cut off from the rest of the country by the barrier of the Vosges mountain range, and separated from neighbouring Germany by the mighty Rhine. Most people speak a guttural language based on Old German, but some understand only the modern version or French. The local cuisine has a variety of influences, but is essentially German.

The colourful combination of cultures is the result of the wars and border squabbles that have plagued the ancient province since the Treaty of Westphalia ended the Thirty Years War in 1648. This gave the French sovereignty over Alsace, and royal edicts issued in 1662, 1682 and 1687 proffered free land to anyone willing to restore it to full productivity. As a result, hordes of Swiss, Germans, Tyroleans and Lorrainers poured into the region.

In 1871, at the end of the Franco-Prussian War, the region once again came under German control, and remained so until the end of the First World War. At this juncture Alsace began to reorganize the administration of its vineyards in line with the new French AOC system, but Germany reclaimed the province in 1940 before the process was complete. Thus it was not until after the Second World War that the quest for AOC status could be resumed, and another seventeen years before it was actually realized in 1962.

The *Grands Crus* of Alsace

The first *Grand Cru* legislation was introduced in 1975, but it was not until 1983 that the first list of twenty-five *Grand Cru* sites was published. Three years later a further twenty-three were added. There are now fifty-one *Grands Crus*, including Kaefferkopf in Ammerschwihr, the most recent addition. There are those who feel that this number is too high and that many of the sites are not truly great growths. On the other hand, just because some of the *Grand Crus* do not have great reputations historically, it does not necessarily follow that the wine they produce is not

Hugel's headquarters, above
The small wine shop, cellars and offices of the merchants Hugel are marked by a typically Alsatian sign in Riquewihr.

La Petite Venise, Colmar, above
Not only can the town boast a strong association with the wine trade, but also many architectural delights and a canal district of great charm.

HOW TO READ ALSACE LABELS

Grape variety
The first thing to look for–in this case Riesling. Another name, in addition to the grape variety, will most probably be a brand name, but could refer to a village or vineyard, as is the case here. The Schlossberg vineyard stretches across the south-facing slopes of Kaysersberg and Kientzheim. If there is no grape variety specified, the wine will either be *Crémant d'Alsace*, which is a good quality *méthode champenoise* sparkling wine, or a blend of different grape varieties, which may or may not refer to itself as an *Edelzwicker.*

Producer and vintage
The label may reveal both. In this case, 1983 is a great vintage and Blanck a fine producer who owns some superbly located vineyards referred to collectively as "Domaine des Comtes de Lupfen", also mentioned. The small print at the base of the label clearly states that the wine was bottled on the domaine by the proprietor, and gives the address of the proprietor, which is obligatory, as is the country of origin, if the wine is for export, and the bottle capacity.

Appellation
All Alsace wines are made within the appellation of Alsace, and are labelled so. If the vineyard is classified as *grand cru*, this information is incorporated with the appellation.

(Label reads:) ALSACE GRAND CRU — BLANCK — Domaine des Comtes de Lupfen — APPELLATION ALSACE GRAND CRU CONTRÔLÉE — Riesling Schlossberg 1983 — 70 cl — Mise en Bouteilles au Domaine des Comtes de Lupfen. Propriété de Paul Blanck et ses fils à Kientzheim (Kaysersberg) Haut-Rhin - France

---

Other information regarding style or quality may also be present:

Medaille d'Or
The medals of Colmar, Mâcon and Paris have been devalued by the growing number of "winners". Many excellent wines are to be found bearing the gold medal stickers, but they are now so common that their presence has become practically meaningless. However, one medal that is definitely well worth looking out for is the "Sigillé de Qualité", which is issued by the Confrèrie Saint Etienne.

Vendange Tardive
A late-harvested wine that is rich and powerful, and may be sweet.

Sélection de grains nobles
A relatively rare, intensely sweet, yet remarkably elegant, botrytized wine.

Elevé en fûts
This indicates that the wine has been aged in cask and should have a certain oakiness to the nose or palate.

Sélection, Réserve, Spéciale Cuvée
These terms suggest, and quite often mean, superior wine.

of true *Grand Cru* quality today. From exhaustive tastings, I am confident for example, that Furstentum will become one of the greatest of all *Grands Crus*. Furthermore, who knows what will happen in the other growths over the next 30 years, as a new generation of young winemakers eager to express their *terroir* build on their experiences?

One can argue about numbers, but without doubt the most stupid aspect of the *Grand Cru* regulations is their limitation to pure varietal wines of just four grapes – Muscat, Riesling, Gewürztraminer and Tokay-Pinot Gris. This not only denies the famous Sylvaner wines of Zotzenberg in Mittelbergheim and Sonnenglanz in Beblenheim the *Grand Cru* status they deserve, but it also robs us of the opportunity to drink the finest possible quality of Pinot Noir, Pinot Blanc, Sylvaner and Chasselas. Even if they might not be in the same quality league, why make a law preventing their cultivation for AOC *Grand Cru* Alsace when the economic reality of the market will in any case force most growers to plant the four classic varieties in their most prized *Grand Cru* sites, because they automatically fetch the highest prices?

The wines of Lorraine

When the *départements* of Meurthe-et-Moselle and Moselle were part of the old Province of Lorraine, their vineyards covered some 30,000 hectares (74,000 acres), more than twice that of neighbouring Alsace today. They currently cover a mere 70 hectares (173 acres), virtually all of which are in the Meurthe-et-Moselle. The viticultural outcrops of the Moselle are particularly sparse and make a sorry sight compared to their former glory; nowadays it is the *Route de la Mirabelle*, not the *Route du Vin*, that is flourishing. Growing damsons, it would seem, is far less risky than growing vines, although most people find that working in the industrialized town of Metz is more profitable.

FACTORS AFFECTING TASTE AND QUALITY

Location
The northeast corner of France, flanked by the Vosges mountains and bordered by the Rhine and Germany's Black Forest. Six rivers rise in the fir-capped Vosges, flowing through the 97 kilometre (60 mile) strip of Alsatian vineyards to feed the river Ill.

Climate
Protected from the full effect of Atlantic influences by the Vosges mountains, these vineyards are endowed with an exceptional amount of warm sunshine and a very low rainfall. The rain clouds tend to shed their load on the western side of the Vosges as they climb over the mountain range.

Aspect
The vineyards nestle on the lower east-facing slopes of the Vosges at a relatively high altitude of about 180 to 360 metres (600 to 1200 ft), and at an angle of between 25° on the lower slopes to 65° on the higher ones. The best vineyards have a south or southeast aspect, but many good growths are also found on north and northeast facing slopes. In many cases the vines are cultivated on the top as well as the sides of a spur, but the best sites are always protected by forested tops. Too much cultivation of the fertile plains in the 1970s has led to recent over-production problems. However, some vineyards on the plains do yield very good quality wines due to favourable soil types.

Soil
Alsace has the most complex geological and solumological situation of all the great wine areas of France. The three basic morphological and structural areas are: the siliceous edge of the Vosges; limestone hills; and the hydrous alluvial plain. The soils of the first include: colluvium and fertile sand over granite, stony-clay soil over schist, various fertile soils over volcanic sedimentary rock and poor, light sandy soil over sandstone; of the second, dry stony brown alkaline soil over limestone, brown sandy-calcareous soils over sandstone and limestone, heavy fertile soils over clay-limestone, brown alkaline soil over chalky-marl; and the third, sandy-clay and gravel over alluvium, brown decalcified loess and dark calcareous soils over loess.

Viticulture and vinification
The vines are trained high on wires to avoid spring ground frost. Traditionally, the wines are fermented as dry as possible, although residual sugar can sometimes be found in *Vendanges Tardives*. The rare *Sélection de Grains Nobles* is intensely sweet, although it is fermented to as high as 16-17 per cent alcohol.

Grape varieties
Chasselas, Sylvaner, Pinot blanc, Pinot gris, Pinot noir, Auxerrois, Gewürztraminer, Muscat blanc à petits grains, Muscat rosé à petits grains, Muscat ottonnel, Riesling, Chardonnay

---

ALSACE GRANDS CRUS

In the complete list of *Grands Crus* below, the sites that are asterisked are the relatively few that can historically establish a pedigree for the grape varieties indicated (in *italic*).

Altenberg de Bergbieten

Altenberg de Bergheim*: *Gewürztraminer*

Altenberg de Wolxheim

Brand*, Turckheim: *Tokay-Pinot Gris*

Bruderthal, Molsheim

Eichberg*, Eguisheim: *Gewürztraminer*

Engelberg, Dahlenheim

Florimont, Ingersheim

Frankstein, Dambach-la-Ville

Froehn, Zellenberg

Furstentum, Kientzheim-Sigolsheim

Geisberg*, Ribeauvillé: *Riesling*

Gloeckelberg, Rodern-St.-Hippolyte

Goldert, Gueberschwihr

Hatschbourg, Hattstatt-Voegtlinshoffen

Hengst, Wintzenheim

Kaefferkopf*, Ammerschwihr: *Riesling* and *Gewürztraminer*

Kanzlerberg*, Bergheim: *Riesling and Gewürztraminer*

Kastelberg, Andlau

Kessler, Guebwiller: Kitterlé, Wanne

Kirchberg de Barr*: *Gewürztraminer*

Kirchberg de Ribeauvillé

Kitterlé, Guebwiller: *Clevner*

Mackrain, Bennwihr

Mambourg, Sigolsheim

Mandelberg*, Mittelwihr: *Riesling*

Moenchberg, Andlau-Eichhoffen

Muenchberg, Nothalten

Ollwiller, Wuenheim

Osterberg, Ribeauvillé

Pfersigberg*, Eguisheim: *Gewürztraminer*

Pfingstberg, Orschwihr-Kientzheim

Praelatenberg, Orschwiller

Rangen*, Thann-Vieux Thann: *Tokay-Pinot Gris*

Rosacker*, Hunawihr: *Riesling*

Saering, Guebwiller

Schlossberg, Kaysersberg-Kientzheim

Schoenenbourg*, Riquewihr: *Riesling and Muscat*

Sommerberg, Niedermorschwihr-Katzenthal

Sonnenglanz*, Beblenheim: *Sylvaner*

Spiegel, Bergholtz-Guebwiller

Sporen*, Riquewihr: Gewürztraminer and *Tokay*

Steinert, Pfaffenheim

Steingrubler, Wettolsheim

Steinklotz, Marlenheim

Vorbourg, Rouffach-Westhalten

Wiebelsberg, Andlau

Wineck-Schlossberg, Katzenthal

Winzenberg, Blienschwiller

Zinnkoepflé*, Westhalten-Soultzmatt: *Gewürztraminer, Tokay-Pinot Gris*

Zotzenberg*, Mittelbergheim: famous for *Sylvaner*

Inspecting vines, above
Emile Boeckel, an important merchant in Alsace, checks grape development at his Mittelbergheim vineyards.

After the harvest, above
Wooden tubs used for transporting grapes are given a hosedown in picturesque Eguisheim.

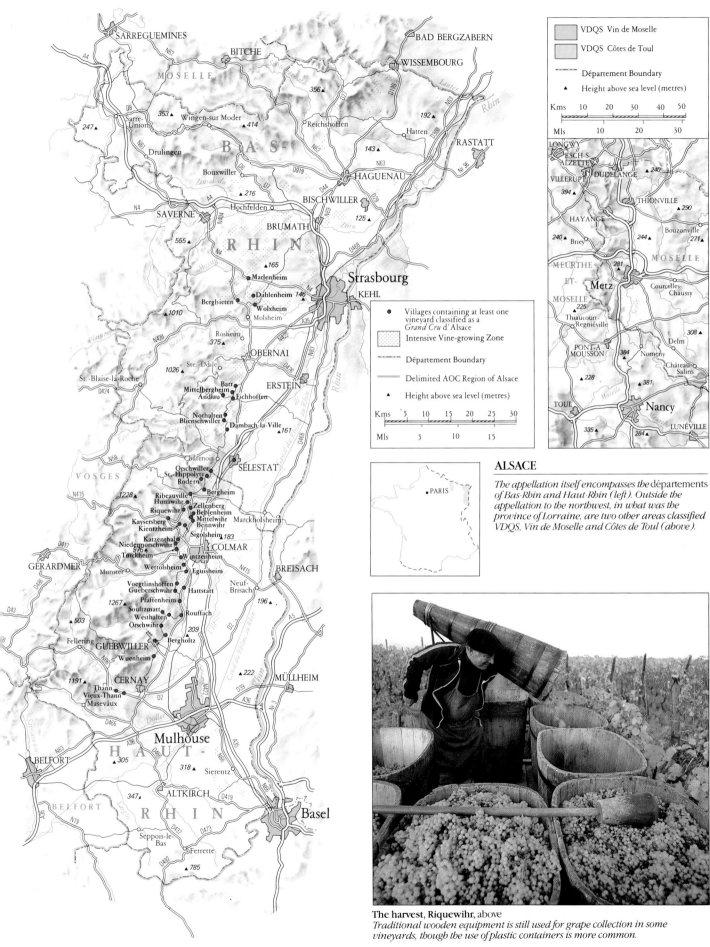

SARREGUEMINES

BITCHE

BAD BERGZABERN

WISSEMBOURG

MOSELLE

356 ▲

353 ▲ Wingen-sur Moder

414 ▲

Reichshoffen

192 ▲

Hatten

RASTATT

247 ▲ Sarre-Union

B A S

Drulingen

143 ▲

Bouxwiller

HAGUENAU

216 ▲

N4 SAVERNE Hochfelden

BISCHWILLER

125 ▲

555 ▲

BRUMATH

R H I N

165 ▲

Marlenheim

Strasbourg

146 ▲ KEHL

Dahlenheim

Bergbieten Wolxheim

1010 ▲ Molsheim

Rosheim

375 ▲

OBERNAI

1026 ▲ Ste.-Odile

St.-Blaise-la-Roche

ERSTEIN

Barr

Mittelbergheim

Andlau Eichhoffen

Nothalten

Blienschwiller

Dambach-la-Ville 161 ▲

Châtenois

V O S G E S

Orschwiller SÉLESTAT

St.-Hippolyte

Rodern

1228 ▲ Ribeauvillé Bergheim

Hunawihr

Riquewihr Zellenberg

Beblenheim Marckholsheim

Kaysersberg Mittelwihr

Kientzheim Bennwihr

Katzenthal Sigolsheim 183 ▲

976 ▲ Niedermorschwihr

Turckheim COLMAR

Wintzenheim

Munster Wettolsheim

Eguisheim

Voegtlinshoffen BREISACH

Gueberschwihr Hattstatt Neuf-Brisach

1267 ▲ Pfaffenheim

Soultzmatt 196 ▲

Westhalten Rouffach

503 ▲ Orschwihr

209 ▲

Bergholtz

Fellering GUEBWILLER

Wuenheim

222 ▲

CERNAY MÜLLHEIM

1191 ▲ Thann

Vieux-Thann

Masevaux

Mulhouse

H A U T -

BELFORT 305 ▲

318 ▲ Sierentz

BELFORT 347 ▲ ALTKIRCH

R H I N Basel

Seppois-le-Bas

Ferrette

785 ▲

LONGWY

ESCH-S.-ALZETTE

DUDELANGE 240 ▲

VILLERUPT

394 ▲ THIONVILLE 290 ▲

HAYANGE

240 ▲ Briey 244 ▲ Bouzonville 271 ▲

MEURTHE- M O S E L L E

ET- 281 ▲

MOSELLE Metz Courcelles-Chaussy

225 ▲

Thiaucourt- 308 ▲

Regniéville Delm

PONT-A- 384 ▲ Nomeny

MOUSSON Château-Salins

228 ▲ 381 ▲

TOUL

335 ▲ Nancy

284 ▲ LUNÉVILLE

• Villages containing at least one vineyard classified as a *Grand Cru* d'Alsace

Intensive Vine-growing Zone

Département Boundary

Delimited AOC Region of Alsace

▲ Height above sea level (metres)

Kms 5 10 15 20 25 30

Mls 5 10 15

• PARIS

ALSACE

The appellation itself encompasses the départements *of Bas-Rhin and Haut-Rhin (left). Outside the appellation to the northwest, in what was the province of Lorraine, are two other areas classified VDQS, Vin de Moselle and Côtes de Toul (above).*

The harvest, Riquewihr, above

Traditional wooden equipment is still used for grape collection in some vineyards, though the use of plastic containers is more common.

Major wine firms of Alsace

LEON BEYER
2 rue de la 1ère Année,
68420 Eguisheim

Production: *20,000 cases*
Vineyards: *20 ha (50 acres)
including 4 ha (10 acres) of
Grands Crus Eichberg and
Pfersigberg*

This great house is famous for its ultra-dry wines that are made to accompany food, not win medals.

☆ Riesling ("Cuvée les Ecaillers", "Cuvée Particulière"), Tokay-Pinot Gris ("Cuvée Particulière", "Sélection de Grains Nobles"), Gewürztraminer ("Cuvée des Comtes d'Eguisheim", "Sélection de Grains Nobles")

PAUL BLANCK
32 Grand-rue,
Kientzheim, 68240 Kaysersberg

Production: *20,000 cases*
Vineyards: *27 ha (67 acres),
including 9 ha (22 acres) of
Grands Crus Schlossberg and
Furstentum.*

Marcel Blanck and his nephew, who together run this top-class firm, spend a lot of time and effort encouraging the cream of local growers to produce wines that are truly expressive of their *terroir.*

☆ Pinot Noir (Furstentum), Riesling (Furstentum Grand Cru, Schlossberg Grand Cru after 10 years, Sélection de Grains Nobles), Tokay-Pinot Gris (Furstentum Grand Cru, Altenbourg, Sélection de Grains Nobles), Gewürztraminer (Furstentum Grand Cru, Altenbourg Vendange Tardive, Sélection de Grains Nobles)

DOMAINE MARCEL DEISS
15 route du Vin,
68750 Bergheim

Production: *12,500 cases*
Vineyards: *20 ha (50 acres),
including 3 ha (7 acres) of Grands
Crus Altenberg de Bergheim and
Schoenenbourg*

Run by young Jean-Michel Deiss, this small house has some of the most stunning wines in Alsace. All of the wines are from Deiss's own 50 acres (20 ha) of vineyards.

☆ Pinot Blanc ("Bennwihr"), Riesling ("Bennwihr", "Bergheim Engelgarten", "Schoenenbourg Grand Cru", "Altenberg de Bergheim Grand Cru"), Tokay-Pinot Gris ("Bergheim")

DOPFF "AU MOULIN"
68340 Riquewihr

Production: *200,000 cases*
Vineyards: *58 ha (143 acres),
including 13 ha (32 acres) of
Grands Crus Sporen, Schoenenbourg
and Brand*

This house is responsible for making sparkling Alsace wines a commercial success, but it also makes excellent still wines, especially those from its own domaine.

☆ Crémant d'Alsace ("Blanc de Noirs", "Cuvée Bartholdi"), Sylvaner and, from its own domaine: Sylvaner ("Riquewihr"), Tokay-Pinot Gris ("Riquewihr"),

Riesling ("Schoenenbourg Grand Cru"), Gewürztraminer ("Riquewihr", "Brand Grand Cru", "Sélection de Grains Nobles")

DOPFF & IRION
68340 Riquewihr

Production: *300,000 cases*
Vineyards: *30 ha (74 acres)
including 5 ha (12.5 acres) of
Grand Cru Schoenenbourg*

This house was established in 1945, but shares the same heritage as Dopff "au Moulin". Dopff and Irion's single-vineyard wines of "Les Sorcières", Les Maquisards" "Les Murailles", and "Les Amandiers" have the greatest finesse.

☆ Muscat ("les Amandiers"), Tokay-Pinot Gris ("les Maquisards", "Sélection de Grains Nobles), Gewürztraminer ("Seigneur d'Alsace", "Les Sorcières", "Vendanges Tardives", "Sélection de Grains Nobles"), Riesling ("Les Murailles") and the new "La Cuvée René Dopff" range

HUGEL
68340 Riquewihr

Production: *100,000 cases*
Vineyards: *25 ha (62 acres),
including 12 ha (30 acres) of
Grands Crus Sporen and
Schoenenbourg*

This one house was responsible for opening Alsace wines' modern export markets. At a tasting in June 1987, Pierre Trimbach, the winemaker of Hugel's arch enemy Maison Trimbach, described the Hugel 1961 Gewürztraminer "Sélection de Grains Nobles" as "the closest to perfection, if perfection exists".

☆ Pinot Noir ("Réserve Personnelle"), Tokay-Pinot Gris ("Cuvée Tradition Sélection Jean Hugel"), Riesling ("Réserve Personnelle", "Vendange Tardive Sélection Jean Hugel"), Gewürztraminer ("Vendange Tardive Sélection Jean Hugel"), Sporen

ANDRÉ KIENTZLER
50 route de Bergheim,
68150 Ribeauvillé

Production: *6,000 cases*
Vineyards: *10 ha (25 acres),
including 2.5 ha (6 acres) of
Grands Crus Geisberg and Kirchberg*

André Kientzler makes exceedingly fine wines, including an Auxerrois that is the finest example of oak-aged white wine in Alsace. He also regularly produces and sells a pure Chasselas wine and he makes a *vin de glâce,* a sort of French *Eiswein.* All of André Kientzler's wines are from his own vineyards.

☆ Auxerrois ("Réserve", "Elevé en Fûts de Chêne"), Sylvaner ("Réserve"), Chasselas ("Réserve"), Tokay-Pinot Gris ("Réserve", "Geisberg Grand Cru", "Vendange Tardive", "Sélection de Grains Nobles"), Riesling ("Geisberg Grand Cru", "Geisberg Grand Cru Vendange Tardive", "Geisberg Grand Cru Sélection de Grains Nobles", "Geisberg Grand Cru—Vin de Glâce"), Gewürztraminer ("Vendange Tardive", "Sélection de Grains Nobles"), Muscat ("Kirchberg de Ribeauvillé Grand Cru")

DOMAINE KLIPFEL
6 avenue de la Gare,
67140 Barr

Production: *100,000 cases*
Vineyards: *35 ha (86 acres),
including, 8.5 ha (21 acres) of
Grands Crus Kastelberg and
Kirchberg de Barr (including the
famous Clos Zisser)*

Established in 1824, this is a large and underrated house with excellent vineyards.

☆ Pinot Noir ("Rouge de Barr Elevé en Fûts de Chêne"), Muscat ("Côtes de Barr"), Gewürztraminer ("Clos Zisser")

MARC KREYDENWEISS
12 rue Deharbe,
Andlau, 67140 Barr

Production: *4,500 cases*
Vineyards: *10 ha (25 acres)
including 2 ha (5 acres) of Grands
Crus Kastelberg, Wiebelsberg and
Moenchberg*

Marc Kreydenweiss' fine Kritt Sylvaner is probably the second best oak-aged white wine of Alsace behind Kientzler's Auxerrois. All the wines are from Marc Kreydenweiss' own vineyards.

☆ Crémant d'Alsace, Sylvaner ("Kritt–Elevé en Barrique"), Muscat ("Clos Rebgarten"), Gewürztraminer ("Kritt", "Kritt–Vendange Tardive"), Riesling (Wiebelsberg Grand Cru", "Kastelberg Grand Cru"), Tokay-Pinot Gris ("Moenchberg Grand Cru Vendange Tardive")

KUENTZ-BAS
14 route du Vin,
Husseren-les-Châteaux,
68420 Herrlisheim près Colmar

Production: *25,000 cases*
Vineyards: *12 ha (30 acres),
including 2 ha (5 acres) of Grands
Crus Eichberg and Pfersigberg*

The origins of this small but very high-quality house can be traced back to 1795. It produces "harvest-dated", genuinely late-harvested wines. The Vendanges Tardives also bear the date of harvest, a good lead that other quality-conscious producers should follow.

☆ Crémant d'Alsace ("Brut de Chardonnay"), Pinot Noir ("Rouge d'Alsace"), Tokay-Pinot Gris (generic and "Vendange Tardive"), Riesling ("Réserve Personnelle" and harvest-dated *cuvées*), Muscat ("Réserve Personnelle"), Gewürztraminer ("Réserve Personnelle", "Cuvée Caroline – Vendange Tardive")

MAISON MICHEL LAUGEL
102 rue du Général de Gaulle,
67520 Marlenheim

Production: *300,000 cases*
Vineyards: *7 ha (17.5 acres)*

Judged on its cheapest products, the wines of this house are not impressive, but it does produce some very good prestige *cuvées.*

☆ Crémant d'Alsace ("Rosé"), Pinot Noir ("Pinot Rouge de Marlenheim"), Tokay-Pinot Gris ("Cuvée Jubilaire"), Gewürztraminer ("Wangen", "Sélection de Grains Nobles")

GUSTAVE LORENTZ
35 Grand-rue,
68750 Bergheim

Production: *170,000 cases*
Vineyards: *26 ha (64 acres),
including 12 ha (30 acres) Grands
Crus Altenberg de Bergheim and
Kanzlerberg*

This house is situated just a few doors from the superb "Winstub du Sommelier", where the local dishes are cooked with the finesse of *haute cuisine,* and the quality of the carafe wine is better than the most expensive wines at other *winstubs.*

☆ Tokay-Pinot Gris ("Réserve", "Cuvée Particulière"), Riesling ("Réserve", "Altenberg de Bergheim Grand Cru"), Gewürztraminer ("Cuvée Particulière", "Altenberg de Bergheim Grand Cru", "Sélection de Grains Nobles")

JOS MEYER
76 rue Clémenceau,
Wintzenheim, 68000 Colmar

Production: *33,000 cases*
Vineyards: *8 ha (20 acres),
including 2 ha (5 acres) of Grands
Crus Hengst and Brand, plus 4 ha
(10 acres) of rented vineyards*

Founded in 1854 by Aloyse Meyer, the house is today run by Jean Meyer, whose passion for quality verges on anarchy. "If I want to grow Chasselas on the Hengst" says Jean Meyer, "why should a bureaucrat in Paris tell me I must not put Chasselas Hengst *Grand Cru* on the label?"

☆ Chasselas (consumed locally), Pinot Blanc ("Les Lutins"), Auxerrois ("H-Vieilles Vignes"), Muscat ("Les Fleurons"), Riesling ("Hengst Grand Cru", "Herrenweg", "Herrenweg Vendange Tardive", "Les Pierrets"), Tokay-Pinot Gris ("Cuvée du Centenaire-Vieille Vignes"), Gewürztraminer ("Hengst Grand Cru", "Herrenweg")

MURÉ and CLOS ST.-LANDELIN
Route du Vin,
RN 83, 68250 Rouffach

Production: *60,000 cases*
Vineyards: *21 ha (52 acres)
including 16 ha (40 acres) of
Grand Cru Vorbourg*

The Muré label wines are rich and mature quickly; the Clos St.-Landelin are reticent when young, but have excellent longevity and attain great finesse.

☆ Crémant d'Alsace ("Riesling Brut O"), Tokay-Pinot Gris (generic and "Clos St.-Landelin"), Riesling ("Clos St.-Landelin") Muscat ("Clos St.-Landelin"), Gewürztraminer (generic, "Zinnkoepflé Grand Cru", "Clos St.-Landelin"), Pinot Noir ("Clos St.-Landelin–Vielli en Pièces de Chêne")

DOMAINE OSTERTAG
87 rue Finkwiller,
67680 Epfig

Production: *6,000 cases*
Vineyards: *8 ha (20 acres),
including 1.5 ha (3.5 acres) of
Grand Cru Muenchberg*

Established in 1966 by Adolphe Ostertag, this domaine is now run by André Ostertag. He makes fine wines that seem to get better with each new vintage. He partly vinifies his Pinot blanc and fully vinifies his Tokay-Pinot Gris in small oak barrels.

☆ Pinot Blanc, Riesling ("Muenchberg Grand Cru"), Tokay-Pinot Gris ("Barrique"), Riesling ("Fronholz", "Muenchberg Grand Cru"), Gewürztraminer ("Fronholz", "Fronholz Vendange Tardive")

JEAN PREISS-ZIMMER
42 rue du Général De Gaulle, 68340 Riquewihr

Production: 20,000 cases
Vineyards: 9 ha (22 acres), including 2.5 ha (6 acres) of Grand Cru Schoenenbourg

This very friendly family firm, which was established in 1848, is located in the centre of picturesque Riquewihr. Almost opposite is the Preiss-Zimmer's equally friendly winstub "Au Tiré Bouchon".

☆ Riesling ("Réserve Comte de Beaumont" and "Réserve Année Exceptionnelle"), Gewürztraminer ("Réserve Année Exceptionnelle", "Réserve Cuvée Personnelle J.-J. Zimmer"), Muscat ("Réserve")

ROLLY GASSMANN
1-2 rue de l'Eglise, Rorschwihr, 68590 St.-Hippolyte

Production: 12,500 cases
Vineyards: 17 ha (42 acres)

Nearly all the wines from this small and ancient house are from its own domaine. The Gassmanns have a reputation for producing wines of exceptional richness and quality.

☆ Sylvaner ("Réserve Millésime"), Pinot Blanc (generic), Auxerrois ("Moenchreben"), Tokay-Pinot Gris ("Réserve Rolly Gassmann"), Riesling ("Réserve Millésime", "Pflaenzereben",

"Kappelweg Réserve Rolly Gassmann"), Muscat ("Moenchreben"), Gewürztraminer (generic, "Kappelweg", "Réserve Rolly Gassmann", "Cuvée Anne")

DOMAINES SCHLUMBERGER
100 rue Théodore Deck, 68500 Guebwiller

Production: 85,000 cases
Vineyards: 140 ha (346 acres), including 58 ha (143 acres) of Grands Crus Kitterlé, Saering, Kessler and Spiegel

This great domaine represents the largest estate of vineyards under single ownership in Alsace. It is famous for its "Cuvée Christine".

☆ Pinot Blanc (generic), Tokay-Pinot Gris ("Réserve Spéciale"), Riesling ("Saering Grand Cru", "Kitterlé Grand Cru"), Gewürztraminer ("KesslerGrand Cru", "Cuvée Christine Schlumberger", "Cuvée Anne Schlumberger")

LOUIS SIPP
5 Grand-rue, 68150 Ribeauvillé

Production: 100,000 cases
Vineyards: 31 ha (77 acres) including 4 ha (10 acres) of Grands Crus Kirchberg de Ribeauvillé and Osterberg

A large and important négociant. Its wines are made in a firm vin de garde style, and with this its Rieslings mature to a beautiful lemony "petrol" character, the hallmark of a classic Riesling.

☆ Riesling ("Kirchberg Grand Cru", Tokay-Pinot Gris ("Vendanges Tardives"), Gewürztraminer ("Osterberg Grand Cru" and "Vendange Tardive")

PIERRE SPARR
2 rue de la Première Armée, 68240 Sigolsheim

Production: 175,000 cases
Vineyards: 30 ha (74 acres), including 4 ha (10 acres) of Grands Crus Mambourg and Brand

The house style is for rich and ripe wines that age gracefully, yet appeal in their youth.

☆ Pinot Blanc ("Réserve"), Tokay-Pinot Gris ("Cuvée Particulière"), Riesling ("Sparr Prestige Tête de Cuvée", "Cuvée Particulière SPS", "Altenberg Cuvée Centenaire", "Altenberg Vendange Tardive"), Gewürztraminer ("Brand Grand Cru", "Sparr Prestige Tête de Cuvée"), "Kaefferkopf" (blend 80% Gewürztraminer and 20% Tokay)

F. E. TRIMBACH
15 route de Bergheim, 68150 Ribeauvillé

Production: 80,000 cases
Vineyards: 14 ha (35 acres) including 4 ha (10 acres) of Grands Crus Geisberg, Osterberg and Rosacker (which includes the superb Clos Ste.-Hune)

The style of Trimbach is one of firm malic strength that can appear to be too dry and austere in the first five years, but eventually develops into a wine of great finesse and depth of flavour. "Clos Ste.-Hune" is the greatest Riesling in Alsace.

☆ Riesling ("Cuvée Frédéric Emile", "Clos Ste.-Hune"), Gewürztraminer ("Cuvee des Seigneurs de Ribeaupierre"), Pinot Noir ("Réserve Personnelle"), Tokay-Pinot Gris ("Réserve Personnelle")

DOMAINE WEINBACH
Clos des Capucins, 68240 Kaysersberg

Production: 13,000 cases
Vineyards: 25 ha (62 acres), including 2 ha (5 acres) of Grand Cru Schlossberg (Kientzheim)

A director of a famous Alsace house once said to me "I am not sure what

magic Colette Faller puts into her vats, but she always manages to produce wines of the most stunning quality". The fact is that Jean Mercky makes the wines, but he is left with no doubts in his mind as to what Madame Faller requires of him! Domaine Weinbach's "Tokay-Pinot Gris 1983 Quintessence de Grains Nobles" is the single-most phenomenal Alsace wine I have ever tasted.

☆ Pinot (i.e., Pinot Blanc, "Réserve"), Riesling ("Cuvée Théo", "Cuvée Ste.-Catherine", "Schlossberg Grand Cru", "Vendange Tardive"), Muscat (generic), Tokay-Pinot Gris ("Réserve Particulière", "Cuvée Ste.-Catherine", "Vendange Tardive", "Quintessence de Grains Nobles"), Gewürztraminer ("Réserve Particulière", "Cuvée Théo", "Cuvée Laurence", "Vendange Tardive", "Quintessence de Grains Nobles")

DOMAINE ZIND HUMBRECHT
34 rue Maréchal Joffre, 68000 Wintzenheim

Production: 18,000 cases
Vineyards: 30 ha (74 acres) including 7.5 ha (18 acres) of Grands Crus Brand, Goldert, Hengst and Rangen

Léonard Humbrecht is fanatical about quality and has long fought to reduce yields and increase quality. All who know him or know of him greatly respect his knowledge, expertise and opinion.

☆ Muscat ("Goldert Grand Cru"), Tokay-Pinot Gris (generic, "Clos St.-Urban", "Rotenberg Sélection de Grains Nobles"), Riesling ("Clos Haüserer", "Brand Grand Cru", "Clos St.-Urban"), Gewürztraminer ("Herrenweg", "Heimbourg Vendange Tardive", "Hengst Vendange Tardive", "Goldert Vendange Tardive", "Heimbourg Sélection de Grains Nobles", "Clos St.-Urban Sélection de Grains Nobles")

Important Alsace coopératives

CAVE VINICOLE DE PFAFFENHEIM-GUEBERSCHWIHR
5 rue du Chai, BP 33, 68250 Pfaffenheim

Production: 190,000 cases
Vineyards: 200 ha (494 acres), including 40 ha (99 acres) of Grand Cru Goldert

This coopérative produces a superb range of Crémant d'Alsace under the "Hartenberger" label, of which the Tokay-Pinot Gris is the most stunning. Its wines are also found under the "E. Wein" brand.

☆ Crémant d'Alsace (entire range), Edelzwicker ("Message d'Alsace", "Gentil d'Alsace"), Pinot Blanc (this grape has a Tokay character when grown at Pfaffenheim – look for one with a "Medaille d'Or J Colmar"), Tokay-Pinot Gris ("Steinert Grand Cru"), Gewürztraminer ("Goldert Grand Cru")

CAVE VINICOLE DE TURCKHEIM
16 rue des Tuileries, 68230 Turckheim

Production: 220,000 cases
Vineyards: 280 ha (690 acres), including 15 ha (37 acres) of Grands Crus

I rate this coopérative as the third best in Alsace. With a name like "Mayerling" for its Crémant, you might expect it to be made from Tokay, but it is in fact 50/50 Pinot blanc and Auxerrois.

☆ Crémant d'Alsace ("Mayerling"), Pinot Blanc ("Côtes du Val St.-Grégoire"), Klevner ("Pinot d'Alsace"), Pinot Noir ("Cuvée à l'Ancienne"), Tokay-Pinot Gris ("Brand Grand Cru", "Vendange Tardive", "Sélection de Grains Nobles"), Riesling ("La Décapole", "Brand Grand Cru", "Vendange Tardive"), Gewürztraminer ("Hengst Grand Cru", "Brand Grand Cru", "Vendange Tardive")

WOLFBERGER – CAVE VINICOLE EGUISHEIM
6 Grand-rue, 68420 Eguisheim

Production: 900,000 cases
Vineyards: 505 ha (1248 acres), including 40 ha (99 acres) of Grands Crus Hengst, Pfersigberg, Eichberg, Steingrubler and Spiegel, plus the vineyards of two subsidiary Coopératives: Cave Vinicole de Dambach-la-Ville with 362 ha (895 acres), and Cave Vinicole de Soultz-Wuenheim with 100 ha (247 acres)

This is not only the largest coopérative in Alsace, it is also the best. It produces consistently the best oak-aged red, has a superb range of special cuvées in the "Bouteilles Armouries" range and offers some spectacular one-off Grands Crus. And yet, because of its high Crémant d'Alsace profile, most people only think of Wolfberger as a sort of coopérative Dopff "au Moulin". In addition to its famous "Wolfberger"

brand, which accounts for 80 per cent of its total production, this coopérative also uses "Rotgold", "Meierheim" and "Aussay".

☆ Crémant ("Prestige", "Millésime" and "Rosé Brut"), Pinot Noir ("Rouge d'Alsace" with Noak cartoon label), plus the entire Grands Crus range and all the "Bouteilles Armouries"

Note: good wines are also made by the coopératives at Ingersheim, Kientzheim-Kaysersberg, Ribeauvillé and Westhalten. The mature vintage crémants of Kientzheim-Kaysersberg and the famous Clos du Zahnacker of Ribeauvillé deserve special mention. Clos du Zahnacker is a single site planted with equal quantities of Pinot gris, Riesling and Gewürztraminer, and the wine is a true vin de garde capable of lasting 20 years or more.

The wines of Alsace and Lorraine

ALSACE AOC

This appellation covers all the wines of Alsace (with the exception of Alsace *Grand Cru* and *Crémant d'Alsace*), but 95 per cent of the wines are often sold according to grape variety. This practice effectively creates several "varietal" AOCs under the one umbrella appellation' and these are listed separately.

ALSACE GRAND CRU AOC

The current production of *Grand Cru* wine is approximately 2.5 per cent of the total volume of AOC Alsace. Because every *cru*, or growth, makes a wine of a specific character, then interpreted by the style of each grower, it is impossible to give a generalized description.

WHITE *See* the *Grands Crus* of Alsace (page 149), major wine firms of Alsace (page 152) and, in this section, consult the various entries according to the grape variety.

🍇 Muscat, Riesling, Gewürztraminer, Pinot gris

ALSACE SÉLECTION DE GRAINS NOBLES AOC

These rare and sought-after wines are made from botrytis-affected grapes, but unlike Sauternes, Alsace is no haven for "noble rot". It occurs haphazardly and in much reduced concentrations, and the wines are therefore produced in tiny quantities and sold at very high prices. It is one of the world's greatest wines.

WHITE It is impossible to generalize about the taste and character of a range of totally unique wines, but all of the finest examples do have one quality in common: the most amazing finesse and balance for wines of such concentration; intense sweetness and alcoholic strength. The figures given with the different grape varieties indicate each one's minimum sugar content, the equivalent Oechsle level and the potential alcohol level.

🍇 Gewürztraminer (279 g/l, 120°, 16·4%), Pinot gris (279 g/l, 120°, 16·4%), Riesling (256 g/l, 110°, 14·3%), Muscat (256 g/l, 110°, 14·3%)

🍷 1985, 1986, 1988, 1989, 1990

🍂 Between 7-30 years

ALSACE VENDANGE TARDIVE AOC

Vendange Tardive is inconsistent in quality and character. In spirit this wine should be the product of late-harvested grapes, which have a

different chemical composition to normally-harvested grapes. The regulations need to stipulate the date of harvest because many growers make wines of the correct technical standard from normally-harvested grapes. Another aspect that requires some sort of control is the relative sweetness of the wine. *Vendange Tardive* covers a sugar level that might end up dry or sweet. Wines should be made to carry slightly different appellations according to their sugar-acidity ratio. The figures given with the different grape varieties, below, indicate each one's minimum sugar content, the Oechsle level and the potential alcohol level.

WHITE Whether bone dry, dry, medium-sweet or sweet, this relatively full-bodied wine should always have the true character of *passerillage*, the result of the complex chemical changes that occur inside a ripe grape that has remained on the vine until November or December.

🍇 Gewürztraminer (243 g/l, 105°, 14·3%), Pinot gris (243 g/l, 105°, 14·3%), Riesling (220 g/l, 95°, 12·9%), Muscat (220 g/l, 95° 12·9%)

🍷 1985, 1986, 1988, 1989, 1990

🍂 Between 5-20 years

AUXERROIS AOC

Theoretically this designation is not permitted, but it does exist and is tolerated by the authorities. *See* also Pinot Blanc AOC.

CHASSELAS AOC

Rarely seen, but when it is, it is usually commercialized as Chasselas rather than Gutedel.

WHITE Generally dull, thin and characterless wines, but the mouth-wateringly delicious samples tasted straight from the vat make one wonder if the few growers who still specialize in these wines should not bottle them *sur lie*.

🍇 Chasselas

🍷 1985, 1986, 1988

🍂 Immediately

☆ Kientzler, Robert Schoffit

CLAIRET AOC

The regulations specify this designation for Pinot noir wines that have been vinified in the *clairet* style. *See* Pinot Noir AOC.

CLEVNER AOC

See Pinot blanc AOC.

CÔTES DE TOUL VDQS

Part of the once-flourishing vineyards of Lorraine, these *côtes* are located in eight communes west of Toul, in the Meurthe-et-Moselle *département*.

RED The Pinot noir is the most successful and is usually sold as a pure varietal. It can have surprisingly good colour for wine from such a northerly region and good cherry-Pinot character.

🍇 Pinot meunier, Pinot noir

🍷 1982, 1983, 1985, 1989, 1990

🍂 Within 1-4 years

WHITE These wines represent less than two per cent of the VDQS, just 76 hectolitres (844 cases). Nevertheless, the Auxerrois is the best grape, its fatness making it ideal for such a northerly area with a calcareous soil.

🍇 Aligoté, Aubin, Auxerrois

🍷 1985, 1986, 1988, 1989, 1990

🍂 Within 1-3 years

ROSÉ Most Côtes de Toul is made and sold as *vin gris*, a pale rosé that is delicious when young.

🍇 Gamay, Pinot meunier, Pinot noir, plus a maximum of 15% Aligoté, Aubin and Auxerrois

🍷 1985, 1986, 1988, 1989, 1990

🍂 Immediately

☆ Marcel Gorny, Laroppe Frères, Lelièvre Frères, Yves Masson, Fernand Poirson, Societé Vinicole du Toulouis, Michel Vosgien

CRÉMANT D'ALSACE AOC

This AOC was introduced in 1976 for *méthode champenoise* wines. The quality is good and will improve as producers gain experience and become willing to grow grapes specifically for *crémant*.

WHITE Although the Pinot blanc has perfect acidity for this sort of wine, it can lack sufficient richness, and after intensive tastings I have come to the conclusion that the Pinot gris has the right acidity and richness.

🍇 Pinot blanc, Pinot gris, Pinot noir Auxerrois, Chardonnay, Riesling

🍷 1982, 1983, 1985, 1986, 1987

🍂 Between 5-8 years

ROSÉ Delightful wines that can possess a finer purity of perfume and flavour than many pink Champagnes.

🍇 Pinot noir

🍷 1983, 1985, 1986, 1987

🍂 Between 3-5 years

☆ Jean-Claude Buecher, Paul Buecher, Joseph Cattin, Ehrhart, Jean Freyburger, Frey-Sohler, Jérôme Geschickt, Willy Gisselbrecht, Bernard Haegi, Paul Scherer, H. & J. Heitzmann, Raymond Klein, Denis Fernand Meyer

EDELZWICKER AOC

This appellation is reserved for wines blended from two or more of the authorized grape varieties. *Edel* means "noble", *zwicker* means "blend", thus this should be a "noble blend" and, indeed, it once was. Since the cosmetic removal of the AOC Zwicker, however, this appellation has become so debased that many producers prefer to sell their cheaper AOC Alsace wines under brand names rather than put the dreaded *Edelzwicker* name on the label.

WHITE Essentially, dry, light-bodied wines that have a clean flavour and are best drunk young. Most *Edelzwickers* are either Sylvaner- or Pinot blanc-based, with better or slightly more expensive products having a generous touch of Gewürztraminer to fatten up the blend. The only truly exceptional, ultra-high quality example of this wine I have come across is Edelzwicker 1985 Ehrhart ("Ammerschwihr") though it was a total anomaly.

🍇 Chasselas, Sylvaner, Pinot blanc, Pinot gris, Pinot noir, Auxerrois, Gewürztraminer, Muscat blanc à petits grains, Muscat rosé à petits grains, Muscat ottonnel, Riesling

🍷 1983, 1985, 1986, 1987

🍂 Immediately (between 2-10 years for Ehrhart 1985)

GEWÜRZTRAMINER AOC

This grape is usually the first Alsace wine people taste. Its voluptuous, up-front style is immediately appealing.

WHITE The fattest and most full-bodied of Alsace wines, classic renditions of this grape have the aroma of banana when young and develop a rich gingerbread character when mature. Traditionally this is a dry wine, but many examples today have a surprisingly high level of sugar, which together with low acidity, can make them far too fat and blowzy.

🍇 Gewürztraminer

🍷 1981, 1983, 1985

🍂 Between 3-10 years (great examples will continue for 20 or 30 years)

☆ Baumann et Fils, J.-P. Bechtold, Dirler, Jérôme Geschickt, André-Rémy Gresser, Frédéric Mallo, Muhlberger, René Schaefle, Gerard Schueller, Bruno Sorg, Fernand Stentz, Lucien Albrecht, Bott Frères, Brucker, Joseph Cattin, Théo Cattin, Domaine Viticole de la Ville de Colmar, Dietrich, R. Faller, Fleith, Willy Gisselbrecht, Jean Sipp, Maison Wiederhirn, Adam, J Hauller & Fils, Charles Wantz, Alsace Willm

GUTEDEL AOC

See Chasselas AOC.

KLEVENER DE HEILIGENSTEIN AOC

An oddity in Alsace for three reasons. Firstly, the wine is made from a grape variety that is native to the Jura further south and is not found anywhere else in Alsace. Secondly, of all the famous village appellations (Rouge d'Ottrott, Rouge de Rodern, Rosé de Marlenheim etc), only Klevener de Heiligenstein is specifically defined in the regulations. Thirdly, it is the only grape that is confined by law to a geographical area within Alsace, namely the village of Heiligenstein. Its name should not be confused with the common synonym for the Pinot blanc, the Klevner, which is always spelt without the middle "e".

WHITE Dry, light-bodied wines of subdued, spicy aroma and delicate, fruity flavour.

🍇 Savagnin rosé

📅 1983, 1985, 1988, 1989, 1990

🍷 Between 2-4 years

KLEVNER AOC
See Pinot Blanc AOC.

MUSCAT AOC

Some growers believe that the best Muscat wine is made by the so-called Muscat d'Alsace, a synonym that covers both the white and pink versions of the rich and full Muscat à petits grains. Others are convinced that the lighter, more floral, Muscat ottonel is best. A blend of the two is probably preferable. These wines are better in average years, or at least in fine years that have good acidity, rather than in truly "great" vintages.

WHITE These are dry, aromatic wines with fine floral charateristics that often smell of orange-flower water and taste of peaches. A top quality Muscat that is expressive of its *terroir* is a great wine by any standard.

🍇 Muscat blanc à petits grains, Muscat rosé à petits grains, Muscat ottonel

📅 1984, 1985, 1986, 1987, 1989

🍷 Immediately

☆ Becker, Paul Ginglinger, Kuehn, Frédéric Mochel, Bruno Sorg, Maison Wiederhirn

PINOT AOC
See Pinot Blanc AOC.

PINOT BLANC AOC

The Auxerrois, which is allowed in this appellation, has more fat than the Pinot blanc and it is therefore used more in the north of the region where the Pinot blanc can be too light in its pure form. The Auxerrois, however, can become too fat, and an overripe Auxerrois is not only flabby but has a distinctly "foxy" flavour.

WHITE The Pinot Blanc boom has encouraged producers to care about quality and character. Some wines are still spineless and lack character, but many have a delightful plumpness and a really ripe, juicy flavour.

🍇 Pinot blanc, Auxerrois, Pinot noir (vinified white), Pinot gris

📅 1985 for Pinot blanc; 1986 for Auxerrois; 1988, 1989, 1990

🍷 Between 2-4 years

☆ Jean-Pierre Bechtold, Brucker, Théo Cattin, Jean-Paul Eckle, Ehrhart, Kuehn, René Schaefle, Schleret, Jean Sipp

PINOT GRIS AOC
See Tokay-Pinot Gris AOC.

PINOT NOIR AOC

Ten years ago most of these wines were made in the rosé style, but the trend in red nowadays is towards much deeper coloured wines that have been matured in small casks with 25-50% new oak.

RED Of the oak-aged style, the most consistent in quality and character is Wolfberger's "Rouge d'Alsace", which is also one of the most reasonably priced.

🍇 Pinot noir

📅 1983, 1985

🍷 Between 2-6 years (12 years for exceptional *cuvées*)

ROSÉ At its best, this dry, light-bodied wine has a deliciously fragrant aroma and flavour reminiscent of strawberries, raspberries or cherries.

🍇 Pinot noir

📅 1985, 1986, 1988, 1989, 1990

🍷 Between 1-2 years

Recommended for red wine only:
☆ Adam, Paul Bluecher et Fils, André-Rémy Gresser, Charles Koehly, Schaetzel, Fernand Stentz; Rosé: Jérôme Fritsch, Mosbach, Joseph Cattin, Théo Cattin, Charles Wantz

RIESLING AOC

Riesling is the most susceptible to differences in soil: clay soils give fatness and richness; granite Riesling is also rich, but firmer and with more finesse; limestone has obvious finesse but less richness; and volcanic soil makes for powerfully flavoured wine.

WHITE In youth, fine Rieslings can be so firm and austere that they will be far from pleasant to drink and give no hint of the beautiful wines into which they will evolve. Trimbach's "Clos Ste.-Hune" is, for me, consistently the greatest of all Alsace Rieslings.

🍇 Riesling

📅 1983, 1985, 1988, 1989, 1990

🍷 Between 4-20 years

☆ Albert Boxler et Fils, Brucker, Joseph Cattin, Dirler, Roger et Roland Geyer, Paul Ginglinger, André-Rémy Gresser, Jean-Pierre Klein et Fils, Frédéric Mallo, Frédéric Mochel, Mochel-Lorentz, Muhlberger, Marcel Mullenbach, Michel Nartz, Edgar Schaller, Maurice Schoech, Robert Schoffit, Seltz, Sick-Dreyer, Bruno Sorg, A. Zimmermann, Lucien Albrecht, Théo Cattin, Erhart, Egard Schaller, Jean Sipp, Maison Wiederhirn, Adam, J Hauller & Fils, Kuehn, Preiss-Henny, Ringenbach-Moser, Alsace Willm

SCHILLERWEIN AOC

The regulations specify this Germanic designation for Pinot noir wines vinified as rosés. It harks back to the days when many Germanic terms like Spitlese and Auslese were in common use. *See* Pinot Noir AOC.

SYLVANER AOC

Hugh Johnson once aptly described the Sylvaner as the "local tap-wine", and by the tap is exactly how it should be served – direct from the megalitre stainless-steel vat, with all the zip and zing of natural carbonic gas that is inevitably filtered out during the bottling process. Like the Muscat, it does not suit the heat of the greatest vintages, and is thus a wine to buy in poorer years.

WHITE Typically, an Alsace Sylvaner is not as fat as a Rheinpfalz Sylvaner, nor as spicy-earthy as a Franconian Silvaner *(sic).* It is an unpretentious, dry, light- to medium-bodied wine with fragrance rather than fruitiness. It is best drunk young, but, like the Muscat, exceptionally long-living examples can always be found. Marc Kreydenweiss makes a very unusual oak-aged Sylvaner that would defy any Master of Wine to identify in a blind tasting.

🍇 Sylvaner

📅 1982, 1984, 1986, 1987, 1988

🍷 Immediately

☆ Boeckel, Raymond Engel, J. Hauller & Fils, Jean-Pierre Klein et Fils

TOKAY D'ALSACE AOC

Technically this name has not been permitted since the Euro-bureaucratic decision to ban it, but many growers deliberately flouted this EEC regulation because they have used Tokay d'Alsace for 400 years. A deal has been struck enabling the old name to be used providing it is always accompanied by the words "Pinot Gris". *See* Tokay-Pinot Gris AOC.

TOKAY-PINOT GRIS AOC

This designation is now the most common way of commercializing wine from the rich Pinot gris grape. For me, this is the greatest of all Alsace wines.

WHITE This dry, medium- to full-bodied wine is decadently rich, but has excellent acidity, and its fullness of flavour never tires the palate. A young Tokay can taste or smell of banana, but it develops into a totally different, honey-rich and succulent wine.

🍇 Pinot gris

📅 1983, 1985, 1988, 1989, 1990

🍷 Between 5-10 years

☆ Landmann-Ostholt, Bruno Sorg, Lucien Albrecht, Bott Frères, Joseph Cattin, Théo Cattin, Dietrich, Ehrhart, R. Faller, Fleith, Willy Gisselbrecht, Maison Wiederhirn, Kuehn, Preiss-Henny, Ringenbach-Moser, Edgar Schaller, Schleret, Jean Sipp

VIN D'ALSACE AOC
See Alsace AOC.

VIN DE MOSELLE VDQS

Although many restaurants persist in listing German Mosel as "Moselle", the river and the wine it produces is called the Mosel in Germany, but when it crosses the border into France, it becomes the Moselle.

RED The few I have come across have been unimpressive.

🍇 A minimum of 30% Gamay, plus Pinot meunier, Pinot noir

📅 1983, 1985, 1988, 1989, 1990

🍷 Immediately

WHITE Light, dry and insubstantial wines.

🍇 Auxerrois, Pinot blanc, Pinot gris, Riesling, Gewürztraminer, a maximum of 30% Sylvaner and, until it is replaced by other varieties, a maximum of 20% Ebling

📅 1985, 1986, 1988, 1989, 1990

🍷 Immediately

The Loire Valley

In winemaking terms, the Loire valley is best imagined as a long ribbon with crisp white wines at either end and fuller wines of all types in the middle.

FROM ITS SOURCE IN THE CÉVENNES Mountains, the Loire flows through about 1000 kilometres (625 miles) and twelve *départements* of green, peaceful countryside, ancient towns and fine châteaux before reaching the Atlantic. It is the longest river in France, and the variations in soil, climate and grape varieties found along its banks and those of its tributaries are reflected in the wide range of wines grown in the four major wine-producing districts. Running east from the Bay of Biscay, the districts are Nantes, Anjou-Saumur, Touraine and the Central Vineyards.

Red, white and rosé, still, *pétillant* and fully sparkling, some sixty different appellations ranging in style from bone-dry to intensely sweet, are strung out across half of France. The two crisp white wines at either end of the Loire are the Muscadet wines of Nantes and the Sauvignon wines of Sancerre and Pouilly Fumé in the Central Vineyards, while the fuller wines of all types are to be found in the centre districts of Anjou-Saumur and Touraine: Anjou Rosé, sparkling Saumur and Vouvray, the rich, sweet wines of Bonnezeaux and Quarts-de-Chaume in the Coteaux du Layon, and the red wines of Bourgueil, Chinon and Champigny.

THE LOIRE'S MOST IMPORTANT GRAPE

The Chenin blanc grape produces four distinctly different styles of wine – dry, semi-sweet, sweet and sparkling. This is due to traditional practices that have been forced on growers by the vagaries of climate. This grape has abundant natural acidity and, if it receives enough sun, a high sugar content. But the Loire is considered a northern area in viticultural terms, and the vine grower must contend with late frosts, cold winds and variable summers. Given a sunny year, the grower's natural inclination is to make the richest wine possible with this sweet and tangy grape, but in many vintages, only a medium or a dry style can be achieved. Apart from exceptions like Savennières, dry Chenin blanc wines are all too often thin, harsh and acidic.

These wines do little to enhance the reputation of the Loire, but they do have similar characteristics to the wines of Champagne in that they are disappointing when still, yet glamorous when sparkling. It is little wonder then, that as the Champagne trade rapidly evolved in the nineteenth century, so the seeds of a sparkling wine industry were sown in Saumur, and today the Loire boasts the largest such market outside of Champagne itself.

THE LOIRE VALLEY

The longest river in France is bordered intermittently with different appellations, those at either end producing crisp white wines, those in the centre wines of variety tending to be fuller in body.

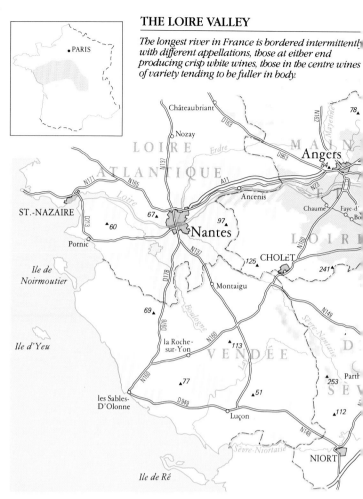

Vineyards at Vouvray, above
In sunny years the area just to the east of Tours produces sweet, slow-maturing wines, valued for their longevity.

The Loire from Champtoceaux, left
From well above the river the hillside town provides a panoramic view of the surrounding countryside.

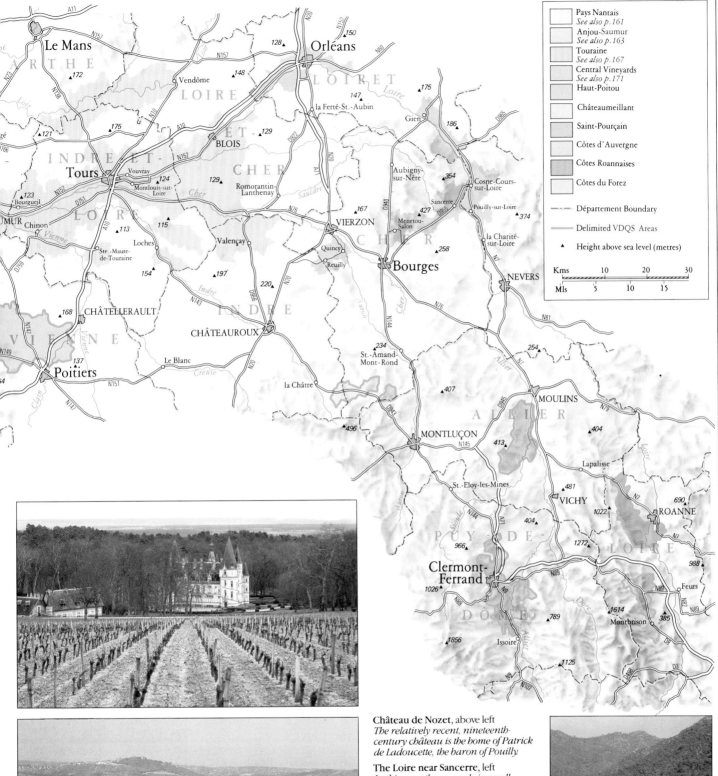

Pays Nantais
See also p.161
Anjou-Saumur
See also p.163
Touraine
See also p.167
Central Vineyards
See also p.171
Haut-Poitou

Châteaumeillant

Saint-Pourçain

Côtes d'Auvergne

Côtes Roannaises

Côtes du Forez

–∙– Département Boundary

— Delimited VDQS Areas

▲ Height above sea level (metres)

Kms   10   20   30
Mls   5   10   15

Château de Nozet, above left
The relatively recent, nineteenth-century château is the home of Patrick de Ladoucette, the baron of Pouilly.

The Loire near Sancerre, left
In this area the ground rises well above the river and the neighbouring vineyards.

The source of the Loire, right
The river begins its journey high up in the Cévennes Mountains, embarking on a route north to Orléans, then west to Nantes and the Atlantic ocean.

Major wine firms of the Loire

ACKERMANN-LAURANCE
St.-Hilaire,
St.-Florent,
49416 Saumur

Sales: *650,000 cases*

Established in 1811, Ackermann-Laurance is the oldest and largest sparkling wine house in the Loire. It also produces a large range of other Loire wines, but the bubblies are best.

☆ Saumur d'Origine "1811" Brut, Cuvée Privée Brut

PIERRE ARCHAMBOULT
Caves la Perrière,
Verdigny,
18300 Sancerre

Sales: *55,000 cases*

A small but good-quality *négociant* whose main brands are red and white Sancerre under the "Caves du Clos de la Perrière" label.

AUBERT FILS
La Varenne,
49270 St.-Laurent des Autels

Sales: *400,000 cases*

This firm owns vineyards in Muscadet and Anjou, and belongs to Bordeaux *négociant* Louis Eschenauer.

☆ Domaine des Joutières Muscadet des Coteaux de la Loire, Domaine des Hardières Coteaux du Layon

ALBERT BESOMBES
"Moc-Baril",
49404 Saumur

Sales: *30,000 cases*

A small family-run *négociant* producing acceptable sparkling Saumur and Vouvray, interesting, slightly *pétillant* wines, and good still wines from various Loire appellations.

☆ Quincy Domaine de Maison Blanche, Cabernet d'Anjou "Moc-Baril"

PIERRE BONNET
La Bronière,
44330 Vallet

Sales: *120,000 cases*

A fairly large Muscadet *négociant* operating under the P. Brévin label, but which also produces a large range of other wines using various labels.

☆ Chinon Séraphin Roze

BOUVET LADUBAY
St.-Hilaire,
St.-Florent,
49416 Saumur

Sales: *130,000 cases*

Founded in 1851 and one of the oldest sparkling Saumur houses, it is now owned by the Champagne house of Taittinger and run by Patrice Monmousseau. Bouvet is one of the few firms that use only Chenin blanc grapes for all except its Saumur Rosé. The other sparkling wines produced include a *Brut* and a *Blanc de Blancs*. (*See also* Taittinger, p.147.)

☆ Saumur Rosé, vintage Crémant Blanc de Blancs, Tressor

COMPAGNIE FRANÇAISE DES GRANDS VINS
77220 Tournon-en-Brie

Sales: *2.5 million cases*

Large-scale sparkling wine producer, owned by St. Raphaël, the aperitif firm, and best known for its Cadre Noir Saumur Brut, which is named after the town's famous cavalry school. They also sell vast quantities of non-AOC *vins mousseux* under various labels, including "Opéra", "Montparnasse", "Grand Impérial", "Aubel" and "Les Monopoles Alfred Rothschild" (nothing to do with the Champagne brand "Alfred Rothschild" sold by Marne et Champagne of Epernay).

DONATIEN BAHUAUD
La Loge,
44330 La Chapelle-Heulin

Sales: *800,000 cases*

One of the oldest and best *négociants* in the Loire Valley, Donatien Bahuaud claims that the vineyard of Château de la Cassemichère was the first to be planted with the Muscadet vine in 1740. But Donatien Bahuaud also produces a large range of other Loire wines, including sparkling Vouvray and Saumur sold under the "Comte de Montesonge" label, and perhaps its most interesting venture outside Muscadet, a much-improving *vin de pays* called "Le Chouan" ("La Colombe" in some markets), made from a small vineyard planted entirely with Chardonnay vines. Experimental plantation of Chardonnay began in the later 1960s. The first wines were marketed as *vins de pays* "Loire Atlantique", but since 1987, the wine has been sold as a "Vin de Pays du Jardin de la France" (*see also* p.200). Presumably the swap to a wider appellation will allow for an increase in production, but currently this wine is produced entirely from a 5ha (12.3 acre) vineyard within the locality of Château de la Cassemichère.

☆ Muscadet de la Cassemichère, Muscadets Cuvée des Aigles, Muscadets Domaine de Fief-Joyeux, Muscadets Le Master de Donatien,

Fringant Muscadet, Pouilly Fumé Les Chaumes, Sancerre Coteaux de Maimbray, Vouvray Domaine des Giraudières, "Le Chouan" ("La Colombe")

LA FRANÇAISE D'EXPORTATION
Route de Saumur,
49260 Montreuil-Bellay

Sales: *670,000 cases*

Part of a very large wine company with an annual worldwide turnover of 3.4 million cases from various French regions, with sales in bulk under numerous labels.

GRATIEN, MEYER & SEYDOUX
Château de Beaulieu,
49401 Saumur

Sales: *125,000 cases*

In 1864 Alfred Gratien established a Champagne house in Epernay and a sparkling wine firm at Saumur. Gratien, Meyer & Seydoux own 20 ha (49.4 acres) of vineyards, and have an agreement to buy grapes from about 200 private growers in the Anjou-Saumur district. Sparkling wines that are made under Saumur, Anjou and Crémant de Loire appellations are sold only when they have been aged for 18 to 24 months, instead of the minimum nine months. Wines are also sold under "Henri d'Arlan" and "Rosset" brands.

☆ Crémant de Loire, Saumur Cuvée Flamme

MONMOUSSEAU
41401 Montrichard

Sales: *175,000 cases*

This house was founded in 1986 by Alcide Monmousseau and, like Bouvet, is today owned by Taittinger. Although it produces a large range of Loire wines, the firm's 70 ha (173 acres) of vineyard enables it to excel in the limited production of prestige *cuvées*. The basic Monmousseau Touraine Brut and the Brut de Mosny are extremely well made.

☆ Cuvée J.M. 93, Cuvée J.M. Rosé

DE NEUVILLE
St.-Hilaire,
St.-Florent,
49416 Saumur

Sales: *250,000 cases*

A large range of well-made, if generally unexciting, Val de Loire wines made by this *négociant* with some contribution from its 45 ha (111 acre) estate.

☆ Saumur Rosé Brut

REMY-PANNIER
Rue Léopold Palustre,
St.-Hilaire,
St.-Florent,
49400 Saumur

Sales: *2.2 million cases*

Founded in 1885, this house produces vast volumes of reliable wines from every AOC in the Loire.

☆ Chinon, Saumur Crémant Brut

MARCEL SAUTEJEAU
Domaine de l'Hyvernière,
44330 Le Pallet

Sales: *900,000 cases*

This large, family-run *négociant* markets a wide range of Loire Valley wines, but is best known for its Muscadet.

☆ Muscadet Clos des Orfeuilles, Muscadet Domaine de l'Hyvernière

SAUVION & FILS
Château du Cléray,
44330 Vallet

Sales: *25,000 cases*

Ernest Sauvion purchased Château du Cléray in 1935, and it is now run by his son and three grandsons. This family concern not only produces some of the finest Muscadets available, it also represents the most progressive force in the district today. Sauvion exports to countries all over the world.

☆ All Sauvion Muscadets, especially Château du Cléray, Cardinal Richard and those found under the "Découverte" label

ANTOINE SUBILEAU
6 rue St Vincent,
44330 Vallet

Sales: *420,000 cases*

Substantial-sized Nantes house producing fine Muscadet.

☆ Muscadet Domaine des Montys, Muscadet Château Fromenteau

LES VINS TOUCHAIS
25 avenue du Maréchal Leclerc,
49700 Doué la Fontaine

Founded in 1947 by a family of growers with 190 ha (469 acres) of vineyards in Anjou-Saumur. The bulk of its production is in the mainstream, high-volume, generic AOC wine business, although most publicity centres on its justifiably famous Moulin Touchais—an exceptional wine that can be found under both Anjou and Coteaux du Layon appellations.

Important Loire coopératives

UNION VINICOLE DU VAL DE LOIRE
23 rue Fouquet,
St.-Hilaire,
St.-Florent,
49400 Saumur

Sales: *550,000 cases*

This company was established in 1877 by Marcel Goblet and today sells a large range of standard-quality wines under the "Jacques Goblet" label.

CIE. DE LA VALLÉE DE LA LOIRE
Montreuil-Bellay,
Route de Loudon,
49260 Cedex 48

Sales: *1.6 million cases*

Founded 20 years ago by Henri Verdier, this firm has a vast production sold under many labels including: "Sebastien Aubert" (Bourgueil), "Monique Verdier" (Muscadet), "Georges Verdier" (Vouvray), "Alban St Pré" and "Jean Monfermy" (Anjou), "Jean Monfermy" (Anjou), "Jean Montbray" (Touraine), and "Veuve Béranger" (Sancerre).

CLAUDE VERDIER
Boulevard Jean Moulin,
49401 Saumur

Sales: *750,000 cases*

"Claude Verdier" appears on this firm's Muscadet, Anjou and Vouvray labels; while "Lecluse et Claude Verdier" is used for its Saumur Brut, and "Nicolas Verdier" for the Crémant de Loire.

☆ Nicolas Verdier Crémant de Loire

VEUVE AMIOT
19-21 rue Jean Ackerman,
St.-Hilaire,
St.-Florent,
49416 Saumur

Sales: *200,000 cases*

Established in 1884 by Elisa Amiot, this company is now owned by Martini & Rossi.

☆ Crémant de Loire, Saumur Haute Tradition

ANDRÉ VINET
10 rue de Prugres,
Vallet

Sales: *450,000 cases*

Large Muscadet *négociant* whose wines are more often seen in France than abroad. Wines from other districts include a Saumur Brut.

☆ Muscadet Domaine Guerande, Muscadet Château Guerande, Muscadet Château La Cormerais, Muscadet Château La Touche

LA VINICOLE DE TOURAINE
Cour-Cheverny

Sales: *2.2 million cases*

Huge production of generally undistinguished AOC Touraine and bulk *vins de table*.

CAVE COOPÉRATIVE CÔTES DE FOREZ
Trelins,
42130 Boen

Sales: *120,000 cases*
Members: *About 260*
Vineyards: *450 ha (1,112 acres)*
Established: *1962*

Most of the members cultivate the Gamay, and produce either the VDQS Côtes de Forez or the Vin de Pays d'Urfe.

CAVE COOPÉRATIVE DU HAUT-POITOU
32 rue Alphonse Plault,
Neuville de Poitou

Sales: *900,000 cases*
Members: *About 1,200*
Vineyards: *Over 1,000 ha (2,470 acres)*

Progressive marketing by this technically well-equipped *coopérative* has led to a wide distribution and acceptance of its wines. The sparkling Chardonnay, Diane de Poitiers, is superb and ages well, but has no official appellation. A rosé version is made from a blend of Cabernet sauvignon and Cabernet franc. The still VDQS Chardonnay is unexciting but improving every year.

☆ Vin du Haut-Poitou Sauvignon, Vin du Haut-Poitou Cabernet, Vin du Haut-Poitou Gamay, Diane de Poitiers

VIGNERONS DE LA NOËLLE CANA
44150 Ancenis

Sales: *200,000 cases*
Members: *380*
Vineyards: *450 ha (1,112 acres)*
Established: *1955*

This *coopérative* produces various AOC, VDQS and Vin de Pays wines.

☆ Prime de la Noëlle Crémant de Loire

LES CAVES DE LA LOIRE
49380 Thouarce

Sales: *1.1 million cases*
Members: *About 500*
Vineyards: *Over 2,000 ha (4,924 acres)*

With establishments at Brissac, Beaulieu and Tigné, this is a union of three *coopératives*, producing a large range of wines, much of which is sold in bulk.

☆ Comte de Treillière Crémant de Loire

CAVE DES VIGNERONS DE SAUMUR A SAINT CYR EN BOURG
49260 Montreuil-Bellay

Sales: *350,000 cases*
Vineyards: *About 800 ha (1,977 acres)*

The members of this *coopérative* produce a wide variety of still and sparkling wines.

☆ Saumur Cuvée Spéciale

LA CONFRÉRIE DES VIGNERONS DE OISLY ET THESÉE
Oisly,
41700 Contres

Sales: *150,000 cases*

This *coopérative* produces attractive, well-made, elegantly balanced wines.

☆ Touraine Gris, Oisly et Thesée Cuvée Prestige Crémant de Loire, Baronnie d'Aignan Blanc, Baronnie d'Aignan Rouge

UNION DE VIGNERONS
Quai de la Ronde,
03500 St.-Pourçain-sur-Sioule

Sales: *150,000 cases*
Members: *350*
Vineyards: *350 ha (865 acres)*

Owning an average of 1 ha (2.5 acres) each, these growers produce red, white and rosé St-Pourçain-sur-Sioule VDQS wines. The style is clean and correct; the quality good and improving.

Generic wines of the Loire

CRÉMANT DE LOIRE AOC
An underrated *méthode champenoise* appellation that often shows greater consistency than other more famous Loire sparkling wines because it can be blended from Anjou-Saumur and Touraine wines. A *crémant* is less fizzy than a fully sparkling or *mousseux* wine, with a pressure of 3.5 atmospheres as opposed to between 5 and 6 atmospheres.

SPARKLING WHITE The better-balanced of these dry to semi-sweet, light- to medium-bodied wines are normally a blend of Chenin blanc, Cabernet franc and Chardonnay. The French invest millions of francs cultivating the Pinot noir and Chardonnay abroad, yet ignore the potential of these vines in the Loire, where the climate, soil and regulations are so inviting.
The Perry de Malleyrand Brut Tradition is an immaculately produced wine with a slowly unfolding sparkle and delicate combination of flavours.

Chenin blanc, Cabernet franc, Cabernet sauvignon, Pineau d'Aunis, Pinot noir, Chardonnay, Arbois and Grolleau noir

[19] Usually non-vintage

Within 1-3 years

SPARKLING ROSÉ The best of these light- to medium-bodied wines are *brut*, and usually contain a high proportion of Cabernet franc and Grolleau noir grapes—but a pure Pinot noir *crémant* rosé would be interesting to taste, and it could easily be made.

Chenin blanc, Cabernet franc, Cabernet sauvignon, Pineau d'Aunis, Pinot noir, Chardonnay, Arbois and Grolleau noir

[19] Usually non-vintage

Most are best drunk immediately, although some benefit if kept 1-2 years

☆ Alain Arnault, Perry de Malleyrand Brut Tradition (Michel Lateyron), Noel Pinot

ROSÉ DE LOIRE AOC
A dry rosé wine introduced in 1974 to exploit the international marketing success of Rosé d'Anjou and to take advantage of the trend for drier styles. The result has been very disappointing.

ROSÉ Dry, light- to medium-bodied rosé from the Loire that could (and should) be the most attractive wine of its type. A few growers, such as Pierre and Philippe Cady and M. Aguilas-Gaudard, try; but most do not. Domaine des Varinelles is consistently good.

Pineau d'Aunis, Pinot noir, Gamay, Grolleau and at least 30% Cabernet franc and Cabernet sauvignon

[19] 1983, 1985, 1988, 1989, 1990

Immediately

☆ Clos de l'Abbaye, Aguilas Gaudard, Domaine de Beillant, Domaine des Varinelles

Other wines of the Loire

CHÂTEAUMEILLANT VDQS

An area on the border of the Cher and Indre *départements,* around Bourges. The wine-growing traditions stretch back to the twelfth century, but this is very much a forgotten area nowadays. Although only red-wine grapes are grown, white wine of some standing used to be made here, and its production is still permitted in the regulations.

RED Grown on volcanic soils, the Gamay grape usually dominates these ruby-coloured reds. They are dry and usually light-bodied, yet firm. They should be drunk as young as possible.

🍇	Gamay, Pinot gris, Pinot noir
📅	1983, 1985, 1988, 1989, 1990
🍷	Within 6-12 months

ROSÉ The best of Châteaumeillant's wines are these dry, light-bodied *vins gris.* Produced from free-run juice (see p.21), they are fresh, grapey and delicately balanced.

🍇	Gamay, Pinot gris, Pinot noir
📅	1983, 1985, 1988, 1989, 1990
🍷	Within 6-12 months

☆ Maurice Lanoix, Henri Raffinat

CÔTES ROANNAISES VDQS

Red and rosé wines made from a localized Gamay clone called Gamay Saint-Romain. Grown on south- and southwest-facing slopes of volcanic soil on the left bank of the Loire some 40 kilometres (25 miles) west of the Mâconnais district of Burgundy. The appellation has long deserved promotion to full AOC status.

RED Some of these dry, medium- to full-bodied wines are produced using a form of *macération carbonique,* and a few are given a little maturation in cask. The result can vary between well-coloured wines that are firm, distinctive and oaky, and fruity Beaujolais-type versions for quaffing when young.

🍇	Gamay
📅	1983. 1985, 1988, 1989, 1990
🍷	Between 1-5 years

ROSÉ Dry, medium-bodied, well-made wines that are crisp, dry and fruity.

🍇	Gamay
📅	1983, 1985, 1988, 1989, 1990
🍷	Within 2-3 years

☆ Chargros, Desormières, Pierre Gaume, Maurice Lutz, Robert Serol, Villeneuve

CÔTES D'AUVERGNE VDQS

An appellation south of Saint-Pourçain and west of Côtes-du-Forez on the edge of the Massif Central. This is the most remotely situated of all the outer areas that officially fall within the Loire region. The wines from certain villages are superior and have been given the right to use the following communal appellations: Côtes d'Auvergne-Boudes (villages of Boudes, Chalus and St-Hérant); Côtes d'Auvergne-Chanturgues (villages of Clermont-Ferrand and Cézabat [part]); Côtes d'Auvergne-Châteaugay (villages of Châteaugay and Cézabat [part]); Côtes d'Auvergne-Corent (villages of Corent, Les Martres-de-Veyre, La Sauvetat and Veyre-Monton); and Côtes d'Auvergne-Madargues (village of Riom).

RED The best of these dry, light-bodied and fruity wines carry the Chanturgues appellation. Most are made from the Gamay, a grape that has traditionally been grown in the area, and are very much in the style of Beaujolais.

🍇	Gamay, Pinot noir
📅	1983, 1985, 1988, 1989, 1990
🍷	Within 1-2 years

WHITE These dry, light-bodied wines made from Chardonnay have been overlooked but are surely a marketable commodity in view of the Chardonnay's upmarket status.

🍇	Chardonnay
📅	1983, 1985, 1989, 1990
🍷	Within 1-2 years

ROSÉ Dry, light-bodied wines with an attractive cherry flavour are made in the village of Clermont-Ferrand and carry the Chanturgues appellation.

🍇	Gamay, Pinot noir
📅	1983, 1985, 1986
🍷	Within 1 year

☆ Caves des Coteaux, Pierre Lapouge

CÔTES DU FOREZ VDQS

This wine is like a VDQS Beaujolais, produced in the Loire *département* adjacent to Lyons. The wines are improving through the efforts of the *coopérative* and a few quality-conscious growers, but they could still be better.

RED Dry, light-bodied wines with some fruit, which are best drunk young and at a cool temperature.

🍇	Gamay
📅	1983, 1985, 1988, 1989, 1990
🍷	Immediately

ROSÉ Simple, light-bodied, dry rosés that make attractive, unpretentious picnic wines.

🍇	Gamay
📅	1985, 1986, 1988, 1989, 1990
🍷	Immediately

☆ Paul Gammon

HAUT-POITOU AOC

Eighty kilometres (50 miles) south-west of Tours, in a hot and dry climate, on land more suited to arable farming than to viticulture, the wines of the Poitiers district have achieved a remarkable reputation.

RED This is a wine to watch: although the really successful reds have until now been few and far between and confined to Cabernet, there is a definite feeling that a general breakthrough is imminent. The quality of the entire appellation is likely to rise significantly, and there is promise of some exciting, pure varietal reds that are about to emerge.

🍇	Pinot noir, Gamay, Merlot, Malbec, Cabernet franc, Cabernet sauvignon and a maximum of 20%, for each grape, of Gamay de Chaudenay and Grolleau
📅	1983, 1985, 1988, 1989, 1990
🍷	Within 3 years

WHITE Dry, light- to medium-bodied, varietal wines. Those made from pure Sauvignon are softer and more floral than most of their more northern counterparts, yet retain the freshness and vitality that is so important to this grape variety. They have been very consistent in quality since 1978, whatever the conditions of the vintage. The Chardonnay has so far been a disappointment, but it does produce a superb non-appellation *méthode champenoise* "Diane de Poitiers".

🍇	Sauvignon blanc, Chardonnay, Pinot blanc and up to a maximum of 20% Chenin blanc
📅	(Sauvignon) 1982, 1983, 1984, 1985, 1986, 1989, 1990
🍷	Within 1 year

ROSÉ Dry, light- to medium-bodied wines that are fresh and fruity. The *coopérative* produces a vivid raspberry-coloured Cabernet that is a bit too obvious, but other more subtle versions can be found.

🍇	Pinot noir, Gamay, Merlot, Malbec, Cabernet franc, Cabernet sauvignon and a maximum of 20% for each grape, of Gamay de Chaudenay and Grolleau
📅	1985, 1986, 1988, 1989, 1990
🍷	Within 3 years

☆ Cave Coopérative du Haut-Poitou (Sauvignon and *méthode champenoise* "Diane de Poitiers"), Robert Champalou, Gérard Descoux, Fournier Frères

SAINT-POURÇAIN VDQS

The Saint-Pourçain area covers nineteen communes southeast of the Bourges appellations of the Central Vineyards in the Allier *département.* The growers are quite ambitious, and many people are enthusiast about these wines, and think that they have a particularly promising future. There are 500 hectares (1,235 acres) of vineyards.

RED Dry, light- to medium-bodied wines which, depending on the grape varieties in the blend, can vary from very light Beaujolais look-alikes to imitations of Bourgogne Passe-tout-grains.

🍇	Gamay, Pinot noir and up to a maximum of 10% Gamay teinturier
📅	1983, 1985
🍷	Within 1-2 years

WHITE Dry, light- to medium-bodied wines. The Tressallier grape (which is known as the Sacy in Chablis), when blended with Chardonnay and Sauvignon, produces a crisp, toasty, full-flavoured wine that does have some merit.

🍇	A maximum of 50% Tressallier and 10% Saint-Pierre-Foré, plus Aligoté, Chardonnay and Sauvignon blanc
📅	1984, 1985, 1986
🍷	Within 1-2 years

ROSÉ Crisp, dry, light- to medium-bodied wines that have a fragrance that is reminiscent of soft summer fruits. The rosés are generally more successful than the red wines of the area but both styles are particularly refreshing and thirst-quenching.

🍇	Gamay, Pinot noir and up to a maximum of 10% Gamay teinturier
📅	1983, 1985, 1986
🍷	Within 1-2 years

☆ Jean Cherillat, Maurice Faure, Joseph Laurent, Jean Ray

Pays Nantais

Nantais is Muscadet country. The richest Muscadet comes from the Sèvre-et-Maine, while that from the Coteaux de la Loire to the north has extra acidity. Elsewhere, wines of very ordinary quality prevail.

SOUTHEAST OF NANTES ARE THE VINEYARDS of Muscadet. The best are those of the Sèvre-et-Maine district, named after two rivers, which is much hillier than the surrounding countryside and protected from northwesterly winds by Nantes itself. Sèvre-et-Maine accounts for one-quarter of the general appellation area, yet produces 85 per cent of all Muscadet. Only in unusually hot or dry years, when they contain extra natural acidity, can the Muscadet grapes grown further north in the Coteaux de la Loire sometimes surpass those from Sèvre-et-Maine.

THE MUSCADET GRAPE AND ITS WINES

Exactly when the Muscadet grape, also known as the Melon de Bourgogne and the Gamay blanc, was first planted in the area is uncertain. There is a plaque at Château de la Cassemichère that claims that the first Muscadet vine was transplanted there from Burgundy in 1740, but Pierre Galet, the famous ampelographer (vine botanist), tells us that "following the terrible winter of 1709, Louis XIV ordered that the replanting of the frozen vineyards of Loire-Atlantique be with Muscadet blanc".

The wine produced by the Muscadet grape is neutral in flavour and bears no hint of the muskiness its name implies. It must be harvested early to preserve acidity, and yet, in doing so, the grower runs the risk of making a wine that lacks fruit. But if the wine is left in contact with its sediment and bottled *sur lie* – off the lees – the operation enhances the fruit, adds a yeasty dimension of depth and, by retaining more of the carbonic gas created during fermentation, imparts a certain liveliness and freshness. Until recently there was no control on the use of the term, and unscrupulous producers would simply describe an ordinary filtered wine as *sur lie* and ask a higher price. Now a Muscadet *sur lie* must remain in contact with its sediment for one winter, and may not be bottled before February 15 following the harvest. It must be bottled directly off its lees, and must not be racked or filtered. Some growers would like the term *sur lie* applied only to wines kept in wooden barrels, arguing that the effect of keeping a wine in contact with its lees in huge vats is negligible.

FACTORS AFFECTING TASTE AND QUALITY

 Location
The Pays Nantais lies in the coastal area and the westernmost district of the Loire Valley, with vineyards occupying parts of the Loire-Atlantique and the Maine-et-Loire *départements*.

 Climate
Mild and damp, but winters can be harsh and spring frosts troublesome. Summers are generally warm and sunny, although they are also rainy.

Aspect
Some of the vineyards are found on the flat land around the mouth of the Loire southwest of Nantes. There are rolling hills in the Sèvre-et-Maine and Coteaux de la Loire, with the best vineyards on gentle riverside slopes. Some of the smaller valleys are actually too steep for viticulture, and the vines in these areas occupy the hilltops.

 Soil
The best vineyards of the Sèvre-et-Maine are light and stony, with varying proportions of sand, clay and gravel above a granulated schistous and volcanic subsoil that is rich in potassium and magnesium. These soils provide good drainage, which is essential for such a damp growing district.

Viticulture and vinification
The Muscadet is a frost-resistant, early-ripening grape that adapts well to the damp conditions of the Pays Nantais. It is harvested early (mid- to late September) to preserve its acidity. The best Muscadet is left in vat or barrel on its sediment – *sur lie* – until it is bottled. This imparts a greater depth and fruitiness, and a faint prickle of natural carbonic gas.

Primary grape varieties
Muscadet, Folle blanche

Secondary grape varieties
Gamay, Gamay de Chaudenay, Gamay de Bouze, Négrette, Chardonnay, Cabernet franc, Cabernet sauvignon, Pinot noir, Chenin blanc, Groslot gris

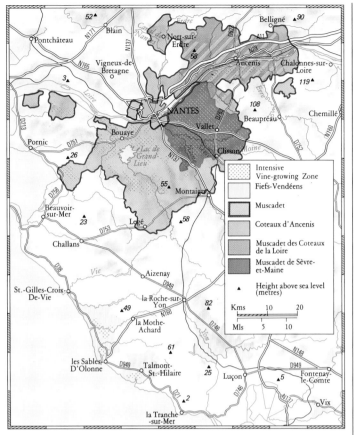

PAYS NANTAIS see also p.156

The areas to the east of Nantes, Sèvre-et-Maine and Coteaux de la Loire, produce the region's finest wines, Muscadet from the former the most famous, only bettered in hot years by wine made from more acidic grapes grown further north.

Nantes, above
The charm of the old quarter contrasts with the urban sprawl of the modern-day city, the gateway to the Loire valley.

Muscadet vines, above
In the heart of Muscadet country, to the southeast of Nantes, the village of St.-Fiacre-sur-Maine overlooks the surrounding vineyards.

The wines of Nantais

COTEAUX D'ANCENIS VDQS

Varietal VDQS wines from the same area as Muscadet Coteaux de la Loire that deserve AOC status.

RED Bone-dry to dry, light- to medium-bodied wines that include Cabernets, made from both Cabernet franc and Cabernet sauvignon grapes. Surprisingly they are not as successful as the juicy Gamay wines which represent no less than 80 per cent of the total production of this appellation.

🍇 Cabernet sauvignon, Cabernet franc, Gamay and up to a combined total of 5% Gamay de Chaudenay and Gamay de Bouze

🍷 1985, 1986, 1988, 1989, 1990

🍷 Within 2 years

WHITE Dry to medium-dry, light-bodied wines. The Pinot gris, also sold as "Malvoisie", is not as alcoholic as its Alsatian cousin, yet can possess a light richness that will linger in the mouth. The Chenin blanc, known locally as "Pineau de la Loire", rarely sparkles.

🍇 Chenin blanc, Pinot gris

🍷 1983, 1985, 1986, 1989, 1990

🍷 Within 12 to 18 months

ROSÉ Bone-dry to dry, light- to medium-bodied wines, some of which are fresh, firm and lively. Gamay is the most popular grape variety.

🍇 Cabernet sauvignon, Cabernet franc, Gamay and up to a combined total of 5% Gamay de Chaudenay and Gamay de Bouze

🍷 1985, 1986, 1988, 1989, 1990

🍷 Within 2 years

☆ Domaine des Genaudières, Jacques Guindon

FIEFS VENDEENS VDQS

A *Vin de Pays* as recently as 1984, this appellation has been steadily improving and deserves its VDQS status. The regulations controlling the grape varieties permitted for this appellation are unique. They determine the proportion of each variety that must be represented in the vineyard, yet there is no control of the grapes contained in the final blend; thus blends and pure varietals are allowed despite the percentages laid down by law of grapes that must be cultivated.

RED The communes of Vix and Mareuil-sur-Lay-Disais produce the best wines. They are dry, medium-bodied and firm, but not long-lived.

They can have a grassy character, derived from the Cabernet franc that is the predominant grape grown in both these two villages.

🍇 A minimum of 50% Gamay and Pinot noir plus Cabernet franc, Cabernet sauvignon, Négrette and up to a maximum of 15% Gamay de Chaudenay

🍷 1985, 1986, 1988, 1989, 1990

🍷 Within 18 months

WHITE Bone-dry to dry, light-bodied wines which, apart from those of Vix and Pissotte, are of lesser quality. This could be because the Chenin blanc rarely ripens properly in a northerly coastal area. If some of the other permitted grape varieties were grown over a much wider area, quality might improve.

🍇 A minimum of 50% Chenin blanc, plus Sauvignon blanc and Chardonnay. A maximum of 20% Melon de Bourgogne in the communes of Vix and Pissotte and a maximum of 40% (reducing to 30% by 1994) Groslot gris in the coastal vineyards around Les Sables d'Olonne

🍷 1985, 1986, 1989, 1990

🍷 Immediately

ROSÉ Dry, light- to medium-bodied wines. The best wines of Vix and Mareuil-sur-Lay-Disais are soft, delicate and underrated. They are worth looking out for.

🍇 A minimum of 50% Gamay and Pinot noir plus Cabernet franc, Cabernet sauvignon, Négrette and up to a maximum of 15% Gamay de Chaudenay. A maximum of 40% (reducing to 30% by 1994) Groslot gris in the coastal vineyards around Les Sables d'Olonne

🍷 1985, 1986, 1988, 1989, 1990

🍷 Within 18 months

☆ Domaine de la Chaignée, Philippe & Xavier Coirer, Michel Paupion, Arsène Rambaud, Domaine des Rochettes

GROS PLANT or GROS PLANT NANTAIS VDQS

Gros plant is the local synonym for the Folle blanche—one of the grapes used to make Cognac.

WHITE Gros Plant is normally so dry, tart and devoid of fruit and body that it seems tough and sinewy to taste. If bottled *sur lie* it can have sufficient depth to match its inherent bite, in much the same way as Muscadet, *see* Muscadet de Sèvre-et-Maine AOC.

🍇 Gros plant

🍷 1985, 1986, 1988, 1989, 1990

🍷 Usually immediately

☆ Clos-des-Rosiers, Domaine du Bois-Bruley, Joseph Hallereau, La Cuvée de Marquisat, Domaine de la Seigneurie du Cléray

MUSCADET AOC

This basic appellation covers the whole Muscadet area, yet the wines produced under it account for only ten per cent of the total production of the appellation.

WHITE Bone-dry, very light-bodied wines which, with very few exceptions, are ordinary wines at best, and often lack balance.

🍇 Muscadet

🍷 1986, 1987, 1988, 1989, 1990

🍷 Immediately

☆ Domaine de la Garanderie, Domaine des Genaudières, Domaine des Herbanges

MUSCADET DES COTEAUX DE LA LOIRE AOC

The Coteaux de la Loire is the most northerly wine area on the French coast. Above this point it is very difficult to grow grapes of sufficient ripeness for winemaking. The combination of its northerly coastal situation with a chalky soil and numerous north-facing slopes is responsible for the characteristically high acidity of the wines produced in the area.

WHITE Bone-dry, light-bodied wines of variable quality that are usually

lacking in fruit, but can be the best balanced of all Muscadets in very hot years.

🍇 Muscadet

🍷 1982, 1985, 1988, 1989, 1990

🍷 Immediately

☆ Chateau la Berrière "Clos Saint-Roch", Domaine de la Garanderie, Jacques Guindon, Domaine des Herbauges, Château de la Roulière

MUSCADET DE SÈVRE-ET-MAINE AOC

Classic Muscadet from a small area containing most of the best wines. Some 45 per cent of this appellation is bottled and sold as *sur lie,* having remained in contact with its sediment for at least one winter before bottling.

WHITE Bone-dry to dry, light-bodied wines. The best should have both fruit and acidity, plus a depth that can be reminiscent of a modest white Burgundy.

🍇 Muscadet

🍷 1986, 1987, 1988, 1989, 1990

🍷 Within 2 years, although some may last 3 or 4

☆ Domaine de la Bigotière, Domaine de la Blanchetière, Domaine de Bois-Bruley, Domaine de la Botinière, Domaine de Bourguignon, André-Michel Bregeon, Château de la Bretesche, Fief de la Brie, Château de la Cantrie, Domaine de Chasseloir, Domaine des Chausselières, Domaine de la Février, Domaine de la Forchetière, Domaine de la Hautière, La Foilette, Marquis de Goulaine, Les Mesnil, Château de la Mercredière, Coupe "Louis Métaireau", Cuvée Millénaire Goulaine, Château de Moutonnière, Château la Nöe, Château de l'Oiselinière, Château l'Oiselinière de la Ramée, Clos des Roches Gaudinières, Clos des Rosiers, Le Soleil Nantais Guibaud Frères

Anjou-Saumur

Anjou-Saumur is a microcosm of the entire Loire Valley, producing virtually every style of wine imaginable, from almost every grape available in the Loire.

ANGERS, THE ANCIENT CAPITAL OF ANJOU, is as important for its textile industry as it is for its wines. Its attractions include a ninth-century castle, twelfth-century cathedral and the thirteenth-century Hôpital St-Jean, which accommodates the small Anjou Wine Museum.

The only other town of major interest in the district is Saumur, the Loire's sparkling wine centre, to which tourists flock in the summer to visit the numerous cellars hewn out of the solid tufa subsoil. The magnificent white tufa-stone castle that overlooks the town was built in the fourteenth century. It is regarded as one of the finest of the Loire châteaux, and is used by the Confrérie des Chevaliers du Sacavins (one of Anjou's several wine fraternities) for various inaugural ceremonies and celebrations.

THE WINES OF ANJOU

Although rosé is on the decline, it still represents up to 55 per cent of the total output. However, because it is essentially a blended wine based on minor grapes such as the Grolleau and Pineau d'Aunis, the most famous grape of Anjou is a white-wine producer called the Chenin blanc. This vine has been cultivated in the area for well over a thousand years. It has many synonyms, from "Pineau de la Loire" to "Franc-blanc", but its principal name, Chenin blanc, stems from Mont-Chenin in fifteenth-century Touraine. Under other names it can be traced as far back as 845, to the abbey of Glanfeuil (south of the river in the Anjou district).

The distinctive tang of the Chenin blanc grape comes from its inherently high tartaric acid content and this, combined with a naturally high extract, makes for unacceptably tart and often bitter styles of dry and medium-dry white. Exceptions to this rule are few and mostly confined to the four sun-blessed, southeast-facing slopes of Savennières. Anjou growers go by the rule rather than

the exception, and the common practice has always been to leave the harvest of this variety until as late as possible. This invites the risk of rain, but by going over the vines several times in the time-honoured tradition of *tries*, picking only the ripest and healthiest grapes on each and every sweep of the vineyard, a miraculous wine may be made. Although a time-consuming and labour-intensive operation, the unique quality of overripe grapes produced can result in the most succulent and immaculately balanced of sweet wines. Unlike poor and boring dry Chenin blanc wines that only deteriorate with age, these treasures are vinous investments that are capable of great maturity and can achieve wonderfully complex honeyed characteristics.

THE SPARKLING SAUMUR INDUSTRY

With the rapid growth of the Champagne market in the nineteenth century, producers in the Loire began to copy the effervescent winemaking practices of their northern cousins, believing that at long last here was a potential outlet for the surplus of thin and tart Chenin blanc wines with which even the most quality-conscious growers were often lumbered. The first sparkling Loire wine was produced by Jean Ackermann. In 1811 he founded the house of Ackermann-Laurance, which monopolized the market for almost forty years. Sparkling Saumur eventually turned into the largest French sparkling wine industry outside of Champagne itself.

In many parts of the Loire the Chenin blanc grape has the perfect acidity for a quality sparkling wine, although devotees of the true yeasty character of Champagne can find its bouquet strangely sweet, maintaining that its flavour is simply too distinctive to be properly transmuted by the *méthode champenoise*. However, the wines are enormously popular, and the admixture of Chardonnay and other neutral varieties can greatly improve the overall blend. Even the most ardent admirer of Champagne has been known to fall prey to the charms of a superior pure Chenin blanc bubbly from this region.

ANJOU-SAUMUR see also p.156

Boasting sparkling wine, and more, from Saumur and a range of wines from Angers' environs, Anjou-Saumur produces most types of wine found in the Loire as a whole.

Bottling Saumur-Champigny, above
The appellation produces some of the Loire valley's finest red wines.

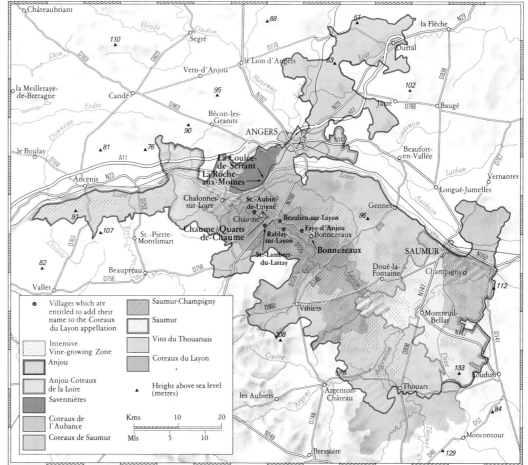

THE REGION'S RED WINES

It is in Anjou, especially in the villages south of Saumur, that the Cabernet franc emerges as the Loire's best red-wine grape. But beyond the neighbouring district of Touraine, its cultivation rapidly diminishes. The Loire is the largest wine region in France, yet surprisingly it boasts just three classic red wines; Saumur-Champigny, Bourgueil and Chinon. The fact that the vineyards producing these wines are clustered together in one tiny part of the region is less surprising, and is also no coincidence. They share a compact area around the confluence of the Vienne and the Loire – two rivers that long ago established the gravel terraces so prized for growing the Cabernet franc today. Good wines are produced from vines cultivated on the higher chalk-tufa slopes, but the best come from the terraces. Most of the slopes and terraces face south, benefitting greatly from the extra exposure to the sun, and giving added protection from northerly winds, resulting in a relatively low rainfall.

THE FUTURE OF ANJOU-SAUMUR

The potential of Anjou looks more rosy than rosé, as it desperately tries to bury a past that has made its name synonymous with cheap, cloying, pink plonk. In this endeavour it deserves to succeed and probably will. The future of Anjou-Saumur lies not only in its sparkling wine industry, but in the continuing development of its red wine production.

FACTORS AFFECTING TASTE AND QUALITY

Location
West-central district with mostly left bank vineyards situated between Angers and Saumur.

Climate
A gentle Atlantic-influenced climate with light rainfall, warm summers and mild autumns, but frost is a problem in Savennières.

Aspect
Soft, rolling hills which hold back the westerly winds. The best sites are the south-facing rocky hillsides of Savennières, and the steep-sided valley of the river Layon.

Soil
In the west and around Layon, the soil is schist with a dark, shallow topsoil that stores heat well and helps ripen the grapes, but some colder clay-soil areas produce heavier wines. The chalk-tufa soil in the east of the district around Saumur produces lighter wines, while the shale and gravel in Saumur-Champigny favours Cabernet franc.

Viticulture and vinification
The Chenin blanc is a particularly slow-ripening grape that is often left on the vine until November, particularly in the Coteaux du Layon. The effect of the autumn sun on the dew-drenched, overripe grapes can encourage "noble rot", particularly in Bonnezeaux and Quarts-de-Chaume. In good years, pickers go through the vineyards several times, selecting only the ripest or most rotten grapes – a tradition known as *tries*. Most wines are bottled in the spring following the vintage, but wines produced from such richly sweet grapes take at least three months to ferment and might not be bottled until the following autumn.

Primary grape varieties
Chenin blanc, Cabernet franc, Gamay, Grolleau

Secondary grape varieties
Chardonnay, Sauvignon blanc, Cabernet sauvignon, Pineau d'Aunis, Malbec

Saumur, above
The castle towers above the town, the buildings distinguished by the brilliant white tufa-stone typical of the area.

Vineyards, Coteaux du Layon, left
In favourable sites, the vines are sometimes attacked by "noble rot". The area is famous for its sweet white wines.

Tufa sub-soil cellars, below
The tufa-stone not only dominates the architecture; the subsoil is ideal for the sparkling-wine cellars.

The wines of Anjou-Saumur

ANJOU AOC

The Anjou district encompasses the vineyards of Saumur; thus Saumur may be sold as Anjou, but not vice versa. The red wines are by far the best, the whites the worst, and the rosé wines, although waning in popularity, remain the most famous. Because *"mousseux"* has "cheap fizz" connotations, the wines officially designated as Anjou Mousseux appellation are often marketed simply as "Anjou".

RED Dry, medium- to full-bodied wines, made mostly from pure Cabernet franc or with a touch of Cabernet sauvignon. These delightful wines are best drunk young, although the odd oak-aged wine of some complexity can be found.

🍇	Cabernet franc, Cabernet sauvignon, Pineau d'Aunis
🗓	1983, 1985, 1988, 1989, 1990
🍷	Within 1-3 years

☆ Domaine des Charbottières, Clos de Coulain, Domaine de la Croix des Loges, Château de Fesles, Logis de la Giraudière, Domaine des Rochelles

WHITE Although these wines vary from dry to sweet and from light- to full-bodied types, there are too many aggressively acid-dry or simply mediocre medium-sweet Chenin blanc wines in the appellation. Some improvement has been made by growers maximizing the 20 per cent Chardonnay and Sauvignon allowance, and shining examples like Moulin Touchais show what can be achieved if quality is put before quantity.

🍇	A minimum of 80% Chenin blanc and a maximum of 20% Chardonay and Sauvignon blanc
🗓	1985, 1986, 1989, 1990
🍷	Immediately

☆ Domaine des Hauts-Perrays, Domaine de Montchenin, Moulin Touchais, "Chauvigné" Richou Père & Fils

ROSÉ Once a marketing miracle, Anjou Rosé sells less well in today's increasingly sophisticated markets. These medium-sweet, light-to medium-bodied, coral pink wines can be delicious in the early spring following the vintage, but quickly tire in the bottle.

🍇	Predominately Grolleau, with varying proportions of Cabernet franc, Cabernet sauvignon, Pineau d'Aunis, Gamay, Malbec
🗓	1983, 1985, 1988, 1989, 1990
🍷	Immediately

ANJOU COTEAUX DE LA LOIRE AOC

A rare, white-only appellation southwest of Angers. Production is small and will dwindle even further as vineyards are replanted with Cabernet for the increasingly popular Anjou Rouge appellation.

WHITE Although currently produced in dry through to medium styles, this was originally legally defined in 1946 as a traditionally sweet wine. Today producers following the trend for drier styles are hampered by out-of-date regulations that set the alcoholic strength too high and the yield too low.

🍇	Chenin blanc
🗓	1985, 1989, 1990
🍷	Within 1 year

☆ Boré Frères, Cuvée Vieille Sève

ANJOU GAMAY AOC

Gamay is only allowed in AOC Anjou wines if the name of the grape is added to the appellation on the label.

RED Dry to medium-dry, light-bodied wines that are rarely of great interest.

🍇	Gamay
🗓	1983, 1985, 1988, 1989, 1990
🍷	Immediately

☆ Alain Arnault, Domaine Cady

ANJOU MOUSSEUX AOC

This *méthode champenoise* wine is softer, but less popular than its Saumur equivalent, although it may come from the communes within Saumur itself.

WHITE A dry to sweet, light- to medium-bodied wine that desperately needs a change of regulation to allow a little Chardonnay in the blend.

🍇	A minimum of 60% Chenin blanc plus Cabernet sauvignon, Cabernet franc, Malbec, Gamay, Grolleau, Pineau d'Aunis
🗓	Mostly non-vintage
🍷	Within 1-2 years

ROSÉ If you want to know what Anjou Rosé tastes like with bubbles, try this light- to medium-bodied wine, which is mostly sold as *demi-sec*.

🍇	Cabernet sauvignon, Cabernet franc, Malbec, Gamay, Grolleau, Pineau d'Aunis
🗓	Mostly non-vintage
🍷	Immediately

☆ Château de Beaulieu, Domaine Cady, Château Montbenault

ANJOU PÉTILLANT AOC

Little-used appellation for gently sparkling *méthode champenoise* wines with a minimum of nine months bottle-age, which must be sold in ordinary still wine bottles with regular corks.

SPARKLING WHITE Dry to *demi-sec*, light-bodied sparkling wines. Considering the variable quality of Anjou Blanc, many producers might be better advised to fizz it up and sell it under this appellation.

🍇	A minimum of 80% Chenin blanc and a maximum of 20% Chardonnay and Sauvignon blanc
🗓	Mostly non-vintage
🍷	Immediately

SPARKLING ROSÉ Dry to medium, light-bodied wines, which may be labelled "Anjou Pétillant", "Anjou Rosé Pétillant" or "Rosé d'Anjou Pétillant".

🍇	Grolleau, Cabernet franc, Cabernet sauvignon, Pineau d'Aunis, Gamay, Malbec
🗓	Mostly non-vintage
🍷	Immediately

ANJOU ROSÉ AOC
See Anjou AOC

BONNEZEAUX AOC

Grown on three south-facing river slopes of the commune of Thouarcé in the Coteaux du Layon, this is one of the undisputed great sweet wines of France. The grapes must be harvested in *tries* with the pickers, collecting only the ripest fruit, taking up to two weeks.

WHITE Intensely sweet, richer and more full-bodied than Quarts-de-Chaume, the other great growth of the Layon valley. This wine has a higher minimum sugar content than Sauternes or Barsac, but more acidity.

🍇	Chenin blanc
🗓	1983, 1985, 1989, 1990
🍷	Up to 20 years or more

☆ Domaine des Charbottières, Domaine de la Croix des Loges, Château de Fesles, Château des Gauliers, Domaine des Rochelles

CABERNET D'ANJOU AOC

This appellation includes Saumur, and it was a Saumurois named Taveau who, in 1905, was the first person to make an Anjou Rosé from Cabernet grapes. Despite its classic Cabernet content and an extra degree of natural alcohol, this is not as superior to Anjou Rosé as it should be because bulk sales at cheap prices have devalued its reputation.

ROSÉ Good examples of these medium to medium-sweet, medium-bodied wines produced by the best domaines have a clean and fruity character with aromas of raspberries.

🍇	Cabernet franc, Cabernet sauvignon
🗓	1983, 1985, 1988, 1989, 1990
🍷	Immediately

☆ Domaine de Bablut, Château de Breuil, Domaine des Maurières

CABERNET DE SAUMUR AOC

All Cabernet de Saumur wines have the right to claim the appellation Cabernet d'Anjou, but those sold as Saumur are usually finer in quality.

ROSÉ A delicate, medium-sweet, light- to medium-bodied wine with a hint of straw to its pink colour and a distinctive raspberry aroma.

🍇	Cabernet franc, Cabernet sauvignon
🗓	1983, 1985, 1988, 1989, 1990
🍷	Immediately

☆ Domaine de Champteloup, Jean-Pierre Charruau

COTEAUX DE L'AUBANCE AOC

Made from old vines grown on schistous banks of the river Aubance. Because these grapes must be well ripened and harvested by *tries*, a labour-intensive system that is not cost-effective, much of this area produces Cabernet d'Anjou.

WHITE A few growers still make this rich and semi-sweet medium- to full-bodied wine that is of excellent longevity and exceptional.

🍇	Chenin blanc
🗓	1983, 1985, 1989, 1990
🍷	Between 5-10 years

☆ Domaine Richou Père et Fils, Domaine des Rochelles, Domaine des Rochettes

COTEAUX DU LAYON AOC

The sweet white wines of this area have been justifiably famous since the fourth century. In favourable sites the vines are sometimes attacked by "noble rot", but in all cases the grapes must be extremely ripe and harvested by *tries* to a minimum of 12° of alcohol from a maximum 30 hectolitres per ha (134 cases per acre). Due to the relatively low price this appellation commands, harvesting by *tries* is viable only for the top domaines.

WHITE Green-gold to yellow-gold coloured, soft textured, sweet, medium-to full-bodied wines, rich in fruit and potentially long-lived.

🍇	Chenin blanc
🗓	1982, 1983, 1985, 1989, 1990
🍷	Between 5-15 years

☆ Château de Fesles, Domaine de la Martereaux, Moulin Touchais, Logis du Prieuré, Clos des Rochettes, Château de la Roulerie, Clos de Sainte Catherine

COTEAUX DU LAYON-CHAUME AOC

This appellation is separated from the previous one by its higher minimum alcoholic content of 13° and from that below by its lower maximum yield of 25 hectolitres per ha (112 cases per acre).

WHITE Sweet, medium- to full-bodied, fine, viscous wines that rank above those of the basic Coteaux-du-Layon appellation.

🍇 Chenin blanc

🗓 1983, 1985, 1988, 1989, 1990

🥂 Between 5-15 years

☆ Château de la Guimonière, Château du Plaisance, Château de la Roulerie *Les Aunis*

COTEAUX DU LAYON VILLAGES AOC

Historically these six villages have consistently produced the cream of all the wines in the Coteaux du Layon, and thus have the right to add their names to the basic appellation.

WHITE These sweet wines are medium- to full-bodied. According to the Club des Layon Villages, Beaulieu-sur-Layon has a soft, light aroma; Faye d'Anjou has a scent reminiscent of brushwood; Rablay-sur-Layon is big, bold and round; Rochefort-sur-Loire is full-bodied, tannic and matures well; Saint-Aubin-de-Luigné has a delicate aroma that develops; and Saint-Lambert-du-Lattay is robust yet round.

🍇 Chenin Blanc

🗓 1983, 1985, 1988, 1989, 1990

🥂 Between 5-15 years

☆ Domaine d'Ambinois (Beaulieu), Jean-Pierre Chené (Beaulieu), Domaine de la Motte (Rochefort)

COTEAUX DE SAUMUR AOC

Since the EEC ban on the term *méthode champenoise* there have been moves to develop this little-used appellation as the principal still wine of the Saumur district in order to promote AOC Saumur as an exclusively sparkling wine.

WHITE Relatively rare, semi-sweet, medium- to full-bodied wines that are richly flavoured and worth seeking out.

🍇 Chenin blanc

🗓 1983, 1985, 1989, 1990

🥂 Between 5-10 years

☆ Château de Brézé, Domaine des Hautes-Vignes

QUARTS-DE-CHAUME AOC

Grown on the plateau behind the village of Chaume in the Coteaux-du-Layon commune of Rochefort-sur-Loire. The vineyards of Quarts-de-Chaume used to be run by the abbey of Ronceray, whose landlord drew a quarter of the vintage as rent.

WHITE Semi-sweet to sweet, medium- to full-bodied wines. Although harvested by *tries* and produced in the same manner as Bonnezeaux, Quarts-de-Chaume is more northerly and thus slightly lighter in body. It also tends to have a touch less sweetness.

🍇 Chenin blanc

🗓 1983, 1985, 1988, 1989, 1990

🥂 Up to 15 years or more

☆ Domaine des Baumard, Château de Belle Rive, Château de l'Echarderie, Château de Surronde Vieilles Vignes

ROSÉ D'ANJOU AOC
See Anjou AOC.

ROSÉ D'ANJOU PÉTILLANT AOC
See Anjou Pétillant AOC.

SAUMUR AOC

Saumur, situated within the borders of the Anjou appellation, is regarded as the Pearl of Anjou. Its wine may be sold as Anjou, while Anjou does not automatically qualify as Saumur. Unless made from Cabernet grapes, all rosé wines must adopt the Anjou Rosé appellation. Like Anjou, its white wines are variable, yet its red wines are excellent.

RED These fine bone-dry to dry, medium- to full-bodied wines are often similar to the red wines of Anjou, although they can vary from light and fruity to deep-coloured and tannic.

🍇 Cabernet franc, Cabernet sauvignon, Pineau d'Aunis

🗓 1983, 1985, 1989, 1990

🥂 Between 1-10 years according to style

☆ Lycée d'Enseign Prof. Agricole, Clos de l'Abbaye, Château de Montreuil-Bellay, Domaine des Nerleux, Château de Passavent, Château de Targé, Reserve des Vignerons

WHITE Varying from bone-dry to sweet and from light- to full-bodied, these wines have a style more akin to Vouvray than Anjou, due to the limestone and the tufa soil. In poor-to-average years, however, a Saumur is easily distinguished by its lighter body, leaner fruit and a tartness of flavour that can sometimes have a metallic edge on the aftertaste.

🍇 A minimum of 80% Chenin blanc and a maximum of 20% Chardonnay and Sauvignon blanc

🗓 1985, 1986, 1989, 1990

🥂 Immediately

☆ Jean-Pierre Charruau, Domaine des Hauts de Sanziers, Château de Villeneuve

SAUMUR-CHAMPIGNY AOC

For many people, the vineyards southeast of Saumur, which are entitled to add the village name of Champigny to the appellation, produce the best red wine in the Loire.

RED Bone-dry to dry, full-bodied wines with a distinctive deep colour and full and fragrant raspberry aromas, often tannic and long-lived.

🍇 Cabernet franc, Cabernet sauvignon, Pineau d'Aunis

🗓 1983, 1985, 1988, 1989, 1990

🥂 Between 5-10 years

☆ Domaine Filliatreau, Domaine des Roches Neuves, Alain Sanzay, Domaine des Varinelles

SAUMUR PÉTILLANT AOC

Little-used appellation for gently sparkling *méthode champenoise* wines with a minimum of nine months bottle-age, which must be sold in ordinary still wine bottles with regular corks.

SPARKLING WHITE These dry to *demi-sec*, light-bodied and fruity wines are not dissimilar to the fine wines of the Montlouis Pétillant appellation and should be revived.

🍇 A minimum of 80% Chenin blanc and a maximum of 20% Chardonnay and Sauvignon blanc

🗓 Mostly non-vintage

🥂 Immediately

SAUMUR MOUSSEUX AOC

Fully sparkling white and rosé wines made by the *méthode champenoise* and often sold simply as Appellation Saumur Contrôlée. A significant amount of red *méthode champenoise* is also produced, but this cannot claim AOC status.

WHITE Although the production per hectare of the bone-dry to sweet medium-bodied white Saumur Mousseux is one-third more than for its Anjou equivalent, Saumur is better in quality and style due to its Chardonnay content and the tufa-limestone soil.

🍇 Chenin blanc plus a maximum of 20% Chardonnay and Sauvignon blanc and up to 60% Cabernet sauvignon, Cabernet franc, Malbec,

Gamay, Grolleau, Pineau d'Aunis, Pinot noir

🗓 Mostly non-vintage

🥂 Within 3-10 years

☆ Bouvet Vintage Crémant Saumur, Saumur Cuvée Spéciale – Cave Coopérative des Vignerons De Saumur

ROSÉ Apart from a few delicious exceptions, these dry to sweet, medium- to full-bodied wines are little better than Anjou Rosé Mousseux.

🍇 Cabernet sauvignon, Cabernet franc, Malbec, Gamay, Grolleau, Pineau d'Aunis, Pinot noir

🗓 Mostly non-vintage

🥂 Immediately

☆ Jean Douet, Domaine des Nerleux, de Neuville Saumur Brut, Noël Pinot

SAVENNIÈRES AOC

When this small portion of Anjou-Coteaux-de-la-Loire produced only sweet wines the AOC regulations set a correspondingly low maximum yield. This concentrates the wines on four southeast-facing slopes of volcanic debris that produce the world's greatest dry Chenin blanc.

WHITE Bone-dry to dry wines, although some of the semi-sweet types that used to be popular are making a comeback.

🍇 Chenin blanc

🗓 1983, 1985

🥂 Between 5-8 years

☆ Château de la Bizolière, Domaine du Closel, Château d'Epiré, Clos du Papillon, La Roche-aux-Moines (Domaine de la Bizolière or Château de Chamboureau), Coulée de Serrant

VINS DU THOUARSAIS VDQS

Michel Gigon is the sole producer of Vins du Thouarsais, a wine that could once boast over a hundred growers.

RED Dry, light- to medium-bodied fruity reds, sometimes reminiscent of cherries and other stone fruit.

🍇 Cabernet franc, Cabernet sauvignon, Gamay

🗓 1983, 1985, 1988, 1989, 1990

🥂 Within 1-2 years

WHITE A lighter-bodied but far more fragrant version of dry and semi-sweet Anjou blanc.

🍇 Chenin blanc plus up to 20% Chardonnay

🗓 1983, 1984, 1985, 1989, 1990

🥂 Immediately

ROSÉ This is a splendid dry, light- or light- to medium-bodied picnic wine.

🗓 1983, 1985, 1989, 1990

🥂 Immediately

☆ Michel Gigon

Touraine

The wine growing district around Tours dates back to Roman times, as does the town itself. Tours was a place of pilgrimage as early as the sixth century and famous for its production of silk in the fifteenth and sixteenth centuries.

THE CABERNET FRANC, KNOWN LOCALLY as the Breton, was flourishing in the vineyards of the abbey of Bourgueil a thousand years ago and, as recently as five hundred years ago, the Chenin blanc – today's predominant Touraine grape – acquired its name from Mont Chenin in the south of the district.

TOURAINE'S WINE REGIONS

With the possible exception of Saumur-Champigny, the best red wines in the Loire come from the appellations of Chinon and Bourgueil which face each other across the river Loire, just west of Tours. Made predominantly from Cabernet franc, good vintages aged in oak may be complex and comparable to claret, while the more everyday wines have the fresh-picked aromas of strawberries and raspberries and can be drunk young and cool. To the east of Tours, Vouvray and Montlouis produce rich, sweet long-lived wines from overripe Chenin blanc grapes in sunny years. North of Tours, the wines produced in Jasnières are from the same grape, but the dry style is distinctly different. Jasnières is a singular white sub-appellation within a wider red, white and rosé AOC called the Coteaux du Loir. The Loir is not a typographical error for Loire, but a confusingly spelt tributary of the great river. Also grown on the banks of the Loir, the larger VDQS area Coteaux du Vendômois produces the full spectrum of wine styles, as does Cheverny to the east, including a distinctive dry white wine from the obscure *Romorantin* grape. In addition to its still red, white and rosé, Cheverny also produces sparkling red, white and rosé, the only VDQS *méthode champenoise*. Touraine Sauvignon blanc makes a good alternative to Sancerre, while the fruity Gamay makes attractive reds and rosés. Other reds are made from the local Grolleau, or from the Pineau d'Aunis. The Chenin blanc is still the most dominant variety and, as in Anjou-Saumur, the tradition has been to produce naturally sweet wines in great years when these grapes are full of sugar. But with the demand for lighter wines, production of drier styles is growing.

TOURAINE see also p.156

Surrounded by different appellations, the ancient city of Tours is the focal point of an area rich in the variety of its wines.

FACTORS AFFECTING TASTE AND QUALITY

Location
East-central district with most of its vineyards in the *département* of Indre-et-Loire, but they also extend into those of Loir-et-Cher, Indre and Sarthe.

Climate
Touraine falls under some Atlantic influence, but the climate is less maritime than in the Nantes district and Anjou-Saumur. Protected from northerly winds by the Coteaux du Loir. Warm summer, low October rainfall.

Soil
Clay and limestone over tufa subsoil east of Tours around Vouvray and Montlouis. Tufa is chalk boiled by volcanic action. It is full of minerals, retains water and can be tunnelled out to make large, cool cellars for storing wine. Sandy-gravel soils in low-lying Bourgueil and Chinon vineyards produce fruity, supple wines; the slopes or *coteaux* of sandy-clay produce firmer wines.

Aspect
Attractively rolling land, flatter around Tours itself, hillier in the hinterland. Vines are planted on gently undulating slopes, which are often south-facing, at between 40-100 metres (130-330ft) above sea level.

Viticulture and vinification
White wine fermentation takes place at low temperatures and lasts for several weeks for dry wines, several months for sweet wines. The reds undergo malolatic fermentation. Some Bourgueil and Chinon is aged for up to 18 months in oak casks before bottling.

Primary grape varieties
Chenin blanc, Cabernet franc, Sauvignon blanc, Grolleau

Secondary grape varieties
Cabernet sauvignon, Pinot noir, Meslier, Gamay, Gamay teinturier, Pineau d'Aunis, Romorantin, Arbois, Chardonnay, Malbec

Azay-le-Rideau, above
The sixteenth-century château was acquired by Francis I after financial scandal forced the original owner to leave France.

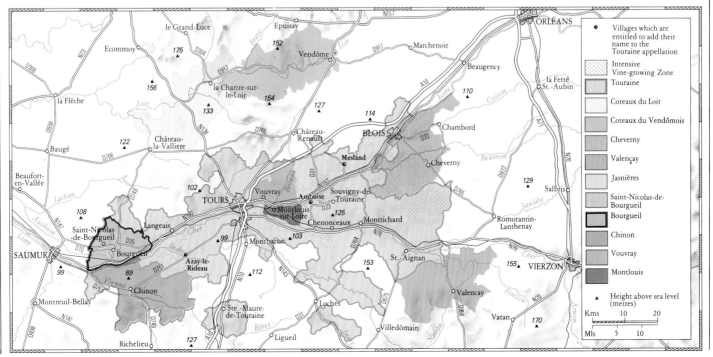

Villages which are entitled to add their name to the Touraine appellation

Intensive Vine-growing Zone

Touraine

Coteaux du Loir

Coteaux du Vendômois

Cheverny

Valençay

Jasnières

Saint-Nicolas-de-Bourgueil

Bourgueil

Chinon

Vouvray

Montlouis

▲ Height above sea level (metres)

The wines of Touraine

BOURGUEIL AOC

Most of the vines are grown on a sand and gravel plateau or *terrasse* by the river and make wines of a pronounced fruity character that are delicious to drink when less than six months old. Those grown on the south-facing clay and tufa slopes, or *coteaux,* ripen up to ten days earlier and produce more full-bodied, longer-lived wines.

RED Bone-dry to dry, medium-bodied, lively wines full of soft fruit flavours that are often aged in cask. They are very easy to quaff when less than six months old; many close up when in bottle and need time to soften. Wines from the *terrasse* vineyards are best drunk young, while those from the *coteaux* repay keeping. Many wines are blended in order to provide a balance.

🍇	Cabernet franc with up to 10% Cabernet sauvignon
🍷	1983, 1985, 1988, 1989, 1990
🌡	Within 6 months or after 6 years

ROSÉ Bone-dry to dry, light- to medium-bodied wines that are very fruity with aromas of raspberries and blackberries and good depth of flavour. They deserve to be better known.

🍇	Cabernet franc with up to 10% Cabernet sauvignon
🍷	1983, 1985, 1988, 1989, 1990
🌡	Within 2-3 years

☆ Claude Ammeux, Robert Caslot, Max Cognard, Paul Gambier, Pierre Grégoire, Lamé-Delille-Boucard, Anselme & Marc Jamet, Pierre Jamet, Paul Poupineau, Joel Taluau, Jean-Baptiste Thouet.

CHEVERNY VDQS

Good-value, crisp and fruity wines that deserve promotion to appellation status. They are usually varietal wines and the label should indicate from which grapes they are made.

RED Dry, light- to medium-bodied wines. The smaller growers mostly produce pure Gamay wines of very acceptable quality, although the addition of ten per cent or more Pinot noir gives a smoother wine.

🍇	Gamay with Cabernet franc, Cabernet sauvignon, Pinot noir, Malbec and up to 15% Gamay teinturier de Chaudenay
🍷	1983, 1985, 1988, 1989, 1990
🌡	Within 1-2 years

WHITE The obscure Romorantin grape makes the most interesting white Cheverny. They are dry, light-bodied, modest wines with a fine, flowery nose, delicate flavour and crisp balance.

🍇	Primarily Sauvignon blanc, Chenin blanc and Romorantin, but Arbois and Chardonnay may also be used
🍷	1985, 1988, 1989, 1990
🌡	Within 1-2 years

ROSÉ Only small quantities are produced but the wines are agreeably dry and light-bodied and very consistent in quality.

🍇	Gamay, Pineau d'Aunis and Pinot gris
🍷	1983, 1985, 1988, 1989, 1990
🌡	Within 1-2 years

SPARKLING RED A small quantity of these poor-quality, dry to *demi-sec*, medium-bodied wines is produced.

🍇	Mainly Cabernet franc and Cabernet sauvignon, but also may contain Chenin blanc, Arbois, Chardonnay, Meslier, Saint-François and Pineau d'Aunis
🍷	Usually non-vintage
🌡	Immediately

SPARKLING WHITE Sparkling Cheverny is the only *méthode champenoise* VDQS in France. The wines, which can be dry or sweet, are made in small amounts for local consumption.

🍇	Cabernet franc and Cabernet sauvignon, but may also contain Chenin blanc, Arbois, Chardonnay, Meslier, Saint-François and Pineau d'Aunis
🍷	Usually non-vintage
🌡	Within 2-3 years

SPARKLING ROSÉ Dry to medium-sweet, medium-bodied wines that are rarely seen.

🍇	Mainly Cabernet franc, Cabernet sauvignon and Pineau d'Aunis, but may also contain Chenin blanc, Arbois, Chardonnay, Meslier and Saint-François
🍷	Usually non-vintage
🌡	Within 1-2 years

☆ Michel Cadoux, Bernard Cazin, Gilbert Chesneau, André Coutoux, Claude Locquineau, Le Chai des Vignerons.

CHINON AOC

The appellations of Chinon and Bourgueil produce the best red wine in Touraine using the Cabernet franc grape, known locally as "le Breton". Chinon wines are generally lighter and more delicate than those of Bourgueil, but those from the tufa hill slopes have greater depth and flavour and age well.

RED Bone-dry to dry, light- to medium-bodied wines that are lively, soft and delicate. Most growers use small oak casks for aging and produce wines of very good quality.

🍇	Cabernet franc with up to 10% Cabernet sauvignon
🍷	1983, 1985, 1988, 1989, 1990
🌡	Within 2-3 years

WHITE A tiny production of clean, dry, light- to medium-bodied wines which are strangely aromatic for Chenin blanc.

🍇	Chenin blanc
🍷	1985, 1989, 1990
🌡	Within 1-2 years

ROSÉ These are dry, fairly light-bodied, smooth and fruity wines which, like Bourgueil rosés, deserve to be better known.

🍇	Cabernet franc with up to 10% Cabernet sauvignon
🍷	1981, 1983, 1985, 1989, 1990
🌡	Within 2-3 years

☆ Guy Caille, G & D Chauveau, Jean-Marie Dozon, P-J Druet, Charles Joguet, Pierre Manzagol, Jean-François Olek, Plouzeau & Fils, Sergé Sourdais, Mme Jean Spelty.

COTEAUX DU LOIR AOC

An area that had extensive vineyards in the nineteenth century. Production has since declined and the wines are generally unexciting.

RED Dry, medium-bodied wines that can have a lively character and good extract in sunny years.

🍇	Minimum of 30% Pineau d'Aunis with Gamay, Pinot noir, Cabernet franc and Cabernet sauvignon
🍷	1983, 1985, 1988, 1989, 1990
🌡	Within 1-2 years

WHITE Bone-dry to dry, light bodied wines that are high in acidity and that can be mean and astringent.

🍇	Chenin blanc
🍷	1985, 1989, 1990
🌡	As early as possible

ROSÉ Dry, fairly light-bodied wines—a few are fruity and well-balanced.

🍇	Pineau d'Aunis, Cabernet franc, Gamay and Malbec with up to 25% Grolleau
🍷	1983, 1985, 1988, 1989, 1990
🌡	Within 1 year

☆ André Fresneau

COTEAUX DU VENDOMOIS VDQS

A steadily improving district producing palatable attractive, well-made wines on both banks of the Loir, upstream from Jasnières.

RED Dry, fairly light-bodied wines that are full of soft-fruit flavours and very easy to drink.

🍇	Minimum of 30% Pineau d'Aunis with Gamay, Pinot noir, Cabernet franc and Cabernet sauvignon.
🍷	1983, 1985, 1988, 1989, 1990
🌡	Within 1-2 year

WHITE Dry, fairly light-bodied wines which, when made from pure Chenin blanc, have a tendency to be very astringent. Growers who blend Chardonnay with the Chenin blanc produce better-balanced wines.

🍇	Primarily Chenin blanc with up to 20% Chardonnay
🍷	1984, 1985, 1989, 1990
🌡	Within 1 year

ROSÉ
☆ Minier & Fils, Jean-Baptiste Pinon

JASNIÈRES AOC

The best area of the Coteaux du Loir whose wines can, in hot years, achieve a richness that compares well to those of Savennières in Anjou (*see* p.166).

WHITE Medium-bodied wines that can be dry or sweet. They are elegant and age well in good years, but can be unripe in poor years.

🍇 Chenin blanc

📅 1983, 1985, 1989, 1990

🍷 Within 2-4 years

☆ André Fresneau, Domaine Gigou, Domaine Legreau, André Paul, Jean-Baptiste Pinon

MONTLOUIS AOC

Like its more famous neighbour Vouvray, Montlouis produces wines that can be dry, medium-dry or sweet depending on the vintage. The wines are very similar in style to those of Vouvray but whereas Vouvray is probably overrated, Montlouis is by comparison most certainly underrated.

WHITE Light- to medium-bodied wines that can be dry or sweet. They are softer and more forward than the wines of Vouvray but can have the same honeyed flavour in fine years. Sweet Montlouis is aged in cask, but the best medium-dry styles are clean-fermented in stainless steel.

🍇 Chenin blanc

📅 1983, 1985, 1988, 1989, 1990

🍷 Within 1-3 years for medium-dry, up to 10 years for sweeter wines

☆ Berger Frères, Guy Deletang & Fils, Claude Levasseur, Daniel Mosny, Dominique Moyer

MONTLOUIS MOUSSEUX AOC

In poor vintages the grapes are used to make sparkling *méthode champenoise* versions of Montlouis. The medium-dry *(demi-sec)* styles of the Mountlouis Mousseux AOC are very popular in France.

SPARKLING WHITE These light- to medium-bodied wines can be *brut, sec, demi-sec* or *moelleux.* The last two styles are only made in those years that are particularly sunny.

🍇 Chenin blanc

📅 Usually non-vintage

🍷 Immediately

MONTLOUIS PÉTILLANT AOC

These gently sparkling white wines are consistently some of the most successful in France.

SEMI-SPARKLING WHITE Light- to medium-bodied wines that can be dry or sweet. They are very consistent in quality and have a rich, fruity flavour balanced by a delicate *mousse* of fine bubbles.

🍇 Chenin blanc

📅 Usually non-vintage

🍷 Immediately

☆ Domaine de la Bigarrière, Jean Chaneveau, Guy Deletang & Fils, Alain Joulin, Maurice Lelarge

ST-NICOLAS-DE-BOURGUEIL AOC

A commune with its own appellation in the northwest corner of Bourgueil. The soil is sandier that that of surrounding Bourgueil and the wines are lighter but certainly the equal in terms of quality. These are some of the finest red wines in the Loire.

RED Bone-dry to dry, medium-bodied wines that age well and have greater finesse than the wines of Bourgueil.

🍇 Cabernet franc with up to 10% Cabernet sauvignon.

📅 1983, 1985, 1988, 1989, 1990

🍷 After 5-6 years

ROSE A small amount of dry, medium-bodied rosé with firm, fruity flavour is produced.

🍇 Cabernet franc with up to 10% Cabernet sauvignon

📅 1985, 1988, 1989, 1990

🍷 Immediately

☆ Claude Ammeux, Robert Caslot, Max Cognard, Paul Gambier, Pierre Grégoire, Lamé-Delille-Boucard, Marc & Anselme Jamet, Pierre Jamet, Paul Poupineau, Joel Taluau, Jean-Baptiste Thouet

TOURAINE AOC

A prolific appellation covering still and sparkling dry, medium-dry and sweet white, red and rosé wines from all over Touraine. Most are varietal wines and the label should indicate from which grape varieties they have been made.

RED Dry, light- to medium-bodied wines. Those made from Gamay are particularly fresh and fruity.

🍇 Primarily Gamay and Cabernet franc but may also contain Cabernet sauvignon, Malbec, Pinot noir, Pinot meunier, Pinot gris and Pineau d'Aunis

📅 1981, 1983, 1985, 1989, 1990

🍷 Within 3 years

WHITE Bone-dry to dry, medium-bodied wines that, when made from pure Sauvignon, are fresh, aromatic and fruity. Good Touraine Sauvignon is better than average Sancerre.

🍇 Primarily pure Sauvignon blanc, but may also contain Chenin blanc, Arbois and a maximum of 20% Chardonnay.

📅 1983, 1984, 1985, 1989, 1990

🍷 Within 1-2 years

ROSE Dry, light- to medium-bodied wines. Those made from Pineau d'Aunis are drier and more subtle than Anjou rosé.

🍇 Cabernet franc, Gamay, Grolleau and Pineau d'Aunis with up to 10% Gamay teinturier de Chaudenay or Gamay de Bouze

📅 1983, 1985, 1989, 1990

🍷 Within 1-2 years

☆ Maurice Barbou, Jean-Claude Bodin, Jacques Delaunay, Joel Delaunay, Michel Lateyron, Lucien Launay, Jean Louet, René Pinon, Jean-Jacques Sard, Etienne Saulquin, Hubert Sinson, J-P Trouve, Closerie du Val-de-la-Leu

TOURAINE-AMBOISE AOC

Modest white wines and light reds and rosés are produced by a cluster of eight villages surrounding, and including, Amboise. The vines are grown on both sides of the Loire adjacent to the Vouvray and Montlouis areas.

RED Dry, light-bodied wines that are mostly blended—those containing a high proportion of Malbec are the best.

🍇 Cabernet franc, Cabernet sauvignon, Malbec and Gamay

📅 1983, 1985, 1989, 1990

🍷 Between 2-3 years

WHITE Bone-dry to dry, light-bodied Chenin Blancs that are usually uninspiring; the rosés are superior.

🍇 Chenin blanc

📅 1983, 1985, 1989, 1990

🍷 Immediately

ROSE These dry, light-bodied, well-made wines are mouth-watering.

🍇 Cabernet franc, Cabernet sauvignon, Malbec and Gamay

📅 1983, 1985, 1989, 1990

🍷 Within 1 year

☆ Hubert Denay, Dutertre & Fils, Michel Lateyron, Yves Moreau, Château de Pocé

TOURAINE AZAY-LE-RIDEAU AOC

Good-quality wines from eight villages on either side of the river Indre, a tributary of the Loire.

WHITE Delicate, light-bodied wines that are usually dry but may be *demi-sec.*

🍇 Chenin blanc

🍷 1983, 1985, 1989, 1990

🍷➤ Within 1-2 years

ROSÉ Attractive, refreshing, dry wines that are coral-pink in colour and have an aroma of strawberries.

🍇 Malbec and Gamay

🍷 1983, 1985, 1989, 1990

🍷➤ Within 1-2 years

☆ Château d'Aulée, Gaston Pavy, Gaston Pibaleau

TOURAINE-MESLAND AOC

Wines from the vineyards of Mesland and five surrounding villages on the right bank of Loire, just upstream from Amboise. The reds and rosés of this appellation are definitely well worth looking out for.

RED These dry, medium- to full-bodied wines are the best of the appellation and, in some cases, they are just as good as those of Chinon or Bourgueil.

🍇 Cabernet franc, Cabernet sauvignon, Malbec and Gamay

🍷 1981, 1983, 1985, 1989, 1990

🍷➤ Within 1-3 years

WHITE Dry, light-bodied wines with a high acidity, which are best in sunny years.

🍇 Chenin blanc

🍷 1983, 1985, 1989, 1990

🍷➤ Within 1-2 years

ROSÉ These dry, medium-bodied wines have more depth and character than those of Touraine-Amboise.

🍇 Cabernet franc, Cabernet sauvignon, Malbec and Gamay

🍷 1982, 1983, 1985, 1989, 1990

🍷➤ Within 1-3 years

☆ Philippe Brossillon, José Chollet, François Girault, Yves Moreau, André Rediguère

TOURAINE MOUSSEUX AOC

Very good-value *méthode champenoise* red, white and rosé wines. While the grapes for the white and rosé versions can come from the entire AOC Touraine area, those for red Touraine Mousseux may only come from the following areas: Bourgueil; St.-Nicolas-de-Bourgueil and Chinon.

SPARKLING RED Dry, light- to medium-bodied wines that are fruity and refreshing

🍇 Cabernet franc

🍷 Usually non-vintage

🍷➤ Immediately

SPARKLING WHITE These light- to medium-bodied wines are made in dry and sweet styles, and are consistent in quality because the large production area allows complex blending.

🍇 Primarily Chenin blanc but may also include Arbois and up to 20% Chardonnay and a combined maximum of 30% Cabernet, Pinot noir, Pinot gris, Pinot meunier, Pineau d'Aunis, Malbec and Grolleau

🍷 Usually non-vintage

🍷➤ Immediately

SPARKLING ROSÉ Light- to medium-bodied wines that are attractive when *brut*, though a bit cloying if sweeter.

🍇 Cabernet franc, Malbec, Noble, Gamay and Grolleau

🍷 Usually non-vintage

🍷➤ Within 1-2 years

☆ J-M Beaufreton, Dutertre Père et Fils, Prince Poniatowski

TOURAINE PÉTILLANT AOC

Refreshing, slightly effervescent white and rosé wines made from the same grape varieties as Touraine Mousseux. None are exported and they are mostly drunk in the locality.

SEMI-SPARKLING RED Red and medium-dry, light-bodied wines that are not very popular.

🍇 Cabernet franc

🍷 Usually non-vintage

🍷➤ Immediately

SEMI-SPARKLING WHITE Well-made, refreshing, light-bodied wines that are made in dry and sweet styles.

🍇 Chenin blanc, Arbois, Sauvignon blanc and up to 20% Chardonnay

🍷 Usually non-vintage

🍷➤ Immediately

SEMI-SPARKLING ROSÉ Attractive, light, quaffing wines that are made in dry and sweet styles.

🍇 Cabernet franc, Malbec, Noble, Gamay and Grolleau

🍷 Usually non-vintage

🍷➤ Immediately

☆ *See* Touraine Mousseux

VALENÇAY VDQS

Well-made, attractive wines from vineyards in the southeast of Touraine around the river Cher. Although these wines more than deserve their VDQS status they are rarely seen outside France.

RED Dry, light-bodied, fragrant wines that when made from pure Malbec—labelled under the local synonym of Cot—are very smooth and full of character.

🍇 Cabernet franc, Cabernet sauvignon, Malbec, Gamay and up to 25% Gascon, Pineau d'Aunis and a maximum of 10% Gamay de Chaudenay

🍷 1983, 1985, 1989, 1990

🍷➤ Within 1-2 years

WHITE Simple, dry, light-bodied wines that are improved by the addition of Chardonnay or Romorantin to the blend.

🍇 Arbois, Chardonnay, Sauvignon blanc and a maximum of 40% Chenin blanc and Romorantin

🍷 1983, 1984, 1985, 1989, 1990

🍷➤ Within 1-2 years

ROSÉ Dry to medium-dry, light-bodied wines that can be full of ripe soft-fruit flavours. They are superior to many AOC Loire rosés.

🍇 Cabernet franc, Cabernet sauvignon, Malbec, Gamay and up to 25% Gascon, Pineau d'Aunis and a maximum of 15% Gamay teinturier de Chaudenay

🍷 1983, 1985, 1989, 1990

🍷➤ Immediately

☆ Jacky Augis, Julienne Beschon, Hubert Sinson

VOUVRAY AOC

White wines that may be dry, medium-dry or sweet depending on the vintage. In sunny years, the classic Vouvray made from overripe grapes affected by the "noble rot" is still produced by some growers. In cooler years, the wines are correspondingly drier and more acid, and greater quantities of sparkling wine are produced.

WHITE At its best, sweet Vouvray can be the richest of all the Loire sweet wines. In good years, the wines are very full bodied, rich in texture and have the honeyed taste of ripe Chenin blanc grapes.

🍇 Chenin blanc but may also contain Arbois

🍷 1983, 1985, 1988, 1989, 1990

🍷➤ Usually 2-3 years, the sweeter wines can last up to 50 years.

☆ Chevreau-Vigneau, Bernard Courson, Alain Ferrand, Jean-Pierre Freslier, Germain Gautier-Peltier, Sylvain Goudron, Gaston Huet, Jean-Pierre Laisement, Mme Henrie Laisement, Jean-Baptiste Pinon, Prince Poniatowski

VOUVRAY MOUSSEUX AOC

In years when the grapes do not ripen properly they are converted into sparkling wine, using the *méthode champenoise,* and are blended with reserve wines from better years to ensure that they are of consistent quality.

SPARKLING WHITE Medium- to full-bodied wines that are made in both dry and sweet styles; they are richer and softer than sparkling Saumur but have more edge than sparkling Montlouis.

🍇 Chenin blanc and Arbois

🍷 1983, 1985, 1988, 1989, 1990

🍷➤ Non-vintage 2-3 years, vintage *brut* and *sec* 3-5 years, vintage *demi-sec* 5-7 years.

☆ Bernard Courson, Alain Ferrand, Jean-Pierre Freslier, Sylvain Gaudron, Germain Gautier-Peltier, Jean-Pierre Gilet, Claude Metivier, Prince Poniatowski, Viticulteurs de Vouvray (Tête de Cuvée)

VOUVRAY PÉTILLANT AOC

These are stylish and consistent semi-sparkling versions of Vouvray, but very little is produced.

SEMI-SPARKLING WHITE Medium-to full-bodied wines that are made in dry and sweet styles. They should be drunk young as they lose their freshness in bottle.

🍇 Chenin blanc and Arbois

🍷 Usually non-vintage

🍷➤ Immediately

☆ *See* Vouvray Mousseux

Central Vineyards

The Central Vineyards are so-called because they are in the centre of France (not the centre of the Loire Valley), which graphically illustrates how far the Loire Valley is stretched out.

IN THIS DISTRICT OF SCATTERED VINEYARDS, the classic wines – dry variations of the Sauvignon blanc – are all white. While it might not be so surprising to discover that the vineyards of Sancerre are quite close to Chablis, can they really be nearer to the Champagne region than to Tours? And who could discern by taste alone that Sancerre is equidistant between the production areas of such diverse wines as Hermitage and Muscadet?

Most well-known of all the towns in this district is Orléans, famous for its liberation by Joan of Arc from the English in 1429. The other important town is Bourges, which is situated in the south between the wine villages of Reuilly, Quincy and Menetou-Salon, and was once the capital of the Duchy of Berry. To the west is Romorantin, which gives its name to one of the Loire's more obscure grape varieties.

THE REGION'S SAUVIGNON BLANC WINES

The Sauvignon blanc is to the Central Vineyards what Muscadet is to the Pays Nantais. It produces the classic wine of the district and, like Muscadet, this also happens to be both white and dry. But two dry white wines could not be more different in style and taste. In the best Muscadet *sur lie* there should be a yeasty fullness, which can sometimes be misread as the Chardonnay character of a modest Mâcon. In Central Vineyard Sauvignons, however, whether they come from Sancerre or Pouilly – or even from one of the lesser-known, but certainly not lesser quality, villages around Bourges – the aroma is so striking it sometimes startles. The rasping dryness of the wine's flavour catches the breath and can only come from one grape variety.

When grown in a cool climate like that of the Loire, the classic varietal characteristic of the Sauvignon blanc is the aroma and flavour of gooseberries. Sometimes this attribute is less pronounced and the bouquet may be more reminiscent of grass or fresh straw. Some of these wines may evoke wet woolly socks, a damp dog, cat's pee or elderflower (which is a polite way of saying cat's pee when in a grower's cellar).

Same grape, different wines

All the white wines of this district are a variation on one theme – the clean, crisp, sometimes green and aggressive varietal character of Sauvignon blanc; but there are some discernible differences. A Sancerre has a concentrated flavour, while the best Pouilly-Fumé has great finesse. More often than not, Menetou-Salon is fresh and floral, Reuilly lighter but not lesser, and Quincy pure and supremely supple. That said, the styles can vary more from grower to grower than from village to village. The effect of the same vintage on each village is different: even those who generally like Pouilly-Fumé more than Sancerre can prefer the greener quality of the latter in very hot years.

SANCERRE VARIATIONS

There are fourteen communes in the AOC area of Sancerre, each producing not one but various styles of wine according to the location, exposure and the soil on which the vines grow. In the commune of Sancerre itself, which includes the hamlet of Chavignol (a name that is creeping on to many labels), the vineyards with the greatest reputations are Clos Beaujeu, Clos du Paradis and Les Monts Damnés. Four kilometres (two-and-a-half miles) southwest, Bué consistently produces the very best Sancerres of the entire appellation from the vineyards of Clos du Chêne Marchand and Le Grand Chemarin. The superbly sited Clos de la Poussie in Bué should make a strikingly good wine, but regularly fails to achieve its potential. Clos de la Poussie has just one owner – a firm named Cordier, which is renowned for the high quality and good value of its Bordeaux wines, yet manages, year after year, to turn out a Sancerre totally lacking the vitality expected from the Sauvignon blanc grape.

A BURGUNDIAN INFLUENCE

Historically this region was part of the Duchy of Burgundy, which explains the presence of Pinot noir vines. After the scourge of phylloxera, the area under vine shrunk and that which was brought back into production was mostly replanted with Sauvignon blanc, which began to dominate the vineyards, but isolated spots of Pinot noir were maintained. Some of the wines they produce today can be very good, although they are extremely delicate in style; however fine the quality, they are but a shadow of the Burgundian Pinot.

FACTORS AFFECTING TASTE AND QUALITY

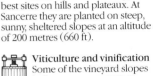

Location
The most easterly vineyards of the Loire are situated in the centre of France, chiefly in the *départements* of Cher, Nièvre and Indre.

Climate
More continental than areas closer to the sea; the summers are shorter and hotter and the winters longer and colder. Spring frosts and hail are particular hazards in Pouilly. Harvests are irregular.

Soil
The soils are dominated by clay or limestone, topped with gravel and flinty pebbles. When mixed with chalk-tufa, gravelly soils produce lighter, finer styles of Sauvignon wines; when combined with Kimmeridgean clay, the result is firmer and more strongly flavoured.

Aspect
Chalk hills in a quiet green landscape. Vines occupy the best sites on hills and plateaux. At Sancerre they are planted on steep, sunny, sheltered slopes at an altitude of 200 metres (660 ft).

Viticulture and vinification
Some of the vineyard slopes in Sancerre are very steep, and cultivation and picking are done by hand. Most properties are small and use the traditional wooden vats for fermentation, but some growers have stainless-steel tanks.

Primary grape varieties
Sauvignon blanc, Pinot noir

Secondary grape varieties
Chasselas, Pinot blanc, Pinot gris, Cabernet franc, Chenin blanc, Gamay

CENTRAL VINEYARDS see also p.156.

The Loire's most easterly vineyards, and the country's most central, are famous for wines made from the Sauvignon blanc grape.

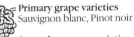

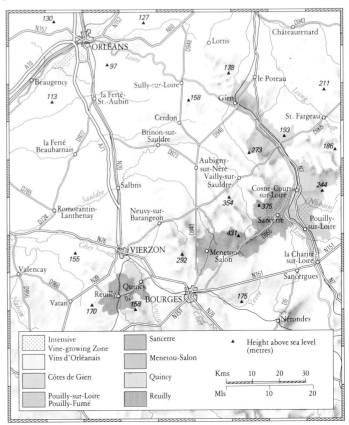

Intensive Vine-growing Zone	Sancerre		▲ Height above sea level (metres)
Vins d'Orléanais	Menetou-Salon		
Côtes de Gien	Quincy		Kms 10 20 30
Pouilly-sur-Loire Pouilly-Fumé	Reuilly		Mls 10 20

The wines of the Central Vineyards

BLANC FUMÉ DE POUILLY
and
BLANC FUMÉ DE POUILLY-SUR-LOIRE AOC
See Pouilly Fumé AOC

COTEAUX DU GIENNOIS VDQS

This once well-known appellation could boast nearly a thousand growers when it covered forty times the size of today's vineyards at the turn of the century.

RED Dry, light-bodied red wines that often have less colour than many rosés.

🍇	Gamay, Pinot noir
19	1983, 1985, 1989, 1990
⌛	Within 1-2 years

WHITE Dry, light-bodied wines that are very basic and lack interest.

🍇	Sauvignon blanc, Chenin blanc
19	1983, 1985, 1986, 1989, 1990
⌛	Within 1 year

☆ Domaine Balland-Chapuis, René Berthier, Paul Paulat & Fils, Poupat & Fils, Station Viticole INRA

COTEAUX DU GIENNOIS COSNE-SUR-LOIRE VDQS

Of the 16 communes in the départements of Nièvre and Loiret which produce Coteaux du Giennois, only eight villages in the Nièvre are entitled to add Cosne-sur-Loire to the appellation.

RED Dry, bright ruby-coloured wines. Often full-tasting, but rarely with the body to match and sometimes more tannic than the basic appellation reds.

🍇	Gamay, Pinot noir
19	1983, 1985, 1989, 1990
⌛	Within 1-2 years

WHITE Dry, medium-bodied, curiously aromatic white wines that are mainly Sauvignon and have a full, toasty flavour.

🍇	Sauvignon blanc, Chenin blanc
19	1983, 1985, 1989, 1990
⌛	Within 1-4 years

☆ René Berthier, Paul Paulat & Fils, Station Viticole INRA

CÔTES DE GIEN
and
CÔTES DE GIEN COSNE-SUR-LOIRE VDQS
See Coteaux du Giennois Cosne-sur-Loire VDQS

MENETOU-SALON AOC

This is an underrated appellation covering the village of Menetou-Salon and nine surrounding villages.

RED Dry, light-bodied, crisp and fruity wines with fine varietal aroma. They are best drunk young, although some oak-matured examples can age well.

🍇	Pinot noir
19	1983, 1985, 1989, 1990
⌛	Within 2-5 years

WHITE Bone-dry to dry wines that are fuller than the red. They are definitely Sauvignon in character, but the flavour can have an unexpected fragrance.

🍇	Sauvignon blanc
19	1983, 1984, 1985, 1989, 1990
⌛	Within 1-2 years

ROSÉ Extremely good-quality, dry, light-bodied wines that are aromatic, and full of straightforward fruit.

🍇	Pinot noir
19	1983, 1985, 1989, 1990
⌛	Within 1 year

☆ Domaine de Chatenoy, Denid de Chavignol, Jacques Couer, Paul & Jean-Paul Gilbert, Alphonse Mellot, Henry Pellé, Jean Teiller

POUILLY BLANC FUMÉ AOC
See Pouilly Fumé AOC

POUILLY FUMÉ AOC

The world's greatest Sauvignon blanc wine. In Pouilly-sur-Loire and its six surrounding communes, only pure Sauvignon wines have the right to use "Fumé" in the appellation name, a term that evokes the grape's gunsmoke character.

WHITE Crisp, bone-dry to dry, medium-bodied wines with a hint of green and the classic gooseberry flavour of Sauvignon. Even in the hottest years the intrinsic finesse and delicacy of these wines prevent them turning fat, although a perfect ripeness, sweet to taste, can come through.

🍇	Sauvignon blanc
19	1983, 1984, 1986, 1989, 1990
⌛	Between 2-5 years

☆ Baron de L (Patrick de Ladoucette), Michel Bailly, Guy Baudin, Jean-Claude Chatelain, Paul Corneau, Patrick Coulbois, Didier Dagueneau, Sergé Dagueneau, Thibault André Dezat, Gitton Père & Fils, George Guyot, Jean-Claude Guyot, Les Loges-aux-Moines, Masson-Blondelet, Raymond & Patrick Moreux, Roger Pabiot, Robert Pesson, Michel Redde, Domaine Saget, Château de Tracy

POUILLY-SUR-LOIRE AOC

This wine comes from the same area as Pouilly Fumé, but is made from the Chasselas grape, although Sauvignon blanc is allowed for blending. Chasselas is a good dessert grape but makes very ordinary wine.

WHITE Dry, light-bodied wines. Most are neutral, tired or downright poor.

🍇	Chasselas, Sauvignon blanc
19	1985, 1989, 1990
⌛	Immediately

☆ Paul Figeat, Robert Pesson

QUINCY AOC

These vineyards, on the left bank of the Cher, are situated on a gravelly plateau. Although located between two areas producing red, white and rosé wines, Quincy only produces white wine from Sauvignon blanc.

WHITE Bone-dry to dry, quite full-bodied wines in which the varietal character of the Sauvignon is evident. There is a purity that rounds out the flavour and seems to remove the rasping finish expected in this type of wine.

🍇	Sauvignon blanc
19	1983, 1985, 1989, 1990
⌛	Within 1-2 years

☆ Brisset-Surtel, Claude Houssier, Domaine de Maison Blanche, Raymond Pipet, Maurice Rapin

REUILLY AOC

The high lime content in the soil of Reuilly gives wines of a higher acidity than those found in Quincy.

RED Dry, medium-bodied wines. Some are surprisingly good, although tasting more of strawberries or raspberries than the more characteristic redcurrant flavour of Pinot noir.

🍇	Pinot noir, Pinot gris
19	1983, 1985, 1989, 1990
⌛	Within 2-5 years

WHITE Bone-dry to dry, medium-bodied wines of good quality with more of a grassy than a gooseberry flavour, yet possessing a typically austere dry finish.

🍇	Sauvignon blanc
19	1983, 1985, 1989, 1990
⌛	Within 1-2 years

ROSÉ This bone-dry to dry, light-bodied wine is a pure Pinot gris wine, although simply labelled Pinot.

🍇	Pinot gris
19	1983, 1985, 1989, 1990
⌛	Within 2-5 years

☆ Henri Beurdin, Robert & Gerard Cordier, Claude Lafond, Guy Malblète, Didier Martin, Gilbert Roussie, Sorbe & Fils

SANCERRE AOC

An appellation famous for its white wines, although originally its reds were better known. Recently the reds and rosés have become fashionable.

RED These wines have been more variable in quality than the whites, but the consistency is improving rapidly. They are dry, light-to medium-bodied with a pretty floral aroma and a delicate flavour.

🍇	Pinot noir
19	1982, 1983, 1985, 1989, 1990
⌛	Mostly between 2-3 years, but some can improve for up to 8

WHITE Bone-dry to dry, medium- to full-bodied wines that are concentrated in flavour and highly aromatic. Classic Sancerre has a rich taste of gooseberries in a great year, but in lean years – when some growers tend to overproduce – it can be a miserable little wine.

🍇	Sauvignon blanc
19	1983, 1985, 1989, 1990
⌛	Within 1-3 years

ROSÉ Attractive, dry, light-bodied rosés with strawberry and raspberry flavours.

🍇	Pinot noir
19	1984, 1985, 1986, 1989, 1990
⌛	Within 18 months

☆ Pierre Archambault, Bernard Bailly-Reverdy, Domaine Balland-Chapuis*, Philippe de Benoist, Henri Bourgeois, Lucien Crochet Vincent Delaporte, André Dezat*, Pierre Girault, Sergé Lalou*, Alphonse Mellot, Georges Millerioux, Henry Natter, Lucien Picard, Pierre Prieur & Fils, Paul Prieur & Fils, Bernard Reverdy, Jean Reverdy, Pierre & Etienne Riffault*, Georges Roblin, Jean-Max Roger, Maurice Roger, Michel Thomas*, Jean Vacheron*, Jean Vatan*
* Particularly recommended for red Sancerre

VINS DE L'ORÉANAIS VDQS

These wines have been made for centuries, but only one-third of the appellation is worked today.

RED Dry, medium-bodied, fresh and fruity wines that are given a short maceration, producing a surprisingly soft texture. They are usually sold as pure varietal wines: the Pinot can be delicate the Cabernet franc is fuller.

🍇	Pinot noir, Pinot meunier, Cabernet franc
19	1983, 1985, 1989, 1990
⌛	Within 1-2 years

WHITE Very small quantities of interesting wines are made from Chardonnay, known locally as Auvernat blanc. They are dry, medium-bodied and surprisingly smooth and fruity.

🍇	Auvernat blanc (Chardonnay), Auvernat gris (Pinot gris)
19	1983, 1985, 1989, 1990
⌛	Within 1-2 years

ROSÉ The local speciality is a dry, light- to medium-bodied rosé known as Meunier Gris – an aromatic *vin gris* with a crisp, dry finish.

🍇	Pinot noir, Pinot meunier, Cabernet franc
19	1983, 1985, 1989, 1990
⌛	Within 1 year

☆ Coopérative Covifruit, Arnold Javoy, Jacky Legroux, Cave Coopérative Mareau-des-Prés, Roger Montigny

The Rhône Valley

Primarily famous for its full, fiery and spicy-rich red wines, the Rhône Valley also produces a small quantity of rosé, made in the south, a tiny amount of white produced throughout the region, and some sparkling and fortified wines.

STRETCHING FROM VIENNE TO AVIGNON, the Côtes-du-Rhône appellation occupies a 200-kilometre (124-mile) length of the banks of the river Rhône. These vineyards in southeast France do not, however, represent the sole source of Rhône wines. The banks of this mighty European river are clad with vines all the way from the Valais vineyards of Visp, which are just 50 kilometres (31 miles) from the Rhône's glacial origins in the Swiss Alps, to the *vin de pays* vineyards of the Bouches-du-Rhône, set amid the Rhône delta just west of Marseilles, where the river finally and sluggishly runs into the Mediterranean.

Just a tiny patch of vineyards in the very north of this region are located within the Rhône *département*, a geographic misnomer that actually accounts for 70 per cent of Burgundy's output. The contrasting character of the wines of the Rhône *département*, i.e. those that bear Rhône AOCs as opposed to those that have Burgundy AOCs, should have a humbling effect on all those (myself included) who glibly talk about regional styles. For example, what could be further apart than a rich, classic Condrieu and a fresh, light Mâcon, or an intense, ink-black Côte Rôtie (Condrieu's northern neighbour), and a quaffing, cherry-coloured Beaujolais?

The cost of Rhône wines

Over the last twenty years, numerous writers have pointed out how ludicrously cheap Rhône wines have been compared to those of Bordeaux and Burgundy. In recent times, however, prices have escalated, making the Rhône a bargain basement no longer. Yet, such was the original undervaluation, the region still remains a source of good value, and the further up-market you go, the better value the wines are. How long this will be the case is debatable, particularly as American wine guru Robert Parker has recently turned his attention from Bordeaux to the Rhône, and seems to be generating an increasing enthusiasm for the Rhône's wines.

A region divided

In terms of grape variety, the Rhône divides neatly into two – the Syrah-dominated north and the Grenache-influenced south – although there are those who unnecessarily confuse the issue by separating the southernmost section of the northern district and calling it the Middle Rhône. The contrasts between north and south are not, however, merely viticultural; both the terrain and climate differ dramatically and the social, cultural and gastro-nomical differences are also marked.

THE RHÔNE VALLEY

The wine district of the Rhône valley covers a large area of southern central France, running from Vienne, just south of Lyon, into the heart of Provence.

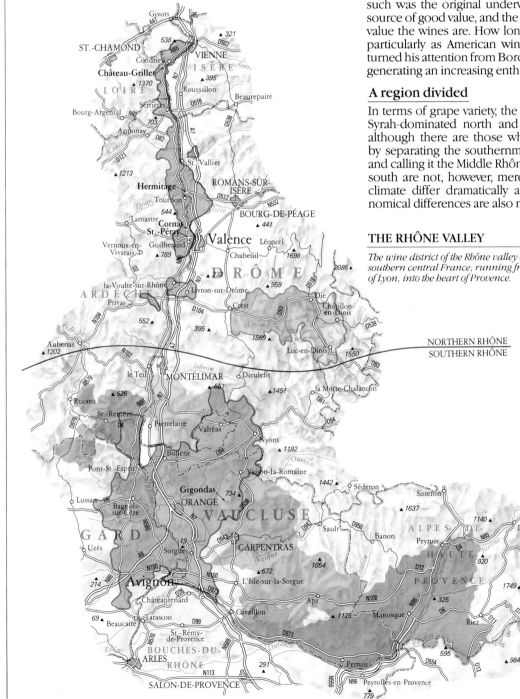

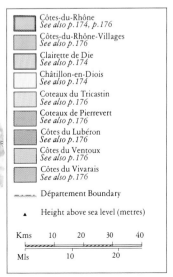

	Côtes-du-Rhône *See also p.174, p.176*
	Côtes-du-Rhône-Villages *See also p.176*
	Clairette de Die *See also p.174*
	Châtillon-en-Diois *See also p.174*
	Coteaux du Tricastin *See also p.176*
	Coteaux de Pierrevert *See also p.176*
	Côtes du Lubéron *See also p.176*
	Côtes du Ventoux *See also p.176*
	Côtes du Vivarais *See also p.176*
------	Département Boundary
▲	Height above sea level (metres)

The Northern Rhône

The Northern Rhône is dominated by the ink-black wines of the Syrah, the Rhône's only truly classic black grape. A small amount of white wine is also produced and, in the south of the district, at St.-Péray and Die, it is sparkling.

THE NORTHERN RHÔNE MIGHT BE THE GATEWAY to the south, but it has more in common with its northern neighbours than it does with the rest of the region, even though its wines cannot be compared to those from any other area. Indeed, it would be perfectly valid to isolate the north as a totally separate region called the Rhône, which would therefore allow the Southern Rhône to be more accurately defined as a high-quality extension of the Midi.

The quality of the Northern Rhône

The ink-black classic wines of Hermitage and Côte Rôtie stand shoulder to shoulder with the *crus classés* of Bordeaux in terms of pure quality, and the elite, the Hermitage of Chave and Jaboulet, or the Côte Rôtie of Guigal and Jasmin, for example, deserve the respect given to First Growths such as Latour, Mouton or Lafite. Cornas is even bigger and blacker than Hermitage and Côte Rôtie, and a great vintage from Auguste Clape rivals the best of its better-known neighbours. While the fine, dry white wines of Condrieu and Château Grillet are unique in character, the presence of such a style in this part of France is not as surprising as that of the sparkling white wines of St.-Péray and Die, particularly the latter, which Francophiles would describe as a superior sort of Asti Spumante!

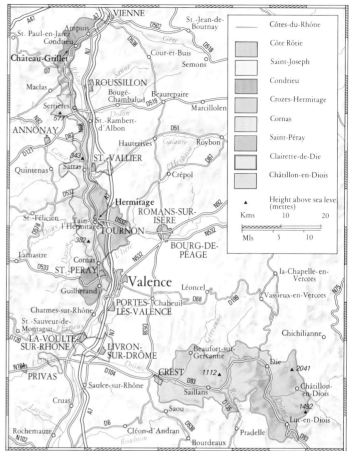

FACTORS AFFECTING TASTE AND QUALITY

 Location
The narrow strip of vineyards that belong to the Northern Rhône commences at Vienne, just south of Lyon, and extends southwards to Valence.

Climate
The effect of the Mediterranean is certainly felt in the Northern Rhône, but its climate has a distinctly continental influence. This results in the pattern of warmer summers and colder winters, which is closer to the climate of southern Burgundy, to the north, than to that of the Southern Rhône to the south. The climatic factor that the area does have in common with the southern half of the Rhône is the *mistral*, a bitterly cold wind that can reach up to 145 kilometres per hour (90 miles per hour) and is capable of denuding a vine of its leaves, shoots and fruit. As a result many *mistral*-prone vineyards are protected by poplar and cyprus trees. The wind can, however, have a welcome drying effect in humid harvest conditions.

Aspect
The countryside is generally less harsh than that of the southern Rhône, with cherry, peach, chestnut and other deciduous trees in evidence. The valley vineyards are cut far more steeply into the hillsides than they are in areas further south.

Soil
The Northern Rhône's soil is generally light and dry, granitic and schistous. More specifically, it is made up of: granitic-sandy soil on the Côte-Rôtie (calcareous-sandy on the Côte Blonde and ruddy, iron-rich sand on the Côte Brune); granitic-sandy soil at Hermitage and Condrieu with a fine overlay of decomposed flint, chalk and mica, known locally as *arzelle;* heavier soil in Crozes-Hermitage with patches of clay; granitic sand with some clay between St.-Joseph and St.-Péray, getting stonier towards the southern end of the region, with occasional outcrops of limestone; and limestone and clay over a solid rock base in the area that surrounds Die.

Viticulture and vinification
Unlike the Southern Rhône, most Northern Rhône wines are produced entirely or predominantly from a single grape variety and, despite the long list of grapes that are occasionally used (*see* Secondary grape varieties, below), that variety is the Syrah.
Viticultural operations are labour-intensive in the northern stretch of the district and, owing to the cost, the vineyards were once under the threat of total abandonment. Since that threat we pay much more for Côte Rôtie, but at least it has remained available. Vinification techniques are very traditional and, when wines are aged in wood, there is less emphasis on new oak than in Bordeaux or Burgundy.

Primary grape varieties
Syrah, Viognier

Secondary grape varieties
Aligoté, Bourboulenc, Calitor, Camarèse, Carignan, Chardonnay, Cinsault, Clairette, Counoise, Gamay, Grenache, Marsanne, Mauzac, Mourvèdre, Muscardin, Muscat blanc à petits grains, Pascal blanc, Picardan, Picpoul, Pinot blanc, Pinot noir, Roussanne, Terret noir, Ugni blanc, Vaccarèse

THE NORTHERN RHÔNE
See also p. 173

This is the home of great red wines such as Hermitage and Côte Rôtie. At its heart, the towns of Tain and Tournon face each other across the river.

Château Grillet, left
Owned by André Neyret-Cachet, Château Grillet's delightful white wine has been domaine-bottled since 1830. Straddling two communes that belong to Condrieu, it is often perceived as a sort of Grand Cru *of that appellation.*

Ampuis under snow, below
The precariously perched, southeast-facing vineyards of Côte Rôtie form a dramatic stretch of scenery on the west bank of the Rhône, some nine kilometres (five miles) south of Vienne.

The wines of the Northern Rhône

CHÂTEAU GRILLET AOC

Château Grillet is the only single-estate appellation in France. Despite its well-justified fame as one of the world's great white wines, I believe that it has yet to achieve its full potential.

WHITE A pale-gold coloured wine, with an entrancing floral bouquet, a lingering, delicate flavour and an elegant, peachy aftertaste. A wine of great finesse and complex character.

🍇 Viognier

🍷 1984, 1985, 1988, 1989, 1990

🥂 Between 4-8 years

☆ Château Grillet

CHÂTILLON-EN-DIOIS AOC

A wine raised to full AOC status in 1974, although it is hard to fathom out what merited such an elevation.

RED Light in colour and body, thin in fruit with little discernible character.

🍇 Gamay, plus up to 25% Syrah and Pinot noir

WHITE Sold as pure varietal wines, the light and fresh, gently aromatic Aligoté is as good as the richer, fuller and rather angular Chardonnay.

🍇 Aligoté, Chardonnay

ROSÉ I have not encountered any.

🍇 Gamay, plus up to 25% Syrah and Pinot noir

☆ UPVF du Diois

CLAIRETTE DE DIE AOC

This dry sparkling wine must be made by the *méthode champenoise*.

SPARKLING WHITE A relatively neutral sparkling wine of moderate quality.

🍇 At least 75% Clairette, plus Muscat à petits grains

🍷 Mostly non-vintage

🥂 Within 1-3 years

☆ Buffardel Frères, UPVF du Diois, Domaine de Magord, Georges Raspail, Caves Salabelle

CLAIRETTE DE DIE DEMI-SEC AOC

See Clairette de Die Tradition AOC

CLAIRETTE DE DIE MOUSSEUX AOC

An alternative name for the Clairette de Die appellation.
See Clairette de Die AOC.

CLAIRETTE DE DIE TRADITION AOC

Wines from this appellation are made by the *méthode dioise,* which involves only one fermentation, as opposed to the two required by the *méthode champenoise*.

SPARKLING WHITE A deliciously ripe and peach-flavoured wine.

🍇 At least 50% Muscat à petits grains, plus Clairette

🍷 Mostly non-vintage

🥂 Immediately

☆ Archard-Vincent, Buffardel Frères, UPVF du Diois, Domaine de Magord, Georges Raspail, Caves Salabelle

CONDRIEU AOC

Together with Château Grillet, which is made in the same style from the same grape and may be considered, unofficially at least, as the same wine, this is the greatest white wine in the entire Rhône valley.

WHITE The trend used to be to produce sweet and medium-sweet wines. Today, Condrieu's pale gold-coloured wines are essentially dry, have a fine, floral aroma of may-blossom and violets, and a combination of fatness, freshness and finesse that develops into an elegant, peachy character.

🍇 Viognier

🍷 1984, 1985, 1988, 1989, 1990

🥂 Between 4-8 years

☆ André Dézormeaux, Pierre Dumazet, Pierre et André Perret, Château du Rozay, Georges Vernay

CORNAS AOC

The sun-trap vineyards of Cornas produce the best value of all the Rhône's quality red wines.

RED Ink-black, full-bodied, strong-flavoured, pure Syrah wines lacking only a little finesse.

🍇 Syrah

🍷 1983, 1985, 1988, 1989, 1990

🥂 Between 7-20 years

☆ Auguste Clape, Guy de Barjac, Paul Jaboulet Aîné, Marcel Juge, Jean Lionnet, Robert Michel, Noël Verset, Alan Voge

CÔTES-DU-RHÔNE AOC

Although generic to the entire region, relatively little Côtes-du-Rhône is made in this district. *See* the Côtes-du-Rhône entry in Wines of the Southern Rhône.

CÔTE RÔTIE AOC

The terraces and low walls of the "burnt" or "roasted" slopes of Côte Rôtie must be tended by hand, but the reward is a wine of great class that vies with Hermitage as the world's finest example of Syrah.

RED A garnet-coloured wine of full body, fire and power, made fragrant by the addition of Viognier grapes. The result is a long-living and complex wine with nuances of violets and spices, and great finesse.

🍇 Syrah, plus up to 20% Viognier

🍷 1982, 1983, 1985

🥂 Between 10-25 years

☆ Pierre Barge, Domaine de Boisseyt, Bernard Burgaud, Emile Champet, Edmund Duclaux, Gentaz-Dervieux, E. Guigal, Paul Jaboulet Aîné, Joseph Jamet, Georges & Robert Jasmin, Vidal-Fleury

CROZES-ERMITAGE AOC
See Crozes-Hermitage AOC.

CROZES-HERMITAGE AOC

Crozes-Hermitage is produced from a relatively large area surrounding Tain.

RED These well-coloured, full-bodied wines are similar to Hermitage, but they are generally less intense and have a certain smoky-rustic-raspberry flavour that only deepens into blackcurrant in the hottest years.

🍇 Syrah

🍷 1983, 1985, 1988, 1989, 1990

🥂 Between 6-12 years (between 8-20 years for top wines and great years)

WHITE These improving dry white wines are gradually acquiring more freshness, fruit and acidity.

🍇 Roussanne, Marsanne

🍷 1984, 1985, 1986, 1989, 1990

🥂 Within 1-3 years

☆ Cave des Clairmonts, Domaine des Entrefaux, Domaine des Voussieres

ERMITAGE AOC
See Hermitage AOC.

HERMITAGE AOC

One of the great classic French red wines, produced entirely from Syrah grapes in virtually all cases, although a small amount of Marsanne and Roussanne may be added. The vines are grown on a magnificent south-facing slope overlooking Tain.

RED These wines have a deep and sustained colour, a very full body, and lovely, plummy, lip-smacking, spicy, silky, violety, blackcurrant fruit. A truly great Hermitage has boundless finesse, despite the weighty flavour.

🍇 Syrah, plus up to 15% Roussanne and Marsanne

🍷 1983, 1985, 1988, 1989, 1990

🥂 Between 12-30 years

WHITE These big, rich and dry white wines have a full, round, hazelnut and dried-apricot flavour. The wines have improved recently but are really no more than curiosities.

🍇 Roussanne, Marsanne

🍷 1983, 1985, 1988, 1989, 1990

🥂 Between 6-12 years

☆ Max Chapoutier, Jean-Louis Chave, E. Guigal, Jean-Louis Grippat, Paul Jaboulet Aîné, Marc Sorrel

HERMITAGE VIN DE PAILLE AOC

In 1974 Gérard Chave made the last *vin de paille* of Hermitage, a wine that is now confined to the Jura vineyards of eastern France. Monsieur Chave declares he made the wine "for amusement". Considering its success, it is extraordinary that some enterprising grower has not taken advantage of this appellation.

L'ERMITAGE AOC
See Hermitage AOC.

L'HERMITAGE AOC
See Hermitage AOC.

ST.-JOSEPH AOC

I have yet to be excited by wines from this appellation.

RED A medium-bodied, fruity red wine with a pepperyness reminiscent of the Southern Rhône.

🍇 Syrah, plus up to 10% Marsanne and Roussanne

🍷 1983, 1985, 1988, 1989, 1990

🥂 Between 3-8 years

WHITE At their best, clean, rich and citrussy-resinous dry wines.

🍇 Marsanne, Roussanne

🍷 1984, 1985, 1986, 1989, 1990

🥂 Within 1-3 years

☆ Jean-Claude Boisset, Jean-Louis Chave, Pierre Coursodon, Philippe Faury, Bernard Gripa, Jean-Louis Grippat, Alain Paret, Coopérative de St.-Désirat-Champagne

ST.-PÉRAY AOC

A white-wine-only village curiously out of step with the rest of the area.

WHITE Firm and fruity, with good acidity for a wine from the south of the region, but usually lacking charm.

🍇 Marsanne, Roussanne

🍷 1984, 1985, 1986, 1989, 1990

🥂 Within 1-3 years

☆ J.-F. Chaboud

ST.-PÉRAY MOUSSEUX AOC

A *méthode champenoise* sparkling wine made from the wrong grapes grown on the wrong soil.

SPARKLING WHITE An overrated, dry sparkling wine with a coarse *mousse*.

🍇 Marsanne, Roussanne

The Southern Rhône

While the mellow warmth of the Grenache is found in most Southern Rhône wines, this district does not revolve round one variety. It is a blender's paradise, with a choice of up to 23 grapes, and, as a result, numerous red, white, rosé and fortified wines of various styles and qualities are produced.

THE SOUTHERN RHÔNE IS A DISTRICT dominated by herbal scrubland, across which blows a sweet, spice-laden breeze. This is a far larger district than the slender northern *côtes*, and its production is, not unnaturally, much higher. Allowing the north a generous 10 per cent of the generic Côtes-du-Rhône appellation, the southern Rhône still accounts for a staggering 95 per cent of all the wines produced in the region. Whereas the Northern Rhône is merely a few hundred metres wide in parts, the southern section is 60 kilometres (37 miles) across at its widest point.

Wines of the Midi or Provence?

There is no doubt that at least half of Southern Rhône is in what was once called the Midi, an area generally conceded to cover the *départements* of the Aude, Hérault and Gard. This fact is never mentioned by those intent on marketing the Rhône's image of quality, because the Midi was infamous for its huge production of *vin ordinaire*. The Rhône river marks the eastern border of the Midi and the most famous appellations of Châteauneuf-du-Pape, Muscat de Beaumes-de-Venise and Gigondas are geographically part of Provence, further east. Viticulturally, however, these areas do not possess the quasi-Italian grape varieties that dominate the vineyards of Provence and may therefore be more rationally defined as a high-quality extension of the Midi. Grenache and Mourvèdre are typical of the grapes that reign supreme.

THE SOUTHERN RHÔNE, see also p. 173

The wider southern part of the Rhône valley area stretches its fingers down towards Provence and eastwards to the Alps. It contains the reliable Côtes-du-Rhone Villages appellation as well as the illustrious Châteauneuf-du-Pape.

FACTORS AFFECTING TASTE AND QUALITY

Location
The Southern Rhône commences at Viviers, some 50 kilometres (31 miles) south of Valence, and runs south to Avignon.

Climate
The Southern Rhône's climate is unmistakably Mediterranean and its vineyards are far more susceptible to sudden change and abrupt, violent storms than are those of the Northern Rhône. The one common factor is the *mistral*, a bitterly cold wind that can reach up to 145 kilometres per hour (90 miles per hour) and is capable of denuding a vine of its leaves, shoots and fruit. Because of this, many *mistral*-prone vineyards are protected by poplar and cyprus trees. The wind can, however, have a welcome drying effect in humid harvest conditions.

Aspect
The terrain in the south is noticeably Mediterranean, with olive groves, lavender fields and herbal scrub amid rocky outcrops.

Soil
The limestone outcrops that begin to appear in the southern area of the Northern Rhône become more prolific and are often peppered with clay deposits, while the topsoil is noticeably stonier. Châteauneuf-du-Pape is famous for its abundance of creamy-coloured drift boulders, which range in size according to location, vary in depth from several inches to a few feet, and may or may not cover reddish alluvial soil. Stone-marl soils persist at Gigondas and weathered-grey sand in Lirac, Tavel and Chusclan, where the soils also incorporate limestone rubble, clay-sand, stone-clay, calcareous clay and large pebbles.

Viticulture and vinification
The vines are traditionally planted at an angle leaning into the wind so that the *mistral* may blow them upright by the time they mature. The south is a district where blends reign supreme. Even Châteauneuf-du-Pape is a blend – usually of four or five varieties, although as many as 13 may be used. Traditional methods of vinification are used on some estates, but modern techniques are an everyday occurrence.

 Primary grape varieties
Carignan, Cinsault, Grenache, Mourvèdre, Muscat blanc à petits grains, Muscat rosé à petits grains

Secondary grape varieties
Aubun, Bourboulenc, Calitor, Camarèse, Clairette, Clairette rosé, Counoise, Gamay, Grenache blanc, Grenache gris, Maccabéo, Marsanne, Mauzac, Muscardin, Oeillade, Pascal blanc, Picardan, Picpoul blanc, Picpoul noir, Pinot blanc, Pinot noir, Roussanne, Syrah, Terret noir, Ugni blanc, Vaccarèse, Viognier

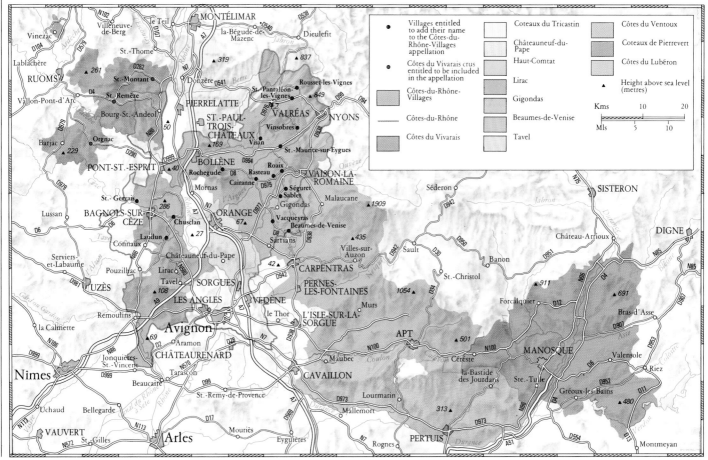

The wines of the Southern Rhône

CHÂTEAUNEUF-DU-PAPE AOC

The name Châteauneuf-du-Pape dates from the time of the dual Papacy. The appellation is well known for its amazingly stony soil. This reflects at night the heat stored during the day, but the size, type, depth and distribution of the stones varies enormously, as does the aspect of the vineyards. These variations, plus the innumerable permutations of the 13 grape varieties that may be used account for the diversity of its styles. In the early 1980s some growers began to question the hitherto accepted concepts of *encépagement* and vinification; winemaking in Châteauneuf-du-Pape is still in an evolutionary state. The steady decline of the traditionally dominant Grenache has speeded up as more growers are convinced of the worth of the Syrah and Mourvèdre. The Cinsault and Terret noir are still well appreciated, and the Counoise is beginning to be appreciated for its useful combination of fruit and firmness. The use of new oak is under experimentation and it already seems clear that white wine is better suited to it than red. If new oak is to have a role to play in Châteauneuf-du-Pape, it will probably have to be used in conjunction with stainless steel, not old oak, as the blending of wines matured in new and old wood can be disastrous.

The regulations for this appellation have a unique safeguard designed to ensure that only fully-ripe grapes in the healthiest condition are utilized. Between five and 20 per cent of the grapes harvested within the maximum yield for this AOC must be rejected and may only be used to make *vin de table*. This process of exclusion is known as *le rapé*.

RED It is impossible to describe a typical Châteauneuf-du-Pape, but it is warmer and spicier than the greatest wines of Hermitage and Côte Rôtie.

🍇 Grenache, Syrah, Mourvèdre, Picpoul, Terret noir, Counoise, Muscardin, Vaccarèse, Picardan, Cinsault, Clairette, Roussanne, Bourboulenc

🍷 1986, 1987, 1988, 1989, 1990

🥂 Between 6-25 years

WHITE Progress has encouraged fermentation temperatures to drop, so these full, rich, dry white wines have improved enormously in terms of freshness, crispness and quality.

🍇 Grenache, Syrah, Mourvèdre, Picpoul, Terret noir, Counoise, Muscardin, Vaccarèse, Picardan, Cinsault, Clairette, Roussanne, Bourboulenc

🍷 1986, 1987, 1988, 1989, 1990

🥂 Within 1-3 years (Between 4-10 years in exceptional cases)

Note: for my personal selection of the best wines of Châteauneuf-du-Pape *see* p.179.

COTEAUX DE PIERREVERT VDQS

Some 400 hectares (990 acres), best suited to the production of rosé.

RED Dull, uninspiring wines with little original character to commend them.

🍇 Carignan, Cinsault, Grenache, Mourvèdre, Oeillade, Syrah, Terret noir

🍷 1983, 1985, 1988, 1989, 1990

🥂 Between 2-5 years

WHITE Unspectacular, light, dry white wines with more body than fruit.

🍇 Clairette, Marsanne, Picpoul, Roussanne, Ugni blanc

🍷 1985, 1986, 1988, 1989, 1990

🥂 Within 1-3 years

ROSÉ Well-made wines with a blue-pink colour and a crisp, light, fine flavour.

🍇 Carignan, Cinsault, Grenache, Mourvèdre, Oeillade, Syrah, Terret noir

🍷 1985, 1986, 1988, 1989, 1990

🥂 Within 1-3 years

☆ Domaine de la Blaque

COTEAUX DU TRICASTIN AOC

An excellent appellation (for red wines), Tricastin was established as a VDQS in 1964, upgraded to AOC in 1973, and is now beginning to get the attention it deserves.

RED Very good wines, especially the deeply-coloured, rich, pepper-blackcurrant, pure Syrah wines that are a delight after a few years in bottle.

🍇 Grenache, Cinsault, Mourvèdre, Syrah, Picpoul noir, Carignan, and a maximum of 20% (in total) of Grenache blanc, Clairette, Bourboulenc and Ugni blanc

🍷 1983, 1985, 1988, 1989, 1990

🥂 Between 2-7 years

WHITE Produced in tiny quantities, these wines cannot be recommended.

🍇 Grenache blanc, Clairette, Picpoul, Bourboulenc and a maximum of 30% Ugni blanc

ROSÉ A small production of fresh and fruity dry rosé that occasionally yields an outstandingly good wine.

🍇 Grenache, Cinsault, Mourvèdre, Syrah, Picpoul noir, Carignan and a maximum of 20% (in total) of Grenache blanc, Clairette, Picpoul blanc, Bourboulenc and Ugni blanc

🍷 1985, 1986, 1988, 1989, 1990

🥂 Immediately

☆ Le Cellier de Templiers, Domaine de la Grangeneuve, Domaine Pierre Labeye, Domaine de la Tour d'Elyssas, Domaine du Vieux Micocoulier, Vignerons Ardéchois

CÔTES DU LUBÉRON VDQS

This wine is ripe for promotion to full AOC status. Much of the credit for this must go to millionaire Jean-Louis Chancel: his 125 hectares (310 acres) of vineyards at Château Val-Joanis are still very young, but the promise is such that this property has been described as the jewel in Lubéron's crown.

RED Bright, well-coloured wines with plenty of fruit and character, improving with every vintage.

🍇 Grenache, Syrah, Mourvèdre, Cinsault, Counoise, plus up to 50% Carignan and a maximum of 20% (total) Pinot noir, Gamay and Picpoul

🍷 1983, 1985, 1988, 1989, 1990

🥂 Between 3-7 years

WHITE The best white wines contain a small, but increasing, amount of Chardonnay, a grape not allowed in the regulations. This is an oversight that the legislators should amend if and when Lubéron is upgraded.

🍇 Clairette, Bourboulenc and a maximum of 30% (in total) of Grenache blanc, Pascal blanc, Roussanne and Ugni blanc

🍷 1984, 1985, 1988, 1989, 1990

🥂 Within 1-3 years

ROSÉ These attractively coloured, fresh and fruity wines are much better quality than most Provence rosé.

🍇 Grenache, Syrah, Mourvèdre, Cinsault, Counoise, plus up to 50% Carignan and a maximum of 30% (total) Pinot noir, Gamay and Picpoul

🍷 1983, 1985

🥂 Immediately

☆ Château la Canorgue, Château de l'Isolette, Clos Mirabeau, Château Val-Joanis

CÔTES-DU-RHÔNE AOC

A generic appellation that covers the entire Rhône region, although the vast bulk of wines actually comes from vineyards in the Southern Rhône. There are some superb Côtes-du-Rhônes, but there are also some disgusting products. The quality and character varies to such an extent that it would be unrealistic to attempt any generalized description. The red wines are the most successful, however, and many of the best rosés are superior in quality to those from the more expensive Rhône appellations. The white wines have improved tremendously in the last few years and continue to do so in encouraging fashion.

The varieties and percentages of grapes permitted are the same for red, white and rosé: Grenache, Clairette, Syrah, Mourvèdre, Picpoul, Terret noir, Picardan, Cinsault, Roussanne, Marsanne, Bourboulenc, Viognier, plus up to 30% Carignan and a maximum of 30% (in total) of Counoise, Muscardin, Vaccarèse, Pinot blanc, Mauzac, Pascal blanc, Ugni blanc, Calitor, Gamay and Camarèse

🍷 1983 (red and rosé), 1984 (white), 1985, 1988, 1989, 1990

🥂 Between 2-8 years (red), within 1-3 years (white and rosé)

☆ Domaine de Bel-Air, Brézème (Jean-Marie Lombard), Domaine de la Berthete, Coopérative Vinicole "Comtadine Dauphinoise", Cave des Vignerons Rasteau, Cave Coopérative de Vénéjan, Cave Coopérative "la Vigneronne", Château du Domazan, Château de Fonsalette, Château du Grand Moulas, Domaine de la Grand'Ribe, La Reviscoulado, Château du Prieuré, Domaine Rabasse-Charavin, Domaine de la Renjardière, Domaine du Roure, Château St.-Estève, Domaine du Vieux Chêne

CÔTES-DU-RHÔNE-VILLAGES AOC

Compared to the generic Côtes-du-Rhône, these wines generally have greater depth, character and quality. The area covered by the appellation is entirely within the Southern Rhône. If the wine comes from one commune only, then it has the right to append that name to the appellation. Gigondas, Cairanne, Chusclan and Laudun were the four villages that formed the original Côtes-du-Rhône-Villages appellation. Gigondas achieved its own AOC in 1971, but other villages have been added from time to time: there are now no less than 17 in the AOC.

RED These wines are mostly excellent.

🍇 A maximum of 65% Grenache, plus a minimum of 25% Syrah, Mourvèdre and Cinsault, and up to 10% (in total) of Clairette, Picpoul, Terret noir, Picardan, Roussanne, Marsanne, Bourboulenc, Viognier, Carignan, Counoise, Muscardin, Vaccarèse, Pinot blanc, Mauzac, Pascal blanc, Ugni blanc, Calitor, Gamay and Camarèse

🍷 1985, 1986, 1988, 1989, 1990

🥂 Between 3-10 years

WHITE These are improving (Vieux Manoir du Frigoulas being the best).

🍇 A minimum of 80% Clairette, Roussanne and Bourboulenc, plus up to 10% of Grenache blanc and a maximum of 10% (in total) of Grenache, Syrah, Mourvèdre, Picpoul, Terret noir, Picardan, Cinsault, Bourboulenc, Viognier, Carignan, Counoise, Muscardin, Vaccarèse, Pinot blanc, Mauzac, Pascal blanc, Ugni blanc, Calitor, Gamay and Camarèse

🍷 1985, 1986, 1988, 1989, 1990

🥂 Within 1-3 years

Continued overleaf

ROSÉ Rosé bearing the Côtes-du-Rhône Villages AOC can be very good.

A maximum of 60% Grenache and 10% Carignan, plus a minimum of 10% Camarèse and Cinsault and up to 10% (in total) of Clairette, Picpoul, Terret noir, Picardan, Roussanne, Marsanne, Bourboulenc, Vaccarèse, Pinot blanc, Mauzac, Pascal blanc, Ugni blanc, Calitor, Gamay, Syrah and Mourvèdre

1985, 1986, 1988, 1989, 1990

Within 1-3 years

☆ Domaine de Cabasse, Domaine le Clos des Cazaux, Cave Coopérative St.-Hilaire d'Ozilhan, Domaine Sainte-Anne, Vieux Manoir du Frigoulas

CÔTES-DU-RHÔNE BEAUMES-DE-VENISE AOC

Famous for its delectable, sweet, Muscat wine, Beaumes-de-Venise also produces a pleasant red wine with a good peppery-raspberry fruit flavour. Dry white and rosé wines are produced under the generic AOC.

☆ Château Redortier

CÔTES-DU-RHÔNE CAIRANNE AOC

An excellent source for rich, warm and spicy red wines that age very well. Cairanne and Vacqueras are the top two villages in the appellation.

☆ Cave des Coteaux de Cairanne, l'Oratoire St.-Martin, Domaine Rabasse Charavin, Domaine du Grand-Jas, Domaine des Travers

CÔTES-DU-RHÔNE CHUSCLAN AOC

Chusclan is situated just north of Lirac and Tavel, two famous rosé appellations and makes an excellent rosé. Most of the wines are red, and are in a good, quaffing style. The white is fresh, lively and reliable.

☆ Caves des Vignerons de Chusclan, Domaine du Lindas

CÔTES-DU-RHÔNE LAUDUN AOC

One of the appellation's four original villages, Laudun excels in making fine, fresh and spicy red wines. It also makes the best white wines in the *villages* appellation, and a small amount of delightful rosé.

☆ Cave des Quatre Chemins, Domaine Pelaquié, Domaine Rémy Estournel, Louis Rousseau & Fils

CÔTES-DU-RHÔNE RASTEAU AOC

This village is best known for its sweet Rasteau "Rancio" (see below) yet it produces nearly four times as much dry red, white and rosé. Its red is the best: a deep-coloured, full, rich and spicy wine that can improve for up to 10 years.

☆ Caves des Vignerons de Rasteau, Domaine de la Grangeneuve, Domaine de la Soumade, Domaine des Coteaux des Travers, Francis Vache

CÔTES-DU-RHÔNE ROAIX AOC

I have not encountered these wines but the Cave Coopérative de Roaix-Séguret accounts for most of the production, and Florimond Lambert is reputed to be a good grower.

CÔTES-DU-RHÔNE ROCHEGUDE AOC

Only the red wine of Rochegude may claim the *villages* appellation. I have encountered only the local *co-opérative wine*, but it is very good quality, well-coloured, soft and plummy. As at Beaumes-de-Venise, the white and rosé is sold as generic Côtes du Rhône.

☆ Cave Coopérative Vinicole de Rochegude

CÔTES-DU-RHÔNE ROUSSET-LES-VIGNES AOC

The neighbouring villages of Rousset-les-Vignes and St.-Pantaléon-les-Vignes possess the northernmost vineyards of this appellation. The wine is soft, quaffing and monopolized by the Cave Coopérative Vinicole de St.-Pantaléon.

CÔTES-DU-RHÔNE SABLET AOC

This village's soft, fruity and quick-maturing red and rosé wines are consistent in quality, and always represent good value.

☆ René Bernard, Domaine du Parandou, Paul Roumanille, Château du Trignon

CÔTES-DU-RHÔNE ST.-GERVAIS AOC

The valley vineyards of St.-Gervais are not those of the great river itself, but belong to the Cèze, one of its many tributaries. The red wines are deliciously deep and fruity, and the whites are fresh and aromatic with an excellent, crisp balance for wines from such a southerly location.

☆ Domaine le Baine, Cave Coopérative de St.-Gervais, Domaine St.-Anne

CÔTES-DU-RHÔNE ST.-MAURICE-SUR-EYGUES AOC

Light, easy-drinking red and rosé wines. Production is monopolized by the local *coopérative*.

CÔTES-DU-RHÔNE ST.-PANTALÉON-LES-VIGNES AOC

The neighbouring villages of St.-Pantaléon-les-Vignes and Rousset-les-Vignes possess the most northerly vineyards of this appellation. The wine is soft, quaffing and monopolized by the Cave Coopérative Vinicole de St.-Pantaléon.

CÔTES-DU-RHÔNE SÉGURET AOC

Seguret produces red wine that is firm and fruity with a good, bright colour. A little white and rosé is also made.

☆ Jean-Pierre Brotte, Domaine de Cabasse, Domaine Garancière, Domaine du Sommier

CÔTES-DU-RHÔNE VACQUEYRAS AOC

The rich, robust, warm wines can improve for twelve years or more.

☆ Domaine les Clos des Cazaux, Domaine la Fourmone, Paul Jaboulet Aîné, Domaine de Montuac, Château des Roques, Domaine de Verquière

CÔTES-DU-RHÔNE VALREAS AOC

Fine red wines with plenty of fruit flavour. A little rosé is also made.

☆ Domaine de la Fuzière, Domaine des Grands Devers, Le Val des Rois

CÔTES-DU-RHÔNE VINSOBRES AOC

Firm red wines of good quality and a little passable rosé.

☆ Domaine des Ausellons, Domaine du Coriançon

CÔTES-DU-RHÔNE VISAN AOC

Red wines of good colour and true *vin de garde* character, along with fresh, quaffing white wines.

☆ Cave Coopérative "les Coteaux de Visan", Domaine de la Cantharide, Domaine de la Costechaude, Clos du Père Clément

CÔTES DU VENTOUX AOC

Limestone subsoil produces a lighter wine than is normal for the Rhône.

RED The fresh and fruity, easy-to-drink reds are the best wines in this AOC.

Grenache, Syrah, Cinsault, Mourvèdre, plus up to 30% Carignan and a maximum of 20% (in total) of Picpoul noir, Counoise, Clairette, Bourboulenc, Grenache blanc, Roussanne, Ugni blanc, Picpoul and Pascal blanc

1985, 1986, 1988, 1989, 1990

Between 2-5 years

WHITE A little white is produced, but it is of minimal interest.

Clairette, Bourboulenc, plus up to 30% (in total) of Grenache blanc, Roussanne, Ugni blanc, Picpoul blanc and Pascal blanc

ROSÉ These wines' fresh character and deliciously delicate fruit can be pure joy on a hot sunny day.

Grenache, Syrah, Cinsault, Mourvèdre, plus up to 30% Carignan and a maximum of 20% (total) Picpoul noir, Counoise, Clairette, Bourboulenc, Grenache blanc, Roussanne, Ugni blanc, Picpoul and Pascal blanc

1985, 1986, 1988, 1989, 1990

Immediately

☆ Domaine des Anges, Cave Coopérative des Coteaux du Mont Ventoux, Domaine de Tenon, Domaine St.-Croix, Domaine St.-Saveur, "Vieille Ferme", Château du Vieux-Lazaret

CÔTES DU VIVARAIS VDQS

The *côtes* of Vivarais look across the Rhône to the *coteaux* of Tricastin. Its best *crus* (Orgnac, St.-Montant and St.-Remèze) may add their names.

RED These light, quaffing reds are by far the best wines in the district.

Cinsault, Grenache, Mourvèdre, Picpoul, Syrah and up to 40% (in total) of Aubun and Carignan. To add their names to the VDQS name, the *cru* wines must not contain Picpoul or Aubun, and the Carignan must be restricted to 25%

1985, 1986, 1988, 1989, 1990

Within 1-3 years

WHITE Mostly dull and disappointing, but Domaine Gallety makes a decent fresh and softly dry white wine.

Bourboulenc, Clairette, Grenache, Maccabéo, Marsanne, Mauzac, Picpoul, Ugni blanc. To add their names to the VDQS name, the *cru* wines must not contain Maccabéo, Mauzac or Ugni blanc

1983, 1985, 1989, 1990

Within 1-3 years

ROSÉ These pretty pink dry wines can have a ripe, fruity flavour and are generally better than the whites.

Cinsault, Grenache, Mourvèdre, Picpoul, Syrah and up to 40% (in total) of Aubun and Carignan. To add their names to this appellation, the *cru* wines must not contain Picpoul or Aubun, and only 25% Carignan

1984, 1985, 1986, 1989, 1990

Within 1-3 years

GIGONDAS AOC

An excellent appellation, producing some of the Rhône's most underrated red wines.

RED The best have an intense black-red colour with a full plummy flavour.

A maximum of 80% Grenache, plus at least 15% Syrah and Mourvèdre and a maximum of 10% (in total) of Clairette, Picpoul, Terret noir, Picardan, Cinsault, Roussanne, Marsanne, Bourboulenc, Viognier, Counoise, Muscardin, Vaccarèse, Pinot blanc, Mauzac, Pascal blanc, Ugni blanc, Calitor, Gamay and Camarèse

1986, 1987, 1988, 1989, 1990

Between 7-20 years

ROSÉ Good quality, dry rosé wines.

A maximum of 80% Grenache and a maximum of 25% (in total) of Clairette, Picpoul, Terret noir, Picardan, Cinsault, Roussanne,

Marsanne, Bourboulenc, Viognier, Counoise, Muscardin, Vaccarèse, Pinot blanc, Mauzac, Pascal blanc, Ugni blanc, Calitor, Gamay and Camarèse

🍇	1983, 1985, 1986
🍷	Between 2-5 years

☆ Domaine le Clos des Cazaux, Domaine les Gouberts, Domaine de Grand Montmirail, Domaine de Longue-Toque, Château de Montmirail, l'Oustau Fauquet, Domaine les Palières, Domaine du Pesquier, Domaine Raspail-Ay, De Rocasère, Domaine St.-Gayan

HAUT-COMTAT VDQS

In theory, red and rosé wines may be made from a minimum of 50 per cent Grenache, plus Carignan, Cinsault, Mourvèdre and Syrah.

LIRAC AOC

Once the preserve of rosé wines, the production of red is now very much on the increase.

RED In really great years, the Syrah and Mourvèdre can dominate despite their minority presence. This produces a more plummy and silky-spicy wine.

🍇	A minimum of 40% Grenache and 20% (in total) of Cinsault, Mourvèdre, Syrah, Clairette, Bourboulenc, Ugni blanc, Maccabéo, Picpoul, Calitor, plus up to 10% Carignan
🍇	1983, 1985
🍷	Between 4-10 years

WHITE A fragrant dry white wine.

🍇	A minimum of 33% Clairette, plus up to 25% (each) of Bourboulenc, Ugni blanc, Maccabéo, Grenache, Picpoul and Calitor
🍇	1985, 1986, 1988, 1989, 1990
🍷	Within 1-3 years

ROSÉ Production is declining in favour of red wine, but these dry rosés have a delightful fresh summer-fruit flavour.

🍇	A minimum of 40% Grenache and 20% (in total) of Cinsault, Mourvèdre, Syrah, Clairette, Bourboulenc, Ugni blanc, Maccabéo, Picpoul, Calitor, plus up to 10% Carignan
🍇	1985, 1986, 1988, 1989, 1990
🍷	Within 1-3 years

☆ Domaine de Castel-Oualou, Domaine de Devoy, Domaine les Garrigues, Domaine Maby, Gabriel Roudil & Fils, Château de Ségriès, Philip Testut, Domaine de la Tour de Lirac

MUSCAT DE BEAUMES-DE-VENISE AOC

The most elegant of the world's sweet fortified Muscat wines. Very little sweet Muscat was made prior to the Second World War. When the AOC was granted in 1945, the wine was classified as a *vin doux naturel*. The process by which this is made entails the addition of pure grape spirit, in an operation called *mutage*, after the spirit has achieved five per cent alcohol by natural fermentation. The final wine must contain at least 15 per cent alcohol, plus a minimum of 110 grams per litre of residual sugar. The Coopérative des Vins et Muscats, established in 1956, accounts for a formidable 90 per cent of the wine produced. It is often said that this wine is always non-vintage, but in fact 10 per cent is sold with a vintage on the label.

WHITE/ROSÉ The colour varies between the rare pale gold and the common light apricot-gold, with an aromatic bouquet more akin to the perfume of dried flowers than fruit.

🍇	Muscat blanc à petits grains, Muscat rosé à petits grains
🍇	Vintages mean little in this AOC
🍷	Within 1-2 years

☆ Domaine des Bernadins, Coopérative des Vins et Muscats Beaumes-de-Venise, Dom-ine de Coyeux, Domaine de Durban, Domaine de St.-Saveur

RASTEAU AOC

First made in the early 1930s, and receiving its AOC status on 1st January 1944, this was the first of the Rhône's two *vin doux naturel* appellations. In popularity and quality it is, however, second to Muscat de Beaumes-de-Venise.

RED A rich, sweet, coarse, grapey-flavoured concoction with plenty of grip, a rather awkward spirity aroma and a pithy, apricot-skin aftertaste.

🍇	A minimum of 90% Grenache, Grenache gris or Grenache blanc, plus up to 10% (in total) of Clairette, Syrah, Mourvèdre, Picpoul, Terret noir, Picardan, Cinsault, Roussanne, Marsanne, Bourboulenc, Viognier, Carignan, Counoise, Muscardin, Vaccarèse, Pinot blanc, Mauzac, Pascal blanc, Ugni blanc, Calitor, Gamay and Camarèse
🍇	Usually non-vintage
🍷	Within 1-5 years

WHITE/TAWNY/ROSÉ This wine does not have the grippy character of the red, but a mellower sweetness.

🍇	A minimum of 90% Grenache, (gris or blanc), plus up to 10% (in total) of Clairette, Syrah, Mourvèdre, Picpoul, Terret noir, Picardan, Cinsault, Clairette, Roussanne, Bourboulenc, Viognier, Carignan, Counoise, Muscardin, Vaccarèse, Pinot blanc, Mauzac, Pascal blanc, Ugni blanc, Calitor, Gamay and Camarèse
🍇	Usually non-vintage
🍷	Within 1-5 years

☆ Domaine de Char-à-Vin, Domaine de la Grangeneuve, Domaine de la Soumade, Francis Vache, Caves des Vignerons

RASTEAU "RANCIO" AOC

These wines are similar to the produce of the Rasteau AOC, except they must be stored in oak casks "according to local custom", which often means exposing the barrels to sunlight for a minimum of two years.

For details of Rasteau "Rancio" wines, grape varieties and vintages, *see* the entry for Rasteau AOC.

TAVEL AOC

Tavel is the most famous French dry rosé, but only the very best domaines live up to its reputation.

ROSÉ Some properties still cling to the old-style vinification methods and, frankly, this means the wines are too old before they are sold. The top domaines in the appellation make clean-cut wines with freshly scented aromas and fine fruit flavours.

🍇	A minimum of 15% Cinsault, plus a maximum of 60% (in total) Grenache, Clairette, Clairette rosé, Picpoul, Calitor, Bourboulenc, Mourvèdre and Syrah, and a maximum of 10% Carignan
🍇	1985, 1986, 1988, 1989, 1990
🍷	Within 1-3 years

☆ Château d'Aquéria, Domaine la Forcadière, Domaine de la Genestière, Prieuré de Montezargues, Seigneur de Vaucrose, Le Vieux Moulin de Tavel

A personal selection of the best wines of Châteauneuf-du-Pape

The author's *Premiers Grands Crus*

CHÂTEAU DE BEAUCASTEL

One of only three estates to utilize all 13 grape varieties, its vines are old with a very small yield of highly concentrated fruit. This property also produces the finest white wine in Châteauneuf-du-Pape.

RED Wonderfully deep-coloured, deliciously juicy wines with masses of plummy-ripe, spicy-blackcurrant fruit, capable of great complexity.

🍇	Grenache 30%, Mourvèdre 30%, Syrah 10%, Cinsault 5%, plus 25% admixture of Picpoul, Terret noir, Counoise, Muscardin, Vaccarèse, Picardan, Clairette, Roussanne, Bourboulenc
🍇	1984, 1985, 1986, 1988, 1989
🍷	Between 10-30 years

DOMAINE DU VIEUX TÉLÉGRAPHE

The style of Vieux Télégraphe has changed, but its quality remains high.

RED The warm, mellow, spicy glow of the Grenache is well-balanced by the Syrah and the Mourvèdre.

🍇	Grenache 70%, Syrah 15%, Mourvèdre 10%, Cinsault 5%
🍇	1984, 1985, 1986, 1988, 1989
🍷	Between 8-25 years

The author's *Grands Crus*

CHÂTEAU FORTIA

Formerly the property of Baron le Roy and now run by his son, the château also produces a fine *blanc*.

RED Well-coloured wines with ripe berry-fruit and a clean, spicy aftertaste.

🍇	Grenache 80%, Syrah 10%, Mourvèdre 8%, Counoise 2%
🍇	1981, 1983, 1985, 1986
🍷	Between 8-25 years

DOMAINE LES CAILLOUX

Run by the talented André Brunel, whose name is also worth looking out for on supermarket *cuvées*.

RED Full of colour and flavour, yet not without finesse. They are plummy with lots of smoky Syrah complexity.

🍇	Grenache 70%, Mourvèdre 15%, Syrah 10%, Cinsault 5%
🍇	1984, 1985, 1986, 1988, 1989
🍷	Between 10-30 years

CHANTE CIGALE

These wines are aged for longer than usual in *foudres* prior to bottling.

RED Nicely coloured wines, rich and spicy with a hint of smoky complexity.

🍇	Grenache 80%, Syrah 10%, Mourvèdre 5%, Cinsault 5%
🍇	1982, 1985, 1986, 1988, 1989
🍷	Between 8-20 years

CLOS DU MONT-OLIVET

These traditionally produced wines could be even better if bottling was carried out at the optimum time for every vintage.

RED Beautifully coloured wines with an extravagantly fruity bouquet and lots of elegant, ripe, cedary-sweet fruit.

🍇	Grenache 80%, Syrah 10%, Cinsault 5%, plus 5% of assorted varieties
🍇	1984, 1985, 1986, 1988, 1989
🍷	Between 8-20 years

CHÂTEAU LA NERTHE

Since this famous château was purchased by the Rhône *négociant* David & Foillard in 1985, the vineyard and winery have undergone considerable renovation.

RED These huge, dark, complex wines have a deep, tannic flavour.

Grenache 60%, Mourvèdre 30%, plus a 10% admixture of Syrah, Counoise, Muscardin and Cinsault

[19] 1981, 1983, 1985, 1986, 1988

Between 12-25 years

CLOS DES PAPES

This excellent property regularly produces some of the finest wines.

RED Deep, dark and delicious wines that are rich, ripe, fruity and spicy.

Grenache 70%, Mourvèdre 20%, Syrah 8%, plus 2% admixture of Vaccarèse and Muscardin

[19] 1984, 1985, 1986, 1988, 1989

Between 6-18 years

CLOS PIGNAN

It is unclear whether this is always the second label of Château Rayas, but it has an uncanny resemblance to its famous stable-mate in certain years. *See also* Château Rayas.

[19] 1981, 1983

Between 8-20 years

CHÂTEAU RAYAS

Many consider this to be the finest Châteauneuf-du-Pape. Its unique character can be attributed to its 100 per cent Grenache content, and to the very old vines that produce concentrated fruit.

RED A great Rayas bulges with ripe, spicy, berry-fruit and has a remarkable, sweet, herby-cedary complexity.

Grenache 100%

[19] 1981, 1983, 1985, 1986, 1988

Between 8-20 years

The author's *Premiers Crus*

CUVÉE DU BELVEDÈRE LE BOUCOU

Rarely seen outside the locality.

RED A deep-coloured wine of rich and warming flavour, full of summer fruits.

Grenache 80%, Counoise 15%, Syrah 5%

[19] 1983, 1985, 1986, 1988

Between 8-20 years

BOSQUET DES PAPES

A seldom-encountered, but consistently fine-quality, property.

RED Richly-flavoured wines that are easily accessible when young, but repay keeping.

Grenache 70%, plus 30% admixture of Syrah, Mourvèdre and Cinsault

[19] 1983, 1984, 1985, 1986

Between 7-15 years

DOMAINE DE CABRIÈRES

A very large and well-known estate to the north of Châteauneuf-du-Pape.

RED These wines are precocious and fruity, yet they have finesse and polish.

Grenache 55%, Syrah 10%, Mourvèdre 10%, Cinsault 10%, plus 15% admixture of Counoise and Muscardin

[19] 1981, 1985, 1986

Between 5-12 years

LES CÈDRES

I have encountered more than one *cuvée* of Châteauneuf-du-Pape from Paul Jaboulet Aîné, but this excellent wine is the most consistent.

RED The wine has a lovely warm, spicy-*cassis* fruit and a silky finesse.

[19] 1983, 1985, 1986, 1988, 1989

Between 5-20 years

CLOS DE L'ORATOIRE DES PAPES

This property always used to make an excellent traditional style of Châteauneuf-du-Pape, but its performance has been disappointing of late. I cannot, however, discard my affection for its old vintages and, therefore, grant it *Premier Cru* status on potential.

CHANTE PERDRIX

This property rigidly adheres to the best traditional methods of vinification.

RED Deep and dark-coloured wines that often seem broody in their youth, but blossom into one of the most exuberant of Châteauneuf-du-Papes.

Grenache 80% and Muscardin 20%

[19] 1981, 1983, 1984, 1985, 1986

Between 8-20 years

LES CLEFS D'OR

Fine wines of the traditional school, including a good Châteauneuf-du-Pape *blanc*.

RED Richly-flavoured wines that are colour, an opulent, plummy bouquet, and a distinctive flavour of damsons, cherries and other stone fruits.

Grenache 80%, plus 20% admixture of Syrah, Mourvèdre, Muscardin and Vaccarèse

[19] 1983, 1985, 1986, 1988

Between 8-20 years

DOMAINE DURIEU

A small, well-kept estate producing medal-winning wines.

RED The underlying toasty complexity of this silky-textured, plummy-flavoured wine gives it its character.

Grenache 70%, Syrah 10%, plus Mourvèdre 20% and Counoise

[19] 1983, 1984, 1985, 1986

Between 8-20 years

CHÂTEAU DES FINES-ROCHES

This famous property belongs to the *négociant* firm of Musset. Its quality suffered during the 1970s, but has been rapidly improving since 1981.

RED Fine-coloured wines that aim more for finesse than intensity of fruit.

Grenache 65%, Syrah 15%, plus 20% admixture of Cinsault, Mourvèdre and Counoise

[19] 1983, 1985, 1986, 1988, 1989

Between 6-15 years

DOMAINE FONT DU LOUP

An up-and-coming domaine making a very good traditional style of wine.

RED Well-coloured wines with a mellow bouquet and flavour of cherries, blackcurrants and raspberries.

Grenache 70%, plus 30% admixture of Syrah, Cinsault and Mourvèdre

[19] 1981, 1984, 1985, 1986

Between 7-20 years

DOMAINE FONT DE MICHELLE

A property run by two nephews of Henri Brunier, the owner of Domaine du Vieux Télégraphe.

RED Well-coloured, rich wines with a deep, spicy-blackcurrant bouquet.

Grenache 70%, Syrah 10%, Mourvèdre 10% and Cinsault 10%

[19] 1984, 1985, 1986, 1988, 1989

Between 6-15 years

CHÂTEAU DE LA GARDINE

Not one of the most consistent wines of the AOC, but it is excellent when it excels. The property also produces a fine Châteauneuf-du-Pape *blanc*.

RED Some vintages are light and insubstantial, but the best show a remarkable depth with smoky, plummy, toasty and spicy flavours.

Grenache 60%, Syrah 23%, plus 17% admixture of Mourvèdre, Cinsault and Muscardin

[19] 1980, 1981, 1985, 1986

Between 8-20 years

DOMAINE DE MARCOUX

An up-and-coming wine on export markets. The property also produces a fine Châteauneuf-du-Pape *blanc*.

RED Full, deep and solidly constructed wines with lots of spicy fruit.

Grenache 70%, Cinsault 15%, Mourvèdre 15%

[19] 1981, 1983, 1985, 1986

Between 8-20 years

DOMAINE DE MONT-REDON

This property makes wine of consistent quality, even in bad years.

RED These nicely coloured wines have good fruit, firmness and finesse, and can also possess a fine spicy, peppery, herby complexity in great years.

Grenache 65%, Syrah 15%, Cinsault 10%, Mourvèdre 5%, plus 5% admixture of other varieties

[19] 1984, 1985, 1986, 1988, 1989

Between 7-20 years

DOMAINE DE NALYS

An overrated property that produced a quaffing wine until 1985. It now makes much richer, quality wines.

RED The new style is rich, attractive and ripe, with underlying softness.

Grenache 60%, Syrah 12%, Cinsault 6%, plus 22% admixture of other red varieties

[19] 1981, 1985, 1986, 1988

Between 8-20 years

DOMAINE LE VIEUX DONJON

This is a rarely encountered, but truly exciting wine, from a small domaine.

RED Full, rich and warm wines, with heaps of ripe, blackcurrant flavour, and a delicious smoky, toasty complexity.

Grenache 80%, Syrah 10%, plus 10% admixture of other varieties (primarily Cinsault)

[19] 1981, 1983, 1984, 1985, 1986

Between 8-20 years

Other fine Châteauneuf-du-Papes: Père Caboche, La Reviscoulado, Domaine de la Roquette, Domaine de Monpertuis, Clos St.-Michel, Domaine de Terre Ferme, Cuvée du Vatican.

The Jura and Savoie

White wines dominate the produce of these vineyards set amid the ski slopes of the French Alps. Sparkling wines are the speciality of Savoie, while Jura can boast the rare, sweet *vins de paille* and the amazingly long-lived *vins jaunes.*

THE JURA IS DOMINATED BY the town of Arbois, a little alpine community reigned over by Henri Maire. His infamous sparkling "Vin Fou", or "Mad Wine", has no appellation and comes in various *cuvées:* some are better than others, but many taste the same. Despite the lighthearted approach to its consumption, "Vin Fou" has performed one admirable function; it has introduced drinkers to this district and its many better wines. This could not have been achieved by the *vins de paille* and *vins jaunes,* due to their scarcity and high price. The very sweet *vin de paille* or "straw wine" is so called because the grapes were traditionally dried on straw mats to concentrate the juice into a syrup. The *vin jaune* or "yellow wine" derives its name from the colour that results from its deliberate oxidation under a yeast *flor* when matured in casks that are not topped up for six years.

The vineyards in the area between Lake Geneva and Grenoble, known as the Savoie, should be far more of a sparkling success than they are. I cannot imagine a better way to promote these wines than through the Savoie's built-in winter sports trade. The only obstacle to their greater success is the failure of foreign wine merchants to import the wines in sufficient quantities.

FACTORS AFFECTING TASTE AND QUALITY

Location
Running down the mountainous eastern border of France, the Jura and Savoie are parallel to the Burgundy region.

Climate
The climate is continental, with hot summers and cold winters. The close proximity of two mountain ranges, those of the Jura and the Savoie, can provoke sudden changes, although these may sometimes be mitigated by the calming effect of lakes Geneva and Bourget.

Aspect
The vineyards of the Jura are situated on the lower slopes of the Jura mountains, the vines growing at between 250-500 metres (820-1,640ft) in height. The Savoie vineyards are lower-lying, although those of Bugey can be fairly steep.

Soil
The limestone of the Jura is generally mixed with clay over a subsoil of compacted marl. There are limestone and marl topsoils over a base of sandy and gravelly marls at Arbois and Château-Châlon and a limestone scree, calcareous sand and clayey sand with alluvial deposits at Bugey and Seyssel.

Viticulture and vinification
The Jura is famous for two special techniques: the viticultural practice responsible for *vin de paille* and the vinification procedure required to make *vin jaune.* For *vin de paille,* wicker trays or wire mesh may be used, but in most cases bunches of grapes are hung from the rafters of heated huts, after which the shrivelled-up, super-concentrated, raisin-like grapes produce an amber-coloured sweet wine of great potential longevity. *Vin jaune* is produced entirely from the Savagnin grape which, after a normal fermentation, is left to age in wooden barrels for six years with no topping up. A yeast *flor* develops similar to that in Jerez during the production of *fino* sherry and the result is not dissimilar.

Grape varieties
Aligoté, Cabernet franc, Cabernet sauvignon, Chardonnay, Chasselas, Chasselas roux, Chasselas vert, Etraire de la Dui, Gamay, Gringet, Jacquère, Joubertin, Marsanne, Molette, Mondeuse, Mondeuse blanche, Persan, Pinot blanc, Pinot gris, Pinot noir, Poulsard, Roussette, Roussette d'Ayze, Savagnin, Serène, Trousseau, Verdesse

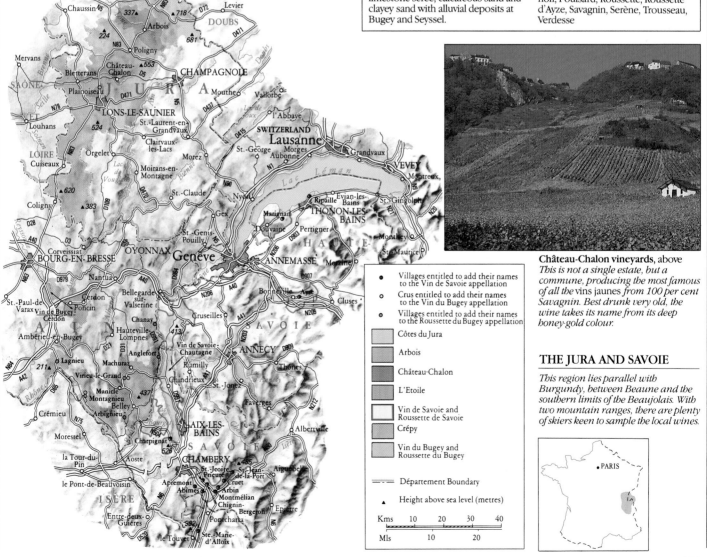

Villages entitled to add their names to the Vin de Savoie appellation

Crus entitled to add their names to the Vin du Bugey appellation

Villages entitled to add their names to the Roussette du Bugey appellation

Côtes du Jura

Arbois

Château-Chalon

L'Etoile

Vin de Savoie and Roussette de Savoie

Crépy

Vin du Bugey and Roussette du Bugey

Département Boundary

▲ Height above sea level (metres)

Kms   10   20   30   40

Mls   10   20

Château-Chalon vineyards, above
This is not a single estate, but a commune, producing the most famous of all the vins jaunes *from 100 per cent Savagnin. Best drunk very old, the wine takes its name from its deep honey-gold colour.*

THE JURA AND SAVOIE

This region lies parallel with Burgundy, between Beaune and the southern limits of the Beaujolais. With two mountain ranges, there are plenty of skiers keen to sample the local wines.

The wines of the Jura and Savoie

ARBOIS AOC

The best-known appellation of the Jura, it covers wines from in and around the town of Arbois.

RED Blended and pure varietal wines: the Trousseau is dark, deep and rich in flavour, with a sturdy, sometimes coarse, construction; the Poulsard is often added to the Trousseau to bring out finesse; wines sold as Pinot may be pure Pinot noir or a blend of both Pinot varieties, but are always light in character, with a rustic charm.

🍇 Trousseau, Poulsard, Pinot noir, Pinot gris

🍷 1983, 1985, 1986, 1989, 1990

🍷 Between 2-8 years

WHITE The light, fresh and fragrant Chardonnay wines are best. The Savagnin has a tendency to oxidize and is best suited to the famous local *vin jaune*.

🍇 Savagnin, Chardonnay, Pinot blanc

🍷 1983, 1985, 1986, 1989, 1990

🍷 Within 1-3 years

ROSÉ The Arbois appellation is famous for its firm and distinctive dry rosé wines made in the pale *vin gris* style.

🍇 Poulsard, Trousseau, Pinot noir, Pinot gris

🍷 1983, 1985, 1986, 1989, 1990

🍷 Within 1-3 years

☆ Lucien Aviet, Domaine de la Grange Grillard, Roger Lornet, Désiré Petit et Fils, Rolet Père et Fils, André & Mireille Tissot

ARBOIS MOUSSEUX AOC

A *méthode champenoise* sparkling wine seldom seen outside Arbois.

SPARKLING WHITE Fresh, honest, dry sparkling wines that show more potential than actual quality.

🍇 Savagnin, Chardonnay, Pinot blanc

🍷 1989, 1990, but often non-vintage

🍷 Within 1-3 years

☆ Fruitière Vinicole D'Arbois

ARBOIS VIN DE PAILLE AOC

Made from grapes that are dried to concentrate the juice, after which fermentation is long and the wine is given up to four years in wood.

WHITE These very sweet wines have old-gold, honey-gold and amber-gold colours, a distinctive and complex bouquet, a powerfully rich and nutty flavour and a surprisingly crisp finish, with a raisiny, apricot-skin aftertaste.

🍇 Savagnin, Chardonnay, Pinot blanc

🍷 1983, 1985, 1986, 1989, 1990

🍷 Between 10-50 (or more) years

☆ Fruitière Vinicole D'Arbois, Rolet Père & Fils

ARBOIS PUPILLIN AOC

A single-commune appellation for red, white and rosé wines made according to the same specification as Arbois AOC. *See* Arbois AOC, Arbois Vin de Paille AOC and Arbois Vin Jaune AOC.

☆ Désiré Petit & Fils, Overnoy-Crinquand, Domaine du Sorbeif

ARBOIS VIN JAUNE AOC

For details of production and style, *see* Château-Chalon AOC.

🍇 Savagnin

🍷 Only made in very good vintages

🍷 Between 10-100 years

☆ Lucien Aviet, Fruitière Vinicole D'Arbois, Roger Lornet, Henri Maire, Rolet Père & Fils

CHÂTEAU-CHALON AOC

The Jura's *vins jaunes* possess a unique style and Château-Châlon, (which is the name of a commune), is its most legendary exponent. It is normally fermented, then left to age in sealed wooden barrels for six years with no topping up. During this time, a *flor* develops – a skin of yeast that floats on top of the wine. The complex changes induced by the *flor* give the acetaldehyde-dominated *vin jaune* an uncanny resemblance to a *fino* Sherry, but the fact that it is not fortified (when Sherry is) and is made from a different grape produces its unique character.

WHITE *Vin jaune* is something of an acquired taste and should be drunk when very old. The vast array of complex nuances of bouquet eventually subdue and transmute the Sherry-like smell of acetaldehyde. It has a rich, fragrance and dry, alcoholic flavour.

🍇 Savagnin

🍷 Only produced in exceptional vintages

🍷 Between 10-100 years

☆ Jean Bourdy, Jean-Marie Coubert, Henri Maire, Château de Muyre, Marius Perron

CÔTES DU JURA AOC

This generic appellation contains some of the most widely encountered Jura wines. Its larger area of production seems to give it an edge over Arbois, the better known smaller AOC that falls within its boundaries.

RED Usually light in colour and body, with elegant fruit and a little finesse.

🍇 Poulsard, Trousseau, Pinot noir, Pinot gris

🍷 1983, 1985, 1986, 1989, 1990

🍷 Between 2-8 years

WHITE Unpretentious dry whites that can make an ideal accompaniment to the local cheese fondue or *raclette*, another melted cheese dish.

🍇 Savagnin, Chardonnay, Pinot blanc

🍷 1983, 1985, 1986, 1989, 1990

🍷 Within 1-3 years

ROSÉ These dry rosés have a fine and fragrant *vin gris* style, with solid fruit.

🍇 Poulsard, Trousseau, Pinot noir, Pinot gris, Savagnin, Chardonnay

🍷 1983, 1985, 1986, 1989, 1990

🍷 Within 1-3 years

☆ Luc Boilley, Jean Bourdy, Cellier des Chartreux de Vaucluse, Gabriel Clerc, Grand Vins de Jura, Caveau des Jacobins, Marius Perron, Rolet Père & Fils, Vichot-Girod

CÔTES DU JURA MOUSSEUX AOC

This the Jura's best sparkling wine appellation.

SPARKLING WHITE The persistent *mousse* of tiny bubbles, the excellent balance and surprising finesse of some of these wines illustrate their potential.

🍇 Savagnin, Chardonnay, Pinot blanc

🍷 1989, 1990, but often non-vintage

🍷 Within 1-3 years

☆ Hubert Clavelin, Gabriel Clerc, Château Gréa, Pierre Richard

CÔTES DU JURA VIN DE PAILLE AOC

Made from grapes that are dried to concentrate the juice, after which fermentation is long and the wine is given up to four years in wood.

WHITE These very sweet wines have old-gold, honey-gold and amber-gold colours, a full, distinctive and complex bouquet, a powerfully rich and nutty flavour and a surprisingly crisp finish, with a raisiny, apricot-skin aftertaste.

🍇 Savagnin, Chardonnay, Pinot blanc

🍷 1983, 1985, 1986, 1989, 1990

🍷 Between 10-50 (or more) years

☆ Rolet Père & Fils, Vichot-Girod

CÔTES DU JURA VIN JAUNE AOC

For details of production and style, *see* Château-Chalon AOC.

🍇 Savagnin

🍷 Only produced in exceptional vintages

🍷 Between 10-100 years

☆ Château d'Arlay, Jean Bourdy, Chantemerle, Hubert Clavelin

CRÉPY AOC

Well known to the skiing set, who enjoy this after a day on the *piste*.

WHITE A light, dry and fruity wine, with a floral aroma and a slight spritz.

🍇 Chasselas roux, Chasselas vert

🍷 1983, 1985, 1986, 1989, 1990

🍷 Within 1-3 years

☆ Goy Frères, Fichard, Mercier & Fils, Georges Roussiaude

L'ETOILE AOC

Named after the star-shaped fossils found in the local limestone.

WHITE These light and dry white wines have an aroma that can often reveal the scents of alpine herbs and bracken.

🍇 Chardonnay, Poulsard, Savagnin

🍷 1983, 1985, 1986, 1989, 1990

🍷 Within 1-3 years

☆ Château l'Etoile, Claude Joly, Domaine de Montbourgeau

L'ETOILE MOUSSEUX AOC

Not quite up to the standard of Côtes du Jura Mousseux, but this *méthode champenoise* has more potential than Arbois Mousseux.

SPARKLING WHITE Domaine de Montbourgeau makes a fine-quality, dry, sparkling wine.

🍇 Chardonnay, Poulsard, Savagnin

🍷 1982, 1983, 1985, 1989, 1990

🍷 Within 1-3 years

☆ Domaine de Montbourgeau

MOUSSEUX DU BUGEY AOC
See Vin du Bugey Mousseux VDQS.

MOUSSEUX DE SAVOIE AOC
See Vin de Savoie Mousseux AOC.

PÉTILLANT DU BUGEY VDQS
See Vin du Bugey Pétillant VDQS.

PÉTILLANT DE SAVOIE AOC
See Vin de Savoie Pétillant AOC.

ROUSSETTE DU BUGEY VDQS

The following villages have the right to add their name to this appellation, if harvested within an extremely low yield – Anglefort, Arbignieu, Chanay, Lagnieu, Montagnieu, Virieu-le-Grand.

WHITE Light, fresh and agreeable off-dry wines with few pretensions.

Roussette, Chardonnay

1983, 1985, 1986, 1989, 1990

Within 1-3 years

☆ Jean Peillot

ROUSSETTE DE SAVOIE AOC

The following villages have the right to add their name to this appellation, if the wine is 100 per cent Roussette: Frangy, Marestel (or Marestel-Altesse), Monterminod, Monthoux.

WHITE Drier than Roussette de Bugey, these wines have fine, tangy fruit.

Roussette, Mondeuse blanche, plus up to 50% Chardonnay

1983, 1985, 1986, 1989, 1990

Within 1-3 years

☆ Claudius Barlet, Marcel Bosson, Cave Coopérative de Chautagne, Noël Dupasquier, Danie Fustinoni, Michel Million-Rousseau, Château Monterminod, Varichon & Clerc

SEYSSEL AOC

Another favourite après-ski wine.

WHITE Delicious when drunk in their native surroundings, these fragrantly dry wines have a refreshing acidity.

Roussette

1983, 1985, 1986, 1989, 1990

Within 1-3 years

☆ Maison Mollex, Clos de la Péclette, Varichon & Clerc

SEYSSEL MOUSSEUX AOC

It was Varichon & Clerc that first carved a niche for Seyssel Mousseux in the export market.

SPARKLING WHITE With its full, yeasty nose, fine *mousse* and elegant flavour, the Royal Seyssel "Private Cuvée" is a yardstick for the rest of the AOC.

Chasselas, plus a minimum of 10% Roussette

1985, 1989, 1990, but often non-vintage

Within 1-3 years

☆ Royal Seyssel

VIN DU BUGEY VDQS

These are often pure varietals. The following villages may add their name: Virieu-le-Grand, Montagnieu, Manicle, Machuraz, Cerdon.

RED Fresh wines that range from the fruity Pinots to the rich Mondeuses.

Gamay, Pinot noir, Poulsard, Mondeuse, plus up to 20% (in total) of Chardonnay, Roussette, Aligoté, Mondeuse blanche, Jacquère, Pinot gris and Molette

1983, 1985, 1986, 1989, 1990

Between 2-8 years

WHITE Off-dry, fresh, light and gently fruity wines of some aromatic character.

Chardonnay, Roussette, Aligoté, Mondeuse blanche, Jacquère, Pinot gris and Molette

1983, 1985, 1986, 1989, 1990

Within 1-3 years

ROSÉ Light and refreshing, dry wines.

Gamay, Pinot noir, Poulsard, Mondeuse, plus up to 20% (in total) of Chardonnay, Roussette, Aligoté, Mondeuse blanche, Jacquère, Pinot gris and Molette

1983, 1985, 1986, 1989, 1990

Within 1-3 years

☆ Cellier de Bel-Air, Caveau Bugiste, Eugène Monin

VIN DU BUGEY CERDON MOUSSEUX VDQS

Only Cerdon may add its name to the Vin du Bugey AOC for *mousseux* wines. They can only be white and made by the *méthode champenoise*.

VIN DU BUGEY CERDON PÉTILLANT VDQS

Only Cerdon may add its name to the Vin du Bugey AOC for *pétillant* wines. They can only be white and made by the *méthode rurale*.

VIN DU BUGEY MOUSSEUX VDQS

These white wines are presumably *méthode champenoise*.

VIN DU BUGEY PÉTILLANT VDQS

Mostly drunk in local restaurants.

SEMI-SPARKLING WHITE Off-dry wines with a lively fizz.

Chardonnay, Roussette, Aligoté, Mondeuse blanche, Jacquère, Pinot gris, Molette

1989, 1990, but often non-vintage

Within 1-3 years

☆ Caveau Bugiste

VIN DE PAILLE D'ARBOIS AOC
See Arbois Vin de Paille AOC.

VIN DE PAILLE DE L'ETOILE AOC
See L'Etoile AOC.

VIN JAUNE D'ARBOIS AOC
See Arbois Vin Jaune AOC.

VIN JAUNE DE L'ETOILE AOC
See L'Etoile AOC.

VIN DE SAVOIE AOC

The wines in this generic appellation are made to a high standard and the following villages have the right to add their name to it: Abymes, Apremont, Arbin, Ayze, Charpignat, Chautagne, Chignin, Chignin-Bergeron or Bergeron (white Roussette only), Cruet, Marignan (Chasselas white only), Montmélian, Ripaille (Chasselas white), St.-Jean de la Porte, St.-Geoire Prieuré, Sainte-Marie d'Alloix.

RED Blends and single-variety wines; the blended wines are usually better.

Gamay, Mondeuse, Pinot noir, Persan, plus Cabernet franc, Cabernet sauvignon (Savoie), and Etraire de la dui, Serène and Joubertin (Isère), plus a maximum 20% (total) of varieties allowed in white Vin de Savoie

1981, 1982, 1983, 1985, 1986

Between 2-8 years

WHITE These dry wines are the best of the appellation, with Abymes, Apremont and Chignin the best villages. They are fine, rich and complex.

Aligoté, Roussette, Jacquère, Chardonnay, Pinot gris, Mondeuse blanche, plus Chasselas (Ain and Haute-Savoie), Gringet and Roussette d'Ayze (Haute-Savoie), Marsanne and Verdesse (Isère)

1983, 1985, 1986, 1989, 1990

Within 1-3 years

ROSÉ Attractive, light and fruity, dry to off-dry rosés made for early drinking.

Exactly as for red Vin de Savoie (*see* above).

1983, 1985, 1986, 1989, 1990

Within 1-3 years

☆ Single-*cru* specialists:
Louis Bouvier, Denise Cochet, Gaston Maurin, Cave Coopérative "le Vigneron Savoyard", Domaine de la Violette (for Abymes), René Bernard, Boniface & Fils, Louis Bouvier, Jean Masson, Jean-Claude Perret, Perceval Frères, La Plantée, Domaine de Rocailles, Cave Coopérative "le Vigneron Savoyard", Domaine de la Violette (for Apremont), Louis Magnin, Cave Coopérative des Vins Fins de Montmélian (for Arbin), Marcel Fert (for Ayze), Coopérative des Vins Fins de Montmélian, Marcel Bosson (for Chautagne), Hubert Girard-Madoux, Coteau De Tormery, Adrien Vacher (for Chignin), Cave Coopérative des Vins Fins de Montmélian, André Quenard & Fils, Raymond Quenard, Coteau de Tormery (for Chignin-Bergeron), Cave Coopérative des Vins Fins de Cruet, André Tiollier (for Cruet), Louis Magnin (for Montmélian)

VIN DE SAVOIE AYZE PÉTILLANT or MOUSSEUX AOC

Very promising, single-commune, *méthode champenoise* wines.

SEMI-SPARKLING WHITE Wispy-light wines with an Alpine-fresh, clean taste.

Gringet, Roussette, plus up to 30% Roussette d'Ayze

1989, 1990, but often non-vintage

Within 1-3 years

☆ Bernard Cailler, Michel Menetrey

VIN DE SAVOIE MOUSSEUX AOC

A very consistent and undervalued generic *méthode champenoise*.

SPARKLING WHITE These dry and delicately fruity wines have a fragrant aroma, fine acidity and a good balance.

Aligoté, Roussette, Jacquère, Chardonnay, Pinot gris, Mondeuse blanche, plus Chasselas (Ain and Haute-Savoie), Molette (Haute-Savoie, Isère), Gringet and Roussette d'Ayze (Haute-Savoie), Marsanne and Verdesse (Isère)

Mostly non-vintage

Within 1-2 years

☆ Cave Coopérative de Cruet

VIN DE SAVOIE PÉTILLANT AOC

A very consistent and undervalued generic *méthode champenoise*.

SEMI-SPARKLING WHITE Attractive, early-drinking dry wines with a gentle, light *mousse* and a fragrant flavour.

Aligoté, Roussette, Jacquère, Chardonnay, Pinot gris, Mondeuse blanche, plus Chasselas (Ain and Haute-Savoie), Gringet, Rousset d'Ayze (Haute-Savoie), Marsanne, Verdesse (Isère)

Mostly non-vintage

Within 1 year

☆ Dominique Allion, Michel Menetrey, Perrier & Fils, Varichon & Clerc

Southwest France

This region comprises many small, scattered areas that combine to produce a wide range of excellent-value wines with discernible stylistic influences from Bordeaux, Spain, Languedoc-Roussillon and the Rhône.

AT THE HEART OF THIS REGION IS GASCONY, the great brandy district of Armagnac. It was from here that d'Artagnan set out in 1630 or thereabouts to seek fame and fortune in the King's Musketeers. The narrow tracks upon which his eventful journey began still wind their lonely way round wooded hills and across bubbling brooks. Little has changed since Alexandre Dumas painted such a colourful picture of these parts, for they remain sparsely populated. Time passes slowly even in the towns, where the square is usually deserted all day long, with the exception of the five o'clock rush-hour that can last for all of ten minutes.

THE DIVERSITY OF THE SOUTHWEST'S APPELLATIONS

The southwest does not have a single wine of truly classic status, yet it probably offers more value for money and is a greater source of hidden bargains than any other French region. From the succulent, sweet Jurançon *moelleux* and Monbazillac, to the fine wines of Bergerac, Buzet and Marmandais, the revitalized "black wines" of Cahors, the up-and-coming Frontonnais, the tannic Madiran and the highly individual Irouléguy of the Basque country, this part of France represents tremendous potential for knowing wine drinkers.

Perhaps because it is a collection of diverse areas, rather than one natural region, the appellations of the southwest at first seem too many and too confusing. Even within one area there appear to be needless duplications. In Bergerac, for example, the dry white wines are relatively easy to understand, there being just two (Bergerac Sec and Montravel), but there are three possibilities for red wines (Bergerac, Côtes de Bergerac and Pécharmant) and a galaxy of sweet and semi-sweet appellations (Côtes de Bergerac Moelleux, Monbazillac, Côtes de Montravel, Haut-Montravel, Rosette and Saussignac). No wonder Bordeaux is such a minefield of confusing minor appellations, when even a comparatively small area such as Bergerac is so littered with them. It would surely be simpler to have a single Bergerac appellation to which certain villages might be allowed to add a communal name; if the same logic were applied throughout the southwest, more of its wines could achieve marketing success, rather than attracting occasional attention as hidden bargains.

SOUTHWEST FRANCE

This diverse region bridges the southwest corner of France. The area is mostly subject to the climatic influence of the Atlantic, but areas like Limoux are more affected by the Mediterranean.

Legend:
- Bergerac
- Pécharmant
- Côtes de St. Mont
- Côtes de Duras
- Côtes du Marmandais
- Cahors
- Côtes de Buzet
- Gaillac
- Irouleguy
- Jurançon
- Limoux
- Other AOC and VDQS Areas
- Département Boundary
- Height above sea level (metres)

Kms 10 20 30 40 50 60
Mls 10 20 30 40

FACTORS AFFECTING TASTE AND QUALITY

 Location
The southwest corner of France, bordered by Bordeaux, the Atlantic, the Pyrenees and the Mediterranean vineyards of Languedoc-Roussillon.

 Climate
The climate of southwestern France is Atlantic-influenced, with wet winters and springs, warm summers and long, sunny autumns. The vineyards of Cahors, Fronton and Gaillac are subject to the greater heat but more changeable characteristics of the Mediterranean.

Aspect
Mostly east- and east-through-to-south-facing slopes, affording protection from the Atlantic, in a varied countryside that can range from rolling and gently undulating to steep and heavily terraced.

 Soil
This collection of diverse areas not unexpectedly has a number of different soils: sandy-calcareous clay over gravel in the best vineyards of Bergerac; sandy soils on the Côte de Duras; calcareous and alluvial soils in the *côtes* of Buzet and Marmandais; gravel-clay and gravel crests over marly bedrock in the hilly hinterland of Cahors and alluvial soils peppered with pebbly quartz, limestone and gravel over a calcareous bedrock in the Lot valley; limestone, clay-limestone and gravel at Gaillac; sandy soils in Madiran, Tursan and Irouléguy; stony and sandy soils in Jurançon, with some limestone and clay at Limoux.

Viticulture and vinification
The viticultural traditions and techniques of vinification of Bergerac, Buzet, Marmandais and, to some extent, Cahors are similar to those of Bordeaux, while those in the other districts of this composite region are very much their own. Limoux still practises the ancient *méthode rurale* (*see* Vin de Blanquette AOC p.188), although the majority of the wines sold are pure *méthode champenoise;* Béarn, Gaillac and Jurançon produce almost every style of wine imaginable by numerous vinification techniques, including a variant of the *méthode rurale* called the *méthode gaillaçoise*, though winemaking in these areas is generally very modern; while the Basque district of Irouléguy remains stoutly traditional, allowing only the introduction of Cabernet sauvignon and Cabernet franc to intrude upon its set ways.

Grape varieties
Abouriou, Arrufiac, Baroque, Cabernet franc, Cabernet sauvignon, Camaralet, Castet, Chardonnay, Chenin blanc, Cinsault, Clairette, Claret de gers, Claverie, Colombard, Courbu blanc, Courbu noir, Cruchinet, Duras, Fer, Folle blanche, Fuella, Gamay, Gros mans[eng], Jurançon noir, Lauzet, Len de l'el, Malbec, Manseng noir, Mauzac, Mauzac rosé, Mérille, Merlot, Milgranet, Mouyssaguès, Muscadelle, Négrette, Ondenc, Petit manseng, Picpoul, Pinot noir, Raffiat, Roussel-lou, Sauvignon blanc, Sémillon, Syrah, Tannat, Ugni blanc, Valdiguié

Carcassonne, above
This impressive town was largely rebuilt during the nineteenth century. Close to the AOC area of Gaillac, its surrounding villages produce a red and rosé vin de pays, Coteaux de la Cité de Carcassonne (see also p. 198).

M. Germain of Château Bellevue-la Forêt, left
The owner of this recommended property, which produces Côtes du Frontonnais, samples the aroma of his fruity red wine, dominated by the round and rich character of the Négrette grape.

Côtes de Buzet vineyards, below
This good-value Bordeaux satellite is barely 15 kilometres (nine miles) from the Gironde département.

The wines of Southwest France

BÉARN AOC

A modest appellation that shines in the local Basque surroundings.

RED Fresh, light and fruity wines with a good balance, but lacking depth.

- A maximum of 60% Tannat, plus Cabernet franc, Cabernet sauvignon, Fer, Manseng noir, Courbu noir
- 1982, 1983, 1985, 1989, 1990
- Within 1-4 years

WHITE Light, dry and aromatic.

- Petit manseng, Gros manseng, Courbu blanc, Lauzet, Camaralet, Raffiat, Sauvignon blanc
- 1984, 1985, 1986, 1989, 1990
- Within 1-2 years years

ROSÉ Simple, fruity dry rosés with a fresh floral aroma.

- Tannat, Cabernet franc, Cabernet sauvignon, Fer, Manseng noir, Courbu noir
- 1983, 1985, 1986, 1989, 1990
- Within 1-2 years

☆ Coopérative Vinicole de Bellocq

BERGERAC AOC

This appellation adjoins Bordeaux; its wines can be mistaken for those from some of its modest appellations.

RED The best reds have a good garnet or ruby colour, fine distinguished fruit and a light and elegant balance.

- Cabernet sauvignon, Cabernet franc, Merlot, Malbec, Fer, Mérille
- 1983, 1985, 1988, 1989, 1990
- Between 2-8 years

ROSÉ Light, easy, attractive dry rosés.

- Cabernet sauvignon, Cabernet franc, Merlot, Malbec, Fer, Mérille
- 1985, 1986, 1988, 1989, 1990
- Within 1-3 years

☆ Domaine des Comberies, Domaine du Denoix, Domaine du Gouyat, Château la Jaubertie, Château la Raye, Domaine de Perreau, Château Puy-Servain, Château Vieil Orme

BERGERAC SEC AOC

These white wines must not exceed four grams per litre of residual sugar.

WHITE Dry Bordeaux-style wines.

- Sémillon, Sauvignon blanc, Muscadelle, Ondenc, Chenin blanc and up to 25% Ugni blanc (on the proviso that the quantity of Sauvignon blanc used is at least equal)
- 1984, 1985, 1986, 1989, 1990
- Within 1-3 years

☆ Château Bellingard, Domaine du Gouyat, Domaine du Grand Vignal, Château la Jaubertie, Domaine de Malfourat, Château Peroudier

BLANQUETTE DE LIMOUX AOC

An exceptionally fine *méthode champenoise* for such sunny southern vineyards.

SPARKLING WHITE These wines have the distinctive aroma of fresh-cut grass and a fine, dry flavour.

- Mauzac, Chardonnay, Chenin blanc
- Mostly non-vintage; vintages that are released are always good
- Within 1-3 years (up to 12 for vintages)

☆ Maison Guinot, Producteurs de Blanquette de Limoux, Domaine de Treilhes

CAHORS AOC

This famous "black wine" got its name from the Malbec, a grape that produced inky-coloured wines. With the introduction of the Merlot and the Tannat, the quality of Cahors improved dramatically after a period of decline, though it can no longer be described as the "black wine" of old.

RED Most Cahors have a deep colour with a blackcurrant tinge. They are full of fruit and have a good plummy, Bordeaux-like taste with a silky texture.

- A minimum of 70% Malbec, plus up to 30% (in total) of Jurançon noir, Merlot and Tannat
- 1983, 1985, 1988, 1989, 1990
- Between 5-12 years (20 in exceptional cases)

☆ Baldes & Fils, André Boulomie, Domaine de la Caminade, Château du Cayrou, Château de Chambert, Domaine Eugénie, Côtes d'Olt, Clos de Gamot, Domaine de la Pineraie, Domaine de Paillas, Domaine du Port, Clos Triguedina

CÔTES DE BERGERAC AOC

Geographically, there are no *côtes*; the only technical difference between this appellation and Bergerac is an extra degree of alcohol.

RED These should be richer and deeper than Bergerac AOC.

- Cabernet sauvignon, Cabernet franc, Merlot, Malbec, Fer, Mérille
- 1983, 1985, 1988, 1989, 1990
- Between 3-10 years

☆ Château Court-les-Muts, Domaine de Fonfrede, Domaine de Golse, Château le Mayne, Château la Plante, Château le Raz, La Tour de Grangemont

CÔTES DE BERGERAC MOELLEUX AOC

These white wines are always sweet.

WHITE Fat and fruity, semi-sweet or sweet wines with a soft balance.

- Sémillon, Sauvignon blanc, Muscadelle, Ondenc, Chenin blanc and up to 25% Ugni blanc (on the proviso that the quantity of Sauvignon blanc used is at least equal)
- 1983, 1985, 1986, 1989, 1990
- Between 3-15 years

☆ Domaine de Grange-Neuve, Les Hauts Perrots, Domaine de la Peyrières, Château de Ségur

CÔTES DE BUZET AOC

This super-value Bordeaux satellite is located on the northern extremity of the Armagnac region.

RED The best are always very good with considerable finesse and charm.

- Merlot, Cabernet sauvignon, Cabernet franc, Malbec
- 1982, 1983, 1985, 1986, 1988, 1989, 1990
- Between 3-10 years (15 in exceptional cases)

WHITE These dry whites are the least interesting wines in this appellation.

- Sémillon, Sauvignon blanc, Muscadelle
- 1984, 1985, 1986, 1989, 1990
- Within 1-3 years

ROSÉ Ripe and fruity, dry rosés.

- Merlot, Cabernet sauvignon, Cabernet franc, Malbec
- 1983, 1984, 1985, 1986, 1988, 1989, 1990
- Within 1-4 years

☆ Vignerons Réunis des Côtes-de-Buzet, Château de Gueyze, Château de Pardère, Château Pierron, Château Sauvagnères

CÔTES DE DURAS AOC

An appellation of increasing interest.

RED Light Bordeaux-style wines.

- Cabernet sauvignon, Cabernet franc, Merlot, Malbec
- 1983, 1985, 1988, 1989, 1990
- Between 2-3 years

WHITE Clean, crisp and dry wines.

- Sauvignon blanc, Sémillon, Muscadelle, Mauzac, Chenin blanc, Ondenc and up to 25% Ugni blanc (on the proviso that the quantity of Sauvignon blanc used is at least equal)
- 1984, 1985, 1986, 1989, 1990
- Within 1-3 years

ROSÉ These attractively coloured, dry, crisp, fruity rosés are firm and fresh.

- Cabernet sauvignon, Cabernet franc, Merlot, Malbec
- 1985, 1986, 1988, 1989, 1990
- Within 1-3 years

☆ Château Bellevue-Haut Roc, Berticot, Domaine de Ferrant, Domaine las Brugues-Mau Michau, Château de Laulan

CÔTES DE MONTRAVEL AOC

This wine must have a minimum of eight grams per litre of sugar and a maximum of 54 grams per litre.

WHITE These fat and fruity wines are usually produced in a *moelleux* style.

- Sémillon, Sauvignon blanc, Muscadelle
- 1983, 1985, 1986, 1989, 1990
- Between 3-8 years

☆ Château du Berny, Jean Bertrand, GAEC du Bloy, Cave Coopérative de Port-Ste.-Foy

CÔTES DE SAINT-MONT VDQS

This appellation is situated within the Armagnac region.

RED Well-coloured wines of full flavour and medium body.

- At least 70% Tannat, plus Cabernet sauvignon, Cabernet franc, Merlot and Fer
  Note: As from 1990, the Fer must constitute one-third of all the grapes other than the Tannat.
- Vintages are unimportant
- Between 2-5 years

WHITE Honest, fruity and dry wines with a soft, tangy finish.

- At least 50% Arrufiac, Clairette and Courbu, plus Gros manseng, Petit manseng
- Vintages are unimportant
- Within 1-2 years

ROSÉ Dry wines with clean, fruity flavour.

- At least 70% Tannat, plus Cabernet sauvignon, Cabernet franc, Merlot and Fer
  Note: As from 1990, the Fer must constitute one-third of all the grapes other than the Tannat.
- Vintages are unimportant
- Within 1-3 years

☆ Producteurs de Plaimont

CÔTES DU BRULHOIS VDQS

This VDQS was elevated from *vin de pays* as recently as November 1984.

RED Decent, if unexciting, Bordeaux-like wine, though more rustic in style.

- Cabernet franc, Cabernet sauvignon, Fer, Merlot, Malbec, Tannat

19 Vintages are unimportant.

↧ Between 2-4 years

ROSÉ Fresh and easy-to-drink dry rosé.

🍇 Cabernet franc, Cabernet sauvignon, Fer, Merlot, Malbec, Tannat

19 Vintages are unimportant.

↧ Within 1-3 years

☆ Coopérative des Côtes du Brulhois

CÔTES DU FRONTONNAIS AOC

An up-and-coming appellation situated just west of Gaillac.

RED These medium- to full-bodied wines have excellent colour and fruit.

🍇 Between 50 and 70% Négrette, up to 25% (in total) of Malbec, Mérille, Fer, Syrah, Cabernet franc and Cabernet sauvignon, plus a maximum of 15% Gamay, Cinsault and Mauzac

19 1983, 1985, 1986, 1989, 1990

↧ Between 2-8 years

ROSÉ Overtly fruity wines.

🍇 Between 50 and 70% Négrette, up to 25% (in total) of Malbec, Mérille, Fer, Syrah, Cabernet franc and Cabernet sauvignon, plus a maximum of 15% Gamay, Cinsault and Mauzac

19 1983, 1985, 1986, 1989, 1990

↧ Within 1-3 years

☆ Château Bel Air, Château Bellevue-la Forêt, Domaine Caze, Château Clos Mignon, Cave Coopérative Côtes-de-Fronton, Château Flotis, Domaine de Joliet, Domaine de la Colombière, Les Dauban

CÔTES DU FRONTONNAIS FRONTON AOC
See Côtes du Frontonnais AOC.

CÔTES DU FRONTONNAIS VILLAUDRIC AOC
See Côtes du Frontonnais AOC.

CÔTES DU MARMANDAIS AOC

Highly successful Bordeaux imitation, upgraded to AOC in 1990.

RED Fresh, clean and impeccably made wines.

🍇 A maximum of 75% (in total) of Cabernet franc, Cabernet sauvignon and Merlot, plus Abouriou, Malbec, Fer, Gamay, Syrah

19 1982, 1983, 1985, 1989, 1990

↧ Between 2-5 years

WHITE Soft, delicious, dry white wines.

🍇 At least 70% Sauvignon blanc, plus Ugni blanc, Sémillon

19 1985, 1986, 1989, 1990

↧ Within 1-2 years

ROSÉ Soft, ripe and fruity dry rosés.

🍇 A maximum of 75% (in total) of Cabernet franc, Cabernet sauvignon and Merlot, plus Abouriou, Malbec, Fer, Gamay, Syrah

19 1983, 1985, 1986, 1989, 1990

↧ Within 1-2 years

☆ Cave Coopérative de Beaupuy, Cave Coopérative de Cocumont, Domaine des Geais

CRÉMANT DE LIMOUX AOC

A provisional sparkling wine appellation introduced in November 1989. Producers will have the choice between this and Blanquette de Limoux (*see* page 186) for a five year period, after which a decision of which to keep will have to be made.

GAILLAC AOC

These vineyards are amongst the oldest in France, yet have only just begun to make their mark.

RED Most are made in the fresh but light, *macération carbonique* style.

🍇 At least 60% Duras, plus Fer, Gamay, Syrah, Cabernet sauvignon, Cabernet franc, Merlot

19 Vintages are unimportant.

↧ Within 1-3 years

WHITE These wines are light-bodied and dry, with a vital, fresh taste.

🍇 At least 15% (each or in total) of Len de l'el and Sauvignon blanc, plus Mauzac, Mauzac rosé, Muscadelle, Ondenc, Sémillon

19 Vintages are unimportant.

↧ Immediately

ROSÉ Honest, light and dry rosés.

🍇 At least 60% Duras, plus Fer, Gamay, Syrah, Cabernet sauvignon, Cabernet franc, Merlot

19 Vintages are unimportant.

↧ Within 1-2 years

☆ Cave de Labastide-de-Levis, Domaine Jean Cros, Domaine de Gradde, Domaine de Labarthe, Mas Pignou, Domaine de Mazou, Domaine de Roucou Cantemerle, Cave Coopérative de Técou

GAILLAC DOUX AOC

Naturally sweet wines that must contain a minimum of 70 grams per litre of residual sugar.

WHITE Sweet to very sweet wines of ripe-peach, or richer, character.

🍇 At least 15% (each or in total) of Len de l'el and Sauvignon blanc, plus Mauzac, Mauzac rosé, Muscadelle, Ondenc, Sémillon

19 1982, 1983, 1985, 1989, 1990

↧ Between 5-15 years

☆ Domaine des Bouscaillous, Domaine de Labarthe, Domaine de Mazou, René Rieux, Domaine de Tres Cantous

GAILLAC LIQUOREUX AOC
See Gaillac Doux AOC.

GAILLAC MOELLEUX AOC
See Gaillac Doux AOC.

GAILLAC MOUSSEUX AOC

Sparkling wine made by *champenoise* and *gaillaçoise* methods.

WHITE Fresh, fragrant and grapey with a fine natural sparkle.

🍇 At least 15% (each or in total) of Len de l'el and Sauvignon blanc, plus Mauzac, Mauzac rosé, Muscadelle, Ondenc, Sémillon

19 Mostly non-vintage.

↧ Within 1-3 years

ROSÉ Attractive, fresh and fruity.

🍇 At least 60% Duras, plus Fer, Gamay, Syrah, Cabernet sauvignon, Cabernet franc, Merlot

19 Mostly non-vintage.

↧ Within 1-2 years

☆ Château Clarès, Domaine Clement Termes, Jean Cros, René Rieux, Domaine des Terrisses, Domaine de Tres Cantous

GAILLAC PREMIÈRES CÔTES AOC

White-only wines from 11 communes. The grapes must be riper than for ordinary Gaillac AOC and the wine must conform to the technical requirements of Gaillac Doux.

☆ Domaine de Tres Cantous

GAILLAC SEC PERLÉ AOC

This style of Gaillac contains a small amount of carbonic gas.

WHITE Light, dry and aromatic wines.

🍇 At least 15% (each or in total) of Len de l'el and Sauvignon blanc, plus Mauzac, Mauzac rosé, Muscadelle, Ondenc, Sémillon

19 The most recent vintage.

↧ Immediately

☆ Domaine Jean Gros, Cave de Labastide-de-Levis, Cave Coopérative de Técou

GAILLAC SEC PRIMEUR AOC
See Gaillac Sec Perlé AOC.

HAUT-MONTRAVEL AOC

This must have at least eight grams per litre of sugar and maximum 54.

WHITE Fat, fruity and *moelleux*.

🍇 Sémillon, Sauvignon blanc, Muscadelle

19 1982, 1983, 1985, 1986

↧ Between 3-8 years

☆ Domaine de Libarde, Paul Marty, Château la Raye, Cave Coopérative de Port-Ste.-Foy

IROULÉGUY AOC

The local *coopérative* has a monopoly over this Basque appellation; luckily the quality is good to excellent.

RED These deep, dark, tannic wines have a rich and mellow flavour, with a distinctive earthy-spicy aftertaste.

🍇 Tannat, plus at least 50% (in total) of Cabernet sauvignon and Cabernet franc

19 1983, 1985, 1986, 1989, 1990

↧ Between 4-10 years

WHITE These modest, dry whites are the least interesting of this appellation.

🍇 Courbu, Manseng

ROSÉ This very fruity, dry rosé is best drunk very young and fresh.

🍇 Grape varieties conform to those for red Irouléguy (see above)

19 1983, 1985, 1986, 1989, 1990

↧ Immediately

☆ Cave Coopérative St.-Etienne-de-Baigorry

JURANÇON AOC

This wine was used at Henri de Navarre's christening in 1553.

WHITE The best have a fine, spicy and tangy bouquet and flavour, and can hint of pineapples and peaches, candied peel and cinnamon.

🍇 Petit manseng, Gros manseng, Courbu, plus up to 15% (in total) of Camaralet and Lauzet

19 1983, 1985, 1986, 1989, 1990

↧ Between 5-20 years

☆ Clos Cancaillau, Domaine Cauhapé, Cave Coopérative de Gran-Jurançon, Cru Lamouroux, A. Lonne, Clos Uroulat

JURANÇON SEC AOC

As for Jurançon, but with less residual sugar. The grapes may be less ripe. It is best drunk young.

☆ Domaine Cauhapé, Clos Mirabel, Cave des Producteurs de Jurançon, Clos Uroulat

LIMOUX AOC

Still version of Blanquette de Limoux.

WHITE Dull, foursquare, dry white wines, the best of which are a bit nervy.

🍇 Mauzac

MADIRAN AOC

Many domaines in this small AOC are trying new oak and there is a trend towards more Cabernet franc.

RED You literally have to chew your way through the tannin in these dark, rich and meaty wines when young.

🍇 At least 40% Tannat, plus Cabernet franc, Fer, Cabernet sauvignon

📅 1983, 1985, 1986, 1989, 1990

🍷 Between 5-15 years

☆ Château d'Aydie, Domaine Barréjat, Château de Gayon, Domaine de Maouries, Château Montus, Ets Nicolas, Cru de Paradis, Château du Perron, Domaine Pichard, Producteurs de Plaimont, Domaine de Teston, Vignerons Réunis du Vic-Bilh

MONBAZILLAC AOC

An excellent-value Sauternes-style appellation of Bergerac.

WHITE These intensely sweet, rich wines are of a very high quality.

🍇 Sémillon, Sauvignon blanc, Muscadelle

📅 1985, 1986, 1988, 1989, 1990

🍷 Between 7-20 years

☆ Château Bellevue, Château la Borderie, Château la Brie, Château Grand-Chemin-Belingard, Repair du Haut-Theulet, Château Monbazillac, Château Treuil-de-Nailhac, Vieux Vignoble du Repaire

MONTRAVEL AOC

The largest of the three Montravel appellations and the only one that can (and must) be dry.

WHITE Dry, crisp and aromatic Sauvignon-dominated wines.

🍇 Sémillon, Sauvignon blanc, Muscadelle, Ondenc, Chenin blanc and up to 25% Ugni blanc (on the proviso that the quantity of Sauvignon blanc used is at least equal)

📅 1984, 1985, 1986, 1989, 1990

🍷 Within 1-2 years

☆ Château de Berny, GAEC du Bloy, Marc Chavant, Château de Libarde, Cave Coopérative de Port-Ste.-Foy, Domaine de la Roche-Marot, Cave Coopérative de St.-Vivien

PACHERENC DU VIC-BILH AOC

A white-only appellation covering the same area as Madiran.

WHITE A wine with exotic floral aromas, a fruit salad of flavours and a soft, off-dry, semi-sweet or sweet finish.

🍇 Arrufiac, Courbu, Gros manseng, Petit manseng, Sauvignon blanc, Sémillon

📅 1985, 1986, 1988, 1989, 1990

🍷 Between 3-7 years

☆ Domaine du Bouscassé, Cave de Crouseilles, Laplace, Domaine de Teston

PÉCHARMANT AOC

The finest red wines of Bergerac.

RED All the characteristics of fine Bergerac, but with a greater concentration of colour, flavour and tannin.

🍇 Cabernet franc, Cabernet sauvignon, Merlot, Malbec

📅 1983, 1985, 1988, 1989, 1990

🍷 Between 4-12 years

☆ Château Champarel, Château Corbiac, Grand-Jaure, Domaine du Haut-Pécharmant, Clos Peyrelevade, Château la Renaudie, Château de Tiregrand

ROSETTE AOC

White wines only; they must contain between eight and 54 grams per litre of residual sugar.

WHITE Château Puypezat has a soft and delicately sweet flavour.

🍇 Sémillon, Sauvignon blanc, Muscadelle

📅 1982, 1983, 1985, 1989, 1990

🍷 Between 4-8 years

☆ Château Puypezat

SAUSSIGNAC AOC

This wine must have a minimum of 18 grams per litre of residual sugar.

WHITE Château Court-les-Muts is a very rich, full, fat and alcoholic wine.

🍇 Sémillon, Sauvignon blanc, Muscadelle, Chenin blanc

📅 1980, 1981, 1983, 1989, 1990

🍷 Between 5-15 years

☆ Château Court-les-Muts

TURSAN VDQS

Nearly all the wines are produced by Les Vignerons du Tursan.

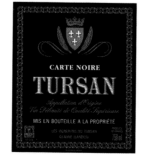

RED Well-coloured, rich and chewy or finer-flavoured and more aromatic depending on the dominant grape.

🍇 Tannat, plus at least 25% (in total) of Cabernet franc, Cabernet sauvignon and Fer

📅 Vintages are unimportant

WHITE Full in body with a solid, somewhat rustic, rich flavour.

🍇 Baroque, plus a maximum (in total) of Sauvignon blanc, Gros manseng, Petit manseng, Claverie, Cruchinet, Raffiat, Claret du gers, Clairette

🍷 Between 2-5 years

ROSÉ An unpretentious dry rosé with good juicy fruit flavour.

🍇 Tannat, plus at least 25% (in total) of Cabernet franc, Cabernet sauvignon and Fer

📅 Vintages are unimportant

🍷 Within 1-3 years

☆ Domaine de Castèle, Les Vignerons du Tursan

VIN DE BLANQUETTE AOC

Still produced by the ancient *méthode rurale*, it is this wine, not Blanquette de Limoux, that was invented by the monks at the Abbey of St.-Hilaire in 1531.

WHITE It is not as fine as Blanquette de Limoux, but it has merit and should be made commercially available.

🍇 Mauzac

VINS DE LAVILLEDIEU VDQS

Situated south of Cahors, this VDQS is eminently superior to the two above.

RED Nicely coloured, medium-bodied wines with a fresh and fruity flavour.

🍇 At least 80% (in total) of Négrette, Mauzac, Mérille, Cinsault, Fuella, plus up to 20% (in total) of Syrah, Gamay, Jurançon noir, Picpoul, Milgranet, Fer

📅 1983, 1985, 1986, 1989, 1990

🍷 Between 3-6 years

WHITE Dry, crisp, aromatic wines.

🍇 Mauzac, Sauvignon blanc, Sémillon, Muscadelle, Colombard, Ondenc, Folle blanche

📅 1983, 1985, 1986

🍷 Within 1-3 years

☆ Hugues de Verdalle

VINS DE MARCILLAC AOC

Rarely encountered wine from the northeastern borderland of the area.

RED Rough and rustic when young, these wines soften and take on a flavour typical of the Fer.

🍇 At least 80% Fer, plus up to 20% (in total) of Cabernet franc, Cabernet sauvignon, Merlot, Malbec, Gamay, Jurançon noir, Mouyssaguès and Valdiguié

📅 Vintages are unimportant

🍷 Between 3-6 years

ROSÉ Full, ripe and attractive dry rosés.

🍇 At least 30% Fer, plus up to 70% (in total) of Cabernet franc, Cabernet sauvignon, Merlot, Malbec, Gamay, Jurançon noir, Mouyssaguès and Valdiguié

📅 Vintages are unimportant

🍷 Within 1-3 years

☆ Le Cros de Cassagnes-Comataux, Pierre Lacombe, Cave Vinicole du Vallon-Valady

VINS D'ENTRAYGUES ET DU FEL VDQS

Rarely encountered wine from the northeastern borderland of the area.

RED Light, rustic reds best consumed locally.

🍇 Cabernet franc, Cabernet sauvignon, Fer, Gamay, Jurançon noir, Merlot, Mouyssaguès, Négrette, Pinot noir

📅 Vintages are unimportant

🍷 Within 1-2 years

WHITE Light, dry and crisp wines.

🍇 Chenin blanc, Mauzac

📅 Vintages are unimportant

🍷 Immediately

ROSÉ Light and fresh dry rosés.

🍇 Cabernet franc, Cabernet sauvignon, Fer, Gamay, Jurançon noir, Merlot, Mouyssaguès, Négrette, Pinot noir

📅 Vintages are unimportant

🍷 Within 1-2 years

☆ Henri Avallon

VINS D'ESTAING VDQS

Rarely encountered wine from the northeastern borderland of the area.

RED Light-bodied, fruity wine.

🍇 Fer, Gamay, Abouriou, Jurançon noir, Merlot, Cabernet franc, Cabernet sauvignon, Mouyssaguès, Négrette, Pinot noir, Duras, Castet

📅 Vintages are unimportant

🍷 Within 1-3 years

WHITE Simple dry white wines with a crisp flavour and a rustic-tangy style.

🍇 Chenin blanc, Roussellou, Mauzac

📅 Vintages are unimportant

🍷 Within 1-2 years

ROSÉ Pleasant and drinkable dry rosé.

🍇 Fer, Gamay, Abouriou, Jurançon noir, Merlot, Cabernet franc, Cabernet sauvignon, Mouyssagues, Négrette, Pinot noir, Duras, Castet

📅 Vintages are unimportant

🍷 Immediately

☆ Le Viala

Languedoc-Roussillon

These Mediterranean vineyards are gradually losing the cheap and not-so-cheerful plonk image, as an increasing number of domaines begin to bottle their own truly expressive wines.

WINE HAS BEEN PRODUCED IN Languedoc-Roussillon for more than 2,000 years, but only over the last ten have its growers seen fit to produce anything of interest apart from the unctuous *vins doux naturels*, once the Midi's only claim to fame. Urged by government schemes to upgrade their wines from *vin de table* to *vin de pays*, a new generation of winemakers began to emerge in the late-1970s. By planting better-quality vines and combining modern technology with the best traditional practices, including the use of some new oak, many exciting new wines filtered through to export markets by the early-1980s. As other growers take note of the increased prices that can be asked for expressive wines, so more and more are turning from selling in bulk to domaine bottling and there is a new-found pride amongst them.

Vineyards at Bages, above
The Mediterranean coastal vineyards of the Côtes du Roussillon, around Perpignan, are reputed to be some of the hottest in France.

FACTORS AFFECTING TASTE AND QUALITY

Location
A crescent of vineyards situated in southern France between the Rhône to the east and the Pyrenees to the southwest.

Climate
The Mediterranean-influenced climate is generally well suited to the vine, although subject to occasional stormy weather. Two winds dominate: the cold and parching *mistral* that blows down from the heights of the Alpine glaciers, and the wet and warm *marin* which comes in from the sea and can cause rot at harvest time. There are many micro-climates and the Coteaux du Languedoc, because it comprises a collection of isolated wine-growing areas, has many micro-climates within its own.

Aspect
Famous for its unending tracts of flat, *vin ordinaire* vineyards that stretch across the vast plains, the best sites of Languedoc-Roussillon, however, mostly occupy south-, southeast- and east-facing *garrigues* and hillsides, or nestle beneath protective overhanging cliffs.

Soil
In general terms, the plains and valleys have rich alluvial soils, while the hillsides are schist or limestone and the *garrigues*, or former moorlands, are comprised of stony, carbonaceous soils over fissured limestone. Within these generalizations specific situations vary enormously.

Viticulture and vinification
This remains the great *vin ordinaire* region of France, where everything is mechanized and the wines of the plain are farmed like wheat or corn. There is a trend towards developing single-domaine vineyards that have potentially expressive *terroirs*, growing classic varieties, combining various traditional methods of fermentation with modern *macération carbonique* techniques and, in an increasing number of instances, giving the wines a certain amount of aging in new oak.

Grape varieties
Aspiran noir, Aspiran gris, Aubun, Bourboulenc, Cabernet franc, Cabernet sauvignon, Carignan, Carignan blanc, Cinsault, Clairette, Counoise, Fer, Grenache, Grenache blanc, Grenache gris, Grenache rosé, Lladoner pelut, Malbec, Malvoisie, Maccabéo, Marsanne, Merlot, Mourvèdre, Muscat d'Alexandrie, Muscat blanc à petits grains, Muscat doré de Frontignan, Muscat rosé à petits grains, Négrette, Oeillade, Palomino, Picpoul, Picpoul noir, Roussanne, Syrah, Terret, Terret noir, Tourbat, Ugni blanc

LANGUEDOC-ROUSSILLON

This is the largest wine-producing region in France, with vineyards stretching from the Camargue to the Spanish border, and including what was the Midi.

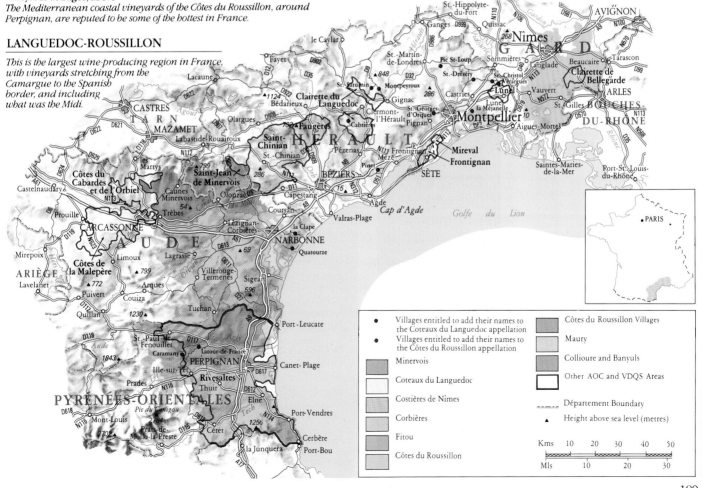

Legend:
- • Villages entitled to add their names to the Coteaux du Languedoc appellation
- • Villages entitled to add their names to the Côtes du Roussillon appellation
- Minervois
- Coteaux du Languedoc
- Costières de Nimes
- Corbières
- Fitou
- Côtes du Roussillon
- Côtes du Roussillon Villages
- Maury
- Collioure and Banyuls
- Other AOC and VDQS Areas
- ----- Département Boundary
- ▲ Height above sea level (metres)

Kms 10   20   30   40   50
Mls   10   20   30

The wines of Languedoc-Roussillon

Note: In the following entries, a wine described as a *vin doux naturel* (or VDN) is made from very ripe grapes and fortified with pure grape spirit after its fermentation has reached five or six per cent. It has the natural sweetness of the grape. To be labelled "Rancio" a VDN must be stored in oak casks "according to local custom", which often means exposing the barrels to direct sunlight for a minimum of two years. This imparts the distinctive *rancio* flavour that is so prized in Roussillon. The "Best recent vintages" (🖳 symbol) for VDNs are omitted because only the best vintages can survive the sort of treatment these wines receive, therefore any vintage offered by the growers listed should be superior of its type.

BANYULS AOC

The most southerly appellation in France, the vineyards of this *vin doux naturel* are literally a stone's throw from those of Spain.

RED The deepest and darkest of all VDNs, a rich, sweet, red Banyuls without too much barrel-age has a porty-fruitiness that is the nearest France gets to the great wines of Portugal's Douro region.

🍷➳ Between 10-40 years

WHITE/ROSÉ/TAWNY Like all VDNs that may be made in red, white and rosé style, they can all turn tawny with time, particularly "rancio" wines.

🍇 All wines: a minimum of 50% Grenache, plus Grenache gris, Grenache blanc, Maccabéo, Tourbat, Muscat blanc à petits grains, Muscat d'Alexandrie, and a maximum 10% (in total) of Carignan, Cinsault and Syrah

🍷➳ Between 10-20 years

☆ Robert Doutres, Cave Coopérative l'Etoile, Domaine du Mas Blanc, Domaine de la Retorie

BANYULS GRAND CRU AOC

As for Banyuls, but a minimum of 75 per cent is required for the primary grape varieties, and Carignan, Cinsault and Syrah are not permitted. The grapes must be destemmed and macerated for a minimum of five days. The wines are similar in basic character to those from the ordinary Banyuls appellation, but with distinctly more finesse.

☆ Hospices de Banyuls, Cellier des Templiers

BANYULS GRAND CRU "RANCIO" AOC
See Banyuls Grand Cru AOC.

BANYULS "RANCIO" AOC
See Banyuls AOC.

CABARDÈS VDQS

An obscure appellation north of Carcassonne.

RED The two wines below are well made, with elegant fruit and balance.

🖳 1983, 1985, 1986, 1989, 1990

🍷➳ Within 3-8 years

ROSÉ I have not encountered any.

🍇 All wines: at least 60% (in total) of Carignan, Cinsault, Grenache, Mourvèdre and Syrah, plus up to 50% Carignan (30% after the harvest of 1979) and maximum 30% (each and not more than 40% in total) of Aubun, Cabernet sauvignon, Malbec, Fer, Merlot, Négrette, Picpoul noir, Terret noir

🍷➳ Between 2-3 years

☆ Union Coopérative du Cabardès, Château de Pennautier

CLAIRETTE DE BELLEGARDE AOC

This appellation does not deserve its AOC status.

WHITE The two domaines below represent the modest height to which these unimpressive dry wines aspire.

🍇 Clairette

🖳 Vintages are unimportant

🍷➳ Before Christmas of the year of production

☆ Domaine de l'Armarine, Domaine St.-Louis-la-Perdrix

CLAIRETTE DU LANGUEDOC AOC

This appellation covers three basic wine types: natural, fortified and "Rancio". The "Rancio" must be aged in sealed casks for at least three years, and comes in both natural and fortified styles.

WHITE The natural wine is fuller and richer than Bellegarde, but has more alcohol and less sweetness in its "Rancio" form. The fortified version is off-dry to medium-sweet, with a resinous flavour that is stronger in "Rancio".

🍇 Clairette

🖳 1983, 1985, 1989, 1990

🍷➳ Between 2-5 years for naturally fermented wines, 8-20 years for fortified wines and "Rancio" wines

☆ Domaine d'Aubepierre, Château de la Condamine-Bertrand

CLAIRETTE DU LANGUEDOC "RANCIO" AOC
See Clairette du Languedoc AOC.

COLLIOURE AOC

This obscure but exciting AOC produces wines from the early-harvested grapes of Banyuls.

RED These deep, dark and powerful wines have a full and concentrated fruit flavour, with a soft, spicy aftertaste.

🍇 Grenache, Mourvèdre, with 25-40% (in total) of Carignan, Cinsault and Syrah

🖳 1982, 1983, 1985, 1989, 1990

🍷➳ Between 3-15 years

☆ Domaine du Mas Blanc, Celliers des Templiers

CORBIÈRES AOC

When this appellation was elevated to full AOC status in December 1985, its area of production was reduced from 42,000 hectares (104,000 acres) to 23,000 hectares (57,000 acres). The top estates often use *macération carbonique*, followed by 12 months or so in new oak and the results can be stunningly successful.

RED These wines have an excellent colour, a full, spicy-fruity nose, and a creamy-clean, soft palate that often hints of cherries, raspberries and vanilla.

🍇 A maximum of 70% Carignan, plus Grenache, Lladoner pelut, Mourvèdre, Picpoul, Terret, Syrah, Cinsault, Maccabéo, Bourboulenc, Grenache gris

🖳 1983, 1985, 1986, 1989, 1990

🍷➳ Between 2-5 years (3-8 years in exceptional cases)

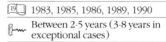

WHITE A soft, almost clinically clean, dry wine that has acquired a more aromatic character in recent vintages, but should be more expressive. There have been some successful experiments with oak-fermented wine.

🍇 Bourboulenc, Clairette, Grenache, Maccabéo, Muscat, Picpoul, Terret

🖳 1985, 1986, 1989, 1990

🍷➳ Within 1-3 years

ROSÉ The best of these dry wines have an attractive colour and a pleasant, floral aroma, but are nothing special.

🍇 Carignan, Grenache, Lladoner pelut, Mourvèdre, Picpoul, Terret, Syrah, Cinsault, Maccabéo, Bourboulenc, Grenache gris

🖳 1983, 1985, 1986, 1989, 1990

🍷➳ Within 1-3 years

☆ Château Aiguilloux, Château la Baronne, Château de Caraguilhes, Château les Ollieux, Château l'Etang des Colombes, Château Hélène, Château de Lastours, Cave Coopérative de Paziols, Château de Quéribus, Château St.-Auriol, Château de Vaugelas, Domaine de Villemajou, Domaine de la Voulte-Gasparets

COSTIÈRES DE NÎMES VDQS

Formerly Costières du Gard, this appellation's average quality is better than many a lacklustre AOC.

RED Simple, light and honestly fruity wines are the norm, yet the best have a round, aromatic and spicy character.

🖳 1983, 1985, 1986, 1989, 1990

🍷➳ Between 2-3 years (average wines), 3-8 years (better *cuvées*)

WHITE Fresh, soft, but uninspiring.

🖳 Vintages are unimportant

🍷➳ Within 1-2 years

ROSÉ Good-value dry rosé with a delightful colour and ripe fruit.

🍇 A maximum of 50% Carignan, plus Terret noir, Aspiran noir, Aspiran gris, Cinsault, Mourvèdre, Grenache, Syrah, Oeillade, Counoise, Clairette, Grenache blanc, Maccabéo, Malvoisie, Marsanne, Muscat blanc, Picpoul, Roussanne, Terret, Ugni blac

🖳 Vintages are unimportant

🍷➳ Within 1-2 years

☆ Domaine de l'Amarine, Château Belle-Coste, Château de Campuget, Cave Coopérative Costières de Beauvoisin, Domaine de Mourier, Ets Nicolas, Domaine St.-Louis-la-Perdrix, Château de la Tuilerie

COTEAUX DU LANGUEDOC AOC

This appellation consists of a collection of areas strung out across three *départements*. The quality is consistent, so the various vintages are of little consequence.

RED Full and honest red wines that make excellent everyday drinking.

🍇 A 50% maximum (each) of Carignan and Cinsault; a 10% minimum (in total) of Mourvèdre and Syrah; a 20% minimum (in total) of Grenache and Lladoner pelut; plus up to 10% (in total) of Counoise, Grenache rosé, Terret noir and Picpoul noir

🍷➳ Within 1-4 years

ROSÉ These dry rosés have good fruit and are far more enjoyable than many a pricey Provence rosé.

🍇 As for the red, plus a maximum 10% (in total) of Picpoul, Bourboulenc, Carignan blanc, Clairette, Maccabéo, Terret blanc and Ugni blanc

🍷➳ Within 1-2 years

☆ Château Carrion-Nizas, domaine de la Coste, Domaine du Daumas Gassac (technically a *vin de pay*, but in reality, one of the greatest wines of France), Domaine de Langlade, Prieuré St.-Jean de Bébian, Château St.-Ferreol

COTEAUX DU LANGUEDOC (VILLAGE NAME) AOC

Except where stated, the wines bearing the names of the following villages conform to the requirements of Coteaux du Languedoc AOC.

CABRIÈRES AOC

A single commune that produces a fine, firm and racy rosé. A little red is also produced. Its *vin vermeil* is best known and so-called because of its vivid vermilion colour.

☆ Coopérative "les Coteaux-de-Cabrières", Domaine du Temple

LA CLAPE AOC

Red, white and rosé wines from five communes in the Aude *département*, including one of the only two white wines allowed under the Coteaux du Languedoc appellation. White Clape can be full, fine and golden or firm, with an attractive Mediterranean spice and capable of aging, while the rosé has a refreshing flavour.

☆ Robert Buttero, Château de Complazens, Château Moujan, Château Pech-Redon, Domaine de la Rivière-le-Haut, Domaine de Vires, Château de Ricardelle de la Clape, Château Rouquette-sur-Mers, Château de Salles, Domaine de Vires

MONTPEYROUX AOC

The fine style of these red and rosé wines is firm and somewhat rustic, but honest and pleasing.

☆ Cave Coopérative "les Coteaux du Castellas"

LA MÉJANELLE AOC

Rosé is permitted, but this AOC produces mostly red wines from an area that covers four communes.

☆ Château de Flaugergues

PIC-ST.-LOUP AOC

Red, rosé and white wines from 12 communes in the vicinity of the *pic*, or peak, in Hérault and one in Gard.

☆ Cave Coopérative Coteaux de Montferrand, Domaine de la Roque, Coopérative de Valflaunes

PINET AOC

Red, white and rosé wines from six communes may be made, although I have only encountered the white. Made from 100 per cent Picpoul it is lively if young, but quickly tires.

☆ Château de Pinet

QUATOURZE AOC

Rather stern red and rosé wines, the best can fill out and soften up with a few years in bottle.

☆ Château Notre Dame

ST.-CHRISTOL AOC

The calcareous-clay soil of St.-Christol produces ripe and well-balanced red and rosé wines that may also be sold as Coteaux de St.-Christol.

☆ Gabriel Martin, Cave Coopérative de St.-Christol

ST.-DRÉZÉRY AOC

Both red and rosé wines are allowed. I have only encountered reds, and these have been modest in quality.

ST.-GEORGES-D'ORQUES AOC

Mostly red wines, which can be well-coloured and fine-flavoured, but also some rosé, produced in an area covering five communes.

☆ Château de l'Engarran, Coopérative de St.-Georges-d'Orques

ST.-SATURNIN AOC

Named after the first bishop of Toulouse, these red and rosé wines come from three communes in the foothills of the Cévennes Mountains. The red is deep-coloured, fine and full-flavoured. A *vin d'une nuit*, macerated for one night only, is also made.

☆ Cave Coopérative de St.-Saturnin

VÉRARGUES AOC

A large production of quaffing, but otherwise unexceptional red and rosé wines from nine communes, four of which also represent the Muscat de Lunel appellation.

CÔTES DE LA MALEPÈRE VDQS

This appellation has a range of permitted grape varieties that is perfectly expressive of its southern location.

RED Well-coloured wines of medium to full body, with elegant, spicy fruit.

🍇 Up to 60% (each) of Merlot, Malbec, and Cinsault, plus a 30% maximum (in total) of Cabernet sauvignon, Cabernet franc, Grenache, Lladoner pelut, Syrah

🍷 1983, 1985, 1986, 1989, 1990

🍴 Between 3-7 years

ROSÉ These attractive dry rosés are totally different to the red, due to the use of the mellow Grenache.

🍇 Cinsault, Grenache, Lladoner pelut, plus a 30% maximum (in total) of Merlot, Cabernet sauvignon, Cabernet franc, Syrah

🍷 1983, 1985, 1986, 1989, 1990

🍴 Within 1-3 years

☆ Domaine de Foucauld, Domaine de Fournery, Château Guilhem, Château de Lamothe, Château de Malvies-Guilhem

CÔTES DU CABARDÈS ET DE L'ORBIEL VDQS
See Cabardès VDQS.

CÔTES DU ROUSSILLON AOC

Situated south of Corbières, this large appellation has begun to shrug off the sort of reputation that typified the wines of the Midi.

RED The best of these wines have a good colour, a full bouquet and a generosity of southern fruit, with just the tiniest hint of vanilla and spice.

🍇 Up to 70% Carignan, at least 10% (in total) of Syrah and Mourvèdre, a maximum of 10% Maccabéo, plus Cinsault, Grenache, Lladoner pelut
Note: No two varieties may exceed 90%

🍷 1980, 1981, 1982, 1983, 1985, 1986, 1989, 1990

🍴 Between 3-8 years

WHITE The best of these fresh and floral wines can be enjoyed for their unctuous fat quality, but lack acidity.

🍇 Maccabéo, Tourbat

🍷 Vintages are unimportant.

🍴 Within 1-2 years

ROSÉ Fresh and attractive dry wines.

🍇 Up to 70% Carignan, at least 10% (in total) of Syrah and Mourvèdre, a maximum of 10% Maccabéo, plus Cinsault, Grenache, Lladoner pelut
Note: No two varieties may exceed 90%.

🍷 Vintages are unimportant

🍴 Within 1-2 years

☆ Cave des Vignerons de Baïxas, Coopérative Vinicole Bélesta, Caves Coopérative les Vignerons Catalans, Cazes Frères, Domaine Jammes, Château de Jau, Jaubert & Noury, SCV de Lesquerde, Montalba-le-Château, Mas Rancoure, Rasigueres, Domaine St.-Luc, Domaine Sarda-Malet, Taichac, Terrassous

CÔTES DU ROUSSILLON VILLAGES AOC

This appellation covers red wines from 25 villages. For grape varieties and vintages *see* Côtes du Roussillon.

RED These wines are good value for money, with more character and finesse than basic Côtes du Roussillon.

☆ Vignerons de Bélesta-de-la-Frontière, Caves Coopérative les Vignerons Catalans, Cazes Frères, Maitres Vignerons de Tautavel, Cave Coopérative de Planezes

CÔTES DU ROUSSILLON VILLAGES CARAMANY AOC

This super-value red wine conforms to the requirements of Côtes du Roussillon Villages.

RED Simply the fullest, richest and longest-living wines of Roussillon.

🍷 1980, 1981, 1982, 1983, 1985, 1986, 1989, 1990

🍴 Between 3-15 years

☆ Caves Coopérative les Vignerons Catalans

CÔTES DU ROUSSILLON VILLAGES LATOUR DE FRANCE AOC

This fine-value red wine conforms to the requirements of Côtes du Roussillon Villages.

RED Full in colour and body, these fine-value wines have a fruity flavour.

🍷 1980, 1981, 1982, 1983, 1985, 1986, 1989, 1990

🍴 Between 3-15 years

☆ Cave Coopérative Latour-de-France

FAUGÈRES AOC

Faugères is a fair-sized, yet obscure and overlooked appellation.

RED These rustic wines have a deep colour and are heavy with the spicy, warm flavours of Cinsault and Carignan.

🍷 1982, 1983, 1985, 1989, 1990

🍴 Between 3-10 years

ROSÉ Small production of attractively coloured, ripe and fruity dry rosés.

🍇 All wines: Cinsault, plus up to 50% Carignan, at least 10% (in total) of Grenache and Lladoner pelut, and a minimum of 5% (in total) of Mourvèdre and Syrah

🍷 1982, 1983, 1985, 1989, 1990

🍴 Between 3-10 years

☆ Domaine de Fraisse, Château Haut-Fabrègues, Cave Coopérative de Laurens

FITOU AOC

Since it was made an AOC in April 1948, Fitou had been fast asleep, but wine buyers beat a path to its desolate door in the early 1980s and it is now the fastest-rising star in the Mediterranean firmament. *Continued overleaf.*

RED Even at the lowest level, these wines have a fine colour and a spicy warmth of Grenache that curbs and softens the concentrated fruit and tannin of low-yielding Carignan.

🍇 Carignan, Grenache, and Lladoner pelut must account for at least 90% of the wine (the Carignan being restricted to 75%), plus up to 10% Cinsault, Maccabéo, Mourvèdre, Syrah, Terret noir

📅 1983, 1985, 1986, 1989, 1990

🍷 Between 3-6 years (4-10 years in exceptional cases)

☆ Caves du Mont-Tauch, Château de Nouvelles, Coopérative Pilote de Villeneuve, Producteurs Réunis VVO, Val d'Orbieu

FRONTIGNAN AOC
See Muscat de Frontignan AOC.

GRAND ROUSSILLON AOC

This should appear in the record books as the largest appellation producing the least wine. Grand Roussillon includes 100 communes, yet produces, in 1985 for example, as little as 30 hectolitres (330 cases). Apparently this appellation is used as a sort of *sous-marque* for the inferior wines produced by the better VDNs within its boundaries.

GRAND ROUSSILLON "RANCIO" AOC
See Grand Roussillon AOC.

MAURY AOC

Despite the long list of possibilities, these fortified wines are mostly pure Grenache.

RED/WHITE/ROSÉ/TAWNY These are grouped together because the reds are pink/tawny and I have not tasted the whites. Pale and intricate wines, they have a curious combination of tangy, toasty berry flavours.

🍇 All wines: at least 50% Grenache noir, plus Grenache gris, Grenache blanc, Muscat à petits grains, Muscat d'Alexandrie, Maccabéo, Tourbat, and a combined maximum of 10% of Carignan, Cinsault, Syrah and Palomino (called Listan in Roussillon)

🍷 Between 10-30 years

☆ Mas Amiel, Cave Jean-Louis Lafage, Les Vignerons de Maury

MAURY "RANCIO" AOC
See Maury AOC.

MINERVOIS AOC

The rocky Minervois area has the typically hot and arid air of southern France. It was elevated to full AOC status in February 1985.

RED At worst, these wines are rough and ready for AOC, but some of the best domaines also produce *vins de pays* that is better than the Minervois of other properties.

🍇 A maximum of 70% (60% as from 1990) Carignan, plus Cinsault, Picpoul noir, Terret noir, Aspiran noir and a minimum of 20% (30% as from 1990) Grenache, Lladoner pelut, Syrah and Mourvèdre (these last two must represent at least 5%, rising to 10% as from 1990)

📅 Vintages are unimportant.

🍷 Within 1-5 years

WHITE Less than one per cent of Minervois is white. A simple, dry and fruity wine fermented at cooler temperatures than was once the norm, it is now fresher and more aromatic.

🍇 Grenache blanc, Bourboulenc, Maccabéo, Picpoul, Clairette, Terret blanc
Note: A minimum of 50% (in total) of Bourboulenc and Maccabéo as from 1990.

📅 Vintages are unimportant.

🍷 Within 1 year

ROSÉ Good-value wines with a pretty strawberry-pink colour, and an honest, dry and fruity flavour.

🍇 A maximum of 70% (60% as from 1990) Carignan, plus Cinsault, Picpoul noir, Terret noir, Aspiran noir and a minimum of 20% (30% as from 1990) Grenache, Lladoner pelut, Syrah and Mourvèdre (these last two must represent at least 5% of the blend, rising to 10% as from 1990), and up to 10% (in total) of Grenache blanc, Bourboulenc, Maccabéo, Picpoul, Clairette, Terret blanc

📅 Vintages are unimportant

🍷 Within 1 year

☆ Château Fabas, Château de Gourgazaud, Domaine des Homs, Cuvée Jacques de la Jugie, Domaine de Mayranne, Château de Paraza, Domaine Ste-Eulalie, Château Villerambert-Julien, Château Villerambert-Moureau

MUSCAT DE FRONTIGNAN AOC

This wine may either be a *vin doux naturel* (VDN) or a *vin de liqueur* (VDL). In the latter the spirit is immediately added to the grape juice preventing any fermentation whatsoever. If the label does not differentiate between the two, the small green tax mark on the cap should bear the letters VDN or VDL.

WHITE The VDNs are delightful, golden-coloured, raisiny-rich, sweet and delicious wines that have a succulent, honeyed aftertaste with a somewhat fatter style than those of Beaumes, although they lack its finesse. The VDLs are much sweeter.

🍇 Muscat doré de Frontignan

🍷 Within 1-3 years

☆ Coopérative Muscat de Frontignan, Château la Peyrade

MUSCAT DE LUNEL AOC

This under-valued VDN approaches Frontignan in terms of pure quality.

WHITE/ROSÉ Fine, fragrant Muscat wines of length, delicacy and balance.

🍇 Muscat blanc à petits grains, Muscat rosé à petits grains

🍷 Within 1-3 years

☆ Coopérative de Lunel

MUSCAT DE MIREVAL AOC

Little-seen VDN appellation.

WHITE Light and sweet wines that often have better balance and acidity than Frontignan, although they may lack its raisiny-rich concentration.

🍇 Muscat blanc à petits grains

🍷 Within 1-3 years

☆ Cave de Rabelais, Cave Coopérative Rabelais

MUSCAT DE RIVESALTES AOC

This should not be confused with the blended Rivesaltes VDNs that bear no mention of the Muscat grape.

WHITE/ROSÉ These rich, ripe, grapey-raisiny wines are consistent in quality.

🍇 Muscat blanc à petits grains, Muscat d'Alexandrie

🍷 Within 1-3 years

☆ Cazes Frères, Cellier des Saints, Château de Jau, Domaine de la Rourède

MUSCAT DE ST.-JEAN-DE-MINERVOIS AOC

Tiny sub-appellation of Minervois producing small quantities of underrated *vin doux naturel*.

WHITE/ROSÉ These delicately golden wines have a finely balanced sweetness and a fresh, apricoty, grapey flavour.

🍇 Muscat blanc à petits grains, Muscat rosé à petits grains

🍷 Within 1-3 years

☆ Domaine de Barroubio, Coopérative de St.-Jean-de-Minervois "le Pardeillan"

RIVESALTES AOC

This appellation represents half of the VDN produced in France.

RED The warm, brick-red glow of these wines belies their astringent-sweet, chocolate/cherry-liqueur flavour and drying, tannic finish.

🍷 Between 10-40 years

WHITE/ROSÉ/TAWNY As much of the red version can be lightened after lengthy maturation in wood, all Rivesaltes eventually merge into one tawny style with time. The whites do not, of course, have any tannic astringency and are more oxidative and raisiny, with a resinous, candied-peel character.

🍇 All wines: Muscat blanc à petits grains, Muscat d'Alexandrie, Grenache, Grenache gris, Grenache blanc, Maccabéo, Tourbat, plus a combined maximum of 10% of Carignan, Cinsault, Syrah and Palomino

🍷 Between 10-20 years

☆ Boudau et Fils, Cazes Frères, Domaine de Garria, Producteurs de la Barnède, Cave Coopérative de Pollestres, Domaine Sarda-Malet St.-Vincent-Tradition

RIVESALTES "RANCIO" AOC
See Rivesaltes AOC.

ST.-CHINIAN AOC

Upgraded from VDQS in May 1982, this excellent-value appellation is the nearest the south, with its native grapes, comes to Bordeaux.

RED Relatively light in colour and weight, these wines have an elegance that belies their Mediterranean origin.

📅 1983, 1985, 1986

🍷 Between 2-6 years

ROSÉ These dry and delicately fruity rosés have a full and fragrant bouquet.

🍇 All wines: Cinsault, a maximum of 50% Carignan, plus at least 10% (20% as from 1990) Grenache and Lladoner pelut and a minimum of 5% (10% as from 1990) Mourvèdre and Syrah
Note: These last four varieties must represent at least 35% by 1990.

📅 Vintages are unimportant

🍷 Within 1-3 years

☆ Cave Coteaux du Rieu-Berlou, Château Cazals Viel, Château Coujan, Domaine des Jougla, Cave Coopérative de Roquebrun

VIN DE FRONTIGNAN AOC
See Muscat de Frontignan AOC.

Provence and Corsica

Provence is famous for its exotic-shaped bottles of rosé wine; it is, however, the lesser-known reds of Provence that should excite the knowledgeable wine drinker, while the modern technology now used in Corsica has turned its plonk into fruity country wines that are a delight to drink.

FOR MOST PEOPLE PROVENCE EVOKES beaches at St.-Tropez or the rich *bouillabaisse*-laden aromas of back-street Marseilles, but there are other experiences to be had in this sun-blessed corner of southern France. For while the wines of Provence may not have the classic status of Burgundy or Bordeaux, they have an abundance of spice-laden flavours that show more than a bit of class.

In Corsica, the advent of France's *vin de pays* system meant that one-third of its vineyards were uprooted and put to better use. If the *vin de pays* system was intended to encourage the production of superior quality wines from the bottom of the market upwards, then here at least it has been successful, for this island is no longer the generous contributor to Europe's "wine-lake" it used to be.

PROVENCE'S ROSÉ WINES

Fancy flasks of Provence pinks used to dominate this wine region, but lost their ground when consumers became sufficiently sophisticated to realize how bad they were. Although few realized that there was any significance in the bottle-shapes, they were in fact designed in the 1930s for a specific purpose—to differentiate between *négociant* and single-domaine wines. The fat-bottom bottle tapering upwards to form a slim and slightly distorted triangle was to be used only by *négociants*, while the curvier bottle could only be used by growers. It was, however, a concept that the consumer was unaware of and because, unlike Bordeaux and Burgundy, Provençal producers use other types of bottle, a bizarre range of shapes, sizes and gaudy colours evolved.

Although sales of rosé have dropped in recent years, they still represent 60 per cent of all Provençal wines produced, and it is fair to say that the quality has soared. Without resorting to such drastic measures as actually acidifying the wines, modern vinification techniques cannot entirely remove the softness verging on flabbiness that is their sunny southern heritage and most growers who are true to their *terroir* would not wish to do so. All that can be done is to produce considerably more aromatic and fragrant wines that remain expressive of their Provençal origins.

FACTORS AFFECTING TASTE AND QUALITY

Location
Provence is situated in the southeast of France, between the Rhône delta and the Italian border. A further 110 kilometres (68 miles) southeast lies Corsica.

Climate
Winters are mild, as are springs, which can also be humid. Summers are hot and stretch into long, sunny autumns. A vine requires 1,300 hours of sunshine in one growing season–1,500 hours is preferable, but in Provence, it luxuriates in an average of 3,000 hours. The close proximity of the Mediterranean, however, is also capable of inducing sharp fluctuations in the weather. Rain is spread over a limited number of days in autumn and winter.

Aspect
The vineyards run down hillsides and onto the plains.

Soil
The geology of Provence is complex. Many ancient soils have undergone chemical changes and numerous new soils have been created. Sand, red sandstone and granite are, however, the most regular common denominators, with limestone outcrops that often determine the extent of superior *terroirs*: the Var *département* has mica-schist, chalky scree and chalky tufa as well as granite hillsides; there are excellent flinty-limestone soils at Bandol; and pudding stones (conglomerate pebbles) that are rich in flint at Bellet. The south of Corsica is mostly granite, while the north is schistous, with a few limestone outcrops and deposits of sandy and alluvial soils in between.

Viticulture and vinification
All the vines used to be individually planted in *gobelet* fashion, but most are now trained on wires. The recent trend towards Cabernet sauvignon has stopped; although many excellent wines are still made from this grape, the current vogue is to re-establish a true Provençal identity by using local varieties only and the laws have been changed to encourage this particular evolution. Red wines from specific appellations such as Bandol and Bellet are on the increase, although 60 per cent of the production is still dry rosé. Much of the rosé has been improved by modern cool-vinification techniques, although much remains tired and flabby. Most is sold to tourists attracted by the bottle shapes.

Grape varieties
Aragnan, Aramon, Aramon gris, Barbarossa, Barbaroux, Barbaroux rosé, Bourboulenc, Braquet, Brun-Fourcat, Cabernet sauvignon, Calitor, Carignan, Castets, Chardonnay, Cinsault, Clairette, Clairette à gros grains, Clairette à petits grains, Clairette de Trans, Colombard, Counoise, Doucillon, Durif, Fuella, Grenache, Grenache blanc, Marsanne, Mayorquin, Mourvèdre, Muscat d'Aubagne, Muscat blanc à petits grains, Muscat de Die, Muscat de Frontignan, Muscat de Hambourg, Muscat de Marseille, Muscat noir de Provence, Muscat rosé à petits grains, Nielluccio, Panse muscade, Pascal blanc, Petit-brun, Picardan, Picpoul, Pignerol, Rolle, Sauvignon blanc, Sémillon, Sciacarello, Syrah, Téoulier, Terret blanc, Terret gris, Terret noir, Terret ramenée, Tibouren, Ugni blanc, Ugni rosé, Vermentino

Sun-drenched rural Provence, left
It might seem financial madness to plant so much as one vine on the sought-after soil of Provence, yet its vineyards flourish and produce no less than 45 million cases of wine annually, from a staggering 58 permitted grape varieties.

Corsican vineyards, above
These vineyards of Domaine de Valrose at Borgo, near the east coast, are typical of the Corsican landscape. The east coast plains are backed by dramatic mountains and palm trees proliferate.

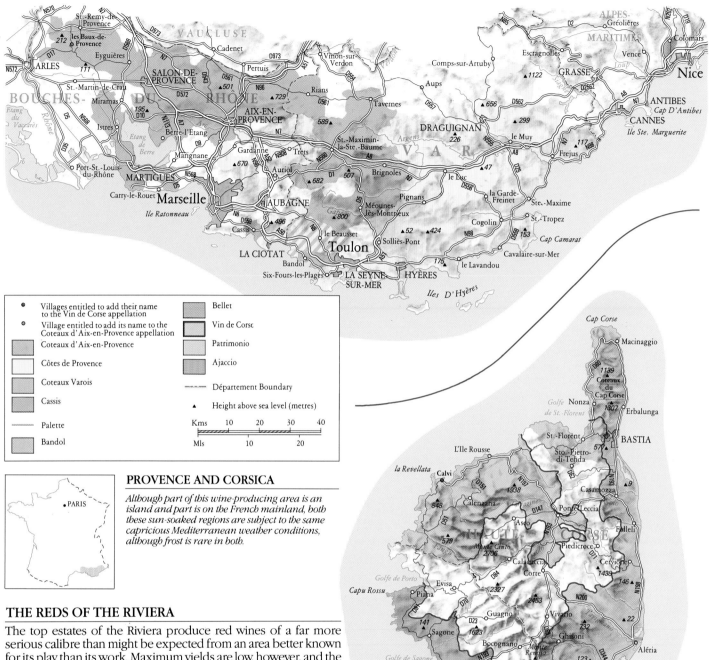

PROVENCE AND CORSICA

Although part of this wine-producing area is an island and part is on the French mainland, both these sun-soaked regions are subject to the same capricious Mediterranean weather conditions, although frost is rare in both.

THE REDS OF THE RIVIERA

The top estates of the Riviera produce red wines of a far more serious calibre than might be expected from an area better known for its play than its work. Maximum yields are low, however, and the potential for quality can be high. The smaller AOCs of Bandol, Bellet and Palette are restricted to a maximum of 40 hectolitres per hectare (180 cases per acre), which is very modest for a region that could easily average more than double this amount. Even the all-embracing AOCs of Côtes de Provence and Coteaux d'Aix-en-Provence are chock-full of fine vineyards capable of producing the exciting red wine that must surely be Provence's future.

CORSICA – "THE ISLE OF BEAUTY"

The days when Corsica's wines were fit only for turning into industrial spirit are long gone, but this is not a potentially fine wine region either. Just 15 per cent of its vineyards are AOC and these yield barely more than five per cent of Corsica's total wine production. This is a fair and accurate reflection of its true potential. Corsica's Vin de Pays de l'Ile de Beauté is typical of the island's essentially unpretentious wines that are a delight to quaff *in situ*, yet sometimes have enough individual character and rustic charm to warrant exporting. It is puzzling that Corsica's only truly classic wine, the succulent sweet Muscat of Cap Corse, is not even recognized, let alone awarded the AOC status it deserves.

The wines of Provence and Corsica

Note: The "Best recent vintages" and "When to drink" are given only in the case of true *vins de garde* for the wines listed below. Vintages in Provence and Corsica are very stable, even more so than those of Southern Rhône, where the quality depends to a large extent on the success or otherwise of the Grenache grape. Even when Provence suffers an excess of good weather, as in 1985 when there was literally too much sun, the best growers manage to produce tremendously good wines. The wines of these two regions are, for the most part, made for early drinking, so it is better to ignore the vintage and buy on name alone. Allow one to three years for white and rosé, two to four years for red.

AJACCIO AOC

A predominantly red-wine appellation on the west coast of Corsica.

RED A mainly Sciacarello wine of good bouquet and medium body.

At least 60% (in total) of Barbarossa, Nielluccio, Sciacarello and Vermentino, plus a maximum of 40% (in total) of Carignan, Cinsault and Grenache
Note: There must also be a minimum of 40% Sciacarello and a maximum of 15% Carignan

WHITE Decently dry and fruity, the best have a good edge of Ugni blanc acidity.

At least 80% Vermentino, plus Ugni blanc

ROSÉ Average to good-quality dry rosé with a typical southern roundness.

At least 60% (in total) of Barbarossa, Nielluccio, Sciacarello and Vermentino, plus a maximum of 40% (in total) of Carignan, Cinsault and Grenache
Note: There must also be a minimum of 40% Sciacarello and a maximum of 15% Carignan

☆ Clos Capitoro, Domaine Peraldi

BANDOL AOC

The red wine of this Provence appellation is a true *vin de garde* and deserves greater recognition.

RED The best of these wines have a dark purple-black colour, a deep and dense bouquet, masses of spicy-plummy Mourvèdre fruit and complex after-aromas that include vanilla, *cassis*, cinnamon, violets and sweet herbs.

Mourvèdre, Grenache, Cinsault (at least two of these must account for a minimum of 80% of the wine), plus Calitor, Carignan, Syrah, Tibouren, Bourboulenc, Clairette, Ugni blanc, Sauvignon blanc

🗓 1982, 1983, 1984, 1985, 1986

🍷 Between 3-12 years

WHITE These dry wines are now made in a fresher, more fragrant style, but they are nothing special compared to the reds.

At least 60% (in total) of Bourboulenc, Clairette and Ugni blanc, plus a maximum of 40% Sauvignon blanc

ROSÉ Well-made and attractive dry rosés that have far more body and structure than most and possess a fine individual character.

Mourvèdre, Grenache, Cinsault (at least two of these three grapes must account for at least 80% of the wine), plus Calitor, Carignan, Syrah, Tibouren, Bourboulenc, Clairette, Ugni blanc, Sauvignon blanc

☆ Domaine du Cagueloup, Domaine le Galantin, Domaine de l'Hermitage, Domaine Lafran-Veyrolles, Domaine de la Laidière, Mas de la Rouvière, Moulin des Costes, Domaine Ott, Domaine de Pibarnon, Château Pradeaux, Domaine des Salettes, Domaine Tempier

BELLET AOC

This tiny Provence appellation is cooled by Alpine winds and produces wines of exceptional fragrance for such a southerly situation.

RED These wines have a good colour and structure, with a well-perfumed bouquet and fine, crisp fruit.

Braquet, Fuella, Cinsault, plus up to 40% (in total) of Grenache, Rolle, Ugni blanc, Mayorquin, Clairette, Bourboulenc, Chardonnay, Pignerol, Muscat à petits grains

🗓 1983, 1985, 1986, 1989, 1990

🍷 Between 4-10 years

WHITE Fine, firm yet fragrant and highly aromatic dry white wines of unbelievable class and finesse.

Rolle, Ugni blanc, Mayorquin, plus up to 40% Clairette, Bourboulenc, Chardonnay, Pignerol, Muscat à petits grains

🗓 1984, 1985, 1986, 1989, 1990

🍷 Between 3-7 years

ROSÉ Fine, floral, dry rosés that are exceptionally fresh and easy to drink.

Braquet, Fuella, Cinsault, plus up to 40% (in total) of Grenache, Rolle, Ugni blanc, Mayorquin, Clairette, Bourboulenc, Chardonnay, Pignerol, Muscat à petits grains

☆ Château de Bellet, Château de Crémat, Clos St.-Vincent

CASSIS AOC

A decent but overpriced Provence appellation located around a beautiful rocky bay, a few kilometres east of Marseilles. In all but a few enterprising estates, these vineyards are on the decline.

RED These solid, well-coloured red wines can age, but do not improve.

Grenache, Carignan, Mourvèdre, Cinsault, Barbaroux, plus up to 10% (in total) of Terret noir, Terret gris, Terret blanc, Terret ramenée, Aramon, Aramon gris

WHITE These dry white wines have an interesting bouquet of herby aromas of gorse and bracken, but are usually flabby and unbalanced on the palate.

Ugni blanc, Sauvignon blanc, Doucillon, Clairette, Marsanne, Pascal blanc

ROSÉ Pleasantly fresh, dry rosés of moderately interesting quality.

Grenache, Carignan, Mourvèdre, Cinsault, Barbaroux, plus up to 10% (in total) of Terret noir, Terret gris, Terret blanc, Terret ramenée, Aramon, Aramon gris

☆ Clos Boudard, Château de Fontblanche, Clos St.-Magdeleine

COTEAUX D'AIX-EN-PROVENCE AOC

This large appellation has many fine estates, several of which have been replanted and re-equipped.

RED The best are deeply coloured *vins de garde* with lots of creamy-*cassis*, spicy-vanilla, plummy and cherry flavours, and capable of some complexity.

Grenache, plus a maximum of 40% of Cabernet sauvignon, Carignan, Cinsault, Counoise, Mourvèdre, Syrah
Note: As from 1995, the maximum for Cabernet sauvignon or Carignan will be 30%

🗓 1983, 1985, 1986, 1989, 1990

🍷 Between 3-12 years

WHITE Dry and fruity white wines of moderate but improving quality.

Up to 70% (in total) of Bourboulenc, Clairette, Grenache blanc, Sauvignon blanc, Sémillon, Ugni blanc and Vermentino
Note: As from the 1991 harvest, the Ugni blanc will be restricted to 40%, Sauvignon blanc and Sémillon to 30%.

ROSÉ Fine-quality dry rosés that are light in body, but bursting with deliciously fresh and ripe fruit.

Grenache, plus a maximum of 50% (in total and falling to 40% as from the 1981 harvest) of Cabernet sauvignon, Carignan, Cinsault, Counoise, Mourvèdre, Syrah
Note: As from 1995, the maximum for both Cabernet sauvignon or Carignan will be 30%

☆ Château Bas, Château de Beaulieu, Château de Beaupré, Château de Calissanne, Commanderie de la Bargemone, Château de Fonscolombe, Château Grand Seuil, Domaine de la Boulangère, Château la Coste, Domaine de la Grande Séouve, les Toques Gourmandes, Château Revelette, Château St.-Jean de l'Hôpital, Château Vignelaure

COTEAUX D'AIX-EN-PROVENCE-LES BAUX AOC

Excellent red, dry white and rosé wines of the same grape varieties and technical requirements as Coteaux d'Aix-en-Provence.

☆ Mas de Gourgonnier, Mas de la Dame, Terres Blanches, Domaine de la Vallongue

COTEAUX VAROIS VDQS

A *vin de pays* until 1985, this VDQS covers an area of pleasant country wines in the centre of Provence.

RED The best have good colour, a deep fruity flavour and some finesse.

Up to 60% Carignan (50% as from the 1988 harvest), plus Cinsault, Grenache, Mourvèdre and Syrah, a maximum of 30% (in total) of Cabernet sauvignon and Tibouren, and no more than 10% (in total) of Bourboulenc, Clairette, Grenache blanc and Ugni blanc

ROSÉ These attractive, easy-to-drink, dry rosés offer better value than some of the more famous pretentious ones.

Up to 60% Carignan (50% as from the 1988 harvest), plus Cinsault, Grenache, Mourvèdre and Syrah, a maximum of 30% (in total) of Cabernet sauvignon and Tibouren, and no more than 10% (in total) of Bourboulenc, Clairette, Grenache blanc and Ugni blanc

Continued overleaf

☆ Domaine de Barbaroux, Domaine du Deffends, l'Abbaye de St.-Hilaire, Domaine du Loou, Domaine St.-Cyriaque, Domaine de St.-Jean

CÔTES DE PROVENCE AOC

While this AOC is famous for its rosés, it is the red wines of Côtes de Provence that have real potential, and they seem blessed with good vintages, fine estates and talented winemakers. Inferior wines are made, but drink the best and you will rarely be disappointed. The major drawback of this all-embracing appellation is its very size. There are, however, several areas with pecul-iarities of soil and specific micro-climates that would make a Côtes de Provence Villages AOC a logical evolution and give the most expres-sive growers something to aim for.

RED There are too many exciting styles to generalize, but the best of all have a deep colour and many show an exuberance of silky Syrah fruit and plummy Mourvèdre. Some have great finesse, others are more tannic and chewy. The typically southern spicy-*cassis* character of Cabernet sauvignon is often present and the Cinsault, Grenache and Tibouren grapes also play important roles.

🍇 Up to 40% Carignan, plus Cinsault, Grenache, Mourvèdre, Tibouren, a maximum of 30% Syrah and a further 30% maximum (in total) of Barbaroux rosé, Cabernet sauvignon, Calitor, Clairette, Sémillon, Ugni blanc and Vermentino

🍴 Between 3-10 years

WHITE Moderate but improving soft, dry, fragrant and aromatic wines.

🍇 Clairette, Sémillon, Ugni blanc and Vermentino

ROSÉ When writers say that a wine does not travel, they quite often mean the ambience of the locality in which they are drunk does not travel and, for me, the Mediterranean sun is integral

to the enjoyment of these wines. They are without doubt wines made to accompany food, but even the best (asterisked below) fail to perform against other rosés under blind conditions. The dry flavour of these wines, conditioned by several days of drinking, can reveal a subtle finesse, but their low acidity makes them seem flat and flabby beside others.

🍇 Up to 40% Carignan, plus Cinsault, Grenache, Mourvèdre, Tibouren, a maximum of 30% Syrah and a further 30% maximum (in total) of Barbaroux rosé, Cabernet sauvignon, Calitor, Clairette, Sémillon, Ugni blanc and Vermentino

☆ Domaine des Aspras, Château Barbeyrolles*, Domaine du Campdummy*, Commanderie de Peyrassol, Château les Crostes, Domaine du Deffends*, Domaine de la Bernarde, Domaine de l'Ile*, Domaine de la Jeannette, Domaine de la Malherbe*, Domaine de Marchandise, Mas de Cadenet, Clos Mireille, Domaine de Peissonnel, Château Réal Martin, Domaine de Rimauresq, Château de Roux*, Domaine St.-André de Figuière, Domaine de St.-Baillon*, Château St.-Martin, Château St.-Pierre, Domaine St.-Roman d'Esclans, Château Ste.-Roseline, Coopérative de Vidauban, Vignerons Presqu'ile St.-Tropez, Vignobles Kennel

PALETTE AOC

Despite its ridiculously long list of permissible grape varieties (and many of them are used), this small AOC is one of the best in Provence. It can be considered the equivalent of a *Grand Cru* of Coteaux d'Aix-en-Provence, standing out from the surrounding vineyards by virtue of its calcareous soil. Three-quarters of this appellation is occupied by just one property – Château Simon.

RED This is a high-quality wine with good colour and firm structure, but not in the blockbusting style. It can achieve finesse and complexity.

🍇 At least 50% (in total) of Mourvèdre, Grenache, and Cinsault, plus Téoulier, Durif, Muscat noir de Provence, Muscat de Marseille, Muscat d'Aubagne, Muscat de Hambourg, Carignan, Syrah, Castets, Brun-Fourcat, Terret gris, Petit-brun, Tibouren, Cabernet sauvignon and up to 15% (in total) of Clairette à gros grains, Clairette à petits grains, Clairette de Trans, Picardan and Clairette rosé, plus Ugni blanc and Ugni rosé, Grenache blanc, Muscat de Frontignan, Muscat de Die, Panse muscade, Picpoul, Pascal, Aragnan, Colombard, Terret-bourret
Note: Within the total 50% minimum, Mourvèdre must represent at least 10%

🍴 Between 7-20 years

WHITE Firm but nervy dry wine with a pleasantly curious aromatic character.

🍇 At least 55% (in total) of Clairette à gros grains, Clairette à petits grains, Clairette de Trans, Picardan and Clairette rosé, plus Ugni blanc and Ugni rosé, Grenache blanc, Muscat de

Frontignan, Muscat de Die, Panse muscade, Picpoul, Pascal, Aragnan, Colombard and a maximum of 20% Terret-bourret

ROSÉ A well-made, but not exceptional wine that is perhaps made too seriously for its level of quality.

🍇 At least 50% (total) of Mourvèdre, Grenache, and Cinsault, plus Téoulier, Durif, Muscat noir de Provence, Muscat de Marseille, Muscat d'Aubagne, Muscat de Hambourg, Carignan, Syrah, Castets, Brun-Fourcat, Terret gris, Petit-brun, Tibouren, Cabernet sauvignon and up to 15% (in total) of Clairette à gros grains, Clairette à petits grains, Clairette de Trans, Picardan and Clairette rosé, plus Ugni blanc and Ugni rosé, Grenache blanc, Muscat de Frontignan, Muscat de Die, Panse muscade, Picpoul, Pascal, Aragnan, Colombard, Terret-bourret
Note: Within the total 50% minimum, the Mourvèdre must represent at least 10%

☆ Château Simon

PATRIMONIO AOC

Small appellation west of Bastia in the north of Corsica.

RED Some fine-quality red wines of good colour, body and fruit are made.

🍇 At least 60% Nielluccio, rising to 75% by 1995 and 90% by 2000, plus Grenache, Sciacarello, Vermentino

WHITE Attractively light and dry wines of a remarkably fragrant and floral character for Corsica.

🍇 At least 80% Vermentino, rising to 90% in 1995 and 100% in 2000, but, in the meantime, a balance of Ugni blanc is allowed

ROSÉ Good-value dry rosés that have a coral-pink colour and an elegant flavour.

🍇 At least 60% Nielluccio, rising to 75% by 1995 and 90% by 2000, plus Grenache, Sciacarello, Vermentino

☆ Clos de Bernardi, Dominique Gentile, Domaine Leccia, Clos Marfisi, Clos de Morta Maio

VIN DE BANDOL AOC
See Bandol AOC.

VIN DE BELLET AOC
See Bellet AOC.

VIN DE CORSE AOC

Generic appellation covering the entire island.

RED These honest wines, full of fruit, are round and clean, with rustic charm.

🍇 At least 50% Nielluccio, Sciacarello and Grenache noir, plus Cinsault, Mourvèdre, Barbarossa, Syrah and a maximum of 20% (in total) of Carignan and Vermentino

WHITE The best are well made, clean and fresh, but not of true AOC quality.

🍇 At least 75% Vermentino, plus up to 25% Ugni blanc

ROSÉ Attractive, dry and fruity, easy-to-drink wines.

🍇 At least 50% Nielluccio, Sciacarello and Grenache noir, plus Cinsault, Mourvèdre, Barbarossa, Syrah and a maximum of 20% (in total) of Carignan and Vermentino

☆ Domaine de Furgoli, Domaine de Maisoleu, Domaine de Pietralba, Ets Nicolas

VIN DE CORSE CALVI AOC

North of Ajaccio, this sub-appellation of Vin de Corse requires the same grape varieties and conforms to the same technical level.

☆ Couvent d'Alzipratu, Clos Landry

VIN DE CORSE COTEAUX DU CAP CORSE AOC

Corsica's northern peninsula is a sub-appellation of Vin de Corse and requires the same grape varieties, except that the Codivarta may be used alongside the Ugni blanc in support of the Vermentino.

☆ Clos Nicrosi

VIN DE CORSE FIGARI AOC

Situated between Sartène and Porto Vecchio, this sub-appellation of Vin de Corse requires the same grape varieties and technical level.

☆ Poggio d'Oro, Domaine de Canella

VIN DE CORSE PORTO VECCHIO AOC

The southeastern edge of Corsica, around Porto Vecchio, is a sub-appellation of Vin de Corse that requires the same grape varieties and technical level.

☆ Fior di Lecci, Domaine de Torraccia

VIN DE CORSE SARTÈNE AOC

South of Ajaccio, this sub-appellation of Vin de Corse requires the same grape varieties and conforms to the same technical level.

☆ Domaine Mosconi

Vins de pays

France's *vins de pays* are an unpretentious group of red, white and rosé wines. They are intended to be quaffing wines that display, in a very rudimentary sense, the broadest characteristics displayed by their region's finest and most famous wines: they should have a rustic charm and be a joy to drink. After all, they are the taste of rural France. Most *vins de pays* are found in Languedoc-Roussillon. This is because the concept of the system is to encourage the production of better-quality wines, from the lowest level upwards, and the *vin ordinaire* of this region, formerly known as the Midi, was once the lowest form of vinous life. Happily, the original concept is working in practice.

THE EXPRESSION "VIN DE PAYS" FIRST APPEARED in the statute books in a decree dated February 8th, 1930. The law in question merely allowed wines to refer to their *canton* of origin provided they attained a certain alcoholic degree; for example "Vin de Pays de Canton X". These *cantons* were not controlled appellations as such: there was no way of enforcing a minimum standard of quality, and the relatively small amounts of these so-called *vins de pays* were often the product of inferior hybrid grapes. It was not until 1973 that the concept of a superior breed of *vins de table*, originating from a defined area and subject to strict controls, was officially born. By 1976, a total of 75 *vins de pays* had been established, but all the formalities were not worked out until 1979, and between 1981 and 1982 every single existing *vin de pays* was redefined and another 20 created. Currently there are 132, though the number fluctuates as *vins de pays* are upgraded to VDQS, or when new *vins de pays* are created.

Officially, a *vin de pays* is a *vin de table* from a specified area that conforms to quality control laws that are very similar, although obviously not quite as stiff as those regulating AOC and VDQS wines. There are three categories: *zonal* (limited to a local area, maybe just one commune), *départemental* (covers an entire *département*), and *regional* (encompassing more than one *département*). There are no official quality differences between these three categories and, although it is not unreasonable to suspect that the zonal *vins de pays* may show more individual character than the wider ranging *vins de pays départementaux*, this is not always so. Furthermore, a grower within a specific zone may decide to sell his wine under a larger, more generic *vin de pays*, for entirely commercial reasons. This often happens in the Loire, for example, where a grower with a vineyard in, say, the Vin de Pays de Retz area finds it difficult to market his wine under that name. He may then elect to sell it as Vin de Pays du Jardin de la France instead, which is a delightful name that even Anglo-Saxons know to be synonymous with the Loire Valley, thus carrying with it an image of quality. The geographical size of the *vins de pays* can be deceiving, with many *vins de pays départementaux* producing relatively little wine compared to some of the more prolific zonal *vins de pays*. For the most part, *vins de pays* are not meant to be overly serious wines, although exceptions, like Bunan's pure Cabernet Sauvignon from the *vin de pays* of Mont Caume, can aspire to extraordinary heights of quality.

The vins de pays of France

All existing *vins de pays* are listed alphabetically over the next three pages, with a brief comment on their respective wines. Each *vin de pays* takes the letter Z, D or R, depending on whether it is zonal (Z), *départemental* (D) or regional (R). Zonal *vins de pays* are also numbered. On the maps on pages 198 and 199 zonal *vins de pays* are thus identified by their numbers, *vins de pays départementaux* are actually named and the three larger, regional *vins de pays* are colour-tinted and identified in the accompanying key (page 199).

To ease location of specific *vins de pays*, all those that appear on the map on page 199 are asterisked in the alphabetical listing, while those that appear on page 198 are not.

Note: percentage figures given in brackets refer to a proportion of the area's annual *vin de pays* output.

Z(1) AGENAIS*
Red, white and rosé wines produced from a combination of classic Bordelais grapes and some rustic regional ones, including the Tannat and Fer.

D AIN*
Crisp white wine, mostly made in Seyssel, with some made in an enclave of vines around Ars, produced in small quantities.

Z(2) ALLOBROGIE*
White wine, dominated by the Jacquère grape, accounts for 95 per cent of the total output. Reds are mostly Gamay- and/or Mondeuse-based. The wines are in a sort of rustic Savoie style.

D ALPES DE HAUTE-PROVENCE*
Roughly two-thirds red and one-third dry white wine, mainly from the southeast of the *département*. Rosé may also be produced.

D ALPES-MARITIMES*
Some 70 per cent red and 30 per cent rosé made from Carignan, Cinsault, Grenache, Ugni blanc and Rolle grapes, mostly from the communes of Carros, Mandelieu and Mougins. White wines may also be produced.

Z(3) ARDAILHOU
Fruity red wine and a little dry rosé, from an area on the Hérault coast.

D ARDÈCHE*
Red and white wines from a range of Rhône and Bordelais grapes, produced on a limited scale.

Z(4) ARGENS*
Red, white and rosé wines in a rustic Provence style.

D AUDE*
Fresh and fruity wine, roughly 75 per cent red and 25 per cent rosé, plus a little white.

Z(5) BALMES DAUPHINOISES*
Dry white (60 per cent), made from the Jacquère and Chardonnay grapes, and red (40 per cent) made from Gamay and Pinot noir. Rosé may also be produced.

Z(6) BÉNOVIE
Red (75 per cent), white (20 per cent) and rosé (five per cent) wines, in a Coteaux du Languedoc style.

Z(7) BÉRANGE
Red and rosé wine from traditional local grapes augmented by the Syrah. White wine may also be produced.

Z(8) BESSAN
Dry, aromatic rosé wines are the best known, but dry white (40 per cent) and a little red is also produced.

Z(9) BIGORRE*
Mostly full, rich, Madiran-type red wine, plus a little good crisp, dry white. Rosé may also be produced.

D BOUCHES-DU-RHÔNE*
Warm, spicy red wine made in the Provence style is predominant. Most of the rest is dry rosé, with just a tiny amount of rather dull, dry white.

Z(10) BOURBONNAIS*
Rare wine from a white-only area in the Loire Valley.

Z(11) CASSAN
Two-thirds red wine, one-third rosé, produced in only modest quantities.

Z(12) CATALAN
Very successful, well-coloured, fruity red wine (70 per cent) made from the Grenache, Carignan and Cinsault grapes, dry rosé (20 per cent) and dry white (10 per cent), with *vins primeurs* a speciality, account for the output of this prolific zone.

Z(13) CAUX
Good, typical, dry and fruity rosé in a Languedoc style. Red (40 per cent) and a little white is also made.

Z(14) CESSENON
Red wines of a rustic St.-Chinian style, plus a little rosé.

Z(15) CHARENTAIS*
Crisp, tangy dry white wines that are really good. Some red and rosé is also made.

D CHER*
Mostly Touraine-like, Gamay-based red wine, plus a small amount of dry rosé in a light *vin gris* style. A little dry white Sauvignon blanc is also produced that can be compared to a sort of rustic Sancerre or Menetou-Salon.

Z(16) COLLINES DE LA MOURE
Red (65 per cent), dry rosé (30 per cent) and dry white (five per cent) wines. The red and rosé are a blend of local grape varieties with those of the southwest; the white wine is basically made from the Ugni blanc.

Z(17) COLLINES RHODANIENNES*
Red wine (95 per cent) from a base of Gamay and Syrah, and Marsanne-dominated dry white wine (five per cent). Rosé may also be produced, and a little *vin primeur* is made.

Z(18) COMTÉ DE GRIGNAN*
Grenache-dominated red wines for the most part, but some rosé and dry white wines may also be produced, the latter from Ugni blanc and a string of Rhône varieties.

R COMTÉ TOLOSAN
Red, white and rosé wines, produced in modest quantities.

Z(19) CÔTE VERMEILLE
Red, white and rosé wines from the Collioure area of Roussillon. The actual *vin de pays* region was created in 1987.

Z(20) COTEAUX DE L'ARDÈCHE*

Particularly successful spicy red wine (90 per cent), rosé (seven per cent) and white (three per cent), made from grapes of Bordelais and Rhône origin. The area has a huge annual production, in excess of two million cases (180,000 hectolitres).

Z(21) COTEAUX DES BARONNIES*

Red (95 per cent) and rosé (five per cent) wines, made from traditional Rhône grapes to which Bordelais varieties may be added. A little white is also made.

Z(22) COTEAUX DE BESSILLES

Red, white and rosé wines from the Hérault *département* of Languedoc-Roussillon. The actual *vin de pays* region was created in 1987.

Z(23) COTEAUX DE LA CABRERISSE

Red (80 per cent) and rosé (20 per cent) wines, with some *vins primeurs.*

Z(24) COTEAUX CÉVENOLS

Red (60 per cent) and dry rosé (40 per cent) wines, both in honest, fruity Languedoc style. Dry white wines may also be produced.

Z(25) COTEAUX DE CÈZE

Approximately two-thirds red and one-third rosé wine, plus a little dry white in basic Côtes-du-Rhône style.

Z(26) COTEAUX CHARITOIS*

White wines from the Loire Valley.

Z(27) COTEAUX DU CHER ET DE L'ARNON*

Reds and *vin gris* rosé made from the Gamay, and dry white wine from the Sauvignon blanc.

Z(28) COTEAUX DE LA CITÉ DE CARCASSONNE

Red (approximately 75 per cent) and rosé (approximately 25 per cent) from 11 communes around the spectacular walled city of Carcassonne, produced from a wide range of grapes. White wine may also be produced.

Z(29) COTEAUX D'ENSERUNE

Two-thirds red and one-third rosé, from primarily Languedoc grapes augmented by the Syrah and some traditional varieties from the southwest.

Z(30) COTEAUX DES FENOUILLÈDES

Red (90 per cent), white (two per cent) and rosé (eight per cent) wines, in a full, rich Roussillon style.

Z(31) COTEAUX FLAVIENS

Red (60 per cent), rosé (30 per cent) and white (10 per cent) wines, from typically Languedoc grape varieties. The *vin de pays* is named after the Roman Emperor Flavius.

Z(32) COTEAUX DE FONTCAUDE

Red (80 per cent) in a light and fresh style, and dry rosé (20 per cent) wines.

Z(33) COTEAUX DE GLANES*

Mainly red, Gamay- and Merlot-dominated wines, plus a little rosé.

Z(34) COTEAUX DU GRÉSIVAUDAN*

Red and rosé Savoie-style wines made from Gamay, Pinot and Etraire de la dui (a local grape variety), and Jacquère-based dry white wines.

Z(35) COTEAUX DE LAURENS

Red, barely any white, but some rosé, made from local traditional grape varieties, augmented by the Syrah.

Z(36) COTEAUX DU LÉZIGNANAIS

Red wine (80 per cent), made from typical Languedoc grapes, dry rosé (20 per cent), and a token amount of white.

Z(37) COTEAUX DU LIBRON

Red (80 per cent) and rosé (20 per cent) made from the traditional grapes of southwest France.

Z(38) COTEAUX DU LITTORAL AUDOIS

Red (up to 85 per cent) and rosé (15 per cent) wines. A little white wine is produced from Grenache blanc and Macabéo grape varieties.

Z(39) COTEAUX DE MIRAMONT

Red wines predominate, made from traditional local grape varieties, plus the Syrah. A little rosé and some *vins primeurs* are also produced.

Z(40) COTEAUX DE MURVIEL

Red (80 per cent) and rosé (20 per cent) wines of typical Languedoc light fruitiness.

Z(41) COTEAUX DE NARBONNE

Red, white and rosé wines from the coastal edge of Corbières.

Z(42) COTEAUX DE PEYRIAC

Full and rustic red wines (85 per cent), made from local grape varieties augmented by the Syrah. The remainder is rosé, plus a little white.

Z(43) COTEAUX DU PONT DU GARD

Typical Languedoc-style red and rosé wines. Dry white is also made, and *vins primeurs* are a local speciality.

Z(44) COTEAUX DU QUERCY*

Richly coloured, full-bodied, but precocious Gamay and Merlot-dominated red wines.

Z(45) COTEAUX DU SALAGOU

Red (80 per cent) and rosé (20 per cent) wines, made from typical Languedoc grape varieties.

Z(46) COTEAUX DU SALAVÈS

Red (80 per cent) and rosé (20 per cent) wines from a large range of Languedoc, southwest and Bordelais grapes. Very small quantities of white *vin primeur* are also produced.

Z(47) COTEAUX DU TERMÉNÈS

Red, white, rosé and *vins primeurs*, produced irregularly, from vines in the centre of Hautes-Corbières.

Z(48) COTEAUX ET TERRASSES DE MONTAUBAN*

Red and rosé wines from the Pays de la Garonne.

Z(49) CÔTES DU BRIAN

Red and rosé wines made from a range of Languedoc grapes in which the Carignan dominates and to which the Syrah may be added.

Z(50) CÔTES CATALANES

Red and rosé wines made from the Cabernets, Gamay, Syrah, Tannat and Jurançon noir grape varieties. White wine may also be made.

Z(51) CÔTES DU CÉRESSOU

Typically light and fruity Languedoc wine produced in fairly large amounts. 60 per cent is red, 15 per cent white and 25 per cent rosé.

Z(52) CÔTES DU CONDOMOIS*

Red wines (60 per cent), dominated by the Tannat grape, and white (40 per cent), made from the Colombard or Ugni blanc. A little rosé is also produced.

Z(53) CÔTES DE GASGOGNE*

Tangy, dry white wines that are the undistilled produce of Armagnac. Wines made from the Colombard grape are the lightest, those from the Ugni blanc are fatter and more interesting, and the Manseng and Sauvignon blanc are also used. Red and rosé wines are also made.

Z(54) CÔTES DE LASTOURS
Mainly red (80 per cent) and rosé (20 per cent) wines. White wines may also be produced and *vins primeurs* are a local speciality.

Z(55) CÔTES DE MONTESTRUC*
Red wines made from the Alicanté bouschet, Cabernets, Malbec, Merlot and Jurançon noir grape varieties, and white wines made from the Colombard, Mauzac and Ugni blanc.

Z(56) CÔTES DE PÉRIGNAN
Mostly red and rosé wines, from the lesser sites of La Clape. White wine may also be produced, and some *vin primeur* is made.

Z(57) CÔTES DE PROUILLE
Red, white and rosé wines, from the Aude *département.*

Z(58) CÔTES DU TARN*
Red, white and rosé wines made from Bordelais and southwestern grape varieties, plus, uniquely for France, the Portugais bleu.

Z(59) CÔTES DE THAU
Red (60 per cent), rosé (35 per cent) and white (five per cent) wines.

Z(60) CÔTES DE THONGUE
Red (70 per cent) and rosé (25 per cent) wines made from local grape varieties. The five per cent of white wine is essentially Ugni blanc-based. The *vins primeurs* of Merlot, Syrah and Carignan are a speciality.

Z(61) CÔTES DU VIDOURLE
Two-thirds red and one-third rosé wines.

Z(62) CUCUGNAN
Essentially red wines, although rosé may be produced.

D DEUX-SÈVRES*
Simple wines of a frank nature, from the vineyards with the richest soil (and thus the poorest as far as wine production is concerned) in the Nantais.

D DORDOGNE*
A rustic Bergerac-style of both red and white wine.

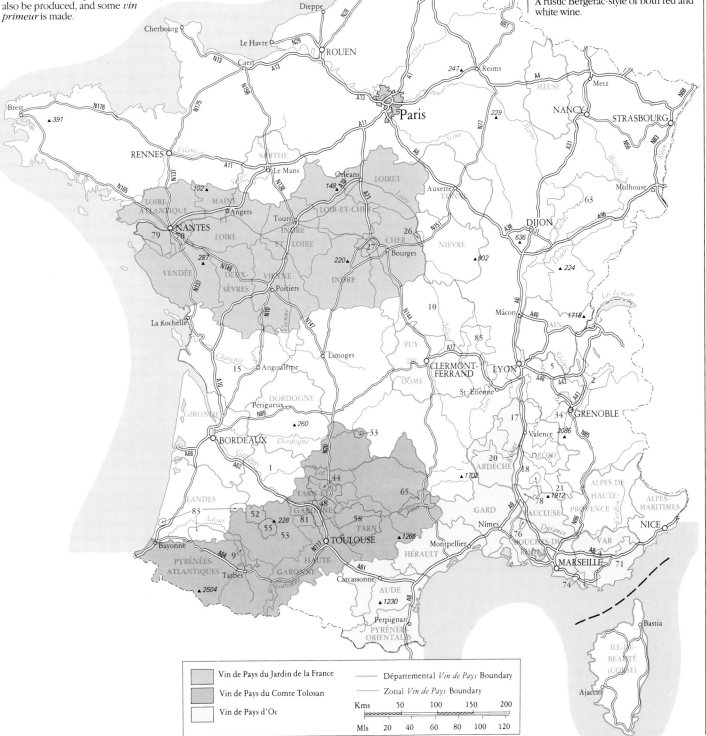

Vin de Pays du Jardin de la France

Vin de Pays du Comte Tolosan

Vin de Pays d'Oc

———— Départemental *Vin de Pays* Boundary

———— Zonal *Vin de Pays* Boundary

| Kms | 50 | 100 | 150 | 200 |

| Mls | 20 | 40 | 60 | 80 | 100 | 120 |

D DRÔME*
Red, white and rosé wines, from typical Rhône grape varieties, similar in style to Coteaux du Tricastin AOC.

Z(63) FRANCHE COMTÉ*
Red, white and rosé wines. The white is of particular note.

D GARD*
Two-thirds red wine and one-third white and rosé. These wines have undergone much improvement since the days of the infamous Midi.

D GIRONDE*
Red and white wines from isolated areas not classified for the production of Bordeaux.

Z(64) GORGES DE L'HÉRAULT*
Red (70 per cent) and rosé (30 per cent) in typical Languedoc style. White wine may also be produced.

Z(65) GORGES ET CÔTES DE MILLAU*
Red wines from the Gamay, Syrah, Cabernets, Malbec and Fer account for nearly all production. *Vin primeur* is a speciality, and a minute amount of white is made. Rosé may also be produced.

D HAUTE GARONNE*
Red and rosé wines made from the Négrette grape in the Fronton area, and from the Merlot, Cabernets, Syrah and Jurançon noir in scattered patches elsewhere. Overall production is very small.

Z(66) HAUTERIVE EN PAYS D'AUDE
Red wine made from a range of typical Languedoc and southwestern grape varieties. A little *vin primeur* is made, and small amounts of white and rosé are also produced.

Z(67) HAUTE-VALLÉE DE L'AUDE
Red wines made from Bordelais grape varieties for the most part, although dry white and rosé wines are also made.

Z(68) HAUTE-VALLÉE DE L'ORB
Mostly red, but also rosé wines, with very limited production.

Z(69) HAUTS DE BADENS
Red and rosé wines in a rustic Minervois style.

D HÉRAULT*
Red (75 per cent), rosé (20 per cent) and white (five per cent) wines. This *vin de pays départemental* yields a staggering nine million cases (810,000 hectolitres) from what was once the heart of Midi mediocrity. Improved viticultural and vinicultural techniques have transformed its production into far better wines.

D ILE DE BEAUTÉ
Red and rosé wines account for 95 per cent, white the other five per cent, of the vast production of Corsica. The grapes used are traditional to the island.

D INDRE*
Red, white and rosé wines, including a pale *vin gris* style, from traditional Loire grape varieties.

D INDRE-ET-LOIRE*
Red, white and rosé wines from traditional Loire grape varieties.

R JARDIN DE LA FRANCE*
Red, white and rosé wines, from this all-embracing *vin de pays*, which covers the entire Loire Valley region. Most of the vast output is dry white and either dominated by the Chenin blanc or Sauvignon blanc.

D LANDES*
Red, white and rosé wines. Approximately 80 per cent is red, and the grapes used are traditional southwestern varieties.

D LOIRE-ATLANTIQUE*
Red and rosé wines, including a pale *vin gris*, are made from the Gamay and Groslot grapes, while Folle blanche and Melon de Bourgogne are used for white, with some interesting developments using Chardonnay.

D LOIRET*
Red and rosé, including a pale *vin gris* style, made from the Gamay grape, plus Sauvignon blanc white account for the small output of this area.

D LOIR-ET-CHER*
Red, white and rosé wines, including a pale *vin gris*, made from traditional Loire grape varieties.

D MAINE-ET-LOIRE*
Red, white and rosé wines made in substantial quantities from traditional Loire grape varieties.

Z(70) MARCHES DE BRETAGNE*
Predominantly Gamay and Cabernet franc red and rosé wines.

Z(71) MAURES*
Approximately two-thirds red wine and one-third rosé, plus a tiny amount of white, account for this area's Provençal-style wines.

D MEUSE*
Red and rosé wines, including a pale *vin gris*, made from Pinot noir and Gamay grapes, and white wine from Chardonnay, Aligoté and Auxerrois.

Z(72) MONT BAUDILE*
Approximately two-thirds red and one-third rosé, plus a little white wine.

Z(73) MONT BOUQUET*
Two-thirds red wine and one-third rosé, produced in a Languedoc style, if a rather full one.

Z(74) MONT CAUME*
Red (55 per cent), rosé (40 per cent) and white (five per cent) wines, produced mostly from traditional Rhône valley grape varieties, although Cabernet sauvignon is used to great effect for some red wines.

Z(75) MONTS DE LA GRAGE
Red and rosé wines in a basic Languedoc style, often beefed-up with Syrah grapes.

D NIÈVRE*
Red, white and rosé wines, production of which is mostly confined to the areas of Charité-sur-Loire, La Celle-sur-Nièvre and Tannay.

R OC*
Red (75 per cent), white (five per cent) and rosé (20 per cent) wines of variable, but usually acceptable, quality. The "Oc" of this regional *vin de pays* is southern dialect for "yes", it being "Oui" elsewhere in France, thus Languedoc, the "tongue of Oc".

Z(76) PETITE CRAU*
Red (70 per cent), white (15 per cent) and rosé (15 per cent) wines, in a style that bridges Rhône and Provence.

Z(77) PÉZENAS*
Roughly 70 per cent red wine and 30 per cent rosé, along with a tiny amount of white and *vins primeurs*.

Z(78) PRINCIPAUTÉ D'ORANGE*
A full red wine, made predominantly from Rhône grape varieties. Rosé may also be produced.

D PUY-DE-DÔME*
Red, white and rosé wines of simple, rustic quality.

D PYRÉNÉES-ATLANTIQUES*
Two-thirds red and one-third white wine, produced from traditional southwestern grape varieties.

D PYRÉNÉES-ORIENTALES*
Full and fruity red, white and rosé wines, produced in large quantities.

Z(79) RETZ*
Rosé wine made from the Groslot grape is predominant, although a little Cabernet franc-based red, and a very tiny amount of white is produced.

Z(80) SABLES DU GOLFE DU LION
Two-thirds red wine, one-third rosé, including a large proportion in pale *vin gris* style, plus a small amount of white wine. The vines belonging to this zonal *vin de pays* are ungrafted and grown on an amazing sand-bar with seawater on both sides.

Z(81) SAINT-SARDOS*
Red, white and rosé wines from a typically southwestern hotchpotch of grape varieties.

D SARTHE*
Red, white and rosé wines may be made, although production of this *vin de pays départemental* is minuscule and, as far as I am aware, limited to just one grower in Marçon.

Z(82) SERRE DU COIRAN
Two-thirds red wine and one-third rosé, with a small amount made as *vins primeurs*. Now called Côtes de Libac.

D TARN-ET-GARONNE*
Mostly red wine, though some rosé is also made.

Z(83) TERROIRS LANDAIS*
A zonal *vin de pays* in Aquitaine and Charentes, created in 1987.

Z(84) TORGAN
Red, white and rosé wines, from the Aude *département* of Languedoc-Roussillon. The *vin de pays* used to be known as Coteaux Cathares.

Z(85) URFÉ*
Red wine for the most part, produced in modest quantities, although white and rosé may also be produced.

Z(86) UZÈGE*
Red (70 per cent), white (10 per cent) and rosé (20 per cent) wines, of good Languedoc style.

Z(87) VAL-DE-CESSE
Red, white and rosé wines from the Aude *département* of Languedoc-Roussillon.

Z(88) VAL-DE-DAGNE
Red, white and rosé wines, produced in substantial quantities.

Z(89) VAL DE MONTFERRAND
Red (70 per cent), white (10 per cent) and rosé (20 per cent) wines, with *vin primeur* and *vin d'une nuit* local specialities, produced in large quantities.

Z(90) VAL D'ORBIEU
Two-thirds red and one-third rosé wines, produced from traditional Rhône grape varieties. White wine may also be produced and *vin primeur* is made.

Z(91) VALLÉE DU PARADIS
Red wine produced in large quantities. A little wine is made as *vin primeur*.

Z(92) VALS D'AGLY
Red (95 per cent), white (one per cent) and rosé (four per cent) wines, along with a little *vin primeur*.

D VAR*
Red (65 per cent), white (five per cent) and rosé (30 per cent) wines, produced in a spicy Provençal style.

D VAUCLUSE*
Red (70 per cent), white (15 per cent) and rosé (15 per cent) wine, in typically southern Rhône style, produced in very large quantities.

Z(93) VAUNAGE
A light red wine that is in typical Languedoc style.

D VENDÉE*
Red, white and rosé wines, produced in small quantities, in a similar style to Fiefs Vendéens (which was a *vin de pays* until it was promoted to VDQS status in December 1984).

Z(94) VICOMTÉ D'AUMELAS
Red (80 per cent) and rosé (20 per cent), plus a tiny amount of white wine. The grapes used are traditional southwestern varieties.

D VIENNE*
Red, white and rosé wines produced in and around the Haut-Poitou district.

Z(95) VISTRENQUE
Red and rosé wines produced in very small quantities. White wine may also be produced.

D YONNE*
White wines only, produced in small quantities.

THE WINES OF
GERMANY

Germany

Efficiency is the key to Germany's winemaking success, and sweetness is its concept of quality. This country possesses just one per cent of the world's vineyards, yet provides 13 per cent of its wines. Every wine is graded by the natural sugar content of its grapes; the more sugar, the higher the quality, and so the greatest German wines are inevitably sweet white wines.

WHEN A GERMAN WINEMAKER BOTTLES A WINE, his aim is to capture the quintessential freshness of the grapes that went into it. From the most modest to the very finest, the secret of successful German wine is the harmony between its sweetness and acidity. With the exception of the top *Trocken* or dry wines, alcohol does not feature in the equation of quality and is generally unobtrusive.

GERMANY'S QUALITY STRUCTURE

Much of German wine law is very precise. In many instances its interpretation leads to a clarity unparalleled in other wine regions, but in others a certain confusion has led to various abuses that would not have occurred in countries with less sophisticated systems. When the EEC produced its laws for regulating wine production, the Germans were obliged to review their own, and in 1971 the so-called "new" German Wine Laws were established. Perhaps the most notable aspect of these revolutionary regulations was the reduction of 25,000 individually named vineyards to some 2,600, and their setting within a framework of quality regions, districts and collective sites. For the export business, the new system made the task of projecting a tangible image far easier, but it contained many basic flaws. To reduce the number of vineyards, they had to be grouped together to form sites approximately ten times larger than the original ones. The most crucial loss was the historical identity of Germany's greatest vineyards and, with it, any chance of setting up a system of lasting prestige.

THE SWEETNESS FACTOR

Germany's wine regime is built on a philosophy that equates ripeness with greatness. In many respects, this is not un-reasonable, for ripe grapes *are* required to make fine wine, but, taken to its ultimate conclusion, the German ideal implies, nonsensically, that a dry wine is inherently inferior to a sweet wine.

The quality categories listed below are linked to the degree of ripeness of the grapes, and therefore to when they are picked. Every German vineyard is picked in stages (equivalent to the *tries* of Sauternes, *see* p71). Because of Germany's northerly climate, these stages begin as soon as the grapes have sufficient sugar to

make *Deutscher Tafelwein* (in the lowest-quality vineyards) or *QbA* (in the better ones).

All German wines are graded according to the sugar content of the grape juice. This is measured in degrees Oechsle by a system that compares the specific gravity of grape juice with that of water. Thus, as water has a specific gravity of 1000, grape juice with

---

THE WINE REGIONS OF GERMANY

Viticulturally, West Germany is made up of four large *Deutscher Tafelwein* regions that encompass eight *Tafelwein* sub-regions, within which there are separate infra-structures for 11 *Qualitätswein* and 15 *Landwein* districts. The *Qualitätswein* areas — called Anbaugebiete — encompass 35 Bereiche or districts, which contain 152 Grosslagen or "collective sites", which in turn encapsulate some 2,600 Einzellagen (single-vineyard sites).

Deutscher Tafelwein Regions	Deutscher Tafelwein Sub-regions	Landwein Regions	Qualitätswein Regions (Anbaugebiete)
Rhein-Mosel	Rhein	Ahrtaler Landwein	Ahr
		Starkenburger Landwein	Hessische Bergstrasse
		Rheinburgen Landwein	Mittelrhein
		Nahegauer Landwein	Nahe
		Altrheingauer Landwein	Rheingau
		Rheinischer Landwein	Rheinhessen
		Pfälzer Landwein	Rheinpfalz
	Mosel	Landwein der Mosel	Mosel-Saar-Ruwer
	Saar	Landwein der Saar	
Bayern	Main	Fränkischer Landwein	Franken
	Donau	Regensburger Landwein	
	Lindau	Bayerischer Bodensee-Landwein	
Neckar	—	Schwäbischer Landwein	Württemberg
Oberrhein	Römertor	Südbadischer Landwein	Baden
	Burgengau	Unterbadischer Landwein	

QUALITY STRUCTURE OVERVIEW

This is a simplistic overview because each category varies according to the grape variety and its area of origin. More detailed analyses are given under each region (*see* Quality Requirements and Harvest Percentages boxes).

Quality category	Minimum Oechsle	Minimum potential alcohol
*Deutscher Tafelwein**	44-50°	5.0-5.9%
*Landwein**	47-55°	5.6-6.7%
*Qualitätswein bestimmter Anbaugebiete (QbA)**	50-72°	5.9-9.4%
Qualitätswein mit Prädikat (QmP):		
Kabinett	67-85°	8.6-11.4%
Spätlese	76-95°	10.0-13.0%
Auslese	83-105°	11.1-14.5%
Beerenauslese	110-128°	15.3-18.1%
Eiswein	110-128°	15.3-18.1%
Trockenbeerenauslese (TBA)	150-154°	21.5-22.1%

* Chaptalization is allowed, and will be necessary if the wine has a potential alcoholic strength of less than 8.5 per cent.

Sampling a maturing Nahe wine, above
This winemaker is examining the progress of a wine from the Mandel Einzellage.

specific gravity of 1050 has an Oechsle of 50°. The warmer the climate, the higher the sugar content and the higher the Oechsle.

The ranges in sweetness and alcohol at each level are made to allow for climatic limitations. It is easier, for example, to achieve greater ripeness, and therefore higher Oechsle levels, in Baden, than it is in other Rhine regions, or the Mosel, for example. However I am not convinced that standards should be dropped to enable certain grape varieties to more easily attain a designated style when grown in specific regions.

Rhein-Mosel Tafelweinregion
- Rhein
- Mosel
- Saar

Bayern Tafelweinregion
- Main
- Donau
- Lindau

Neckar Tafelweinregion

Oberrhein Tafelweinregion
- Römertor
- Burgengau

- – – – State Boundary
- ▲ Height above sea level (metres)

Kms 20 40 60 80
Mls 10 20 30 40 50

Landwein districts

1	Ahertaler Landwein
2	Starkenburger Landwein
3	Rheinburgen Landwein
4	Nahegauer Landwein
5	Altrheingauer Landwein
6	Pfälzer Landwein
7	Rheinischer Landwein
8	Landwein der Mosel
9	Landwein der Saar
10	Fränkischer Landwein
11	Regensburger Landwein
12	Bayerischer Bodensee-Landwein
13	Schwäbischer Landwein
14	Südbadischer Landwein
15	Unterbadischer Landwein

GERMANY

The country's winemaking zones are centred around its major rivers — the world-famous Rhine and Mosel, as well as the Neckar, Nahe, Saar, Ruwer and Main.

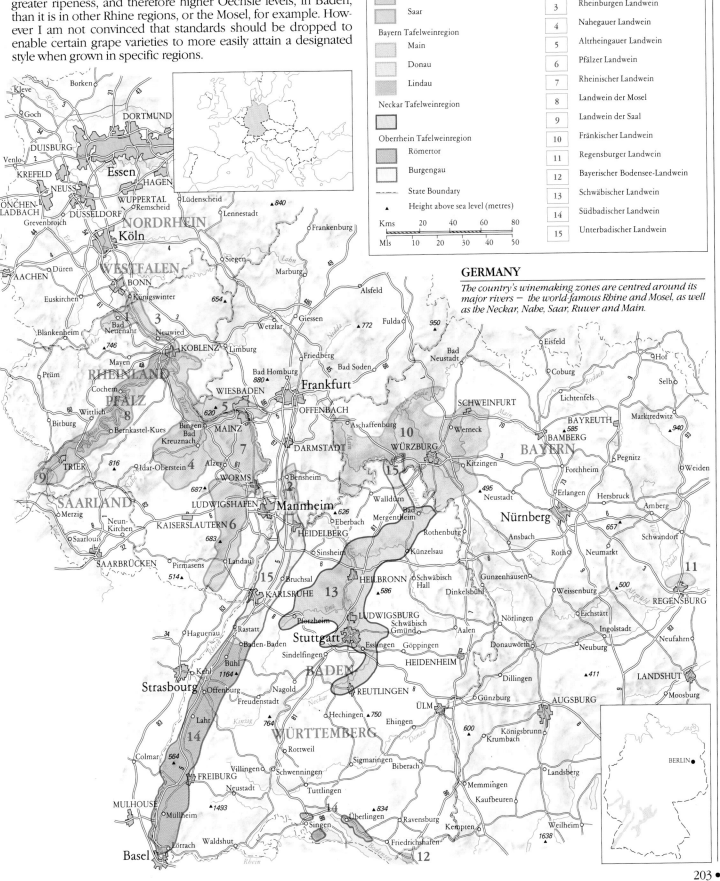

German red wine

If a German "red wine" is served chilled to a person blindfolded, they will nearly always assume it to be white. This is especially true of those wines that have some residual sweetness, whether caused naturally by stopping the fermentation, or through the addition of *Süssreserve*. Sweet *Auslese Rotwein* is common and *Beerenauslese* not unheard of. There is a trend to make drier, sometimes truly dry red wines, but these generally lack the classic structure, body, depth, tannin and colour that the rest of the world considers to be essential requisites for even the most basic red wine.

CHANGING IDEAS ABOUT GERMAN WINES

The modern concept of what German wines to drink, plus when and how to drink them is based on a tradition that is over a hundred years old. Outside Germany itself, the predilection for Rhine and Mosel is essentially a British one; historically, this has always been so. Even two world wars failed to diminish the British fondness for these wines, and Britain remains Germany's biggest customer. America is the second-biggest customer, with 30 per cent of German exports.

At one time, the British, whose tastes influenced the rest of the world, only drank Hock, a name that originally applied only to the wines of Hochheim, but soon became generic for all white Rhein or Rhine wines. Unlike the light, grapey Rhine wines we know now, the passion in the nineteenth century was for mature, full-flavoured, amber-coloured wines. Hock glasses traditionally have brown stems because they were deliberately made to reflect the desired amber colour of age into the wine. The Christie's auction of May 1777 listed "Excellent Genuine Old Hock" of the 1719 vintage, and another London sale offered "Hock Hocheim" 1726 in August of 1792. How a modern Hock might taste in 60 years time is anyone's guess, but mine is that it would not be very pleasant — unless it happened to be a *Trockenbeerenauslese*.

From Hock to Mosel

By the time Mosel wines became popular, the trend was for lighter, younger wines, hence the traditional green-stemmed Mosel glasses, made to reflect the greenness of youth into the wine. Incidentally, "Moselle" is the name of the river in France's most northerly wine area, producing VDQS Vins de Moselle, and as soon as the river crosses the border it becomes "Mosel". Surprisingly, too many English-labelled German wines mistakenly use the spelling "Moselle".

COMPARISON OF GERMAN HARVESTS 1984-1987

Production varies enormously in Germany from as much as 15.39 million hectolitres (171 million cases) in 1982 to as little as 5.2 million hectolitres (58 million cases) in 1985, as does the spread of wines across the range of quality categories, shown by the table below:

Quality category	1984	1985	1986	1987
Tafelwein to *Landwein*	16%	–	6%	4%
QbA	79%	51%	79%	82%
Kabinett	5%	30%	12%	13%
Spätlese	–	16%	3%	1%
Auslese to TBA	–	3%	–	–
Size of harvest				
Millions of hectolitres	7.7	5.2	10.2	–
(Millions of cases)	(85.5)	(58.1)	(113.3)	–
Hectares under vine	92,195	92,858	93,220	–
(Acres)	(227,800)	(229,450)	(230,340)	–
Hectolitres per hectare	83.4	55.9	109.4	–
(Cases per acre)	(375)	(253)	(492)	–

QUALITY REQUIREMENTS AND HARVEST PERCENTAGES

Germany is notorious for the variation of its vintages. As a form of insurance, therefore, most of the crop is harvested early. This secures a minimum income from *Deutscher Tafelwein* and *QbA* wines, with those grapes that remain on the vine providing a possibility of higher-quality wines from later harvests. If, when, and how much these grapes ripen is the most basic indication of the nature of any vintage. The degree of ripeness attained is expressed in degrees Oechsle and the minimum level for each *QmP* can vary according to the region and grape variety in question. Each degree of Oechsle is the equivalent of 2-2.5 grams per litre of sugar. The exact amount of sugar varies according to the level of unfermentable extract also present. For a survey of each region, *see* the individual charts in the regional sections.

UNDERSTANDING AP CODE NUMBERS

All *QbAs* and *QmPs*, including *Deutscher Sekt*, must carry an *AP (Amtliche Prüfnummer)* number. The number proves that a wine has undergone and passed various tasting and analytical tests and its origin has been established to the board's satisfaction. Each time a producer applies for an *AP* number, specially sealed samples of the approved wine are kept by both the board and the producer. Should there be a fault or a fraud enquiry, these samples are analyzed and checked against a sample of the product on the market that has given rise to complaint or investigation. This sounds foolproof, but like all systems it can be abused, simply by printing fictitious *AP* numbers on the label. The penalty for this is imprisonment, plus a ban from operating for the company and large fines.

Understanding the *AP* number can be very useful, particularly if the wine is a non-vintage *QbA* such as a Liebfraumilch and you want some idea of how long it has been in bottle.

1984
"BLUE NUN"
LIEBFRAUMILCH RHEINHESSEN
QUALITÄTSWEIN

4 = Examination Board number

907 = number of the commune where the wine was bottled

189 = the bottler's registered number

013 = the bottler's application number

85 = the year in which the bottler made the application

A.P.Nr.
4 907 189
013/85

The commune and bottler's numbers run into thousands and are of the least significance to the consumer. It is the last two sets of numbers that provide the most accessible and useful information. For the "Blue Nun", the 013 and 85 reveal that this is the thirteenth application that Sichel, the bottler or producer of "Blue Nun", has made in 1985 for the 1984 vintage of its Liebfraumilch Rheinhessen. There must have been twelve other shipments of the same wine earlier in 1985; this bottle would probably therefore taste distinctly fresher than a bottle with, for example, an 001 application number. The number of applications in a year can be helpful in determining the rate of turnover of a specific wine. If the wine happens to be a non-vintage version of something that should be drunk as young as possible, the date of application will be a revelation.

HOW TO READ GERMAN WINE LABELS

Information on the style and origin of wines is available in abundance on German labels.

Mosel-Saar-Ruwer
One of the 11 specified regions or Anbaugebiete, one of which must appear on the label of every *Qualitätswein bestimmter Anbaugebiete (QbA)* and *QmP* wine. In the case of a *Landwein*, one of its 15 regions must be indicated and the term *Deutscher Tafelwein* must also be mentioned.

Zeller Marienburger
This reveals that the wine comes from the commune of Zell on the lower reaches of the Mosel River, between Reil and Bullay. In German, *"-er"* is an adjectival ending added to the name of the place where a wine comes from, in the same way that English-speaking people might add *"-er"* to describe a person from London or New York as a "Londoner" or "New Yorker". Marienburger is the name of an Einzellage (an individual site or vineyard) within Zell.

Qualitätswein mit Prädikat (QmP)
The wine comes from the highest quality category of German wine and will carry one of the predicates that range from *Kabinett* up to *Trockenbeerenauslese*.

Name and address
The name and address of the owner of the estate and bottler of the wine must be shown on every German label. This example clearly shows

Vintage
A wine must be at least 85 per cent a product of the named year. It also carries the adjectival *"-er"* ending.

Grape variety
This is often indicated on German labels. This example states "Riesling" and is in fact 100 per cent pure

Riesling, although it need only be 85 per cent according to the regulations. If more than one grape variety is indicated on the label, then they must be listed in order of their importance in that wine; therefore a Riesling-Kerner contains more Riesling than Kerner.

Kabinett
The predicate appended to the end of this wine's name reveals that it is the lightest and driest of the predicates. The predicate can come either before or after the grape variety.

Amtliche Prüfnummer or Amtliche Prüfungsnummer
The *AP* number, as it is commonly called, is found on all *QbA* and *QmP* wines and is literally the "official proof number". The code is unique to each batch of wine presented to the official examination board and its presence is proof that the wine has passed the statutory origin, tasting and laboratory analysis test. *See* Understanding *AP* Code Numbers, p.204.

Produce (or Product) of Germany
This must be clearly shown on every bottle of exported German wine. If it is not, the wine is made from grapes grown in another country.

Volume
An indication of the liquid contents is mandatory at all levels of quality.

Alcoholic strength
Mandatory for export wines only.

that Kloster Machern is owned by Schneider'sche Weingüterverwaltung Kloster Machern, which is in fact part of Michel Schneider, a small, high-quality export house based in Zell.

Kloster Machern
The name of the estate. This property once belonged to an ancient Cistercian order that dates back to 1238.

Other terms that may appear on a label:

Bereich
If the wine carries the appellation of a Bereich, it will simply state this – "Bereich Zell", for example.

Grosslage
This is one of the main problems of German wine labelling. A Grosslage, or collective site, is a relatively large area (made up of several Einzellagen), under which name fairly modest wines are sold. The problem is that a Grosslage name appears after a commune name in exactly the same way as an Einzellage, of which there are 2,600, and so consumers are constantly led to believe that a Grosslage wine is an Einzellage. This legal mess could easily be rectified if it was incumbent upon producers to print the word "Grosslage" on labels in exactly the same way as it is for them to indicate "Bereich". Until the law is changed there is no simple way of differentiating between these wines.

Indication of sweetness (still wine)
This is permitted, but not mandatory, not even for *Landwein*, which is rather strange as it is a wine that may only be produced in *Trocken* and *Halbtrocken* styles. The terms that might be encountered are:

Trocken Dry – must not contain more than 4 grams per litre of residual sugar, although up to 9 grams per litre is permitted if the acidity is 2 grams per litre or less. *Halbtrocken* Half-dry – must not contain more than 18 grams per litre of residual sugar and 10 grams per litre of acidity. *Lieblich* Medium-sweet – nearer to the French *moelleux* than medium-sweet, this wine may have up to 45 grams per litre of residual sugar. *Süss* Sweet – with in excess of 45 grams per litre of residual sugar, this is a truly sweet wine.

Where applicable, *Rotwein* (red wine), *Weisswein* (white wine) or *Rotling* (rosé wine) must be indicated on the label of any category of *Tafelwein* up to and including *Landwein*. They must also be featured on the label of *QbA* and higher quality wines, but this is not mandatory, except in the case of *Rotling* or Rosé, which must be indicated on the label of *QbA* wines, although this is optional for *QmP*.

Weissherbst
A single-variety rosé produced from black grapes only. The grape variety must be indicated and the minimum quality of what was originally a botrytis wine is now *QbA*. The Spätburgunder can produce a

fine, fresh and mild wine with an attractive, smooth flavour.

Schillerwein
A Württemberg product that is the same as a *Rotling*, which is to say it may be made from a blend of black and white grape varieties.

Badisch Rotgold
A speciality rosé wine made from a blend of Ruländer and Spätburgunder. It must be of at least *QbA* level, and can only be produced in Baden.

Perlwein
Cheap, semi-sparkling wines made by carbonating a still wine. Mostly white, but may be red or rosé.

Schaumwein
With no further qualification, such as *Qualitätsschaumwein*, this indicates the cheapest form of sparkling wine, probably a carbonated blend of wines from various EEC countries.

Qualitätsschaumwein
A "quality sparkling wine" can be produced by any member state of the EEC, but the term should be qualified by the country of origin (of the wine), thus only *Deutscher Qualitätsschaumwein* will necessarily be from Germany.

Deutscher Sekt or Deutscher Qualitätsschaumwein
A sparkling wine made by any method (though probably *cuve close*), that is made from 100 per cent German grapes. It may indicate a maximum of two grape names and should be at least 10 months old when sold.

Deutscher Qualitätsschaumwein or Deutscher Sekt bestimmter Anbaugebiete
A sparkling wine made by any method (probably *cuve close*), that is made from 100 per cent German grapes from one specified region although it may indicate an even smaller area of origin if 85 per cent of the grapes come from that named area.

Flaschengärung
Bottle-fermented *Sekt*, but not necessarily *méthode champenoise*.

Flaschengärung nach dem traditionellen Verfahren
Sekt made by the *méthode champenoise*, although not usually a wine that shows much autolytic character.

Für Diabetiker geeignet
This means "suitable for diabetics". The wines must be *Trocken*, contain less than 1.5 grams per litre of sulphur dioxide (as opposed to 2.25 grams per litre) and no more than 12 per cent of alcohol.

Mosel winery, above
This wine firm's typically attractive premises are at Eller on the inner bend of a 180° loop made by the Mosel near Brem.

SÜSSRESERVE

Süssreserve is sterilized grape juice that may have just one or two degrees of alcohol, but has none if processed before fermentation can commence. It not only contributes the grapey freshness and sweetness for which German wines are famous, but also provides the winemaker with a convenient last-minute ingredient with which he can correct the balance of a wine. The origin of *Süssreserve* must, in essence, be the same as the wine to which it is added. Its quality, or degree of ripeness, should by law be at least the equivalent of the wine itself. The quantity added is not in itself restricted, but is indirectly controlled by the overall ratio of sugar to alcohol.

Quality	Grams/litre of alcohol for every gram/litre of residual sugar	Exceptions	
Tafelwein	3	Franconian red	(5)
Qualitätswein	3	Franconian red	(5)
		Franconian white and rosé	(3.5)
		Württemberg red	(4)
		Rheingau white	(2.5)
Kabinett	no controls	Franconian red	(5)
		Franconian white and rosé	(3)

THE STORY OF LIEBFRAUMILCH

A myriad theories surround the origin of Liebfraumilch (or Liebfrauenmilch), but many agree that it means "milk of Our Lady" and refers to the wine produced from one small and fairly indifferent vineyard in the suburbs of Worms that was once called Liebfrauenkirche or "Church of Our Lady". This is now part of Liebfrauenstift-Kirchenstück, which in turn is part of the 1,000-hectare (2,470-acre) Grosslage Liebfrauenmorgen. The single-vineyard wine that gave birth to the name of Liebfraumilch has no bearing whatsoever on the bulk-blended wine of today, nor, for that matter, any connection with the Liebfraumilch that was sold more than 100 years ago. What is interesting, however, is the nature of those early Liebfraumilch wines that gave the blended product of today its worldwide reputation and huge sales. The generic character of this wine was officially defined by the Worms Chamber of Commerce in 1910, when it stated that Liebfraumilch was merely "a fancy name" that merchants "have made a use of", merely applying it to "Rhine wines of good quality and character". According to German wine expert Fritz Hallgarten, the "fancy name" plunged to greater depths during the following 20 years. Even between 1945 and the advent of the new German wine laws in 1971, one-third of the wines blended into Liebfraumilch came from German regions other than the Rhine.

When the new German regulations specified that Liebfraumilch could be made only from Rheinhessen, Rheinpfalz, Rheingau and Nahe grapes, a great many producers interpreted this literally, considering that the law provided for an umbrella Liebfraumilch designation that entitled it to come from any one or more of the four specified regions. But as a *Qualitätswein*, Liebfraumilch can only come from one specified region. I could not understand why a Liebfraumilch that was a blend of wines from more than one permitted region should not be classified as Liebfraumilch *Tafelwein*, with wines from a single region entitled to *QbA* status. However, Liebfraumilch producers disliked the idea of the *Tafelwein* classification – a misguided view in my opinion, not least because Liebfraumilch sells on its brand name.

Not a wine the Germans drink

More than one-third of all German exported wines are sold as Liebfraumilch, an inexpensive, unpretentious, bulk-blended German wine specifically constructed for the export market. The Germans drink very little Liebfraumilch, maybe less than 0.01 per

cent of the 1.08 million hectolitres (12 million cases) produced each year. In fact virtually 100 per cent goes down non-German throats, with Britain as the largest consumer, followed by America.

Liebfraumilch is a *QbA*, yet many of the cheapest brands come a very poor second when tasted blind against *Deutscher Tafelwein*, and even those that consistently prove to be the best are certainly not fine wines. It nevertheless serves a very useful purpose. Characteristics such as tannin, alcohol and definite dryness can discourage many newcomers to wine, yet they enjoy the fresh, flowery aroma and sweet, grapey taste of Liebfraumilch. It is a very good stepping-stone, and statistics show that the vast majority of seasoned wine-drinkers originally "cut their teeth" on this accessible wine.

What is Liebfraumilch?

Germany's most criticized wine is the only one to be defined by taste and sweetness in its wine laws. According to the regulations, the minimum amount of residual sugar is 18 grams per litre, equivalent to the maximum allowed for a *Halbtrocken*, although few are actually this low, and some are twice as high. Producers have their own idea of what level of sweetness is right for the market and make their wines accordingly. Many buyers insist on a certain ratio of sugar to acidity; most brands contain between 22-35 grams per litre, with 27-28 as a good average.

Liebfraumilch labels must now show one of the four permitted regions; at least 85 per cent of the wine must come from the region stated. On average, the Rheinhessen and the Rheinpfalz produce more than nine out of every ten bottles of Liebfraumilch, while the Nahe makes very little and the Rheingau virtually none.

Any grape permitted for German *QbA* wine may be used for the production of Liebfraumilch, the only control being that at least 51 per cent of the blend must be composed of one or more of the following varieties: Riesling, Silvaner, Müller-Thurgau and Kerner. According to the regulations, the wine should taste of these grapes, although I have met no expert who can either describe or detect a definitive blend of four such different varieties. What I have discovered is that some of the best blends have been denied their *AP* numbers because they have received a beneficial *Süssreserve* of aromatic Morio-muskat. The Liebfraumilch examining board apparently believes these eminently more attractive wines to be untypical of the appellation — I am completely in favour of Liebfraumilch, but let it at least be an honest and attractive wine.

SEKT–GERMANY'S SPARKLING WINE

Germany's *Sekt* or sparkling wine industry is very important. Its output now averages 2.25 million hectolitres (25 million cases) – 50 per cent more than a *bumper* crop of Champagne. Although exports rose from 24,300 hectolitres (270,000 cases) in 1970 to 90,000 hectolitres (1 million cases) by 1987, the Germans essentially make *Sekt* for themselves and resort to imports from Champagne, Italy and elsewhere to quench their annual thirst for 2.7 million hectolitres (30 million cases) of fizzy wine. As *Sekt* is a product designed for German palates, it is not surprising that the style is essentially grapey and inclined to medium sweetness, with no hint of the autolytic character of classic Champagne.

SEKT SWEETNESS CHART

Sweetness rating	Residual sugar (grams per litre)
Extra Herb or *Extra Brut*	0-6
Herb or *Brut*	0-15
Extra Trocken or Extra Dry	12-20
Trocken* or Dry	17-35
Halbtrocken* or *Demi-Sec*	33-50
Süss, Drux, Doux or Sweet	50 +

* Not to be confused with still wine limits, which are no more than 9 grams per litre for *Trocken* and 18 grams per litre for *Halbtrocken*.

GERMANY'S NEW *BARRIQUE* WINES

A new breed of very high-quality wine is beginning to establish itself in Germany. The term *Barrique* has been adopted by a number of growers as a generic tag for essentially (though not necessarily) dry red and white wines that are matured in small, new oak barrels. This innovation began in Baden in the late 1970s with growers such as Benno u. Wolf Dietrich Salwey and Weingut Schwarzer Adler. The most interesting regions for *Barrique* wines are Baden and Württemberg, with excellent potential in hotter years in the Rheingau, Rheinhessen and Nahe.

Grape varieties

The most successful grapes so far have been Burgundian varietals – Weisser Burgunder (Pinot blanc), Grauer Burgunder (Pinot gris) and Spätburgunder. The Württemberg growers place much faith in the local Lemberger grape for red wines, although it has yet to prove sufficiently deep and fine to warrant, and benefit from, the influence of new oak. The Riesling also has relatively few supporters, but its producers tend not to use new oak, or cut down the maturation period. Another common style is a blend of Weisser Burgunder and Chardonnay.

Oak maturation

The size of barrel, length of maturation and proportion of new oak are critical factors in determining the amount of oak influence in the wine. The smaller the barrel, the greater the ratio of wood surface to wine and, therefore, the more influence. Oaky characteristics are also increased by longer maturation and higher proportions of new oak. The majority of *Barrique* wines produced use classic 225-litre *barriques* of Allier, Limousin and Nevers oak, for between three and 15 months. Most of the *barriques* are 100 per cent new oak, but some producers use 50 per cent new oak, and some even use all old-oak barrels. Further variations include using new German oak, totally or partly, and using barrels as small as 125 litres or as large as 600 litres in capacity.

Residual sweetness and quality levels

The majority of white *Barrique* wines can be described as fully fermented and, organoleptically, totally dry. Most contain between less than 1 gram per litre of residual sugar and 2 grams; some may

Picking grapes in the Mosel, above
Harvesting the Riesling in this region's steep vineyards is labour-intensive.

contain between 6 and 7 grams per litre, but this is well below the limit for German *Trocken* wines and would, to all intents and purposes, taste dry to most palates. Red *Barrique* wines are dry to very dry, with less than 2.75 grams per litre of residual sugar.

In general, *Barrique* wines come from grapes with an Oechsle level of between 80° and 105° and are therefore at least of *Spätlese* level. But few of the white wines are labelled as such, although more red wines are labelled as either *QbA* or *QmP*. Any *QmP* white wines are likely to be Rieslings of very restrained *"Barrique"* character. There is a rational reason why the official Examination Boards fail to pass *Barrique* wines for any level of *Qualitätswein;* to be accepted as a *QbA* or *QmP*, the wines must be "typical of their grape and area of origin". The influence of oak changes these characteristics. This automatic rejection of *Barrique* wines is of little consequence to the growers; most no longer submit them for *Qualitätswein* status and are released from its legal constraints.

The future of *Barrique* wines

It is easy to perceive how these intriguingly undersold wines can capture the interest of Germany's more sophisticated wine-drinkers. Most *Barrique* wines are actually pre-sold before the last harvest has been gathered each year. They are easy to sell, and the grower has little cause to lament the inability of Germany's laws to classify them as quality wines.

This situation has long been paralleled in Italy, where so many of the finest wines are sold as table wines for vastly superior prices to those that bear the country's official DOC quality status. If, as I expect, the *Barrique* wines become increasingly successful, this will promote the general impression that many of Germany's finest wines are table wines, while most of its extremely modest and often very poor wines are officially sold as *Qualitätswein*. The answer is to introduce an official category for *Barrique* wines, with controls flexible enough to encourage growers to make the finest red and white, oak-aged wines. Yields could be restricted to promote quality, preventing a deluge of inferior *Barrique* wines.

There are currently 20-30 producers of *Barrique* wines, although these are on the increase. Most are small, high-quality growers whose methods are constantly evolving with experience. Having tasted a fair selection of *Barrique* wines, I find them variable in quality, but generally good and improving. Many need at least five years in bottle to harmonize and the more recent vintages are often intrinsically better than the older ones that are now beginning to peak. There is still much to learn in the area of barrel-maturation, and the greatest amount of experimentation should be directed towards discovering what type of oak is best suited to particular varieties of grape. One other noticeable failing is a certain lack of appreciation of the virtues of putting any oak-influenced wine through its malolactic, in vat or cask.

Major wineries of Germany

BLACK TOWER
See Hermann Kendermann.

BLUE NUN
See H. Sichel Söhne.

DEINHARD
Deinhard Platz 3,
5400 Koblenz

Sales: *2.5 million cases*
Vineyards: *100 ha (247 acres)*
Established: *1794*

A very important, high-quality export house that is best-known for its "Green Label" Moselle (sic), "Hans Christof" *Kabinett* and "Lila Imperial" *Sekt*. Its Wegeler-Deinhard Estate includes the second-largest section of Bernkasteler Doctor, a vineyard that makes Germany's most famous and most expensive wine.

☆ "Lila Imperial" (vintage), Wegeler-Deinhard Estate wines

EWALD THEODOR DRATHEN
Auf der Hill,
5584 Alf-Mosel

Vineyards: *7 ha (17 acres)*
Established: *1860*

A small estate production of competent quality sold on the domestic market, supplemented by substantial sales abroad of cheap generic German and EEC blended wine, including *Sekt*.

GOLDENER OKTOBER
See St. Ursula Weingut

GREEN LABEL
See Deinhard.

LOUIS GUNTRUM WEINKELLEREI
Rheinallee 62,
6505 Nierstein am Rhein

Sales: *250,000 cases*
Vineyards: *65 ha (160 acres)*
Established: *1824*

Originally Dutch, the Guntrum family settled in the Rheinhessen as long ago as the fourteenth century. Hans Joachim Louis Guntrum is delightfully eccentric. He wears a wooden bow-tie and constantly wages war on producers of cheap and inferior Liebfraumilch. The bulk of Guntrum's sales are generic but superior German wines. Where this great house excels is in its own estate wines that succinctly express the Guntrum philosophy that lower yields bring better quality.

☆ Guntrum Estate wines

ARTHUR HALLGARTEN
6222 Geisenheim

Sales: *50,000 cases*
Established: *1933*

A traditional firm that never deviates from its standards of quality. Hallgarten's generic wines are always well made and its "Kellergeist" is one of the best Liebfraumilch. The special selections from independent growers are first-rate.

☆ Generic wines, Special Selections

ADOLPH HUESGEN
Am Bahnhof,
5580 Traben-Trarbach

Sales: *1.2 million cases*
Vineyards: *25 ha (62 acres)*
Established: *1735*

Although Huesgen's large production includes EEC blends and some rather lacklustre generic German wines, its superb, dryish, 1983 Riesling "Silber 250", specially produced to celebrate the firm's 250th anniversary in 1985, clearly demonstrates its potential.

☆ 1983 Riesling "Silber 250"

HERMANN KENDERMANN
Mainstrasse 57,
6530 Bingen

Sales: *1.5 million cases*
Established: *1947*

This large export house is best known for its "Black Tower" Liebfraumilch, one of the largest-selling brands in the world (labelled Rhine wine in some export markets). Kendermann was purchased by European Cellars, the multi-national company owned by Allied-Lyons and Whitbread, in February 1987.

LANGGUTH ERBEN
Dr. Ernst-Spiess-Allee 2,
5580 Traben-Trarbach

Sales: *2.5 million cases*
Vineyards: *100 ha (247 acres)*
Established: *1789*

Langguth owns 11 hectares (27 acres) of its own vineyards, the total holding reflecting its limited partnership with almost 400 growers. Generic wines carry the "FW Langguth" banner and *Prädikat* wines are sold under the "Erben" label. The "Erben" range consistently shows an extraordinary degree of quality and longevity, considering its high volume of production.

☆ "Erben" (particularly *Kabinett*)

LANGENBACH
Alzeyerstrasse 31,
6520 Worms

Sales: *1 million cases*
Vineyards: *7 ha (17 acres)*
Established: *1852*

Another major export house owned by European Cellars, Langenbach owns a substantial plot of Liebfrauenstift, part of the original Liebfraumilch vineyard. Its "Crown of Crowns" is merely adequate, as is its *Sekt* range.

PETER MERTES
Postfach 1360,
5550 Bernkastel-Kues

Sales: *4.5 million cases*
Vineyards: *32 ha (79 acres)*
Established: *1924*

The largest privately-owned producer of generic German wines and one of the most important re-exporters of EEC and foreign wines, particularly Italian. Its aggressive selling technique and price-undercutting has not earned the firm many friends in the trade, but has brought it success. While the pragmatic chairman Michael Willkomm admits that he sells on price, not quality, his "Dr. Willkomm" Liebfraumilch has often fared better in blind tastings than famous Liebfraumilch brands that sell for twice the price. Its estate-bottled production is small, but can provide good-value wines, particularly from Sommerauer Schlossberg.

☆ "Dr. Willkomm" for value, Sommerauer Schlossberg for value and quality

RUDOLF MÜLLER
Postfach 20,
5586 Reil an der Mosel

Sales: *350,000 cases*
Vineyards: *14.5 ha (26 acres), plus contracts with other growers totalling 50 ha (123 acres)*
Established: *1919*

This export house has its own excellent estate, Weingut Rudolf Müller, in the Saar, and close ties with three others: Weingut Gebert, also in the Saar, Kessel Erben in Schwabsburg, near Nierstein, and Wwe Dr. H. Thanisch, which includes the largest part of the world-famous Bernkasteler Doctor, the firm's greatest, yet least-advertised, wine. Rudolf Müller is, however, best known for good-quality, reliable, inexpensive generic wines, especially the fresh, tangy "Bishop of Riesling", its top-selling wine.

☆ Entire range for value, estate-bottled Scharzhofberger for quality

CARL REH
See Günther Reh Group.

FRANZ REH & SOHN KG
Römerstrasse 27,
5559 Leiwen

Sales: *1.5 million cases*
Vineyards: *13 ha (32 acres)*
Established: *1843*

A private firm with a very large production of German generics and some finer wines from its own estate, the vineyards of which have been family-owned since the seventeenth century.

GÜNTHER REH GROUP
Liebfraunstrasse 10,
5500 Trier

Sales: *50,000 cases (estate wines only)*
Vineyards: *75 ha (185 acres)*
Established: *1978*

This large and powerful group encompasses the Faber Sektkellerei and Carl Reh generic wines at one end of the quality spectrum, and such star-performing estates as Reichsgraf von Kesselstatt, Otto van Volxem, Dr. J. B. Hain and Ehses Berres at the other.

☆ Estate wines from: Reichsgraf von Kesselstatt, Otto van Volxem, Dr. J. B. Hain, Ehses Berres

RHEINBERG KELLEREI
Mainzerstrasse 162-170,
6530 Bingen

Sales: *4.25 million cases*
Established: *1939*

Huge exporter of generic wines under many different labels.

SCHOLL & HILLEBRAND
Geisenheimstrasse 9,
6220 Rüdesheim

Sales: *20,000 cases (Weingut G. Breuer 6,000 cases)*
Vineyards: *16 ha (40 acres)*
Established: *1880*

Small, upmarket export house in the Rheingau, with a good generic range that includes Riesling Dry, one of the few truly excellent yet commercial *Trocken* wines. Its top-quality wines come from the underrated Weingut G. Breuer estate.

☆ Scholl & Hillebrand Riesling Dry, all estate wines from Weingut G. Breuer

ST. URSULA WEINGUT
Mainzerstrasse 184,
6530 Bingen

Sales: *2.5 million cases*
Established: *1963*

Owned by Nestlé, the vast production of this firm is mostly marketed under the well-known "Goldener Oktober" label. It is also the sole exporter of the fine wines produced by the Weingut Villa Sachsen.

☆ Weingut Villa Sachsen

G. A. SCHMITT
Wilhelmstrasse 2-4,
6505 Nierstein

Sales: *200,000 cases*
Vineyards: *100 ha (247 acres)*
Established: *1618*

After some difficult times this important export house is back on course producing well-made, very good-value, generic wines. Sweeter QbAs have the edge over *Trocken* styles. There are also some fine estate wines.

☆ Estate wines

H. SICHEL SÖHNE
Werner-von-Siemens-Strasse 14-18,
6508 Alzey

Sales: *2 million cases*
Established: *1857*

The story of Sichel, a company founded by the sprightly 66-year-old Hermann Sichel, is very much the story of its famous Liebfraumilch, "Blue Nun", Germany's largest-selling wine is one that few Germans would recognize,

as virtually all of its production is exported. The first mention of "Blue Nun" appeared on the company's London price list and featured the 1921 vintage. Its launch could not have occurred at a more fortuitous time: Liebfraumilch was already popular and with great quantities of classic *Auslese* wine available for the blend, "Blue Nun" received instant acclaim.

Why it was decided to call the wine "Blue Nun" is still something of a mystery. There were no smiling nuns on the first "Blue Nun" label and, when they did appear, in 1925, they were wearing brown habits and sombre faces. It was not until much later that they developed their blue habits and satisfied smiles.

☆ "Blue Nun Gold", Selected estate wines

CARL SITTMANN
Wormserstrasse 61,
6504 Oppenheim

Sales: *850,000 cases*
Vineyards: *80 ha (198 acres)*
Established: *1879*

A large producer of acceptable, if uninspiring, generic wines, Sittmann truly excels in its estate wines.

☆ Estate wines

DR. WILLKOMM
See Peter Mertes.

ZIMMERMANN-GRAEF
Marientaler Au,
5583 Zell an der Mosel

Sales: *1.3 million cases*
Established: *1886*

Important for generic wines, its better blends are sold under the relatively new "Graef" label. Good estate wines are also produced.

Important German cooperatives

GEBIETS-WINZER-GENOSSENSCHAFT DEUTSCHES WEINTOR eG
6741 Ilbesheim

Production: *1.2 million cases*
Vineyards: *5,000 ha (12,350 acres)*
Members: *1,300*
Established: *1967*

A fast-expanding cooperative near the French border that produces inexpensive, but well-made wines from as many as 50 different grape varieties grown in the Bereich Südliche Weinstrasse.

GEBIETS-WINZERGE-NOSSENSCHAFT FRANKEN eG
8710 Kitzingen-Repperndorf

Production: *1.6 million cases*
Vineyards: *1,800 ha (4,448 acres)*
Members: *7 cooperatives with an aggregate of 2,904 members*
Established: *1959*

This multi-cooperative produces mostly dry or dryish Müller-Thurgau wines, although the traditional Franconian Silvaner is the second-most important variety, accounting for one-quarter of the production.

WINZERGENOSSEN-SCHAFT FRIEDELSHEIM eG
Hauptstrasse 97-99,
6701 Friedelsheim

Production: *250,000 cases*
Vineyards: *150 ha (371 acres)*
Members: *127*
Established: *1911*

A cooperative with a high percentage of Riesling vines and some very good sites in Bereich Mittelhaardt-Deutsche Weinstrasse. However, I have not encountered its wines on any export market.

KAISERSTÜHLER WINZER-GENOSSENSCHAFT IHRINGEN eG
Winzerstrasse 6,
7817 Ihringen

Production: *700,000 cases*
Vineyards: *400 ha (988 acres)*
Members: *950*
Established: *1924*

A small, good-quality cooperative with vineyards in Ihringen, more than 85 per cent of which consist of Silvaner, Müller-Thurgau and Spätburgunder.

WINZERGENOSSEN-SCHAFT MAYSCHOSS-ALTENAHR
Bundesstrasse 42,
5481 Mayschoss

Production: *110,000 cases*
Vineyards: *110 ha (271 acres)*
Members: *280*
Established: *1868*

This small Ahr cooperative is the oldest cooperative in Germany. Mayschoss-Altenahr is well known for its soft, light, red Spätburgunder wines, which account for about 40 per cent of its total production.

WINZERGENOSSENSCHAFT & WEINKELLEREI RHEINGRAFENBERG eG
Naheweinstrasse 63,
6553 Meddersheim

Production: *85,000 cases*
Vineyards: *156 ha (385 acres)*
Members: *120*
Established: *1929*

Small, fine-quality cooperative with more than 55 per cent of its production from the Riesling grape.

GEBIETSWINZERGENOSSENSCHAFT RIETBURG eG
6741 Rhodt u.d. Rietburg

Production: *1.4 million cases*
Vineyards: *1,100 ha (2,718 acres)*
Members: *1,150*
Established: *1958*

Large Rheinpfalz cooperative with a very wide range of wines produced from Müller-Thurgau, Silvaner, Riesling, Ruländer, Kerner and various other varieties grown between Neustadt and Landau. The Rheinpfalz produces more wine than any other German wine region.

RUPPERTSBERGER WINZERVEREIN "HOHEBURG" eG
Uebergasse 23,
6701 Ruppertsberg

Production: *150,000 cases*
Vineyards: *204 ha (504 acres)*
Members: *209*
Established: *1911*

Well-made wines of good to very good quality. Its excellent vineyards have a high proportion of Riesling and are found in the area of Ruppertsberg and surrounding villages in the Rheinpfalz.

WINZERKELLER SÜDLICHE BERGSTRASSE/ KRAICHGAU eG
Bögnerweg 3,
6908 Wiesloch

Production: *500,000 cases*
Vineyards: *1,380 ha (3,408 acres)*
Members: *4,300*
Established: *1935*

A large Baden cooperative with vineyards in nearly 60 villages throughout the Bereich Badische Bergstrasse-Kraichgau. *See also* The wines of Baden, p.239.

WINZERGENOSSENSCHAFT THÜNGERSHEIM eG
Untere Haupstrasse 272a,
8702 Thüngersheim

Production: *200,000 cases*
Vineyards: *217 ha (536 acres)*
Members: *365*
Established: *1930*

This small, high-quality Franconian cooperative consistently produces a range of wines of medal-winning quality.

WINZERGENOSSENSCHAFT VIER JAHRESZEITEN-KLOSTER LIMBURG
Limburgerstrasse 8,
6702 Bad Dürkheim

Production: *420,000 cases*
Vineyards: *322 ha (796 acres)*
Members: *243*
Established: *1900*

A cooperative with a well-established reputation for producing very fine-quality wines from its vineyards in the Bad Dürkheim area, in the Central Rheinpfalz.

WINZERGENOSSENSCHAFT WACHTENBURG-LUGINSLAND eG
6706 Wachenheim a.d. Weinstrasse

Production: *450,000 cases*
Vineyards: *330 ha (815 acres)*
Members: *320*

Riesling features heavily in the very good wines produced by this Rheinpfalz cooperative, with fine vineyards in Bereich Mittelhaardt-Deutscher Weinstrasse.

ZENTRALKELLEREI BADISCHER WINZERGENOSSENSCHAFT eG
Zum Kaiserstuhl 6,
7814 Breisach

Production: *14 million cases*
Vineyards: *12,320 ha (30,000 acres)*
Members: *100 cooperatives with an aggregate membership of 24,000 growers*
Established: *1952*

This super-sized cooperative of co-operatives sells approximately 90 per cent of Baden's total annual wine output under no less than 400-500 different labels. From the basic supermarket blends to the single-estate wines, the winemaking techniques cannot be faulted. However, too many wines lack dash and show similarity of character.

ZENTRALKELLEREI MOSEL-SAAR-RUWER eG
5550 Bernkastel-Kues

Production: *3.6 million cases*
Vineyards: *3,240 ha (8,006 acres)*
Members: *20 cooperatives with an aggregate membership of some 5,200*
Established: *1968*

A very large and rapidly expanding cooperative on the Mosel. Its wide range is mostly of modest quality.

ZENTRALKELLEREI RHEINISCHER WINZERGENOSSENSCHAFT
Wöllsteinerstrasse 16,
6551 Gau-Bickelheim

Production: *3.3 million cases*
Vineyards: *3,000 ha (7,413 acres)*
Members: *6,000*

The best-known product from this huge cooperative with vineyards in the Rheingau and Rheinhessen is its "Little Rhine Bear" Liebfraumilch.

Major *Sekt* brands and houses

BLACK TOWER
The fizzy version of the well-known Liebfraumilch brand made by European Cellars' Hermann Kendermann winery, "Black Tower" is a very commercial *cuve close*.

BLUE NUN
The fizzy version of Sichel Söhne's world-famous "Blue Nun" Liebfraumilch is another straightforward, commercial *cuve close*.

BROGSITTER'S ZUM DOM HERRENHOF
125 Walporzheimerstrasse,
Walporzheim im Ahrtal

Sales: *25,000 cases*
Established: *1600*

An Ahr house that specializes in red *Sekt*, the best-known being "Rotsekt" and "Sankt Peter". These are an acquired taste, to say the least, but

there is an interesting and potentially good *méthode champenoise* Scharzberger Riesling.

BURGEFF
6203 Hochheim/Main

Established: *1836*

A large and competent *cuve close* producer, widely known for its "Burgeff Grün" and "Schloss Hochheim" brands.

CASTELLER HERRENBERG
See Fürstlich Castell'sches Domänenamt.

FÜRSTLICH CASTELL'SCHES DOMÄNENAMT
8711 Castell Unterfranken

Sales: *80,000 cases wine, plus Sekt*
Established: *1258 (wines)*

Franconian *cuve close* sold under the "Casteller Herrenberg" label.

DEINHARD
Deinhard Platz 3,
5400 Koblenz

Established: *1794*

This high-quality export house has a large *Sekt* range. All the wines are made by *cuve close*, from the inexpensive and very commercial "Cabinet", "Tradition" and "Mosel Dry", through the good non-vintage "Lila Imperial", to the excellent Riesling-based vintage "Lila Imperial", which can be stunning in its varietal intensity and usually possesses a fine, creamy *mousse*, showing that the tank-method is as good as *méthode champenoise* for aromatic sparkling wines.

DEUTZ & GELDERMANN
Muggens-Turm-Strasse 26,
7814 Breisach

Sales: *225,000 cases*
Established: *1925*

Most of the sparkling wine made by this offshoot of the famous Champagne *grande marque* firm is Pinot-based *méthode champenoise*, sold under the "Carte Noir" label. "Carte Rouge" is made by the transfer method, as is "Privat Cuvée" Halbtrocken, "Superb" Trocken and "Wappen von Breisach Grande Classé" Extra Trocken. This company also makes other *Sekt* by the *cuve close* method.

EWALD THEODOR DRATHEN
Auf der Hill,
5584 Alf-Mosel

Sales: *6,500 cases*
Established: *1860*

A large range of inexpensive, very commercial, *cuve close* wines, including Schloss Avras, its top-of-the-range *cuvée*.

FABER
27 Niederkircherstrasse,
5500 Trier

Sales: *4.2 million cases*
Established: *1950*

Germany's biggest bottler of bubbles, all *cuve close* and of very ordinary commercial quality, sold under the "Krönung" and "Rotlese" labels.

GEBRÜDER WEISS
See Kessler.

GRÄFLICH VON KAGENECK'SCHE SEKTKELLEREI
35 Muggens-Turmstrasse,
7814 Breisach

Sales: *140,000 cases*
Established: *1974*

A large range of varietal *méthode champenoise* competently made under the auspices of the giant ZBW cooperative in Baden and sold under various labels.

PETER HERRES
Rudolf-Diesel-Strasse 7-9,
5500 Trier a.d. Mosel

Established: *1954*

A rapidly growing firm producing a competent quality of *Sekt* under the "Herres Hochgewächs", "King Lear's", "Graf Artos" and "Römer" labels.

HENKELL
Biebricher Allee 142,
6200 Wiesbaden

Sales: *4 million cases*
Established: *1856*

One of Germany's oldest *Sekt* houses, and probably its most famous. All of Henkell's wines are produced by *cuve close*. Its inexpensive "Henkell Trocken" is rather lacklustre, but does not lack popularity and sales of its "Rüttgers Club" brand alone total 1.25 million cases. Henkell also own Sektkellerei Carstens, producing a range of cheaper *Sekt* under that label.

HAUS HOCHHEIM
Postfach 1145,
6203 Hochheim am Main

Sales: *85,000 cases*
Established: *1884*

Medium-sized house producing commercial *cuve close* wines of modest quality under "Goldlack", "Grünlack", "Rotlack" and "Sonder Cuvée" labels.

KESSLER
7300 Esslingen

Established: *1826*

Founded by George Christian von Kessler, who once worked for the great Veuve Clicquot, this is Germany's oldest *Sekt* house. The firm uses various methods of production, but all those sold under the Kessler label are made by the *méthode champenoise* and are highly regarded on the domestic market. Those produced by

its subsidiary firm Gebrüder Weiss are all *cuve close*.

KLOSS FOERSTER
Postfach 1207,
6220 Rüdesheim

Sales: *84,000 cases*
Established: *circa 1850*

An old-established firm that originated in eastern Germany and today uses both *cuve close* and *méthode champenoise* to make a varied range of *Sekt* at its Rheingau premises. These range from the relatively inexpensive "Wappen Trocken" and "Wappen Rot" brands, through the interesting Bereich Johannisberg Rheingauer Riesling and Rüdesheimer Bischofsberg, both *QbA Sekts*, to the top-of-the-range "Impersonator Brut" label.

KUPFERBERG
19 Kupferberg-Terrasse,
6500 Mainz

Sales: *1 million cases*
Established: *1850*

One of Germany's best-known brands, "Kupferberg Gold" was once *méthode champenoise*, although it has not been made by this process for quite some time. Kupferberg's top-of-the-range "Fürst von Bismarck" brand is a very respectable wine that undergoes fermentation in bottle, after which it is decanted, filtered and re-bottled. This firm, which is part of the very large Racke group, owns Bricout & Koch, a small but very good Champagne house.

LANGENBACH
31 Alzeyerstrasse,
6520 Worms

Sales: *1 million cases*
Established: *1852*

Part of European Cellars, this firm produces a range of commercially acceptable *cuve close* sparkling wines. These include a Waldracher Riesling *QbA Sekt*, "Goldlack Riesling", "Weisslack", "Schloss Dalberg", "Schloss Leutstetten", a red "Purpur" and sparkling versions of "Crown of Crowns" and "Silver Crown".

LILA IMPERIAL
See Deinhard.

MATHEUS MÜLLER
6228 Eltville

Sales: *600,000 cases*
Established: *1836*

One of Germany's oldest *Sekt* houses, Matheus Müller was purchased by the multinational Seagram Company in 1984. The best-known brand belonging to this firm, which uses only *cuve close*, is "MM Extra". Cheaper wines are produced under the "Hoel Diplomat" label by its sister *Sektkellerei*, Gebrüder Hoel (which should not be confused with Gebrüder Weiss, a subsidiary of Kessler).

RUDOLF MÜLLER
Postfach 20,
5586 Reil

Established: *1919*

An excellent export house making *Sekt* under its well-known "Splendid" label. The wine is of modest quality, with the exception of the Mosel Riesling Extra Dry Deutscher Sekt, a wine that ranks amongst the best of its type. There is a Wwe Dr. H. T. Thanisch Bereich Bernkastel Riesling Trocken, a *QbA Sekt*, which has a fine reputation.

RITTERHOF
51 Weinstrasse Nord,
6702 Bad Dürkheim

Sales: *16,000 cases*
Established: *1837*

Small in size, but one of the oldest *Sekt* houses in Germany, Ritterhof makes pure Rheinpfalz *cuve close*, with half of the grapes coming from its own estate. The "Ritterstolz", "Ritterhof Riesling Brut" and "Ritterhof Riesling Trocken" are all respectable, while the red "Dürkheimer Feuerberg Halbtrocken" is very much an acquired taste.

SANKT PETER
See Brogsitter's Zum Dom Herrenhof.

SCHLOSSKELLEREI AFFALTRACH
15 Am Ordensschloss,
7104 Obersulm-Affaltrach

Sales: *50,000 cases*
Established: *1928*

A Württemberg *Sekt* house that produces a decent quality of wine under the "Baumann Riesling" label. Others include "Brillant", and "Diamant", with second wines sold under the "Burg Löwenstein" brand.

SCHLOSS AVRAS
See Ewald Theodor Drathen.

SCHLOSS DALBERG
See Langenbach.

SCHLOSS HOCHHEIM
See Burgeff.

SCHLOSS LEUTSTETTEN
See Langenbach.

SCHLOSS RHEINGARTEN
6222 Geisenheim

Established: *1898*

Well-known *cuve close* sparkler of competent commercial quality.

SCHLOSS SCHÖNBORN
Hauptstrasse 53,
6228 Eltville

Single-estate, vintaged, Rheingau Riesling *méthode champenoise* wine. The house is experimenting with other grape varieties, and a pink Pinot Noir looks likely in the future.

SCHLOSS WACHENHEIM
Postfach 40,
6706 Wachenheim

Good quality, single-estate, vintaged

Riesling *Sekt* made by *méthode champenoise*.

SCHNAUFER
1 Im Mönchswasen,
7262 Althengstett

Sales: *200,000 cases*

A large production of competent commercial *Sekt* made by the *cuve close* method and sold under the "Liechtenstein" label.

SÖHNLEIN RHEINGOLD
Söhnleinstrasse 1-8,
6200 Wiesbaden

Sales: *1 million cases*
Established: *1864*

Most of this firm's production is sold under the Söhnlein "Brillant" label, an inexpensive, commercial *cuve close*. Its prestige "Fürst von Metternich" brand, which is made in part from grapes grown at Prince von Metternich's Schloss Johannisberg estate in the Rheingau, comes a very close second to Deinhard's vintaged "Lila Imperial", with a fine *mousse* and a clean Riesling character.

WAPPEN VON BREISACH GRANDE CLASSÉ
See Deutz & Geldermann.

WINZERSEKT
Erzeugergemeinschaft Rheinhessischer Winzer W.V.
Michel-Mort-Strasse 4,
6555 Sprendlingen

Sales: *2 million cases (wine and Sekt)*
Established: *1981/1982*

An association of 820 growers who contribute part of their output to this *Sekt* house, which was the first to devote its production entirely to *méthode champenoise* wines. It is questionable whether this is worth the extra trouble and expense involved, when the wines are deliberately kept in contact with the yeast for the absolute minimum period allowed by law. Winzersekt wants no hint of autolytic character and wishes to keep the wines as fresh and fruity as possible. This could be achieved more efficiently using *cuve close*, but the public perception is that *méthode champenoise* implies superior quality. The fact that this is only true when an autolysed, neutral-grape character is desired, such as in Champagne, is not yet widely understood and therefore Winzersekt's methods are obviously based on marketing decisions. Having said that, they are evidently very successful.

Generic wines of Germany

Note: The German wine categories below are listed in ascending order of quality, and not in alphabetical order. Only the broadest character can be given for each category. So much depends upon the grape variety. This can even determine the colour of a wine, although some 90 per cent is white. Most grape varieties likely to be encountered, including all the most important crosses, are included in the Glossary of Major grape varieties (*see* pp.24-32).

The area of origin also has a strong influence on the type of wine a particular grape variety will produce. A winemaker can either make the most of what nature brings, or fail. For full details on these two aspects, see the regional chapters in which styles are described and growers recommended.

WEIN

The existence of this term without the qualification of *Tafel-*, indicates a cheap, blended table wine from grapes grown outside the EEC.

TAFELWEIN

Table wine may be a blend from different EEC countries or the wine made in one member country from grapes harvested in another. Known as "Euroblends", these products are sometimes dressed up to look like German wines, but the wine beneath the Gothic writing and German language usually turns out to be an Italian or multi-state blend. This practice, once prolific, now less so, is tantamount to deception and contrary to Article 43 of EEC Regulation 355/79. To be sure of drinking a genuine German product, check that *"Tafelwein"* is qualified by the all-important *"Deutscher"*.

The more successful of these wines are made in years like 1982, when Germany is overburdened by such a huge yield of basic-quality wines that the wineries turn back the convoy of tankers from Italy and dump the excess production in their bulk-selling Euroblends. The best have a good dose of fresh and flowery Morio-Muskat *Süssreserve*. They taste not dissimilar to basic (if anonymous) German wine.

Unimportant, but the odds are improved in any year that follows a really big, but merely modest German vintage

Immediately

DEUTSCHER TAFELWEIN

This is the lowest grade of pure German wine, and normally accounts for between three and five per cent of the country's total production. The wine must be 100 per cent German and if at least 75 per cent comes from any one of the *Tafelwein* regions or sub-regions indicated in the table on page 202, the label is allowed to show that name. These regional names are the most specific geographic location permitted, although, prior to the introduction of *Landwein* legislation, it was permissible sometimes to include the name of a *Bereich*.

A *Deutscher Tafelwein* should convey the basic characteristics of the region from which it comes, so a Rhein, for example, might be expected to have a more flowery aroma, but less acidity than a Mosel. In practice, however, the wines are blended from such a hotch-potch of grape varieties, mostly crosses, that all one can hope for is something fresh and fruity in a medium-dry "Germanic" style!

Most recent, modest years – avoid classic vintages

Immediately

LANDWEIN

Landwein is a *Deutscher Tafelwein* from a more specific region and the label must contain both terms. It is a relatively new category, introduced in 1982 to parallel the French *Vin de Pays* system, although there are significant differences. The 130 or so *Vins de pays* represent a group of wines that aspire to VDQS and, theoretically, AOC status. As such they are far more flexible than *Landwein*. The German category is not a transitional one, it consists of 15 fixed areas that have no hope of achieving anything higher than a "dressed-up" *Tafelwein* sub-region status. It can be discerned from the chart on p.202 that seven *Landwein* areas are, in fact, merely alternative names for seven *Tafelwein* sub-regions. One, *Schwäbischer Landwein*, is identical to a *Tafelwein* region, Neckar, and the remaining seven are divisions of another sub-region, the Rhein.

The potential of *Landwein* can never be the same as that of *Vin de pays*. It is possible for a French winemaker to be proud of his *Vin de pays* status and he can always dream of better things, while a German producer simply uses *Landwein* to dispose of his lesser or excess production, because it is a more marketable appellation than *Deutscher Tafelwein*. The major difference between *Landwein* and *Deutscher Tafelwein* is that the former must be made either as *Trocken* wine, with a maximum of nine grams per litre of residual sugar, or as *Halbtrocken,* with a maximum of 18 grams per litre.

Theoretically, *Landwein* should be the better wine, as it contains less sugar to mask any faults that may be present in the lowest levels of bulk-winemaking and is supposed to have slightly more flavour and character. It is often fresh and delightful to quaff in a *Weinstube* or local café, but, like *Deutscher Tafelwein*, it is not an appellation to be sought out especially. However, if a *Landwein* comes your way, taste it with an open mind and, better still, if it happens to be from a famous estate, snap it up as a cheap and modest introduction to its greater single-vineyard wines.

Most recent, modest years – avoid classic vintages

Immediately

QUALITÄTSWEIN BESTIMMTER ANBAUGEBIETE or QbA

A *QbA* is literally a quality wine from one of the 11 specified regions. These wines may be (and invariably are) chaptalized to increase the alcohol content, and sweetened with *Süssreserve*. Bearing in mind that the legal minimum potential alcoholic strength of a *QbA* is merely 5.9 per cent, it can be understood why the alcohol level is not increased for its own sake, but to give the wine a reasonable shelf-life.

The category includes Liebfraumilch and the vast majority of Niersteiner Gutes Domthal, Piesporter Michelsberg and other generic wines. Most Grosslage and Bereich wines are sold as *QbAs*. There is no technical or legal reason why this may be so, but it makes marketing sense if more specific wines, such as Einzellagen or estate-bottled wines, are sold as more prestigious *QmPs* that can demand higher prices.

Although a *QbA* has a lower Oechsle requirement than a *Kabinett,* it is a more commercial product and distinctly sweeter.

Not too important, although modest years are usually more likely to produce fresher wines than classic vintages

Within 1-3 years (up to 10 years for exceptional wines)

QUALITÄTSWEIN MIT PRÄDIKAT or QmP

This means "a quality wine affirmed (or predicated) by ripeness" and covers the quality categories of *Kabinett, Spätlese, Auslese, Beerenauslese, Eiswein* and *Trockenbeerenauslese*. The grower must give the authorities prior notice of his intention to harvest for any *QmP* wine and, whereas a *QbA* can be blended from grapes gathered from all four corners of an Anbaugebiet, providing it carries only the name of that region, the origin of a *QmP* must be a geographical unit of no greater size than a Bereich. A *QbA* can be chaptalized, but a *QmP* cannot. A certain very highly respected estate owner who believes he could make much better *QmP* wines if he were allowed to chaptalize them, once made the interesting observation that the French chaptalize their best wines, while the Germans chaptalize their poorest! It is, however, permissible to add *Süssreserve*, although many growers maintain that it is not the traditional method and claim that sweetness is best achieved by stopping the fermentation before all the natural grape sugars have been converted to alcohol. *See* the various *QmP* entries.

KABINETT QmP

The term *Kabinett* once referred to wines that were stored for their rare and exceptional qualities, much as "Reserve" is used in some countries today. In this context, it originated at Kloster Eberbach in the Rheingau in the early eighteenth century. The first documented existence of this word appeared as *"Cabernedt"* on an invoice from the Elville master cooper, Ferdinand Ritter, to the Abbot of Eberbach in 1730. Just six years later, another bill in Ritter's hand, refers to the *"Cabinet-Keller"*. The meaning of *"Cabinet"* as a treasured store found its way into the French language as early as 1547, and is found in German literature in 1677. This is the first of the predicates in the Oechsle scale, but not necessarily the lowest for those who enjoy lighter, drier styles. Its grapes must reach an Oechsle level of 67-85°, the exact minimum varying according to the grape variety concerned and its geographical origin. With no chaptalization, this means that the wine has a minimum *potential* alcoholic strength of between 8.6 and 11.4 per cent by volume.

Although made from riper (thus sweeter) grapes than a *QbA*, a *Kabinett* is usually, though not necessarily, made in a slightly drier style. Some producers resolutely refuse to bolster the wine with *Süssreserve*. This makes *Kabinett* the lightest and, for some, the purest of German wine styles.

1986, 1987, 1988, 1989, 1990

Between 2-5 years (up to 10 years in exceptional cases)

SPÄTLESE QmP

Technically *Spätlese* implies that a wine is made from late-harvested grapes, but it is important to remember that "late" is relative to the normal (early) occurrence of a harvest in Germany. As both *QbA* and *Kabinett* are produced from grapes that have not fully ripened, *Spätlese* can more accurately be seen as the first level of German wine to be produced from ripe grapes. The minimum Oechsle level of 76-95°, which would give a minimum *potential* strength of between 10 and 13 per cent by volume, is hardly an indication of overripe grapes.

Although a *Spätlese* is made from grapes that merely have a modest degree of ripeness, the style of wine produced is traditionally sweet, with excellent balancing acidity. This is one of my favourite tasting wines; the grape style is greatly enhanced, but not overwhelmed, by the sugar.

📅 1985, 1986, 1988, 1989, 1990

🍷 Between 3-8 years (up to 15 in exceptional cases)

AUSLESE QmP

This predicated wine is made from bunches left on the vines after the *Spätlese* harvest and as such is truly late-harvested. The regulations state that bunches of fully ripe to very ripe grapes free from disease or damage must be selected for this wine. They must also possess an Oechsle reading of 83-105°, the exact minimum varying according to the grape variety concerned and its geographical origin. With no chaptalization, this means that the wine has a minimum *potential* strength of between 11.1 and 14.5 per cent by volume.

Traditionally this rich and sweet wine is made in exceptional vintages only. There may be some hint of *Edelfäule* or botrytis, especially if the wine comes from a top estate that has a policy of under-declaring its wines and thus might be borderline *Beerenauslese*, but even without *Edelfäule* an *Auslese* is capable of considerable complexity. It is possible to find totally dry *Auslese* wine and this may or may not be labelled *Auslese Trocken*, depending on the whim of the winemaker. *Auslese* is the ideal predicate for *Trocken* wines, because its natural ripeness provides a Burgundy-like degree of body, fullness of fruit and alcohol. Too many export versions of the *Trocken* style have been thin, weak and disappointing, earning this category of wine a very poor reputation which it does not deserve. In Germany itself, it is relatively easy to find delicious examples of *Auslese Trocken* with the correct weight and stature, made

from good *QmP* wines.

📅 1983, 1985, 1988, 1989

🍷 Between 5-20 years

BEERENAUSLESE QmP

A very rare wine made only in truly exceptional circumstances from overripe grapes that have been affected by *Edelfäule*. According to the regulations each berry should be shrivelled, and be individually selected, on a grape-by-grape basis. They must achieve an Oechsle level of 110-128°, the exact minimum varying according to the grape variety concerned and its geographical origin. With no chaptalization, this means that the wine has a minimum *potential* strength of between 15.3 and 18.1 per cent by volume, but only 5.5 per cent need actually be alcohol, with residual sugar accounting for the rest.

These intensely sweet, full-bodied wines are remarkably complex and elegant. I actually prefer *Beerenauslese* to the technically superior *Trockenbeerenauslese* – it is easy to drink and be delighted by the former, whereas the latter requires concentration and analysis.

📅 1983, 1985, 1989

🍷 Between 10-35 years (up to 50 years in exceptional cases)

EISWEIN QmP

Until 1982 this was a qualification used in conjunction with one of the other predicates. It was previously possible to obtain *Spätlese Eiswein*, *Auslese Eiswein* and so on, but *Eiswein* is now a predicate in its own right, with a minimum Oechsle level for its grapes equivalent to *Beerenauslese*. An *Eiswein* occurs through extremely unusual circumstances whereby grapes left on the vine to be affected by *Edelfäule* are frozen by frost or snow. They are harvested, rushed to the winery and pressed in their frozen state. Only the water inside the grape actually freezes; this rises to the top of the vat in the form of ice. The ice is skimmed off, leaving a freeze-condensed juice that is rich, concentrated and capable of producing wines that are the equivalent of, but totally different from, *Beerenauslese* or *Trockenbeerenauslese*.

This icy harvest can be a very late one. It seldom occurs before December and quite often takes place in January of the following year (although it must carry the previous year's vintage). The Oechsle level of an *Eiswein*, which must be at least the equivalent

of a *Beerenauslese*, can be every bit as high as a *Trockenbeerenauslese*. Its quality is also comparable, although of an entirely different character due essentially to its far higher acidity balance. For me, it is the zippy, racy, tangy vitality of this acidity that makes it superior. The finest *Eisweins* have a finesse unequalled by other German wine.

📅 1983, 1985

🍷 Between 10-50 years

TROCKENBEERENAUSLESE QmP or TBA

Germany's legendary *TBA* is produced from heavily botrytized grapes, left on the vine to shrivel into raisin-like berries that must be individually picked. These grapes must reach an Oechsle level of 150-154°. With no chaptalization, the wine will have a minimum *potential* strength of between 21.5 and 22.1 per cent by volume, although only 5.5 per cent need be in the form of alcohol, the rest being residual sugar.

Consulting charts, however, does little to highlight the difference in style that exists between a *Beerenauslese* and a *TBA*, which is every bit as great as that between a *Kabinett* and a *Beerenauslese*. The first noticeable difference is often the colour. Going from *Auslese* to *Beerenauslese* is merely to progress from a light to a rich gold or buttercup yellow. The *TBA* colour range extends from a raisin khaki through various shades of brown, to dark iodine, with some distinctly odd orange-tawny hues in-between. The texture is very viscous and its liqueur-like consistency is just one of many reasons why it is impossible to drink *TBA*. Taking a good mouthful of *TBA* is about as easy as swigging cough mixture – one can merely sip it. Its intensity and complexity, and the profundity of its aromas and flavours really must be experienced. It demands attention and provokes discussion, but is not really a wine to enjoy, and is difficult to relax with.

📅 1983, 1985, 1989

🍷 Between 12-50 years

SPARKLING WINE

SEKT

The common method of production for this anonymous sparkling wine is *cuve close*. It is made from grapes grown outside Germany, usually from Italy or the Loire Valley in France and, until 1986, this could amazingly be called *Deutscher Sekt*. This was because *Sekt* was considered to be a method of production and, so it was argued, if production took place in Germany, it must logically be German or *Deutscher Sekt*. As the vast majority of Germany's huge *Sekt* industry used imported grapes, juice or wine (and still does), this was more a matter of lobbying by those with vested interests, than logic. However, much of the effort to dispose of this false logic came from honourable sectors

within the German wine industry itself. Common sense finally won through on September 1, 1986, when an EEC directive brought this appellation into line with the general philosophy of the Common Market's wine regime. There has been a noticeable upsurge in the number of what are now genuine German *Deutscher Sekt*, although *Sekt* plain and simple still dominates the market.

DEUTSCHER SEKT

An EEC directive ruling of 1986 states that *Deutscher Sekt* must be made from 100 per cent German grapes. The best are usually Riesling-based and do not allow autolysis to interfere with the pure varietal aroma and flavour of the wine, characteristics that are held in the greatest esteem by its producers and the vast majority of its German consumers. See also *Deutscher Qualitätsschaumwein bestimmter Anbaugebiete*.

📅 Most are non-vintage and for those that are vintaged, no discernible pattern has emerged, although it seems doubtful that big years (such as 1983 and 1976) would have the correct acidity balance

🍷 Between 3-8 years

DEUTSCHER SEKT BESTIMMTER ANBAUGEBIETE or DEUTSCHER SEKT bA
See *Deutscher Qualitätsschaumwein bestimmter Anbaugebiete*.

DEUTSCHER QUALITÄTSSCHAUMWEIN BESTIMMTER ANBAUGEBIETE or DEUTSCHER QUALITÄTS-SCHAUMWEIN bA

This *Deutscher Sekt* must be made entirely from grapes grown within one specified wine region and may come from a smaller geographical unit, such as a Bereich, Grosslage or Einzellage, providing that at least 85 per cent of the grapes used come from the area indicated. An alternative appellation is *Deutscher Sekt bestimmter Anbaugebiete*.

📅 Most are non-vintage and for those that are vintaged, no discernible pattern has emerged, although it seems doubtful that big years (such as 1983 and 1976) would have the correct acidity balance

🍷 Between 3-8 years

The Ahr

With black grape varieties such as the Spätburgunder and Portugieser accounting for two in every three vines, it is not surprising that the Ahr's specialities are *Rotwein* and *Weissherbst*. What is surprising is that black varieties should be cultivated here at all, considering Germany is a northern country, and the Ahr is its most northerly region. This is possible because the Ahr is a deep valley, protected by the Hohe Eifel hills, which captures the sun, generates heat and stores it in its rocky, slatey soil. The cumulative effect of this heat allows black grapes to ripen.

THE SECOND-SMALLEST OF GERMANY'S WINE REGIONS, the Ahr takes the name of the river that flows parallel to, and north of, the lower reaches of the Mosel, and joins the Rhine just south of Bonn. It is one of the most beautiful and serene viticultural landscapes in the world, as anyone who has ever travelled along the Rotweinwanderweg, the Ahr's famous red-wine route, will verify. The almost traffic-free route meanders through vineyards and forests, and along peaceful valley slopes that are protected by the Eifel hills.

FACTORS AFFECTING TASTE AND QUALITY

Location
The lower reaches of the Ahr river, ten kilometres (six miles) south of Bonn.

Climate
Despite its northerly position, the deep Ahr valley is sheltered by the surrounding Hohe Eifel hills and maintains temperatures that are favourable for viticulture.

Aspect
The vineyards of the Ahr are sited mainly on inclines and the steeply terraced rocky valley sides.

Soil
Deep, rich, loess soils in the lower Ahr valley and basalt and slatey stone soils with some tufa in the upper Ahr valley.

Viticulture and vinification
Three-quarters of all the vineyards are worked by part-time farmers under labour-intensive conditions. This makes the Ahr's wines much more expensive to produce than those of flat, southern regions like Baden, although more than half of the crop is vinified by a small number of large, technically proficient, cooperatives. Red wines account for 70 per cent of the Ahr's output and used to be made in sweet and semi-sweet styles, but drier versions are more popular today. Pure varietal *Weissherbst*, usually Spätburgunder, is also a speciality.

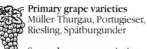
Primary grape varieties
Müller-Thurgau, Portugieser, Riesling, Spätburgunder

Secondary grape varieties
Domina, Dornfelder, Kerner

THE REGION AT A GLANCE

Area under vine: 400 ha (990 acres)

Average yield: 79 hl/ha (355 cases/acre)

Red wine: 70%

White wine: 30%

Infrastructure: Bereich 1; Grosslage 1; Einzellagen 43

Note: The vineyards of the Ahr straddle 11 Gemeinden (communes), the names of which may appear on the label.

THE AHR

The most northerly of Germany's wine-producing regions is made up of districts clustered close to the River Ahr, a tributary of the Rhine.

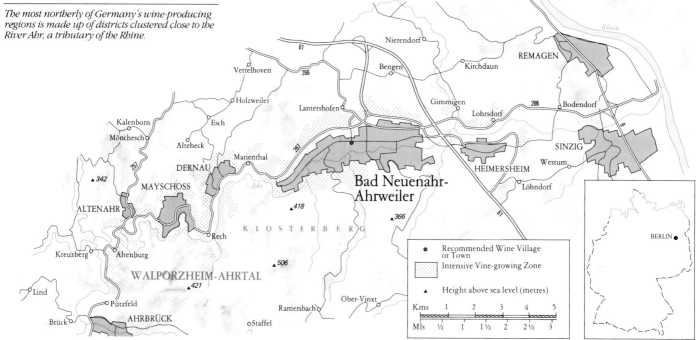

Recommended Wine Village or Town
Intensive Vine-growing Zone
Height above sea level (metres)

Old wine-casks at Mayschoss, above
Beautiful carving depicting grapes and vines on old wooden casks at Mayschoss, upriver from Bad Neuenahr.

Harvesting in the Ahr, left
These steeply sloping vineyards at Marienthal are planted with black grape varieties and 70 per cent of the region's wines are in fact red.

THE RIESLING'S GROWING STATURE

Since the 1950s the Ahr's area under vine has shrunk by one third, and the Spätburgunder is now the most important grape variety, whereas it was once the Portugieser. The Spätburgunder − Germany's name for the Pinot noir − produces a far more distinctive wine than the mild and often neutral Portugieser, but it is still far from being "true" red wine, in any classic sense of the term, and does not possess the varietal intensity of even a basic Burgundian Pinot Noir.

The Ahr's less well-known success is the Riesling, a grape that produces fresh, racy and highly aromatic white wines with fine acidity. While the red wines, and the scenic vineyards from which they come, will always be in demand by the tourists, it is the finer Rieslings that are developing a certain well-deserved reputation. A good deal of Müller-Thurgau is also planted, though, with one or two notable exceptions, the wines are nothing special. Secondary varieties include the Domina, Dornfelder and Kerner.

QUALITY REQUIREMENTS AND HARVEST PERCENTAGES

Minimum Oechsle	Quality Category	Harvest breakdown			
		1984	1985	1986	1987
44°	Deutscher Tafelwein	6%	—	7%	5%
47°	Landwein				
50–60°	*QbA	92%	55%	86%	87%
67–73°	*Kabinett	2%	30%	6%	7%
76–85°	*Spätlese	—	15%	1%	1%
83–88°	*Auslese				
110°	Beerenauslese	—	—	—	—
110°	Eiswein				
150°	Trockenbeerenauslese				

*Minimum Oechsle levels vary according to grape variety, with those that have a naturally lower sugar content allowed to qualify at a correspondingly lower level.

The wines of the Ahr

BEREICH WALPORZHEIM-AHRTAL

The only Bereich in the Ahr district, Walporzheim-Ahrtal produces mostly light-ruby coloured red wines from Spätburgunder and Portugieser grapes. Those areas in the Bereich with slaty soil give quite a vigorous wine, while those with rich loess produce a softer style. The wines used to be fairly sweet, but the trend now is for drier wines. The *Weissherbst* is soft and fruity and the Riesling fresh and racy.

GROSSLAGE KLOSTERBERG

The only Grosslage in the Bereich,

the wines of Klosterberg are thus identical to the wines of Walporzheim-Ahrtal.

NEUENAHR

☆ Vineyard *Sonnenberg*
☆ Grower *Toni Nelles*

HEIMERSHEIM

☆ Vineyard *Landskrone*
☆ Grower *Winzergenossenschaft Heimersheim*

WALPORZHEIM

☆ Vineyard *Gärkammer*
☆ Grower *G. G. Adeneuer*

☆ Vineyard *Himmelchen*
☆ Grower *Winzergenossenschaft Walporzheim*

☆ Vineyard *Pfaffenberg*
☆ Grower *Peter Kriechel*

The Mittelrhein

Saddled with a less than inspiring name, overshadowed by the glamorous Rheingau and possessing precariously perched vineyards that have declined by 40 per cent since 1965, this region, which is all too often overlooked by serious wine drinkers, offers some of Germany's finest and most underrated wines as well as dramatic scenery.

THE SITE OF ONE OF THE OLDEST SETTLEMENTS of man, it was from the Mittelrhein that the Celts spread out across Europe. With such ancient roots, it is not surprising that this region is steeped in so much of Germany's mythical history. It was at Drachenfels in Köningswinter, for instance, that Siegfried slew the dragon and the vineyards in this vicinity produce a red Spätburgunder wine known as *Drachenblut* or "Dragon's blood". The Rhine, which now possesses the Nibelung treasure that once belonged to Siegfried, flows with many such fables, past the many medieval castles and towers of the region, and rushes through the Rhine Gorge, passing the famous "Loreley" rock where the siren attracted many ships to their final and fatal destination.

SHRINKING VINEYARDS, GROWING TOURISM

The difficulty of working the steepest and best of the Mittelrhein's slopes has encouraged many of the workforce to forsake them and seek higher wages for easier work in Germany's booming industrial cities. This has led to a steady decline in the number of vineyards here, but it is by no means a deserted area, as its dramatic beauty makes it one of Germany's favourite tourist spots. It might be best to visit the Mittelrhein out of season, but at least the tourist industry can take the credit for keeping alive the surviving vineyards.

In this region, where many tiny tributaries often provide valley vineyards of a superior natural aspect for viticulture than most of those on the mighty Rhine, the potential for producing high-quality Riesling wine on its slatey soil is evident. There are still quite a few really excellent growers and estates, consistently producing exciting wines that display a vigorous varietal character, intense flavour and truly splendid acidity. The acidity, which is so prized that *Sekt* houses try to purchase as much of the lesser and surplus wines as possible, makes the rare occurrence of *Auslese* and higher *QmP* wines something special.

THE REGION AT A GLANCE

Area under vine: 750 ha (1,853 acres)

Average yield: 79 hl/ha (355 cases/acre)

Red wine: 2%

White wine: 98%

Infrastructure: Bereiche 3; Grosslagen 11; Einzellagen 111

Note: The vineyards of this region straddle 59 Gemeinden (communes), the names of which may appear on the label.

THE MITTELRHEIN

North and south of Koblenz, the Mittelrhein's vineyards run up towards the steep, rocky escarpments that closely border this stretch of the Rhine.

●	Recommended Wine Village or Town
▦	Intensive Vine-growing Zone
┈	Bereich Boundary
—	Grosslage Boundary
▲	Height above sea level (metres)

FACTORS AFFECTING TASTE & QUALITY

Location
A 160-kilometre (100-mile) stretch of the Rhine Valley between Bonn and Bingen.

Climate
The benefits of the sun are maximized by the steep valley sides that also afford protection from cold winds. The river acts as a heat-reservoir, tempering the low night and winter temperatures.

Aspect
Vines are grown on the steep valley sides, benefitting from any available sunshine. North of Koblenz, all the vineyards are on the east bank while to the south, most are on the west bank.

Soil
Slatey soil on a clay base and a conglomerate rock of rounded pebbles and sand called *Greywacke*. There are also small, scattered deposits of loess and,

towards the north, some vineyards are of volcanic origin.

Viticulture and vinification
Virtually all the remaining vineyards in this region have been *flurbereinigt* (modernized by abolishing terraces) and many of the very steep slopes are a patchwork of precarious vineyards. With a high proportion of Riesling grapes giving an average yield that is very low by German standards, the quality is generally high. Approximately 80 per cent of growers are part-time and one-quarter of the harvest is processed by the cooperatives using normal white-wine vinification techniques.

Primary grape varieties
Riesling

Secondary grape varieties
Bacchus, Kerner, Müller-Thurgau, Optima, Scheurebe, Silvaner

QUALITY REQUIREMENTS AND HARVEST PERCENTAGES

Minimum Oechsle	Quality Category	Harvest breakdown			
		1984	1985	1986	1987
44°	Deutscher Tafelwein	29%	—	1%	7%
47°	Landwein				
50–60°	*QbA	70%	57%	70%	75%
67–73°	*Kabinett	1%	32%	22%	15%
76–85°	*Spätlese	—	11%	—	3%
83–88°	*Auslese				
110°	Beerenauslese	—		7%	
110°	Eiswein				
150°	Trockenbeerenauslese				

*Minimum Oechsle levels vary according to grape variety, with those that have a naturally lower sugar content allowed to qualify at a correspondingly lower level.

Mittelrhein vineyards, right
The region's weekend wine-growers have plenty to do to maintain these slopes.

The wines of the Mittelrhein

BEREICH BACHARACH

This west-bank Bereich covers the most heavily cultivated southern sector on the Mittelrhein and is named after the beautiful old market town of Bacharach.

GROSSLAGE SCHLOSS REICHENSTEIN

There are no outstanding villages, vineyards, estates or growers in this Grosslage that faces the Rheingau across the river and neighbours the Nahe to the south, although good wines are made in the village of Niederheimbach, where the vineyard of Froher Weingarten has the best reputation.

GROSSLAGE SCHLOSS STAHLECK

There is perhaps more potential here in the south-facing vineyards that belong to tributaries of the Rhine, than in the east-facing vineyards on the great river itself. Yet it is Posten at Bacharach, encompassing both aspects, that clearly excels.

BACHARACH

☆ Vineyard *Posten*
☆ Growers *Wilhelm Wasum, Fritz Bastian, Karl Heidrich*

BEREICH RHEINBURGENGAU

The largest and most successful of the Mittelrhein's three Bereiche, Rheinburgengau stretches from the second-most-northerly Grosslage to the Rheingau.

GROSSLAGE BURG HAMMERSTEIN

Starting just south of Köningswinter and stretching along the right bank, almost as far as Koblenz, this long, scenic Grosslage is comprised of scattered vineyards, with the only unbroken stretch of fine Riesling vines at Hammerstein.

HAMMERSTEIN

☆ Vineyard *Schlossberg*
☆ Growers *Gräfl. Westerholtsche Gutsverwaltung, Gemeinde Bad Hönningen*

GROSSLAGE BURG RHEINFELS

A village-sized Grosslage on the west bank, with its best vineyards on the southeast-facing banks of a small tributary at Werlau, an Ortsteil of St. Goar.

WERLAU

☆ Vineyard *Ameisenberg*
☆ Grower *Winzergenossenschaft Werlau*

GROSSLAGE GEDEONSECK

A top-performing Grosslage where a bend in the river allows for excellent east- and south-facing vineyards, the best of which are situated within an Ortsteil of Boppard.

BOPPARD HAMM

☆ Vineyard *Ohlenberg*
☆ Growers *August Perll, Familie Splisser, Karl August Stumm, Franz Adolf Lorenz*

☆ Vineyard *Fässerlay*
☆ Grower *August Perll*

GROSSLAGE HERRENBERG

The southeastern end of this right-bank Grosslage abuts the western edge of the Rheingau region, but all of the Einzellagen are located in the north, between Dörscheid and Kaub, just downstream from Bacharach on the opposite bank.

KAUB

☆ Vineyard *Backofen*
☆ Growers *Vereinigung Kauber Weingutsbesitzer, Peter Bahles, Heinrich Weiler*
☆ Vineyard *Rosstein*
☆ Grower *Heinrich Weiler*

GROSSLAGE LAHNTAL

There are no outstanding villages, vineyards, estates or growers in this beautiful hinterland Grosslage and its vineyards have been in a state of decline for many years. However, the Einzellage of Hasenberg at Bad Ems has a certain reputation.

GROSSLAGE LORELEYFELSEN

Some fine Riesling vineyards set amid dramatic scenery that includes the famous "Loreley" rock.

ST. GOARSHAUSEN

☆ Vineyard *Hessern*
☆ Growers *Willi Menges, Fritz Maus*

GROSSLAGE MARKSBURG

The vineyards on the Mittelrhein side of Koblenz have mostly been overtaken by urban sprawl, but one of the best remains in the Ortsteil of Ehrenbreitstein. The others in this Grosslage are located to the north and south of the city. There is naturally a similarity between these wines and those of the lower Mosel.

BRAUBACH

☆ Vineyard *Marmorberg*
☆ Growers *Weingut Priesteroth, Braubacher Winzerverein*

KOBLENZ-EHRENBREITSTEIN

☆ Vineyard *Kreuzberg*
☆ Growers *Klaus Wagner*

GROSSLAGE SCHLOSS SCHÖNBURG

The reputation of the fine Riesling vineyards in this Grosslage very much rests on the high quality of just one grower, Heinrich Weiler.

OBERWESEL

☆ Vineyard *St. Martinsberg*
☆ Grower *Heinrich Weiler*

☆ Vineyard *Römerkrug*
☆ Grower *Heinrich Weiler*

BEREICH SIEBENGEBIRGE

A single-Grosslage Bereich covering the vineyards of Königswinter Siebengebirge, or "Seven Mountains", is the northernmost Bereich in Germany.

GROSSLAGE PETERSBERG

This Grosslage comprises the same area as Bereich Siebengebirge. There are no outstanding villages, vineyards, estates or growers, although good wines are made in the Drachenfels vineyard of Königswinter.

Mosel-Saar-Ruwer

The supreme elegance and tantalizing piquancy of a great Riesling grown in Mosel-Saar-Ruwer is preferred by some to all other German wines. While in cold or wet years the warmer Rhine regions produce more attractive wines, in good and great years no other wine can equal the finesse and vitality of a fine Mosel-Saar-Ruwer.

IF ANY GRAPE IS INTRINSICALLY RACY, it is the vigorous Riesling, and if any region can be singled out for emphasizing this raciness, it must be Mosel-Saar-Ruwer. Grown here, the Riesling combines a relatively high acidity with an irrefutable suggestion of lightness and elegance. But a fine Mosel-Saar-Ruwer is never thin, as these wines have surprisingly high extract levels that, together with the acidity, intensify the characteristics of flavour.

In the hottest vintages, the best *Auslesen* and *Beerenauslesen* come from Mosel-Saar-Ruwer, where the wines remain racy, while those from the other regions appear fat and overblown by contrast. Even the most modest wines retain a freshness and vitality in sunblessed years that will be lacking in those from the warmer regions.

THE GOOD DOCTOR

There are many great vineyards in this region, but none is as famous as the legendary Bernkasteler Doctor, which produces Germany's most expensive wine. The story is that Boemund II, an archbishop of Trier in the fourteenth century, was so ill that his doctors could do nothing for him. A wine-grower from Bernkastel recommended the restorative powers of the wine from his vineyard. Boemund drank some, made a miraculous recovery and declared "The best doctor grows in this vineyard in Bernkastel".

More recently, the Doctor vineyard has been the subject of a lengthy court case. The original vineyard comprised 1.35 hectares (3.34 acres), but in 1971 the new German wine law proscribed a ban on all vineyards of less than 5 hectares (12.35 acres), and the authorities planned to expand the Doctor almost equally to the west (into the Einzellage Graben) and to the east (into an area classified merely as Grosslage Badstube). This would have enabled thirteen different producers to make and sell Bernkasteler Doctor, whereas only three owners of the true Doctor vineyards had existed before. It is not surprising that the three owners of the original Doctor vineyard took their objections to court.

Finally, in 1984, after an exhaustive study had been made of the

FACTORS AFFECTING TASTE AND QUALITY

Location
This region follows the Mosel river from Koblenz south to the border with France. It includes the vineyards of two major tributaries, the Saar and the Ruwer, which flow into the Mosel from the south.

Climate
The moderate rainfall and rapid warming of the steep and protective valley sides provide ideal conditions for vines to flourish and produce grapes with high acidity, even when harvested overripe.

Aspect
The Mosel has more loops and bends than any other German river, providing slopes of every aspect. The valleys have very steep sides where most of the vines grow at an altitude of between 100-350 metres (330-1,150 ft).

Soil
Soils vary from sandstone, shell-limestone and red marl in the upper Mosel, to Devon slate in the middle Mosel, Saar and Ruwer, and clay slate and grey stony soil in the lower Mosel. Alluvial sand and gravel soils are also found in lower sites. Classic Riesling sites are slatey; the Elbling prefers limestone.

Viticulture and vinification
Many of the greatest German wines come from the highest and steepest vineyards in this area, most of which are situated in the upper reaches of the valleys. Tending the vines is unavoidably labour-intensive and this, combined with a longer winter than experienced elsewhere in Germany, accounts for the higher prices asked for fine Mosel-Saar-Ruwer wines. The early onset of winter causes fermentation to take place at very cool temperatures, and when the wines are bottled early they retain more carbonic gas, which emphasizes the crisp, steely character of the Riesling grape. There are about 13,750 growers who own very small plots of land and approximately 60 per cent of the total wine produced is processed and distributed by merchants and shippers. Cooperatives, which sell 15 per cent of the total, and growers and estates, who sell direct and account for 25 per cent, are increasing their sales.

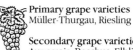

Primary grape varieties
Müller-Thurgau, Riesling

Secondary grape varieties
Auxerrois, Bacchus, Elbling, Kerner, Optima, Ortega

vineyard's *terroir*; the court decided that the Doctor vineyard could legitimately be stretched to include all of the Graben element and a small portion of the Badstube, making a total of 3.26 hectares (8 acres). The ten owners of the Badstube section excluded from the Doctor vineyard found themselves in possession of vineyards that, having for 13 years been accorded the status of Germany's most prestigious wine, were now nameless. They proposed that they should be allowed to use the Einzellage name of Alte Badstube am Doctorberg ("Old Badstube on the Doctor's Hill") and, despite protests from the original owners, this was accepted by the Ministry.

Not only was the expansion of the *terroir* open to question in this case, but the general directive that a single vineyard should be of a stipulated minimum size was sheer folly. It would have been much more effective to have amended the law to allow any genuine vineyard name the right to appear in small print on a label, and to establish a register of perhaps 100 or more (but certainly not 2,600) truly great vineyards that would have the right to appear on the label in a dominant size of print with an appropriate designation of elevated status.

The Bernkasteler Doctor vineyard today, below
The red outline encloses the area of the original vineyard (yellow) and those areas finally adopted in 1984 (light and mid-green). The area excluded in 1984 is pink.

☐ Doctor (ex Graben)	L J. Lauerburg *(0.13 hectares)*
☐ Doctor (original)	D Deinhard *(1.06 hectares)*
☐ Doctor (ex Badstube)	T Dr. H. Thanisch *(1.81 hectares)*
☐ Alte Badstube am Docterberg	G-A Hl. Geist-Armenspende or Holy Spirit Charity Fund *(0.26 hectares)*

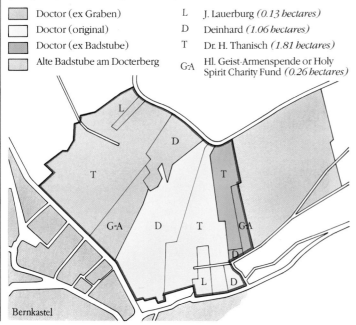

Bernkastel

Bernkastel from the Doctor vineyard, above
Bernkasteler Doctor wines are some of Germany's most prestigious and expensive. Bernkastel lies in the Badstube Grosslage.

QUALITY REQUIREMENTS AND HARVEST PERCENTAGES

Minimum Oechsle	Quality Category	Harvest breakdown 1984	1985	1986	1987
44°	Deutscher Tafelwein	33%	—	4%	8%
47°	Landwein				
50–60°	*QbA	66%	63%	72%	86%
67–73°	*Kabinett	1%	27%	18%	5%
76–85°	*Spätlese	—	8%	6%	1%
83–88°	*Auslese				
110°	Beerenauslese	—	2%	—	—
110°	Eiswein				
150°	Trockenbeerenauslese				

* Minimum Oechsle levels vary according to grape variety, with those that have a naturally lower sugar content allowed to qualify at a correspondingly lower level.

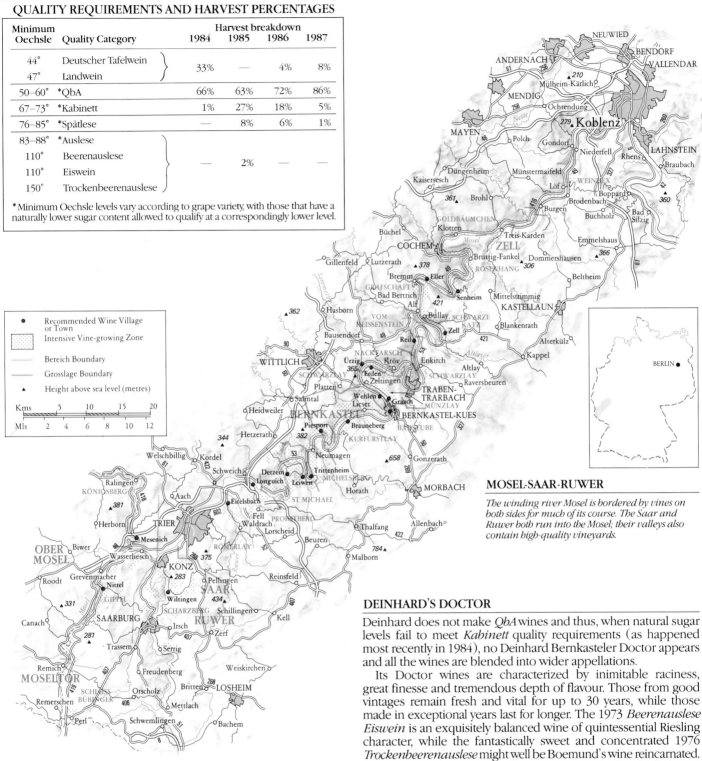

MOSEL·SAAR·RUWER

The winding river Mosel is bordered by vines on both sides for much of its course. The Saar and Ruwer both run into the Mosel; their valleys also contain high-quality vineyards.

DEINHARD'S DOCTOR

Deinhard does not make *QbA* wines and thus, when natural sugar levels fail to meet *Kabinett* quality requirements (as happened most recently in 1984), no Deinhard Bernkasteler Doctor appears and all the wines are blended into wider appellations.

Its Doctor wines are characterized by inimitable raciness, great finesse and tremendous depth of flavour. Those from good vintages remain fresh and vital for up to 30 years, while those made in exceptional years last for longer. The 1973 *Beerenauslese Eiswein* is an exquisitely balanced wine of quintessential Riesling character, while the fantastically sweet and concentrated 1976 *Trockenbeerenauslese* might well be Boemund's wine reincarnated.

The main reason why the Doctor vineyard, which has a south-southwest facing slope, was expanded westwards rather than eastwards, is that these westerly exposures benefit from longer hours of sunshine. The vines commence at a height of 100 metres (330 ft) and rise very steeply to 180 metres (590 ft), the rate of incline being between 54 and 63°, which is very important in a northern region where the sun is relatively low in the sky. This together with its aspect makes the Doctor a veritable suntrap. The Riesling vines, many of which are still ungrafted, are planted on thick, heat-retaining Devon slate soil. Strict pruning techniques restrict the yield to around 70 hectolitres per hectare (315 cases/acre) to give the wine greater concentration.

THE REGION AT A GLANCE

Area under vine: 11,650 ha (28,800 acres)

Average yield: 108 hl/ha (489 cases/acre)

Red wine: None

White wine: 100%

Infrastructure: Bereiche 5; Grosslagen 20; Einzellagen 523

Note: The vineyards of this region straddle 192 Gemeinden (communes), the names of which may appear on the label.

The wines of Mosel-Saar-Ruwer

BEREICH ZELL

The lower Mosel is generally regarded as an area of unexciting wines, yet there are some good wines to be found if you know where to look.

GROSSLAGE GOLDBÄUMCHEN

No outstanding villages, vineyards or growers although good wines are made in the village of Eller.

GROSSLAGE GRAFSCHAFT

Good wines made in the villages of Alf and Bullay, but the Riesling of Neef stands out as a wine of classic quality.

NEEF

☆ Vineyard *Frauenberg*
☆ Grower *Eduard Bremm*

GROSSLAGE ROSENHANG

A promising Grosslage which winds along the right bank of the Mosel downstream from Schwarze Katz.

MESENICH

☆ Vineyard *Abteiberg, Deuslay*
☆ Grower *Rudolf Kochems*

VALWIG

☆ Vineyard *Herrenberg*
☆ Grower *Josef Thielmann*

GROSSLAGE SCHWARZE KATZ

The village of Zell has some good Einzellagen with officially classified slopes that can make fine and aromatic Riesling, but it is best known for its Grosslage label that carries the famous Schwarze Katz or "Black Cat". Originally, the best wines of Zell were chosen in a blind tasting and awarded the insignia of the black cat, but since Merl and Kaimt have been merged with Zell, it is just a blended Grosslage wine.

ZELL

☆ Vineyard *Domherrenberg*
☆ Growers *Hildegard and Peter Thielen*

☆ Vineyard *Petersborn-Kabertchen*
☆ Grower *Heinrich Mager jr.*

GROSSLAGE WEINHEX

No outstanding villages, vineyards or growers in this Grosslage, which extends over both banks of the Mosel and into the suburbs of Koblenz.

BEREICH BERNKASTEL

This covers the entire Mittelmosel, encompassing all of the river's most famous villages and towns, and most of its best vineyards. Much wine is sold under this Bereich appellation, but most of it is disappointing.

GROSSLAGE BADSTUBE

With possibly the greatest and certainly the most famous, of all Einzellagen, the Doctor vineyard, as well as the almost equally well-known Lay, the superb Graben and six other good sites, the Badstube must be the grandest Grosslage in Germany. The quality of even the surplus wine from such great vineyards is so high that it is practically impossible to find poor Badstube, and it is especially good in relatively poor years when grapes from Doctor fail to achieve *Kabinett* level and are included in its other wines.

BERNKASTEL

☆ Vineyard *Doctor*
☆ Growers *Dr. H. Thanisch Wwe., Deinhard, J. Lauerburg*

☆ Vineyard *Lay*
☆ Growers *Dr. H. Thanisch Wwe., J. Lauerburg, Erben Karl Dillinger, Joh. Jos. Prüm, Otto Pauly KG, S. A. Prüm Erben*

GROSSLAGE VOM HEISSEN STEIN

No outstanding villages, vineyards or growers, although good wines are made in the village of Reil.

GROSSLAGE KURFÜRSTLAY

This includes the lesser wines of Bernkastel and the superior wines of Brauneberg, the very best of which come from the south-southeast-facing Juffer hill that rises from the river opposite the village of Brauneberg. Its wines are remarkably racy considering their exceptional fullness of body and some prefer them to those of the Doctor, although I delight in their differences.

BERNKASTEL

☆ Vineyard *Kardinalsberg*
☆ Grower *St. Nikolaus Hospital*

BRAUNEBERG

☆ Vineyard *Juffer*
☆ Growers *Fritz Haag, Christian Karp Schreiber, Paulinshof, P. Licht-Bergweiler Erben, Max. Ferd. Richter, Reichsgraf von Kesselstatt*

☆ Vineyard *Juffer Sonnenuhr*
☆ Growers *Fritz Haag, Christian Karp-Schreiber, Paulinshof, Ferdinand Heng Erben, Max. Ferd. Richter, St. Nikolaus Hospital, Dr. H. Thanisch Wwe.*

GROSSLAGE MICHELSBERG

There *are* great wines made in Piesport, but the thin, characterless Piesporter Michelsberg is not one of them. It is a Grosslage wine that comes not from steep, slatey slopes such as Goldtröpfchen, but from very high-yielding, flat, alluvial land.

PIESPORT

☆ Vineyard *Goldtröpfchen*
☆ Growers *Friedrich-Wilhelm-Gymnasium, Reichsgraf von Kesselstatt, Hubert Kirsten, Bischöfliches Konvikt Trier, Oskar Tobias*

TRITTENHEIM

☆ Vineyard *Apotheke*
☆ Growers *Friedrich-Wilhelm-Gymnasium, Bischöfliches Priesterseminar Trier, Weingut Milz-Laurentiushof*

☆ Vineyard *Altärchen*
☆ Growers *Friedrich-Wilhelm-Gymnasium, Bischöfliches Priesterseminar Trier, Weingut Milz-Laurentiushof*

GROSSLAGE MÜNZLAY

The three villages in this Grosslage may lack the fame of Bernkastel and the popularity of Piesport, but they possess truly superb Mosel vineyards and boast an incomparable number of great growers and estates.

GRAACH

☆ Vineyard *Himmelreich*
☆ Growers *Dr. H. Thanisch Wwe., Reichsgraf von Kesselstatt, Dr. F. Weins Prüm Erben, Joh. Jos. Prüm, Friedrich-Wilhelm-Gymnasium, S. A. Prüm Erben, St. Nikolaus Hospital, Studert-Prüm, Josef Cristoffel Erben, J. Lauerburg, Otto Pauly KG, Max Ferd. Richter, Deinhard*

☆ Vineyard *Josephshöfer*
☆ Grower *Reichsgraf von Kesselstatt*

☆ Vineyard *Domprobst*
☆ Growers *Dr. F. Weins Prüm Erben, Joh. Jos. Prüm, Friedrich-Wilhelm-Gymnasium, P. Licht-Bergweiler Erben, S. A. Prüm Erben, Heribert Kerpen, Studert-Prüm, Josef Christoffel Erben, Otto Pauly KG, Max. Ferd. Richter, Deinhard*

WEHLEN

☆ Vineyard *Sonnenuhr*
☆ Growers *Dr. H. Thanisch Wwe., Prüm-Bergweiler, Weingut Kerpen, Dr. F. Weins Prüm Erben, Joh. Jos. Prüm, P. Licht-Bergweiler Erben, S. A. Prüm Erben, St. Nikolaus Hospital, Studert-Prüm, Josef Christoffel Erben, Otto Pauly KG, Deinhard*

ZELTINGEN

☆ Vineyard *Himmelreich*
☆ Growers *Joh. Jos. Prüm, Frh. von Schorlemer, Geschw. Ehses-Berres, Franz Merrem, Friedrich-Wilhelm-Gymnasium, Karl Weber, Lehmen, Peter Nicolay KG*

☆ Vineyard *Sonnenuhr*
☆ Growers *Reichsgraf von Kesselstatt, Joh. Jos. Prüm, Friedrich-Wilhelm-Gymnasium*

GROSSLAGE NACKTARSCH

No outstanding villages, vineyards or growers.

GROSSLAGE PROBSTBERG

No outstanding villages, vineyards or growers.

GROSSLAGE SCHWARZLAY

Erden and Uerzig are two of the Mittelmosel's most underrated villages. Their spectacular vineyards cling to cliff-like slopes in defiance of gravity and are capable of producing rich, racy wines of stunning intensity and style.

ERDEN

☆ Vineyard *Treppchen*
☆ Growers *St. Johannishof, Dr. Loosen, Rich. Jos Berres, Rob. Eymael, Weingut Schmittger, Schwaab-Scherr, Peter Nicolay KG, Bischöfliches Priesterseminar Trier, Dr. Weins-Prüm Erben, Benedict Loosen Erben*

☆ Vineyard *Prälat*
☆ Growers *St. Johannishof, Dr. Loosen, Peter Nicolay KG, Geschwister Berres, Dr. Weins-Prüm Erben, Benedict Loosen Erben*

UERZIG

☆ Vineyard *Würzgarten*
☆ Growers *Rob Eymael, Peter Nicolay KG, Joh. Jos. Cristoffel Erben, Dr. Weins-Prüm Erben, Benedict Loosen Erben*

GROSSLAGE ST. MICHAEL

Popular but overrated wines come from Klüsserath, whereas those of Detzem and Leiwen, in particular, are better, especially in sunny areas.

DETZEM

☆ Vineyard *Würzgarten*
☆ Grower *Karl Loewen*

LEIWEN

☆ Vineyard *Laurentiuslay*
☆ Growers *Reichsgraf von Kesselstatt, Alfred Lex, Karl Loewen*

BEREICH SAAR-RUWER

This contains two Grosslagen that cover the Mosel's two most famous tributaries, the Saar and the Ruwer. It is easy to remember which Grosslage belongs to which river as Scharzberg is on the Saar and Römerlay on the Ruwer.

GROSSLAGE RÖMERLAY

This covers the vineyards of the Ruwer and incorporates the ancient Roman city of Trier, as well as a few scattered plots on the Mosel, including one on the left bank facing Trier. The Ruwer is much the smaller of the two tributaries, yet it has its share of exceptional vineyards owned by gifted growers who make very aromatic, vital wines that are as racy as any on the Mosel, but not quite as biting as those of the Saar. The quality is extraordinarily high and few wines are seen under the Grosslage appellation.

MAXIMIN GRÜNHAUS

☆ Vineyards *Abtsberg, Bruderberg, Herrenberg*
☆ Grower *Von Schubert*

EITELSBACH

☆ Vineyards *Karthäuserhofberger Kronenberg, Karthäuserhofberger Sang, Karthäuserhofberger Burgberg*
☆ Grower *Eitelsbacher Karthäuserhof*

☆ Vineyard *Marienholz*
☆ Growers *Bischöfliches Konvikt Trier, Bert Simon*

KASEL

☆ Vineyard *Hitzlay*
☆ Growers *Bischöfliches Konvikt Trier, Bert Simon, Deinhard, Reichsgraf von Kesselstatt, Patheiger Erben, Von Beulwitz Erben, Weingut Petershof*

☆ Vineyard *Kehrnagel*
☆ Growers *Deinhard, Reichsgraf von Kesselstatt, Bischöfliches Konvikt Trier, Bert Simon*

☆ Vineyard *Herrenberg*
☆ Growers *Deinhard, Reichsgraf von Kesselstatt, Patheiger Erben, Bert Simon*

GROSSLAGE SCHARZBERG

This covers the Saar and a small section of the Mosel between Konz and Trier to the north. These wines are so racy that they are positively biting and steely in their youth, but age gracefully, harmonizing into exquisitely piquant flavours. Very modest Saar wines can be too thin and unripe to enjoy, but *Kabinett* and higher predicates from great growers are almost sure to please. Unlike the Ruwer's Römerlay, this Grosslage appellation is often used.

WILTINGEN

☆ Vineyard *Scharzhofberger*
☆ Growers *Hohe Domkirche-Trier, Weingut v. Hövel, Vereinigte Hospitien-Trier, Egon Müller, Carl-Friedrich Rautenstrauch, Appolinarius J. Koch, Reichsgraf von Kesselstatt, Staatsdomäne, Von Hövel, Bernd van Volxem*

☆ Vineyard *Braune Kupp*
☆ Growers *Appolinarius J. Koch, Le Gallais, Graf zu Hoensbroech, Bischöfliches Priester Seminar Trier*

☆ Vineyard *Kupp*
☆ Growers *Graf zu Hoensbroech, Hubert Schmitz*

☆ Vineyard *Braunfels*
☆ Growers *Carl-Friedrich Rautenstrauch, Reichsgraf von Kesselstatt, Hubert Schmitz*

FILZEN

☆ Vineyard *Herrenberg*
☆ Grower *Edmund Reverchon*

SERRIG

☆ Vineyard *Herrenberg*
☆ Grower *Bert Simon*

☆ Vineyard *Schloss Saarfelser Schlossberg*
☆ Growers *Vereinigte Hospitien-Trier*

SAARBURG

☆ Vineyard *Rausch*
☆ Growers *Forstmeister Geltz Erben, Freiherr von Solemacher*

KANZEM

☆ Vineyard *Altenberg*
☆ Growers *Maximilian von Othegraven, Bischöfliches Priesterseminar Trier, Edmund Reverchon*

OCKFEN

☆ Vineyard *Bockstein*
☆ Growers *Dr. Fischer, Staatl. Weinbaudomäne, Weingut Forstmeister Geltz Erben, Zilliken, Edmund Reverchon, Adolf Rheinart Erben, Freiherr von Solemacher*

WAWERN

☆ Vineyard *Herrenberg*
☆ Grower *Dr. Fischer*

BEREICH OBERMOSEL

The Obermosel, or Upper Mosel, runs parallel to the Luxembourg border and is planted mostly with Elbling, which has been grown here since Roman times. The wines are thin, acidic and mostly made into *Sekt*.

GROSSLAGE KÖNIGSBERG

No outstanding villages, vineyards or growers.

GROSSLAGE GIPFEL

No outstanding villages, vineyards or growers, although respectable wines are made in the village of Nittel.

BEREICH MOSELTOR

The most southerly Bereich on the Mosel encompasses the upper reaches of the river that flows from its source in the Vosges mountains of France through Luxembourg and into Germany, thus Moseltor or "Mosel gate". Its wines are very light and acid, and of little significance except to the *Sekt* houses.

GROSSLAGE SCHLOSS BÜBINGER

In the village of Perl, Helmut Herber has a good reputation for his *Trocken* wines, particularly from the Auxerrois grape. Alfons Pettgen supplies both the GDR and Saarland State governments for their official functions.

PERL

☆ Vineyard *Hasenberg*
☆ Grower *Helmut Herber*

SEHNDORF

☆ Vineyard *Klosterberg*
☆ Grower *Alfons Pettgen*

The Nahe

A sunny microclimate and varied soils combine to produce wines that have the elegance of a Rheingau, the body of a light Rheinhessen, and the acidity of a Mosel. The perfumed aroma of a Nahe wine is unique to the region, as are its extremely fragrant flavour and soft, smooth style.

DESPITE AN ABUNDANCE OF ROMAN ROADS and villas, viticulture came relatively late to the Nahe, the earliest documented record dating from the eighth century, at least 500 years after the Romans had established a flourishing wine industry in the Mosel valley. As with the rest of Germany, the vineyards underwent a great expansion in the twelfth and thirteenth centuries, and by the last century the Nahe was universally considered to be on a par with the Rheingau. Strangely, by the Second World War it had become Germany's least-known region. This had nothing to do with a loss of either quantity or quality; excellent vineyards like Kupfergrube at Schlossböckelheim, today widely acclaimed as the greatest of all Nahe vineyards, did not even exist before 1900. The decline was probably due instead to the fact that the region was a relatively small area of scattered vineyards, and as such it was difficult to compete with larger, more compact ones. When those larger competitors also became industrialized, they prospered and developed sophisticated transport systems, edging the Nahe further into the cold. As a region with an essentially rural, non-industrialized, mixed-agricultural economy, it looked inwards; its own population could consume most of its production with little trouble and so the Nahe's wines adopted an increasingly lower profile on national and international markets.

FACTORS AFFECTING TASTE AND QUALITY

Location
The region balloons out from between Rheinhessen and the Mittelrhein around the River Nahe, which runs parallel to, and 40 kilometres (25 miles) southeast of, the Mosel.

Climate
A temperate, sunny climate with adequate rainfall and no frosts. Local conditions are influenced by the Soonwald forest to the northeast and heat-retaining, rocky hills to the east. Protected south-facing vineyards enjoy micro-climates that are almost Mediterranean.

Aspect
Vineyards are found on both the gentle and steep slopes of the Nahe and its hinterland of many small tributary river valleys. Vines grow at altitudes of between 100–300 metres (330–985 ft).

Soil
Diverse soils ranging from quartzite and slate along the lower reaches to porphyry (hard rock poor in lime), melaphyry (hard rock rich in lime) and coloured sandstone in the middle and upper reaches. Near Bad Kreuznach, weathered clay, sandstone, loess and loam soil may also be found. The greatest Riesling wines grow on sandstone.

Viticulture and vinification
Since the mid-1960s, cultivation of the Riesling and Silvaner has declined by 20 and 15 per cent respectively. The Müller-Thurgau is now the most important variety, accounting for some 30 per cent, but has not increased significantly; most of the overall change is due to the cultivation of crosses such as Kerner, Scheurebe and Bacchus.
In the cellar, methods remain traditional and very efficient, with technically up-to-date cooperatives processing just 20 per cent of the crop. As much as 40 per cent of all the wine made in this region is processed by small growers who sell direct to passing customers, with the remaining 40 per cent belonging to (or delivered by growers to) the traditional trade and export houses.

Primary grape varieties
Müller-Thurgau, Riesling, Silvaner

Secondary grape varieties
Bacchus, Faberrebe, Kerner, Scheurebe, Ruländer, Weissburgunder

QUALITY REQUIREMENTS AND HARVEST PERCENTAGES

Minimum Oechsle	Quality Category	Harvest breakdown 1984	1985	1986	1987
44°	Deutscher Tafelwein	20%	—	4%	4%
50°	Landwein				
57–60°	*QbA	76%	57%	80%	88%
70–73°	*Kabinett	3%	27%	14%	8%
78–82°	*Spätlese	1%	13%	2%	—
85–92°	*Auslese	—	3%	—	—
120°	Beerenauslese				
120°	Eiswein				
150°	Trockenbeerenauslese				

*Minimum Oechsle levels vary according to grape variety, with those that have a naturally lower sugar content allowed to qualify at a correspondingly lower level.

THE NAHE

Between Rheinhessen and the Mittelrhein nestles the self-contained wine-producing region of the Nahe. Its namesake river has many tributaries running between spectacular overhanging cliffs.

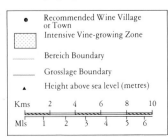

- • Recommended Wine Village or Town
- Intensive Vine-growing Zone
- Bereich Boundary
- Grosslage Boundary
- ▲ Height above sea level (metres)

Kms 2 4 6 8 10
Mls 1 2 3 4 5 6

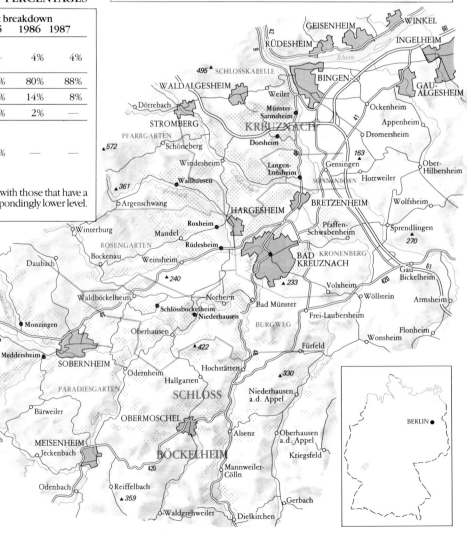

THE REGION AT A GLANCE

Area under vine: 4,300 ha
(10,620 acres)

Average yield: 86 hl/ha
(387 cases/acre)

Red wine: 2%

White wine: 98%

Infrastructure: Bereiche 2;
Grosslagen 7;
Einzellagen 328

Note: The vineyards of this
region straddle 80 Gemeinden
(communes), the names of
which may appear on the label.

A BLEND OF OLD AND NEW

Combining finesse and fragrance with a soft, yet racy character and a capacity to age, the Riesling has always been the Nahe's finest wine. However, it has never been the most important variety, and its production has greatly declined. The Silvaner accounted for as much as 40 per cent of grapes grown until as recently as the mid-1960s, but Germany's ubiquitous Müller-Thurgau has now become the chief variety. New crosses are becoming more important, including the Riesling-like Kerner, and the Scheurebe, which is attractive, aromatic and well balanced at *Auslese* level.

The wines of the Nahe

BEREICH KREUZNACH

This Bereich covers the area once called the Untere Nahe, or Lower Nahe.

GROSSLAGE KRONENBERG

This is not a branded beer, but one of the best Grosslagen in the Nahe, although all its finest wines, invariably Rieslings with a magical blend of perfumed fragrance and soft yet racy acidity, carry Einzellage names.

BAD KREUZNACH

☆ Vineyard *Kahlenberg*
☆ Growers *Graf von Plettenberg, Eckel-Pitthan, Ludwig Herf, Rudolf Peter Anheuser, Oekonomierat August Anheuser, Kreuznacher Weinbauschule, Paul Anheuser*

☆ Vineyard *Krötenpfuhl*
☆ Growers *Graf von Plettenberg, Rudolf Peter Anheuser, Oekonomierat August Anheuser, Carl Finkenauer, Paul Anheuser*

☆ Vineyard *Brückes*
☆ Growers *Graf von Plettenberg, Eckel-Pitthan, Oekonomierat August Anheuser, August Grünewald, Carl Finkenauer, Rudolf Peter Anheuser, Paul Anheuser*

☆ Vineyard *Hinkelstein*
☆ Growers *Günther Schlink, Staatliche Weinbaudomäne, Graf von Plettenberg, Oekonomierat August Anheuser, Paul Anheuser*

☆ Vineyard *Hinkelstein*
☆ Growers *Günther Schlink, Staatliche Weinbaudomäne, Graf von Plettenberg, Oekonomierat August Anheuser, Paul Anheuser*

GROSSLAGE PFARRGARTEN

A relatively small, but intensively cultivated Grosslage west and slightly north of Bad Kreuznach. The wines of Wallhausen are the best.

WALLHAUSEN

☆ Vineyard *Sonnenweg*
☆ Grower *Prinz zu Salm-Dahlberg'sches Weingut*

☆ Vineyard *Felseneck*
☆ Grower *Prinz zu Salm-Dahlberg'sches Weingut*

GROSSLAGE SCHLOSSKAPELLE

Fine, racy Riesling from Münster-Sarmsheim, fuller, richer versions from Dorsheim and excellent-value wines from Windesheim and Guldental.

WINDESHEIM

☆ Vineyard *Sonnenmorgen*
☆ Grower *Konrad Knodel*

MÜNSTER (-SARMSHEIM)

☆ Vineyard *Dautenpflanzer*
☆ Grower *Staatliche Weinbaudomäne*

DORSHEIM

☆ Vineyard *Klosterpfad*
☆ Growers *Schlossgut Diel, Staatliche Weinbaudomäne*

☆ Vineyard *Goldloch*
☆ Grower *Schlossgut Diel*

☆ Vineyard *Burgberg*
☆ Grower *Staatliche Weinbaudomäne*

GULDENTAL

☆ Vineyard *Rosenteich*
☆ Grower *Karl Kruger*

GROSSLAGE SONNENBORN

A one-village Grosslage, the wines of Langenlonsheim are generally interesting and fulsome, but rather rustic.

LANGENLONSHEIM

☆ Vineyard *Steinchen*
☆ Grower *Tesch-Heintz*

BEREICH SCHLOSS BÖCKELHEIM

This is the more famous of the Nahe's two Bereiche. It is named after the region's most important village and boasts its best stretch of south-facing Riesling vineyards, although it also contains many more modest vineyards planted with inferior grape varieties.

GROSSLAGE BURGWEG

Not to be confused with the Grosslagen of the same name in the Rheingau and Franken, this Burgweg produces the Nahe's greatest range of fine Riesling wines, and Schlossböckelheimer Kupfergrube is widely regarded as the best of all. They have a tingling intensity of flavour derived from a combination of great extract and high acidity.

SCHLOSSBÖCKELHEIM

☆ Vineyard *Kupfergrube*
☆ Growers *Staatliche Weinbaudomäne, Ludwig Herf, Graf von Plettenberg*

☆ Vineyard *Königsfels*
☆ Growers *Paul Anheuser, Jacob Schneider, Egon Anheuser*

☆ Vineyard *Felsenberg*
☆ Growers *Staatliche Weinbaudomäne, Graf von Plettenberg, Hans Crusius-Traisen*

☆ Vineyard *Hermannshöhle*
☆ Grower *Staatliche Weinbaudomäne, Oekonomierat August E. Anheuser, Jacob Schneider*

☆ Vineyard *Hermannsberg*
☆ Grower *Staatliche Weinbaudomäne*

☆ Vineyard *Steinberg*
☆ Grower *Staatliche Weinbaudomäne*

BAD MÜNSTER AM STEIN

☆ Vineyard *Rotenfels*
☆ Growers *Staatliche Weinbaudomäne, Hans Crusius-Traisen, Weingut Rotenfels, Voigtländer Fenker*

NORHEIM

☆ Vineyard *Dellchen*
☆ Growers *Oekonomierat August E. Anheuser, Adolf Lötzbeyer, Paul Anheuser, Staatliche Weinbaudomäne*

GROSSLAGE PARADIESGARTEN

A large area of scattered vineyards of variable quality. With the exception of Obermoschel, all its finest wines come from the extreme eastern edge of the Nahe. The relatively unknown wines usually offer excellent value for money.

MONZINGEN

☆ Vineyard *Rosenberg*
☆ Grower *Nahe-Winzerkellereien e.G.*

☆ Vineyard *Frühlingsplätzchen*
☆ Grower *Nahe-Winzerkellereien e.G.*

MEDDERSHEIM

☆ Vineyard *Rheingrafenberg*
☆ Grower *Winzergenossenschaft Rheingrafenberg*

MERXHEIM

☆ Vineyard *Römerberg*
☆ Grower *Winzergenossenschaft Rheingrafenberg*

OBERMOSCHEL

☆ Vineyard *Geissenkopf*
☆ Grower *Weingut Schmidt*

GROSSLAGE ROSENGARTEN

The true, original and famous Rüdesheimer Rosengarten is a great *Rheingau* Riesling from an Einzellage called Rosengarten. The Nahe version may be honest enough, but it is merely a modest Grosslage wine and in all probability, a blend of Müller-Thurgau and Silvaner.

RÜDESHEIM

☆ Vineyard *Goldgrube*
☆ Grower *Graf von Plettenberg*

ROXHEIM

☆ Vineyard *Höllenpfad*
☆ Growers *Graf von Plettenberg, Paul Anheuser*

The Rheingau

Many countries use the synonym Johannisberg Riesling to identify the true Riesling, as opposed to the many inferior varieties that prostitute its name. There can be no doubt that the King of Germany's grapes are more at home in and around the village of Johannisberg than anywhere else.

WHILE I HAVE ENJOYED MORE GREAT RIESLINGS from the Mosel-Saar-Ruwer than from the Rheingau, due to my personal preference for a higher acidity balance, I cannot deny that the Riesling luxuriates on Johannisberg's single sun-blessed slope in a most unique way. This shows through in the relaxed and confident style of the wines that, even at *QbA* level, leave a soft, satisfying and elegant taste of peaches in the mouth and have a youthful, honeyed character that has nothing to do with *Edelfäule*, overripeness or bottle-aging. One can prefer other renditions of this grape, but it is impossible to find finer, more graceful examples.

Viticulture in the Rheingau, above
Over 80 per cent of the vines are Riesling, and it is here that it performs best.

FACTORS AFFECTING TASTE AND QUALITY

Location
A compact region only 36 kilometres (22 miles) long, situated on the northern banks of the Rivers Rhine and Main between Bingen and Mainz.

Climate
Vines are protected from cold by the tempering effect of the river and the shelter provided by the Taunus mountains. The region receives above-average hours of sunshine during the growth period of May to October.

Aspect
The vines grow at an altitude of between 100-300 metres (330-985 ft) on a superb, fully south-facing slope.

Soil
Quartzite and weathered slate-stone in the higher placed sites produce the greatest Riesling, while loam, loess, clay and sandy gravel soils of the lower vineyards give a fuller, more robust style. The blue phyllite-slate around Assmannshausen is traditionally thought to favour the Spätburgunder.

Viticulture and vinification
There are some 500 independent wine estates and approximately 2,600 private growers. Many of these make and market their own wines whilst others supply the region's ten cooperatives. Riesling represents 80 per cent of the vines cultivated and it is traditional to vinify all but the sweetest wines in a drier style than in other regions. Assmannshausen is famous for its red wine, one of Germany's best.

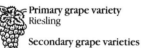 **Primary grape variety**
Riesling

Secondary grape varieties
Kerner, Müller-Thurgau, Ehrenfelser, Silvaner, Spätburgunder

THE REGION AT A GLANCE

Area under vine: 2,750 ha (6,800 acres)

Average yield: 79 hl/ha (355 cases/acre)

Red wine: 6%

White wine: 94%

Infrastructure: Bereich 1; Grosslagen 10; Einzellagen 118

Note: The vineyards of this region straddle 28 Gemeinden (communes), the names of which may appear on the label.

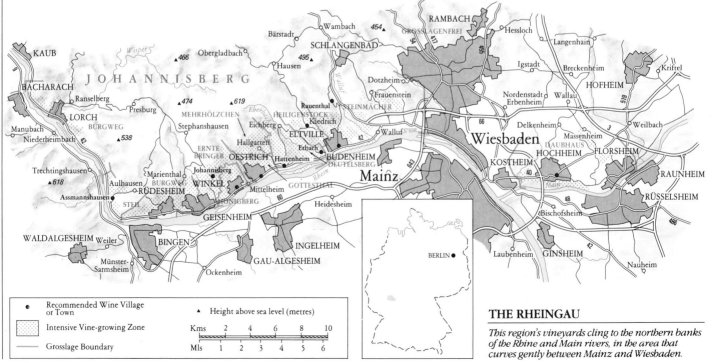

Recommended Wine Village or Town

Intensive Vine-growing Zone

Grosslage Boundary

▲ Height above sea level (metres)

Kms 2 4 6 8 10

Mls 1 2 3 4 5 6

THE RHEINGAU

This region's vineyards cling to the northern banks of the Rhine and Main rivers, in the area that curves gently between Mainz and Wiesbaden.

THE RHEINGAU'S CHARTA FOR QUALITY

In the midst of the excitement generated by Germany's new *Trocken* wines, it became evident to various top Rheingau estates that most of the wines exported were bulk-blended and of low commercial quality. As these properties had traditionally produced naturally drier wines, they believed that a continuance of poor *Trocken* wines could damage their own image, and so banded together to protect it. In 1983, the Association of Charta-Estates was launched to "further the classic Rheingau Riesling style, to upgrade the quality of Rheingau wines, and to make them unique among wines from other growing areas".

Berg Schlossberg vineyards, Rudesheim, above
These south-facing vineyards are blessed with perfect exposure to the sun's rays.

THE CHARTA RULES

Having tasted many Charta-wines, I am convinced that they are indeed superior. Most of the finest wines of the Rheingau are Charta-wines, but it must be emphasized that this includes dry styles only — great *QmP* Rheingau wines of sweeter styles from *Auslese* upwards are not affected by the Charta organization. A Charta-wine may be recognized by its distinctive tall, slim, brown bottle, which is traditional in the Rheingau. All bottles are embossed with a Roman double arch insignia and carry a Charta back-label bearing the same insignia.

1 Charta-wines are examined organoleptically, both before and after bottling. The second examination is made to check the authenticity of the original sample.

2 Wines destined to become Charta-wines must be accompanied by an official analysis (two bottles per type) and must satisfy certain criteria laid down by the Association of Charta-Estates.

3 The wines that are submitted for examination must conform to the following:
a) 100% own-estate production
b) 100% from Riesling grapes
c) a minimum acidity of 7.5 grams per litre
d) between 9 and 18 grams per litre of unfermented sugar
e) higher than the average minimum density of 65° Oechsle for *QbA*, 78° Oechsle for *Kabinett* and 88° Oechsle for *Spätlese*.

The wines must have all the characteristics of a true Riesling, of the vintage and of the vineyard.

4 Examination registration has to be made four weeks prior to the date of examination, indicating the vintage and category.
   As a standard for the examination, normal wines of comparable location and category are blind-tasted alongside the submitted wines. Charta-wines have to surpass the quality of those standard wines in each aspect. The wines for the second tasting, as well as being a check against the original, have to be accompanied by the analysis of the *AP* number examination (see p.204). These are lodged as documents belonging to the Association and can be used for verification purposes in the eventuality of any claims that a member is passing off an inferior or different wine as a Charta-wine.

QUALITY REQUIREMENTS AND HARVEST PERCENTAGES

Minimum Oechsle	Quality Category	Harvest breakdown			
		1984	1985	1986	1987
44°	Deutscher Tafelwein	20%	—	3%	2%
53°	Landwein				
57–66°	*QbA	79%	40%	72%	89%
73–80°	*Kabinett	1%	53%	21%	8%
85–95°	*Spätlese	—	6%	4%	1%
95–105°	*Auslese	—	1%	—	—
125°	Beerenauslese				
125°	Eiswein				
150°	Trockenbeerenauslese				

* Minimum Oechsle levels vary according to grape variety, with those that have a naturally lower sugar content allowed to qualify at a correspondingly lower level

The wines of the Rheingau

BEREICH JOHANNISBERG

This one Bereich covers the entire Rheingau and, trading off the famous village of Johannisberg, situated behind Schloss Johannisberg, lesser wines sell well under it. However, producers have started using Grosslage names on the labels because they do not include the word "Grosslage", and thus suggest the wine might even be from one specific site, and perhaps of better quality.

GROSSLAGE BURGWEG

This is the westernmost Grosslage in the Rheingau. If a wine bears its name on the label and clearly indicates the all-important "Riesling", it may well be quite good, but will not compare with Burgweg's many superb Einzellage wines made by one of the great estates or small growers.

RÜDESHEIM

☆ Vineyard *Bischofsberg*
☆ Growers *Weingut Schloss Groenesteyn, Weingut G. H. von Mumm, Domäne Schloss Schönborn, Deinhard, August Eser, Dr. Heinrich Nägeler, Balthasar Ress*

☆ Vineyard *Drachenstein*
☆ Grower *Dr. Heinrich Nägeler*

☆ Vineyard *Kirchenpfad*
☆ Growers *Weingut Schloss Groenesteyn, Balthasar Ress*

☆ Vineyard *Berg Rottland*
☆ Growers *Weingut Schloss*

Groenesteyn, Weingut G. H. von Mumm, Staatsweingüter, Domäne Schloss Schönborn, Deinhard, Dr. Heinrich Nägeler

☆ Vineyard *Berg Roseneck*
☆ Growers *Weingut Schloss Groenesteyn, Weingut G. H. von Mumm, Deinhard, Dr Heinrich Nägeler, Balthasar Ress, Staatsweingüter*

☆ Vineyard *Berg Schlossberg*
☆ Growers *Weingut Schloss Groenesteyn, Weingut G. H. von Mumm, Domäne Schloss Schönborn, Deinhard, Dr. Heinrich Nägeler, G. Breuer, Balthasar Ress, Staatsweingüter*

☆ Vineyard *Klosterlay*
☆ Grower *Pfarrgut Rüdesheim*

GEISENHEIM

☆ Vineyard *Mönchspfad*
☆ Growers *Schumann-Nägeler, Basting-Gimbel, Weingut G. H. von Mumm, Adam Vollmer*

☆ Vineyard *Mäuerchen*
☆ Growers *Domäne Schloss Schönborn, Schumann-Nägeler, Weingut Freiherr von Zwierlein, Basting-Gimbel, Weingut G. H. von Mumm, Adam Vollmer*

GROSSLAGE DAUBHAUS

The most easterly Grosslage, where the best vines are restricted to a relatively tiny, isolated, but excellent strip at Hochheim. The wines are firm and full, not quite matching the elegance of the Rheingau's very best.

HOCHHEIM

☆ Vineyard *Domdechaney*
☆ Growers *Domdechant Werner'sches Weingut, Domäne Schloss Schönborn, Geheimrat Aschrott'sche Erben, Staatsweingüter*

☆ Vineyard *Kirchenstück*
☆ Growers *Domdechant Werner'sches Weingut, Domäne Schloss Schönborn, Geheimrat Aschrott'sche Erben, Staatsweingüter*

☆ Vineyard *Hölle*
☆ Growers *Domdechant Werner'sches Weingut, Domäne Schloss Schönborn, Geheimrat Aschrott'sche Erben*

GROSSLAGE DEUTELSBERG

This Grosslage encompasses the great Erbach vineyards and the underrated wines of Hattenheim that have great strength and longevity. It also includes the famous Kloster Eberbach and Mariannenau Island vineyard.

HATTENHEIM

☆ Vineyard *Steinberg*
☆ Grower *Staatsweingüter*

☆ Vineyard *Nussbrunnen*
☆ Growers *Schloss Reinhartshausen, Freiherr Langwerth von Simmern, Domäne Schloss Schönborn, Pfarrgut Hattenheim*

☆ Vineyard *Engelmannsberg*
☆ Growers *Domäne Schloss Schönborn, Staatsweingüter, August Eser*

☆ Vineyard *Wisselbrunnen*
☆ Grower *Domäne Schloss Schönborn*

☆ Vineyard *Mannberg*
☆ Growers *Freiherr Langwerth von Simmern, Weingut Reitz, Balthasar Ress, Staatsweingüter*

☆ Vineyard *Hassel*
☆ Grower *Domäne Schloss Schönborn*

☆ Vineyard *Pfaffenberg*
☆ Grower *Domäne Schloss Schönborn*

☆ Vineyard *Schützenhaus*
☆ Grower *Domäne Schloss Schönborn*

GROSSLAGE ERNTEBRINGER

The most often-seen of the Rheingau's Grosslagen, Erntebringer

is also the best, although not comparable to the Einzellagen, particularly the legendary Schloss Johannisberg and the grossly underrated Klaus.

JOHANNISBERG

☆ Vineyard *Schloss Johannisberg*
☆ Grower *Fürstl. Metternich'sches Weingut Schloss Johannisberg*

☆ Vineyard *Klaus*
☆ Growers *Domäne Schloss Schönborn, Weingut G. H. von Mumm, Landgräfl. Hessisches Weingut, Weingut Johannishof-Eser*

GROSSLAGE GOTTESTHAL

It is strange that this Grosslage, sandwiched between the superb Grosslagen of Deutelsberg and Honigberg, should be relatively disappointing. However, some excellent, longlived Riesling can be found.

OESTRICH

☆ Vineyard *Lenchen*
☆ Growers *Deinhard, August Eser, Weingut Hupfeld Erben*

GROSSLAGE HEILIGENSTOCK

The best product of this small Grosslage is the fabulous, peach-and-honey Riesling of Kiedrich. The Grosslage wine can also be good.

KIEDRICH

☆ Vineyard *Sandgrub*
☆ Growers *Winzergenossenschaft Kiedrich, Georg Sohlbach, Schloss Reinhartshausen, Dr. R. Weil, Heinz Nikolai, Weingut Schloss Groenesteyn, H. Tillmanns Erben, Landgräfl. Hessisches Weingut, Freiherr zu Knyphausen, Robert von Oetinger*

☆ Vineyard *Wasseros*
☆ Growers *Winzergenossenschaft Kiedfrich, Georg Sohlbach, Dr. R. Weil, Weingut Schloss Groenesteyn*

☆ Vineyard *Gräfenberg*
☆ Grower *Winzergenossenshaft Kiedrich, Georg Sohlbach, Dr. W. Weil, Staatsweingüter, Weingut Schloss Groenesteyn*

GROSSLAGE HONIGBERG

Wines of great vitality, finesse and all the elegant, mouthwatering, peachy fruit and youthful honey you could expect from top Rheingau.

WINKEL

☆ Vineyard *Schloss Vollrads*
☆ Grower *Graf Matuschka-Greiffenclau*

☆ Vineyard *Jesuitengarten*
☆ Growers *Deinhard, Weingut Johannisberg, Eser, Fritz Allendorf, Baron von Brentano'sche Gutsverwaltung, Landgräfl. Hessisches Weingut*

☆ Vineyard *Hasensprung*
☆ Grower *Domäne Schloss Schönborn, Deinhard, Weingut Johannisberg-Eser, Hof Sonneck, Baron von Brentano'sche Gusverwaltung, Basting-Gimbel, Landgräfl. Hessisches Weingut*

GROSSLAGE MEHRHÖLZCHEN

This Grosslage, which is on higher, steeper slopes than the rest of the Rheingau, is tucked up beneath the Taunus hills and planted almost entirely with Riesling. The best is found around Erbach, the village that dominates this district. The wines are full of fruit, often displaying a unique spicy aroma.

ERBACH

☆ Vineyard *Schlossberg*
☆ Grower *Schloss Reinhartshausen*

☆ Vineyard *Steinmorgen*
☆ Growers *Robert von Oetinger, Schloss Reinhartshausen, H. Tillmanns Erben*

☆ Vineyard *Marcobrunn*
☆ Growers *Freiherr zu Knyphausen, Staatsweingüter, Weingut Schloss Reinhartshausen, Weingut Schloss Schönborn, Freiherr Langwerth von Simmern, Weingut Kohlhaas, Ritter und Edler von Oetinger*

HALLGARTEN

☆ Vineyard *Jungfer*
☆ Growers *Fürst Löwenstein, Heinz Nikolai, Franz Engelmann*

GROSSLAGE STEIL

This tiny Grosslage, which divides the Grosslage of Burgweg, is famous for the red wines of Assmannshausen. These are very soft and have a pure varietal style, but possess neither the body nor the tannin one is accustomed to find to some degree in any red wine. Most of the vineyards are steep and west-facing, but the best, those of Höllenberg, on a tiny tributary, are south-facing.

ASSMANNSHAUSEN

☆ Vineyard *Höllenberg*
☆ Growers *Staatsweingüter, August Kessler, Weingut G. H. von Mumm, Valentin Schlotter*

GROSSLAGE STEINMÄCHER

Its vineyards are less intensive than those of the main body of the Rheingau's vines, but the wines they make are in no way less impressive.

RAUENTHAL

☆ Vineyard *Baiken*
☆ Growers *Staatsweingüter, Gräfl. Eltzsche Gutsverwaltung, Domäne Schönborn, Freiherr Langwerth von Simmern, Christian Sturm-Rauenthal*

☆ Vineyard *Wülfen*
☆ Grower *Schloss Reinhartshausen*

ELTVILLE

☆ Vineyard *Taubenberg*
☆ Growers *Gräfl. Eltzsche Gutsverwaltung, Freiherr Langwerth von Simmern, Weingut J. B. Becker (Niederwalluf), Freiherr zu Knyphausen*

☆ Vineyard *Langenstück*
☆ Grower *Oekonomierat Fischer Erben*

☆ Vineyard *Sonnenberg*
☆ Growers *Gräfl. Eltzsche Gutsverwaltung, Freiherr Langwerth von Simmern, Weingut J. B. Becker (Niederwalluf), Oekonomierat Fischer Erben*

WALLUF

☆ Vineyard *Walkenberg*
☆ Grower *Weingut J. B. Becker (Niederwalluf)*

Rheinhessen

Producer of some 50 per cent of all Liebfraumilch, Rheinhessen has the most vineyards of all Germany's wine regions. This fact, plus the diversity of its soils and grape varieties make it impossible to convey a uniform impression of its wines, which range from mild Silvaner to aromatic, spicy Müller-Thurgau.

RHEINHESSEN IS INDISPUTABLY LINKED with the ubiquitous Liebfraumilch. This is partly because 50 per cent of it comes from this region and partly because the famous, if overrated, Liebfraumilch-Kirchenstück in Worms, is where it all began; furthermore, Sichel brews up its "Blue Nun" at Alzey. Nierstein carries a similar stigma to Liebfraumilch in the minds of many experienced drinkers. This is due to the copious quantities of the cheap Bereich Nierstein and Niersteiner Gutes Domtal that flood the market, downgrading the true Niersteiner Einzellagen.

THE RHINE TERRACE

Despite the high volume of indifferent wines, there are many great growers and estates in this region. For an initial step-up in quality for a modest price, look out for the "Rhein Terrasse" sticker on bottles of Rheinhessen. The Rhine Terrace comprises nine villages on the slopes that descend from Rheinhessen's plateau to the Rhine. These are Bodenheim in the Sankt Alban Grosslage; Nackenheim in the Gutes Domtal Grosslage; Nierstein, which is

shared by the Grosslagen of Gutes Domtal, Spiegelberg, Rehbach and Auflangen; Oppenheim in the Grosslagen of Güldenmorgen and Krötenbrunnen; Dienheim, also in the Krötenbrunnen Grosslage; Guntersblum and Ludwigshöhe, both of which are in the Krötenbrunnen and Vogelsgarten Grosslagen; and Alsheim and Mettenheim, in the Grosslage of Rheinblick.

FACTORS AFFECTING TASTE AND QUALITY

Location
This region is situated between the towns of Bingen, Mainz and Worms, immediately south of the Rheingau.

Climate
Rheinhessen enjoys a temperate climate and is protected from cold winds by the Taunus hills to the north and the Odenwald forest to the east. Vineyards that slope down to the river are protected by the Rhine terrace itself.

Aspect
Vines grow on east- and southeast-facing slopes at an altitude of between 100–200 metres (330–660 ft) on the river slopes of the Rhine Terrace, while those in Rheinhessen's hinterland are found at various heights and with every possible aspect.

Soil
Mainly loess deposited during inter-glacial sandstorms, but also limestone, sandy-marl, quartzite, porphyry-sand and silty-clay. Riesling growers favour heavier marl soil.

Viticulture and vinification
Much of the wine is made from vast vineyard yields, bulk-blended into cheap generic wines such as Bereich Nierstein, and, of course, Liebfraumilch. At the other extreme, small quantities of some fine wines are produced on the best estates.

Primary grape varieties
Müller-Thurgau, Silvaner

Secondary grape varieties
Bacchus, Faberrebe, Huxelrebe, Kerner, Morio-muskat, Portugieser, Riesling, Scheurebe

RHEINHESSEN

One of Germany's largest regions in terms of hectares under vine, it is an area of great variety where several different grapes are grown.

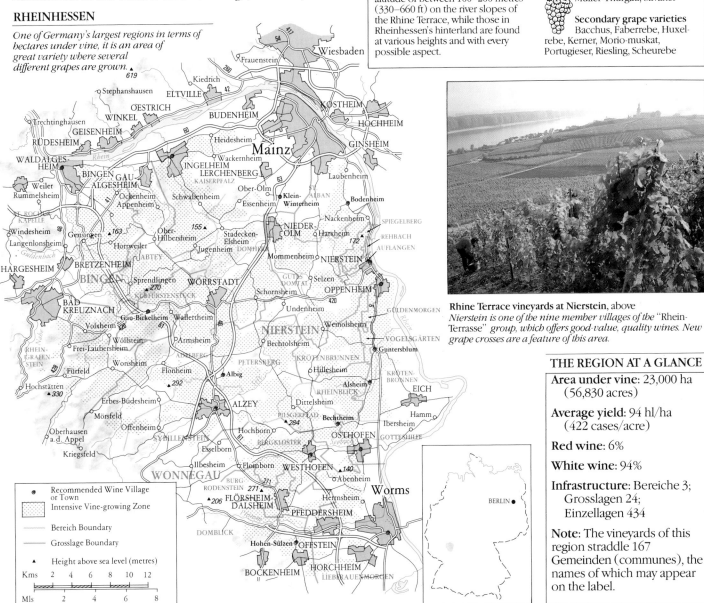

Rhine Terrace vineyards at Nierstein, above
Nierstein is one of the nine member villages of the "Rhein-Terrasse" group, which offers good-value, quality wines. New grape crosses are a feature of this area.

THE REGION AT A GLANCE

Area under vine: 23,000 ha (56,830 acres)

Average yield: 94 hl/ha (422 cases/acre)

Red wine: 6%

White wine: 94%

Infrastructure: Bereiche 3; Grosslagen 24; Einzellagen 434

Note: The vineyards of this region straddle 167 Gemeinden (communes), the names of which may appear on the label.

Legend:
- Recommended Wine Village or Town
- Intensive Vine-growing Zone
- Bereich Boundary
- Grosslage Boundary
- ▲ Height above sea level (metres)

Kms 2 4 6 8 10 12
Mls 2 4 6 8

QUALITY REQUIREMENTS AND HARVEST PERCENTAGES

Minimum Oechsle	Quality Category	Harvest breakdown			
		1984	1985	1986	1987
44°	Deutscher Tafelwein	10%	—	1%	4%
50–53°	Landwein				
60–62°	*QbA	82%	38%	75%	80%
73–76°	*Kabinett	5%	28%	19%	15%
85–90°	*Spätlese	3%	29%	5%	1%
92–100°	*Auslese	—	5%		
120°	*Beerenauslese				
120°	*Eiswein				
150°	Trockenbeerenauslese				

*Minimum Oechsle levels vary according to grape variety, with those that have a naturally lower sugar content allowed to qualify at a correspondingly lower level.

Liebfraumilch country in the spring, right
The village of Grau-Heppenheim, near Alzey, in the large Petersberg Grosslage.

The wines of Rheinhessen

BEREICH BINGEN

Abutting the Nahe region to the west and separated by the Rhine from the Rheingau to the north, this is the smallest of Rheinhessen's three Bereiche and the least important in terms of both quantity and quality.

GROSSLAGE ABTEY

No outstanding villages, vineyards, or growers, although good wines are made in the village of St. Johann.

GROSSLAGE ADELBERG

No outstanding villages, vineyards, or growers, although good wines are made in the village of Wörrstadt.

GROSSLAGE KAISERPFALZ

A Grosslage consisting mainly of a small tributary valley halfway between Bingen and Mainz, with vineyards facing both east and west. Kaiserpfalz produces some of the region's most promising red wines from the Portugieser and Spätburgunder grapes. The village of Ingelheim is one of the places that claim to be the birthplace of Charlemagne.

INGELHEIM (-WINTERHEIM)

☆ Vineyard *Kirchenstück*
☆ Grower *Rotweingut J. Neus*

JUGENHEIM

☆ Vineyard *Hasensprung*
☆ Grower *Adolf Schick*

GROSSLAGE KURFÜRSTENSTÜCK

Gau-Bickelheim is the home of the Rheinhessen's huge central co-operative, but it is good growers or the excellent Staatsdomäne from the Einzellage of Kapelle that produce superior wines.

GAU-BICKELHEIM

☆ Vineyard *Kapelle*
☆ Growers *Weingut Villa Sachsen, Kurt Berger Erben, Espenschied-Heuss, Staatsdomäne*

GROSSLAGE RHEINGRAFENSTEIN

No outstanding villages, vineyards, or growers.

GROSSLAGE SANKT ROCHUSKAPELLE

Bingen is often thought to belong more to the Nahe region than to Rheinhessen, but 14 of its 18 Einzellagen belong to this Rheinhessen Grosslage, which is the best in Bereich Bingen.

BINGEN

☆ Vineyard *Kirchberg*
☆ Grower *Weingut Villa Sachsen*

BINGEN-RÜDESHEIM

☆ Vineyard *Scharlachberg*

☆ Growers *Kommerzienrat P. A. Ohler'sches Weingut, Weingut Villa Sachsen*

☆ Vineyard *Bubenstück*
☆ Grower *Weingut Villa Sachsen*

☆ Vineyard *Rosengarten*
☆ Grower *Weingut Villa Sachsen*

BINGEN-KEMPTEN

☆ Vineyard *Kappellenberg*
☆ Grower *Weingut Villa Sachsen*

☆ Vineyard *Schlossberg-Schwätzerchen*
☆ Growers *Kommerzienrat P. A. Ohler'sches Weingut, Weingut Villa Sachsen*

BEREICH NIERSTEIN

A famous Bereich with many superb sites and great growers, yet the wines sold under its label include some of the most dull, characterless and lacklustre in all Germany. It is best to choose the great Einzellagen or leave these wines alone.

GROSSLAGE AUFLANGEN

The best of the three Grosslagen that encompass parts of Nierstein (the other two are Rehbach and Spiegelberg). Its vineyard area begins in the centre of the town, stretching west to include the south and south-east facing vineyards of the tiny tributary that flows through Schwabsburg, and north to the Kranzberg, which overlooks the Rhine itself.

NIERSTEIN

☆ Vineyard *Heiligenbaum*
☆ Growers *Staatsdomäne, Louis Guntrum, George und Karl Ludwig Schmitt, J. und A.H. Strub, Freiherr Heyl zu Herrnsheim, Geschwister Schuch, Weingut Gute Hoffnungshütte St. Antony, Heinrich Seip*

☆ Vineyard *Kranzberg*
☆ Growers *F.K. Schmitt, Gustav Adolf Schmitt, Geschwister Schuch, Heinrich Seip*

☆ Vineyard *Orbel*
☆ Growers *Staatsdomäne, Louis Guntrum, F.K. Schmitt, Georg und Karl Ludwig Schmitt, J. und A.H. Strub, Freiherr Heyl zu Herrnsheim, Reinhold Senfter, Weingut Gute Hoffnungshütte St. Antony, Heinrich Seip, Eugen Wehrheim*

☆ Vineyard *Oelberg*
☆ Growers *Louis Guntrum, Gustav Adolf Schmitt, Gustav Gessert, J. und H.A. Strub, Freiherr Heyl zu Herrnsheim, Geschwister Schuch, Franz Josef Sander, Heinrich Seip, Eugen Wehrheim*

GROSSLAGE DOMHERR

No outstanding villages, vineyards or growers, although good wines are made in the village of Klein-Winternheim.

GROSSLAGE GÜLDENMORGEN

Güldenmorgen was once a fine Einzellage belonging to Oppenheim, but now encompasses three villages and no longer has any connotation of quality, although five of its individual vineyards do.

OPPENHEIM

☆ Vineyard *Herrenberg*
☆ Growers *Louis Guntrum, Dr. Dahlem Erben, Friedrich Baumann, Carl Koch Erben, Gustav Adolf Schmitt*

☆ Vineyard *Kreuz*
☆ Grower *Louis Guntrum*

☆ Vineyard *Daubhaus*
☆ Grower *Friedrich Baumann*

☆ Vineyard *Sackträger*
☆ Growers *Landes Lehr- und Versuch- sanstalt Oppenheim, Louis Guntrum, Dr. Dahlem Erben, Reinhold Senfter, Staatsdomäne, Carl Sittman, Friedrich Baumann, Carl Koch Erben, Geschwister Schuch*

DIENHEIM

☆ Vineyard *Tafelstein*
☆ Growers *Louis Guntrum, Dr. Dahlem Erben, Carl Sittman, Friedrich Baumann, Carl Koch Erben, Brüder Dr. Becker*

GROSSLAGE GUTES DOMTAL

This district covers a vast area of Rhine hinterland behind the better Grosslagen of Nierstein. Although it encompasses 15 villages, most is sold under the ubiquitous Nier- steiner Gutes Domtal (sometimes Domthal) name. Much is decidedly inferior and cheapens the reputation of Nierstein's truly great wines. The most famous village is Dexheim, because of its so-called Doktor, named after the old spelling of the great Bernkasteler Doctor vineyard. But neither Dexheim generally, nor Dexheimer Doktor specifically, warrant the attention.

GROSSLAGE KRÖTENBRUNNEN

This district contains those parts of Oppenheim's vineyards not included in the Grosslage Güldenmorgen, and the wide-ranging vineyards of Guntersblum.

GUNTERSBLUM

☆ Vineyard *Steinberg*
☆ Grower *Dr. Reinhard Muth*

GROSSLAGE PETERSBERG

This Grosslage lies behind Gutes Domtal and is wedged between the Bereiche of Bingen and Wonnegau. Although large, it has few exciting sites or growers.

ALBIG

☆ Vineyard *Schloss Hammerstein*
☆ Grower *Köster-Wolf*

GROSSLAGE REHBACH

One of the greatest Grosslagen in Rheinhessen, Rehbach consists of a long, thin strip of very steep terraced slopes overlooking the Rhine, just north of Nierstein. Riesling wines from these vineyards are aromatic, intense and delightfully mellow, yet have a definite raciness on the finish.

NIERSTEIN

☆ Vineyard *Hipping*
☆ Growers *Anton Balbach Erben, Franz Karl Schmitt, Louis Guntrum, J. und H.A. Strub, Carl Sittmann, Heinrich Seip, Reinhold Senfter, Georg und Karl Ludwig Schmitt, Geschwister Schuch, Eugen Wehrheim*

☆ Vineyard *Pettenthal*
☆ Growers *Freiherr Heyl zu Herrnsheim, Anton Balbach Erben, Franz Karl Schmitt, Gustav Adolf Schmitt, Heinrich Seip, Geschwister Schuch, Eugen Wehrheim*

☆ Vineyard *Brudersberg*
☆ Grower *Freiherr Heyl zu Herrnsheim*

GROSSLAGE RHEINBLICK

This district produces better-than- average Grosslage wine, plus one or two good grower wines.

ALSHEIM

☆ Vineyard *Frühmesse*
☆ Growers *Dr. Reinhard Muth, Weingut Rappenhof, Carl Sittmann*

GROSSLAGE SANKT ALBAN

Named after the Sankt Alban monastery, which once owned most of the land in this underrated Grosslage situated between Mainz and Nierstein. The Einzellage wines have fine, positive character and usually represent excellent value for money.

BODENHEIM

☆ Vineyard *Hoch*
☆ Growers *Staatlich Weinbaudomäne Mainz-Bodenheim, Oberstltn. Lieb- rechtsche Weingutsverwaltung, Jamin-Kern*

☆ Vineyard *Silberberg*
☆ Growers *Staatlich Weinbaudomäne Mainz-Bodenheim, Oberstltn. Lieb- rechtsche Weingutsverwaltung, Christian Blass, Wendlin Haub*

☆ Vineyard *Westrum*
☆ Growers *H.G. Kerz, Josef Acker, J.B. Riffel*

GROSSLAGE SPIEGELBERG

The largest of Nierstein's riverside districts, its vineyards stretch to the north and south of both the famous town and the Grosslage Auflangen. Ignore the ubiquitous, mild and neutral-flavoured Grosslagen wines and choose the wines of the finer Einzellagen that are situated between Nierstein and Oppenheim.

NIERSTEIN

☆ Vineyard *Hölle*
☆ Growers *Louis Guntrum, J. & H.A. Strub*

☆ Vineyard *Brückchen*
☆ Growers *Jakob Becker, J. & H.A. Strub, Eugen Wehrheim*

☆ Vineyard *Paterberg*
☆ Growers *Louis Guntrum, Heinrich Seip, Kurfürstenhof*

GROSSLAGE VOGELSGARTEN

Not one of the best Rheinhessen districts, although Schmitt-Dr. Ohnacker makes fine, rich, some- times powerful wines that are well worth seeking out.

GUNTERSBLUM

☆ Vineyard *Authenthal*
☆ Grower *Schmitt-Dr. Ohnacker*

BEREICH WONNEGAU

The least-known of Rheinhessen's three Bereiche, yet containing the world-famous (but not world-class) Liebfrauenstift Einzellage, which had the dubious honour of giving birth to Liebfraumilch. Wonnegau means "province of great joy".

GROSSLAGE BERGKLOSTER

No outstanding villages, vineyards or growers, although good wines are made in the village of Westhofen.

GROSSLAGE BURG RODENSTEIN

A large proportion of the wines made in this district are sold under its Grosslage name. Most of it is well above average quality, although not in the same class as its best Einzel- lage wines.

NIEDERFLÖRSHEIM

☆ Vineyard *Frauenberg*
☆ Grower *Scherner-Kleinhanns*

DALSHEIM

☆ Vineyard *Steig*
☆ Growers *Weingut Schales, Müller-Dr. Becker*

☆ Vineyard *Hubacker*
☆ Grower *Weingut Keller*

GROSSLAGE DOMBLICK

No outstanding villages, vineyards or growers, although good wines are made in the village of Hohen-Sülzen and the Grosslage label usually offers sound value.

GROSSLAGE GOTTESHILFE

A tiny district encompassing the excellent wine village of Bechtheim. Very little wine is seen on export markets under the Grosslage label.

BECHTHEIM

☆ Vineyard *Geyersberg*
☆ Growers *Oekonomierat Johann Geil Erben, Brenner'sches Weingut*

☆ Vineyard *Stein*
☆ Growers *Oekonomierat Johann Geil Erben, Brenner'sches Weingut, Jean Buscher*

☆ Vineyard *Gotteshilfe*
☆ Growers *Gerhard und Hugo Koch- Mettenheim*

GROSSLAGE LIEBFRAUENMORGEN

This familiar sounding Grosslage includes the famous Liebfrauenstift- Kirchenstück vineyard in Worms, the birthplace of Liebfraumilch.

GROSSLAGE PILGERPFAD

This Grosslage stretches from the lesser vineyards of Bechtheim to the large Petersberg district in Bereich Nierstein and produces little-seen and generally uninspiring wines.

OSTHOFEN

☆ Vineyard *Liebenberg*
☆ Grower *Weingut Ahnenhof*

GROSSLAGE SYBILLENSTEIN

No outstanding villages, vineyards or growers, although good wines are made in the village of Alzey, and its Kappellenberg vineyard has a certain reputation. Alzey is the location of Sichel, master-blenders of "Blue Nun" Liebfraumilch (*see* p.209).

The Rheinpfalz

Sometimes referred to as the Palatinate, the Rheinpfalz represents 80 kilometres (50 miles) of the sun-blessed vineyards on the crest of the Haardt mountain range and the Pfälzer Wald (forest region). Heavy marl soils in the north tend to make full-bodied, if rather mild-flavoured wines, and the chalk and clay soils to the south yield lighter, fragrant, well-flavoured wines.

RARE PHYSICAL EVIDENCE OF ANCIENT German wines exists in the Rheinpfalz at the Wine Museum at Speyer, where a glass amphora contains genuine, golden 1,600-year-old wine, made by the Romans, beneath a thick layer of foul-looking resin and oil. By the twelfth century, the Bishop of Speyer owned all the best vineyards in the Rheinpfalz and they remained the property of the Church until they were acquired by Napoléon. After the great Corsican emperor left, somewhat reluctantly, the socio-economic compo-sition of the Rheinpfalz changed dramatically and irrevocably. With the restructuring came a considerably less monopolistic form of land ownership.

THE RHEINPFALZ TODAY

The region now has some 25,000 smallholders, each of whom works less than one hectare (about two-and-a-half acres) on average. These smallholders generally tend their vines at the weekends, working in the cities and towns during the week. Many sell their grapes to cooperatives, who process about 25 per cent of the Rheinpfalz's vast output. There are, however, still a large minority of estates, with considerably more land and, of course, their own winemaking facilities. Because of the vast numbers of growers, grapes, soil types and microclimates, a diverse range of wines is made, from 50 per cent of all Liebfraumilch to a wealth of splendidly expressive pure varietals.

Rheinpfalz landscape, above
This region yields more wine than any other in Germany.

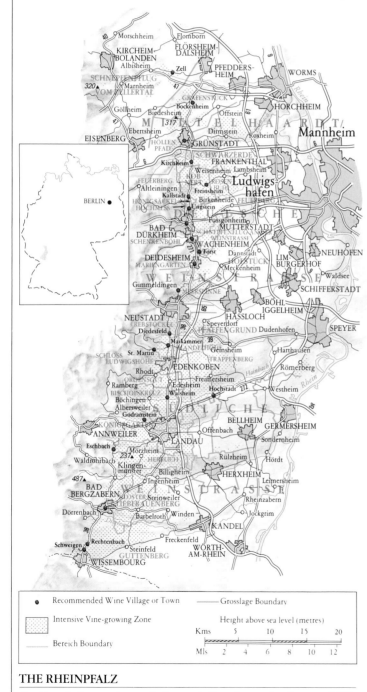

THE RHEINPFALZ

On this region's great plateau, the Romans built an Emperor's palace over 2,000 years ago. From palatium, *the Latin for "palace", the German 'pfalz" is derived.*

THE REGION AT A GLANCE

Area under vine: 20,800 ha (50,400 acres)

Average yield: 116 hl/ha (520 cases/acre)

Red wine: 11%

White wine: 89%

Infrastructure: Bereiche 2; Grosslagen 26; Einzellagen 335

Note: The vineyards of the Rheinpfalz straddle 170 Gemeinden (communes), the names of which may appear on the label.

FACTORS AFFECTING TASTE AND QUALITY

 Location
The second-largest German wine region, stretching 80 kilometres (50 miles) from Rheinhessen to Alsace, bounded by the Rhine on the east and the Haardt Mountains on the west.

Climate
The sunniest and driest wine-producing region in Germany, the Rheinpfalz's climate is enhanced by the sheltering effect of the Haardt and Donnersberg hills.

Aspect
Vineyards are sited mainly on flat land or gentle slopes, at a height of between 100 and 250 metres (330 and 820 ft), overlooked by wooded hills.

 Soil
A great variety of soils, ranging from loam and weathered sandstone to widely dispersed "islands" of limestone, granite, porphyry and clayish slate.

Viticulture and vinification
The Rheinpfalz produces more wine than any other German wine region. The leading estates have a relatively high proportion of Riesling in their vineyards, and produce wines of the very highest quality, although speciality Gewürztraminers and Muskatellers can be extraordinarily good if vinified dry.

 **Primary grape varieties**
Kerner, Müller-Thurgau, Riesling

Secondary grape varieties
Bacchus, Gewürztraminer, Huxelrebe, Morio-muskat, Muskateller, Portugieser, Ruländer, Scheurebe, Silvaner

QUALITY REQUIREMENTS AND HARVEST PERCENTAGES

Minimum Oechsle	Quality Category	Harvest breakdown			
		1984	1985	1986	1987
44°	Deutscher Tafelwein	30%	—	12%	5%
50–53°	*Landwein				
60–62°	*QbA	60%	47%	78%	80%
73–76°	*Kabinett	10%	32%	8%	14%
85–90°	*Spätlese	—	17%	2%	1%
92–100°	*Auslese	—	4%	—	—
120°	*Beerenauslese				
120°	*Eiswein				
150°	Trockenbeerenauslese				

* Minimum Oechsle levels vary according to grape variety, with those that have a naturally lower sugar content allowed to qualify at a corresponding lower level.

Riverside vines, above
A cloak of green vines covers these fertile riverside vineyards.

The wines of the Rheinpfalz

Note: 1. Where I state that there are no outstanding villages, vineyards, estates or growers in a particular Grosslage, excellent estates and growers might well own vineyards there, but the wine produced is not of the highest standard.
2. In the Rheinpfalz, each Grosslage can only be prefixed by a specified village, the name of which appears in brackets after the Grosslage appellation.

BEREICH MITTELHAARDT-DEUTSCHE WEINSTRASSE

The quality of wines produced in this Bereich is so high that few are sold as anything less than Einzellagen.

GROSSLAGE FEUERBERG
(Bad Dürkheim)

Although most of Kallstadt's best Einzellagen come under the Grosslage Kobnert, the most famous, Annaberg, falls within the boundaries of Feuerberg. It is a versatile Grosslage, producing a wide range of wines from full, spicy Gewürztraminers to soft, velvety Spätburgunders.

KALLSTADT

☆ Vineyard *Annaberg*
☆ Grower *K. Fitz-Ritter*

BAD DÜRKHEIM

☆ Vineyard *Nonnengarten*
☆ Growers *Alfred Bonnet, K. Fitz-Ritter, Winzergenossenschaft Vier Jahreszeiten-Kloster Limburg*

GROSSLAGE GRAFENSTÜCK
(Bockenheim)

No outstanding villages, vineyards or growers, although good wines are made in the village of Bockenheim.

GROSSLAGE HOCHMESS
(Bad Dürkheim)

A small, but high-performance Grosslage that includes the best vineyards of Bad Dürkheim, although some fine wines are also produced within the boundaries of Feuerberg and Schenkenböhl. They display a perfect harmony of full flavour and flowery fragrance.

BAD DÜRKHEIM

☆ Vineyard *Spielberg*
☆ Growers *Johannes Karst & Söhne, Bassermann-Jordan, K. Fitz-Ritter, Karl Schaefer/ Dr. Fleischmann, Winzergenossenschaft Vier Jahreszeiten-Kloster Limburg*

☆ Vineyard *Michelsberg*
☆ Growers *Johannes Karst & Söhne, Bassermann-Jordan, K. Fitz-Ritter, Karl Schaefer/ Dr. Fleischmann, Winzergenossenschaft Vier Jahreszeiten-Kloster Limburg*

GROSSLAGE HOFSTÜCK
(Deidesheim)

This Grosslage produces homogeneous, noble and elegant wines, which owe a great deal of their outstanding quality to favourable soil conditions.

DEIDESHEIM

☆ Vineyard *Nonnenstück*
☆ Growers *Reichsrat von Buhl, Josef Biffar*

☆ Vineyard *Hoheburg*
☆ Growers *Bassermann-Jordan, Reichsrat von Buhl, Bürklin-Wolf, Dietz-Mattis, Winzergenossenschaft Hoheburg 1918, Winzerverein 1911, Otto Spindler*

RUPPERTSBERG

☆ Vineyard *Reiterpfad*
☆ Growers *Bassermann-Jordan, Reichsrat von Buhl, Bürklin-Wolf, Deinhard, Dr. Kern*

GROSSLAGE HÖLLENPFAD
(Grünstadt)

Fine wines full of aroma and body.

GRÜNSTADT

☆ Vineyard *Goldberg*
☆ Growers *Helmut Busch, Winzerkeller Leiningerland e.G.*

GROSSKARLBACH

☆ Vineyard *Burgweg*
☆ Grower *Karl Lingenfelder*

GROSSLAGE HONIGSÄCKEL
(Ungstein)

Some full-bodied, fine wines with intense flavour are made here.

UNGSTEIN

☆ Vineyard *Herrenberg*
☆ Growers *Karl Fuhrmann-Weingut Pfeffingen, Bassermann-Jordan, K. Fitz-Ritter, Winzergenossenschaft Herrenberg-Honigsäckel*

GROSSLAGE KOBNERT
(Kallstadt)

Kobnert was a single vineyard prior to the 1971 Wine Law; now it is a Grosslage, but a very good one, particularly in the hands of somebody such as the talented Koehler-Ruprecht.

KALLSTADT

☆ Vineyard *Steinacker*
☆ Growers *Alfred Bonnet, Gg. Henninger IV, Koehler-Ruprecht, Weingut Benderhof*

☆ Vineyard *Saumagen*
☆ Grower *Koehler-Ruprecht*

WEISENHEIM

☆ Vineyard *Mandelgarten*
☆ Grower *Pfleger-Karr*

GROSSLAGE MARIENGARTEN
(Forst an der Weinstrasse)

Nowhere in the entire Rheinpfalz can Riesling wines of such incomparable finesse and intensity be found. Virtually all the great Rheinpfalz producers are here.

FORST AN DER WEINSTRASSE

☆ Vineyard *Jesuitengarten*
☆ Growers *Bassermann-Jordan, Reichsrat von Buhl, Bürklin-Wolf, Weingut Hahnhof, Willhelm Spindler, Winzerverein Forst, Heinrich Spindler, J. L. Wolf Erben, Lindenhof Eugen Spindler, Geschw. Wallbillich*

☆ Vineyard *Kirchenstück*
☆ Growers *Bassermann-Jordan, Reichsrat von Buhl, Bürklin-Wolf, Deinhard, Wilhelm Spindler, Winzerverein Forst, Dr. Herberger, Ferdinand Heinemann*

☆ Vineyard *Ungeheuer*
☆ Growers *Bassermann-Jordan, Reichsrat von Buhl, Georg Mosbacher, Bürklin-Wolf, Georg Sieben Erben, Deinhard, J. L. Wolf Erben, Dr. Kern, Mossbacherhof, Lindenhof Eugen Spindler*

☆ Vineyard *Pechstein*
☆ Growers *Bassermann-Jordan, Reichsrat von Buhl, Bürklin-Wolf, J. L. Wolf Erben, Lindenhof Eugen Spindler, Acham-Magin*

DEIDESHEIM

☆ Vineyard *Hohenmorgen*
☆ Growers *Bassermann-Jordan, Bürklin-Wolf*

☆ Vineyard *Leinhöhle*
☆ Growers *Bassermann-Jordan, Reichsrat von Buhl, Josef Biffar, Deinhard, J. L. Wolf Erben, Dr. Kern, Lindenhof Eugen Spindler*

☆ Vineyard *Grainhübel*
☆ Growers *Bassermann-Jordan, Reichsrat von Buhl, Jul. Ferdinand Kimich, Winzergenossenschaft Deidesheim 1913, Winzerverein Deidesheim 1898, Josef Biffar, Weingut Hahnhof, Deinhard, Wilhelm Spindler, Dr. Kern, Lindenhof Eugen Spindler, Herbert Giessen Erben*

☆ Vineyard *Herrgottsacker*
☆ Growers *Bassermann-Jordan, Bürklin-Wolf, Josef Biffar, Deinhard, J. L. Wolf Erben, Dr. Kern, Mossbacherhof, Lindenhof Eugen Spindler, Acham-Magin*

WACHENHEIM

☆ Vineyard *Gerümpel*
☆ Growers *Bürklin-Wolf, J. L. Wolf Erben, Weingut Probsthof, Karl Schaefer/Dr. Fleischmann*

☆ Vineyard *Goldbächel*
☆ Growers *Reichsrat von Buhl, Bürklin-Wolf, Wilhelm Spindler*

☆ Vineyard *Fuchsmantel*
☆ Grower *Bürklin-Wolf, Karl Schaefer/Dr. Fleischmann*

GROSSLAGE MEERSPINNE
(Neustadt-Gimmeldingen)

Climatically-pampered vineyards on the slopes of, and sheltered by, the Haardt mountains. They produce fine wines, most of which are Riesling.

NEUSTADT-GIMMELDINGEN

☆ Vineyard *Kapellenberg*
☆ Grower *Christmann*

KÖNIGSBACH

☆ Vineyard *Idig*
☆ Growers *Winzerverein Königsbach, Reichsrat von Buhl*

MUSSBACH

☆ Vineyard *Eselshaut*
☆ Grower *Müller-Catoir*

GROSSLAGE PFAFFENGRUND
(Neustadt-Diedesfeld)

Not an exceptional Grosslage, although some Einzellagen can produce very good wines.

DUTTWEILER

☆ Vineyard *Mandelberg*
☆ Growers *Wolfgang Geissler, F. & G. Bergdolt*

GROSSLAGE REBSTÖCKEL
(Neustadt-Diedesfeld)

No outstanding villages, vineyards or growers although good wines are made in the village of Neustadt-Diedesfeld.

GROSSLAGE ROSENBÜHL
(Freinsheim)

Light, attractive, easy-drinking wines that rarely rise into the fine-wine bracket. Reasonable red wines, made from the Portugieser grape, are also produced.

FREINSHEIM

☆ Vineyard *Goldberg*
☆ Grower *Karl Lingenfelder*

GROSSLAGE SCHENKENBÖHL
(Wachenheim)

The third Grosslage to share the vineyards of Bad Dürkheim, this one ranks with Feuerberg – Hochmess being by far the best.

BAD DÜRKHEIM

☆ Vineyard *Fuchsmantel*
☆ Growers *Johannes Karst & Söhne, K. Fitz-Ritter, Winzergenossenschaft Vier Jahreszeiten-Kloster Limburg*

☆ Vineyard *Abtsfronhof*
☆ Grower *K. Fitz-Ritter*

GROSSLAGE SCHNEPFENFLUG AN DER WEINSTRASSE
(Forst an der Weinstrasse)

No outstanding villages, vineyards or growers.

GROSSLAGE SCHNEPFENFLUG VOM ZELLERTAL
(Zell)

No outstanding villages, vineyards or growers, although good wines are made in the village of Zell.

GROSSLAGE SCHWARZERDE
(Kirchheim)

Mediocre Silvaner-based wines are the norm here, but there are a couple of good growers in obscure villages that offer good value.

LAUMERSHEIM

☆ Vineyard *Mandelberg*
☆ Grower *Knipser Johannishof*

DIRMSTEIN

☆ Vineyard *Jesuitenhofgarten*
☆ Grower *Schlossgut Gebr. Janson*

BEREICH SÜDLICHE WEINSTRASSE

The lesser of the two Rheinpfalz Bereiche, Südliche Weinstrasse's wines are dominated by rather dull and neutral Müller-Thurgau, but the younger winemakers are producing better Riesling and cooperative varietals from various grapes that are at worst clean and correct.

GROSSLAGE BISCHOFSKREUZ
(Walsheim)

Most wines are sound, if unexciting, though the two Einzellagen below are capable of producing exceptional wines in capable hands.

WALSHEIM

☆ Vineyard *Silberberg*
☆ Grower *Heinz Pfaffmann*

NUSSDORF

☆ Vineyard *Herrenberg*
☆ Grower *Emil Bauer*

GROSSLAGE GUTTENBERG
(Schweigen)

Jülg and Becker produce excellent, expressive, if rarely encountered, Riesling.

SCHWEIGEN-RECHTENBACH

☆ Vineyard *Sonnenberg*
☆ Growers *Oskar Jülg, Fritz Becker*

GROSSLAGE HERRLICH
(Eschbach)

An area easily capable of producing *QmP* wines. The *Auslese* are nothing special, but get exported and can be astonishingly cheap.

LEINSWEILER

☆ Vineyard *Sonnenberg*
☆ Grower *Thomas Siegrist*

GROSSLAGE KLOSTER LIEBFRAUENBERG
(Bad Bergzabern)

No outstanding villages, vineyards or growers, although good wines are made in the town of Bad Bergzabern.

GROSSLAGE KÖNIGSGARTEN
(Godramstein)

Birkweiler is an obscure wine village, but it possesses several talented winemakers.

BIRKWEILER

☆ Vineyard *Kastanienbusch*
☆ Growers *Karl Wehrheim, Fritz Siener, Dr. Heinz Wehrheim/Hohenberg, Oekonomierat Rebholz*

GROSSLAGE MANDELHÖHE
(Maikammer)

The best estates in this Grosslage produce some pleasant, attractive Rieslings.

MAIKAMMER

☆ Vineyard *Kirchenstück*
☆ Growers *Dieter Ziegler, Ludwig Schneider GmbH*

☆ Vineyard *Immengarten*
☆ Growers *Rassiga-Weegmüller, Ferdinand Gies, Robert Isler Erben, Ludwig Schneider GmbH*

GROSSLAGE ORDENSGUT
(Edesheim)

Only Dr. Bossung appears to excel in this Grosslage.

EDESHEIM

☆ Vineyard *Schloss*
☆ Grower *Dr. Bossung*

GROSSLAGE SCHLOSS LUDWIGSHÖHE
(Edenkoben)

No outstanding villages, vineyards or growers, although good wines are made in the village of St. Martin.

GROSSLAGE TRAPPENBERG
(Hochstadt)

No outstanding villages, vineyards or growers, although good wines are made in the village of Hochstadt.

The Hessische Bergstrasse

At the northern tip of Baden's vineyards is the Hessische Bergstrasse, smallest and least-known of Germany's wine regions. Its wines are fruity and have a pronounced earthy acidity.

THE VINEYARDS OF THE HESSISCHE BERGSTRASSE are planted with a relatively high proportion of Riesling, particularly in the Bereich Starkenburg where the best wines are grown. The vineyards are farmed by more than 1,000 individual growers with the average-sized plot being barely more than one-third of a hectare. Most of these growers are part-timers who tend their plots at weekends.

The vines, which grow on relatively rich soils, produce very fruity wines that have a typical and easily-recognized, earthy acidity, with a style that is richer than most Rheinhessen wines and reminiscent of a somewhat rustic Rheingau. The Müller-Thurgau is not Germany's best, but it can be fragrant; the Silvaner lacks the assertive character found in Franken to the east; but the Gewürztraminer can have a fine, subdued style.

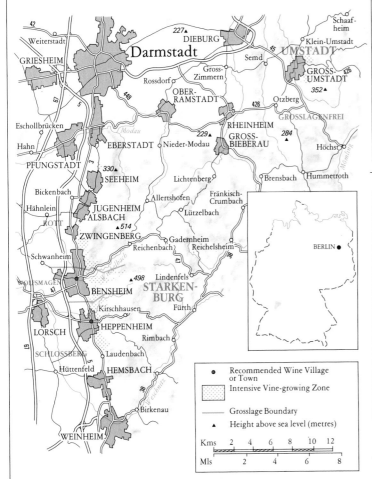

THE REGION AT A GLANCE

Area under vine: 360 ha (890 acres)

Average yield: 77 hl/ha (346 cases/acre)

Red wine: 2%

White wine: 98%

Infrastructure: Bereiche 2; Grosslagen 3; Einzellagen 22

Note: The vineyards of the Hessische Bergstrasse straddle 10 Gemeinden (communes), the names of which may appear on the label.

QUALITY REQUIREMENTS AND HARVEST PERCENTAGES

Minimum Oechsle	Quality Category	Harvest breakdown 1984	1985	1986	1987
44°	Deutscher Tafelwein	15%	—	2%	3%
53°	Landwein				
57–66°	*QbA	83%	30%	71%	86%
73–80°	*Kabinett	2%	55%	25%	11%
85–95°	*Spätlese	—	15%	2%	—
95–105°	*Auslese				
125°	Beerenauslese				
125°	Eiswein				
150°	Trockenbeerenauslese				

* Minimum Oechsle levels vary according to grape variety, with those that have a naturally lower sugar content allowed to qualify at a correspondingly lower level.

FACTORS AFFECTING TASTE AND QUALITY

Location
Between Darmstadt and Heppenheim, beside the Odenwald mountains, with the Rhine to the west and the Main to the north.

Climate
The vineyards on the southern slopes of the valleys flanking the Bergstrasse benefit from an average temperature of over 9°C (48°F). Combined with an annual rainfall of 75.5 centimetres (30 ins), this produces ideal conditions.

Aspect
The best vineyards are on south- and west-facing slopes in Bereich Umstadt, and south- and east-facing slopes in Bereich Starkenburg.

Soil
Most of the soil consists of varying amounts of light, finely-structured loess and basalt.

Viticulture and vinification
The vineyards in this region are not of the modern *Flurbereinigung* type, but are planted rather haphazardly on old-established terraces among orchards. Although a great many individuals grow grapes, more than 80 per cent of the wines are processed in cooperatives.

Primary grape varieties
Müller-Thurgau, Riesling

Secondary grape varieties
Ehrenfelser, Kerner, Ruländer, Scheurebe, Silvaner, Gewürztraminer

THE HESSISCHE BERGSTRASSE

Called "the spring garden of Germany", its vineyards lie between orchards.

Map legend

- Recommended Wine Village or Town
- Intensive Vine-growing Zone
- Grosslage Boundary
- ▲ Height above sea level (metres)

Kms 2 4 6 8 10 12
Mls 2 4 6 8

The wines of the Hessische Bergstrasse

BEREICH STARKENBURG

The larger of this region's Bereiche, and the best in quality terms. Riesling is planted in most vineyards.

GROSSLAGE ROTT

The largest of Starkenburg's three Grosslagen, it includes the northern section of Bensheim, one of the region's two best communes. The finest wine comes from its south-facing Herrnwingert vineyard.

BENSHEIM (-SCHÖNBERG)

☆ **Vineyard** *Herrnwingert*
☆ **Growers** *Staatsweingüter, Bergsträsser Gebiets-Winzergenossenschaft*

GROSSLAGE SCHLOSSBERG

This covers three villages south of Bensheim, including Heppenheim, which rivals Bensheim itself, especially on its steep, southwest-facing Centgericht vineyard, where the wines attain a unique peachiness.

HEPPENHEIM

☆ **Vineyard** *Centgericht*
☆ **Growers** *Staatsweingüter, Bergsträsser Gebiets-Winzergenossenschaft*

GROSSLAGE WOLFSMAGEN

This includes the southern section of Bensheim with the two Ortsteile of Zell and Gronau. The south-facing slope of Streichling is both the largest and best of its Einzellagen.

BENSHEIM

☆ **Vineyard** *Streichling*
☆ **Growers** *Staatsweingüter, Weingut der Stadt Bensheim, Bergsträsser Gebiets-Winzergenossenschaft*

BEREICH UMSTADT

No outstanding villages or vineyards and no Grosslagen, as its six Einzellagen are *Grosslagenfrei*. Müller-Thurgau, Ruländer and Silvaner dominate.

Franken

Classic Franconian Silvaner is distinctly dry with an earthy or smoky aroma and is bottled in the traditional flask-shaped Bocksbeutel. Unfortunately, Silvaner is gradually giving way to Müller-Thurgau and other grape varieties.

THERE IS ALMOST TWICE AS MUCH LAND under vine in Franken than there is in the Rheingau, but the vineyards are scattered over a far greater area and interspersed with meadows and forests. Franken is also a beer-producing region and many say that more pleasure can be had from a *stein* of Würzburger beer than from a glass of Würzburger *Stein*, Franken's most famous wine. Exported wine is invariably from the better estates and relatively expensive, particularly if bottled in the traditional *Bocksbeutel*.

I like this region's Silvaner: its full, sappy taste and distinctive earthy bite make it far more interesting than most other examples of this variety, and exceptional wines attain a degree of smoky complexity. However, my favourite Franconian wine is Riesling because, although it accounts for less than three per cent of the vines grown and often fails to ripen in this region, it is made by some of the best estates into exceptionally racy wines in sunny years. Rieslaner (a *Riesling x Silvaner* cross), Bacchus and Kerner are all successful, particularly as a *QmP*, although it is rare to find a wine above *Auslese* level.

THE REGION AT A GLANCE

Area under vine: 4,700 ha (11,614 acres)

Average yield: 79 hl/ha (355 cases/acre)

Red wine: 23%

White wine: 77%

Infrastructure: Bereiche 3; Grosslagen 17; Einzellagen 171

Note: The vineyards of Franken straddle 125 Gemeinden (communes), the names of which may appear on labels.

FACTORS AFFECTING TASTE AND QUALITY

Location
Situated in Bavaria, Franken is the most north-easterly of Germany's wine regions.

Climate
The most continental climate of Germany's wine regions, with dry warm summers and cold winters. Severe frosts affect yields.

Aspect
Many vineyards face south and are located on the slopes of the valleys of the Main and its tributaries, as well as on sheltered sites of the Steigerwald.

Soil
The three Bereiche have different soil structures: Mainviereck has predominantly weathered coloured sandstone; Maindreieck limestone with clay and loess; and Steigerwald, weathered red marl.

Viticulture and vinification
More than half the vineyards have been replanted since 1954. The classic Franconian vine, the Silvaner, has become less widely planted than the Müller-Thurgau. The region's wines are usually vinified drier than most in Germany and accompany food well. There are 6,000 growers, allowing for a great range of styles, although half the wines are processed by cooperatives.

Primary grape varieties
Müller-Thurgau, Silvaner

Secondary grape varieties
Bacchus, Kerner, Ortega, Perle, Riesling, Scheurebe, Traminer

QUALITY REQUIREMENTS AND HARVEST PERCENTAGES

Minimum Oechsle	Quality Category	Harvest breakdown			
		1984	1985	1986	1987
44°	Deutscher Tafelwein	13%	—	5%	—
50°	Landwein				
60°	QbA	85%	27%	70%	94%
76–80°	*Kabinett	2%	59%	20%	5%
85–90°	*Spätlese	—	11%	5%	1%
100°	Auslese		3%		
125°	Beerenauslese				
125°	Eiswein				
150°	Trockenbeerenauslese				

*Minimum Oechsle levels vary according to grape variety, with those that have a naturally lower sugar content allowed to qualify at a correspondingly lower level.

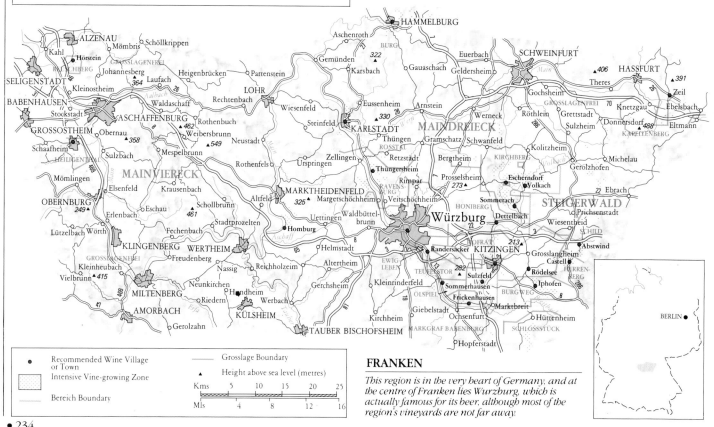

Legend

- ● Recommended Wine Village or Town
- ▨ Intensive Vine-growing Zone
- ─ Bereich Boundary
- ─ Grosslage Boundary
- ▲ Height above sea level (metres)

Kms 5 10 15 20 25
Mls 4 8 12 16

FRANKEN

This region is in the very heart of Germany, and at the centre of Franken lies Würzburg, which is actually famous for its beer, although most of the region's vineyards are not far away.

The wines of Franken

Note: In Franken, certain Grosslagen can only be prefixed by a specified village, the name of which appears in brackets after the Grosslage appellation.

BEREICH STEIGERWALD

Nowhere is the earthy character of Franconian wine more evident than in this Bereich where the heavier soil tends to result in fuller-bodied wines.

GROSSLAGE BURGWEG

This Grosslage (which shares its name with a Grosslage in the Nahe and another in the Rheingau) contains one of Franken's greatest wine villages, Iphofen, which has steep, southwest-facing vineyards.

IPHOFEN

☆ Vineyard *Julius-Echter Berg*
☆ Growers *Würzberger Juliusspital, Hans Wirsching, Ernst Popp KG*

☆ Vineyard *Kronsberg*
☆ Growers *Hans Wirsching, Johann Ruck, Ernst Popp KG*

GROSSLAGE HERRENBERG

There are south-facing vineyards in this Grosslage, but it is the northwest-facing vineyards of Castell that produce the most exceptional wines.

CASTELL

☆ Vineyards *Schlossberg, Kugel-spiel, Hohnart, Kirchberg*
☆ Grower *Fürstlich Castell'sches Domänenamt*

GROSSLAGE KAPELLENBERG

No outstanding villages, vineyards, or growers, although good wines are made in the village of Zeil.

GROSSLAGE SCHILD

No outstanding villages, vineyards, or growers, although good wines are made in the village of Abtswind.

GROSSLAGE SCHLOSSBERG

Underrated Grosslage with excel-lent, sheltered vineyards in Rödelsee.

RÖDELSEE

☆ Vineyard *Küchenmeister*
☆ Growers *Juliusspital, Hans Wirsching, Ernst Popp KG*

☆ Vineyard *Schwanleite*
☆ Grower *Ernst Popp KG*

GROSSLAGE SCHLOSSSTÜCK

No outstanding villages, vineyards, or growers, although good wines are made in the village of Ippesheim.

BEREICH MAINDREIECK

Most of the vineyards in this Bereiche are in the vicinity of Würzburg. Grapes grown on the limestone soils can produce wines of exceptional finesse and clarity of character.

GROSSLAGE BURG
(Hammelburg)

Robust, earthy Silvaners and the lighter, fragrant Müller-Thurgaus are the main attractions of this Grosslage.

HAMMELBURG

☆ Vineyard *Trautlestal*
☆ Growers *Städt. Weingut Schloss Saaleck, Winzergenossenschaft Hammelburg*

SAALECK

☆ Vineyard *Schlossberg*
☆ Grower *Städt. Weingut Schloss Saaleck*

GROSSLAGE EWIG LEBEN

This Grosslage contains the greatest concentration of fine vineyards in Franken. A particularly favourable microclimate helps create wines of a rare harmony. Rieslings from this area possess an original natural charm complemented by a bouquet often reminiscent of peaches.

RANDERSACKER

☆ Vineyard *Sonnenstuhl*
☆ Growers *Staatsweingut Würzburg, Armin Störrlein, Robert Schmitt*

☆ Vineyard *Pfülben*
☆ Growers *Staatsweingut Würzburg, Würzburger Juliusspital, Bürgerspital zum Heiligen Geist, Paul Schmitt, Martin Göbel*

☆ Vineyard *Teufelskeller*
☆ Growers *Staatsweingut Würzburg, Würzburger Juliusspital, Bürgerspital zum Heiligen Geist, St. Kilianskellerei*

GROSSLAGE HOFRAT
(Kintzingen)

One of Franken's few relatively large Grosslagen, where the Einzellagen seldom excel, except for the vine-yards on the lazy bend of the River Main north and south of Sulzfeld.

SULZFELD

☆ Vineyard *Maustal*
☆ Grower *Weingut Zehnthof Theo Luckert*

☆ Vineyard *Cyriakusberg*
☆ Grower *Weingut Zehnthof Theo Luckert*

GROSSLAGE HONIGBERG

No outstanding villages, vineyards, or growers, although good wines are made in the village of Dettelbach.

GROSSLAGE KIRCHBERG
(Volkach)

This Grosslage contains some of Franken's finest vineyards. The recommended growers create delicious fruity or spicy Rieslings.

NORDHEIM

☆ Vineyard *Vögelein*
☆ Growers *Richard und Helmut Christ, Winzergenossenschaft Nordheim*

ESCHERNDORF

☆ Vineyard *Lump*
☆ Growers *Winzergenossenschaft Nordheim, Juliusspital*

SOMMERACH

☆ Vineyard *Katzenkopf*
☆ Grower *Winzergenossenschaft Sommerach*

GROSSLAGE MARKGRAF BABENBERG

No outstanding villages, vineyards, or growers, although good wines are made in the village of Frickenhausen.

GROSSLAGE OELSPIEL

The main feature of this Grosslage is an excellent, southwest-facing strip of vineyards on the right bank of the Main, southeast of Würzburg.

SOMMERHAUSEN

☆ Vineyard *Steinbach*
☆ Grower *Ernst Gebhardt*

GROSSLAGE RAVENSBURG
(Thüngersheim)

Rather downstream from Franken's best vineyards, but excellent wines come from steep west-, southwest- and south-facing vineyards in Retzbach and Thüngersheim.

RETZBACH

☆ Vineyard *Benediktusberg*
☆ Grower *Winzergenossenschaft Thüngersheim*

THÜNGERSHEIM

☆ Vineyard *Johannisberg*
☆ Growers *Winzergenossenschaft Thüngersheim, Juliusspital*

☆ Vineyard *Scharlachberg*
☆ Growers *Winzergenossenschaft Thüngersheim, Staatl. Hofkeller*

GROSSLAGE ROSSTAL
(Karlstadt)

No outstanding villages, vineyards, or growers, although good wines are made around the town of Karlstadt.

GROSSLAGE TEUFELSTOR

A continuation of Ewig Leben, but the wines are not as good.

EIBELSTADT

☆ Vineyard *Kapellenberg*
☆ Grower *Ernst Gebhardt*

RANDERSACKER

☆ Vineyard *Dabug*
☆ Grower *Winzergenossenschaft Randersacker*

GROSSLAGENFREI

Many of the vineyards in Bereich Maindreieck are *Grosslagenfrei* (composed of individual Einzellagen that are not grouped under any Grosslagen) and some are exceptional, such as Würzburger Stein whose superb steep, south-facing site is supposed to be the best in the region and as such has given its name to any Franconian wine in the form of Steinwein. Powerful, noble Rieslings and flinty, earthy Silvaners are produced in the Stein vineyard.

WÜRZBURG

☆ Vineyard *Stein*
☆ Growers *Staatl. Hofkeller, Juliusspital, Bürgerspital zum Heiligen Geist*

☆ Vineyard *Innere Leiste*
☆ Growers *Staatl. Hofkeller, Julius-pital, Bürgerspital zum Heiligen Geist*

HOMBURG

☆ Vineyard *Kallmuth*
☆ Grower *Fürstl. Löwenstein-Wertheim-Rosenbergsches Weingut*

BEREICH MAINVIERECK

The smallest and most westerly of the Bereiche, it produces modest wines.

GROSSLAGE HEILIGENTHAL

No outstanding villages, vineyards, or growers.

GROSSLAGE REUSCHBERG

One village with just two Einzellagen.

HÖRSTEIN

☆ Vineyard *Abtsberg*
☆ Grower *Staatsweingüter*

GROSSLAGENFREI

Most of Mainviereck's vineyards are in *Grosslagenfrei* (individual Einzellagen not grouped under any Grosslagen). There are no out-standing villages, vineyards, or growers, although good red wines are made in the villages of Klingenberg and Miltenberg.

Württemberg

Württemberg is not well known as a wine region, principally because the light red wine and rosé *Schillerwein* produced from the extensive plantings of black grapes are not styles that are much in demand outside the region itself.

WÜRTTEMBERG IS GERMANY'S RED-WINE REGION, with black grape varieties growing in 51 per cent of its vineyards. Almost half are planted with Trollinger, a grape that produces a light, fresh and grapey wine that few people outside of Germany would regard as a true red wine. The most concentrated Trollinger wines are made between Heilbronn and Winnenden, just northeast of Stuttgart, but they do not compare with Baden reds. The red Lemberger is enjoyed locally, but it has an unimpressive, neutral flavour. The rosé

WÜRTTEMBERG

Most of the region's vineyards, in fertile districts near the river Neckar, are interspersed with farmland.

THE REGION AT A GLANCE

Area under vine: 9,600 ha (23,722 acres)

Average yield: 99 hl/ha (445 cases/acre)

Red wine: 51%

White wine: 49%

Infrastructure: Bereiche 6, Grosslagen 17, Einzellagen 206

Note: The vineyards of Württemberg straddle 230 Gemeinden (communes), the names of which may appear on the label.

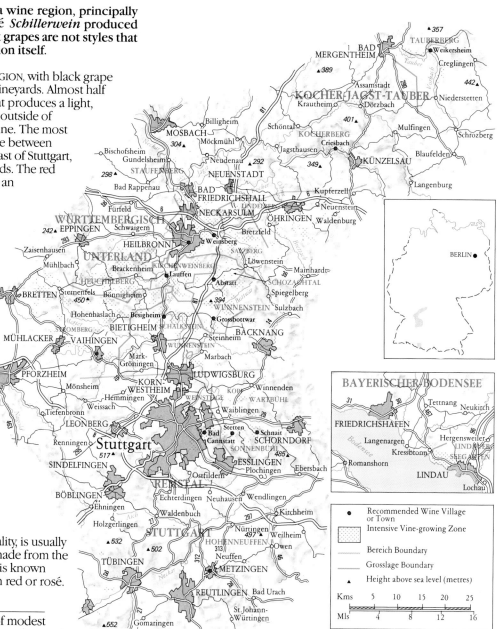

Schillerwein, which is a regional speciality, is usually more characterful than the red wines made from the Pinot meunier, or Schwarzriesling as it is known locally, which makes a better white than red or rosé.

WHITE WINES

White Württemberg wines are usually of modest quality, although there are exceptions, such as robust, intensely flavoured Riesling, with pronounced acidity. The region's other white grape varieties make wines of a very ordinary quality, unless harvested at one of the higher *QmP* categories.

QUALITY REQUIREMENTS AND HARVEST PERCENTAGES

Minimum Oechsle	Quality Category	Harvest breakdown			
		1984	1985	1986	1987
40°	Deutscher Tafelwein				
50°	Landwein	8%	—	4%	1%
57–63°	*QbA	90%	63%	92%	93%
72–78°	*Kabinett	2%	25%	3%	6%
85–88°	*Spätlese	—	11%	1%	—
95°	Auslese				
124°	Beerenauslese				
124°	Eiswein	—	1%	—	—
150°	Trockenbeerenauslese				

* Minimum Oechsle levels vary according to grape variety, with those that have a naturally lower sugar content allowed to qualify at a correspondingly lower level.

FACTORS AFFECTING TASTE AND QUALITY

Location
Situated on the eastern edge of Germany's wine-growing land, between Frankfurt to the north and Lake Constance to the south.

Climate
Sheltered by the Black Forest to the west and the hilly Swabian Alb to the east, this area has a specially warm growing season.

Aspect
The vineyards are fairly widely scattered either side of the River Neckar, on the gentle slopes of various river valleys.

Soil
Soils vary widely, but red marl, clay, loess and loam dominate, with scatterings of shell-limestone in the main Neckar Valley area and at the confluences of its tributaries. The topsoils are deep and well drained, producing full wines – in a German sense – with a firm acidity.

Viticulture and vinification
There are 16,500 growers; most have tiny plots and tend them part-time, taking their grapes to the cooperatives that process and market the wines. Although more than half of the area is planted with black grapes 70 per cent of the wine is white (i.e. many black grapes are vinified white).

Primary grape varieties
Müllerrebe, Müller-Thurgau, Riesling, Trollinger

Secondary grape varieties
Kerner, Lemberger, Pinot meunier, Portugieser, Ruländer, Silvaner, Spätburgunder

The wines of Württemberg

BEREICH REMSTAL-STUTTGART

The second largest Bereich, covering some 1,600 hectares (3,954 acres).

GROSSLAGE HOHENNEUFFEN

No outstanding villages, vineyards, or growers, although good wines are made in the village of Metzingen.

GROSSLAGE KOPF

No outstanding villages, vineyards, or growers, although good wines are made in the village of Grossheppach.

GROSSLAGE SONNENBÜHL

No outstanding villages, vineyards, or growers.

GROSSLAGE WARTBÜHL

Squeezed between the two quite unremarkable Grosslagen of Kopf and Sonnenbühl, these wines are superior. With very little to choose between the aspect, soil and microclimate the only factor that distinguishes Wartbühl is its selection of grape varieties, all white and with a high percentage of Riesling.

STETTEN

☆ Vineyard *Brotwasser*
☆ Grower *Wurttemburgische Hofkammer*

☆ Vineyard *Lindhälder*
☆ Grower *Karl Haidle*

REMSHALDEN-GRUNBACH

☆ Vineyard *Klingle*
☆ Grower *Jürgen Ellwanger*

GROSSLAGE WEINSTEIGE

No outstanding vineyards or growers, although wines made in the Ortsteil of Bad Cannstadt on the terraces of the Einzellage Zuckerle produce Riesling, Trollinger and Spätburgunder that regularly win medals.

BEREICH WÜRTTEMBERGISCH UNTERLAND

This Bereich encompasses more than 70 per cent of Württemberg's vineyards throughout its nine Grosslagen near the town of Heilbronn.

GROSSLAGE HEUCHELBERG

From the rich limestone soil of this area west of Heilbronn come some of Württemberg's finest Rieslings.

NEIPPBERG

☆ Vineyard *Schlossberg*
☆ Grower *Weingut Graf von Neippberg*

STOCKHEIM

☆ Vineyard *Altenberg*
☆ Grower *Weingärtnergenossenschaft Dürrenzimmern-Stockheim*

MELMSHEIM

☆ Vineyard *Katzenöhrbrle*
☆ Grower *Ernst Dautel*

CLEEBRONN

☆ Vineyard *Michaelsberg*
☆ Grower *Weingärtnergenossenschaft Cleebronn-Güglingen-Frauenzimmern*

GÜGLINGEN

☆ Vineyard *Michaelsberg*
☆ Grower *Weingärtnergenossenschaft Cleebronn-Güglingen-Frauernzimmern*

GÜGLINGEN

☆ Vineyard *Michaelsberg*
☆ Grower *Weingärtnergenossenschaft Cleebronn-Güglingen-Frauenzimmern*

GROSSLAGE KIRCHENWEINBERG

Mostly black grapes grow in this Grosslage, where the Pinot meunier (Schwarzriesling) dominates. Kirchenweinberg includes the Einzellage of Katzenbeisser at Lauffen, which at 456 hectares (1,267 acres) is not only larger than Bereiche such as Kocher-Jagst-Tauber, but bigger than the Hessische Bergstrasse or the Ahr.

FLEIN

☆ Vineyard *Eselsberg*
☆ Growers *Weingut Wolf, Weingärtner-genossenschaft Flein-Talheim*

LAUFFEN

☆ Vineyard *Katzenbeisser*
☆ Grower *Weingärtnergenossenschaft Lauffen*

GROSSLAGE LINDELBERG

A small, scattered area east of Heilbronn. *Barrique*-matured Lemburger red is making a name for itself, but fine, elegant Rieslings are still the mainstay of this mini Grosslage.

VERRENBERG

☆ Vineyard *Verrenberg*
☆ Grower *Fürst zu Hohenlohe-Oehringen'sche Schlosskellerei*

GROSSLAGE SALZBERG

This area, sandwiched between Heilbronn and the Grosslage of Lindelberg, produces fine Rieslings on the steepest section of the south-southeast-facing slope of Eberstadt's Eberfürst vineyard.

EBERSTADT

☆ Vineyard *Eberfürst*
☆ Grower *Weingärtnergenossenschaft Eberstadt*

GROSSLAGE SCHALKSTEIN

The south-facing *Käsberg* vineyard is the finest in an area that specializes in red wines of a darker and fuller style than is normal in this region.

MUNDELSHEIM

☆ Vineyard *Käsberg*
☆ Grower *Württembergische Hofkammer*

GROSSLAGE SCHOZACHTAL

Mostly white wines, with fine Riesling from the village of Abstatt. Some encouraging experiments have been made with wood-matured Lemberger and Spätburgunder.

ABSTATT

☆ Vineyard *Burg Wildeck*
☆ Grower *Staatliche Weinbau Lehr-und Versuchsanstalt Weinsberg*

GROSSLAGE STAUFENBERG

This covers the town of Heilbronn, its Ortsteile and several outlying villages. Not only are there excellent Einzellagen, but some fine wines are sold under the Grosslage appellation.

HEILBRONN

☆ Vineyard *Stiftsberg*
☆ Grower *Drautz-Able*

GUNDELSHEIM

☆ Vineyard *Himmelreich*
☆ Grower *Staatliche Weinbau Lehr-und Versuchsanstalt Weinsberg*

WEINSBERG

☆ Vineyard *Schemelsberg*
☆ Grower *Staatliche Weinbau Lehr-und Versuchsanstalt Weinsberg*

GROSSLAGE STROMBERG

A predominantly black-grape area, with Lemberger as the most common.

MAULBRONN

☆ Vineyard *Eilfinger Berg*
☆ Grower *Württembergische Hofkammer Kellerei*

GROSSLAGE WUNNENSTEIN

Excellent wines are produced by Schloss Shaubeck in the very south of this area. Graf Adelmann's superb Brüssele Riesling should also be tasted.

KLEINBOTTWAR

☆ Vineyard *Süssmund*
☆ Growers *Graf Adelmann, Schloss Schaubeck*

BEREICH KOCHER-JAGST-TAUBER

Although this small Bereich specializes in white wines, they rarely excel.

GROSSLAGE KOCHERBERG

No outstanding villages, vineyards, or growers, although good wines are made in the village of Criesbach.

GROSSLAGE TAUBERBERG

This encompasses the River Tauber, which flows through the vineyards of Baden just northwest of Bad Mergentheim. Excellent results have been achieved with Rieslings, Traminers and Muscats.

WEIKERSHEIM

☆ Vineyard *Schmecker*
☆ Grower *Weingüter Fürst Hohenlohe-Langenburg*

BEREICH OBERER NECKAR

A tiny Bereich in the south of the main viticultural area, with no outstanding villages, vineyards, or growers.

BEREICH WÜRTTEMBERGISCH BODENSEE

There are no outstanding vineyards or growers in this one-Einzellage Bereich on Lake Constance (Bodensee).

BEREICH BAYERISCHER BODENSEE

This contains one Grosslage consisting of four Einzellagen. Climatic conditions are not favourable enough for the growth of Riesling, the small production consisting mainly of Müller-Thurgau whites, robust Spätburgunder reds and Spätburgunder *Weissherbst*.

GROSSLAGE LINDAUER SEEGARTEN

No outstanding villages, vineyards, or growers.

Baden

Sunny Baden is widely described as Germany's most southerly wine region, but it is not so much one region as a political hotchpotch of several diverse districts that once produced wine in the now defunct grand duchy of Baden. The great variation of geographical, geological and climatical conditions across these diverse districts produces a wide range of wines, from mild Silvaner, through light, spicy Gutedel, to the full-bodied Ruländer, not forgetting the attractive pink-coloured *Weissherbst* (a speciality of the region), and a good deal of red wine – Baden being the second-largest red-wine-producing region in Germany.

BADEN IS CURRENTLY CONSIDERED one of Germany's newest wine regions, yet it was actually its largest up until 1800, when it possessed more than 27,000 hectares (66,700 acres) of vines, almost twice the amount grown today. Ironically, it was when Germany acquired a wealthy and viticulturally prolific Alsace in 1871, as one of spoils of the Franco-Prussian War, that Baden's vineyards began to decline. The downward trend continued, despite the formation of the Baden Wine Growers' Association by Heinrich Hansjakob, a winegrowing priest, at Hagnau in 1881. Even after the return of Alsace to French Sovereignty in 1918, Baden's wine production continued to decline, primarily through lack of investment, and in the 1920s production was adversely affected by inheritance laws that split Baden's vineyards into even smaller units. By 1950, with barely 6,000 hectares (14,800 acres) of vines, Baden's wine industry was at its lowest ebb.

THE REGION AT A GLANCE

Area under vine: 14,900 ha (36,800 acres)

Average yield: 84 hl/ha (377 cases/acre)

Red wine: 23%

White wine: 77%.

Infrastructure: Bereiche 7; Grosslagen 16; Einzellagen 306

Note: The vineyards of Baden straddle 315 Gemeinden (communes), the names of which may appear on the label.

QUALITY REQUIREMENTS AND HARVEST PERCENTAGES

Minimum Oechsle	Quality Category	Harvest breakdown			
		1984	1985	1986	1987
50–55°	Deutscher Tafelwein	10%	—	6%	1%
55°	Landwein				
60–72°	*QbA	85%	61%	90%	73%
76–85°	*Kabinett	4%	29%	3%	25%
86–92°	*Spätlese	1%	9%	1%	1%
100–105°	*Auslese		1%	—	—
128°	Beerenauslese				
128°	Eiswein				
154°	Trockenbeerenauslese				

* Minimum Oechsle levels vary according to grape variety, with those that have a naturally lower sugar content allowed to qualify at a correspondingly lower level.

BADEN

This huge wine-producing region's vineyards are mostly spread along a strip extending beside the western boundary of the Black Forest, between it and the border with France. Inset is the northerly area of the Bereich *of Badisches Frankenland.*

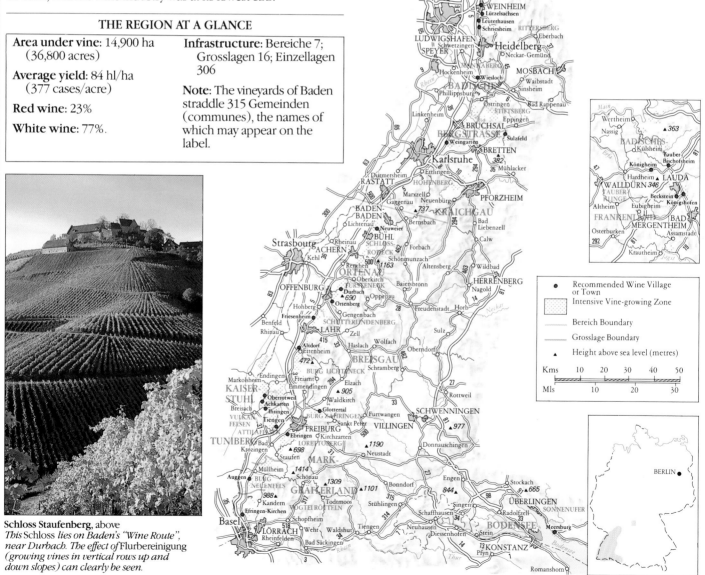

Schloss Staufenberg, above
This Schloss *lies on Baden's "Wine Route", near Durbach. The effect of* Flurbereinigung *(growing vines in vertical rows up and down slopes) can clearly be seen.*

The resurgence of Baden's wine industry began in 1952 with the formation of the Zentralkellerei Kaiserstuhler Winzergenossenschaften (Central Winery of Kaiserstuhl), which two years later expanded into the Zentralkellerei Badischer Winzergenossenschaften (Central Winery of Baden), or ZBW for short. ZBW built a £25 million vinification and storage plant at Breisach that helped to raise quality standards throughout the region and adopted an aggressive marketing policy on the domestic scene. Baden established itself as Germany's third-largest wine producing region, yet its wines were virtually unknown outside the country until ZBW made a serious effort to export its products in the early-1980s. Sadly, Baden is now a victim of its own success, for ZBW, which accounts for some 90 per cent of the region's output, has established such a clear-cut identity for its wines that Baden *per se* is generally perceived to produce one style of well-made, but rather basic and characterless wine. The truth is that while this one style represents the bulk of ZBW's, and thus Baden's, production, both ZBW and the region's independent producers have a wealth of other wines that are seldom seen or spoken about outside their locality. It is now time for ZBW to turn its marketing expertise to the relatively small number of very high-quality wines within its region.

FACTORS AFFECTING TASTE AND QUALITY

Location
The longest Anbaugebiet, Baden stretches for approximately 400 kilometres (250 miles), from Franken in the north, past Württemberg and Badische Bergstrasse to Bodensee, or Lake Constance, the most southerly of Germany's vineyards.

Climate
Compared to the rest of Germany, the bulk of Baden's vineyards have a sunny and warm climate, due in part to the shelter afforded by the Black Forest and the Odenwald Mountains.

Aspect
Most vineyards are on level or gently sloping ground. However, some are to be found higher up the hillsides, and these avoid the frosts of the valley floors.

Soil
Baden's soils are rich and fertile, varying from heat-retaining gravel near Lake Constance, through limestone, clay, marl, loam, granite and loess deposits to limestone and Keuper, a sandy-marl, in the Kraichgau and Taubergrund. Volcanic bedrock forms the main subsoil structure throughout most of the region.

Viticulture and vinification
The relatively flat and fertile vineyards of this region are easily mechanized. Although the geographical spread and variety of soils has led to a large number of different, traditional styles of wine, they are over-shadowed by the mild and neutrally fruity, bulk-produced Baden *QbA* marketed by ZBW. More than 90 per cent of the winemaking in Baden is conducted by its 54 cooperatives, but there are several independent and top-quality estates amongst the region's 26,000 growers. A speciality that is unique to Baden is Badisch Rotgold, a rosé made from pressing Ruländer and Spätburgunder grapes together.

Primary grape varieties
Müller-Thurgau, Ruländer, Spätburgunder

Secondary grape varieties
Gutedel, Kerner, Nobling, Riesling, Silvaner, Traminer, Weissburgunder

Bodensee (Lake Constance), above
South Baden vines at Meersburg, the best village of the Sonnenufer Grosslage.

The wines of Baden

BEREICH BADISCHES FRANKENLAND

The most northerly of Baden's vineyards, this Bereich bridges Franken and Württemberg. The wines have a similar style to those produced in both regions. If anything, the crisp, dry, aromatic and slightly earthy Müller-Thurgau and Silvaner wines lean nearer to Franken than to Württemberg. Only that part of the Bereich outside of Franken itself is allowed to use Franken's famous *Bocksbeutel.*

GROSSLAGE TAUBERKLINGE

No outstanding villages, vineyards or growers, although good wines are made in the villages of Beckstein, Königheim, Königshofen and Tauberbischofsheim.

BEREICH BADISCHE BERGSTRASSE-KRAICHGAU

This Bereich has four Grosslagen, two in the Badische Bergstrasse north and south of Heidelberg and two in the Kraichgau, a larger but sparsely cultivated area further south. Only one Grosslage, Stiftsberg, in the Kraichgau, has any reputation at all. Half of the Bereich is planted with Müller-Thurgau, but it makes mostly dull and lacklustre wine. When successful, the best wines are Ruländer and Riesling.

GROSSLAGE HOHENBERG

No outstanding villages, vineyards or growers, although good wines are made in the village of Weingarten.

GROSSLAGE MANNABERG

No outstanding villages, vineyards or growers, although good wines are made in the village of Wiesloch.

GROSSLAGE RITTERSBERG

No outstanding villages, vineyards or growers, although good wines are made in the villages of Leutershausen, Lützelsachsen, Schriesheim and Weinheim.

GROSSLAGE STIFTSBERG

Situated in the Kraichgau, east of the Mannaberg, this is the Bereich's most successful Grosslage. Nearly half of its vineyards are classified as "steep", which officially means sloping at more than 20 degrees, and this contributes to the extreme fruitiness of the Ruländer and the relatively racy character of the Riesling.

SULZFELD

☆ **Vineyard** *Burg Ravensburger*
☆ **Grower** *Freiherr von Gölertsche Gutsverwaltung*

MICHELFELD

☆ **Vineyard** *Himmelberg*
☆ **Growers** *Weingut Burg Hornberg, Weingut Reichsgraf & Marquis zu Hoensbroech*

BEREICH ORTENAU

Sheltered by the high hills of the Black Forest, the two Grosslagen of this Bereich produce some of Baden's greatest wines. These are generally full, fruity and often very spicy. The Riesling, known locally as Klingelberger, is extremely fine for such a powerful and spicy variation of this normally racy variety. Müller-Thurgau is particularly good and full, and successful Ruländer-Spätburgunder Badisch Rotgold is also produced. Confusingly, the Gewürztraminer is often called Clevner, usually a synonym for Pinot blanc.

Continued overleaf

GROSSLAGE FÜRSTENECK

This Grosslage sports some of Baden's finest estates. The range of grape varieties is greater here than anywhere else within Baden and the wines include Rieslings that range from firm and spicy to fine and delicate; powerful Gewürztraminer; some of Germany's best Müller-Thurgau; and some extraordinarily good Gutedel. Many of the wines are made in increasingly drier styles, although some estates are famous for their sweeter, late-harvested products.

DURBACH

☆ Vineyard *Schlossberg*
☆ Grower *Grafl. Wolff-Metternich'sche Gutsverwaltung*

☆ Vineyard *Schloss Grohl*
☆ Grower *Grafl. Wolff-Metternich'sche Gutsverwaltung*

☆ Vineyard *Schloss Staufenberg*
☆ Grower *Max Markgraf von Baden*

☆ Vineyard *Plauelrain*
☆ Growers *Freiherr von Neveusche Gutsverwaltung, Winzergenossenschaft Durbach, A. Laible*

ORTENBERG

☆ Vineyard *Schlossberg*
☆ Grower *Freiherr von Neveusche Gutsverwaltung*

ZELL

☆ Vineyard *Abtsberg*
☆ Grower *Winzergenossenschaft Zell-Weierbach*

GROSSLAGE SCHLOSS RODECK

In addition to the excellent cooperative recommended below, which specializes in *Rotwein,* and makes some of Germany's best ''Barrique'' QmP Spätburgunder, very good wines are produced by several growers in the Mauerberg vineyard, also at Neuweier, Stich den Buben at Steinbach, Betschgräber at Eisental, Alde Gott at Sasbach-walden, and in Hex vom Dasenstein at Kappelrodeck.

NEUWEIER

☆ Vineyard *Heiligenstein*
☆ Grower *Affentaler Winzergenossenschaft*

BEREICH BREISGAU

Strangely, the old city of Breisgau is not part of the Bereich that takes its name,

it is in fact situated within the Bereich of Kaiserstuhl-Tuniberg to the south. The wines of this Bereich do not compare with its famous southern neighbour, although they can be attractive and easy to drink. There is a mild, fruity, off-dry Müller-Thurgau; a full and juicy Ruländer; and a popular *Weissherbst* made from Spätburgunder.

GROSSLAGE BURG LICHTENECK

No outstanding villages, vineyards or growers, although good wines are made in the village of Altdorf.

GROSSLAGE BURG ZÄHRINGEN

No outstanding villages, vineyards or growers, although good wines are made in the village of Glottertal.

GROSSLAGE SCHUTTER-LINDENBERG

No outstanding villages, vineyards or growers, although good wines are made in the village of Friesenheim.

BEREICH KAISERSTUHL-TUNIBERG

The two Grosslagen of this Bereich produce a third of all Baden wines, including many of its best. It is a copybook example of *Flurbereinigung,* which is the name given to the national reorganization of vineyards, whereby traditionally terraced slopes are transformed into efficient wire-trained vines that run vertically up and down the hills. This is especially evident on the immaculately manicured slopes of the Kaiserstuhl, the famous extinct volcano that dominates the Bereich.

To the south of the mighty Kaiserstuhl is the far less awesome sight of the Tuniberg, another volcanic outcrop, that provides the Bereich's only other topographical and viticultural relief. The Tuniberg's steeper, west-facing slopes are cultivated, but neither its reputation nor its bulk can match those of Kaiserstuhl.

Though the warmest and driest Bereich in Germany, there are several microclimates that favour certain sites protected by the Kaiserstuhl. It is from these Einzellagen that some of Baden's best wines come, although the bulk of the wine produced is sold under the Bereich name, usually with the grape name attached. Bereich Kaiserstuhl-

Tuniberg Müller-Thurgau dominates. It is, however, the very full white Ruländer and the assertive *Weissherbst* Ruländer that are responsible for the reputation of the Bereich. Some fine, rich Spätburgunder are also produced, wines that enhance this reputation.

GROSSLAGE ATTILAFELSEN

No outstanding villages, vineyards or growers in this Grosslage, which covers the smaller volcanic outcrop of Tuniberg, although good wines are made in the village of Tiengen.

GROSSLAGE VULKANFELSEN

The largest and most successful of Kaiserstuhl-Tuniberg's two Grosslagen, Vulkanfelsen covers the superior volcanic vineyards of the Kaiserstuhl mound itself. Above all else, it is the full, fiery intensity of Ruländer wines from the Kaiserstuhl that give this district its reputation.

ACHKARREN

☆ Vineyard *Schlossberg*
☆ Growers *Winzergenossenschaft Achkarren, Weingut Ihringer zum Falken, Adolf Hauser*

IHRINGEN

☆ Vineyard *Winklerberg*
☆ Growers *Dr. Heger, Rudolf Stigler, Gebr. Müller, H. Glattes, Ihringer Winzergenossenschaft*

BICKENSOHL

☆ Vineyard *Steinfelsen*
☆ Grower *Winzergenossenschaft Bickensohl*

OBERROTWEIL

☆ Vineyard *Eichberg*
☆ Growers *Weingut von Gleichenstein, Kaiserstühler Winzerrerein Oberrotweil*

☆ Vineyard *Henkenberg*
☆ Growers *Weingut von Gleichenstein, Kaiserstühler Winzerverein Oberrotweil*

BÖTZINGEN

☆ Vineyard *Lasenberg*
☆ Grower *Winzergenossenschaft Bötzingen*

OBERBERGEN

☆ Vineyard *Bassgeige*
☆ Grower *Winzergenossenschaft Oberbergen*

BURKHEIM

☆ Vineyard *Schlossgarten*
☆ Grower *Winzergenossenschaft Burkheim*

BEREICH MARKGRÄFLERLAND

This is the second most important Bereich in Baden. The principal grape variety is, unusually, the Gutedel, which makes a light, dryish and neutral wine

that benefits from a slight spritz and can be most attractive when very youthful. Other prominent varieties include the Nobling, an up-and-coming cross between the Gutedel and Silvaner, that makes a more characterful wine than the light Müller-Thurgau. The latter can be attractive nevertheless. The Spätburgunder can be full and successful, and the Gewürztraminer also fares well.

GROSSLAGE BURG NEUENFELS

The vast majority of vineyards are officially classified as "steep" (i.e. sloping at more than 20 degrees) in this Grosslage, which makes some of the most delicious Gutedel.

AUGGEN

☆ Vineyard *Schäf*
☆ Grower *Weingut Blankenhorn*

GROSSLAGE LORETTOBERG

No outstanding villages, vineyards or growers, although good wines are made in the village of Ebringen.

GROSSLAGE VOGTEI RÖTTELN

Although much of the wine is sold under the Grosslage name, there are two exceptional vineyards here that are best known for Gutedel and, to a lesser extent, Spätburgunder.

EFRINGEN-KIRCHEN

☆ Vineyard *Kirchberg*
☆ Grower *Bezirkskellerei Markgräflerland*

BLANSINGEN

☆ Vineyard *Wolfer*
☆ Grower *Bezirkskellerei Markgräflerland*

BEREICH BODENSEE

In the Hochrhein of Bodensee, or the Upper Rhine of Bodensee, better known in English-speaking countries as Lake Constance, the wines are not great, but can be very acceptable. They range from the fruity and lively Müller-Thurgau to both *Rotwein* and *Weissherbst* from the Spätburgunder.

GROSSLAGE SONNENUFER

No outstanding villages, vineyards or growers, although good wines are made in the village of Meersburg.

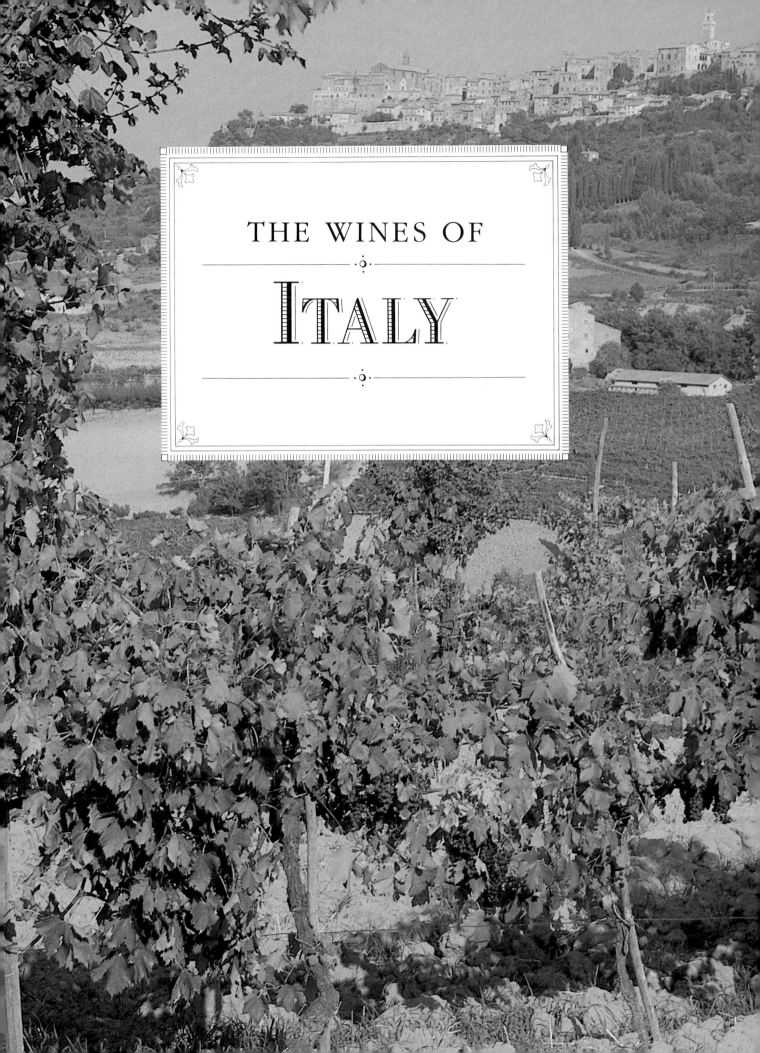

THE WINES OF
ITALY

Italy

Italy is the largest wine-producing country in the world, with an output averaging 77 million hectolitres (856 million cases) each year, amounting to 33 per cent of all European production and 25 per cent of world production.

ITALY HAS BEEN MAKING WINE for at least 2,500 years and has as much potential as France for fine wine, but during the last 25 years the quality of its wines has declined seriously. I am a friend of good Italian wine, but not of bland, poor or oxidized products that tarnish their own reputation and through it that of Italian wines as a whole. Italy still has many great winemakers, both traditional and innovative, and there are fine wines produced in virtually every famous appellation and in many theoretically lesser ones. However, they are heavily outweighed by the majority.

ITALY'S WINE LAWS

The blame for the decline in the quality of Italian wines lies partly with the 1963 wine laws. The inefficiency of its large and complex wine trade, and the lack of any cohesive marketing image, prompted Italy to introduce its *Denominazione di Origine Controllata* legislation, which is the equivalent of the French AOC laws. The number of wines granted this status quickly grew from a workable amount of classic and relatively well-known names to an unmanageable quantity of relatively obscure and often undeserving ones. The law failed to distinguish good from bad and therefore did not become a guarantee of quality.

Montalcino, below
With its famous Brunello vines in the foreground, Montalcino basks in Tuscan sunshine. Viticulturally, the surrounding area is highly prestigious; its tannic red wines generally need at least 10 years maturation.

Quantity versus quality

Since the 1960s, wine production in terms of yield per hectare has increased at a rate virtually proportionate to the decline in overall quality. The DOC law set its permitted yields much too high and so encouraged a very poor basic standard. For example, Chianti's yields are set at 87.5 hectolitres per hectare (393 cases per acre) and those for Soave at 98 hectolitres per hectare (440 cases per acre), compared to 50 hectolitres per hectare (225 cases per acre) for generic Bordeaux.

Another factor instrumental in encouraging an emphasis on quantity was the decline in Italy's *per capita* consumption of wine in the early 1970s, which led the industry to woo export markets. Feeling unable to compete in quality terms with the French, Italian producers concentrated on the bottom end of the market. The proliferation of two-litre (half-gallon), screw-top bottles that

ITALIAN WINE AND CUISINE

Italian wines should be judged in the context of the provincial cuisine that goes hand in hand with the traditional styles of the country wines. Regional cooking is often simple, and many of the most popular wines are not meant to be taken too seriously. These wines should, however, be fresh, clean and fruity, not dirty nor oxidized. The higher than normal levels of acidity and tannin found in many of them complement the flavours and textures of local dishes. In areas where the cooking is more sophisticated there will always be a correspondingly more complex wine capable of considerable quality.

resulted did little to enhance the image of any DOC. Then, having sold their wines initially at very low prices to buy their way into the market, the producers were reluctant to raise the price for fear of losing that market. Their solution to the problem of how to continue to produce large quantities of cheap wine was to lower the quality still further. They encouraged growers to move out of the lower-yielding, hilly, *classico* areas, on to the higher-yielding, rich, alluvial plains and to cultivate the most prolific-cropping grape varieties allowed within the DOC laws.

As a result, the DOC designation became so devalued that the theoretically inferior *Vino da Tavola* (table wine) category was – and still is – used for some of Italy's greatest wines. (*Vino da Tavola* [VT] wines also have no restrictions on grape varieties,

so many of Italy's fine, usually Cabernet-based, blends also come into the VT category.) The *vin ordinaire* image of DOC wines was so evident by the late-1970s that a higher quality category was put into effect – the *Denominazione di Origine Controllata e Garantita* or DOCG. Although this tightened up some of the regulations, it did not go far enough, and while the first red wines to be granted DOCGs are worthy, or potentially worthy, of this elevated status, the first white DOCG is Albana di Romagna, an unremarkable and virtually unknown wine.

THE FUTURE

Italy's *per capita* consumption of wine has continued to drop (from 110 litres [147 bottles] in 1970 to 82 litres [109 bottles] in

ITALY

As might be expected of a nation so geographically and culturally diverse, Italy produces a vast array of different types of wine. Away from the mainland, the islands of Sicily and Sardinia both have thriving wine industries.

	Northwest Italy *See also p.245*
	Northeast Italy *See also p.250*
	Central Italy-West *See also p.255*
	Central Italy-East *See also p.260*
	Southern Italy and the Islands *See also p.263*
	Provincia Boundary
▲	Height above sea level (metres)

Kms 50 100 150 200
Mls 20 40 60 80 100 120

1985) and exports began to slow down in the mid-1980s. Faced with a shrinking market, but an increased demand for higher-quality wines, the way forward must be for Italy to reduce the quantity and improve the standard of its production. Only when the country is producing considerably less wine than France will it be on the way to building a similar viticultural reputation. This can only be done through legislation that will hurt the pockets of some of the most powerful of Italy's winemakers. I suggest that the following measures should be implemented: all DOC yields to be cut by one-third and all DOCG yields by 15 per cent; no DOC or DOCG wines to be grown on alluvial plains; and no DOC wines to be blended with wines from outside the production zone, but the cultivation of up to 15 per cent of any *vinifera* grape variety to be allowed in DOC areas. I would also like to see a special vineyard appellation for some of Italy's greatest wines, such as Sassicaia, Sammarco, Tignanello and Torcolato.

THE WINES OF ITALY: USING THE TASTE GUIDE LISTINGS

In the listings that follow the introduction to each region of Italy, wines are divided into "fine" and "other", regardless of whether they are DOCG, DOC, VT, generic or branded. If a region has few or no "fine" wines, the listing is headed "The wines of . . The best wines of those not classified as "fine", and those that are occasionally good are asterisked.

Where the wine described – either in the "fine" or "other" sections – is from a single producer, its name is printed in *italics* beneath that of the wine.

In most "fine wine" sections there is also a list of the area's best sparkling wines and best Cabernet-based wines. In the case of the latter, the name of the wine is given first, followed by the producer in *italics*, and then the grape varieties.

HOW TO READ ITALIAN WINE LABELS

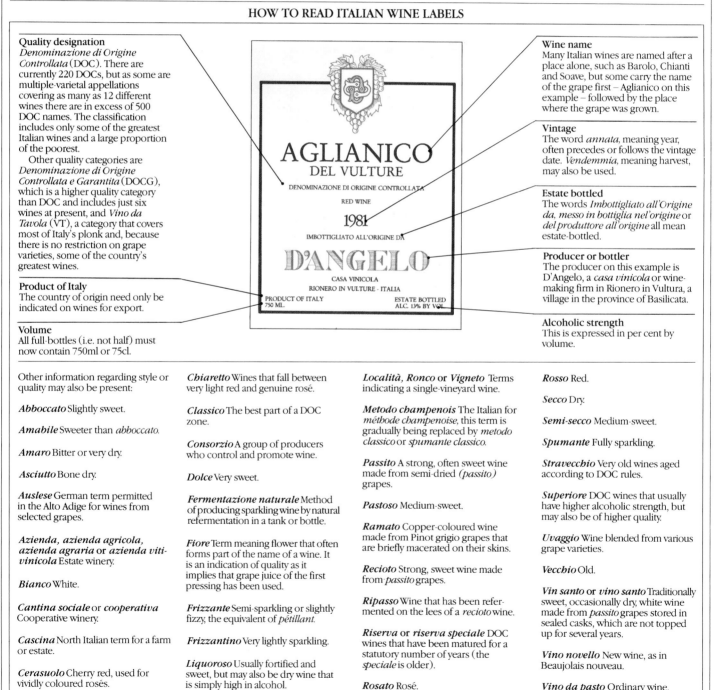

Quality designation
Denominazione di Origine Controllata (DOC). There are currently 220 DOCs, but as some are multiple-varietal appellations covering as many as 12 different wines there are in excess of 500 DOC names. The classification includes only some of the greatest Italian wines and a large proportion of the poorest.

Other quality categories are *Denominazione di Origine Controllata e Garantita* (DOCG), which is a higher quality category than DOC and includes just six wines at present, and *Vino da Tavola* (VT), a category that covers most of Italy's plonk and, because there is no restriction on grape varieties, some of the country's greatest wines.

Product of Italy
The country of origin need only be indicated on wines for export.

Volume
All full-bottles (i.e. not half) must now contain 750ml or 75cl.

Wine name
Many Italian wines are named after a place alone, such as Barolo, Chianti and Soave, but some carry the name of the grape first – Aglianico on this example – followed by the place where the grape was grown.

Vintage
The word *annata*, meaning year, often precedes or follows the vintage date. *Vendemmia*, meaning harvest, may also be used.

Estate bottled
The words *Imbottigliato all'Origine da, messo in bottiglia nel'origine* or *del produttore all'origine* all mean estate-bottled.

Producer or bottler
The producer on this example is D'Angelo, a *casa vinicola* or wine-making firm in Rionero in Vultura, a village in the province of Basilicata.

Alcoholic strength
This is expressed in per cent by volume.

Other information regarding style or quality may also be present:

Abboccato Slightly sweet.

Amabile Sweeter than *abboccato*.

Amaro Bitter or very dry.

Asciutto Bone dry.

Auslese German term permitted in the Alto Adige for wines from selected grapes.

Azienda, azienda agricola, azienda agraria or ***azienda viti-vinicola*** Estate winery.

Bianco White.

Cantina sociale or ***cooperativa*** Cooperative winery.

Cascina North Italian term for a farm or estate.

Cerasuolo Cherry red, used for vividly coloured rosés.

Chiaretto Wines that fall between very light red and genuine rosé.

Classico The best part of a DOC zone.

Consorzio A group of producers who control and promote wine.

Dolce Very sweet.

Fermentazione naturale Method of producing sparkling wine by natural refermentation in a tank or bottle.

Fiore Term meaning flower that often forms part of the name of a wine. It is an indication of quality as it implies that grape juice of the first pressing has been used.

Frizzante Semi-sparkling or slightly fizzy, the equivalent of *pétillant*.

Frizzantino Very lightly sparkling.

Liquoroso Usually fortified and sweet, but may also be dry wine that is simply high in alcohol.

Località, Ronco or ***Vigneto*** Terms indicating a single-vineyard wine.

Metodo champenois The Italian for *méthode champenoise*, this term is gradually being replaced by *metodo classico* or *spumante classico*.

Passito A strong, often sweet wine made from semi-dried (*passito*) grapes.

Pastoso Medium-sweet.

Ramato Copper-coloured wine made from Pinot grigio grapes that are briefly macerated on their skins.

Recioto Strong, sweet wine made from *passito* grapes.

Ripasso Wine that has been refer-mented on the lees of a *recioto* wine.

Riserva or ***riserva speciale*** DOC wines that have been matured for a statutory number of years (the *speciale* is older).

Rosato Rosé.

Rosso Red.

Secco Dry.

Semi-secco Medium-sweet.

Spumante Fully sparkling.

Stravecchio Very old wines aged according to DOC rules.

Superiore DOC wines that usually have higher alcoholic strength, but may also be of higher quality.

Uvaggio Wine blended from various grape varieties.

Vecchio Old.

Vin santo or ***vino santo*** Traditionally sweet, occasionally dry, white wine made from *passito* grapes stored in sealed casks, which are not topped up for several years.

Vino novello New wine, as in Beaujolais nouveau.

Vino da pasto Ordinary wine.

Northwest Italy

This area includes the great wine region of Piedmont as well as the regions of Liguria, Lombardy and Valle d'Aosta.

FEW AREAS ENCOMPASS SUCH CONTRASTING topography as the northwest of Italy, from the alpine *pistes* of the Valle d'Aosta and the Apennines of Liguria to the alluvial plains of the river Po. Contrast is also evident in the character of its two most famous wines: the big, black and tannic Barolo and the light, water-white, effervescent and grapey-sweet Asti.

PIEDMONT (PIEMONTE)

Piedmont is dominated by three grapes: Nebbiolo, Barbera and Moscato. It is Nebbiolo which is responsible for the magnificently rich and smoky Barolo and the elegant, more feminine, yet sometimes more powerful Barbaresco. The softer Barbera has a much greater yield than Nebbiolo but is potentially almost as fine; it excels around Alba. Piedmont also produces Asti, which is Italy's most popular fine wine. Made from the Moscato grape, its light, succulently sweet and grapey character makes Asti *spumante* undeniably the world's best sparkling wine for accompanying dessert.

LOMBARDY (LOMBARDIA)

Northeast of Piedmont, Lombardy stretches from the flat plains of the Po Valley to snow-clad Alpine peaks. The region's finest wines include Franciacorta's full reds and excellent *spumante classico*, and Valtellina's red Sassella. These wines are still relatively unknown compared to Piedmont's Barolo or Barbaresco and are good value.

LIGURIA

One of Italy's smallest regions, Liguria is more famous for its Riviera, which is set against the dramatic and beautiful backdrop of the Maritime Alps, than it is for its wines. The best-known Ligurian

FACTORS AFFECTING TASTE AND QUALITY

Location
Flanked to the north and west by the Alps and by the Ligurian Sea to the south, Northwest Italy contains the provinces of Piedmont, Lombardy, Liguria and Valle d'Aosta.

Climate
The winters are severe with frequent inversion fogs rising out of the valleys. Summers are hot, though not excessively so, but hail can damage the grapes at this time of year. Long autumns enable the late-ripening Nebbiolo grape to be grown very successfully.

Aspect
This area covers mountains, foothills (Piedmont means foothills) and the valley of Italy's longest river, the Po. Grapes are grown on hillsides that provide good drainage and exposure to the sun. In classic areas such as Barolo, every south-facing hillside is covered with vines, while in Lombardy many vineyards extend down to the rich, alluvial plains of the Po Valley.

Soil
A wide range of soils with many local variations, the predominant type is calcareous-marl which may be interlayered or intermingled with sand and clay.

Viticulture and vinification
The great red wines of the region have suffered in the past from long aging in large wooden vats, as many growers only bottled their wine when they sold it. This practice dried up the fruit and oxidized the wine. Now, many wines are bottled at the optimum time although there is still no consensus about the best aging vessels.

The use of *cuve close* for sweet, grapey styles of wine from Asti has been very successful and these wines sell well internationally. Some of the same *spumante* houses have developed dry *spumante* from Pinot and Chardonnay grapes, utilizing the *méthode champenoise*, to produce fine-quality sparkling wines.

Primary grape varieties
Barbera, Nebbiolo, Moscato

Secondary grape varieties
Arneis, Bonarda, Brachetto, Brugnola, Cabernet franc, Cabernet sauvignon, Chardonnay, Chiavennasca (Nebbiolo), Cortese, Croatina, Dolcetto, Erbaluce, Favorita, Freisa, Gamay, Grenache, Grignolino, Marzemino, Merlot, Ormeasco, Petit rouge, Pigato, Pignola Valtellina, Pinot bianco, Pinot grigio, Pinot nero, Riesling, Rossese, Rossola, Trebbiano, Ughetta, Uva rara, Vermentino, Vespolina

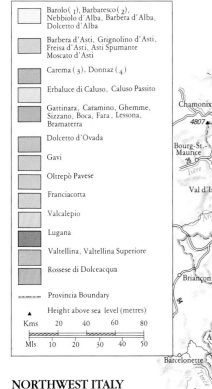

Barolo (₁), Barbaresco (₂),
Nebbiolo d'Alba, Barbera d'Alba,
Dolcetto d'Alba

Barbera d'Asti, Grignolino d'Asti,
Freisa d'Asti, Asti Spumante
Moscato d'Asti

Carema (₃), Donnaz (₄)

Erbaluce di Caluso, Caluso Passito

Gattinara, Caramino, Ghemme,
Sizzano, Boca, Fara, Lessona,
Bramaterra

Dolcetto d'Ovada

Gavi

Oltrepò Pavese

Franciacorta

Valcalepio

Lugana

Valtellina, Valtellina Superiore

Rossese di Dolceacqua

- - - Provincia Boundary

▲ Height above sea level (metres)

Kms 20 40 60 80

Mls 10 20 30 40 50

NORTHWEST ITALY

The presence of the Alps gives this largely hilly region a hot growing season and a long autumn. The finest wines come from the foothills of Piedmont, which provide ideal growing conditions for the late-ripening Nebbiolo grape.

wine is named after of Cinque Terre (five villages), above which the steep, intricately terraced vineyards tower like some Aztec pyramid. Most wines come in the category of pleasant holiday drinking.

VALLE D'AOSTA

Up in the Alps is the Valle d'Aosta, Italy's smallest and most mountainous wine region. Its high-altitude vineyards are pretty and produce some enjoyable wines but none that are truly fine.

AVERAGE ANNUAL PRODUCTION

Region	DOC production	Total production
Piedmont	1 million hl (11 million cases)	4 million hl (44 million cases)
Lombardy	400,000 hl (4 million cases)	2 million hl (22 million cases)
Liguria	7,000 hl (78,000 cases)	400,000 hl (4 million cases)
Valle d'Aosta	500 hl (5,550 cases)	30,000 hl (350,000 cases)

Percentage of total Italian production: Piedmont, 5.2%; Lombardy, 2.6%; Liguria, 0.52%; Valle d'Aosta, 0.04%.

Pergola-trained vines, above
These Nebbiolo vines, grown near Carema in Piedmont, are trained on a pergola Piemontese. They are made into a fragrant, medium-bodied wine.

Fine wines of Piedmont

ARNEIS DEI ROERI VT

These wines are produced from the ancient Arneis grape variety grown in the hills north of Alba.

WHITE The best are amazingly rich and full-flavoured, yet soft, deftly balanced with a fine *frizzantino*.

Arneis

1984, 1985, 1986, 1988, 1989

Between 3-5 years

☆ Castello di Neive, Bruno Giacosa, Vietti

ASTI or ASTI SPUMANTE DOC

Italy's greatest sparkling wine, and one of the most famous wines in the world, is produced by *cuve close* from grapes grown in 52 communes throughout the provinces of Asti, Cuneo and Alessandria.

SPARKLING WINE The *cuve close* method produces wines with a fresh, grapey appeal. The best Asti has a fine *mousse* of tiny bubbles, a luscious sweetness and a light, delicately rich fruitiness that hints at peaches.

Muscat

Mostly non-vintage

Within 1-2 years

☆ Villa Banfi, Barbero, Bersano, Luigi Bosca, Cantina Sociale Canelli, Villa Carlotta, Cinzano, Giuseppe Contratto, Cora, Duca d'Asti, Fontanafredda, Gancia, Kiola, Martini, Sperone, Tosti

BARBARESCO DOCG

Produced from Italy's greatest indigenous grape variety. The wines must be aged for a minimum of two years, one of which must be in oak or chestnut casks.

RED Generally more feminine and elegant than Barolo, Barbaresco has a suppler structure, softer fruit and a more obvious charm.

Nebbiolo

1982, 1983, 1985, 1986

Between 5-20 years

☆ Accademia Torregiorgi, Castello di Neive, Bruno Ceretto, Pio Cesare, Fratelli Cigliuti, Giuseppe Cortese, Angelo Gaja, Bruno Giacosa, Marchese di Gresy, Produttori di Barbaresco

BARBERA D'ALBA DOC

Barbera is the most prolific Piedmont vine and, as such, has a somewhat lowly image. It is, in fact, one of Italy's great grapes.

RED At their best these wines are magnificently rich and flavourful.

Barbera and up to a maximum of 15% Nebbiolo

1983, 1985, 1986, 1988, 1989

Between 5-12 years

☆ Elio Altare, Pio Cesare, Aldo Conterno, Giacomo Conterno, Damonte, Renato Ratti, Vietti

BAROLO DOCG

Great Barolo is incomparable.

RED Deep, sometimes inky-deep, in colour and powerfully built, top-quality Barolos are capable of great smoky-complexity and surprising finesse for such weighty wines. Barolo's image is only dented by the many poorly produced, oxidized or even foul wines that are allowed, quite reprehensibly, to carry this great and famous appellation.

Nebbiolo

1983, 1985, 1986, 1988, 1989

Between 8-25 years

☆ Elio Altare, Fratelli Barale, Giacomo Borgogno, Cavalotto, Ceretto, Clerico, Aldo Conterno, Giacomo Conterno, Paolo Cordero, Fontanafredda, Franco-Fiorina, Fratelli Oddero, Bruno Giacosa, Valentino Migliorini, Marchesi di Barolo, Giuseppe Mascarello, Renato Ratti, Giuseppe Rinaldi, Cantina Sociale Terre del Barolo, Vietti

BRICCO MANZONI VT

Valentino Migliorini

This Nebbiolo and Barbera blend gets better with each vintage.

RED A deep-coloured, full-bodied, rich and beautifully balanced wine.

Barbera, Nebbiolo

1982, 1985

Between 5-10 years

CARAMINO VT

Up-and-coming wines from vineyards in the Novara foothills.

RED Elegant, full-bodied wines that gain considerable finesse with age.

Nebbiolo

1983, 1985, 1986, 1988, 1989

Between 4-12 years

☆ Luigi Dessilani

CORTESE DI GAVI or GAVI DOC

The quality and character of these fashionable wines is very uneven.

WHITE At best, soft-textured, dry white wines with a slight *frizzantino* when young, they develop a honey-rich flavour after a couple of years in bottle. Some examples may be definitely *frizzante*.

Cortese

1982, 1983, 1985, 1986

Between 2-3 years

☆ Gavi dei Gavi, Pio Cesare, Fontanafredda

GATTINARA DOC

Wines from the right bank of the river Sésia in northern Piedmont.

RED Gattinara is a fine wine if it is not–atypically–overcropped. When young the fruit can be chunky or rustic, but a fine, silky-textured flavour and a graceful, violet-perfumed finesse can develop when mature.

Nebbiolo and up to a maximum of 10% Bonarda

🍷 1983, 1985, 1986, 1988, 1989

🕰 Between 6-15 years

☆ Mario Antoniolo, Augustino Brugo, Luigi Dessilani, Fontanafredda, Antonio Vallana

GHEMME DOC

Produced on the bank opposite Gattinara, Ghemme is usually regarded as the inferior of the two DOCs, but its wines are not over-cropped and are more consistent.

RED Although just as full in colour, body and flavour as Gattinara, Ghemme starts off with a much finer bouquet and more elegant fruit.

🍇 Nebbiolo 60-85%, Vespolina 10-30% and up to a maximum of 15% Bonarda novarese

🍷 1983, 1985, 1986, 1988, 1989

🕰 Between 4-15 years

☆ Antichi Vignetti di Cantelupo, Augustino Brugo, Luigi Dessilani

MOSCATO D'ASTI or MOSCATO D'ASTI SPUMANTE DOC

Wines similar in flavour to Asti Spumante, but with a minimum pressure of three atmospheres, as opposed to five. Still or just slightly *frizzantino* Moscato d'Asti (or Moscato d'Asti Spumanti) should carry the Moscato Naturale d'Asti appellation, but the name on the label often drops the "Naturale". For details of grape variety, best recent vintages and when to drink times, *see* Moscato Naturale D'Asti.

MOSCATO NATURALE D'ASTI DOC

Sometimes simply labelled Moscato d'Asti, these wines are bottled with a high level of residual sugar and may continue to ferment inside the bottle.

WHITE These wines are occasionally still, but sometimes show the barest hint of a prickle and may be *frizzantino or frizzante*. They are always, however, rich and succulently sweet.

🍇 Muscat

🍷 Current vintage

🕰 Immediately

☆ Ascheri, Braida, Cantina Sociale Canelli, Duca d'Asti, Fontanafredda, I Vignaili di S. Stefano, Vietti

MOSCATO DI STREVI VT

These wines are as good as Moscato d'Asti. For details of grape variety, best recent vintages and when to drink times, *see* Moscato Naturale D'Asti DOC.

NEBBIOLO D'ALBA DOC

Pure Nebbiolo wines come from an area between those of Barolo and Barbaresco.

RED Most wines are fine, full, rich and fruity. Sweet and sparkling versions are allowed.

🍇 Nebbiolo

🍷 1983, 1985, 1986, 1988, 1989

🕰 Between 4-10 years

☆ Ascheri, Ceretto, Pio Cesare, Aldo Conterno, Giacomo Conterno, Angelo Gaga, Bruno Giacosa, Giuseppe Mascarello, Vietti

SPANNA VT

Spanna is the local name for the Nebbiolo and this *Vino da Tavola* should merely represent the most basic wines from this grape variety. In the hands of some specialists, however it can rival all but the best Barolos and Barbarescos.

🍇 Spanna (Nebbiolo)

🍷 1983, 1985, 1986, 1988, 1989

🕰 Between 3-6 years (4-10 years in exceptional cases)

☆ Antonio Brugo, Luigi Dessilani, Antonio Vallana

The best dry sparkling wines of Piedmont

STEFANO BARBERO

CONTRATTO BRUT

LUIGI BOSCA BRUT NATURE

These wines are all made by the méthode champenoise.

Other wines of Piedmont

BARBERA D'ASTI* DOC

Similar in character to Barbera d'Alba, but softer, simpler and more supple.

BARBERA DEL MONFERRATO* DOC

Most wines are lesser versions of Barbera d'Asti. Semi-sweet or *frizzante* styles may also be made.

BAROLO CHINATO DOC

Barolo aromatized with quinine.

BOCA* DOC

Medium- to full-bodied, spicy red Nebbiolo wines; can be good value.

BRACHETTO D'ACQUI DOC

Sweet, *frizzante* and sparkling red wines with grapey, Muscat-like characteristics.

BRACHETTO D'ALBA VT

Non-DOC Brachetto wine from Alba.

BRACHETTO D'ASTI VT

Non-DOC Brachetto wine from Asti.

BRAMATERRA* DOC

Full-bodied red wines.

BRICCO DEL DRAGO* VT

Cascina Drago

A well-balanced Dolcetto and Nebbiolo blend.

CALUSO PASSITO* DOC

Full-bodied, sweet white wines made from *passito* Erbaluce grapes.

CAMPO ROMANO VT

Fruity, red *frizzante* wines.

CAREMA* DOC

Soft, medium-bodied, Nebbiolo wines that are grown on the mountainous slopes close to the border with Valle d'Aosta. They are good, reliable but not exciting.

COLLI TORTONESI DOC

Robust and rather rustic, full-bodied reds and crisp, dry, sometimes *frizzante,* whites

CORTESE DELL'ALTO MONFERRATO DOC

Dry, crisp, still, semi-sparkling and sparkling white wines.

DOLCETTO* VT

Many examples of Piedmont's famous Dolcetto wines are produced in non-classified areas and do not qualify for DOC status.

DOLCETTO D'ACQUI* DOC

Dolcetto is a plump grape with a low acid content that is traditionally used to make cheerful, Beaujolais-type wines that are deep purple in colour and best enjoyed young.

DOLCETTO D'ALBA* DOC

Soft, smooth, juicy wines that should be drunk within three years.

DOLCETTO D'ASTI DOC

Lighter versions of Dolcetto d'Alba.

DOLCETTO DI DIANO D'ALBA* DOC

Slightly fuller and grapier than most other Dolcetto wines.

DOLCETTO DI DOGLIANI DOC

Young, fresh and fruity Dolcetto from Dogliani.

DOLCETTO DELLE LANGHE MONREGALESI DOC

These rarely encountered wines are produced in tiny quantities by a handful of growers. They are reputed to have an exceptionally fine aroma.

DOLCETTO DI OVADA DOC

The fullest and firmest of Dolcettos that can last for as long as 10 years.

ERBALUCE DI CALUSO DOC

Fresh, dry, light-bodied, white wines. A *passito* version exists; *see* Caluso Passito DOC.

FARA DOC

Underrated, enjoyable, fruity wines with a spicy-scented character.

FAVORITA VT

Popular, dry, very crisp white wines.

FREISA D'ASTI DOC

Fruity, dry and semi-sweet red wines; also sparkling and *frizzante* reds.

FREISA DI CHIERI DOC

The same styles of wine as Freisa d'Asti from just outside Turin.

GABIANO* DOC

Full-bodied, red Barbera wines of promising quality.

GRECO VT

Light, sharp white wines from a variant of the Erbaluce grape.

GRIGNOLINO D'ASTI DOC

Lightly tannic red wines with a slightly bitter aftertaste.

GRIGNOLINO DEL MONFERRATO CASALESE DOC

Light, crisp, fresh Grignolino from the Casale Monferrato area.

LESSONA* DOC

Red wines that can be delightfully scented, with rich fruit and some finesse.

MALVASIA DI CASORZO D'ASTI DOC

Slightly aromatic, sweet, red and rosé wines that may also be sparkling.

MALVASIA DI CASTELNUOVO DON BOSCO DOC

Slightly aromatic, sweet, red, still and sparkling wines.

NEBBIOLO DEL PIEMONTE VT

Mostly simple red wines, but exceptionally fine examples are sometimes made in great years by the best Barolo and Barbaresco producers.

PICCONE VT

Sella Lessona

Robust red wines made from a Gattinara-like blend in the Vercelli hills north of the Po.

ROERO* DOC

These sometimes successful, dry white wines are a blend of ancient Arneis and classic Nebbiolo. They used to be sold as Bianco dei Roeri, a *Vino da Tavola*.

RUBINO DI CANTAVENNA* DOC

Full-bodied red wines that are a blend of mostly Barbera, Grignolino and sometimes Freisa.

SIZZANO* DOC

Good, full-bodied, red wines produced from a Gattinara-like blend on a bank of the river Sésia, just south of Ghemme.

Fine wines of Lombardy

FRANCIACORTA DOC

Produced on hilly slopes near Lake Iseo northeast of Milan, Franciacorta has been a DOC since 1967.

RED Well-coloured, medium- to full-bodied wines that are capable of great richness and some finesse.

- Cabernet franc 40-50%, Barbera 20-30%, Merlot 10-15% and up to a maximum of 15% of any other variety
- 1982, 1983, 1985, 1986
- Between 3-8 years

WHITE These do not have the same record for consistency and quality as the reds, but their smooth, dry, fruity character shows promise.

- Pinot bianco, Chardonnay
- 1986, 1988, 1989
- Within 1-3 years

SPARKLING WHITE Using the *méthode champenoise*, with extended aging on the lees, Franciacorta has already demonstrated its potential for producing fine, biscuity, *brut* styles.

- Pinot bianco, Chardonnay and up to a maximum of 15% Pinot grigio and Pinot nero
- Mostly non-vintage
- Between 2-5 years

SPARKLING ROSÉ The exceptional Cà del Bosco has a light richness of ripe fruit, strong *mousse* and soft balance.

- Pinot bianco, Chardonnay and up to a maximum of 15% Pinot grigio
- Mostly non-vintage
- Between 2-5 years

☆ Barboglio de Gaiocelli, Bellavista, Berlucchi, Cà del Bosco, Longhi-de Carli

GRUMELLO DOC
See Valtellina Superiore DOC.

INFERNO DOC
See Valtellina Superiore DOC.

MAURIZIO ZANELLA VT

Cà del Bosco

Named after the owner of Cà del Bosco and considered to be the finest Bordeaux-style blend produced so far in Italy.

RED A full, rich, well-coloured wine with obvious finesse. Its delicious, juicy-fruitiness comes from the small proportion of *macération carbonique* wine that is added to the blend.

- Cabernet sauvignon 40%, Cabernet franc 30%, Merlot 30%
- 1981, 1982, 1983, 1984, 1985, 1986
- Between 3-10 years

MOSCATO DI SCANZO VT

According to the Italian wine expert Burton Anderson this is a great wine of exquisite richness.

NARBUSTO VT

Angelo Ballabio

A wine that has an extraordinary depth and richness of fruit despite spending eight years in wood.

OLTREPÒ PAVESE DOC

The Oltrepò Pavese is a large production area covering 42 communes south of the river Po. Only 17 per cent of the wine is sold under this DOC, the rest finds its way to specialist wineries in Piedmont, who turn it into non-DOC *spumante* by *cuve close* and, increasingly, *méthode champenoise*. Many styles of wine are produced, including nine pure varietals, asterisked below, which usually represent quite good value.

There are also three geographical sub-district appellations: Oltrepò Pavese Barbacarlo, occasionally sweet, but usually dry, robust, red, *frizzante*; Oltrepò Pavese Buttafuoco, deep-coloured, normally dry red wines that are rustic, but always show plenty of fruit; and Oltrepò Pavese Sangue di Giuda, soft, sweet, red *spumante* called the "blood of Judas". Basic reds and rosés that are not varietals, nor special geographic sub-appellations, are also made in a great range of styles with equal variation in quality.

- Barbera*, Bonarda* (Croatina), Cortese*, Moscato bianco* (a pure varietal *liquoroso* is also produced), Pinot bianco, Pinot grigio*, Pinot nero*, Riesling Italico*, Riesling Renano*, Ughetta, Uva rara
- 1982, 1983, 1985, 1986
- RED: Between 2-5 years
  WHITE AND ROSÉ: Within 1-3 years

☆ Giacomo Agnes, Angelo Ballabio, Bianchina Alberici, Maga Lino

SASSELLA DOC
See Valtellina Superiore DOC.

VALGELLA DOC
See Valtellina Superiore DOC.

VALTELLINA SUPERIORE DOC

A narrow strip of vineyards on the north bank of the river Adda near the Swiss border, whose wines must contain a minimum of 12 per cent alcohol, as opposed to 11 per cent for Valtellina. Most of the wines come from four sub-districts: Grumello, Inferno, Sassella (the best) and Valgella – the most productive but least good. *Sfursat* or *Sforzato*, which literally means "strained", is a dry, concentrated Valtellina Superiore that has a minimum of 14.5 per cent alcohol.

RED The richness of these wines is belied by their elegance. They have good colour and are capable of developing exquisite finesse after several years in bottle.

- A minimum of 95% Chiavennasca (Nebbiolo), Pinot nero, Merlot, Rossola, Brugnola, Pignola Valtellina
- 1983, 1985, 1986, 1988, 1989
- Between 5-15 years

☆ Enologica Valtellinese, Fondazione Fojanini, Nino Negri, Nera, Rainoldi, Tona

Lombardy's best dry sparkling wines

BELLAVISTA CUVÉE BRUT

BELLAVISTA GRAN CUVÉE PAS OPERÉ

BERLUCCHI BRUT CUVÉE IMPÉRIALE

BERLUCCHI BRUT CUVÉE IMPÉRIALE MILLESIMATO

BERLUCCHI BRUT CUVÉE IMPÉRIALE MAX ROSÉ

CÀ DEL BOSCO FRANCIACORTA PINOT BRUT

CÀ DEL BOSCO FRANCIACORTA PAS DOSE

CÀ DEL BOSCO FRANCIACORTA CRÉMANT BRUT

DORIA PINOT BRUT

VILLA MAZZUCCHELLI BRUT

VILLA MAZZUCCHELLI PAS DOSE

All these wines are made by the méthode champenoise.

Other wines of Lombardy

BOTTICINO* DOC

Full-bodied, Barbera-based red wines with a good level of alcohol and a light tannic structure.

CANNETO VT

Vinous red wines with a bitter after-taste that can be good value.

CAPRIANO DEL COLLE DOC

Rarely encountered red wines from the Sangiovese blended with Marzemino, Barbera and Merlot and tart, white wines from the Trebbiano.

CELLATICA* DOC

Vinous red wines that can be aromatic and flavoursome. They have a slightly bitter aftertaste.

CLASTIDIO* VT

Angelo Ballabio

Wines from Casteggio in the heart of the Oltrepò Pavese area. Medium-bodied, full-flavoured red and rosé wines from a blend of Barbera, Cratina and Uva rara grapes and crisp, fresh Riesling and Pinot bianco white wines are made.

CLASTIDIUM* VT

Angelo Ballabio

What used to be a very rich, medium-sweet to sweet, golden-white wine that aged beautifully and had a legendary reputation. Gradually it became drier, but the wine still maintained its extraordinary long-evity and quality. Since the ownership of Angelo Ballabio changed hands in the late-1970s, most vintages have been a shadow of former ones.

COLLE DEL CALVARIO* VT

Castello di Grumello

A steadily improving, well-structured red wine with good potential longevity. The white is attractively fresh and fruity.

COLLI MORENICI MANTOVANI DEL GARDA DOC

Dry, light-bodied, red, white and rosé.

GROPPELLO VT

Medium-bodied, fruity red wines often in the *amarone* style.

LAMBRUSCO MANTOVANO VT

These *frizzante* red wines, which may be dry or sweet, are produced on the plains of Mantua (Mantova).

LUGANA* DOC

Soft, dry white Trebbiano wines made on Lake Garda's shore.

RIVIERA DEL GARDA BRESCIANO DOC

On the opposite bank of Lake Garda to Valpolicella, this area produces light, fruity, vinous, slightly bitter, red wines and soft rosé wines.

RONCO DI MOMPIANO* VT

M. Pasolini

Marzemino and Merlot are blended to make aromatic and smooth red wines.

SAN COLOMBANO AL LAMBRO or SAN COLOMBANO DOC

Robust, rustic red wines made from Croatina, Barbera and Uva rara.

TOCAI DI SAN MARTINO DELLA BATTAGLIA DOC

Dry, full-flavoured white wines with a flowery aroma and slightly bitter aftertaste.

VALCALEPIO* DOC

Up-and-coming appellation for well-coloured, deeply flavoured red wines made of a blend of 55-70% Merlot and 25-45% Cabernet sauvignon, and light, dry and delicate white wines made from 55-70% Pinot bianco and 25-45% Pinot grigio.

VALTELLINA* DOC

This generic appellation encompasses 19 communes of the province of Sondrio in the north of Lombardy. Most products are light-scented, medium-bodied red wines of simple, although often pleasing, character. The finest Valtellina wines are virtually all *superiore. See* Valtellina Superiore DOC.

VINO NOVELLO DI ERBUSCO VT

Fruity red wines best drunk within a few months of the harvest.

The wines of Liguria

BARBERA DI LINERO VT

Rather ordinary, medium-bodied red wines from a variety that does much better a little further north in Piedmont.

BUZZETTO DI QUILIANO VT

Buzetto is the local name for the ubiquitous Trebbiano and its light, dry white wines are lacklustre and acidulously dry.

CINQUE TERRE* DOC

Delicate, dry white wines and Cinque Terre Sciacchetrà, which is a medium-sweet, *passito,* white wine.

LUMASSINA VT

Dry, rather neutral white wines.

RIVIERA LIGURE DI PONENTE* DOC

Four former *vini da tavola* are grouped together under this appellation which covers the western riviera of Liguria. These are: Ormeasco, bright, cherry-red wines with juicy, raspberry, Dolcetto fruit; Pigato, full-flavoured yet precocious red wines; Rossese, well-scented, characterful reds; and Vermentino, rich, full and dry white wines.

ROSA DI ALBENGA VT

Liguria's best-known rosés are vividly coloured, dry and characterful.

ROSSESE DI DOLCEACQUA or DOLCEACQUA DOC

Red wines that are capable of rich, lush fruit, a soft texture and spicy-aromatic aftertaste.

The wines of Valle d'Aosta

AYMAVILLE* VT

Crisp, fruity wines from Aymaville, southwest of Aosta.

BLANC DE COSSAN VT

Fresh, tart, *blancs de noir* from Cossan, just outside Aosta.

BLANC DE MORGEX VT

Dry, sharp white wines that are low in alcohol, from the slopes above Morgex, close to La Salle.

BLANC DE LA SALLE VT

Lightly-scented, fresh white wines that include *méthode champenoise* sparkling wines.

CHAMBAVE ROUGE* VT

Attractively-scented, crisp red wines from Barbera, Dolcetto and Gros vien grapes grown at Chambave.

CREME DU VIEN DE NUS* VT

Don Augusto Pramotton

Rich, fragrant red wine made by the village priest of Vien de Nus.

DONNAZ* DOC

Soft, well-balanced red wines with a slightly bitter aftertaste.

ENFER D'ARVIER DOC

Low-key, medium-bodied, soft and fairly rich red wines.

GAMAY DELLA VALLE D'AOSTA VT

Fruity, Beaujolais-type wines.

GAMAY-PINOT NERO VT

Light and fruity *passetoutgrains*-type of blended wines.

LA COLLINE DE SARRE ET CHESALLET* VT

Fresh and fruity red wines.

MALVOISIE DE COSSAN VT

Semi-sweet, smooth and slightly bitter white wines.

MALVOISIE DE NUS VT

Don Augusto Pramotton

This rich, white dessert wine is made by the village priest in tiny quantities. It is long-lived and expensive.

MOSCATO DI CHAMBAVE* VT

Dry, well-perfumed, full-flavoured, white wines.

PASSITO DI CHAMBAVE* VT

Sweet, golden and long-lived, these aromatic white wines are made from traditional *passito* or semi-dried grapes.

PETIT ROUGE* VT

Deep, dark and highly perfumed red wines.

SANG DES SALASSES VT

Fruity but slightly bitter red wines from the Pinot noir.

TORRETTE* VT

Deep in colour, bouquet and body, these wines are made from the Petit rouge grape.

Northeast Italy

Freshness, crisp acidity and purity of varietal character personify the wines of the northeastern regions of Trentino-Alto Adige, Friuli-Venezia Giulia and the Veneto.

THIS IS A MORE MOUNTAINOUS AREA than the northwest (with the exception of Valle d'Aosta), with just over half the land occupied by the Dolomites and their precipitous foothills. Some of the finest wines are grown in the lush, verdant vineyards of the South Tyrol in the Alto Adige, just over the border from Austria. A great deal of wine is exported; the bulk of it unexciting Soave and Valpolicella. Locally there is much greater variety and value to be had – a number of French and German grapes are grown in addition to the local varieties and dedicated producers continue to experiment.

TRENTINO-ALTO ADIGE

This is the most westerly and spectacular of the three regions, with more than 90 per cent of the area covered by mountainous countryside. It comprises two autonomous provinces, the Italian-speaking Trento in the south and the German-speaking Bolzano or South Tyrol in the north, where the wines may possess alternative German names and can carry a *QbA* designation.

The generic Alto Adige DOC (Südtiroler QbA) is remarkably good and accounts for 30 per cent of the region's total DOC output. There are also a number of fine wines produced in these cool, high vineyards.

THE VENETO

Stretching from the river Po to the Austrian border and sandwiched between Trentino-Alto Adige to the west and Friuli-Venezia Giulia to the east, the majority of the Veneto's wines are grown on the alluvial plains in the south of the region. This is one

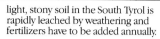

FACTORS AFFECTING TASTE AND QUALITY

Location
The northeast of Italy is bounded by the Dolomites to the north and the Adriatic Sea to the south.

Climate
Similar to the northwest in that summers are hot and winters cold and harsh, but fog is less of a problem and hail more frequent. There are unpredictable variations in the weather from year to year so vintages are important, particularly for red wines.

Aspect
Vineyards are found on a variety of sites ranging from the steep, mountainous slopes of Trentino-Alto Adige to the flat, alluvial plains of the Veneto and Friuli-Venezia Giulia. The best vineyards are always sited in hilly countryside.

Soil
Most vineyards are on glacial moraine – a gritty mixture of sand, gravel and sediment deposited during the Ice Age. Most are clayey or sandy clay and the best sites are often marly and rich in calcium. The light, stony soil in the South Tyrol is rapidly leached by weathering and fertilizers have to be added annually.

Viticulture and vinification
The northeast has led Italy's move towards more modern vinification techniques and experimentation with foreign grape varieties. It was the first area to use cold fermentation and, initially, the wines produced were so clean that they lacked natural character. There is now much experimentation into how to increase intensity of flavour through the use of new oak.

Grape varieties
Cabernet franc, Cabernet sauvignon, Chardonnay, Cortese, Corvina, Durello, Garganega, Gewürztraminer, Lagrein, Limberger, Malbec, Malvasia, Marzemino, Merlot, Moscato, Nosiola, Petit verdot, Picolit, Pinot bianco, Pinot grigio, Pinot nero, Prosecco, Raboso, Refosco, Ribolla, Riesling, Sauvignon blanc, Schiava, Schioppettino, Tazzelenghe, Teroldego, Terrano, Tocai, Trebbiano, Verduzzo, Vespaiolo

NORTHEAST ITALY

The variety of sites offered by the mountains and the hills of this area enables many grape varieties to be grown in addition to local ones. The most exciting wines come from the high vineyards of the South Tyrol, the hills of Friuli and around Vicenza in the Veneto.

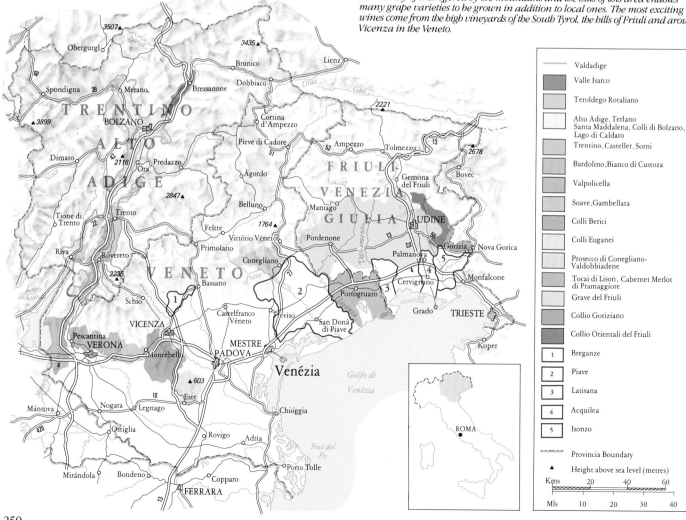

	Valdadige
	Valle Isarco
	Teroldego Rotaliano
	Alto Adige, Terlano, Santa Maddalena, Colli di Bolzano, Lago di Caldaro
	Trentino, Casteller, Sorni
	Bardolino, Bianco di Custoza
	Valpolicella
	Soave, Gambellara
	Colli Berici
	Colli Euganei
	Prosecco di Conegliano-Valdobbiadene
	Tocai di Lison, Cabernet Merlot di Pramaggiore
	Grave del Friuli
	Collio Goriziano
	Collio Orientali del Friuli
1	Breganze
2	Piave
3	Latisana
4	Acquilea
5	Isonzo

---- Provincia Boundary

▲ Height above sea level (metres)

Kms 20 40 60
Mls 10 20 30 40

of the most exciting hunting grounds for Italian Bordeaux-type blends. Maculan of Breganze, in the western province of Vicenza, produces the best Cabernet-based blends, although such is the rate of development in this style of wine that several other producers may reach the same quality in the near future.

FRIULI-VENEZIA GIULIA

Situated in the northeastern corner of Italy, this largely mountainous region has grown many non-Italian varieties since phylloxera wiped out its vineyards in the late-nineteenth century. The naturally innovative Friulians (and South Tyrolians) used the opportunity to replant their vineyards with several better-quality foreign grapes, starting with the Merlot, which was brought to this region by Senator Pecile and Count Savorgnan in 1880. Over the last 100 years, the northeast has consistently demonstrated that the use of superior grape varieties and relatively lower yields can produce wines of dramatically improved quality.

Friuli is the home of some of the country's best wines, including many of its most complex Cabernet blends. Girolamo Dorigo's "Montsclapade", which is the best of an exceptionally fine group of wines, is a typically Friulian blend of both Cabernets, Merlot and Malbec. The Malbec is a rare variety on this side of the Alps, but it fares well in Friuli and might well be the key to the complexity of these wines. A few rather unconventional blends are found, the most unusual being Abbazia di Rosazzo's multi-national Ronco dei Roseti, which mixes the four Bordeaux varieties with the German Limberger, the Italian Refosco and the obscure Tazzelenghe.

Another Abbazia di Rosazzo wine, Ronco delle Acacie, is a rare masterpiece in the new Italian school of "super-deluxe" *Vini da Tavola* white wines. This category of dry white Italian wine is expensive but mostly disappointing.

The largest volume of fine wines comes from one of Friuli's two Colli or "hilly" areas, Colli Orientali del Friuli, which is close to the Yugoslav border and encompasses many varietal wines. They are well worth looking out for – all except for the Picolit, a grossly overrated and horrendously overpriced sweet wine. This one is the only Picolit in Italy to have DOC status, but the wine is no better than other examples found throughout the country.

Bardolino vineyards, above
Ripening grapes adorn rows of vines in the Veneto's Bardolino area, which has a good reputation for its light, dry red and rosé wines.

AVERAGE ANNUAL PRODUCTION

Region	DOC production	Total production
Veneto	1.5 million hl (17 million cases)	10 million hl (111 million cases)
Trentino-Alto Adige	700,000 hl (8 million cases)	1.5 million hl (17 million cases)
Friuli-Venezia Giulia	420,000 hl (5 million cases)	1.6 million hl (13 million cases)

Percentage of total Italian production: Veneto, 13%; Trentino-Alto Adige, 2%; Friuli-Venezia Giulia, 1.5%.

Fine wines of Trentino-Alto Adige

ALTO ADIGE (SÜDTIROLER) DOC

This generic appellation covers the entire Alto Adige or South Tyrol, which is in the northern province of Bolzano. It is remarkably consistent in terms of quality, considering that it represents some 30 per cent of the region's total production. With the exception of Alto Adige *spumante,* all the wines are pure varietals and must contain at least 95 per cent of the grape indicated (as opposed to 85 per cent else-where in Italy). Alternative German names are given in brackets.

RED There are six varietals in this category. **Cabernet** covers either Cabernet sauvignon or Cabernet franc, or both, and ranges from simple, but delightful, everyday wines to deeper-coloured, fuller-bodied, richer wines that become warm, mellow and spicy after five to ten years. **Lagrein Dunkel (Lagrein Scuro)** is made from an underrated, indigenous grape variety and can have a fine, distinctive character and good colour. **Malvasia** or **Malvasier** is produced here as a red wine, but it would be better made into white or rosé. **Merlot** can be simply

light and fruity or attain greater heights, with a good spicy, sweet-pepper aroma and fine, silky texture. **Pinot Nero (Blauburgunder)** is a most difficult varietal to perfect, but those from Mazzon are good and a speciality of this region (they will have Mazzoner on the label). **Schiava (Vernatschs)** accounts for one in five bottles produced under this appellation and is the most popular tavern wine.

🍷 1983, 1985, 1986, 1988, 1990

🍾 Between 2-10 years

Südtiroler
Grauvernatsch
DENOMINAZIONE DI ORIGINE CONTROLLATA · QUALITÄTSWEIN b.A.
Schiava Grigia dell'Alto Adige

Abgefüllt in Tramin von · Imbottigliato in Termeno da
WEINGUT · WEINKELLEREI · CANTINA
J·Hofstätter
TERMENO · TRAMIN
11.5 % vol   ITALIA   e 75 cl.
(542/82)

WHITE There are no less than ten different varietals in this category. **Chardonnay** can range from light and neutral to delicately fruity, and even *frizzantino* or verging upon *spumante.* The fuller versions can have recognizable varietal characteristics, but still lack the weight and intensity of flavour of even basic Burgundy. **Moscato Giallo (Goldenmuskateller)** is made into delicious dessert wines. **Pinot bianco (Weissburgunder)** is the most widely planted of all the white grape varieties and produces most of Alto Adige's finest white wines. **Pinot grigio (Ruländer)** is potentially as successful as Pinot bianco, but does not always occupy the best sites. **Riesling Italico (Welschriesling)** is insignificant in both quantity and quality. **Riesling Renano (Rheinriesling)** is fine, delicate and attractive at the lowest level, but can be extraordinarily good in exceptional vintages. *Riesling x Silvaner* (Müller-Thurgau) is relatively rare – a pity because planted here it achieves a lively spiciness. **Sauvignon** was very scarce in the early 1980s, but as the vogue for this grape spread so its cultivation increased and sufficient success has been achieved to earmark the crisp, dry and varietally pure Alto

Adige Sauvignon as the wine of the 1990s. **Silvaner** is made mostly to be drunk young and fresh. **Traminer aromatico (Gewürztraminer)** is more restrained than the classic Alsace version, but its delicate aroma and understated flavour has a charm of its own.

🍷 1983, 1984, 1986, 1988, 1990

🍾 Within 1-5 years

ROSÉ Only three varietal *rosato* wines are allowed. **Lagrein Rosato (Lagrein Kretzer)** is overtly fruity in a very round and smooth style. **Pinot Nero** or **(Blauburgunder)** is more successful as a rosé than as a red. **Moscato rosa (Rosenmuskateller)** makes very flamboyant, semi-sweet to sweet wines with an unusually high natural acidity, intense floral perfume and an exaggerated Muscat flavour.

🍷 1983, 1985, 1986, 1988, 1990

🍾 Within 1-3 years

SPARKLING WHITE Pure or blended Pinot bianco, Pinot grigio, Pinot nero and Chardonnay turned into *spumante*

Continued overleaf

by either *cuve close* or *méthode champenoise.*

| 🔟 | Mostly non-vintage |
| 🍷 | Within 2-5 years |

☆ Bellendorf, Josef Hofstätter, Kettmeir, Alois Lageder, Schloss Sallegg, Tiefenbrunner

TERLANO (TERLANER) DOC

Soft, dry, blended white wines and five varietals from five communes near Bolzano. The quality and character is very similar to the Alto Adige DOC. *See* that entry for best recent vintages and when to drink.

☆ Alois Lageder, Cantina Sociale Terlano

TRENTINO DOC

Although many Trentino wines are softer and less racy than those from Alto Adige, their general character is similar. In addition to all the varietals that qualify for Alto Adige, this appellation also includes Nosiola, a grape variety used for both the disappointing, sweet *vin santo* and dull, dry wine with a typically bitter aftertaste. Cabernet franc and Cabernet sauvignon are used for pure varietals as well as blends. A local variety, Marzemino, produces a pleasant, medium-bodied wine, with a fruit-and-bitter-almond flavour. *See* Alto Adige for best recent vintages and when to drink.

☆ Barone de Cles, Riccardo Battitotti, Guerrieri Gonzaga, Conti Bossi Fedrigotti, Conti Martini, Pojer & Sandri, De Tarczal, Armando Simoncelli, Zeni

VALLE ISARCO (EISACKTALER) DOC

The varietal whites made from Gewürztraminer, Pinot grigio, Silvaner and Müller-Thurgau are similar to those of the Alto Adige. Another variety, Veltliner, produces a mild, clean, fruity, dry wine for quaffing. *See* Alto Adige for best recent years and when to drink.

☆ Alois Lageder, Klosterkellerei Eisacktaler, Stiftskellerei Neustift

The best Cabernet-based wines of Trentino-Alto Adige

These wines are not quite as successful as similar blends in the neighbouring Veneto and Friuli regions, but some improve with each new vintage. The finest Bordeaux-style wines of Trentino may improve for ten years or more.

CASTEL SAN MICHELE, *Istituto Agrario Provincale San Michele all'Adige*
Cabernet franc, Cabernet sauvignon, Merlot

FOIANEGHE, *Conti Bossi Fedrigotti*
Merlot, Cabernet sauvignon

MASO LODRON, *Letrari*
Cabernet franc, Cabernet sauvignon, Merlot

MORI VECIO, *Lagariavini*
Cabernet franc, Cabernet sauvignon, Merlot

SAN LEONARDO, *Guerrieri Gonzaga*
Cabernet franc, Cabernet sauvignon, Merlot

SAN ZENO, *La Vinicola Sociale Aldeno*
Merlot, Cabernet franc, Cabernet sauvignon

The best dry sparkling wines of Trentino-Alto Adige

EQUIPE 5 BRUT RISERVA

EQUIPE 5 BRUT ROSÉ

FERRARI BRUT

FERRARI BRUT DE BRUT

FERRARI BRUT ROSÉ

FERRARI NATURE

FERRARI RISERVA GIULIO FERRARI

These wines are all made by the méthode champenoise. They are all VT and not necessarily made from grapes grown within the region.

Other wines of Trentino-Alto Adige

CALDARO or LAGO DI CALDARO (KALTERERSEE) DOC

Soft, fruity, red wines that are easy to drink.

CASTELLER DOC

Dry or semi-sweet, red and rosé wines for everyday drinking.

COLLI DI BOLZANO (BOZNER LEITEN) DOC

Soft, fruity, red wines that are best drunk very young.

DE VITE* VT

Josef Hofstätter

Dry white wine with a fragrant flavour.

KOLBENHOFER* VT

Josef Hofstätter

A more serious version of Caldaro from a vineyard above Tramin.

MERANESE DI COLLINA (MERANER HÜGEL) DOC

Light, delicately-scented red wines from Merano, northwest of Bolzano.

SANTA MADDALENA (SANKT MAGDALENER*) DOC

Drinkable, full-bodied, smooth, vinous red wines from an appellation that was undeservedly ranked by Mussolini as one of Italy's greatest.

SORNI* DOC

This steadily improving appellation makes soft red wines and light, fresh, delicate whites.

TEROLDEGO ROTALIANO* DOC

Full-bodied red wines made from the Teroldego grape. There is also a fuller, more concentrated *Superiore* version and an attractive rosé.

VALDADIGE (ETSCHTALER) DOC

Crisp, dry and semi-sweet white and red wines.

Fine wines of Friuli-Venezia Giulia

COLLI GORIZIANO or COLLIO DOC

A large range of predominantly white wines from a hilly area close to the Yugoslav border.

RED These three varietals can reach very high standards.

🍇	Merlot, Cabernet franc, Pinot nero
🔟	1983, 1985, 1986, 1988, 1990
🍷	Within 1-4 years

WHITE In addition to a blended, dry, white wine that can be slightly *frizzantino,* there are eight dry white varietals.

🍇	Riesling Italico, Tocai Friulano, Malvasia, Pinot bianco, Pinot grigio, Ribolla, Sauvignon, Traminer
🔟	1983, 1986, 1988, 1990
🍷	Within 1-3 years

☆ Borgo Conventi, Livio Felluga, Marco Felluga, Conti Formentini, Gradmir Gradnik, Jermann, Doro Pricnic, Radikon, Russiz Superiore, Mario Schiopetto

COLLI ORIENTALI DEL FRIULI DOC

A larger, more prestigious area than its neighbour Colli Goriziano.

RED With the exception of the Pinot nero, red varietals are more successful here than they are in Colli Goriziano.

| 🍇 | Merlot, Cabernet franc, Cabernet sauvignon, Pinot nero, Refosco |

| 🔟 | 1983, 1985, 1986, 1988, 1990 |
| 🍷 | Between 3-8 years |

WHITE All these wines are pure varietals made in a dry style, with the exception of Verduzzo, which is an interesting, full-flavoured wine that may be dry or semi-sweet, and the famous, but overrated and overpriced, Picolit. (This is the only Picolit in Italy to have its own DOC.)

| 🍇 | Picolit, Pinot bianco, Pinot grigio, Ribolla, Riesling Renano, Sauvignon, Tocai Friulano, Verduzzo |

Sauvignon, Tocai Friulano, Verduzzo

[19] 1983, 1986, 1988, 1990

Within 1-3 years

☆ Abbazia di Rosazzo, Girolamo Dorigo, Giovanni Dri, Livio Felluga, Valle, Volpe Pasini

PICOLIT DOC
See Colli Orientali del Friuli DOC.

RONCO DELLE ACACIE VT
Abbazia di Rosazzo

This brilliant *barrique*-aged blend is 100 per cent Italian in style.

WHITE An aromatic bouquet combined with mouth-watering fruit flavours, finesse and beautifully understated new oak on the finish.

Pinot bianco, Ribolla, Malvasia, Tocai Friulano

[19] 1984, 1985, 1986, 1988, 1990

Between 3-7 years

SCHIOPPETTINO VT

An ancient Friulian variety, Schioppettino was nearly extinct until these wines suddenly became fashionable in the 1980s.

RED Very ripe and round wines with a fine, spicy-scented bouquet and rich fruit flavour that only attains great finesse with maturity.

Schioppettino

[19] 1983, 1985, 1986, 1988, 1990

Between 5-15 years

☆ Ronchi di Cialla, Ronco del Gmeniz, Giuseppe Toti

VINTAGE TUNINA VT
Jermann

One of Italy's greatest "super-deluxe" white wines. Whilst others in this style are disappointing and expensive, this wine justifies its price.

WHITE This wine has an aroma and flavour that is akin to a fine Alsatian Pinot Blanc and there is also the hint of a white Burgundy, but it also has a slightly bitter-sweet finish that is distinctly Italian.

Chardonnay, Pinot bianco, Sauvignon blanc, Picolit

[19] 1983, 1985, 1986, 1988, 1990

Between 5-10 years

The best Cabernet-based wines of Friuli-Venezia Giulia

DRAGARSKA VT, *Drufovka*
Cabernet franc, Cabernet sauvignon, Merlot

MONTSCLAPADE VT, *Girolamo Dorigo*
Cabernet franc, Cabernet sauvignon, Merlot, Malbec

RONCO DEL GMENIZ (COLLI ORIENTALI DOC)
Cabernet franc, Cabernet sauvignon, Merlot, Malbec

RONCO DEI ROSETI VT, *Abbazia di Rosazzo*
Cabernet franc, Cabernet sauvignon, Merlot, Limberger, Refosco, Tazzelenghe

Other wines of Friuli-Venezia Giulia

AQUILEA* DOC

A wide-ranging appellation of four varietal red wines and one blended one (Merlot, Cabernet, Cabernet Franc, Cabernet Sauvignon, Refosco dal Peduncolo Rosso); seven white varietals (Tocai Friulano, Pinot Bianco, Pinot Grigio, Riesling Renano, Sauvignon, Traminer, Verduzzo Friulano); and a rosé that must be at least 70 per cent Merlot. All are generally light, crisply-balanced wines, although some producers excel in better years.

CARSO* DOC

Basic Carso must be made from at least 70 per cent Terrano, which is the Mondeuse of France, while Terrano del Carso must be from a minimum of 85 per cent; both are deep, full, red wines. Malvasia del Carso is a rich and spicy, dry white wine.

FRANCONIA (BLAUFRÄNKISCH) VT

This is made from the Limberger of Germany in a fuller, darker style than is possible in its homeland, yet it still possesses the same light, fruity flavour.

GRAVE DEL FRIULI* DOC

This large appellation spreads out either side of the river Tagliamento between Sacile in the west and Cividale di Friuli in the east. It accounts for more than half of Friuli's total production. It is a large and complicated, multi-varietal DOC and although the overall quality of its wines does not allow it a place in the "fine" wine section, several wine-makers regularly produce fine wines. There are six red varietals (Merlot, Cabernet, Cabernet Franc, Cabernet

Sauvignon, Refosco, Pinot Nero); eight white varietals (Chardonnay, Tocai Friulano, Pinot Bianco, Pinot Grigio, Verduzzo, Riesling Renano, Sauvignon, Traminer Aromatico) and a Cabernet franc-dominated *rosato* blend.

ISONZO* DOC

A small area south of Colli Goriziano, but not quite in the same class. The two red varietals (Merlot, Cabernet) are most successful and, of the eight white varietals, the Sauvignon is the most promising.

LATISANA DOC

An area that stretches from the central section of the Grave del Friuli to the Adriatic coast at Lignano Sabbiadoro. The red varietals are Merlot, Cabernet and Refosco

and the white are Tocai Friulano, Pinot Bianco, Pinot Grigio and Verduzzo Friulano.

LISON-PRAMAGGIORE DOC

This DOC of Veneto overlaps part of Friuli. *See* Fine wines of the Veneto.

TACELENGHE or TAZZELENGHE VT

This red wine's name is the local dialect for *tazzalingua,* which means a sharpness on the tongue, and is indicative of the wine's tannic nature. However, it does soften after five or six years in bottle.

TERRANO DEL CARSO VT

See Carso DOC.

Fine wines of the Veneto

LISON-PRAMAGGIORE DOC

This new DOC, in the very east of the Veneto, has combined the three DOCs of Cabernet di Pramaggiore, Merlot di Pramaggiore and Tocai di Lison into one and expanded the appellation.

RED The Cabernet is a fine, chocolatey blend that can attain significant finesse after five or six years in bottle; the prolific Merlot is more serious in Pramaggiore than in any other area of the Veneto, especially when given structure by the addition of 10 per cent Cabernet.

Cabernet franc, Cabernet sauvignon, Merlot, Pinot gris, Refosco dal Peduncolo Rosso

[19] 1983, 1985, 1986, 1988, 1990

Between 3-8 years

WHITE Tocai Italico, as the Tocai di Lison is now called, is a pleasant, refreshingly dry, fruity, white wine with a light richness. The new varietals have yet to establish a reputation.

Pinot bianco, Riesling Italico, Sauvignon, Tocai Italico and Verduzzo

[19] 1983, 1985, 1986, 1988, 1990

Within 1-3 years

☆ Paolo de Lorenzi, La Frattoria, Santa Margherita, Tenuta Sant'Ana, Torresella

PRATO DI CANZIO (BREGANZE DOC)
Maculan

One wine stands out in the Breganze DOC as exceptional by any standards.

WHITE This wine has a rich, tangy

flavour, some spice, an excellent balance of fruit and acidity and a hint of sweet oak on the nose and aftertaste.

Tocai, Pinot bianco, Riesling

[19] 1985, 1986, 1988, 1990

Within 2-5 years

RECIOTO DI SOAVE DEI CAPITELLI (RECIOTO DI SOAVE DOC)
Anselmi

This wine is a revelation. It has a gloriously golden colour; a luxuriant bouquet suggestive of honey, flowers, nuts and molasses; a fabulously rich, sweet and complex flavour of honeyed-spicy fruit and a fine, smoky-creamy oak finish. I recommend any vintage. The wines should be drunk between 3-10 years.

SOAVE DOC

Most examples of this over-produced wine are thin and acidic, but there are a few enjoyable wines from the central, hilly, *classico* area.

🍇	Minimum of 70% Garganega, and a maximum of 30% Trebbini
🗓	1982, 1983, 1985, 1988, 1990
🍷	Within 1-4 years

☆ Bolla's Vignetti di Frosca, Masi's "Col Baraca", Pieropan's "La Rocca", Santi's "Monteforte", Anselmi's "Capitel Foscarino" and "Monteforte"

SOAVE CLASSICO CAPITEL FOSCARINO (SOAVE CLASSICO DOC)

Anselmi

If this wine is indicative of how classic Soave once tasted, then there is little wonder that it achieved such widespread fame. Its rich, crisp fruit can only be obtained from moderate yields of perfectly ripe, healthy grapes. Roberto Anselmi cuts off whole bunches of grapes during the summer to limit the potential harvest. I recommend any vintage to be drunk at between 2-4 years of age.

SOAVE CLASSICO MONTEFORTE (SOAVE CLASSICO DOC)

Anselmi

This Soave is full of the vanilla aroma of new oak and, although I would not like to see all Soave made in this style, such expressive and innovative winemaking is only to be encouraged. I recommend any vintage. The wine should be drunk between two and four years.

TORCOLATO VT

Maculan

Torcolato is made from *passito* grapes and is very rich and succulently sweet at the same time. This version is the most elegant *passito* wine I have encountered.

🍇	Tocai, Vespaiolo
🗓	1980, 1982, 1983, 1986
🍷	Between 5-10 years

"VALPOLICELLA" RIPASSO VT

This style of wine has long been traditional in the Veneto. The best young Valpolicella is pumped into tanks or barrels previously used for *recioto* that still contain its lees. When mixed with the young wine, active yeast cells remaining in this sediment precipitate a second fermentation. This increases the alcohol content of the wine and gives it some of the *recioto* character. Once the wines have gone through this process, they cannot bear the Valpolicella appellation and are thus sold as *Vino da Tavola* under various brand names.

🗓	1981, 1983, 1985, 1986, 1988
🍷	Between 6-15 years

☆ Allegrini's "La Grola", Boscaini's "Le Cane", Fratelli Tedeschi's "Capitel San Rocco", Masi's "Campo Fiorin", Bertani's "Catullo"

The best Cabernet-based wines of the Veneto

BRENTINO (BREGANZE DOC), *Maculan*
Cabernet franc, Cabernet sauvignon, Merlot

CAPO DEL MONTE VT, *Fattoria di Ogliano*
Cabernet franc, Marzemino

CASTELLO DI RONCADE VT, *Barone Ciani Bassetti*
Cabernet franc, Cabernet sauvignon, Merlot, Malbec, Petit verdot

LA RIVE ROSE (COLLI BERICI DOC), *Villa dal Ferro-Lazzarini*
Cabernet franc, Cabernet sauvignon

VENEGAZZU DELLA CASA VT, *Conte Loredan-Gasparini*
Cabernet franc, Cabernet sauvignon, Merlot, Malbec

VIGNETO FRATTA (BREGANZE DOC), *Maculan*
Cabernet sauvignon, Cabernet franc

Other wines of the Veneto

BARDOLINO* DOC

Dry, sometimes *frizzante,* light reds and rosé *(chiaretto)* wines that can be interesting.

BIANCO DI CUSTOZA* DOC

Scented, dry white wines with a smooth aftertaste and sparkling white wines from various grapes grown on the shores of Lake Garda.

BIANCO TOARA VT

Dry, scented white wines made around the village of Toara in the Colli Berici district.

BREGANZE* DOC

Vinous, slightly tannic, blended red wines and dry, fresh white wine blends. There are two red varietals (Cabernet, Pinot Nero) and three white ones (Pinot Bianco, Pinot Grigio, Vespaiolo).

CAPITEL SAN ROCCO* VT

Fratelli Tedeschi

A red wine that is Tedeschi's equivalent of Masi's "Campo Fiorin"

(*see* "Valpolicella" *ripasso*) and a more interesting white – a dry, aromatic and characterful version of Soave.

COLLI BERICI DOC

Three red varietals (Merlot, Tocai Rosso, Cabernet) and four white (Garganega, Tocai Bianco, Sauvignon, Pinot Bianco), produced in an area immediately south of Vicenza. The Cabernet can be rich and grassy with chunky-chocolatey fruit, the red Tocai is unusual and interesting, but the others are unexciting.

COLLI EUGANEI DOC

Bordering Colli Berici to the southeast, this area produces soft, full-bodied, dry or semi-sweet red wine blends and Cabernet and Merlot varietals. There are four white varietals and smooth, dry or semi-sweet white blends. The basic blended *rosso* is the most consistent wine.

GAMBELLARA DOC

Scented, dry or sometimes semi-sweet, white wines and fruity, semi-sweet, still, semi-sparkling or sparkling white *recioto*. There is also a sweet, smooth *vin santo*.

LESSINI DURELLO DOC

This is a new appellation for dry white wine from the Durello grape grown between Verona and Vicenza.

MASIANCO VT

Masi

Dry and fruity white wine made from Garganega, Trebbiano and Durello grapes.

MONTELLO E COLLI ASOLANI DOC

Red varietals (Merlot, Cabernet) and white varietals including Prosecco.

PIAVE or VINI DEL PIAVE* DOC

A large area to the west of Lison-Pramaggiore producing four red varietals (Merlot, Cabernet, Pinot Nero, Raboso) and four white varietals (Tocai, Verduzzo, Pinot Bianco, Pinot Grigio). The Cabernet and Raboso can be really quite good.

PROSECCO DI CONEGLIANO-VALDOBBIADENE DOC

Dry and semi-sweet, fizzy, white wines that have large bubbles and a coarse, dull flavour. A still version is also produced.

RABOSO* DOC

The indigenous Raboso grape has long produced excellent-value *Vino da Tavola* red wines that are full of sunny fruit and capable of improving after two to three years in bottle, but it has only recently acquired DOC status.

RECIOTO BIANCO DI CAMPOCIESA* VT

Soft, sweet, well-scented, golden-coloured white wines made from *passito* grapes.

RECIOTO DI SOAVE DOC

Naturally sweet, *liquoroso* or *spumante* Soave made from *passito*

grapes. The one outstanding wine is made by Anselmi. *See* Recioto di Soave dei Capitelli, p.253.

RECIOTO DELLA VALPOLICELLA DOC

These wines, which are made from *passito* grapes, have a very deep colour and a powerful Port-like flavour. Dry *amarone* and *spumante* styles are also produced.

VALPANTENA DOC

Single-village Valpolicella or Recioto della Valpolicella.

VALPOLICELLA DOC

The American wine writer Robert Parker describes most Valpolicella as "insipid industrial garbage" and I would agree with him. Exceptions are made by Quintarelli, Alighieri, and also include Bolla's Vigneti di Jago. Valpolicella at its best is full of juicy, cherry-fruit flavours.

Central Italy – West

This area of Italy is totally dominated by the red Sangiovese wines from the hills and tiny valleys of central Tuscany, between Florence and the Umbria-Latium border. There are few other wines of any repute produced in the region and little to connect them.

TUSCANY (TOSCANA)

PROUD POSSESSOR OF THREE OF ITALY'S SIX DOCGs, Tuscany is also a centre of experimental winemaking. The powerful red Vino Nobile di Montepulciano was the very first of Italy's DOCGs and was followed by another Sangiovese clone, Brunello di Montalcino. More recently, Chianti was made DOCG, with Carmignano tipped for future classification. These are the most famous names in Tuscany, but although many of the region's finest wines bear them, not all do and the quality of the wines granted DOCG status can be very variable – notably Chianti. This fact was recognized by the Tuscan producers themselves, who actively sought the ideal solution of a DOCG for the best of Chianti. Two basic approaches towards achieving this aim were to either apply DOCG to the Chianti Classico area, where most of the finest wines have traditionally been made, and leave the rest as DOC Chianti, or, recognizing that some exceptional estates exist outside this central zone, grant DOCG status to the best 10 per cent of the production, regardless of origin. Unfortunately

FACTORS AFFECTING TASTE AND QUALITY

Location
Located between the Apennines to the north and east and the Tyrrhenian Sea to the west.

Climate
Summers are long and fairly dry and winters are less severe than in northern Italy. Heat and lack of rain can be a problem throughout the area during the growing season.

Aspect
Vineyards are usually sited on hillsides for good drainage and exposure to the sun.
Deliberate use is made of altitude to offset the heat, with red grapes growing up to 550 metres (1,800 ft) and white grapes up to 700 metres (2,275 ft). The higher the vines, the longer the ripening season and the greater the acidity of the grapes.

Soil
Very complex soils with gravel, limestone and clay outcrops predominating. In Tuscany a rocky, schistous soil known locally as *galestro* covers most of the best vineyards.

Viticulture and vinification
Recent years have seen much experimentation, particularly in Tuscany, with classic French grapes, especially Cabernet sauvignon. These have been used with traditional grape varieties such as Sangiovese and on their own. The results, whilst atypical of the area, are perhaps the most stunning of any region in Italy for this sort of wine, with great wines such as Sassicaia and Tignanello widely acclaimed to be world class.
A traditional speciality is the sweet, white *vin santo* made from *passito* grapes dried on straw mats in attics. It is aged for up to six years, often in a type of *solera* system (*see* p.285).

Primary grape varieties
Sangiovese, Malvasia, Trebbiano

Secondary grape varieties
Aglianico, Barbera, Cabernet sauvignon, Canaiolo, Cesanese, Chardonnay, Colorino, Gamay, Grechetto, Mammolo, Merlot, Pinot bianco, Pinot grigio, Roussane, Sagrantino, Sauvignon blanc, Sémillon, Verdello, Vermentino, Vernaccia

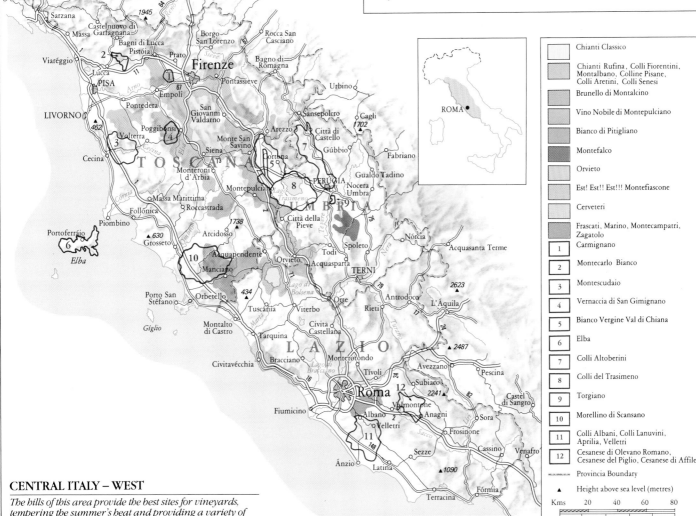

	Chianti Classico
	Chianti Rufina, Colli Fiorentini, Montalbano, Colline Pisane, Colli Aretini, Colli Senesi
	Brunello di Montalcino
	Vino Nobile di Montepulciano
	Bianco di Pitigliano
	Montefalco
	Orvieto
	Est! Est!! Est!!! Montefiascone
	Cerveteri
	Frascati, Marino, Montecampatri, Zagatolo
1	Carmignano
2	Montecarlo Bianco
3	Montescudaio
4	Vernaccia di San Gimignano
5	Bianco Vergine Val di Chiana
6	Elba
7	Colli Altoberini
8	Colli del Trasimeno
9	Torgiano
10	Morellino di Scansano
11	Colli Albani, Colli Lanuvini, Aprilia, Velletri
12	Cesanese di Olevano Romano, Cesanese del Piglio, Cesanese di Affile

Provincia Boundary

▲ Height above sea level (metres)

CENTRAL ITALY – WEST

The hills of this area provide the best sites for vineyards, tempering the summer's heat and providing a variety of microclimates suitable for classic French grape varieties as well as the traditional ones.

those responsible for drawing up the new regulations applied DOCG status to the whole area and to all Chianti wines. It is still theoretically possible for Chiantis to be refused DOCG, and a few awful wines are, but the selection by tasting is a public sham. Any system that does not recognize that the majority of Chianti is mediocre is doomed.

The largest number of exceptional Tuscan wines are the "new" *barrique*-aged ones. Their origins stretch back to 1948, when a vineyard for the now famous Sassicaia wine first planted by Incisa della Rochetta with Cabernet sauvignon vines reputedly from Château Lafite-Rothschild. This became so successful that a new red wine called Tignanello was introduced by Antinori in the wake of the 1971 vintage. This wine was a compromise between Tuscany and Bordeaux, with Sangiovese used as the base and 20 per cent of Cabernet sauvignon blended in. Until Tignanello appeared, nobody truly appreciated the harmony that could be achieved between these two grapes: it is akin to the natural balance of Cabernet and Merlot, only the Cabernet adds weight to the Sangiovese, and provides balance through satisfying flavour. Tignanello sparked off the current new-wave of Tuscan wines.

UMBRIA

Orvieto is Umbria's best-known and best-forgotten wine. Next to Frascati and Soave, it is the most used and abused name in the Italian restaurants of the world. While there are a few exciting Orvietos, such as Bigi's Vigneto Torricella, they are in a lamentably small minority. One of Umbria's few deservedly famous names is Lungarotti's "Rubesco" Torgiano, whose reputation led to the establishment of the Torgiano DOC. Lungarotti is also the clear leader when it comes to producing Umbria's excellent new-wave wines. These utilize numerous grape varieties, both native and French, and are thus produced in numerous styles, but they are nearly always aged in new-oak *barriques*.

LATIUM (LAZIO)

One of the country's largest regions, Latium appropriately boasts one of its largest selling wines, Frascati, the Latin Liebfraumilch. Unfortunately for a region that can boast one of the classic wines of antiquity, Falernum, it has few quality wines. However, Latium's only two fine wines, Boncompagni Ludovisi's "Fiorano" and Cantina Colacicchi's "Torre Ercolana", both innovative Cabernet-Merlot blends, are very good indeed.

AVERAGE ANNUAL PRODUCTION

Region	DOC production	Total production
Tuscany	1 million hl (11 million cases)	4 million hl (44 million cases)
Umbria	165,000 hl (2 million cases)	1.7 million hl (18 million cases)
Latium	540,000 hl (6 million cases)	6 million hl (67 million cases)

Percentage of total Italian production: Tuscany, 5.2%; Umbria, 2.2%; Latium, 7.8%.

Tradition and innovation, above
This tranquil landscape appears to have remained unchanged for many centuries, but, while Tuscan winemaking is steeped in tradition, the area is now also experimenting with different grape varieties and barrique *aging.*

Vernaccia vines in autumn, above
These vines grow exclusively around the medieval Tuscan town of San Gimignano, whose impressive towers can be seen in the distance. From good producers, the white Vernaccia is a deliciously crisp, fruity dry wine.

Fine wines of Tuscany

BARRIQUE WINES VT

Without doubt, the new-wave of pure varietal or blended wines aged in small new oak *barriques* is the most exciting development in the recent history of Tuscan wines. The best are listed below, followed by their producers, in *italic*.

Pure Sangiovese

BORGO AMOROSA, *Amorosa*

BORRO CEPPARELLO, *Isole e Olena*

CAPANELLE ROSSO, *Capanelle*

CEPARELLO, *Isole e Olena*

LA CORTE, *Castello di Querceto*

FLACCIANELLO DELLA PIAVE, *Fontodi*

GROSSO SENESE, *Podere Il Palazzino*

PALAZZO ALTESI, *Altesino*

LE PERGOLE TORTE, *Monte Vertine*

QUERCIAGRANDE, *Podere Capaccia*

SANGIOVETO DI COLTIBUONO, *Badia a Coltibuono*

VINATTIERI ROSSO, *Vinattieri*

Pure Cabernet sauvignon

SASSICAIA, *Marchesi Incisa della Rochetta*

TAVERNELLE, *Villa Banfi*

50/50 Sangiovese and Cabernet sauvignon

BRUNO DI ROCCA, *Vecchie Terre di Montefili*

Sangiovese-dominated blends

CABREO PODERE IL BORGO, *Ruffino*

COLTASSALA, *Castello di Volpaia*

I COLTRI, *Melini*

I GRIFI, *Avignonesi*

CONCERTO, *Castello di Fonterutoli*

I SODI DI SAN NICCOLO, *Castellare di Castellina*

SOLATIO BASILICA, *Villa Cafaggio*

TIGNANELLO, *Marchesi Antinori*

VIGORELLO, *San Felice*

Cabernet sauvignon-dominated blends

GHIAIE DELLA FURBA, *Villa de Capezzana*

MORMORETO, *Marchesi Frescobaldi*

SAMMARCO, *Castello dei Rampolla*

SOLAIA, *Marchesi Antinori*

Pure Chardonnay

CABREO VIGNETO LA PIETRA, *Ruffino*

COLLINE DI AMA, *Castello di Ama*

FONTANELLE, *Villa Banfi*

VILLA DI CAPEZZANA, *Contini Bonacossi*

White *liquoroso* blends

SASSOLATO, *Villa Cilnia*

Other *bianco* blends

TORRICELLA, *Barone Ricasoli*

BRUNELLO DI MONTALCINO DOCG

One of Italy's most prestigious wines, made from Brunello, a localized clone of the Sangiovese. Many of the relatively unknown producers offer truly classic wines.

RED The general notion is that these wines should be so thick with harsh tannins that they must be left for at least 20 years. If these are ripe skin tannins and there is sufficient fruit, this can be a formula for a wine of classic stature. However, too many Brunello wines are macerated for too long, often not destalked and the majority of tannins found in even the most expensive are incapable of softening.

The producers recommended below all make wines that require at least 10 years maturation, but they are packed with fruit that will develop into layers of rich, complex, smoky-spicy, plummy-fruit flavours.

🍇 Brunello

🍷 1982, 1983, 1985, 1988, 1990

🍶 Between 10-25 years

☆ Altesino, Campogiovanni, Caprilli, Castelgiocondo, Constanti, Lisini, Pertimali, Poggio Attico, Talenti, Tenuta Carpazo, Tenuta Il Poggione, Val di Suga

CARMIGNANO DOC

A tiny appellation west of Florence, it is the classic Carmignano *rosso* that is a fine wine and may be awarded DOCG status. A fresh and fruity *rosato* and a *vin santo* are also made.

RED Very much like medium-bodied Chianti, but with less acidity, which, with its Cabernet content gives a chocolatey-finesse to the fruit.

🍇 45-65% Sangiovese, 10-20% Canaiolo nero, 6-10% Cabernet sauvignon, 10-20% Trebbiano, Canaiolo bianco, Malvasia, and up to a maximum of 5% Mammolo, Colorino

🍷 1982, 1983, 1985, 1988, 1990

🍶 Between 4-10 years

☆ Fattoria di Artimino, Fattoria di Bacchereto, Contini Bonacossi (Villa di Capezzana, Villa di Trefiano), Fattoria Il Poggiolo

CHIANTI DOCG

When Chianti was granted DOCG status the yields were reduced, the amount of white grapes allowed in Chianti *classico* was cut down and up to 10 per cent Cabernet sauvignon was permitted in the blend. However, the DOCG was applied to the entire Chianti production area and thus has failed to be a guarantee of quality.

RED The best basic Chianti is ruby to garnet coloured, medium bodied, and full of juicy cherry and plummy fruit flavours. It is enjoyable to quaff but is not of DOCG standard.

The finest wines are usually sold as Chianti Classico (from the original Chianti area), Chianti Rufina (from a small area northeast of Florence) or Chianti Colli Fiorentini (which bridges the Classico and Rufina areas).

🍇 75-90% Sangiovese, 5-10% Canaiolo nero, 5-10% (or 2-5% if *classico*) Trebbiano, Malvasia, and up to a maximum of 10% Cabernet and other specified varieties

🍷 1982, 1983, 1985, 1988, 1990

🍶 Within 3-5 years (inexpensive, everyday drinking), between 4-8 years (more serious Chianti), between 6-20 years (finest *classico*)

☆ Badia a Coltibuono, Capanelle, Castello di Ama, Castello Gabbiano, Castello Querceto, Castello di Rampolla, Castello di San Paolo in Rosso, Castello Vicchiomaggio, Castello di Volpaia, Fattoria Il Paradiso, Fattoria di Vetrice, Marchesi Frescobaldi (Montesodi, Castello di Nipozzano, Poggio a Remole), Fontodi, Fossi, Il Palazzino, Isole e Olena, Lamole di Lamole, Monsanto Il Poggio, Monte Vertine, Nozzole, Pasolini, Podere Emilio Constanti, Podere Il Palazzino, Barone Ricasoli Brolio, Rocca delle Macie, Ruffino (Aziano, Riserva Ducale), Selvapiana, Tenuta di Capezzana, Tenuta di Poggio, Villa Antinori (Santa Christina, Riserva del Marchese), Villa Cafaggio, Villa Cilnia

ROSSO DI MONTALCINO DOC

This appellation is for lesser or declassified wines of Brunello di Montalcino or wines made from young vines. As a rule they are more accessible in their youth than Brunello.

🍇 Brunello

🍶 Between 8-25 years

☆ Altesino, Campogiovanni, Castelgiocondo, Lisini, Tenuta Carpazo, Tenuta Il Poggione, Val di Suga

VINO NOBILE DI MONTEPULCIANO* DOCG

Made largely from Prugnolo gentile, a clone of Sangiovese, these wines come from Montepulciano, a part of Chianti that used to be called Colli Senesi prior to the introduction of Chianti DOCG. A few Vino Nobile producers make wines that deserve DOCG status, but they are generally overrated and overpriced.

RED The finest wines resemble fine *riserva* Chianti Classico, but have a more exuberant character, with generous ripe-fruit flavours of cherry and plum.

🍇 50-70% Prugnolo gentile, 10-20% Canaiolo, 10-20% Malvasia, Trebbiano, and up to a maximum of 5% Grechetto bianco (known locally as Pulcianculo) or Mammolo

🍷 1982, 1983, 1985, 1988, 1990

🍶 Between 6-25 years

☆ Avignonesi, Podere Boscarelli, Fratelli Bologna Buonsignori, Tenuta Sant' Agnese-Fanetti, Fassati

Tuscany's best dry sparkling wines

BRUT DI CAPEZZANA

VILLA BANFI PINOT OLTREPÒ BRUT

VILLA BANFI BRUT

These wines are all made by the méthode champenoise.

Other wines of Tuscany

ALEATICO* VT

Rare, rich, sweet red wines.

ALICANTE* VT

Erik Banti

A fat, juicy-rich and spicy, medium-bodied red wine.

BIANCO DELLA VAL DI NIEVOLE DOC

Dry, slightly *frizzante* white wines and soft, white *vin santo.*

BIANCO DI PITIGLIANO* DOC

Delicate, dry, reasonably characterful white wines.

BIANCO PISANO DI SAN TORPÉ DOC

Dry, vinous, white wines and dry or semi-sweet *vin santo.*

BIANCO VERGINE DELLA VALDICHIANA DOC

Rich, slightly sweet white wines with a bitter aftertaste.

BOLGHERI DOC

Delicate, dry white wines and dry, slightly scented, Sangiovese *rosato.*

CANDIA DEI COLLI APUANI DOC

Delicate, slightly aromatic, dry or semi-sweet white wines.

CERTINAIA* VT

Castello di San Paolo in Rosso

Although I have not tasted this relatively new wine, it has such a good reputation that it should be recommended. It is produced in Chianti from black grapes only and aged in conventional large Slavonian oak casks.

ELBA* DOC

Made from the same grapes as Chianti, the reds are very similar in style. The dry white wines are very ordinary and *spumante* red and white wines are also produced.

GALESTRO* VT

Ultra-clean, light, fresh and delicately fruity, dry white wines produced by a *consorzio* of wineries to agreed standards, including minimum alcoholic strength.

GRATTAMACCO* VT

Podere di Grattamacco

Moreish red wine based on Colorino and Sangiovese grapes, and a dry, fruity white wine.

MAREMMA* VT

Well-made, light and fruity, dry, red, white and rosé wines from the coastal Maremma hills.

MONTE ANTICO* VT

Various red and white Chianti-like wines from the hills close to Montalcino.

MONTECARLO* DOC

Some interesting dry white wines are beginning to appear in this area, which is halfway between Carmignano and the coast. Although based on the bland Trebbiano, supplementary varieties (Sémillon, Pinot grigio, Pinot bianco, Sauvignon blanc, Roussane and Vermentino) may account for 30-40 per cent of the blend, thus allowing growers to express their own individual styles, from light and delicate to full and rich, either with or without *barrique* aging.

MONTESCUDAIO DOC

Vinous dry white wine; soft, slightly fruity, red wine; and soft, white, *vin santo.*

MORELLINO DI SCANSANO* DOC

Some good Brunello-like wines from 100 per cent pure Sangiovese.

MOSCADELLO DI MONTALCINO DOC

Aromatic, sweet, still and *frizzante,* white Muscat wines and sweet, fortified, white wines.

PARRINA* DOC

Soft, Sangiovese-based red wines with attractively delicate fruit and less interesting dry white wines from the tiniest, most southerly DOC in Tuscany.

POMINO* DOC

This Pinot bianco, Chardonnay and Trebbiano blend from within the Chianti Rufina was first commercialized by Marchesi de' Frescobaldi and has now been made a DOC. It includes a fine red Sangiovese, Canaiolo and Cabernet sauvignon blend and a semi-sweet red and white *vin santo.*

ROSATO DELLA LEGA CT

Dry rosé wines made by members of the Chianti Classico *consorzio.*

ROSSO DELLA LEGA VT

Everyday red wines made by members of the Chianti Classico *consorzio.*

ROSSO DELLE COLLINE LUCCHESI* DOC

Soft, Chianti-like reds and dry white Trebbiano wines.

VAL D'ARBIA DOC

Dry, fruity, white wines and dry to sweet *vin santo.*

VERNACCIA DI SAN GIMIGNANO* DOC

Dry, fresh white wines, some of which can be deliciously crisp and full of vibrant, characterful fruit.

VIN SANTO* VT

A red or white *passito* wine that may be sweet, semi-sweet or dry.

VINO DELLA SIGNORA VT

Poggio al Sole

Smooth, aromatic, dry white wine.

Fine wines of Umbria

Umbria does not have Tuscany's reputation for new-wave wines, but there are some exciting *Vini da Tavola* that make more interesting drinking than most DOCs. The best wines are listed below, be they *Vino da Tavola* or DOC.

Red

RUBESCO TORGIANO, *Lungarotti*
Sangiovese, Canaiolo

RUBESCO TORGIANO RISERVA VIGNA MONTICCHIO, *Lungarotti*
Sangiovese, Canaiolo

CABERNET SAUVIGNON DI MIRALDUOLO, *Lungarotti*
Cabernet sauvignon

CASTELLO DI MONTORO, *Marchesi Patrizi Montoro*
Sangiovese, Merlot, Barbera, Montepulciano

DECUGNANO DEI BARBI ROSSO, *Decugnano dei Barbi*
Sangiovese, Montepulciano

ROSSO D'ARQUATA, *Adanti*
Barbera, Canaiolo, Merlot

RUBINO, *Colle del Sole-Polidori*
Sangiovese, Merlot

SAN GIORGIO, *Lungarotti*
Sangiovese, Canaiolo, Cabernet sauvignon

White

CASTELLO DELLA SALA, *Marchesi Antinori*
Trebbiano, Verdello, Grechetto, Sauvignon blanc, Pinot bianco

CERVARO DI MIRALDUOLO, *Lungarotti*
Chardonnay

GRECHETTO, *Bigi*
Grechetto

TORGIANO BIANCO RISERVA TORRE DI GIANO, *Lungarotti*
Trebbiano, Grechetto

Other wines of Umbria

COLLI ALTOTIBERINI DOC

This DOC is in the hilly upper Tiber valley area, where interesting, dry whites, firm but fruity reds and dry, slightly fruity rosés are produced. The reds are a blend of Sangiovese and Merlot.

COLLI DEL TRASIMENO DOC

A very large DOC area on the Tuscan border, with vineyards in the hills and on the lakeside slopes of the impressive Lake Trasimeno. The dry and off-dry whites are ordinary, but the reds in which the bitter edge of Sangiovese is softened with Gamay, are more interesting.

COLLI PERUGINI DOC

Dry, slightly fruity, Trebbiano-based white wines; full-bodied red wines and dry, fresh rosé wines, from primarily Sangiovese grapes, produced in a large area between Colli del Trasimeno and the Tiber, covering six communes in the province of Perugni and one in the province of Terni.

GRECHETTO or GRECO* VT

Clean, fresh, dry and sweet white wines that have a pleasant floral aroma but seldom excel, the exception being Bigi's Grechetto, which is aged in oak.

This popular, widely exported, dry or semi-sweet wine is generally very disappointing, but Bigi's Vigneto Torricella is outstanding, and there are other very respectable wines from various producers. The best semi-sweet or *abbocato* style will include a small proportion of botrytized grapes.

TORGIANO DOC

This DOC was built on the back of the reputation of one wine, Lungarotti's Rubesco Torgiano, which is rated under "Fine wines of Umbria" with its sister white wines. Both red and dry white wines are allowed in the DOC.

VIN SANTO VT

Umbria's ubiquitous *passito* wine which is similar to Tuscan examples.

The wines of Latium

Cabernet-based wines

There are only two of any real quality in Latium and they are also the region's two finest wines.

FIORANO, *Boncompagni Ludovisi*
Cabernet sauvignon, Merlot

TORRE ERCOLANA, *Cantina Colacicchi*
Cabernet sauvignon, Merlot, Cesanese

APRILIA DOC

The uninspiring wines in this DOC include two red varietals (Merlot, Sangiovese) and one white (Trebbiano). The washed-out flavours indicate that official yields are far too high.

BIANCO CAPENA DOC

A large DOC northeast of Rome producing dry and semi-sweet white wines.

CASTELLI ROMANI VT

Rarely exciting dry and semi-sweet white, red and rosé wines.

CECUBO VT

Cantine Cenatiempo

Deep-coloured, sturdy red with rustic charm.

CERVETERI DOC

Rustic reds, dry and semi-sweet white wines of decent, everyday quality grown along the coast northwest of Rome.

CESANESE DEL PIGLIO DOC

This DOC covers a complicated range of basically simple red wines, from grapes grown in a hilly area southeast of Rome. The styles include dry, off-dry, medium-dry, semi-sweet and sweet, and may be still, *frizzantino, frizzante* or *spumante*.

CESANESE DI AFFILE DOC

The same styles as Cesanese del Piglio from a neighbouring area.

CESANESE DI OLEVANO ROMANO DOC

A smaller DOC covering the same styles as Cesanese Del Piglio.

COLLE PICCHIONI* VT

Paola Di Mauro

A robust and characterful red wine made from Merlot, Cesanese and Sangiovese grapes grown on volcanic soil in the Castelli Romani region.

COLLI ALBANI DOC

Soft and fruity, dry and semi-sweet white wines that can be *spumante*.

COLLI LANUVINI* DOC

Smooth, white wines that may be dry or semi-sweet.

CORI DOC

Little-seen and rarely exciting, dry, semi-sweet, or sweet white wines and smooth, vinous reds.

EST! EST!! EST!!! DI MONTEFIASCONE DOC

The name is the most memorable thing about these dry or semi-sweet white wines made of Trebbiano and Malvasia. The story as to why the

wine is so named goes something like this: in the twelfth century a gluttonous German bishop by the name of Johann Fugger was ordered to go to Rome for the coronation of Henry V. In order to drink well on his journey, he despatched ahead of him his major-domo with orders to visit all the inns along the route and mark those offering the best wine with the word *"Est"*, short for *"Vinum est bonum"*. When he arrived at Montefiascone, he so enjoyed the local wine that he chalked *"Est! Est!! Est!!!"*. Fugger must have been in full agreement because, as soon as he tasted the wine, he gave up his journey and remained in Montefiascone until his death. It is uncertain how much truth there is to this story, although a tomb in the village church bears Fugger's name. However, whose body it contains and whether it is indeed seven hundred years old, is open to speculation.

FALERNO or FALERNUM VT

Cantine Cenatiempo

Falernum was the famous wine of ancient Rome. Its modern equivalent is a typically dark-coloured and rustically rich Aglianico wine, the best of which must be the Villa Matilde *riserva*, which has a full aroma and a better balance than most. A dry white also exists.

FRASCATI DOC

In the past these wines were invariably flabby or oxidized. Improvements in vinification techniques have made a difference, but today most are no more than light, dry and bland. The only exceptions to this in my experience come from Colli di Catone, Villa Simone and, occasionally, Fontana Candida's Vigneti Santa Teresa. The wines are mostly dry, but semi-sweet, sweet and *spumante* styles are also made. Frascati is from Trebbiano and Malvasia grapes.

MARINO* DOC

Typically light and unexciting Trebbiano and Malvasia blend that may be dry, semi-sweet or *spumante*. Paola di Mauro's deliciously rich and caramelized "Oro" stands out due to its relatively high proportion of Malvasia grapes, and the fact that it receives a prefermentation on its skins and is matured in *barriques*.

MONTECOMPATRI-COLONNA DOC

These dry or semi-sweet, Malvasia-based white wines may bear the name of one or both of the above towns.

VELLETRI DOC

Uninspiring, dry or semi-sweet white wines and vinous reds from the Castelli Romani area.

ZAGAROLO DOC

Tiny production of dry or semi-sweet white wines from grapes grown east of Frascati.

Central Italy – East

This long area comprises the regions of Emilia-Romagna, the Marches, the Abruzzi and Molise. The best wines come from the Marches and the Abruzzi but Emilia-Romagna's Lambrusco is exported in vast quantities.

IF THIS REGION, WHICH EXTENDS ACROSS almost the entire width of northern Italy into Piedmont, appears geographically to wander off its central-east designation, it certainly does not topographically, for every hectare lies east of the Apennines on initially hilly ground that flattens out into alluvial plains that stretch towards the Adriatic.

EMILIA-ROMAGNA

Emilia-Romagna is protected on its western flank by the Apennines, from which seven major and many minor rivers rise. The rich soil results in abundant production of grapes, the three most prolific varieties being Lambrusco, Trebbiano and Albana, which produces rustic white wines that have, unaccountably, been given Italy's first DOCG for a white wine. Emilia-Romagna does, however, have some genuinely outstanding wines.

THE ABRUZZI (ABRUZZO)

The Abruzzi has only one fine wine – Montepulciano d'Abruzzo – but its hills offer such a range of microclimates and soils that

FACTORS AFFECTING TASTE AND QUALITY

 Location
This area stretches along the Adriatic coast, from Molise in the south right up to Emilia-Romagna.

Climate
The influence of the Mediterranean provides generally hot and dry summers, which get progressively hotter as one travels south, and cool winters. In hilly regions microclimates are created by the effects of altitude and aspect.

 Aspect
The best vineyards are invariably to be found on well-drained, foothill sites, but viticulture is spread across every imaginable type of terrain, with a heavy concentration on flat plains, particularly along the Po Valley in Emilia-Romagna, where grapes are produced in abundance.

Soil
Mostly alluvial, with outcrops of granite and limestone.

Viticulture and vinification
A wide variety of viticultural practices and vinification techniques are used. Much bulk-blended wine originates here, but some producers retain the most worthwhile traditions and augment them with modern methods.

Grape varieties
Albana, Barbarossa, Barbera, Bianchello, Bonarda, Cabernet franc, Cabernet sauvignon, Cagnina, Chardonnay, Ciliegiolo, Lambrusco, Maceratino, Malvasia, Merlot, Montepulciano, Ortrugo, Pagadebit, Pinot bianco, Pinot grigio, Pinot nero, Riesling Italico, Sangiovese, Sauvignon, Toscano, Trebbiano, Verdicchio, Vernaccia

AVERAGE ANNUAL PRODUCTION

Region	DOC production	Total production
Emilia-Romagna	600,000 hl (6.6 million cases)	11 million hl (122 million cases)
Abruzzi	250,000 hl (2.7 million cases)	4.5 million hl (50 million cases)
Marches	275,000 hl (3 million cases)	2.5 million hl (28 million cases)
Molise	450,000 (5 million cases)	550,000 hl (6 million cases)

Percentage of total Italian production: Emilia-Romagna, 14%; Abruzzi, 6%; Marches, 3%; Molise, 0.7%.

it should be capable of producing a variety of them. But winemakers are conservative here and only one producer, Santoro Corella, is experimenting with different varieties.

THE MARCHES (MARCHE)

Tourism has been a factor in the success of the Marches's wines. This hilly region has a beautiful Adriatic coastline where holidaymakers quench their thirst with the local white – the pale, dry Verdicchio. There are, however, more exciting wines to be found in the exceptionally fine DOCs of Rosso Cònero and Rosso Piceno and, in a few isolated circumstances, Sangiovese dei Colli Pesaresi, together with excellent *Vini da Tavola* such as Rosso di Corinaldo and Tristo di Montesecco.

MOLISE

This is a poor region with high unemployment and a badly equipped wine industry. Until 1963 it was combined with the Abruzzi and did not gain its first DOC until 1983. The Italian wine expert Burton Anderson believes that it may one day provide wines of real class, but, if greater potential does exist, it will take substantial investment to exploit it.

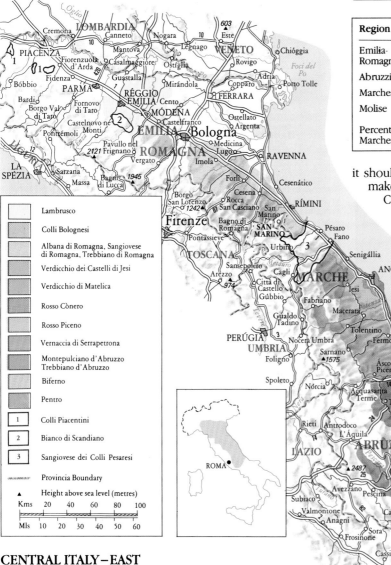

CENTRAL ITALY–EAST

With the Appennines forming the region's western border, the eastern part of central Italy is dominated by their foothills and the plains that stretch towards the Adriatic.

Fine wines of Emilia-Romagna

RONCO CASONE VT

Gian Matteo Baldi

The toughest of Baldi's three *barrique*-aged Sangiovese, it would benefit from the addition of some Cabernet sauvignon and, perhaps, Merlot.

RED Deep-coloured, very firm and austere wine that softens with age.

🍇 Sangiovese

📅 1980, 1981, 1982, 1983, 1985, 1986, 1988, 1990

🍷 Between 8-15 years

RONCO DEI CILIEGI VT

Gian Matteo Baldi

The best of Baldi's Sangiovese wines.

RED Well-coloured with an elegant bouquet, this wine has rich, silky fruit, obvious finesse and a supple tannin structure that is nicely underscored by a restrained use of oak.

🍇 Sangiovese

📅 1980, 1981, 1982, 1983, 1985, 1986, 1988

🍷 Between 5-15 years

RONCO DELLE GINESTRE VT

Gian Matteo Baldi

The lightest of Baldi's wines.

RED A fine, medium-bodied wine that opens up quickly and has a well-balanced flavour.

🍇 Sangiovese

📅 1980, 1981, 1982, 1983, 1985, 1986

🍷 Between 4-12 years

ROSSO ARMENTANO* VT

Fratelli Vallunga

A well-established and successful blend of French and Italian grape varieties.

RED A soft, finely scented, ruby-coloured wine that is tight when young, but gains finesse when mature.

🍇 Sangiovese, Cabernet franc, Pinot nero

📅 1982, 1983, 1985, 1986, 1988

🍷 Between 6-10 years

TERRE ROSSE CHARDONNAY VT

Vallania

This wine is a thousand times better than the best Albana di Romagna.

WHITE A dry, medium-bodied wine of fine depth and flavour that has the perfect balance between true varietal character and authentic Italian style. It combines the grape's natural richness and buttery character with an almost ethereal quality that can only be Italian, yet it does not have an ounce of bitterness.

🍇 Chardonnay

📅 1983, 1985, 1986, 1988

🍷 Within 2-5 years

Other wines of Emilia-Romagna

ALBANA DI ROMAGNA* DOCG

Very straightforward, fruity, dry and semi-sweet white wines that can also be *spumante*.

BARBAROSSA DI BERTINORO* VT

Fattoria Paradiso

This is one of Emilia-Romagna's better red wines.

BIANCO DI SCANDIANO DOC

Full-bodied, dry and semi-sweet white wines that may also be *spumante* and *frizzante*.

BOSCO ELICEO or ROSSO DEL BOSCO VT

Cantina Sociale Bosco Eliceo

Full-bodied, alcoholic, fruity red.

CAGNINA VT

Sweet, fruity red wines.

COLLI BOLOGNESI* DOC

Also known as Colli Bolognesi dei Castelli Medioevali or Colli Bolognesi di Monte San Pietro, this appellation covers three red varietals and five white. The Sauvignon is best, but the Pinot Bianco can also be good.

COLLI DI PARMA DOC

Solid, slightly *frizzante* red wines; and two white varietals – Malvasia and Sauvignon.

COLLI PIACENTINI DOC

A wide range of wines: two dry or semi-sweet, still, *frizzantino, frizzante* or *spumante* white *uvaggi* bearing the sub-appellations of Val Nure and Monterosso Val d'Arda; three dry or off-dry, still or *frizzante* red varietals (Barbera, Bonarda, Pinot Noir); and five dry or semi-sweet, still or *spumante* white varietals (Malvasia, Ortrugo, Pinot Grigio, Sauvignon, Trebbiano Val Trebbia).

GUTTURNIO DEI COLLI PIACENTINI* DOC

Solid red wines made from Barbera and Bonarda grapes, grown in the Piacenza hills where Julius Caesar's father-in-law made a wine that was traditionally drunk from a large vessel called a *gutturnium*. A semi-sweet, *frizzante* version is occasionally produced.

LAMBRUSCO* VT

Most Lambrusco produced, and nearly all that which is exported, is non-DOC. This is usually because it is packaged in screw-top bottles, which are illegal under DOC law.

Traditionally, Lambrusco is an off-dry, cherry-red, frothy wine that tastes of ripe, cherry-flavoured fruit and is low in alcohol; exported wines are mostly sweet. *Rosato* and *bianco* styles are also made and the degree of sparkle varies from barely *frizzantino* to virtually *spumante*. (DOC Lambrusco must be naturally sparkling).

LAMBRUSCO GRASPAROSSA DI CASTELVETRO DOC

Dry or semi-sweet, vinous, *frizzantino* red wines that are usually superior to non-DOC versions, but do not quite match the Lambrusco di Sorbara.

LAMBRUSCO REGGIANO DOC

Dry or semi-sweet, *frizzante* red and rosé wines that are the lightest DOC Lambruscos.

LAMBRUSCO SALAMINO DI SANTA CROCE* DOC

These dry or semi-sweet, vinous, semi-*spumante* red wines are the most aromatic of Lambruscos and can come up to the standard of the Lambrusco di Sorbara.

LAMBRUSCO DI SORBARA* DOC

Mostly dry, although occasionally semi-sweet, medium-bodied, *frizzantino* red wines that have more body and depth of flavour than most.

MÜLLER THURGAU DI ZIANO VT

Dry, crisp, white wines that are the most successful of various local Müller-Thurgau.

PAGADEBIT* VT

Dry and semi-sweet white wines that can have some delicacy.

PICOL ROSS* VT

Moro

This dry, well-scented and quite fruity, red *frizzante* wine is the best non-DOC Lambrusco available.

ROSSO DELLA BISSERA* VT

Bruno Negroni

Deep in colour and rich in rustic, chunky fruit, Bissera has the potential to be a fine wine.

SANGIOVESE DI ROMAGNA* DOC

These solid, red wines rarely excite, unless from exceptional vineyards such as Fattoria Paradiso's Vigneti delle Lepri.

SCORZA AMARA* VT

Scorza Amara is a local variant of the Lambrusco grape and is produced in a *frizzante* form that is slightly fuller than most Lambrusco.

TREBBIANO DI ROMAGNA DOC

Dry, neutral white wines that are also made in dry, sweet and semi-sweet *spumante* versions.

The wines of the Abruzzi

MONTEPULCIANO D'ABRUZZO* DOC

The Abruzzi's only fine wines.

RED There are two styles, both very deep in colour. Some are full of soft, fat, luscious fruit, others are firmer, certainly more tannic with a silky-violety aftertaste.

🍇 Montepulciano and up to a maximum of 15% Sangiovese

🍷 1983, 1985, 1986, 1988, 1990

🍷 Between 4-8 or 8-20 years.

ROSÉ Fresh, light, dry rosés of modest quality, unless produced by Illuminati, when they can be fine indeed.

🍇 Montepulciano and up to a maximum of 15% Sangiovese

🍷 1980, 1981, 1982, 1983, 1985, 1986, 1988, 1990

🍷 Within 1-3 years

☆ Soft and fruity: Cantina Sociale di Tollo (Collo Secco), Tenuta S. Agnese. Firm and tannic: Valentini, Emidio Pepe, Illuminati

RUBINO VT

Tenuta S. Agnese

Firm, finely-scented, red wine.

SPINELLO VT

Tenuta S. Agnese

Light, dry white wine.

TREBBIANO D'ABRUZZO* DOC

Usually dry, neutral and mediocre white wines although they can be delicately scented and velvety in texture.

VAL PELIGNA VT

Santoro Colella

Dry, red and white wine from various grape varieties.

Fine wines of the Marches

ROSSO CÒNERO DOC

Fine wines that improve with *barrique*-aging.

RED Deep-coloured, rich and full-bodied wines.

🍇 Montepulciano, and up to a maximum of 15% Sangiovese

🍷 1982, 1985, 1986, 1988, 1990

🍷 Between 6-15 years

☆ Garofoli's vigna Piancarda, Umani Ronchi's "Cà Sal di Serra", Marchetti "Le Terrazze", Mecvini

ROSSO DI CORINALDO VT

Cantina Sociale Val di Nevola

A consistently well-made wine.

RED Good-quality, medium-bodied wine that shows an exuberance but retains the grape's spicy elegance.

🍇 Merlot

🍷 1983, 1985, 1986, 1988, 1990

🍷 Between 4-8 years

ROSSO PICENO DOC

Rapidly improving wines from just south of the Rosso Cònero DOC. *Superiore* wines come from a restricted area and are aged for at least one year.

RED Fine, firm, ruby-coloured wines with smooth, juicy fruit that sometimes has *barrique* characteristics.

🍇 Sangiovese 60%, Montepulciano 40%

🍷 1983, 1985, 1986, 1988, 1990

🍷 Between 4-10 years

☆ Tattà, Villa Pigna

SANGIOVESE DEI COLLI PESARESI DOC

Some wines from this DOC can be heartily recommended.

RED The best are richly-coloured, deep-flavoured wines with obvious class and finesse.

🍇 A minimum of 85% Sangiovese, with Montepulciano and Ciliegiolo

🍷 1983, 1985, 1986, 1988, 1990

🍷 Between 3-8 years

☆ Constanini's "La Torraccia", Tattà, Umani Ronchi, Vallone, Villa Pigna

TRISTO DI MONTESECCO VT

Fattoria di Montesecco

An unusual but delightful blended wine matured in new oak.

WHITE A vivacious, dry wine that projects well-balanced fruit against a deliciously soft and creamy background.

🍇 Malvasia di Candia, Pinot grigio, Riesling Italico, Toscano, Trebbiano

🍷 1985, 1986, 1988, 1990

🍷 Within 2-4 years

Other wines of the Marches

BIANCHELLO DEL METAURO DOC

Dry, delicate, white wines.

BIANCO DEI COLLI MACERATESI DOC

Dry, white, Trebbiano-based wines.

FALERIO DEI COLLI ASCOLANI DOC

Dry, lightly-scented white wines.

FONTANELLE* VT

Tattà

Scented, smooth, dry white wine.

LACRIMA DI MORRO DOC

Soft, medium-bodied red wines.

MONTEPULCIANO DELLE MARCHE* VT

Rich and rustically fruity red wines that are not quite in the same class as Montepulciano d'Abruzzo.

ROSATO DELLE MARCHE VT

Dry, rosé wines from Sangiovese and Montepulciano.

ROSATO DI MONTANELLO* VT

Villamagna, Campagnucci-Compagnoni

Light, dry and fruity, rosé wines.

SANGIOVESE DELLE MARCHE VT

Simple, locally-consumed, red wines that are usually better than run-of-the-mill Chianti.

VERDICCHIO DEI CASTELLI DI JESI DOC

Popular wines whose quality has declined. *Spumante* and *frizzante* versions are also made.

VERDICCHIO DI MATELICA* DOC

Made within a hilly zone in the centre of the Verdicchio area.

VERNACCIA DI SERRAPETRONA DOC

Dry and sweet *spumante* reds.

The wines of Molise

BIANCO DEL MOLISE VT

The dry white wine of the region.

BIFERNO DOC

Smooth, slightly tannic, red wines; dry, lightly aromatic, white wines and dry and fruity rosé wines.

MONTEPULCIANO DEL MOLISE* VT

Smooth, well-coloured, full-bodied red wines that are usually good value.

MONTEPULCIANO CERASUOLO DEL MOLISE VT

Cherry-coloured wines that are usually drunk young and fresh.

PENTRO or PENTRO DI ISERNIA DOC

Smooth, slightly tannic reds; dry, fresh whites; and dry, fruity rosés.

RAMITELLO* VT

Masseria di Majo Norante

Full-bodied red wine from Sangiovese and Montepulciano grapes; medium-bodied Trebbiano and Malvasia white wine; and red and white *frizzante*.

ROSATO DEL MOLISE VT

Everyday, dry, local *rosato* made from Montepulciano and Sangiovese grapes.

ROSATO DEL MOLISE-FIORE VT

Slightly more characterful *rosato* made in the province of Campobasso.

ROSSO DEL MOLISE VT

The region's basic *rosso* is an unexciting *uvaggio* that can be blended from many grapes, though Montepulciano and Sangiovese dominate.

Southern Italy and the Islands

Hot and largely hilly, with volcanic soils, southern Italy is an ancient and prolific wine-growing area. While overproduction continues to be a problem, there are an increasing number of well-made wines.

JUTTING OUT INTO THE BLUE WATERS of the Mediterranean, the vineyards of southern Italy receive very little natural moisture and bake rather than bask in unrelenting sunshine. This factor provides for deep-coloured wines with strong flavours and high alcoholic levels. These heavy wines do not suit modern tastes and even though southern Italy continues to produce a glut of this almost unsaleable wine, the region is subtly changing course. Its small but growing volume of cleaner, finer, more expressive wines may enable it to establish an identity capable of thriving in ever more sophisticated world-wine markets. The biggest obstacle to achieving this is the poverty which has for so long blighted southern Italy.

APULIA (PUGLIA)

Apulia's exceptionally fertile plains make it one of Italy's largest wine-producing regions, but until the 1970s most of its wines were seen fit only for blending or for making Vermouth. Because of this, most Apulian producers decided to try to rid themselves of this lowly reputation, bringing about a radical transformation of their industry. A great number of very ordinary wines are still produced, but various changes have greatly improved the situation. Irrigation schemes, the introduction of lower-yielding, higher-quality grape

AVERAGE ANNUAL PRODUCTION

Region	DOC production	Total production
Apulia	198,000 hl (2.2 million cases)	11 million hl (122 million cases)
Sicily	270,000 hl (3 million cases)	10 million hl (111 million cases)
Sardinia	260,000 hl (3 million cases)	2.5 million hl (28 million cases)
Calabria	33,000 hl (367,000 cases)	1.2 million hl (13 million cases)
Basilicata	6,300 hl (70,00 cases)	420,000 hl (4.6 million cases)
Campania	12,500 hl (139,000 cases)	2.5 million hl (27.7 million cases)

Percentage of total Italian production: Apulia, 14%; Sicily, 13%; Sardinia, 3.3%; Calabria, 1.6%; Basilicata, 0.6%; Campania, 3.3%.

SOUTHERN ITALY AND THE ISLANDS

An enormous area geographically, southern Italy produces massive quantities of wine. Apulia, Italy's "heel", makes the most distinguished, while wines from Sardinia are notably well made. Elsewhere, quality is patchy.

ROMA

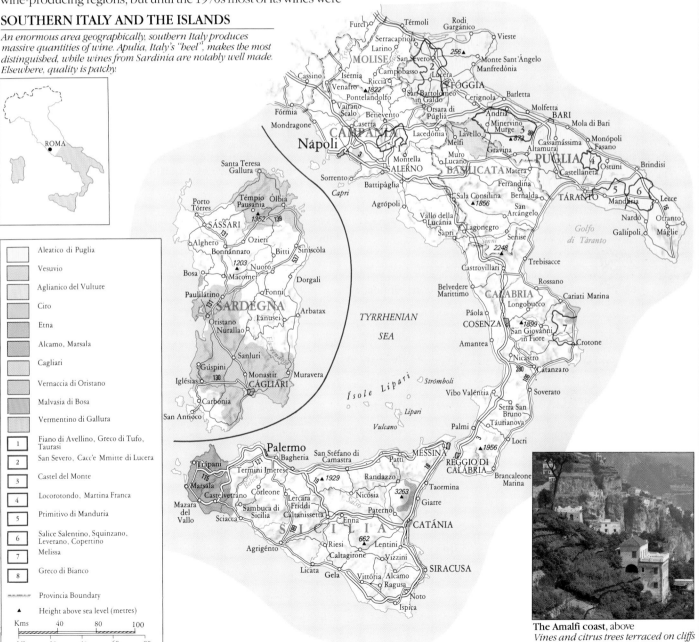

Legend:
- Aleatico di Puglia
- Vesuvio
- Aglianico del Vulture
- Ciro
- Etna
- Alcamo, Marsala
- Cagliari
- Vernaccia di Oristano
- Malvasia di Bosa
- Vermentino di Gallura
- 1 — Fiano di Avellino, Greco di Tufo, Taurasi
- 2 — San Severo, Cacc'e Mmitte di Lucera
- 3 — Castel del Monte
- 4 — Locorotondo, Martina Franca
- 5 — Primitivo di Manduria
- 6 — Salice Salentino, Squinzano, Leverano, Copertino
- 7 — Melissa
- 8 — Greco di Bianco
- ----- Provincia Boundary
- ▲ Height above sea level (metres)

Kms 40 80 100
Mls 20 40 60 80

The Amalfi coast, above
Vines and citrus trees terraced on cliffs typical to the area.

varieties (including many classic French ones) and a move away from the single-bush cultivation, known as *alberello*, to modern wire-trained systems, have led to both new wines gaining favour and some traditional ones showing renewed promise. Now the two most important grape varieties are the Primitivo, which has been identified as the Zinfandel of California and is the earliest-ripening grape grown in Italy, and the Uva di Troia, which has no connection with the town of Troia in Apulia's northern province of Foggia, but refers to ancient Troy, from where the grape originates. It was brought to the region by the first Greeks to settle in the Taranto area.

CAMPANIA

Campania Felix, as the Romans called it, is well-known for "Lacryma Christi", a wine that today is not bad enough to bring a tear to the eye of Christ, but which is certainly not a fine wine. Little else produced here is of interest.

BASILICATA

Basilicata is a dramatic and wild region dominated by the extinct volcano Mount Vulture. Manufacturing industry is scarce here, accounting for less than one per cent of the region's output, and the mountainous terrain makes mechanized agriculture extremely difficult. Lacking investment finance and with two in every three inhabitants unemployed, Basilicata has not had the means nor the incentive to modernize its wine industry. Consequently, with the exception of the first class, if idiosyncratic, Aglianico dèl Vulture DOC by Fratelli d'Angelo, there is very little here of interest.

CALABRIA

The decline in Calabria's viticultural output since the 1960s has been for the better in terms of quality. Since then the most unsuitable land has been abandoned, and the eight current DOCs, located in hilly and mountainous terrain, may eventually prove to be a source of quality wine. At the moment, however, improvement in wine technology is slow and, with the exception of Umberto Ceratti's succulent Greco di Bianco, a world-class dessert wine that is a relic of the past, this region also has little in the way of interesting wine.

SICILY (SICILIA)

Sicily is the largest island in the Mediterranean and, in terms of quantity, one of Italy's most important wine regions, annually producing a quantity roughly equal to Veneto or Emilia Romagna.

FACTORS AFFECTING TASTE AND QUALITY

 Location
An area including the southern mainland regions of Apulia, Campania, Basilicata and Calabria as well as the islands of Sicily, further south, and Sardinia, across the Tyrrhenian Sea to the west.

Climate
By far the hottest and driest region of Italy, although the coastal areas and islands are tempered by maritime winds.

Aspect
Most of the region is either mountainous or hilly, although vineyards are to be found on the flat land and gentle slopes of Apulia. The best sites are always found on the north-facing, higher slopes of hillsides where the vines receive less sun and benefit from the tempering effect of altitude, thus ensuring a longer growing season.

Soil
Predominantly volcanic and granitic, but with some isolated outcrops of clay and chalk.

 **Viticulture and vinification**
This area, together with the Midi in France, is the principal source of Europe's infamous "wine lake". Nevertheless producers using better quality grape varieties grown on higher sites are making wines of a standard and style that deserve wider recognition.

Grape varieties
Aglianico, Aleatico, Barbera, Bianco d'Alessano, Bombino bianco, Bombino nero, Cabernet franc, Cannonau, Carignano, Catarratto, Chardonnay, Coda di Volpe, Falanghina, Fiano, Frappato, Gaglioppo, Greco, Grillo, Inzolia, Malbec, Malvasia, Malvasia nera, Monica, Montepulciano, Moscato, Nasco, Negroamaro, Nerello mantello, Nerello mascalese, Nero d'Avola (Calabrese), Nuragus, Olivella, Perricone, Piedirosso, Pinot bianco, Pinot nero, Primitivo, Sangiovese, Sauvignon, Torbato, Trebbiano, Trebbiano Toscano, Uva di Troia, Verdeca, Vermentino, Vernaccia

Many of the island's wines are consumed locally, although the branded wine "Corvo" has a fairly high export profile. Sicily's once popular classic wine, Marsala, now finds itself out of favour with modern tastes, although there is a determined effort to re-establish it by dropping the flavoured versions and concentrating on the lighter *vergine* style.

SARDINIA (SARDEGNA)

Whilst virtually all styles of wine are still produced in Sardinia, its wine industry has undergone a radical modernization since the late-1970s. Its wines are now vinified in stainless steel at cool temperatures and, as a result, the majority of Sardinia's wines are fresh and clean, with good fruity flavours. Although it produces no "fine" wine, in the classic sense, the wines are generally well made and easy to enjoy.

Note: for reasons of space, only those VT wines of sufficient quality to merit inclusion are listed in the Southern Italy and Islands taste guides.

Fine wines of Apulia

ALEATICO DI PUGLIA DOC

Produced throughout the region, but in tiny quantities, this wine is rarely encountered on export markets.

RED Opulent and aromatic wines with a full, warming, smooth and exotic flavour, ranging from very sweet and fortified (*liquoroso* or *liquoroso dolce naturel*) to medium-sweet and unfortified (*dolce naturel*). A *riserva* must be aged for at least three years from the date of harvest or, in the case of *liquoroso*, the date of fortification.

🍇 Aleatico and up to a maximum of 15% in total of Negroamaro, Malvasia nera and Primitivo

📅 1984, 1985, 1986, 1988, 1990

🍷 Immediately

☆ Felice Botta, Nuova Vinicola Picardi

IL FALCONE (CASTEL DEL MONTE RISERVA DOC)

Rivera

This is Apulia's greatest red wine and a fine wine by any standards.

RED A well-coloured, full-bodied, flavoursome wine with a very fine and deeply scented bouquet that is dominated by Montepulciano.

🍇 Uva di Troia, and up to a maximum of 35% Montepulciano, Sangiovese and Bombino nero

📅 Any

🍷 Between 8-20 years

FAVONIO VT

Attilio Simonini

These wines come from an estate on the Capitanata plain, east of Foggia, in northern Apulia. Although the land would seem to be too flat, hot and dry for native French varieties, the wines are remarkably successful.

RED A notably good Pinot Nero, with fine varietal character, and both a straight and an oak-aged Cabernet Franc, the latter being extraordinarily good.

🍇 Cabernet franc, Pinot nero

📅 1983, 1985, 1986, 1988, 1990

🍷 Between 3-10 years

WHITE Crisp, fruity Pinot Bianco, improving Chardonnay, sometimes oak-aged, and racy Trebbiano, all dry and light to light-to-medium bodied.

🍇 Pinot bianco, Chardonnay, Trebbiano

📅 1982, 1983, 1985, 1986, 1990

🍷 Within 1-3 years

ROSA DEL GOLFO VT

Giuseppe Calo

One of Italy's finest rosés, this wine is made by the "teardrop" system of soft crushing and minimal maceration.

RED A fragrantly scented, light-bodied, delightfully dry and well-balanced, cherry-pink wine, with a fresh and gentle, fruity flavour.

🍇 Negroamaro, Malvasia nera

📅 Any

🍷 Within 1-2 years

Other wines of Apulia

ALEZIO* DOC

Alcoholic, slightly tannic red wines, also sold as Doxi Vecchio, and dry, soft, flavourful rosés, also sold as Lacrima di Terra d'Otranto.

APULIA* VT

Full-bodied, robust red wines.

BRINDISI DOC

Smooth, vinous red wines and dry, light and fruity rosés.

CACC'E MMITTE DI LUCERA DOC

The name of this full-bodied red *uvaggio*, which is made from seven different grape varieties, loosely means "knock it back".

CASTEL MITRANO* VT

Austere, tannic and alcoholic red wines.

CASTEL DEL MONTE* DOC

The region's best-known wine is named after the thirteenth-century castle built by Emperor Frederick von Hohenstaufen. With the exception of a *riserva* made by Rivera, which is sold as "Il Falcone", the wines are less lofty than their name: vinous, slightly tannic reds; delicate, dry whites; dry, fruity, scented rosés.

COPERTINO* DOC

Smooth, rich, red wines and dry, finely scented rosés.

DONNA MARZIA* VT

Full-bodied, alcoholic red wines and dry white wines.

GRAVINA DOC

Dry or semi-sweet, fresh white wines. Dry and semi-sweet, *spumante*, white wines.

LEVERANO DOC

Vinous, alcoholic red wines; dry, soft, white wines and fresh and fruity rosés.

LOCOROTONDO* DOC

Lightly fruity, dry white wines that can also be *spumante*.

MARTINI or MARTINI FRANCA DOC

Vinous, dry white wines that can be *spumante*.

MATINO DOC

Dry, robust red and slightly vinous rosé wines.

MOSCATO DI TRANI* DOC

Smooth, sweet whites and sweet, *liquoroso*, fortified wine.

NARDO DOC

Robust, alcoholic, red wines.

ORTA VOVA DOC

Full-bodied, vinous red wines and dry rosé wines.

OSTUNI or BIANCO DI OSTUNI DOC

Delicate, dry white wines.

OSTUNI OTTAVIANELLO DOC

Vinous, light red wines.

PORTULANO* VT

Giuseppe Calo

A full-bodied red wine of ample flavour that is capable of maturing well for up to eight years.

PRIMITIVO DI MANDURIA DOC

Dry to semi-sweet, full-bodied red wines which may also be naturally sweet, fortified and naturally sweet, and fortified and dry.

ROSSO BARLETTA DOC

Medium-bodied, ruby-coloured, everyday-quality red wines usually consumed locally when very young.

ROSSO CANOSA DOC

Vinous, slightly tannic red wines.

ROSSO DI CERIGNOLA* DOC

Full, rustic and robust red wines.

ROSSO DI SAVA* VT

Vinicola Amanda

Dry and sweet red wines from the Primitivo grape. It is possible for these wines to qualify as Primitivo di Manduria DOC.

SALICE SALENTINO* DOC

Full-bodied, alcoholic, rich red wines and smooth, alcoholic rosé wines.

SAN SEVERO DOC

Dry, vinous red and rosé wines and dry, fresh white wines.

SQUINZANO DOC

Full-bodied, robust red wines and lightly scented, smooth rosé wines.

TORRE ALEMANNA* VT

Riforma Fondiaria

Deep-coloured, full-bodied red wine from various grapes including the Malbec.

TORRE QUARTO* VT

Crillo-Farrusi

Full-bodied, fruity red wine from various grapes including the Malbec, and dry white and rosé wines.

The wines of Campania

CAPRI DOC

Easy-to-drink, medium-bodied red and light-bodied, dry, white wines seldom seen beyond the Isle of Capri.

CILENTO* VT

Cantina Sociale di Cilento

Various dry, semi-sweet, still and *spumante*, red and rosé wines. The red is based on the Primitivo grape, known as Zinfandel in California.

FALERNO* VT

Falernum, the wine so enjoyed in ancient Rome, was made in the northwest of Campania and Latium. The deep-coloured, full-bodied and rustically robust Aglianico can be one of this region's better red wines. A dry white is also produced.

FIANO DI AVELLINO* DOC

Mastroberardino's Vignadora is the best wine in this unusual, but well above average, dry white wine DOC.

GRECO DI TUFO* DOC

Delicate, dry and soft, white wines that may sometimes be *spumante*.

ISCHIA DOC

Vinous, medium-bodied red wines; low-key, dry white wines and a dry white *superiore* which is lightly aromatic.

LETTERE* VT

Soft and round, blended red wines that can be good value.

RAVELLO* VT

The full-bodied red wines made from a blend of Aglianico, Merlot and other grapes are the best wines. Dry whites and dry rosés are also produced.

SOLOPACA* DOC

Smooth red and soft, dry white wines that are sometimes of interest.

TAURASI* DOC

A wine that requires long aging but which may last for 20 years. Mastroberardino produces the best, with the Taurasi *riserva* the top of the range.

VESUVIO DOC

Red, dry white, rosé, *spumante* and sweet fortified wines from the volcanic slopes of the still active Mount Vesuvius.

The wines of Basilicata

AGLIANICO DEL VULTURE* DOC

The finest Aglianico wines in Italy come from the slopes of Mount Vulture and the surrounding hills. They are Basilicata's only fine wines. If described as *vecchio*, the wine will have had a minimum of three years aging, while *riserva* will have had five; both will have been aged for two years in wood. This wine may also be sold as a semi-sweet, *spumante* red.

RED Big, but balanced wines of fine deep colour and rich, chocolate-cherry fruit and firm tannin structure. Slightly rustic in youth, these wines develop a true silky finesse with age.

🍇 Aglianico
🍷 1981, 1985, 1986, 1988
🍴 Between 6-20 years

☆ Fratelli d'Angelo, Paternosta

AGLIANICO DEI COLLI LUCANI* VT

Vinicola Miali

Robust, dry and semi-sweet red wines. *Spumante* red wines are also made.

MOSCATO DEL VULTURE* VT

Sweet, white, dessert wines that are usually *spumante*.

MONTEPULCIANO DI BASILICATA* VT

Cantina Sociale del Metapontino

Full-bodied, scented red wine.

The wines of Calabria

GRECO DI BIANCO DOC

Made on the very tip of Calabria, around Bianco, these are simple *passito* wines. The finest producer, Umberto Ceratti, harvests tiny, already shrivelled grapes and, apparently, plunges them into boiling water immediately after picking! Ceratti's Greco di Bianco is unequivocally the region's finest wine.

WHITE Deceptively strong, succulently sweet and smooth, *liquoroso* wines with a vivacious bouquet, exuberant fruit and a luscious, silk finish.

🍇 Greco, and up to a maximum of 5% of other varieties

🗓 1981, 1983, 1985, 1986

🍷 Between 3-5 years

☆ Umberto Ceratti

CERASUOLO DI SCILLA VT

Dry and semi-sweet, cherry-coloured *uvaggio*.

CIRO DOC

Strong, alcoholic red, white and rosé wines that were famous in antiquity.

DONNICI DOC

Dry, fruity red and rosé wines that are best drunk young.

LAMEZIA DOC

Light, delicately fruity red wines.

MELISSA DOC

Full-bodied reds and crisp, dry whites.

POLLINO DOC

Full, fruity, *chiaretto* wines.

SANT'ANNA DI ISOLA CAPO RIZZUTO DOC

Vinous red and rosé wines from the Ionian hills.

SAVUTO* DOC

Pleasant, light, red or rosé wines.

The wines of Sicily

ALCAMO or BIANCO ALCAMO DOC

Dry, slightly fruity, white wines.

CERASUOLO DI VITTORIA DOC

Cherry-coloured wines from the southeastern corner of Sicily.

CORVO* VT

Duca di Salaparuta

The brand name for red, white, *spumante* and fortified "Stravecchio di Sicilia" wines that are probably the most famous in Sicily. The consistent, full, smooth and fruity red is by far the most successful.

ETNA* DOC

According to Homer, this is the wine that Ulysses used to intoxicate the Cyclops. There are three basic styles: a full red; a fruity rosé; and a soft, but bland, dry white.

VILLAGRANDE
ETNA ROSSO
vino a denominazione d'origine controllata
12,50%/VOL.   R.I. N° 119 CT   N: 182776   ITALIA E·75 CL

FARO DOC

Ruby-coloured, medium-bodied red wines from the Nerello grape grown around Messina.

MALVASIA DELLE LIPARI DOC

Sweet, aromatic, *passito* white wines.

MARSALA* DOC

Dry, semi-sweet and sweet, fortified, golden (*oro*), amber (*ambra*) and red (*rubino*) wines. *Fine* is the basic category, with just one year's aging for *rubino*, none for *oro* or *ambra*; *Superiore* is aged for at least two years, four if *riserva*; *Vergine*, the lightest, and *Solera* must have at least five years aging, unless they are *stravecchio* or *riserva*, in which case the minimum will be 10 years.

MOSCATO DI NOTO DOC

Still, *spumante* or fortified semi-sweet and sweet Moscato wines.

MOSCATO DI PANTELLERIA* DOC

Sicily's best still, *spumante* and fortified semi-sweet and sweet Moscato wines.

MOSCATO DI SIRACUSA DOC

Sweet, smooth white wines.

REGALEALI* VT

Conte Tasca d'Almerita

These rich, full-bodied, soft, red wines and dry, crisp whites and rosés are some of Sicily's best.

SOLICCHIATO BIANCO DI VILLA FONTANE* VT

Giuseppe Coria

Characterful, semi-sweet, amber-coloured dessert wine made from sun-dried grapes.

STERI* VT

Giuseppe Camilleri

The deep-coloured, full-bodied, rich, red wines are quite good, while the crisp and dry white is passable.

The wines of Sardinia

ANGHELU RUJU* VT

Sella & Mosca

An interesting, rich, deep-coloured, sweet, red dessert wine.

ARBOREA DOC

New DOC for Sangiovese red and dry or semi-sweet, Trebbiano white.

CAMPIDANO DI TERRALBA or TERRALBA DOC

Soft, full-bodied, Boval-based red wines.

CANNONAU DI SARDEGNA* DOC

A DOC of variable quality that throws up the occasional gem, Cannonau encompasses dry, semi-sweet or sweet red, white, rosé and *liquoroso* wines.

CARIGNANO DEL SULCIS DOC

Vinous, smooth, dry red and rosé wines.

GIRÒ DI CAGLIARI DOC

Smooth, alcoholic, dry and sweet, red wines and dry and sweet, fortified wines.

MALVASIA DI BOSA* DOC

Rich, sweet and dry, full-bodied, white wines, and sweet and dry *liquoroso* wines.

MALVASIA DI CAGLIARI DOC

Dry and sweet, alcoholic, white wines and dry and sweet, *liquoroso* wines.

MALVASIA DI PLANARGIA* VT

Emilio & Gilberto Arru

Unfettered by DOC regulations, this is a sort of superior Malvasia di Bosa.

MANDROLISAI DOC

Dry, scented, red and rosé wines with a bitter aftertaste.

MONICA DI CAGLIARI DOC

Delicately scented, smooth, dry and sweet red wines, and sweet and dry *liquoroso* wines.

MONICA DI SARDEGNA DOC

Dry, medium-bodied, fragrant red wines.

MOSCATO DI SORSO-SENNORI DOC

Sweet, rich, white Moscato and sweet, aromatic *liquoroso*. The wines are fuller and more luscious than Moscato di Cagliari.

NASCO DI CAGLIARI DOC

Finely scented, delicate, dry and sweet white wines that can also be *liquoroso*.

NURAGUS DI CAGLIARI DOC

A large production of dry, semi-sweet and *frizzante* white wines.

TORBATO DI ALGHERO* VT

Sella & Mosca

Dry, crisp white wine with a fine, fruity balance.

VERMENTINO DI GALLURA DOC

Dry, light-bodied, soft to flabby, but always clean white wines.

VERNACCIA DI ORISTANO* DOC

Dry, lightly bitter white wines, Sherry-like in style, and *liquoroso* sweet and dry wines.

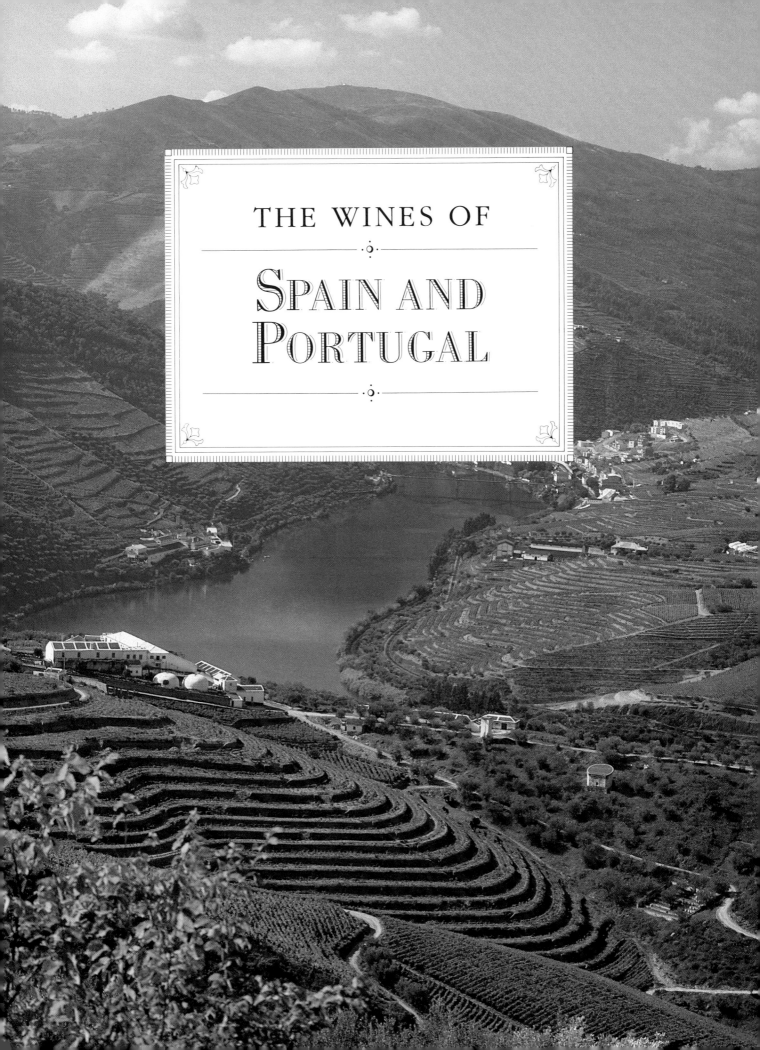

THE WINES OF

SPAIN AND PORTUGAL

Spain

Europe's second-best wine-producing country, Spain has a wine industry blessed with a special blend of tradition and innovation that will propel it to the forefront of the fine-wine scene in the 1990s. At present it is an ideal hunting ground for budget-conscious appreciators of good wine.

AS RECENTLY AS THE EARLY 1970S, almost 95 per cent of all exported Spanish wine was purchased in bulk and shipped by tanker. One was more likely to imagine that the liquid being pumped into awaiting road-tankers was destined for the petro-chemical industry rather than for human consumption. Also, the importers invariably added great amounts of sulphur dioxide to the wine in an attempt to halt oxidation, which had usually set in at an alarming rate due to poor vinification standards in Spain.

THE NADIR OF THE SPANISH WINE INDUSTRY

At this time most Spanish wine was awful. The whites were generally the product of the Airén, an inferior grape grown throughout the country, but mostly on the plains. The same blended wine lurked behind the many different labels: if bottled in its straight form, the importer would call it "Chablis"; given a touch of grape concentrate it would become "Graves"; a larger amount of concentrate would make it "Entre-Deux-Mers", and with masses it became "Barsac" or "Sauternes", although the latter might have a fraction more sweetness than the former. The wines were, without exception, dull, flabby and horrendously over-sulphured. The reds tended to be dark, heavy and reeking of alcohol and oxidation. The more intense these characteristics were, the more likely it was that the wine would be labelled as Spanish "Burgundy", which says a lot about true Burgundy at that time!

RIOJA AND SPAIN'S WINE RENAISSANCE

Exports have dropped steadily since the 1970s, and more than 90 per cent of what is not exported is sold in bottle. Nobody, particularly not the Spanish, is mourning the loss of the bulk-produced, low-margin, high-migraine, mass-produced wines. Spain's wines are now a safe bet for quality and value, a change brought about largely through the quest for international

---

HOW TO READ SPANISH WINE LABELS

Appellation
First establish where the wine comes from, as this should give you some indication of its quality and style. In this case it is Rioja, and the designation beneath this reveals that Rioja is a "Denominación de Origen" or controlled-quality wine region. Not all DO wines carry this designation, which is unfortunate because whereas many people might have heard of Rioja, what proportion of consumers know all of the other DOs?

Wine style
The *rosado seco* on this label tells us that the wine is dry rosé. There are various other indications of style: *blanco* (white wine); *Cava* (a sparkling DO wine made by the *méthode champenoise*); *clarete* (mid-way between light-red and dark rosé, although this term is being superceded by *tintillo*); *cosechero* (a wine of the year or, as in *vin de l'année*, generally synonymous with *nuevo*, below); *espumoso* (sparkling wine made by any method); *generoso* (fortified or dessert wine); *nuevo* (fresh, fruity "new" or *nouveau* style); *tintillo* (light-red wine similar to a *clarete*); *tinto* (red wine); *viejo* (a term that should mean old, but its use is not controlled by law); *vino de aguja* (a semi-sparkling or *pétillant* wine); *vino de mesa* (literally "table wine", this is likely to be found on ordinary and inexpensive wines); and *vino de pasto* (an ordinary, inexpensive and often light style of wine).

Vintage
Until the late 1970s, when bottled wines began to assume more importance in export markets, the vintages indicated on many Spanish wines were known as "telephone numbers", to indicate their lack of importance. If 1964 was highly regarded on the domestic market, only new wines bearing that year would be sold and Spanish consumers either did not notice, or did not want to notice, that there were no 1963s nor 1965s. Vintages are now what they appear to be, or are at least as authentic as those produced in other EEC markets, where by law a bottle must contain a minimum of 85 per cent of wine produced in the year indicated. The term *Cosecha* (harvest or vintage) often appears with the year.

Name
This may be the brand name, or could relate to a specific vineyard, or might simply be the bodega that produced the wine. The following should help you to untangle who did what on the most complex of labels: *Anejado por* ("aged by"); *Bodega* (literally a "wine cellar", commonly used as part of the name of a wine firm, as in Bodegas Carrion, for example); *Criado por* ("blended" and/or "matured by"); *Elaborado por* (as *criado por* but also may be "made by"); *Embotellado por* ("bottled by"); *Viña* or *Viñedo* (literally "vineyard", but often merely part of a brand name, nothing to do with a specific vineyard).

Sweetness
The sweetness of white wines is often indicated on Spanish labels, something many French producers might benefit from doing. The terms used are: *brut* (bone-dry to dry, a term usually used for sparkling wines); *seco* (dry); *semi-seco* (medium-dry); *abocado* (medium-sweet); *dulce* (sweet).

Consejo Regulador stamp
The stamps of the various *Consejo Reguladors*, or regulating bodies, that guarantee the origin of a wine may be found on the label or capsule (*see* p.270).

Other information regarding style or quality may also be present:

Sin crianza
A wine without wood-aging. This category includes all the cool-fermented, early-bottled "new-wave" white wines and most rosés.

Con crianza or **Crianza**
A wine that has been aged in wood for a minimum of one year if red, six months if white or rosé.

Reserva
In good years, the best wines of a region are sold as *Reservas*. These are given a minimum maturation of three years for red wines and two years for white and rosé wines. The reds must spend at least one year in oak, the whites and rosés six months. In Rioja, Spain's greatest quality region, only seven per cent of the wines sold are *Reserva*.

Gran Reserva
Usually reserved for *cuvées* of *Reserva* wines from the very best years that are considered capable of enduring even further aging. For red wines, the minimum is two years in oak and three in bottle, or vice-versa. White and rosé *Gran Reservas*, although less common, require four years aging, of which at least six months must be in oak. Even in Rioja, barely five per cent of the wine sold is *Gran Reserva*.

Doble pasta
This term refers to red wines that have been macerated with double the normal proportion of grape skins to juice during fermentation (*see* How wine is made, p.18). Such wines are opaque, with an intense colour, and may be sold either by the bottle in their pure form, or used in bulk to blend with other lighter wines.

SPAIN

The south of Spain has long been famed for its Sherry, but the last 20 years have seen amazing progress in non-fortified, bottled wines, both still and sparkling, produced in regions all over the country.

Map legend:
- Rioja and Navarra *See also p. 271*
- Catalonia *See also p. 277*
- Jerez *See also p. 283*
- Cava *See also p. 271, p. 277*
- Ribera del Duero
- La Mancha
- Valdepeñas
- Valencia
- Montilla
- Other DO Areas
- Provincial Boundary
- ▲ Height above sea level (metres)

Kms 50 100 150 200
Mls 40 80 120

respect. If anything, Rioja was *too* successful and the Spanish are now desperately trying to convince consumers that the country has other wine regions. Sherry, of course, maintains its classic status and, since the advent of Rioja, we have seen the rise of Navarra and the classic Catalonian wines of Penedés, the latter's emergence led by Miguel Torres, one of the wine world's greatest innovators. Catalonia is also the centre of Spain's Cava industry, and the excellence of its sparkling wines almost caught out its Common Market competitors in the mid-1980s. The EEC had been trying to develop an acceptable definition for the term *méthode champenoise* for almost three years when certain people realized that Spain, whose Cava wines represent the single largest *méthode champenoise* appellation in the world, was but a few months away from joining the EEC. It was no coincidence that a ban on the term was rushed through in the last months of 1985.

Spain's best wine regions

Spain's greatest and, of course, most expensive wine is Vega Sicilia, made in the Ribera de Duero. This area has been a DO since 1982, and in it a handful of wineries produce some incredible red wines. Ribera de Duero is set to rival Rioja as Spain's most exciting top-quality red-wine area.

I optimistically believe that even some of Spain's most unimpressive wine areas are capable of producing delightful wines as and when the right people devote their attention to these parts of the country. If baking hot vineyards in Australia and South Africa, with the wrong soil for viticulture, can produce strikingly fresh wines with clear-cut varietal characteristics, then one wonders what a genius like Miguel Torres (*see* Catalonia, p.277) could achieve in Spain's poorest areas, which are not as difficult or demanding.

SPAIN'S APPELLATIONS

The Denominación de Origen (DO) is Spain's equivalent of the French AOC system. Its regulations, though, authorize grape varieties for appellations, not for specific styles of wine within them, as in France. Whilst the DO system has its faults, it is not as bad as various critics make it out to be. Some point out that DOs cover as much as 62 per cent of Spain's vineyards, compared with Italy's DOCs, which account for just 10 per cent of that country's area under vine. But, whereas the DO system does recognize too many very ordinary wine areas, it does not spread this status over 500 individual and mostly forgettable wines with more than 5,000 names, as the Italian DOC system does. The Spanish system certainly has a future, if developed with careful consideration.

On February 22 1988, a Royal Decree outlined the conditions under which Spanish DOs can achieve Denominación de Origen Calificada or DOCa, a higher status similar to, but, one hopes, far more meaningful than Italy's DOCG. Although it is possible that a few municipalities in some DOs could be registered for DOCa status before 1990, no significant reclassifications are expected for some time.

CONSEJO REGULADOR STAMPS

Every current DO possesses its own stamp, which usually appears somewhere on the label. These can be very attractive, and offer a guarantee of authenticity.

Harvesting Bobal grapes, above
This is the chief variety for red and rosé wines at Utiel-Requena DO in Valencia.

Sampling Sherries using a *venencia*, right
The development of a cask of Sherry is of crucial importance in determining its eventual style.

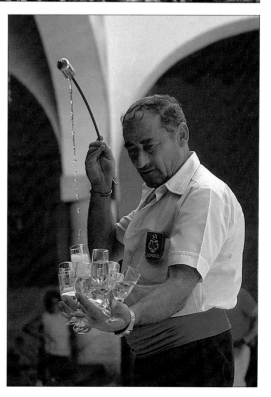

Rioja's Terra Alta, above
The hilly country of the largest of Rioja's districts produces the smoothest of its red wines.

Rioja and Navarra

Spain's greatest fine-wine regions, Rioja and Navarra, produce mostly red wines, and both whites and reds are renowned for their oaky character. The best wines come from the Rioja's Alta and Alavesa districts in the west, the former having great fruit, the latter more finesse. Most wines are not, however, purely from a single district and the stockier, coarser wines of Rioja's arid Baja district in the east can be very useful for adjusting the balance of blends.

ONLY A SHORT DRIVE FROM THE SHABBY SUBURBS of the commercial city of Bilbao, and the dramatic beauty of an upland valley becomes apparent, rich with architectural treasures of the twelfth century, isolated hilltop *pueblos,* a philanthropic people, a generous tradition and a hearty cuisine. This is rural Spain, far from the docks, factories and office blocks of an industrialized country, and the "fish'n'chips" and pressurized beer of the tourist centres. Here, the land twists and turns in a way peculiar to this area of Spain, with mounds suddenly rising, as if from nowhere, and spectacular rock formations forcing themselves upon the surrounding countryside. And, strewn about the place at random are castles, looking more like churches that could collapse if burdened by a congregation. Yet small towns boast massive fortifications called churches, seemingly strong enough to withstand a full-scale onslaught by the Moors!

RIOJA

I have heard many French *vignerons* grumble that Rioja is giving Spanish wine a good name, so it is ironical that French *vignerons* originally blessed the region with its unmistakable sweet-vanilla-oak identity that has so effectively captured the imagination of wine drinkers the world over. As early as the eighteenth century, a few enlightened Riojanos had looked to France generally, and Bordeaux in particular, to improve their winemaking techniques. The changes that resulted were subtle compared to the total revolution of the industry in the wake of phylloxera's devastation of French vineyards in the 1860s, when a number of *vignerons,* mostly Bordelais but some Burgundian, gave up all hope of reviving their own vineyards and descended upon Rioja to set up new bodegas.

While there is no denying that it was this Gallic influence that originally spurred the region to its place of ascendancy, there is now a local conviction that Rioja is intrinsically superior to all other Spanish wines and this belief is enough to make it fact. The only factor that would seem to threaten further progress is the legal requirement that a bodega must have a minimum stock of 500 *barriques* before it is allowed to export any wine. If this law was applied in Burgundy it would stop nearly all of its best wines leaving France.

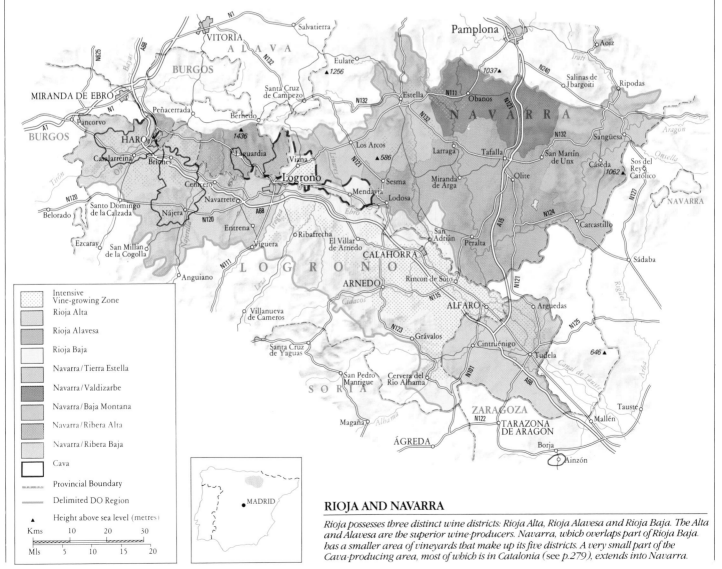

RIOJA AND NAVARRA

Rioja possesses three distinct wine districts: Rioja Alta, Rioja Alavesa and Rioja Baja. The Alta and Alavesa are the superior wine-producers. Navarra, which overlaps part of Rioja Baja. has a smaller area of vineyards that make up its five districts. A very small part of the Cava-producing area, most of which is in Catalonia (see p.279), extends into Navarra.

Sans-Chêne red wine

Oak cask-aging is of prime importance to the character of Rioja's wines. You cannot visit the region without encountering Bordeaux-sized, 225-litre *barriques* by the thousand. Some bodegas, however, seem to go to extraordinary lengths to remove all trace of the oak's influence. They steam-clean the aldehydes, mostly vanillin, from the wood and then use the barrels to store lesser wines before using them for *Reservas* and *Gran Reservas*. Only a very few Riojas made in this way have sufficient character to be successful. Such wines derive extra concentration from lower yields, but they are not Rioja in the classic sense.

Rioja's classic styles

The region has justly achieved world-wide fame for its ability to produce fine-quality red wines that are distinctly oaky and competitively priced. The story for whites is a little different, because, given the equivalent oak-aging of a Rioja *tinto*, a Rioja *blanco* loses its fruit and freshness, rapidly oxidizes and leaves a sharp, acid taste in the mouth. This is how all white Riojas once tasted, but it is interesting to note that, starting with the 1978 vintage, even Marqués de Murrieta *blanco*, perhaps the most traditional of white Riojas, began to change its spots: first a touch of fruit, then some freshness, and now a modest balance of both. Much white wine is still made in the traditional style, but virtually every major exporting house at least offers an alternative, in the form of "new-wave" white wine.

Rioja's "new-wave" whites

Unlike the *sans-chêne* reds, the ultra-clean "new-wave" whites deserve a place in today's market, where trends are for lighter, fresher and drier wines. Headed by the Marqués de Cáceres *blanco*, a steely-crisp and clean wine that can be reminiscent of Sauvignon blanc, although made from 100 per cent Viura grapes, this category is firmly established with consumers. Whereas these wines are enjoyable, they do not, as yet, possess any distinctive generic characteristics that identify them as Rioja. The whites that manage to combine the best of the old and the new have more distinct regional characteristics. Olarra's "Añares Blanco Seco", Franco-Españolas' "Diamante" and CVNE's "Monopole", for example, manage to combine the creamy-vanilla oak character that is the hallmark of Rioja, with superb freshness and heaps of creamy, lemony fruit.

RIOJA'S DISTRICTS

Rioja's 37,500 hectares (92,665 acres) of vineyards are located along the Ebro Valley, between Haro and Alfaro, and throughout its hinterland, with vines clustered around many of the Ebro's tributaries, one of which, the Oja River, gave its name to the region. An average of 12 million cases (1,080,000 hectolitres) of wine is produced every year, some 70 per cent of which is red, 15 per cent white and 15 per cent rosé, called *rosado*. Most Rioja is blended from wines or grapes originating from the region's three districts: Rioja Alta, Rioja Alavesa and Rioja Baja.

Rioja Alta

Vineyards: *16,130 hectares (39,860 acres)*
Grape varieties: *Tempranillo 60%, Mazuelo 10%, Garnacha 10%, Graciano 2%, Viura 15%, Malvasia 2%, Others 1%*

The principal towns of Rioja, Logroño and Haro, are both in the Rioja Alta. Logroño is a very big town by Spanish standards, but Haro, at the western edge of the region, is a much smaller, far more charming, older and traditional enclosed hilltop community. The area's wine is Rioja's fullest in terms of fruit and concentration, which can be velvety smooth. Bodegas Muga makes fine examples of pure Rioja Alta, as do CVNE – in the form of their "Imperial" range – in nine years out of every ten.

Rioja Alavesa

Vineyards: *8,035 hectares (19,855 acres)*
Grape varieties: *Tempranillo 80%, Garnacha 5%, Viura 10%, Others 5%*

There are no large towns in the Alavesa, a district that is similar in climate to the Alta. The wines produced here are Rioja's fullest in body and reveal a much firmer character than those of the Alta and Baja, with greater acidity. It was to the Alavesa that Pedro Domecq came, after years of intensive research, to plant a vast estate of 400 hectares (985 acres), cultivating his vines on wires as opposed to using the bush method traditional to the region. Apart from Domecq Domaine, which is obviously a pure Alavesa wine, Remelluri's "Labista de Alava" and Laserna's "Viñedos del Contino", two single-vineyard Alavesas, and CVNE's "Real" range (although not quite 100 per cent Alavesa), are all typical of the district.

Rioja Baja

Vineyards: *13,335 hectares (32,950 acres)*
Grape varieties: *Tempranillo 2%, Garnacha 90%, Viura 3%, Others 5%*

A semi-arid area influenced by the Mediterranean, it is hotter, sunnier and drier than the Alta and Alavesa, with rainfall that varies throughout the region, averaging between 38 and 43 centimetres (15 and 17 inches) per year, but falling as low as 25 centimetres (10 inches) at Alfaro in the south. Some 20 per cent of the vines growing in Rioja Baja come within, and can claim, the Navarra appellation. The wines are deep-coloured and very alcoholic, sometimes as strong as 18 per cent, but lack acidity, aroma and finesse, and are best used for blending.

GRAPE VARIETIES

As Rioja wines are almost invariably blended, their character and quality depend to a large extent upon the producer's own house style. In addition to blending the various strengths, bodies and different styles of *terroir* from relative areas, there is usually an attempt to balance the various varietal characteristics of one or more of the seven grapes that are permitted in Rioja. These grape varieties are: Tempranillo, Garnacha, Graciano, Mazuelo, Viura, Malvasia and the little-utilized Garnacha blanca.

A typical red Rioja blend
Tempranillo 70% for a distinctive bouquet, good acidity and aging characteristics. The grape ripens some two weeks before the Garnacha (*temprano* means "early") and is also known as the Cencibel, Tinto fino or Ull de Llebre in other parts of Spain.
Garnacha 15% for body and alcohol – too much can make the wine coarse. This is the Grenache of the Rhône, also known as the Lladoner and Aragonés. It is the dominant grape of the Rioja Baja, where it regularly produces wines of 16 per cent alcohol.

Graciano 7.5% for freshness, flavour and aroma. A singular variety with the unusual property of thin, yet tough black skin.

Mazuelo 7.5% for colour, tannin and good aging characteristics. This is the Carignan of southern France and is known as the Cariñena in other parts of Spain. To the above a small proportion of white grapes, perhaps five or ten per cent of Viura, may sometimes be added.

A typical white Rioja blend
Viura 95% for freshness and fragrance. This grape has reasonable acidity and a good resistance to oxidation. It is also known as the Macabéo and Alcañon in other parts of Spain.
Malvasia 5% for richness, fragrance, acidity and complexity. Also known as the Rojal blanco and Subirat, this grape has a tendency to colour a patchy red when ripe, so pressing must be quick to avoid tainting the juice. Most white wines are pure Viura, although some contain up to 50 per cent Malvasia.

NAVARRA

Not quite in the same league as Rioja, yet capable of producing some very fine wines that are usually exceptional value, the wine-growing region of Navarra lies south of Pamplona, overlapping part of Rioja Baja. It consists of 26,500 hectares (65,500 acres), of which 18,000 hectares (44,500 acres) are classified as DO Navarra. Recent marketing successes have reversed a certain decline in the area that had driven some growers to plant asparagus and artichokes rather than vines. This revival has encouraged some ambitious experiments with classic foreign grape varieties. Cabernet sauvignon has been an authorized variety on an experimental basis for some years, but several others are now being investigated by the Estación de Viticultura y Enología de Navarra (EVENSA), Spain's most advanced viticultural and oenological research station. It is based in Olite, in the Ribera Alta, and has a number of sub-stations situated throughout all the districts of Navarra. Merlot is likely to become an approved variety and others under consideration include Chardonnay, Pinot noir, Gamay, Syrah, Chenin blanc, Gewürztraminer, Sangiovese, Barbera, Rhine riesling and even Ruby cabernet, the Californian cross.

Navarra's wine industry

Navarra has 84 bodegas, of which no less than 52 are cooperatives, but only 16 have any record of exporting their products and, of these, just four actually vinify and age the wines on their own premises. One of these four is, however, the central Unión Territorial de Cooperativas de Campo, or UTECO for short, which could profitably extend its export activities to all 52 of its member cooperatives.

FACTORS AFFECTING TASTE AND QUALITY

Location
Situated in Northern Spain in the upper valley of the River Ebro, Rioja and Navarra are bounded to the northeast by the Pyrenees and to the southwest by the Sierra de la Demanda. Navarra has the most northerly vineyards in Spain.

Climate
The Cantabrian Mountains, a range that is modest in elevation yet impressive in structure, provide a major key to the quality of Rioja, protecting the region from the devastating winds whipped up over the Bay of Biscay and holding in precarious check the influence of the Atlantic and Mediterranean. That of the former is at its strongest in Navarra, and the latter in the Rioja Baja. Temperature rises and rainfall decreases as one moves eastwards towards the Mediterranean. The Pyrenees also provide shelter from the north, but winters can be cold and foggy, particularly in Navarra. Rioja can suffer from hailstorms and the hot, dry *solano* wind.

Aspect
Vineyards are variously located, from the highest in the foothills of the Pyrenees in Navarra to those on the flatter lands of the Rioja Baja in the southeast. Generally, the best vineyards are in the central hill country of the Rioja Alta and Alavesa.

Soil
Although soils do vary, the common denominator is limestone. In Navarra, limestone contains between 25 and 45 per cent "active" lime, and is coated by a layer of silty-alluvium near the Ebro or weathered limestone and sandstone topsoil in drier areas. Limestone with either sandstone or calcareous clay and slatey deposits dominate the Rioja Alavesa and Alta, while a ferruginous-clay and a silty-loam of alluvial origin cover a limestone base in the Rioja Baja.

Viticulture and vinification
Most wines are a blend of at least three grapes from different areas; very few are 100 per cent pure varietal or single-estate wines. The traditional vinification process, which is still used to produce the local *vino nuevo*, is a crude form of *macération carbonique* carried out in open vats, and trodden after the first few days of inter-cellular fermentation. This is much as the Beaujolais wines used to be made, but the result here is much coarser, with a dark-damson colour and lots of youthful tannin.
Most wines are, however, vinified in the normal manner, but aged longer than other commercial wines. Although recent trends favour shorter oak-aging and longer bottle-maturation, the character of Rioja still relies heavily on oak, and it is essential for its future that it should remain so.

Primary grape varieties
Tempranillo, Viura

Secondary grape varieties
Garnacha, Garnacha blanca, Graciano, Muscat blanc à petits grains, Mazuelo, Malvasia, Cabernet sauvignon

NAVARRA'S DISTRICTS

The region is divided into five districts:

Baja Montana
Vineyards: *4,000 hectares (9,884 acres)*
Grape varieties: *Garnacha, Tempranillo 50%, Others 50%*

Situated in the Montana foothills, Baja Montana is the highest and wettest area of Navarra and the vintage is considerably later here than in the south of the region. Extra rain means the grape yield is between 50 and 100 per cent higher than in any of the other four areas. The district produces some of Navarra's best rosés, fresh and fruity in aroma and flavour.

Ribera Alta
Vineyards: *8,100 hectares (20,015 acres)*
Grape varieties: *Viura 40%, Tempranillo 25%, Garnacha 15%, Malvasia 10%*

The largest of Navarra's five districts, Ribera Alta borders the Rioja Alta and produces some of the region's finest wines. The rosés are smooth and aromatic, the reds soft and fruity and the whites are soft, dry and fresh.

Ribera Baja
Vineyards: *8,000 hectares (19,768 acres)*
Grape varieties: *Garnacha 45%, Viura 30%, Malvasia 10%, Muscat à petits grains 10%, Others 5%*

This very hot and dry region includes approximately 20 per cent of Rioja's Baja district and produces typically deep-coloured, full and robust red wines and a few sweet Moscatels.

Tierra Estella
Vineyards: *4,000 hectares (9,884 acres)*
Grape varieties: *Tempranillo 55%, Garnacha 15%, Mazuelo, Graciano 20%, Others 10%*

Climatically similar to Valdizarbe in the north of the area, though getting gradually drier further south, the Tierra Estella makes pleasant, fruity reds and rosés from the Tempranillo, but those from the Garnacha tend to oxidize. Some crisp white wines from the Viura are also produced.

Valdizarbe
Vineyards: *2,500 hectares (6,177 acres)*
Grape varieties: *Tempranillo 45%, Garnacha 45%, Mazuelo, Graciano and others 10%*

A district with a slightly drier climate than the Baja Montana. Excellent value red and rosé wines from the Tempranillo are produced here, although some have a tendency to oxidize.

Tierra Estella, Navarra, above
The picturesque village of Maneru is situated near Estella, southwest of Pamplona. Tempranillo is the main variety grown in the area's vineyards.

The wines of Rioja and Navarra

NAVARRA DO

The temperate climate, alluvial covered limestone soil, grape varieties, good winemakers and fine traditions combine to produce a truly classic wine region. Like Rioja, the appellation has built its reputation on oaky red wines and is now augmenting them with fresh, fruity and surprisingly crisp whites and rosés.

🔖 **ALL WINES Primary:** Tempranillo, Graciano, Viura **Secondary:** Garnacha, Mazuela, Garnacha blanca, Malvasia, Palomino, Moscatel, Cabernet sauvignon (authorized experimental grape variety)

RED The emphasis of these fine, ruby-coloured, full-bodied, well-flavoured red wines has switched from Garnacha to Tempranillo since the early-1980s and the wines now have better balance.

📖 1981, 1982, 1983, 1985, 1986, 1987, 1989

🍷 Between 3-10 years

WHITE Fresh, fruity and well-made dry white wines.

📖 1982, 1983, 1984, 1985, 1989

🍷 Within 1-2 years

ROSÉ Attractively coloured dry wines with a fresh aroma and fruity flavour.

📖 1981, 1982, 1983, 1985

🍷 Within 1-4 years

☆ *See* The best bodegas of Navarra, p.276.

RIOJA DO

Indubitably Spain's greatest wine region in that it produces far and away the largest quantity of the country's finest wines.

🔖 **ALL WINES Primary:** Tempranillo, Viura **Secondary:** Garnacha, Graciano, Mazuela, Malvasía de Rioja, Garnacha blanca

RED Typically garnet-coloured, medium- to full-bodied, rich, mellow and oaky wines that are still amazing value despite the inevitable price increases that have occurred as the fame of Rioja spreads.

📖 1981, 1982, 1985, 1986, 1989

🍷 Between 3-8 years (*Vino de Crianza*), between 5-30 years (*Reserva*), between 8-30 years (*Gran Reserva*), and up to 50 years or more in exceptional cases

WHITE Three basic styles of Rioja can be identified: "traditional" (very oaky, ranging from clean and fruity to unmistakably oxidized), "new-wave" (no oak, lighter, very fresh and delicate fruit), and "in-between" (very clean and fruity with tangy-oak on the aftertaste). Most wines (all the best) are dry, although some semi-sweet and sweet wines can be found.

📖 1981, 1982, 1985, 1989

🍷 Within 1-3 years (unless you like the oxidized traditional style, in which case the wine gives increasing pleasure the longer it is kept)

ROSÉ An underrated category of Rioja, these wines are mostly dry, very fresh and intensely fruity.

📖 1981, 1982, 1985, 1989

🍷 Within 1-3 years

☆ *See* The best bodegas of Rioja, below and The best of the rest, p.275.

The best bodegas of Rioja

BODEGAS EL COTO
Oyón, Alava

Production: *180,000 cases*
Vineyards: *140 ha (345 acres)*
Established: *1973*

These wines have immaculate style, grace and finesse. I have put them into blind tastings against some of the best Riojas, and they have usually been placed in the top three or four.

☆ El Coto, Coto de Imaz Reserva

BODEGAS MARTÍNEZ BUJANDA
Oyón, Alava

Production: *105,000 cases*
Vineyards: *200 ha (495 acres)*
Established: *1890*

This high-tech winery produces a pure, fresh *blanco* and fine, firm *tintos*.

☆ "Valdemar" (*blanco*, and Reserva and Gran Reserva *tinto*)

BODEGAS MUGA
Barrio de la Estación, Haro, Alta

Production: *33,000 cases*
Vineyards: *22 ha (55 acres)*
Established: *1932*

Top-class *tintos* are made here. The "Prado Enea" is in the rich, mellow Burgundian style, with generous plummy-spicy fruit and a lovely smoky complexity. The basic Muga is obviously much younger and fresher, but can be aged to obtain a similar elegance and the seductive, silky finish found in the "Prado Enea". Isaac Muga also produces a *blanco*, a *rosado* and a Cava.

☆ Muga *tinto*, "Prado Enea" (Reserva and Gran Reserva)

BODEGAS OLARRA
Polígono de Cantabria, Logroño

Production: *400,000 cases*
Vineyards: *None*
Established: *1972*

This ultra-modern, "Y"-shaped bodega houses a high-tech winery that nevertheless incorporates tradition where Olarra want it. The wines are all very good to excellent. I have never tasted one that could be ranked as one of the greatest Riojas produced, but I have not come across another bodega to which I could give carte blanche approval. This extends to the fresh, fruity, nouveau-style white.

☆ "Añares" and "Cerro Añon" ranges Second label: "La Catedral"

BODEGAS RIOJANAS
Estación 1, Cenicero

Production: *170,000 cases*
Vineyards: *200 ha (495 acres)*
Established: *1890*

This bodega has built its reputation on red wines, particularly the Reserva and Gran Reserva versions of the oaky Viña Albina and the plummy Monte Real.

☆ "Canchales" *tinto*, "Monte Real" *tinto* Reserva, "Viña Albina" *tinto*

LA CATEDRAL
See Bodegas Olarra.

CERRO AÑON
See Bodegas Olarra.

COMPAÑÍA VINÍCOLA DEL NORTE DE ESPAÑA
See CVNE.

CONSTANILLA
See Marqués de Cáceres.

CONTINO
Sociedad Vinícola Laserna, Finca San Rafael, Laserna, Laguardia, Alava

Production: *10,000 cases*
Vineyards: *45 ha (110 acres)*
Established: *1974*

Partly owned by CVNE, the wine has an excellent, deep colour, an aromatic bouquet and a creamy-rich vanilla and fruit flavour, with a voluptuous finish.

☆ Contino Rioja Reserva

CUNE
See CVNE.

CVNE
(Compañía Vinícola del Norte de España)
Avenida Costa del Vino 21, Haro

Production: *333,000 cases*
Vineyards: *470 ha (1,160 acres)*
Established: *1879*

The "Imperial" wines show finesse in the traditional sense, the "Viña Real" is in a plummier, fatter style, the "Monopole" *blanco* combines freshness of fruit with creamy new oak and the "Cune" wines are the freshest of all.

☆ "Viña Real", "Cune" ("Lanceros" and *rosado*), "Monopole" *blanco*, "Imperial" (Reserva and Gran Reserva)

GRANDEZA
See Marqués de Cáceres.

LA GRANJA NUESTRA SEÑORA DE REMÉLLURI
See Remélluri.

GRAN VENDEMA
See Marqués de Cáceres.

IMPERIAL
See CVNE.

LABASTIDA DE ALAVA
See Remélluri.

LÓPEZ DE HEREDIA VIÑA TONDONIA
See Viña Tondonia.

MARQUÉS DE CÁCERES
Union Viti-Vinícola de Logroño, Carretera de Logroño, Cenicero

Production: *350,000 cases*
Established: *1970*

Of these wines, the *tinto* style is quite light, yet firm, with the potential for great finesse (the wines always benefit from extra time in bottle). The *blanco* is the market-leader in new-wave dry whites; and the *rosado* is fragrant, dry and quite delicious.

☆ Marqués de Cáceres Second labels: "Constanilla", "Gran Vendema", "Grandeza", "Rivarey"

MARQUÉS DE MURRIETA
Ygay, Logroña, Alta

Production: *75,000 cases*
Vineyards: *150 ha (370 acres)*
Established: *1848*

The Rioja *blanco* from this bodega is sought out by those who adore the old oxidized style. I can just about tolerate the youngest *crianzas,* which have shown a little more fruit and freshness since 1978, but the *blanco* Reserva tastes like a cup of tea that has been brewed in a new oak barrel. To be totally objective, however, one cannot criticize Marqués de Murrieta for producing the wine, as it is considered by many to be the epitome of the genre. Where the bodega really excels, though, is in its red wines and the remarkable range of old vintages that remain commercially available. Its *pièce de résistance* is the remarkable Castillo Ygay Reserva Especial *tinto.* The vintage available at the time of writing was the 1942. This is, in fact, a relatively recent introduction, the 1934 being available up until 1983!

☆ "Castillo" Ygay Reserva Especial, Ygay *tinto* "Etiqueta Blanca", Ygay *tinto* Reserva

MONTE REAL
See Bodegas Riojanas.

PRADO ENEA
See Bodegas Muga.

REMÉLLURI
La Granja Nuestra Señora de Remélluri,
Labastida, Alava

Production: *11,500 cases*
Vineyards: *32 ha (80 acres)*
Established: *1967*

With the exception of the rather awkward 1979 vintage, the exquisite balance, elegance and finesse of this single-vineyard Labastida de Alava belies its great richness of fruit and long creamy-vanilla oak finish.

☆ "Labastida de Alava"

LA RIOJA ALTA
Avenida Vizcaya,
Haro

Production: *120,000 cases*
Vineyards: *125 ha (310 acres)*
Established: *1890*

The Viña Alberdi is an excellent introduction to these wines, but the serious business begins with the elegant Viña Ardanza, a remarkably complex wine considering that it accounts for more than half of the firm's production. The Reserva 904 is an exceptionally concentrated and classy wine and Reserva 890 is a rare product indeed, with eight years in wood and six in bottle.

☆ "Viña Alberdi" *tinto,* "Viña Ardanza" Reserva, Reserva "904", Reserva "890"

RIVAREY
See Marqués de Cáceres.

SOCIEDAD VINÍCOLA LASERNA
See Contino (usual name).

UNION VITI-VINÍCOLA DE LOGROÑO
See Marqués de Cácares (usual name).

VALDEMAR
See Bodegas Martínez Bujanda.

VIÑA ALBERDI
See La Rioja Alta.

VIÑA ARDANZA
See La Rioja Alta.

VIÑA BOSCONIA
See Viña Tondonia.

VIÑA CUBILLO
See Viña Tondonia.

VIÑA TONDONIA
López de Heredia Viña Tondonia
Avenida de Vizcaya 3,
Haro

Production: *130,000 cases*
Vineyards: *170 ha (420 acres)*
Established: *1877*

Just up the hill from the very traditional Bodegas Muga is Tondonia, an old-fashioned firm that makes Muga look high-tech. It is impossible to find a more traditional bodega, from the massive cobwebs in the tasting room, to the religious dipping into wax of all bottle ends as if they contained Port. The style here is rich and oaky, and the wines are capable of great age. Tondonia is the finest wine, Bosconia the fattest and Cubillo the youngest.

☆ "Viña Tondonia" *(blanco* and *tinto),* "Viña Bosconia" *tinto,* "Viña Cubillo" *tinto*

VINEDOS DEL CONTINO
See Contino (usual name).

YGAY
See Marqués de Murrieta.

The best of the rest

AGE BODEGAS UNIDAS
See Félix Azpilicueta Martínez (usual name).

AGESSIMO
See Félix Azpilicueta Martínez.

FÉLIX AZPILICUETA MARTÍNEZ
Barrio de la Estación,
Fuenmayor

Production: *1.7 million cases*
Vineyards: *50 ha (124 acres)*
Established: *1881*

☆ "Marqués del Romeral" Reserva, "Fuenmayor" Reserva
Second labels: "Agessimo", "Credencial"

BODEGAS ALAVESAS
Carretera de Elciego,
Laguardia, Alava

Production: *22,000 cases*
Vineyards: *90 ha (220 acres)*
Established: *1970*

☆ Solar de Samaniego

BODEGAS BERBERANA
Carretera Elciego,
Cenicero

Production: *1.8 million cases*
Vineyards: *55 ha (135 acres)*
Established: *1877*

☆ "Carta de Plata" *tinto,* "Carta de Oro" *(blanco* and *tinto),* Gran Reserva

BODEGAS BERONIA
Carretera Ollauri-Nájera,
Ollauri

Production: *72,000 cases*
Vineyards: *10 ha (25 acres)*
Established: *1974*

☆ Beronia 5° año *tinto,* Reserva

BODEGAS BILBAÍNAS
Particular del Norte 2,
Bilbao

Production: *230,000 cases*
Vineyards: *250 ha (620 acres)*
Established: *1901*

☆ Vendimia Especial, Viña Pomal *tinto,* Viña Zaco *tinto,* Viña Pomal Reserva

BODEGAS CAMPILLO
The Second Label range of Faustino Martínez, often better than the principal label because Faustino uses these wines to break in new barrels.
See Bodegas Faustino Martínez.

BODEGAS CAMPO VIEJO
Gustavo Adolfo Bécquer 3,
Logroño

Production: *2 million cases*
Vineyards: *260 ha (640 acres)*
Established: *1959*

☆ Reserva, Gran Reserva (on export markets), "Marqués de Villamagna" Gran Reserva, Crianza *tinto*
Second labels: Bodegas Castillo, "San Asensio"

BODEGAS CARLOS SERRES
Avenida Santo Domingo 40,
Haro

Production: *110,000 cases*
Vineyards: *None*
Established: *1896*

☆ Carlomagno *tinto* Reserva, Carlos Serres *tinto* Gran Reserva

BODEGAS CASTILLO SAN ASENSIO
See Bodegas Campo Viejo.

BODEGAS CORRAL
Carretera de Logroño,
Navarrete

Production: *100,000 cases*
Vineyards: *40 ha (100 acres)*
Established: *1898*

☆ "Don Jacobo" *tinto*

BODEGAS DOMECQ
Villabuena,
Elciego, Alava

Production: *250,000 cases*
Vineyards: *400 ha (985 acres)*
Established: *1973*

☆ Domecq Domain Reserva, Gran Reserva
Second Label: "Marqués de Arienzo"

BODEGAS FAUSTINO MARTÍNEZ
Carretera de Logroño,
Oyón, Alava

Production: *300,000 cases*
Vineyards: *350 ha (865 acres)*
Established: *1860*

☆ Faustino I

BODEGAS FRANCO ESPAÑOLAS
Cabo Noval 2,
Logroño

Production: *550,000 cases*
Vineyards: *Insignificant*
Established: *1890*

☆ "Viña Soledad" *blanco,* Rioja "Bordon" *tinto*

BODEGAS GURPEGUI
San Adrián
(This firm also has cellars at Bodegas Berceo, Calle de las Cuevas 32, Haro)

Production: *825,000 cases*
Vineyards: *200 ha (495 acres)*
Established: *1872*

☆ "Viña Berceo", "Dominio de la Plana", "Gonzalo de Berceo" *tinto*

BODEGAS MARTÍNEZ LACUESTA
La Ventilla 71,
Haro

Production: *220,000 cases*
Vineyards: *None*
Established: *1895*

☆ "Campeador" Gran Reserva, Reserva Especial

BODEGAS LAGUNILLA
Carretera Vitoria,
Fuenmayor

Production: *250,000 cases*
Vineyards: *None*
Established: *1885*

☆ "Viña Herminia" (*tinto* and *tinto* Reserva and Gran Reserva)

BODEGAS LAN
Paraje de Buicio,
Fuenmayor

Production: *220,000 cases*
Established: *1970*

☆ Lan *blanco*, Lan *tinto*, "Viña Lanciano" *tinto* Gran Reserva

BODEGAS MARQUÉS DEL PUERTO
López Agós y Cia,
Fuenmayor

Production: *132,000 cases*
Vineyards: *40 ha (100 acres)*
Established: *1972*

☆ Marqués del Puerto Reserva

BODEGAS MONTECILLO
San Cristóbal 34,
Fuenmayor

Production: *220,000 cases*
Vineyards: *None*
Established: *1874*

☆ Montecillo (*tinto* and *blanco*), "Viña Monty", "Viña Cumbrero" *tinto*

BODEGAS MURÚA
Carretera de Laguardia,
Elciego, Alava

Vineyards: *None*
Established: *1974*

☆ 5° Años, Reserva

BODEGAS MUERZA
Pl. de Vera Magallón 1,
San Adrián, Navarra

Production: *48,000 cases*
Vineyards: *25 ha (64 acres)*
Established: *1882*

☆ Rioja Vega Gran Reserva

BODEGAS PALACIO
San Lázaro 1,
Laguardia, Alava

Production: *83,000 cases*
Vineyards: *10 ha (25 acres)*
Established: *1894*

☆ "Glorioso", "Bodas de Oro", "Palacio" Tinto

BODEGAS RAMÓN BILBAO
Carretera Casalarreina, Haro

Production: *77,000 cases*
Vineyards: *10 ha (25 acres)*
Established: *1924*

☆ "Viña Turzaballa" *tinto*

BODEGAS RIOJA SANTIAGO
Barrio de la Estación,
Haro

Production: *150,000 cases*
Vineyards: *None*
Established: *1870*

☆ "Condal", "Condal" Reserva, Gran "Condal" Reserva

CREDENCIAL
See Félix Azpilicueta Martínez.

COVIAL
Laguardia, Alava

A bottle of the Bastarrica 1985, tasted in 1986, was the most delicious *macération carbonique* Rioja I have ever found.

☆ "Bastarrica"

LÓPEZ AGÓS Y CIA
Bodegas Marqués del Puerto

MARQUÉS DE ARIENZO
See Bodegas Domecq.

MARQUÉS DE RISCAL
Torres 1,
Elciego, Alava

Production: *250,000 cases*
Vineyards: *200 ha (495 acres)*
Established: *1860*

The red wines from Rioja's most famous bodega have an unpleasant musty-mushroom character.

FEDERICO PATERNINA
Avenido Santo Domingo 11,
Haro

Production: *1 million cases*
Vineyards: *None*
Established: *1898*

☆ "Rinsol" *blanco*, "Banda Azul" *tinto*, "Viña Vial" Gran Reserva

THE BEST COOPERATIVES OF RIOJA

Note: Cooperatives are not as important in Rioja, in terms of quality and export potential, as they are in, say, France, but recommended wines of those below are worth listing.

COOPERATIVA VINÍCOLA DE LABASTIDA
Labastida, Alavesa

☆ "Gastrijo" Reserva, "Castillo" Labastida Gran Reserva

SOCIEDAD COOPERATIVA "COSECHEROS ALAVESES"
Laguardia, Alava

☆ "Artadi"

The best bodegas of Navarra

AGRONAVARRA CENAL
Ciudadela 5,
Pamplona

Established: *1983*

☆ "Campo nuevo" *tinto*, "Principe de Viana" *tinto*

BODEGAS SIMÓN CAYO
Murchante

☆ "Monte Cierzo", "Viña Zarcillo"

BODEGAS JULIÁN CHIVITE
Ribera,
Cintruénigo

Established: *1860*

☆ "Viña Marcos" *tinto*, "125 Anniversario" *tinto*, "Parador Chivite" *tinto*, "Gran Feudo" *tinto*, "Cibonero Reserva", Chivite *blanco*

BODEGAS IRACHE
Irache I,
Ayegui

☆ "Gran Irache", "Viña Irache" *tinto*, "Viña Ordoiz" *tinto*

BODEGAS OCHOA
Carretera Zaragoza 21,
Olite

Established: *1845*

☆ Ochoa *tinto*, "Viña Chapitel" *tinto*

BODEGAS VILLAFRANCA DE NAVARRA
Carretera Pamplona,
Villafranca

Established: *1921*

☆ "Monte Ory" *tinto*

SEÑORIO DE SARRÍA
Puente la Reina

Established: *1952*

☆ Gran Vino del Señorío de Sarría *tinto*, "Viña del Perdon" *tinto*, "Viña Ecoyen" *tinto*, Blanco *seco*, Rosado

VINÍCOLA NAVARRA
Carretera Pamplona-Zaragoza,
Campanas

Established: *1880*

☆ "Bandeo" *tinto*, "Castillo de Tiebas" Reserva, "Las Campanas" *tinto*

THE BEST COOPERATIVES OF NAVARRA

COOPERATIVA "CIRBONERA"
Ribera,
Cintruénigo

☆ "Campolasierpe" *rosado*

SOCIEDAD COOPERATIVA "NUESTRA SEÑORA DEL ROMERO"
Carretera Tarazona,
Cascante

☆ "Nuevo Vino" *tinto*, "Señor de Cascante" *tinto*, "Torrecilla" *tinto*

Catalonia

The most famous name in Catalonia is Penedés. There are essentially two reasons why this wine district has risen to stardom so rapidly since the early 1980s – the success of Cava, Spain's only DO *méthode champenoise* wine, and the winemaking genius of Miguel Torres Jnr.

THE TORRES WINE BUSINESS HAS BEEN HANDED DOWN from father to son since 1870, but the firm's true potential only emerged under the present Miguel Torres Snr., who began travelling the international markets just after the war. He became renowned for spreading the gospel of Spain's fine bottled wines and his stout refusal to supply Sangria, however lucrative the offers. It was, however, his son Miguel Torres Jnr. who put Torres on the fine-wine map through his innovative ideas that have stimulated the entire Spanish wine trade.

THE CONTRIBUTION OF MIGUEL TORRES

After reluctantly agreeing with his father to study oenology and viticulture in France, it was another two years before Miguel Jnr. became dedicated to a winemaking career, but in 1962, he returned home to put his theory into practice. His first move was to plant classic French and German grape varieties. This was considered bizarre by the then very traditional Spanish trade, and even Miguel now admits that when he began these experiments he had no idea of the true nature of the Penedés climate. He attributes the success of the Cabernet sauvignon at the family's estate at Pachs to pure luck. I would simply add that to have such luck requires an inquisitive mind and the willingness to take risks.

Miguel Torres was the first to introduce cool-fermentation techniques to Spain, perhaps the greatest catalyst in the transformation of its image as a source of cheap wines to that of a fine-wine producing country. He has also exported his intensive-cultivation techniques (*see* Viticulture, p.15) to California, and I have no doubt that these will be as widely practised as cool-fermentation in the world's hot and arid areas in the 1990s. The clean, oaky character of his highly respected top wines has

FACTORS AFFECTING TASTE AND QUALITY

Location
Lying in the northeast corner of Spain, where the River Ebro enters the Mediterranean, this area includes Alella, Penedés, Tarragona, Priorato and Terra Alta.

Climate
A mild Mediterranean climate prevails in Alella and Penedés, becoming more continental (hotter summers and colder winters) moving westwards and inland towards Terra Alta. In the same way, problems with fog in the northeast are gradually replaced by the hazard of frost towards the southwestern inland areas. In the high vineyards of Alto Penedés, white and aromatic grape varieties are cultivated at greater altitudes than traditional ones; they benefit from cooler temperatures.

Aspect
Vines are grown on all types of land ranging from the flat plains of the Campo de Tarragona, through the 400-metre (1,300-ft) high plateaux of Terra Alta to the highest vineyards in the Alto Penedés which reach an altitude of 800 metres (2,620 ft). For every 100 metres (330 ft) rise in altitude, the temperature drops 1°C (0.56°F).

Soil
There is a wide variety of soils ranging from granite in Alella, through limestone-dominated clay, chalk and sand in Penedés, to a mixture of mainly limestone and chalk with granite and alluvial deposits in Tarragona. The soil in Priorato is an unusual reddish slate with particles of reflective mica.

Viticulture and vinification
Catalonia is a hot-bed of experimentation. Ultra-modern winemaking techniques have been pioneered by Cava companies such as Codorníu and fine-wine specialists like Torres.

With the exception of very traditional Priorato, viticultural and vinification practices are usually quite modern throughout Catalonia. This is especially so at the Raimat Estate in Lérida, where the technology ranges from the latest and most efficient "Sernagiotto" continuous press for bulk production to the "Potter gravity crusher". Described as the simplest press ever designed, this extracts no more than 50 to 60 per cent of the grape's potential juice.

Primary grape varieties
Cariñena, Garnacha, Macabéo, Malvasia, Monastrell, Parellada, Xarello

Secondary grape varieties
Cabernet franc, Cabernet sauvignon, Chardonnay, Chenin blanc, Colombard, Garnacha blanca, Garnacha peluda, Gewürztraminer, Merlot, Moscatel, Muscat, Pansá rosada, Pedro Ximénez, Pinot noir, Riesling, Samsó, Subirat parent, Syrah, Tempranillo

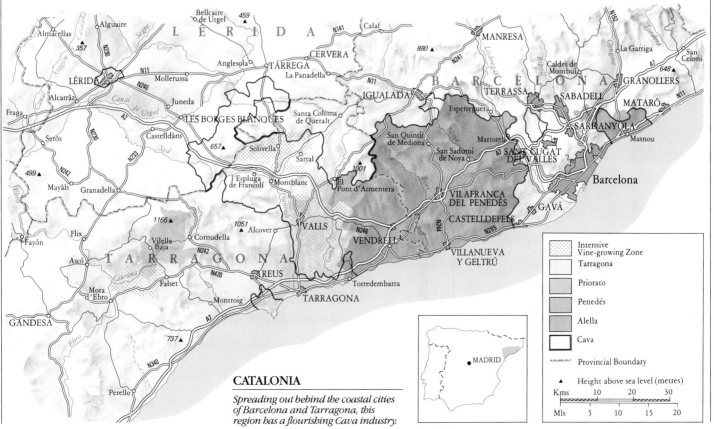

CATALONIA
Spreading out behind the coastal cities of Barcelona and Tarragona, this region has a flourishing Cava industry.

Intensive Vine-growing Zone
Tarragona
Priorato
Penedés
Alella
Cava
- - - Provincial Boundary
▲ Height above sea level (metres)
Kms 10 20 30
Mls 5 10 15 20

encouraged a swing away from long-term maturation in old barrels to limited aging in new oak. Two other Catalonian producers now produce wines of a quality that can be compared with Torres': the Californian-based Jean León, also in the Penedés, and the Raimat Estate, Codorníu's high-performance Lérida vineyard; but as yet these do not have the range and proven consistency of Torres.

PENEDÉS

Prior to phylloxera, which struck in the Penedés in 1876, more than 80 per cent of the vineyards were planted with black grape varieties. When the vines were grafted onto American rootstock, white varieties were given priority due to the growing success of sparkling wines. Today, this region covers approximately 45,000 hectares (111,120 acres), of which some 25,000 hectares (61,775 acres) are classified as Denominación de Origen Penedés. It is easy to recognize the classic varieties in the vineyard because they are invariably trained along wires, whereas traditional Spanish vines grow in little bushes. Production averages 1.5 million hectolitres (16.7 million cases) of wine per year; 80 per cent is white.

Fermentation tanks at Torres, above
The headquarters of Torres' operation is to be found at Vilafranca del Penedés. Here Miguel Torres Jnr. has pioneered modern vinification techniques.

Medio Penedés vineyards, below
East of San Sadurní de Noya, the centre of the region's Cava industry, rows of vines stretch peacefully towards the Sierra de Montserrat.

PENEDÉS DISTRICTS

The region of Penedés can be divided into three district areas, Bajo Penedés, Medio Penedés and Penedés Superior:

Bajo (or Baix) Penedés

Grape varieties: *Monastrell, Malvasia, Garnacha, Cariñena and various other, mostly black, grapes.*

This is the coastal strip and is the warmest of all three areas, being equivalent to Regions III, IV and V, using the Californian heat summation system. The land is low and flat, with vines growing on limestone, clay and sandy soil. This area increasingly produces full-bodied reds such as Torres' "Tres Torres Sangredetoro", "Tres Torres Gran Sangredetoro" and "Gran Sangredetoro".

Medio Penedés

Grape varieties: *Mostly Xarello and Macabéo; this is also the best area for Tempranillo, Cabernet sauvignon, Merlot and Monastrell.*

The middle section of the Penedés is slightly hilly, occasionally flat land at an altitude of some 200 metres (660 ft) in the foothills west of Barcelona, on a soil of mostly limestone and clay. It has a cooler climate than the Bajo area, with most areas averaging Regions II and III. This is essentially Cava country, but it also produces the best of the new-style reds, and Torres' "Coronas", "Gran Coronas" and "Gran Coronas Black Label" wines.

Penedés Superior

Grape varieties: *Almost exclusively white and mostly Parellada, plus Riesling, Gewürztraminer and Muscat. A little Pinot noir is also grown.*

This area is furthest inland of the three and the grapes grow on chalky foothills at an altitude of between 500 to 800 metres (1,640 to 2,620 ft). Climatic conditions are the coolest in the Penedés, equivalent to Regions I and II. It is so cool that Cabernet sauvignon will not ripen here and almost all the wines produced are white. However the area is well suited to Pinot noir, grown at San Marti by Torres for its "Viña Magdala" blend. Most pure Penedés Superior wines are of the fresh, cool-fermented type and can show remarkably fine aroma and acidity. Other Torres wines are "Viña Esmeralda", "San Valentin", "Waltraud", "Viña Sol", "Gran Viña Sol" and "Gran Viña Sol Green Label".

The wines of Catalonia

ALELLA DO

Tiny, predominantly white appellation just north of Barcelona, where grapes grow on windy granite hills. After a period of decline in the 1970s, these wines gained in favour and the vineyards expanded in the early 1980s; further progress is now threatened by urban development.

ALL WINES, Primary: Xarello, Garnacha blanca
Secondary: Tempranillo, Garnacha, Garnacha peluda, Pansá rosada

RED Wines with a good colour, medium body and a soft, fruity flavour.

1982, 1983, 1984, 1986, 1990

Within 1-5 years

WHITE Light-bodied, pale-coloured, fresh and delicately fruity dry whites that have good acidity when made with grapes from the best north-facing slopes. Wines made from grapes grown on fully exposed south-facing slopes are sweeter, fatter and richer.

1982, 1983, 1984

Within 1-2 years (dry), within 1-4 years (sweet)

ROSÉ Fresh, dry and light-bodied with light fruit and a fragrant finish.

1982, 1983, 1984, 1990

Within 1-2 years

☆ Alta Alella Chardonnay, Marqués de Alella, Marfil, Alellasol

AMPURDÁN-COSTA BRAVA DO

At the foot of the Pyrenees, this is the closest wine area to France. Some 70 per cent of its produce is rosé.

ALL WINES, Primary: Garnacha
Secondary: Cariñena, Macabéo, Xarello

RED Deep, cherry-red wines, medium- to full-bodied, with crisp fruit.

1982, 1983, 1985, 1986, 1990

Between 2-5 years

WHITE Pale, greenish-yellow coloured wines that are fruity, slightly sweet and often *pétillant*.

1982, 1983, 1985, 1986, 1990

Within 1 year

ROSÉ Dry, medium-bodied, fruity wines.

1982, 1983, 1985, 1986, 1990

Within 1 year

☆ Oliveda, Convinosa, Cavas de Ampurdán

CAVA DO

Originally Cava had no fixed geographical origin, being an appellation of method– *méthode champenoise*– rather than origin. Since Spain became a member of the Common Market, it has had to comply with the EEC's wine regime, which is based on integrity of origin.

Because of the regulations, the Spanish simply drew borders around each and every Cava producer, irrespective of location. In actual fact, more than 90 per cent of all Cavas are produced in Catalonia.

Of the grape varieties authorized, just three are important: Xarello gives alcohol, firmness and acidity; Macabéo supplies fruit and freshness, and generally "lifts" a blend; and Parellada softens the Xarello and imparts a distinctive aromatic quality.

ALL WINES Macabéo, Xarello, Parellada, Chardonnay, Malvasia, Riojana, Monastrell, Garnacha

SPARKLING WHITE A top-quality Cava has an unmistakable toasty aroma, a firm *mousse* of small- to pin-prick-size bubbles, and a fresh, clean palate of distinctive fruit. The toasty aroma is the autolysed character of native Spanish grapes and may be taken as a sign of good bottle-age prior to disgorging.

Mostly non-vintage, and almost all vintages will be superior

Within 1-3 years (4-8 years for vintage and deluxe *cuvées*)

SPARKLING ROSÉ These seldom-encountered wines represent the less serious branch of the Cava business.

Mostly non-vintage

Within 1-3 years

☆ *See* Major bodegas of Catalonia

CONCA DE BARBERÁ DO

Little-known wines, mostly white and rosé, from the hilly hinterland of Penedés.

ALL WINES Macabéo, Parellada, Trepat, Sumoll, Ull de Llebre, Garnacha

RED Lacklustre, medium-bodied wines that I do not recommend.

WHITE Pale-coloured, light-bodied everyday-drinking dry white wines of between nine and 11 per cent of alcohol.

1981, 1982, 1984, 1985, 1990

Immediately

ROSÉ These light, dry, fresh, delightfully aromatic and delicately fruity wines are the best in the appellation.

1982, 1985

Within 1-2 years

COSTERS DEL SEGRE DO

This appellation encompasses four areas of different viticultural character within the province of Lérida: les Garrigues and Valls de Riu Corb, which are primarily white-grape districts, Artesa, which is planted almost entirely with black grapes, and Raimat, which is dominated by foreign grape varieties and has quickly assumed classic status in Spanish wine's recent history. The following assessment is based entirely on Raimat, which is owned by the Raventos family of Codorníu fame.

☆ Raimat (especially Chardonnay, "Abadia", Cabernet Sauvignon, Tempranillo)

PENEDÉS DO

Although Penedés is the heart of the Cava industry, this appellation is reserved for the excellent still wines that would be famous if just one wine maker existed – Miguel Torres Jnr.

ALL WINES Garnacha, Cariñena, Monastrell, Tempranillo, Macabéo, Xarello, Parellada, Subirat parent, Chardonnay, Cabernet sauvignon, Merlot, Riesling

RED The styles range from light and fresh to full and smooth, youthful to mature, oak-matured to oak-free.

1980, 1982, 1985, 1986

Within 1-3 years (for light styles), up to 20 (for great wines like Torres' "Gran Coronas Black Label")

WHITE The styles range from light to full, oaky-rich to varietally aromatic and ultra-dry to medium-sweet.

1981, 1982, 1984, 1985, 1990

Within 1 year (for very fresh and aromatic wines like Torres' "Esmeralda"), between 3-8 years (for classics like Jean Léon's Chardonnay)

ROSÉ Fresh, dry and fruity wines.

1982, 1985, 1990

Within 1-2 years

FORTIFIED WHITE Sweet, raisiny, full-bodied dessert wines made from Malvasia and Moscatel grapes that are left on the vine to shrivel. Fermentation is arrested with pure alcohol.

Mostly non-vintage

Immediately (for a fresh style), but may be left for two to five years to acquire *"rancio"* character

RANCIO Oxidized and maderized fortified wines, now very rare.

☆ *See* Major bodegas of Catalonia

PRIORATO DO

An area with a dry climate and poor soil in which the vines' roots spread everywhere in search of moisture. The popular saying is that the people of Priorato can get wine out of a stone!

ALL WINES Primary: Garnacha **Secondary:** Garnacha peluda, Cariñena, Garnacha blanca, Macabéo, Pedro Ximénez

RED/WHITE/ROSÉ These table wines must have an alcoholic level of between 13.75 and 18 per cent. Most are nearer to 18, and that is without any form of fortification. With the possible exception of the red Novell, the wines cannot be taken seriously.

FORTIFIED RED/GOLD Sweet and semi-sweet wines of between 14 and 18 per cent alcohol, of which at least eight per cent must be by natural fermentation.

RANCIO TAWNY/BROWN The lacklustre fortified wines above gain very little from the Mediterranean's beloved *rancio* process, other than increased alcohol and a typical oxidized and maderized character.

☆ Scala Die "Novell", "Cartoixa"

TARRAGONA DO

The largest appellation in Catalonia, the coastal vineyards of Tarragona are located just south of Penedés.

ALL WINES Garnacha, Mazuela, Tempranillo, Macabéo, Xarello, Parellada, Garnacha blanca

RED Full-bodied, robustly flavoured wines with high alcohol content.

1982, 1984, 1985, 1986

Between 2-5 years

WHITE Sturdy, aromatic wines with good fruit, but often lacking freshness.

1982, 1984, 1985, 1990

Immediately

ROSÉ The dry rosés have a surprisingly pale colour and some delicacy of fruit.

1982, 1984, 1985, 1990

Within 1 year

FORTIFIED WHITE/TAWNY Known as Tarragona *classico*, these wines are reputed to be of high quality and have a character somewhere between a good tawny Port and a fine old *oloroso*. I have not tasted these rare wines.

RANCIO I have not tasted these wines, but, if true to form, the *rancio* will be an oxidized, maderized version.

☆ Celler Cooperativa de Valls, Cooperativa Agrícola, José Lopez Beltran (Don Beltran), Pedro Masana (non-DO wines), De Muller (Moscatel Seco)

TERRA ALTA DO

Terra Alta is situated in the highlands well away from the coast. Vintages make little difference and any reasonable wine should be drunk immediately.

ALL WINES Primary: Garnacha blanca **Secondary:** Macabéo, Cariñena, Garnacha, Garnacha peluda

RED Robust wines with a lot of colour and body, not yet of serious quality.

WHITE The best, like Pedro Rovira's "Alta Mar" are fresh, fruity, slightly sweet and pleasantly aromatic.

ROSÉ Alcoholic, full-bodied and coarse.

RANCIO Fortified Garnacha with up to 30 grams per litre of residual sugar and a minimum of 15 per cent alcohol.

☆ Cooperativa Agricola la Hermandad, Pedro Rovira (Alta Mar)

Major bodegas of Catalonia

MASÍA BACH
Carretera Martorell-Capellades, San Esteve Sesrovires, Barcelona

Production: *200,000 cases*
Established: *1920*

Renowned more for its sweet, oak-aged white "Extrísimo Bach", than for its reds, which havè always been merely soft and acceptable. I realized this Codorníu-owned firm had begun to take its red-winemaking seriously when it released a stunning 1985, simply labelled "Masía Bach".

☆ Masía Bach *tinto* Reserva, "Viña Extrísima", "Viña Extrísima" Reserva

RENÉ BARBIER
San Sadurní de Noya, Barcelona

Production: *500,000 cases*
Established: *1880*

Owned by Freixenet, this firm operates from the Segura Viudas premises.

☆ René Barbier *rosado*, Kraliner *blanco*

CASTELLBLANCH
Avenida Casetas Mir, San Sadurní de Noya

Production: *1 million cases*
Established: *1908*

This firm, owned by Freixenet, produces a remarkably consistent Cava wine.

☆ "Brut Zero", "Lustros"

CELLER JOSEP MARÍA TORRES I BLANCO
See Mas Rabassa (usual name).

CODORNÍU
644 Avenida Gran Via, Barcelona

Production: *5 million cases*
Established: *1551*

This firm founded the Spanish sparkling wine industry under the auspices of Don José Raventos. It is the most innovative firm in Spain's Cava industry, and its production dwarfs even that of Moét & Chandon. Codorníu invented the *girasol* or sunflower apparatus that enables *remuage* to be performed by the pallet-load (*see* Champagne, p.139).

☆ "Non Plus Ultra", "Gran Codorníu", "Anne de Codorníu", Chardonnay Cava

FREIXENET
San Sadurní de Noya

Production: *3 million cases*
Established: *1889*

Freixenet produces probably the most

famous of Cavas – "Cordon Negro". Once a firm favourite of mine, it has lacked depth and character since the 1975 vintage; I now prefer the cheaper *brut* "Carta Nevada"; the other *prestige cuvées* are even more superior.

☆ "Cuvée DS", "Brut Nature", "Carta Nevada", "Brut Barroco"

JEAN LEÓN
Francisco Cambó, Barcelona

Production: *20,000 cases*
Established: *1962*

These firm wines have a full flavour and a somewhat Californian style. The Cabernet is good, but not consistent; the Chardonnay is always stunning.

☆ Cabernet Sauvignon, Chardonnay

MARQUÉS DE MONISTROL
Monistrol, San Sadurní de Noya

Production: *250,000 cases*
Established: *1882*

This competent Cava company, owned by Martini & Rossi, also produces a fine Reserva red Penedés wine.

☆ Vin Nature Blanc de Blancs, Blanco Seco, Brut Nature, Gran Reserva *tinto*

MAS RABASSA
Celler Josep María Torres i Blanco, Barrio La Serreta, Olerdola Barcelona

I am most impressed with these fresh, delicious, new-style wines.

☆ Mas Rabassa Xarello and Macabéo

MESTRES
Plaza del Ayuntamiento 8, San Sadurní de Noya

Production: *10,000 cases*
Established: *1928*

Small, very traditional, family-owned Cava business producing numerous wines of fine autolytic character.

☆ Mestres Brut, "Clos Nostre Senyor", "Mas-Via"

MONT MARCAL
Castellvi de la Marca, Penedés

Production: *50,000 cases*
Established: *1975*

Very charracterful, well-made Cava produced by private family firm.

☆ Mont Marcal Brut, Gran Reserva

RAIMAT
Raimat, Lérida,

Production: *750,000 cases*
Established: *1920*

This estate owned by Codorníu utilizes highly innovative equipment to produce an excellent range of fine wines using classic French grapes.

☆ Raimat ("Abadia", "Clamor", Cabernet Sauvignon, Chardonnay Blanc de Blancs Cava Brut)

SEGURA VIUDAS
Carretera de San Sadurní a la Llacuna, San Sadurní de Noya

Production: *2 million cases*
Established: *1954*

Now part of the huge Freixenet group, this is the best Cava house in Spain. Its wines all have the true biscuity character of fine, mature Cava.

☆ Cava (NV Brut, Vintage Brut, Blanc de Blancs Brut, Reserva "Heredad")

TORRES
**Miguel Torres
Comercio 22,
Vilafranca del Penedés**

Production: *1.2 million cases*
Established: *1870*

The gifted but modest Miguel Torres Jnr. is responsible both for the exceptional international success of these wines, and, by reflected glory, for those of the whole Penedés area.

Perhaps the most effective way of conveying the achievement of Miguel Torres Jnr. is to reveal the triumph of his very first "Gran Coronas Black Label". His father had seen the commercial value of releasing small quantities of fine *reserva* wines and had introduced the "Gran Coronas" label, a step up from his "Coronas", for this purpose. In 1970 Miguel Jnr. went one step further by producing an even tinier amount of "Gran Coronas" that contained Cabernet sauvignon, and that was given a limited aging in new oak. This wine took all the prizes at Gault-Millau's 1979 "Wine Olympics", coming top of its category and beating Château Latour 1970, Château Pichon-Lalande 1964 and Château La Mission Haut-Brion 1961!

The second most striking feature of this contest, after the examination of quality alone, was a comparison of the prices, the "Gran Coronas Black Label" selling at the time for 29 French francs, compared to 150 for the Latour, 83.70 for the Pichon and 138 for the Mission Haut-Brion.

Because of its unique place in the Penedés wine industry and the quality and originality of its wines, the Torres range deserves a detailed appraisal:

SAN VALENTIN

Virtually the same wine as Viña Sol, except that the fermentation is stopped before all the grape sugars are consumed, making a medium-sweet version.

🍇 Parellada 100%

VIÑA SOL

This deliciously fresh and fruity white wine, with its impeccably clean, dryish finish should be drunk young.

🍇 Parellada 100%

GRAN VIÑA SOL

A fuller, rounder version of the Viña Sol with a barely discernible three months in new *limousin* oak, Gran Viña Sol is capable of improving in bottle for two or three years.

🍇 Parellada 48%, Chardonnay 52%

GRAN VIÑA SOL RESERVA

Sometimes referred to as "Green Label", this is made from a different grape mix from the standard Gran Viña Sol and is given the benefit of a very noticeable six months' maturation in new American oak. A richly flavoured wine, it is beautifully balanced with good acidity and a dry finish, and can improve in bottle for up to five years.

🍇 Parellada 70%, Sauvignon blanc 30%

VIÑA ESMERALDA

When this wine was first launched, it was 40 per cent Muscat, 60 per cent Gewürztraminer, but the emphasis has gradually changed and the grape proportions are now reversed. This is super quaffing wine – very fruity and aromatic, light in body, with an interesting amalgam of two varietal flavours and a luscious, medium-sweet finish. Just one warning: drink before 12 months old, because it quickly tires and, in the process, takes on an unnerving "split personality".

🍇 Muscat 60%, Gewürztraminer 40%

WALTRAUD

A wine with a penetrating aroma that is more spicy and raisiny than any of the classic German renditions of this grape. It has an elegant blend of delightful fruit flavours and a perfect balance of acidity and residual sugar. It is best drunk within one to two years.

🍇 Riesling 100%

MILMANDA

Hellishly expensive Chardonnay that was not originally worth the price (dark, maderized and over-oaked), but it has evolved into a wine of classic quality since the 1988 vintage.

🍇 Chardonnay 100%

SANGRE DE TORO
or TRES TORRES SANGREDETORO

A mellow, full-bodied red wine that is aged for 12 months in old oak and for a further period in large, old vats. It can improve for up to six years or so.

🍇 Garnacha 70%, Cariñena 30%

**GRAN SANGRE DE TORO RESERVA
or GRAN SANGREDETORO**

The best Sangre de Toro wines are reserved after fermentation and aged in new oak for six months and for a further period in old oak. This produces a richer, oakier wine of greater depth and complexity that improves in bottle for up to six or eight years after the harvest.

Garnacha 70%, Cariñena 30%

VIÑA MAGDALA

The varietal character of the Pinot noir is overwhelmed by the Tempranillo

and 18 months in American oak (six of which are in new oak), but it is an elegantly rich and fine red wine in its own right, and has the capacity to age for between five and eight years.

Pinot noir 50%, Tempranillo 50%

CORONAS

The most basic of Torres' three famous Coronas wines is an excellent-value, full-bodied, soft and fruity red wine with a slight pepperyness that has been mellowed out by 15 months in old American oak. It improves for

up to eight years in bottle.

Tempranillo 100%

GRAN CORONAS RESERVA

Heaps of vanilla-oak underline the rich Cabernet flavour in this full-bodied, well-balanced red wine. It receives 18 months in American oak (six of which are in new oak), improves in bottle for upwards of ten years, and is a classy wine by any standard.

Cabernet sauvignon 70%, Tempranillo 30%

GRAN CORONAS RESERVA

Distinguished from the other Gran Coronas Reserva by its distinctive black label, this is consistently the greatest red wine produced in Spain. It has an immense concentration of classic Cabernet character that is perfectly underpinned by smoky-vanilla oak, and is capable of improving for up to 25 years.

Cabernet sauvignon 90%, Cabernet franc 10%

The best of the rest

BODEGAS BOSCH-GUELL
Vilafranca del Penedés, Barcelona

Established: *1886*

☆ Blanco *selecto* "Rómulo", Clarete *fino* "Rómulo", Rosado *seco* "Rómulo"

BODEGAS J. FREIXEDAS
87-89 Calvo Sotelo, Vilafranca del Penedés

Established: *1886*

☆ "Santa Marta", Special Reserva "Castilla", "La Torre" Cava Brut

BODEGAS ROBERT
Sitges, Barcelona

One of the few remaining producers of Sitges, a fortified Malvasia and Moscatel wine made a few kilometres south of the outskirts of Barcelona, from grapes that are allowed to shrivel on the vine.

☆ Sitges

CASTELL DEL REMEI
Penelles, Lérida

☆ Reserva *blanco*, Reserva *tinto*, Castell de Remei *rosado*, "Extra Cep" Sémillon, "Extra Cep" Cabernet

CAVA LLOPART
Industria 46, San Sadurní de Noya, Barcelona

Established: *1887*

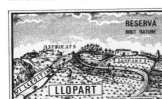

☆ Llopart Reserva *Brut Nature Cava*

CAVAS DEL AMPURDÁN
Plaza del Carmen 1, Perelada, Gerona

Established: *1925*

☆ Tinto "Cazador", Reserva "Don Miguel"

CAVAS DEL CASTILLO DE PERELADA
P° de San Antonio 1, Perelada, Gerona

Established: *1925*

☆ "Gran Claustro"

CAVAS FERRET
Guardiola de Font-Rubí, Barcelona

☆ Ferret Blanco, Ferret Rosado

CAVAS HILL
Bonavista 1, Mojá, Vilafranca del Penedés

Established: *1887*

☆ "Penedés Reserva"

CAVAS NADAL
El Pla del Penedés, Barcelona

Established: *1945*

☆ Nadal Brut

CAVAS TORELLO
Can Martí de Baix, San Sadurní de Noya

Established: *1953*

☆ "Blanc Tranquille", "Torello" Brut

CELLER HISENDA MIRET
San Martín Sarroca, Barcelona

☆ "Viña Toña Xarel-lo", "Viña Toña Parellada"

COMPAÑÍA VINÍCOLA DEL PENEDÉS
Vilafranca del Penedés, Barcelona

☆ "Viña Franca" *blanco*

CONDE DE CARALT
Carretera de San Sadurnía la Llacuna, San Sadurní de Noya

Established: *1954*

Another Freixenet-owned Cava firm on the Segura Viudas premises.

☆ Conde de Caralt (Reserva, Brut Nature)

COVIDES
Vilafranca del Penedés, Barcelona

☆ "Duc de Foix"

DE MULLER
Real 38, Tarragona

Established: *1851*

☆ Moscatel "Añejo", "Aureo", Moscatel Rancio, "Pajarete", Priorato de Muller

JOSÉ FERRER MATEU
Avda. Penedés 27, Santa Margarita y Monjous, Barcelona

☆ "Viña Laranda" *tinto*

JUVÉ & CAMPS
14 Apartado de Correos, San Sadurní de Noya, Barcelona

Established: *1921*

☆ Reserva de la Familia Juvé & Camps

MASCARÓ
Casal 9, Vilafranca del Penedés, Barcelona

Established: *1947*

☆ Mascaró Brut

MASIA VALLFORMOSA
La Sala 45, Vilovi del Penedés

Established: *1932*

☆ "Vall Fort" Gran Vino *tinto*, "Vallformosa" Brut Nature

PARXET
Torrente 38, Tiana, Barcelona

Production: *42,000 cases*
Established: *1920*

A refined sparkling wine.

☆ Parxet Cava Brut Nature, Parxet Cava Brut Reserva

JEAN PERICO
Can Ferrar del Mas, San Sadurní de Noya

This Freixenet-owned Cava company based on the Segura Viudas premises makes an inexpensive product. It is consistently good, and excellent value.

☆ Jean Perico Brut

CELLERS DE SCALA DEI
Plaza Priorat 3, Scala Dei

Established: *1973*

Top Priorato producer.

☆ "Cartoixa Scala Dei"

IMPORTANT COOPERATIVES

COOPERATIVA "AGRÍCOLA DE GANDESA"
Gandesa, Tarragona

Established: *1919*

☆ Gandesa Blanc Gran Reserva, Gandesa Blanc Especial

COOPERATIVA DE "MOLLET DE PERELADA"
Alt Empordà, Perelada, Gerona

☆ "Vi Novell" *tinto*

Southern Spain

This region is justly famous for Jerez de la Frontera's Sherry, one of the world's great fortified wines. Sherry produced in and around Sanlúcar de Barrameda is called Manzanilla. The region also includes Málaga, home of a classic yet most underrated dessert wine, Montilla, and Condado de Huelva, an obscure area producing both light and dessert wines, most of which are consumed locally.

THE VINOUS ROOTS OF SHERRY PENETRATE 3,000 years of history, back to the Phoenicians who founded Gadir, today Cadiz, in 1100 BC. They quickly deserted Gadir because of the hot, howling *levante* wind that is said to drive men mad, and established a town called Xera further inland; this may be the Xérès or Jerez of today. It is believed that the Phoenicians introduced viticulture to the region. If they did not, then the Greeks certainly did, and it was the Greeks who brought with them their *hepsema*, the precursor of the *arropes* and *vinos de color* that add sweetness, substance and colour to modern-day sweet or cream Sherries.

THE DEVELOPMENT OF SHERRY

In the Middle Ages, the Moors introduced an Arab invention called an *alembic*. With this simple pot-still, the inhabitants of Jerez were able to turn their excess production into grape spirit and add it, with the *arrope* and *vino de color*, to their new wines each year to produce the first crude but true Sherry.

The repute of these wines gradually spread throughout the civilized world, not least by virtue of the English merchants who established wine-shipping businesses in Andalucía at the end of the thirteenth century. After Henry VIII broke with Rome, Englishmen in Spain were under constant threat from the Inquisition. The English merchants were rugged individualists, and survived, as they did, remarkably, when Francis Drake set fire to the Spanish fleet in the Bay of Cadiz in 1587. Described as the day he "singed the king of Spain's beard", it was the most outrageous of all Drake's raids, and when he returned home, he took with him a booty of 2,900 casks of Sherry. The exact size of these casks is not known, but the total volume is estimated to be well in excess of 150,000 cases, which makes it a vast shipment of one wine for that period in history. It was, however, eagerly consumed by a relatively small population that had been denied its normal quota of Spanish wines during the war. England has been by far the largest market for Sherry ever since.

Sherry's classic grape varieties

British Sherry expert Julian Jeffs believes that as many as 100 different grape varieties were once traditionally used to make Sherry and, in 1868, Diego Parada y Barreto listed 42 then in current use. Today only three varieties are authorized: Palomino, Pedro Ximénez and Moscatel fino. The Palomino is considered the classic Sherry grape and, as the lists of wines under each bodega show, (*see* pp.287-290), most Sherries are in fact 100 per cent Palomino, although they may be sweetened with Pedro Ximénez for export markets. There are two sub-varieties of Palomino, the Palomino fino and the Palomino de Jerez. Although a few Sherries contain a significant proportion of Pedro Ximénez, or PX as it is often called, and a small number of pure PX wines exist, its primary use is for sweetening.

THE UNIQUENESS OF JEREZ SHERRY

It is the combination of its soil and climate that makes Jerez de la Frontera uniquely equipped to produce Sherry, a style of wine that is attempted in many countries around the world, but never truly accomplished. In this respect, Sherry has much in common with Champagne, for it is by an accident of nature that the region is inherently superior to all others in its potential to produce a specific style of wine. The parallel can be taken further: both Champagne and Sherry are produced from neutral and unbalanced base wines that are uninspiring to drink before they undergo the elaborate process that turns them into high-quality, perfectly balanced, finished products.

The famous *albariza* soil

Jerez's *albariza* soil, which derives its name from its brilliant white surface, is not chalk but a soft marl of organic origin formed by the sedimentation of diatom algae in the Triassic period. Diatoms are still found in huge numbers in plankton today and past depositions have resulted in such diverse natural products as diatomaceous earth and have even contributed to oil reserves. The *albariza* becomes yellow in colour at a depth of about one metre (3ft 4ins) and turns bluish after five metres (16ft 5ins). It crumbles and is super-absorbent when wet, but extremely hard when dry. This is the key to the exceptional success of *albariza* as a vine-growing soil.

Jerez is a region of baking heat and drought from autumn to

FACTORS AFFECTING TASTE AND QUALITY

 Location
Andalucía's vineyards stretch from Condado de Huelva near the Portuguese border in the west, via Jerez on the coast to Málaga in southern Spain.

Climate
This is the hottest wine region in Spain. Generally, the climate is Mediterranean, but towards the Portuguese border, the Atlantic influence comes into play and, further inland, around Montilla-Moriles, it becomes more continental. The Atlantic-driven *pontete* wind produces the *flor* of *fino* Sherry.

Aspect
Vines are grown on all types of land, from the virtually flat coastal plains producing Manzanilla, through the slightly hillier Sherry vineyards rising to 100 metres (330 ft), to the higher gentle inland slopes of Montilla-Moriles and the undulating Antequera plateau of Málaga at some 500 metres (1,640 ft).

Soil
The predominant soil in the Jerez is a deep lime-rich variety known as *albariza* that soaks up and retains moisture. Its brilliant white colour also reflects sun on to the lower parts of the vines.

Sand and clay soils also occur but although suitable for vine-growing, they produce lesser-quality Sherries. The equally bright soil to the east of Jerez is not *albariza*, but a schisto-calcareous clay.

Along the southeast coastal section of Málaga, the soils are mostly slatey, with an admixture of sand, clay and mica, while limestone with very fine sand dominates in the northwest. Condado de Huelva has reddish soils, with darker alluvium places.

 **Viticulture and vinification**
Vinification is the key to the production of the great fortified wines for which this area is justly famous. Development of a yeast *flor* and oxidation by deliberately underfilling casks are vital components, as, of course, is the *solera* system that ensures a consistent product over the years. Montilla is vinified using the same methods as for Sherry, but is naturally strong in alcohol, not fortified.

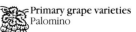 **Primary grape varieties**
Palomino

Secondary grape varieties
Baladí, Garrido fino, Laynen, Listan, Mantúo, Moscatel fino, Pedro Ximénez, Torrontés, Zalema

Jerez landscape, above
*Southwest of Jerez de la Frontera, the
Los Barrios district is typical of the
gently sloping Sherry vineyards. Not
all Sherry is grown on white albariza
soil; sand and clay are also to be
found.*

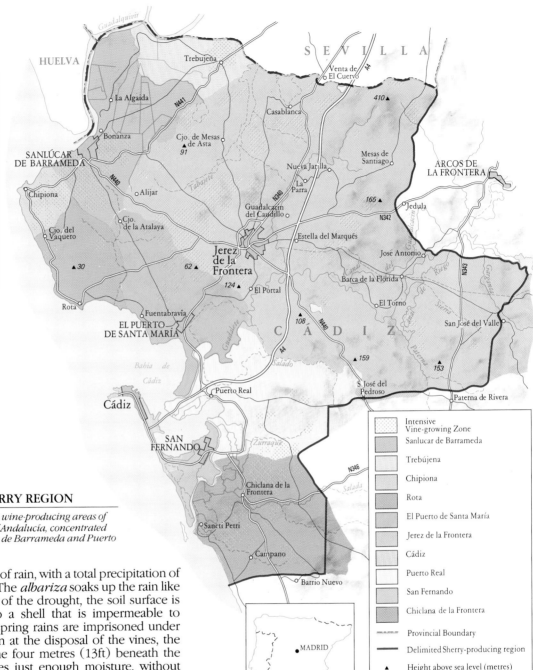

Legend:
- Intensive Vine-growing Zone
- Sanlúcar de Barrameda
- Trebújena
- Chipiona
- Rota
- El Puerto de Santa María
- Jerez de la Frontera
- Cádiz
- Puerto Real
- San Fernando
- Chiclana de la Frontera
- – – – Provincial Boundary
- ——— Delimited Sherry-producing region
- ▲ Height above sea level (metres)

Kms 4 8 12 16
Mls 2 4 6 8 10

SOUTHERN SPAIN: THE SHERRY REGION

*By far the most important sector of the wine-producing areas of
Southern Spain is the Sherry region of Andalucía, concentrated
round Jerez de la Frontera, Sanlúcar de Barrameda and Puerto
de Santa Maria.*

spring; there are about 70 days of rain, with a total precipitation of
some 50 centimetres (20 ins). The *albariza* soaks up the rain like
a sponge, and with the return of the drought, the soil surface is
smoothed and hardened into a shell that is impermeable to
evaporation. The winter and spring rains are imprisoned under
this protective cap, and remain at the disposal of the vines, the
roots of which penetrate some four metres (13ft) beneath the
surface. The *albariza* supplies just enough moisture, without
making the vine too lazy or over-productive. The high active-lime
content encourages the ripening of grapes with a higher acidity
level than would otherwise be the norm for such a hot climate.
This acidity assists the fermentation, provides a fresher base wine
and safeguards against unwanted oxidation prior to fortification
(as opposed to the deliberate oxidation after fortification).

The *levante* and *pontete* winds

The hot, dry *levante* is one of Jerez de la Frontera's two alternating
prevailing winds. This easterly wind "blow-dries" and "vacuum-
cooks" the grapes on their stalks during the critical ripening stage.
This results in a dramatically different metabolization of fruit
sugars, acids and aldehydes, that produces a wine with an unusual
balance peculiar to Jerez. Alternating with the *levante* is the wet
Atlantic *pontete* wind. This is of fundamental importance, as it
allows the growth of *Saccharomyces beticus* in the microflora of
the Palomino grape. This is the poetically named Sherry *flor* (*see
p.284*), without which there would be no *fino* in Jerez.

HOW GREAT SHERRY IS MADE

The Harvest

Twenty or more years ago, it was traditional to begin the grape
harvest in the first week of September. After picking, Palomino
grapes were left in the sun for 12 to 24 hours, PX and Moscatel for
10 to 21 days. Older vines were picked before younger ones, and
PX and Moscatel picked first of all as they required longer sunning
than Palomino. At night, the grapes were covered with *esparto*
grass mats as a protection against dew. This sunning is called the
soleo, and its primary purpose is to increase sugar content, while
reducing the malic acid and tannin content. Although some
producers still carry out the *soleo*, most harvest in the second week

of September and forgo the *soleo* for all but PX and Moscatel used in the sweetest Sherry. In this case the grapes are left in the sun for much less than the traditional 10 to 21 days.

The *yeso*

Prior to pressing, the stalks are removed and a small proportion of *yeso* (gypsum) is added to precipitate tartrate crystals and increase tartaric acid levels. This traditional practice may have evolved when growers noticed that grapes covered by *albariza* dust produced better wine than clean ones. *Albariza* has a high calcium carbonate content that would crudely accomplish the task.

The pressing

Traditionally four labourers called *pisadores* were placed in each *lagar* (open receptacle) to tread the grapes, not barefoot but wearing *zapatos de pisar*, heavily nailed cow-hide boots to trap the pips and stalks undamaged between the nails. Each man tramped 58 kilometres (36 miles) on the spot during a typical session lasting from midnight to noon.

Automatic horizontal presses are now in common use and it is debatable whether single-load presses, usually pneumatic, are superior to continuous presses. Advocates of single-load presses point to the fact that continuous pressing increases the level of undesirable tannin, while decreasing the level of desirable tartaric acid in the juice, so that the resulting wines invariably lack the freshness and delicacy essential for a *fino*; also that continuous presses extract too much juice and cannot separate the first pressing. Some big firms are increasingly dependent on continuous presses, and claim that they do not affect the quality of their wine. But the small, historic, family firm of Valdespino, for example, will probably dispose of its continuous press. While the regulations demand that each bodega should distil 10 per cent of its production, Valdespino found that some of its wine was so poor that it had to distil 11 per cent!

Fermentation

Small Sherry houses still ferment their wine in small oak casks purposely filled only to 90 per cent capacity. After approximately 12 hours, the fermentation starts and continues for between 36 and 50 hours at temperatures that vary between 25-30°C (77-86°F), by which time as much as 99 per cent of available sugar is converted to alcohol; after a further 40 or 50 days, the process is complete. Current methods often use stainless-steel fermentation vats, and yield wines that are approximately one per cent higher in alcohol due to an absence of absorption and evaporation. Selected yeast cultures are added and oak casks are used only for

HOW THE FERMENTED SHERRY DEVELOPS

The larger bodegas like to make something of a mystery of the *flor*, declaring they have no idea whether or not it will develop in a specific cask. There is some justification for this – one cask may have a fabulous froth of *flor* (like dirty soap-suds), while the cask next to it may have none. Any cask with good signs of dominant *flor* will invariably end up as Fino, but others with either no *flor* or ranging degrees of it may develop into one of many different styles. There is no way of guaranteeing the evolution of the wines, but it is well known that certain zones can generally be relied on to produce particular styles.

Zone	Style	Zone	Style
Añina	*fino*	Madroñales	*Moscatel/sweet*
Balbaina	*fino*	Miraflores	*fino/Manzanilla*
Carrascal	*oloroso*	Rota	*Moscatel/sweet*
Chipiona	*Moscatel/sweet*	Sanlúcar	*fino/Manzanilla*
Los Tercios	*fino*	Tehigo	colouring wines
Macharnudo	*amontillado*	Torrebreba	*Manzanilla*

maturation. With the exception of PX and Moscatel, all wines are fermented totally dry, whether by traditional or modern methods.

THE MAGICAL *FLOR*

There are several different styles of Sherry. Ranging from the driest and lightest to the sweetest and fullest, the basic types are: Fino and Fino Manzanilla, Amontillado, Oloroso and Cream. For the majority of Sherry drinkers, Fino is the quintessential Sherry style. It is a natural phenomenon called *flor* that determines whether or not a Sherry will become a Fino.

Flor is a grey-white film that is a strain of yeast called *Saccharomyces beticus*. This occurs naturally in the microflora of the Palomino grape grown in the Jerez district. It is found to one degree or another in every butt or vat of   ting Sherry and Manzanilla, but whether or not it can dominate the wine and develop as a *flor* depends upon the strength of the *Saccharomyces beticus* and the biochemical conditions. The effect of *flor* on Sherry is to absorb remaining traces of sugar, diminish glycerine and volatile acids and greatly increase esters and aldehydes.

To flourish, *flor* requires:
- An alcoholic strength between 13.5 and 17.5 per cent. The optimum is 15.3 per cent, the level at which vinegar-producing *acetobacter* is killed off.
- A temperature of between 15-30°C (59-86°F).
- A sulphur dioxide content of less than 0.018 per cent.
- A tannin content of less than 0.01 per cent.
- A virtual absence of fermentable sugars.

CASK-CLASSIFICATION IN THE CELLAR

Chalk mark	Character of wine	Probable style of Sherry	Action to take
First cask-classification			
/ *una raya*	light and good	*fino/amontillado*	fortify up to 15.5%
/' *raya y punto*	slightly less promising	undecided	fortify up to 15.5%
// *dos rayas*	less promising	*oloroso*	fortify up to 18%
/// *tres rayas*	coarse or acid	–	usually distilled
Ve *vinegar*	–		immediately removed to avoid infection
Second cask-classification			
Y *palma*	a wine with breeding	has *flor*	–
/ *raya*	fuller	no *flor*	–
// *dos rayas*	tending to be coarse	no *flor*	–
# *gridiron*	no good at all	no *flor*	–
Further cask-classifications			
Y *palma*	light and delicate	a *fino* sherry	–
⩩ *palma cortada*	fuller than a *fino*	*fino-amontillado* or *amontillado*	–
+ *palo cortado*	no *flor*, but exceptional, full bodied, and delicate	*Palo cortado*	–
/ *raya*	darker, fuller, not breeding *flor*	medium-quality *oloroso*	–
// *dos rayas*	darker and fuller but coarser	low-quality *oloroso*, for blending cheap Sherries that are usually sweetened	–
✓ *pata de gallina*	*raya* that has developed the true fragrance of a fine *oloroso*	top-quality *oloroso*, to be aged and kept dry	–

FIRST CASK-CLASSIFICATION AND FORTIFICATION

The cellarmaster's job is to sniff all the casks of Sherry and mark on each one in chalk how he believes it is developing, according to a recognized cask-classification system (*see* box, left). At this stage, the lower-grade wines (those that have little or no *flor*) are fortified to 18 per cent to kill off the *flor*, thus determining their character once and for all and protecting the wine from the dangers of acetification. The *flor* itself is a protection against the *acetobacter* that threaten to turn wine into vinegar, but it is by no means invincible and will be at great risk until fortified to 15.3 per cent, or above, the norm for *fino*, and is not truly safe until it is bottled. The *raya y punto* mark is now virtually obsolete; such uncertainties are classed as *dos rayas* and fortified accordingly.

In Jerez, it is believed that the addition of very strong alcohol to wine is unwise, and causes a violent reaction, so a fifty-fifty mixture known as *mitad y mitad, miteado* or *combinado* (half pure alcohol, half grape juice) is used for fortification. Some producers prefer to use mature Sherry instead of grape juice. This seems to run contrary to the principle of diluting the spirit in order to avoid an unwanted reaction with the wine. In fact, I consider any worries to be unfounded – the addition of neat spirit to wine is achieved with little fuss in the production of Port, and causes no violent reaction in Muscat de Beaumes de Venise, for example.

SECOND CASK-CLASSIFICATION

The wines will often be racked prior to fortification, and always after. Some two weeks later, they undergo a second, more precise classification (see chart, left), but no further fortification, or other action, may take place.

FURTHER CASK-CLASSIFICATION

The wines are allowed to develop in their own way for between nine and 36 months, during which time they are classified regularly (see chart, left) to determine their final style.

THE *SOLERA* BLENDING SYSTEM

Once the style of the Sherry has been established, the wines are fed into fractional-blending systems called *soleras*. These utilize casks at various stages of maturation that are regularly refreshed with younger wine to produce a continuous quantity of a consistently identical Sherry.

The *solera* system consists of a stock of wine in cask, split into graduated units of equal volume, each of a different maturation. The final and oldest stage is called the *Solera;* each of the more youthful stages that feed it are *criaderas*, or the "nursery". There are often as many as seven *criaderas* in a *solera* system, up to fourteen in a Manzanilla *solera*.

Usually up to one-third of the *Solera* is drawn off for blending.

and bottling. This is the maximum allowed per year by law, although older *soleras* of very high quality may be restricted to one-fifth by conscientious bodegas. It should be noted that the legal maximum applies to each individual cask, not one of which may be reduced by more than one-third in any one year. The amount drawn off from the mature *Solera* stage is immediately replenished by an equal volume taken from the first *criadera*, which in turn is topped up by the second *criadera* and so on. When the last *criadera* is emptied of its one-third, it is refreshed by an identical quantity of *añada*, or new wine. This is comprised of like-classified Sherries from the current year's production, aged up to 36 months, depending on the style and exactly when they are finally classified.

The final blend

Pure *Soleras* are classic Sherries: absolutely dry and potentially of the finest quality. In addition to these relatively rare wines, a proportion of Sherry may be drawn off from a *solera* such as the one described above to refresh a much older and far smaller one. A Sherry from a *solera* laid down in 1914, for example, may be a classic wine, but it will have very little of the 1914 vintage left in it. After 10 years of annually tapping off one-third of the wine, less than two per cent of the original vintage remains. After 20 years, every bottle drawn off should contain approximately one-thousandth of a 5 ml spoonful! Few Sherries are, however, pure *Soleras*, and most, whether shipped in bulk or bottle, are not only a blend of various different *soleras* (and *añada* wine for cheap Sherries), but also contain one or more of the following agents.

GRAPE-BASED SWEETENING AND COLORING AGENTS

PX The most traditional and most important sweetening agent in the production of Sherry, although gradually giving way to other less expensive ones. After the *soleo* (*see* p.283), the sugar content increases from around 23 per cent to between 43 and 54 per cent. The PX is pressed and run into casks containing pure grape spirit, after which it has an alcohol level of about nine per cent and contains some 430 grams per litre of sugar. This mixture is tightly bunged and left for four months, during which it undergoes a slight fermentation, increasing the alcohol by about one degree and reducing the sugar by some 18 grams per litre. Finally the wine undergoes a second muting, raising the alcoholic strength to a final 13 per cent but reducing the sugar content to about 380 grams per litre. Other sweetening agents are:

Moscatel
This is prepared in exactly the same way as PX, but the result is not as rich and its use, which has always been less widespread, is technically not permitted under DO regulations.

Dulce pasa
As for PX and Moscatel, but using Palomino, which can achieve a 50 per cent sugar concentration prior to muting, and is on the increase. This must not be confused with *dulce racimo* or *dulce apagado*, sweetening agents that were once brought in from outside the region and are now illegal.

Dulce de almibar or dulce blanco
A combination of glucose and laevulose blended with *fino* and matured, this agent is used to sweeten pale-coloured sherries.

Sancocho
A dark-coloured, sweet and sticky non-alcoholic syrup made by reducing unfermented local grape

juice to one-fifth its original volume by simmering over a low heat. It is used in the production of *vino de color* – a "colouring wine".

Arrope
This dark-coloured, sweet and sticky non-alcoholic syrup, made by reducing unfermented local grape juice to one-fifth its original volume, is also used in the production of *vino de color*.

Color de macetilla
The finest *vino de color* produced by blending two-parts *arrope* or *sancocho* with one-part unfermented local grape juice. This results in a violent fermentation and, when the wine falls bright it has an alcoholic strength of 9 per cent and a sugar content of 235 grams per litre. Prized stocks are often matured by *solera*.

Color remendado
Cheaper and more commonly used *vino de color* made by blending *arrope* or *sancocho* with local wine.

THE EVOLUTION OF SHERRY STYLES

The tree shows the course taken by each Sherry to become one of the well-known styles by which it is sold.

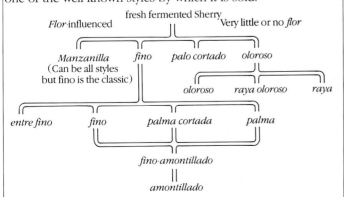

THE STYLES OF SHERRY

Manzanilla
Although *fino* is the most classic form of this wine made in the Sanlúcar de Barrameda area, there is the equally famous *pasada* and it, too, has its *fino-amontillados* (called *pasadas*), *amontillados*, *olorosos* and equivalent intermediary styles.

Manzanilla *fina*
A relatively modern, early-picked, *fino* made in Sanlúcar de Barrameda. Its production differs from that of a traditional *fino* in that its casks are allowed more ullage, the proportion of *flor* per cask is greater and grows more vigorously, the fortification is lower and the *solera* system is more complex. A true Manzanilla *fina* is pale, light-bodied, dry and delicate with a definite *flor* nose and a slightly bitter, sometimes distinctly saline, aftertaste. These wines are usually 100 per cent Palomino with an alcoholic strength of 15.5 to 17 per cent.

Manzanilla *pasada*
When a Manzanilla begins to age, it loses its *flor*, gains alcoholic strength, and becomes the equivalent of a *fino-amontillado*, known in Sanlúcar de Barrameda as a *pasada*. These wines are invariably 100 per cent Palomino with an alcoholic strength of up to 20.5 per cent.

Fino
A *palma* is the highest quality of *fino* Sherry and may be graded in a rising scale of quality: *dos palmas, tres palmas, cuatro palmas*. A *palma cortada* is a *fino* that has developed more body, has a very dry, but smooth almondy flavour, and is veering towards *amontillado*. An *entre fino* has little merit. Few *finos* remain *fino* with age in cask, which is why genuine "Old Fino Sherry" is rare. A *fino* is light, dry and delicate with a *flor* nose that should overpower any acetaldehyde. The

wines are invariably 100 per cent Palomino with an alcoholic strength of between 15.5 and 17 per cent.

Amontillado
With age, a *fino* develops an amber colour in cask and becomes a *fino-amontillado* then, after at least eight years, a proper *amontillado*, when it takes on a "nutty" character and acquires more body. A true *amontillado* is completely dry, with between 16 and 18 per cent alcohol.

Oloroso
Oloroso means "fragrant" and when genuinely dry, rich and complex from age, I find it certainly has the greatest finesse and is the most rewarding wine in Jerez. Much of its character is due to the higher fortification and generous glycerine content that develops without the aid of *flor*. The alcoholic strength usually ranges between 18 and 20 per cent.

Palo cortado
This wine cannot be deliberately made, nor even encouraged (a *palo cortado solera* is extremely difficult to operate), and only one butt in a thousand turns into a true *palo cortado*. A law unto itself, it is a naturally dry wine with a style between *amontillado* (on the nose) and *oloroso* (on the palate). Like *palma*, *palo cortado* may be graded; *dos cortados, tres cortados, cuatro cortados*.

Note: The development of a Sherry can be natural, so that a *fino* can, without the help of increased fortification, turn into an *oloroso* (thus a natural *oloroso* may have developed with the aid of *flor*). A *palo cortado* can develop from either an *amontillado* or an *oloroso*. A genuine old *fino* sherry can suddenly turn into an *oloroso*.

SHERRY AND THE EEC

When the Spanish opted to join the Common Market on January 1, 1986, they had no idea that it would refuse to acknowledge the uniqueness of their Sherry. Indeed, they had every reason to expect that the 3,000-year pedigree of their classic aperitif would be protected, because the EEC Commission had specifically proposed that this should be so; the definition, respect and defence of appellations is woven into the very fabric of the EEC's wine regime. But there is a basic flaw in the system that allows just two dissenting nations to hold up or veto the collective decision of all the rest. Britain and Ireland joined forces to block the Commission's proposals on Sherry. Now Spain finds that the EEC is committed to defend the name of its cheap, everyday-drinking wines, but not that of Sherry, its most famous wine!

The wines of Southern Spain

CONDADO DE HUELVA DO

Sandwiched between the Sherry district and the Algarve of Portugal, the sweet dessert wines of this area were mentioned by Chaucer in the *Canterbury Tales*. Light, dry wines are a more recent phenomenon and most are consumed locally.

ALL WINES Primary: Zalema
Secondary: Garrido fino, Palomino, Pedro Ximénez, Moscatel, Mantúo

WHITE Clean, dry, everyday-drinking wines.

Vintages are unimportant

Immediately

FORTIFIED WHITE/TAWNY There are two basic types, *pálido* (young, pale-straw colour, dry, austere wines, with 14-17 per cent alcohol) and *viejo* (*solera*-matured, mahogany hued, both dry and sweet wines that are deliberately oxidized, containing 15-23 per cent alcohol).

Vintages are unimportant

Within 1-3 years

JEREZ-XÉRÈS-SHERRY DO
See Sherry DO.

MÁLAGA DO

Just northeast of Jerez in southern Spain, the coastal vineyards of Málaga produce one of the most underrated classic dessert wines in the world. Most is matured by the *solera* system, involving some six scales (*see* Sherry, p.285) and may be blended in a Sherry-like manner with various grape-based colouring and sweetening agents, such as *arrope, vino de color, vino tierno* and *vino maestro*.

Moscatel, Pedro Ximénez

FORTIFIED GOLD/TAWNY/ BROWN/RED The colour depends on the style of Málaga, its age and method of maturation, its degree of sweetness and the grape variety used. It may be any one of the following:
Dulce color is a dark-coloured, medium-bodied Málaga that has been sweetened with *arrope*.
Lágrima is made from free-run juice only, and is the most luscious of all Málaga styles.
Moscatel is a sweet, rich, raisiny, medium-to-full bodied wine that is similar to the Jerez version, only more luscious.
Old Solera has the most finesse, depth and length of all Málagas and is capable of complexity rather than lusciousness. It is medium- to full-bodied, still sweet yet with a dry finish.

Oscuro is a dark, sweet Málaga that has been sweetened with *arrope* and coloured by *vino de color*.
Pajarette is darkish in colour, and less sweet, but more alcoholic than other Málagas.
Pedro Ximénez is a smooth, sweet, deliciously rich varietal wine with an intense flavour, which is similar in character to the Jerez version.
Seco is a pale, dry, tangy wine with a creamy hazelnut character.

Mostly non-vintage or *solera*-aged

Immediately (though it can last, but not improve, for several years)

☆ Scholtz Hermaoz, Pérez Texeira, Larios

MANZANILLA DO
See Sherry pp.282-286.

MONTILLA-MORILES DO

Sherry-like, but theoretically unfortified aperitif wines from the hottest and driest part of Córdoba. The vineyards are on pale-grey, lime-rich soil and the fully fermented, totally dry wines reach a natural alcohol content of 15 per cent or more before entering a *solera* system. They may have a little

sweetening wine added, particularly the wines that are to be exported.

Primary: Pedro Ximénez
Secondary: Moscatel, Airén, Baladí

WHITE The term *amontillado* originated in Jerez, describing a Sherry with characteristics similar to those of Montilla. Literally the word means "a montilla style". Ironically *amontillado* is not seen on Montilla bottles, but the range of wines here is exactly the same as those from Jerez describing themselves as *amontillado*. They even produce a *Palo Cortado*.

All non-vintage or *solera*-aged

Immediately

☆ Marqués de la Sierra, Alvear, Bodegas Mora Chacon, Gracia Hermanos, Perez Barquero, Rodriguez Chiachio

SHERRY DO

One of the world's classic fortified wines, the name of its appellation may be Jerez-Xérès-Sherry, Jerez, Xérès or, by far the most popular, Sherry. For more details *see* Sherry, pp.282-286.

Major Sherry and Manzanilla bodegas

Note: Where known, the grape variety and strength of a Sherry are indicated in brackets. These may vary slightly in some export countries, where strength or sweetness may be adjusted according to local preferences or regulations.

The Sherry bouquet is dominated by acetaldehyde, a compound I find objectionable. Furthermore, *fino* Sherry is distinguished by its *flor* character, another aroma I dislike. While I can wholeheartedly and enthusiastically recommend genuine old, dry *oloroso* and rare *palo cortado* Sherries, I have had to rely on others for the rest of the recommendations in this section.

ALLIED-LYONS

The giant Allied-Lyons group has two areas of interest in the Sherry market. On one hand (and most importantly), it owns the Jerez firms of Harveys (including Harveys of Bristol), Terry and Palomino & Vergara, plus an estimated 45 per cent of Pedro Domecq and a 10 per cent slice of Barbadillo. On the other hand, through its UK production of brands such as "VP" and "QC", it is the dominant force in the production of "British Sherry". It is not simply a matter of being involved in two opposing markets, but of being on two sides of a dispute concerning basic principles, which must cause problems for its Jerez-based directors. *See* Harveys.

BARBADILLO
Antonio Barbadillo
Luis de Eguilas 11,
Sanlúcar de Barrameda

Vineyards: *1,000 ha (2,470 acres)*
Established: *1821*

The leading Manzanilla house, it has a fine reputation and accounts for 70 per cent of all Manzanilla produced.

Wines: *Manzanilla:* "Eva" (Palomino 15.5°), "Etiqueta Blanca" (Palomino, 15.5°), Manzanilla Fina* (Palomino, 15.5°), "Pastora" (Palomino, 15.5°), "Sirena" (Palomino, 15.5°), "Solear"* (Palomino, 15.5°)
Fino: "De Balbaina" (Palomino, 16°), "Etiqueta Amarilla" (Palomino, 16°), "Tio Rio" (Palomino, 17°), "Viña Del Cuco" (Palomino, 16°)
Amontillado: "Cuco" (Palomino, 17°), "Etiqueta Blanca" (Palomino, 17°), "Principe" (Palomino, 17°)
Oloroso: "Cuco" (Palomino, 18°), "Etiqueta Amarilla" (Palomino, 18°), "San Rafael" (Palomino, 18°)
Sweet: "Cuco Cream" (Palomino, 18°), "Eva Cream"* (Palomino, 18°), "Fruta Laura" (Moscatel, 18°), "Paso Evora" (Moscatel, 18°), Pedro Ximénez (Pedro Ximénez, 18°), Sanlucar Cream*

BERTOLA
See Bodegas Internacionales.

HIJOS DE AGUSTÍN BLÁQUEZ
Julio Ruiz de Alda 42,
Jerez de la Frontera

Established: *1795*

This historic old firm is best known for its "Carta Blanca" *fino* and now belongs to Pedro Domecq.

Wines: Fino: "Carta Blanca" (Palomino, 16.5°), "Balfour" Fino
Dry Amontillado: "Carta Plata", "Carta Oro"*
Medium Amontillado: "Balfour" Amontillado
Dry Oloroso: "Carta Roja" (Palomino, 19°)
Medium Oloroso: "Don Paco" (Palomino, 19°)
Palo Cortado: "Capuchino" (Palomino, 20°)
Sweet: "Carta Azul" (Pedro Ximénez, 17°), "Medal Cream" (Palomino, 20°), "Balfour Cream", "Balfour Pale Cream"

BODEGAS INTERNACIONALES
Carretera Madrid-Cadiz,
Jerez de la Frontera

Established: *1974*

The huge premises that houses this bodega was built in 1977 and is the largest edifice in Jerez.

Wines: *Manzanilla:* "Victoria"
Fino: "Duke of Wellington" (17.5°), "Bertola" (15.5°)
Dry Amontillado: "Pemartin"
Medium Amontillado: "Duke of Wellington" (17.8°), "Varela"
Dry Oloroso: "La Novia"
Medium Oloroso: "Duke of Wellington"
Sweet: "Duke of Wellington Pale Cream" (17.8°), "Bertola Cream", "Bertola Pale Cream"

JOHN WILLIAM BURDON
Puerto de Santa María

Established: *1821*

This firm was established by its namesake, a successful nineteenth-century shipper, and has been owned by Luis Caballero since 1932.

Wines: *Fino:* Dry, "Puerto Fino Superior" Dry (Palomino, 16.5°)
Amontillado: Medium, "Don Luis" Fine Old Amontillado
Oloroso: "Heavenly Cream" Rich Old Oloroso
Sweet: Pale Cream, Rich Cream

LUIS CABALLERO
San Francisco 32,
Puerto de Santa María

Established: *1830*

One of the largest firms in Jerez, Luis Caballero owns La Cuesta and John William Burdon.

Wines: *Manzanilla:* "Macarena"
Fino: "Caballero Pavon"
Dry Amontillado: "Tio Benito"
Medium Amontillado: "Benito", "Caballero"
Dry Oloroso: "Caballero Oloroso Real"
Medium Oloroso: "Caballero"
Sweet: "Benito Pale Cream", "Benito Cream", "Caballero", "Caballero Oloroso Mayoral"

CAYD
Puerto 21,
Sanlúcar de Barrameda

Established: *1870s*

This company, which is of Italian descent, is part of Campo Virgen de la Caridad, a cooperative with about 1,000 members.

Wines: Manzanilla: "Bajo De Guia" (Palomino, 15.5°), "La Sanluqueña" (Palomino, 15.5°), "Saeta" (Palomino, 15.5°)
Fino: Cayd (Palomino, 15.5°)
Oloroso: Cayd Medium (Palomino, 18°)
Sweet: Cayd Cream (Palomino, 18°)

CROFT
Rancho Croft,
Carretera Circunvalación 636,
Jerez de la Frontera

Production: *2.75 million cases*
Vineyards: *485 ha (1,200 acres)*
Established: *1968*

Shippers of port since 1678, Croft was acquired in 1911 by W. & A. Gilbey, a British firm that had been shipping Sherries since 1860. W. & A. Gilbey formalized its Jerez interests under the name of Croft Jerez S.A. in 1968 and built a large, traditional-style, yet computer-controlled bodega called Rancho Croft.

Wines: *Fino:* "Croft Delicado" (Palomino, 17.5°)
Amontillado: "Croft Classic" (Palomino, 17.5°), "Croft Particular", "Don Gaspar"
Oloroso: "Doña Gracia" (Palomino, 17.5°)
Palo Cortado: Croft Palo Cortado (Palomino, 17.5°)
Sweet: "Croft Original Pale Cream" (Palomino, 18°)

CUVILLO
José Moreno de Mora 15,
Puerto de Santa María

Established: *1773*

This firm once supplied Harveys with top-quality sweet Sherry that was sold under the "Bristol Cream" label. Sweet Sherries are still its forte.

Wines: *Fino:* "Basileo" (Palomino, 17°), "Naviero" (Palomino, 20°)
Amontillado: "Basileo" (Palomino, 17°), "Solero Santa Isabel" (Palomino, 20°)
Oloroso: "Sangre" (Palomino, 19°), "Trabajadero"* (Palomino, 19°)
Palo Cortado: Palo Cortado*
Sweet: "Corona Cream"* (Palomino, 20°), "Cuvillo Cream"* (Palomino, 18°), Pedro Ximénez (Pedro Ximénez, 18°)

DELGADO ZULETA
Carmen 32,
Sanlúcar de Barrameda

Established: *1744*

One of the oldest bodegas, Delgado Zuleta is best known for its light, crisp Manzanilla *pasada* "La Goya".

Wines: *Manzanilla:* "La Goya"*

(Palomino, 15.5°), "Barbiana" (Palomino, 15.5°)
Fino: "Don Tomas" (Palomino, 15.5°)
Amontillado: "Quo Vaddis" (Palomino, 18°)
Oloroso: "Puerto Lucero" (Palomino, 18°)
Sweet: "Monteagudo Cream" (Palomino, 17.5°) Pedro Ximénez (Pedro Ximénez, 17°)

DÍEZ-MÉRITO
Cervantes 3,
Jerez de la Frontera

Vineyards: *200 ha (500 acres)*

Established: *1854*

In line with popular trends, certain "Don Zoilo" Manzanilla and Fino blends have recently been reduced to 15.5° on some export markets.

Wines: *Manzanilla:* "Don Zoilo", "La Torera", "Diez Hermanos"
Fino: "Candido" (Palomino), "Don Zoilo"* (Palomino, 17°), "Imperial" (Palomino, 18°), "Diez Hermanos" Palma (Palomino, 16.7°)
Dry Amontillado: "Don Zoilo" (Palomino, 19°), "Mérito"
Medium Amontillado: "Don Zoilo", "Mérito", "Figaro Diez Hermanos"
Dry Oloroso: "Don Zoilo" (98% Palomino and 2% Pedro Ximénez, 19°), "Victoria Regina"* (Palomino, 21°), "Mérito", "Realengo"
Medium Oloroso: "Diez Hermanos Favorito"
Sweet: "Don Zoilo Cream" (75% Palomino and 25% Pedro Ximénez, 19°), "Don Zoilo" Medium (90% Palomino and 10% Pedro Ximénez, 19°), "Don Zoilo" Moscatel (Moscatel, 18°), "Don Zoilo Pale Cream" (Palomino and Moscatel, 17.5°), "Don Zoilo" Pedro Ximénez (Pedro Ximénez), "Diez Hermanos Favorito Cream" (75% Palomino and 25% Pedro Ximénez, 18.5°), Pedro Ximénez XXX (Pedro Ximénez, 12.5°), "Mérito Cream", "Mérito Pale Cream"

PEDRO DOMECQ
San Ildefonso 3,
Jerez de la Frontera

Vineyards: *1,050 ha (2,600 acres)*

Established: *1730*

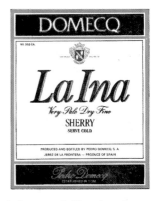

The largest and oldest Sherry firm in the business, it owns more than 75 bodegas in the region and, apart from its standard range, occasionally releases limited editions of rare *solera* wines.

Continued overleaf

Wines: *Fino:* "Botaina" (Palomino, 17.5°), "La Ina"*, "Double Century" *Amontillado:* Amontillado "51a" (Palomino, 17.5°) *Dry Amontillado:* "Botaina"* (Palomino, 17.5°) *Medium Amontillado:* "Double Century" *Oloroso:* "Decano Napoleon" (85% Palomino, 15% Pedro Ximénez, 19°), "Double Century" (90% Palomino, 10% Pedro Ximénez, 18°), "La Raza", (92% Palomino, 8% Pedro Ximénez, 18.5°), "Rio Viejo"* (Palomino, 18.5°) *Palo Cortado:* "Sibarita" (95% Palomino, 5% Pedro Ximénez, 18.5°) *Sweet:* "Celebration Cream"* (75% Palomino, 25% Pedro Ximénez, 18°), "Venerable"* (Pedro Ximénez, 16°), "Viña 25" (Pedro Ximénez, 18°), "Double Century"*

DON ZOILO
See Díez-Mérito.

DUFF GORDON
Fernán Caballero 6,
Puerto de Santa María

Established: *1768*

Founded by the British Consul in Cadiz, James Duff, and his nephew William Gordon, this historic old firm was managed by Thomas Osborne in the early nineteenth century and it was absorbed into the house of Osborne in 1872.

Wines: *Fino:* "Feria" (Palomino, 17.5°) *Amontillado:* "El Cid" (Palomino, 18-19°) *Sweet:* "Santa Maria Cream" (Palomino and Pedro Ximénez, 19°), "PX 1827"*

DUKE OF WELLINGTON
See Bodegas Internacionales.

GARVEY
Divina Pastora 3,
Jerez de la Frontera

Vineyards: *300 ha (740 acres)*
Established: *1780*

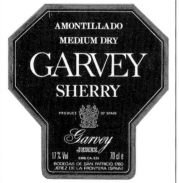

This historic firm and former Rumasa bodega now belongs to the German cooperative AG. I like this story of a young Englishman visiting Jerez. He knew of only one Sherry — Harveys — and asked a local where its bodega was. Harveys having no bodega at the time and the Englishman speaking no Spanish, the local, who spoke no English, directed him to Garvey, considering it the next best thing. The Englishman, having been royally

entertained, later wrote to the Consul in Cadiz praising the hospitality of Harveys — "but how odd they should spell it with a 'G' in Spain".

Wines: *Manzanilla:* "La Lidia" *Fino:* "San Patricio"* (Palomino, 17°) *Amontillado:* "Tio Guillermo" *Dry Oloroso:* "Ochavico" *Medium Oloroso:* "Long Life" *Sweet:* "Long Life" (Palomino, 18.5°), "Sandrita", "Flor de Jerez", Pedro Ximénez (Pedro Ximénez)

Second label: "Pedro Rodriguez"

GONZÁLEZ BYASS
Manuel M. Gonzalez 12,
Jerez de la Frontera

Vineyards: *2,000 hectares (4,940 acres)*

Established: *1870*

One of the great Jerez firms. "Tio Pepe" is the world's top-selling *fino*.

Wines: *Manzanilla:* "Fina Piedra" (Palomino, 17°) *Fino:* "Elegante" (Palomino, 17.5°), "Tio Pepe" (Palomino, 16.8°) *Dry Amontillado:* "Viña AB" (Palomino, 17.5°) *Medium Amontillado:* "Caballero" (Palomino, 17.5°), "La Concha" (Palomino, 17.5°), "Amontillado del Duque"* (Palomino, 17.5°) *Dry Oloroso:* "Alfonso" (Palomino, 19°) *Medium Oloroso:* "Nutty Solera" (Palomino, 19°), "Matusalem Muy Viejo"* (Palomino, 19°), Oloroso "Dulce Solera 1847" (Palomino, 19°) *Sweet:* "San Domingo Pale Cream" (Palomino, 19°), "Sedoso Bristol Milk" (Palomino, 19°), "Nectar Cream" (Palomino, 19.5°), "Diamond & Jubilee" (Palomino, 19.5°), "Romano Cream" (Palomino, 19.5°)

HARVEYS
John Harvey & Sons (España)
Arcos 53,
Jerez de la Frontera

Production: *17% of world sales*
Vineyards: *1,215 ha (3,000 acres)*
Established: *1970*

Although relatively recently established in Jerez, the British-based John Harvey & Sons, which dates back to 1796, has long been involved in the Sherry business, and accounts for 17 per cent of world sales.

Wines: *Manzanilla:* Harveys, "1796" *Fino:* "Luncheon Dry", "Tico" (the mixer), "1796" Superior Fino *Dry Amontillado:* Fine Old Amontillado, "1796" Fine Old Amontillado

Medium Amontillado: Club Amontillado *Palo Cortado:* Palo Cortado*, "1796" Palo Cortado* *Sweet:* "Bristol Cream" (Palomino, 17.7°), "Finesse"

LUSTAU
Emilio Lustau
Plaza del Cubo 4,
Jerez de la Frontera

Established: *1896*

The quality of these Sherries is very consistent, from a very important BOB business to its exceptional Almacenista range. The firm also owns Tomás Abad.

Wines: Manzanilla, Fino, Jerez Fino, Dry Amontillado, Medium Amontillado, Dry Oloroso*, Medium Oloroso, Palo Cortado*, Pale Cream, Cream, "Old East India" and its prestigious Almacenista* and Reserva* ranges.

MARQUÉS DEL REAL TESORO
See Real Tesoro.

MÉRITO
See Díez-Mérito.

OSBORNE
Fernàn Caballero 3,
Puerto de Santa María

Established: *1772*

In "Bailen", a true dry Oloroso, this firm produces a superb wine that may be appreciated even by those who generally dislike the Sherry style. Osborne has owned Duff Gordon, another historic Sherry bodega, since 1872.

Wines: *Fino:* "Quinta" (Palomino, 17-19°) *Amontillado:* "Conquinera" (Palomino, 17-19°) *Dry Oloroso:* "Bailen" (Palomino, 17-19°) *Medium Oloroso:* "10 RF" (Palomino, 17-19°) *Sweet:* Moscatel (Moscatel, 19°), Osborne Cream, (Pedro Ximénez and Palomino, 17-19°), Pedro Ximénez (Pedro Ximénez, 19°)

PALOMINO & VERGARA
Colon 1,
Jerez de la Frontera

Established: *1765*

This historic and former Rumasa company now belongs to Allied-Lyons.

Wines: *Fino:* "Tio Mateo*" (Palomino, 17°), Palomino & Vergara *Dry Amontillado:* "Buleria" *Medium Amontillado:* Palomino & Vergara

Dry Oloroso: "Los Flamencos" *Medium Oloroso:* Palomino & Vergara *Sweet:* Pale Cream, "Solera Cream 1895"

HIJOS DE RAINERA PÉREZ MARÍN "LA GUITA"
Banda de la Playa 28,
Sanlúcar de Barrameda

Established: *1859*

Small firm famous for its "La Guita" Manzanilla *pasada*.

Wines: *Manzanilla:* "La Guita"* (Palomino, 16°), "Hermosilla" *Fino:* "Bandera" (Palomino, 16°)

REAL TESORO
Pajarete 3,
Jerez de la Frontera

The first Marquis of "Royal Treasure" acquired his title after melting his own silver for cannon-balls for the fleet!

Wines: *Manzanilla:* "La Bailadora", "La Capitana"* *Fino:* "Ideal" (Palomino, 17°) *Amontillado:* Real Tesoro (Palomino, 17°), Viejo*, Medium Dry *Oloroso:* "Almirante" (Palomino, 17°) *Sweet:* Pedro Ximénez Real Tesoro (Pedro Ximénez, 17°), Real Tesoro Cream (Palomino, 17°), "Solera 1850" (Palomino, 17°)

LA RIVA
Alvar Nuñez 44,
Jerez de la Frontera

Established: *1776*

This historic old firm is now owned by Pedro Domecq.

Wines: *Fino:* Tres Palmas*, "Copa" Fino *Dry Amontillado:* "Guadalupe Superior" *Medium Amontillado:* Copa Amontillado *Oloroso:* Reserva, "Viña Sabel" *Palo Cortado:* "La Riva" *Sweet:* "Royal Cream", "Copa Cream"

PEDRO RODRIGUEZ
See Garvey.

SANDEMAN
Calle Pizarro 10,
Jerez de la Frontera

Vineyards: *650 ha (1,600 acres)*
Established: *1790*

Although more famous for Port, this firm always produces good Sherries.

Wines: *Fino:* "Don Fino" (Palomino, 17.5°), Dry Fino Seco *Dry Amontillado:* Bone Dry Old Amontillado *Medium Amontillado:* Medium Dry, "Royal Esmeralda" *Oloroso:* Dry Old Oloroso *Medium Oloroso:* "Character Amoroso", "Royal Corregidor"*, "Imperial Corregidor"* *Palo Cortado:* "Royal Ambrosante"*, Dry Old Palo Cortado* *Sweet:* "Armada Cream*"* (Palomino and Pedro Ximénez, 17.5°), "Character Amoroso" (Palomino and Pedro Ximénez, 17.8°), Oloroso, Light Oloroso

TERRY
Bodegas Terry
Santísima Trinidad 2,
Puerto de Santa María

Established: *1883*

This firm is owned by Allied-Lyons.

Wines: *Fino:* "Camborio" (Palomino, 16.5°), "Maruja" (Palomino, 16.5°), "Savory & James Carrera"
Medium Amontillado: "Camborio" (Palomino, 18°), "Savory & James Carrera"
Medium Oloroso: "Camborio" (Palomino, 18°), "Savory & James Carrera"
Sweet: "Amoroso Cream" (Palomino and Pedro Ximénez, 17.5°), "Camborio" (Palomino and Pedro Ximénez, 18°), "Savory & James Carrera"

VALDESPINO
Paseo del Olivar 16,
Jerez de la Frontera

Production: *400,000 cases*
Established: *1430*

The oldest bodega in Jerez, still family-owned and producing greatly respected, classic cask-fermented Sherries. Favours traditional methods.

Wines: *Manzanilla:* "Montana", "Deliciosa"
Fino: "Inocente" (Palomino, 16°), "Cuesta Alta"
Dry Amontillado: "Tio Diego", "Don Tomas"*
Medium Amontillado: "Martial", "Matador", Old Dry, Classic
Dry Oloroso: Rare
Medium Oloroso: "Solera 1842", "Don Gonzalo"*
Palo Cortado: "Tres Palos Cortados"
Sweet: "Matador Pale Cream", Jerez Cream, Pedro Ximénez "Solera Superior"*

WILLIAMS & HUMBERT
Nuno del Canas 1,
Jerez de la Frontera

Established: *1877*

Producer of Dry Sack (derived from the sixteenth-century British term for dry Spanish wine) and launched as a commercial Sherry brand by Williams & Humbert in 1908.

Wines: *Fino:* Pando (Palomino, 17°)
Amontillado-Oloroso blend: "Dry Sack" (95% Palomino and 5% Pedro Ximénez, 19.5°)
Palo Cortado: Dos Cortados*
Sweet: "Canasta Cream" (Palomino, 19.5°), "Walnut Brown", "Topaz Extra Pale Cream", "Tintilla"

Other Sherry and Manzanilla bodegas

TOMÁS ABAD
Muro de la Merced 28,
Jerez de la Frontera

Now owned by Emilio Lustau.

Wines: Tomás Abad *(Manzanilla, Fino, Dry Amontillado, Medium Amontillado, Dry Oloroso, Medium Oloroso, Palo Cortado, Sweet)*

ALAMEDA
Miguel M. Gómez,
Avenida Libertad, Puerto Santa María

Wines: *Manzanilla, Fino, Dry Amontillado, Medium Amontillado, Oloroso, Pale Cream, Cream*

HEREDEROS DE ARGÜESO
Mar 8, Sanlúcar de Barrameda

Established: *1822*

Wines: *Manzanilla:* Argüeso (Palomino, 15.5°), Manzanilla Extra (Palomino, 15.5°), "San Leon" Pasada (Palomino, 15.5°)
Amontillado: Amontillado Viejo (Palomino and Listán, 18°), Argüeso, (Palomino, 17.5°)
Oloroso: Argüeso (Palomino, 18°)
Sweet: Moscatel Fruta (Moscatel, 17°)

MANUEL DE ARGÜESO
Pozo Olivar, Jerez de la Frontera

Wines: *Manzanilla:* "Señorita", "Santa Ana"
Fino: "Colombo"
Dry Amontillado: "Coliseo"
Medium Amontillado: "Torre Verde"
Dry Oloroso: Very Old
Medium Oloroso: Argüeso
Palo Cortado: "Banda Playa"
Sweet: Argüeso Pale Cream, "Damas Cream"

HEREDEROS DE MANUEL BARÓN
Banda de la Playa 21,
Sanlúcar de Barrameda

BOBADILLA
Bodegas Manuel Fernández
Carretera Circunvalación,
Jerez de la Frontera

Established: *1872*

Wines: *Fino:* "Victoria" (Palomino, 17°), "Abanico" (Palomino, 17°)
Medium Amontillado: "Alcazar" (Palomino, 18°)
Dry Oloroso: "Capitan" (Palomino, 19°)
Sweet: "La Merced Cream", "Sadana Pale Cream"
Also produced: Manzanilla, Medium Oloroso, Palo Cortado

BODEGAS INFANTES DE ORLEANS BORBON
Baños 1, Sanlúcar de Barrameda

Established: *1943*

Wines: *Manzanilla:* Manzanilla Especial (Palomino, 15.5°), Manzanilla Fina (Palomino, 15.5°), "Torre Breva" (Palomino, 15.5°)
Fino: "Alvaro" (Palomino, 16°)
Amontillado: "Botanico" (Palomino, 17°)
Oloroso: "Fenicio" (Palomino, 18°)
Sweet: "Orleans 1884" (Palomino, 18°), Moscatel "Pasa Atlantida" (Moscatel, 18°), Pedro Ximénez "Carla" (Pedro Ximénez, 18°)

BODEGAS RAYÓN
Rayón 1-3, Jerez de la Frontera

Established: *1926*

Wines: *Manzanilla:* "Pisanova"
Fino: "Ampo"
Dry Amontillado: "La Viga"
Medium Amontillado: "Rayón"
Oloroso: "Fusco"
Sweet: "Adul Pale Cream", Rayón Cream

JOSÉ BUSTAMANTE
San Francisco Javier 3,
Jerez de la Frontera

Established: *1892*

Wines: *Fino:* "Betis" (Palomino, 17.5°), Bustamante (Palomino, 17.5°), "Reverencia" (Palomino, 17.5°)
Amontillado: Bustamante (Palomino, 17.5°), "Chambergo" (Palomino, 17.5°), "Reverencia" (Palomino, 17.5°)
Sweet: Bustamante Cream (Palomino and Pedro Ximénez 17.5°), "Reverencia Cream" (Palomino and Pedro Ximénez, 17.5°)

LA CONDESA
M. Gil Galán
Ferrocarril 14, Jerez de la Frontera

Established: *1872*

Wines: Fino, Amontillado, Oloroso, Cream

CONQUEROR
See Luis Páez.

CONQUISTADOR
See Viñas SA.

LA CUESTA
San Francisco 32,
Puerto de Santa María

Owned by Luis Caballero.

Established: *1843*

Wines: *Fino:* "Troubador" Pale Dry
Amontillado: "Troubador" Medium Dry
Oloroso: "Troubador Cream"

DEPORTIVO
See M. Gil Luque.

DON DIEGO
See Portalto.

JOSÉ ESTÉVEZ
Cristal 4, 6 and 8, Jerez de la Frontera

Wines: *Manzanilla:* "Greta", "El Tutor"
Fino: "Don Felix", "Dique", "Casanova"
Dry Amontillado: "Tocayo"
Medium Amontillado: "Don Felix", "Casanova", "Tocayo"
Oloroso: "Don Pancho"
Palo Cortado: "Ruiz"
Sweet: "Don Felix", "Greta", "El Tutor" Pale Cream, "Don Pancho", "Dique" Cream

J. FERRIS M.
See Las 3 Candidas (usual name).

FERNANDO GARCÍA-DELGADO
See Savory & James (usual name).

FRANCISCO GARCÍA DE VELASCO
See Los Angeles (usual name).

M. GIL GALÁN
See La Condesa.

M. GIL LUQUE
Carretera Arcos, Jerez de la Frontera

Established: *1900*

Wines: *Fino:* "Deportivo" (Palomino, 17°)
Amontillado: Medium "Deportivo" (Palomino, Pedro Ximénez, 18°)
Oloroso: "Deportivo Cream" (Palomino and Pedro Ximénez, 18°)

MIGUEL M. GÓMEZ
See Alameda.

LUIS G. GORDON
Huerta Pintada 20, Jerez de la Frontera

Established: *1754*

Wines: *Manzanilla:* "La Giralda" (Palomino, 17°)
Fino: "Manola" (Palomino, 17°), "Neluco"
Dry Amontillado: "Altanero"
Medium Amontillado: "Galante"
Dry Oloroso: "Tambor" (Palomino, 18°)
Medium Oloroso: "Senador"
Sweet: "Tambor Cream" (Palomino, 19°), "Acoso Pale Cream", "Royal Crescent Cream"

EMILIO M. HIDALGO
Clavel 29, Jerez de la Frontera

Established: *1874*

Wines: *Manzanilla:* Hidalgo
Fino: "Panesa" (Palomino, 16.5°), Hidalgo
Dry Amontillado: "Tresillo" (Palomino, 18°)
Medium Amontillado: "Don Emilio"
Oloroso: "Gobernador" (Palomino, 18°)
Sweet: "Magistral Cream" (Palomino and Pedro Ximénez, 18°)

VINÍCOLA HIDALGO
Banda de la Playa 24,
Sanlúcar de Barrameda

Established: *1792*
Continued overleaf

Wines: *Manzanilla:* "La Gitana"
(Palomino, 15.5°)
Fino: Hidalgo
Amontillado: "Napoleon"
(Palomino, 18°)
Oloroso: Hidalgo
Palo Cortado: Hidalgo
Sweet: Hidalgo Pale Cream, Hidalgo
Cream

HOOTER
See Portalto.

B. M. LAGOS
Banda Playa 46,
Sanlúcar de Barrameda

Established: *1910*

Wines: *Manzanilla:* "Benitez",
"Lagos", "Señero"
Fino: "Benitez", "Lagos", "Señero"
Amontillado: "Benitez", "Lagos",
"Señero"
Oloroso: "Benitez", "Lagos", "Señero"
Sweet: "Benitez", "Lagos", "Señero"
(Pale Cream and Cream)

LAS 3 CANDIDAS
J. Ferris M.
Carretera Puerto-Sanlúcar,
Puerto de Santa María

Established: *1957*

Wines: *Fino:* "Las 3 Candidas"
(Palomino, 17°)
Amontillado: "Las 3 Candidas"
(Palomino, 18°)
Sweet: "Las 3 Candidas Cream"
(Palomino, 17.5°)

LOS ANGELES
Francisco García de Velasco,
Sebastian Elcano 2,
Sanlúcar de Barrameda

Established: *1803*

Wines: Manzanilla, Fino, Amontillado,
Oloroso, Pale Cream, Cream

JOSÉ MEDINA
Banda de la Playa 46-50,
Sanlúcar de Barrameda

Wines: *Manzanilla:* Medina
(Palomino, 15°), Medina Especial,
"Solera 54"
Fino: Medina (Palomino, 17°), Medina
Especial, "Solera 54"
Amontillado: Medina (Palomino, 18°),
Medina Especial, "Solera 54"
Oloroso: Medina (Palomino, 18°),
Medina Especial, "Solera 54"
Sweet: Medina Pedro Ximénez (Palomino and
Pedro Ximénez, 22°), Medina Pedro
Ximénez (Pedro Ximénez, 22°),
"Solera 54 Cream"

ANTONIO NUÑEZ
Ronda del Caracol,
Jerez de la Frontera

Wines: *Manzanilla:* "Rompecopa"
Fino: "Santacuna"
Dry Amontillado: "Mundial"
Medium Amontillado: "Santacuna"
Dry Oloroso: "Arrumbador"
Medium Oloroso: "Collarin"
Sweet: "Santacuna Cream" and "Pale
Cream"

CARLOS DE OTAOLAURRUCHI
Cristo de las Aguas,
Sanlúcar de Barrameda

Wines: *Manzanilla:* "Victoria"
(Palomino, 17°)
Fino: "Otaola" (Palomino, 17°)
Sweet: "Otaola Cream"
(Palomino, 18°)

LUIS PÁEZ
Banda de la Playa 46,
Sanlúcar de Barrameda

Wines: *Manzanilla:* "Conqueror",
"Rey de Oro"
Fino: "Conqueror", "Rey de Oro"
Amontillado: "Conqueror", "Rey de
Oro"
Sweet: "Conqueror Pale Cream",
"Conqueror Cream", "Rey de Oro
Cream"

ANTONIO PARRA GUERRERO
Apartado 501,
Jerez de la Frontera

Wines: *Fino:* "Patrimonio"
Dry Amontillado: "Los Mellizos"
Medium Amontillado: "India" Medium
Dry Oloroso: "Rey Sol"
Medium Oloroso: "Tonipor"
Sweet: "Irene II Pale Cream", "India
Cream"

JOSÉ PEMARTÍN
Pizarro 17, Jerez de la Frontera

Wines: *Fino:* Pemartín Dry (Palomino,
17°), Vina Pemartín (Palomino, 17°)
Oloroso: Solera Pemartín (Palomino,
18°)
Sweet: Moscatel Pemartín (Moscatel,
18°), Pemartín Cream (Palomino,
18°)

PÉREZ MEGÍA
Hijos de A Pérez Megía
Fariñas 60,
Sanlúcar de Barrameda

Wines: *Manzanilla:* "Alegria"
Fino: "Salome"
Dry Amontillado: "Jalifa"
Medium Amontillado: Pérez Megía
Oloroso: Pérez Megía
Palo Cortado: Pérez Megía
Sweet: Pérez Megía Pale Cream,
"Miguel Angel Cream"

PORTALTO
Cervantes 38, Puerto de Santa María

Wines: Fino, Amontillado, Oloroso
and Cream produced under the
"Portalto", "Don Diego", "Ward
Brothers", "Sharps", and "Hooter"
labels.

RAFAEL REIG
Sebastin Elcano 2,
Sanlúcar de Barrameda

Wines: *Manzanilla:* "Langostino"
Fino: "Langostino"
Amontillado: "Langostino"
Oloroso: "Langostino"
Sweet: "Langostino"

REY DE ORO
See Luis Páez.

ROMATE
Sanchez Romate
Lealas 26,
Jerez de la Frontera

Established: *1781*

Wines: *Manzanilla:* "Viva La Pepa"
(Palomino, 17.5°), "Petenera"
Fino: "Cristal" (Palomino, 17.5°),
"Marismeño", (Palomino, 17.5°, 16.5°
in some markets), Romate (Palomino,
17.5°)
Amontillado: "N.P.U." (Palomino,
17.5°), Romate (Palomino, 17.5°)
Dry Oloroso: "Don Jose" (Palomino,
17.5°), "El Cesar", "Carlos V"
Medium Oloroso: Romate, "Don
Antonio"
Palo Cortado: Romate
Sweet: "Iberia Cream" (Palomino and
Pedro Ximénez, 17.5°), Romate
Cream (Palomino and Pedro Ximénez,
17.5°), Romate Pale Cream

PEDRO ROMERO
Trasbolsa 60,
Sanlúcar de Barrameda

Established: *1850*

Wines: *Manzanilla:* "Aurora"
(Palomino, 15.5°), "Viña El Alamo"
(Palomino, 15.5°)
Fino: "Vinã El Alamo" (Palomino,
16°)
Amontillado: "Viña El Alamo"
(Palomino, 18°)
Oloroso: "Viña El Alamo" (Palomino,
18°)
Sweet: "Viña El Alamo Cream"
(Palomino, 18°), Moscatel "Viña El
Alamo" (Moscatel, 19°), Pedro
Ximénez "Viña El Alamo" (Pedro
Ximénez, 19°)

SAVORY & JAMES
Fernando García-Delgado
Sancho Vizacíano 20,
Jerez de la Frontera

Wines: Manzanilla, Fino, Amontillado,
Pale Cream, Cream

SHARPS
See Portalto.

JOSÉ DE SOTO
M. Antonio Jesús Tirado 6,
Jerez de la Frontera

Established: *1888*

Wines: *Fino:* "Campero" (Palomino,
16.5°), "Soto" (Palomino, 17°)
Dry Amontillado: "La Uvita"
(Palomino, 18°)
Medium Amontillado: "Don Jaime"
Dry Oloroso: "La Espuela" (Palomino,
18°)
Medium Oloroso: Medium Dry
Palo Cortado: "Soto"
Sweet: Cream Sherry (Palomino, 18°)

CARLOS Y JAVIER DE TERRY
Valdés 5, 7 and 9,
Puerto de Santa María

Established: *1783*

Wines: *Manzanilla:* "501"
Fino: "501 Marinero" (Palomino,
16.5°)
Amontillado: "501 Miranda"
Oloroso: "501 Tercios" (Palomino,
18°)
Sweet: "501 Zurbarán Cream"

JUAN VICENTE VERGARA
Carretera Cartuja,
Jerez de la Frontera

Established: *1765*

Totally owned by José Medina, but run
under its own separate identity.

Wines: *Manzanilla:* "JV"
Fino: "El Patio" (Palomino, 17.8°),
"Fiverlac", "Fernando", "De Liñan"
Dry Amontillado: "JV"
Medium Amontillado: "Amalia"
(Palomino, 17.8°), "JV", "Fiverlac",
"Fernando", "De Liñan"
Oloroso: "JV" (Palomino, 17.8°)
Sweet: "Ronda Cream" (Palomino,
17.8°), "Royal Wedding Pale Cream"
(Palomino, 17.8°)

VIÑA EL ALAMO
See Pedro Romero.

VIÑAS SA
Lealas 28,
Jerez de la Frontera

Wines: Manzanilla, Fino, Amontillado,
Oloroso, Palo Cortado, Pale Cream,
Cream under the "Conquistador"
label.

WARD BROTHERS
See Portalto.

WISDOM & WARTER
Pizarro 7,
Jerez de la Frontera

Established: *1854*

Wines: *Manzanilla:* "La Guapa",
Wisdom
Fino: "Olivar" (Palomino, 17.5°),
Palma, Wisdom
Dry Amontillado: "Royal Palace"
(Palomino, 17.5°), Fine Amontillado
Dry Oloroso: "Merecedor"
Sweet: "Wisdom's Choice" Cream
(Palomino, 17.5°), "Feliciano Pale
Cream", "Cream of the Century",
Wisdom Cream, Wisdom Pale Cream

Other Spanish wines

Note: Regions or provinces in which DOs are located are given in *italics* beneath the DO heading

ALICANTE DO
Valencia

These mild-climate red and rosé wines are grown on dark limey soil in the hills behind Alicante. A little non-DO white wine is also made.

Primary: Monastrell
Secondary: Garnacha, Bobal

RED Naturally deep in colour and, when made as *doble pasta*, can be ink-black and astringent wines. Made in the old Spanish style, they are full-bodied, high in alcohol and robust.

1981, 1982, 1985, 1986, 1989

Between 6-12 years (up to 20 in exceptional cases)

ROSÉ Full and alcoholic wines that lack the grace required of a dry rosé.

Mostly non-vintage.

Immediately

☆ "Hijo de Luis Garcia Poveda" (Costa Blanca)

ALMANSA DO
Castilla-La Mancha

North of Jumilla and Yecla, this appellation bridges the heights of the central plains of La Mancha and the lowlands of Valencia.

Monastrell, Garnacha tintorera, Merseguera

RED Full in body and richly coloured, the best can be smooth and fruity.

1980, 1982, 1985, 1986

Between 3-10 years (up to 20 in exceptional cases)

ROSÉ Good examples can be fruity and clean.

1980, 1982, 1985, 1986

Within 1-3 years

☆ Alfonso Abellan, Bodegas Carrion, Bodegas Piqueras

BIERZO DO
Castilla-León

This recent appellation (1990) is one of the more exciting of Spain's new DOs. Encompassing red, white and rosé wines from six different grapes, it is the red that should stand out. It must be made from a minimum of 70 per cent Mencía, a variety that is capable of producing attractive, aromatic wines.

☆ Bodega Commercial Cooperativa Viños del Bierzo, Bodegas Palacio de Arganza

CAMPO DE BORJA DO
Aragón

The name derives from the notorious Borgia family, who used to run things here at the height of their power in the late fifteenth century.

ALL WINES, Primary: Garnacha
Secondary: Macabéo, Garnacha blanca

RED Full, robust and alcoholic.

1982, 1983, 1985, 1986

Between 3-8 years

ROSÉ Too big and coarse for the style, although the Cooperativa Agrícola de Borja makes some successful rosés.

1982, 1983, 1985, 1986

Immediately

☆ Bodegas Bordeje, Cooperativa Agrícola de Borja, Cooperativa del Campo Union Agraria del Santo Cristo, Cooperativa del Campo San Juan Bautista.

CARIÑENA DO
Aragón

Cariñena's low rainfall accounts for the high alcohol content of the whole range of wines, often as high as 18 per cent.

ALL WINES, Primary: Garnacha
Secondary: Macabéo, Cariñena, Juan Ibáñez, Bobal, Monastrell and Garnacha blanca

RED Robust, deep-coloured, pungently fruity and aromatic wines. The better-quality wines are more balanced.

1982, 1983, 1985, 1986

Between 3-8 years

WHITE These wines range from pale, dry, light and fruity, to buttercup-yellow, full, rich and sweet.

ROSÉ Both traditional rosé and deeper coloured *clarete* styles are produced.

1982, 1983, 1985, 1986

Immediately

RANCIO This category is for red, white and rosé wines that are over 14 per cent in alcohol and given at least two years' maturation in oak. They have a deliberate oxidized, maderized and literally rancid character.

Vintages are unimportant.

Usually sold when old, and does not improve in bottle.

☆ Cooperativa Agrícola de Borja, Bodegas San Valero

JUMILLA DO
Murcia

The high, hilly vineyards of Jumilla were not affected by phylloxera and 90 per cent of vines are ungrafted.

ALL WINES, Primary: Monastrell
Secondary: Airén, Garnacha tintorera

RED Comprises 94 per cent of the wines produced under the Jumilla and Jumilla Monastrell appellations. The wine is generally lacklustre unless made as a *doble pasta*.

1980, 1981, 1986

Within 1-3 years (up to 6 for *doble pasta*)

WHITE Mostly very ordinary, full- to medium-bodied wines, although the producers recommended below manage something far fresher, fruitier and more aromatic.

1980, 1981, 1986

Immediately

ROSÉ Dry, *clarete* and true rosé styles of dry wine that can be acceptable.

1980, 1981, 1986

Immediately

☆ Bodegas Bleda, Bodegas Señorio del Condestable, Jumilla Union Vitivinícola

JUMILLA MONASTRELL DO

In Jumilla, red, rosé and *doble pasta* wines made entirely from Monastrell grapes may use this appellation.

Monastrell

RED These wines are generally fuller than straightforward Jumilla DO wines and tend to improve with age. They can be smooth, fruity and very aromatic. The *doble pasta* are even fuller bodied.

1980, 1981, 1986

Between 3-8 years

☆ Asensio Carcelen (Sol y Luna), Bodega Cooperativa San Isidro, Bodegas Señorio del Condestable, Jumilla Union Vitivinícola

LA MANCHA DO
Castilla-La Mancha

The wine-land of Don Quixote has improved tremendously since the early-1980s. Output remains enormous, but many producers now harvest much earlier and so achieve fresher, lighter, more aromatic wines.

ALL WINES, Primary: Airén, Garnacha, Cencibel
Secondary: Moravia, Pardillo, Verdoncho, Macabéo.

RED Flavoursome, well-balanced wines of medium and full body, with good, clean fruit.

1980, 1982, 1986

Between 2-6 years

WHITE If chosen well, these wines, which span the entire sweetness spectrum from dry to dessert, can be fresh and aromatic.

1980, 1982, 1986

Immediately

ROSÉ It is now possible to find some elegant styles of dry rosé in La Mancha, and the Cooperativa Nuestra Señora de Manjavacas makes a fresh, clean, delightful and intensely fruity wine.

1980, 1982, 1986

Immediately

☆ Cooperativa Nuestra Señora de Manjavacas, Vinícola de Castilla, Julián Santos, Bodegas Ayuso

MÉNTRIDA DO
Castilla-La Mancha

Cheap wine, consumed locally.

ALL WINES, Primary: Garnacha
Secondary: Cencibel, Tinto Madrid

RED Deep-coloured, full-bodied, coarse wines. Not recommended.

ROSÉ Strong, alcoholic and too full-bodied for rosé. Not recommended.

RIAS BAIXAS DO
Galicia

This appellation covers various red, white and rosé wines, but the best-known and most enjoyable wines are the soft, perfumed whites made from low-yielding Albariño grapes, which can have some real depth of fruit and a fresh, lively acidity.

☆ Albariño do Salnes, Bodegas Cardallal, Bodegas del Palacio de Feiñanes, Bodegas de Vilariño-Cambados, Morgadio-Agromiño

RIBEIRO DO
Galicia

Due to the Atlantic-influenced climate of northwest Spain, the style of Ribeiro reflects that of Portugal's Vinhos Verdes.

ALL WINES, Primary: Caiño,
Secondary: Garnacha, Ferrol, Sousón, Mencía, Tempranillo, Brancellao, Jerez, Torrontés, Godello, Macabéo, Albilla, Loureira and Albariño

RED Well-coloured red wines, which have crisp fruit, high acidity and sometimes a degree of *pétillance*.

Vintages are unimportant

Within 1 year

WHITE Very fresh and fruity dry white wines, often with a good *pétillance*.

Vintages are unimportant

Within 1 year

ROSÉ Pale, light-bodied, delicately fruity rosés with a hint of *pétillance*.

Vintages are unimportant

Within 1 year

☆ Bodegas Rivera, Cooperativa del Ribeiro

RIBERA DEL DUERO DO
Castilla-León

From the upper reaches of the Douro comes Vega Sicilia Unico Reserva, reputedly Spain's greatest red wine. I do not entirely subscribe to this view; I think it is potentially the best, but its 10 or more years in wood takes its toll on the fruit, as can be demonstrated by tasting it alongside the same vintage of Vega Sicilia's "Valbuena" 3 año and 5 año. These are the estate's lesser wines, drawn off and bottled after three and five years respectively. The "Valbuena" is not quite as fine, and certainly not as complex, but it possesses a vivacity of fruit that the

Vega Sicilia Unico Reserva lacks. In fact, it is nothing short of miraculous that the latter wine is as good as it is after so long in wood (a treatment that would destroy many of the greatest wines of Bordeaux).

Since this area was granted DO status in 1982 a number of other good, great and even spectacular wines have appeared.

🐝 ALL WINES, **Primary**: Tinto del Pais,
Secondary: Garnacha, Cabernet sauvignon, Malbec, Merlot

RED The best wines have a truly dense colour, are full-to-massive in body, and are packed solid with rich, oaky-sweet and abundant plummy-fruit flavours. Beneath the obvious finesse there is an undeniable complexity of flavours.

🗓 1982, 1983, 1985, 1986, 1989

🍷— Between 5-25 years

ROSÉ These fresh, dry, fruity wines are made in the *clarete* (*claros*) style.

🗓 1982, 1983, 1985, 1986, 1989

🍷— Within 1-2 years

☆ Bodegas Alejandro Fernandez (Tinto Pesquera), Ismael Arroya, Bodegas Mauro, Hermanos Pérez (Viña Pedrosa), Cooperativa Ribera del Duero (especially Protos), Vega Sicilia

RUEDA DO
Castilla-León

A small district down-river from Ribeiro del Duero, known mainly for its white wines made almost entirely from the Verdejo grape. However, Bodegas de Crianza Castilla la Vieja produces a stunning Cabernet-Merlot wine under its "Marqués de Griñon" label, but it does not qualify for DO Rueda, although the white wine under the same label does.

🐝 ALL WINES, **Primary**: Verdejo
Secondary: Palomino, Fino, Viura

WHITE The "Marqués de Griñon" is a fine, clean, dry wine with an elegant, creamy, Chardonnay-like character, while the Marqués de Riscal Sauvignon is fuller and crisper.

🗓 1980, 1981, 1982, 1983, 1984, 1985, 1986, 1989

🍷— Within 1-3 years

FORTIFIED WHITE/TAWNY There are two types: *pálido*, which is obviously pale and supposed to be aged with *"flor"* as in sherry; and *dorado*, a mahogany-coloured, oak-aged wine of slightly higher alcohol content. To my mind they are both dull, flabby and oxidized.

☆ Agricola Castellana, Bodegas de Crianza Castilla la Vieja (especially non-DO red "Marqués de Griñon"), Marqués de Riscal (especially its Sauvignon)

SOMONTANO DO
Aragón

One of Spain's most recent DOs,

Somontano is situated between Penedés and Navarra.

🐝 ALL WINES, Monastrell, Garnacha, Parraleta, Macabéo, Garnacha blanca, Alicoñon

RED Light-to medium-bodied wines that show a fragrant, lively fruit.

🗓 1982, 1983, 1985, 1986

WHITE The best are simple, pale, dry and fruity, but beware the inferior wines made from Macabéo that can contain a thumping 16 per cent alcohol.

🗓 1982, 1983, 1985, 1986

🍷— Within 1 year

ROSÉ Fresh, dry, light-bodied rosés with a delicate aroma.

🗓 1982, 1983, 1985, 1986

🍷— Within 1-2 years

☆ Cooperativa Somontano de Sobrarbe (Montesierra, Senorio de Lazan), Lalanne

TORO DO
Castilla-León

Predominantly red wines that often undergo considerable oak-aging.

🐝 ALL WINES, Tempranillo, Malvasia, Albillo, Palomino, Verdejo, Garnacha

RED Successful, well-coloured, full-bodied wines that have a rich fruity-oak balance.

🗓 1985, 1986, 1989

🍷— Between 4-8 years

WHITE Successful, dry, medium-bodied, fruity and well-balanced. wines, made from the Malvasia grape.

🗓 1985, 1986

🍷— Within 1-3 years

ROSÉ Smooth, dry and very fruity wines.

🗓 1985, 1986

🍷— Within 1-3 years

☆ Luis Mateos Toro, Bodegas Frutos Villar, Bodegas Fariña

UTIEL-REQUENA DO
Valencia

A large and important essentially red-wine district situated in the extreme west of the province of Valencia. Distilling wine and *doble pasta* were once the area's forte but recently the emphasis has been placed on producing more characterful wines.

🐝 ALL WINES, **Primary**: Bobal
Secondary: Garnacha, Tempranillo

RED Some wines are developing fine fruity flavours, some elegance and softness.

🗓 1981, 1982, 1983, 1984, 1986

🍷— Between 2-5 years

ROSÉ Dry rosés that have an attractive colour and a fresh and fruity character.

🗓 1981, 1982, 1983, 1984, 1986

🍷— Within 1 year

☆ Augusto Egli (Casa Lo Alto)

VALDEORRAS DO
Galicia

One or two producers are making this an up-and-coming district. Vines are planted on the terraced hillsides that flank the river Sil. Valdeorras' northern, wet, Atlantic-influenced climate allows for the production of wines that are not overburdened with alcohol.

🐝 ALL WINES, **Primary**: Garnacha, Mencía, Godello
Secondary: Grao negro, Maria Ardonña, Merenzao, Palomino, Valenciana

RED Aromatic, medium-bodied attractive wines that have soft-fruit flavours and a smooth finish.

🗓 1985, 1986

🍷— Within 1-4 years

WHITE These wines can be fresh, dry, and aromatic, with a clean, fruity finish.

🗓 1985, 1986

🍷— Within 1 year

ROSÉ A successful light-red/dark-rosé *clarete* wine.

🗓 1985, 1986

🍷— Within 1 year

☆ Cooperativa 0 Barco (Mencino), Bodega Jesus Nazareno

VALDEPEÑAS DO
Castilla-La Mancha

This is La Mancha's solitary fine-wine area. Despite the torrid heat, some terrific wines are being made here and they are very good value. The rich, red, stony soil hides a water-retentive limestone base that helps offset the lack of rainfall.

🐝 ALL WINES, **Primary**: Airén
Secondary: Tempranillo

RED The best wines are medium-to full-bodied and have a wonderfully rich yet well-balanced flavour.

🗓 1981, 1983, 1984, 1986, 1989

🍷— Between 2-6 years

WHITE Pale, light, dry and smooth.

🗓 1981, 1983, 1984, 1986, 1989

🍷— Within 1 year

ROSÉ Smooth and fruity wines, with a dry finish.

🗓 1981, 1983, 1984, 1986, 1989

🍷— Within 1-2 years

☆ Viña Albali Reservas, Bodegas Los Llanos, Bodegas Felix Solis

VALENCIA DO
Valencia

An area renowned for its low-quality table wines, plus the occasional fine Moscatel. However, some very good lighter wines are now being made.

🐝 ALL WINES, **Primary**: Pedro Ximénez, Monastrell, Moscatel
Secondary: Merseguera, Planta fina, Tortosí, Malvasia, Garnacha, Común, Garnacha tintorera and Forcayat

RED Fine-flavoured, fruity wines.

🗓 1983, 1984, 1985, 1986, 1989

🍷— Between 2-5 years

WHITE Light-bodied, dry white wines.

🗓 1983, 1984, 1985, 1986, 1989

🍷— Within 1 year

ROSÉ Fresh, dry wines with gentle fruit.

🗓 1983, 1984, 1985, 1986, 1989

🍷— Within 1 year

FORTIFIED WHITE Delicious, ultra-sweet raisiny Moscatel.

🍷— Immediately

☆ Antonio Arraez, Cooperativa Agrícola de Villar, Vincente Gandia, Augusto Egli (particularly good value Moscatel), Vincente Grandía Pla, Cavas Murviedro, Bodegas Tierra Hernández

YECLA DO
Murcia

Stony-limestone vineyards located between Alicante and Jumilla.

🐝 ALL WINES, **Primary**: Monastrell
Secondary: Verdil, Merseguera

RED Either ink-black (*doble pasta*) or cherry-coloured wines with body, good fruit and balance.

🗓 1980, 1981, 1986

🍷— Between 2-5 years

WHITE At best fresh, clean and fruity.

🗓 1980, 1981, 1986

🍷— Immediately

ROSÉ A dry, *clarete*-style rosé with clean, cherry-flavoured fruit.

🗓 1980, 1981, 1986

🍷— Within 1-2 years

☆ Bodegas Castano "Las Gruesas", Ochoa Palao "Cuvee Prestige"

Portugal

Portugal is the home of two classic fortified wines, Port and Madeira, as well as the popular, fresh and deliciously unpretentious white wine, Vinho Verde. Alongside these, it would be unthinkable not to mention the phenomenal marketing success of "Mateus", the famous pink *pétillant* wine, and its rival, "Lancers". For a long time, this was, incredibly, the extent of Portugal's repertoire in terms of international recognition. However, since its entry into the EEC, the country's wine is experiencing an upsurge in quality and interest.

AS THE SEVENTH-LARGEST WINEMAKING country in the world, Portugal has great potential and could offer so much more, yet, with very few exceptions, the "old guard" of its wine industry has hitherto been content stubbornly to defend what it perceives as traditional Portuguese styles of wine, but which are more accurately described as tannic and ungenerous, with too little fruit and too much oxidation. Interestingly, these problems have been paralleled in Spain.

THE TURNAROUND IN PORTUGAL'S WINE INDUSTRY

Until the mid-1970s, the Spanish, like the Portuguese, had also used jargon like "traditional values" to excuse poor standards of winemaking. Finally, a new generation of winemakers admitted

Vineyards, Setúbal, above
The area's Moscatel vines produce a celebrated fortified wine that has its own Região Demarcada (RD).

that the problem was essentially poor vinification, and that the drinking attitudes of a society that knew nothing better were hardly sufficient to justify its continuation. Winemaking in Spain changed quickly and radically, but it appeared as if old habits would linger on forever in Portugal. Until, that is, the country joined Europe's Common Market in January 1986, an event that can now be seen as the catalyst to Portugal's coming of age in the international world of fine wine.

Contrary to the spirit of its earlier history, Portugal has tended to look inwards throughout this century, but since 1986 it has actively engaged in trying to be part of the outside world. For wine drinkers, this means that the complacency based on old-fashioned wine styles has been replaced with a desire to make wines that everyone can enjoy. It means that we can look forward to Dão *with* fruit, to Bairrada fulfilling its potential as Portugal's most exciting red-wine area, to the development of new classic wines on the one hand and the generation of a new breed of clean, simple, fruity wines at the base of the industry on the other.

PORTUGAL

It is in the north of the country that the most famous wines – Port and Vinho Verde – are produced, along with the most upwardly mobile, those from Bairrada and Dão.

Demarcated regions

- Vinho Verde
  See also p. 295
- Port
  See also p. 295
- Bairrada
  See also p. 303
- Dão
  See also p. 303
- Colares
- Carcavelhos
- Bucelas
- Moscatel de Setúbal
- Algarve

Other wine regions

- Lafões
- Pinhel
- Estremadura
- Ribatejo
- Alentejo

- - - - - International Boundary
───── Provincial Boundary
▲ Height above sea level (metres)

Kms 20 40 60 80 100
Mls   20   40   60

PORTUGAL'S WINE PRODUCTION

Portugal exports some 15 million cases of wine each year, but the wines the world sees are a misleading reflection of what is actually produced. Fortified wines and rosé account for 75 per cent of its exports, yet less than 15 per cent of production. Vinho Verde, which represents just five per cent of exports, accounts for 20 per cent of the total production. And the Vinho Verde that is exported is sweetened so that it does not resemble the true product. Nearly all the Vinho Verde actually produced in Portugal is red, but 99.9 per cent of Vinho Verde exported is white. The red versions, which have an unripe fruit flavour and taste strangely metallic and malic, are not suited to export markets and are only appreciated by the tough Portuguese peasant palate.

Wine	Hectolitres	(Cases)
Algarve (total)	7,650	(85,000)
Bairrada (red)	540,000	(6,000,000)
Bairrada (white)	55,800	(620,000)
Bucelas (white)	4,950	(55,000)
Colares (red)	2,250	(25,000)
Dão (red)	229,500	(2,550,000)
Dão (white)	49,500	(550,000)
Douro (red)	540,000	(6,000,000)
Douro (white)	229,500	(2,550,000)
Madeira (total)	19,800	(220,000)
Port (total)	675,000	(7,500,000)
Ribatejo (red)	720,000	(8,000,000)
Ribatejo (white)	63,000	(700,000)
Vinho Verde (red)	1,200,000	(13,350,000)
Vinho Verde (white)	495,000	(5,500,000)
Other wines	4,170,000	(46,295,000)
Total production	9,001,950	(100,000,000)

Overhead vines, Aveleda, Minho, right
Vines grown for the Minho's famous Vinho Verde are trained high to allow for other crops underneath.

HOW TO READ PORTUGUESE WINE LABELS

Style of the wine
Various terms found on Portuguese labels are descriptive of the wine's style. The *branco* on this example means white. Other possible terms include *adamado* sweet; *aperitivo* apéritif; *bruto* Portuguese adaption of the French *brut*, used to describe a dry sparkling wine; *clarete* Bordeaux-style; *claro* new or "nouveau" wine; *doce* sweet; *espumante* sparkling wine that may be made by any method unless qualified by another term; *generoso* an apéritif or dessert wine rich in alcohol and usually sweet; *licoroso* a fortified wine; *maduro* literally "matured", it refers to a wine that has been kept in a vat (sometimes concrete). To the Portuguese consumer, a dried-out, oxidized wine is *maduro* and they prefer it that way; *quinado* tonic wine; *rosado* rosé; *séco* dry; *tinto* red.

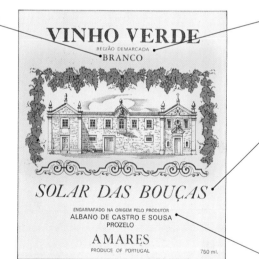

VINHO VERDE
REGIÃO DEMARCADA
BRANCO

SOLAR DAS BOUÇAS

ENGARRAFADO NA ORIGEM PELO PRODUTOR
ALBANO DE CASTRO E SOUSA
PROZELO

AMARES
PRODUCE OF PORTUGAL   750 ml.

Região demarcada (RD)
This indicates that the wine comes from one of Portugal's legally demarcated areas. In this example, the wine is Vinho Verde from near Amares, in the Minho.

Name of the property
The use of words such as *Casa*, *Palacio* and *Solar* in the name of a wine may also indicate a single-vineyard wine. This wine is made at Solar das Bouças, and the presence of the term *Engarrafado na origem* confirms that it has been estate-bottled. However, it should be remembered that the Portuguese have not yet realized the importance that is placed on estate-bottling on international markets and consequently many vineyards are not equipped to make and bottle wine, so that these functions may well be carried out elsewhere. *Vinha* means vineyard. *Adega*, literally "Cellar", is commonly used as part of the name of a company or cooperative, much in the way that the Spanish employ "Bodega", their equivalent term.

Bottled on the property
Engarrafado means bottled at, or by, and is followed by the name of the bottler. In this case, it is Albano de Castro e Sousa. *Engarrafado na origem* indicates that wine is estate-bottled and is one of the most useful, yet least encountered, terms on a Portuguese label. "Quinta", as part of a wine's name, should indicate that it is the product of a single farm or estate. Like the French term "château", it has been somewhat abused in the past, but is now 95 per cent reliable and is to be the subject of continuous tightening up under the auspices of the EEC wine regime.

Other important and interesting terms on Portuguese labels:

Carvalho Oak

Casta Grape variety. Grape varieties are often indicated on Vinhos Verdes and the most common of these are: Alvarinho, Avesso, Azal, Loureito, Pederña, and Trajadura. *Casta Predominante* refers to the major grape variety used in a wine.

Colheita This means "Vintage" and is followed by the year of harvest.

Concurso Nacional National competition for wines organized annually by the *Junta Nacional do Vinho*. A wine boasting this should be superior, according to Portuguese standards.

Garrafeira This term may only be used for a vintage-dated wine that possesses an extra 0.5 per cent of alcohol above the minimum requirement. Red wines must have a minimum of three years' maturation including one year in bottle; white wines one year including six months in bottle. The wine may come from a demarcated region, but does not have to; it could well be blended from various areas.

Reserva Can only be used to qualify a vintage year of "outstanding quality", where the wine has an alcoholic strength of at least 0.5 per cent above the minimum requirement. The wine may come from a demarcated region, but does not have to; it could well be blended from various areas.

Selo de Origem The seal of origin that guarantees the authenticity of a demarcated wine.

Velho Literally "old", this term used not to have any legal definition – now it can only be applied to wines with a minimum age of three years for reds and two years for white.

Vinho de mesa Table wine. Without an all-important indication of a specific RD or Garrafeira, the wine will simply be a cheap blend.

The Douro and the Minho

No two neighbouring districts could produce more contrasting wines than the Douro's deep-coloured, rich, warm and spicy fortified Port, and the Minho's light, water-white, semi-sparkling Vinho Verde.

"IT SHOULD FEEL LIKE LIQUID FIRE in the stomach . . . it should burn like inflamed gunpowder . . . it should have the tint of ink . . . it should be like the sugar of Brazil in sweetness and like the spices of India in aromatic flavour . . ." This vivid impression of Port was written in 1754 by the agents for the Association of Port Wine Shippers, yet remains a fair description of the great after-dinner wine we know today.

THE ORIGIN OF PORT

It is hard to imagine how such a wonderful winter-warming drink as Port could ever have been conceived in such a hot and sunny country as Portugal. Harder still, while traipsing through the steeply terraced vineyards of the Upper Douro in ninety degrees of heat. As Port is best suited for privileged tables and colder climes, why on earth did the Portuguese bother to invent it? The popular belief is that it was not the Portuguese but the British; however this is not entirely accurate. We can thank the Portuguese for dreaming up this most classic of fortified wines, although it was the British who capitalized on the idea.

In 1678, two English gentlemen were sent by a Liverpool wine merchant to Viana do Castello, north of Oporto, to learn the wine trade. Holidaying up the Douro River, they were regally entertained by the Abbot of Lamego. Finding his wine "very agreeable, sweetish and extremely smooth", they asked what made it exceptional among all others tasted on their journey. The Abbot finally confessed to doctoring the wine with brandy, but the English gentlemen were so pleased with the result that they purchased the entire stock and shipped it home.

The development of the Port trade

The ancient house of C. N. Kopke & Co had been trading in Douro wines for nearly 40 years and, since 1670, an Englishman named John Clark had been busy building up a business that would become Warre & Co. In the same year as the encounter with the Abbot of Lamego, the firm of Croft & Co was established, and this was followed by Quarles Harris in 1680 and Taylor's in 1692. When the Methuen Treaty of 1703 gave Portuguese wines preferential rates of duty in Britain, many English and Scottish firms flocked to Oporto to set up trade. Firms of other nationalities – Dutch, German, even French, followed, but it was the British shippers who virtually monopolized the trade and they frequently abused their power. In 1755, the Marquis of Pombal, who had assumed almost dictatorial powers over Portugal some five years before, put a curb on their activities through the Board of Trade. This was achieved by restricting the privileges enjoyed by British merchants under two 100-year-old treaties. He also established the Oporto Wine Company, endowing it with the sort of powers to which the British had been accustomed. This infuriated the British, but their protests were to no avail and Pombal went on to instigate many worthy, if unpopular, reforms, including the limiting of the Douro's production area to the finest vineyards, the outlawing of manure, which reduced yields but greatly improved quality, and the banning of elderberries for colouring the wine.

The production of Port at this time had not been perfected. Fifty years after the encounter with the Abbot of Lamego, the trade had widely accepted the practice of brandying, but the importance of when, and in what quantity, to administer the brandy was too subtle a sophistication for the times. Ironically, the Abbot's wine was superior because he had added the brandy during, and not after the fermentation, thus interrupting the process (muting) with a natural sweetness that had so attracted the two Englishmen.

Grape pickers near Amarante,
southern Minho, above
Ladders with buckets fixed to them are
needed to pick the overhead bunches.

THE DOURO AND THE MINHO

These two northern areas produce the celebrated Port and Vinho
Verde. The river Douro has long been crucial to the Port trade.

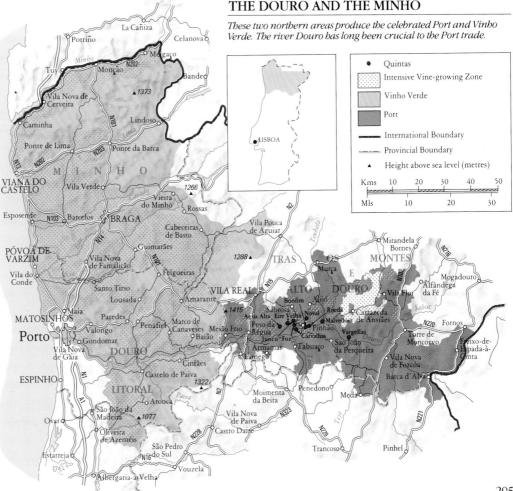

Legend:
- • Quintas
- Intensive Vine-growing Zone
- Vinho Verde
- Port
- International Boundary
- Provincial Boundary
- ▲ Height above sea level (metres)

PORT GRAPE VARIETIES

There are 48 grape varieties permitted in the production of Port. This simple fact goes a long way to explaining the great variation in quality and character of Ports within the same basic style. The official classification of the grapes is as follows:

Very good black grapes
Bastardo, Donzelinho tinto, Mourisco, Tinta roriz, Tinta Francisca, Tinta cão, Touriga Francesa, Touriga nacional

Good black grapes
Cornifesto, Malvasia preta, Mourisco de Semente, Periquita, Rufete, Samarrinho, Sousão, Tinta amarela, Tinta da barca, Tinta barroca, Tinta carvalha, Touriga Brasileira

Average black grapes
Alvarelhão, Avesso, Casculho, Castela, Coucieira, Moreto, Tinta Bairrada, Tinto martins

Very good white grapes
Donzelinho, Esgana-cão, Folgosão, Gouveio (or Verdelho), Malvasia fina, Malvasia rei, Rabigato, Viosinho

Good white grapes
Arinto, Boal, Cercial, Côdega, Malvasia corada, Moscatel galego

Average white grapes
Branco sem nome, Fernão pires, Malvasia parda, Pedernã, Praça, Touriga branca

The six best Port grape varieties

The six grape varieties currently considered by growers and winemakers to be the best are:

Touriga nacional Almost universally agreed to be the very best of all Port grapes, Touriga nacional has tiny berries and produces pitch-black wine with intense aromatic properties, great extract and high tannin content. It prefers hotter situations, but is a poor pollinator and does not yield a large crop. Cloning is under way to increase production by 15 per cent and sugar content by 10 per cent, the most successful clone so far being R110.

Tinta cão This variety can add finesse and complexity to a blend, but it enjoys a cooler environment and requires training on wires to produce a decent crop. As traditional cultivation methods make it a poor producer, growers are not over-keen to cultivate it; the grape's survival will depend upon the willingness of Port shippers to maintain the variety on their large, managed estates.

Tinta roriz Not really a member of the Tinta family, this grape is sometimes simply called the Roriz. It is in fact the well-known Spanish variety, Tempranillo, the mainstay of Rioja. In the Douro it likes heat and fares best on the sunniest front rows of terraces cut into south- or west-facing slopes. Its dark grapes have

thick skins, high sugar content and low acidity, providing great colour, tannin and succulence in a blend. Some believe this to be better than the Touriga nacional.

Tinta barroca The wine produced by this grape variety is quite precocious and is therefore useful in younger-drinking Ports, or to dilute wines that are too tannic and distinctive. Like Tinta cão, this grape variety prefers cooler situations and particularly enjoys north-facing slopes.

Touriga Francesa A member of the Touriga family, this grape has no connection whatsoever with the similarly named Tinta Francisca, a member of the Tinta family. According to Bruce Guimaräens of Fonseca and Taylor's, this high-quality variety is useful for "filling in the gaps" in vineyards between those areas occupied by vines that like either hot or cool situations. It contributes fruit and aroma to a blend.

Tinta amarela This grape variety is dark-coloured and very productive. Its importance has been on the increase in recent years. Susceptible to rot, this high-quality vine performs best in the hottest, driest areas.

HOW PORT IS MADE

If any wine is perceived as having been "trodden", then it is Port, perhaps because the pressing and winemaking traditionally takes place in the vineyards where, until relatively recently, affairs were conducted on farms in a rather rustic style. Nowadays, few Ports are trodden, although several houses have showpiece *lagars* for tourists.

Many houses have "autovinificators" – rather antiquated devices that rely on the build-up of pressure from carbonic gas given off during fermentation to force the juice up and over the *manta* of grape skins. The object is to extract the maximum amount of colouring matter from the skins, because so much of this is eliminated by fortification. However there are other, far simpler, yet more advanced, vats capable of this and several types have been installed throughout the industry.

FACTORS AFFECTING TASTE AND QUALITY

 Location
The Douro and Minho regions are located in the north of Portugal. Port is made in the Cima Corgo, Baixo Corgo and Douro Superior districts of the Douro Valley, and Vinho Verde in the Minho province, which falls between the Douro River and Minho River valleys.

Climate
The summers are dry and hot and the winters mild and wet in the Minho region, becoming more continental in the upper Douro Valley, where the summers are extremely hot, rainfall is high – 52 centimetres (20.8 ins) – and winters can be very cold.

Aspect
Vines are planted on generally hilly land that becomes very steep in parts of both areas, although much of the bulk Vinho Verde production comes from flat, mixed farming land.

Soil
Most Vinho Verde is produced on the weathered granite soil that dominates the Minho, although some vines grow in a band of Silurian schist soils between the Lima and Cavado rivers. The Douro is a patchwork of hard, sun-baked, granite and schist soils, with the finest Ports originating from the schist vineyards that dominate further upriver. Because of the importance of schist to Port production, Douro table wines are relegated to granite soils.

Viticulture and vinification
Terracing in the Douro is widespread to maximize the use of the land, although the current trend is to make wider terraces, thus enabling mechanization. Some of the less precipitous slopes are now cultivated in vertical rows. Steep terraces mean labour-intensive viticulture, and the hard Douro soil often requires blasting to enable planting.
Port wines are made and fortified in the Douro, but most are blended and bottled at lodges in Vila Nova de Gaia. Vinho Verde is made from red and white grapes traditionally trained high. The wine is vinified dry, with a deliberate *pétillance*.

 Primary grape varieties
Alvarelhão, Alvarinho, Espadeiro, Loureiro, Tinta amarela, Tinta barroca, Tinta cão, Tinta Francisca, Touriga Francesa, Touriga nacional, Vinhão

Secondary grape varieties
Arinto, Avesso, Azal branco, Bastardo, Boal, Borraçal, Brancelho, Cercial, Côdega, Cornifesto, Donzelinho, Donzelinho branco, Donzelinho tinto, Esgano cão, Fernão pires, Folgosão, Malvasia, Malvasia corada, Malvasia fina, Malvasia parda, Malvasia preta, Moscatel galego, Mourisco de semente, Mourisco tinto, Perdernã, Periquita, Rabigato, Rabo de ovelha, Rufete, Samarrinho, Sousão, Tinta barca, Tinta carvalha, Tinta roriz, Touriga Brasileira, Trajadura, Verdelho, Viosinho

Fermentation and fortification

The initial fermentation phase of Port differs little from that which is encountered elsewhere in the world, except that vinification temperatures are often as high as 32°C (90°F). This obviously has no detrimental effect on this particular style of wine and probably accounts for its chocolatey, high pH complexity. When approximately six to eight per cent of alcohol has been achieved, the wine is fortified, unlike Sherry, where the fermentation process is allowed to complete its natural course. This is because Port derives its sweetness from unfermented sugars, whereas sweet Sherries are totally dry wines to which a syrupy concentrate has been added. The timing of the addition of brandy is based on the sugar reading, not on the alcohol level. When the sweetness of the fermenting juice has dropped to 6° Beaumé, approximately 90 grams per litre of sugar, the alcoholic strength will normally be between six and eight per cent, but this varies according to the richness of the juice, which in turn is dependent on the grape variety, where it is grown and the year in question.

The use of the word "brandy" is somewhat misleading. It is not, in fact, brandy in any common sense of the word, but a clear and flavourless grape-distilled spirit of 77 per cent alcoholic strength, known in Portugal as *aguardente*. This adds alcoholic strength to a Port, but never aroma or flavour. The *aguardente* is produced either from wines made in the south of Portugal, or from excess production in the Douro itself. Its price and distribution to each shipper are strictly rationed. The amount added averages 110 litres for every 440 litres of wine, making a total of 550 litres, which is the capacity of a Douro *pipe,* a specific size of cask used for shipping wine from the valley to the lodges at Vila Nova de Gaia. A drier Port has a slightly longer fermentation and requires less than 100 litres of *aguardente*, while a particularly sweet (or *geropiga*) Port is muted very early with as much as 135 litres.

If gauged correctly, the brandy added to arrest the fermentation will eventually harmonize with the fruit and the natural sweetness of the wine. The concept of Port's balance between fruit, alcohol and sweetness is, of course, greatly affected by what we are used to drinking, and thus conditioned to expect. In the deepest Douro a local farmer is likely to use a far higher proportion of alcohol for the Port drunk by himself and his family, than for the Port he makes under the auspices of a shipper. Generally the British shippers prefer more fruit and less brandy than the Portuguese, but all commercial shippers, British or Portuguese, would consider the domestic port of a Douro farmer to have insufficient body to match the brandy.

Maturation and blending

Until 1986, all Port was required by law to be matured and bottled at Vila Nova de Gaia on the left bank of the Douro estuary opposite Oporto. At some 75 kilometres (47 miles) from the region of production, this was like insisting that all Champagne be blended, bottled and disgorged at Le Havre. It was also restrictive, preventing small growers who could not possibly afford a lodge at Vila Nova de Gaia from exporting their wine. All this has changed, and although most Ports do still come from the big shippers' lodges, many new Ports now find their way on to the market direct from privately owned Douro *quintas*.

THE QUINTA CLASSIFICATION

The Douro Valley covers 243,000 hectares (600,000 acres), of which 24,000 (60,000 acres) are cultivated; within this area, there are approximately 80,000 individual vineyards owned by 29,620 growers. Each vineyard is classified according to a points system allocated for the categories listed below. The better the classification, the higher official price a vineyard receives for its grapes and the greater its permitted production.

Category	Minimum	Maximum
Location	−50	+600
Aspect	−1,000	+250
(Altitude; lowest best	−900	+150)
(Gradient; steepest best	−100	+100)
Soil	−350	+100
(Schist	N/A	+100)
(Granite	−350	N/A)
(Mixture	−150	N/A)
Microclimate; sheltered best	0	+60
Vine varieties; official classification	300	+150
Age of vines; oldest best	0	+60
Vine density; lowest best	−50	+50
Productivity; lowest best	−900	+120
Vineyard maintenance	−500	+100
Total	−3,150	+1,490

The vineyards are classified from A, for best, to F, for worst, as follows:
Class A (1,200 points or more); Class B (1,001 – 1,199 points); Class C (801 – 1,000 points); Class D (601 – 800 points); Class E (401 – 600 points); Class F (400 points or below).

Aciprestes
Class A, (Royal Oporto)

Agua Alta
Class not disclosed, (Churchill)

Alegria
Class not disclosed, (Santos)

Aradas
Class A-B, (Noval)

Atayde
Class A, (Cockburn)

Avidagos
Class A-B, (Da Silva)

Boa Vista
Class A, (Offley Forrester)

Bomfim
Class A, (Dow)

Bom-Retiro
Class A, (Ramos-Pinto)

Carvalhas
Class A, (Royal Oporto)

Carvalheira
Class A, (Cálem & Filho)

Carvoeira
Class B, (Barros, Almeida)

Casal
Class D, (Sandeman)

Casa Nova
Class A-B, (Borges & Irmao)

Cavadinha
Class A, (Warre)

Confradeiro
Class D, (Sandeman)

Côtto
Class not disclosed, (Champalimaud)

Corte
Class A, (privately owned, managed by Delaforce)

Corval
Class A, (Royal Oporto)

Cruizeiro St. Antonio
Class A, (Guimarães)

Dona Matilde
Class B, (Barros, Almeida)

Eira Velha
Class A, (privately owned, managed by Cockburn)

Ervamoira
Class A, (Ramos-Pinto)

Ferradosa
Class A-B, (Borges & Irmao)

Fontela
Class A, (Cockburn)

Fonte Santa
Class A, (Kopke)

Foz
Class A, (Cálem & Filho)

Granja
Class C, D and E, (Royal Oporto)

Hortos
Class A-B, (Borges & Irmao)

Junco
Class A-B, (Borges & Irmao)

Laranjeira
Class B, (Sandeman)

La Rosa
Class A, (privately owned, managed by Robertson Bros)

Leda
Class A-B, (Ferreira)

Lobata
Class A, (Barros, Almeida)

Madalena
Class A, (Warre)

Malvedos
Class A, (Graham)

Marco
Class A-B, (Noval)

Meao
Class A-B, (Ferreira family)

Mesquita
Class A, (Barros, Almeida)

Monte Bravo
Class A, (privately owned, managed by Dow)

Nova
Class A, (privately owned, managed by Warre)

Noval
Class A-B, (Noval)

Panascal
Class A, (Guimaraens)

Passa Douro
Class A, (Sandeman)

Porrais
Class C, (Ferreira family)

Porto
Class A-B, (Ferreira)

Quartas
Class C, (Pocas)

Roeda
Class A, (Croft)

Sagrado
Class A, (Cálem & Filho)

San Domingos
Class B, (Ramos-Pinto)

Santo Antonio
Class A, (Cálem & Filho)

Seixo
Class A-B, (Ferreira)

Sibio
Class A, (Royal Oporto)

Sidro
Class C and D, (Royal Oporto)

Silho
Class A-B, (Borges & Irmao)

Silval
Class A-B, (Noval)

Soalheira
Class A-B, (Borges & Irmao)

Sta Barbara
Class B-C, (Pocas)

St. Luiz
Class A, (Kopke)

Terra Feita
Class A, (Taylor's)

Tua
Class A, (Cockburn)

Urqueiras
Class A-B, (Noval)

Urtiga
Class B, (Ramos-Pinto)

Valado
Class C, (Ferreira family)

Vale de Mendiz
Class A, (Sandeman)

Vale Dona Maria
Class A, (Smith Woodhouse)

Vargellas
Class A, (Taylor's)

Vedial
Class A, (Cálem & Filho)

Velho Roncao
Class A-B, (Pocas)

Vezuvio
Class A-B, (Ferreira family)

Zimbro
Class A, (privately owned, managed by Dow)

VINTAGES "DECLARED" SINCE 1945

Any year may be "declared" by any shipper. All the firm needs to do is submit samples to the Instituto do Vinho do Porto for approval and, if accepted, bottle the wine within the two-year limit. Some years have been declared by just one solitary shipper: 1951 (Feuerheerd), 1962 (Quinta do Noval), and 1972 (Dow); while others are almost universally declared: 1963, 1970, 1975, 1977, 1983 and 1985 – the last vintage to be declared at the time of writing, which was "declared by more shippers than any other previous vintage" according to one source. The following summary is a comprehensive listing of small and large shippers, famous and obscure, existing and no longer operative (but still available at auction).

Adams 1945, 1947, 1948, 1950, 1955, 1960, 1963, 1966

Barros, Almeida 1975, 1980, 1982, 1983, 1985

Borges 1963, 1970, 1980, 1982, 1983, 1985

Burmester 1945, 1948, 1954, 1955, 1958, 1960, 1963, 1970, 1977, 1980

Butler, Nephew 1945, 1947, 1948, 1955, 1957, 1958, 1960, 1970, 1975

Cálem 1947, 1948, 1955, 1958, 1960, 1963, 1975, 1977, 1980, 1983, 1985

Cockburn 1947, 1950, 1955, 1960, 1963, 1967, 1970, 1975, 1983, 1985

Croft 1945, 1950, 1955, 1960, 1963, 1966, 1970, 1975, 1977, 1982, 1985

Quinta do Noval 1945, 1947, 1948, 1950, 1955, 1958, 1960, 1962, 1963, 1966, 1969, 1970, 1972, 1975, 1978, 1980, 1982, 1985

Da Silva C. 1970, 1977, 1978, 1982, 1985

Delaforce 1945, 1947, 1950, 1955, 1958, 1960, 1963, 1966, 1970, 1975, 1977, 1982, 1985

Diez 1970, 1975, 1977, 1980

Douro Wine Shippers 1970, 1980, 1982, 1983, 1985

Dow 1945, 1947, 1950, 1955, 1960, 1963, 1966, 1970, 1972, 1975, 1977, 1980, 1983, 1985

Feist 1970, 1980, 1982, 1983

Ferreira 1945, 1955, 1960, 1963, 1966, 1970, 1975, 1977, 1980, 1983, 1985

Feuerheerd 1945, 1951, 1955, 1957, 1960, 1963, 1966, 1970, 1980

Fonseca 1945, 1948, 1955, 1960, 1963, 1966, 1970, 1975, 1977, 1980, 1983, 1985

Gonzalez Byass 1945, 1955, 1960, 1963, 1967, 1970, 1975

Gould Campbell 1955, 1960, 1963, 1966, 1975, 1977, 1980, 1983, 1985

Graham 1945, 1948, 1955, 1960, 1963, 1966, 1970, 1975, 1977, 1980, 1983, 1985, 1988

Guimarães 1963, 1966, 1970

Hutcheson 1970, 1980, 1982, 1983

Kopke 1945, 1948, 1950, 1952, 1955, 1958, 1960, 1963, 1966, 1970, 1977, 1982, 1983, 1985

Mackenzie 1945, 1947, 1948, 1950, 1952, 1954, 1955, 1957, 1958, 1960, 1963, 1966, 1970, 1975, 1982

Martinez 1945, 1955, 1958, 1960, 1963, 1967, 1970, 1975, 1982, 1983, 1985

Messias 1970, 1975, 1980, 1982, 1983, 1985

Morgan 1948, 1950, 1955, 1960, 1963, 1966, 1970, 1975, 1977, 1982

Niepoort 1945, 1970, 1980, 1982, 1983, 1985

Offley Forrester 1950, 1954, 1960, 1962, 1963, 1966, 1967, 1970, 1972, 1975, 1977, 1980, 1982, 1983, 1985

Osborne 1970

Pinto dos Santos 1955, 1957, 1958, 1960, 1963, 1966, 1970, 1974, 1975, 1985

Poças 1967, 1970, 1975, 1977, 1982, 1983, 1985

Quarles Harris 1945, 1947, 1950, 1955, 1958, 1960, 1963, 1966, 1975, 1977, 1980, 1983, 1985

Ramos Pinto 1945, 1955, 1970, 1980, 1982, 1983, 1985

Real Vinicola 1945, 1947, 1950, 1955, 1960, 1980, 1982, 1983, 1985

Rebello Valente 1955, 1960, 1963, 1966, 1975, 1980, 1983, 1985

Robertson Bros 1945, 1947, 1955, 1970, 1977

Royal Oporto 1945, 1958, 1960, 1962, 1963, 1967, 1970, 1975, 1977, 1983, 1985

Rozes 1983

Sandeman 1945, 1947, 1950, 1955, 1957, 1958, 1960, 1962, 1963, 1966, 1967, 1970, 1975, 1977, 1980, 1982, 1985

Smith Woodhouse 1945, 1947, 1950, 1955, 1960, 1963, 1966, 1970, 1975, 1977, 1980, 1983, 1985

Sociedade Constantino 1945, 1947, 1950, 1958, 1966

Taylor, Fladgate & Yeatman 1945, 1948, 1955, 1960, 1963, 1966, 1970, 1975, 1977, 1980, 1983, 1985

Tuke, Holdsworth 1945, 1947, 1950, 1955, 1960, 1963, 1966

Vasconcellos 1982

Viera de Souza 1970, 1980, 1983

Warre 1945, 1947, 1950, 1955, 1958, 1960, 1963, 1966, 1970, 1975, 1977, 1980, 1983, 1985

Wiese & Krohn 1947, 1950, 1952, 1960, 1967, 1970, 1982, 1985

BARON JOSEPH FORRESTER

Born in England in 1809, Joseph Forrester arrived in Oporto in 1831 and busied himself with every aspect of the Port trade. In 1848 he anonymously published *A Word or Two on Port*, which became a best-seller in both Oporto and London, with eight rapid reprints. The book did not endear Forrester to his colleagues in the trade, but through its success, public opinion forced many of his reforms on them. Not all of the practices he complained about would necessarily be considered abuses today. One "malpractice" he fortunately was unsuccessful in stopping was the addition of brandy!

Forrester's most famous contribution to the improvement of the Port trade was his detailed mapping of the river bed in the Upper Douro, showing the rapids and making the river much safer for navigation. Ironically, it was the treachery of this river that brought about his end. In May 1862, after lunch at Quinta da Vargellas, the Baron took a trip downriver, accompanied by two ladies. The boat hit a submerged rock in the rapids and its hull split open. The Baron drowned but the two ladies were much luckier, literally bobbing safely to the shore due to the buoyancy of the hoops in their crinolines.

The historic *barco rabelo*, above
Based on the Viking warship, these flat-bottomed boats, loaded with pipes of Port, would sail for Oporto on the hazardous journey from the Upper Douro.

VINHO VERDE

Vines that virtually grow on trees, trellises, up telegraph poles and along fences – on anything, in fact, to take them above the ground – produce the grapes that make Vinho Verde, *the* wine of the Minho. Training the vine in such a way enables the smallholders – and there are more than 60,000 of them in the Minho – to grow the cabbages, maize and beans that the families survive on, and to produce grapes, which are either sold to large wineries such as Sogrape or Aveleda, or made into wine locally and sold to tourists. In addition to these smallholdings, there are a growing number of professionally run *quintas*, where the vines are neatly trained on *cruzeta* trellises, seven or eight feet above the ground. Only in the Minho can one see pickers going to the harvest with ladders, a sight more reminiscent of hop-picking.

How Vinho Verde is made

When picked, the grapes should not be fully ripe, for Vinho Verde has a low alcohol content (about nine per cent) and high acidity, which is why it is called *verde* or "green". Bottling takes place very early to retain as much freshness as possible and to encourage a malolactic fermentation in the bottle, which results in some degree of *pétillance*, though this can be anything from a semi-sparkle to barely a prickle. More red Vinho Verde is made than white, but virtually all of that exported is white and, more often than not, fizzed up (sparged) and sweetened.

The wines of the Douro and the Minho

DOURO RD

Known principally for its Port, the Douro Valley in fact makes as much table wine as fortified wine. Because the finest Port is produced on schist soils, most table wines are relegated to areas of the region's other dominant soil, granite. I am surprised that the Syrah, which thrives in the Northern Rhône's hot, granite soil, has not been tried here – perhaps it is because the wines already have good fruit and surprising elegance. The region's quality potential is highlighted by Barca Velha, Portugal's most expensive table wine made by Ferreira at Quinta do Vale de Meão. Across the Spanish frontier is Vega Sicilia, Spain's most expensive wine.

RED There is nothing "Porty" about these wines, as some writers suggest. They can range from the lighter, claret types to the fuller, richer Burgundian style, but all the successful ones share clean fruit and good balance. Quinta do Côtto's "Grande Escolha" is the first of a new breed to use new oak, and the result is absolutely stunning.

Tinta Francisca, Tinta roriz, Tinta cão, Touriga nacional, Touriga Francesa, Tinta barroca, Tinta amarela, Mourisco tinto, Bastardo, plus up to 40% Cornifesto, Donzelinho, Malvasia, Periquita, Rufete, Tinta barca, Alvarelhão, Donzelinho tinto, Malvasia preta, Morisca de semente, Sousão, Tinta carvalha, Touriga Brasileira.

1983, 1984, 1985, 1989, 1990

Between 2-10 years (up to 25 for Barca Velha)

WHITE Quinta do Côtto produces a delightful, fresh and fruity wine with a light, honeyed aftertaste. Sogrape makes a rich, honeyed-fruit-flavoured "Planalto", and experiments are being made with Chardonnay, Riesling, Gewürztraminer and Sauvignon blanc.

Esganacão, Folgosão, Verdelho, Malvasia fina, Rabigato, Viosinho, Donzelinho branco, plus up to 40% Arinto, Boal, Cercial, Côdega, Malvasia corada, Moscatel galego, Donzelinho branco, Samarrinho, Fernão pires, Malvasia parda, Moscatel galego, Rabo de ovelha

1980, 1983, 1984, 1985

Between 2-5 years

☆ Ferreira (Barca Velha, Reserva Especial), Côtto Grande Escholha, Quinta da Pacheca, Douro Santa Marta, Douro Mesão Frio

PORT RD

The two basic styles of Port, from which all variants stem (*see* below), with the exception of White Port, are Ruby and Tawny. Ruby is bottle-aged, fruity and includes Vintage Port at the top of its scale, while Tawny is cask-aged and mellow, with Fine Old Tawny as its epitome.

See Port grape varieties, p.296

See Vintages "declared" since 1945 and Great Port houses

See Great Port houses

☆ *See* Great Port houses and The best of the rest, p.301

STYLES OF PORT

Crusted Port or Crusting Port
This is a blend of very high-quality wines from two or more years, given up to four years in cask and, ideally, at least three years in bottle prior to sale. It is thus a more forward style of Port than Vintage, yet throws a similar deposit in the bottle, hence the name.

Fine Old Tawny Port
By constant racking over a period of 10, 20 years or more, the wine assumes a tawny colour, falls bright and will throw no further deposit. It assumes a smooth, silky texture, a voluptuous, mellow, nutty flavour and great finesse, with complex after-aromas that can include freshly ground coffee, chocolate, raisins, nutmeg and cinnamon.

Fine Old Ruby Port
These good-quality Ports blended from various years with approximately four years in cask are ready to drink when sold. They have the fruity-spice character of a young Ruby, but the mixture of grape and spirit is more homogenous, with no fiery edges.

Late-Bottled Vintage Port (LBV)
A pure vintage Port from a generally undeclared year*, given between four and six years in cask before bottling. LBVs are ready for drinking when sold, but usually continue to improve in bottle for another five or six years.
* At the time of writing, Taylor's has caused consternation by releasing an LBV from the universally declared 1983 vintage, a big, classic year.

Ruby Port
The cheapest red Ports are youthful Rubies that have had less than a year in cask and possess a basic, grapey fruit flavour that can be quite fiery.

Single-quinta Port
A wine from a single vineyard: this may be a classic Vintage Port from an established house, as in the case of Quinta do Noval; a special release from a non-classic vintage, such as Quinta de Vargellas (a property that is normally the heart of Taylor's Vintage Port, but also produces fine wines in ordinary years); a non-vintage FOT, such as Ramos Pinto's Quinta do Bom-Retiro "20 year Old"; or a Vintage-dated Tawny like Borges' Quinta do Junco.

Tawny Port
Basic Tawny Ports are often a blend of red and white Ports. This is contrary to the EEC regulations to which Portugal has made itself subject since its entry in January 1986, but, as with Champagne, the Port industry can prove that this blending method is traditional to the area. Some skilful blends can have even the most experienced Port tasters guessing whether they are Tawny by definition or by blending.

Vintage Port
By law, a Vintage Port must be bottled within two years; most are bottled within 18 months. Maturation in bottle is more reductive than cask-aging and the wine that results has a certain fruitiness that will not be found in any Fine Old Tawny, however great it may be. When mature, a fine Vintage Port is a unique taste experience with a heady bouquet and a sultry flavour. A warming feeling seems to follow the wine down the throat – more of an "afterglow"

than an aftertaste. The grape and spirit are totally integrated and the palate is near to bursting with warm, spicy-fruit flavours.

Vintage Character Port
The suggestion that these wines, which are blended from various years and matured in cask for up to four years, have a "Vintage" character is misleading. They may be fine Ports, but the character is that of a Fine Old Ruby, and not of a Vintage Port.

Vintage-dated Tawny Port
These excellent-value, often sublime, wines are FOTs, but with a vintage. They may have 20 or 50 years in cask and should not be confused with the plumper, fruitier Vintage Ports that have less than three years in cask. There should be an indication of when the wine was bottled or a term such as "Matured in Wood". Some firms simply label Vintage Ports "Vintage" and Tawnies "Colheita". Other clues on the label include "Reserve", "Reserva", or "Bottled in" dates.

White Port
Most dry White Ports taste like flabby Sherry, but there are some interesting sweet ones such as Ferreira's "Superior White", which is creamy-soft and delicious.

VINHO VERDE RD

Genuine Vinho Verde is totally dry, although it may be delicately dry or rasping dry. It will always have a refreshing tang and may have a certain "mineral" aftertaste.

White wine varieties: Azal branco, Loureiro, Trajadura, Perdernã, Avesso, Alvarinho. **Red wine varieties:** Azal tinto, Borraçal, Espadeiro, Vinhão, Rabo de ovelha, Brancelho

Particular vintages are unimportant, but knowing the year the wine was produced, and hence if it will be fresh, is.

As young as possible, usually not older than 12-18 months.

☆ *See* The best single-quinta Vinhos Verdes, The best of the rest and Good commercial blended Vinhos Verdes, pp.301-2.

Great Port houses

COCKBURN
Rua das Coradas,
4401 Vila Nova de Gaia

Vineyards: *200 ha (494 acres)*
Established: *1815*

Founded by Robert Cockburn, who married Mary Duff, a lady much admired by Lord Byron, this house was purchased by Harveys of Bristol,

which has since come under the auspices of Allied-Lyons. Its Vintage Ports have good colour and depth, fine fruit, silky texture and a chocolatey complexity. Cockburn also controls Martinez Gassiot.

1983, 1985

Between 15-30 years

☆ "Special Reserve", "Director's Reserve", "10 Year Old Tawny", "20 Year Old Tawny"

CROFT
Largo Joaquim Magalhães,
4400 Vila Nova de Gaia

Vineyards: *80 ha (198 acres)*
Established: *1678*

To many Croft is best known for its Sherries, yet it is one of the oldest Port houses. In all but a few years, its Ports are lighter than most, two exceptions being 1975 and 1985, when its great concentration made it one of the top wines. This house is now owned by IDV (International Distillers and Vintners).

1985

Between 12-25 years

☆ "LBV", "Distinction", Quinta da Roêda

DELAFORCE
Largo Joaquim Magalhães,
4401 Vila Nova de Gaia

Established: *1868*

Although owned by IDV (International Distillers and Vintners) since 1968, and thus a sister company to Croft and Morgan, this is still very much a family-run firm, with fifth-generation David Delaforce in day-to-day control. Its style is very much on the lighter-bodied side, which particularly suits "His Eminence's Choice", an exquisite old Tawny with a succulent balance and a lingering fragrance. I find the light touch of Delaforce inadequate for Vintage Ports, although they do have a following.

☆ "His Eminence's Choice Superb Old Tawny"
Continued overleaf

DOW & CO.
Silva & Cosens,
Travessa Barão de Forrester,
4401 Vila Nova de Gaia

Vineyards: *40 ha (99 acres)*
Established: *1798*

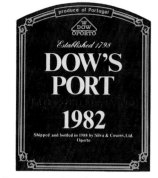

Cosens came into the company in the mid-nineteenth century and the Dow's connection was made in 1877, when James Ramsay Dow was made a partner and his firm, Dow & Co., was merged with Silva & Cosens. Dow's is now one of the many brands belonging to the Symington family. Its typically big, black and backward Vintage is consistently one of the very best; a concentrated wine that has a great depth of spicy-chocolatey fruit and a complex, tannic, somewhat drier character than most.

19	1980, 1983, 1985
⏳	Between 18-35 years

☆ "Boardroom", "20 Year Old Tawny", "Vintage Character", "Late Bottled Vintage" and "Crusted Port"

FERREIRA
Rua da Cavalhosa 19-103,
4400 Vila Nova de Gaia

Vineyards: *110 ha (271 acres), plus access to 210 ha (519 acres) belonging to members of the Ferreira family*
Established: *1761*

Now the Portuguese brand leader, the house of Ferreira did not establish its present reputation until the mid-nineteenth century, when it was under the helm of Dona Antonia Adelaide Ferreira, the "Veuve Clicquot" of Oporto. She built up the largest estate of vineyards in the Douro and left a fortune, valued at £3.4 million, when she died, aged 85, in 1896.
Ever mindful of its Portuguese roots, it is not surprising that tawny Port is Ferreira's forte. Equally expected is the lighter style of its Vintage Port, a wine that is typically smooth and mellow. It has a fruitiness that can only be captured by early bottling, but it is not as plump and concentrated as the Port produced by British houses. The house is a brand leader in Portugal, and was taken over in 1988 by European Cellars.

19	1982, 1983 (Vintage and Quinto do Seixo)
⏳	Between 15-30 years

☆ "Dona Antonia", "Quinta do Porto 10 Year Old Tawny", "Duque de Bragança 20 Year Old Tawny", "Superior White"

FONSECA
Guimaraens Vinhos,
Quinta Dom Prior,
4401 Vila Nova de Gaia

Vineyards: *50 ha (124 acres)*
Established: *1822*

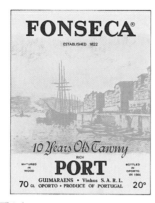

This house was originally called Fonseca, Monteiro & Co., but changed its name when purchased by Manuel Pedro Guimaraens in 1822. It has been part of Taylor, Fladgate & Yeatman since 1948. Fonseca has always been the major brand, but occasionally wines are shipped under the Guimaraens label. Its Vintage Port, although not as massive as Taylor's, is very much of the same style; deep-coloured, with a deliciously rich and ripe flavour, and a sensual chocolatey-raisiny complexity that puts it among the best.

19	1980, 1983, 1985
⏳	Between 15-30 years

☆ "Bin 27" and any Fine Old Tawnies

W. & J. GRAHAM & CO.
Rua Rei Ramiro 514,
4401 Vila Nova de Gaia

Vineyards: *45 ha (111 acres)*
Established: *1820*

Graham's was founded as a textile business and only entered the Port trade when, in 1826, its Oporto office accepted wine in payment of a debt. Or so the story goes. Now it is yet another piece of the Symington Port empire. It is the Vintage Port that has earned this house its reputation – big, black, beautifully sweet and long-lived wines.

19	1980, 1983, 1985, 1988
⏳	Between 18-40 years

☆ "Six Grapes" and any Fine Old Tawnies

GUIMARAENS
See Fonseca.

NOVAL
Rua Cândido dos Reis 575,
4401 Vila Nova de Gaia

Vineyards: *85 ha (212 acres)*
Established: *1813*

This was originally a Portuguese house, having been founded by Antonio José da Silva, but has been controlled by the Dutch van Zeller family for four generations. Since 1973, it has been officially known as Quinta do Noval SARL, being named after its beautiful estate set high above Pinhão in the Upper Corgo district, but it is careful to market most of its products under the name of "Noval", reserving "Quinta do Noval" for its own-vineyard Vintage Port. This property's most famous wine is Quinta do Noval "Naçional", a deep and dense-coloured, powerfully structured, super-concentrated wine that retains the grace and finesse for which this house is renowned, made from 5,000 pre-phylloxera vines. Only 250 cases are made and it is not commercially available, unless you buy 50 cases of regular vintage Quinta do Noval, when the house will traditionally offer six bottles as a gift. "Naçional" can occasionally be obtained at auction, but it is very expensive – the legendary 1931 has fetched £1,250 a bottle at auction, the highest price for any Port.

19	1982, 1983, 1985
⏳	Between 20-35 years

☆ "LB", "20 Year Old", "40 Year Old"

SANDEMAN
Largo Miguel Bombarda 3,
4401 Vila Nova de Gaia

Vineyards: *280 ha (692 acres)*
Established: *1790*

Sandeman took over Robertson's and Rebello Valente in 1881 and has since added the houses of Diez Hermanoz, Offley Forrester and Rodriguez Pinho, and is itself now controlled by Seagram. Vintage Port sold under the Sandeman brand is usually firm, fruity and of good, but not deep, colour.

19	1982, 1985
⏳	Between 15-30 years

☆ "Founders Reserve", "Imperial 20 Year Old Tawny"

SILVA & COSENS
See Dow & Co.

TAYLOR, FLADGATE & YEATMAN
Rua Choupelo 250,
4401 Vila Nova de Gaia

Vineyards: *125 ha (309 acres)*
Established: *1692*

Founded by Job Bearsley, this house underwent no less than 21 changes of title before adopting its present one, which derives from the names of various partners: Joseph Taylor in 1816, John Fladgate in 1837, and Morgan Yeatman in 1844. At one time the firm was known as Webb, Campbell, Gray & Cano (Joseph Cano was, as it happens, the only American ever to be admitted into the partnership of a Port house). In 1744, Taylor's became the first shipper to buy a property in the Douro, but its most famous acquisition was Quinta de Vargellas in 1890, a prestigious property that provides the heart and soul of every vintage of Taylor's Port, the darkest, deepest and most massive of all Vintage Ports and the highest-valued on the auction market. A pure Quinta de Vargellas is more ethereal, with a noticeable influence of oak.

19	1980, 1983, 1985
⏳	Between 20-40 years

☆ "10 Year Old Tawny", "20 Year Old Tawny", Quinta de Vargellas

WARRE & CO.
Travessa Barão de Forrester,
4401 Vila Nova de Gaia

Vineyards: *45 ha (111 acres)*
Established: *1670*

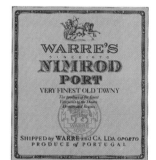

Only the German-founded house of C. N. Kopke can claim to be older than Warre's, although the firm only assumed its present name in 1729 when William Warre entered the business. This house, which now belongs to the entrepreneurial Symington family, normally vies with Graham's as producer of the darkest and most concentrated Vintage Port style after that of Taylor's. Warre's Quinta da Cavadinha, in the pure form, is fragrant, elegant and ethereal, contrasting with the Vintage Port, of which it forms a part.

19	1980, 1983, 1985
⏳	Between 18-35 years

☆ "Warrior", "Nimrod", "Grande Reserve" vintage-dated Fine Old Tawnies

The best of the rest

CÁLEM
Avenida Diogo Leite,
4400 Vila Nova de Gaia

Vineyards: *50 ha (123 acres)*
Established: *1859*

The largest of the family-owned Port houses.

🗓 1983, 1985

🎚 Between 15-25 years

☆ "10 Year Old Tawny", Quinta de Foz

CHURCHILL
4100 Oporto

Established: *1981*

These Ports have excellent colour, intense fruit and classic structure.

🗓 1982, 1985

🎚 Between 12-25 years

☆ "Crusted", "Vintage Character", Quinta de Agua Alta

GOULD CAMPBELL
Travessa Barão de Forrester,
4401 Vila Nova de Gaia

Established: *circa 1797*

This firm, now part of the Symington group, produces fine Vintage Ports.

🗓 1980, 1983

🎚 Between 12-25 years

MORGAN
Largo Joaquim Magalhães,
4401 Vila Nova de Gaia

Established: *1715*

Purchased by Croft in 1952 and now owned by IDV, this house produces pleasant, plummy Port.

🗓 1982

🎚 Between 12-20 years

OFFLEY FORRESTER
Rua Guilherme Braga,
4400 Vila Nova de Gaia

Established: *1737*

Once the firm of Baron Forrester, (*see* p.298), this house is now owned by Seagram and makes an elegant style of Vintage Port and a deeper-coloured single-quinta wine.

🗓 1982, 1983

🎚 Between 12-25 years

☆ "Baron Forrester" vintage-dated Tawnies, "Boa Vista"

POÇAS
Rua Visconde das Devesas,
4401 Vila Nova de Gaia

Established: *1918*

The only Port house to win the government "Caravela Portuguesa" award for export in two consecutive years, 1979 and 1980.

🗓 1982, 1983

🎚 Between 12-25 years

QUARLES HARRIS
Rua Barão de Forrester,
4401 Vila Nova de Gaia

Established: *1680*

The second-largest Port house in the 1790s, it is now one of the smallest. The style is dark, plummy and smooth, with a spicy-raisiny bouquet.

🗓 1980, 1983, 1985

🎚 Between 12-25 years

QUINTA DO CÔTTO
Montez Champalimaud,
Regua

Established: *pre-1300*

The fastest-rising star amongst the new wave of single-grower Ports.

🗓 1982

🎚 Between 12-25 years

RAMOS-PINTO
Avenida Ramos-Pinto,
4401 Vila Nova de Gaia

Vineyards: *99 ha (245 acres)*
Established: *1880*

Adriano Ramos-Pinto was just 20 years old when he started this firm, but he laid firm foundations for what is now one of the most respected Portuguese houses, producing rich and well-rounded Ports.

🗓 1982, 1983

🎚 Between 12-25 years

☆ Single-quinta and old vintage-dated Tawnies

ROYAL OPORTO
Real Companhia Vinícola do Norte de Portugal,
Rua Azevedo Magalhães,
4400 Vila Nova de Gaia

Vineyards: *1,235 ha (3,051 acres)*
Established: *1756*

Founded by the Marquis de Pombal to regulate the Port trade, this is now a privately owned source of good, inexpensive Vintage Port.

🗓 Quinta das Carvalhas 1983, Quinta do Sibio 1983

🎚 Between 12-25 years

REBELLO VALENTE
See Robertson Brothers and Co.

ROBERTSON BROTHERS AND CO.
Rua Dr. António Granjo,
4400 Vila Nova de Gaia

Established: *1881*

A small house best known for its Tawnies and, under the famous Rebello Valente label, very traditional Vintage Ports. It is now a subsidiary of Sandeman and owned by Seagram.

🗓 1983, 1985 (Rebello Valente)

🎚 Between 12-25 years

☆ Tawny Ports

SMITH WOODHOUSE
Travessa Barão de Forrester,
4401 Vila Nova de Gaia

Vineyards: *25 ha (62 acres)*
Established: *1784*

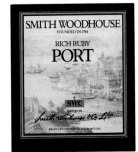

The products of this famous British-founded Port house are not all that highly thought of in Portugal, which is surprising because the entire export range is very respectable.

🗓 1980, 1983, 1985

🎚 Between 12-25 years

☆ Entire range

The best single-quinta Vinhos Verdes

Note: All wines included are white, dry to some degree, and slightly *pétillant*, unless otherwise stated.

ALVARINHO DE MONÇÃO – CEPA VELHA

Produced from Alvarinho grapes grown at Monção on the Spanish border, this wine is slightly richer and firmer than most Vinhos Verdes, with a stronger, almost fat-fruit, flavour that retains its freshness for up to two years in bottle.

CASA DA CALÇADA

A very dry, correctly tart Vinho Verde with little *pétillance* from Amarante, east of Oporto.

CASA DE COMPOSTELA

A light, fresh and fruity, cool-fermented wine made mostly from the Pedernã grape, blended with Loureiro and Trajadura, grown at Requião, near Famalicão.

CASA DE SEZIM

This wine, made on an estate that has been owned by the same family since 1375, has a good aroma and more weight than most. Made from the Loureiro grape and blended with Trajadura, Pedernã and a little Azal branco, many find this the second-best Vinho Verde, after Palácio da Brejoeira.

PAÇO DE TEIXEIRÓ

Set in the foothills of Serra do Marão, this single-vineyard Vinho Verde has belonged to the innovative Champalimaud family of Quinta do Côtto since the thirteenth century. It is a distinctive and fragrant dry wine, made predominantly from Avesso grapes.

PALÁCIO DA BREJOEIRA

The vast neo-classical Palácio da Brejoeira at Pinheiros, near Monção on the Spanish border, is famous. The vineyards that surround it produce Portugal's finest and most prestigious Vinho Verde, made from the Alvarinho grape. It is a wine that has finesse (a term I would not apply to other Vinhos Verdes, no matter how enjoyable they might be), a delicately tangy acidity and great length. It is a deliciously dry white wine and, most remarkable of all, it has the capacity to remain fresh and vital for up to four years.

QUINTA DA AVELEDA

A fine, fragrant and dryish wine with a barely discernible *pétillance*.

QUINTA DO CRASTO

A traditionally produced Vinho Verde with a delicate and aromatic character, made predominantly from Pedernã, Azal and Avesso grapes grown on the slopes of the River Paiva at Travanca, near Cinfães.

QUINTA DA LIVRAÇÃO

A light, fragrant, cool-fermented Vinho Verde produced from a blend of grape varieties grown on the slopes of the River Tâmega, at Livração, near Marcos de Canaveses. Its delicate character remains fresh for up to a year or two in bottle.

QUINTA DO TAMARIZ

An estate-bottled Vinho Verde since 1939, this fine, fresh and well-balanced wine is the product of Loureiro and Trajadura grapes grown at Carreira, on south-facing slopes. •

SOLAR DAS BOUÇAS

A pure Loureiro wine from a small estate at Prozelo, near Amares. It has a characteristically light aroma, a correctly crisp flavour, a very slight *pétillance* and a perfumed aftertaste reminiscent of orange-flower water.

SOUTO VEDRO

An excellent, crisp and definitely dry wine with a fine *verde* tartness and a strong *pétillance*, from the slopes of the River Tâmega in Amarante.

TORMES

A pure Avesso Vinho Verde from a single estate at Vila Nova, this refreshing wine has a full aroma and a fragrant, deliciously dry and tangy flavour.

The best of the rest

CASA DE CABANELAS

A light, dry, aromatic wine made from Azal, Loureiro, Trajadura and Pedernã grapes grown at Bustelo.

CASA DOS CUNHAS

Light, dry, aromatic Loureiro wine and a red from Espadeiro and Vinhão grapes, made at Quintado Belinho.

CASA DO LANDEIRO

Good, typical Vinho Verde, made from Loureiro and Trajadura grapes grown at Carreira, near Barcelos.

CASA DE PENELA

A well made, aromatic and distinctive wine produced from Loureiro and Trajadura grapes, grown at Adaúfe.

CASA DE RENDUFE

An Avesso-based, fruity wine with a delicate aroma, from the south bank of the River Douro at Resende.

CASA DE SANTA LEOCÁDIA

A fine, aromatic Vinho Verde, with the fruity character of the Loureiro grape, made at Geraz do Lima.

CASA DA TAPADA

A pure Loureiro Vinho Verde grown on southwest-facing slopes at Fiscal.

CASA DE VILA BOA

Fresh, light and distinctive, this wine is made predominantly from Azal grapes grown at Vila Boa de Quires.

CASA DE VILACETINHO

A fresh, delicate and elegant wine made from a blend of Azal, Loureiro and Pedernã grown at Alpendurada.

CASA DE VILA NOVA

A predominantly Avesso wine with up to 20 per cent Pedernã, grown at Santa Cruz do Douro, near Baião.

CASA DE VILAVERDE

A light, clean and aromatic Vinho Verde made from a blend of Loureiro, Pedernã and Azal grapes grown at Caíde de Rei.

CONVENTO DE ALPENDURADA

Traditionally vinified red Vinho Verde made from various varieties grown on south-facing slopes above the River Douro at Alpendurada. The vineyard belongs to a convent that dates back to 1024.

MONTEFARO

A delicately aromatic wine produced at Quinta de Seara in Esposende. Of the two styles made, the one marked *meio seco* is drier.

MOURA BASTO

A predominantly Azal wine with good *pétillance* and delicate flavour.

PAÇO D'ANHA

A fresh, dry, fruity wine dominated by Loureiro and Trajadura grown at Anha, near Viana do Castelo.

POINTE DE LIMA

One of the few red Vinhos Verdes that non-Portuguese palates appreciate, this wine has a very fresh, dry and slightly tannic fruit flavour.

QUINTA DO CRUZEIRO

A typical Vinho Verde produced from Loureiro, Trajadura and Avesso grapes, grown at Modelos.

QUINTA DE CURVOS

A typical Vinho Verde, with a good "mineral" taste, from the coastal vineyards of Esposende.

QUINTA DO MIOGO

A light wine with a delicate aroma made from Loureiro grapes grown on the hills at Guimarães.

QUINTA DO OUTEIRO DE BAIXO

A light, fine and fruity wine made from Azal and Pedernã grapes grown near Amarante. The red is made from Espadeiro grapes.

QUINTA DA PORTELA

A typical Vinho Verde grown on southwest-facing slopes at Carreira.

QUINTA DA QUINTÃO

A dry, aromatic wine from Santo Tome de Negrelos, near Santo Tirso.

QUINTA DE SANTO CLAUDIO

A pure Loureiro wine from a terraced, south-facing vineyard at Curvos.

SOLAR DE RIBEIRO

A medium-dry Vinho Verde, with a fuller flavour than most, from Santo Lourenço do Douro.

TÂMEGA

On the few occasions I have tasted this wine, it has always been a fine strong-flavoured Vinho Verde.

GOOD COMMERCIAL BLENDED VINHOS VERDES

AGULHA

Dry Vinho Verde, with only a faint *pétillance*, sold in a stone bottle.

AVELEDA

A pleasant commercial wine made near Penafiel, it has a good *pétillance*. *See also* "Casal Garcia", "Grinalda" and Quinta de Aveleda.

CASAL GARCIA

Aveleda's best commercial Vinho Verde. A fresh wine with less acidity than some, but a good off-dry flavour.

CASALINHO

A very light Vinho Verde that has an off-dry taste and a good *pétillance*.

CASAL MENDES

A lively, medium-dry, white Vinho Verde and a popular, semi-sweet non-DO rosé produced by Aliança.

DOM FERRAZ

A semi-dry wine with a fullish aroma, and typical "mineral" fruit.

GAMBA

A commercial-style, off-dry Vinho Verde, with good *pétillance*.

GATÃO

The largest-selling Vinho Verde in the world, "Gatão" can have a flowery-fresh aroma when young.

GAZELA

A well-made, quite stylish, Vinho Verde with a definite *pétillance*.

GRINALDA

One of the best commercial blends, from Aveleda's own vineyards throughout the Minho. It has a fragrant nose and a crisp Vinho Verde flavour.

LAGOSTA

Well-known on export markets, Lagosta has a gassy *pétillance* and fuller, fatter flavour than most.

MEIRELES

A good commercial wine with a refreshing flavour and sparkle.

MIRITA

A slightly sweeter semi-sparkling commercial blend made by Aliança.

TRES MARIAS

A sweetish wine produced by Vizela.

Bairrada and Dão

Dão is Portugal's classic red wine, and the neighbouring region of Bairrada is the pretender to its crown, but the truth is that the potential of both regions is higher than the quality of the wines currently produced. Portugal's two most important red wines are grown in adjacent areas of similar climate.

BAIRRADA

TO THE OUTSIDE WORLD, BAIRRADA IS ONE of Portugal's new wines. But in fact it is one of its oldest, with a viticultural history dating back to the tenth century. Since it achieved Região Demarcada status in 1979, all of its wines have had to be bottled in the region of production and this has helped it secure a good reputation quickly. Bairrada's vineyards cover 18,000 hectares (44,500 acres) in the districts of Aveiro and Coimbra.

Production averages 600,000 hectolitres (6.6 million cases) and 90 per cent of the wine is red. Six cooperatives account for 40 per cent of this output and private companies 25 per cent, with small growers making up the remaining 35 per cent. The major

grape variety is the Baga. Eighty per cent of all grapes grown in the region are of this variety and it must account for at least 50 per cent of any particular red Bairrada produced. However, Bairrada also has a growing reputation for its sparkling white wines.

Cellar, Hotel Bussaco, above
Situated in the Beiras VR area, this legendary and luxurious hotel near Coimbra makes excellent red wines.

Vineyard, Bairrada, below
Increasingly good red wines are being produced in the flattish coastal vineyards of this area.

FACTORS AFFECTING TASTE AND QUALITY

Location
These two regions are situated between the Vinho Verde and Port regions to the north and Estremadura and Beira-Baixato in the south.

Climate
The climate comes strongly under the maritime influence of the Atlantic, with high rainfall and relatively short, dry summers. The temperature often drops rapidly in the autumn, usefully slowing up the fermentation of the wine.

Aspect
In the coastal area of Bairrada, vineyards are scattered on low-lying, fairly flat land, whereas in the Dão the best vines are generally found on slopes at an altitude between 200 and 500 metres (660-1,640 ft), though vines are grown up to 2,000 metres (6,600 ft) above sea level.

Soil
The soil is fairly homogeneous in each area. In Bairrada the most important vines are grown on clay soil known locally as "barros". The soil is almost entirely granitic in Dão, with small areas of schist that favour white grapes rather than the dominant red varieties of this area.

Viticulture and vinification
The more mountainous areas of the Dão require extensive terracing and work is therefore labour-intensive. Smaller producers normally leave the red skins and stalks with the must for fermentation, producing a deep-coloured, coarse, tannic wine, while larger wineries usually destalk the grapes and give the wines a shorter maceration on the skins.

Primary grape varieties
Baga, Touriga nacional

Secondary grape varieties
Agua santa, Alfrocheiro preto, Alvarelhão, Arinto, Assario branco, Barcelo, Bastardo, Bical, Borrado das moscas, Castelão, Cercial, Cercialinho, Chardonnay, Encruzado, Jaen, Maria Gomez, Preto de mortagua, Rabo de ovelha, Terrantez, Tinta amarela, Tinta cão, Tinta pinheira, Tinta roriz, Trincadeira, Uva cão, Verdelho

BAIRRADA AND DÃO

These two predominantly red-wine areas fall between the main northern and southern wine-producing areas of Portugal. The river Dão flows through the coastal Beira Littoral districts of Bairrada into the heart of higher, hotter Dão in the Beira Alta.

Intensive Vine-growing Zone
Bairrada
Dão
Provincial Boundary
▲ Height above sea level (metres)

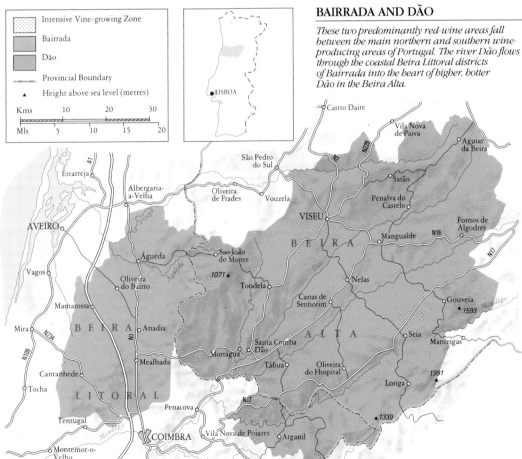

DÃO

This region covers an area of 376,400 hectares (930,000 acres), but only 20,000 hectares (49,400 acres) are under vine. This area produces 270,000 hectolitres (three million cases) of wine per year, of which 90 per cent is red, although modern vinification techniques look set to increase the profile of Dão white wines. Dão has some 40,000 smallholders with half-a-hectare (one acre) of land each, and there are ten cooperatives, which have a combined production equivalent to 40 per cent of the region's total output. They concentrate almost entirely on production of Dão's dry, hard red wine.

With the superstar Touriga nacional grape as Dão's major red-wine variety, and a wealth of vineyards with excellent *terroirs*, the region has obvious fine-wine potential, and to be fair, the producers are not entirely responsible for failing to exploit it. Much of the blame can be placed on the shoulders of the official tasting commission that consistently and obstinately refuses to approve wines for their RD status because they are fresh and taste "too young".

Dão vineyards, above
Betweeen rocky outcrops, the lush green hillside is terraced with vines; the predominant variety in the Dão's red wines is the Touriga nacional.

Castro Daire, Lafoẽs, above
Vineyard terraces fall sharply away from the attractive hilltop town strung along the ridge. Unlike in the Minho, vines are trained on a low system.

The wines of Bairrada and Dão

BAIRRADA RD

This area produces one of Portugal's two most important red wines and is gaining a better reputation for its still and sparkling white wines.

RED The best have a deep colour and good tannin, but also a generous amount of rich fruit, with a capacity to soften with age and develop a fine, perfumed bouquet.

▧ At least 50% Baga, plus Castelão, Tinta pinheira and up to 20%

Alfrocheiro preto, Bastardo, Preto de mortagua, Trincadeira, Jaen, Agua santa

[19] 1980, 1983, 1985, 1987, 1989

🍷 Between 5-12 years, but some can improve for up to 25 years

WHITE Bairrada's Research Station has produced some interesting white wines, the best from either Rabo de ovelha or Cercial grapes, but the commercial wineries have yet to demonstrate their potential for these wines.

▧ Rabo de ovelha, Sercial, Bical, Maria Gomez, plus up to 40% Arinto, Cercial, Chardonnay and Cercialinho

SPARKLING WHITE One of Portugal's few decent *méthode champenoise* wines is produced here – the single-vineyard Vinho Espumante Natural Bruto from Quinta do Ribeirinho. This is of an unusually high quality in what is by no means a natural sparkling-wine area.

▧ Bical

☆ Caves São João, Quinta do Ribeirinho, Caves Primavera, Bairrada Marques de Graciosa, Luis Pato

DÃO RD

This is the finest red-wine area for devotees of Portugal's old-fashioned, dried-out wines. Despite regular rumours that Dão wines are being produced with more fruit and less tannin, once tasted they tell a different story, stubbornly remaining ungenerous products of outmoded vinification methods.

RED The best have sufficient fruit to match the tannin and can improve for up to 15 years.

▧ A minimum 20% of Touriga nacional, plus a maximum total 80% of Alfrocheiro preto, Bastardo, Jaen, Tinta pinheira and Tinta roriz, and a maximum 20% of Alvarelhão, Tinta amarela and Tinta cão

[19] 1980, 1982, 1983, 1985

🍷 Between 5-15 years (best wines)

WHITE The best can be clean and fresh, but none are anything special

▧ Encruzado 20%, plus up to 80% Assario branco, Barcelo, Borrado das moscas, Cercial, Verdelho, including a maximum 20% Rabo de ovelha, Terrantez and Uva cão

🍷 Within 1-3 years

☆ Conde de Santar, Quinta da Insua, Vinicola Ribalonga, Terras Altas, Dão Grão Vasco, Dão Caves de Solar de São Domingos, José Marguès Agostinho Dão Garrafeira

Madeira

The island of Madeira gives its name to the world's most exotic dessert wine, the only wine that has to be baked in an oven! Madeira is part of the Funchal archipelago, located some 600 kilometres (370 miles) west of the Moroccan coast. The story of its discovery is a bit bizarre and spiced no doubt, with exaggeration and embellishment.

PRINCE HENRY THE NAVIGATOR sent Captain Jão Gonçalves Zarco, who was also known as "Zarco the Cross-eyed" to claim the island for Portugal in 1418. When Zarco landed on Madeira, he found it so densely wooded that he failed to penetrate inland, but his solution was simple – set fire to the island, sit back and wait for a clearing to emerge. Zarco had to wait a long time, so the story goes, for the fire raged for seven years, consuming every bit of vegetation and infusing the permeable volcanic soil with potash, so rendering it particularly suitable for vine-growing.

THE ORIGIN OF MADEIRA'S DISTINCTIVE WINE

As a source of fresh food and water, the island soon became a regular port of call for east-bound ships, which would often transport barrels of Madeira wine for sale in the Far East or Australia. As the ships journeyed through the tropics the wine was heated to a maximum of 45°C (113°F) and cooled again in the six-month voyage, giving the wine a very distinctive and desirable character. The winemakers on Madeira were, of course, totally unaware of this until one unsold shipment returned to the island. Since that point, special ovens, called *estufas*, have evolved in order that this heating and cooling can be replicated in the *estufagem* process. All Madeiras undergo a normal fermentation prior to the *estufagem* process. Drier wines are fortified prior to *estufagem*, the sweeter styles after.

FACTORS AFFECTING TASTE AND QUALITY

Location
The island of Madeira is approximately 50 by 20 kilometres (30 by 12 miles) in size and is situated in the Atlantic 600 kilometres (370 miles) from the Moroccan coast at a latitude of 33 degrees.

Climate
The rainfall on the island is heavy because of its position in the Atlantic and its mountainous geography. Because of its latitudinal position, summers are hot and winters very warm.

Aspect
Land is at a premium, and vineyards are located on small terraces of the steep cliffs, rising from the water's edge to some 914 metres (3,000 ft) above sea level in places. The best grapes come from vines grown on the southern slopes of the island, which receive the most sunshine.

Soil
The soil is fertile, being light red in colour, porous and of volcanic origin infused with potash.

Viticulture and vinification
Vines are trained high to allow other crops to grow beneath them because of the lack of available land. Despite the high rainfall, irrigation must be practised via a network of aqueducts because of the steep slopes and porous soil. After fermentation, wine is placed in a heated store-room called an *estufa*, and gradually heated to 45°C (113°F). Some eighteen months after cooling, the wine enters a *solera* system (*see* p.285). All wines are fortified.

Primary grape varieties
Bual, Malmsey, Sercial, Verdelho

Secondary grape varieties
Bastardo, Terrantez, Tinta negra mole, Moscatel.

View from Cabo Girão, left
Neat pockets of vines co-exist with sugar cane and vegetables.

Coastal view, Madeira, above
Terraced vineyards cling to Madeira's rocky terrain in coastal areas.

MADEIRA

The island of Madeira, in the Atlantic Ocean, is famed for its fortified wine. Funchal is the capital, where most of the wine lodges are found.

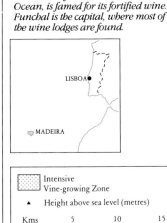

LISBOA

MADEIRA

Intensive Vine-growing Zone

▲ Height above sea level (metres)

Kms   5   10   15
Mls 2   4   6   8

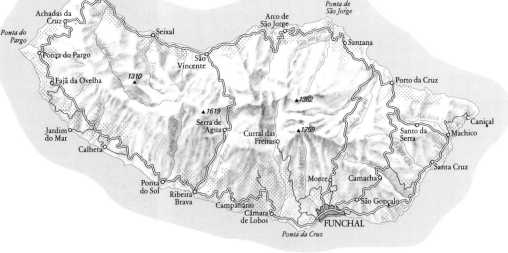

Porto do Moniz
Achadas da Cruz
Ponta do Pargo
Ponta do Pargo
Fajã da Ovelha
Jardim do Mar
Calheta
Seixal
São Vicente
1310
1619
Serra de Agua
Ponta do Sol
Ribeira Brava
Campanário
Câmara de Lobos
Ponta da Cruz
Curral das Freiras
1362
1769
Monte
Camacha
São Gonçalo
FUNCHAL
Arco de São Jorge
Ponta de São Jorge
Santana
Porto da Cruz
Santo da Serra
Santa Cruz
Caniçal
Machico

STYLES OF MADEIRA

There are four basic types of Madeira, each named after the grape from which it is made. These are: Sercial, which was once thought to be the Riesling grape and makes the lightest and driest Madeira; Verdelho, which is a tangy medium-sweet wine, with somewhat more body; Bual, a definitely sweet style that has a baked, smoky complexity; and Malmsey, my own favourite, a lusciously rich, sweet and honeyed wine.

All Madeiras once bore a vintage, but this is unusual today, most being blends or products of *solera* systems. If a pure vintage from the 1980s were to be released, this would not happen until the first decade of the twenty-first century. Any such vintage should, by definition, be superior. When it is sold, be it vintage or not, Madeira should be ready to drink. Due to a combination of high alcohol and the *estufagem* baking process, however, it has a virtually infinite shelf-life. I have been fortunate enough to taste several 100 to 200-year-old Madeiras; all were still perfectly healthy.

Viticulture in Madeira: *Every small hillock is terraced and planted with vines, often grown on overhanging arbours to permit other planting beneath. One plant that cannot be grown underneath or between vines is the banana. It demands its own space and because Portugal's mainland imports as many bananas as Madeira can produce, valuable vineyard space is gradually being eroded by the more profitable banana plantations.*

The best Madeira houses

BARBEITO

Wines: *"Island Dry Special"*, *"Rainwater Dry" Madeira Wine*, *"Island Rich"* *, *"Crown" Malmsey* *, 25 year Old Bual* *

BLANDY BROTHERS

Wines: *"Duke of Sussex" Sercial*, *"Duke of Cambridge" Verdelho*, *"Duke of Cumberland" Bual*, *"Duke of Clarence" Malmsey* *, 10 Year Old Malmsey* *, Solera Gran Cama de Lobos 1864, Solera Malmsey 1863* *

COSSART GORDON

Wines: *"Good Company" (Sercial [Dry], Bual, Malmsey)*, *"Rainwater"*, *"Finest Old" (Sercial, Bual, Malmsey*)*, *"Duo Centenary Celebration" (Sercial*, Bual*)*, Bual Reserve Over 5 Years* *, *"Finest Old" Malmsey Reserve Over 5 Years* *, *"Finest Old" Sercial Over 5 Years Reserve* *, *"Finest Old" Bual Over 5 years* *, Solera Sercial 1860* *

HARVEYS

Wines: *"Superior Dry" Sercial*, *"Superior Old" Bual*, *"Superior Old" Rich Malmsey* *

LEACOCK

Wines: *"St. John Reserve" (Sercial, Verdelho, Bual)*, *"Special Reserve" (Malmsey* *, Bual*)*

LOMELINO

Wines: *"Tarquinio" ("Reserve" Sercial, Rich Bual, Dessert Malmsey)*, *"Imperial" ("Finest Delicate" Sercial, "Superior Golden" Verdelho, "Choice Old" Bual, "Rare Old" Malmsey* *)*

POWER, DRURY & CO

Wines: *"Reserve" Verdelho*, *"Special Reserve" Malmsey* *, 1954 Vintage Malmsey* *, 1952 Verdelho* *, 1910 Bual* *

RUTHERFORD & MILES

Wines: *"Old Trinity House" Bual*, *"Reserve" Sercial Over 5 Years Old*, *"Special Reserve Special Dry" Over 10 Years Old*, *"Reserve" Bual Over 5 Years Old* *, *"Special Reserve Bual Medium Sweet" Over 10 Years Old*, *"Reserve" Malmsey Over 5 Years Old*, *"Special Reserve" Malmsey Sweet Over 10 Years Old* *, *"Reserve" Malmsey* *, *"Reserve" Verdelho* *

Other Portuguese wines

Note: RD = Região Demarcada
Portugal's equivalent of France's AOC, Spain's DO etc.
VR = Vinho Região These named regions are hoping for demarcation, although, at the time of writing, only parts of Alentejo and Ribatejo seem likely to receive full RD status within the near future.

ALENTEJO VR

The Alentejo Province covers approximately one-third of Portugal, stretching up from the Algarve, and its wines may be labelled with the following districts: Portalegre, Borba, Redondo, Reguengos (Reguengos de Monsaraz), Moura, Vidigueira, Evora and Granja.

Alentejo is producing some outstanding one-off wines from both indigenous and imported grape varieties. Potentially one of Portugal's greatest fine-wine regions, it is at present in a state of flux, making it impossible to describe individual regional styles for the moment.

Arinto, Assario, Boal, Cabernet sauvignon, Castelão, Monvedro, Moreto, Pendura, Periquita, Rabo de ovelha, Roupeiro, Tamaez, Tinta caiada, Touriga nacional, Trincadeira

Between 4-15 years (full-bodied, oak-aged reds); within 1-3 years (whites); within 1 year (rosés)

☆ Mouchão, José de Sousa Rosado, Fernandes Tinto Velho, Tapada de Chaves, Esporão, Tinto da Anfora, Quinta de Pancas, Quinta do Carmo

ALENQUER
See Estremadura VR.

ALCOBAÇO
See Estremadura VR.

ALGARVE RD

Although this large region is known more for its tourism than for its wine, it has had its own RD since 1978.

RED Ruby-coloured and alcoholic wines with low acidity and little charm. Not recommended.

Bastardo, Crato preto, Monvedro, Moreto, Negra mole, Pau ferro, Periquita, Pexém, Trincadeira

WHITE Dry, alcoholic and a bit flabby. Not recommended.

Crato branco, Boais, Manteudo, Tamarez, Sabro, Perrum

ALMEIRIM
See Ribatejo VR.

ARRABIDA
See Estremadura VR.

ARRUDA
See Estremadura VR.

AZEITÃO
See Estremadura VR.

BAIRRADA RD
See Bairrada and Dão, p.304.

BEIRAS VR

This region is located in the north of Portugal, in the Beira Alta, between the Vinho Verde and Dão areas. It includes the following districts: Castelo Rodrigo, Cova de Beira, Moimenta da Beira (or Tavora), Lafões, Lamego, Pinhel and Tarouca.

Virtually every style of wine is made, and quality varies enormously. Lafões, for example, produces light, acidic, red and white wines in a small area that straddles part of the Vinho Verde and Dão regions, while Pinhel makes the region's only rosé and a dry, full and rather earthy-tasting white. "Raposeira", Portugal's most popular *méthode champenoise* wine, is made by Seagram at Lamego from Chardonnay, Pinot noir and Pinot blanc varieties that are restricted to the production of sparkling wine. The incredible red wine of Bussaco (Buçaco), near Coimbra, deserves its own RD.

Alva, Alverelhão, Arinto, Baga, Bastardo, Castelão, Cercial, Codo, Fontegal, Malvasia, Martágua, Marufo, Moreto, Mourisco, Polgazão, Rufete, Tamarez, Tinta amarela, Tinta carvalha, Touriga varieties, Trincadeira

☆ Buçaco, Raposeira

BORBA
See Alentejo VR.

BUCELAS RD

The Arinto grape grows particularly well on the loam soil of this small district, but the antiquated wine-making methods are holding back what is obviously a potentially fine appellation. Cool fermentation, early bottling and a delicate touch of new oak would make this wine an international superstar.

WHITE
A lacklustre, dry white wine that has a dried-out, acidic, lemony flavour. Not recommended until new technology arrives!

Arinto, plus a maximum of 25% Cercial, Esganacão, Rabo de ovelha

CARCAVELOS RD

Famous in Portugal itself since the late eighteenth century when the Marquis of Pombal owned a large vineyard and winery here, Carcavelos did not acquire any international repute until the Duke of Wellington's officers developed a certain passion for it.

Viticulturally this area has now shrunk to just one vineyard, Quinta do Barão, between Lisbon and the popular holiday resort of Estoril, and production seldom exceeds 1,000 cases. The wine, fortified to between 18 and 20 per cent of alcohol and containing up to 15 grams per litre of sugar, is rarely seen on export markets.

FORTIFIED AMBER A topaz-coloured, off-dry wine with a nutty aroma, a delicate almondy flavour and a velvety texture.

Primary: Arinto, Galego dourado, Espadeiro, Negra mole, Preto martinho, Santarém
Secondary: Boais, Cercial, Rabo de ovelha

1980, 1983, 1985, 1987, 1989

Between 5-20 years

CARTAXO
See Ribatejo VR.

CASTELO RODRIGO
See Beiras VR.

CHAMUSCA
See Ribatejo VR.

CHAVES
See Trás-os-Montes VR.

COLARES RD

This small, historic wine area is famous for its ungrafted, phylloxera-free Ramisco vines that are planted in trenches dug out of the sandy dunes of Sintra in order to protect them from the salt-blighting Atlantic winds. Growers wear special baskets on their heads to protect them from suffocation should the sides of the trenches fall in.

RED These well-coloured, full-bodied wines have so much tannin that they are dry to the point of being astringent. With great age, they attain an aroma of sweet violets and smooth out to a silky finish.

A minimum of 80% Ramisco, plus Molar, Parreira matias, Santarém

1980, 1983, 1985, 1987, 1989

Between 15-30 years

WHITE Very traditional *maduro*-style dry white wines that are not recommended for non-Portuguese palates.

A minimum of 80% Malvasia, plus Arinto, Galego dourado, Janapal

☆ Colares-Chivite

CORUCHE
See Ribatejo VR.

COVA DE BEIRA
See Beiras VR.

DÃO RD
See Bairrada and Dão, p.304.

DOURO RD
See The Douro and the Minho, p. 299.

ENCOSTAS DA AIRE
See Estremadura VR.

ENCOSTAS DA NAVE
See Trás-os-Montes VR.

ESTREMADURA VR

From Lisbon, Estremadura stretches north to the Bairrada region. Its wines may be labelled with the following districts: Alcobaço, Alenquer, Arrabida, Arruda, Azeitão, Encostas da Aire, Gaeiras and Torres (or Torres Vedras).

This is Portugal's largest wine-producing region. As such it is generally perceived as a source of cheap, uninteresting wine, yet the Adega Cooperativa Estremadura has demonstrated that fresh, clean and fruity wines can be produced at even the cheapest level of *vinho de mesa*. Estremadura has three RDs, Bucelas, Carcavelos and Colares, within its regional borders and boasts some very exciting non-demarcated wines, such as Periquita, Pasmados and Camarate.

RED The most basic of these wines have a soft, clean and fruity flavour. The very best have more concentration, lots of ripe berry-fruit flavours and are usually aged in wood.

Baga, Camarate, Castelão, Castelino, Periquita, Tinta miuda, Tinta muera

1980, 1983, 1985, 1987, 1989

Between 2-4 years (4-10 years for better wines)

Continued overleaf

WHITE Pale straw-coloured wines, fresh and gently fruity with a light, crisp, dry finish, sometimes very slightly *pétillant*.

🍇 Arinto, Bual, Chardonnay, Esgaña, Fernão pires, Jampal, Malvasia, Rabo de ovelha, Vital

19 1980, 1983, 1985, 1987, 1989

🍷 Within 1-3 years

☆ Pasmados, Camarate, Periquita, Quinta da Folgorosa, Adega Co-operativa do Arruda (selected *cuvées*), Adega Cooperativa do Torres Vedras (selected *cuvées*)

EVORA
See Alentejo VR.

GARRAFEIRA

This uniquely Portuguese concept (*see also* p.294) can include a blend of wines from different regions or one wine from one region, and single-vineyard Garrafeiras are expected in the future. There is no restriction on the grape varieties used unless the Garrafeira also carries an RD. (The origin and grape varieties of José-Maria da Fonseca Garrafeiras are coded into mysterious letters boldly printed next to the vintage: "TE", "CO", "DA" and "P".)

A Garrafeira wine must be "of good quality" and aged in wood for at least two years (one year for white), followed by one year in bottle (six months for white). For recommended RD Garrafeiras, see the entry for the specific appellation in question. *See also* Ribatejo VR, which also produces Garrafeiras.

☆ Casal do Castelão Garrafeira, José-Maria da Fonseca TE Garrafeira, Borlido Garrafeira, Caves Velhas (Caves Velhas Garrafeira, Romeira Garrafeira), Quinta d'Abrigada Garrafeira, Evelita Garrafeira

GAEIRAS
See Estremadura VR.

GRANJA
See Alentejo VR.

LAFÕES
See Beiras VR.

LAMEGO
See Beiras VR.

MADEIRA RD
See Madeira, p.305

MOIMENTA DA BEIRA
See Beiras VR.

MOSCATEL DE SETÚBAL RD

This style of fortified Muscat wine is believed to have been created by José-Maria da Fonseca, the old-established company that has a quasi-monopoly over its production today. There are three styles: six-year-old (usually vintaged), 20-year-old (not normally vintaged, replacing the 25-year-old that was vintaged), and a 50-year-old Moscatel called Setúbal Apoteca, which is occasionally encountered at auction. These ages indicate the length of time spent in oak. Once bottled, a Moscatel de Setúbal is considered ready for drinking.

FORTIFIED AMBER All Moscatel is sweet to intensely sweet, full-bodied and silky-textured. The six-year-old is the best style to choose for freshness and the grapey-apricoty varietal character of the Muscat. If complexity is paramount, the darker-coloured, rich, intense, raisiny-nutty-apricot 20-year-old is a superior choice.

🍇 Moscatel do Douro, Moscatel Roxo, Moscatel de Setúbal, plus up to 30% Arinto, Boais, Diagalves, Fernão pires, Malvasia, Olho de lebre, Rabo de ovelha, Roupeiro, Tália, Tamarez, Vital

19 1980, 1982, 1983, 1985, 1987

🍷 Immediately

MOURA
See Alentejo VR.

PINHEL
See Beiras VR.

PORT RD
See The Douro and the Minho, p.299.

PORTALEGRE
See Alentejo VR.

REDONDO
See Alentejo VR.

REGUENGOS or REGUENGOS DE MONSARAZ
See Alentejo VR.

RIBATEJO VR

This large province is sandwiched between Estremadura and Alentejo, northeast of Lisbon, and includes the following inner districts: Almeirim, Cartaxo, Chamusca, Coruche, Santarem, Tomar and Valada do Ribatejo.

The temperate climate and rich alluvial plains of the River Tagus encourage high yields, making this the second most important wine region in Portugal. Some very good wines are made here.

RED Deep-coloured, full-bodied wines that are very fruity (often black-curranty) and tannic when young, but soften with age and develop a fine, spicy bouquet.

🍇 Camarate, Castelão, Mortágua, Periquita, Preto martinho, Tinta miuda, Trincadeira

19 1980, 1983, 1985, 1987, 1989

🍷 Between 5-15 years

WHITE Most of the dry white wines produced in this region are dull. Occasionally one comes across a *vinho licoroso* that can be reminiscent of a Verdelho Madeira. Not a category to recommend until attitudes and technology change.

🍇 Boais, Fernão pires, Jampal, Rabo de ovelha, Terrantez

☆ Serradayres, Dom Luis de Margaride (Dom Hermano, Convento da Serra, Casal Monteiro), Ribatejo Garrafeira, Carvalho Ribeiro & Ferreira, Romeira Garrafeira, Adega Cooperativa d'Almeirim

ROSÉ VR

Production of Portuguese sparkling wine began with Mateus at Vila Real and was later extended to Beira Alta, Bairrada and the Setúbal Peninsula. These wines reached the height of their popularity in the mid-1970s and, although a declining force in the market, they still account for one-quarter of all exports. At the time of writing, the vast majority bear no origin, and as such are classified as *vinho de mesa,* but they will eventually have to comply with regulations that insist that all rosé wines come from one of four Vinho Regiãos and should be made from at least 60 per cent of certain named grape varieties. These are: **Trás-os-Montes VR** Alvarelhão, Tinta amarela, Tinta cão, Tinta francisca, Touriga varieties **Beiras VR** Alvarelhão, Baga, Marufo, Rufete, Tinta amarela, Tinta carvalha, Touriga varieties **Ribatejo VR** Camarate, Castelão, Preto martinho, Tinta miuda, Trincadeira **Algarve VR** Bastardo, Monvedro, Moreto, Negra mole, Pau ferro, Pexem, Trincadeira

SANTAREM
See Ribatejo VR.

SETÚBAL

The non-Moscatel wines of the Setúbal Peninsula do not, as yet, have their own RD, yet they produce some of Portugal's best table wines, including the outstanding American-owned, Australian-made, Portuguese-marketed Quinta da Bacalhôa. This wine is made from Cabernet sauvignon plus a little Merlot, and aged in new oak.

RED The Quinta da Bacalhôa has a deep colour and a rich blackcurrant flavour that is well edged with supple tannin, supported by good oak and capable of considerable development in bottle.

🍇 Cabernet sauvignon, Merlot, Periquita, and many others

19 1982, 1983, 1985, 1987, 1989

🍷 Between 4-12 years

WHITE One of the most exciting white Setúbal wines is Palmela, made by João Pires from early-picked Muscat grapes. It is a ravishingly fresh and vital wine that makes the most of all the exaggerated flowery, peachy character of the Muscat grape. Experiments are under way with Chardonnay and various other varieties.

🍇 Chardonnay, Muscat and many others

19 1982, 1983, 1985, 1987, 1989

🍷 Within 1-3 years

☆ Quinta da Bacalhôa, João Pires Palmela

TAROUCA
See Beiras VR.

TAVORA
See Beiras VR.

TOMAR
See Ribatejo VR.

TORRES or TORRES VEDRAS
See Estremadura VR.

TRÁS-OS-MONTES VR

This province is situated in the northeastern corner of Portugal and encompasses the following inner districts: Chaves, Encostas da Nave, Valpacos and Vila Real.

The style of wine ranges from light and industrial in the higher altitude vineyards of Botticas and Carrazedo, to full-bodied, very alcoholic and rather coarse in the Valpaços district. The most important wine made in this region is the semi-sparkling, semi-sweet, Portuguese rosé that crops up on virtually every export market. The well-known Mateus, Trovador and others come from Trás-os-Montes.

🍇 Alvarelhão, Bastardo, Bual, Côdega, Gouveio, Moreto, Terrantez, Tinta amarela, Tinta cão, Tinta carvalha, Tinta Francisca, Touriga varieties

VALADA DO RIBATEJO
See Ribatejo VR.

VALPAÇOS
See Trás-os-Montes VR.

VIDIGUEIRA
See Alentejo VR.

VILA REAL
See Trás-os-Montes VR.

VINHO VERDE RD
See The Douro and the Minho, p.299.

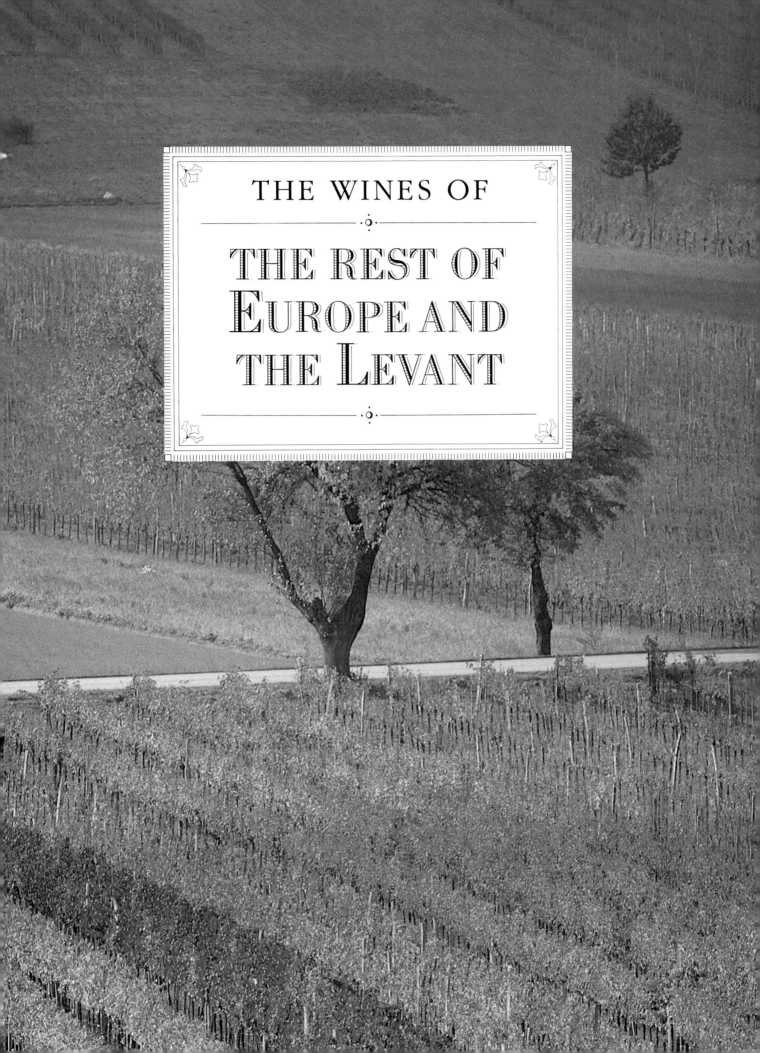

THE WINES OF

THE REST OF EUROPE AND THE LEVANT

Great Britain

Wine in Great Britain is destined to remain a cottage industry. This is not because the country does not have its serious and successful winemakers, it is because at least 90 per cent of the country's most suitable wine-growing sites are under concrete and asphalt. Perhaps part of the charm of these wines is knowing that they are developing and emerging, yet will always be limited in production.

WINEMAKING IN BRITAIN IS NOT NEW, but dates back to the Romans. The Domesday Book reveals the existence of some 40 vineyards during the reign of William the Conqueror and by medieval times the number had risen to 300, most of which were run by monks. The Black Death took its toll in the mid-fourteenth century and, almost one hundred years later, the dissolution of the monasteries virtually brought an end to English winemaking.

THE RESURGENCE OF ENGLISH WINE

The modern English wine boom began in the late-1960s and was at its height in the early 1970s. Few of the new vineyards could reasonably expect more than an average of 800 degree-days Celsius (1,440 degree-days Fahrenheit), which was well below the accepted minimum of 1,000 degree-days Celsius, so even the best-situated risked failure. Fortuitously, just as many of the wine-boom vineyards began to bear fruit, the exceptionally hot summer of 1975 was followed in 1976 by a drought. Fully ripe grapes with high sugar levels gave the growers heart to persevere although, with no chilling equipment and very little experience, many had difficulty in fermenting their excessively hot juice and, despite the euphoria of the harvest, a lot of wines were poorly made.

The next really hot year was 1982 and, although weather in the intervening years had ranged from ordinary to fairly poor, English wines steadily improved. The initially impetuous growers soon discovered that they were operating under a constant barrage of climatic calamities. Many failed, but the strong, the capable and creative survived and were all the better for having struggled.

FUTURE TRENDS

It seems obvious to me that the wine industry, small-scale though it is, will undergo a natural reorganization in the future. Contrary to the experience of potentially powerful wine producers like California and Australia, Britain will not see a flood of "boutique" wineries. Over the next ten years, the number of wineries will actually reduce, although the size of their vineyards will increase. (The small vineyards with established reputations and loyal customers will, of course, have their place in the market, but many will disappear as labels preferring the financial security of selling their grapes or bulk wine to larger concerns). The fewer, but increasingly larger wineries will in turn be able to guarantee a continuity of supply to their high-volume customers.

BRITISH OR ENGLISH?

The distinction between British and English wines is an important one: British wine is anything but British, it is produced from reconstituted grape concentrate and should not be confused with English or Welsh wine, made from freshly harvested grapes grown in England or Wales.

British wines originate from places as far apart as Cyprus, Germany, Spain and South Africa. The production process is similar to home-winemaking, where tap water is added to a thick, sweet slurry of concentrate and a packet of yeast. Many people want to drink these products, so producers should be free to make and sell them. They should not, however, be allowed to do so "under a false flag"; the term "British Wine" should be abolished and the products accurately labelled.

FACTORS AFFECTING TASTE AND QUALITY

 Location
Most vineyards are located in England and Wales, south of a line drawn through Birmingham and the Wash.

Climate
Great Britain is at the northerly extreme of climates suitable for the vine, but the warm Gulf Stream tempers the weather sufficiently to make viticulture possible. Rainfall is relatively high and conditions vary greatly from year to year, making harvests unreliable. High winds can be a problem, but winter frosts are less troublesome than in many wine regions.

Aspect
Vines are planted on all types of land, but the best sites are usually sheltered, south-facing slopes with the consequent microclimate advantages that can be crucial for wine production in this marginal viticultural region.

 Soil
Vines are grown on a wide variety of soils ranging from granite, through limestone, chalk and gravel to clay.

Viticulture and vinification
The British climate is not favourable for growing black grapes, and the vast majority of British wines are white. Of the two styles, the most economically viable is the so-called "German style". This is a quaffing wine, easy to produce from high-cropping grapes and relies on the addition of *süssreserve* for its fresh, grapey sweetness. The more expensive style is drier, more charactorful, and made from higher-quality, lower-yielding grapes.

Grape varieties
Auxerrois, Bacchus, Blauberger, Blauer Portugieser, Cabernet sauvignon, Chardonnay, Chasselas, Dornfelder, Dunkelfelder, Ehrenfelser, Faber (Faberebe), Gagarin blue, Gewürztraminer, Gutenborner, Huxelrebe, Kanzler, Kerner, Léon Millot, Madeleine Angevine, Müller-Thurgau, Optima, Ortega, Perle, Pinot blanc, Pinot gris, Pinot meunier, Pinot noir, Scheurebe, Seyval blanc, Regner, Reichensteiner, Riesling, Sauvignon blanc, Schönburger, Seibel, Siegerrebe, Triomphe d'Alsace, Wrotham pinot, Würzer, Zweigeltrebe

Wootton Vineyard, Somerset, above
This prize-winning vineyard lies in lush, rolling countryside near Shepton Mallet. Somerset has one of the highest production levels in the country.

Major vineyards of Great Britain

Notes: The top recent award-winning wines from the English Wine of the Year Competition are mentioned in the entries below. Unlike so many similar events, this one does not award medals lightly. Only those wines that have been awarded Gold Medals (GM) or the prestigious President's Cup (PC) (for the best limited-production wine), the Gore-Browne Trophy (GB) (for the best wine of any category from the previous year) and the newly established Jack Ward Memorial Salver (JW) (for the best wine of any category and year) are mentioned.

1 ADGESTONE
Upper Road, Adgestone, Isle of Wight

Vineyards: *3.6 ha (9 acres) of Müller-Thurgau, Seyval blanc and Reichensteiner*

Good-quality, dryish blend.

1979 Competition: Adgestone 1978 GM, GB
1982 Competition: Adgestone 1980 GM

2 ALDERMOOR
Picket Hill, Ringwood, Hampshire

3 ASCOT
Ascot Farm, Ascot, Berkshire

4 ASTLEY
The Crundels, Astley, Stourport on Severn, Worcestershire

Vineyards: *1.8 ha (4.5 acres) of Müller-Thurgau, Kerner, Huxelrebe and Madeleine Angevine*

A maturing vineyard established on *crundel*, an Old-English name for a south-facing sandstone bank, that is renowned for its fine Kerner and also makes an excellent "Huxelvaner" from Huxelrebe and Müller-Thurgau.

1986 Competition: Astley Kerner 1985 GM, PC

5 AVONWOOD
Seawalls Road, Sneyd Park, Bristol, Avon

6 BARDINGLEY
Babylon Lane, Hawkenbury, Kent

7 BARKHAM MANOR VINEYARD
Piltham, Uckfield, Sussex

Vineyards: *9.3 ha (23 acres) of Müller-Thurgau, Kerner, Huxelrebe, Schönburger and Bacchus*

8 BARNSGATE MANOR VINEYARDS
Heron's Ghyll, Uckfield, Sussex

Vineyards: *8 ha (20 acres) of Müller-Thurgau, Chardonnay, Kerner, Reichensteiner, Pinot noir and Seyval blanc*

9 BARTON MANOR
Whippingham, East Cowes, Isle of Wight

Vineyards: *2.3 ha (5.7 acres) of Müller-Thurgau, Seyval blanc, Huxelrebe, Reichensteiner, Zweigeltrebe and Gewürztraminer*

Very good blended wines that sometimes possess a slight spritz are sold under "Barton Manor" and "Wight Wine" labels.

1984 Competition: Barton Manor Dry 1983 GM, GB

10 BEAULIEU
Beaulieu, Nr Brockenhurst, Hampshire

11 BEENLEIGH MANOR
Beenleigh Manor, Harbertonford, Devonshire

Vineyards: *0.4 ha (1 acre) of Cabernet sauvignon and Merlot*

12 BERWICK GLEBE
Frensham Cottage, Berwick, Sussex

Vineyards: *0.8 ha (2 acres) of Müller-Thurgau and Reichensteiner*

13 BIDDENDEN
Little Whatmans, Biddenden, Kent

Vineyards: *9.7 ha (24 acres) of Ortega, Müller-Thurgau, Dornfelder, Reichensteiner, Scheurebe and Huxelrebe*

Since the early 1980s, this vineyard has consistently produced some of England's finest wines, from the basic but spicy Müller-Thurgau, through attractive Pinot Noir Rosé, to the Ortega, which is definitely its top-performing style.

1984 Competition: Ortega 1983 GM
1987 Competition: Ortega 1986 GM, GB

BODENHAM
See Broadfield.

BODIAM CASTLE
See Castle Vineyards.

14 BOOKERS
Foxhole Lane, Bolney, Sussex

Wines are sold under the "Bolney" label.

15 BOTHY
The Bothy, Frilford Heath, Oxfordshire

16 BOYTON VINEYARDS
Boyton End, Stoke-by-Clare, Suffolk

17 BRANDESTON PRIORY
The Priory, Brandeston, Suffolk

18 BREAKY BOTTOM
Northtease, Rodwell, Sussex

Vineyards: *1.6 ha (4 acres) of Seyval blanc and Müller-Thurgau*

Clean, crisp, expressive wines of high quality.

19 BRUISYARD
Church Road, Bruisyard, Suffolk

Vineyards: *4 ha (10 acres) of Müller-Thurgau*

Very fat and distinctive wines sold under the "Bruisyard St Peter" label.

20 BROADFIELD
Broadfield Court Estate, Bodenham, Herefordshire

Vineyards: *4 ha (10 acres) of Reichensteiner, Huxelrebe, Müller-Thurgau and Seyval blanc*

Wines are sold under the "Bodenham" label.

21 BROADWATER
Broadwater, Framlingham, Suffolk

22 BRYMPTON D'EVERCY
Ponsonby-Fane, Yeovil, Somerset

23 CANE END
Cane End Farm, Cane End, Oxfordshire

24 CAPTON
Capton, Nr Dartmouth, Devonshire

25 CARR TAYLOR
Westfield, Hastings, Sussex

Vineyards: *8.5 ha (21 acres) of Reichensteiner, Gutenborner, Schönburger, Kerner and Huxelrebe*

One of the most enterprising producers, Carr Taylor wines are usually Germanic in style and excellent value. The range includes one of the few English *méthode champenoise*, unusually round and fruity. In 1986, Carr Taylor produced one of the best-ever English Reichensteiners.

26 CASTLE CARY
Honeywick House, Castle Cary, Somerset

27 CASTLE VINEYARDS
Bodiam, Robertsbridge, Sussex

Vineyards: *1 ha (2.5 acres) of Reichensteiner, Blauberger, Faber, Bacchus, Pinot noir and Regner*

Wines are sold under the "Bodiam Castle" label.

28 CAVENDISH MANOR
Cavendish, Sudbury, Suffolk

Vineyards: *4 ha (10 acres) of Müller-Thurgau*

Dryish style of Müller-Thurgau, with a flowery aroma and a spicy flavour.

29 CHALKHILL
Knowle Farm, Bowerchalke, Wiltshire

Vineyards: *2.6 ha (6.5 acres) of Müller-Thurgau, Bacchus and Kerner*

Wines ranging from sweetish everyday blends, such as "Special Selection", to top-quality varietals, the finest being very dry and aromatic. The winemaker is Mark Thompson, a gifted young man who is also consultant to the ambitious Wellows project. His seering, Sauvignon-like Chalkhill Vineyard Müller-Thurgau, with its distinctive gooseberry flavour, is a great success. Wines are sold under "Chalkhill" and "Chalke Valley" labels.

CHALKLANDS
See Chilsdown.

CHALKE VALLEY
See Chalkhill.

30 CHANCTONBURY
Nash Hotel, Steyning, Sussex

31 CHARLES VINEYARD
Willingale, Ongar, Essex

Vineyards: *0.4 ha (1 acre) of Zweigeltrebe*

Wines are sold under the "Roding Valley Red" label

32 CHICKERING
Chickering Hall, Hoxne, Suffolk

33 CHIDDINGSTONE
Vexour Farm, Chiddingstone, Kent

Vineyards: *2.6 ha (6.5 acres) of Pinot noir, Kerner, Chasselas and Pinot blanc*

34 CHILFORD HUNDRED
Chilford Hall, Linton,
Cambridgeshire

Vineyards: 7.2 ha (18 acres) of
Müller-Thurgau, Huxelrebe,
Siegerrebe, Ortega and
Schönburger

Just one wine is made, an estate-
bottled blend, which is dry, has fine
acidity and a racy character.

35 CHILSDOWN
The Old Station House,
Singleton, Sussex

Vineyards: 4.2 ha (10.5 acres) of
Müller-Thurgau, Reichensteiner
and Seyval blanc

Dry, full, well-made wines sold under
"Chilsdown", "Chalklands" and
"Grapple" labels.

36 CHILTERN VALLEY
Old Luxters Farm, Hambleden,
Henley-on-Thames, Oxfordshire

COGGESHALL VILLAGE
See Coggeshall Vineyard.

37 COGGESHALL
VINEYARD
Claremont, Coggeshall,
Essex

Vineyards: 0.4 ha (1 acre) of Faber

Wines are sold under the "Coggeshall
Village" label.

38 CONGHURST
Conghurst Oast,
Hawkhurst, Kent

39 COXLEY
Church Farm, Coxley,
Somerset

40 CRANMORE
Solent Road, Cranmore,
Isle of Wight

Vineyards: 4.8 ha (12 acres) of
Müller-Thurgau, Würzer and
Gutenborner

CRAZIES
See Joyous Garde Vineyard.

CRAZIES HENLEY
RESERVE
See Joyous Garde Vineyard.

41 CROFFTA
Groes-Faen, Pontyclun,
Glamorgan

Vineyards: 1.2 ha (3 acres) of
Müller-Thurgau, Seyval blanc and
Madeleine Angevine

This very commendable blended wine
suggests that Wales could be a good
hunting-ground for new vineyards in
the future.

42 CROFT CASTLE
Croft Castle (National Trust),
Nr Leominster, Herefordshire

CUCKMERE
See Flexerne.

THE CULM MEASURE
See Prospect Vineyard.

DEERHURST
See Tapestry.

43 DENBY'S
Denby's Farm, Dorking, Surrey

A recently established vineyard.

44 DEVIL'S CAULDRON
VINEYARD
Ashford Road, High Halden,
Kent

45 DITCHLING
Claycroft, Ditchling,
Sussex

Vineyards: 2 ha (5 acres) of Müller-
Thurgau, Reichensteiner and Ortega

Excellent, racy and stylish wines,
including a particularly good Müller-
Thurgau.

DOMESDAY
See Saint George's Waldron.

46 DOWNERS
Clappers Lane,
Fulking, Sussex

47 EGLANTINE
Ash Lane, Costock,
Nottinghamshire

48 ELHAM VALLEY
Breach, Barham, Kent

Not to be confused with Elmham Park.

49 ELMHAM PARK
Elmham House,
North Elmham, Norfolk

Vineyards: 3 ha (7.5 acres) of
Müller-Thurgau, Madeleine
Angevine, Kerner and Huxelrebe

Attractively packaged, well-made wines
that have fresh, fragrant aromas,
elegant fruit and a fine, racy finish.

50 ELMS CROSS
Bradford-on-Avon, Wiltshire

51 ENGLISH WINE
CENTRE
Valley Wine Cellars,
Alfriston, Sussex

Vineyards: 0.4 ha (1 acre) of
Müller-Thurgau, plus 1.8 ha (4.5
acres) under contract.

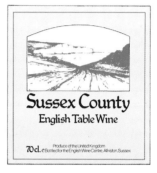

This enterprising venture sells a large
range of English wines from other
vineyards and is the venue for the
English Wine Festival.

52 ESSEX CROWN
VINEYARDS
Ardleigh, Colchester, Essex

FELSTAR
See Felsted Vineyards.

53 FELSTED VINEYARDS
Crix Green, Felsted, Essex

Vineyards: 4.2 ha (10.5 acres) of
Müller-Thurgau, Pinot noir,
Madeleine Angevine, Chardonnay
and Seyval blanc

In 1966 this became Essex County's
first vineyard since the Middle Ages.
Ten years later it produced England's
first méthode champenoise wine. Its
biggest-selling wine is an unusual
Chardonnay & Seyval Blanc blend, and
its wines are sold under "Felstead" and
"Felstar" labels.

1978 Competition: Felstar Müller-
Thurgau and Sieger GM

54 FENLANDIA
VINEYARDS
48 High Street, Harlton,
Cambridgeshire

55 FINN VALLEY
VINEYARD
Otley, Ipswich, Suffolk

Vineyards: 4 ha (10 acres) of
Müller-Thurgau and Pinot noir

56 FIVE CHIMNEYS
Five Chimneys Farm,
Hadlow Down, Sussex

57 FLEXERNE
Fletching Common,
Newick, Sussex

Vineyards: 2 ha (5 acres) of
Müller-Thurgau

Wines are sold under the "Cuckmere"
label.

58 FLINTS
Hambleden,
Henley-on-Thames,
Oxfordshire

59 FONTHILL
The Old Rectory,
Fonthill Gifford, Wiltshire

60 FRITHSDEN
38 Crouchfield,
Boxmoor, Hertfordshire

Vineyards: 1 ha (2.5 acres) of
Müller-Thurgau, Pinot noir, Kerner,
Siegerrebe and Reichensteiner

Light, fresh, Müller-Thurgau.

61 FRYARS VINEYARD
West Chiltington,
Pulborough, Sussex

62 GAMLINGAY
VINEYARD
Gamlingay, Nr Sandy, Bedfordshire

Vineyards: 3.6 ha (9 acres) of
Scheurebe, Faber, Müller-Thurgau
and Reichensteiner

An excellent, medium-sweet, fragrant
and spicy wine from the Scheurebe
grape.

63 GRAISELOUND
Haxey, Doncaster, Yorkshire

GRAPPLE
See Chilsdown.

64 GREAT SHOESMITHS
FARM
Wadhurst, Sussex

Vineyards: 6.8 ha (17 acres) of
Regner, Huxelrebe, Kerner,
Schönburger, Seyval blanc and
Müller-Thurgau

65 HAMBLEDON
VINEYARD
Mill Dow, Hambledon,
Hampshire

Vineyards: 2.8 ha (7 acres) of
Chardonnay, Pinot noir and Seyval
blanc

The oldest commercial vineyard in
England.

66 HAMSTEAD
Yarmouth, Isle of Wight

67 HARBLEDOWN &
CHAUCER
Isabel Mead Farm,
Harbledown, Kent

Vineyards: 0.8 ha (2 acres) of
Regner, Reichensteiner and Müller-
Thurgau

68 HARBOURNE
High Halden, Ashford, Kent

Vineyards: 1.2 ha (3 acres) of
Müller-Thurgau, Blauer
Portugieser, Reichensteiner and
Pinot noir

69 HARDEN FARM
Grove Road, Penshurst, Kent

Vineyards: 7.3 ha (18 acres) of
Schönburger, Bacchus,
Reichensteiner, Regner, Faber and
Huxelrebe

EVA QUALITY SEAL

Although technically recognized by the EEC as merely the equivalent of Vins de Pays, distinctive wines are produced by many of the vineyards. An excellent guide to higher-quality English wines is the English Viticultural Association (EVA) Quality Seal. Wines are awarded this seal on an annual basis after being subjected to tests that are tougher than those applied by Germany's *QbA* boards (*see* Germany p.204). The EVA seal is by no means universally utilized, but more and more vineyards are submitting their wines and its appearance on a bottle is a good indication of quality.

70 HENDRED VINEYARD
East Hendred, Wantage, Oxfordshire

71 HEYWOOD
Holly Farm, Diss, Norfolk

72 HIGHFIELD
Long Drag, Tiverton, Devon

73 HOLLYBUSH
Holly Bush Farm, Brockenhurst, Hampshire

Vineyards: *1.6 ha (4 acres) of Seyval blanc, Schönburger, Pinot blanc, Huxelrebe and Reichensteiner*

74 THE HOLT
Woolton Hill, Newbury, Berkshire

Vineyards: *0.6 ha (1.5 acres) of Müller-Thurgau, Madeleine Angevine and Siegerrebe*

Wines are sold under the "Woodhay" label.

75 HOOKSWAY
Hooksway, North Mardon, Sussex

76 HORTON VINEYARD
Three Legged Cross, Wimborne, Dorset

77 HRH VINEYARD
The Willows, Stoke St Gregory, Somerset

Vineyards: *3.2 ha (8 acres) of Müller-Thurgau, Reichensteiner, Bacchus, Siegerrebe, Huxelrebe, Auxerrois and Pinot noir*

GREAT BRITAIN

In 1985 there were 430 hectares (1,062 acres) of vineyards in Great Britain of which 325 (803 acres) were in production. In 1988 the total production area under vine had risen to 500 hectares (1,236 acres) of vines, with 323 known vineyards in England and Wales.

•	Vineyard
	County Boundary
▲	Height above sea level (metres)

78 IGHTHAM
Mote Road, Ivy Hatch, Kent

Vineyards: *1.2 ha (3 acres) of Müller-Thurgau*

Good, grapey, Germanic-style Müller-Thurgau.

79 ISLE OF ELY
Twentypence Road, Wilburton, Cambridgeshire

Vineyards: *1 ha (2.5 acres) of Müller-Thurgau, Chardonnay and Madeleine Angevine*

This winery makes a dryish blended white wine under the "St Etheldreda" label that has added backbone from the use of some Chardonnay. Wines are also sold under "Isle of Ely" label.

80 JOYOUS GARDE VINEYARD
Crazies Hill, Wargrave, Berkshire

Vineyards: *1 ha (2.5 acres) of Bacchus, Müller-Thurgau, Schönburger and Huxelrebe*

Vibrant, fruity wines with a slight spritz that often go well in blind tastings are sold under "Crazies" and "Crazies Henley Reserve" labels.

81 KENTS GREEN
Taynton, Gloucestershire

Vineyards: *0.2 (0.5 acre) of Müller-Thurgau and Huxelrebe*

1986 Competition: Kents Green 1985 GM

82 KINGS GREEN
Bourton, Gillingham, Dorset

Vineyards: *1.6 ha (4 acres) of Pinot noir, Gamay noir, Zweigeltrebe and Gewürztraminer*

83 KINGSLAND
North Trade Road, Battle, Sussex

84 KINVER
Dunsley House, Kinver, Worcestershire

85 LAMBERHURST
Ridge Farm, Lamberhurst, Kent

Vineyards: *19.4 ha (48 acres) of Müller-Thurgau, Seyval blanc, Reichensteiner, Schönburger and Chasselas*

One of the largest and best English vineyards, Lamberhurst also vinifies and bottles wine for up to 30 other vineyards.

1983 Competition: Huxelrebe 1982 GM, GB, Schönburger 1982 GM

86 LANGHAM VINEYARD
Langham, Colchester, Essex

87 LEEDS CASTLE
Leeds Castle Foundation, Maidstone, Kent

88 LEEFORD VINEYARDS
Whatlington, Battle, Sussex

Vineyards: *6.9 ha (17 acres) of Reichensteiner, Schönburger, Kerner and Huxelrebe*

Wines are sold under the "Saxon Valley" label.

89 LEXHAM HALL
Lexham Hall, Nr Litcham, Norfolk

Vineyards: *3.2 ha (8 acres) of Müller-Thurgau, Madeleine Angevine, Scheurebe and Reichensteiner*

Some fine, fragrant and flavoursome wines in a delicately dry style.

90 LODDISWELL
Lilwell, Loddiswell, Devonshire

Vineyards: *1.6 ha (4 acres) of Müller-Thurgau, Huxelrebe, Bacchus, Reichensteiner and Siegerrebe*

This vineyard's wines are rarely encountered, but its 1983 Huxelrebe was stunningly successful.

91 LODGE FARM
Hascombe, Godalming, Surrey

92 LYMINGTON
Winsford Road, Pennington, Hampshire

93 LYMINSTER
Lyminster Road, Nr Arundel, Sussex

Vineyards: *0.6 ha (1.5 acres) of Schönburger, Reichensteiner and Pinot noir*

MAGDALEN
See Pulham.

94 MEON VALLEY VINEYARD
Swanmore, Southampton, Hampshire

Vineyards: *2 ha (5 acres) of Müller-Thurgau, Seyval blanc, Pinot meunier, Madeleine Angevine and Zweigeltrebe*

Wines are sold under "Hillgrove" and "Meon Wara" labels.

MOORLYNCH
See Spring Farm.

95 MORTON MANOR VINEYARD
Morton Manor, Brading, Isle of Wight

Vineyards: *0.6 ha (1.5 acres) of Müller-Thurgau, Seyval blanc, Reichensteiner, Huxelrebe, Madeleine Angevine, Zweigeltrebe and Pinot noir*

96 NEVARDS
Nevards, Boxted, Essex

97 NEW HALL VINEYARDS
Purleigh, Chelmsford, Essex

Vineyards: *11.9 ha (29.5 acres) of Bacchus, Chardonnay, Huxelrebe, Müller-Thurgau, Pinot noir, Pinot gris, Reichensteiner and Zweigeltrebe*

Good, commercial style of Müller-Thurgau and a particularly successful, slightly sweet Huxelrebe

98 NORTONS FARM
Sedlescombe, Battle, Sussex

99 NUTBOURNE MANOR
Nr Pulborough, Sussex

100 PENBERTH VALLEY VINEYARD
Chynance, St. Buryan, Cornwall

Vineyards: *0.6 ha (1.5 acres) of Triomphe d'Alsc   Siegerrebe, Cabernet sauvig.   , Chardonnay and Pinot noir*

101 PENSHURST
Grove Road, Penshurst, Kent

Vineyards: *4.9 ha (12 acres) of Müller-Thurgau, Reichensteiner, Seyval blanc, Scheurebe and Ehrenfelser*

102 PILTON MANOR
Pilton, Shepton Mallet, Somerset

Vineyards: *2.6 ha (6.5 acres) of Seyval blanc, Müller-Thurgau and Huxelrebe*

This winery makes a commercial Müller-Thurgau, good Seyval Blanc, even better Huxelrebe and interesting *méthode champenoise*.

1975 Competition: Riesling-Sylvaner 1973 GB
1976 Competition: Riesling-Sylvaner 1975 GB

103 POLMASSICK
St Ewe, St. Austell, Cornwall

104 PROSPECT VINEYARD
Uffculme, Cullompton, Devonshire

Vineyards: *0.3 ha (0.75 acres) of Madeleine Angevine and Triomphe d'Alsace*

Wines are sold under "The Culm Measure" label.

105 PULHAM
Mill Lane, Pulham Market, Norfolk

Vineyards: *2.4 ha (6 acres) of Auxerrois, Bacchus, Chardonnay, Müller-Thurgau and Zweigeltrebe*

Pulham's first vintage won the coveted Gore-Browne Trophy and it has since produced an interesting Auxerrois and a fine, crisp, smoky Chardonnay. Wines are sold under the "Magdalen" label.

1977 Competition: Magdalen Rivaner 1976 GB
1980 Competition: Magdalen Rivaner 1979 GB

PURLEY
See Westbury Vineyard.

106 QUEEN COURT
17 Court Street, Faversham, Kent

107 ROCK LODGE
Scayne's Hill, Sussex

Vineyards: *1.4 ha (3.5 acres) of Müller-Thurgau and Reichensteiner*

Rarely encountered wines from grapes grown in a sheltered, south-facing plot.

RODING VALLEY RED
See Charles Vineyard.

108 ROWNEY
Rowney Farm, Chasseways, Hertfordshire

109 SAINT ANNE'S
Wain House, Oxenhall, Gloucestershire

110 SAINT GEORGE'S WALDRON
Waldron Village, Nr Heathfield, Sussex

Vineyards: *2 ha (5 acres) of Müller-Thurgau, Reichensteiner, Pinot noir, Seyval blanc and Schönburger*

Wines under the patriotic "St George's" label, including a super Müller-Thurgau, are sold in the House of Commons. Other labels are "Tudor Rose" and "Domesday".

111 SAINT NICHOLAS OF ASH
Moat Farm House, Ash, Kent

SAXON VALLEY
See Leeford Vineyards.

112 SEDLESCOMBE
Staple Cross, Robertsbridge, Sussex

Vineyards: *4 ha (10 acres) of Gewürztraminer, Gutenborner, Müller-Thurgau, Ortega and Reichensteiner*

Formerly known as Pine Ridge, this was Britain's first, and is currently its largest, organic vineyard.

113 SEYMOURS
Forest Road, Horsham, Sussex

114 SHERSTON EARL
Sherston, Nr Malmesbury, Wiltshire

SILVER SNIPE
See Snipe.

115 SNIPE
Snipe Farm Road, Clopton, Suffolk

Vineyards: *0.6 ha (1.5 acres) of Müller-Thurgau*

Wines are sold under the "Silver Snipe" label.

SPOTS FARM
See Tenterden.

116 SPRING BARN VINEYARD
Laughton, Nr Lewes, Sussex

117 SPRING FARM
Moorlynch, Bridgwater, Somerset

Vineyards: *4.9 ha (12 acres) of Madeleine Angevine, Seyval blanc, Würzer, Müller-Thurgau and Schönburger*

Wines are sold under the "Moorlynch" label.

118 STANLAKE PARK
Stanlake Park, Twyford, Berkshire

Vineyards: *6.9 ha (17 acres) of Schönburger, Scheurebe, Kerner,*

Ortega, Regner, Reichensteiner, Seyval blanc, Müller-Thurgau and Pinot varieties

119 STAPLE
Church Farm,
Staple, Kent

Vineyards: *2.8 ha (7 acres) of Müller-Thurgau, Reichensteiner and Huxelrebe*

Wines are sold under the "Staple St. James" label.

STAPLE ST. JAMES
See Staple.

120 STAPLECOMBE
Burlands Farm, Staplegrove,
Somerset

ST CUTHMANS
See Steyning Vineyards.

ST ETHELDREDA
See Isle of Ely.

121 STEYNING VINEYARDS
Horsham Road,
Steyning, Sussex

Vineyards: *3.6 ha (9 acres) of Müller-Thurgau, Schönburger and Ortega*

Wines are sold under the "St. Cuthmans" label.

ST. GEORGE'S
See Saint George's Waldron.

122 STITCHCOMBE
Stitchcombe, Marlborough,
Wiltshire

Vineyards: *2 ha (5 acres) of Müller-Thurgau, Reichensteiner and Siegerrebe*

123 STOCKS VINEYARD
Stocks Farm, Suckley,
Hereford & Worcester

Vineyards: *4 ha (10 acres) of Müller-Thurgau*

124 SWIFTSDEN
Swiftsden House,
Hurst Green, Sussex

Vineyards: *1.2 ha (3 acres) of Müller-Thurgau and Reichensteiner*

125 SYNDALE VALLEY
Lady's Wood, Newnham, Kent

Vineyards: *3.6 ha (9 acres) of Müller-Thurgau, Reichensteiner, Zweigeltrebe, Ortega, Seyval blanc, Pinot blanc, Würzer and Wrotham pinot*

126 TAPESTRY
Well Farm, Apperley,
Gloucestershire

Vineyards: *1.2 ha (3 acres) of Madeleine Angevine and Chardonnay*

Wines are sold under the "Deerhurst" label.

127 TENTERDEN
Spots Farm, Tenterden, Kent

Vineyards: *4 ha (10 acres) of Müller-Thurgau, Dunkelfelder, Seyval blanc, Reichensteiner, Pinot noir, Gutenborner and Schönburger*

This vineyard is expertly run by Stephen Skelton, whose Seyval Blanc drew a myriad of superlatives from wine writers when it won the Gore-Browne Trophy in 1981. Since then, other varieties have also proved successful and the wine to watch in the future is Schönburger, which is well suited to Tenterden's fine, sandy soil. Wines are sold under the "Tenterden" and "Spots Farm" labels.

1981 Competition: Spots Farm Seyval Blanc 1980 GB
1983 Competition: Spots Farm 1982 GM; Spots Farm Müller-Thurgau Dry 1982 GM; Spots Farm Gutenborner Dry 1982 GM

128 THORNBURY CASTLE VINEYARD
Thornbury, Bristol, Avon

129 THREE CHOIRS
Fairfield Fruit Farm,
Newent, Gloucestershire

Vineyards: *8 ha (20 acres) of Reichensteiner, Schönburger, Huxelrebe, Seyval blanc and Bacchus*

An excellent standard of wines made in a full, ripe and satisfying style, including a very fine Late Harvest Huxelrebe.

1986 Competition: Seyval-Reichensteiner 1984 GM
1987 Competition: Three Choirs 1984 Medium GM, JW

130 THREE CORNERS
Beacon Lane, Woodnesborough,
Kent

Vineyards: *0.6 ha (1.5 acres) of Siegerrebe, Ortega and Reichensteiner*

Wines are sold under the "Tricorne" label.

131 TINTERN PARVA
Parva Farm, Tintern, Gwent

Vineyards: *1.6 ha (4 acres) of Müller-Thurgau, Bacchus, Pinot noir, Reichensteiner and Ortega*

TRICORNE
See Three Corners.

TUDOR ROSE
See Saint George's Waldron.

132 TYTHERLEY
The Garden House,
West Tytherley, Wiltshire

133 WELLOW
East Wellow, Romsey, Hampshire

Vineyards: *32 ha (80 acres) of Auxerrois, Bacchus, Chardonnay, Faber, Huxelrebe, Kerner, Müller-Thurgau, Ortega and Reichensteiner*

In 1985, Andy Vining purchased Wellow, which has an exceptionally favourable microclimate, and within two years had planted 20 hectares (50 acres) with vines. In 1986, a few acres produced a light crop of grapes, unusual for one-year-old vines, and Andy actually made his first 27 bottles of wine. A year later, I found it to be light, fresh and fruity in a medium-sweet Germanic style. Nothing exceptional, but well made (as it should be with Mark Thompson of Chalkhill as consultant), and it certainly augurs well for the future. Wellow yielded 2,000 bottles in 1987 and by 1992, with 40 hectares (100 acres) in full production, expects to be the largest producer of English wine.

134 WESTBURY VINEYARD
Purley-on-Thames,
Reading, Berkshire

Vineyards: *5 ha (12.5 acres) of Müller-Thurgau, Seyval blanc, Pinot noir, Siegerrebe, Reichensteiner, Madeleine Angevine and Schönburger*

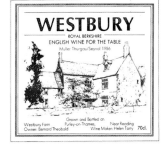

The irrepressible Bernard Theobold has forthright and optimistic views about the potential of English wine and he can carry these to excess in some of his rather strange "red" wines. His range of styles is large, and there are a number of happy discoveries to be made.
Wines are sold under the "Westbury" and "Purley" labels.

1984 Competition: Westbury Müller-Thurgau-Seyval 1982 GM; Westbury Müller-Thurgau 1981 GM

135 WHATLEY
Old Rectory, Whatley,
Somerset

136 WHITMOOR HOUSE
Ashhill, Cullompton,
Devonshire

137 WHITSTONE
Bovey Tracey,
Nr Newton Abbot,
Devonshire

Vineyards: *0.6 ha (1.5 acres) of Müller-Thurgau and Madeleine Angevine*

Clean, well-made, dry white wines, blended from two grape varieties and vinified by Colin Gillespie at Wootton.

138 WICKENDEN
Cliveden Road, Taplow,
Buckinghamshire

WIGHT WINE
See Barton Manor.

139 WILLOW GRANGE
Street Farm, Crowfield,
Suffolk

WOODHAY
See The Holt.

140 WOOTTON
North Wootton,
Shepton Mallet, Somerset

Vineyards: *2.4 ha (6 acres) of Müller-Thurgau, Schönburger, Auxerrois and Seyval blanc*

I have great memories of Wootton's wonderfully rich 1976 Schönburger, a variety with which this vineyard has always been successful.

1979 Competition: Müller-Thurgau 1978 GM
1982 Competition: Schönburger 1981 GM, GB
1986 Competition: Seyval 1985 GM, GB

141 WRAXALL
Shepton Mallet, Somerset

Vineyards: *2.4 ha (6 acres) of Auxerrois, Gagarin blue, Kerner, Müller-Thurgau, Madeleine Angevine, Pinot noir, Seyval blanc, Siegerrebe, Zweigeltrebe and Wrotham pinot*

The owner believes that a good light red wine can be made at Wraxall.

142 YEARLSTONE
Chilton, Bickleigh,
Devonshire

Vineyards: *0.6 ha (1.5 acres) of Madeleine Angevine, Siegerrebe, Riesling and Chardonnay*

Switzerland

Swiss wines at their best are as fresh and clean as Alpine air. Although many varieties are cultivated, the most famous is the Chasselas. In France this is viewed as a table grape, yet the Swiss make it into a light, dry, spritzy and delicately delicious wine that is the perfect partner to their much-loved cheese fondue.

SWITZERLAND'S FAVOURITE CHASSELAS GRAPE can be found under the guise of the Dorin in the Vaud, the Perlan in Geneva and Neuchâtel and, most famous of all, the Fendant in the Valais. Switzerland also produces a surprising amount of red wine, usually from Pinot noir or Gamay, sometimes both. The Pinot noir is a grape that likes to

be pampered and, although the Swiss cannot produce a Pinot noir vine that bears even the remotest resemblance to a Burgundy, in favoured situations it is capable of making simple, attractive, fruity wines that do honour to this noble variety. But the best red wines of Switzerland are certainly the deeper-coloured, more serious Merlot wines from the Italian-speaking canton of Ticino in the south of the country.

FACTORS AFFECTING TASTE AND QUALITY

Location
Situated between the south of Germany, north of Italy and the central-east French border.

Climate
Continental alpine conditions prevail, with local variations due to altitude, the tempering influence of lakes and the sheltering effects of the various mountain ranges. Some areas, such as the Valais in the south, are very dry. Spring frosts are a perennial threat in most areas.

Aspect
Vines are grown in areas ranging from valley floors and lake shores to the steep alpine foothill sites, which, just south of Visp, reach an altitude of nearly 1,200 metres (3,940 ft) and are the highest vineyards in Europe. The best sites are found on south-facing slopes, which maximize exposure to sun.

Soil
Mostly a glacial moraine of decomposed slate and schist,

often with limestone over sedimented bedrock of limestone, clay and sand.

Viticulture and vinification
Terracing is required on the steeper sites, and so too is irrigation in dry areas such as the Valais. Most vineyard work is labour-intensive, except in a few more gently sloping vineyards such as those around Lake Geneva, where mechanical harvesting is practical. Careful vinification and chaptalization produce remarkably high yields.

The last three decades have seen a growth in the production of red wine in what is generally a white-wine-dominated region.

Grape varieties
Aligoté, Amigne, Arvine, Chardonnay, Chasselas, Gamay, Humagne, Marsanne, Merlot, Müller-Thurgau, Muscat à petits grains, Païen, Pinot gris, Pinot noir, Rèze, Riesling, Sylvaner.

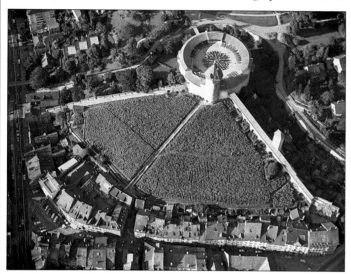

Schaffhausen vineyards, above
The Munot vineyard, situated in Schaffhausen itself, is one of the finest in this German-speaking Swiss canton. The orderly rows of vines reflect the characteristic well-known Swiss neatness.

SWITZERLAND

Switzerland is divided into three basic areas – French-speaking, German-speaking and Italian-speaking. Some of the wine-producing cantons cross these "international" boundaries and possess alternative names. This mountainous country's vineyards are polarized near its lakes and rivers.

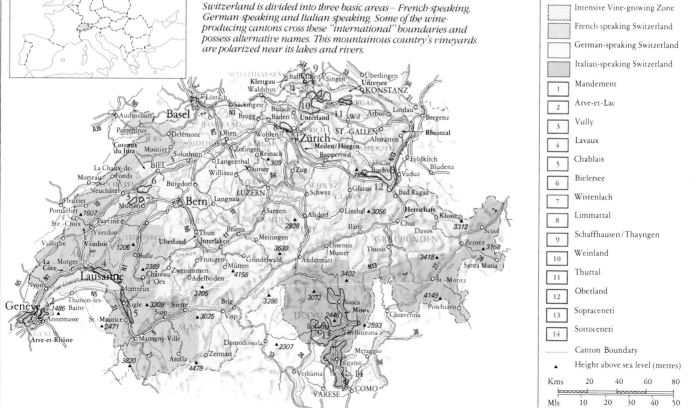

	Intensive Vine-growing Zone
	French-speaking Switzerland
	German-speaking Switzerland
	Italian-speaking Switzerland
1	Mandement
2	Arve-et-Lac
3	Vully
4	Lavaux
5	Chablais
6	Bielersee
7	Wistenlach
8	Limmattal
9	Schaffhausen / Thayngen
10	Weinland
11	Thurtal
12	Oberland
13	Sopraceneri
14	Sottoceneri
	Canton Boundary
▲	Height above sea level (metres)

Kms   20   40   60   80
Mls   10   20   30   40   50

HOW TO READ SWISS WINE LABELS

There are few ground rules useful for the reading of Swiss wine labels; they may be in one of three languages, French, German or Italian, and bear few special regulatory terms. Any Swiss wine that is not completely dry must be labelled *Légèrement Doux* (gently or lightly sweet) or *Avec sucre residuel* (literally "with residual sugar"). The term *Premier Cru* has no connotation of quality whatsoever; it may be used by any wine estate, domaine or château. The vintage year can be relied on, and the name and address of the producer will be evident on the label. If the wine is to be exported to EEC countries, it must conform to the Community regulations that insist upon such terms as "Produce of Switzerland" and demand that alcoholic strength and volume be clearly shown on the label.

Terraced vines, Lake Geneva, above
The smallest canton in Switzerland has gently sloping vineyards of high quality. Mandement is the best district and Santigny the best-known village.

The grapes and wines of Switzerland

Note: Although Switzerland has no strict wine regime such as the French AOC system, there are certain protected names that may only be used in specific localities under certain conditions and these are indicated below by the use of OA (Official Appellation).

AMIGNE

An old Valais variety that gives a full, rustic, smooth white — usually dry.

ARVINE

Another old Valais variety that makes an even richer, yet more rustic, dry white.

BLAUBURGUNDER

Synonym for Pinot noir used in German-speaking Switzerland.

CHASSELAS

The most important grape variety in Switzerland, its wines can be nicely flavoured if not overcropped. Bottling *sur lie* provides *pétillance*. The wine is called Fendant in the Valais, Dorin in the Vaud and Perlan in Geneva and Neuchâtel.

DÔLE OA

Protected name for a light red blend of Pinot noir and Gamay, grown in the Valais, with a minimum Oechsle of 85°.

DORIN OA

Protected name for white Chasselas wine grown in the Vaud.

ELBLING

This rarely-seen variety is in decline. It is merely of light, neutral character.

FENDANT OA

Protected name for white wines produced from Chasselas grapes grown in the Valais.

GAMAY

Grown mostly in the Valais and Vaud, this famous Beaujolais grape makes red wines of little distinction in its pure varietal form. Blended with Pinot noir to make Dôle, or as a pale rosé, it can be quite successful.

GORON OA

As for Dôle, but for grapes that fail to reach the minimum 85° Oechsle level.

HERMITAGE BLANC

A synonym for the old Rhone variety, Marsanne, used in the Valais. It makes full, rich, sometimes quite refined, dry white wines.

HUMAGNE

An old Valais variety, this dark-skinned grape is used to make both red and white wines of full, rustic charm.

JOHANNISBERG

Synonym used for Sylvaner wine produced in the Valais.

KLEVNER

Synonym of Pinot noir, used for wines produced in German-speaking Switzerland, particularly in and around Zurich.

MALVOISIE OA

This synonym for the Pinot gris is used to identify sweet wines, often from the Valais.

MERLOT

The outstanding red grape of Ticino in Italian-speaking Switzerland.

MÜLLER-THURGAU

This most prolific *Riesling x Sylvaner* cross was created in 1882 by Dr. Müller, from the canton of Thurgau.

MUSCAT

The Muscat à petits grains is traditionally grown in the Valais, in very small quantities. The dry white wine it makes is very light in body, but has the grape's unmistakable varietal flowery aroma.

NOSTRANO

Inexpensive red-wine blend of *vin ordinaire* quality, produced in the Italian-speaking canton of Ticino.

OEIL DE PERDRIX

Literally "partridge eye", this traditional French term is used for pale rosé wines, most often encountered in Neuchâtel.

PAÏEN

Local variant of the Gewürztraminer, grown in the Valais where it makes dry, aromatic white wines.

PERLAN OA

Protected name for white wine produced from Chasselas grapes grown in Geneva and Neuchâtel.

PETITE ARVINE

Synonym for the Arvine. *See* Arvine.

RÄUSCHLING

Synonym for the Elbling. *See* Elbling.

RÈZE

Rarely encountered ancient Valais variety.

RIESLING-SYLVANER

See Müller-Thurgau.

SALVAGNIN OA

Red-wine blend of Pinot noir and Gamay found in the Vaud.

TWANNER

Overrated, light red wine from the village of Twann on the northwestern shore of Lake Bienne (Bielersee) in the canton of Berne.

VITI OA

Controlled appellation for quality Merlot wine from the Italian-speaking canton of Ticino.

The wine areas of Switzerland

FRENCH-SPEAKING SWITZERLAND

Although French-speaking Switzerland represents just one-sixth of the country, it boasts more than 80 per cent of its vineyards, some 10,115 hectares (25,000 acres), with an average annual production of 1,035 million hectolitres (11.5 million cases). It includes Geneva, Neuchâtel, Valais and Vaud.

GENEVA

Wine districts: *Arve-et-Lac, Arve-et-Rhône, Mandement*

The smallest canton produces light, dry, gently aromatic and lively white wines with a hint of *pétillance* from the Chasselas, known locally as Perlan. There are also various light, fruity reds.

🍇 Aligoté, Chardonnay, Chasselas, Gamay, Müller-Thurgau, Pinot gris, Pinot noir

☆ Chasselas "Etoile de Peissy", "Perlan" Coteau de Rougemont, Pinot Noir "Le Vieux Clocher"

NEUCHÂTEL

Wine districts: *Coteaux du Jura, Vully*

Sheltered by the Jura Mountains, these vineyards are capable of producing some of Switzerland's choicest wines, particularly from the Pinot noir grape, which makes a light red wine, a pale pink "Oeil de Perdrix" and an even more delicate *blanc de noir*. The dry white Chasselas can have a refreshing prickle. Slightly fuller, more serious styles are produced from the up-and-coming Chardonnay.

🍇 Chardonnay, Chasselas, Pinot gris, Pinot noir

☆ Château de Vaumarcus, André Ruedin

VALAIS

Wine districts: *No specified districts*

The oldest, most famous and by far the most intensively cultivated of Switzerland's cantons, the Valais boasts more than one-third of the country's vineyards, although some fall within the German-speaking sector. A large range of interesting and very individual wines is produced here, the best-known being "Dôle", red-wine blends of Pinot noir and Gamay. Any wine bearing the name "Goron" is declassified "Dôle". Red wines from the Humagne are also worth exploring.

The Valais "Fendant" is a smooth, and sometimes slightly effervescent, dry white Chasselas wine. Riesling is rare, but can be fine in a light, racy and dry style. Sylvaner, which may be sold as "Johannisberg" is dry and fat, with a flavour of unripe tomatoes. The Païen makes aromatic white wines, usually dry, and "Malvoisie" is made from late-picked grapes into a semi-sweet, rich and quite luscious white wine.

Armigne, Arvine, Chasselas, Gamay, Humagne, Marsanne (locally Hermitage blanc), Muscat à petits grains, Païen, Pinot gris (locally Malvoisie), Pinot noir, Riesling, Sylvaner

☆ Bonvin Fils "Brûlefer", Caves de Riondaz, Château Lichten Dôle "Selection Or", Dôle "Clos du Château", Domaine du Mont d'Or "Gout du Conseil", Charles Favre ("Dame de Sion", "Reserve de Tous Vents"), Maurice Gay (Armigne, Muscat, "Reserve Fendant") Alphonse Orsat "Ermitage du Prévot", Louis Vuignier (Arvine, Humagne, "Malvoisie")

VAUD

Wine districts: *Chablais, La Côte, Lavaux, Vaudois*

The Vaud encompasses almost one-quarter of Switzerland's vineyards, making it the second-most intensively cultivated canton in the country. Chasselas accounts for eight out of every ten bottles produced and the wines, which are sold as "Dorin", are dry, light and elegant, with a delicate, fruity character. The popular local reds sold as "Salvagnin" are a sort of rustic version of "Dôle", pleasantly fruity and

relatively full-bodied. Rare Rieslings of a very vital and surprisingly well-flavoured character are sometimes encountered. The Chablais district specializes in tangy-dry, rich and smooth-textured white Chasselas wines, which are particularly good from around Aigle, and red *nouveau* Gamay wines made by *macération carbonique* for current drinking. The best district is Lavaux, its finest villages Rivaz and Treytorrens.

Chasselas, Pinot gris, Pinot noir, Riesling

☆ Henri Badoux "Aigle les Murailles", Château d'Allaman, Château de Châtagnéréaz, Château Maison Blanche, Château de Vinzel, Clos de la George, Dézaley "La Tour de Marsens" ("Dorin", Pinot Noir), Domaine de la Lance, Domaine du Martheray, Domaine de Riencourt, Robert Isoz (Pinot Gris, Gewürztraminer), Gérard Pignet Dézaley "Renard", J & P Dézaley "l'Arbalète"

GERMAN-SPEAKING SWITZERLAND

By far the largest of the three cultural divisions, German-speaking Switzerland covers two-thirds of the country, yet encompasses only one-sixth of its total viticultural area, some 2,033 hectares (5,000 acres), with an average annual production of 207,000 hectolitres (2.3 million cases).

AARGAU

Wine districts: *No specified districts*

Best-known for its red wines, the villages of Netteler, Goldwand and Brestenberger are the best known. Off-dry, light, fragrant white wines of low alcohol content are also produced.

Müller-Thurgau, Pinot noir

BASEL

Wine districts: *No specified districts*

The wines of white-wine-only Basel, are mostly grown on the banks of the Birs River, a tributary of the Rhine. The most celebrated vineyard is the tiny Im Schlipf.

Chasselas, Müller-Thurgau

BERN

Wine districts: *Bielersee, Oberland*

Although some rather thin and mean red wines are produced in this canton, most grapes grown are white, and produce wines that are fragrant and lively, with refreshing acidity. They are easy to drink when young.

Chasselas, Müller-Thurgau, Pinot noir

FRIBOURG

Wine districts: *Wistenlach (or Vully)*

Fribourg is mainly French-speaking, but its vineyards are located in the

German-speaking area. Mostly white wines, they are typically dry, light and fresh with fruity acidity.

Chasselas, Pinot noir

GRAUBÜNDEN (or GRISONS)

Wine districts: *Herrschaft*

On these vineyards of the Rhine's upper reaches, the Pinot noir is favoured by the warm southern wind that urges grapes to ripen well and provides wines with comparatively good colour and body, which are well balanced, have fine varietal aroma and a smooth flavour. Completer is a rare grape of ancient origin that makes an interesting, rich, *Auslese* style of wine.

Blauburgunder, Completer, Müller-Thurgau,

☆ "Adelheid von Randenburg", "Graaf von Spiegelberg", Hans Schlatter

SAINT-GALLEN

Wine districts: *Rheintal, Oberland*

This canton encompasses the upper reaches of the Rhine just south of Lake Constance (Bodensee). Most wines are red and the best are grown on the Buchenberg, a vineyard known as "the pearl of Rheintal".

Pinot noir (locally Blauburgunder)

SCHAFFHAUSEN

Wine districts: *Klettgau, Thayngen*

The vines in this canton grow between the Rhine, with its famous falls, and the foothills of the Jura Mountains. Most of the wines produced are red Pinot noir, with the finest wines grown on the Im Hintere Waatelbuck vineyard of Hallauer and the Munot vineyard at Schaffhausen itself.

Elbling, Müller-Thurgau, Pinot gris (locally Malvoisie), Pinot noir, Sylvaner

THURGAU

Wine districts: *Thurtal, Untersee*

The home of the famous Dr. Müller, who left his indelible mark on world viticulture with his prolific Müller-Thurgau cross. Inevitably the grape grows here. However, more than 80 per cent of the vines cultivated are Pinot noir and the delicately fruity wines this grape produces are far superior.

Müller-Thurgau, Pinot noir

WALLIS

Wine districts: *No specified districts*

The German-speaking part of the Valais. *See* Valais.

ZÜRICH

Wine districts: *Horgen, Meilen, Limmattal, Unterland, Weinland*

The most important winemaking canton in German-speaking Switzerland produces some of the most expensive, least impressive wines in the entire country. This is due to a climate that is less suitable for viticulture, particularly in the spring when frosts can be devastating. Grown on sheltered slopes with a good exposure to the sun, the Pinot noir produces attractive fruity wines.

Müller-Thurgau, Pinot noir, Rauschling

☆ Château de Thun

ITALIAN-SPEAKING SWITZERLAND

The vineyards of this region cover some 1,215 hectares (3,000 acres) and produce approximately 90,000 hectolitres (1 million cases) per year of primarily red wines.

GRISONS (or GRAUBÜNDEN)

Wine district: *Misox*

The Italian-speaking part of Graubünden. *See* Graubünden.

TICINO

Wine districts: *Sopraceneri, Sottoceneri*

Totally different to Zürich, this canton consistently provides some of the best and least expensive wines in Switzerland. The Merlot is by far the most successful grape. It makes well-coloured red wines of good depth, body and character, that often carry the official "VITI" (Merlot from Ticino) classification. "Nostrano" is an anonymous red-wine blend of grapes.

Merlot, plus various local, French and Italian varieties

☆ Cantina Sociale Giubiasco, Figli fu Alberto Daldini, Tenuta Montalbano, Vigneto Roncobello di Morbio

Austria

A predominantly white-grape-cultivating country, Austria is a winemaking "clone" of Germany, with the Riesling its most classic, yet under-exploited, variety. Grown in the right vineyard to a sensible yield, the country's most popular grape, the ubiquitous Grüner veltliner, is also capable of producing a very distinguished and distinctive wine.

EAST OF VIENNA, THE ANCIENT SETTLEMENT of Carnuntum was once known as "Rome on the Danube" and, although the history of winemaking in Austria dates back to pre-Roman times, it was Probus, the gardener's son who became Emperor of Rome, who laid the foundation of this country's viticulture when in 280 AD he rescinded Emperor Domitian's ban on the planting of vineyards anywhere except Italy.

THE MODERN AUSTRIAN WINE TRADE

By the late-1970s, production was on the increase, while domestic consumption was declining, and the industry began to build up the largest wine-lake outside the EEC. Austria's wine industry was designed chiefly for exports to Germany, traditionally its only significant customer. After a succession of bumper harvests, both in Germany and Austria, sales to the former dried up and the overproduction continued until the so-called "anti-freeze" scandal broke. This had a devastating effect on what little export trade Austria had.

The scandal did, however, make people consider the state of the industry, and most Austrians came to realize that production must be dropped and quality raised. Cabernet sauvignon and Chardonnay are now being cultivated, pruning systems are changing and new oak *barriques* are being purchased for the maturation of a new wave of upmarket varietal wines that will revitalize the Austrian wine industry in the 1990s.

AUSTRIA'S GREAT WINE SCANDAL IN PERSPECTIVE

The innocent majority of Austria's 40,000 wine producers still wonder if their exports will ever recover from the so-called "anti-freeze" scare publicized by the world's press in the summer of 1985. It was reported that quantities of Austrian wine had been

AUSTRIA

Austria's vineyards are concentrated in the east. Niederösterreich (Lower Austria, north and south of Vienna), and Burgenland (on the Hungarian border, southeast of Vienna) are the most important both for quality and quantity.

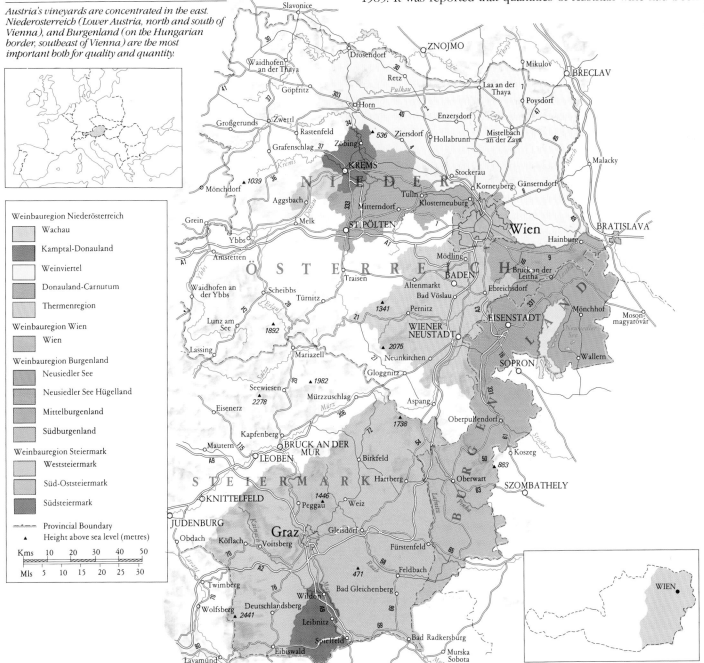

Weinbauregion Niederösterreich
- Wachau
- Kamptal-Donauland
- Weinviertel
- Donauland-Carnutum
- Thermenregion

Weinbauregion Wien
- Wien

Weinbauregion Burgenland
- Neusiedler See
- Neusiedler See Hügelland
- Mittelburgenland
- Südburgenland

Weinbauregion Steiermark
- Weststeiermark
- Süd-Oststeiermark
- Südsteiermark

Provincial Boundary
▲ Height above sea level (metres)

Kms 10 20 30 40 50
Mls 5 10 15 20 25 30

artificially sweetened with "anti-freeze", later named as *diethylene glycol*, and described as highly poisonous.

In fact, although the substance used was indeed *diethylene glycol*, this is not anti-freeze. Anti-freeze is *ethylene glycol*, which is three times more poisonous. The media failed to acknowledge that natural wine alcohol is more toxic than *diethylene glycol* and, of course, is found in wine in far greater concentrations. Had the news stories pointed out that it is legal to add relatively huge quantities of more toxic pure alcohol to fortify wines such as Sherry and Port, this would have allayed many unnecessary fears.

Why add *diethylene glycol*?

Even the reason for the presence of *diethylene glycol* (widely believed to be for sweetening a wine, but actually of little practical use in this application) was not appreciated by the media. The Austrian tricksters had learned from the mistakes of their German counterparts, who had often tried to illegally sweeten or "stretch" wines with sugar. This practice had always been detected by routine laboratory tests that highlight unnaturally low sugar-free dry extract levels. During the ripening of a grape, its sugar-free dry extract increases in direct relation to its production of sugar, so when the Germans added sugar to wine, whether to sweeten or to illegally chaptalize it, the sugar-free dry extract levels were conspicuously low. Adding accurate amounts of glycerine as well as sugar was found to increase the sugar-free extract reading to the appropriate level. However glycerine, a common ingredient in wine, was also routinely measured and the practice again detected because wine that had correct sugar-free extract levels had a suspiciously high glycerine content. Then a clever Austrian biochemist hit on the idea of using *diethylene glycol*. This had the same effect on the extract readings, did not show up as glycerine and was a substance that nobody would dream of specifically looking for in wine. So sugar was illegally used to sweeten or "stretch" the Austrian wines, and *diethylene glycol* was added to "hide" the sugar.

Although I certainly do not condone this illegal practice, it constituted a financial fraud, not a health scare. The Austrian wine industry as a whole is as innocent as that found in any other country. The damage done to the country's wine trade is an unfortunate case of the whole industry taking the blame for the actions of a few individuals.

The Wachau, above
Much of Austria is very picturesque, making it a popular holiday destination; here the lush vineyards complement this typical Lower Austrian landscape.

FACTORS AFFECTING TASTE AND QUALITY

Location
Austria's vineyards are found in the east of the country, north and south of Vienna, bordering Czechoslovakia, Hungary and Yugoslavia.

Climate
The climate is a warm, dry continental type with annual rainfall varying between 57–77 centimetres (23-31 ins), the hottest and driest area being Burgenland, where, in the warm autumns, mists rising from the Neusiedler See help promote botrytis cinerea (the "noble rot" beloved by wine-growers).

Aspect
Vines are grown on all types of land from the plains of the Danube to its valley sides that are often very steep and terraced, and from the hilly Burgenland to the slopes of mountainous Styria.

Soil
Soils vary from generally stony schist, limestone and gravel (though occasionally loamy) in the north, through predominantly sandy soils on the shores of the Neusiedler See in Burgenland, to mainly clay with some volcanic soils in Styria.

Viticulture and vinification
Austria's methods are, not surprisingly, similar to those of Germany. But although modern techniques have been introduced here, far more Austrian wine is produced by traditional methods than is the case in Germany.

More than 85 per cent of the country's vines are cultivated by the Lenz Moser system, which trains the vines to twice normal height, achieving a higher ratio of quality to cost, by enabling the use of mechanized harvesting. This system brought fame to its Austrian inventor, the late Lenz Moser, and has been adopted by at least one grower in most winemaking countries.

Grape varieties
Blauberger, Blauer Portugieser, Blauer wildbacher, Blaufränkisch, Bouviertraube, Cabernet franc, Cabernet sauvignon, Chardonnay, Frühroter veltliner (Malvasia), Furmint, Gewürztraminer, Goldburger, Grüner veltliner, Pinot blanc, Pinot noir, Merlot, Müller-Thurgau, Muskateller, Muskat-ottonel, Neuburger, Pinot gris, Roter veltliner, Rotgipfler, Sauvignon blanc, Scheurebe, St. Laurent, Silvaner, Trollinger, Riesling, Welschriesling, Zierfandler, Zweigelt.

AUSTRIA VERSUS GERMANY

Both countries operate wine regimes that base levels of quality on degrees of ripeness by measuring the amount of sugar found in the grapes at the time of harvest. As in Germany, Austrian wines range from *Tafelwein*, through *Qualitätswein* to *Trockenbeerenauslese*. The overview below shows that most Austrian wines conform to higher minimum standards than their German counterparts. More significant, however, is the fact that the minimum level for each category is rigid, so it has a distinctive style. This gives the consumer a clear idea of what to expect, whereas a German category varies according to the variety of grape and its area of origin. In Germany, only experience can reveal that a Mosel *Auslese*, for example, tastes no sweeter than *Spätlesen* from other regions. The Austrian classification could be improved if it incorporated a rising sugar level for wines of increasing degrees of acidity. A sliding scale of sugar/acidity ratios would give a sharper definition to each category, for the more acidity a wine contains, the less sweet it tastes.

MINIMUM OECHSLE LEVELS

Quality Category	Austria	Germany
Tafelwein	63°	44-50°
Landwein	63°	47-55°
Qualitätswein	73°	50-72°
Kabinett	83.5°	67-85°
Spätlese	94°	76-95°
Auslese	105°	83-105°
Beerenauslese	127°	110-128°
Eiswein	127°	110-128°
Ausbruch	138°	N/A
Trockenbeerenauslese	156°	150-154°

HOW TO READ AUSTRIAN WINE LABELS

Country of origin
All Austrian wines, whether domestic or for export, must state *Osterreichischer Wein, Wein aus Osterreich, Osterreich* or a foreign-language equivalent of "Austrian Wine". All bottles carrying such a term are guaranteed by the Austrian government to be made from 100 per cent Austrian-grown grapes.

Grape variety
If included on the label, the wine must be made from at least 85 per cent of the grape variety indicated. In this case it is Blaufränkisch.

Sweetness
The degree of sweetness must also be indicated by *Trocken* or *Suitable for diabetics* (4 grams per litre or less of residual sugar), *Halbtrocken* (5-9 grams per litre), *Halbsüss* (10-18 grams per litre) or *Süss* (higher levels). This example is a *Trocken* (dry) style.

WEIN AUS ÖSTERREICH

1986

BLAUFRÄNKISCH
KABINETT

trocken   12% Alk. Vol.

WEINBAUGEBIET NEUSIEDLER SEE - HÜGELLAND

WEINKELLEREI MOORHOF — ALEX UNGER
7062 ST. MARGARETHEN — BURGENLAND

The vintage
This must be shown on all *Prädikatswein* and guarantees that at least 85 per cent of the wine comes from grapes harvested in the year indicated.

Alcoholic strength by volume
This must be shown on all Austrian wines.

Specific origin
It is permitted to include the name of a wine-growing region, district, village or vineyard on a label, providing that 100 per cent of the wine originates from the specific area indicated. In this case the wine area (*Weinbaugebiet*) is Neusiedler See-Hügelland in the Burgenland region.

Name and address of the dealer, bottler or producer
Obligatory

Quality category
The label must show one of Austria's quality categories. These are similar to those of neighbouring Germany, but some carry different stipulations:
Tafelwein or *Tischwein* The lowest category, this may not be exported. It may well be blended from various regions and may not give any specific area of origin.
Landwein This is *Tafelwein* with a very wide area of origin and may not be exported. Only political regions

such as Niederösterreich, Burgenland or Kartens may be indicated. The wine must have a maximum alcoholic strength of 11.5 per cent and not more than six grams per litre of residual sugar.
Qualitätswein For this category and *Landwein* above, all wines may be exported and only specified grape varieties may be used.
Kabinett Chaptalization is forbidden for this category and above; unlike its German equivalent, an Austrian

Kabinett is not classified as a *Prädikatswein*. This is more logical because a *Prädikatswein* should be a wine that is predicated with a special or super degree of ripeness and *Kabinett* is merely harvested at normal ripeness. (Wines in this category may not contain more than nine grams per litre of residual sugar).
Prädikatswein Apart from *Ausbruch* (see box, below), all *Prädikatswein* possess similar characteristics to their German equivalents and conform to

approximately the same standards, except that the addition of *süssreserve* is not allowed (whereas it is commonly used up to and including *Auslese* in Germany); mechanical harvesting is not allowed except in the case of *Spätlese* or *Eiswein; Spätlese* may not be sold until after March 1 following the harvest, and all other *Prädikatswein* wines may not be sold until after May 1.

Other terms which may also be found on Austrian labels include:

Bergwein A "mountain wine" produced from grapes grown on terraced vineyards or slopes with in excess of 26 per cent incline.
Erzeugerabfüllung Bottled by the producer.

Originalabfüllung Estate-bottled.

Perlwein A *spritzig* wine of between 0.5 and 2 atmospheres pressure and with less than 12 per cent alcohol.

Reid Single-site vineyard, equivalent to the German *lage*.

Schaumwein Fully sparkling wine. Most are made by *cuve close*. Schlumberger Blanc de Blancs (*méthode champenoise*) is the only good-quality Austrian sparkling wine I have tasted.

Weingarten, Weingut Wine estate.

Banderol
The capsule must be sealed over with a red and white sticker bearing the company's registration number. Only very small wine companies and growers may be exempt from this.

AUSBRUCH — A RELIC OF THE AUSTRO-HUNGARIAN EMPIRE

Ausbruch is a still-popular style of wine that harks back to the days of the Austro-Hungarian Empire (and is also still produced in Hungary today). At 138° Oechsle, *Ausbruch* officially falls between the sweetness levels of *Beerenauslese* (127°) and *Trockenbeerenauslese* (150°). In terms of character, however, *Ausbruch* should be totally different from either a *Beerenauslese* or *Trockenbeerenauslese*. The name means "to break up"; the wine is made traditionally from the richest and sweetest botrytized grapes that are so shrivelled and dried-out that to press them is virtually impossible without first moistening the mass (breaking it up) with a more liquescent juice (the regulation stipulates *Spätlese* quality). A true *Ausbruch* is overwhelmed by an intensely raisiny aroma and flavour that may be even more botrytis in character than a *Trockenbeerenauslese*, yet the wine itself need not necessarily be as rich.

An aerial view of some of Austria's most steeply terraced vineyards.

The grapes and wines of Austria

BLAUBURGER

Area planted: *100 ha (247 acres)*

RED A *Blauer Portugieser x Blaufränkisch* cross that produces a well-coloured wine of little distinction, but with a certain capacity to improve in bottle.

- Between 2-5 years

BLAUER BURGUNDER

See Pinot noir.

BLAUER PORTUGIESER

Area planted: *3,090 ha (7,630 acres)*

RED Austria's most widely planted black grape variety accounts for just over five per cent of the vines grown and makes a light-bodied, but well-coloured red wine with a mild flavour.

- Within 1-2 years

BLAUER WILDBACHER

Area planted: *176 ha (435 acres)*

RED/ROSÉ Otherwise known as Schilcher, this traditionally produces a light, dry, crisp and fruity, pale rosé wine.

- Within 1-2 years

BLAUFRÄNKISCH

Area planted: *2,570 ha (6,350 acres)*

RED This variety, known as the Lemberger in Germany and the Kékfrankos in Hungary, is popular in Burgenland, where it produces a tart, fruity wine.

- Between 2-4 years

BOUVIER

Area planted: *607 ha (1,500 acres)*

WHITE An early-ripening table grape that has a low natural acidity and is often used for high-quality *Prädikatswein*.

- QUALITÄTSWEIN: between 1-3 years
- PRÄDIKATSWEIN: between 2-8 years

CABERNET

See Cabernet franc.

CABERNET FRANC

Area planted: *No official statistics*

RED This variety, simply called Cabernet in Austria, is cultivated by Schlumberger at Bad Vosläu in the Thermenregion. Schlumberger uses it in "Privat-Keller", a Cabernet-Merlot blend that is one of Austria's few serious red wines.

- Between 3-5 years

CABERNET SAUVIGNON

Area planted: *No official statistics*

RED A very small amount of this variety is grown by Schlumberger at Bad Vosläu and, in 1982, Lenz Moser received special permission to cultivate 2.5 hectares (6 acres) at Mailberg, the first Cabernet sauvignon in Lower Austria.

The first vintage of Lenz Moser's wine was 1986. The wine is maturing in small casks of new Limousin oak and, when it is released, will probably be Austria's first fine-quality red wine.

- QUALITÄTSWEIN: between 5-6 years
- PRÄDIKATSWEIN: between 10-15 years

CHARDONNAY

Area planted: *50-100 ha (125-250 acres)*

WHITE Traditional Austrian names for this variety include Morillon and Feinburgunder, although more and more wine from this classic grape is being sold by its internationally known name.

A medium-bodied, dry wine of increasingly better quality, it still requires greater varietal intensity; some examples could benefit from a restrained use of new oak.

- Between 2-5 years

FEINBURGUNDER

See Chardonnay.

FRÜHROTER VELTLINER

Area planted: *1,128 ha (2,790 acres)*

WHITE Sometimes labelled as Malvasia, this normally dry, white wine has more alcohol and body than Austria's most widely grown white wine, Grüner Veltliner, but less distinctive character.

- Within 1-2 years

FURMINT

Area planted: *No official statistics*

WHITE This is a rarely encountered Hungarian dry, medium-to-full bodied, rich and fruity varietal that does particularly well at Rust in Burgenland.

- Between 3-5 years

GEWÜRZTRAMINER

Area planted: *870 ha (2,150 acres)*

WHITE Usually labelled Traminer or Roter Traminer, this variety ranges from light and floral to intensely aromatic. The wine may be dry or have one of various shades of sweetness. It makes the fullest, richest and most pungent of *Trockenbeerenauslesen*.

- Between 3-6 years

GOLDBURGER

Area planted: *500 ha (1,235 acres)*

WHITE A *Welschriesling x Orangetraube* cross that produces white wines of a neutral character, used for blending purposes.

- Within 1-3 years

GRAUER BURGUNDER

See Pinot gris.

GRÜNER VELTLINER

Area planted: *19,775 ha (48,865 acres)*

WHITE The Danube is the best area for great Grüner Veltliner, the finest examples of which have a fiery flavour that attacks the palate with a distinctive burning sensation clearly reminiscent of freshly ground pepper. This may not be to everyone's taste, but it certainly is not the ubiquitous, bland *vin ordinaire* produced by this grape in virtually every other wine-growing area of Austria.

- QUALITÄTSWEIN: within 1-4 years
- PRÄDIKATSWEIN: between 3-10 years

JUBLINÄUMSREBE

Area planted: *10 ha (25 acres)*

WHITE Another *Blauer Portugieser x Blaufränkisch* cross, this variety is allowed for *Prädikatswein* only, as its mild character is transformed by botrytis.

- Between 3-7 years

KLEVNER

See Pinot blanc.

MALVASIA

See Frühroter veltliner.

MERLOT

Area planted: *No official statistics*

RED Small amounts are grown in Krems, Mailberg and Furth in Lower Austria, plus in a few scattered plots in Burgenland. This variety has potential in Austria, but is under-exploited.

- QUALITÄTSWEIN: within 1-3 years
- PRÄDIKATSWEIN: between 3-5 years

MORILLON

See Chardonnay.

MÜLLER-THURGAU

Area planted: *5,760 ha (14,230 acres)*

WHITE Often labelled as *Riesling x Silvaner*, this is Austria's second-most prolific grape variety. Austrian exporters should realize the value of Müller-Thurgau for adding fat to their Grüner Veltliners, most of which do not have the bite found in the best examples and lack a depth of fruit. Outside Austria, the international taste is for a less peppery and more fruity style.

The best of Austria's pure varietal Müller-Thurgaus have a fine, spicy character that is superior to the average German version.

- Within 1-2 years

MUSKATELLER

Area planted: *176 ha (435 acres)*

WHITE An under-exploited variety that makes some of Burgenland's finest *Prädikatswein* and excels in the sheltered sites of Styria.

- QUALITÄTSWEIN: within 1-3 years
- PRÄDIKATSWEIN: within 2-10 years

MUSKAT-OTTONEL

Area planted: *1,074 ha (2,654 acres)*

WHITE Less weighty than the Muskateller, this variety has more immediate aromatic appeal and is best drunk when young.

- Between 2-4 years

MUSKAT-SILVANER

See Sauvignon blanc.

NEUBURGER

Area planted: *1,780 ha (4,400 acres)*

WHITE An Austrian variety that excels on chalky soil, producing full-bodied wines with a typically nutty flavour in all categories of sweetness.

- QUALITÄTSWEIN: between 2-4 years
- PRÄDIKATSWEIN: between 3-8 years

PINOT BLANC

Area planted: *1,970 ha (4,870 acres)*

WHITE Often called Klevner or Weisser Burgunder, this produces a fresh, light-bodied, easy-to-drink wine at lower quality levels. In exceptional years it can develop a fine spicy-richness in the upper *Prädikatswein* categories.

- QUALITÄTSWEIN: between 2-4 years
- PRÄDIKATSWEIN: between 3-8 years

PINOT GRIS

Area planted: *420 ha (1,038 acres)*

WHITE More commonly sold as Ruländer or Grauer Burgunder, this grape is a fuller, spicier version of Pinot blanc that has a typical nutty richness.

QUALITÄTSWEIN: between
2-4 years

PRÄDIKATSWEIN: between
3-8 years

PINOT NOIR

Area planted: *352 ha (870 acres)*

RED This is labelled Blauer
Burgunder, Blauer Spätburgunder or
Blauburgunder in different parts of
Austria. It often produces a
disappointing wine, although a few
growers do excel in specific locations.

Between 2-5 years

RIESLING

Area planted: *1,180 ha (2,916
acres)*

WHITE The wine from this grape
should be sold as Weisser riesling or
Rheinriesling, to distinguish it from
Welschriesling. Wachau and Kremser
Riesling can be compared with fine
German examples.

QUALITÄTSWEIN: between
2-6 years

PRÄDIKATSWEIN: between
4-12 years

RIESLING X SILVANER
See Müller-Thurgau.

ROTER TRAMINER
See Gewürztraminer.

ROTER VELTLINER
Area planted: *320 ha (865 acres)*

WHITE A rather neutral wine that is
usually blended into light, dry wines.

Within 1-3 years

ROTGIPFLER

Area planted: *188 ha (790 acres)*

WHITE A robust, full-bodied, spicy
wine of not dissimilar character to the
Zierfandler, that is often made into a
dry style.

Between 3-7 years

RULÄNDER
See Pinot gris.

ST. LAURENT

Area planted: *592 ha (1,463 acres)*

RED A typically Austrian red-wine
variety that has a light, mild, quaffing
character.

Between 2-5 years

SAUVIGNON BLANC

Area planted: *106 ha (1,463 acres)*

WHITE Usually called Muskat-silvaner
(or occasionally Weisser sauvignon),
this variety grown in Styria normally
makes an austere, dry style, but can
really excel at the higher levels of
Prädikatswein.

QUALITÄTSWEIN: between
2-4 years

PRÄDIKATSWEIN: between
4-10 years

SCHEUREBE

Area planted: *300 ha (740 acres)*

WHITE Not too pleasant at
Qualitätswein level, this variety
develops a beautiful aromatic character
at higher levels of *Prädikatswein.*

Between 2-4 years

SCHILCHER
See Blauer wildbacher.

SILVANER

Area planted: *40 ha (99 acres)*

WHITE Seldom seen, tomato-tasting
varietal.

Within 1-2 years

TRAMINER
See Gewürztraminer.

TROLLINGER

Area planted: *No official statistics*

ROSÉ A light, dry, mild and fruity wine.

Within 1-3 years

WEISSER BURGUNDER
See Pinot blanc.

WEISSER SAUVIGNON
See Sauvignon blanc.

WELSCHRIESLING

Area planted: *4,610 ha (11,390
acres)*

WHITE Austria's third-most prolific
variety makes very ordinary dry wines,
but can be rich and stylish at upper
levels of *Prädikatswein.*

QUALITÄTSWEIN: within
1-3 years

PRÄDIKATSWEIN: between
2-8 years

ZIERFANDLER

Area planted: *126 ha (311 acres)*

WHITE Also known as the Spätrot, this
variety is known for its full-bodied and
well-flavoured dry wine. It has good
longevity.

Between 3-7 years

ZWEIGELT

Area planted: *2,756 ha (6,810
acres)*

RED Another typically light, mild and
fruity red-wine variety, this grape is
sometimes called Blauer zweigelt or
Rotburger.

Between 2-5 years

The wine regions of Austria

BURGENLAND

Austria's easternmost region is also
its warmest and consistently
provides overripe grapes, almost
guaranteeing a substantial
production of *Prädikatswein* each
year. The Mittelburgenland and
Südburgenland are Austria's most
important red-wine areas, with black
varieties accounting for some 75
per cent of the vines cultivated.

NEUSIEDLER SEE

These vineyards and those of
Neusiedler See-Hügelland are situated
within the area of influence of the
Neusiedler See, a vast, shallow pan of
water barely two metres (six and one-
half feet) deep. Its unique microclimate regularly produces more
botrytized grapes than any other
wine area in the world.

☆ Villages *Apetlon, Illmitz, Podersdorf*

NEUSIEDLER SEE-HÜGELLAND
See Neusiedler See
☆ Villages *Donnerskirchen, Rust*

MITTELBURGENLAND

This was part of the old Rust-
Neusiedler See district and although it
also produces *Prädikatswein,* it is
physically separated from the
Neusiedler See's influence by the
Sopron wine area of Hungary. The
Mittelburgenland wines are more
passerillage than botrytis in character.
This is, however, a red-wine district,
with some 75 per cent of the
production coming from varieties such
as Blaufränkisch and Zweigelt. The
wines do not possess the body, tannin
and acidity balance normally associated with even modest red wines.

☆ Villages *Deutschkreuz, Horitschon,
Neckenmarkt*

SÜDBURGENLAND

Uninspiring red wines, mainly
Blaufränkisch, but some surprisingly
fine *Prädikatswein* from the modest
Welschriesling.

☆ Eisenberg, Rechnitz

Grüner veltliner 19%,
Blaufränkisch 12%, Müller-
Thurgau 9%, Zweigelt 5%, Muskat-
ottonel 5%, Weissburgunder 5%,
Neuburger 5%, plus Traminer, Riesling,
Goldburger, Chardonnay, Frühroter
veltliner, St. Laurent, Blauer Burgunder,
Blauer Portugieser, Welschriesling

1986, 1987, 1988, 1989, 1990

☆ Paul Achs, Burgenlandischer
Winzerverband, Esterhazy'sche
Schlosskellerei, Gangl, Franz Heiss,
Ladislaus Torok, Klosterkeller
Siegendorf, Alexander Unger, Weinbau
Wilhelm Schröck, Weingut Elfenhof,
Weingut Feiler, Weingut
Heidelbodenhof — Siegfried Tschida,
Weingut Sepp Hold, Weingut
Marienhof, Weingut Romerhof,
Ladislaus und Robert Wenzel,
Winzergenossenschaft St. Martinus

LOWER AUSTRIA or
NIEDERÖSTERREICH

This is Austria's premier dry wine
region, famous for the powerfulness
of its peppery Grüner Veltliners and
the elegance of its Rieslings. Top
Rieslings can be light and airy in
their youth, but they attain a
richness after a few years in bottle
and can achieve a fine, racy balance
comparable to some of the best
German Rieslings. *Kabinett* is the
style that dominates the classic
wines of this region, although
Spätlese and, occasionally, *Auslese*
wines are made in the hottest years.

WACHAU

On a par with Kamtal-Donauland as
Lower Austria's top-performing
district, the Wachau produces many
fine varietals including Grüner
veltliner, the most important, and
Riesling, the best.

☆ Villages *Durnstein, Loiben, Spitz.*

KAMTAL-DONAULAND

As for the Wachau except that, if anything, it produces better Rieslings.

☆ Villages *Krems, Langenlois, Strass*

DONAULAND-CARNUNTUM

An area of historic, rather than intrinsic, importance, the wines are good value, but not top-class. Its winemaking fame extends back to Roman times. It boasts the world's oldest viticultural college at Klosterneuburg, and at Göttelsbrunn a 200-year-old Brauner veltliner vine is to be found. Believed to be the oldest in Europe, it produces an astonishing five hectolitres (55 cases) in a good vintage.

☆ Villages *Kirchberg, Klosterneuburg.*

WEINVIERTEL

This very large area is a combination of two former districts of Retz (which is the hinterland of Kamtal-Donauland) and Falkenstein, a totally separate area north of Vienna. Both areas extend northwards as far as the border with Czechoslovakia. Some red wines are produced, but most are white and although few could be said to have any class, they are very well made, highly drinkable and represent great value for money.

☆ Villages *Falkenstein, Retz*

THERMENREGION

As its name suggests, this is one of Austria's warmest regions. This is an area of both red and white wines, with the Blauer Portugieser and Neuburger dominating. Zierfandler and Rotgipfler are specialities of Gumpoldskirchen, where the grapes ripen to *Spätlese* or *Auslese* levels in most years.

☆ Villages *Bad Vöslau, Gumpoldskirchen*

🍇 Gruner veltliner 45%, Müller-Thurgau 10%, Blauer Portugieser 9%, Zwiegelt 4%, Welschriesling 4%, plus Frührote veltliner, Riesling, Weisser Burgunder, Neuburger, Rotgipfler, Zierfandler, Roter veltliner, St. Laurent, Traminer, Muskat-ottonel, Goldburger, Chardonnay, Blauer Burgunder, Blaufränkisch, Cabernet sauvignon, Cabernet franc, Merlot

🗓 1986, 1987, 1988, 1989, 1990

☆ Abensperg-Traun'sches Schloss-weingut, Deutsch-Ordens-Schloss-kellerei-Lerei Gumpoldskirchen, Freigut Thallern, Domäne Baron Geymüller, Kelleramt Chorherrenstift Klosterneuburg, Lenz Moser, Hof-kellerei des Fürsten von Liechtenstein, Metternich'sche Weingüter, Schloss Gobelsburg, Schlumberger, Karl Schober, Weingut Bründlmayer, Weingut Karl Grabner — Sepp Schierer, Weingut Gunter Haimer, Weingut Franz Hirtzberger, Weingut Josef Jamek, Khevenhüller Metsch'sches Weingut, Weingut Manfred Biegler, Weingut Mantlerhof, Weingut Nikolaihof, Weingut Franz Prager, Weingut Schwamberg, Starhemberg'sches Weingut, Weingut Undhof — Fritz Saloman, R. Zimmermann, Verband Niederöster-reichischen Winzergenossenschaften, Winzergenossenschaft Gumpold-skirchen, Winzergenossenschaft

Krems, Winzergenossenschaft Dinstlgut Loiben, Winzergenossenschaft Wachau

STYRIA or STEIERMARK

Situated in the southeastern corner of Austria, this region's continental climatic influences are challenged by those of the Mediterranean, and high rainfall is interspersed with exceptional levels of sunshine and warmth. The region produces red and very dry white wines and, although few particularly fine-quality wines are encountered, there are many interesting local special-ities. The most famous is *Schilcher*. Made from the obscure Blauer wild-bacher grape, it is a sort of blush-wine that results from the briefest maceration on the grape skins that must cease before fermentation. There are three wine districts:

SÜDSTEIERMARK

The very best wines of this area have Styria's naturally high acidity, but this is combined with delicate and pure fruit flavours, making for exceptional finesse, particularly in varieties such as Gewurztraminer, Chardonnay (known locally as Morillon) and Riesling.

☆ Villages *Arnfels, Leibnitz, Leutschach*

WESTSTEIERMARK

Some 70 per cent *Schilcher* wine, *Zwiebelschilcher* is an onion-skin-coloured *Schilcher* grown on the slopes above Stainz. Another speciality is Sauvignon blanc, known locally as Muskat-Silvaner, a somewhat mystifying synonym since the seeringly dry wines it produces in these vineyards (and elsewhere for that matter) have no hint of either Muskat or Silvaner.

☆ Villages *Stainz*

SÜD-OSTSTEIERMARK

The Müller-Thurgau and Welschriesling are surprisingly successful here and the Gewürztraminer can be the most expressive in Austria.

☆ Villages *Kloch*

🍇 Welschriesling 20%, Müller-Thurgau 19%, Weisser Burgunder 8%, Traminer 5%, plus Blauer

wildbacher, Scheurebe, Blauer zweigelt, Blauburger, Blaufränkisch, Rheinriesling, St. Laurent, Morillon (Chardonnay), Ruländer (Pinot gris), Muskat-Silvaner (Sauvignon blanc), Muskateller, Goldburger

☆ Friedrich Frühwirth, Prinz Liechtenstein'sches Weingut, Schloss Kapfenstein, Schlosskellerei Uhlheim, Rudoph Schuster, Eduard Tscheppe, Weingut Sattlerhof

VIENNA or WIEN

The only capital city in Europe to have its own wine-growing region, most of Vienna's wines are sold by the pitcher as Wiener *Heuriger*, in the city's many bars called *heurigen*. The wine is less than one year old when sold. As much as 28 per cent is blended, but pure varietals of classic grapes are on the increase. There are no inner districts, but there are several wine villages within the city limits, of which the most famous is Grinzling.

🍇 Grüner veltliner 26%, Riesling 8%, Müller-Thurgau 6%, Weisser Burgunder 6%, Zweigelt 4%, plus St. Laurent, Blauer Portugieser, Neuburger and Traminer

🗓 1986, 1987, 1988, 1989, 1990

☆ Diem, Johann Kattus, Martin Kierlinger, Weingut Franz Mayer, Weingut Nussdorf, Schlumberger (Osterreichischer Sekt)

Other wine areas of Austria

KÄRNTEN

The wines of Kärnten are confined to a small area immediately to the west of Weststeiermark (Western Styria), comprising a few vineyards scattered between the towns of Klagenfurt and St. Andrä (not the St. Andrä in Südsteiermark). Red, white, *Schilcher* and *Bergwein* wines are produced and sold by one or two small firms, but the quality of the wines is very modest.

OBERÖSTERREICH

This is a large region to the west of the

Wachau, but with just 85 hectares (210 acres) of vineyards in the vicinity of Linz. To my knowledge, all the wines are sold under the "Weinbauer" brand in a *gasthof* at Hofkirchen.

TIROL

The Zirler Weinhof produces some 135 hectolitres (1,500 cases) of very ordinary wine from just 1.5 hectares (3.7 acres) of Müller-Thurgau, Blauer Portugieser and Zweigelt at Zirl. This might be the last place to plant a vineyard, if not for the fact that it is

conveniently placed on the tourist route to popular Seefeld.

VORARLBERG

The westernmost region of Austria used to boast 100 hectares (247 acres) of vines, but only six (15 acres) exist today, strung out between Bregenz, on Lake Constance (Bodensee), and Frastanz, close to Liechtenstein. The quality is very ordinary, but about half-a-dozen growers sell their wines commercially.

Müller-Thurgau, Grüner veltliner and Blauer Portugieser account for 80 per cent of the grapes grown, with Chasselas, Weisser Burgunder, Bouvier and Blauer Burgunder making up the balance.

Bulgaria

Although the Bulgarians have been cultivating vines for more than 3,000 years, winemaking came to a halt under Turkish Muslim rule between 1396 and 1878. After this it was not until 1918 that winemaking began again in earnest, and only in the 1970s that the Bulgarians made any real effort to export their wines. Since then, however, they have hardly made a mistake in improving, adapting and marketing wines to suit an increasingly sophisticated international market.

DURING THE MID-1970s CABERNET SAUVIGNON was the most fashionable wine grape. At the same time, economic depression meant that wine drinkers were on the lookout for cheaper alternatives to Bordeaux. Cabernet Sauvignon from Bulgaria's Suhindol region was not simply cheap, it was extraordinarily well made, had a deep colour, full body, soft fruit, rich, blackcurrant varietal flavour, and just a hint of wood-aging on the finish. It was almost a computerized assessment of what consumers wanted. Spurred on by the success of this wine, Bulgaria has become the fourth-largest exporter of wines in the world, with State subsidies allowing for attractive prices.

BULGARIA'S WINE LEGISLATION

In 1960, four basic viticultural regions, encompassing 18 micro-regions, were defined by ministerial decree. Between 1960 and 1985 Bulgaria's vineyards trebled in size and now cover 182,105 hectares (450,000 acres). A fifth region, called the Sub-Balkan Region, was established in 1985 and a sophisticated infrastructure of 119 appellations now exists. The Bulgarian Wine Law of July 1978 established three basic levels of wine:

● **Standard Quality**, divided into two categories: Table Wine, which may not indicate an area of origin more specific than that of Bulgaria, and Country Wine, which carries a district appellation.

● **High Quality**, also split into two categories: wines of Declared Geographical Origin or DGOs, which carry sub-regional,

FACTORS AFFECTING TASTE AND QUALITY

 Location
Bulgaria's eastern border is formed by the Black Sea, while its neighbour to the north is Romania, to the west Yugoslavia; those to the south are Greece and Turkey. Most vineyards are concentrated in the valleys of the Danube and Maritsa Rivers.

Climate
The climate is warm continental, although it is cooler in the north and more temperate towards the east due to the influence of the Black Sea. Rainfall averages between 47 and 95 centimetres (19 and 38 inches).

Aspect
Vines are grown largely on the flat valley floors and coastal plains.

Soil
Predominantly fertile alluvium in the valleys, with dark-grey and brown forest soils in the northern region, rich, black carbonate soils in the southern region, becoming sandy in the vineyards of the southeast coastal area.

 Viticulture and vinification
Until 1944, Bulgaria's vineyards were very fragmented, but cooperative farms then formed a cohesive industry that in its infancy decided to cultivate classic French varieties alongside native ones. The average yield per hectare for DGO wines is a very modest 42.5 hectolitres per hectare (190 cases per acre) and the maximum for *Controliran* wines ranges between 27.5 and 45 hectolitres per hectare (124 and 202 cases per acre), depending on the grape variety and origin. *Controliran* and DGO wines aged in wood may be classified as "Reserve". This term guarantees a minimum maturation in wood of four years for red *Controliran* wines, three years for red DGO and white *Controliran* wines, and two years for white DGO wines. Initially, "Reserve" wines must be stored in 200-litre (44-gallon) barrels of Bulgarian or American oak, one-third of which should be new. After the first year they are transferred to 1700-litre (374-gallon) wooden vats made from oak from the Strandja region.

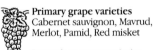 **Primary grape varieties**
Cabernet sauvignon, Mavrud, Merlot, Pamid, Red misket

Secondary grape varieties
Aligoté, Cabernet franc, Chardonnay, Dimiat, Fetjaska, Gamay, Gewürztraminer (Traminer)*, Italianski riesling, Kadarka (Gamza), Muscat (Muskat ottonel), Pinot Gris, Pinot noir, Sylvaner, Rkatsiteli, Rhein riesling, Sauvignon blanc, Shiroka Melnishka loza, Tamianka, Ugni blanc

* Brackets indicate local synonym

BULGARIA

Situated in the centre of the Balkan Peninsula, Bulgaria has an extremely varied landscape, many different soil types and an attractive climate. The Danube forms the natural border with Romania to the north. In the south it is bordered by Greece and Turkey, to the east by the Black Sea, and to the west by Yugoslavia.

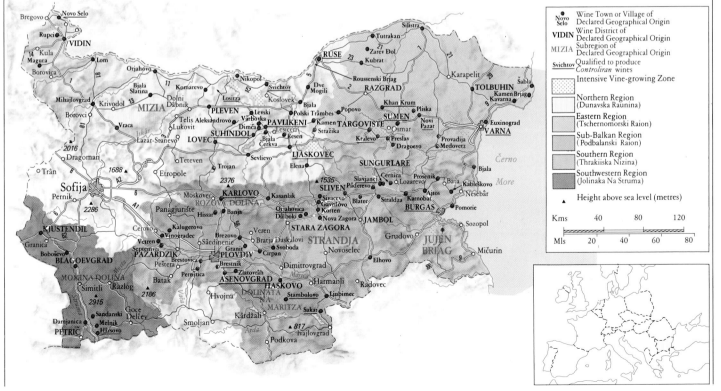

district, town or village appellations, and *Controliran* wines, the highest quality category, which have to be made from specified grape varieties grown in certain DGOs.

● **Special Quality**, which is confined to fortified wines that are seldom seen outside Bulgaria.

HOW TO READ BULGARIAN WINE LABELS

Butiliram To bottle

Bjalo vino White wine

Cherveno vino Red wine

Desertno Dessert or sweet wine

Iskriashto vino Sparkling wine

Kolektziono Reserve

Lozia Vineyard

Lozova prachka Vine or vine variety.

Naturalno Natural

Sladko vino Sweet wine

Sostatachna zakar Semi-dry or medium wine

Suho vino Dry wine

Traditzioni Regionalni Vino Country Wine

Vino Kontrolirano Naimenovanie za Proizhod Controliran wine

Vino ot Deklariran Geografski Wine of declared geographical origin (DGO)

Vinoproizvoditel Wine producer

Vinimpex State commercial enterprise, controlling Bulgaria's entire wine export trade

Bottling Cabernet Sauvignon, above
The Cabernet Sauvignon produced in the state wineries at Suhindol is exceptionally well-made, inexpensive and justifiably popular.

The wines of Bulgaria

NORTHERN REGION (DUNAVSKA RAUNINA)

Controliran wines: *Ljaskovetz Aligoté, Lositza Cabernet Sauvignon, Novo Selo Gamza, Pavlikeni Gamza, Ruse Riverside White, Suhindol Gamza, Svichtov Cabernet Sauvignon*

This region accounts for 35 per cent of Bulgaria's vineyards and encompasses one sub-regional, seven district and 28 town or village DGOs. Suhindol's reputation is based on Bulgaria's best-selling Cabernet Sauvignon, but two others from the district are worth trying; the attractive, grapey-oak Gamza, which is a *Controliran* wine, and the interesting, soft-textured Merlot-Gamza blend, which is of equal quality, but only a DGO. Cabernet Sauvignon from the Svichtov region is so rich and ripe it might be better used to pep-up lesser Cabernets.

🍇 Cabernet sauvignon, Chardonnay, Gamza, Gamay, Muskat ottonel, Pinot noir, Red misket, Rkatsiteli, Sauvignon blanc, Traminer, Vrachanski misket

SOUTHERN REGION (THRAKIISKA NIZINA)

Controliran wines: *Asenovgrad Mavrud, Brestnik Wine,*

Oriahovica Cabernet-Merlot, Sakar Merlot, Stambolovo Merlot

This region accounts for 22 per cent of Bulgaria's vineyards and encompasses two sub-regional, seven district and 25 town or village DGOs. Asenovgrad is justly famous for its dark, plummy, spicy Mavrud wine that can age well for 10 or more years. Plovdiv makes fine, firm, blackcurranty Cabernet Sauvignon as does Stara Zagora, a district that boasts a superb Cabernet Sauvignon-Merlot *Controliran* wine from Oriahovica. Oriahovica also makes a Cabernet Sauvignon Reserve that has a lot of class. From the Strandja region comes Sakar Mountain Cabernet, a wine that has established itself on many export markets as a classic, although it is the Merlot from the region that has *Controliran* status.

🍇 Aligoté, Cabernet sauvignon, Dimiat, Gamay, Mavrud, Merlot, Pamid, Pinot noir, Red misket, Sauvignon blanc

EASTERN REGION (TSCHERNOMORSKI RAION)

Controliran wines: *Khan Krum Gewürztraminer, Kralevo Treasure, Novi Pazar Chardonnay, South Coast (or Jujen Briag) Rosé, Varna Chardonnay*

ESTATE BOTTLED e 70 cl
Bulgarian
Chardonnay

PRESLAV REGION
A fine white wine
Produce of Bulgaria   12% vol
Sole importer in the UK BULGARIAN VINTNERS Co Ltd. London EC1R 3AD

This region accounts for 30 per cent of Bulgaria's vineyards and encompasses one sub-regional, six district and 22 town or village DGOs. The Sumen district is particularly noted for its white wines; its Riesling and Sauvignon are both very commercial and fresh-flavoured, and in recent years there has been a noticeable improvement in the Chardonnays, particularly those from Khan Krum. Although Khan Krum claims *Controliran* status for its Gewürztraminer, outside Bulgaria it is best known for its fine, toasty-oak Chardonnay, a wine that repays keeping for a year or two after purchase. Two other well-known Sumen Chardonnays come from Novi Pazar and Preslav. Although the wines have been disappointing to date, they will improve. The South Coast Rosé is an off-dry Cabernet Sauvignon blush wine from Burgas, an underrated district that produces many inexpensive yet very drinkable Country Wines such as Burgas Aligoté.

🍇 Cabernet sauvignon, Chardonnay, Dimiat, Traminer, Red misket, Rhein riesling, Sauvignon blanc, Tamianka, Ugni blanc, Varneski misket

SOUTHWESTERN REGION (JOLINAKA NA STRUMA)

Controliran wines: *Harsovo Melnik*

This region accounts for six per cent

of Bulgaria's vineyards and encompasses one sub-regional, three district and five town or village DGOs. The most famous wine is Melnik, which is made from the Shiroka Melnishka loza grape. The name means "broad vine of Melnik" and the grape is often simply called "Melnik". The wine itself is generally well-coloured, rich and warm, and may be tannic or soft, depending on how it is made. Damianitza Melnik is very smooth and rich, but I have not tasted the *Controliran* Harsovo Melnik.

🍇 Cabernet sauvignon, Chardonnay, Shiroka Melnishka loza, Tamianka

SUB-BALKAN REGION (PODBALANSKI RAION)

Controliran wines: *Rose Valley (or Rozova Dolina) Misket, Sungurlare Misket*

This region accounts for seven per cent of Bulgaria's vineyards and encompasses one sub-regional, two district and eight town or village DGOs. The Rose Valley Misket is made in the Karlovo district and Sungurlare Misket in Slaviantzi. Both are typical light-golden, floral-scented, musky wines. The first Bulgarian sparkling wine to gain any significant penetration of export markets comes from the Sub-Balkan region. Called "Balkan Crown Brut", it is made by the *cuve close* method from a blend of Chardonnay, Ugni blanc and Riesling, and is at least as good as 95 per cent of the *cuve close* produced in classic winemaking countries such as France and Germany. This surely augurs well for the advent of Bulgarian *méthode champenoise* wines, which are made, but not as yet exported. Pure Chardonnay and Riesling versions are also exported, but I have not tasted them.

🍇 Chardonnay, Red misket, Riesling, Ugni blanc

Czechoslovakia and Hungary

Czechoslovakia exports few wines and, not surprisingly, none has any sort of international reputation, while Hungary is famous for its "Bull's Blood" and Tokay, but little else. Both countries have the potential to achieve much more.

CZECHOSLOVAKIA

THOSE WINES FROM CZECHOSLOVAKIA that are occasionally encountered on export markets are invariably blended brands, which is a pity because the country does produce many fine, fresh and fruity varietal wines, mainly white and in dry and medium styles, that display commercially attractive characteristics.

Of Czechoslovakia's 45,670 hectares (112,850 acres) of vineyards, which annually produce some 2 million hectolitres of wine, more than two-thirds are situated in Slovakia, although the best of these unobtainable wines come from Moravia, where most of the remaining vines are cultivated.

HUNGARY

While Hungary has little – beyond its Tokay – to excite the wine-drinker at present, it has considerable potential, but can only exploit it if and when its winemakers adopt a more innovative attitude. At present most of Hungary's wines are dull and lacking in any individual expression. Only when people want to make something interesting will they, because no matter how great the potential of the *terroir*, lacklustre wines will be made if there is no winemaking imagination or inspiration. Hungary will produce more imaginative wines, I think, because its dabbling with a mixed economy has given rise to a number of increasingly affluent inhabitants since the early 1980s, many of whom have second homes around Lake Balaton. They will make higher demands on Hungary's own wine industry because of their growing experience

of fine wines from other countries. The revolution in the country's wine industry will also be prompted by the high level of its cuisine. Hungary's restaurants are blessed with many creative young chefs who combine the best elements of Hungary's great culinary traditions with their new ideas to excellent effect. Pressure to match its fine food with fine wine will eventually have its effect, benefitting not only fellow countrymen, but also the tourist trade.

The legendary "Bull's Blood" of Eger

The legend of Egri Bikavér – "Bull's Blood" – dates from 1552 when the fortress of Eger, fiercely defended by István Dobó and his Magyars, was besieged by the numerically superior force of the Turkish Army led by Ali Pasha. It is said that, throughout the battle, the Magyars drank copious quantities of the local wine and that when the Turks saw the red-wine stained beards of their ferocious enemies, they ran in terror, thinking that all Magyars gained their strength by drinking the blood of bulls. Hence the name of this wine was born, Egri Bikavér or "Bull's Blood" of Eger. It was never a pretentious wine, but the robust structure and fiery flavour that made it so popular rarely emerges these days.

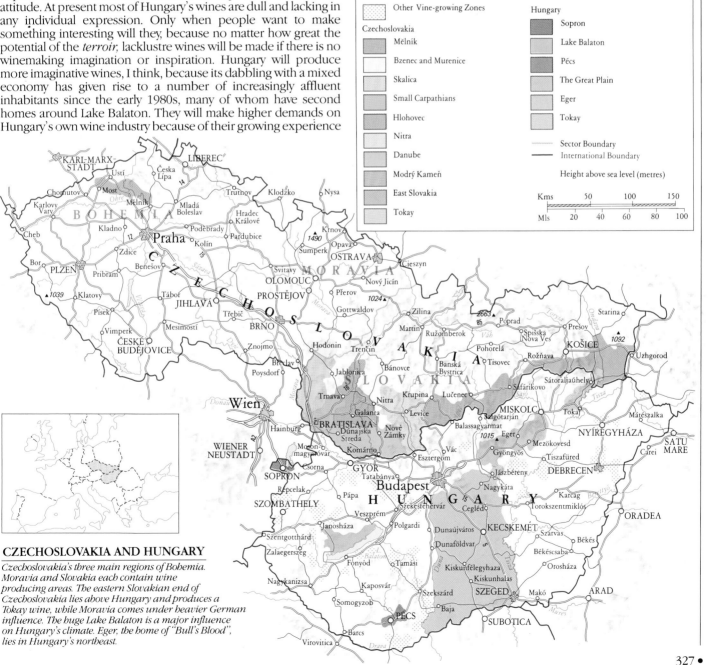

	Other Vine-growing Zones		Hungary
	Czechoslovakia		Sopron
	Mělník		Lake Balaton
	Bzenec and Murenice		Pécs
	Skalica		The Great Plain
	Small Carpathians		Eger
	Hlohovec		Tokay
	Nitra		
	Danube		Sector Boundary
	Modrý Kameň		International Boundary
	East Slovakia		Height above sea level (metres)
	Tokay		

Kms 50 100 150
Mls 20 40 60 80 100

CZECHOSLOVAKIA AND HUNGARY

Czechoslovakia's three main regions of Bohemia, Moravia and Slovakia each contain wine producing areas. The eastern Slovakian end of Czechoslovakia lies above Hungary and produces a Tokay wine, while Moravia comes under heavier German influence. The huge Lake Balaton is a major influence on Hungary's climate. Eger, the home of "Bull's Blood", lies in Hungary's northeast.

Tokay

The most famous Hungarian wine is, of course, Tokay (also spelt Tokaji). The most celebrated wine is Imperial Tokay, or Tokay Aszú Essencia, a drink surrounded by legend – an elixir so prized by the Tsars of Russia that they maintained a detachment of Cossacks solely for the purpose of escorting convoys of the precious liquid from Hungary to the royal cellars at St. Petersburg. Reputed to last at least three hundred years, it must surely have been thought of as an elixir of eternal youth. Until the last war, Fukier, the ancient wine merchants of Warsaw, had 328 bottles of Tokay 1606 but, to my knowledge, none has emerged at auction since 1945. What is sold today as Tokay Aszú and Tokay Aszú Essencia is not the same, but can still be great wine.

How Tokay is made

As with all great sweet wines, Tokay owes its quality and character to semi-dried, extremely rich grapes (Furmint and Hárslevelü) that have been affected by botrytis cinerea, or "noble rot". These shrivelled grapes, called Aszú (prounounced ossu) by the Hungarians, are put into a wooden hod called a *putton* for six to eight days, during which time a highly concentrated juice collects at the bottom of the container. This juice is pure Essencia, in its fermented and matured form the closest thing to the legendary drink of the past. This is made for sweetening purposes, though not sold. Each *putton*, which holds 25 kilograms (50 pounds) of Aszú grapes, yields only a quarter of a pint of pure Essencia. After the Essencia is removed, the *putton* of Aszú grapes is kneaded into paste and added to a 140-litre (30-gallon) cask, called a *gönc*, of dry base wine. This base wine is made from a blend of non-botry-tized Furmint and Hárslevelü grapes (wines labelled Muskotály Aszú will contain 100 per cent Muskotály grapes). The *gönc* is deliberately not filled up, an air-space being left to encourage the oxidized side of Tokay's character. Naturally the sweetness of the wine depends on how many *puttonyos* (plural of *putton*) are added to the dry base wine: today's Tokay Aszú Essencia contains about eight *puttonyos*.

Pure Essencia, the wine of old still made for sweetening, is so rich in sugar it requires a special strain of yeast to ferment and even then it can take many decades to reach five or six per cent of alcohol. I was lucky enough to taste pure Essencia at the state cellars at Tolcsva. It had been fermenting for 13 years, yet had achieved less than two per cent of alcohol! With 640 grams per litre of residual sugar, it poured like oil, but had the most incredible bouquet, like the scent of a fresh rose in full morning bloom. But for the 38 grams per litre of acidity, it would have been like drinking syrup. It was intensely sweet, clean and very grapey.

It is not just Aszú wines that are made in Tokay. Szamorodni, which comes in two styles – dry *(száraz)* and sweet *(édes)* – is a product of the same blend of Furmint and Hárslevelü, but the grapes are seldom botrytized. Three pure varietal Tokay wines – Tokay Furmint, Tokay Hárslevelü and Tokay Muskotályos – are made in *száraz* and *édes* styles.

RESIDUAL SUGAR LEVELS OF TOKAY WINES

Wine style	Residual sugar	Minimum years aging in wood
Száraz	0–4 grams per litre	2
Edes	20–50 grams per litre	2
Aszú 2 *puttonyos**	50–60 grams per litre	4
Aszú 3 *puttonyos*	60–90 grams per litre	5
Aszú 4 *puttonyos*	90–120 grams per litre	6
Aszú 5 *puttonyos*	120–150 grams per litre	7
Aszú 6 *puttonyos*	150–180 grams per litre	8
Azzú *Essencia* (approx 8 *puttonyos*)	200–240 grams per litre	10

* Aszú 2 *puttonyos* is allowed but never made

FACTORS AFFECTING TASTE AND QUALITY

Location
Situated in central Europe, both countries have Austria and Germany to the west, Romania and the USSR to the east, with Poland to the north and Yugoslavia to the south. The largest wine-growing areas are on the plain of the Danube in central Hungary, and in the central southern part of Slovakia and the northern area of Moravia in Czechoslovakia. Hungary's Tokay region is in the northeast of the country, near the borders with the Soviet Union and Czechoslovakia.

Climate
Conditions are warm, dry and fully continental, with the only local variations confined to the tempering effects of altitude, or in the case of central Hungary, the presence of Lake Balaton, which is Europe's largest lake. In the Tokay area of the Carpathian foothills, northeast Hungary, long misty autumns encourage botrytis.

Aspect
The vast majority of vines are grown on the flat or gently undulating river plains in both countries, but the better vineyards are often found on sloping hilly sites, such as those of Somló, north of Lake Balaton.

Soil
The soils of Hungary range from slate, basalt, clay and loess in the west, through the sandy soil of the central Great Plain, to the clay and volcanic rock of the higher northeast, and volcanic, slate and sand soils at Pécs in the south. Loess predominates in the wine-growing areas of Czechoslovakia.

Viticulture and vinification
The most famous wine is Tokay, which necessitates the harvesting of carefully selected botrytized grapes through several *tries*. The production methods of this wine are fully described opposite. Otherwise red and white wines are made by standard vinification techniques in both countries, with no exceptional practices. Technology is quasi-modern, with old and new systems often operating in tandem and nothing that could be described as state-of-the-art in either country. With the exception of Tokay, Czechoslovakia seems to produce cleaner wine from its equipment.

**Grape varieties
Czechoslovakia**
Ezerjó, Gewürztraminer (Traminer), Grüner veltliner, Leányka, Limberger, Müller-Thurgau, Muscat ottonel, Neuberger, Pinot blanc, Pinot gris (Rulander, Rulandské), Pinot noir (Spätburgunder), Portugieser, Rhine riesling (Rýnski rizling), St. Laurent, Sauvignon blanc, Sylvaner (Silván), Welschriesling (Vlasskyrizling, Welschrizling)

Hungary
Ezerjó, Feherburgundi, Furmint, Gewürztraminer (Tramini), Grüner veltliner (Veltlini), Hárslevelü, Kadarka, Kékfrankos, Kéknyelyü, Kovidinka, Leanyka, Merlot (Médoc noir), Mézesfeher, Muskotály, Pinot noir (Nagyburgundi), Szilváni, Szürkebarát, Welschriesling (Olaszrizling)

* Brackets indicate local synonym

Old Tokay in mould-covered casks, above
It is worth travelling to Hungary just to experience the delights hidden in its ancient cellars.

HOW TO READ CZECHOSLOVAKIAN WINE LABELS

Very little information appears on Czechoslovakian labels. Most labels simply state the grape variety, a brand name or the name of a producer. Wines rarely carry a vintage.

Biele víno White wine

Červené víno Red wine

Dezertné korenené víno Aromatized dessert wine

Dezertné víno Dessert wine

Dia Suitable for diabetics (no sugar)

Koospol Ltd State monopoly export company

Odrodové Vína Grape variety

Obsah cukru Sugar content

Polosladké Semi-sweet

Ružové víno Rosé wine

Sladké Sweet

Suché Dry

Šumivé víno Sparkling wine

Vinárskych Závodov Wine producer

Víno Wine

Zvyškovym cukrom Residual sugar

HOW TO READ HUNGARIAN WINE LABELS

Asztali bor Table wine

Aszú Overripe grapes for sweetening Tokay – the equivalent of German Auslese

Borkülönlegessége szölögazdaságának A speciality from the vineyards of the region named

Édes Sweet

Fehér White

Habzó Sparkling

Kímert bor Ordinary wine

Magyar Allami Pincegazdaság Hungarian state cellars

Minösegi bor Top-quality wine

Palackozott Bottled

Szamorodni Literally "as it comes" – the term often refers to Tokay that has not been specially treated with Aszú and is therefore usually dry, though it can be used for other wines.

Száraz Dry

Vörös Red

The wines of Czechoslovakia

Note: Vintages are irrelevant as the wines seldom bear one.

MORAVIA

Vineyards: *14,500 ha (35,800 acres)*

Moravia accounts for one-third of Czechoslovakia's vineyards, with two major areas of production, Hustopěce-Hodonin, on the River Morava, and Znojmo-Mikulov, on the River Dyje, the latter ranking as the country's third most important wine district. There is a high level of winemaking expertise in Moravia and its aromatically fresh, light and varietally elegant wines rank amongst the best in the country. Most are, however, consumed locally, which is a great pity. Sparkling wines are produced in the towns of Mikulov and

Bzenec by both *cuve close* and continuous methods.

Pinot blanc, Rülander, Spät-burgunder, Sauvignon blanc, Traminer

BOHEMIA

Vineyards: *570 ha (1,400 acres)*

This region northeast of Prague accounts for less than 1.25 per cent of Czechoslovakia's vineyards. It is based around Melnik and Velke Zernoseky, with most vines grown on the banks of the rivers Ohře and Labe (which becomes the Elbe in Germany) or their immediate hinterland. The wines have a natural affinity with those of Germany, but are rarely encountered on export markets.

Limberger, Neuberger, Pinot blanc, Pinot noir, Portugieser, Rýnski Silván, Welschrizling

SLOVAKIA

Vineyards: *30,600 ha (75,600 acres)*

This is Czechoslovakia's greatest viticultural region, accounting for two-third's of the country's output, with most wines produced in the Little Carpathians and Nitra districts. Sparkling wines have been made since 1825 at Sered, east of Bratislava in the Danube district and are still marketed under the "Hubert" brand, but quality is not particularly high. Other important wine districts are East Slovakia, Hlohovec-Trnava, Modrý Kaměn, Skalica-Záhorie, and, in part of the

Tokay district that is Czechoslovakian, wines similar to the famous Hungarian version are reputed to be made.

Ezerjó, Grüner veltliner, Leányka, Müller-Thurgau, Muscat ottonel, Rulandské, Rýnski rizling, Silván, Tráminer, Vlásskyrizling

The wines of Hungary

Note: Vintages appear to make little difference to these wines.

EGER

Located halfway between Budapest and Tokay, this region is famous for its Egri Bikavér or "Bull's Blood of Eger". This traditionally unpretentious, robust, Kadarka-based red wine has been notoriously variable in both quality and character since the early 1980s. Other wines include the gold-coloured, medium-sweet Egri Leányka.

Hárslevelü, Kadarka, Leányka, Médoc noir, Olaszrizling

THE GREAT PLAIN

Fresh, flowery, medium-sweet Muscat from Kiskunhalas stands out amid a sea of dull, dry Olaszrizlings.

Ezerjó, Kadarka, Kövidinka, Mézesfeher, Leányka, Olaszrizling

LAKE BALATON

The area surrounding the largest lake in

Europe benefits from the moderating effect the lake has on the climate and thus on the conditions for viticulture, although many of the wines are spoiled by unimaginative winemaking. The most important, Olaszrizling and Furmint, are both made in medium-dry to medium-sweet styles and are, at best, medium quality.

Furmint, Kéknyelyü, Olaszrizling, Szilváni, Szürkebarát

PÉCS

Standard, semi-sweet Olaszrizling and full-flavoured, if rather heavy, Nagyburgundi. The best wines come from Vilány and include dark, spicy Kadarka and greatly improving, but variable-quality Cabernet Sauvignon.

Feherburgundi, Furmint, Kadarka, Nagyburgundi, Olaszrizling

SOPRON

A potentially fine-wine region in the west of Hungary, jutting into Austria's Burgenland. Too much emphasis is given to the light red wines of the

Kékfrankos grape, but the Tramini can be superb in a rich, fat botrytized style.

Kékfrankos, Tramini, Veltelini

TOKAY

There is no hiding the Sherry-like aroma of the great sweet wines of this region, nor would the Hungarians wish to do so because they are very proud of their "unique Tokay character". This aroma builds up, quite predictably, over the first five years, gradually acquiring subtle nuances of caramel, toffee, mint and vanilla, rather than the nuttiness commonly found in a mature Sherry. Tokay assumes an even greater caramel richness between five and

15 years, becoming more "raisiny" in character as the bouquet increases in complexity and the flavour deepens, but the tell-tale Sherry-like hint of acetaldehyde is always noticeable. These developments, although quite spectacular, are how one might expect the maturation of such a wine to proceed. Between 15 and about 30 years little seems to happen, but then a dramatic change occurs. It is as if the acetaldehyde suddenly disappears, to reveal a rejuvenated, outstandingly elegant, very clean wine. Of course, it would be impossible for the acetaldehyde to actually disappear: what really happens is that it is buried beneath an avalanche of many other powerful aromatics that, having built-up for three decades, now suddenly emerge. Any remaining Sherry-like character is transformed and enhanced. A pot-pourri of rose petals, violets and other pure aromas of spring miraculously appear. A Tokay over 30 years of age is an amazingly fresh and beautifully balanced wine: liquorous in texture; full of soft and ripe fruit flavours; and with a lingering finish that has the richness of honey.

Furmint, Hárslevelü, Muskotály

Romania

Viticulturally, Romania has at least as much potential as any other Eastern-bloc country. Tradition in Romania has been balanced by technology, the appreciation of which has enabled the country to keep alive the variety of its wines, but we have been misled about Romania's true potential by the mediocrity of its well-known Banat Riesling.

THE WINEMAKING COLLECTIVES OF THIS COUNTRY care passionately about the individual character of most of the 7.5 million hectolitres (83 million cases) of wine they produce annually, and are committed to establishing the highest levels of quality, demonstrating a true understanding of the criteria for producing wines of an internationally acceptable standard. Yet, strangely, these wines consistently fail to make any impact on export markets. This may be due to a lack of marketing skills and unimaginative importers who opt for the very cheapest wines when, for a few cents more, they could stock a large range of truly expressive wines.

FACTORS AFFECTING TASTE AND QUALITY

Location
The main wine areas spread from Iaşi in the northeast down through the Carpathian foothills to the Danube Valley.

Climate
The climate is continental, with hot summers and cold winters, tempered slightly in the southeast by the Black Sea.

Aspect
Vines are grown on all types of land from plains through the plateau land of Dobrudja to the slopes of the Carpathian foothills.

Soil
A wide variety of soils are planted with vines, including the generally sandy-alluvial plains and stony, hillside soils of Banat,

the limestone of Dobrudja, the oolitic limestone of Mutenia's Pietroasele vineyards, and the stony fringes of the Carpathians.

Viticulture and vinification
The State does not have such a tight control on the winemaking industry in Romania as it does, for example, in Bulgaria. This has enabled wines of greater individuality to be produced.

Grape varieties
Băbească (Băbească neagră), Cabernet sauvignon, Chardonnay, Fetească albă, Fetească neagră, Fetească regală, Galbenă, Gewürztraminer (Traminer), Grasă, Kadarka (Cadarca), Merlot, Muscat ottonel, Mustoasă, Pinot gris, Pinot noir, Riesling, Tămîîoasă, Welschriesling

New vineyards, above
Against a background of gently rolling countryside, an army of recently planted stakes wait to support new vines.

ROMANIA

While the Carpathian Mountains occupy a good deal of Romania, the principal winemaking areas are scattered about randomly, either in the Carpathian foothills, on the plateau lands of Dobrudja, or on the plains. The country's best wines are made in Transylvania.

Legend:
- Vine-growing Zone
- Winemaking Areas
- Transylvania
- Moldavia
- Banat
- Oltenia
- Mutenia
- Dobrudja
- State Boundary
- ▲ Height above sea level (metres)

HOW TO READ ROMANIAN WINE LABELS

Cules la Innobilarea (C.I.B.) Boabelor, equivalent to *Beerenauslese* or above (minimum of 112° Oechsle)

Cules la Maturiate (C.M.D.) Deplina, similar to a high *Spätlese* (minimum 95° Oechsle)

Cules la Maturiate (C.M.I.) Innobilarea, similar to a high *Auslese* (minimum 100° Oechsle)

Dulce Sweet

Edelbeerenlese equivalent to *Beerenauslese* or above (minimum of 112° Oechsle)

Edelreiflese equivalent to *Auslese* or above (minimum of 100° Oechsle)

Imbuteliat Bottled

I.V.V. This stands for Cooperative and should be followed by its name or location.

Pivnită Cellar

Recolta Vintage

Sec Dry

Spumos Sparkling

Strugure Grape

Vie Vine

Viile Vineyard

Vin alb White wine

Vin de masă Table wine

Vinexport Exporting agency of the Government

Vin rose Rosé wine

Vin rosu Red wine

Vin superior Superior wine

Vin usor Light wine

Vollreiflese similar to a high *Spätlese* (minimum 95° Oechsle)

V.S.O. Basic quality wine designation

V.S.O.C. Categorized-quality wine designation similar to Germany's *QmP* and covering *Edelbeerenlese* (*C.I.B.*), *Edelreiflese* (*C.M.I.*) and *Vollreiflese* (*C.M.D.*).

Vine training, above
A rickety appearance belies Romania's sensible use of modern technology.

The wines of Romania

BANAT

Wine districts: *Minis, Recas-Tirol, Teremia*

This region is in the east of the country, close to the border with Yugoslavia and Hungary. The sandy plain of the Teremia district is best known for its large production of eminently drinkable white wines, while the hilly Minis area provides excellent, inexpensive reds from the Cardarca, Pinot noir, Cabernet and Merlot grapes, grown on stony terraces. The mountain slopes of Recas-Tirol produce "Valea Lunga", a pleasant, light-bodied, red wine.

Cabernet sauvignon, Fetească regală, Cadarca, Merlot, Mustoasă, Pinot noir, Riesling

DOBRUDJA

Wine districts: *Murfatlar, Saricia-Niculitel*

Murfatlar is the most important and most ancient winemaking district in Dobrudja, with well-organized vineyards on hills close to the Black Sea and an experimental state research station that has introduced many classic western varieties. Once reliant on its prestigious past, the wines used to be too old, oxidized and heavy, but

they are now clean and well balanced, with the lovely, late-harvested, softly sweet and stylish Gewürztraminer a good example of this new style.

Cabernet sauvignon, Chardonnay, Gewürztraminer, Muscat ottonel, Pinot gris, Pinot noir, Riesling

MOLDAVIA

Wine districts: *Cotnari, Dealurile-Moldovei, Odobesti (sub-districts: Cotesti, Nicoresti), Tecuci-Galati*

The vineyards of Odobesti surrounding the industrial town of Focsani produce large quantities of rather ordinary red and white wine. There are, however, exceptions in this district due to the diversity of soils. Cotesti, for example, has a good reputation for Pinot noir and Merlot, while Nicoresti is known for its full-coloured, spicy, red wine produced from the Băbească grape. The vineyards of Cotnari, near Iaşi are the most famous in Romania; their reputation dates back to the fifteenth century. The wine produced is a rich dessert wine, not unlike Tokay but rather less intense and not as complex. The Bucium hills of Visan and Doi Peri overlook the city of Iaşi and the cool climatic conditions are reflected in Cabernet Sauvignon wines that have crisp, leafy characteristics.

Băbească, Cabernet sauvignon, Fetească albă, Fetească neagră, Grasă, Merlot, Pinot noir, Welschriesling

MUTENIA

Wine districts: *Dealul Mare (sub-district: Pietroasele)*

North of Bucharest is the Dealul Mare district, which stretches across the

lower, southeast-facing slopes of the Carpathian Mountains, and is famous for its red wines, "Valea Calugareasca", or "Valley of the Monks" and "Tohani".

There is a small area of chalky soil within this district that has a special microclimate best suited to the production of sweet white wines with fine balancing acidity, and it is here that the prestigious vineyards of Pietroasele are situated. The area's Tămîîoasă or "frankincense" grape is a Muscat-related variety that makes a lusciously sweet, gold-coloured wine of very expressive quality. One of the most remarkable Romanian wines I have tasted was a beautiful, botrytized "Rosé *Edelbeerenlese*" version of the normally lacklustre Fetească neagră grape.

Băbească neagră, Cabernet sauvignon, Fetească neagră, Fetească regală, Galbenă, Merlot, Pinot gris, Pinot noir, Riesling, Tămîîoasă

OLTENIA

Wine districts: *Arges-Stefănesti, Drăgăsani, Drobeta-Turnu, Severin, Segarcea*

The town of Simburesti in the Drăgăsani district produces Oltenia's best reds. This station, which sells its wines on the open market, has a reputation for a full, dry red wine from the Fetească neagră grape, as well as the Cabernet sauvignon, which is appreciated throughout Romania. Interesting, sweet wines are found on the west side of the River Oltul. Arges-Stefănesti vineyards are planted close to the River Arges and produce mainly white wines. Segarcea is a red-wine district south of the city of Craiova. The Pinot noir is good here, although not as well known as the Cabernet sauvignon.

Cabernet sauvignon, Fetească neagră, Fetească regală, Muscat ottonel, Pinot noir, Riesling, Sauvignon, Tămîîoasă

TRANSYLVANIA

Wine districts: *Alba Iulia-Aiud, Bistrita-Năsăud, Tirnave (Trnave)*

Of all the wine-growing regions of Romania, Transylvania is perhaps the most exciting. The crisp fruit and good acidity of its white wines is somewhere between the style of Alsace and South Tyrol. The steep, sloping Tirnave vineyards lie between the two Tirnave rivers, where they produce good-quality white wines with more than a hint of Germanic style and delicacy. Not surprisingly, German settlers introduced many of their own grape varieties. The native Fetească grape is also successful in this area.

Fetească albă, Fetească regală, Muscat ottonel, Pinot gris, Riesling, Sauvignon blanc, Traminer, Welschriesling

Yugoslavia

In the 1960s and early 1970s, the ubiquitous Yugoslav Laški Riesling was the first stepping-stone for young wine-drinkers, who tended to progress to Liebfraumilch, eventually aspiring to the sophisticated heights of Mateus Rosé. If it all seems a bit *passé* now, this has not filtered back to Ljubljana, where they blithely continue to make the same mediocre wines, ignoring their beautiful country's potential for fine-quality wines.

TRADITIONALLY, IT IS THE FERTILE LOWLANDS of Vojvodina and Serbia in the east, where the vineyards drain into the mighty Danube, that have provided most of Yugoslavia's wine. The steeper slopes of Slovenia in the north, where the climate is cooler than anywhere else in the country, bar the as-yet uncultivated highlands of Yugoslavia's coastal mountain range, have always produced the country's finest wines. Yugoslavia has absorbed migrants from Croatia to the south, Italy, Romania and Hungary to the east, and Austria to the north. In turn, French and German traders travelling up the Danube have spilled out into Croatia, Dalmatia, Serbia and beyond. Through these ethnic influences, the vineyards of Yugoslavia have been filled with such diverse grape varieties as Cabernet sauvignon, Merlot and Sémillon from France; Grüner veltliner from Austria; Barbera, Refosco and Gewürztraminer (via Austria) from Italy; Kadarka and Furmint from Hungary; and Blatina, Plavać mali, Zilavka and others from Bulgaria.

HOW TO READ YUGOSLAVIAN WINE LABELS

Bijelo vino White wine	*Proizvedeno u viastitoj vinariji poljoprivredne zadruge...* Made in the cellars of the cooperative named...
Biser vino Sparkling wine	
Crno vino Red wine	
Čuveno vino Selected wine	*Punjeno u...* Bottled at...
Desertno vino Dessert wine	*Ružica vino* Rosé wine
Kvalitetno vino Quality wine	*Slatko* Sweet
Polsubo Medium-dry	*Stolno vino* Table wine
Prirodno Natural	*Suho* Dry
Proizvedeno u vinariji... Produced at...	*Visokokvalitetno* High quality

FACTORS AFFECTING TASTE AND QUALITY

Location
Vines are grown throughout the coastal plain and nearby islands in the west and in eastern inland areas. They stretch from the northernmost parts of the country to the Greek border in the south.

Climate
The warm Mediterranean climate of coastal Yugoslavia becomes progressively hotter further south, while continental influences become more dominant inland, where the cooler northern districts favour white wine production.

Aspect
Vineyard sites vary from tiny patches on small, rocky islands, through the largely flat valley plains of the southern and eastern inland areas, to the hillsides in northeast Yugoslavia.

Soil
Fine, sandy loess with limestone dominates the soils of the southeastern and central valleys where over half of Yugoslavia's wines are produced. Its finest white wines are made from vines grown on the lime and marl soils of Slovenia in the north. The coastal vineyards contain very rocky soils over limestone, with those of coastal Slovenia marked by their *terra rossa* soils.

Viticulture and vinification
In the early 1960s, this was the first East-European country to modernize its wine industry and aggressively market its products abroad. Since Tito's death, however, progressive attitudes in the wine trade have been replaced by more apathetic ones and, whereas the country remains capable of an acceptable standard of wine, the styles produced are not fulfilling this potential.

Grape varieties
Babić, Banat riesling (Kreaca), Barbera, Blatina, Bogdanuša, Cabernet franc (Cabernet), Cabernet sauvignon, Debit-Grk, Dobričić, Ezerjó, Furmint (Sipon), Gamay, Gewürztraminer (Traminac, Traminer), Grenache, Kadarka, Kratošija, Krstač, Kujundžuša, Malvasia (Malvazija), Maraština, Merlot, Mondeuse noire (Teran), Pinot blanc, Pinot noir, Plavać mali, Plemenka, Plovdina, Prokupac, Refosco (Refško), Ribolla gialla (Rebula), Riesling, Sauvignon blanc, Sémillon (Semijon), Smederevka, Silvaner (Sylvaner), Tocai (Tokay), Trebjac, Vranac, Vugava, Welschriesling (Banatski rizling, Kreaca, Graševina, Vraski rizling), Zilavka, Zlahtina.
Note: Varieties in brackets are local synonyms.

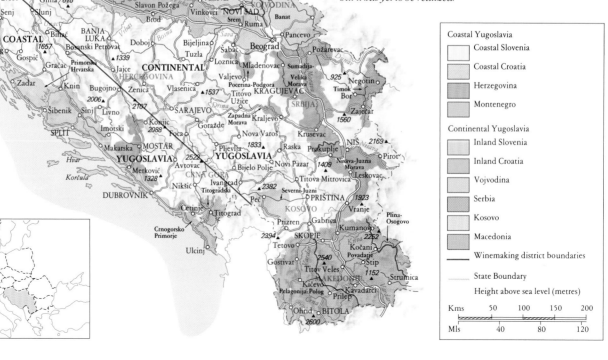

YUGOSLAVIA

The regions in the north of the country, Slovenia and Croatia, produce the finest wines. Elsewhere there is certainly potential, but it has yet to be realized.

Coastal Yugoslavia
- Coastal Slovenia
- Coastal Croatia
- Herzegovina
- Montenegro

Continental Yugoslavia
- Inland Slovenia
- Inland Croatia
- Vojvodina
- Serbia
- Kosovo
- Macedonia

— Winemaking district boundaries
— State Boundary
Height above sea level (metres)

Kms 50 100 150 200
Mls 40 80 120

LOST OPPORTUNITIES AND UNFULFILLED POTENTIAL

With such a variety of climatic, topographic, ampelographic and solumologic conditions worked by an ethnic mix of people armed with French and German expertise, Tito saw a great potential for his country's wine industry. In the immediate post-war period he implemented a programme of viticultural reconstruction and initiated the building of fifty modern wineries, strategically situated throughout the wine-producing areas. By the 1960s Yugoslavia boasted one of the most modern and efficient wine industries in Europe. Sadly this impetus was lost in the 1970s, when the time was opportune for Yugoslavia to instigate an appellation system that would simplify its jumble of generic, geographic, varietal and branded wine names.

Across the board, Yugoslav wines are more successful than those of Greece, and certainly a lot less oxidized, but they should be far better. One-fifth of Greek vineyards are potentially capable of producing fine wine, as and when the producers become quality-conscious, but at least three times as many Yugoslav vineyards have the same potential. If only the industry could shake itself free of its lethargy and rekindle the spark of innovation it had in the heyday of Tito, it could be producing a sparkling range of crisp, refreshing white wines and soft, fruity reds, including plenty of top-quality products.

The wines of Coastal Yugoslavia

COASTAL CROATIA

Winegrowing district: *Primorska Hrvatska*
Vineyards: 33,000 ha (81,540 acres)

It is the black Plavać mali grape that makes the finest wines in this region. The best-known wine is Dingač, grown on the Pelješac peninsula. This deep-coloured, full-bodied red wine was the first Yugoslav appellation to be protected by law. Other wines made from Plavać mali include Postup, also from Pelješac, Faros, from Hvar island, and Bolski Plavać from Brač island.

The most commonly encountered wine on the Istrian Peninsula, the oldest vinegrowing region of Yugoslavia, is Motovunski Teran, a light-red wine.

Babić, Bogdanuša, Debit-Grk, Dobričić, Malvazija, Merlot, Plavać mali, Teran, Trebjac, Vranac, Vugava, Zlahtina

COASTAL SLOVENIA

Winegrowing district: *Primorska Slovenija*
Vineyards: 5,000 ha (12,355 acres)

This region is in the south of Slovenia, close to the Italian border. The climate is of mild Mediterranean type, except in Vipara and Briški Okoliš, both of which come under the moderating influence of the Alps. This is hilly country, with plateaux and valleys crammed between the Alps and the coastal mountains. Of local repute is Kraški Teran, a ruby-coloured wine.

Barbera, Cabernet sauvignon, Merlot, Rebula, Teran, Tocai

HERZEGOVINA (HERCEGOVINA)

Vineyards: 5,000 ha (12,355 acres)

Situated in the southern part of the Central Balkans, Herzegovina's climate and rocky soil have favoured two varietal wines, Zilavka, a white wine, and Blatina, a red wine.

Blatina, Kujundžuša, Smederveka, Vranac, Zilavka

MONTENEGRO (CRNA GORA)

Winegrowing districts: *Crnogorsko, Titogradski, Primorje*
Vineyards: 2,500 ha (6,180 acres)

The best-known vineyards of this region are those of Crnogorsko on the terraced southern slopes of Lake Skadar. In the nineteenth century, this wine was called Crmničko Crno and was made from Vranac and Kratošija grapes, and was expensive. Today it is made entirely from Vranac grapes, is known as Crnogorski Vranac and fetches a far more modest price.

Kratošija, Krstač, Vranac

The wines of Continental Yugoslavia

INLAND CROATIA

Winegrowing district: *Kontinentalna Hrvatska*
Vineyards: 38,000 ha (93,900 acre)

This region boasts a fine amphitheatre of terraced vineyards set amid gently undulating landscape. The Kutjevačka Graševina is a pale-straw-coloured wine from the Kutjevo. It has a hint of youthful green and the fruity aroma of ripe grapes. Interesting Traminer, Muscat Ottonel and Pinot Blanc are also produced and the best come from the slopes of Baranja.

Traminer, Muscat ottonel, Pinot blanc, Pinot noir, Riesling, Sauvignon blanc, Sylvaner, Graševina

MACEDONIA

Winegrowing districts: *Povadarje, Plina-Osogovo, Pelagonija-Polog*
Vineyards: 30,000 ha (74,130 acres)

Phylloxera, which devastated European vineyards in the late-nineteenth century, did not reach Macedonia until 1912. During the European scourge, the French and Germans drank Macedonian wines as a substitute and the habit has survived, particularly in Germany. Most popular is Kratošija, a deep-coloured red wine made from native Vranac and Kratošija varieties. It has a distinctive taste and aroma, full body and a smooth flavour. It is bottled in its second year, when the bouquet is at its fullest, and is best drunk immediately.

Grenache, Kratošija, Plovdina, Prokupac, Vranac

KOSOVO

Winegrowing districts: *Severni, Juzni*
Vineyards: 3,000 ha (7,410 acres)

This small region produces Amselfelder Kosovsko Vino, the result of successful cooperation between Yugoslav producers and German marketeers.

The Amsfelder Kosovsko wines are mostly red and come in dry and semi-sweet styles, with dry white and rosé accounting for just 10 per cent each and very small amounts of dry red Cabernet franc and Spätburgunder.

Cabernet franc, Gamay, Pinot noir, Riesling

SERBIA (SRBIJA)

Winegrowing districts: *Sumadija-Velika Morava, Nišava-Južna Morava, Pocerina-Podgora, Timok, Zapadna Morava*
Vineyards: 72,000 ha (177,910 acres)

This is the largest vinegrowing region in Yugoslavia, and Sumadija-Velika Morava is easily the largest district with some 28,000 hectares (69,190 acres).

The vineyards around Župa have the best reputation in Serbia. Prokupac is the leading grape variety, and is used to make Županska Ružica, a light-bodied, dry rosé. A Pinot Noir and Gamay blend is also produced. The Smederevka is said to originate from Smederevo, southeast of Belgrade, where it accounts for 90 per cent of grapes grown and makes mild, fruity, medium-sweet white wines.

Gamay, Pinot noir, Plemenka, Plovdina, Prokupac, Riesling, Smederevka

INLAND SLOVENIA (KONTINENTALNA SLOVENIJA)

Winegrowing districts: *Podravina, Posavina*
Vineyards: 19,000 ha (46,950 acres)

This region produces the best Yugoslavian white wines from steep, hilly, vine-clad slopes that are on the same latitude as central France. By far the most famous wines come from Lutomer. While the medium-sweet Lutomer Welschriesling (formerly Lutomer Laški Riesling), is ubiquitous, and the best-known Yugoslav wine on international markets, other varieties offer more interest. Lutomer Gewürztraminer, for example, provides a pleasant, spicy edge to its popular medium-sweet style, while Lutomer Sauvignon Blanc is in the dry mould, with fine, crisp and fruity varietal character, providing it is drunk as young as possible. Lutomer Cabernet Sauvignon can be as good as the better-known Bulgarian versions.

Cabernet sauvignon, Sipon, Traminer, Pinot blanc, Rhine Riesling, Sauvignon blanc, Welschriesling

VOIVODINA (VOJVODINA)

Winegrowing districts: *Banat, Srem Subotica, Pescara*
Vineyards: 23,000 ha (56,830 acres)

The Welschriesling is called the Kreaca here and sold as Banatski Rizling. These are fruity wines similar to those of Lutomer – honest, but far from exciting, with Traminer again making a far more interesting alternative and the soft, fruity Merlot a good buy for red-wine drinkers.

Ezerjó, Traminer, Kadarka, Merlot, Rhine riesling, Sauvignon blanc, Sémillon, Graševina, Kreaca, Vraski rizling

The USSR

With an annual production of some 40 million hectolitres (445 million cases), the USSR is now the third-largest wine-producing country in the world, just ahead of Spain.

THE OCCASIONAL CRIMEAN RED AND "KRIM" sparkling wines had surfaced on export markets, but it was not until the mid-1980s that the USSR decided to market a limited range of wines on an international basis. As yet the wines are not acceptable by western standards, and there is little or no perception of the quality criteria for sophisticated wine drinkers.

THE USSR'S WINE EXPORTS

The USSR's half-hearted export efforts can be understood in the context of a country that consumes more wine than it actually produces, especially in view of the government policy of encouraging its people to drink even more wine. The government is promoting wine because the excessive consumption of vodka is a very serious problem in the USSR.

The expansion of its vineyards has rapidly made the USSR the second-largest vine-growing country in the world, and it is set to be the largest by the mid-1990s, when it can look forward to taking a more active role in exporting its products. Its modest move into the international market in the mid-1980s can therefore be seen as part of a Soviet 10-year-plan to acquaint us with some of its unfamiliar terminology. It can also be seen as a period of adjustment for the USSR. A decade is certainly not too long for what will be the world's largest wine industry to come to grips with the needs of a quality-based market. There is much to learn, as can be gleaned from the 1986 harvest in Georgia, where officials declared the vintage to be so good that only grapes with a minimum of 19 per cent potential alcohol could be accepted for the production of wine. This was done in the name of "Perestroika" to raise the quality to international standards! But what will be required, however, is the spirit of "Glasnost" – to effect a cultural exchange with oenologists in countries such as France and Australia, who can provide the benefit of their experience in advising on the numerous traditional and modern approaches that can achieve premium-quality products.

FACTORS AFFECTING TASTE AND QUALITY

Location
Vines are grown in the south-western states of the USSR, fanning out from the northern and eastern shores of the Black Sea, and stretching to the western and northwestern coastal areas of the Caspian Sea. Viticultural developments in the Central Asian Republics of Uzbekistan, Tadzhikistan and Kirgiz have also been reported.

Climate
The USSR's climate is something of an obstacle to vinegrowing. Throughout the vinegrowing area, the winters are generally very cold, often − 30°C (− 22°F) and the summers very hot and dry. If it were not for the tempering effect of the Black and Caspian Seas, climatic conditions would probably make it impossible for viticulture. Georgia, protected by the Caucasus Mountains, enjoys a favourable microclimate.

Aspect
Most of the vines are grown on flat or gently sloping coastal and valley land, but some hilly areas are planted, for example around Simferopol in the Crimea.

Soil
Virtually the complete range of soils is encountered in the USSR.

Viticulture and vinification
In many regions, vines have to be buried in the earth to survive the bitterly cold winters. As viticulture has increased fourfold since 1950, so has efficiency, but the emphasis has been on quantity rather than quality.

In the mid-1950s, a system that has become known as the "Russian Continuous Flow Method" was developed for producing sparkling wine cheaply, easily and quickly by a natural second fermentation. Base wine is fed under pressure into a series of large, specialized, stainless-steel tanks. This meets a continuous feed of sugar and yeast, slowly passing through various filtering, fining, pasteurizing and stabilizing tanks to emerge, three weeks later, with bubbles onto a bottling line that operates continuously.

Grape varieties
Aleatico (Aleatika), Alexandreuli, Aligoté, Bastardo, Bayan shirei, Cabernet franc (Caberne, Cabernet), Cabernet sauvignon (Caberne sovinyon), Chardonnay, Chilar, Chinuri, Ekim kara, Fetiaska (Fetjasko, Fetjaska), Furmint, Goruli, Grasnostok zolotovskij, Gurdzhaani, Machuli-Tetra, Magarach, Malbec, Matrassa, Merlot, Mtsvane, Mudzhuretuli, Muscadine (white and pink), Muscat (Muscatel), Ochshaleschi (Adzhaleschi), Pinot blanc, Pinot gris (Grey pinot), Pinot noir, Plechistik, Riesling (Rhein riesling, Risling, Rizling), Rkatsiteli, Sary pandas, Saperavi, Sercial (Sersial), Sylvaner (Silvaner), Tasitska, Tavkveri, Tsimlyansky (Tsimljanskoje), Tsinandali, Tsolikouri, Verdello (Vardeljo, Verdels), Voskeat, Welschriesling (Italianskirizling)

THE USSR

The wine regions of the USSR form an arc around the Black Sea. Spreading eastwards, they also reach the Caspian's shores.

Vine-growing Zone
Moldavia
Ukraine
Russia
Georgia
Armenia
Azerbaijan
– – – International Boundary
——— State Boundary
▲ Height above sea level (metres)

Kms 100 200 300 400 500
Mls 100 200 300

Dessert winemaking, Krym (Crimea), right
Rows of large wooden barrels undergo inspection at a "Madeira" winery.

The wines of the USSR

ARMENIA

This mountainous republic south of Georgia specializes in high-strength, red table wines and, from Muscadine and Saperavi grapes cultivated in the Ararat region, strong dessert wines. In the Echmiadzin region, wineries produce fine, high-strength wines of "Madeira", "Port" and "Sherry" types from such grape varieties as Chilar, Sersial, Vardeljo and Voskeat; white and pink Muscadine are used to make dessert wines. "Echmiadzin" are reputed to be the best white table wines, "Norashen" the best reds.

Chilar, Muscadine, Muscatel, Sersial, Vardeljo, Voskeat

AZERBAIJAN

East of Armenia, Azerbaijan's largest wine-growing zone spreads over from Kirovabad to Akstafa. Wines are produced from local grape varieties such as Bayan shirei, Tavkveri and others. The best-known table wines of Azerbaijan are "Sadilly", dry white wines and "Matrassa", soft, spicy, red wines. "Akstafa" and "Alabashly" are both high-strength, "Port" types and various dessert wines of local repute include "Mil", "Shamakhy", "Kjurdamir" and "Kara-Chanakh".

Bayan shirei, Matrassa, Tavkveri

KAZAKHSTAN

This state is situated on the northeastern shores of the Caspian Sea, well to the north of the rest of the USSR's wine regions. This area has a certain fame for its "Ak-Bulak", "Kazakhstan", "Kyzyl-Tan" and "Violet Muscatel" dessert wines. The still white wines include Riesling "Issyk" and "Chilikskoje".

GEORGIA

With numerous valleys, each with their own different, but favourable, micro-climates, this state is the largest, oldest and most traditional of Russia's wine regions. About 1,000 different grape varieties are grown in Georgia. Tsinandali is a white grape that grows on the right bank of the Alasan valley in Kakhetia, the southeastern region of the main Caucasian range. Its wines are dry and often blended with those of Mtsavane and Rkatsiteli grapes. After a long fermentation, the wine is matured in oak casks for three years and bottled in the fourth.

The Gurdzhaani grape, which is grown in the same area as the Tsinandali, makes wines that are light gold in colour with a unique, subtle, bitter taste.

"Mukuzani", wines made from the Saperavi grape, are a dark ruby colour, with a powerful bouquet and a smooth taste. Those originating from Kakhetia are very tannic. "Napareuli" wines are also made from the Saperavi grape, grown on the left bank of the Alasan valley, but are much lighter in body than the "Mukuzani". Both are matured for three years and bottled in the fourth. "Akhasheni", made from the Saperavi grape, are semi-sweet, full-bodied wines that are the colour of a dark pomegranate. "Ochschaleschi" are dark red, semi-sweet wines. "Khvanchkara" wines are grown on the southern slopes of the Rioni gorge and made from a blend of Alexandreuli and Mudzhuretuli grapes. They have a very strong bouquet and are semi-sweet in taste with a raspberry flavour. Local sparkling wines are made by the *méthode champenoise* from Chinuri, Goruli, Mtsvane and Tasitska grapes.

1,000 grape varieties are grown in Georgia, but the most important are Saperavi, Tsinandali, Gurdzhaani, Tsolikouri, Chinuri, Murkhranuli and Tasitska

MOLDAVIA

The southern and central regions of the Moldavian republic specialize in making white table wines and sparkling wines. The same regions are also known for dessert and high-strength wines. Of particular note is "Negru de Purkar", a deep-coloured, firm-structured, red-wine blend of Cabernet and Saperavi. Red table wines are mostly made in the south.

Aligoté, Cabernet, Fetjaska, Furmint, Malbec, Merlot, Muscadine, Pinot blanc, Grey pinot, Pinot noir, Rkatsiteli, Rhine riesling, Saperavi

RUSSIA

Wine districts: *Checheno-Ingush, Dagestan, Krasnodar, Rostov-na-Donu, Stavropol*

This state concentrates on white wines and sparkling wines in the north and west, and red in the south and east.

Krasnodar's most reputable vineyards are on southwest-facing coastal slopes overlooking the Black Sea. Abrau is known for its dry Rizling, Caberne and sweet sparkling wines. Anapa, just along the coast to the north, also makes Rizling, while down the coast at Gelendzhik, Aligoté is the local speciality.

To the east of Krasnodar and north of the Caucasus, Stavropol is known for its dry Rizling and Silvaner, as well as the strong dessert wines, Muscatel Praskoveiski. Other dessert wines are the spicy "Mountain Flower".

Rostov-na-Donu, located around the confluence of the rivers Don and Kan and Taganrogskiy Zaliv estuary, is famous for its rich "Ruby of the Don" dessert wines. Plechistik is a grape used to give backbone to Tsimlyansky (which is a place in Rostov-Don, a grape and a wine – red or sparkling red, white or rosé!) and, throughout the state, also makes decent, dry red wines.

On the east-facing slopes of the Caucasus Mountains, overlooking the Caspian Sea, are the vineyards of the republic of Dagestan. This is a black-grape area that is known for the full body and flavour of its dry red wines, with the best coming from Derbent in the south of the region.

Checheno-Ingush is another republic with vineyards on the Caucasus, but these are found inland, along its northern slopes, to the southeast of Stavropol. Most of the wines produced in this area are of the "Port"-type.

Aligoté, Caberne, Muscatel, Grey pinot, Pinot noir, Plechistik, Pukhljakovsky, Rizling, Rkatsiteli, Silvaner, Tsimlyansky

UKRAINE

Wine districts: *Krym (Crimea), Nikolayev-Kherson, Odessa*

The state's wine industry is mainly concerned with producing still white wines, although red, and white sparkling wines are also produced in the Crimea and, as with every wine region in the USSR, dessert wines are always a local speciality.

Krym (Crimea) is the famous peninsula that encloses the Sea of Azov. It was here, in the villages of Alushta and Sudak, that L. S. Golitsin made the first Russian sparkling wine in 1799. Sparkling "Krim" is a *méthode champenoise* wine made in five styles, from *Brut* through to Sweet, and in a semi-sweet red version. The grapes used include Chardonnay, Pinot noir, Rizling, Aligoté and Caberne. The wines are coarse and the old-fashioned addition of brandy does not help, but the *Brut* and *Demi-Sec* Red are widely available in export markets and sell on novelty value. The "Ruby of Crimea", which is a blend of Saperavi, Matrassa, Aleatika, Caberne and Malbec, is a robust, rustic, full-bodied red that is quite commonly encountered in various countries.

Nikolayev-Kherson, just northeast of Krym, and Odessa, near the Moldavia state border, produce various white, sparkling and dessert wines. The best-known local wines are "Perlina Stepu", "Tropjanda Zakarpatja" and "Oksamit of Ukraine".

Aleatika, Aligoté, Bastardo, Caberne, Chardonnay, Chorny doktor, Ekim kara, Fetjasko, Magarach, Malbec, Matrassa, Muscadine, Muscatel, Grey pinot, Riesling, Rkatsiteli, Sary pandas, Sersial, Solnechnaya dolina, Saperavi, Verdels

Greece

Between the thirteenth and eleventh centuries BC, long before a single vine existed in what are now the most famous wine regions of the world, Greek viticulture was at its peak and, together with wheat and olives, was of fundamental importance to the economy.

THE CLASSIC WINES OF ANCIENT GREECE were great wines indeed, relative to their era, and worthy of note in the writings of Hippocrates, Homer, Plato, Pliny, Virgil and many others. Sources like these show how sophisticated the viticulture was. Vines were trained in parallel rows, just as they are today, with care taken to ensure proper spacing between each plant, and at least six different methods of pruning and training were employed, depending upon the variety of grape, type of soil and wind strength.

It was the Greeks who taught the Romans all they knew about wine and who spread the concept of commercial viticulture. But with the decline in the Greek civilization went the famous wines of antiquity. No longer the economic foundation of a great civilization, Greek wines now represent a mere two per cent of the gross national product.

THE GREEK WINE TRADE TODAY

A few years ago I asked wine producer John Boutaris why Greek wines were invariably oxidized, maderized or sometimes simply bad. He stretched, raised a gentle smile and replied that most Greeks like oxidized wines. He believes that if Greek producers

turned out respectable wines, they would not be able to sell them on the domestic market and would have to export them, but doubts that foreigners would go out of their way to buy Greek wines. He claims that outside Greece, wine drinkers only know about Retsina. Even so, at Boutaris' spotless production centre at Steinmacho in the Naoussa district, he turns out clean, well-made wines that range from the cheap but cheerful "Rotunda" range to Naoussa, Boutari Cava and Boutari Grande Reserve, which are consistently three of the best wines produced in Greece.

There are few Greek appellations worth investigating, and the number of quality-conscious producers is pitifully low. The Côtes de Meliton is the only fine, all-round appellation in Greece; there is not one respectable dry white appellation; the sweet liqueur Muscat wines are very reliable and the finest, Samos, is high quality indeed. As for red-wine appellations, only the full, rich Naoussa and Nemea stand out, although the lighter Goumenissa and the smooth, sweet Mavrodaphne of Patras may also be recommended. As for the producers, Boutari and Tsantali make fresh, clean and fruity wines throughout their ranges; Genka, whose wines sell under the "Cellar" label, makes clean wines, but with the excellent exception of its "Cellar Cava", they are so clean that the flavours have been washed out; Calliga of Cephalonia, which has received enthusiastic reviews from some of my colleagues, is no more than adequate in my opinion, and a far more promising enterprise on Cephalonia, if a very much smaller one, is Gentilini. Other fine wines are made by Caviros, and Chateau Semeli and Chateau Harlaftis make good Cabernet Sauvignon wines. More than half of all Greek wine is processed by cooperatives, and these are responsible for most of the worst examples, although good (even fine) wines are made by Ioánnina, Nemea "Herculese", Patras, Limnos, Samos and CAIR.

GREECE

The myriad mainland areas and islands that is modern-day Greece provides for a plethora of wine regions. The cooler northern regions, particularly Macedonia, produce the best wines, while the island of Samos produces great sweet wines.

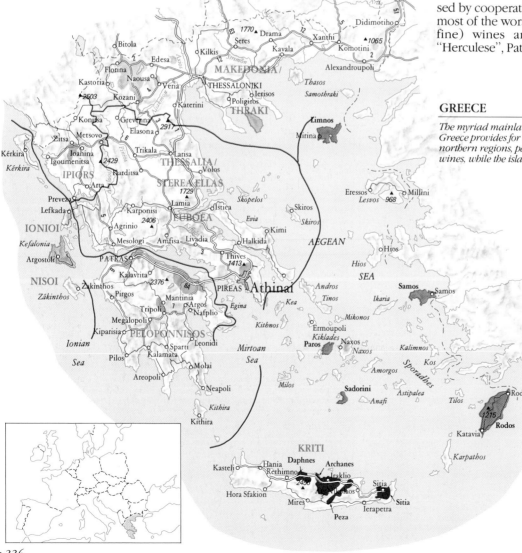

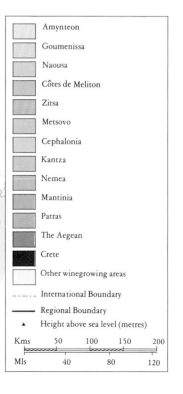

	Amynteon
	Goumenissa
	Naousa
	Côtes de Meliton
	Zitsa
	Metsovo
	Cephalonia
	Kantza
	Nemea
	Mantinia
	Patras
	The Aegean
	Crete
	Other winegrowing areas
- - -	International Boundary
——	Regional Boundary
▲	Height above sea level (metres)

Kms   50   100   150   200

Mls   40   80   120

FACTORS AFFECTING TASTE AND QUALITY

 Location
Vines are grown throughout mainland Greece and on many of its islands, but the majority are located in the northern region of Macedonia, and the Peloponnese in the south.

Climate
This consists of mild winters and sub-tropical summers, with most Greek vineyards tempered by seasonal sea-breezes called *meltemi* and bathed in an average of 3,000 hours of sunshine every year. There are, however, great variations; from the coolest mountain vineyards of Macedonia, where grapes can fail to ripen, to Crete, where the summer brings five months of intense heat and drought, which is tempered only by the sea-breezes.

Aspect
Vines are grown on all types of land; relatively flat coastal sites, river valleys, steep hillsides and at altitudes rising to 610 metres (2,000 ft) at Amynteon in the Macedonian mountains. Less than 15 per cent of the land mass of the Ionian islands is flat and 23 per cent rises sharply between 305 and 610 metres (1,000 and 2,000 ft). To avoid overripening, the best vineyards often face north, contrary to most classic wine areas in the Northern Hemisphere where vines hug south-facing slopes.

Soil
Mainland soils are mostly limestone, while those of the islands are rocky and volcanic.

Viticulture and vinification
The general quality of Greek wines is disappointing, with oxidation being a major fault. At least 50 per cent of the wines produced are resinated; the technique was originally used to prevent oxidation, and Greeks gradually grew to like the distinctive taste. Some better-quality wines are now emerging, particularly from cooler northern areas. The sweet Muscat wines from the island of Samos are the most famous traditional Greek wines of quality.

 Grape varieties
Agiorgitiko, Aidani, Amorgiano, Assyrtiko, Athiri, Batiki, Cabernet franc, Cabernet sauvignon, Chardonnay, Cinsault, Debina, Goustoldi, Grenache, Korintiaki, Kotsifali, Krassato, Liatiko, Limnio, Mandilaria, Mavrodaphne, Merlot, Messenikola, Monemvassia, Moschophilero, Muscat, (Muscat blanc à petits grains, Muscat d'Alexandrie, Traini muscat, White muscat), Negoska, Pavlos, Petite sirah, Pinot noir, Rhoditis, Robola, Romeiko, Rozaki, Sauvignon blanc, Savatiano, Skiadopoγlo, Stavroto, Sykiotis, Thymiatiko, Tssaoussi, Ugni blanc, Vertzami, Vilana, Xynomavro

Pressing grapes by hand, left
Traditional, non-mechanized viticultural methods still prevail throughout much of Greece today.

HOW TO READ GREEK WINE LABELS

ΟΙΝΟΣ (or ΚΡΑΣΙ)
Οινοσ (or κρασι) Wine

ΛΕΥΚΟΣ
Λευκοσ White

Strength and Volume
The alcoholic strength is expressed in per cent by volume and the capacity in litres or centilitres

ΜΙΝΩΣ
ΚΑΒΑ

e 70 CL · ΕΛΛΗΝΙΚΟΝ ΠΡΟΙΟΝ · PRODUCT OF GREECE 12% VOL

ΟΙΝΟΣ ΚΡΗΤΙΚΟΣ ΛΕΥΚΟΣ ΞΗΡΟΣ ΟΙΝΟΣ ΕΠΙΤΡΑΠΕΖΙΟΣ "CRETAN WHITE DRY WINE,, TABLE WINE

ΠΑΡΑΓΩΓΗ-ΕΜΦΙΑΛΩΣΗ
ΑΦΟΙ ΜΗΛΙΑΡΑΚΗ Ο.Ε. «ΜΙΝΩΣ»
ΕΞΑΓΩΓΙΚΗ ΕΤΑΙΡΙΑ ΟΙΝΩΝ ΚΡΗΤΗΣ
ΠΕΖΑ ΗΡΑΚΛΕΙΟΥ ΚΡΗΤΗΣ
ΑΔ. ΕΜΦ. 1/62 Γ.Χ.Κ. ΗΡΑΚΛΕΙΟ ΚΡΗΤΗΣ

PRODUCED AND BOTTLED BY:
CRETAN WINE EXPORT Co "MINOS.
MILIARAKIS BROTHERS
PEZA-IRAKLION-CRETE

ΕΛΛΗΝΙΚΟ ΠΡΟΪΟΝ
Ελληνικο Προιον Produce of Greece

ΕΠΙΤΡΑΠΕΖΙΟΣ ΟΙΚΟΣ
Επιτραπεζιοσ Οικοσ Table wine

ΞΗΡΟΣ
Ξηροσ Dry

Other information regarding style or quality may also be present on Greek labels:

ΑΦΡΩΔΗΣ ΟΙΝΟΣ, ΗΜΙΑΦΡΩΔΗΣ
Αφρωδησ Οινοσ, Ημιαφρωδησ
Sparkling wine, semi-sparkling

ΕΡΥΘΡΟΣ Ερυθροσ
Red

ΡΟΖΕ Ροζε
Rosé

ΗΜΙΞΗΡΟΣ Ημιξηροσ
Dry, semi-dry

ΓΛΥΚΟΣ, ΗΜΙΓΛΥΚΟΣ
Γλυκοσ, Ημιγλυκοσ
Sweet, semi-sweet

ΡΕΤΣΙΝΑ Ρετσινα
Retsina – many carry no appellation of origin and may therefore be blended

ΡΕΤΣΙΝΑ ΑΤΤΙΚΗΣ
Ρετσινα Αττικησ
Retsina with appellation of origin from Attica

ΡΕΤΣΙΝΑ ΕΥΒΟΙΑΣ
Ρετσινα Ευβοιασ
Retsina with appellation of origin from Evia

ΟΝΟΜΑΣΙΑ ΚΑΤΑ ΠΑΡΑΔΟΣΗ
Ονομασια Κατα Παραδοση
Traditional appellation (reserved for Retsina only)

ΟΝΟΜΑΣΙΑ ΠΡΟΕΛΕΥΣΕΩΣ ΑΝΩΤΕΡΑΣ ΠΟΙΟΤΗΤΟΣ
Ονομασια Προελευσεωσ Ανωτερασ Ποιοτητοσ
Appellation of origin of high quality. Most wines bearing this appellation are of modest, not high quality. Greece has a long way to go before its appellation system will carry any connotation of quality. In the meantime, specifically recommended producers are the best pointers for quality

ΟΙΝΟΠΟΙΕΙΟΝ Οινοποιειον
Winery

ΟΙΝΟΠΑΡΑΓΩΓΟΣ
Οινοπαραγωγοσ
Wine-producer

ΠΑΡΑΓΩΓΗ ΚΑΙ ΕΜΦΙΑΛΩΣΙΣ
Παραγωγη Και Εμφιαλωσισ
Produced and bottled by..

Vintage
As Greece belongs to the EEC, the vintage should mean that at least 85 per cent of the wine comes from the year indicated

RETSINA—BOON OR BURDEN?

Retsina is wine, usually white, to which pine resin is added during fermentation. This practice dates back to antiquity, when wine was stored in jars and *amphorae*. As they were not airtight, the wines rapidly deteriorated. In the course of time, people learned to seal the jars with a mixture of plaster and resin and the wines naturally lasted longer. This increased longevity was attributed to the antiseptic effect of resin, the aroma and flavour of which quickly tainted the stored wine. It was, of course, a false assumption, but in the absence of Pasteur's discoveries (then some twenty-five centuries in the future), it appeared to be supported by the fact that the more resinous the wine, the less it deteriorated. Within a short time, the resin was being added directly to the wine and the only difference between modern and ancient Retsina is that the resin is now added directly to the wine during fermentation, rather than after. The best Retsina is said to come from three areas, Attica, Evia and Viota, and the best resin, which must be from the Alep or Aleppo pine, comes from Attica.

Most of the Greek wine exported is Retsina. Because of this, and because it is mainly Retsina that is encountered in Greek *tavernas*, many mistakenly believe that all Greek wines are resinated. This has always been a bone of contention for quality-conscious producers: should they spearhead their export drive with Retsina because it is the one internationally recognized wine, or should they concentrate on promoting their lesser-known, clean, well-made wines?

Until now, most exporters have taken the easy option of basing their export sales on Retsina, but I think this should change. Strictly speaking Retsina is *not* wine. It would be if its pine character were the result of maturation in pine casks (that is a thought!) but having pine resin added makes it an aromatized wine, such as Vermouth. If it could be marketed as such by the Greek wine industry, then Retsina could continue to be an important export product, without confusing or endangering the image of other Greek wines. This would have the effect of encouraging higher standards for unresinated wines and, hopefully, encourage more firms to develop pride in the quality of the wines they make and sell.

Overhead vines, Crete, above
Ripening grapes hang from trellised vines at Skalani. The shade from the vine's foliage often provides welcome protection.

The wines of Greece

Note: Vintages may vary in character from lighter to fuller styles, but have little impact on the wine's quality. A good producer will make good-quality wines, whatever the year.
AO = Appellation of Origin
TA = Traditional Appellation

MACEDONIA AND THRACE

The most northerly section of Greece is, without doubt, the source of most of the country's best wines today.

AGIORITIKOS

AT CHROMITSA, AN AREA NEAR THE MONASTERY OF ST PANTELEIMON, AT THE HOLY MOUNTAIN OF AGION OROS, WE PLANTED OUR VINEYARDS OF THE FINE GREEK GRAPE VARIETIES OF ASYRTIKO, ATHIRI AND RODITIS.

FROM THESE VARIETIES WE PRODUCE OUR WINE, AGIORITIKOS, WITH RESPECT TO THE TRADITION OF GOOD WINEMAKING.

CONTAINS SULFITES

This excellent wine comes from 60 hectares (148 acres) of vineyards on Mount Athos (Agioritikos), the third peninsula of Halkidiki, immediately east of Sithonia. Leased from the Hourmistas monastery by the Tsantali winery, the vines are tended by Russian monks under the direction of the firm's vineyard manager. The best wine is the fine, dry, full-bodied red, which is made from Cabernet sauvignon and Limnio. There is also a dry and a medium-dry white wine, both fresh, clean and fruity, and a delicious, dry rosé.

🞕 Cabernet sauvignon, Limnio, Sauvignon blanc

AMYNTEON AO

The most northerly of Greek appellations, the vines are grown at a height of 650 metres (2,130 ft) and the grapes are seldom overripe. The quality is sporadic, with a strangely blowzy brew from the local cooperative, but there are occasional gems that clearly indicate its true potential.

🞕 Xynomavro

CÔTES DE MELITON AO

DOMAINE CARRAS

CÔTES DE MELITON
APPELLATION D' ORIGINE DE QUALITE SUPERIEURE
Grand Vin Rouge
1979
ELEVE ET MIS EN BOUTEILLE SUR LE DOMAINE
TOYPIΣTIKH · ΓΕΩΡΓΙΚΗ · ΕΞΑΓΩΓΙΚΗ Α.Ε.
ΣΙΘΩΝΙΑ · ΕΛΛΑΣ
12,5% e 0,75L

This appellation covers the red, white and rosé wines of Sithonia, the middle of Halkidiki's three peninsulas. They are made to a consistently high standard because all the wines are from the excellent Domaine Porto Carras, the brainchild of the late John Carras. Made by modern vinification methods, the

wines are generally light, elegant and best enjoyed young. The exception is the top-of-the-range Chateau Carras, which is a deep-coloured, full-bodied, rich-flavoured, red wine of true *vin de garde* quality.

🞕 Assyrtico, Athiri, Cabernet franc, Cabernet sauvignon, Cinsault, Grenache, Limnio, Petite sirah, Rhoditis, Sauvignon blanc, Savatiano, Ugni blanc, Xynomavro

🍷 Within 1-2 years (Chateau Carras: between 5-8 years for lighter vintages; 10-20 years for bigger ones)

GOUMENISSA AO

A light-bodied red wine from the Goumenissa district northeast of Naoussa. Usually a wine of good fruit and a certain elegance, the best undergo a light maturation in cask and can be relatively rich in flavour.

🞕 Xynomavro, Negoska

🍷 Between 3-8 years

☆ Boutari

NAOUSA AO

These generally reliable wines are grown west of Thessalonika, at a height of 350 metres (1,150 ft) on the southeastern slopes of Mount Velia. Although I can only give three rock-solid recommendations, of which Boutari and Chateau Pegasus are by far the best, I cautiously suggest that any Naousa could be worth the gamble; the local growers take a pride in their wine that can be lacking elsewhere. Good Naousa is well-coloured, rich and aromatic on the nose, with heaps of spicy fruit on the palate and a long finish.

🍇 Xynomavro

🍷 Between 4-15 years

☆ Boutari, Chateau Pegasus, Tsantali

EPIRUS

There are relatively few vineyards in this mountainous area on the Albanian border.

METSOVO AO

Apparently the production of Cabernet sauvignon has been expanding in this mountainous area to the east of Zitsa, but as Metsovo is so far off the beaten track, I have not tasted it.

🍇 Cabernet sauvignon

ZITSA AO

Dry and semi-sweet, slightly *spritzy,* clean and delicately fruity white wine from six villages around Zitsa, northwest of Ioánnina, where the vines grow at an altitude of some 600 metres (1,970 ft). Most of the production is processed by the Union of Agricultural Cooperatives of Ioánnina and I recommend it wholeheartedly.

🍇 Debina

🍷 Immediately

☆ Union of Agricultural Cooperatives of Ioánnina

THE PELOPONNESE

Separated from mainland Greece by the sheer-sided Corinth canal, the Peloponnese is well known for its intensive viticulture, which produces vast quantities of currants and sultanas as well as wine.

MANTINIA AO

A dry white wine from mountain vineyards surrounding the ancient ruins of Mantinea in the centre of the Peloponnese. The vines grow at a height of 650 metres (2,130 ft) and although there are some very fresh, young wines with nice lively fruit, the quality is not consistent and I have not encountered the wines on export markets.

🍇 Moschophilero

🍷 Immediately

MAVRODAPHNE OF PATRAS AO

A rich, sweet, red liqueur wine with a velvety smooth, sweet-oak finish. Often compared to a Recioto della Valpolicella, a good Mavrodaphne is to my mind far better. One delightful aspect of this wine is that it can be drunk with equal pleasure when it is either young and fruity or smooth and mature.

🍇 Mavrodaphne

🍷 Within 1-20 years

☆ Andrew P. Cambas, Achaia Clauss, Union of Agricultural Cooperatives of Patras

MUSCAT OF PATRAS AO

An attractive, gold-coloured, sweet, liqueur Muscat wine that can be delicious in its typically raisiny way.

🍇 Muscat blanc à petits grains

🍷 Immediately

☆ Union of Agricultural Cooperatives of Patras "Moschato"

MUSCAT RION OF PATRAS AO

Similar to Muscat of Patras by all accounts, but I have not tasted or even seen it.

🍇 Muscat blanc à petits grains

NEMEA AO

This is a relatively reliable appellation and I believe for the same reason as Naoussa – local pride. Grown in the Corinth district at a height of between 250 and 800 metres (820 and 2,620 ft), the Agiorgitiko grape provides a deep-coloured, full and spicy red wine that is sometimes spoilt by dried-out fruit, or a lack of fruit. Known locally as the "Blood of Hercules", because his blood was shed when he killed the Nemean lion, it has been produced for 2,500 years.

🍇 Agiorgitiko

🍷 Between 5-20 years

☆ Andrew P. Cambas "Lion of Nemea", Achaia Clauss, Cooperative Winery of Nemea "Herculese", Kourtakis

PATRAS AO

A light, dry white wine from the hilly hinterland of Patras. I have only tasted the local cooperative product and have found the wine both dull and flabby. However, the cooperative itself is capable of good quality, as evinced by its first-class Mavrodaphne and Muscat.

🍇 Rhoditis

CENTRAL GREECE

The most important wine-growing areas in this region are the provinces of Attica (or Attiki), the area around Athens; Viotia (or Voiotia), immediately northwest of Attica; and Evia (or Evvoia, or Euboea), a large island off the east coast.

KANTZA AO

This dry white wine from the province of Attica is Retsina without the pine-resin. The only one I have tasted is from Andrew P. Cambas and, although clean, I did not find it special.

🍇 Savatiano

RETSINA TA

Although rosé is not unknown, Retsina is almost invariably white, with 85 per cent of the blend coming from the Savatiano grape. It may be blended from various areas or can have a specific, usually superior, origin, but in every case Retsina carries the unique "Traditional Appellation". This designation recognizes the ancient practice of resinating wine and the EEC has confined its use to Greece.

There are degrees of resination, from relatively light to heavy, and the quality of the pine resin itself can range from poor to fine; the better-quality pine resin makes better-quality Retsina. Despite its penetrating aroma and flavour, pine resin cannot hide a tired, flabby, oxidized or, simply, bad wine. Personally, I do not like Retsina, but I have to admit that the aroma of fine pine resin is refreshing and I also agree that this aromatized wine has a useful "cutting" quality when drunk with oily Greek food!

🍇 Rhoditis, Savatiano

🍷 As young and as fresh as possible.

☆ Appellations of Origin: Attica, Evia, Viota, Thebes; Brands: "Marco", "Pikermi", "Thives"

THE IONIAN ISLANDS

Corfu, which almost touches the Albanian coast, is the most northerly of this group of islands off the west coast of Greece that includes Lefcas, Cephalonia and, just off the Peloponnese, Zante.

GENTILINI

This exciting venture has been achieved by a young, quality-conscious winemaker, Nicholas Cosmetatos. While waiting for his own vineyard to mature, he has demonstrated a fastidious wine-making approach blending locally purchased Tssaoussi and Robola grapes to produce fine, clean, crisp

Continued overleaf

and dry white wines of an encouraging quality. His latest addition to the range is Gentilini Fumé, which contains no Sauvignon blanc, despite the name, and is in fact the same Tssaoussi/Robola blend, but with two to three months in oak, which adds a little depth. By 1991, when his two-and-a-half-hectare (six-acre) vineyard is in full production, Gentilini will be all domaine-produced and bottled. The wines envisaged are three qualities of blended white wine, plus a limited edition of pure varietal wine from Tssaoussi, Sauvignon blanc and Chardonnay grapes, aged in new Limousin oak *barriques* (not too much, I trust).

It all sounds very exciting and I desperately hope that Nicholas Cosmetatos is the first of a new generation of dedicated Greek winemakers.

🍇 Chardonnay, Sauvignon blanc, Tssaoussi

MAVRODAPHNE OF CEPHALONIA AO

I have not tasted this sweet red liqueur wine; it should, however, be similar to the Mavrodaphne of Patras, which comes from the nearby Peloponnese.

🍇 Mavrodaphne

MUSCAT OF CEPHALONIA AO

One of the lesser-known, sweet liqueur wines from the Muscat grape. I tasted it once and found it acceptable, but cannot comment on its consistency.

🍇 Muscat blanc à petits grains

ROBOLA OF CEPHALONIA AO

A dry white wine that can be fresh and floral, with an almost racy nose and a tangy, lightly rich, delicate lemon-fruity flavour. However, it is all too often spoilt by sloppy winemaking.

🍇 Robola

🍷 Within 1-2 years

SANTA MAVRA

Deep-coloured, full-bodied red wine of local repute grown on terraces up to an altitude of 800 metres (2,620 ft) on the island of Lefcas. Although I have encountered this wine only once, it was clean and tasted like raspberry juice with tannin.

🍇 Vertzami

VERDEA

An astringent, often oxidized, dry white wine made on the island of Zante, where it is famous for its delicate bouquet.

🍇 Pavlos, Skiadopoylo

THESSALY

This region covers the central eastern sector of the mainland.

ANCHIALOS AO

Medium-bodied, dry white wine from the Nea Anchialos area on the Gulf of Pegassitikos near Volos. The local "Demetra" cooperative wine is clean, though unexciting.

🍇 Savatiano, Rhoditis, Sykiotis

RAPSANI AO

I have driven past these red-wine regions in the vicinity of Mount Olympus, but have not had the opportunity to try the wine.

🍇 Xynomavro, Krassato, Stavroto

THE AEGEAN

The most important wine-growing islands in this region are, in order of importance, Samos, Lesbos and Lemnos.

LEMNOS (LIMNOS) AO

A soft and flowery dry white wine with clean fruit and an attractive Muscat character from the island of Lemnos. The local cooperative version is consistently well made.

🍇 Limnio

🍷 Immediately

☆ Union of Agricultural Cooperatives of Lemnos

LESBOS

This island's wines are consumed locally, none are exported.

MUSCAT OF LEMNOS AO

A superior liqueur Muscat wine that is richer and sweeter than Patras, though not in the class of Samos.

🍇 Muscat d'Alexandrie

🍷 Immediately

☆ Union of Agricultural Cooperatives of Lemnos

MUSCAT OF SAMOS AO

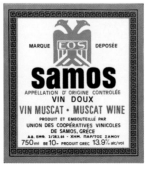

One of the great sweet wines of the world, the local cooperative's Samos and Samos Nectar are both superb, perfectly balanced, rich and mellifluous wines. It also produces a deliciously dry and fresh, non-appellation version called "Samena", which is as clean as a whistle, with a delightful orange flower-water aroma and delicate fruit.

🍇 Muscat blanc à petits grains

🍷 Immediately

☆ Union des Cooperatives Vinicoles de Samos

THE CYCLADES

The cradle of Greek wines in ancient times, the most important wine-growing islands of the Cyclades today are Paros and Thera. The Aegean *meltemi* can blow across this region so violently that the vines have to be trained in a low *gobelet* in order to keep the fruit on the bush!

PAROS AO

Deep-coloured, light-bodied, red wine from the Mandilaria grape that I have tasted only once. My notes record a "very strange taste". A rich, dry, white wine from the Monemvassia grape (which some believe to be the original Malvasia), is also produced, but I have not tasted it.

🍇 Mandilaria, Monemvassia

SANTORINI AO

This full-bodied, dry white wine grown on Thera can have as much as 17 per cent natural alcohol, plus a surprisingly high acidity level. The wine is interesting and unusual, though, in my opinion, not particularly enjoyable. A sweet straw-wine called Santorini *liastos* (made in a similar way to the French ''vin de paille'') is also produced, which seems a far more sensible way of processing such unusual grapes.

🍇 Assyrtiko, Aidani

🍷 Between 2-5 years

THE DODECANESE

Within this region, only Rhodes is of any significance in terms of wine-making, although a small amount of wine is made on Cos, the island of Hippocrates.

MUSCAT OF RHODES AO

A good-quality, rich and sweet, golden, liqueur Muscat wine that I consider to be on a par with the Muscat of Patras.

🍇 Muscat blanc à petits grains, Traini muscat

🍷 Immediately

☆ CAIR

RHODES AO

Of the wines produced by the CAIR, the local cooperative, I have tasted a dull, oily, dry white wine called "Ilios"; a strong, but coarse, dry and sweet *méthode champenoise* sparkling wine; and a well-balanced, sweet, red Muscat wine called "Amandia". Various other wines are also produced, but I have not tasted them.

🍇 Amorgiano, Athiri

🍷 Immediately

☆ CAIR

CRETE

The largest Greek island, Crete is divided by a high mountain range that acts as a barrier between the south, which faces Africa, and the north, which faces the Aegean.

ARCHANES AO

I have tasted the local cooperative's "Armanti" table wine, but I have not had the opportunity to taste this red appellation wine, which is apparently aged in old oak barrels.

🍇 Kotsifali, Mandilaria

DAPHNES AO

Dry red and sweet, red, liqueur wines that I have not tasted.

🍇 Liatiko

PEZA AO

From my experience, based purely on the local cooperative's wines, great benefit could be gained if the malolactic process was prevented in the production of its "Regalo" dry white wine and if the "Mantiko" reds were bottled and sold much younger.

🍇 Kotsifali, Mandilaria, Vilana

SITIA AO

Deep-coloured, robust, dry red and sweet red liqueur wines.

🍇 Liatiko

The Levant

With the exception of one outstanding wine, Chateau Musar from Lebanon's war-torn Bekaa Valley, fine wine is non-existent in the Levant. However, honestly made wines are produced in the Israeli-held Golan Heights and on the island of Cyprus.

IT IS BELIEVED THAT WINE HAS BEEN produced in the Levant since at least 4,000 BC, when it was reputedly first made on any significant scale in Mesopotamia, an area that was roughly equivalent to modern-day Iraq. In recent history, however, most vineyards in the Levant have been used for the production of table grapes, sultanas and currants. The success of Serge Hochar at Chateau Musar is beginning to change this; he has completely confounded our perception of the potential of wine in certain microclimatically privileged parts of the Levant. Peace permitting, more wines in the Musar class might emerge.

TURKEY

Wine districts: *Thrace-Marmara; Ankara; Mediterranean Coast; Black Sea Coast; Central Anatolia; Central-south Anatolia*

This country has the fifth-largest area under vine in the world, but because its population is predominantly Muslim, most vines produce either table grapes, sultanas or currants.

The wines that are produced in Turkey are generally flabby, too alcoholic, heavy, over-sulphured and can often be oxidized. Most well known are "Trakya" (dry white Sémillon from Thrace), "Trakya Kirmisi" (a red blend of native grapes, also from Thrace), the amusingly named "Hosbag" (red Gamay, also from Thrace), and "Buzbag" (Turkey's most famous red wine made from native grapes grown in southeast Anatolia), but despite their fame they should all be avoided. The best Turkish wine is "Villa Doluca", a clean, well made, nicely balanced, pure red Gamay from Thrace.

THE LEVANT

Among the disparate group of countries that forms the area known as the Levant, only Lebanon can boast a "fine" wine.

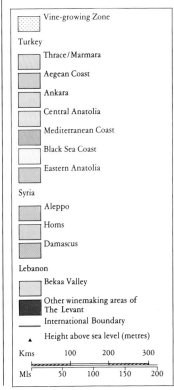

	Vine-growing Zone
Turkey	
	Thrace / Marmara
	Aegean Coast
	Ankara
	Central Anatolia
	Mediterranean Coast
	Black Sea Coast
	Eastern Anatolia
Syria	
	Aleppo
	Homs
	Damascus
Lebanon	
	Bekaa Valley
	Other winemaking areas of The Levant
	International Boundary
▲	Height above sea level (metres)

Kms 100 200 300
Mls 50 100 150 200

CYPRUS

Wine districts: *Marathassa Afames, Pitsilia, Maheras Mountains. Troödos Mountains, Mesaoria*

Wines have been made on this beautiful island for at least 4,000 years and Cyprus' most famous wine, "Commanderie St. John" is one of a handful that claim to be the world's oldest. It can be traced back to 1191, when Richard the Lionheart, King of England, acquired the island during the Crusades. He subsequently sold it to the Order of the Knights of the Temple, who established themselves as *Commanderies* and later became known as the Knights of the Order of St. John. "Commanderie St. John" is a *solera*-matured, sweet dessert wine, which is made from a blend of black and white grapes that have been left in the sun for 10 to 15 days after the harvest, to shrivel and concentrate the sugars. It used to be rich and luscious with a fine toasty fullness, but there is nothing special about the wine produced today.

In recent years Cyprus has experienced more than its fair share of political difficulties, and against this turbulent background the island's wine trade has also suffered two damaging blows. The EEC banned Cyprus Sherry when Spain joined the Community in 1986, which was crippling because the entire Cypriot wine industry was built on this high-volume-selling wine. The second blow came when General Secretary Gorbachov cut off all imports into Russia in a crusade against alcohol abuse, because Cypriot

Cypriot vineyards, above
One of the island's thriving winemaking areas is situated in the foothills of the Troödos Mountains.

FACTORS AFFECTING TASTE AND QUALITY

Location
The eastern Mediterranean area generally known as the Middle East, also including Cyprus.

Climate
Hot and dry for the most part. The microclimates enjoyed by the minority of good-quality vineyards are created by proximity to the Mediterranean and by altitude, which tempers the heat and usually means higher rainfall.

Aspect
Vines are grown on all types of land from the flat, coastal plains close to the Mediterranean to the higher mountain slopes of Cyprus, Turkey, Israel and Lebanon.

Soil
Soils vary greatly, from those of volcanic origin on Cyprus, through the alluvial river and sandy coastal soils throughout the area, to the Lebanon's gravel over limestone.

Viticulture and vinification
Sweet, heavy, fortified wines are still made in large quantities, but the emphasis is definitely moving to lighter table wines. Vineyards are now being planted on higher mountain sites, grapes are being harvested at lower sugar levels and are being fermented at cooler temperatures, and wines are being bottled earlier to maximize freshness and fruit.

Grape varieties
Turkey
Adakarasi, Altintas, Aramon, Beylerce, Cabernet sauvignon, Carignan, Chardonnay, Cinsault, Cubuk, Dimrit, Hasandede, Gamay, Irikira, Kalecik, Karalhana, Karasakiz, Kuntra, Muscat, Papazkarasi, Pinot noir, Riesling, Sémillon, Sylvaner, Tokmark, Yapincak

Cyprus
Cabernet franc, Cabernet sauvignon, Carignan, Chardonnay, Grenache, Malvasia grossa, Maratheftikon, Mataro, Mavro, Muscat Hamburg, Palomino, Riesling, Riesling Italico, Sémillon, Ugni blanc, Zynisteri

Lebanon
Aramon, Cabernet sauvignon, Carignan, Chardonnay, Chasselas, Cinsault, Muscat à petits grains, Pinot noir, Sauvignon blanc, Ugni blanc

Israel
Cabernet sauvignon, Clairette, Grenache, Muscat d'Alexandrie, Sauvignon blanc, Sémillon

Egypt
Chardonnay, Chasselas, Fayumi, Gamay, Guizaki, Muscat Hamburg, Pinot blanc, Pinot noir, Rumi

Note: as Syria and Jordan have no developed wine "industry", it is not possible to compile a listing of their grape varieties.

exports were mostly high-strength or fortified wines and spirits. The Cypriots not only took all this in their stride, but also managed to revamp their wine industry at the same time, accurately projecting the needs of the 1990s. Early harvesting, temperature-controlled stainless-steel vats and various modern vinification techniques have revolutionized the Cypriot approach to table wines, making much lighter, cleaner and crisper products.

Some names to look for that will make an enjoyable drink are: Domaine d'Ahera (light, dry red); "Bellapais" (spritzy, semi-sweet, fruity white); "Thisbe" (an alternative to Liebfraumilch) from Keo; Carignan Noir (dry red varietals); Grenache Noir (dry red varietals); and "Avra" (dry, white *méthode champenoise*) released by the wine company Sodap in 1986-7.

SYRIA

Wine districts: *Aleppo, Homs, Damascus*

Approximately 90,000 hectares (222,000 acres) of vines in Syria produce mostly table grapes, sultanas and currants and wine production rarely exceeds 8,000 hectolitres (90,000 cases) a year. The wine-growing districts are all on lower mountain slopes.

LEBANON

Wine district: *Bekaa Valley*

The Lebanon's leading winemaker, Serge Hochar of Chateau Musar, performs a minor miracle in the Bekaa Valley. How he can be so cheerful, when in the past his vineyards have had to contend with the presence of Syrian tanks and Israeli jets, is remarkable.

The wine is made from Cabernet sauvignon, Cinsault and Syrah grapes grown at a cool climatic height of 1,000 metres (3,300 ft), on hillside slopes of gravelly soil over limestone bedrock. These vines receive no less than 300 days of sunshine per year and receive no rain during the harvest. If the wine tastes like a good claret, then it is because Hochar trained at Bordeaux; the wine is made predominantly from Cabernet sauvignon grapes and also according to traditional Bordelais methods. Sometimes however, a vintage hints more of the Rhône than Bordeaux, although Rhône varieties are in the minority. Hochar explains that this is because it is sometimes impossible to predict the eventual varietal power of the Cinsault grape. Whether Rhône- or Bordeaux-biased, Chateau Musar is always, to one degree or another, full-bodied and full-flavoured, with a good structure of supple tannin and a rich, plummy, spicy-sweet flavour that is generous, but never fat. The wines all achieve a remarkable complexity and finesse. In my experience, high quality is guaranteed in every year that is released. Some vintages will be drinking well between five and eight years after the harvest, others, like 1970 and 1972, are still improving.

Of other Lebanese wines, Domaine des Tourelles and Domaine de Kefraya are pleasantly drinkable, but most producers still use very crude methods.

ISRAEL

Wine districts: *Zefat, Zichron-Jacob, Richon-le-Zion, Allab, Beersheba*

Although I have tasted Israeli wines periodically since the 1960s, it was not until 1987 that clean, expressive wines started to appear. Most notable of these are Gamla Cabernet Sauvignon and Yarden Sauvignon Blanc, both from high-altitude vineyards planted in the Golan Heights where temperatures, even in the middle of summer, rarely rise above 25° (77°F). Both wines are full of vibrant fruit flavours.

JORDAN

Wine district: *Amman-Zarqua*

A country where the vine once flourished, Jordan now has rapidly diminishing vineyards that cover just 3,000 hectares (7,400 acres), with only a small percentage of these responsible for its wine production, which averages just 6,000 hectolitres (67,000 cases) a year. Jordanians are not noted wine drinkers, preferring Arrack instead, the aniseed-flavoured spirit that is ubiquitous in the Levant.

EGYPT

Wine districts: *Abu Hummus*

Travelling to the Nile Delta, you are advised to refuse the ice, and the same advice should also apply to the foul-tasting Egyptian wine that should be avoided at all costs. There are about 20,000 hectares (50,000 acres) of land under vine in Egypt, producing roughly 15,000 hectolitres (170,000 cases) of wine a year.

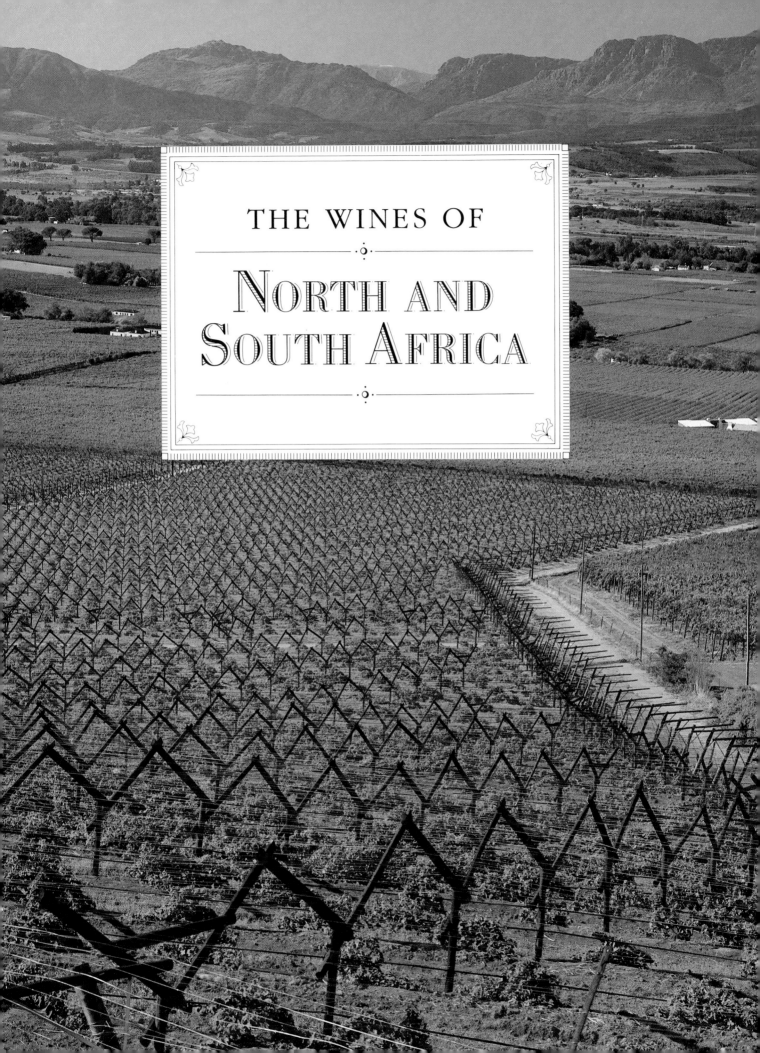

THE WINES OF
NORTH AND
SOUTH AFRICA

North Africa

The wine industries of Algeria, Morocco and Tunisia, and the appellation systems within which they work, are all based on the structure left behind by the colonial French. Today the governments of each country play active roles in the further development of their wine industries, but a combination of governmental commitment to improve quality and Muslim influence has brought about a decline in yields. No "fine wines" are produced, but the quality can be good. The best wines are invariably Moroccan reds and Tunisian Muscats.

ALGERIA

Wine districts of the Department of Oran: *Coteaux de Mascara, Coteaux de Tlemcen, Monts du Tessalah, Mostaganem, Mostaganem-Kenenda, Oued-Imbert*
Wine districts of the Department of Alger: *Aïn-Bessem-Bouira, Coteaux du Zaccar, Haut-Dahra, Médéa*

In 1830, Algeria was the first to be colonized by the French, and with this head-start, has always dominated North African viticulture in terms of quantity, if not quality. The demise of the country's wine industry after independence made it clear that the cynical remarks about the use of its wine in bolstering Burgundies were true, but the ironic fact is that both the  Moroccan and the Burgundian wines benefitted from being blended together. It was never the best Burgundies that were enhanced with dark Algerian red, it was the poorest, thinnest, and least attractive wines. After the blending, they were not Burgundian in character, but were superior to the original Burgundy.

Since independence, Algeria's vineyards have shrunk by almost one-half and the red wines produced that are unblended with French wines have not shown much improvement. The white and rosé wines, however, have improved enormously and are getting fresher with each new vintage. Of the few reds that can be honestly recommended, the best are from Coteaux de Mascara, where they are made in a solid, rustic, slightly coarse style.

Berber women working in a Tunisian vineyard, above
The best and most reliable AOC wines in Tunisia are Muscats.

NORTH AFRICA

Morocco, Algeria and Tunisia are all wine-producing countries to one degree or another, with most of the vineyards being concentrated along the coastal Mediterranean and Atlantic belts.

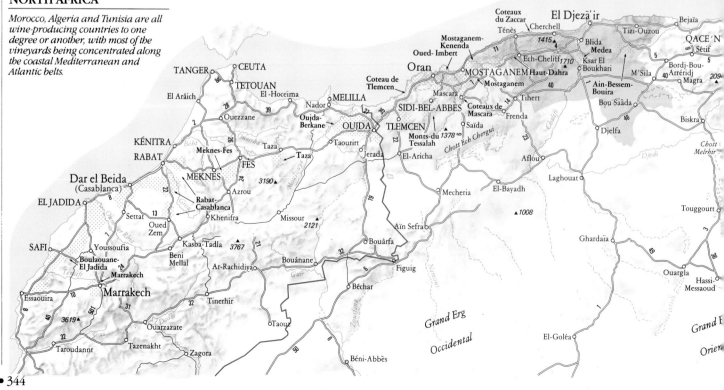

FACTORS AFFECTING TASTE AND QUALITY

Location
The coastal belt of Algeria, Morocco and Tunisia, adjacent to the western Mediterranean and the Atlantic.

Climate
Hot and dry, as one would expect in a region that is at the southern extreme of the Northern Hemisphere's vinegrowing belt. Conditions become a little less severe moving westwards through Morocco, where the Atlantic exerts a tempering influence, but the cooling effect of altitude is extremely important in vineyard areas throughout North Africa.

Aspect
Vines are still grown on the flat coastal plains, although vast areas have been pulled up. Most remaining vines and new plantings are on hill sites a little further inland. In such areas vineyards can be found at altitudes of up to 1,200 metres (3,900 ft), as in the Medea Hills of Algeria, for example.

Soil
Sand, marl and rich alluvial soils are found along the coastal plain. Calcareous-gravel over intervening layers of limestone, marl and sand characterize many inland mountain areas. In the foothills, vines are grown on silica, clay, gravel, sand and volcanic soils.

Viticulture and vinification
When Morocco, Tunisia and Algeria gained independence from France in the late 1950s and early 1960s, the trade in wine between the former colonist and all three countries virtually ceased. Since then they have concentrated on raising the quality of the wines rather than the quantity, hence the removal of many of the vineyards on the coastal plains and the development of the cooler mountain areas.

Grape varieties
Algeria
Alicante Bouschet, Aramon, Cabernet sauvignon, Carignan, Cinsault, Clairette, Faramon, Farhana, Gamay, Grenache, Grilla, Hasseroum, Macabeo, Merseguera, Morastel, Mourvèdre, Pinot noir, Syrah, Ugni blanc

Morocco
Alicante Bouschet, Beni-Sadden, Cabernet sauvignon, Carignan, Cinsault, Clairette, Grenache, Mourvèdre, Muscat, Pedro Ximenez, Rafsai, Sais, Syrah, Ugni blanc, Zerkhoun

Tunisia
Alicante Bouschet, Alicante-grenache, Beldi, Cabernet franc, Carignan, Cinsault, Clairette, Merseguera, Morastel, Mourvèdre, Muscat, Nocera, Pedro Ximenez, Pinot noir, Reldei, Ugni blanc

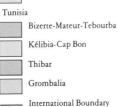

Intensive Vine-growing Zone

Algeria

Oran

Alger

Tunisia

Bizerte-Mateur-Tebourba

Kélibia-Cap Bon

Thibar

Grombalia

— International Boundary

▲ Height above sea level (metres)

Kms 50 100 150 200 250
Mls 50 100 150

MOROCCO

Wine districts: *Meknès-Fez, Rabat-Casablanca, Oujda-Berkane, Marrakech*

Wines were made here during Roman times, but under sole Muslim influence viticulture died out. In 1912, however, most of Morocco came under either French or Spanish control (with an international zone encompassing Tangiers) and it once more became an active winemaking country. When Morocco gained independence in 1956, the new government introduced a quality control regime similar to the French AOC system and, in 1973, it nationalized the wine industry. Since then, the area under vine has declined to 22,000 hectares (54,000 acres), which is about one-quarter of their pre-nationalization size. Few wines carry the official Appellation d'Origine Garantie (AOG) designation. Some pale rosés sold as *vin gris* can be pleasant when chilled but the best wines are red, the most successful being two "Les 'Trois Domaines" wines, called "Tarik" and "Chante Bled" on most export markets. These wines are made from Carignan, Cinsault and Grenache grapes grown in the Meknès-Fez district. Of the two, the "Tarik" is bigger, the "Chante Bled" smoother.

TUNISIA

Wine districts: *Grombalia, Bizerte-Mateur-Tebourba, Kélibia-Cap Bon, Thibar*

Wines were first made around the Carthage area in Punic times, but production was forbidden for 1,000 years under Muslim rule. After French colonization in 1881 viticulture resumed; by independence in 1955 the foundations of a thriving industry had been laid. At this time two basic appellations had been established – Vin Supérieur de Tunisie, for table wines, and Appellation Contrôlée Vin Muscat de Tunisie, for liqueur Muscat. These designations did not, however, incorporate any controls to safeguard origin, and in 1957 the government introduced a classification system that established four levels: Vins de Consommation Courante (VCC), Vins Supérieurs (VS), Vins de Qualité Supérieure (VDQS), and Appellation d'Origine Contrôlée (AOC). Although vineyards have been reduced to some 75,000 hectares (185,000 acres), little more than half their pre-nationalization size, this is a positive step towards better quality. The best Tunisian wines are Muscat, ranging from the lusciously sweet, rich, viscous Vin de Muscat de Tunisie, to fresh, delicate, dry Muscats such as the Muscat de Kelibia. There are also a few good red wines, such as "Château Feriani", "Domaine Karim" and "Royal Tardi".

Vineyards at Binzert, northern Tunisia, above

South Africa

It is not easy to write about South Africa's wines without reflecting on the social and political difficulties that have dogged this rich and beautiful country. Many people of various shades of skin work in South Africa's wine trade; for their sake and for ours as consumers, I hope the fine-wine estates survive intact the troubled times ahead, just as the great Bordeaux châteaux weathered the French Revolution.

VIRTUALLY ALL OF SOUTH AFRICA'S VINEYARDS are located within a 160-kilometre (100-mile) sweep of Cape Town. This is roughly the same area cultivated by Jan van Riebeek, the Commander of the first Dutch settlement, who on February 2, 1659, recorded the now famous words, "Today, praise be to the Lord, wine was made for the first time from Cape grapes".

The first vines had been planted four years earlier and if van Riebeek's words heralded the answer to a desperate prayer, the wines were not, by all accounts, particularly successful. Simon van der Steel, who arrived in the Cape some 17 years after van Riebeek had left, complained about the "revolting sourness" of the local wines. He proceeded to remedy the situation by founding Groot Constantia, the most illustrious wine farm in the country's history.

THREE CENTURIES OF WINEMAKING

The arrival of French Huguenots, with their viticultural and winemaking expertise, greatly improved the quality of Cape wines, and by the early 1700s they were beginning to be held in high esteem. When French Revolutionary forces entered Holland, the British occupied the Cape and, cut off from supplies of French wines, began exporting South African wine to the many corners of their Empire, enhancing its growing reputation. By 1859, the

WINE OF ORIGIN SEAL

The seal of the Wine of Origin legislation is not necessarily seen on all South African wines. Known as the "bus ticket" on the domestic market, it carries up to three coloured bands: blue (origin: guarantees that 100 per cent of the wine comes from the region, district or ward indicated); red (vintage: certifies that at least 75 per cent of the wine is made from grapes harvested in the year indicated); and green (cultivar: certifies that at least 75 per cent of the wine is made from the variety of grape indicated). Since 1982 there has been a gold for wines that have been awarded "Superior" status. At the time of writing, the Wine of Origin legislation, and in particular the future of its Seal, was under review. Most speculation is centred on whether to drop the "Superior" designation or introduce a third, intermediary, level called "Premium".

Two obvious shortcomings of the present system are its 75 per cent minimum for vintage and cultivar, which should be raised to at least 85 per cent, and the fact that the contents of a blend – of genuine interest to the consumer – may not be revealed, let alone guaranteed.

HOW TO READ SOUTH AFRICAN WINE LABELS

Night Harvested
This means that the grapes were picked at night, when they are coolest, under floodlight, or by miner's lamp. This implies that we might expect a fresher, more aromatic and livelier wine than one produced from normally harvested grapes.

Style of the wine
The Afrikaans *semi-soet* is thoughtfully translated into semi-sweet.

The bottler
The small print at the bottom of the label reveals that the wine was not bottled on the estate itself, but at Gilbeys' main winery in Stellenbosch. Although many people in the industry would like to see it made obligatory for estates to bottle their own wines on the premises, I believe all that is required is to allow those who already do this the added prestige of a strictly controlled "Estate-bottled" term.

Vintage
This is clearly stated as 1987.

(label text) NIGHT HARVESTED · Est. · 1710 · VINTAGE 1987 · TWEE JONGEGEZELLEN · ESTATE · WYN VAN OORSPRONG TULBAGH · Night Harvest · 750ml · SEMI-SWEET · SEMI-SOET · Grown and made on the Estate Twee Jongegezellen, Tulbagh and bottled by Gilbey Distillers & Vintners (Pty) Ltd., Stellenbosch. · ESTATE WINE

Origin of the wine
The Wine of Origin Seal is not a substitute for information given on the label, but may simply be seen as authenticating it. From the example shown, we can see that the wine comes from the Wine of Origin (or *Wyn van Oorsprong*) district of Tulbagh. The Twee Jongegezellen Estate is well known for its high quality of white wines.
No variety or cultivar is stated. In this case the wine is actually a Riesling-Sauvignon-Chenin-based blend. The pity is that the system does not allow the contents of a blend to be revealed on a label, let alone guarantee it, as these blends may well vary slightly from year to year.

Volume
The contents, here a regular 750ml bottle-size, is obligatory, but the wine's alcoholic strength is not, although most export labels carry this information, which must be expressed in percentage by volume.

Other terms found on South African wine labels:

Edel laat-oes (Noble Late Harvest)
This usually, but not necessarily, implies that some botrytized grapes have been used. The wine must not be fortified; there is no minimum natural alcoholic strength, but a minimum of 50 grams per litre of residual sugar is stipulated.

Edelkeur
Literally "noble rot".

Fortified or liqueur wine
This must have an alcoholic strength of no less than 16.5 per cent by volume but no more than 22 per cent. The category includes "Port"

and "Sherry", plus such uniquely South African wines as Jerepigo.

Gebottel in... Bottled in...

Geproduser en Gebottel in... Produced and bottled in...

Geproduser en Gebottel in die Republiek van Sud-Africa
Produced and bottled in the Republic of South Africa.

Gekweek en gemaak op...
Grown and made on... (ie, not bottled on).

Gekweek, gemaak en gebottel op...
Grown, made and bottled on... (ie, estate-bottled).

Jerepigo
A very sweet liqueur wine with at least 160 grams per litre of residual sugar. Jerepigo Muscadel is very popular.

Koöperatiewe, Koöperatieve, Koöperasie, Koöperatief
Cooperative

Landgoedwyn
Estate-wine

Laat-oos
Late Harvest. This must not be fortified and must have a minimum natural alcoholic strength of 10 per cent and between 10 and 30 grams per litre of residual sugar.

Moskonfyt
Concentrated grape juice

Oesjaar
Vintage

Spesiale laat-oes
Special Late Harvest: usually, but not necessarily, implies that some botrytized grapes have been used; it must not be fortified; there is a minimum natural alcoholic strength of 10 per cent by volume; between 20 and 50 grams per litre of residual sugar.

Stein
A semi-sweet style of wine that is normally Chenin-based.

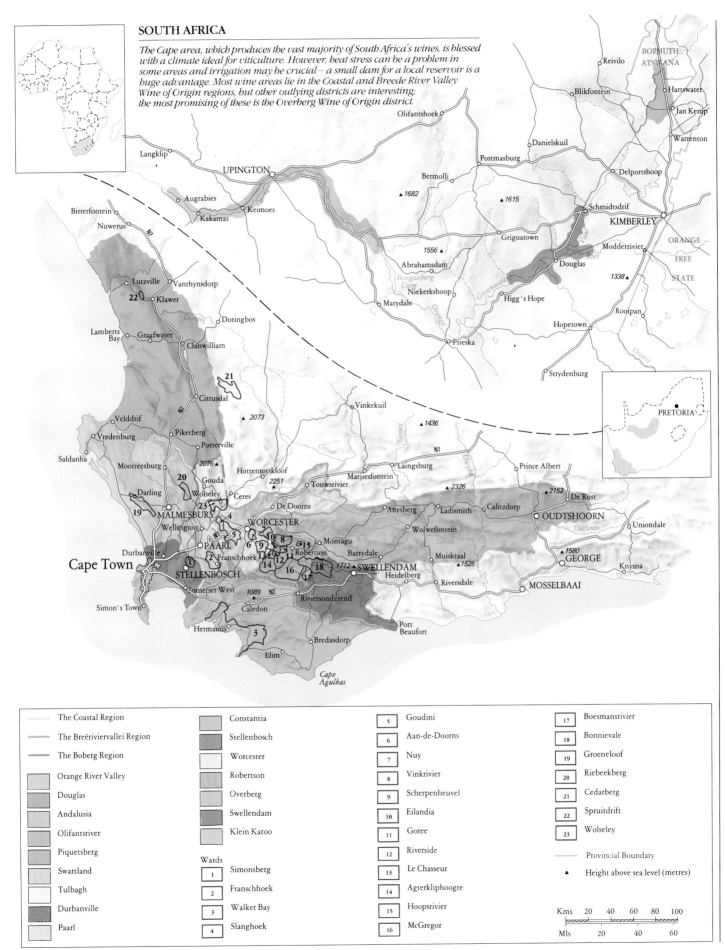

SOUTH AFRICA

The Cape area, which produces the vast majority of South Africa's wines, is blessed with a climate ideal for viticulture. However, heat stress can be a problem in some areas and irrigation may be crucial – a small dam for a local reservoir is a huge advantage. Most wine areas lie in the Coastal and Breede River Valley Wine of Origin regions, but other outlying districts are interesting; the most promising of these is the Overberg Wine of Origin district.

Map labels:

BOPHUTH-ATSWANA
Reivilo
Blikfontein
Hartswater
Jan Kemp
Olifantshoek
Danielskuil
Warrenton
Langklip
UPINGTON
Postmasburg
Delportshoop
Augrabies
Bermolli
▲ 1682
▲ 1615
Schmidtsdrif
Kakamas
Keimoes
KIMBERLEY
Bitterfontein
Nuwerus
Griquatown
Moddterivier
ORANGE
1556 ▲
Abrahamsdam
Douglas
FREE
Lutzville
Vanrhynsdorp
Niekerkshoop
Higg's Hope
Rooipan
STATE
22
Klawer
Marydale
Doringbos
Lamberts Bay
Graafwater
Hopetown
Clanwilliam
Prieska
1338 ▲
21
Strydenburg
Citrusdal
Vinkekuil
Velddrif
▲ 2073
▲ 1436
PRETORIA
Vredenburg
Piketberg
Porterville
Laingsburg
Prince Albert
Saldanha
Moorreesburg
▲ 2076
Hottentotskloof
Matjiesfontein
N1
20
Gouda
2251 ▲
Touwsrivier
▲ 2326
▲ 2152
De Rust
Darling
Wolseley
Ceres
De Doorns
Anysberg
Ladismith
Calitzdorp
OUDTSHOORN
Uniondale
19
23
MALMESBURY
4
WORCESTER
Wolwefontein
Durbanville
Wellington
7 6
10
8
Montagu
Muiskraal
▲ 1580
GEORGE
Cape Town
9
15
Robertson
Barrydale
▲ 1526
Knysna
2
PAARL
13 5
11
18
1712
SWELLENDAM
1 STELLENBOSCH
Franschhoek
14 12
16
17
Heidelberg
MOSSELBAAI
Somerset West
1089 N2
Riviersonderend
Riversdale
Simon's Town
Caledon
Port Beaufort
Hermanus
3
Bredasdorp
Elim
Cape Agulhas

Legend:

— The Coastal Region
— The Breërivervallei Region
〜 The Boberg Region

Orange River Valley
Douglas
Andalusia
Olifantsriver
Piquetsberg
Swartland
Tulbagh
Durbanville
Paarl

Constantia
Stellenbosch
Worcester
Robertson
Overberg
Swellendam
Klein Karoo

Wards
1 Simonsberg
2 Franschhoek
3 Walker Bay
4 Slanghoek

5 Goudini
6 Aan-de-Doorns
7 Nuy
8 Vinkrivier
9 Scherpenheuvel
10 Eilandia
11 Goree
12 Riverside
13 Le Chasseur
14 Agterkliphoogte
15 Hoopsrivier
16 McGregor

17 Boesmansrivier
18 Bonnievale
19 Groeneloof
20 Riebeekberg
21 Cedarberg
22 Spruitdrift
23 Wolseley

— Provincial Boundary
▲ Height above sea level (metres)

Kms 20 40 60 80 100
Mls 20 40 60

Vineyard near Franschhoek, Cape Province, above
A flat valley floor provides a typical site for these vines in the Paarl WO area.

export of Cape wines to Britain alone had reached one million gallons. However, in Britain, Cobden (the "apostle of the free market"), and Gladstone secretly negotiated a commercial treaty with the French that had a devastating effect on this trade. In 1860, Cape wine exports fell to half a million gallons, the next year this dropped to 126,000 gallons; by 1865 it was as low as 93,000 gallons.

A time of struggle for South African wine

Despite this setback to the wine trade, production was not checked. In fact, the large influx of immigrants attracted by the discovery of gold and diamonds in the late nineteenth century prompted a rapid expansion of vineyards in anticipation of a vastly increased demand. But the sudden wealth of these immigrants sparked off the Boer War, and sales of wine decreased at home and abroad. Yet farmers continued to make wine they could not sell.

In 1905, the Cape Government encouraged the formation of cooperatives, but nothing constructive was done either to reduce production or stimulate demand. Thus, when the Ko-öperatiewe Wijnbouwers Vereniging, or KWV as it is now known, was formed in 1918 with government-backed powers, its decision to distil half the country's annual wine production into brandy immediately and very effectively improved the quality of Cape wines. Its policy of blending the rest of the surplus into marketable export products did no less than save the South African wine industry.

A new trend in white wines

The launch of a low-cost, medium-dry white wine, "Lieberstein", by the Stellenbosch Farmers' Winery (SFW) in the late-1950s created a dramatic breakthrough on the home market that was to have a direct effect upon exports. Other producers followed suit when they saw sales of "Lieberstein" increase a thousandfold within five years, and soon people who had never even considered drinking wine developed the habit. The 1960s saw further growth, coinciding with quality improvements caused by the widespread introduction of cold-fermentation techniques. The South Africans were at this point ahead of other New World countries in wine technology and, having signed an agreement in 1935 to ban the use of French names, were in much the best position to grab a good share of the international market that was opening up for lighter, drier, fresher, more aromatic white wines. Although it took even serious-quality producers in America and Australia a few years to realize that they had to sell their wines on their own reputation, rather than on the back of traditional French ones, the South Africans failed to make inroads. This was because South Africa's bureaucracy obstructed the cultivation of fashionable grape varieties and failed to provide a centralized campaign to build a generic image for Cape wines. While California took just one year to switch from unfashionable varieties to international favourites simply by chip-budding the new varieties to well-

FACTORS AFFECTING TASTE AND QUALITY

Location
The southernmost tip of the African continent.

Climate
Generally mild Mediterranean type, but coastal areas have a much higher rainfall and are cooler than inland parts in spring and autumn. All coastal areas are cooled to some degree by sea breezes. The coolest district is Overberg, which rates as Region I on the Winkler scale, followed by Constantia and Stellenbosch, both low Region III. Little Karoo, Tulbagh, Olifants River and parts of Paarl (Dal Josaphat) are the hottest, falling between high Region IV and low Region V.

Aspect
Most vines are cultivated on relatively flat or gently undulating valley floors. More recently, higher slopes have been increasingly cultivated, but much has still to be done to fulfil potential.

Soil
Soils range from gravel and heavy loams of sandstone, shale and granitic origin on the coastal plain, to the deep alluvial, sandy and lime-rich, red-shale soils of Little Karoo and other river valleys.

Viticulture and vinification
Contrary to popular belief, Cape vineyards sometimes fail to even ripen their grapes, although there are, of course, many hot areas where vines may suffer from heat-stress and grapes can quickly overripen. Irrigation is often necessary and successful cultivation depends on the availability of water.

Where the heat factor is critical, wealthier estates may conduct the harvest at night, under floodlight, as this enables grapes to be picked at their optimum maturity, and yet conveyed to the press-house at the coolest temperature possible. While Cape winemakers have been quick to adopt such revolutionary practices as will produce fresh, aromatic and vital white wines in areas normally considered too hot for winemaking, they have been slow to cultivate the higher and cooler slopes. South Africa also has a history of overproduction, a disadvantage with some grapes, notably the Pinotage.

Primary grape varieties
Cabernet sauvignon, Chardonnay, Chenin blanc (Steen), Muscat d'Alexandrie (Hanepoot), Pinotage, Sauvignon blanc, Syrah (Shiraz)

Secondary grape varieties
Alicante bouschet, Auxerrois, Barbarossa, Barbera, Bastardo, Bourboulenc, Bukettraube, Cabernet franc, Carignan, Cinsault, Clairette blanche, Colombard, Cornichon, Cornifesto, Crouchen (Cape riesling), Emerald riesling, False Pedro, Ferdinand de Lesseps, Fernão Pires, Flame tokai (Vlamkleur tokai), Folle blanche, Gamay, Gewürztraminer, Grenache (Rooi grenache), Hárslevelü, Malbec, Merlot, Morio muscat, Muscadel, Muscat de Hambourg, Muscat ottonel, Palomino, Pedro Ximénez, Petit verdot, Pinot gris, Pinot noir, Riesling (Rhine/Weisser riesling), Sémillon (Greengrape), Souzão, Tinta amarela (Malvasia rey), Tinta barocca, Tinta Francisca, Tinta roriz, Ugni blanc, Zinfandel

established root-systems, South Africa's ludicrous regulations impounded incoming vines for up to 15 years before they were released to farmers.

THE LACK OF RESTAURANT SALES

Many other obstacles have slowed the Cape's progress towards making top-quality wines. Few South African restaurants can boast talented or original cuisine, and relatively few have a licence. All restaurants allow customers to bring their own and most tend to bring inexpensive wine-boxes. People are conditioned by cheap supermarket prices and unused to paying for recognized international classics. Without the habit of drinking more expensive wines, there is a reluctance to pay the premium required by wine estates to fund lower yields and the purchase of new-oak casks. Amazingly, though, more and more Cape winemakers are managing to break out of this vicious circle.

NEW WINE AREAS

Stellenbosch and Paarl are traditionally viewed as the country's two greatest wine districts, but with the establishment of Hamilton Russell's top-performing vineyard at Hermanus, the Walker Bay area of Overberg to the southeast is now seen by many as potentially much finer. Most surprising of all is the even more recent establishment of Buitenverwachting and Klein Constantia, in 1985 and 1986 respectively, for these two estates have completed the cycle of exploration and development in South Africa's winelands. Constantia, once merely the site of an historic wine, is now the most exciting white-wine area in all South Africa.

Other African wines

Although Kenya and Zimbabwe are obviously not part of South Africa geographically, politically or culturally, for reasons of space and convenience they are included here.

KENYA

It was with utter amazement that I learned of the first Kenyan grape wines, produced by the D'Olier family in 1986. In an equatorial country the production of native wine is something of a gamble, but the D'Oliers, who in 1985 won a silver medal at Lisbon for their papaya wine, have produced two, a white from the family's D'Olier Naivasha estate and a red from Ol Donyo Keri. These Kenyan wines are the world's first commercially available equatorial wines and I look forward to tasting them.

ZIMBABWE

This country has as much as 500 hectares (1,200 acres) of vineyard, and the area under vine is increasing, although there are just three wine companies (profiled below). The industry is very young, having been established as recently as the mid-1960s, and virtually all of its exports are to neighbouring African states. The quality of Zimbabwean wine is only adequate by international standards at present, but exports have begun, albeit in a trickle, and technology is available locally to raise standards should increased exports prove viable.

Of the many grape varieties grown, the most significant are: Cabernet, Clairette blanche, Colombard, Chenin blanc (sometimes called Steen), Hanepoot (red and white), Cinsault (known locally as Hermitage), Servan blanc (known locally as Issor), Muscatel (red and white), Muscat d'Hambourg, Pinotage, Riesling and Seneca.

African Distillers

This company, which is also known as Afdis, produces 11,250 hectolitres (125,000 cases) of wine per year. It owns vineyards at Worringham near Bulawayo, Green Valley near Mutare, and Bertrams at Gweru. The estates are large, but the total area under vine is just 110 hectares (270 acres). Afdis is experimenting with several classic and new grape varieties, and supplements its needs with grapes grown by five privately owned estates, which have vineyards totalling 130 hectares (320 acres).

Monis Wineries

This company has 100 hectares (250 acres) of vineyards, which are situated south of a village called Marondera, 100 kilometres (62 miles) east of Harare. Grapes from these are complemented by purchases from three independently owned vineyards, and processed at Monis's Mukuyu winery. According to Monis, Professor Becker at Germany's Geisenheim research station classifies their level of winemaking as "of international standards", but the company is still seeking to improve its techniques. I have not tasted the wines, but the most interesting appear to be the "Mukuyu" Blanc Fumé, which is matured in French oak and produced in limited quantities only, "Mukuyu" Cabernet, which I assume to be Cabernet Sauvignon, "Mateppe" Late Harvest, which is apparently a rich, semi-sweet wine, and "Veritas" Dry red, which is made in a Burgundy style.

Philips

Although all Philips wines are made and bottled by either African Distillers or Monis, they occupy a unique position at the top end of the Zimbabwean wine market. Under the "Flame Lily" brand, they sell well on the African Continent and have recently begun appearing elsewhere. Sales, both domestic and export, average 3,600 hectolitres (40,000 cases) a year. Domaine-bottled wines are due in the future from a small, young vineyard in the Enterprise district, 36 kilometres (22 miles) from Harare, where Philips currently has six hectares (15 acres). This area is being modestly expanded on an annual basis, and the varieties grown in it include Gewürztraminer, Bukettraube, Chenin blanc, Colombard and Riesling. With deep alluvial and red loam soils, an altitude of 1,050 metres (3,440 ft) and an annual rainfall of 100 centimetres (40 inches), the vineyard sounds promising indeed.

The wines of South Africa

Note: Wines may carry the more specific appellation of a ward (sub-district), if one is classified, and if the wine is made from grapes grown entirely within the ward indicated.

THE COASTAL REGION WO

As the majority of wines exported from South Africa are either "KWV", "Nederburg" or "Fleur du Cap" blends, this is the most frequently encountered appellation. It comprises six districts: Constantia, Durbanville, Paarl, Stellenbosch, Swartland and Tulbagh.

CONSTANTIA WO

Wards: *none*

The vineyards of this district are situated on the eastern, red-granitic slopes of Constantia Mountain, south of Cape Town. Bordered by sea on two sides, the climate is very moderate, of Mediterranean character, with up to 85 centimetres (34 ins) annual rainfall. This is traditionally red-wine country, but Buitenverwachting, which means "beyond expectation", and Klein Constantia have demonstrated its great potential for Sauvignon blanc and Rhine riesling.

DURBANVILLE WO

Wards: *none*

The vineyards of this district are located in the lowlands of the Tygerberg hills and, although the rainfall is less than half that of Constantia, the deep well-weathered, red, granite-based soils have a good water-retention, with the vines cooled and dried by sea-breezes from False Bay. This is generally a red-wine district, with the Pinotage and Shiraz of Meerendale classics of their type.

PAARL WO

Wards: *Franschhoek WO*

This district embraces the fertile Berg River valley and includes the towns of Franschhoek, Wellington and Paarl itself. The vineyards are located on three main types of soil: granite in the Paarl district, Table Mountain sandstone along the Berg River, and Malmesbury slate to the north. The climate is Mediterranean with wet winters and hot, dry summers. Average annual rainfall is about 65 centimetres (26 ins), but this declines towards the northwest of the district. Although mainly a white-wine area, high-lying vineyards are often well-suited to the production of fine quality reds and the many excellent estates include Backsberg and Boschendal.

STELLENBOSCH WO

Wards: *Simonsberg-Stellenbosch WO*

This district is situated between False Bay to the south and Paarl to the north. There are three types of soil; granite-based in the east (considered best for red wines), Table Mountain sandstone in the west (favoured for white wines), and alluvial soils around the Eerste River. With warm, dry summers, cool, moist winters and an average annual rainfall of 50 centimetres (20 ins), irrigation is usually unnecessary, except in some situations at the height of the summer season. This district has the greatest concentration of South Africa's finest wine estates, which include: Alto, Blaauwklippen, Delheim, Goede Hoop, Jacobsdal, Kanonkop, Le Bonheur, Meerlust, Middelvlei, Overgaauw, Simonsig, Spier and Uitkyk.

SWARTLAND WO

Wards: *Riebeekberg WO, Groenekloof WO*

This replaced the old Wine of Origin district of Malmesbury. Of the vast area covered by Swartland, most is arable land, with viticulture confined to the southern section around Darling, Malmesbury and Riebeek. The soils are Table Mountain sandstone and Malmesbury slate, with rainfall light, at around 24 centimetres (10 ins), making irrigation generally necessary. In this primarily red-wine country, there is only one classic wine estate – Allesverloren, with vineyards superbly sited on the slopes of the Kasteelberg near Riebeek West.

TULBAGH WO

Wards: *none*

This district is situated north of Paarl, on the eastern border of Swartland. Although Wolseley is geographically within this district, viticulturally it is part of the Breede River Region. The vineyards of the Tulbagh basin are surrounded by high mountains and located on sandy and shale-based soils. The climate is hot and relatively dry, with some 35 centimetres (14 ins) of annual rainfall, making irrigation necessary, although vines closer to the mountain slopes receive a higher rainfall. This district is well known for its white wines, as its two most famous estates, Theuniskraal and Twee Jongezellen, testify.

THE BOBERG REGION WO

This fortified-wine region is situated within the Coastal Region itself, encompassing the catchment areas of the Berg River and the Klein Berg River in Paarl and Tulbagh districts.

THE BREERIVIERVALLEI or BREEDE RIVER VALLEY REGION WO

This region consists of the three districts of Robertson, Swellendam, and Worcester through which the great Breede River flows, plus Wolseley, which viticulturally forms part of this region. The vineyards in this region depend on irrigation.

ROBERTSON WO

Wards: *Agterkliphoogte WO, Boesmansriver WO, Bonnievale WO (part overlaps Swellendam district), Le Chasseur WO, Eilandia WO, Goree WO, Hoopsrivier WO, McGregor WO, Riverside WO, Vinkrivier WO*

This district is bordered to the south by the Riversonderend Mountains and to the north by Langeberg Range. The soil, climate and topography are, for the most part, similar to those of the Karoo. The top wine estates are Bon Courage, De Wetshof, Rietvallie, Weltevrede, and Zandvliet.

SWELLENDAM WO

Wards: *Bonnievale WO (part overlaps Robertson district)*

The Swellendam district comprises bulk-wine producing vineyards operated by the members of some half-a-dozen cooperatives of mostly average performance, with the occasional excellent winery.

WORCESTER WO

Wards: *Nuy WO, Goudini WO, Slanghoek WO, Scherpenheuvel WO, Aan-de-Doorns WO*

On the western edge of Little Karoo and adjoining the eastern border of Paarl, the Worcester district is richly cultivated with vines in the Breede River catchment area. The soils are derived from Table Mountain sandstone and the fertile red shale of Little Karoo, and the hot climate is tempered in the west by high rainfall, while in the eastern Karoo-influenced section it is very low. Although there are a few wine estates in Worcester, including the excellent Bergsig, the real stars of this district are the high-performing cooperatives that make exceptionally fine white and fortified wines, particularly Nuy Koöp Wynkelder at Nuy, which must be South Africa's finest cooperative.

OTHER NON-REGIONAL DISTRICTS

ANDALUSIA WO

Situated 80 kilometres (50 miles) north of Kimberley, this former ward of Vaalharts has been declared a district in its own right. The one local cooperative, Vaalharts Landboukoöp-erasie, is situtated at Hartswater.

BENEDE ORANJE WO

Small, 10-kilometre (six-mile) stretch of the Orange River near Augrabies. The local cooperative, the Oranjerivier Wynkelders Koöperatief, has centres at Groblershoop, Grootdrink, Kakamas, Keimoes and Upington.

DOUGLAS WO

This district southwest of Kimberley was granted its own Wine of Origin status as recently as 1981. The local cooperative, Douglas Koöp Wynmakery, is in Douglas itself.

LITTLE KAROO or KLEIN KAROO WO

Wards: *none*

A long, narrow strip that stretches from Montagu in the west to De Rust in the east. The vineyards require irrigation to survive the hot and arid climate. The famous red, shale-based Karoo soil and the deep alluvium closer to the various rivers, are very fertile and well-suited to the Jerepigo, Muscadel and other dessert wines for which this area is known. Most of the production is processed by cooperatives, although two wine estates exist and one, Boplaas, is of the very highest standard.

OLIFANTS RIVER or OLIFANTSRIVIER WO

Wards: *Spruitdrift WO, Cedarberg WO*

A long, narrow district with vines growing on sandstone or lime-rich alluvial soil. The climate is hot and dry, with rainfall averaging just 26 centimetres (10.4 ins) and decreasing closer to the coast. There are no wine estates, the grapes grown being processed by some half-a-dozen cooperatives.

THE ORANGE RIVER or ORANJERIVIER REGION WO

Also known as the Lower Orange River, this northernmost viticultural area is totally divorced from the rest of the country's vineyards. The climate is hot and dry, irrigation is essential and the fertile soils are capable of high yields. No estate wines are produced here; all the grapes are processed by local cooperatives.

OVERBERG WO

Wards: *Walker Bay WO*

Overberg replaces the old Wine of Origin district that used to be called Caledon. It consists of a very large, though little-cultivated, area southeast of Paarl and Stellenbosch. There is just one estate, Hamilton Russell Vineyards in the Walker Bay ward, but it is one of South Africa's most exciting; suggesting this district could be ripe for future viticultural development.

PICKETBERG or PIQUETBERG WO

Wards: *none*

A large district sandwiched between Swartland and Tulbagh to the south and Olifants River district to the north. With very hot temperatures and rainfall as low as 17.5 centimetres (7 ins) in places, it is not suited to viticulture.

Major South African wine firms and ranges

ALPHEN WINES

Originally an estate with a history almost as old as that of Groot Constantia, Alphen today markets a range of wines made by Gilbeys from several Stellenbosch vineyards.

☆ Cabernet Sauvignon

BELLINGHAM

A range made and marketed by the Union Wine Group of Wellington. There is in fact a Bellingham estate in Groot Drakenstein, but few of the Bellingham wines are made exclusively from grapes grown on the original farm.

☆ Cabernet Sauvignon, Shiraz, Bukettraube, Special Late Harvest (Chenin-based)

THE BERGKELDER

This Stellenbosch-based organization belongs to the Oude Meester Group and is responsible for the maturation, bottling and marketing of wines from 19 member estates. Some of these estates are owned by the Bergkelder, some are privately, others jointly owned. They consist of Allesverloren, Alto, Bonfoi, La Bonheur, Goede Hoop, Hazendal, Jacobsdal, Koopmanskloof, Meerendal, Meerlust, Middelvlei, Mont Blois, La Motte, L'Ormarins, Rietvallei, Theuniskraal, Uitkyk, De Wetshof and Zandvliet. The Bergkelder markets its own wines under the "Fleur du Cap" and "Stellenryck" labels.

BERTRAMS WINES

The Gilbey-owned Bertrams range is produced at Stellenbosch. Its red wines do not undergo malolactic fermentation, yet win many awards. All Bertrams label wines are made from grapes on Gilbey's Devon Valley estate.

☆ Cabernet Sauvignon, Shiraz, "Director's Reserve Bin F6" Zinfandel

CHATEAU LIBERTAS

This is not an individual estate wine, but a blend of Cabernet, Shiraz and Cinsault from various locations. Its reputation suffered in the 1970s when Cabernet sauvignon came into vogue and supplies of this grape dried up, but the wine has now regained its former rich flavour and fine quality.

CULEMBORG WINES

A range made and marketed by the Union Wine Group of Wellington. They are further down-market than Union's Bellingham range, but are technically well made and extremely good value.

FLEUR DU CAP

This range, made and marketed by the Bergkelder at Stellenbosch, has established a high basic standard of quality and produces the occasional spectacular wine.

☆ Cabernet Sauvignon, Sauvignon Blanc, Gewürztraminer, Special Late Harvest (Chenin blanc)

GILBEYS

The South African arm of IDV, Gilbeys is part-owned by Anton Rupert's large company, Rembrandt. It produces the Alphen, Bertrams, Valley and Vredenburg wine ranges, owns the Hartenberg and Klein Zalze estates, and markets the wines of Spier and Twee Jongegezellen estates.

KWV
Ko-öperatiewe Wijnbouwers Vereniging,
Suider-Paarl 7624

With the enormous volume of wine it receives, the national cooperative organization is obviously capable of making some very good wines. None of its products are allowed to be sold in South Africa, although a trip to one of its international airports is all that is required for any citizen to stock up on his favourite brand.

☆ Cabernet, "Cape Forêt" (oak-matured Chenin blanc), Shiraz, Pinotage, "Roodeberg" (Cabernet-Shiraz-Pinotage-Tinta barocca), "La Concorde Roodevallei" (Cabernet-based), "Laborie White" (Riesling-based), Weisser Riesling, Noble Late Harvest

NEDERBURG WINES

This range of wines, made and marketed by the Stellenbosch Farmers' Winery (SFW), is named after an estate that was renamed Johann Graue in 1972 to honour its first winemaker. Only wines bearing the "Nederburg Johann Graue" label are true estate wines, but under the internationally renowned Günter Brözel, Nederburg has produced a remarkably diverse range of good to very good and sometimes near-miraculous wines, particularly the botrytis Edelkeur and Noble or Special Late Harvest.

☆ Paarl Cabernet Sauvignon, Chardonnay (Auction), "Edelrood" (Cabernet-Shiraz), "Eminence" (light botrytized Muscadel), Gewürztraminer "Special Vintage", Rhine Riesling, Riesling Edelkeur, Shiraz (Auction), Special Late Harvest, Steen Nobel, "Private Bin Nos"

NEIL ELLIS VINEYARD SELECTION
Stellenbosch 7601

A relatively recent project involving the Californian concept of buying grapes on a "select only" basis.

☆ Cabernet Sauvignon, Rhine Riesling, Sauvignon Blanc

OUDE LIBERTAS WINES

These Stellenbosch Farmers' Winery wines have been discontinued as a range, but the label will still appear on limited releases from time to time.

OUDE MEESTER GROUP

This group wholly owns a dozen wine and spirit companies including the Bergkelder, which produces the "Fleur du Cap" and "Stellenryck" ranges and markets the wines of some 19 associate estates.

J. C. LE ROUX

This label is used by the Bergkelder for its production of sparkling wines. The full yet light, yeasty-rich, Pinot Noir, which is made from grapes grown on

the Alto and Meerlust estates, is the best so far.

☆ "J. C. le Roux" Pinot Noir

STELLENBOSCH FARMERS' WINERY or SFW

The opposite number to the Oude Meester Group, SFW owns half-a-dozen different companies and makes and markets Chateau Libertas and the Nederburg and Zonnebloem ranges.

STELLENRYCK COLLECTION

A range of very high-quality and individually characterful wines made and marketed by the Bergkelder as a sort of upmarket "Fleur du Cap".

☆ Stellenryck Collection Cabernet Sauvignon, Rhine Riesling, Blanc Fumé, Gewürztraminer

UNION WINE GROUP

An independent wine group that is not in the same division as Oude Meester or SWF, but ranks with Gilbeys. It produces the Bellingham and Culemborg ranges. *See* Bellingham, Culemborg.

VALLEY WINES

A modestly priced range made and marketed by Gilbeys. The Cabernet Sauvignon is exceptional value.

☆ Valley Cabernet Sauvignon

VREDENBURG

An inexpensive range of Gilbey wines.

ZONNEBLOEM WINES

This upmarket range of wines is owned by SFW.

☆ Cabernet Sauvignon, Shiraz, Sauvignon Blanc, Special Late Harvest (normally blended), Noble Late Harvest (normally blended)

The best wine estates of South Africa

ALLESVERLOREN ESTATE
Riebeek West 6800, Swartland

Vineyards: *150 ha (370 acres; not irrigated)*

Traditionally one of the Cape's greatest Port producers, owner Fanie Malan now makes fine non-fortified wines that have a deep colour and flavour.

☆ Cabernet Sauvignon, Tinta barocca, "Swartland Rood" (Shiraz, Suzão and Pinotage), "Port" (80% Tinta barocca)

ALTO ESTATE
Stellenbosch 7600

Vineyards: *95 ha (235 acres; not irrigated)*

Once the property of Fanie Malan, now of Hempies du Toit, the Alto style is big and muscular and benefits from as long as 10 or 15 years in bottle.

☆ Cabernet Sauvignon, Alto Rouge (Cabernet-Shiraz)

ALTYDGEDACHT ESTATE
Durbanville 7550

Owned by Oliver Parker, who learned his winemaking skills in California and New Zealand. There is the promise of Chardonnay, Sauvignon blanc and Merlot in the near future.

☆ "Tintoretto" (Barbera-Shiraz), Bukettraube

BACKSBERG ESTATE
Klapmuts 7625, Paarl

Vineyards: *160 ha (395 acres; irrigation available)*

This estate is owned by Sydney Back, three times Champion Estate Winemaker. In 1985, Back hired Steve Dooley, a young American oenologist with experience in Napa, California. The wines combine richness, finesse and complexity with great success.

☆ Cabernet Sauvignon, "Klein Babylonstoren" (Cabernet-Merlot matured in new oak), Pinot Noir, Shiraz, Dry Red, Chardonnay, Sauvignon Blanc, Blanc Fumé, "John Martin" (cask-fermented Sauvignon blanc), Bukettraube, Special Late Harvest (Chenin blanc)

BERGSIG ESTATE
Breede River 6858, Worcester

Vineyards: *320 ha (790 acres; irrigated)*

One of the largest wine estates, known for its light, elegant, oaky style.

☆ Cabernet Sauvignon, Pinotage, Noble Late Harvest (Chenin blanc), "Port" (Tinta amarela-Tinta barocca-Cinsault)

BLAAUWKLIPPEN
Stellenbosch 7600

Vineyards: *92 ha (227 acres; approximately one-third irrigated)*

Winemaker Walter Finlayson, who was one of the pioneers of maturation in new oak, is generally considered one of the Cape's great innovators. This estate has a wide range of high-quality wines, with a well-oaked Reserve that is often compared to a fine Médoc.

☆ Cabernet Sauvignon, "Reserve" (Cabernet sauvignon), Pinot Noir, Zinfandel, Shiraz, Red Landau, White Landau, Special Late Vintage, "Barouche" (Pinot and Chardonnay *méthode champenoise*)

BON COURAGE
Robertson 6705

Vineyards: *156 ha (385 acres)*

The wines from this estate used to be sold in bulk and have only been available since the mid-1980s, yet owner Andre Bruwer was Champion Estate Winemaker in 1985 and 1986.

☆ Kerner Special Late Harvest, Noble Late Harvest (Buckettraube)

BONFOI
Vlottenburg 7580, Stellenbosch

Vineyards: *148 ha (366 acres; not irrigated)*

Eight grape varieties are grown, but only one, Chenin blanc, is bottled under the estate label.

☆ "Cuvée Agée" (oak-matured Chenin Blanc)

LE BONHEUR ESTATE
Klapmuts 7625, Stellenbosch

Vineyards: *62 ha (153 acres; not irrigated)*

Owner and winemaker Mike Woodhead is a soil scientist. His Blanc Fumé is widely considered one of the Cape's finest, his Cabernet Sauvignon and recently introduced Chardonnay are just as classy and far more complex.

☆ Cabernet Sauvignon, Blanc Fumé, Chardonnay

BOPLAAS ESTATE
Calitzdorp 6660, Klein Karoo

Vineyards: *50 ha (123 acres)*

It is the deliberate cutting of yields that helps make Boplaas wines so flavoursome. Reds are also intensified by running off one-third of the free-run juice prior to fermentation.

☆ Cabernet Sauvignon, Merlot, Special Late Harvest, "Port" (mostly Tinta barocca)

BOSCHENDAL ESTATE
Groot Drakenstein 7680,
Paarl

Vineyards: *250 ha (618 acres; all but the mountain slopes are irrigated)*

Although this very large estate is best-known as the Cape's pioneering *méthode champenoise* producer, it also produces other exciting wines.

☆ Chardonnay, Cabernet Sauvignon, "Lanoy" (oaky Cabernet-Shiraz), Shiraz, "Blanc de Noir" (Cabernet-Pinotage-Shiraz), "Grand Vin Blanc" (Sauvignon-Riesling-Crouchen), Riesling, "Le Bouquet" (Gewürz-traminer), "Vin d'Or (Riesling-Chenin), Boschendal Brut (variable blend, *méthode champenoise*)

BUITENVERWACHTING
Cape Town 8000, Constantia

Vineyards: *70 ha (173 acres)*

A recently renovated and replanted property that is already showing promise.

☆ Blanc Fumé, Rhine Riesling

CLOS CABRIÈRE ESTATE
Franschhoek 7690

Vineyards: *18 ha (44 acres)*

This estate belongs to Achim von Arnim, the winemaker at Boschendal who, not surprisingly, specializes in fine *méthode champenoise*.

☆ "Pierre Jourdan"

CLOS DE CIEL
Somerset West 7130, Stellenbosch

South Africa's top wine writer, John Platter, has now purchased this small-holding where he intends to grow Chardonnay.

DELAIRE VINEYARDS AND WINES
Stellenbosch 7602

Vineyards: *25 ha (62 acres)*

Wine writer, John Platter set himself up as an easy target when he purchased this property (originally named Avondour) and turned his hand to winemaking. Its cool climate and decomposed granite soil proved ideal, and after replanting the existing vineyards, Platter turned out to be every bit as good at making fine wine as criticizing it. Platter sold Delaire in 1987 and moved to a smallholding called Clos de Ciel. The wines below are recommended on the basis of the standard set by Platter. Future releases will have to be assessed on their own merit.

☆ Rhine Riesling, "Grande Cuvée" (cask-fermented Sauvignon-Riesling), "Cuvée Rouge" (oak-matured Cabernet-Pinotage), Blanc de Blanc (similar to "Grande Cuvée" but without oak), Blanc de Noir (similar to "Cuvée Rouge" but without oak)

DELHEIM WINES
Koelenhof 7605, Stellenbosch – Simonsberg

Vineyards: *120 ha (296.5 acres; irrigation available)*

Delheim's winemaker Kevin Arnold was named South Africa's Champion Winemaker in 1986. His red wines are deep, smoky and beautifully underpinned with new-oak complexity, while his whites, which are often cask-fermented, combine remarkable richness with great finesse. The decadently rich, beautifully balanced botrytis wines are a world-class speciality.

☆ "Grand Reserve" (oak-matured Cabernet sauvignon), Cabernet Sauvignon, Pinot Noir, Pinotage Rosé, Blanc Fumé, "Heerenwijn" (Colombard-Chenin), Gewürz-traminer, "Spatzendreck" Late Harvest (Chenin blanc), Special Late Harvest, "Edelspatz" Noble Late Harvest

EIKENDAL VINEYARDS
Stellenbosch 7600

Vineyards: *70 ha (173 acres)*

Owned by Swiss company A.G. Für Plantagen. Wines made under the "Duc de Berry" label are not quite up to the standard of Eikendal.

☆ Cabernet Sauvignon

FAIRVIEW ESTATE
Suider-Paarl 7625

Vineyards: *130 ha (321 acres; not irrigated)*

This estate is now run by Cyril Back, whose brother Sydney runs the Backs-berg Estate. Fairview is best regarded for its reds. These are firm, rich and powerfully flavoured wines, packed with ripe fruit but not lacking in finesse.

☆ Cabernet Sauvignon, Shiraz, Pinot Noir, "Charles Gerard" (Sauvignon blanc)

GOEDE HOOP ESTATE
Kuils River 7580, Stellenbosch

Vineyards: *80 ha (198 acres; not irrigated)*

Only one wine is produced, a full, smoky-rich, excellent-value, blended red called "Vintage Rouge".

☆ "Vintage Rouge" (Cabernet-Shiraz-based blend)

GROOT CONSTANTIA ESTATE
Constantia 7848

Vineyards: *135 ha (333 acres; not irrigated)*

This government-run property is part of the original Constantia farm, the oldest and most famous of Cape estates. The Cabernet Sauvignon has finesse and freshness and ages very well. The Gewürztraminer has an intense citrus-spice tang, heady bouquet and a luscious, sweet finish.

☆ Cabernet Sauvignon, Shiraz, Pinotage, "Heerenrood" (Cabernet-Shiraz), Weisser Riesling, Stein, Sauvignon Blanc, Gewürztraminer, Constantia Blanc (Chenin-Hárslevelü-Pinot gris-Fernão pires)

HAMILTON RUSSELL VINEYARDS
Hermanus 7200, Overberg

Vineyards: *60 ha (148 acres; irrigation available)*

Situated in the Hemel-en-Aarde Valley behind Hermanus, this is Africa's most southerly vineyard. Owner Tim Hamilton Russell has spared no expense to ensure that it will also become the finest, and Peter Finlayson, his gentle giant of a winemaker, is fastidious in his efforts to make that dream come true.

☆ "Grand Vin Noir" (oak-matured Pinot noir), "Grand Crû Noir" (oak-matured Cabernet-Merlot), Chardon-nay, Sauvignon Blanc, Hemel-en-Aarde Valley Blanc de Blanc (oak-matured Chenin blanc-Colombard-based)

HARTENBERG VINEYARDS
Koelenhof 7605, Stellenbosch

Vineyards: *110 ha (272 acres)*

Formerly known as Montagne, this estate has been purchased by Gilbeys, who renamed it Hartenberg, a strange choice in view of the fact that Gilbey had previously sold a range of lesser-quality wines under the same name. However, the quality of the new Hartenberg wines launched in 1985 is very good.

☆ Cabernet Sauvignon, Shiraz

JACOBSDAL ESTATE
Kuils River 7580, Stellenbosch

Vineyards: *117 ha (289 acres; not irrigated)*

Although several other vine varieties are grown here, only Pinotage is bottled under the estate label. This is not my favourite grape, but the wine from Jacobsdal's low-yielding, bush-trained vines has greater richness, character and complexity, with a less robust, rustic and high-tone character than other versions.

☆ Pinotage

KANONKOP ESTATE
Muldersvlei 7606, Stellenbosch

Vineyards: *128 ha (316 acres; not irrigated)*

Winemaker Beyers Truter is generally considered to be one of the greatest Stellenbosch red-wine exponents.

☆ Cabernet Sauvignon, "Paul Sauer Fleur" (Cabernet-based), Pinot Noir, Pinotage, Sauvignon Blanc

KLEIN CONSTANTIA ESTATE
Constantia 7845

Vineyards: *85 ha (210 acres)*

The first vines were planted here as recently as 1982, but by 1986 its Sauvignon Blanc had picked up the country's premier white-wine prize.

☆ Sauvignon Blanc, Rhine Riesling

LANDSKROON ESTATE
Suider-Paarl 7624

Vineyards: *280 ha (692 acres; not irrigated)*

A very large estate of low-yielding, bush-trained vines that produce full, soft smooth wines.

☆ Cabernet Sauvignon, Pinot Noir, Cinsault, "Bouquet Rouge" (Cinsault-Shiraz)

LEMBERG ESTATE
Tulbagh 6820

Vineyards: *5 ha (12.3 acres; not irrigated)*

Janey Muller's tiny estate is run like a Californian "boutique" winery.

☆ "Vinum Arum" Sauvignon Blanc, "Hommage" Sauvignon Blanc, Sauvignon Blanc, Hárslevelü

LIEVLAND
Klapmuts 7625, Stellenbosch

Vineyards: *70 ha (173 acres; not irrigated)*

Named after one of its former owners, the Russian Baroness of Lievland.

☆ Cabernet, Shiraz, "Rood" (Cabernet-Cinsault-Shiraz)

MEERENDAL ESTATE
Durbanville 7550

Vineyards: *115 ha (284 acres; not irrigated)*

Kosie Stark produces wines of depth and character, which are only let down by the reluctance of the Bergkelder, which represents this estate, to add a touch of new oak.

☆ Shiraz, Pinotage

MEERLUST ESTATE
Faure 7131, Stellenbosch

Vineyards: *280 ha (692 acres; 90 per cent can be irrigated)*

Owner Nico Myburgh is the eighth generation of his family to own and work this farm, one of the Cape's most consistent wine estates.

☆ Cabernet Sauvignon, Pinot Noir, "Rubicon" (Cabernet-Merlot), Merlot

MIDDELVLEI ESTATE
Stellenbosch 7600

Vineyards: *162 ha (400 acres); only Tinta barocca and Clairette blanche are irrigated*

Amiable "Stiljan" Momberg made his reputation with the Pinotage. Since 1981, "Stiljan" has applied equal attention and care to producing stunning Cabernet Sauvignon.

☆ Cabernet Sauvignon, Pinotage

MONT BLOIS ESTATE
Robertson 6705

Vineyards: *120 ha (296 acres; irrigated)*

A consistent winner of gold medals for its famous fortified Muscadel at various local and national wine shows.

☆ Muscadel

NEETHLINGSHOF ESTATE
Stellenbosch 7600

Vineyards: *138 ha (341 acres; 40 per cent irrigated)*

Until 1985, this estate belonged to "Jan Bek" Momberg, the cousin of Middelvlei's "Stiljan" Momberg; most of the wines recommended below are his. However, new owner Hans Schreiber is sparing no expense and there is no drop in quality.

☆ "Lord Neetling" Rouge (Cabernet-Tinta barocca matured in new oak), Colombard, Weisser Riesling Special Late Harvest, Gewürztraminer, Gewürztraminer Special Late Harvest

L'ORMARINS ESTATE
Groot Drakenstein, Paarl

Vineyards: *175 ha (432 acres; irrigated)*

This estate is run by Toni Rupert, the son of Anton Rupert, the second-richest man in South Africa and the most powerful influence in the country's wine industry. L'Ormarins has quickly risen to the top ranks of South African wine estates through the unbeatable combination of Toni's boyish enthusiasm, unlimited finance and a superbly situated vineyard. Night harvesting, to bring in the grapes at their coolest and optimum ripeness, is a speciality.

☆ Cabernet Sauvignon, Shiraz, Chardonnay, Blanc Fumé, Sauvignon Blanc, Rhine Riesling, Bukettraube Noble Late Harvest, Chenin Blanc Noble Late Harvest

OVERGAAUW ESTATE
Vlottenburg 7604, Stellenbosch

Vineyards: *75 ha (185 acres; 60 per cent irrigated)*

A technically superior operation that produces exciting wines with lots of class but very little sulphur dioxide.

☆ "Tria Corda" (oak-matured Cabernet-Merlot), Cabernet Sauvignon, "Overtinto" (Tintas barocca, Francisca and amarela, plus Cornifesto and Souzão, wood-matured "Port" style), Chardonnay, Vintage "Port" (similar grapes to "Overtinto", but aged in bottle, not wood)

RIETVALLEI ESTATE
Robertson 6705

Vineyards: *128 ha (316 acres; irrigated)*

Specialist producer of medal-winning sweet, fortified, red Muscadel wine.

☆ Rietvallei Rooi Muskadel

RUSTENBERG
Stellenbosch 7600

Vineyards: *80 ha (198 acres; less than one-tenth irrigated)*

Although only 80 hectares (198 acres) are under vine, this huge estate encompasses some 1,000 hectares (2,470 acres).

☆ Cabernet Sauvignon, Pinot Noir, "Rustenberg" (Cabernet-Shiraz)

RUST-EN-VREDE ESTATE
Stellenbosch 7600

Vineyards: *31 ha (77 acres; not irrigated)*

Owned by Jannie Engelbrecht, a former Springbok, who produces only wines he likes to drink. He has taste!

☆ Cabernet Sauvignon, Shiraz

SIMONSIG ESTATE
Koelenhof 7605, Stellenbosch

Vineyards: *180 ha (445 acres; 70 per cent irrigated)*

The estate is owned by Frans Malan, one of the Cape's pioneers in *méthode champenoise* wines.

☆ Cabernet Sauvignon, Chardonnay, Shiraz, Morio Muscat, Gewürztraminer, Weisser Riesling, Noble Late Harvest (various different blends), "Kaapse Vonkel" (Chenin-based *méthode champenoise*, soon due to become a Chardonnay-Pinot noir blend)

SPIER ESTATE
Vlottenburg 7604, Stellenbosch

Vineyards: *250 ha (618 acres; irrigated)*

Its wines marketed by Gilbeys, this estate is owned and run by Chris Joubert and his father Niel, who are direct descendents of founder Pierre Joubert, a Huguenot *vigneron* from the Loire Valley.

☆ Cabernet Sauvignon, Shiraz, Colombard, Special Late Harvest, Chenin Blanc Special Late Harvest

THEUNISKRAAL ESTATE
Tulbagh 6820

Vineyards: *150 ha (370 acres; irrigated)*

A white-wine specialist estate that consistently wins awards and medals. The Riesling is the most famous Theuniskraal wine, the Gewürztraminer the most popular, and the Sémillon the most serious.

☆ Riesling, Gewürztraminer, Sémillon

TWEE JONGEGEZELLEN ESTATE
Tulbagh 6820

Vineyards: *274 ha (677 acres; irrigated)*

This vast estate used to make as many as a dozen different wines, but this was reduced to just five, all white, in the mid-1980s.
No other estate can claim to produce so much white wine of such a consistently high standard. The owner, N. C. Krone, is a great innovator.

☆ "TJ 39 Grand Prix; (Muscat-Riesling, plus up to 15 other varieties), "Schanderl" (Muscat-Gewürztraminer-Riesling-based blend), "TJ Light" (Gewürztraminer-Müller Thurgau-Pinot gris-based, low-alcohol blend), "TJ Night Harvest" (Riesling-Sauvignon-Chenin-based blend), "Engeltjiepipi" (light botrytis style, various varieties)

UITKYK ESTATE
Muldersvlei 7606, Stellenbosch

Vineyards: *165 ha (408 acres; two-thirds irrigated)*

This estate, whose name is pronounced "ate-cake", owes its current reputation to more than two decades of effort on the part of its winemaker, Harvey Illing.

☆ "Carlonet" (Cabernet sauvignon-Shiraz-Cinsault-Pinotage blend), "Carlsheim" (Sauvignon-based)

VON LOVEREN
Klaasvoogds 6707, Robertson

Vineyards: *107 ha (264 acres)*

The wines from this estate are relatively new, but very promising.

☆ Noble Late Harvest (Riesling-Chenin blend)

VERGENOEGD ESTATE
Faure 7131, Stellenbosch

Vineyards: *130 ha (321 acres; irrigation available)*

An historic estate with a very traditional reputation. Its conservative approach ensures that consistently excellent wines are made.

☆ Cabernet Sauvignon, Shiraz, Cinsault

VILLIERA ESTATE
Koelenhof 7605, Paarl

Vineyards: *95 ha (235 acres)*

A rapidly rising star on the Cape wine scene, Villiera has gained something of a reputation for its excellent value-for-money *méthode champenoise* and various other innovative styles of wine.

☆ "Crû Monro" (Merlot-Cabernet), "Private Reserve" (Cabernet-based blend), Rhine Riesling, Sauvignon Blanc, Tradition Charles de Fère (*méthode champenoise* Pinotage-Chenin-Pinot noir)

VRIESENHOF
Stellenbosch 7600

Vineyards: *15 ha (37 acres; not irrigated)*

A small estate run by another ex-Springbok, Jan "Boland" Coetzee, whose interests in things Burgundian have led him to turn *négociant-éleveur* in a small way.

☆ "Private Reserve" (Cabernet sauvignon), Chardonnay

WELGEMEEND ESTATE
Klapmuts 7625, Paarl

Vineyards: *13 ha (32 acres; not irrigated)*

Small, high-quality, red-wine estate.

☆ "Estate Wine", Cabernet Sauvignon, "Amadé", "Douelle"

WELTEVREDE ESTATE
Bonnievale 6730, Robertson

Vineyards: *110 ha (272 acres; irrigated)*

Weltevrede means "well satisfied", an apt comment on the wines.

☆ Rhine Riesling, Gewürztraminer, Noble Late Harvest (Chenin-Riesling-based blend), Muscat de Hambourg

DE WETSHOF ESTATE
Robertson 6705

Vineyards: *120 ha (297 acres; irrigated)*

Specialist in well-made white wines.

☆ Rhine Riesling, Chardonnay, Sauvignon Blanc, Edeloes (botrytis)

ZANDVLIET ESTATE
Ashton 6715, Robertson

Vineyards: *131 ha (324 acres; irrigated)*

Famous for its Shiraz, but Pinot Noir might well be its future star.

☆ Pinot Noir, Shiraz

ZEVENWACHT
Kuils River 7580, Stellenbosch

Vineyards: *200 ha (494 acres; not irrigated)*

Zevenwacht has grown rapidly and makes fresh, frank and aromatic wines.

☆ Cabernet Sauvignon, Rhine Riesling, Gewürztraminer

Important South African Cooperatives

AAN DE DOORNS KOÖP WYNKELDER
Worcester 6850

Established: *1955*

This cooperative produces fine, well-balanced Cabernet Sauvignon and medal-winning dry Chenin Blanc.

☆ Cabernet Sauvignon, Chenin Blanc

BADSBERG KOÖP WYNKELDER
Rawsonville 6845, Worcester

Established: *1951*

This cooperative has a great reputation for its immensely rich and luscious, honey-gold, Hanepoot dessert wine.

☆ Hanepoot

BOLANDSE KOÖP WYNKELDER
Huguenot 7645, Paarl

Established: *1948*

Highly-praised cooperative, incorporating the Paarlvallei Koöp Wynkelder.

☆ Cabernet Sauvignon, Riesling, Late Vintage

BOTHA KOÖP WYNKELDER
Botha 6857, Breede River, Robertson

Regular medal-winning wines.

☆ Cabernet Sauvignon

BOTTELARY KOÖP WYNKELDER
Koelenhof 7605, Stellenbosch

This cooperative has a reputation for its white wines in particular.

☆ Cabernet Sauvignon, Colombard, Weisser Riesling, Gewürztraminer

DU TOITSKLOOF KOÖP WYNKELDER
Rawsonville 6845, Worcester

This cooperative has produced several award-winning wines since 1968.

☆ Cinsault, Bukettraube

EERSTERIVIER VALLEISE KOÖP WYNKELDER
Vlottenburg 7604, Stellenbosch

Eersterivier Valleise regularly wins awards, particularly for white wines.

☆ "Hanseret" Rouge (Cabernet-based blend), Chenin Blanc, "Hanseret" Dry White (Colombard-Clairette), "Hanseret" Semi-Sweet (Chenin-based)

FRANSCHHOEK VINEYARD KOÖP WYNKELDER
Franschhoek 7690

Another cooperative with a reputation for white wines.

☆ "La Cotte" Sauvignon Blanc, "La Cotte" Rhine Riesling

HELDERBERG KOÖP WYNKELDER
Firgrove 7110, Stellenbosch

A large range of above-average wines.

☆ Cabernet Sauvignon

NORDALE KOÖP WYNKELDER
Bonnievale 6730, Swellendam

A small range of very good-quality wines. Although established as recently as 1950, Nordale is the oldest winery in the area.

☆ Colombard, Red Muscadel Jerepigo

NORTH WESTERN WINE MERCHANTS
See Vredendal Koöperatiewe Wynkelder.

NUY KOÖP WYNKELDER
Nuy 6700, Worcester

South Africa's finest cooperative produces wines that can compete with the best estate-produced wines.

☆ Colombard, Colombard Effe Soet, Bukettraube, "Chant de Nuy" (Colombard-Chenin-based blend), Red Muscadel, White Muscadel

OLIFANTSRIVIER KOÖP WYNKELDER
See Vredendal Koöp Wynkelder.

PAARLVALLEI KOÖP WYNKELDER
See Bolandse Koöp Wynkelder.

ROBERTSON KOÖP WYNKELDER
Robertson 6705

Winemaker Pon van Zyl, who retired as recently as 1985, is still affectionately known as the "father of the Colombard".

☆ Colombard, Bukettraube, Steen Special Late Harvest, "Soet" Muskadel, "Baron du Pon" (upmarket, low-key Colombard)

ROMANSRIVIER KOÖP WYNKELDER
Wolseley 6830, Breede River, Robertson

One of the most successful medal-winning cooperatives in the country.

☆ Cabernet Sauvignon, "Vin Blanc Special Reserve", Colombard Effe-soet, Edel Laatoes

ROODEZANDT KOÖP WYNKELDER
Robertson 6705

A top-performing cooperative that is beginning to use small new-oak *barriques* to mature selected wines.

☆ Cabernet Sauvignon, Emerald Riesling, Muscat d'Alexandrie, Soet Hanepoot, Hanepoot Jerepigo, White Muscadel

ROOIBERG KOÖP WYNKELDER
Robertson 6705

Another medal-winning cooperative.

☆ Blanc Fumé, "Vinkrivier" Steen, Muscadel Red, Muscadel White

SIMONSVLEI KOÖP WYNKELDER
Suider Paarl 7624

This cooperative has a 40-year-old reputation for producing fine wines.

☆ Cabernet Sauvignon, Shiraz, Chenin Blanc, Muscadel Jerepigo

SLANGHOEK KOÖP WYNKELDER
Rawsonville 6845, Worcester

This cooperative has a very good reputation for its white wines.

☆ Colombard, Soet Hanepoot

SPRUITDRIFT KOÖP WYNKELDER
Vredendal 8160, Olifants River

A medal-winning cooperative with a reputation for talented winemakers such as Giel Swiegers and, currently, Johann Rossouw.

☆ Nags Pars, Special Late Harvest, Hanepoot Jerepigo

VLOTTENBURG KOÖP WYNKELDER
Vlottenburg 7604, Stellenbosch

This medal-winning cooperative excels with its white wines.

☆ Riesling, Weisser Riesling, Special Late Harvest (blend)

VREDENDAL KOÖPERATIEWE WYNKELDER
Vredendal 8160, Olifants River

Established: *1948*

Formerly known as Olifantsrivier Koöp Wynkelder, this is South Africa's largest and fastest-improving cooperative. Its wines are marketed under the "North Western Wine Merchants" label.

☆ Hanepoot Jerepigo

WABOOMSRIVIER KOÖP WYNKELDER or WAGONBOOM WINES
Breërivier 6858, Worcester

The label of these medal-winning wines features the flower of *waboom*, from whose wood wagon-wheels used to be made locally.

☆ Cabernet Sauvignon, Ruby Cabernet, Sweet Hanepoot Jerepigo

WELMOED KOÖP WYNKELDER
Lynedoch 7603, Stellenbosch

These wines were made by Kobus Rossouw prior to his move to the Simonsvlei Koöp Wynkelder.

☆ Cabernet Sauvignon, Shiraz, Rouge Sec, Weisser Riesling, Sauvignon Blanc, Noble Late Harvest, Sweet Hanepoot

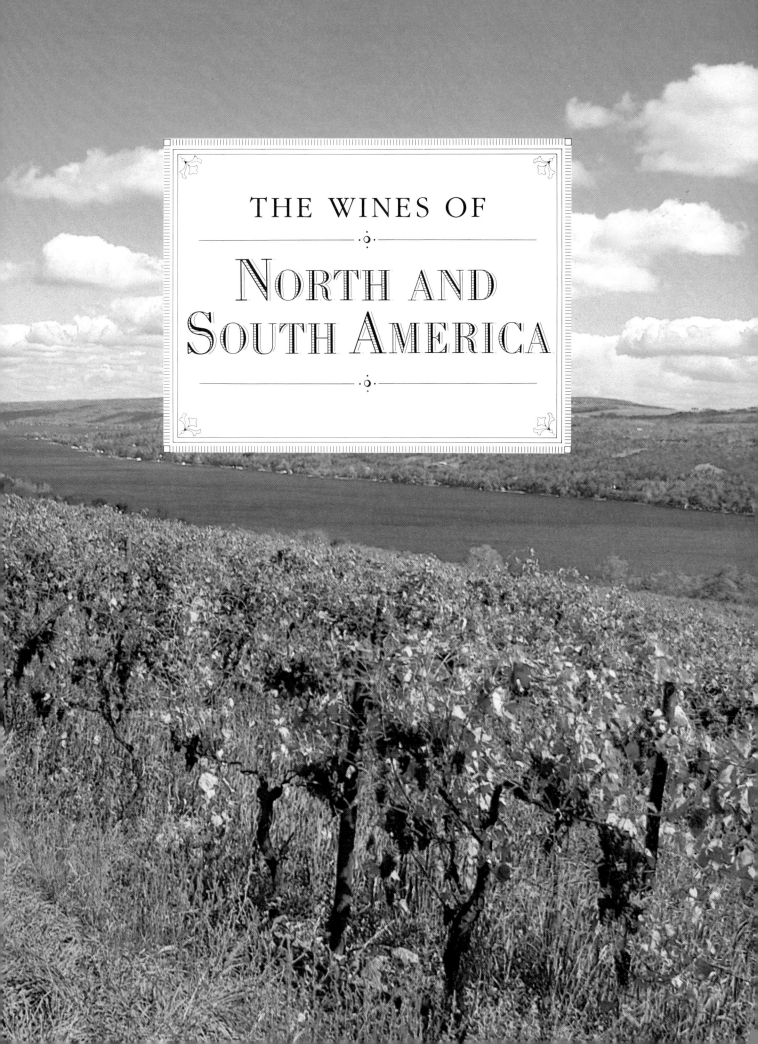

THE WINES OF

NORTH AND SOUTH AMERICA

North America

To talk of North American wine is not to discuss California alone. Although California would rank as the sixth-largest wine-producing nation in the world (if it were a nation), it is but one of 40 wine-producing states within the United States, and the vineyards of North America also encompass those of Ontario and British Columbia in Canada (*see* p.402), and the Baja California and Sierra Madre in Mexico (*see* p.400).

IN 1521, WITHIN ONE YEAR OF INVADING Mexico, the Spanish conquistadors planted vines and set about making the first North American wines. Fourteen years later, when French explorer Jacques Cartier sailed down the St. Lawrence to New France, he discovered a large island overrun by wild vines and decided to call it the Ile de Bacchus. He had second thoughts, however, and later renamed it the Ile d'Orleans, a calculated move in view of the fact that the then Duke of Orleans was the son of King Francis I of France. It is assumed that, circa 1564, the Jesuit settlers who followed in the wake of Cartier's explorations were the first winemakers in what was to become Canada. The earliest wines made in what is now the United States of America came from Florida. Between 1562 and 1564, French Huguenot settlers produced wines from native Scuppernong grapes growing on a site that would become Jacksonville.

NATIVE NORTH AMERICAN GRAPE VARIETIES

All classic grape varieties belong to one species, *Vitis vinifera*, but North America's native varieties belong to several different species, not one of which happens to be *Vitis vinifera* (*see* Grape variety, p.10). There were plenty of native vines growing wild wherever the early settlers travelled, and so they came to rely on them for their initial wine production. The Australian settlers, on the other hand, were forced to wait for precious shipments of classic European vines before they could plant vineyards. Although various European varieties were taken across the Atlantic in the nineteenth century, nearly all North American wines outside of California remained the product of native varieties until relatively recently.

The most common native North American species, *Vitis labrusca*, has such a distinctive aroma and flavour that it seems truly amazing that those pioneers who were also winemakers did not pester their home countries for supplies of more acceptable vines. The *labrusca* character, commonly referred to as "foxy", makes the most aromatic of Muscats appear almost neutral by comparison, and it is generally not appreciated by European and

Australian palates. The "foxy" aroma is so exotic and treacle-sweet that it pervades every aspect of the flavour and makes the aftertaste cloy and linger at the back of the throat.

PROHIBITION IN THE UNITED STATES

Although total Prohibition in the United States was confined to 1920-1933, the first "dry legislation" was passed as early as 1816, and the first state to go completely dry was Maine, in 1846. By the time the 18th Amendment to the Constitution was put into effect in 1920, forbidding "the manufacture, sale or transport of intoxicating liquors", more than 30 states were already totally dry.

The result of Prohibition was chaos. It denied the government legitimate revenue and encouraged bootleggers to amass fortunes. The number of illicit stills multiplied quicker than the authorities could find and dismantle them, and the speakeasy became a way of life in the cities. Not only did the authorities often realize that it was much easier to turn a blind eye to what was going on, the federal government actually found it useful to open its own speakeasy in New York! Many vineyards were uprooted, but those grapes that were produced were often concentrated, pressed and sold as "grape bricks". These came complete with a yeast capsule and instructions to dissolve the brick in one gallon of water, but warned against adding the yeast because it would start a fermentation. This would turn the grape juice into wine "and that would be illegal", the warning pointed out.

Prohibition and the wine industry

By the mid-to-late nineteenth century, the Californian wine industry had such a reputation that great French wine areas, such as Champagne, began to form *syndicats* to protect themselves, in part, from the potential of California's marketing threat. However, the thirteen years of Prohibition coincided with a vital point in the evolution of wine, and its effect was to set the Californian wine industry back a hundred years.

In Europe, the First World War had robbed every industry of its young, up-and-coming generation, but the rich tradition of the wine industry enabled it to survive until the arrival of a new generation. The early 1900s were also the era of the foundation of the French Appellation Controlée laws, a quality control system that all other serious winemaking countries would eventually copy. The United States also lost much of one generation in the First World War, but it had less of a winemaking tradition to fall back on and, come 1920, there was virtually no wine industry whatsoever to preserve. After Prohibition came one of the worst economic depressions in history, followed by a Second World War that took yet another generation of bright young minds. It was, therefore, little wonder that by the late 1940s the wine industry of the United States was so out of date. It had lost touch with European progress and resorted to the production of awful *labrusca* wines that had been the wine drinker's staple diet in pre-Prohibition days. California produced relatively little *labrusca* compared to the eastern states, but its winemakers also resorted to old-fashioned styles, making heavy, sweet, fortified wines. The fact that Californian wine today is a match for the best of its European counterparts and that its industry is healthy, growing fast and looking to compete on foreign markets, clearly proves that in the United States opportunity is obviously boundless.

Mount Pleasant Vineyards, Missouri, above
In Augusta, America's first Approved Viticultural Area, are the Mount Pleasant Vineyards, a reminder that there is more to American wine than California.

ANNUAL NORTH AMERICAN WINE PRODUCTION

Country	Cases (Hectolitres)	Hectares (acres) under vine
Canada	3,000,000 (270,000 hectolitres)	10,100 (25,000)
USA	220,000,000 (19,800,000 hectolitres)	405,000 (1,000,000)
Mexico	2,500,000 (225,000 hectolitres)	58,000 (143,000)

NORTH AMERICA

Across the continent of North America, in Canada, the United States and Mexico, wine is produced, be it from native grapes or vinifera *varieties, with winemakers working in enormously varied conditions according to climate. One could be forgiven for forgetting that, legally if not geographically, sun-blessed Hawaii (left) is part of North America. Maui Island boasts the state's one winery.*

Legend:
- California *See also p.363*
- Pacific Northwest *See also p.389*
- Atlantic Northeast *See also p.392*
- Canada-British Columbia *See also p.402*
- Canada-Ontario *See also p.402*
- Ozark Highland
- Ozark Mountain
- Other winemaking areas

— International Boundary
State/Provincial Boundary
▲ Height above sea level (metres)

• Winery
▲ Height above sea level (metres)

Kms 100 200 300 400 500
Mls 100 200 300

Kms 200 400 600 800 1000
Mls 200 400 600

THE APPELLATION SYSTEM OF THE UNITED STATES

Every state, from Hawaii to Alaska, and each of the counties it contains, is recognized in law by the Department of Treasury's Bureau of Alcohol, Tobacco and Firearms (BATF), as its own individual appellation of origin, but other generic appellations are also recognized. The appellations are categorized as follows:

American Wine Appellation

A wine from anywhere, blended or otherwise, within the United States of America, including the District of Columbia and the Commonwealth of Puerto Rico. Irrationally, as with wine from EEC countries, this is classed as *vin de table* that must not carry a vintage. It is the only appellation allowed for wines shipped in bulk to other countries.

Multi-state Appellation

A wine from any two or three contiguous states. The percentage of wine from each state must be clearly indicated on the label.

State Appellation

A wine from any state; at least 75 per cent of grapes must come from grapes grown within the one state indicated. Thus wine claiming the appellation of California may contain up to 25 per cent produce of one other, or a variety of several other, state(s). The same principle applies to County Appellations.

County Appellation

A wine from any county within any state, at least 75 per cent of the wine must come from grapes grown within the one county indicated.

Note: For the purposes of the above appellations, the definition of "state" also includes the District of Columbia and the Commonwealth of Puerto Rico.

The effects of the system

The possible permutations of multi-county appellations alone are so daunting that not even the BATF has been able to compile a complete list of all the appellations that are permitted under the law it administers. The law itself is sympathetic to the American ideal of its citizens being free to make an honest living wherever, whenever and however they can, and as such is admirable. However the all-encompassing appellation system, which guarantees the origin of a product from anywhere, is worse than useless in my opinion, because it only serves to complicate and confuse. To be of practical use to the consumer, a system has to guarantee the origin of products from areas that have some degree of repute for that product. For example: when buying coffee, it is useful to know that the beans come from Brazil or Kenya, but what would be the point of coffee beans carrying a guarantee of Appellation Rwanda Contrôlée? Rwanda certainly does produce coffee, but it is a coffee that has no international prestige and is best sold under a brand name of a reputable coffee blender on export markets, as indeed it is.

THE APPROVED VITICULTURAL AREAS OF THE UNITED STATES

During the mid-1970s, the BATF considered the concept of specific controlled appellations, and in September 1978 published its first laws and regulations designed to introduce a system of Approved Viticultural Areas (AVAs), to supplement the old appellation system. As a result, in order to establish an Approved Viticultural Area, interested parties have to supply the following, and I quote:

● Evidence that the name of the viticultural area is locally or internationally known.

● Historical or current evidence that the boundaries of the viticultural area are as specified in the appellation.

● Evidence relating to the geographical features (climate, soil, elevation, physical features, and the like) that distinguish the viticultural features of the proposed area from those of surrounding areas.

● The specific boundaries of the viticultural area, based on the features that can be found on United States Geological Survey (USGS) maps of the largest applicable scale.

● A copy of the appropriate USGS map with the boundary prominently marked.

Vineyards, Upstate New York, above
Rows of vines combine to form an emerald-green patchwork on the gently sloping countryside near Hammondsport. In the distance is Keuka Lake, one of the finger-shaped lakes that have a moderating influence on the area's climate.

Jekel Vineyards, California, right
An irrigation pipe skirts rows of vines in one of the drier parts of Monterey County. Conditions are a far cry from those around the Finger Lakes.

The status of AVAs

If only because of their defined geographical boundaries, the AVAs of the United States bear some relation to the AOCs of France. However, because the AVAs are such a recent innovation, they have not yet evolved to a point where anything sensible can be said about each specific one in terms of styles of wine, grape varieties, vintage differences, and the like. In the sections on the AVAs of particular areas, I have therefore given details of geographical, climatic and soil factors that affect quality and distinguish one AVA from another, or from the surrounding, unclassified, areas. These factors will obviously affect styles of wine.

Because many AVAs have yet to establish a "wine identity", the American maps show wine regions – not necessarily with AVA status – whose wine has established a reputation. Regions that are not AVAs may not even have applied for AVA status.

THE AVAs OF THE UNITED STATES

The number of AVAs is set to rise. The current total is 109, with a further two pending.

Alexander Valley (California, established 23rd November 1984)

Altus (Arkansas, established 29th June 1984)

Anderson Valley (California, established 19th September 1983)

Arkansas Mountain (Arkansas, established 27th October 1986)

Arroyo Grande Valley (California, established 5th February 1990)

Arroyo Seco (California, established 16th May 1983)

Augusta (Missouri, established 20th June 1980)

Bell Mountain (Texas, established 10th November 1986)

Ben Lomond Mountain (California, established 8th January 1988)

California Shenandoah Valley (California, established 27th January 1983)

Carmel Valley (California, established 15th January 1983)

Catoctin (Maryland, established 14th November 1983)

Cayuga Lake (New York, established 25th March 1988)

Central Coast (California, established 25th November 1985)

Central Delaware Valley (Pennsylvania and New Jersey, established 18th April 1984)

Chalk Hill (California, established 21st November 1983)

Chalone (California, established 14th July 1982)

Cienega Valley (California, established 20th September 1982)

Clarksburg (California, established 22nd February 1984)

Clear Lake (California, established 7th June 1984)

Cole Ranch (California, established 16th March 1983)

Columbia Valley (Oregon and Washington, established 13th December 1984)

Cumberland Valley (Maryland and Pennsylvania, established 26th August 1985)

Dry Creek Valley (California, established 6th September 1983)

Edna Valley (California, established 11th June 1982)

El Dorado (California, established 14th November 1983)

Fennville (Michigan, established 19th October 1981)

Fiddletown (California, established 3rd November 1983)

Finger Lakes (New York, established 1st October 1982)

Fredericksburg (Texas, established 22nd December 1988)

Grand River Valley (Ohio, established 21st November 1983)

Guenoc Valley (California, established 21st December 1981)

Herman (Missouri, established 10th September 1983)

Howell Mountain (California, established 30th January 1984)

Hudson River Region (New York, established 6th July 1982)

Isle St. George (Ohio, established 20th September 1982)

Kanawha River Valley (West Virginia, established 8th May 1986)

Knights Valley (California, established 21st November 1983)

Lake Eric (New York, Pennsylvania and Ohio, established 21st November 1983)

Lake Michigan Shore (Michigan, established 14th November 1983)

Lancaster Valley (Pennsylvania, established 11th June 1982)

Leelanau Peninsula (Michigan, established 29th April 1982)

Lime Kiln Valley (California, established 6th July 1982)

Linganore (Maryland, established 19th September 1983)

Livermore Valley (California, established 1st October 1982)

Lodi (California, established 7th March 1986)

Loramie Creek (Ohio, established 27th December 1982)

Los Carneros (California, established 19th September 1983)

Madera (California, established 7th January 1985)

Martha's Vineyard (Massachusetts, established 4th February 1985)

McDowell Valley (California, established 4th January 1982)

Mendocino (California, established 16th July 1984)

Merritt Island (California, established 16th June 1983)

Mesilla Valley (New Mexico and Texas, established 18th March 1985)

Middle Rio Grande Valley (New Mexico, established 2nd February 1988)

Mimbres Valley (New Mexico, established 23rd December 1985)

Mississippi Delta (Louisiana, Mississippi and Tennessee, established 1st October 1984)

Monterey (California, established 16th July 1984)

Monticello (Virginia, established 22nd February 1984)

Mt. Harlan (California, established 5th February 1990)

Mt. Veeder (California, established 22nd March 1990)

Napa Valley (California, established 27th February 1981)

North Coast (California, established 21st October 1983)

Northern Fork – George Washington Birthplace (Virginia, established 31st May 1987)

Northern Sonoma (California, established 17th June 1985)

North Fork of Long Island (New York, established 10th November 1986)

North Fork of Roanoke (Virginia, established 16th May 1983)

Noth Yuba (California, established 30th August 1985)

Ohio River Valley (Indiana, Ohio, West Virginia and Kentucky, established 7th October 1983)

Old Mission Peninsula (Michigan, established 8th July 1987)

Ozark Highlands (Montana, established 30th September 1987)

Ozark Mountain (Arkansas, Missouri and Oklahoma, established 1st August 1986)

Pacheco Pass (California, established 11th April 1984)

Paicines (California, established 15th Sepbember 1982)

Paso Robles (California, established 3rd November 1983)

Potter Valley (California, established 14th November 1983)

Rocky Knob (Virginia, established 11th February 1983)

Rogue Valley (Oregon, pending approval)

Russian River Valley (California, established 21st November 1983)

San Benito (California, established 4th November 1983)

San Lucas (California, established 2nd March 1987)

San Pasqual Valley (California, established 16th September 1981)

San Ysidro District (California, pending approval)

Santa Clara Valley (California, established 28th March 1989)

Santa Cruz Mountains (California, established 4th January 1982)

Santa Maria Valley (California, established 4th September 1981)

Santa Ynez Valley (California, established 16th May 1983)

Shenandoah Valley (Virginia and West Virginia, established 27th January 1983)

Sierra Foothills (California, established 18th December 1987)

Solano County Green Valley (California, established 28th January 1983)

Sonoita (Arizona, established 26th November 1984)

Sonoma Coast (California, established 13th July 1987)

Sonoma County Green Valley (California, established 21st December 1983)

Sonoma Mountain (California, established 22nd February 1985)

Sonoma Valley (California, established 4th January 1982)

South Coast (California, established 23rd December 1985)

Southeastern New England (Connecticut, Rhode Island and Massachusetts, established 27th April 1984)

Stag's Leap District (California, established 27th January 1989)

Suisun Valley (California, established 27th December 1982)

Temecula (California, established 23rd November 1984)

The Hamptons, Long Island (New York, established 17th June 1985)

Umpqua Valley (Oregon, established 30th April 1984)

Virginia Eastern Shore (Virginia, established 2nd January 1991)

Walla Walla Valley (Washington and Oregon, established 7th March 1984)

Warren Hills (New Jersey, established 8th August 1988)

Western Connecticut Highlands (Connecticut, established 9th February 1988)

Wild Horse Valley (California, established 30th November 1988)

Willamette Valley (Oregon, established 3rd January 1984)

Willow Creek (California, established 9th September 1983)

Yakima Valley (Washington, established 4th May 1983)

York Mountain (California, established 23rd September 1983)

THE LAW AND AMERICAN WINE LABELS

American law permits brand names that convey "no erroneous impressions as to the age, origin, identity, or other characteristics of the product". The law is not, however, quite as reasonable as it seems, because it allows American winemakers to label their products with "generic" and "semi-generic" names and lists these as:
Generic: Vermouth, Sake
Semi-generic: Angelica, Burgundy, Claret, Chablis, Champagne, Chianti, Haut Sauterne, Hock, Malaga, Marsala, Madeira, Moselle, Port, Rhine Wine, Sauterne, Sherry, Tokay
The Act then proceeds to list "non-generic" names that cannot be used on American wine labels:
Non-generic: Aloxe-Corton, Alsace, Alsation *(sic)*, Anjou, Anjou-Saumur, Beaujolais, Beaune, Bordeaux, Bordeaux Blanc, Bordeaux Rouge, Bourgogne des Environs de Chablis *(sic)*, Chambertin, Chambolle-Musigny, Chassagne-Montrachet, Château Lafite, Château Margaux, Châteauneuf-du-Pape, Château Yquem *(sic)*, Côte Beaujolaise *(sic)*, Côte de Beaune, Côte Mâconnaise *(sic)*, Côte de Nuits, Côte du Rhône, Côte Rôtie, Coteaux du Layon, Coteaux de la Loise *(sic)*, Deidesheimer, Flagey-Echézeaux, Forster *(sic)*, Gevrey-Chambertin, Grand Chablis *(sic)*, Graves, Graves Barsac *(sic)*, Hermitage, Lacryma Christi, Lagrima *(sic)*, Liebfraumilch, Loire *(sic)*, Mâcon, Mâconnais, Margaux, Médoc, Meursault, Montrachet, Morey, Mosel, Mosel-Saar-Ruwer, Nuits, Nuits-St.-Georges, Pomerol, Pommard, Puligny-Montrachet, Rhône, Rudesheimer, Santenay, Saumur, Savigny, Schloss Johannisberger, St.-Emilion, St.-Julien, Suisse, Swiss, Tavel, Touraine, Volnay, Vosne-Romanée, Vouvray

Wine-label law and the future

It is easy to understand that when early settlers produced wines they would liken them to "Old World" wines they knew, hence the usage of terms such as "sherry" or "port". However, it is an irrational law that permits an American winemaker to produce Burgundy but not Bordeaux, Chablis but not Grand Chablis (that does not exist anyway) and Moselle but not Mosel! How the BATF lists of "generic", "semi-generic" and "non-generic" names grew is one of America's great legal mysteries, but the current situation is as ludicrous as the thought of the EEC sanctioning French producers the use of "semi-generics" such as Napa Valley, Sonoma County and Washington State. Now that American law recognizes and protects American viticultural areas, perhaps it will honour and respect foreign appellations by revoking the law that permits their abuse. Under the present system, as the saying goes, the law is an ass.

HOW TO READ AMERICAN WINE LABELS

Winery
By law, both the producer's name and address must be on the label. The latter is at the label's base. Wagner is one of New York State's leading pure varietal producers.

Appellation
The appellation is always the first thing to look for on a label. Unfortunately, the law does not insist that any AVA indicated should be followed by the term "Approved Viticultural Area". As a result, who is to know if Finger Lakes has any official connotation whatsoever? It would also surely be sensible for county appellations to be followed by the term "County Appellation" (plus the state in which the county is located) and, if only for the benefit of export markets, it would do no harm to add the term "State Appellation" where appropriate.

Estate Bottled
This term may only be used for wines from within an AVA. The wine must be 100 per cent from the property named on the label and neither the grapes nor the wine may leave the estate between the harvest and the time of bottling.

Grape variety
Most Californian wines, and some east coast products such as this Finger Lakes' Chardonnay, are pure varietals, though until 1983 this meant using only 51 per cent of the grape variety indicated on the label. Since 1983 it has had to be at least 75 per cent, and the figure is higher in many wines, though those made from any *Vitis labrusca* variety are an anomaly because they may still contain only 51 per cent of the variety indicated. This is because the "foxy" character of *labrusca* is so strong that even a small amount totally dominates a wine and, in my view, 51 per cent is far too much! A wine made from two or three grape varieties may only bear their names if they are all revealed together with the percentage of the wine derived from each variety.

Estate Bottled

WAGNER
VINEYARDS

1984
Reserve
Finger Lakes
Chardonnay

ALCOHOL 13.0% BY VOLUME
PRODUCED & BOTTLED BY WAGNER VINEYARDS, LODI, N.Y.

Vintage
At least 95 per cent of the wine must be from the vintage indicated. Until the early 1970s, BATF regulations demanded that the figure was 100 per cent, but winemakers, particularly those producing higher-quality wines aged in small oak barrels, petitioned for a limited margin to enable topping-up, and this was granted.

Alcoholic strength
This must be stated by law.

Other information regarding style or quality may also be present:

Table wine or Light wine
A wine with an alcohol level not in excess of 14 per cent by volume.

Natural wine
A wine may only be called "natural" if it has not been fortified with grape brandy or alcohol.

Dessert wine
A wine with an alcoholic content of at least 14 per cent by volume, but not in excess of 24 per cent. Wines designated as "sherry" must contain at least 17 per cent and those bearing the names of "angelica", "madeira", "muscatel" or "port" must have a minimum of 18 per cent. If any of the aforementioned types of wine have an alcoholic strength in excess of 14 per cent, but less than 18 per cent (or 17 per cent in the case of "sherry"), they must be prefixed with the term "light", as, for example, in "light sherry" or "light madeira".

Volume
This must be stated by law, somewhere on the bottle.

Sparkling wine
This term may be used to describe "carbonated", *cuve close*, "bottle fermented" or *méthode champenoise* wine. If the label bears no other information, the consumer should fear the worst (carbonated or *cuve close*). However the label may refer to the wine by any of the following terms, without actually stating that it is sparkling.

Champagne
A sparkling wine derived through a second fermentation in "glass containers of not greater than one (US) gallon capacity". "Champagne" could be "fermented in this bottle" (which means it must be *méthode champenoise* though, ironically, it might not describe itself as "champagne") or "bottle fermented".

Bottle fermented
As for "champagne", though not necessarily produced by *méthode champenoise*. This term usually refers to a wine that has undergone a second fermentation inside a bottle, after which it is decanted and filtered under pressure before rebottling.

Crackling wine
As for "champagne", though the wine has a lesser degree of effervescence and may also be called "pétillant", "frizzante" or "crémant".

Carbonated wine
Still-wine made bubbly through the addition of CO_2 from a bottle of gas, the method used to produce fizzy drinks such as lemonade or cola.

Note: for information on Mexican labels, see p.400.

California

According to most Californians, America's Golden State has always been a natural home for classic grape varieties and has constantly produced an abundance of world class wines. Since the early 1980s, and the winemaking revolution that has seen overblown flavour being usurped by finesse and style, these claims have assumed increasing credibility. The 1990s look set to be California's golden era.

CALIFORNIA WAS FIRST SETTLED by the Spanish in 1769 and formed part of Mexico until 1848, when it was ceded to the United States, becoming a State of the Union in 1850. The first Californian wine was made in 1782 at San Juan Capistrano, by Fathers Pablo de Mugártegui and Gregorio Amurrió. Mission vines, brought to California by Don José Camacho on the San Antonio, which docked at San Diego on 16th May 1778, were used to make the wine. However, it was not until 1883 that Bordelais Jean-Louis Vignes established California's first commercial winery. He was the first Californian winemaker to import European vines and, in 1840, he became the first to export Californian wines.

THE AMAZING HARASZTHY

Eight years before California passed from Mexican to American sovereignty, a certain Agoston Haraszthy de Mokesa, a Hungarian political exile, settled in Wisconsin. Haraszthy was a colourful, flamboyant entrepreneur in the mould of Barnum or Champagne Charlie. Among other things, he founded a town in Wisconsin and modestly called it Haraszthy (it was later renamed Sauk City), ran a Mississippi steamboat and cultivated the first vineyard in Wisconsin — all within two years of beginning a new life in a strange country.

In 1849, Haraszthy moved to San Diego, leaving his business interests in the hands of a partner who promptly took advantage of a rumour that Haraszthy had perished during his trans-continental trek, selling all the business and properties and vanishing with the money. Haraszthy was broke, yet within less than six months was farming his own 65-hectare (160-acre) fruit and vegetable ranch. Within a few more months he had acquired a butchers shop and a livery stable in Middleton, a part of San Diego

that still boasts an Haraszthy Street. In addition, he ran an omnibus company, started a construction business, was elected the first sheriff of San Diego, was made a judge and became a Lieutenant in the volunteer militia. He also began importing cuttings of numerous European vine varieties.

Napa Valley vineyards, above
Of all California's winemaking regions Napa is the best known and its wines are the most sought after. The first vines were planted here in 1838, and today the valley boasts a vast area under vine and a bewildering array of grape varieties.

The harvest, Phelps Vineyards, above
Established in 1973, the Phelps Vineyards have become one of California's most prestigious wineries. Based in the Napa Valley, they produce over 6,300 hectolitres (70,000 cases) of high-quality wine per year.

EVOLUTION OF CALIFORNIAN WINERIES 1981-1985

COUNTY	1981	1985	DIFFERENCE	COUNTY	1981	1985	DIFFERENCE
Alameda	21	24	+3	San Benito	7	6	−1
Amador	13	15	+2	San Bernardino	15	7	−8
Butte	0	3	+3	San Diego	4	8	+4
Calaveras	2	3	+1	San Francisco	4	3	−1
Contra Costa	4	9	+5	San Joaquin	21	21	−
El Dorado	4	9	+5	San Luis Obispo	12	25	+13
Fresno	22	21	−1	San Mateo	9	6	−3
Humboldt	3	7	+4	Santa Barbara	14	18	+4
Kern	10	10	−	Santa Clara	49	42	−7
Lake	2	6	+4	Santa Cruz	16	19	+3
Los Angeles	11	15	+4	Shasta	1	1	−
Madera	8	7	−1	Solano	5	5	−
Marin	7	8	+1	Sonoma	93	129	+36
Mendocino	16	29	+13	Stanislaus	5	7	+2
Merced	1	1	−	Trinity	0	1	+1
Monterey	9	15	+6	Tulare	3	5	+2
Napa	118	148	+30	Tuolumne	2	2	−
Nevada	0	1	+1	Ventura	2	5	+3
Orange	5	3	−2	Yolo	7	10	+3
Placer	1	2	+1	Yuba	1	1	−
Riverside	9	16	+7	**Total**	**540**	**676**	**+136**
Sacramento	4	3	−1				

The Buena Vista winery

Having imported no less than 165 different vine varieties from Europe, in 1857 Haraszthy purchased 227 hectares (560 acres) of land near the town of Sonoma, in an area called the Valley of the Moon, built a winery which he named Buena Vista and dug six cellars out of the sandstone hill. With north California's first significant wine estate, Haraszthy won several awards and attracted much publicity for both his vineyard and his wine. This venture drew so much attention that, in 1861, the governor of California commissioned Haraszthy to visit Europe and report on its wine-growing areas. Haraszthy's trip took him to every wine region in France, Germany, Italy, Spain and Switzerland, where he interviewed thousands of wine-growers, took copious notes, consulted foreign literature and so accumulated a library of invaluable reference material. He returned to the United States with a staggering 100,000 cuttings of 300 different vine varieties, only to have the state Senate plead poverty when he presented them with a bill for 12,000 dollars for his trip, although the cuttings alone were worth three times that amount. He was never reimbursed for his trouble and many of the cuttings, which he had expected to be distributed among the state's other wine-growers, simply rotted away.

Haraszthy was not deterred: within seven years he managed to expand Buena Vista to 2,430 hectares (6,000 acres). In doing so, he totally changed the course of Californian viticulture, transferring the focus of attention from the south of the state to the north. At the height of its fame Buena Vista had offices in San Francisco, Philadelphia, Chicago, New York and London, but this success was superficial, for the vineyard was described in 1864 as "the largest wine-growing estate in the world and the most unprofitable". Haraszthy also suffered losses on the stock exchange and was faced with a new tax on brandy that resulted in loss of income. A fire at the winery then destroyed much of his stock and the bank cut off his credit. Enough was enough, even for Agoston Haraszthy de Mokesa. He left California for Nicaragua, where he obtained a government contract to distil rum from sugar. An enigmatic character to the end, Haraszthy disappeared altogether in 1869, presumed drowned while trying to cross an alligator-infested stream on his plantation.

THE VARIETAL BOOM

After Prohibition, most winemakers returned to their regular habit of selling under various officially designated "semi-generic" names, such as Californian Chablis, Champagne, Sauterne (sic) or Sherry. In 1939, however, Frank Schoonmaker, a New York writer and wine importer, started a revolution when he decided to add domestic American wines to his range, but refused to sell anything bearing these so-called "semi-generic" names and insisted that the wines be labelled as varietals. It was not the first time that Californian wines had been sold under varietal labels; examples of Cabernet, Riesling and Zinfandel were known in the nineteenth century. Such wines were, however, a relatively rare commodity. Schoonmaker increased the range of varietal wines by including Chardonnay, Pinot Noir, Grenache Rosé and many, many more, but the key to his success was the superb quality of the wines he selected. He did not "order" the wines, he simply tasted everything he could until he found the very best available. These wines were gems and very popular with knowledgeable drinkers. The mass market followed suit, equating this new-found exciting quality with the varietal name. An increasing number of wineries realized what was happening and jumped on the varietal bandwagon. Regrettably, Californian Chablis remained on the market, but the change of direction helped some wineries to establish a native identity of their own.

"BOUTIQUE" AND "HIPPY" WINERIES

During the 1940s the Californian wine industry was invaded by large distilleries, but most deserted the scene in the following decade, leaving the field to Seagram, the Canadian-based firm that had purchased the Paul Masson Winery. History was to repeat itself twenty years later, the distillers coming and going with only Seagram remaining loyal to the industry. The mergers and takeovers reduced the number of wineries to an all-time low in the early 1960s. But, at the same time, imperceptibly at first, a number of small, one-man wineries were opening up. Known as "boutique" wineries, these were in fact the first of California's (now many) small domaines, run by a hotch-potch of newcomers, from ex-football stars to doctors, lawyers and teachers. Some wineries were run by people who had become disillusioned with their professional life and had "dropped out". As a result, a new term, "hippy" wineries, enjoyed an ephemeral popularity. Whether "boutique" or "hippy", these small outfits proved to be as much a turning point in the evolution of Californian wine as Schoonmaker's varietal boom. Each small domaine was established by an individual who had sought out a specific *terroir* into which to pour his new-found passion. Many people were never successful, but today some of California's greatest wines are made by those who served their winemaking apprenticeship in the flower-power era.

CALIFORNIA'S CLIMATIC REGIONS

The areas suited to growing vines can be divided into five climatic regions, based on heat summation during the growing season (measured in "degree days"), ranging from Region I, the coolest, to Region V, the hottest. The pioneering work in establishing these areas was carried out by the University of California at Davis in the 1950s and 1960s, and the research continues to be a valuable source of information for growers wanting to know whether specific grape varieties will thrive in particular areas.

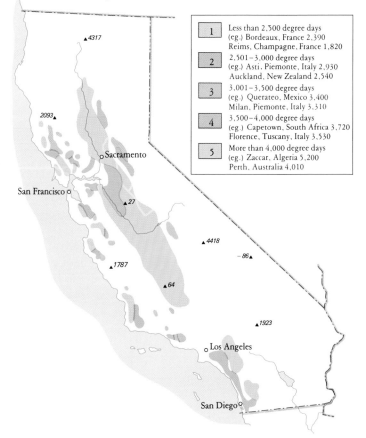

1	Less than 2,500 degree days (eg.) Bordeaux, France 2,390 Reims, Champagne, France 1,820
2	2,501–3,000 degree days (eg.) Asti, Piemonte, Italy 2,930 Auckland, New Zealand 2,540
3	3,001–3,500 degree days (eg.) Quereteo, Mexico 3,400 Milan, Piemonte, Italy 3,310
4	3,500–4,000 degree days (eg.) Capetown, South Africa 3,720 Florence, Tuscany, Italy 3,530
5	More than 4,000 degree days (eg.) Zaccar, Algeria 5,200 Perth, Australia 4,010

CALIFORNIAN WINERIES AND PRODUCTION 1945-85

YEAR	WINERIES	PRODUCTION (CASES)
1945	415	46,884,000
1955	334	60,345,000
1965	227	79,370,000
1975	321	138,714,000
1985	676	173,000,000

THE FRENCH INVASION

The first purchase of Californian vineyards by a French company was the acquisition of some 324 hectares (800 acres) at Yountville in the Napa Valley, by the great Champagne house of Moët & Chandon in 1973. Moët & Chandon was convinced of California's potential in the 1960s, 10 to 20 years earlier than other French firms. It foresaw the future demand for quality sparkling wine in the United States long before Americans actually fulfilled the prophecy. It was seven years before another French company, again from Champagne, followed Moët & Chandon's lead; Piper-Heidsieck established its Piper-Sonoma winery in 1980, although in 1979 the German wine company, A. Racke, had taken over the Buena Vista winery and Baron Philippe de Rothschild had collaborated with Robert Mondavi to produce an outlandishly expensive Médoc-style Californian red wine, called "Opus One". In 1981 European influence again increased when Moët & Chandon's parent company, Moët-Hennessy, purchased its New York-based importer, Schieffin & Company, and also acquired the Simi winery in Sonoma. Then, in 1983, Christian Moueix of Château Pétrus teamed up with the two daughters of the late John Daniels to produce "Dominus", a wine that challenges "Opus One". The various other foreign companies that have entered the Californian wine scene include: Bollinger, Maison Deutz, Louis Roederer, Torres of Spain, Antinori of Italy and Suntory of Japan.

CALIFORNIA

Wines of higher quality and with greater finesse are produced in those areas of California cooled by sea and bay winds and the great coastal fog bank. The very hot Central Valley yields the bulk of California's jug-wine, mass-produced vin ordinaire, which, with the aid of cool fermentation, is clean, fruity and well made.

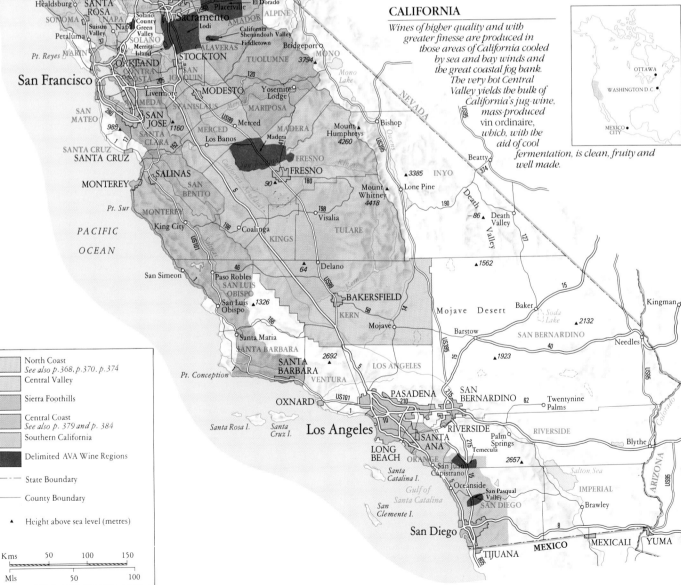

Legend:
- North Coast *See also p. 368, p. 370, p. 374*
- Central Valley
- Sierra Foothills
- Central Coast *See also p. 379 and p. 384*
- Southern California
- Delimited AVA Wine Regions
- State Boundary
- County Boundary
- ▲ Height above sea level (metres)

Kms   50   100   150
Mls   50   100

The grapes and wines of California

There are almost 300,000 hectares (740,000 acres) of vines in California, but less than half this total encapsulates "wine" grape varieties. The breakdown of vines in 1985 was as follows:

138,833 hectares (343,056 acres) wine grape varieties

117,826 hectares (291,147 acres) raisin grape varieties

37,675 hectares (93,094 acres) table grape varieties

372 hectares (920 acres) rootstock

294,705 hectares (728,217 acres) all vines

The breakdown by colour and recent evolution (between 1975 and 1985) of wine grape varieties is as follows:

GRAPE COLOUR	1975 HECTARES (ACRES)	1975 %	1985 HECTARES (ACRES)	1985 %
Black	52,886 (130,681)	62%	59,811 (147,792)	43%
White	31,880 (78,775)	38%	79,022 (195,264)	57%
All	84,766 (209,456)	100%	138,833 (343,056)	100%

Details on all but the most minor grape varieties and their wines, are listed alphabetically below, under "Black grape varieties" and "White grape varieties". Wines can be grouped this way because virtually all quality Californian wines are pure varietals. For recommended wines, see the "Major wineries" of each region. It is extremely difficult to recommend "Best Recent Vintages" and "When to Drink" times. These details only appear if and where they are feasible.

Black grape varieties

Of approximately 60,000 hectares (145,000 acres) of black grape varieties cultivated in California today, over 59,000 hectares (148,700 acres) are represented on this and the following two pages. The balance consists of numerous other varieties with an insufficient area under vine to warrant inclusion in the listing.

BLACK GRAPE OVERVIEW

Barbera	10%	Rubired	5%
Cabernet sauvignon	15%	Ruby cabernet	7%
Carignan	11%	Zinfandel	17%
Grenache	10%	Others	20%
Pinot noir	5%		

ALEATICO

Area planted: _21 ha (53 acres)_

Believed to be a black variant of the Muscat family, this grape is best known for the rich, sweet and fragrant dessert wines produced in Italy. It is shy-bearing and therefore rarely produced as a pure varietal wine in California.

ALICANTE BOUSCHET

Area planted: _1,299 ha (3,210 acres)_

A favourite of Prohibition days, when the coloured juice of this _teinturier_ grape enabled bootleggers to stretch its wine with water and sugar, cultivation of the Alicante bouschet has dropped to little more than two per cent of all California's black grapes.

BARBERA

Area planted: _5,999 ha (14,825 acres)_

Accounting for 10 per cent of California's black varieties, this Italian grape is mostly cultivated in the Central Valley, where its high natural acidity makes it useful for blending purposes. This said, more than thirty wineries produce a pure varietal Barbera in one form or another.

- 🍷 1980, 1984, 1985
- ⌕ Between 3-6 years (up to 10 in exceptional cases)

BLACK MALVOISIE

Area planted: _97 ha (239 acres)_

According to American viticultural literature, the Black malvoisie is the Hermitage of South Africa, which is the Cinsault of France. Its robust, well-coloured wines are useful for blending.

CABERNET FRANC

Area planted: _260 ha (643 acres)_

California's cultivation of this Bordeaux variety has tripled since 1983, primarily for use in effecting better-balanced Cabernet sauvignon blends. Some fine Cabernet franc rosés are also produced in the North Coast area.

- 🍷 1984, 1985, 1986, 1987, 1990
- ⌕ Within 1-3 years (rosé)

CABERNET SAUVIGNON

Area planted: _9,153 ha (22,617 acres)_

This grape accounts for 15 per cent of California's black grape varieties and, although the Chardonnay has inevitably stolen the limelight since the trend towards dry white wines, the Cabernet sauvignon remains California's finest red-wine grape.

Yet the Californian wine industry has been in a state of flux. Because of this, a confusing range of Cabernet Sauvignons have been produced: the massive, ink-black, tannic blockbusters of the 1950s and early-1960s; the high-tech, 100 per cent new oak wines in the late-1960s, which were welcome in that they were very clean and precise, with supple tannin replacing harsh tannin, but which were blatantly too rich and too oaky; the experiments to achieve better balance and finesse that appeared to pay off in the vintages of 1980 and 1981, but not in 1982 and 1983, when it appeared that the fruity, voluptuous feel of this sunny state had been sacrificed in the search for finesse; and the excellent 1984 vintage, which clearly demonstrated that California had not forsaken its sun-blessed character, and the truly magnificent 1985, the best wines since 1974, which proved the quest for finesse was not folly.

The wines now have the deliciously ripe, blackcurranty flavour, with the velvety texture and violet and mint after-aromas that must surely represent the true character of Californian Cabernet sauvignon. In addition to this, oak is now used far more intelligently, and some of the most exciting wines are blended with Merlot and Cabernet franc, as they are in Bordeaux. Perhaps varietal bottling has served its purpose as far as Cabernet sauvignon is concerned? Certainly most of the more exciting wines in the future will be labelled as multi-varietal appellations or may well carry upmarket brand names.

- 🍷 1980, 1981 (but tread carefully), 1982 (Napa and Sonoma only), 1984, 1985, 1986, 1987, 1990
- ⌕ Between 3-5 years (inexpensive); 5-12 years (top wineries); 8-25 (or more) years (exceptional wines)

CARIGNAN

Area planted: _6,613 ha (16,341 acres)_

The Carignan represents 11 per cent of the state's black grape varieties and provides a high yield of well-coloured, strong-flavoured, coarse and tannic wine that is useful for blending both in California and in its native south of France, where it is one of the 13 grapes permitted in Châteauneuf-du-Pape. It has a less harsh character in California's coastal districts, where some wineries produce a pure varietal version. In California is it often spelt "Carignane".

- 🍷 1980, 1984, 1985, 1990
- ⌕ Between 3-6 years (up to 10 years in exceptional cases)

CARNELIAN

Area planted: _644 ha (1,592 acres)_

This _Carignan x Cabernet sauvignon x Grenache_ cross was created by the leading viticulturalist, Professor Olmo, as long ago as 1936, yet it was not released from the UC-Davis nursery until 1972.

Whether this variety will eventually prove itself depends on what the aims for it are. If it is intended to be accepted as capable of producing a pure varietal wine in the Central Valley, then its chance of success is debatable − the last significant new planting was in 1979 and, to my knowledge, the only winery producing a pure varietal Carnelian is Giumarra Vineyards. If the aim is more modest − to improve the basic character and quality of Central Valley jug wines − then it has already succeeded.

CENTURION

Area planted: _240 ha (592 acres)_

This _Carignan x Cabernet sauvignon x Grenache_ crossing was also created by Professor Olmo and was released from the UC-Davis nursery a few years after the Carnelian (see above). It produces fuller, darker wines.

CHARBONO

Area planted: _34 ha (84 acres)_

This variety is the Corbeau, an almost extinct French variety that is also known as the Charbonneau. It produces a wine similar in style to that of the Barbera. Indeed, the first winery to make a pure varietal wine from this grape, Inglenook Vineyards, labelled it as Barbera until Dr Winkler of the UC-Davis nursery identified it as Charbono. Inglenook continues to make the best Charbono varietal wine.

EARLY BURGUNDY

Area planted: *87 ha (214 acres)*

This grape has as much in common with Burgundy as Californian Chablis. It is a synonym for the Abouriou, a blending grape used in southwest France. Although really nothing more than a blending grape in California, the Trentadue Winery in Sonoma does produce a pure varietal Early Burgundy.

GAMAY

Area planted: *992 ha (2,452 acres)*

Also called the Napa gamay, this grape has nothing to do with the Gamay Beaujolais. In comparison, it is later-ripening; may be cultivated in a wider range of climates, especially hotter ones; is more productive; has a thinner skin and makes a lighter, lesser-quality wine.

19 | 1980, 1981, 1984, 1985, 1986

⌛ Between 1-4 years

GAMAY BEAUJOLAIS

Area planted: *1,022 ha (2,526 acres)*

This has been officially recognized as a Pinot noir clone and its identifiers categorically state that it is not the Gamay. But there could still be a connection, as there is a serious theory that many centuries ago the Gamay itself originated from an ancient clone of the Pinot noir. Californian law allows a pure varietal wine from this grape to be labelled either Gamay Beaujolais (which most is) or Pinot noir. The wine is fuller and fruitier than that of the Gamay or Napa gamay, but it lacks the richness and definition of a classic Pinot noir wine and has a distinctly peppery character in comparison. Many wineries use *macération carbonique* techniques, though some mature in oak.

19 | 1981, 1984, 1985, 1986, 1987

⌛ Within 1-3 years (*nouveau* style); 3-6 years (oak-matured)

GRENACHE

Area planted: *6,354 ha (15,701 acres)*

This Rhône variety accounts for more than 10 per cent of California's black grapes and makes medium-dry rosé and tawny port-type dessert wines, although pale red *nouveau* styles are also produced. Its wine is tart and fruity, with an aroma that has an unusual, ethereal character.

19 | 1984, 1985, 1986, 1987, 1990

⌛ Within 1-3 years

GRIGNOLINO

Area planted: *21 ha (52 acres)*

Only a handful of wineries make pure varietal wine from this grape, which produces a basically fruity wine of uneven quality and character. This variation is due to the fact that there are many different clones of this variety in Napa and Santa Clara, despite the tiny number of acres planted.

MALBEC

Area planted: *26 ha (65 acres)*

This grape has never really caught on in California. The existing small area under vine is experimental and used for blending with Cabernet sauvignon to produce a better-balanced wine, as in Bordeaux.

MATARO

Area planted: *202 ha (499 acres)*

This grape is none other than the Mourvèdre, the Rhône variety. I have heard that the brilliant Bonny Doon Vineyard in Santa Cruz has released a pure varietal Mourvèdre (marketed as Mourvèdre, not Mataro), but I have not yet tasted it.

MERLOT

Area planted: *1,101 ha (2,721 acres)*

Wines produced from this grape are often blended with up to 15 per cent Cabernet sauvignon. This gives added structure on which to hang the Merlot's luxurious flavours and the results have been very promising indeed. It is sometimes labelled as Merlot Noir.

MERLOT NOIR
See Merlot.

MISSION

Area planted: *936 ha (2,314 acres)*

California's first *vinifera* grape, the Mission was planted by the Franciscans throughout the south of the state. It is a pity that the large purple grapes borne by this historic vine yield such a poor and indistinctly flavoured wine. Mission grapes are traditionally used to make Angelica, a fortified grape-juice drink similar in production to Ratafia de Champagne and Pineau de Charente, but nearer in style to a dark blending Sherry that never sees the light of commercial day.

MUSCAT HAMBURG

Area planted: *25 ha (63 acres)*

The only Californian varietal wine, that I know of, produced from this black Muscat grape is from Novitiate Wines, an enterprise owned and run by The Society of Jesus.

NAPA GAMAY
See Gamay.

PETITE SIRAH

Area planted: *2,066 ha (5,105 acres)*

Perhaps ignorance is bliss, for it seems that ever since this underrated grape was identified as the lowly Durif of France, its popularity has nonsensically plummeted. It may be unfashionable to say so, but there are many wineries in California that regularly produce fine wines from this grape and a few that occasionally make something outstanding. The Petite Sirah from the Ridge Winery at York Creek is probably the very finest example.

19 | 1984, 1985, 1986, 1987, 1990

⌛ Between 4-8 years

PINOT NOIR

Area planted: *3,163 ha (7,816 acres)*

This famous Burgundian grape represents just over five per cent of the black varieties cultivated in California, and I cannot help but wonder if this is five per cent too much. California has a long way to go before it will convince even the most optimistic of critics that the potential quality of its Pinot noir is even a fraction of that already achieved with Burgundy's other classic vine, the Chardonnay. The difficulty has always been to extract the elegance of the Pinot noir's clean, vibrant fruit. This has been hampered by the fact that, unlike wines of much richer grapes (Chardonnay or Cabernet sauvignon, for example), its silky-textured, redcurrant flavour has a particularly delicate floral finesse that is sensitive to maturation in new oak. Whereas excessive oakiness can hide the faults of other wines, it cannot hide the faults of a fine Pinot noir wine without obscuring its varietal definition. There are, however, several wineries that are making headway with this problematical grape: Robert Mondavi (Reserve), Smith-Madrone, Trefethen and Saintsbury, in Napa, and La Crema Vinera, in Sonoma, have all produced wines that would rank among California's best Pinot Noirs; Calera's Jensen and Selleck vineyards probably have the best potential, but its tendency to go overboard on elegance can result in overly "pretty" renditions; and Kalin in Marin, Joseph Swan and Iron Horse in Sonoma, and Congress Springs in the Santa Cruz Mountains are also good and improving fast.

19 | 1980, 1984, 1985, 1986, 1988

⌛ Between 3-7 years

PINOT ST. GEORGE

Area planted: *58 ha (143 acres)*

This grape has no connection whatsoever with the Pinot family; Pinot St. George is a synonym for the Négrette grape of southwest France used, most notably, in Côtes du Frontonnais. In the 1960s the Christian Brothers won quite a few medals with their wine from this grape. It was labelled Red Pinot and the style was much darker and fuller than is normal today. Some pure varietal late-harvest wines are also produced.

ROYALTY

Area planted: *473 ha (1,169 acres)*

This *Aramon rupestris ganzin No.4 x Alicante bouschet x Trousseau* hybrid is a red-juice *teinturier* developed by Professor Olmo as a "port" wine variety and released by the UC-Davis nursery in 1958.

RUBIRED

Area planted: *3,268 ha (8,076 acres)*

This *Aramon rupestris ganzin No.4 x Alicante bouschet x Tinta cão* hybrid is a red-juice *teinturier* developed by Professor Olmo as a "port" wine variety and released by the UC-Davis nursery in 1958. It now accounts for just over five per cent of all the black grapes grown in California.

RUBY CABERNET

Area planted: *4,280 ha (10,576 acres)*

Another of the prolific Professor Olmo's brainchilds, this *Carignan x Cabernet sauvignon* cross was developed in 1936. The theory was to produce a grape with the quality and character of Cabernet sauvignon, yet the climatic tolerance and high yield of Carignan. In a modest way Olmo succeeded, although the variety's Cabernet character is admittedly low-key. At least 20 wineries spasmodically produce this as a varietal wine.

SALVADOR

Area planted: *510 ha (1,262 acres)*

This obscure *teinturier* grape, used for blending in Central Valley jug wines, is, according to Jancis Robinson, a *rupestris x vinifera* hybrid with "gelatinous" juice.

ST. MACAIRE

Area planted: *20 ha (50 acres)*

A minor variety from Bordeaux, where it is also known as the Bouton blanc and the Moustouzère. To my knowledge the St. Macaire has never been used in California to produce a pure varietal wine.

SYRAH

Area planted: *45 ha (110 acres)*

It is surprising that this classic Rhône grape is not more widely planted. Joseph Phelps produces a lovely, ripe, fruity wine from the Syrah, but Bonny Doon's stunning, rich and concentrated wine is in a different class altogether. When will others try to follow his lead?

TINTA MADEIRA

Area planted: *67 ha (172 acres)*

Some people question whether or not this is the Portuguese variety, and in California it is used for "ruby port" wines, not "madeiras". The East-Side Winery in San Joaquin makes an interesting pure varietal in "tawny port" style.

VALDEPENAS

Area planted: *390 ha (966 acres)*

Thought to be the Tempranillo of Rioja fame, this grape is used mostly for blending into jug wines, although one or two pure varietals have been made.

ZINFANDEL

Area planted: *10,266 ha (25,367 acres)*

White Zinfandel
CALIFORNIA

This was once thought to be America's only indigenous *Vitis vinifera* grape, but was positively identified by Isozyme "finger printing" (a method of recording the unique pattern created by the molecular structure of enzymes found within specific varieties) as the Primitivo grape of southern Italy. There may yet be a twist to the story, for the earliest records of Primitivo in Italy date from the late nineteenth century and yet the Zinfandel is documented in the nursery catalogue of William Prince of Long Island, USA, in 1830. Furthermore, Italian growers have often referred to their Primitivo as a foreign variety.

Depending on the way it is vinified, Zinfandel produces many different styles of wine, from rich and dark to light and fruity, or *nouveau* style, from dry to sweet, white to rosé, dessert wine or sparkling! In my opinion, the best are produced in the rich and well-coloured style, with ripe, balanced fruit, preferably aged with a little oak and perhaps blended with Petite sirah for increased backbone. In this category my favourites include Grgich Hills Cellars, Heitz, Ravenswood (particularly Old Hill Vineyard) and Ridge (Geyserville of Lytton Springs, not Paso Robles).

🗓 1980, 1981, 1984, 1985, 1986

🍷 Between 5-15 years (for the above recommended style)

White grape varieties

Of approximately 80,000 hectares (197,000 acres) of white-wine grape varieties cultivated in California today, over 75,000 hectares (185,000 acres) are represented on this and the following page. The balance consists of numerous other varieties with an insufficient area under vine to warrant inclusion in the listing.

WHITE GRAPE OVERVIEW			
Chardonnay	14%	Sauvignon blanc	8%
Chenin blanc	21%	White riesling	5%
French colombard	38%	Others	14%

BURGER

Area planted: 934 ha (2,307 acres)

This all-American-sounding grape operates under various names in France, including Monbadon, Grand blanc d'Orléans and Castillone à Montendre, but, confusingly, has no connection with the Burger of Alsace and Switzerland, which is the Elbling. Occasionally one encounters pure varietal Burger wines, but they are of little consequence. The variety has an immensely prolific yield and the neutral flavour of its wine is best used to pad out cheap blends.

CHARDONNAY

Area planted: *11,204 ha (27,241 acres)*

Chardonnay
SONOMA COUNTY 1986 VINTAGE
WINDSOR VINEYARDS
PRODUCED AND BOTTLED BY WINDSOR VINEYARDS
WINDSOR, CALIF. ALCOHOL 13.4% BY VOLUME. CONTAINS SULFITES

When, I wonder, will California's golden grape go out of fashion? There have always been great Californian Chardonnays, even when the trend was for massive, blockbusting wines positively reeking of oak, but there were also far too many that were simply too fat and too blowzy during that era. Now the grapes are harvested earlier, the acidity is up, the pH down and, generally, the standards are much, much higher; "finesse" has become a new buzz-word in Californian wine circles. Wineries have even swung too far towards perfecting the acidity levels and they have neglected the quota of ripe fruit flavour that must also be present to effect the correct balance. Others have completely deserted maturation in oak and have used their high-tech equipment so "expertly" that they end up with wines that are clinically clean and washed-out of natural flavours.

It might sound odd to describe great wines as delicious, but that is exactly what great Californian Chardonnays are. They are bursting with every kind of fruit imaginable, from the perfumed products of the tropics to the succulence of Mediterranean peaches and the malic acidity of green northern apples. These wines may be very exotic or simply elegant, can be crisp and positively firm or full and buttery.

🗓 1980, 1981, 1982 (Napa, Sonoma and Monterey, tread carefully), 1983 (Sonoma only, tread carefully), 1984, 1985, 1986, 1987, 1988, 1990

🍷 Between 2-8 years (25 or more years in very exceptional cases)

CHAUCHE GRIS
See Gray riesling.

CHENIN BLANC

Area planted: *16,779 ha (41,462 acres)*

This Loire Valley grape is famous for such wines as the sweet, honey-rich Vouvray and the searingly dry, but stunningly flavoured, Savennières. In California it covers more than one-fifth of the state's white grape vineyards and, although the recent trend to improve the acidity balance has improved the wines made from this variety, it fares less well than in France. As I admit to being less than fond of all but the greatest wines made from this grape, it is hard for me to work up any excitement for the Chenin blanc in California.

🗓 1980, 1981, 1984, 1985, 1986

🍷 Between 1-4 years

CHEVRIER
See Sémillon.

COLOMBARD
See French colombard.

EMERALD RIESLING

Area planted: *1,185 ha (2,928 acres)*

This *Muscadelle x Riesling* cross was Professor Olmo's first viticultural offspring, and some say his most successful. In the Central Valley it not only produces grapes of a comparable acidity level to that of the French colombard, it also achieves this task whilst producing huge crops. Because far too many pure varietal Emerald Riesling wines were marketed in the 1960s, it has been judged out of context; its true position in the scheme of things is to enliven the acidity and improve the character of Central Valley bulk blends.

FEHER SZAGOS

Area planted: *53 ha (130 acres)*

To my knowledge, this Hungarian grape has never been made into a pure varietal wine. It has a high natural sugar content and is mostly blended into dessert wines.

FLORA

Area planted: *139 ha (343 acres)*

This *Sémillon x Gewürztraminer* cross was developed by Professor Olmo to provide Gewürztraminer-like wine under California's hot sun. It has a slightly better acidity level than Gewürztraminer and its yield is a little higher, but the spiciness of the wine it makes is somewhat muted. The majority of winemakers believe it to have too little or no advantage over the classic Gewürztraminer. A couple of wineries produce a pure varietal Flora, but its quality is nothing special.

FOLLE BLANCHE

Area planted: *91 ha (226 acres)*

A grape that is not widely planted in California. Louis B. Martini makes a pure varietal Folle Blanche, but I have never tasted it.

FRANKEN RIESLING
See Sylvaner.

FRENCH COLOMBARD

Area planted: *29,460 ha (73,241 acres)*

Accounting for almost 38 per cent of all California's white grape vineyards, the French colombard has always been more than adequate as a jug wine's main ingredient. But its true potential was only realized with the advent of cool fermentation. A pure varietal French colombard is by no means a fine-quality wine, in any classic sense of the term, but it is superb value, totally unpretentious and absolutely delicious.

🗓 1984, 1985, 1986, 1988, 1990

🍷 Within 1 year

FUMÉ BLANC
See Sauvignon blanc.

GEWÜRZTRAMINER

Area planted: *1,612 ha (3,983 acres)*

1986
Chateau St. Jean
SONOMA COUNTY
Gewürztraminer

If the French Colombard is one of California's most underrated varietal wines, then Gewürztraminer must be amongst its most overrated. The hype surrounding California's Gewürztraminers baffles me — most lack the crisp varietal definition I expect of a classic grape and have a strange softness and attenuated flavour.

GRAY RIESLING

Area planted: *986 ha (2,346 acres)*

This pink-skinned variety is sometimes spelt as Grey riesling, and the grape may also be called the Chauche gris. Thought to be the Trousseau gris of France, it makes mild, fruity varietal wine that often has a little sweetness and slight spiciness. It is unspectacular, but cheap and popular.

GREEN HUNGARIAN

Area planted: *146 ha (362 acres)*

Souvrain Cellars produced the first varietal wine from this obscure grape in 1945. Most Green Hungarian wines are neutral in flavour and slightly sweet. The most interesting thing about this variety is that nobody knows how it received its name.

JOHANNISBERG RIESLING
See White Riesling.

MALVASIA BIANCA

Area planted: *745 ha (1,842 acres)*

The Malvasia bianca has a fine spicy-flowery character, but it is under-appreciated in California, where it is mostly blended into dessert wines. A few wineries produce a light, off-dry and semi-sweet, pure varietal wine.

MONTEREY RIESLING
See Sylvaner.

MOSCATO CANELLI
See Muscat blanc.

MUSCAT CANELLI
See Muscat blanc.

MUSCAT DE FRONTIGNAN
See Muscat blanc.

MUSCAT BLANC

Area planted: *670 ha (1,657 acres)*

Also known as Muscat de Frontignan, Muscat canelli and Moscato canelli, this grape is surprisingly successful in California, producing some delightfully perfumed, flowery-flavoured wines in off-dry through to very sweet and dessert styles. Bonny Doon's 1986 Muscat Canelli *vin de glace* is reputedly stunning.

🖹 1980, 1984, 1985, 1986

🍷 Within 1 year

PALOMINO

Area planted: *1,093 ha (2,702 acres)*

This classic Sherry grape is the variety that dominates the Central Valley's "sherry" production.

PEDRO XIMENES

Area planted: *26 ha (64 acres)*

This classic Jerez grape makes the thick, concentrated and treacly wine used to sweeten up California's "sherry" type wines. It has very occasionally been marketed as a pure varietal "sherry".

PEVERELLA

Area planted: *166 ha (409 acres)*

This rather obscure grape variety produces a wine that is essentially neutral, but for a mildly peppery finish.

PINOT BLANC

Area planted: *917 ha (2,265 acres)*

When grown with care and barrel-fermented, it is virtually impossible to tell a Pinot Blanc wine from a Chardonnay, particularly the examples from Napa, Monterey and Sonoma. There are some excellent, very serious makers of pure varietal Pinot Blancs, but essentially this is one of California's most under-exploited varieties.

SAUVIGNON BLANC

Area planted: *6,225 hectares (15,383 acres)*

Also known as the Fumé blanc, almost eight per cent of California's white grape vineyards are occupied by this variety. Sauvignon Blanc wines have such upfront appeal that it is all too easy to tire of even the greatest examples. While they can last a few years in bottle, they also seldom improve — perhaps another factor in their decline in popularity since the early 1980s.

🖹 1980, 1982 (Napa, Sonoma and Monterey only, tread carefully), 1984, 1985, 1986, 1988, 1990

🍷 Within 1-3 years

SAUVIGNON VERT

Area planted: *95 ha (234 acres)*

This grape has no connection with the Sauvignon vert of France. It is, apparently, the Muscadelle of Bordeaux, although the Californian variant appears to have more acidity. Kirigin Cellars, in Santa Clara, and the Nichelini Vineyard, in Napa, produce rare varietal wines from this grape, but I have not tasted them.

SÉMILLON

Area planted: *1,230 ha (3,039 acres)*

Also known as the Chevrier, this grape has long been a favourite among California's winemaking fraternity, but not, it would appear, with the consumer. This might change now that America's wine guru, Robert Parker Jnr., has declared Sémillon to be an up-and-coming varietal. Excellent oak-fermented dry wines have been made, often blended with a little Sauvignon blanc. Some succulent sweet botrytis styles have also been produced.

SONOMA RIESLING
See Sylvaner.

ST. EMILION

Area planted: *475 ha (1,174 acres)*

This is the Ugni blanc of France and the Trebbiano of Italy. It is mostly used for bulk-blended jug wines.

SYLVANER

Area planted: *499 ha (1,233 acres)*

In California this classic Franconian variety is also known as the Franken riesling, Monterey riesling or the Sonoma riesling. The wines tend to be off-dry and rather neutral in flavour.

WHITE RIESLING

Area planted: *4,066 ha (10,046 acres)*

Also known as the Johannisberg riesling, this grape covers more than five per cent of California's white grape vineyards. Apart from the sensational tangy-dry exceptions produced with great consistency by Jekel Vineyards and Chateau St.-Jean, only the wonderfully sweet, botrytis or latè-harvest Rieslings aspire to truly fine-wine status in California.

🖹 1982, 1983 (dry, off-dry and early-harvest wines only), 1984, 1985, 1986 (sweet wines only), 1988, 1990

🍷 Between 1-3 years (dry and off-dry early harvest styles); 2-7 or more years (sweet)

The regional appellations of California

CALIFORNIA AO

This state appellation may be used for any wine, at least 75 per cent of which must be made from grapes grown anywhere in California.

CENTRAL COAST AVA

Established: *25th November 1985*

Stretching from Oakland to Santa Barbara, this sprawling appellation covers some 560 kilometres (350 miles) of coastal vineyards. Flanked by the California Coastal Ranges, it straddles the counties of Alameda, Monterey, Santa Cruz, Santa Clara, San Benito, San Luis Obispo and Santa Barbara, and encompasses 14 smaller Approved Viticultural Areas: Arroyo Seco, Carmel Valley, Chalone, Cienega Valley, Edna Valley, Lime Kiln Valley, Livermore Valley, Monterey, Pacheco Pass, Paicines, Paso Robles, Santa Maria Valley, Santa Ynez and York Valley.

NORTH COAST AVA

Established: *21st May 1983*

This appellation covers 12,170 square kilometres (4,700 square miles), and straddles the counties of Napa, Sonoma, Mendocino, Solano, Lake and Marin, encompassing 20 smaller Approved Viticultural Areas: Alexander Valley, Anderson Valley, Chalk Hill, Clear Lake, Cole Ranch, Dry Creek Valley, Guenoc Valley, Howell Mountain, Knights Valley, Los Carneros, McDowell Valley, Mendocino, Napa Valley, Northern Sonoma, Potter Valley, Russian River Valley, Solano Green Valley, Sonoma Green Valley, Sonoma Valley and Suisun Valley.

SOUTH COAST AVA

Established: *23rd December 1983*

California's South Coast regional appellation engulfs an area of approximately 4,660 square kilometres (1,800 square miles) and is located along the Pacific coastline between Los Angeles and the Mexican border. It overlaps two counties, Orange and San Diego, and encompasses two smaller Approved Viticultural Areas, Temecula and San Pasqual Valley.

Mendocino County

An up-and-coming wine area, all Mendocino's best vineyards are located on forks of the Navarro and Russian rivers in the south of the county.

MENDOCINO COULD WELL BE THE BUZZ-WORD of the 1990s for top-quality Californian sparkling wine, if the huge investment by the great French Champagne house of Louis Roederer pays off. In the early 1980s Roederer sunk some 15 million dollars into a 200-hectare (500-acre) vineyard and winery in the Anderson Valley, where the climate is considerably cooler than that of surrounding areas. Relying on traditional Champenois grapes, Chardonnay and Pinot noir, one third of the land was planted in 1982, another third in 1983 and the balance in 1984. The first crop was harvested in 1986, and is due for release in 1988. I suspect it will be worth the wait; this wine could bring Mendocino the glamour and increased public interest it needs for its vineyards to be truly opened up.

THE GROWTH OF MENDOCINO'S WINE INDUSTRY

Because parts of Mendocino are too hot for classic wine production, there was a tendency in the past to plant highly productive vines for jug-wine blends. However, the county has a complex climate, and there are some areas where coastal

influences dominate and cooler Region I and II climates (*see* p.362) prevail. This has been recognized by the rise in the number of wineries in the area, from 16 in 1981 to 29 in 1985, and by the substantial amount of premium-quality varietal planted in the late 1970s. Since the early 1980s there has been an increasing trend towards even higher-quality varietals, with a large expansion of Cabernet sauvignon vineyards and a huge increase in the planting of Chardonnay and Sauvignon blanc.

FACTORS AFFECTING TASTE AND QUALITY

Location
160 kilometres (100 miles) northwest of San Francisco, Mendocino is the most northerly of the major viticultural coastal counties of California.

Climate
The mountain ridges surrounding the Upper Russian and the Navarro rivers climb as high as 1,070 metres (3,500 ft) and form a natural boundary that creates the reputed "transitional" climate of Mendocino. This climate is unusual in that either coastal or inland influences can dominate for long or short periods, but is generally reflected by warmer winters and cooler summers. This provides for a growing season with many warm, dry days and cool nights. The Ukiah Valley has the shortest but warmest growing season north of San Francisco.

Aspect
The vines are planted mainly on flat ground at the bottom of the valleys or on the gentle, lower slopes at a height of between 76 to 445 metres (250 to 1,460 ft), with some rising to as high as 490 metres (1,600 ft). The vines generally face east, though just south of Ukiah they face west.

Soil
Deep, diverse alluvial soils in the flat riverside vineyards, gravelly-loam in parts of the Russian River Valley and a thin scree on the surrounding slopes.

Viticulture and vinification
The average growing season is 268 days, compared to 308 in Sonoma (where bud-break is 10 days earlier than in Mendocino), and 223 days in Lake County. One of California's potentially great wine districts, production in Mendocino is geared towards providing the high-quality premium varietals.

Primary grape varieties
Cabernet sauvignon, Carignan, Chardonnay, Chenin blanc, French colombard, Sauvignon blanc, Zinfandel

Secondary grape varieties
Barbera, Burger, Cabernet franc, Charbono, Early Burgundy, Flora, Folle blanche, Gamay, Gamay Beaujolais, Gewürztraminer, Grenache, Grey riesling, Green Hungarian, Malvasia bianca, Merlot, Muscat blanc, Palomino, Petite sirah, Pinot blanc, Pinot noir, Ruby cabernet, Sauvignon vert, Sémillon, Sylvaner, Syrah, White riesling

Fetzer Vineyards Ranch, above
A spectacular gateway marks the entrance to this winery specializing in Chardonnay and Zinfandel.

Vineyard landscape, below
These typically flat Mendocino vineyards belong to Parducci Wine Cellars – a large firm producing a wide range of fine wines.

MENDOCINO, see also p.363
The area's northerly location does not necessarily mean harsher micro-climates. Inland regions are protected by the surrounding mountains although the Anderson Valley is cooler.

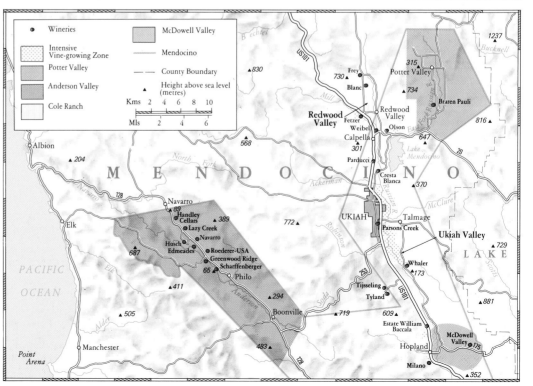

The AVAs of Mendocino

ANDERSON VALLEY AVA

Established: *23rd March 1983*

This area consists of some 23,300 hectares (57,600 acres), a mere 240 (600) of which have been planted with vines. The valley's coastal-influenced microclimate is cooler than the "transitional" climate that prevails in the rest of Mendocino. The valley's soil is made up of more than 20 alluvial soils.

COLE RANCH AVA

Established: *16th May 1983*

Situated in a small, narrow valley, this appellation consists of a mere 25 hectares (61 acres) of Cabernet sauvignon, Chardonnay and Johannisberg riesling vineyards, all owned by the Cole family. The vines grow on soils ranging from deep, gravelly-clay-loam to shallow, gravelly-silty clay.

McDOWELL VALLEY AVA

Established: *4th January 1982*

The McDowell Valley enjoys the natural protection of the mountains that encircle it. All the vineyards are restricted to the gravelly-loam soils found at approximately 300 metres (1,000 ft), the surrounding soils being unsuitable for vines. There is a microclimate here that warms up when other Mendocino areas are experiencing spring frosts. It is, however, slightly cooler during the growing season.

MENDOCINO AVA

Established: *16th July 1984*

This appellation may only be used for wines produced from grapes grown in the southernmost third of the county. It encompasses Mendocino's four other, smaller, approved viticultural areas plus surrounding and intervening vineyards.

MENDOCINO COUNTY AO

This appellation, which is not an AVA, covers the wines from anywhere within the entire county of Mendocino.

POTTER VALLEY AVA

Established: *14th November 1983*

An appellation consisting of 11,130 hectares (27,500 acres) situated northwest of Clear Lake, some 4,450 hectares (11,000 acres) of which are under vine. Vines grow on the valley floor and are protected by the surrounding hills.

Major wineries of Mendocino

WILLIAM BACCALA
Highway 101, Hopland, CA 95449

This relatively new winery produces excellent Chardonnay wines.

☆ Chardonnay

BLANC VINEYARDS
10200 West Road, Redwood Valley, CA 95470

A family-owned operation that consists of 61 hectares (150 acres) of Redwood Valley's vineyards.

BRAREN PAULI WINERY
12507 Hawn Creek Road, Potter Valley, CA 95469

Founded by Larry Braren and Bill Pauli, who produce Zinfandel, Chardonnay and Sauvignon Blanc wines.

CRESTA BLANCA
2399 North State Street, Ukiah, CA 95482

A winery founded at Livermore, Alameda County, by Charles Wetmore, a journalist and one of the pioneers of the Californian wine industry. From vines taken from Château d'Yquem as cuttings, he produced the first American wines to win medals at the Paris Exposition.

☆ Chardonnay, Petite Sirah, Zinfandel

EDMEADES VINEYARDS
5500 California State Highway 128, Philo, CA 95466

A small winery that produces good-quality varietal wines.

☆ Cabernet Sauvignon, Chardonnay, Pinot Noir, Zinfandel

FETZER VINEYARDS
1150 Bel Arbres Road, Redwood Valley, CA 95470

Fetzer has built up a reputation for exceptional value-for-money wines.

☆ Cabernet Sauvignon, Chardonnay, Fumé Blanc, Gamay Beaujolais, Gewürztraminer, Petite Sirah, Pinot Blanc, Sauvignon Blanc, White Riesling, Zinfandel

FREY VINEYARDS
14000 Tomki Road, Redwood Valley, CA 95470

A family business that has nearly 12 hectares (30 acres) of vineyards.

GREENWOOD RIDGE VINEYARDS
Box 1090 Star Route, Philo, CA 95466

These vineyards, in the Anderson Valley, were planted in 1972. Greenwood Ridge did not, however, begin to sell its own estate-bottled wines until 1980.

☆ White Riesling

HANDLEY CELLARS
Philo, CA 95466

This winery specializes in Chardonnay and *méthode champenoise* wines.

HUSCH VINEYARDS
4900 Star Route, Philo, CA 95466

Founded by Tony Husch, this winery was sold in 1979 to Hugo Oswald, the current owner and winemaker. It has large vineyard holdings in the Anderson and Ukiah Valleys, and consistently produces good-quality, medal-winning, varietal wines.

☆ Chardonnay, Gewürztraminer, Pinot Noir, Sauvignon Blanc, Sweet Gewürztraminer

LAZY CREEK VINEYARD
4610 Highway 128, Philo, CA 95466

Owned and run by the Kobler family, who have 8 hectares (20 acres) planted with Chardonnay, Pinot noir and Gewürztraminer.

☆ Pinot Noir

McDOWELL VALLEY VINEYARDS
3811 Highway 175, Hopland, CA 95449

This is a large, high-quality and ambitious family concern that consists of some 162 hectares (400 acres) planted with 12 different grape varieties.

☆ Cabernet Sauvignon, Chardonnay, Petite Sirah, Syrah, Zinfandel

MILANO WINERY
14594 South Highway 101, Hopland, CA 95449

A small winery that produces some interesting, full-flavoured wines. The Chardonnay is particularly good value.

☆ Cabernet Sauvignon, Chardonnay, Gewürztraminer, Johannisberg Riesling, Late Harvest Johannisberg Riesling, Zinfandel

MOUNTAIN HOUSE WINERY
38999 Highway 128, Cloverdale, CA 95425

Ron Lipp, a lawyer from Chicago, spent three years looking at potential properties before he settled on Mountain House.

☆ Chardonnay

NAVARRO VINEYARDS
5601 Highway 128, Philo, CA 95466

A white wine specialist and one of California's best Gewürztraminer producers.

☆ Chardonnay "Private Reserve", Gewürztraminer, Late Harvest Gewürztraminer, Sweet White Riesling

OLSON VINEYARDS
3620 Road B, Redwood Valley, CA 95470

This winery was founded 11 years after its vineyards, in 1982. The varietal range is quite large.

PARDUCCI WINE CELLARS
501 Parducci Road, Ukiah, CA 95482

A large winery, with over 142 hectares (350 acres). Parducci was actually founded in Sonoma in 1918, and after Prohibition, in 1931, the business was re-established at Ukiah. The wines are clean and fruity, with a good depth of flavour. They are well-exported and are good value-for-money.

☆ Cabernet Sauvignon, Cabernet Merlot, Chardonnay, Chenin Blanc, Gamay Beaujolais, Johannisberg Riesling, Muscat Canelli, Petite Sirah, Pinot Noir, Sauvignon Blanc, Zinfandel

PARSONS CREEK WINERY
3001 South State Street, Ukiah, CA 95482

An up-and-coming winery that has no vineyards but obviously buys in grapes very well.

☆ Chardonnay, Gewürztraminer, Johannisberg Riesling, NV Brut, Sweet Gewürztraminer

ROEDERER USA
2211 McKinley Avenue, Berkeley CA 94704

Owned by the French Champagne house, Louis Roederer, the first *méthode champenoise* wines are due to be released in 1988.

SCHARFFENBERGER CELLARS
307 Talmage Road, Ukiah, CA 95482

These wines also appear under the "Eaglepoint" label. I have not tasted them.

TIJSSELING
2150 McNab Ranch Road, Ukiah, CA 95482

A successful "champagne" vineyard.

☆ Brut NV, Brut Blanc de Blancs, Brut Blanc de Noirs

TYLAND VINEYARDS
2200 McNab Ranch Road, Ukiah, CA 95482

☆ Cabernet Sauvignon

WHALER VINEYARDS
6200 Eastside Road, Ukiah, CA 95482

A small, fine-quality winery specializing in Zinfandel.

☆ Zinfandel

Sonoma County

Six fertile valleys combine to make Sonoma California's most prolific wine-producing county, with an output comprised of equal quantities of red and white wine, and a reputation fast approaching that of Napa County.

BECAUSE OF THE VOLUME OF ITS PRODUCTION, Sonoma County was classed as little more than a source of blending wine until the late-1960s. It produced better-quality blending wine than the Central Valley, admittedly, but that wine was still nothing more than pep-up fodder for the bulk-produced anonymous generics. Then, in 1969, Russell Green, a former oil mogul and owner of a fast-growing vineyard in the Alexander Valley, purchased Simi, a once-famous winery founded in 1876, but at the time in decline. Green had ambitious plans for Simi, many of which he carried out, but soaring costs forced him to sell up in 1973. During those four brief years, however, he managed to restore the pre-Prohibition reputation of the old winery by creating a new genre of high-quality varietal Sonoma wines. With this achievement, he made other winemakers in the district ambitious.

Not only did the established Sonoma wineries re-evaluate what they were doing, with a pleasing plethora of interesting, expressive vinous delights as a result, but Green's activity also attracted new blood to the area. In 1970 the pre-Prohibition winery of Grand Cru in Glen Ellen was opened up and, in Kenwood, a new one, appropriately called Kenwood Vineyards, was established. Vina Vista was founded in 1971, Jordan and Dry Creek in 1972; Chateau St. Jean, Hacienda, Fisher and Sausal in 1973; and Clos du Bois, Landmark, Mark West, Rafanelli and Sotoyome in 1974.

The price and quality of Sonoma wines available today is still as variable as the county's climate, but the old wineries now have a new sense of purpose and the influx of other winemakers with fresh ideas has made this a most exciting wine district. Sonoma is capable of producing some of California's greatest wines, especially from grapes grown in its coolest areas on the higher and steeper slopes.

Vineyards, Dry Creek Valley, above
Sonoma's Dry Creek lies close to the Russian River, of which Dry Creek is a tributary. Moist and fertile, the valley has a gravelly soil unique to the area, enabling it to claim AVA status.

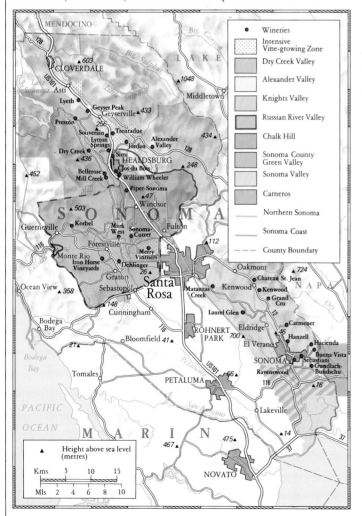

SONOMA COUNTY, see also p.363
One of California's most important wine-producing areas, Sonoma boasts a varied climate plus many different soils, producing a broad spectrum of wines.

Map legend:
- • Wineries
- Intensive Vine-growing Zone
- Dry Creek Valley
- Alexander Valley
- Knights Valley
- Russian River Valley
- Chalk Hill
- Sonoma County Green Valley
- Sonoma Valley
- Carneros
- Northern Sonoma
- Sonoma Coast
- County Boundary

FACTORS AFFECTING TASTE AND QUALITY

Location
The largest wine-producing county north of San Francisco, located between the Napa Valley and the Pacific Ocean.

Climate
Extremes of climate range from warm (Region III) in the north of the county to cool (Region I) in the south, where the refreshing effect of ocean breezes is significant, though progressively diminishing the further inland one goes. Fog penetration is more prevalent in the southern sectors around Petaluma, but rarely penetrates the Sonoma Mountains that protect Sonoma Valley in the southeast of the county.

Aspect
There are two major valley systems with significantly different orientations: Sonoma Valley, whose creek drains into the San Francisco Bay, and the Russian River, which flows directly into the Pacific Ocean. The vines grow at a height of approximately 120 metres (400ft) on flat land, particularly in the sector encompassing the AVAs of Russian River Valley, Alexander Valley and Dry Creek, or on the gentle lower slopes. Slightly steeper slopes are gradually being cultivated in the Sonoma Valley.

Soil
The soil situation varies greatly, from low-fertile loams in the Sonoma Valley and Santa Rosa areas, to highly fertile alluvial soils in the Russian River Valley, with limestone at Cazadera, a gravelly soil, known as Dry Creek Conglomerate, in Dry Creek and vent-based volcanic soils within the fall-out vicinity of Mount St. Helena.

Viticulture and vinification
Bulk winemaking is still important in the Russian River Valley, but "boutique" wineries specializing in premium varietals are now taking over.

Primary grape varieties
Cabernet sauvignon, Chardonnay, Chenin blanc, French colombard, Gewürztraminer, Merlot, Petite sirah, Pinot noir, Pinot blanc, Sauvignon blanc, White riesling, Zinfandel

Secondary grape varieties
Aleatico, Alicante bouschet, Barbera, Black malvoisie, Cabernet franc, Carignan, Chasselas doré, Early Burgundy, Folle blanche, Gamay, Gamay Beaujolais, Gray riesling, Green Hungarian, Grenache, Malbec, Malvasia bianca, Mission, Muscat blanc, Palomino, Pinot St. George, Ruby cabernet, Sauvignon vert, Sémillon, Sylvaner, Syrah

The AVAs of Sonoma County

ALEXANDER VALLEY AVA

Established: *23rd November 1984*

Located in the northeast of the county, this appellation extends from the banks of the Russian River into the foothills of the Mayacamus Mountains. In August 1986 its boundaries were extended so it now overlaps the Russian River AVA.

CHALK HILL AVA

Established: *21st November 1983*

This appellation covers 85 square kilometres (33 square miles) and encompasses 648 hectares (1,600 acres) of vineyards rising in altitude from 61 to 405 metres (200 to 1,330 ft). There is no chalk here, the soil's whiteness in fact derived from volcanic ash with a high quartzite content. Emitted by Mount St. Helena over many centuries, it has mixed with local sandy and silty loams to provide a deep soil that is not particularly fertile. This area is protected by a thermal belt that promotes a September harvest, compared to October in surrounding areas.

DRY CREEK VALLEY AVA

Established: *6th September 1983*

This appellation faces that of the Alexander Valley across the Russian River. Its climate is generally wetter and warmer than surrounding areas, with a longer growing season than the Russian River appellation to the south.

KNIGHTS VALLEY AVA

Established: *21st November 1983*

An area of approximately 142 square kilometres (55 square miles) containing 405 hectares (1,000 acres) of vineyards, with vines growing on rocky and gravelly soil of low fertility at altitudes that are generally higher than those in the adjacent AVAs.

LOS CARNEROS AVA

Established: *12th September 1983*

The Los Carneros, or simply Carneros, appellation covers an area of low, rolling hills that straddle the counties of Sonoma and Napa. This was originally sheep country, but the cool sea-breezes that come off San Pablo Bay to the south provide an excellent fine-wine growing climate.

NORTHERN SONOMA AVA

Established: *17th June 1985*

This large appellation completely encapsulates six other AVAs, those of Alexander Valley, Chalk Hill, Dry Creek Valley, Knights Valley, Russian River Valley and Sonoma County Green Valley, and is separated from the Sonoma Valley appellation to the south by the city of Santa Rosa.

RUSSIAN RIVER VALLEY AVA

Established: *21st November 1983*

The name Russian River began appearing on wine labels as recently as 1970, although its vineyards date from the nineteenth century. The early morning coastal fog provides a cooler growing season than that of neighbouring areas.

SONOMA COAST AVA

Established: *13th July 1987*

An appellation covering 1,940 square kilometres (750 square miles), made up of the area directly inland from the length of Sonoma's Pacific coastline – the AVA's western boundary. It is significantly cooler than other areas owing to the persistent fog that envelops the Coast Ranges, the mountains that are within sight of the Pacific Ocean.

SONOMA COUNTY GREEN VALLEY AVA

Established: *21st December 1983*

Originally it was proposed that this area within the Russian River Valley AVA be called, simply, Green Valley, but in line with a ruling to add Solano County to that county's Green Valley appellation, it was decided to add "Sonoma County". The climate here is one of the coolest in the Russian River Valley and the soil is mostly fine sandy loam.

SONOMA MOUNTAIN AVA

Established: *22nd February 1985*

A tiny appellation within the Sonoma Valley AVA. Sonoma Mountain has a thermal belt phenomenon that drains cold air and fog from its steep terrain to the slopes below, creating a climate characterized by more moderate temperatures than the surrounding areas.

SONOMA VALLEY AVA

Established: *4th January 1982*

The first grapes were planted here in 1825 by the Mission San Francisco de Sonoma. Rainfall is lower than elsewhere in the county and fog rarely penetrates the Sonoma Mountains.

Major wineries of Sonoma

ALEXANDER VALLEY VINEYARDS
8644 Highway 128, Healdsburg, CA 95448

Underrated wines in a full, rich style.

☆ Cabernet Sauvignon, Chardonnay, Johannisberg Riesling

BELLEROSE VINEYARD
435 West Dry Creek Road, Healdsburg, CA 95448

The unique "Cuvée Bellerose" is comprised of Cabernet sauvignon, Merlot, Cabernet franc, Petit verdot and Malbec.

☆ "Cuvée Bellerose"

BUENA VISTA WINERY
27000 Ramal Road, Sonoma, CA 95476

Haraszthy's original winery, now German-owned, makes good wines.

☆ Cabernet Sauvignon, Chardonnay, Fumé Blanc

CARMENET VINEYARD
1700 Moon Mountain Drive, Sonoma, CA 95476

A new operation, under the auspices of Chalone Vineyards of Monterey.

☆ Sauvignon Blanc, Sonoma Red

CHATEAU ST. JEAN
8555 Sonoma Highway, Kenwood, CA 95452

This prestigious winery is now owned by the Japanese firm Suntory, and the quality of its wines, particularly its speciality wines, is as high as ever.

☆ Chardonnay "Robert Young Vineyard", Late Harvest and Selected Late Harvest Johannisberg Riesling, Muscat Canelli, Sauvignon Blanc, Late Harvest Sémillon-Sauvignon

CLOS DU BOIS
5 Fitch Street, Healdsburg, CA

With its massive 405 hectares (1,000 acres) of vineyards and more medals than any other winery, Clos du Bois can boast a rare achievement in combining quantity with quality.

☆ Cabernet Sauvignon, Chardonnay (particularly Flintwood), Merlot, Sauvignon Blanc Barrel-Fermented

DEHLINGER WINERY
6300 Guerneville Road, Sebastopol, CA 95472

A small winery producing wines of finesse and excellent style.

☆ Cabernet Sauvignon, Chardonnay, Pinot Noir, Zinfandel

DRY CREEK VINEYARD
3770 Lambert Bridge Road, Healdsburg, CA 95448

David Stare's vineyard has a high reputation for Fumé Blanc, but also produces a splendid red "Reserve".

☆ Chardonnay, "David Stare Reserve", Fumé Blanc

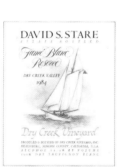

GEYSER PEAK WINERY
22281 Chianti Road, Geyserville, CA 95441

Since the Trione family purchased this winery in 1982, some fine wines have been made. Nervo Winery is a second label.

☆ "Trione" Cabernet Sauvignon

GRAND CRU VINEYARDS
1 Vintage Lane, Glen Ellen, CA 95442

A high-quality operation on the site of the original Grand Cru winery.

☆ Cabernet Sauvignon, Chenin Blanc, Gewürztraminer, Sauvignon Blanc, Sweet Gewürztraminer, Zinfandel

GUNDLACH-BUNDSCHU WINERY
3775 Thornberry Road, Sonoma, CA 95487

High-quality winery owned and run by the fifth generation of the family of the founder, Jacob Gundlach.

☆ Cabernet Sauvignon, Gewürztraminer, Merlot, Riesling, White Riesling

HACIENDA WINERY
1000 Vineyard Lane, Sonoma, CA 95476

This high-quality winery owns part of Haraszthy's original vineyard.

☆ Cabernet Sauvignon, Chardonnay ("Claire de Lune"), Gewürztraminer

HANZELL VINEYARDS
18596 Lomita Avenue, Sonoma, CA 95476

Well-known, highly individual winery.

☆ Chardonnay, Pinot Noir

IRON HORSE VINEYARDS
9786 Ross Station Road, Sebastopol, CA 95472

This small winery makes a fine, neat, racy Chardonnay and superb *méthode champenoise*.

☆ Blanc de Noirs, Sparkling Brut, Brut Late Disgorged, Sonoma County Green Valley Chardonnay

JORDAN VINEYARD & WINERY
1474 Alexander Valley Road,
Healdsburg, CA 95448

An exciting Cabernet Sauvignon.

☆ Cabernet Sauvignon

KENWOOD VINEYARDS
9592 Sonoma Highway,
Kenwood, CA 95452

Concentrated wines with good attack.

☆ Cabernet Sauvignon, Chardonnay,
Chenin Blanc, Gewürztraminer,
Zinfandel

KORBEL CHAMPAGNE CELLARS
13250 River Road,
Guerneville, CA 95446

California's leading sparkling wine
specialist in the popular sector.

☆ Blanc de Noirs Champagne, Natural
Champagne

LAUREL GLEN VINEYARD
P.O. Box 548,
Glen Ellen, CA 95442

Laurel Glen makes succulent Cabernet
Sauvignon.

☆ Cabernet Sauvignon

LYETH VINEYARD & WINERY LTD.
24625 Chianti Road,
Geyserville, CA 95441

An exciting new winery, producing
red and white typical Bordeaux blends.

☆ Red Table Wine, White Table Wine

LYTTON SPRINGS WINERY
650 Lytton Springs Road,
Healdsburg, CA 95448

Producer of some high-quality wines.

☆ Zinfandel

MARK WEST VINEYARDS
7000 Trenton-Healdsburg Road,
Forestville, CA 95436

Owned by Pan-Am pilot Bob Ellis, this
vineyard is named after a small
creek bordering Ellis' ranch. The style
is elegant and fine, but can lapse.

☆ Chardonnay, Johannisberg Riesling,
Pinot Noir Blanc

MATANZAS CREEK WINERY
6097 Bennett Valley Road,
Santa Rosa, CA 95404

A small winery producing fine, rich,
elegant wines with good fruit-acidity.

☆ Cabernet Sauvignon, Chardonnay,
Merlot, Sauvignon Blanc

THE MERRY VINTNERS
3339 Hartman Road,
Santa Rosa, CA 95401

A winery founded by Merry Edwards,
who established Matanzas Creek Winery.

☆ Vintage Preview Chardonnay, Barrel-
Fermented Chardonnay

MILL CREEK VINEYARDS
1401 Westside Road,
Healdsburg, CA 95448

James Kreck aims for elegance and
finesse in his fine quality wine.

☆ Cabernet Sauvignon, Cabernet
Blush, Chardonnay

PIPER SONOMA
P.O. Box K,
Windsor, CA 95492

Piper-Heidsieck, the Reims-based
grande marque Champagne house,
joined forces with Sonoma Vineyards
to fund this venture and now owns it.

☆ Blanc de Noirs, Brut, Tête de Cuvée

PRESTON VINEYARDS
9282 West Dry Creek Road,
Healdsburg, CA 95448

A 51-hectare (125-acre) vineyard
capable of making high-quality wines.

☆ Chardonnay, Cuvée de Fumé,
Zinfandel

RAVENSWOOD
21415 Broadway,
Sonoma, CA 95476

Joel Peterson is the master when it
comes to Zinfandel and also produces
some stunning Merlots.

☆ Merlot, Zinfandel

SEBASTIANI VINEYARDS
389 Fourth Street East,
Sonoma, CA 95476

Despite a huge production, the wines
have been inconsistent in the 1980s.

☆ Cabernet Sauvignon,
Gewürztraminer, Muscat, Zinfandel

SIMI WINERY
16275 Healdsburg Avenue,
Healdsburg, CA 95448

For a winery with a huge production,
Simi produces some stunning wines,
particularly its power-packed, ripe,
oaky Chardonnays.

☆ Chardonnay, Muscat Canelli, Rosé de
Cabernet, Sauvignon Blanc

SONOMA-CUTRER VINEYARDS
4401 Slusser Road,
Windsor, CA 95492

Specialist producing three totally
different, equally stunning Chardonnays.

☆ Cutrer Vineyard, "Les Pierres" and
"Russian River Ranches" Chardonnays

SOUVERAIN WINERY
P.O. Box 528,
Geyserville, CA 95441

A large production of inexpensive
wines that can be really good, if rarely
exciting.

☆ Cabernet Sauvignon, Colombard

TORRES VINEYARDS
11480 Graton Road,
Sebastopol, CA 95472

In 1982 Miguel Torres planted eight
hectares (20 acres) of his 23 hectares
(56 acres) with Chardonnay and one
experimental acre with his native
Parellada. In doing so, he used four
times as many vines per acre than is
the norm. High-density cultivation
causes competition between the vines,
yielding less fruit per vine. But with
four times the number, the total
volume per acre is the same. The vines
obviously cost more to plant and tend,
but the reduced yield per vine
provides better-quality fruit. The first
wines are due to be released in 1990.

TRENTADUE WINERY
19170 Redwood Highway,
Geyserville, CA 95441

An 81-hectare (200-acre) vineyard in
the Alexander Valley producing a
characterful selection of varietal wines
that are rarely, if ever, filtered.

☆ Gamay Rosé, Late Harvest Zinfandel,
Nebbiolo, Petite Sirah and, for interest:
Aleatico, Carignane, White Carignane

WILLIAM WHEELER WINERY
130 Plaza Street,
Healdsburg, CA 95448

Producer of some fine wines from 71
hectares (175 acres) of Dry Creek
vineyards planted with Cabernet Sauvignon, Chardonnay and Sauvignon blanc.

☆ Cabernet Sauvignon, Chardonnay

The best of the rest

ADLER FELS WINERY
5325 Corrick Lane,
Santa Rosa, CA 95405

Owner David Coleman was bitten
by the wine bug when designing the
labels for Chateau St. Jean.

☆ Fumé Blanc

ALDERBROOK VINEYARDS
2306 Magnolia Drive,
Healdsburg, CA 95448

An old prune farm, replanted with
Chardonnay, Sauvignon blanc and
Sémillon. Specialist in barrel-fermented
whites.

BALVERNE WINERY & VINEYARDS
10810 Hillview Road,
Windsor,
CA 95492

This winery has 101 hectares (250
acres) of hillside vineyards and was the
first to make a Californian Scheurebe.

BANDIERA WINERY
155 Cherry Creek Road,
Cloverdale,
CA 95425

This improving winery is now making
good, if rarely exciting, wines. It is
owned by the Californian Wine
Company.

☆ Cabernet Sauvignon

Bandiera
Cabernet Sauvignon 1984
North Coast
Made & Bottled by Bandiera Winery, Cloverdale, CA

BLACK MOUNTAIN VINEYARD
See J. W. Morris Winery.

CAMBIASO VINEYARDS
1141 Grant Avenue,
Healdsburg, CA 95448

A Thai-owned winery with a large
production of inexpensive "generics"
and improving varietals.

☆ Cabernet Sauvignon, Chenin Blanc,
Petite Sirah, Sauvignon Blanc

CHALK HILL WINERY
10300 Chalk Hill Road,
Healdsburg, CA 95448

This operation was known as Donna
Maria Vineyards when the owner only
grew and sold grapes, but became
Chalk Hill Winery when it began to
make and sell wines in 1981.

CORDTZ BROTHERS CELLARS
28237 River Road,
Cloverdale, CA 95425

The building itself is pre-Prohibition, but was totally re-equipped in 1980.

☆ Zinfandel

H. COTURRI & SONS LTD
6725 Enterprise Road,
Glen Ellen, CA 95442

Oak-matured varietals are the speciality.

DE LOACH VINEYARDS
1791 Olivet Road,
Santa Rosa, CA 95401

A winery best known for its rich, buttery, lemony Chardonnays.

☆ Chardonnay, Fumé Blanc, White Zinfandel

DOMAINE LAURIER
8075 Martinelli Road,
Forestville, CA 95436

A 12-hectare (30-acre) vineyard planted with Cabernet sauvignon, Chardonnay, Pinot noir and Sauvignon blanc.

FIELD STONE WINERY
10075 State Highway 128,
Healdsburg, CA 95448

An underrated, underground winery producing fresh and fruity wines.

☆ Cabernet Sauvignon, Johannisberg Riesling, Petite Sirah, Spring Cabernet

FISHER VINEYARDS
6200 St. Helena Road,
Santa Rosa, CA 95404

The first vintage here was a 1979 Chardonnay. The vineyards are in the Mayacamas Mountains and Napa.

☆ Cabernet Sauvignon "Coach Insignia"

FOPPIANO VINEYARDS
12707 Old Redwood Highway,
Healdsburg, CA 95448

A family-run winery that makes an interesting range of varietal wines.

☆ Cabernet Sauvignon, Chardonnay, Petite Sirah, "Riverside Farm" Fumé Blanc and White Cabernet Sauvignon

FRITZ CELLARS
24691 Dutcher Creek Road,
Cloverdale, CA 95425

A 36-hectare (90-acre) vineyard supplies most of this winery's needs.

☆ Fumé Blanc

FULTON VALLEY WINERY
875 River Road,
Fulton, CA 95439

With Rod Berglund (La Crema Vinera's winemaker for five years), heading the winemaking of this new operation, Fulton Valley should be worth looking out for.

GLEN ELLEN WINERY
1883 London Ranch Road,
Glen Ellen, CA 95442

These wines are usually very good value.

☆ Cabernet Sauvignon, Chardonnay, Fumé Blanc

HAYWOOD WINERY
18701 Gehricke Road,
Sonoma, CA 95476

☆ Chardonnay, White Riesling

HOP KILN WINERY
Griffin Vineyards,
6050 Westside Road,
Healdsburg, CA 95448

This winery, a National Historic Landmark, produces good wines.

☆ "A Thousand Flowers", Petite Sirah, Gewürztraminer, Primitivo Zinfandel

HULTGREN & SAMPERTON
P.O. Box 1026,
Healdsburg, CA 95448

A six-hectare (14-acre) vineyard in the Alexander and Dry Creek Valleys.

☆ Petite Sirah

JOHNSON'S ALEXANDER VALLEY WINES
8333 Highway 128,
Healdsburg, CA 95448

All wines are estate-bottled, vintaged, 100 per cent varietals.

☆ Cabernet Sauvignon, Johannisberg Riesling, White Pinot Noir

KISTLER VINEYARDS
Nelligan Road,
Glen Ellen, CA 95442

An improving winery with 16 hectares (40 acres) of vineyard.

☆ Chardonnay

LAMBERT BRIDGE
4085 West Dry Creek Road,
Healdsburg, CA 95448

Distribution is by Seagram, and the quality ranges from good to high.

☆ Cabernet Sauvignon, Chardonnay

LANDMARK VINEYARDS
9150 Los Amigos Road,
Windsor, CA 95492

Landmark's best wines are sold under its own label. It has 32 hectares (80 acres) of vineyards in the Sonoma and Alexander valleys.

J. W. MORRIS WINERY
101 Grant Avenue,
Healdsburg, CA 95448

Originally a "port" specialist, now placing more emphasis on its varietal wines from its Black Mountain vineyards in the Alexander Valley.

PAT PAULSEN VINEYARDS
25510 River Road,
Cloverdale, CA 95425

In addition to his winemaking talent, Pat Paulsen's activities range from would-be Presidential candidate to comedian, theatre-owner and film star.

☆ Muscat Canelli

J. PEDRONCELLI WINERY
1220 Canyon Road,
Geyserville, CA 95441

Good-value wines with an improving range of varietals.

☆ Chardonnay, Pinot Noir, Gewürztraminer, Zinfandel, Zinfandel Rosé

POMMERAIE VINEYARDS
10541 Cherry Ridge Road,
Sebastopol, CA 95472

Specialist in Cabernet Sauvignon and Chardonnay with a tiny production.

☆ Cabernet Sauvignon

A. RAFANELLI
4685 West Dry Creek Road,
Healdsburg, CA 95448

A small vineyard with a good reputation, producing Zinfandel and Gamay.

RIVER OAKS VINEYARDS WINES
5 Fitch Street,
Healdsburg, CA 95448

A large winery producing good, commercial-quality wine.

J. ROCHIOLI VINEYARDS
6192 Westside Road,
Healdsburg, CA 95448

An old-established vineyard that has recently ventured into estate-bottling.

☆ Chardonnay

SAUSAL WINERY
7370 Highway 128,
Healdsburg, CA 95448

A winery whose best wine to date has been Zinfandel.

SEA RIDGE WINERY
P.O. Box 287,
Cazadero, CA 95421

A winery that specializes in Pinot noir and Chardonnay, grown on limestone.

SELLARDS WINERY
6400 Sequoia Circle,
Sebastopol, CA 95472

Tiny Chardonnay, Cabernet Sauvignon and Sauvignon Blanc specialist.

SOTOYOME WINERY
641 Limerick Lane,
Healdsburg, CA 95448

Producer of some good-quality varietal wines.

☆ Cabernet Sauvignon, Petite Sirah

ROBERT STEMMLER WINERY
3805 Lambert Bridge Road,
Healdsburg, CA 95884

Tiny vineyard augmented by grapes purchased on a select basis.

☆ Chardonnay, Fumé Blanc

RODNEY STRONG VINEYARDS
11455 Old Redwood Highway,
Windsor, CA 95492

Strong has made some rich Cabernet Sauvignon and soft-styled Chardonnay, but he lacks consistency and some wines lack flavour.

☆ Cabernet Sauvignon, Chardonnay

JOSEPH SWAN VINEYARDS
2916 Laguna Road,
Forestville, CA 95436

Tiny amount of Zinfandel, plus Chardonnay and Pinot Noir.

TOPOLOS RUSSIAN RIVER VINEYARDS
5700 Gravenstein Highway,
North Forestville, CA 95436

Good varietals from vineyards around the winery and on Sonoma Mountain.

☆ Petite Sirah

TOYON WINERY & VINEYARDS
9643 Highway 128,
Healdsburg, CA 95448

Good commercial-quality varietals, produced from vineyards in the Alexander Valley and grapes purchased on a select basis.

☆ Cabernet Sauvignon

VALLEY OF THE MOON
777 Madrone Road,
Glen Ellen, CA 95442

A winery that built its reputation on generic wines, but which also produces estate-bottled varietals from its own 81-hectare (200-acre) vineyard.

VINA VISTA
Chianti Road,
Geyserville, CA 95441

Ex-electrical engineer Keith Nelson produces various varietal wines that have a certain following.

STEPHEN ZELLERBACH VINEYARD
14350 Chalk Hill Road,
Healdsburg, CA 95448

A 28-hectare (70-acre) vineyard in the Chalk Hill area producing white and red Cabernet Sauvignon, Merlot and Chardonnay.

Napa County

Napa County, and most particularly the Napa Valley within it, is the heart and soul of the Californian wine industry. Its vineyards are the most concentrated in the state, it has more wineries than any other county, and they produce the greatest number and variety of fine wines in the entire North American continent.

IT IS HARD TO BELIEVE THAT NAPA WAS PLANTED after Sonoma, but it was, and by some 13 years; in 1838 a trapper from North Carolina by the name of George Yount acquired a few Mission vines from General Mariano Vallejo's Sonoma vineyard and planted them outside his log cabin, three kilometres (two miles) north of present-day Yountville. He merely wished to make a little wine for his own use. Little did he know that the entire Napa Valley would one day be carpeted with a lush green sea of vines. Within six years Yount himself was harvesting an annual average of 900 litres (200 gallons); by the turn of the decade various other vineyards had sprung up and, in 1859, Samuel Brannan, an ex-Mormon millionaire, purchased eight square kilometres (three square miles) of rich valley land and planted cuttings of various European vine varieties he had collected during his travels abroad. Within a further 20 years there were more than 7,285 hectares (18,000 acres) of vineyard in the county, more than half the amount currently cultivated and almost twice the area of vines now covering Mendocino.

Today, the Napa Valley's vinous reputation is well established throughout the world. Napa wines, particularly Chardonnay and Cabernet Sauvignon, continue to be the most sought-after and highly prized wines in the American continent, and will continue to be so for the the foreseeable future at least.

Napa vineyards, above
In this, the most famous of all Californian wine regions, vines grow mostly on the fertile valley floors, with wooded hills providing a backdrop.

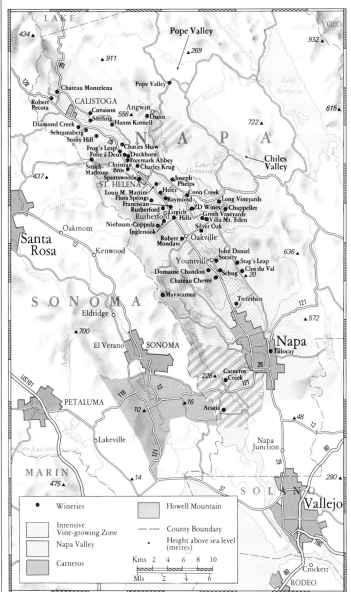

Legend:
- Wineries
- Intensive Vine-growing Zone
- Napa Valley
- Carneros
- Howell Mountain
- — — County Boundary
- ▲ Height above sea level (metres)

Kms 2 4 6 8 10
Mls 2 4 6

FACTORS AFFECTING TASTE AND QUALITY

Location
Starting alongside San Francisco Bay, Napa runs 54 kilometres (34 miles) north and west to the foothills of Mount St. Helena. Flanking it are the Sonoma Valley to the west and Lake Berryessa to the east.

Climate
This ranges from cool (Region I) near the Bay, in the often foggy Carneros District, to warm (Region III) in the northern section of the Napa Valley and in Pope Valley.

Aspect
Vines are mostly planted on the valley floors but some are cultivated on slopes. Although flat, the altitude of the valley floors ranges from barely five metres (17 ft) above sea level at Napa itself, to 70 metres (230 ft) at St. Helena in the middle of the valley, and 122 metres (400 ft) at Calistoga in the north. The wooded western slopes provide afternoon shade, which adds to the tempering effect of altitude and so favours white grapes, whereas the eastern slopes favour red varieties.

Soil
Fertile clay and silt loams in the south, gravel loams of better drainage and lower fertility in the north.

Viticulture and vinification
There is a vast range of wineries, from a small number of large firms employing the latest high-tech methods, to an increasing number of small boutique wineries. The latter have limited production based on traditional methods, although often with the help of judicious use of modern techniques. The great wines from this valley have established California's vinous reputation throughout the world.

Primary grape varieties
Cabernet sauvignon, Chardonnay, Chenin blanc, Merlot, Pinot noir, Sauvignon blanc, White riesling, Zinfandel

Secondary grape varieties
Aleatico, Alicante bouschet, Barbera, Black malvoisie, Burger, Cabernet franc, Carignan, Early Burgundy, Flora, Folle blanche, French colombard, Gamay, Gamay Beaujolais, Gewürztraminer, Gray riesling, Green Hungarian, Grenache, Malbec, Malvasia bianca, Mataro, Mission, Muscat blanc, Palomino, Petite sirah, Pinot blanc, Pinot St. George, Ruby cabernet, Sauvignon vert, Sémillon, Sylvaner, Syrah

NAPA COUNTY, see also p.363

The intensive wine-growing areas of this illustrious Californian district occupy a long, narrow strip running roughly parallel to those of Sonoma County. Many famous names are crowded around Route 29.

The AVAs of Napa County

CARNEROS AVA

Also known as Los Carneros, this AVA overlaps Napa and Sonoma counties. *See* Los Carneros, Sonoma, p.371.

HOWELL MOUNTAIN AVA

Established: *30th January 1984*

The relatively flat table-top of Howell Mountain is a sub-appellation of the Napa Valley, covering 57 square kilometres (22 square miles) and encompassing some 81 hectares (200 acres) of vineyards at an altitude of between 420 and 890 metres (1,400 and 2,200 ft). Vines were first planted here in 1880.

NAPA COUNTY AO

An appellation that covers grapes grown anywhere in the entire county.

NAPA VALLEY AVA

Established: *27th February 1981*

This AVA includes all of the county with the exception of the area around Putah Creek and Lake Berryessa. The Napa Valley appellation is 40 kilometres (25 miles) long and between 12 and 16 kilometres (eight and ten miles) wide, sheltered by two parallel mountain ranges. The vast majority of vineyards occupy the flat valley floor in an almost continuous strip from Napa to Calistoga, although the slopes are beginning to be cultivated.

STAG'S LEAP DISTRICT AVA

Established: *27th January 1989*

Major wineries of Napa County

ACACIA WINERY
2750 Las Amigas Road,
Napa, CA 94559

Burgundian varietal specialist.

☆ Chardonnay, Pinot Noir

CARNEROS CREEK WINERY
1285 Dealy Lane, Napa, CA 94559

This high-quality winery went through a dull patch in the early 1980s, but seems to be back on course.

☆ Cabernet Sauvignon, Chardonnay, Merlot, Pinot Noir

CAYMUS VINEYARDS
8700 Conn Creek Road,
Rutherford, CA 94573

A high-quality winery with a stunning range of Cabernet Sauvignons. A second label is "Liberty School".

☆ Cabernet Sauvignon, Petite Sirah, Pinot Noir Blanc

CHAPPELLET VINEYARDS
1581 Sage Canyon Road,
St. Helena, CA 94574

An excellent winery with a range of skilfully produced wines that show great finesse.

☆ Cabernet Sauvignon, Chardonnay, Chenin Blanc, Johannisberg Riesling, Merlot

CHATEAU CHEVRE WINERY
2030 Hoffman Lane,
Yountville, CA 94599

A winery producing a magnificent Merlot and a soft Sauvignon Blanc.

☆ Merlot, Sauvignon Blanc

CHATEAU MONTELENA WINERY
1429 Tubbs Lane,
Calistoga, CA 94515

The style of this small, prestigious winery has changed over the years, but the quality has always been high.

☆ Cabernet Sauvignon, Chardonnay, Zinfandel

THE CHRISTIAN BROTHERS
4411 Redwood Road,
Napa, CA 94558

All too often lacklustre wines. There has, however, been a marked improvement since the mid-1980s.

☆ Cabernet Sauvignon, Sauvignon Blanc, Zinfandel

CLOS DU VAL
5330 Silverado Trail, Napa, CA 94558

A small winery with a well-deserved reputation for quality and complexity.

☆ Cabernet Sauvignon Reserve, Merlot, Zinfandel

CONN CREEK WINERY
8711 Silverado Trail,
St. Helena, CA 94574

Best known for Cabernet Sauvignon.

☆ Cabernet Sauvignon, Chardonnay, Johannisberg Riesling, Zinfandel

CUVAISON
4550 Silverado Trail,
Calistoga, CA 94515

The assertive style of this Swiss-owned winery best suits its Chardonnay. Its second label is "Calistoga Cellars".

☆ Chardonnay

THE JOHN DANIEL SOCIETY
Napa, CA 94558

Christian Moueix of Château Pétrus has joined forces with the daughters of John Daniel to produce "Dominus", an excellent Bordeaux-like blend.

☆ "Dominus"

DIAMOND CREEK VINEYARDS
1500 Diamond Mountain Road,
Calistoga, CA 94515

A tiny specialist winery producing great Cabernet Sauvignons.

☆ Cabernet Sauvignon (Red Rock Terrace, Volcanic Hill and Gravelly Meadow)

DOMAINE CHANDON
California Drive,
Yountville, CA 94599

The most consistent French-financed Californian venture so far.

☆ Chardonnay, Napa Blanc de Noirs, Napa Brut NV, 10th Special Anniversary

DUCKHORN VINEYARDS
3027 Silverado Trail,
St. Helena, CA 94574

Superb wines with a cult following.

☆ Cabernet Sauvignon, Merlot (Three Palms), Sauvignon Blanc

DUNN VINEYARDS
805 White Cottage Road,
Angwin, CA 94508

Randy Dunn makes a tiny quantity of top-quality Cabernet Sauvignon from his Howell Mountain vineyard.

☆ Cabernet Sauvignon (especially Howell Mountain)

FLORA SPRINGS WINE COMPANY
1978 Zinfandel Lane W.,
St. Helena, CA 94574

The exciting new "Trilogy" is a blend of Merlot with the two Cabernets.

☆ Chardonnay (Barrel-Fermented) "Trilogy"

FOLIE À DEUX
3070 St. Helena Highway,
St. Helena, CA 94574

A tiny production of sought-after Cabernet Sauvignon, Chardonnay and Chenin Blanc.

☆ Chardonnay

FRANCISCAN VINEYARDS
1178 Galleron Road,
Rutherford, CA 94573

Although production is growing fast, the wine continues to be good.

☆ Burgundy, Cabernet Sauvignon, Charbono, Chardonnay

FREEMARK ABBEY WINERY
3020 St. Helena Highway North,
St. Helena, CA 94574

The immaculately produced offerings of this prestigious winery are always snapped up by knowledgeable buyers.

☆ Cabernet Bosché, Chardonnay, "Edelwein Gold" (Johannisberg Riesling), Petite Sirah

FROG'S LEAP WINERY
3358 St.Helena Highway,
St. Helena, CA 94574

These wines show great finesse.

☆ Cabernet Sauvignon, Chardonnay

GRGICH HILLS CELLAR
1829 St. Helena Highway,
Rutherford, CA 94573

Owned and run by Miljenko Grgich, once winemaker at Chateau Montalena, this winery produces intense, rich and vibrant styles of high-quality wine.

☆ Cabernet Sauvignon, Chardonnay, Johannisberg Riesling, Zinfandel

GROTH VINEYARDS & WINERY
750 Oakville Crossroad,
Oakville, CA 94562

In a very short time this winery has established a reputation for producing some of the finest wines in California.

☆ Cabernet Sauvignon, Chardonnay

HEITZ WINE CELLARS
500 Taplin Road,
St. Helena, CA 94574

This winery has made its name on its brilliant Martha's Vineyard wine.

☆ Cabernet Sauvignon (Bella Oaks Vineyard and Martha's Vineyard), Zinfandel

INGLENOOK VINEYARDS
PO Box 19, Rutherford, CA 94573

One of California's top wineries under John Daniels in the 1960s, the quality has slipped somewhat since then, although the Cabernet Sauvignon and, strangely, the Charbono have consistently performed well.

☆ Cabernet Sauvignon, Charbono

HANNS KORNELL CHAMPAGNE CELLARS
1091 Larkmead Lane, St. Helena, CA 94574

A *méthode champenoise* specialist, highly regarded by some, but I have not been impressed by its range.

CHARLES KRUG
2800 St. Helena Highway, St. Helena, CA 94574

Purchased by the Mondavi family in 1943, this winery is best known for its high-quality Cabernet Sauvignon, but most of the production is jug wine and generics sold under a second label — "C.K.Mondavi".

☆ Cabernet Sauvignon "Cesare Mondavi Selection"

LONG VINEYARDS
PO Box 50, St. Helena, CA 94574

High-quality, estate-bottled wines.

☆ Cabernet Sauvignon, Chardonnay, Johannisberg Riesling

LOUIS M. MARTINI
PO Box 112, St. Helena, CA 94574

The high-quality reputation of this winery is only justified for some of its Cabernet Sauvignon and Merlot wines. I have not had the opportunity to taste its non-vintage Moscato Sparkling.

☆ Cabernet Sauvignon, Merlot

MAYACAMAS VINEYARDS
1155 Lokoya Road, Napa, CA 94558

A prestigious small winery.

☆ Cabernet Sauvignon, Chardonnay, Sauvignon Blanc

ROBERT MONDAVI WINERY
7801 St. Helena Highway, Oakville, CA 94562

1986
Napa Valley
JOHANNISBERG RIESLING
ALCOHOL 10.5% BY VOLUME
PRODUCED AND BOTTLED BY
ROBERT MONDAVI WINERY
OAKVILLE, CALIFORNIA

The new Mondavi Woodbridge Winery label is a good, inexpensive introduction to Californian wine. Its Cabernet Sauvignon Reserve ranks among the very best the state can produce. "Opus One" is the product of Mondavi's collaboration with Baron Philippe de Rothschild. A Cabernet-Merlot blend, the quality is good and has improved with each vintage, but it is expensive.

☆ Cabernet Sauvignon, Fumé Blanc, Johannisberg Riesling, Moscato d'Oro, "Opus One", Pinot Noir Reserve

NIEBAUM-COPPOLA ESTATE
1460 Niebaum Lane, Rutherford, CA 94573

This venture has been funded by Hollywood movie director Francis Ford Coppola, and the results so far have undeniable class and quality.

☆ "Rubicon"

ROBERT PECOTA WINERY
3299 Bennett Lane, Calistoga, CA 94515

An underrated winery that produces some ravishing white wines.

☆ Chardonnay, Gamay Beaujolais, Muscato di Andrea

JOSEPH PHELPS VINEYARDS
200 Taplin Road, St. Helena, CA 94574

Joseph Phelps Vineyards
A Napa Valley Red Wine produced and bottled by
Joseph Phelps Vineyards, St. Helena, California from
Cabernet Sauvignon (60%), Merlot (20%) and Cabernet Franc (20%)

A prestigious winery with a large range of wines that are top-quality.

☆ Cabernet Sauvignon (Backus, Eisele or Insignia vineyards), "Delice de Sémillon", Gewürztraminer, Johannisberg Riesling Late Harvest, Sauvignon Blanc, Scheurebe Late Harvest, Zinfandel

RAYMOND VINEYARD AND CELLAR
849 E. Zinfandel Lane, St. Helena, CA 94574

The Raymond family has a solid reputation for uncompromising quality.

☆ Cabernet Sauvignon, Chardonnay, Chenin Blanc, Johannisberg Riesling Late Harvest, Zinfandel

RUTHERFORD VINTNERS
1673 St. Helena Highway, Rutherford, CA 94573

Some 70 per cent of the production is estate bottled. Chateau Rutherford is the reserve Cabernet Sauvignon. Wines are also sold under the "Leo Cellars" label.

☆ Cabernet Sauvignon, Merlot

SCHRAMSBERG VINEYARDS
Schramsberg Road, Calistoga, CA 94515

A very prestigious winery that deserves its reputation for its Blanc de Blancs. I am less impressed with its Cuvée de Pinot and Blanc de Noirs.

☆ Blanc de Blancs

SCHUG CELLARS
6204 St. Helena Highway, Napa, CA 94558

Founded by the talented Walter Schug, ex-winemaker at Joseph Phelps. The first wines were released in 1983 and show great potential.

☆ Chardonnay (Beckstoffer Vineyard), Pinot Noir (Beckstoffer and Heineman Vineyards)

CHARLES SHAW
1010 Big Tree Road, St. Helena, CA 94574

In 1982 Chuck and Lucy Shaw wisely hired Ric Forman, the talented winemaker who added a *nouveau* Gamay to the range and oversaw the introduction of Chardonnay and Fumé Blanc. A second label is "Bale Mill Cellars".

☆ Chardonnay, Fumé Blanc, Napa Valley, Gamay Nouveau

SILVER OAK CELLARS
915 Oakville Crossroad, Oakville, CA 94562

Silver Oak Cellars concentrates solely on one variety — Cabernet Sauvignon. The wines have great finesse.

☆ Cabernet Sauvignon

SMITH-MADRONE
4022 Spring Mountain Road, St. Helena, CA 94574

Some 16 hectares (40 acres) of high-altitude vines producing a small, high-quality range.

☆ Chardonnay, Johannisberg Riesling

SPOTTSWOODE VINEYARD & WINERY
1401 Hudson Avenue, St. Helena, CA 94574

A tiny production of powerful Cabernet Sauvignon, made for keeping, and excellent Sauvignon Blanc.

☆ Cabernet Sauvignon, Sauvignon Blanc

STAG'S LEAP WINE CELLARS
5766 Silverado Trail, Napa, CA 94558

A most prestigious winery, which has built its reputation on special releases of Cabernet Sauvignons.

☆ Cabernet Sauvignon (Stag's Leap Vineyard Special Cask or Lot selections), Chardonnay, Johannisberg Riesling

STERLING VINEYARDS
1111 Dunaweal Lane, Calistoga, CA 94515

An astonishing high-quality winery in the mid-1970s, Sterling's standards dropped after Coca-Cola purchased it in 1978. However, since becoming owned by Seagrams in 1983 there has been a slow but undeniable revival.

☆ Cabernet Blanc, Cabernet Sauvignon ("Diamond Mountain"), Chardonnay, Sauvignon Blanc

STONY HILL VINEYARD
PO Box 308, St. Helena, CA 94574

Eleanor McCrea's Chardonnays are world-class, but her Gewürztraminer, Riesling and Sémillon du Soleil are also good.

☆ Chardonnay, Gewürztraminer, Riesling, Sémillon de Soleil

TREFETHEN VINEYARDS
1160 Oak Knoll Avenue, Napa, CA 94558

This winery combines high quality and consistency with good value.

☆ Cabernet Sauvignon, Chardonnay, "Eshcol Red", "Eshcol White", Johannisberg Riesling

TULOCAY WINERY
1426 Coombsville Road, Napa, CA 94558

A small, low-key, high-quality winery.

☆ Cabernet Sauvignon, Pinot Noir

VILLA MT. EDEN WINERY
620 Oakville Crossroad, Oakville, CA 94562

VILLA MT. EDEN
ESTABLISHED 1881
Estate 1985 Bottled Napa Valley
Dry
Chenin Blanc
PRODUCED AND BOTTLED BY
VILLA MT. EDEN WINERY - OAKVILLE, CALIFORNIA, U.S.A.
ALCOHOL 12.0% BY VOLUME

A winery established on a vineyard originally planted in 1881. The quality is consistently high and Ranch Red and Ranch White are good value.

☆ Cabernet Sauvignon, Chenin Blanc, Chardonnay, Ranch Red, Ranch White

ZD Wines
8383 Silverado Trail, Napa, CA 94558

Pronounced "Zee Dee", this winery makes variable Cabernet Sauvignons, but fine Burgundian varietals, especially Chardonnays.

☆ Chardonnay, Pinot Noir

The best of the rest

ALTA VINEYARD CELLAR
1311 Schramsberg Road,
Calistoga,
CA 94515

A winery on the site of the original Alta Vineyard, described by Robert Louis Stevenson in *The Silverado Squatters* (1883), from which comes "The smack of Californian earth shall linger on the palate of your grandson".

☆ Chardonnay, Gamay

AMIZETTA VINEYARDS
1099 Greenfield,
St. Helena, CA 94574

A Sauvignon specialist.

S. ANDERSON VINEYARD
1473 Yountville Crossroad,
Napa,
CA 94558

A small winery producing Chardonnay and *méthode champenoise* wines.

ARTISAN WINES LTD
6666 Redwood Road,
Napa,
CA 94558

Michael Fallow is both president and winemaker of this establishment in the Mount Veeder area. Specializing in Cabernet Sauvignon and Chardonnay, there are two labels: "Michael's" (for estate-bottled wine) and "Ultravino".

BEAULIEU VINEYARD
1960 St. Helena Highway,
Rutherford,
CA 95473

Owned by the Grand Metropolitan group since 1987, this was the centre of Californian innovation under the legendary André Tchelistcheff. It now leads the way in clonal research.

☆ Cabernet Sauvignon "Georges de Latour", Sauvignon Blanc

BELL CANYON
See Burgess Cellars.

BERINGER VINEYARDS
2000 Main Street,
St. Helena, CA 94574

Although all the products from this Nestlé-owned winery are consistently good, it is worth paying extra for the best.

☆ Cabernet Sauvignon (especially "Private Reserve"). Chardonnay (especially "Gamble Ranch" and "Private Reserve")

BOUCHAINE VINEYARDS
1075 Buchli Station Road,
Napa, CA 94558

A small winery concentrating almost entirely on Burgundian varietals.

☆ Chardonnay

BUEHLER VINEYARDS INC
820 Greenfield Road,
St. Helena, CA 94574

Estate-bottled Cabernet Sauvignon, Pinot Blanc and Zinfandel.

BURGESS CELLARS
1108 Deer Park Road,
St. Helena,
CA 94574

Owner Tom Burgess and winemaker Bill Sorenson often produce wines of the highest quality. A second label is "Bell Canyon".

☆ Cabernet Sauvignon, Chardonnay, Zinfandel

CAIN CELLARS
3800 Langtry Road,
St. Helena, CA 94574

Jerry Cain produces Cabernet Sauvignon, Chardonnay, Malbec, Merlot and Sauvignon Blanc.

CAKEBREAD CELLARS
8300 St. Helena Way,
Rutherford,
CA 94573

Bruce Cakebread has quietly gained a good reputation.

☆ Cabernet Sauvignon, Chardonnay, Sauvignon Blanc

CASA NUESTRA
3473 Silverado Trail North,
St. Helena, CA 94574

A small winery producing Cabernet, Chenin Blanc and Tinto.

CASSAYRE-FORNI CELLARS
1271 Manley Lane,
Rutherford,
CA 94573

Owned by Jim and Paul Cassayre, and winemaker Mike Forni.

☆ Cabernet Sauvignon

CHATEAU BOSWELL WINERY
3468 Silverado Trail,
St. Helena, CA 94574

A Cabernet Sauvignon specialist.

CHATEAU CHEVALIER WINERY
3101 Spring Mountain Road,
St. Helena,
CA 94574

This 24-hectare (60-acre) vineyard was originally planted in the 1870s. The quality is good and improving.

☆ Cabernet Sauvignon, Chardonnay, Pinot Noir

COSTELLO VINEYARDS
1200 Orchard Avenue,
Napa, CA 94558

Estate-bottled Chardonnay, Gewürztraminer and Sauvignon Blanc.

DEER PARK WINERY
1000 Deer Park Road,
St. Helena, CA 94576

Tiny vineyard producing Zinfandel, Chardonnay and Sauvignon Blanc.

DE MOOR WINERY
7481 Highway 29,
Oakville,
CA 94562

Originally called Napa Wine Cellars. The winemaker here is Aaron Mosley, who was assistant to Mike Grgich at Chateau Montalena and Grgich Hills.

☆ Chardonnay, Sauvignon Blanc

EHLERS LANE WINERY
3222 Ehlers Lane,
St. Helena,
CA 94574

Cabernet Sauvignon, Chardonnay and Sauvignon Blanc varietals, some sold under the "Rainbow Vineyards" label.

EVENSEN VINEYARDS & WINERY
8254 St. Helena Highway,
Oakville,
CA 94562

A winery that produces a tiny amount of fine-quality wine from its three-hectare (eight-acre) vineyard planted entirely with Gewürztraminer.

☆ Gewürztraminer

FALCON CREST
See Spring Mountain Vineyards.

FAR NIENTE
PO Box 327, Oakville,
CA 94562

A revitalized pre-Prohibition winery making its mark with fine Chardonnay.

☆ Chardonnay

FORMAN VINEYARDS
1501 Big Rock Road,
St. Helena, CA 94575

A small winery producing classic yet opulent wines.

☆ Cabernet Sauvignon, Chardonnay

GARRISON FOREST
See St. Clement Vineyards.

GIRARD WINERY
7717 Silverado Trail,
Oakville, CA 94562

Wines that show a rare ability to balance richness with finesse.

☆ Cabernet Sauvignon, Chardonnay

GREEN & RED VINEYARD
3208 Chiles Pope Valley Road,
St. Helena, CA 94574

Chardonnay and Zinfandel from vineyards planted on Chiles Canyon and Chiles Valley hillsides.

GREENWOOD CELLARS
See Villa Helena Winery.

WILLIAM HILL WINERY
1775 Lincoln Avenue,
Napa,
CA 94558

The Chardonnays are good and getting better, but the Cabernet Sauvignons excel here. As you might expect, "Gold Label" is better than "Silver Label".

☆ Cabernet Sauvignon, Chardonnay

JACABELS CELLARS
See Whitehall Lane Winery.

JOHNSON TURNBULL VINEYARDS
8210 St. Helena Highway,
Oakville,
CA 94562

A small winery owned by Reverdy and Marta Johnson and William Turnbull, that specializes in Cabernet Sauvignon.

☆ Cabernet Sauvignon

ROBERT KEENAN WINERY
3660 Spring Mountain Road,
St. Helena, CA 94574

A renovated 1904 winery that produces Cabernet Sauvignon, Chardonnay and Merlot.

LAKESPRING WINERY
2055 Hoffman Lane, Napa,
CA 94558

Chardonnay is the best of the various varietals produced at Lakespring by winemaker Randy Mason.

☆ Chardonnay

MARKHAM VINEYARDS
2812 N. St. Helena Highway,
St. Helena, CA 94574

Various wines, mostly varietal, from Napa Valley vineyards at Calistoga, Yountville and Oak Knoll.

☆ Chenin Blanc, Gamay Blanc

JOSEPH MATHEWS WINERY
1711 Main Street, Napa, CA 94558

A recently renovated winery known in the past for its sherries but now concentrating on premium varietals.

MICHAEL'S
See Artisan Wines.

**LOUIS K. MIHALY
VINEYARD**
3103 Silverado Trail, Napa,
CA 94558

Chardonnay, Pinot Noir and Sauvignon
Blanc wines that are fairly well
distributed in the USA

MONT ST. JOHN CELLARS
5400 Old Sonoma Road,
Napa,
CA 94558

White estate-bottled varietals from
Napa's Carneros district, plus blended
wines.

MONTICELLO CELLARS
4242 Big Ranch Road,
Napa,
CA 94558

Better for whites than reds, although
recent releases of Cabernet Sauvignon
and Pinot Noir have been exciting.

☆ Cabernet Sauvignon (Jefferson),
Chardonnay (Jefferson), Chevrier,
Pinot Noir.

MOUNT VEEDER WINERY
1999 Mount Veeder Road,
Napa, CA 94558

Cabernet Sauvignon and Chardonnay,
produced on Mount Veeder.

NAPA CREEK WINERY
1001 Silverado Trail,
St. Helena, CA 94558

A quietly expanding winery, with eight
hectares (20 acres) of Napa vineyards
and a small range of varietal wines.

NAPA VINTNERS
See Don Charles Ross Winery.

NAPA WINE CELLARS
See De Moor Winery.

NEWTON VINEYARDS
2555 Madrona Avenue,
St. Helena,
CA 94574

A winery whose products very
successfully combine oak with fruit
and structure.

☆ Cabernet Sauvignon, Merlot,
Sauvignon Blanc

PEJU PROVINCE WINERY
8466 St. Helena Highway,
Rutherford,
CA 94573

A winery that produces Cabernet
Sauvignon, Chardonnay and Sauvignon
Blanc wines. I have not tasted them.

ROBERT PEPI WINERY
7585 St. Helena Highway,
Oakville, CA 94562

Mostly Sauvignon Blanc, plus a little
Chardonnay and Cabernet Sauvignon.

PINE RIDGE WINERY
5901 Silverado Trail, Napa, CA 94558

Interesting reds, disappointing whites.

☆ Cabernet Sauvignon (Andrus
Reserve and Rutherd Cuvée), Merlot
Selected Cuvée

PLAM VINEYARDS
6200 St. Helena Highway,
Napa, CA 94558

A small Chardonnay specialist.

**PRAGER WINERY AND
PORT WORKS**
1281 Lewelling Lane,
St. Helena, CA 94574

A family-run winery. In addition to
Cabernet Sauvignon and Chardonnay,
three varietal "ports" are produced –
Cabernet Sauvignon, Petite Sirah and
Pinot Noir. I have not tasted them.

QUAIL RIDGE
1055 Atlas Peak Road,
Napa, CA 94558

Adequate but unexciting wines.

RAINBOW VINEYARDS
See Ehlers Lane Winery.

ROMBAUER VINEYARDS
St. Helena, CA 94574

According to some critics, an up-and-
coming winery. It specializes in
Cabernet Sauvignon and Chardonnay.

**DON CHARLES ROSS
WINERY**
7121-C Action Avenue,
Napa, CA 94558

Cabernet Sauvignon, Chardonnay,
Sauvignon Blanc and Zinfandel wines
sold under the "Don Charles Ross"
and "Napa Vintners" labels.

ROUND HILL CELLARS
1097 Lodi Lane,
St. Helena, CA 94574

This winery is capable of good to
excellent quality, but its wines tend to
be inconsistent.

☆ Cabernet Sauvignon, Chardonnay

**RUTHERFORD HILL
WINERY**
Rutherford Hill Road,
Rutherford, CA 94574

A good range of flavoursome wines.

☆ Cabernet Sauvignon, Chardonnay,
Gewürztraminer, Merlot

RUTHERFORD RANCH
See Round Hill Cellars.

ST. CLEMENT VINEYARDS
2867 St. Helena Highway,
St. Helena,
CA 94574

Sauvignon Blanc, Chardonnay and
Cabernet Sauvignon and "Garrison
Forest" Chardonnay and Merlot.

☆ Chardonnay ("St. Clement"),
Sauvignon Blanc

SAINTSBURY
1500 Los Carneros Avenue,
Napa,
CA 94559

An impressive winery specializing
in Burgundian varietals.

☆ Chardonnay, Pinot Noir

V. SATTUI WINERY
White Lane, St. Helena,
CA 94574

The wines have a loyal following, but
I have not tasted them.

**SEQUOIA GROVE
VINEYARDS**
8338 St. Helena Highway,
Napa,
CA 94558

Cabernet Sauvignon from Stag's Leap
and Alexander Valley, Chardonnay
from other locations.

☆ Chardonnay (Estate)

SHAFER VINEYARDS
6154 Silverado Trial, Napa,
CA 94558

The quality seems a bit erratic, but this
winery certainly has potential.

☆ Cabernet Sauvignon (Hillside Select
and Reserve), Chardonnay

SHOWN & SONS
8514 St. Helena Highway,
Rutherford, CA 94573

Since its first vintage in 1978, various
varietals have been produced, but I
have not tasted any.

SILVERADO VINEYARDS
6121 Silverado Trail, Napa, CA 94558

This winery is owned by the Walt
Disney family, but its clean wines are
by no means Mickey Mouse products.

☆ Chardonnay, Sauvignon Blanc

**SPRING MOUNTAIN
VINEYARDS**
2805 Spring Mountain Road,
St. Helena, CA 94574

Known to millions as "Falcon Crest"
this winery can produce wines that
require aging and develop finesse.

☆ Cabernet Sauvignon, Chardonnay

STONEGATE WINERY
1183 Dunaweal Lane,
Calistoga, CA 94515

Cabernet Sauvignon; Chardonnay;
Merlot; and Sauvignon Blanc.

☆ Cabernet Sauvignon, Sauvignon
Blanc

**STORYBOOK MOUNTAIN
VINEYARDS**
3835 Highway 128,
Calistoga, CA 94515

I have not tasted the wines from this
Zinfandel specialist's 15-hectare (36-
acre) vineyard, originally established
by Adam and Jacob Grimm in 1880.

**SULLIVAN VINEYARDS
WINERY**
1090 Galleron Road,
Rutherford, CA 94573

James and Jo Sullivan produce
Cabernet Sauvignon, Chardonnay,
Chenin Blanc and Zinfandel, estate-
bottled.

SUTTER HOME WINERY
277 St. Helena Highway South,
St. Helena, CA 94574

Zinfandel accounts for 95 per cent of
the vast production.

☆ White Zinfandel, Zinfandel

TUDAL WINERY
1015 Big Tree Road,
St. Helena, CA 94574

A small winery with a four-hectare
(10-acre) Cabernet sauvignon
vineyard. Chardonnay is also produced.

ULTRAVINO
See Artisan Wines

VICHON WINERY
1595 Oakville Grade,
Oakville, CA 94562

Cabernet Sauvignon, Chardonnay and
Chevrignon (50/50 Sémillon/Sauvig-
non) wines that I have not tasted.

VILLA HELENA WINERY
1455 Inglewood Avenue,
St. Helena, CA 94574

A tiny, relatively new winery specializing
in Chardonnay and Sauvignon Blanc.
"Greenwood Cellars" is a second label.

**WHITEHALL LANE
WINERY**
1563 St. Helena Highway,
St. Helena, CA 94574

A winery that produces Blanc de Pinot
Noir, Cabernet Sauvignon, Chardonnay,
Merlot and Sauvignon Blanc.
The second label is "Jacabels Cellars".

The North-Central Coast

A district where a small number of big companies traditionally produce a vast quantity of inexpensive wines, the North-Central Coast can also boast a large number of relatively new wineries that specialize in tiny quantities of premium varietal.

WINEMAKING IN THE NORTH-CENTRAL Coast district dates from at least as far back as the 1830s, and all but three of the biggest wineries that now control the production of the district were established between 1852 and 1883. Today five wineries dominate the North-Central Coast in terms of output: Almadén Vineyards; Paul Masson Vineyards; Taylor California Cellars; Weibel Champagne Vineyards; and Wente Bros. When the big companies were established virtually all the vineyards were located in and around Santa Clara County, and this remained the situation until almost 30 years after Prohibition. In the late-1950s and early-1960s, however, the growing urban sprawl of San Jose forced the wine industry to search out new areas for vine-growing. Happily, this search coincided with the publication of a climatic report based on heat-summation by the University of California. This pinpointed cooler areas further south, particularly in Monterey, that should support fine-wine vineyards.

The move to Monterey

In 1957, two companies, Mirassou and Paul Masson, were the first to make the move, purchasing some 530 hectares (1,300 acres) in the Salinas Valley. In the ensuing rush to plant the land, some areas were used that were too cool or exposed to excessive coastal winds. These failures were not the fault of the heat-summation maps, but were due to producers who could not conceive that grapes would not ripen in California.

In October 1966, the two authors of the heat-summation study, Professors Winkler and Amerine, were honoured at a special luncheon where a toast was made to "the world's first fine-wine district established as the direct result of scientific temperature research". Though this might have seemed premature, it has been substantiated by Monterey's viticultural growth and the increasing number of exciting, high-quality wines the county yields.

Jekel Vineyards, above
Oak barrels wait to be filled at one of the North-Central Coast's leading wineries. Behind them the vineyards stretch out across the Salinas Valley, more famous for its salad vegetables.

AREA UNDER VINE

Between 1977 and 1987, about 4,000 hectares (10,000 acres) of vineyards have been planted in Monterey, the area under vine in Alameda has doubled and, although San Mateo can boast a mere 18 hectares (45 acres), this represents a five-fold increase. The current county wine-grape areas under vine are: **Contra Costa**, 378 hectares (934 acres); **Alameda**, 800 hectares (1,976 acres); **San Mateo**, 18 hectares (45 acres); **Santa Cruz**, 32 hectares (78 acres); **Santa Clara**, 560 hectares (1,385 acres); **San Benito**, 986 hectares (2,437 acres); and **Monterey**, 12,259 hectares (30,291 acres).

FACTORS AFFECTING TASTE AND QUALITY

 Location
The Central Coast's northern sector stretches from the San Francisco Bay area to Monterey.

Climate
Generally warm (Region III), but with variations such as the cooler (Region I) areas of the Santa Cruz Mountains and the northern part of the Salinas Valley. Low rainfall in the south necessitates much irrigation, but there are micro-climates with higher rainfall.

Aspect
Vines are planted mainly on the flat and sloping lands of the various valleys. Variations are found: on the steep slopes of the Santa Cruz Mountains and the high benchland of the Pinnacles above Soledad, for example.

 Soil
A wide variety of gravel loams, often high in stone content and rich in limestone, in the Livermore Valley; clay and gravel loams in Santa Clara; sandy and gravelly loams over granite or limestone in San Benito; and gravelly, well-drained low-fertility soils in Monterey.

Viticulture and vinification
A small number of big companies produce a vast quantity of inexpensive wines utilizing high-tech, production-line methods. The number of small wineries is growing. Many of these are quality-conscious and some are justifiably famous. Their methods are constantly changing.

 Grape varieties
Cabernet sauvignon, Pinot noir, Zinfandel, Petite syrah, Chenin blanc, Riesling, Chardonnay, Sauvignon blanc, Gamay, Gewürztraminer, Carignan, French colombard, Grey riesling, Sémillon

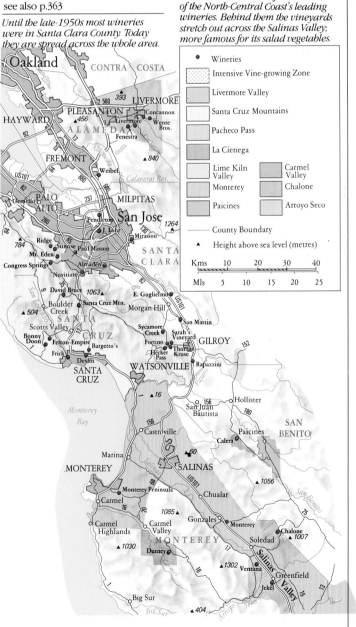

THE NORTH-CENTRAL COAST,
see also p.363

Until the late-1950s most wineries were in Santa Clara County. Today they are spread across the whole area.

- • Wineries
- Intensive Vine-growing Zone
- Livermore Valley
- Santa Cruz Mountains
- Pacheco Pass
- La Cienega
- Lime Kiln Valley
- Monterey
- Paicines
- Carmel Valley
- Chalone
- Arroyo Seco
- County Boundary
- ▲ Height above sea level (metres)

The AVAs of the North-Central Coast

ALAMEDA COUNTY AO

An appellation covering grapes grown anywhere within Alameda County.

ARROYO SECO AVA
(Monterey County)

Established: *16th May 1983*

A 73-square-kilometre (28-square-mile), triangular-shaped area of sloping benchland adjacent to the Arroyo Seco Creek, a tributary of the Salinas River. Its vineyards are free from frost and adequately drained. The prominent soil is a coarse sandy loam, with a low lime content.

BEN LOMOND MOUNTAIN AVA
(Santa Cruz County)

Established: *8th January 1988*

An area covering 155 square kilometres (60 square miles) on Ben Lomond Mountain, northwest of Santa Cruz, and encompassing 28 hectares (70 acres) of vines. The AVA's establishment is a revival of an old area.

CARMEL VALLEY AVA
(Monterey County)

Established: *15th January 1983*

An appellation covering 78 square kilometres (30 square miles) around the Carmel River and Cachagua Creek. The valley's higher elevation and its protective northeastern Tularcitos Ridge, which curbs the intrusion of marine fog and provides more sunny days than is usual in the county, creates a distinctive microclimate.

CHALONE AVA
(Monterey County)

Established: *14th July 1982*

An area covering 35 square kilometres (13.5 square miles) of benchland between the North and South Chalone Peaks, 503 metres (1,650 feet) above

sea level, with volcanic and granitic soils of high limestone content. It is hotter than the Salinas Valley, and is not affected by maritime fog and so has more sunny days.

CIENEGA VALLEY AVA
(San Benito County)

Established: *20th September 1982*

The valley is located at the base of the Gabilan (or Gavilan) Mountain Range, where the Pescadero Creek is used artificially to augment the area's rainfall. The soil is loamy, generally well drained and often underlain by weathered granite.

CONTRA COSTA COUNTY AO

An appellation covering grapes grown anywhere within Contra Costa County.

LIME KILN VALLEY AVA
(San Benito County)

Established: *6th July 1982*

Although part of the Cienega Valley, Lime Kiln Valley is significantly different in its climate, with an annual rainfall ranging between 41 centimetres (16 ins) on the eastern valley floor to 102 centimetres (40 ins) in the mountainous western area, and in its soils, which are sandy and gravelly loams over a bedrock of limestone, with a high magnesium carbonate content.

LIVERMORE VALLEY AVA
(Alameda County)

Established: *1st October 1982*

This is one of the coastal inter-mountain valleys surrounding San Francisco. The appellation has a moderate climate, cooled by sea breezes and morning fog, though with very little spring frost. Virtually all its annual 38 centimetres (15 ins) of rain falls in the winter and early spring. The South Bay Aqueduct, however, provides overhead sprinkler irrigation.

MONTEREY AVA
(Monterey County)

Established: *16th July 1984*

This AVA is confined to the Monterey Bay area and the Salinas Valley, where the various sandy and gravelly loams are of an alluvial origin and differ from those of surrounding areas. It is also distinguished by a very dry climate that yields barely 25 centimetres (10 ins) of rain a year, although the watersheds of the Santa Lucia, Gabilan and Diablo Mountain Ranges provide sufficient water, through the presence of underground aquifers, to irrigate the vineyards.

MONTEREY COUNTY AO

An appellation covering grapes grown anywhere within Monterey County.

PACHECO PASS AVA
(San Benito County)

Established: *11th April 1984*

The terrain sets this area apart from its neighbours. It is a small valley, with a flat or gently sloping topography that contrasts with the rugged hills of the Diablo Range to the east and west. The climate is moderate and wetter than that of the Hollister Basin to the south.

PAICINES AVA
(San Benito County)

Established: *15th September 1982*

Here the days are warm and the nights cool, and the annual rainfall ranges between 30 and 38 centimetres (12 and 15 ins).

SAN BENITO AVA
(San Benito County)

Established: *4th November 1987*

Not to be confused with San Benito County, this AVA encapsulates the smaller AVAs of Paicines, Cienega Valley and Lime Kiln Valley.

SAN BENITO COUNTY AO

An appellation covering grapes grown anywhere within San Benito County.

SAN LUCAS
(Monterey County)

Established: *2nd March 1987*

This AVA consists of a 17-kilometre (10-mile) segment of the Salinas Valley between King City and San Ardo, in the southern section of Monterey County. The soils are mostly alluvial loams.

SAN MATEO COUNTY AO

An appellation covering grapes grown anywhere within San Mateo County.

SANTA CLARA COUNTY AO

An appellation covering grapes grown anywhere within Santa Clara County.

SANTA CLARA VALLEY AVA
(Santa Clara County)

Established: *28th March 1989*

SANTA CRUZ MOUNTAINS AVA
(Santa Clara County)

Established: *4th January 1982*

The name Santa Cruz Mountains was first recorded in 1838. Its climate is influenced in the western section by ocean breezes and maritime fog movements, while the eastern area is moderated by the San Francisco Bay. Cool air coming down from the mountains forces warmer air up, lengthening the growing season to a full 300 days. The soils are forms of shale that are peculiar to the area.

Major wineries of the North-Central Coast

ALMADÉN VINEYARDS
(Santa Clara County)
1530 Blossom Hill Road,
San Jose,
CA 95118

The best wines from this bulk-wine producer are sold under the Charles Lefranc label. This winery was purchased by the Grand Metropolitan group in 1987.

☆ Cabernet Sauvignon (Charles Lefranc), Chardonnay (Charles Lefranc), Pinot Noir (Charles Lefranc)

BONNY DOON VINEYARD
(Santa Cruz County)
10 Pine Flat Road,
Santa Cruz,
CA 95060

One of California's newest and brightest stars, the wines are

electrifying in their brilliance, finesse and sheer style. Winemaker Randall Grahm specializes in Rhône varieties, makes sublime Pinot Noir and even produces a *vin de paille*.

☆ All wines

CALERA WINE COMPANY
(San Benito County)
11300 Cienega Road,
Hollister,
CA 95023

One of California's premier pioneers in the continuing quest for perfect Pinot Noir. Potentially, it is probably the best, though its pursuit of elegance can produce a certain "prettiness" of style. Its Zinfandels should not be overlooked.

☆ Pinot Noir (especially Jensen and Selleck), Zinfandel, Zinfandel Essence

CHALONE VINEYARD
(Monterey County)
Stonewall Canyon Road,
Soledad,
CA 93960

This winery has 63 hectares (155 acres) of vineyard, with its own AVA, and is dedicated to, and astonishingly successful at producing fine, rich and complex wines of the most exquisite style.

☆ Chardonnay, Chenin Blanc, Pinot Blanc, Pinot Noir

CONGRESS SPRINGS VINEYARD (Santa Clara County)
23600 Congress Springs Road,
Saratoga, CA 95070

A small winery making top-quality wines with vibrant fruit, lots of toasty-oak flavours and a voluptuous texture.

☆ Cabernet Sauvignon, Chardonnay (especially Private Reserve), Pinot Noir, Sémillon

JEKEL VINEYARD
(Monterey County)
40155 Walnut Avenue,
Greenfield, CA 93927

Very impressive white wines overshadow the good, but not outstanding, red wines.

☆ Chardonnay, Johannisberg Riesling (especially Late Harvest), Muscat Canelli, Pinot Blanc

CHARLES LEFRANC CELLARS
See Almadén Vineyards.

PAUL MASSON VINEYARDS (Santa Clara County)
13150 Saratoga Avenue,
Saratoga, CA 95070

Founded by a Burgundian, this winery is one of the great American success stories. Its jug-wines are cleaner and easier to drink than many of Europe's cheapest *vins de table* and its better wines, under the Pinnacles Estate label, are good and improving.

☆ Pinnacles Estate wines

MEV
See Mount Eden Vineyards.

MIRASSOU VINEYARDS
(Santa Clara County)
3000 Aborn Road,
San Jose,
CA 95135

This company is known for its good-value jug-wines. Its White Burgundy, made primarily from Pinot blanc, can also be quite good. Otherwise it produces reliable, if unexciting, Cabernet Sauvignon.

☆ Cabernet Sauvignon (Harvest Reserve), White Burgundy

MOUNT EDEN VINEYARDS
(Santa Clara County)
22020 Mt. Eden Road,
Saratoga,
CA 95070

This winery produces just three varietals, all of which are fine in quality. The Chardonnay excels and the Pinot Noir is definitely second. The second label, MEV, is especially good value for Chardonnay.

☆ Cabernet Sauvignon, Chardonnay (including MEV), Pinot Noir

RIDGE VINEYARDS, INC.
(Santa Clara County)
17100 Monte Bello Road,
Cupertino, CA 95015

Those who wonder about the long-term maturation potential of Californian wines should taste these stunning wines that improve for between 10-20 years in bottle.

☆ Cabernet Sauvignon (Howell Mountain, Monte bello and York Creek), Petite Sirah (York Creek), Zinfandel (Dusi Ranch, Geyserville, Lytton Springs and York Creek)

TAYLOR CALIFORNIA CELLARS (Santa Clara County)
13150 Saratoga Avenue,
Saratoga, CA 95070

Owned by Vintners International, this massive winery produces 5.5 million cases (495,000 hectolitres) of wine a year.

WEIBEL VINEYARDS
(Santa Clara County)
1250 Stanford Avenue,
Mission San Jose, CA 94538

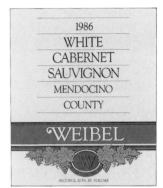

This winery produces sparkling wines sold under many labels.

☆ Pinot Noir, White Cabernet Sauvignon, White Zinfandel

WENTE BROS.
(Alameda County)
5565 Tesla Road,
Livermore, CA 94550

These wines can range from overtly fruity to distinctly dull. However, they are always inexpensive and those recommended can be good value.

☆ Arroyo Seco Riesling, Chardonnay, Petite Sirah, Sauvignon Blanc

The best of the rest

BARGETTO'S SANTA CRUZ WINERY (Santa Cruz County)
3535 North Main Street,
Soquel, CA 95018

☆ Chenin Blanc, Johannisberg Riesling

DAVID BRUCE
(Santa Cruz County)
21439 Bear Creek Road,
Los Gatos, CA 95031

☆ Chardonnay, Zinfandel

CONCANNON VINEYARD
(Alameda County)
4590 Tesla Road,
Livermore, CA 94550

☆ Petite Sirah, Rkatsiteli (for interest), Sauvignon Blanc, Zinfandel Rosé

CYGNET CELLARS
(San Benito County)
11736 Cienega Road,
Hollister, CA 95023

☆ Zinfandel

DURNEY VINEYARD
(Monterey County)
P.O. Box 22016,
Carmel Valley, CA 93922

☆ Cabernet Sauvignon, Chenin Blanc

FELTON-EMPIRE VINEYARDS
(Santa Cruz County)
379 Felton-Empire Road,
Felton, CA 95018

☆ White Riesling

FENESTRA WINERY
(Alameda County)
83 E. Vallecitos Road,
Livermore, CA 94550

☆ Petite Sirah, Sauvignon Blanc

FORTINO WINERY
(Santa Clara County)
4525 Hecker Pass Highway,
Gilroy, CA 95020

☆ Barbera, Charbono, Petite Sirah

GEMELLO WINERY
(Santa Clara County)
2003 El Camino Real,
Mountain View, CA 94040

☆ Zinfandel

E. GUGLIELMO WINERY (EMILE'S WINES)
(Santa Clara County)
1480 East Main Avenue,
Morgan Hill, CA 95037

☆ Petite Sirah

J. LOHR WINERY
(Santa Clara County)
1000 Lenzen Avenue,
San Jose, CA 95126

☆ Johannisberg Riesling, Petite Sirah

MONTEREY PENINSULA WINERY (Monterey County)
467 Shasta Avenue,
Sand City, CA 93955

☆ Cabernet Sauvignon, Zinfandel

THE MONTEREY VINEYARD
(Monterey County)
800 South Alta Street,
Gonzales, CA 93926

☆ Botrytis Sauvignon Blanc, December Harvest Zinfandel, Pinot Blanc

OBESTER WINERY
(San Mateo County)
12341 San Mateo Road,
Half Moon Bay,
CA 94019

☆ Johannisberg Riesling

PENDLETON WINERY
(Santa Clara County)
499 Aldo Avenue,
Santa Clara,
CA 95050

☆ Pinot Noir

ROSENBLUM CELLARS
(Alameda County)
1401 Stanford Avenue,
Emeryville,
CA 94608

☆ Zinfandel

ROUDON-SMITH VINEYARDS
(Santa Cruz County)
2364 Bean Creek Road,
Santa Cruz,
CA 95066

☆ Chardonnay, Pinot Blanc, Zinfandel

Continued overleaf

SAN MARTIN WINERY
(Santa Clara County)
12900 Monterey Road,
San Martin, CA 95046

VINTAGE 1986

Domain
San Martin

MONTEREY COUNTY

Johannisberg Riesling

PRODUCED AND BOTTLED BY
SAN MARTIN WINERY, SAN MARTIN, CA
ALCOHOL 11.5% BY VOLUME

☆ Chardonnay, Fumé Blanc, Soft
Johannisberg Riesling, Petite Sirah

**SANTA CRUZ MOUNTAIN
VINEYARD**
(Santa Cruz County)
2300 Jarvis Road,
Santa Cruz, CA 95065

☆ Cabernet Sauvignon, Pinot Noir

SARAH'S VINEYARD
(Santa Clara County)
4005 Hecker Pass Highway,
Gilroy, CA 95020

☆ Johannisberg Riesling

SUNRISE WINERY
(Santa Clara County)
13100 Montebello Road,
Cupertino, CA 95014

☆ Cabernet Sauvignon

**SYCAMORE CREEK
VINEYARDS**
(Santa Clara County)
12775 Uvas Road,
Morgan Hill, CA 95037

☆ Johannisberg Riesling, Zinfandel

**VENTANA VINEYARDS
WINERY** (Monterey County)
P.O. Box G, Soledad, CA 93960

VENTANA VINEYARDS

1987
MONTEREY
SAUVIGNON BLANC
VENTANA VINEYARDS

PRODUCED AND BOTTLED BY VENTANA VINEYARDS
SOLEDAD, CALIFORNIA B.W. 4847 · ALCOHOL 13.4% BY VOLUME
PRODUCE OF U.S.A. · CONTAINS SULFITES

☆ Chardonnay, Johannisberg Riesling,
Petite Sirah, Sauvignon Blanc

Other wineries of the North-Central Coast

Note: many of the following wineries are just beginning to establish a reputation and may well become deserving of a place in the "Best of the rest" and "Major wineries" sections with the passing of time. Others are well-established, but have yet to excel.

AHLGREN VINEYARD
(Santa Cruz County)
P.O. Box 931,
Boulder Creek, CA 95006

BAY CELLARS
(Alameda County)
1675 Tacoma Avenue,
Berkeley, CA 94707

CANNERY WINE CELLARS
(San Francisco County)
2801 Leavenworth Street,
San Francisco, CA 94133

CARROUSEL CELLARS
(Santa Clara County)
2825 Day Road, Gilroy, CA 95020

CHATEAU JULIEN
(Monterey County)
8940 Carmel Valley Road,
Carmel Valley, CA 93923

COOK-ELLIS WINERY
(Santa Cruz County)
2900 Buzzard Lagoon Road,
Corralitos, CA 95076

CRESCINI WINES
(Santa Cruz County)
2621 Old San Jose Road,
Soquel, CA 95073

CRONIN VINEYARDS
(San Mateo County)
11 Old La Honda Road,
Woodside, CA 94062

DEVLIN WINE CELLARS
(Santa Cruz County)
2815 Porter Street Highway 1,
Soquel, CA 95073

ENZ VINEYARDS
(San Benito County)
Limekiln Road, Hollister, CA 95023

THOMAS FOGARTY WINERY
(San Mateo County)
19501 Skyline Boulevard,
Portola Valley, CA 94025

FRETTER WINE CELLARS
(Alameda County)
805 Camelia Street,
Berkeley, CA 94710

FRICK WINERY
(Santa Cruz County)
303 Potrero Street,
Santa Cruz, CA 95060

J. H. GENTILI WINES
(San Mateo County)
60 Lowell Street,
Redwood City, CA 94062

GROVER GULCH WINERY
(Santa Cruz County)
7880 Glen Haven Road,
Soquel, CA 95073

HECKER PASS WINERY
(Santa Clara County)
4605 Hecker Pass Highway,
Gilroy, CA 95020

**KATHRYN KENNEDY
WINERY**
(Santa Clara County)
13180 Pierce Road,
Saratoga, CA 95070

KIRIGIN CELLARS
(Santa Clara County)
11550 Wastonville Road,
Gilroy, CA 95020

THOMAS KRUSE WINERY
(Santa Clara County)
4390 Hecker Pass Road,
Gilroy, CA 95020

**LIVERMORE VALLEY
CELLARS**
(Alameda County)
1508 Wetmore Road,
Livermore, CA 94550

McHENRY VINEYARD
(Santa Cruz County)
Bonny Doon Road,
Santa Cruz, CA 95060

MORGAN WINERY
(Monterey County)
19301 Creekside Circle,
Salinas, CA 93908

**THE MOUNTAIN VIEW
WINERY**
(Santa Clara County)
2402 Thaddeus Drive,
Mountain View, CA 94043

OZEKI SAN BENITO
(San Benito County)
249 Hillcrest Road,
Hollister, CA 95023

PAGE MILL WINERY
(Santa Clara County)
13686 Page Mill Road,
Los Altos Hills, CA 94022

PEDRIZZETTI WINERY
(Santa Clara County)
1645 San Pedro Avenue,
Morgan Hill, CA 95037

RAPAZZINI WINERY
(Santa Clara County)
4350 Monterey Highway,
Gilroy, CA 95020

MARTIN RAY
(Santa Clara County)
Saratoga, CA 95070

RIVER RUN VINTNERS
(Santa Cruz County)
65 Rogge Lane,
Watsonville, CA 95076

SAN BENITO VINEYARDS
(San Benito County)
251 Hillcrest Road,
Hollister,
CA 95023

SHERRILL CELLARS
(Santa Clara County)
1185 Skyline Boulevard,
Woodside, CA 94062

**SILVER MOUNTAIN
VINEYARDS**
(Santa Cruz County)
Box 1695, Los Gatos, CA 95031

SUMMERHILL VINEYARDS
(Santa Clara County)
3920 Hecker Pass Highway,
Gilroy, CA 95020

TAKARA SAKE USA INC
(Alameda County)
708 Addison Street,
Berkeley, CA 94710

**ROBERT TALBOTT
VINEYARDS**
(Monterey County)
P.O. Box 267,
Carmel Valley, CA 93924

**VILLA PARADISO
VINEYARDS**
(Santa Clara County)
1830 West Edmundson Avenue,
Morgan Hill, CA 95037

WALKER WINES
(Santa Cruz County)
Van Allen Ridge, P.O. Box Fl,
Felton, CA 95018

WOODSIDE VINEYARDS
(San Mateo County)
340 Kings Mountain Road,
Woodside, CA 94062

YERBA BUENA WINERY
(San Francisco County)
Pier 33, San Francisco, CA 94111

The South-Central Coast

An up-and-coming wine district, the South-Central Coast continues to attract many small "boutique" wineries, most of which specialize in either Chardonnay, Pinot Noir, Cabernet Sauvignon or Zinfandel.

PASO ROBLES, IN SAN LUIS OBISPO COUNTY, was originally planted with vines in the late-eighteenth century; the Santa Ynez Valley, in Santa Barbara County, had a flourishing wine industry in pre-Prohibition times and the town of Santa Barbara itself was once dotted with vineyards. Yet both of the counties were virtually void of vines in the early-1960s, and it was not until Estrella, in Paso Robles, and Firestone, in the Santa Ynez Valley, had established very successful vineyards in 1972, that others began to follow. Since 1977 the area under vine has almost tripled. Interestingly, the region has no large wineries, the largest being Firestone with an annual production of merely 76,000 cases (6,840 hectolitres). The current county areas under vine (wine-grape vineyards only) are: San Luis Obispo, 2,252 hectares (5,566 acres) and Santa Barbara, 3,745 hectares (9,253 acres).

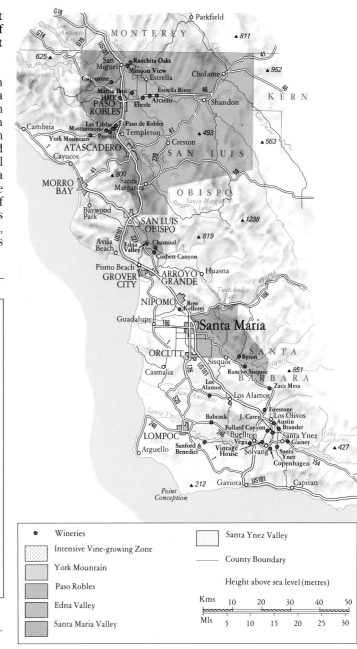

FACTORS AFFECTING TASTE AND QUALITY

Location
The southern sector of the Coastal Region, which stretches southwards along the coast from Monterey, and includes the counties of San Luis Obispo and Santa Barbara.

Climate
Generally warm (Region III), except for areas near the sea, particularly around Santa Maria in the middle of the region where Regions I and II prevail because of the regular incursion of the tail of the great coastal fog bank. Annual rainfall ranges from 25 centimetres (10 ins) to 114 centimetres (45 ins).

Aspect
Most vines grow on hillsides in San Luis Obispo and on southern-facing benchland in Santa Barbara County, at altitudes that range from 37-180 metres (120-600 ft) in the Edna Valley, to 180-305 metres (600-1,000 ft) in Paso Robles

and 460 metres (1,500 ft) on York Mountain.

Soil
Mostly sandy, silty or clay loams, but the soil can be more alkaline, as in the gravelly lime soils found on the foothills of the Santa Lucia Mountains.

Viticulture and vinification
Since the 1970s, a small number of premium-quality wineries have been established. The cooler areas have invited experimentation with premium varieties. Wines that challenge the best that California can produce are now being made.

 Grape varieties
Cabernet sauvignon, Zinfandel, Chardonnay, Chenin blanc, Sauvignon blanc, Riesling, Gewürztraminer, Pinot noir.

THE SOUTH-CENTRAL COAST, see also p.363

Based on San Luis Obispo and Santa Barbara counties, this area has a fine reputation for top-quality premium varietals.

Map legend:
- • Wineries
- Intensive Vine-growing Zone
- York Mountain
- Paso Robles
- Edna Valley
- Santa Maria Valley
- Santa Ynez Valley
- County Boundary
- Height above sea level (metres)

Kms 10 20 30 40 50
Mls 5 10 15 20 25 30

The AVAs of the South-Central Coast

EDNA VALLEY AVA
(San Luis Obispo County)

Established: *11th June 1982*

This elongated valley is located just south of Paso Robles. It covers 91 square kilometres (35 square miles) and is well defined by the Santa Lucia Mountains to the northeast, the San Luis Range to the southwest and a low hilly complex to the southeast. In the northwest it merges with the Los Osos Valley, forming what is, in effect, a wide-mouthed funnel that sucks in ocean air from Morro Bay. This marine air flows unobstructed into the valley, where it is captured by its pocket of mountains and hills, providing a moderate summer climate that

differentiates it from surrounding areas. The vines grow at a height of between 37-90 metres (120-300 ft) on the valley floor, rising to 120 metres (600 ft) in the Santa Lucia Mountains, on soils that are mostly sandy-clay loam, clay loam and clay.

PASO ROBLES AVA
(San Luis Obispo County)

Established: *3rd November 1983*

This area was given its name in the eighteenth century, when travellers passed through it on their way from the San Miguel to the San Luis Obispo missions. It is one of California's oldest wine-growing regions: grapes have

been harvested in this area of rolling hills and valleys since circa 1797. It is bounded by the Santa Lucia Mountains to the north and west, the Chalone Hills to the east and the Santa Margarita Lake to the south. There is no penetration by coastal winds or marine fog and, consequently, there is the equivalent of an additional 500-1,000 degree-days here compared to viticultural areas to the west and east. This obviously has a considerable effect on grape ripening patterns. The Paso Robles vineyards are located at a height of between 180-305 metres (600-1,000 ft), on generally fertile and well-drained soils of alluvial nature on the flats and colluvial construction on the terraces.

SAN LUIS OBISPO AO

An appellation covering grapes grown anywhere within the entire county of San Luis Obispo.

SANTA BARBARA AO

An appellation covering grapes grown anywhere within the entire county of Santa Barbara.

SANTA MARIA VALLEY AVA
(Santa Barbara County)

Established: *4th September 1981*
Continued overleaf

The Pacific winds blow along this funnel-shaped valley, causing cooler summers and winters, with warmer autumns than in surrounding areas. The terrain climbs from 61-244 metres (200-800 ft), with most vineyards concentrated at 91 metres (300 ft). The soil is sandy and clay loam, and is free from the adverse effects of salts.

SANTA YNEZ VALLEY AVA
(Santa Barbara County)

Established: *16th May 1983*

European settlers named the mission established here in 1804 "Santa Ynez". The area under vine before Prohibition was in excess of 2,000 hectares (5,000 acres), but viticulture in the valley only really began to pick up again in the 1970s. However, there was still only a mere 486 hectares (1,200 acres) when the appellation was established in 1983, even though its boundaries enclosed 738 square kilometres (285 square miles). The Santa Ynez Valley is bounded by mountains to the north and south, by Lake Cachuma and Los Padres National Forest to the east, and by a series of low hills to the west. This topography, combined with the close proximity of the ocean, serves to moderate the weather. Maritime fog plays an important role in lowering temperatures, but with the Santa Rita Hills blocking penetration of the coldest sea winds, the Valley does not have the coolest of coastal climates: Solvang, in its centre, has 2,680 degree-days, while Lompoc, just three kilometres (two miles) outside the appellation's western boundary, has 1,970 and Santa Barbara, to the south, has 2,820. The vineyards are located at an altitude of 60-120 metres (200-400 ft) in the foothills of the San Rafael Mountains, on soils that are mostly well drained, sandy, silty, clay and shale loam.

TEMPLETON
(San Luis Obispo County)

Templeton is situated within Paso Robles. It is not an AVA, but I have included it for the purposes of clarification, because various sources have stated that it is. Even official publications from California's Wine Institute have made the error.

WILD HORSE VALLEY AVA
(San Luis Obispo County)

Established: *30th November 1988*

YORK MOUNTAIN AVA
(San Luis Obispo County)

Established: *23rd September 1983*

This small appellation is just 11 kilometres (seven miles) from the sea, situated at an altitude of 450 metres (1,500 ft) in the Santa Lucia Mountains, close to the western border of Paso Robles. Its Region I climatic classification, and 114 centimetres (45 ins) of rain per year, set it apart from the warmer and considerably drier surrounding areas.

Major wineries of the South-Central Coast

EDNA VALLEY VINEYARD
(San Luis Obispo County)
2585 Biddle Ranch Road,
San Luis Obispo, CA 93401

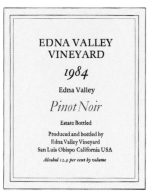

Originally a joint venture with Chalone Vineyard (*see* p.380), this Burgundian varietal specialist makes some superbly rich and toasty Chardonnays and very good Pinot Noirs. Other labels include Richard Graff Winery.

☆ Chardonnay, Pinot Noir

ESTRELLA RIVER WINERY
(San Luis Obispo County)
Highway 46 East,
Paso Robles,
CA 93447

Pronounced "eh-STRAY-yuh", this excellent winery is built on a knoll overlooking its 324 hectares (800 acres) of vines.

☆ Blanc de Blancs Brut, Chardonnay, Muscat Canelli

THE FIRESTONE VINEYARD
(Santa Barbara County)
Zaca Station Road,
Los Olivos, CA 93441

A very conscientious winery that makes fine wines. Although they can occasionally lapse, the wines are usually rich, ripe and magnificent.

☆ Cabernet Sauvignon, Johannisberg Riesling, Merlot

RICHARD GRAFF WINERY
See Edna Valley Vineyard.

ZACA MESA WINERY
(Santa Barbara County)
Zaca Station, Foxen Canyon Road,
Los Olivos, CA 93441

Fine wines from ungrafted vines in phylloxera-free vineyards.

☆ Chardonnay, Johannisberg Riesling, Pinot Noir

The best of the rest

Note: many of the following wineries are just beginning to establish a reputation and may well become deserving of a place in the "Major wineries" section in the future.

BALLARD CANYON WINERY
(Santa Barbara County)
1825 Ballard Canyon Road,
Solvarg, CA 93463

☆ Chardonnay, Johannisberg Riesling

J. CAREY CELLARS
(Santa Barbara County)
1711 Alamo Pintado Road,
Solvang, CA 93463

☆ Sauvignon Blanc

MASTANTUONO
(San Luis Obispo County)
Vineyard Drive and Highway 46 W,
Paso Robles, CA 93446

☆ Zinfandel

PESENTI WINERY
(San Luis Obispo County)
2900 Vineyard Drive,
Templeton, CA 93465

☆ Zinfandel

RANCHITA OAKS WINERY
(San Luis Obispo County)
Cross Canyon Vineyards
Estrella Route Box 4790,
San Miguel, CA 93451

☆ Zinfandel

SANFORD & BENEDICT VINEYARDS
(Santa Barbara County)
5500 Santa Rosa Road,
Lompoc, CA 93436

☆ Chardonnay, Pinot Noir

SANTA BARBARA WINERY
(Santa Barbara County)
202 Anapaca Street,
Santa Barbara, CA 93101

☆ Late Harvest Zinfandel

SANTA YNEZ VALLEY WINERY
(Santa Barbara County)
343 North Refugio Road,
Santa Ynez, CA 93460

☆ Chardonnay, Sauvignon Blanc

VEGA VINEYARDS WINERY
(Santa Barbara County)
9496 Santa Rosa Road,
Buellton, CA 93427

☆ White Riesling

YORK MOUNTAIN WINERY
(San Luis Obispo County)
York Mountain Road,
Templeton, CA 93465

☆ Zinfandel

The Central Valley

California's coastal areas are perhaps its most famous wine districts; they are certainly its most capable when it comes to producing fine wines, but they are not significant in terms of quantity. The baking-hot, flat and dry Central Valley accounts for 80 per cent of all Californian wine.

WHILE FINE-WINE PRODUCTION MAY HAVE BEEN on the increase in California over the last ten years, the output of cheap jug-wine has been positively soaring. The area under vine in Madera, the valley's most prolific county, has doubled, while that in Fresno and Kern has increased by 5,260 hectares (13,000 acres) apiece, San Joaquin by 4,050 (10,000), Stanislaus by 2,800 (7,000) and Merced by 2,400 (6,000). The current county wine-grape vineyard areas are: Shasta, 15 hectares (36 acres);Tehama, 61 hectares (151 acres); Glenn, 585 hectares (1,445 acres); Colusa, 59 hectares (146 acres); Yolo, 550 hectares (1,363 acres); Butte, 74 hectares (184 acres); Yuba, 140 hectares (348 acres); Sacramento, 1,445 hectares (3,570 acres); San Joaquin, 14,430 hectares (35,652 acres); Stanislaus, 6,919 hectares (17,097 acres); Merced, 6,127 hectares (15,142 acres); Madera, 16,166 hectares (39,947 acres); Fresno, 15,430 (38,129 acres); Kings, 522 hectares (1,290 acres); Tulare, 5,923 hectares (14,637 acres); and Kern, 14,507 hectares (35,849 acres).

THE VALLEY OF THE GIANTS

With nine companies, below, annually producing one million cases (90,000 hectolitres) or more, the Central Valley is truly the Valley of the Giants and E. & J. Gallo a Goliath amongst giants. Its production is almost double that of all the other eight companies put together and represents 35 per cent of all Californian wines produced.

E. & J. Gallo Winery (Stanislaus County)	60 million cases (5,400,000 hl)
Delicato Vineyards (San Joaquin County)	8 million cases (720,000 hl)
LaMont Winery (Kern County)	8 million cases (720,000 hl)
Franzia Winery (San Joaquin County)	5 million cases (450,000 hl)
Giumarra Vineyards (Kern County)	5 million cases (450,000 hl)
Guild Wineries (San Joaquin County)	3 million cases (270,000 hl)
Gibson Wine Company (Fresno County)	2 million cases (180,000 hl)
Papagni Vineyards (Madera County)	1.6 million cases (144,000 hl)
Noble Vineyards (Kern County)	1 million cases (90,000 hl)

FACTORS AFFECTING TASTE AND QUALITY

Location
The viticultural area of this huge fertile valley stretches 644 kilometres (400 miles) from Redding in the north to Bakersfield in the south, running between the Coastal Ranges to the west and the Sierra Nevada to the east.

Climate
Generally homogenous from end to end, warming steadily from Region IV in the north to Region V in the south. The area around Lodi is the only exception, being cooled by sea air sweeping up the Sacramento River.

Aspect
The vines are grown on the vast flat area of the valley floor.

Soil
Very fertile sandy loam dominates the length and breadth of the valley.

Viticulture and vinification
Production of vast quantities of reliable quality jug-wine, using the latest techniques of mechanization and irrigation, and a virtually continuous fermentation and bottling process. Somewhat higher-quality Zinfandel and sweet dessert wines are produced around Lodi.

Grape varieties
French colombard, Cabernet sauvignon, Chenin blanc, Barbera, Carignan, Grenache, Ruby cabernet, Zinfandel

Harvested Cabernet sauvignon, above
The Central Valley's huge output does not prohibit premium varietal quality.

The AVAs of the Central Valley

CLARKSBURG AVA
(Sacramento County)

Established: *22nd February 1984*

A large area south of Sacramento in the Central Valley, covering 259 square kilometres (100 square miles) and encompassing the AVA of Merritt Island. The average annual rainfall is 41 centimetres (16 ins), which is greater than the precipitation experienced in areas to the south and west, but less than that which occurs north and east.

LODI AVA
(Sacramento and San Joaquin Counties)

Established: *17th March 1986*

An inland area that is comprised of alluvial fan, plains that are prone to flood and lower and higher terrace lands. Although the land both north and south of the area has some similar

soil structures, it is the combination of these soils with the climatically moderating effect from the San Francisco Bay that makes the area distinctive. The Sierra Nevada foothills and the more upland soils are on the eastern boundary.

MADERA AVA
(Madera and Fresno Counties)

Established: *7th January 1985*

A viticultural area not to be confused with Madera County. It is located in both the Madera and Fresno Counties and contains approximately 1,800 square kilometres (700 square miles) and more than 14,500 hectares (36,000 acres) of wine grapes, plus substantial areas of raisin and table grapes. Its growing season averages between 260–270 days, with periodic freezing temperatures during the winter that trigger vine dormancy. To the east, the growing season is 220

days, while to the west, it averages 285 days a year.

MERRITT ISLAND AVA
(San Joaquin County)

Established: *16th June 1983*

An island bounded on the west and north by Elk Slough, by Sutter Slough on the south, and the Sacramento River on the east. Its climate is tempered by cooling southwesterly breezes from the Carquinez Straits, near San Francisco, which reduce the temperature substantially compared to that of the City of Sacramento, located just six miles north. Fog from the San Francisco Bay is rarely a problem since Merritt Island is the northernmost island in the Sacramento Delta. The soil is primarily sandy loam, while areas to the west have clay-type soil, and to the south, an organically structured peat dirt that is moderately fertile.

NORTH YUBA AVA
(Yuba County)

Established: *30th August 1985*

An area in the Central Valley that is 11 kilometres (seven miles) long and five to ten kilometres (three to six miles) wide on the middle and upper foothills of Yuba County, immediately west of the Sierra Nevada and north of the Yuba River. The 609-metre (2,000-ft) contour line of the Sierra Nevada Mountains forms the eastern and northern portions of the AVA's boundary, and the 304-metre (1,000-ft) contour line north of the Yuba River Canyon forms the southern portion of the boundary. The eastern bank of Woods Creek forms part of the western portion of the boundary. This area escapes both the early frosts and the snow of higher elevations in the Sierra Nevadas and the heat, humidity and fog common to the Sacramento Valley lowlands, and is therefore relatively temperate compared to the rest of the AVA.

Major wineries of the Central Valley

AMBASSADOR
See LaMont Winery.

BRECKENRIDGE CELLARS
See Giumarra Vineyards.

CALIFORNIA VILLAGES
See Gibson Wine Company.

CAPISTRO
See LaMont Winery.

R & J COOK WINERY
(Yolo County)
Netherlands Road,
Clarksburg, CA 95612

☆ Chenin Blanc, Petite Sirah

COOKS CHAMPAGNES
See Guild Wineries.

CRIBARI
See Guild Wineries.

DELICATO VINEYARDS
(San Joaquin County)
12001 South Highway 99,
Manteca, CA 95336

A gigantic production of inexpensive wine that includes Barberone (ie of Barbera type), Chianti Light, Green Hungarian and Pink Chablis! I like the idea of its "Indelicato" label, but is it tongue in cheek?

DI GIORGIO VINEYARDS
See LaMont Winery.

FICKLIN VINEYARDS
(Madera County)
30246 Avenue 7½,
Madera, CA 93637

California's leading "port" wine specialists.

☆ Tinta Port

FRANZIA WINERY
(San Joaquin County)
17000 E. Highway 120
Ripon, CA 95366

A large production of inexpensive, often overtly fruity wines. The better varietals, such as Cabernet Sauvignon, can be very sweet indeed. Other labels include Tribuno.

E. & J. GALLO WINERY
(Stanislaus County)
600 Yosemite Boulevard,
Modesto, CA 95353

As California's largest winery, Gallo has a production equivalent to four times the annual output of the entire Champagne region of France, and is the largest wine producer in the world. It is an oenological miracle for any one firm to produce such mega-quantities and keep the wine drinkable, but Gallo do a bit more than that. These are not fine wines, but they are well made and about as good as you can get for the cheap price.

☆ Chablis Blanc, Hearty Burgundy, Johannisberg Riesling, Sauvignon Blanc

GIBSON WINE COMPANY
(Sacramento County)
9750 Kent Street,
Elk Grove, CA 95624

A cooperative winery, with about 150 members, producing a vast amount of primarily "generic" wines. Its other labels include California Villages, Romano and Silverstone Cellars.

GIUMARRA VINEYARDS
(Kern County)
Edison Highway,
Edison, CA 93303

This giant operation was founded by "Papa Joe" Giumarra, a Sicilian immigrant who made his money in the Prohibition era. It is still very much a family organization and despite its huge production of mostly jug-wines, they are well made and offer good value. Other labels include Breckenridge Cellars, Ridgecrest Cellars and Maison Dominique.

☆ Zinfandel

GOLD BELL
See Oak Ridge Vineyards.

GUASTI
See LaMont Winery.

GUILD WINERIES
(San Joaquin County)
One Winemasters Way,
Lodi, CA 95240

This is the central bottling and blending facility for the San Francisco-based Guild Wineries cooperative. There are in excess of 1,000 members, they own the Roma and Cribari wineries and part of the cooperative's vast production is sold under various other labels, including Tavola, Vintners Choice, Mendocino Vineyards and Cooks Champagnes.

HARBOR WINERY
(Sacramento County)
610 Harbor Boulevard,
West Sacramento, CA 95691

☆ Chardonnay, Zinfandel

INDELICATO
See Delicato Vineyards.

LAMONT WINERY
(Kern County)
1 Bear Mountain Winery Road,
Di Giorgio, CA 93217

This operation produces an enormous quantity of value-for-money jug-wine, some of which can be surprisingly good. Other labels include Di Giorgio Vineyards, Capistro, Guasti, Ambassador and Mission Valley.

☆ French Colombard, Zinfandel

MAISON DOMINIQUE
See Giumarra Vineyards.

MENDOCINO VINEYARDS
See Guild Wineries.

MISSION BELL
See Oak Ridge Vineyards.

MISSION VALLEY
See LaMont Winery.

NOBLE VINEYARDS
(Fresno County)
P.O. Box 31,
Kerman, CA 93630

A huge winery with a vast output of inexpensive wines, including Barbera, Burger, Chenin Blanc and French Colombard.

OAK RIDGE VINEYARDS
(San Joaquin County)
6100 East Highway 12,
Lodi, CA 95240

A winery that produces large amounts of inexpensive wines. The Oak Ridge label is reserved for varietals and premium blends from its own vineyards, while the Royal Host and Gold Bell labels are used for standard table and dessert wines. Other brands include Mission Bell.

PAPAGNI VINEYARDS
(Madera County)
31754 Avenue 9,
Madera, CA 93838

Despite a huge output, this operation produces some fine wines. Angelo Papagni's Alicante Bouschet is not to be missed.

☆ Alicante Bouschet, Chardonnay, Moscato d'Angelo

QUADY WINERY
(Madera County)
13181 Road 24,
Madera, CA 93637

☆ Vintage Port

RIDGECREST CELLARS
See Giumarra Vineyards.

ROMA
See Guild Wineries.

ROMANO
See Gibson Wine Company.

ROYAL HOST
See Oak Ridge Vineyards.

SILVERSTONE CELLARS
See Gibson Wine Company.

TAVOLA
See Guild Wineries.

TRIBUNO
See Franzia Winery.

VINTNERS CHOICE
See Guild Wineries.

Other winemaking areas of California

This section is a round up of Californian wine areas not dealt with in the preceding pages. Quality wines come from the Sierra Foothills, which are east of the Central Valley, on a more northerly latitude to the San Francisco Bay area. The wines of Southern California, from between the Mexican Border and the southern extremity of the Central Coast region, are suddenly in vogue, and there are of course excellent wines made in the Lake County area, which falls within the North Coast AVA.

Note: many wineries included in the "Other wineries" section for their relevant area are just beginning to establish a reputation, and may well become deserving of a place in the "Major wineries" section in due course.

SIERRA FOOTHILLS

This was California's gold-rush country and, since the 1970s, scores of new wineries have opened up here, most being of the "boutique" ilk. The Sierra Foothills is a quality wine area, definitely not another Central Valley (see p.385). It attracts the specialists who are content to produce limited quantities. Zinfandel has been the big, blockbusting, spicy star in the region, with Sauvignon Blanc rapidly making ground. The current county wine-grape vineyard areas are: Placer, 50 hectares (123 acres); El Dorado, 185 hectares (456 acres); Amador 664 hectares (1,640 acres); and Calaveras 73 hectares (181 acres).

Sierra Foothills AVAs

CALIFORNIA SHENANDOAH VALLEY AVA
(Amador County)

Established: *27th July 1983*

The famous Shenandoah Valley is, of course, in Virginia (it received its AVA status in January 1983) and this one, set amid the Sierra Foothills, was so-named by Virginian settlers who migrated to California during the gold rush. Vines were grown here in 1881 when the diggers ran out of gold and turned to making wine, and the area today covers just over 38 square kilometres (15 square miles). The vines grow on well-drained, moderately deep soils, consisting mostly of coarse sandy loams formed from weathered granitic rock with a heavy, often clayey, loam subsoil.

EL DORADO AVA
(El Dorado County)

Established: *14th November 1983*

This gold-rush-country appellation is limited to areas at altitudes between 365 and 1,067 metres (1,200 and 3,500 ft) in the Sierra Foothills.

FIDDLETOWN AVA
(Amador County)

Established: *3rd November 1983*

The Fiddletown viticultural area is located in the eastern Sierra Foothills of Amador County. It differs from the neighbouring Shenandoah Valley of California area because of its higher elevations, colder night-time temperatures and more rainfall. Summer daytime temperatures range from 27-38°C (80-100°F). Nights are cool because of the mountain breezes. Grapes are grown without any irrigation and the vineyards are located on deep, moderately well-drained, sandy loams.

Major wineries of the Sierra Foothills

AMADOR FOOTHILL WINERY
(Amador County)
12500 Steiner Road,
Plymouth, CA 95669

The wines from this winery, with its small Shenandoah Valley vineyards, are made by owner and ex-NASA chemist Ben Zeitman.

☆ Fumé Blanc, Zinfandel

ARGONAUT WINERY
(Amador County)
Willow Creek Road,
Ione, CA 95640

☆ Zinfandel

BOEGER WINERY
(El Dorado County)
1709 Carson Road,
Placerville, CA 95667

The first modern-day winery to re-open the pre-Prohibition Sierra Foothill vineyards, Boeger has since established itself as a reliable producer of good-value wines.

☆ Cabernet Sauvignon, Chenin Blanc, Hangtown Red, Johannisberg Riesling

HARVEST CELLARS
See Stevenot Winery.

KARLY WINES
(Amador County)
11076 Bell Road,
Plymouth, CA 95669

This underrated winery makes high-quality wines that are quietly packed with flavour and show extraordinary finesse.

☆ Sauvignon Blanc, Zinfandel

KENWORTHY VINEYARDS
(Amador County)
10120 Shenandoah Road,
Plymouth, CA 95669

☆ Zinfandel

MADRONA VINEYARDS
(El Dorado County)
P.O. Box 454, Gatlin Road,
Camino, CA 95709

☆ Zinfandel

MONTEVIÑA
(Amador County)
20680 Shenandoah School Road,
Plymouth, CA 95669

A good and steadily improving Zinfandel specialist, with vineyards in the Shenandoah Valley.

☆ Fumé Blanc, White Zinfandel

SHENANDOAH VINEYARDS
(Amador County)
12300 Steiner Road,
Plymouth, CA 95669

Producers of powerful wines.

☆ Zinfandel Reserve, Zinfandel Port

STEVENOT WINERY
(Calaveras County)
2690 San Domingo Road,
Murphys, CA 95247

San Luis Obispo County
MUSCAT CANELLI
1986

Stevenot

PRODUCED AND BOTTLED BY
STEVENOT WINERY
MURPHYS, CALAVERAS COUNTY, CALIFORNIA
ALCOHOL 10% BY VOLUME   B.W. 4839

A medium-sized winery producing some impressive white wines. A second label is Harvest Cellars.

☆ Chardonnay, Fumé Blanc, Muscat Canelli

Other wineries of the Sierra Foothills

D'AGOSTINI WINERY
(Amador County)
14430 Shenandoah Road,
Plymouth, CA 95669

BALDINELLI VINEYARDS
(Amador County)
10801 Dickson Road,
Plymouth, CA 95669

BEAU VAL WINES
(Amador County)
10671 Valley Drive,
Plymouth, CA 95669

CHISPA CELLARS
(Calaveras County)
Main Street and Murphys Grade
Road, Murphys, CA 95247

EL DORADO VINEYARDS
(El Dorado County)
3551 Carson Road,
Camino, CA 95709

FITZPATRICK WINERY & VINEYARDS
(El Dorado County)
6881 Fairplay Road,
Somerset, CA 95684

GERWER WINERY
(El Dorado County)
8221 Stoney Creek Road,
Somerset, CA 95684

GRANITE SPRINGS WINERY & VINEYARDS
(El Dorado County)
6060 Granite Springs Road,
Somerset, CA 95684

GREENSTONE WINERY
(Amador County)
Highway 88 at Jackson Valley Road,
Ione, CA 95640

SANTINO WINERY
(Amador County)
12225 Steiner Road,
Plymouth, CA 95669

STONERIDGE
(Amador County)
13862 Ridge Road East,
Sutter Creek, CA 95685

STORY VINEYARD
(Amador County)
10851 Bell Road,
Plymouth, CA 95669

TKC VINEYARDS
(Amador County)
Shenandoah Valley Road,
Plymouth, CA 95669

SOUTHERN CALIFORNIA

Much smaller in size than even the Sierra Foothills, Southern California, site of the state's very first vineyards, has also undergone a revival since 1977. The current county wine-grape vineyard areas are: Ventura, 0.5 hectares (1 acre); Los Angeles, 0.5 hectares (1 acre); Orange, 13 hectares (33 acres); San Bernardino, 1,412 hectares (3,489 acres); Riverside, 1,233 hectares (3,047 acres); and San Diego 53 hectares (131 acres).

Southern California AVAs

SAN PASQUAL AVA
(San Diego County)

Established: *16th September 1981*

The San Pasqual Valley lies 16-24 kilometres (10-15 miles) east of the

Continued overleaf

Pacific Ocean and is in the normally hotter southern section of California. It possesses, however, a soil, climate and topography that sets it apart. It is a natural valley located in the Santa Ysabel watershed, the elevation of the valley floor is from 90-150 metres (300-500 ft) above sea level, and it is surrounded on three sides by low mountain ranges rising to 460 metres (1,500 ft). The valley is fed by natural streams that feed the San Diequito River, and is substantially affected by coastal influences. Temperatures are warm in the summer, but seldom over 35°C (95°F). Ocean breezes cool the area and night-time temperatures are normally below 18°C (65°F). The surrounding areas have climates ranging from tropical, through desert-like, to mountainous.

TEMECULA AVA
(Riverside County)

Established: *23rd November 1984*

Temecula is located in Riverside County, Southern California, and includes Murrieta and Rancho California, two areas that have had their own AVA petitions rejected by the BATF (*see* p.358). Marine breezes entering the area through the Deluz and Rainbow Gaps cool the area to moderate temperatures. There are some 800 hectares (2,000 acres) of vineyards currently cultivated in this AVA, with Sauvignon blanc and Chardonnay the most widely planted varieties and Chenin blanc and Cabernet sauvignon the least successful.

WILLOW CREEK AVA
(Humboldt County)

Established: *9th September 1983*

An area influenced primarily by two major climatic forces; the Pacific Ocean and the warmer climate of the Sacramento Valley 161 kilometres (100 miles) to the east, which create easterly winds that give Willow Creek fairly cool temperatures in the summer and infrequent freezes in the winter. The area to the east of Willow Creek experiences colder temperatures in winter and hotter temperatures in summer.

Major wineries of Southern California

AHERN WINERY
(Los Angeles County)
715 Arroyo Avenue,
San Fernando, CA 91340

☆ Zinfandel

CALLAWAY VINEYARD & WINERY
(Riverside County)
32720 Rancho California Road,
Temecula, CA 92390

One of the first wineries to prove that parts of southern California have exceptionally good microclimatic conditions for producing fine-wine grapes.

☆ Chardonnay, Sauvignon Blanc, Fumé Blanc, "Sweet Nancy" Chenin Blanc

CILURZO VINEYARD & WINERY
(Riverside County)
41220 Calle Contento,
Temecula, CA 92390

This was the first vineyard in the Temecula AVA.

FILSINGER VINEYARDS & WINERY
(Riverside County)
39050 De Portola Road,
Temecula, CA 92360

☆ Chardonnay

LEEWARD WINERY
(Ventura County)
2784 Johnson Drive,
Ventura, CA 93003

☆ Chardonnay

MOUNT PALOMAR WINERY
(Riverside County)
33820 Rancho California Road,
Temecula, CA 92390

☆ White Riesling

SAN PASQUAL VINEYARDS
(San Diego County)
13455 San Pasqual Road,
Escondido, CA 92025

SAN PASQUAL
VINTAGE 1985

Mac Gregor Vineyard
EDNA VALLEY
CHARDONNAY

PRODUCED & BOTTLED BY SAN PASQUAL VINEYARDS
SAN DIEGO, CALIFORNIA ALCOHOL 13.1% BY VOLUME

☆ Charbono, Gamay, Muscat Canelli, Sauvignon Blanc

Other wineries of Southern California

BRITTON CELLARS
(Riverside County)
40620 Calle Contento,
Temecula, CA 92390

JOHN CULBERTSON WINERY
(San Diego County)
2608 Via Rancheros,
Fallbrook, CA 92020

THE DAUME WINERY
(Ventura County)
270-D Aviador,
Camarillo, CA 91310

J. FILIPPI VINTAGE CO.
(San Bernardino County)
Mira Loma, CA 91752

GLEN OAK HILLS WINERY
(Riverside County)
40607 Los Ranchos Circle,
Temecula, CA 92390

HART WINERY
(Riverside County)
P.O. Box 956,
Temecula, CA 92390

THE MARTIN WINERY
(Los Angeles County)
11800 West Jefferson Boulevard,
Culver City, CA 90230

PICONI WINERY, LTD.
(Riverside County)
33410 Rancho California Road,
Temecula, CA 92390

POINT LOMA WINERY
(San Diego County)
3655 Poe Street,
San Diego, CA 92106

RANCHO DE PHILO
(San Bernardino County)
10050 Wilson Avenue,
Alta Loma, CA 91701

SOUTH COAST CELLAR
(Los Angeles County)
12901-B Budlong Avenue,
Gardena, CA 90247

LAKE, MARIN AND SOLANO COUNTIES

The only other counties of any real repute or significance are Lake, Marin and Solano, all of which are part of the North Coast AVA. Lake has 1,292 hectares (3,194 acres) of wine-grape vineyards. Marin has four (11) and Solano 477 (1,178).

Lake, Marin and Solano Counties AVAs

CLEAR LAKE AVA
(Lake County)

Established: *7th June 1981*

Located between the Mayacamas Mountains and the Mendocino National Forest, Clear Lake's large water-mass moderates the AVA's climate.

GUENOC VALLEY AVA
(Lake County)

Established: *21st December 1981*

An appellation south of McCreary Lake and east of Detert Reservoir. Situated within the North Coast AVA, the valley has a lower rainfall and less severe fog than the nearby Middletown area, and also has a more extreme climate.

SOLANO COUNTY GREEN VALLEY AVA
(Solano County)

Established: *28th February 1983*

Green Valley is sandwiched between the Napa Valley to the west and the Suisun Valley to the east. The soil here is a clay loam and the climate is influenced by the cool, moist winds that blow inland from the Pacific and San Francisco Bay almost continuously from spring through to autumn.

SUISUN VALLEY AVA
(Solano County)

Established: *27th December 1982*

Adjacent to Solano County Green Valley, this AVA enjoys the same cool, moist winds that blow from spring through to autumn. The soils consist of various forms of clay, and silty and sandy loams.

Major wineries of Lake, Marin and Solano Counties

KALIN CELLARS
(Marin County)
61 Galli Drive, Novato, CA 94947

The style of these ultra-high-quality wines is deep, full and rich, with great finesse and a fine smoky complexity.

☆ Cabernet Sauvignon (Reserve), Chardonnay, Sauvignon Blanc, Sémillon

KENDALL-JACKSON VINEYARDS AND WINERY
(Lake County)
600 Matthews Road,
Lakeport, CA 95453

A winery that has had its own label only since 1983, but has rapidly gained a very good reputation.

☆ Cabernet Sauvignon, Chardonnay, Muscat Canelli, Sauvignon Blanc

Other wineries of Lake, Marin and Solano Counties

GUENOC WINERY
(Lake County)
21000 Butts Canyon Road,
Middletown, CA 95461

KONOCTI WINERY
(Lake County)
P.O. Box 890
Kelseyville, CA 95451

LOWER LAKE WINERY
(Lake County)
P.O. Box 950, Highway 29,
Lower Lake, CA 95457

PACHECO RANCH WINERY
(Marin County)
5494 Redwood Highway,
Ignacio, CA 94947

SUSINÉ CELLARS
(Solano County)
301 Spring Street,
Suisun City, CA 94585

The Pacific Northwest

The northwestern states of Oregon, Washington and Idaho have significantly cooler climates than those of California. These conditions favour the cultivation of aromatic grapes such as Pinot noir, Riesling, Gewürztraminer and Sauvignon blanc, and produce wines that have less alcohol and more acidity, and which are in a more ethereal style than those of California.

THE PACIFIC NORTHWEST IS THE BRIGHTEST of America's new, quality-wine regions and it is also the second largest, although with the equivalent of merely six per cent of California's vineyards, the gap between first and second is an almighty one.

The first *vinifera* vines were planted in Oregon's Rogue River Valley as early as 1854. These and other *vinifera* vineyards were still in existence at the time of Prohibition, but the Northwest wine industry as a whole relied almost entirely on *labrusca* grapes of the Concord variety until the 1970s. American Wine Growers, Seattle's largest winery, had established experimental vineyards of various classic European varieties in the 1950s, and a limited number of pioneering wine-growers followed suit in the early and mid 1960s. The real revolution began later in the decade, after the Napa Valley's legendary winemaker and wine-consultant, André Tchelistcheff, gave Washington's wine industry an unexpected but much needed boost of confidence. In 1967 he was asked to evaluate the state's quality potential, and had almost concluded that it had very little when he came across a homemade wine produced from grapes grown in the Yakima Valley. The wine was, he pronounced, the finest Gewürztraminer that had ever been made in the USA. This discovery prompted the move away from *labrusca* towards premium varietals, with Tchelistcheff himself actively helping American Wine Growers to develop their fairly well-established *vinifera* vineyards. He improved pruning techniques, cut yields and produced their first commercial varietal wines under the Ste. Michelle label.

Slowly other Pacific Northwest winemakers took up the premium varietal challenge, but it was not until the end of the 1970s that the rest of the world really began to take notice. What fired the imagination was the extraordinary success achieved by one of Oregon's earliest pioneers, David Lett, with perhaps the most difficult of all European grape varieties − the Pinot noir. Lett entered a 1975 vintage into a blind tasting competition in Paris in 1979. It was organized by Robert Drouhin and won, not undeservedly, by his own superb 1959 Chambolle-Musigny, but Lett's Eyrie Vineyard 1975 Pinot Noir came second, demolishing the reputation of some very prestigious Burgundies in the process of making the world aware of Oregon's potential.

THE PACIFIC NORTHWEST

Encompassing thousands of square miles, the Pacific Northwest is a collection of well-dispersed winemaking areas. The ocean forms the length of its western border, from where northern California meets Oregon to where Washington meets Canada. The sea moderates the climate although its effects on inland Idaho are obviously minimal, where continental influence prevails.

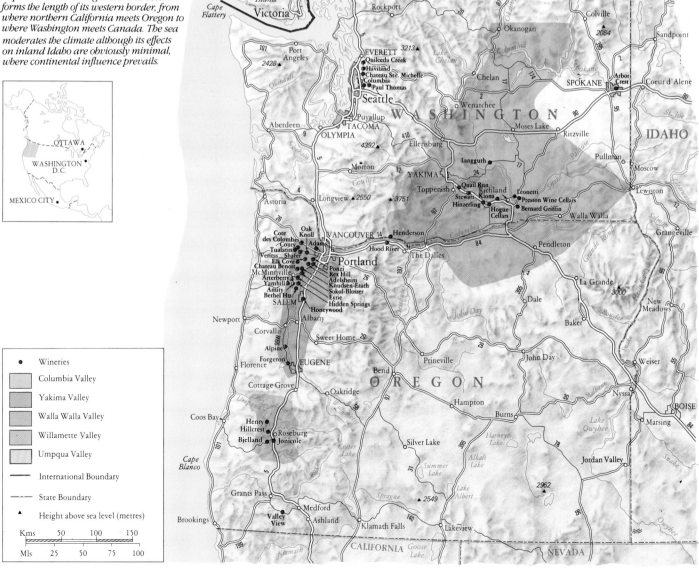

Wineries
Columbia Valley
Yakima Valley
Walla Walla Valley
Willamette Valley
Umpqua Valley
International Boundary
State Boundary
Height above sea level (metres)

Kms 50 100 150
Mls 25 50 75 100

IDAHO

The smallest winemaking state in the northwest, Idaho's high-altitude vineyards are very sunny and produce wine that has an unusual combination of high acidity and high alcohol. With so small an area under vine, it is impossible to contemplate the direction of Idaho's embryonic industry, let alone predict the potential quality of its wines.

OREGON

The oldest and coolest of the three northwestern states, Oregon's grapes often struggle to ripen, and its fine, crisp and often delicate

wines are the most far-removed in style from those of California. Richard Sommer was the first to reinstate *vinifera* vines in this state after Prohibition when he planted Riesling at his Hillcrest Vineyard in Umpqua Valley in 1961. Since 1977, Oregon has had sufficient pride in the identity of its own products to outlaw the use of "generic" names such as "Chablis", "Burgundy", etc. When, I wonder, will other states have sufficient maturity and self-respect to follow?

WASHINGTON

The largest winemaking state in the Pacific Northwest, Washington now has more *vinifera* vineyards than any other American state with the exception of California. Various varieties are performing well and it will be interesting to see which ones consistently fare best in which areas. I believe, however, that Washington's greatest potential may not be in a particular variety, but in a specific style of wine — high-quality *méthode champenoise*.

FACTORS AFFECTING TASTE AND QUALITY

Location
An arbitrary grouping of three northwestern states: Washington, Oregon and Idaho. The Yakima Valley, running through Washington, is at roughly the same latitude as northern Bordeaux and southern Burgundy.

Climate
The temperatures generated by continental air masses are moderated in Washington and Oregon by westerly winds from the Pacific Ocean. Oregon is the coolest state, Washington the wettest (though with plentiful sunshine, averaging over 17 hours per day in June), with crisp, cool nights during the critical ripening period. Western Washington is notoriously wet, with 254 centimetres (100 ins) of rain on the coastline each year. This drops to 101 centimetres (40 ins) a little further inland, and in eastern Washington, which is protected by the Cascade Mountains, it can be as low as 20 centimetres (seven or eight ins), although the Yakima and Columbia rivers and their tributaries assure adequate irrigation. Climatic conditions are generally more continental towards Idaho.

Aspect
The vines are located in valleys, usually planted on low-lying slopes, but also on the valley floors.

Soil
The soils are deep, fertile, light-textured, silty, sandy or clay loams over volcanic bedrock. Most of Washington's viticultural areas are phylloxera-free.

Viticulture and vinification
Washington vines are ungrafted, irrigation is widely practised, with the oldest wines protected by cutting off the water supply prior to winter, thus allowing them to become dormant before the cold sets in. Rapid development is taking place throughout the entire Pacific Northwest, concentrating on the production of top-quality wines made from classic grape varieties.

Grape varieties
Chardonnay, Riesling, Sauvignon blanc, Gewürz-traminer, Sémillon, Chenin blanc, Cabernet sauvignon, Pinot noir, Zinfandel, Gamay, Merlot, Muscat ottonel, Pinot gris

Irrigation, Washington, above
Although the state has a notoriously wet climate, some drier areas in eastern Washington, where most of the vineyards are located, rely on irrigation.

The AVAs of the Pacific Northwest

COLUMBIA VALLEY AVA
(Oregon and Washington)

Established: *13th December 1984*

An appellation consisting of a large, treeless basin surrounding the Yakima, Snake and Columbia rivers. Its undulating surface is cut by these rivers and broken-up by long, sloping, basaltic uplifts. The growing season averages 150 days and the annual rainfall is 38 centimetres (15 ins) or less.

UMPQUA VALLEY AVA
(Oregon)

Established: *30th April 1984*

This appellation comprises the lowland section between the basin of the Umpqua River and the slopes of the surrounding mountains, with the vines growing up to a maximum altitude of 300 metres (1,000 ft). The annual rainfall is high, the winters are cool and the summers warm, with a

slightly greater annual temperature range than surrounding areas such as the Willamette Valley.

WALLA WALLA VALLEY AVA
(Washington and Oregon)

Established: *7th March 1984*

An area called the Walla Walla Valley since it was settled in the 1850s, before the creation of Oregon and Washington, this AVA overlaps the two states. The area has long been famous for its sensational onions, known as "Walla Walla Sweets" because they are deliciously sweet, but it is fast acquiring an agricultural reputation that extends to wine, particularly wine made from Cabernet sauvignon and Merlot grapes. The Walla Walla Valley receives 25-50 centimetres (10-20 ins) of rainfall each year, whereas the Columbia Basin, to the west and north, receives less than 25 centi-

metres (10 ins) and the Blue Mountains, to the east and southeast, receive 63-114 centimetres (25-45 ins).

WILLAMETTE VALLEY AVA
(Oregon)

Established: *3rd January 1984*

The boundaries of this viticultural area encompass in excess of 12,900 square kilometres (5,000 square miles) and contained some 800 hectares (2,000 acres) of vineyards and 27 wineries at the time it was granted AVA status. It is enclosed by the Columbia River to the north, the Coast Range Mountains to the west, the Calapooya Mountains to the south, and the Cascade Mountains to the east. The vines grow on silty loam and clay loam in the Willamette Valley, rather than the mountain soils that are the result of dense coniferous vegetation and heavier winter precipitation on the steeper surrounding slopes.

YAKIMA VALLEY AVA
(Washington)

Established: *4th May 1983*

Eastern Washington is characterized by a series of basaltic uplifts that occurred millions of years ago and created a large number of valleys with distinct northern and southern boundaries and slopes. Yakima Valley is one of these, and has been used as an unofficial appellation of origin for wines made from Yakima Valley grapes since 1967. The valley derived its name from the Yakima Nation, a loose confederation of Indian tribes that once controlled a vast portion of eastern Washington. At the time the AVA was created, it contained in excess of 8,900 hectares (22,000 acres) of vines, but only 1,400 hectares (3,500 acres) were of *vinifera* varieties, the balance consisting of Concord, White Diamond and Island Belle, all American varieties.

Major wineries of the Pacific Northwest

IDAHO

STE. CHAPELLE
Caldwell, ID 83605

Named after the Gothic Ste. Chapelle in Paris, Idaho's leading winery has set a fine standard for others to follow.

☆ Blanc de Noirs Brut, Riesling, Chardonnay

OREGON

ADAMS VINEYARD
Portland, OR 97209

A winery that has quickly established a reputation for beautifully balanced Burgundian-like varietals.

☆ Chardonnay (especially Reserve), Pinot Noir

ADELSHEIM VINEYARD
Newberg, OR 97132

Fine wines across the range, and one of the most successful Pinot noir wines produced outside of Burgundy.

☆ Chardonnay, Pinot Gris, Merlot (Layne Vineyards Grant's Pass), Pinot Noir, Sauvignon Blanc

AMITY VINEYARDS
Amity, OR 97101

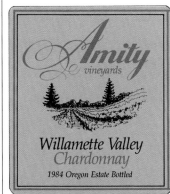

This winery produces a wide and fascinating range of wines, very few of which are disappointing.

☆ Chardonnay, Pinot Noir (Nouveau, Estate, Winemaker's Reserve)

ARTERBERRY WINERY
McMinnville, OR 97128

Essentially a sparkling-wine specialist, the winery also produces a deliciously plump Pinot noir red.

☆ Arterberry Brut, Arterberry Naturel, Pinot Noir

CHATEAU BENOIT
Carlton, OR 97111

Producer of an eclectic, but interesting, range of varietals. Some are quite fine.

☆ Müller-Thurgau, Sauvignon Blanc, NV Brut

THE EYRIE VINEYARDS
McMinnville, OR 97128

The state's Pinot noir pioneer. The rest of David Lett's entire range is also top-quality.

☆ Chardonnay, Muscat Ottonel, Pinot Gris, Pinot Noir (especially Reserve)

KNUDSEN ERATH WINERY
Dundee, OR 97115

One of the best wineries in Oregon, producing Pinot Noirs that have few worthy rivals.

☆ Chardonnay, Pinot Noir (Vintage Select)

OAK KNOLL WINERY
Hillsboro, OR 97123

This winery produces one of the finest Pinot noir wines in Oregon, from bought-in grapes.

☆ Pinot Noir

PONZI VINEYARDS
Beaverton, OR 97007

One of Oregon's top-performing wineries.

☆ Chardonnay, Pinot Gris, Pinot Noir, Dry White Riesling

REX HILL VINEYARDS
Newberg, OR 97132

Producer of good Chardonnay and a variety of fine Pinot noir wines.

☆ Chardonnay, Pinot Noir, Pinot Noir Blanc

SOKOL BLOSSER WINERY
Dundee, OR 97115

A large winery by Oregon standards, but small enough to be staunchly quality-conscious.

☆ Chardonnay, Pinot Noir

TUALATIN VINEYARDS
Forest Grove, OR 97116

A winery that produces blockbusting Chardonnay and elegant Pinot Noir.

☆ Chardonnay, Pinot Noir

The best of the rest

ALPINE VINEYARDS
☆ Chardonnay, Pinot Noir (Vintage Select)

BETHEL HEIGHTS VINEYARD
☆ Pinot Noir

CAMERON WINERY
☆ Chardonnay (Reserve), Pinot Noir

ELK COVE VINEYARDS
☆ Chardonnay, Pinot Noir, Riesling Late Harvest

GIRARDET WINE CELLARS
☆ Chardonnay

HIDDEN SPRINGS WINERY
☆ Pinot Noir

HOOD RIVER VINEYARDS
☆ Zinfandel

SHAFER VINEYARDS
☆ Chardonnay, Pinot Noir Blanc

VERITAS VINEYARD
☆ Chardonnay

YAMHILL VALLEY VINEYARDS
☆ Chardonnay, Pinot Noir

WASHINGTON

ARBOR CREST
Spokane, WA 99207

Formerly a cherry winery, Arbor Crest is owned by the Mielke brothers, third generation farmers. With the help of Scott Harris, their fastidious winemaker, Arbor Crest has become one of the best wineries in the state.

☆ Cabernet Sauvignon, Chardonnay, Merlot, Sauvignon Blanc

CHATEAU STE. MICHELLE
Woodinville, WA 98072

Some of the still wines from this winery may have disconcerting vegetal character, but the Fumé Blanc is clean and fine, and the sparkling wines show great potential.

☆ Blanc de Noirs Brut, Fumé Blanc

COLUMBIA WINERY
Bellevue, WA 98005

Formerly Associated Vintners, these wines are made by British Master of Wine David Lake, whose first Gewürztraminer brought him instant acclaim.

☆ Cabernet Sauvignon (Red Willow Vineyard), Chardonnay, Sémillon

THE HOGUE CELLARS
Prosser, WA 99350

After rearing cattle and growing spearmint for chewing-gum, Warren Hogue embarked upon running this ambitiously sized, yet family-run, vineyard and winery. The quality is high and it deserves to succeed.

☆ Cabernet Sauvignon (Reserve), Chardonnay, Merlot (Reserve)

LEONETTI CELLAR
Walla Walla, WA 99362

Owner Gary Figgins' wines have been winning medals since his 1978 vintage was judged the Best Cabernet Sauvignon in the USA by *Winestate Wine Buying Guide* in 1982.

☆ Cabernet Sauvignon

PRESTON WINE CELLARS
Pasco, WA 99301

Bill Preston has turned his retirement home into the largest privately owned winery in the Pacific Northwest. The quantity is high, but so is the quality.

☆ Chardonnay, White Riesling Ice Wine, Select Harvest Riesling

The best of the rest

KIONA VINEYARDS
☆ Chardonnay

BERNARD GRIFFIN
☆ Chardonnay

HAVILAND VINTNERS
☆ Cabernet Sauvignon

HINZERLING VINEYARDS
☆ Gewürztraminer

QUAIL RUN
☆ Chardonnay

QUILCEDA CREEK VINTNERS
☆ Cabernet Sauvignon

STEWART VINEYARDS
☆ Johannisberg Riesling (Late Harvest)

PAUL THOMAS WINERY
☆ Cabernet Sauvignon

WOODWARD CANYON WINERY
☆ Chardonnay

The Atlantic Northeast

The most intensively viticultivated region east of the Rockies, the Atlantic Northeast has a wine industry traditionally based on native American grapes. Since Prohibition it has become increasingly dependent on French-American hybrids, but *vinifera* varieties are rapidly gaining ground, particularly amongst smaller, quality-conscious growers.

WINES HAVE BEEN MADE IN AMERICA'S NORTHEAST since the middle of the seventeenth century, when vineyards were first established on Manhattan and Long Island. The emphasis, however, has always been on the notoriously "foxy" *labrusca* varieties. *Vinifera* vines were not cultivated until as recently as 1957, although the series of events that were to culminate in this most important development in the Atlantic Northeast's quest for quality wines began in 1934.

Immediately after Prohibition, Edwin Underhill, the President of Gold Seal Vineyards, went to Champagne and persuaded Charles Fournier, the *chef de cave* at Veuve Clicquot, to return with him to the United States. He arrived in 1934 and, being accustomed to the classic concept of Champagne whereby the neutral base wines are enhanced by yeast autolysis, Fournier found the *labrusca* grape varieties planted in New York State's Finger Lake vineyards far too aromatic. Persuaded by local wine-growers that *vinifera* vines could not survive the harsh winters, he began planting hybrid vines (crosses between French and native American varieties). These were initially shipped from France, and then acquired from a winemaker by the name of Philip Wagner, who had already established a considerable collection of hybrids at his Boordy Vineyard in Maryland.

In 1953 Fournier heard that a Ukrainian by the name of Konstantin Frank had been criticizing the entire industry for not planting *vinifera* vines. Frank had arrived in America in 1951 with no money. Unable to speak English, he washed dishes to support his wife and three children. As soon as he could speak a little of the native tongue, he applied for a job at the New York State viticultural research station at Geneva, telling his prospective employers that he had studied viticulture at Odessa, organized collective farms in the Ukraine, taught viticulture and oenology at an agricultural institute and, after the war, managed farms in Austria and Bavaria for the occupying forces. When told that the winters were too harsh for European vines, he instantly dismissed the idea as absurd. "Cold?" he would say, "Where I come from, it's so cold, spit freezes before it hits the ground." He had apparently cultivated *vinifera* vines where temperatures drop to 40°C below freezing (−40°F) and where entire vineyards had to be buried under several feet of soil every year before the winter set in. He argued that if *vinifera* grapes could grow successfully in Russia, then their failure to do so in New York State must be due to diseases or pests that could be controlled, rather than winter temperatures. The staff at Geneva thought he was crazy and set him to work, hoeing blueberries!

THE ATLANTIC NORTHEAST

Of the states that form the Atlantic Northeast, New York has been the most prominent in establishing the area's reputation for vinifera *wines. All the other states have wine industries, if ones dominated by native* labrusca.

Catoctin

Lake Michigan Shore

Lake Erie

Northern Neck George Washington Birthplace

Finger Lakes

Hudson River Region

Ohio River Valley

Cumberland Valley

Southeastern New England

Shenandoah Valley

Kanawha River Valley

Monticello

North Fork of Roanoke

Delimited AVA Wine Region

International Boundary

State/Provincial Boundary

Height above sea level (metres)

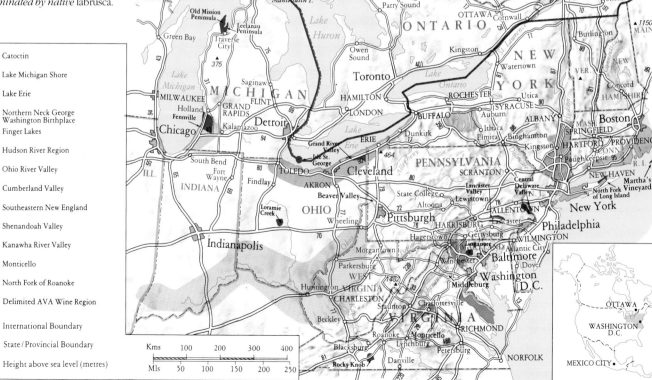

Two years later, when Fournier heard Frank's claims, he employed him, taking the chance that his theory would prove correct. Frank's claims were justified, particularly after the great freeze of February 1957. Later that year some of the hardiest *labrusca* vines failed to bear a single grape, yet less than ten per cent of the buds on Frank's Riesling and Chardonnay vines were damaged and they produced a bumper crop of fully ripe grapes.

In the 1980s Frank was still battling with the Geneva viticultural station. *Vinifera* had not taken off in New York State, despite Frank's success. He blamed this on the "Genevians", who maintained that *vinifera* was too risky to be cultivated by anyone other than an expert. Frank had, however, become very articulate in his new language: "The poor Italian and Russian peasants with their shovels can do it, but the American farmer with his push-button tools cannot."

FACTORS AFFECTING TASTE AND QUALITY

 Location
An arbitrary group of states situated between the Great Lakes and the Atlantic Ocean.

Climate
Despite severe winters, the tempering influence exerted by large masses of inland water, such as the Finger Lakes, Lake Michigan and Lake Erie, creates microclimates that makes cultivation of *vinifera* vines possible.

 Aspect
Many of the vineyards are planted on flat ground around the various lake shores, and on the nearby lower slopes of the various mountain ranges.

Soil
New York: shale, slate, schist and limestone in the Hudson River Region; Virginia: silty loam and gravel at Rocky Knob, limestone and sandstone at North Fork of Roanoke; Michigan: glacial scree in Fennville; Ohio: shallow drift soil over fissured limestone bedrock on Isle St. George; Pennsylvania: deep limestone-derived soils in the Lancaster Valley.

Viticulture and Vinification
In many areas, despite some advantageous microclimates, *vinifera* vines can only survive the harsh winters by being buried under several feet of earth before the winter arrives. Sparkling wines are a speciality of New York State and of the Finger Lakes in particular. Through very careful vineyard practices, the use of the latest sprays, and the aid of new technology in vinification, the number of *vinifera* varietals produced is increasing and their reputation growing.

 Grape varieties
Native *labrusca* grapes such as Concord, Catawba, Delaware and Ives predominate; French-American hybrids such as Vidal blanc, Seyval blanc, Chelois, Baco noir, Maréchal Foch and Aurore are becoming increasingly important; and the quantity of *vinifera* varieties, such as Chardonnay, Riesling, Cabernet sauvignon and Gewürztraminer, is small but growing.

Concord vines, Ohio, left
Although one or two wineries in Ohio do produce vinifera *wines, most of the state's produce is made from hybrids or native varieties such as Concord.*

Mechanical harvesting, below
Grapes are picked by machine at vineyards belonging to the Taylor Wine Company. Based at Hammondsport, the winery is one of New York State's most successful.

The AVAs of the Atlantic Northeast

CATOCTIN AVA
(Maryland)

Established: *14th November 1983*

Situated west of the town of Frederick, this AVA covers 686 square kilometres (265 square miles) within Frederick and Washington Counties. The specific *terroir* of the area was well known before the AVA was established, due to the fact that it roughly coincides with the boundaries of the Maryland Land Resource Area No. 130. These areas are determined by the US Soil Conservation Service on the basis of identifiable patterns of soil, climate, water availability, land use and topography.

CAYUGA LAKE AVA
(New York)

Established: *25th March 1988*

CENTRAL DELAWARE VALLEY AVA
(Pennsylvania and New Jersey)

Established: *18th April 1984*

An appellation covering 388 square kilometres (150 square miles), although very little of this area is planted with vines. The Delaware River modifies the climate.

CUMBERLAND VALLEY AVA (Maryland and Pennsylvania)

Established: *26th August 1985*

Situated between the South Mountains and the Allegheny Mountains, the Cumberland Valley is 128 kilometres (80 miles) long and bends in a northeasterly direction from the Potomac River in Washington County, Maryland, to the Susquehanna River in Cumberland County, Pennsylvania. The AVA encompasses approximately 3,100 kilometres (1,200 square miles), but vines are confined to a collection of small areas where the soil, drainage, rainfall and protection from lethal winter temperatures permit viticulture. Vineyards are found on high terraces along the north bank of the Potomac River, the hills and ridges in the basin of the valley, and upland areas along the slopes of South Mountain.

FENNVILLE AVA
(Michigan)

Established: *19th October 1981*

Lake Michigan has a moderating effect on this area's climate, providing slightly warmer winters and cooler summers than other areas within a 30-mile radius. Fennville covers 310 square kilometres (120 square miles) and has a history dating back more than 100 years for the cultivation of various fruits, including grapes for wine production. The soil is mostly scree of glacial origin.

FINGER LAKES AVA
(New York)

Established: *1st October 1982*

The name is derived from 11 finger-shaped lakes in west-central New York State. Climatic conditions are tempered by this mass of inland water, added to which the topography of the surrounding land creates "air drainage", moderating extremes of temperature in winter and summer. The appellation, which incorporates the pending AVA of Cayuga Lake, has an average 143-day growing season, whereas the area immediately northeast is 170-180 days and the district southwest diminishes to 110-120 days.

GRAND RIVER VALLEY AVA (Ohio)

Established: *21st November 1983*

This AVA is located in Lake, Geauga, and Ashtabula Counties. Since Lake Erie's effect on climate is the overriding factor affecting viticulture in northeast Ohio, the Grand River Valley AVA is confined to that portion of the valley located within the Lake Erie AVA. The lake protects vineyards from frost damage and forces a longer growing season than that experienced in inland areas. The river valley increases "air drainage", giving this AVA a sufficiently different microclimate to warrant its distinction from the Lake Erie AVA.

HUDSON RIVER REGION AVA (New York)

Established: *6th July 1982*

This AVA encompasses all of Columbia, Dutchess and Putnam Counties, the eastern portions of Ulster and Sullivan Counties, nearly all of Orange County and the northern portions of Rockland and Westchester Counties. The Hudson River Region has been referred to as one of the most complex geological divisions in the world. Its vineyards area is located on a geological division known as the Taconic Province, where glacial deposits of shale, slate, schist and limestone form the soil.

ISLE ST. GEORGE AVA
(Ohio)

Established: *20th September 1982*

An island of nearly 2 square kilometres (one square mile) that is located entirely within Ottawa County. The northernmost of the Bass Islands, Isle St. George has a history of grape growing dating back to 1853, and today 142 hectares (350 acres) of vines cover more than half of it. Its climate is moderated by Lake Erie, but it is significantly different from that found on the lake-influenced Ohio mainland vineyards. It is cooler in the spring and summer, warmer in the winter and frost-free for 206 days a year, which is longer than any other area in Ohio. The shallow drift soil over fissured limestone bedrock is well suited to viticulture.

KANAWHA RIVER VALLEY AVA (West Virginia)

Established: *8th May 1986*

This approved viticultural area consists of approximately 2,600 square kilometres (1,000 square miles), yet contains barely 15 acres of vines and has one bonded winery.

LAKE ERIE AVA
(New York, Pennsylvania and Ohio)

Established: *21st November 1983*

Approximately 150 square kilometres (60 square miles), overlapping three states, make up this viticultural area, which also encompasses the AVAs of Isle St. George and Grand River Valley. Lake Erie itself exerts a moderating influence on the climate and is the fundamental factor that permits viticulture.

LAKE MICHIGAN SHORE AVA (Michigan)

Established: *14th November 1983*

Located in the southwest corner of the state of Michigan, this AVA encompasses the counties of Berrien and Van Buren, in addition to portions of Allegan, Kalamazoo and Cass. It is a geographically and climatically uniform region, although it does encapsulate smaller, very specific *terroirs* such as Fennville, which has its own AVA.

LANCASTER VALLEY AVA
(Pennsylvania)

Established: *11th June 1982*

Lancaster County has a grape-growing history dating back to the early nineteenth century, but this has been of purely local interest until relatively recently. The vineyards are located on a virtually level valley floor, at an average elevation of 120 metres (400 ft). The valley's deep, limestone-derived soils are well drained, yet have good moisture retention, are highly productive and differ sharply from those found in the surrounding hills and uplands.

LEELANAU PENINSULA AVA (Michigan)

Established: *29th April 1982*

There are four wineries and approximately 61 hectares (150 acres) of French hybrid and *vinifera* grapes in this area. Lake Michigan delays fruit development beyond the most serious frost period in the spring, and prevents sudden temperature drops in the Fall. It is situated on the western shore of Lake Michigan, northwest of Traverse City.

LINGANORE AVA
(Maryland)

Established: *19th September 1983*

Maryland's first viticultural area, which lies east of the town of Frederick. The Linganore viticultural area is generally warmer and wetter than the areas to the east, and slightly cooler and dryer than the areas to the west.

LORAMIE CREEK AVA
(Ohio)

Established: *27th December 1982*

An area of merely 1,460 hectares (3,600 acres) in Shelby County, west-central Ohio. Moderate-to-poor drainage means vines must be grown on slopes and ridges to prevent "wet feet".

MARTHA'S VINEYARD AVA
(Massachusetts)

Established: *4th February 1985.*

Martha's Vineyard AVA is an island in Massachusetts and should not be confused with the legendary Martha's Vineyard of the Heitz Wine Cellars in California's Napa Valley. The island is surrounded on the north by Vineyard Sound, on the east by Nantucket Sound, and on the south and west by the Atlantic Ocean. The boundaries of the viticultural area include an area known as Chappaquiddick, which is connected to Martha's Vineyard by a sandbar. Climate distinguishes the area from those surrounding it; ocean winds delay the beginning of spring and make for a cooler autumn, extending the growing season to an average of 210 days, compared to 180 days on mainland vineyards.

MONTICELLO AVA
(Virginia)

Established: *22nd February 1984*

Monticello is well known as the home of Thomas Jefferson and there are many historical references to Jefferson planting wine grapes here. The area's average annual rainfall is 107 centimetres (42 ins), while that of the nearby North Fork of Roanoke is 99 centimetres (39 ins) and the neighbouring Shenandoah Valley has a broader range of 97 to 124 centimetres (38 to 49 ins).

NORTHERN NECK GEORGE WASHINGTON BIRTHPLACE AVA
(Virginia)

Established: *21st May 1987*

A 160-kilometre-(100-mile) long peninsula, lying between the Potomac and Rappahannock rivers in the tidewater district of Virginia, which runs from the Chesapeake Bay in the east to within a few miles of Fredericksburg to the west. The vines grow on sandy clay soils on the slopes and hills, and on alluvial soils in the river flats. The climate is favourable, moderated by the surrounding water mass, with excellent air-drainage.

NORTH FORK OF LONG ISLAND AVA (New York)

Established: *10th November 1986*

This AVA consists of almost 420 square kilometres (160 square miles) within the townships of Riverhead, Shelter Island and Southold, including all mainland and island areas. The climate is classified as "humid continental", but the sea that surrounds North Fork makes it a distinct grape-growing area and renders it more temperate than many other places of the same latitude in the interior of the country. The growing season averages between one and three weeks longer in North Fork than it does in the South Fork of the Island and, in general, the sandy soils contain a smaller percentage of silt and loam, but are slightly higher in natural fertility.

NORTH FORK OF ROANOKE AVA
(Virginia)

Established: *16th May 1983*

A valley protected from destructive storms and excessive rainfall in the growing season by the Allegheny mountain ridges of the Eastern Continental Divide to the west, and Fort Lewis Mountains to the east. The vines are planted on the limestone southeast-facing slopes and limestone-interbedded-with-sandstone north-facing slopes. These soils are significantly different from those that are found in the surrounding hills and ridges.

OHIO RIVER VALLEY
(Indiana, Ohio, West Virginia and Kentucky)

Established: *7th October 1983*

A vast AVA covering 67,340 square kilometres (26,000 square miles), overlapping four states and encompassing some 240 hectares (600 acres) of vineyards. In 1859 Ohio was the nation's leading wine-producing state, but neglect throughout the Civil War enabled black rot and powdery mildew to take grip and destroy nearly all of Ohio's vineyards.

OLD MISSION PENINSULA AVA
(Michigan)

Established: *8th July 1987*

An area bounded on three sides by the waters of Grand Traverse Bay, and connected to the mainland at Traverse City. The surrounding waters, coupled with warm southwesterly winds, provide a unique climate that makes cultivation of *vinifera* vines possible.

ROCKY KNOB AVA
(Virginia)

Established: *11th February 1983*

Located within the scenic Blue Ridge Mountains, this area is colder in the spring than surrounding areas, so the vines flower late. This enables them to survive the erratic and very cold early spring temperatures and causes a late fruit-set, extending the growing season by about one week. The silty-loam and gravel soil provides good drainage.

SHENANDOAH VALLEY AVA
(Virginia and West Virginia)

Established: *27th January 1983*

The beautiful Shenandoah Valley is situated between the Blue Ridge Mountains, and the Allegheny Mountains.

SOUTHEASTERN NEW ENGLAND AVA
(Connecticut, Rhode Island and Massachusetts)

Established: *27th April 1984*

An area distinguished from its surrounds in New England and New York by the moderate climate, caused by its proximity to various coastal bodies of water. The annual rainfall is 112 centimetres (44 ins), the daily mean temperature is –1°C (30°F) in January and 21°C (70°F) in July, with a growing season that lasts 180 days.

WARREN HILLS AVA
(New Jersey)

WESTERN CONNECTICUT HIGHLANDS AVA
(Connecticut)

Major wineries of the Atlantic Northeast

CONNECTICUT

CROSSWOOD VINEYARDS
North Stonehingham, CT 06359

Established in 1981, this winery has five hectares (12 acres) of Chardonnay, Gamay, Gewürztraminer, Johannisberg riesling, Pinot noir and Vidal blanc vines.

☆ Gewürztraminer, Johannisberg Riesling
Second label: Scrimshaw

HAIGHT VINEYARDS
Litchfield, CT 06759

☆ Chardonnay, Riesling

HAMLET HILL VINEYARDS
Pomfret, CT 06258

☆ Seyval Blanc

HOPKINS VINEYARDS
New Preston, CT 06777

☆ Ravat Blanc (sweet)

SCRIMSHAW
See Crosswood Vineyards.

DELAWARE

The retail sale of wine is not allowed in Delaware, but one winery exists, Northminster Winery, selling solely to restaurants.

MARYLAND

BASIGNANI

I know little about this new winery other than it is producing Cabernet Sauvignon and Merlot of sufficient quality to attract a lot of attention.

BOORDY VINEYARDS
Hydes, MD 21082

This is where journalist Philip Wagner introduced hybrids to the Atlantic Northeast, a turning point in America's viticultural history. Wagner retired in 1980 and his old winery is now owned by Rob Derford.

BYRD VINEYARDS
Myersville, MD 21773

A pioneering *vinifera* establishment that produces medal-winning wines, some of which are absolutely stunning.

☆ Cabernet Sauvignon, Chardonnay, Sauvignon Blanc

CATOCTIN VINEYARDS
Brookeville, MD 20729

☆ Chardonnay, Johannisberg Riesling

ELK RUN VINEYARD
Mount Airy, MD 21771

☆ Chardonnay

MONTBRAY WINE CELLARS
Westminster, MD 21157

In 1974, Montbray became the first winery in the USA to produce a Riesling "ice wine".

☆ Chardonnay, Johannisberg Riesling, Seyval Blanc

MASSACHUSETTS

CHICAMA VINEYARDS
West Tisbury, MA 02575

The first commercial winery in Massachusetts and the first to establish *vinifera* vines on Martha's Vineyard.

COMMONWEALTH WINERY
Plymouth, MA 02360

A winery with no vineyards. It purchases grapes from both in-state and out-of-state sources.

☆ Riesling

MICHIGAN

BOSKYDEL VINEYARD
Lake Leelanau, MI 49653

The first vineyard to be established on the Leelanau Peninsula.

BRIARWOOD
See Fenn Valley Vineyards.

BRONTE WINERY
See Tabor Hill Bronte Wines.

CHATEAU GRAND TRAVERS
12239 Center Road, Traverse City, MI 49684

Michigan State's only 100-per-cent *vinifera* vineyard.

☆ Chardonnay, Johannisberg Riesling

FENN VALLEY VINEYARDS
6130 122nd Avenue, Fennville, MI 49408

The first winery to produce wines under the Fennville AVA.

☆ Vidal Blanc
Second label: Briarwood

LAKESIDE VINEYARD
13581 Red Arrow Highway, Harvert, MI 49115

This was originally called the Molly Pitcher Winery, but was renamed Lakeside Vineyard when it changed hands in 1975. It was sold again in 1983 and is now run by Leonard Olson, former owner of Tabor Hill Vineyards.

☆ Chardonnay, Johannisberg Riesling
Second label: Molly Pitcher Winery

LEELANAU WINE CELLARS
Omena, MI 49674

Appreciated locally for Baco Noir, and showing promise with *vinifera* wines.

☆ Chardonnay

LEMON CREEK WINERY
Lemon Creek Road, Berrien Springs, MI 49103

Michigan's largest grower of Vidal blanc produces a very agreeable Riesling-Vidal blanc blend.

MOLLY PITCHER WINERY
See Lakeside Vineyard.

ST. JULIAN WINE COMPANY
716 South Kalamazoo Street,
Paw Paw, MI 49079

Founded by an Italian, this was originally a Canadian winery called Meconi Wine Cellars, but became American when it moved to Detroit, and changed its name to the Italian Wine Company. In 1938 it moved to its current location and became the St. Julian Wine Company. Its sparkling wines are well thought of.

TABOR HILL BRONTE WINES
82807 Country Road 687,
Hartford, MI 49057

Originally founded in Detroit as the Bronte Winery, which was the first firm to commercialize "Cold Duck", an awful carbonated-Concord concoction that enjoyed an extraordinary vogue in the 1960s. With such an ignominious history, it is little wonder that the firm moved to a different neighbourhood and assumed another identity!

TABOR HILL VINEYARDS
Mt. Tabor Road, Buchanan, MI 49107

Under the ownership of Leonard Olson and Carl Banholzer, this was Michigan's first *vinifera* operation and gained much respect for its wines. Olson and Banholzer sold out in 1979, but the quality has been maintained.

☆ Chardonnay

WARNER VINEYARDS
706 South Kalamazoo Street,
Paw Paw, MI 49079

The largest winery in the state. Warner sees the commercial necessity of cultivating hybrids but it is heartening to see that more than 75 per cent of its vineyards is planted with *vinifera*.

NEW JERSEY

BERNARD D'ARCY WINES
See Gross Highland Winery.

GROSS HIGHLAND WINERY
Absecon Highlands, NJ 08201

These wines are sold under the "Bernard D'Arcy Wines" label.

☆ Ronay Blanc, Vidal Blanc

RENAULT WINERY
Egg Harbor City, NJ 08215

Founded by Louis-Nicholas Renault, the representative of Champagne Montebello at Mareuil-sur-Aÿ.

TEWKSBURY WINE CELLARS
Lebanon, NJ 08833

☆ Chardonnay

NEW YORK

BENMARL WINE COMPANY LTD
Highland Avenue,
Marlboro, NY 12542

One of the state's most successful wineries. Benmarl is Gaelic for the vineyard's slate-marl soil.

☆ Seyval Blanc

THE BRIDGEHAMPTON WINERY
Box 979,
Bridgehampton, NY 11932

☆ Chardonnay, Première Cuvée Blanc, Sauvignon Blanc, Johannisberg Riesling

BROTHERHOOD WINERY
35 North Street,
Washingtonville, NY 10992

The oldest winery in continuous operation, established by a shoemaker called Jean Jacques, who initially sold wine to the First Presbyterian Church. Of the wines, which are very much of the old school, some critics rate the "Ports" very highly.

BULLY HILL VINEYARDS INC.
Greyton H. Taylor Memorial Drive,
Hammondsport, NY 14840

Walter Taylor, owner and winemaker, says that hybrids are "the greatest innovation since the wine bottle".

CANANDAIGUA WINE COMPANY
116 Buffalo Street,
Canandaigua, NY 14424

In the language of the Seneca Indians, Canandaigua means "chosen place". This firm has a huge production, in

excess of 8 million cases (720,000 hectolitres). It has recently gone into producing premium varietals and is highly thought of for its sweet and sparkling Muscat wines.

Second labels: Richards, J. Roget, Virginia Dare

CASA LARGA VINEYARDS
2287 Turk Hill Road,
Fairport, NY 14450

Promising winery which has had some success with *vinifera* wines.

☆ Chardonnay, Johannisberg Riesling

CHATEAU ESPERANZA WINERY
Bluff Point, NY 14417

After a rather uneven start, the quality of wines from this winery is settling down. Locals say good things about late-harvested, botrytized Ravat.

CLINTON VINEYARDS
Schultzville Road,
Clinton Corners, NY 12514

This specialist winery makes one of the best Seyval Blancs in the state.

☆ Seyval Blanc

FINGER LAKES WINE CELLARS
Italy Hill Road,
Branchport, NY 14418

These cellars produce a good Chardonnay and a promising Riesling.

☆ Chardonnay

CHARLES FOURNIER
See Gold Seal Vineyards.

GLENORA WINE CELLARS
Glenora-on-Seneca,
Dundee, NY 14837

Named after the nearby Glenora waterfall, this winery consistently produces stunningly successful, crisp and stylish wines.

☆ Chardonnay, Johann Blanc, Seyval Blanc

GOLD SEAL VINEYARDS
Hammondsport, NY 14840

Originally called the Imperial Winery, this historic firm built its reputation on "New York Champagne". The quality of this sparkling wine was based on 100 years of true Champagne expertise, in the form of Charles le

Breton of Louis Roederer, Jules Crance of Moët & Chandon, Charles Fournier of Veuve Clicquot and Guy Davaux of Marne et Champagne, who all worked at the vineyards. It was Charles Fournier who really made Gold Seal unforgettable when he pioneered hybrids and, ignoring local experts, employed New York's champion of *vinifera* vines, the irrepressible Konstantin Frank.

☆ Chardonnay, Charles Fournier Blanc de Blancs, Johannisberg Riesling
Second label: Henri Marchant

GREAT RIVER VINEYARDS
See Windsor Vineyards.

GREAT WESTERN WINERY
Old Bath Road,
Hammondsport, NY 14840

Another historic winery, Great Western is now a subsidiary of The Taylor Wine Company. Its wines are more old school and less innovative, despite the occasional good *vinifera*.

☆ Johannisberg Riesling, Sweet Gewürztraminer

HARGRAVE VINEYARD
See Long Island Vineyard.

HERON HILL VINEYARDS
Middle Road,
Hammondsport, NY 14840

Fine-quality, vibrant wines.

☆ Chardonnay, Johannisberg Riesling, Seyval Blanc
Second label: Otter Springs

HIGH TOR VINEYARDS
South Mountain Road,
New City, NY 10956

Vines have grown here since the eighteenth century.

PATRICIA & PETER LENZ
Main Road, Peconic, NY 11958

☆ Chardonnay

LONG ISLAND VINEYARD
Route 48, Cutchogue, NY 11935

After considering the potential of wine areas nationwide, including California, the Hargraves family set up this establishment on Long Island and have since proved consistently that wines of great finesse can be produced here.

☆ Cabernet Sauvignon, Chardonnay, Sauvignon Blanc
Second label: Hargrave Vineyard

HENRI MARCHANT
See Gold Seal Vineyards.

MANISCHEWITZ
See Monarch Wine Company.

MARLBORO CHAMPAGNE
See Windsor Vineyards.

McGREGOR VINEYARDS
5503 Dutch Street,
Dundee, NY 14837

☆ Riesling

MONARCH WINE COMPANY
Brooklyn, NY 11232

Producers of 3 million cases (270,000 hectolitres) per annum of Kosher wines.

Second labels: Pol d'Argent, Chateau Laurent, Manischewitz, Le Premier Cru

OTTER SPRINGS
See Heron Hill Winery.

PINDAR VINEYARDS
Peconic, NY 11958

Improving Gewürztraminer and Johannisberg Riesling, among others.

☆ Chardonnay

PLANE'S CAYUGA VINEYARD
6799 Cayuga Lake Road,
Ovid, NY 14521

Robert Plane has quickly established an extraordinary reputation for his Chardonnay. His hybrids are also worthy of interest.

☆ Chardonnay

POL D'ARGENT
See Monarch Wine Company.

LE PREMIER CRU
See Monarch Wine Company.

RICHARDS
See Canandaigua Wine Company.

J. ROGET
See Canandaigua Wine Company.

ROYAL KEDEM WINERY
Milton, NY 12547

Vast quantities of Kosher wines.

SCHAPIRO'S WINERY
New York, NY 10002

The only winery left in Manhattan, Schapiro's produces Kosher wines.

THE TAYLOR WINE COMPANY
Old Bath Road,
Hammondsport, NY 14840

From the huge success of this firm sprang Taylor California Cellars. The two are now owned by Vintners International, the Taylor Wine Company also selling under the Gold Seal and Great Western labels.

VINIFERA WINE CELLARS
Hammondsport,
NY 14846

A fascinating range of impressive, often exciting, *vinifera* wines.

☆ Chardonnay, Johannisberg Riesling

VIRGINIA DARE
See Canandaigua Wine Company.

WAGNER VINEYARDS
Route 414, Lodi, NY 14860

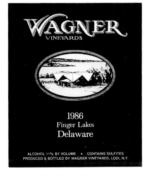

Consistently high-quality wines.

☆ Chardonnay, Gewürztraminer, Riesling, Seyval Blanc

WALKER VALLEY VINEYARDS
Oregon Trail Road,
Walker Valley, NY 12588

Producers of an interesting Maréchal Foch and improving Chardonnay.

HERMANN J. WEIMER VINEYARD
Dundee, NY 14837

While working for a certain hybrid aficionado, Weimer produced some outstanding *vinifera* wines from his own vineyard. They received rave reviews, and he has not looked back.

☆ Chardonnay, Johannisberg Riesling

WICKHAM VINEYARDS, LTD
Hector, NY 14841

Sometime-producers of an agreeable Johannisberg Riesling

WINDSOR VINEYARDS
104 Western Avenue,
Marlboro, NY 12542

A winery owned by Rodney Strong Vineyards, which is now part of Seagrams, the great Canadian-owned multi-national drinks company. Its Cabernet Sauvignon, Merlot, Sauvignon Blanc and Gewürztraminer show promise.

☆ Chardonnay
Second labels: Great River Vineyards, Marlboro Champagne

WOODBURY VINEYARDS
South Roberts Road,
Dunkirk, NY 14048

The Woodburys are one of many traditional, American grape-growing families converted by the simple wisdom of Konstantin Frank.

☆ Chardonnay, Johannisberg Riesling, Seyval Blanc

OHIO

CHALET DEBONNÉ
7743 Doty Road,
Madison, OH 44057

☆ Chablis, Vidal Blanc

GRAND RIVER WINE CO.
Madison, OH 44057

☆ Seyval Blanc

MARKKO VINEYARD
Ridge Road, Conneaut, OH 44030

Owned by Arnulf Esterer, the first of Konstantin Frank's followers to plant *vinifera* in Ohio. The wines are the best this state has produced to date.

☆ Cabernet Sauvignon, Chardonnay

PENNSYLVANIA

ALLEGRO VINEYARDS
Sechrist Road, Brogue, PA 17309

Producers of exciting Chardonnay and promising Cabernet Sauvignon.

☆ Cabernet Sauvignon, Chardonnay

CHADDS FORD WINERY
Chadds Ford, PA 19317

Run by Eric Miller, son of the gifted owners of New York State's Benmarl Winery. It is too early to pass judgement, but these wines are well worth following.

☆ Chardonnay

MAZZA VINEYARDS
North East, PA 16428

☆ Johannisberg Riesling

NAYLOR WINE CELLARS
Stewartstown, PA 17363

Owners Robert and Audrey Naylor make some of the finest wines in Pennsylvania.

☆ Cabernet Sauvignon, Johannisberg Riesling

NISSLEY VINEYARDS
Brainbridge, PA 17502

☆ Chardonnay, Johannisberg Riesling

RHODE ISLAND

PRUDENCE ISLAND VINEYARDS
Prudence Island, RI 02872

☆ Chardonnay

SAKONNET VINEYARDS
Little Compton, RI 02837

The first winery to open on Rhode Island after Prohibition.

☆ America's Cup White, Chardonnay, White Riesling, Vidal Blanc

VIRGINIA

MEREDYTH VINEYARDS
Middleburg, VA 22117

☆ Chardonnay

OASIS VINEYARD
Hume, VA 22639

☆ Cabernet Sauvignon

PIEDMONT VINEYARDS & WINERY INC
Middleburg, VA 22117

Mrs Furness runs this winery, the best in the state, and her finest wine is the rich, crisp and stylish Chardonnay.

☆ Chardonnay

PRINCE MICHEL VINEYARDS
200 Lovers Lane,
Culpeper, VA 22701

☆ White Riesling

WEST VIRGINIA

WEST-WHITEHILL WINERY LTD
Keyser, West VA 26726

☆ Seyval Blanc

Other winemaking areas of the United States

Note: where wineries are simply listed at the end of each state, those marked with a * symbol grow classic European *vinifera* varieties. In some states, rather than provide a listing of wineries, certain wineries are accompanied by an address and profile because the quality of their wines merits such attention.

ALABAMA

The first commercially cultivated vines were planted in Alabama in the 1830s and the state had a flourishing wine industry prior to Prohibition. However, as much as half its counties remained "dry" until as recently as 1975, and legislation licensing farm wineries was not passed until 1978.

Alabama wineries

BRASWELL'S WINERY
PERDIDO VINEYARDS

ARIZONA

Surprisingly, table grapes have long thrived in the irrigated Arizona deserts and, more recently, a few classic wine grape varieties have been cultivated on the 1,220-metre (4,000-ft) high vineyards of this state's solitary AVA at Sonoita, southeast of Tucson.

The AVA of Arizona

SONOITA AVA

Established: *26th November 1984*

The Santa Rita, Huachuca and Whetstone mountain ranges isolate this AVA from its surrounds. Geologically, this AVA is a basin rather than a valley, because it comprises the head-waters for three distinct drainages: Sonoita Creek to the south, Cienega Creek to the north and the Babocamari River to the east.

Arizona winery

R. W. WEBB WINERY *

ARKANSAS

More than one hundred wineries sprang up in Arkansas after Prohibition, but these producers had more moonshining traditions than winemaking skills, and barely half a dozen wineries survived. The potential quality is, however, very high.

The AVAs of Arkansas

ALTUS AVA

Established: *29th June 1984*

An area that covers approximately 52 square kilometres (20 square miles), extending for approximately eight kilometres (five miles) along a plateau situated between the Arkansas River bottom lands and the climatically protective high peaks of the Boston Mountains.

ARKANSAS MOUNTAIN AVA

Established: *27th October 1986*

A huge area in the mountainous region of Arkansas, containing about 11,650 square kilometres (4,500 square miles), and encompassing some 480 hectares (1,200 acres) of vineyards north and south of the Arkansas River. The Arkansas mountains moderate winter temperatures and provide shelter from violent northerly winds and sudden changes in temperature. Classic European grape varieties are grown in Arkansas Mountain, but cannot survive in the area immediately south because of Pierce's disease, a vine-destroying condition associated with warm climates that attacks *Vitis vinifera*.

OZARK MOUNTAIN AVA

Established: *1st August 1986*

An area covering 142,450 square kilometres (55,000 square miles), and containing 1,780 hectares (4,400 acres) of vines and some 36 wineries. Five major rivers make up its boundaries: the Mississippi, the Missouri, the Osage, the Neosho, and the Arkansas, and the AVA includes Mt. Magazine, the highest mountain in Arkansas. The land is hilly-to-mountainous and the soils are stony, well-drained and contain clay from deeply weathered, well-consolidated sedimentary volcanic rocks. The AVA also covers parts of Missouri and Oklahoma.

Arkansas winery

WIEDERKEHR WINE CELLARS
Altus, AR 72821

Not only is this the state's oldest winery, but its owner, UC-Davis-trained Al Wiederkehr, is its most successful winemaker, producing fine wines. Total annual production is 650,000 cases (58,500 hectolitres).

☆ Cabernet Sauvignon, Moscato

COLORADO

The growing season in most of Colorado is too short to permit grape-growing, but at least two wineries have successfully cultivated vines, and *vinifera* ones at that.

Colorado wineries

COLORADO MOUNTAIN
  VINEYARDS *
PIKES PEAK VINEYARDS *

FLORIDA

Not surprisingly, a lot of "orange wine" is grown in the semi-tropical climate of this state. A rather odd concoction it might be, yet it is certainly superior to the wine made from the local *muscadine* grapes, which are able to survive the humidity and Pierce's disease.

Florida wineries

ALAQUA VINEYARDS WINERY
FLORIDA HERITAGE WINERY
FRUIT WINES OF FLORIDA
LAFAYETTE VINEYARDS AND
  WINERY *

GEORGIA

Grapes have been cultivated in Georgia since 1733. Based on native *muscadine* grapes, Georgia was the sixth-largest wine-growing state by 1880. Today the emphasis is on *vinifera*.

Georgia winery

CHATEAU ELAN LTD
Braselton, GA 30517

☆ Chardonnay

HAWAII

Only Alaska seems a less likely wine-producing state. Vines were first planted here in 1814

Hawaii winery

TEDESCHI VINEYARD AND WINERY
Ulupalakua, Maui 96790

Sparkling *méthode champenoise* produced from a *vinifera* vineyard perched 610 metres (2,000 ft.) up on the volcanic slopes of Maui Island.

☆ Blanc de Noirs Brut

ILLINOIS

Until as recently as 1980, the wine-making importance of Illinois was vastly exaggerated because of the two-million-case David Morgan Corporation, which has now moved to New York.

Illinois wineries

GEM CITY VINELAND CO INC
LYNFRED WINERY *
THOMPSON WINERY CO

INDIANA

Winemaking was important in Indiana from the beginning of the nineteenth century, but it was destroyed by Prohibition. Not until 1971 was it possible for commercial farm wineries to operate.

Indiana wineries

THE BLOOMINGTON WINERY INC
CHATEAU THOMAS WINERY
EASLEY WINERY
HUBER ORCHARD WINERY
OLIVER WINE COMPANY INC
POSSUM TROT VINEYARDS
ST WENDEL CELLARS INC
VILLA MILAN VINEYARD

IOWA

Iowa saw most of its vineyards destroyed in 1980 by the use of "2, 4-D" pesticide on neighbouring crops. After initial gloom, they are now being replanted and the prospects are good.

Iowa wineries

CHRISTINA WINE CELLARS
EHRLE BROTHERS INC
HERITAGE WINE AND CHEESE
  HOUSE
OKOBOJI WINERY
OLD STYLE COUNTRY WINERY INC
OLD WINE CELLAR WINERY
PRIVATE STOCK WINERY
SANDSTONE WINERY INC
VILLAGE WINERY

KENTUCKY

Much of this state still thinks it is in the Prohibition era, many counties remaining dry.

Kentucky winery

THE COLCORD WINERY

LOUISIANA

See Mississippi Delta AVA, Mississippi.

MINNESOTA

Vineyards have to be buried beneath several feet of earth in order to survive the harsh winters. These have restricted cultivation to hybrids, except for the Johannisberg riesling grown at the Alexis Bailly Vineyard.

Minnesota wineries

ALEXIS BAILLY VINEYARD *
J. BIRD
LAKE SYLVIA VINEYARD
SCENIC VALLEY WINERY INC

MISSISSIPPI

The pattern here is very similar to that in Kentucky. However, heavy and restrictive taxes were reduced in 1984 and the Mississippi Delta was granted its own AVA.

The AVA of Mississippi

MISSISSIPPI DELTA AVA

Established: *1st October 1984*

A fertile alluvial plain of some 15,500 square kilometres (6,000 square miles), with loess bluffs that abruptly rise 30 metres (100 ft) along the entire eastern side of the delta that also covers parts of Louisiana and Tennessee.

Mississippi wineries

ALMARLA VINEYARDS
CLAIRBORNE VINEYARDS
OLD SOUTH WINERY
THE WINERY RUSHING

MISSOURI

The first wines were produced in Missouri in the 1830s and the state had a flourishing wine industry in the mid-eighteenth century. However, today there is little tangible evidence of fine wine coming from the state.

The AVAs of Missouri

See also Ozark Mountain AVA, Arkansas.

AUGUSTA AVA

Established: *20th June 1980*

Grape-growing in Augusta, the first AVA, dates from 1860. The bowl-like ridge of hills to the west, north, and east, and the Missouri River on the southern edge of the viticultural area, provide a microclimate that separates Augusta from that of the surrounding areas.

HERMANN AVA

Established: *19th September 1983*

In 1904, this area furnished 97 per cent of the wine produced in Missouri. The soils are well drained, have a high water capacity and are deep enough to provide good root development.

OZARK HIGHLANDS AVA

Established: *30th September 1987*

Located within the much larger Ozark Mountain AVA (see the AVAs of Arkansas), this area is confined to all counties within Missouri. The climate is frost-free and relatively cool during spring and autumn, compared to surrounding areas.

Missouri wineries

HERMANNHOF WINERY
Nelson, MO 65347

☆ Brut "Champagne"

MT. PLEASANT VINEYARDS
101 Webster, Augusta, MO 63332

☆ Seyval Blanc, Villard Noir (Private Reserve)

NEW MEXICO

Only Florida can claim an older wine-making history than New Mexico; its industry dates back to the early 1600s, but its future is modest at best.

The AVAs of New Mexico

MESILLA VALLEY AVA

Established: *18th March 1985*

An area that follows the Mesilla Valley along the Rio Grande River from an area just north of Las Cruces, New Mexico (where most of its vineyards are situated) to El Paso, Texas. Soils are alluvial, stratified, deep and well drained.

MIDDLE RIO GRANDE VALLEY AVA

Established: *2nd February 1988*

MIMBRES VALLEY AVA

Established: *23rd December 1985*

An area covering 2,577 hectares (995 square miles), which follows the Mimbres River southward from north of Mimbres to south of Columbus.

New Mexico wineries

ANDERSON VALLEY VINEYARDS
Albuquerque, NM 87107

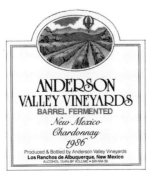

☆ Chardonnay, Chenin Blanc

LA VINA WINERY
Chamberino, NM 88027

☆ Zinfandel

NORTH CAROLINA

There are no AVAs established or planned for North Carolina as yet. The hot climate dictates that most wines are produced from the hardy, native Scuppernong. It produces large, cherry-like grapes that make an unusual wine.

BILTMORE ESTATE WINERY
One Biltmore Plaza,
Ashville, NC 28803

I have not tasted these wines, which are produced by Frenchman Philippe Jourdain, but have heard good reports of them.

OKLAHOMA

Prohibitive winery licence fees make this state unimportant in wine terms.

Oklahoma wineries

CIMMARRON CELLARS *
PETE SCHWARZ WINERY

SOUTH CAROLINA

Winemaking began here as long ago as 1764, but it has never really recovered from Prohibition.

South Carolina wineries

FOXWOOD WINE CELLARS
TENNER BROTHER INC
TRULUCK VINEYARDS *

TENNESSEE

Although Tennessee still has some "dry" counties, the state has relatively recently passed legislation easing the founding of farm wineries. Tiegs and Smoky Mountain wineries have a strong local following.

The AVA of Tennessee

See Mississippi Delta AVA, Mississippi.

Tennessee wineries

HIGHLAND MANOR WINERY *
LAUREL HILL VINEYARD *
SMOKY MOUNTAIN VINEYARD
TENNESSEE VALLEY WINERY *
TIEGS VINEYARDS

TEXAS

The Franciscan missions were making wines here at least 130 years before the first vines were grown in California and the first commercial Texan winery, Vel Verde, was established before the first Californian one, albeit by only two years, in 1881. I think the potential is still there.

The AVAs of Texas

See also Mesilla Valley AVA, New Mexico

BELL MOUNTAIN AVA

Established: *10th November 1986*

Located in Gillespie County, north of Fredericksburg, this AVA contains some 18 hectares (45 acres) of vines on the southern and southwestern slopes of Bell Mountain. The area is drier than the Pedernales Valley to the south and the Llano Valley to the north, and also cooler due to its elevation and its constant breezes. Its soils are non-calcareous, sandy-loam soils, with light, sandy-clay subsoil.

FREDERICKSBURG AVA

Established: *22nd December 1988*

Texas wineries

LLANO ESTACADO WINERY
Lubbock, TX 79413

This is the top-performing winery in Texas. Its wines are stylish and deserve to be well known on export markets.

☆ Chardonnay, Gewürztraminer, White Cabernet

Second label: Staked Plains

PHEASANT RIDGE WINERY
Lubbock, TX 79401

I hear good reports about this winery, although I have not tasted their wines.

SANCHEZ CREEK VINEYARDS
Weatherford, TX 76086

Under its founder, journalist Lyndol Hart, this winery developed a reputation for producing Rhône-style blends dominated by Grenache and Carignan. The winery was sold to Ron Weatherington in 1983.

☆ Ruby Cabernet

STAKED PLAINS
See Llano Estacado Winery.

WISCONSIN

A state that has a bigger reputation for its cherry, apple and other "wines" (not serious in any true wine sense) than for those made from grapes.

Wisconsin winery

WOLLERSHEIM WINERY INC
Prairie du Sac, WI 53578

This winery was built in 1858 by the Kehl family, from Nierstein in Germany. It was re-established in 1972 by Robert and Joann Wollersheim.

☆ Baco Noir, Seyval Blanc

Mexico

It was the Spanish who brought wine to Mexico, the oldest wine-producing country in the Americas. By 1521, just one year after invading Mexico, the conquistadors had planted vines and began making wine soon after, the very first in the entire North American continent.

IN 1524, THE GOVERNOR OF NEW SPAIN (MEXICO), Hernando Cortez, ordered all Spanish residents who had been granted land and given Indians for forced labour, annually to plant "one thousand vines per hundred Indians" for a period of five years. By 1595 the country was almost self-sufficient in wine, and shipments of domestic Spanish wine had dwindled to such an extent that producers in the home country pressured Philip II into forbidding the planting of further vineyards in the New World.

The original "Tequila Sunrise"

When the Spanish encountered a strange, milky-white Aztec cactus wine called "pulque", they were not very impressed. In a bid to utilize the local product, however, they tried distilling it: the crystal-clear, colourless spirit that resulted was far more to their taste, and was named "tequila", after *Agave tequilana,* the variety of cactus used. Today tequila is one of Mexico's most important exports, and vast quantities of pulque are still produced and consumed by native Mexicans.

Modern Mexican wine

There are nearly 60,000 hectares (148,300 acres) of vines in Mexico, but almost 40 per cent produce table grapes or raisins, and the bulk wines are distilled and used for the manufacture of brandy. Of the average annual harvest of 638,000 tons of grapes, just six per cent ends up as wine, giving a typical production of approximately 225,000 hectolitres (2.5 million cases).

It was not long ago that the best grape wines tasted little better than pulque, but a combination of foreign investment and local demand for more sophisticated products has meant significant improvements. Many international oenologists are very optimistic about Mexico's potential as a producer of good-quality wines.

FACTORS AFFECTING TASTE AND QUALITY

 Location
Eight of the country's states grow grapes, from Baja California in the north to San Juan del Rio, just north of Mexico City in the south.

Climate
Half of Mexico lies south of the Tropic of Cancer, but altitude moderates the temperature of the vineyards. Most are situated on the high central plateau and some are cooled by the nearby ocean. Principal problems include extreme fluctuation of day and night temperatures, and the fact that most areas have either too little or too much moisture. The dry areas often lack adequate sources of water for irrigation, and the wet districts suffer from too much rain during the growing season.

Aspect
In the states of Aguascalientes, Querétaro and Zacatecas, vines are grown on flat plateau lands and the sides of small valleys, at altitudes of 1,600 metres (5,300 ft), rising to nearly 2,100 metres (7,000 ft) in Zacatecas State. In Baja California, vines are located in valley and desert areas at much lower heights of 100-335 metres (330 -1,100 ft).

 Soil
The soils of Mexico can be divided into two wide-ranging categories: slope or valley soils are thin and low in fertility, while plains soils are of variable depth and fertility. In the Baja California, the soils range from a poor, alkaline sandy soil in Mexicali, to a thin spread of volcanic soil intermixed with gravel, sand and limestone to provide excellent drainage. In Sonora, the soils of Caborca are similar to those found in Mexicali, but those in Hermosillo are very silty and of alluvial origin. The high plains of Zacatecas have mostly volcanic and silty-clay soils. In the Aguascalientes, the soil in both valley and plains is of a scarce depth with a thin covering of calcium. The volcanic, calcareous sandy-clay soil in Querétaro has a good depth and drainage and is slightly alkaline, while in La Laguna the silty-sandy alluvium is very alkaline.

Viticulture and vinification
Irrigation is widely practised in dry areas such as Baja California and Zacatecas. Most wineries are relatively new and staffed by highly trained oenologists.

Grape varieties
Barbera, Bola dulce, Cabernet sauvignon, Cardinal, Carignan, Chenin blanc, French colombard, Grenache, Malaga, Malbec, Merlot, Mission, Muscat, Nebbiolo, Palomino, Perlette, Petite sirah, Rosa del Perú, Ruby cabernet, Sauvignon blanc, Trebbiano, Valdepeñas, Zinfandel

HOW TO READ MEXICAN WINE LABELS

Many terms found on Mexican wine labels are the same as, or similar to, those seen on Spanish labels, *see* How to read Spanish wine labels, p.268. Common terms are:

Vino tinto Red wine

Vino blanco White wine

Variedad Grape variety

Contenido neto Contents

Hecho en Mexico Made in Mexico

Cosechas Seleccionadas Special blend

Viña Vineyard

Espumoso Sparkling

Seco, Extra Seco Dry, extra dry

Vino de Mesa Table wine

Bodega Winery

Pedro Domecq Winery, above
This firm produces a variety of red, white and rosé wines at its modern winery where temperature-controlled stainless-steel fermentation vats are used.

Vineyards, Calafia Valley, Baja California, above
Some 13 different grapes are grown by Domecq in this valley where the soil is of volcanic origin with some gravel, sand and limestone providing excellent drainage.

AREAS UNDER VINE IN MEXICO

State	Hectares	(Acres)
Sonora	26,200	(64,700)
Querétaro	2,500	(6,100)
Aguascalientes	6,500	(16,000)
Durango	1,700	(4,200)
Coahuila	4,300	(10,600)
Zacatecas	5,800	(14,300)
Baja California Norte	7,500	(18,500)
Chihuahua	3,500	(8,600)
Total	58,000	(143,000)

Harvest in the Calafia Valley *Pedro Domecq harvests all its grapes by hand.*

Major wineries of Mexico

ALAMO
See Vinicola de Aguascalientes.

BODEGAS DE SANTO TOMÁS, S.A.
Lago Alberio No. 424, Col. Anáhuac, Delegación Miguel Hidalgo, C.P. 11320

Established: *1888*
Wines: *Cabernet Sauvignon, Carignan, Chardonnay, Chenin Blanc, Grenache, Pinot Noir*

Founded next to the ruins of the Santo Tomás Mission by an Italian goldminer, who sold it to General Rodriguez in 1920. Rodriguez went on to become President of Mexico and, in 1962, hired Dimitri Tchelistcheff, son of the legendary André Tchelistcheff, doyen of the Napa Valley. The winery now belongs to an importer in Mexico City, Elias Pando, but Tchelistcheff is still the winemaker. The firm is gradually increasing the range and size of its classic European vines, and its finest wines from these grapes are some of the best in the country.

CASA MADERO
Amberes No. 4 P.H., Delegación Cuauhtémoc, C.P. 06600

Established: *1626*
Wines: *"San Lorenzo", "Varietales Madero"*

This is the second-oldest winery on the American continent, comprising 400 hectares (1,000 acres) of vineyards.

CASA MARTELL
Av. Río Churubusco No. 213, Col. Granjas México

Wines: *"Clos San José", "Chatillón", "Martell" Cabernet Sauvignon, "Martell Chatillón", "Domaine San José", "Hammerhaus"*

Owned and run by the Martell Cognac firm of France.

CASA PEDRO DOMECQ
Av. Mexico No. 337, Col. del Carmen Coyoacán, C.P. 04100

Wines: *"Chateau Domecq", Cabernet Sauvignon "X-A", Zinfandel "X-A", Cariñan "X-A", Blanc de Blancs "X-A", Chenin Blanc "X-A", Riesling "X-A", Calafia", "Los Reyes", "Padre Kino", "Fray Junípero"*

The only winery in Mexico that has been purpose-built exclusively to make quality wines from premium varietals. The famous Sherry house of Domecq is considered Mexico's finest wine-producer.

CAVAS DE SAN JUAN (VINOS HIDALGO)
Profesora Eulalia Guzmán No. 185, Col. Atlampa, Delegación Cuauhtémoc, C.P. 06450

Wines: *"Hidalgo", "San Isidro", Blanc de Blancs, Riesling Traminer, Cabernet Sauvignon, Pinot Noir*

The mile-high Cavas de San Juan is the highest winery in Mexico and owns some 250 hectares (625 acres) of vines.

L.A. CETTO
Antonio M. Rivera No. 25, Col. Industrial Tlanepantla, C.P. 54030, Tlanepantla

Wines: *Fumé Blanc, Cabernet Sauvignon, Petite Sirah, Zinfandel, Chenin Blanc, Riesling*

DISTRIBUIDORA VALLE REDONDO
Serapio Rendón No. 125, 1er. piso, Col. San Rafael, Delegación Cuauhtémoc, C.P. 06470

ANTONIO FERNANDEZ Y CIA
Av. Progreso No. 190, Col. Industrial Tlanepantla, C.P. 54030 Tlanepantla

Wines: *"Etiqueta de Oro" Semillón, "Etiqueta de Oro" Riesling, "Etiqueta de Oro" Chenin Blanc, "Etiqueta de Oro" Rubí Cabernet, "Etiqueta de Oro" Sauvignon Blanc, "Etiqueta de Oro" Sylvaner*

FORMEX IBARRA
Poniente 146 No. 658, Col. Industrial

Vallejo, Delegación Azcapotzalco, C.P. 02300

Wines: *"Urbinón"*

MARQUÉS DE AGUAYO
Ramos Arizpe No. 195, Hacienda el Rosario, Parras, Coahuila

Established: *1593*

The oldest winery in the entire American continent, it is now solely engaged in the distillation of brandy.

PINSON HNOS.
Camino del Desierto de los Leones No. 4152, Col. San Angel Inn, Delegación Alvaro Obregón, C.P. 01060

Wines: *"Don Eugenio", "Alcadle", "Foylenmilch", "Marisquero", Cabernet, Barbera, Chenin Blanc, "Sauternes", Blanc de Blancs*

PRODUCTOS DE UVA
Antonio M. Rivera No. 25, Tlanepantla

Wines: *"Marqués del Valle", "Castillo del Rhin", "Castillo de Aranjuez", "Bacco Nebbiolo", "Bacco Moscato", "Bacco Cold-Duck", "Chambrulé" Brut, "Chambrulé" Blanc de Blancs, "Chambrulé" Reserva Limitada*

VINICOLA DE AGUASCALIENTES
Avenue Copilco No. 164, Col. Óxtopulco

Wines: *"Champ d'Or"*
Second label: *Alamo*

The largest wine firm in Mexico and proprietors of 10 per cent of all the vineyards in the country. Most of the production is brandy. This company also owns Vinicola del Vergel.

VINICOLA DEL VERGEL
Calle San Luis Tlatilco No. 19, Parque Industrial Naucalpan

Wines: *"Mesón de la Hacienda", "Viña Santiago", "Vergel", "Verdizo", "Noblejo"*

Canada

Canada's wine industry is at a turning point: up until now it has been heavily dependent on hybrids and hampered by archaic liquor laws and its misleading use of names like "Chablis" and "Champagne". This has resulted in a lack of identity, unity and direction, but a small number of highly motivated, quality-conscious winemakers are trying seriously to ensure its future.

WINE HAS BEEN MADE COMMERCIALLY in Canada since at lease 1860. For the first hundred years, Canadian palates preferred the sweet styles produced by the native *labrusca* grape varieties. Canada endured prohibition, as did America, but for 11 years, not 13. Both still have isolated dry areas, but, unlike America, Canada's experience has lingered on in the form of a state liquor control system based on the monopoly system operated in Sweden.

CANADA'S LIQUOR CONTROL BOARDS

The Provincial Liquor Boards determine what may be sold and at what price. They also control the import of all alcoholic drinks. This form of protectionism not only affects foreign competition, it also restricts the development and progress of domestic Canadian wine. For even Canadian wine may not be sold without the appropriate Liquor Board's permission. Such draconian measures are unhelpful; they put Canada's domestic wine industry a giant step behind America's. Like America, Canada is handicapped by hiding behind so-called "generic" names (although "Champagne" is banned in the province of Quebec), thereby preventing any hope of creating a true national identity. Because of the variation in their regulations, Canada's Liquor Boards divide what should be one unified industry, pitching provinces against each other, and presenting a poor image to potential export markets. This is a hard cross to bear for those who are striving to prove that Canada can produce quality wines.

The number of wines that may be sold varies greatly from province to province, but even the largest range is a drop in the ocean compared with the many tens of thousands of wines available in free markets such as America and Great Britain. In France, it is possible to purchase 10,000 different Bordeaux wines alone. Ironically, the "Statement of Purpose" of the Liquor Control Board of Ontario (a typical example) declares that *"The LCBO is committed to providing the people of this province with a wide variety of quality products from around the world."*

ONTARIO GRAPE EVOLUTION 1976 – 1986

Grape Variety	1976 Hectares (acres)	1981 Hectares (acres)	1986 Hectares (acres)
Aligoté	–	6 (15)	2 (6)
Chardonnay	34 (83)	79 (195)	123 (304)
Gamay	25 (61)	27 (67)	31 (77)
Gewürztraminer	–	–	23 (57)
Johannisberg riesling	17 (41)	139 (344)	256 (634)
Pinot noir	–	–	17 (41)
(Major *Labrusca* varieties)			
Concord	3,678 (9,088)	2,800 (6,918)	2,412 (5,960)
Niagara	1,186 (2,931)	756 (1,868)	626 (1,548)
Others (mostly hybrids)	4,195 (10,367)	5,039 (12,452)	5,754 (14,219)
Total	9,134 (22,571)	8,846 (21,859)	9,245 (22,846)

CANADA

The southern Niagara district is the most important area of Canada's chief wine-producing province of Ontario, climatically influenced to a large extent by Lake Erie. Other provinces that produce pleasant wines are British Columbia, Alberta, Nova Scotia and Quebec.

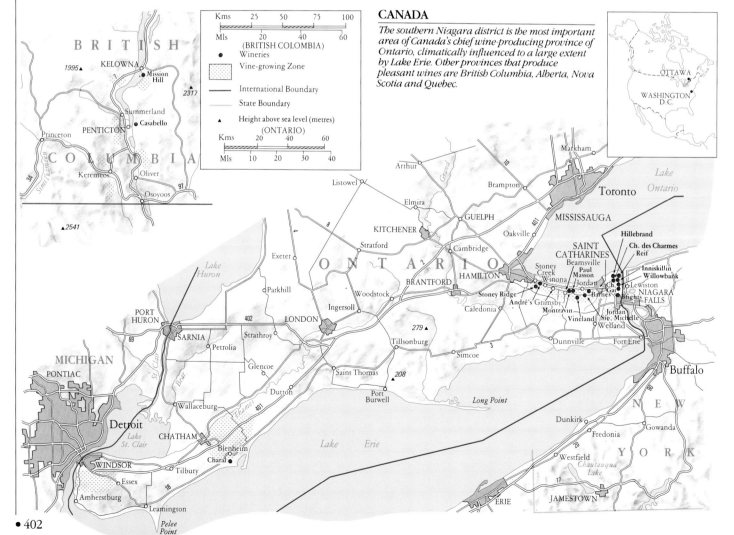

CANADA'S QUALITY POTENTIAL

The evolution of Canada's wine industry is no different to that of America's Atlantic Northeast, to which Ontario's vineyards are geographically appended. Both industries have been built on native *labrusca* wines, both took to hybrids after Prohibition, and both are now having isolated successes with classic *vinifera* vines. But in terms of size and success, Canada's wine industry lags far behind. Although America still has, in general, a long way to go, it is encouraged and led by the runaway success of California. Canada has no California to show the way, which is why it is only potentially on a par with America's Atlantic Northeast.

This is Canada's big disadvantage. I believe that the only solution for survival is to dismantle the archaic Liquor laws. It would not, however, be necessary to disband the Boards themselves; they are well equipped to play numerous policing and promotional roles. These could include ensuring the authenticity of domestic and foreign products; helping to combat fraud; establishing a much-needed appellation system and developing education and marketing campaigns to inform the consumer and improve exports.

By removing the provincial listing procedure, the Canadian market would be exposed not simply to more imported wines, but to all shades of the best and the worst the world has to offer. For the first time this would give Canadians a true price-quality yardstick against which they could judge their own domestically produced wines. And with laws to encourage small wine farm operations, the range and quality of wines would increase significantly.

FACTORS AFFECTING TASTE AND QUALITY

Location
The chief areas are the Niagara Peninsula of Ontario in the east and the Okanagan Valley of British Columbia some 3,218 kilometres (2,000 miles) away, west of the Rocky Mountains. Vines also grow in Alberta and Nova Scotia.

Climate
Europeans tend to imagine Canada as the cold north, but 85 per cent of Canada's vines are grown in Ontario on the same latitude as the dusty southern French vineyards of Provence and the Chianti hills of Tuscany in central Italy. The microclimate of Ontario is the vital factor here; with the temperature-moderating influence of Lakes Erie and Ontario, and the wind-break effect of the Niagara Escarpment, the vines are protected from winter wind and frost damage.

The Okanagan Valley of British Columbia is on a more northerly latitude, some 49° to 50°N and approximately in line with Champagne and the Rheingau, but the area is technically a desert, with as little as 15 centimetres (six ins) of rain in the south. The summers are consistent, with fierce daytime heat that rapidly builds up the grape sugars, followed by cold nights that allow the grapes to retain high acid levels. The glacial Okanagan lake provides a moderating effect, but winter quickly sets in and grapes do not develop beyond mid-October.

Aspect
The vines in both Ontario and British Columbia are mostly grown on lakeside slopes. Those in Ontario are sheltered by the Niagara Escarpment, and the better grape varieties are grown on the steep north-facing slopes.

Soil
Ontario soils cover a wide range from sandy loams to gravel and sand.

Viticulture and vinification
Methods range from the traditional to the use of the latest advances in vinous technology. There are few quality or authenticity regulations in Canada, although at least 80 per cent of the grapes used must be from the province indicated on the label (85 per cent in the case of Ontario). The balance is often made up from Californian grapes, because the minimum government-guaranteed price for Canadian-grown grapes is more than three times the cost of buying Californian grapes and transporting them to Canada in refrigerated trucks as grapes, juice or wine.

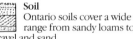
Grape varieties
Agawam, Alden, Aligoté, Aurore, Auxerrois, Baco noir, Buffalo, Cabernet franc, Cabernet sauvignon, Canada muscat, Catawba, Chambourcin, Chancellor, Chardonnay, Chasselas Chelois, Chenin blanc, Commandant, Concord, De Chaunac, Delaware, Dutchess, Elvira, Fredonia, Gamay, Gewürztraminer, Johannisberg riesling, Kerner, Léon Millot, Maréchal Foch, Merlot, New York muscat, Niagara, Okanagan riesling, Patricia, Petite sirah, Pinot blanc, Pinot gris, Pinot noir, President, Rosette, Rougeon, Seyval blanc, Siegfried rebe, Seyve villard, Van Buren, Vee blanc, Veeport, Ventura, Verdelet, Vidal blanc, Villard noir, Vincent, Zinfandel

ONTARIO – THE MOST IMPORTANT WINE REGION

Accounting for approximately 85 per cent of the country's vines and wines, Ontario is of paramount importance; how it develops will determine the future evolution of Canadian wine. Native *labrusca* vines (mostly Concord, plus Agawam, Alden, Buffalo, Catawba, Delaware, Elvira, Niagara and President) are generally on the decline, although they still occupy as much as 50 per cent of the vineyards and the cultivation of one variety, Elvira, is actually growing. *Labrusca* remains important for sparkling and dessert wine production and one variety, Concord, still accounts for more than 20 per cent of all the vines cultivated.

The hybrid situation is polarizing, with three varieties representing the most important growth area between 1981 and 1986: Vidal blanc increased by 470 per cent, Seyve villard by 350 per cent and Vee blanc by 250 per cent. Baco noir, New York muscat, Seyval blanc, Ventura and Villard noir have all witnessed increases of between 15 and 40 per cent, but Chelois, Himrod, Van Buren, Veeport and Verdelet are all on a downward trend.

The growth of *vinifera* vines

The first *vinifera* vines introduced into Canada – Chardonnay, Johannisberg riesling and Pinot noir – were planted at Brights Ontario vineyard in 1946 by a French chemist called Adhemar de Chaunac. Prior to 1972, there were insufficient *vinifera* vines for official statistical records They are now increasing steadily, but because they are responsible for most of the best wines and all of the newest, most exciting ones, the rate of this increase has often been exaggerated. It would be misleading to state their increase in percentage terms because they start from such a low base, therefore a ten-year evolution of surface area planted is given in the chart, *see* p.402. Those varieties not included in the chart (Auxerrois, Cabernet sauvignon, Chasselas, Chenin blanc, Merlot, Petite sirah, Pinot blanc, Pinot gris and Zinfandel) are cultivated in parcels too tiny to warrant inclusion in the official statistics.

Crushing grapes, Niagara, right
Vinification methods vary hugely in Canada's wine-producing districts. Vinifera grape varieties are still less cultivated than Labrusca, but are happily on the increase.

Night harvest, Inniskillin Wines, below
This tractor is being used to harvest grapes for this Niagara winery's "Icewine". It is unique in that the six other producers of this style all call their product "Eiswein".

THE NIAGARA WINE DISTRICT OF ONTARIO

Ontario would benefit from an appellation system in Niagara, where 94 per cent of its vines grow. The following is a rough breakdown of the district into seven identifiable areas and an outline of their basic geography, topography and climate.

Lake Ontario is the major influence, storing massive amounts of heat and releasing it when the surrounding land and air temperature drops below its own. Cold air drains away where there are slopes and accumulates on flat ground and in depressions, making frost and winter-cold damage more likely.

Lakeshore

Best grape varieties: *Chardonnay, Gamay, Gewürztraminer, Johannisberg riesling, Pinot noir, Seyval blanc, Seyve villard, Vidal blanc, Villard noir*

The shoreline vineyards are found in a strip of land some 40 kilometres (25 miles) long. As warm air rises from the ground, cool air is drawn in from over the lake, which changes temperature very slowly. This moderating lake breeze retards the growing season in spring and mid-summer. In winter, the reverse happens, with warmth convected from the lake to the land. This protects the shoreline vineyards from the harshest effects of the bitterly cold Ontario winters and permits the growing of *vinifera* varieties.

Flat plain between lakeshore and escarpment

Best grape varieties: *Baco noir, De Chaunac, Maréchal Foch, Ventura*

This is the largest geographical sector of Niagara; it stretches for some 32 kilometres (20 miles) from its widest width of eight kilometres (five miles) by the Niagara River, tapering to a thin wedge at Beamsville Spa. Cold air tends to settle here, making the vineyards prone to winter cold and spring frosts, so that the most successful varieties are quite hardy and early-maturing.

Base of escarpment and steep slopes east of St. Catharines

Best grape varieties: *Baco noir, De Chaunac, Maréchal Foch, Seyval blanc, Seyve villard, Vidal blanc, Villard noir*

Once the beach of a glacial lake, these slopes are easy enough to cultivate with machinery and pose no erosion problems, yet the degree of steepness is sufficient on clear, chilly nights to encourage cold air to drain onto the flat plain beneath, where it accumulates. This is the most intensively cultivated area.

Steep north-facing escarpment slopes in western Niagara

Best grape varieties: *Chardonnay, Gamay, Gewürztraminer, Johannisberg riesling, Pinot noir, Seyval blanc, Seyve villard, Vidal blanc, Villard noir*

These slopes are only found in the sector west of St. Catharines. Some areas are too steep to cultivate, but slopes of four to ten per cent incline between Beamsville and Rockway are prime sites for high-quality *vinifera* varieties. There is good air-drainage and summer temperatures are warmer than those in the Lakeshore vineyards.

Gentle slopes above the escarpment

Best grape varieties: *De Chaunac, Maréchal Foch, Seyval blanc, Seyve villard, Ventura, Vidal blanc, Villard noir*

This area extends along the ridge of the escarpment and includes all the highest points. It is generally suitable for vines, but the risk of cold-damage is higher than in the four preceding zones.

Flat, rolling land south of escarpment

High cold-damage risk; only the hardiest hybrids and native vines are suitable, none of which make anything worth drinking.

Fonthill kame

This is a large gravel and sand hill in the middle of the flat lands south of the escarpment; only "foxy" native varieties can survive.

Major wineries of Canada

Note: only Canadian wines are discussed or recommended below, although many wineries blend and sell wines made entirely, or in part, from imported grapes, juice or concentrate. Official records list the following import sources in order of importance in 1986: USA, Chile, Spain, Italy, Mexico, South Africa and others. Some Canadian producers even import from Crete!

ALBERTA

ANDREW WOLF WINE CELLARS
Cochrane

BRITISH COLUMBIA

ANDRES WINES
Port Moody
See Andres Wines (Ontario).

BRIGHTS HOUSE OF WINE
Oliver
See Brights Wines (Ontario).

CALONA WINES LTD
1125 Richter Street,
Kelowna, V1Y 2K6

Established: *1932*

This winery's semi-sweet German-style Schloss Laderheim became Canada's best-selling wine in 1981. It occasionally produces good premium varietal under the "Winemaster's Selection" label.

☆ Maréchal Foch, Chenin Blanc

EAGLE RIDGE
See Andres Wines (Ontario).

GRAY MONK CELLARS
Okanagan Centre

Vineyards: *9.5 ha (24 acres) of Auxerrois, Gewürztraminer, Johannisberg riesling, Kerner and Pinot gris*
Established: *vineyard in 1972, winery in 1982*

This small, improving, unpretentious winery strives for finesse in its wines.

☆ Pinot Auxerrois (Kabinett)

JORDAN & STE.-MICHELLE CELLARS
See Jordan & Ste.-Michelle Cellars (Ontario).

PACIFIC COAST CELLARS
See Andres Wines (Ontario).

Other wineries

CASABELLO WINES (Labatt's)
DIVINO
GEHRINGER BROTHERS
MISSION HILL VINEYARDS
ST.-CLARE WINES
SUMAC RIDGE ESTATE WINERY
UNIACKE ESTATE WINES

NOVA SCOTIA

ANDRES WINES (ATLANTIC)
See Andres Wines (Ontario).

GRANDE PRÉ WINES
Grand Pré

Vineyards: *10 ha (25 acres) of some 65 varieties, but mostly Maréchal Foch, Michurnitz and Severnyi*

Roger Dial, the owner and winemaker, called his best wine "Cuvée d'Amur" after the Amur River that forms the Sino-Siberian frontier. The reason is that the wine is made from Michurnitz, a hardy grape of the species *Vitis amurensis*. It is also a play on the word "amour".

☆ "Cuvée d'Amur"

ONTARIO

ANDRES WINES
Winona, L0R 2L0

Vineyards: *121 ha (300 acres)*
Established: *1961 (in British Columbia)*

This is the winery that introduced Canada to the delights of "Baby Duck", a popular and much-imitated sweet pink or red fizzy Labrusca wine. The name is derived from the German "Kalte Enke" (Cold Duck), which was made from the dregs of both red and white wines, to which some Sekt was added to liven it up. The company has however, a large range of more serious wines and is upgrading its image. Andres still operates its original winery in Port Moody and owns a winery in

Nova Scotia. It produces Ontario and British Colombia wines.

☆ "Domaine d'Or", Vidal

Second labels: "Eagle Ridge", "Pacific Coast Cellars"

BARNES WINES
St Catharines, L2R 6S4

Established: *1873*

Originally called The Ontario Grape Growing and Wine Manufacturing Company, Barnes is Canada's oldest continuously run winery. It was purchased by Reckitt & Colman in 1973, then sold in 1981 to a private company called Keewhit, who in turn sold a 49 per cent holding to Gilbeys, a subsidiary of IDV.

☆ Gewürztraminer, Johannisberg Riesling "Limited Edition"

BRIGHTS WINES
4887 Dorchester Road,
Niagara Falls, L2E 6V4

Vineyards: *486 ha (1,200 acres)*
Established: *1874*

This winery produced the first Canadian bottle-fermented sparkling wine, "Brights President", in 1949 and the first Canadian *vinifera* varietal (a Chardonnay) in 1956. It also owns Brights Wines in British Columbia and Les Vins Brights in Quebec. In 1986 it purchased Jordan & Ste.-Michelle Cellars.

☆ Baco Noir, Cabernet Sauvignon, "Entre-Lacs Dry White", Pinot "Champagne"

CHÂTEAU DES CHARMES
St. Davids, L0S 1P0

Vineyards: *28 ha (68 acres)*
(vinifera *only*)
Established: *1978*

Considered by many to be the finest winery in the country, Château des Charmes produces wines that are the nearest to the French style. Its black label denotes that the wine comes from the Château des Charmes estate while its white label indicates that the wine is a blend or made from bought in grapes. Winemaker Paul Bosc has been described by Leon Adams, the doyen of American wine writers, as "the best winemaker in Canada".

☆ Chardonnay (black label), "Sentinel Blanc"

CHATEAU-GAI WINES
2625 Stanley Avenue,
Niagara Falls, L2E 6T8

Established: *1941*

Formerly known for its sparkling wines, which prompted court action by the French government in 1967, because of the use of the term "Champagne". The best products from this winery were limited editions of *vinifera* varietals made by Paul Bosc before he established Château des Charmes. It is now known principally for its wine and fruit coolers.

COLIO WINES
Harrow, Essex County

Vineyards: *121 ha (300 acres)*
Established: *1980*

This winery was founded by a group of Italian businessmen who wanted to import Italian wines from their twin-town of Udine in the Friuli-Venezia Giulia, but found it easier to build a winery and make their own.

☆ "Riserva Bianco Secco", Villard Noir

HILLEBRAND ESTATES WINES
Niagara-on-the-Lake, L0S 1J0

Vineyards: *14 ha (35 acres) of Chardonnay, Gewürztraminer, Johannisberg riesling, Kerner, Morio muscat, Müller-Thurgau, Baco noir and Seyval blanc*
Established: *1979*

Initially called Newark (the original name of Niagara-on-the-Lake), the title of this winery changed when it was purchased by Scholl & Hillebrand of Rüdesheim in 1983. Since then the emphasis of style has moved from dry French to off-dry German wines, and Müller-Thurgau and Kerner wines have been added to the vineyard.

☆ Newark Gewürztraminer, "Schloss Hillebrand", Vidal

INNISKILLIN WINES
Niagara-on-the-Lake, L0S 1J0

Vineyards: *30 ha (74 acres) of Chardonnay, Gewürztraminer, Johannisberg riesling, Gamay, Pinot noir, Vidal, De Chaunac, Chancellor and Zweigeltrebe*
Established: *1974*

The winery is co-owned by Don Ziraldo, (an agronomist and one of Canada's greatest wine publicists) and the winemaker, Karl Kaiser, is a highly respected oenologist, whose recent introduction of Icewine has attracted

a lot of excited comment. Inniskillin's best wines are often sold under its "Limited Edition" label.

☆ Cabernet Sauvignon, Chardonnay Blanc de Blancs Brut, Chardonnay "Reserve", Maréchal Foch, Pinot Noir, Vidal (especially Late Harvest *Beerenauslese* and Icewine from the Brae Burn Estate)

JORDAN & STE.-MICHELLE CELLARS
120 Ridley Road,
St Catharines, L2R 7E3

Vineyards: *65 ha (160 acres)*

A bewildering history of takeovers provides as many as seven different foundation dates for this winery and a confusing cacophony of continuously changing company names. The oldest date on record is 1870, when an apple-drying business was set up by Clark Snure and, eventually, two wineries – Jordan and Ste.-Michelle – were merged. They then took over the Growers' Wine Company in Surrey, British Columbia. The result is one of the largest wineries in Canada, producing mostly inexpensive hybrid blends, although better-quality varietals are promised from its experimental vineyards.

LONDON WINERY
560 Wharncliffe Road South,
London, N6J 2N5

Established: *1925*

Founded by two brothers from Nassau in the Bahamas, who began making wine for medicinal purposes during Prohibition. They cleverly built up stocks of mature wine in readiness for the Repeal they knew would come.

☆ Cuvée Supérieur (red)

MONTRAVIN CELLARS
1233 Ontario Street,
Beamsville, L0R 1B0

Established: *1973*

Hungarian-born Karl Podamer gained his sparkling wine skills in Champagne prior to emigrating to Canada. Originally called Podamer Champagne Cellars, the company changed its name in 1983, when it expanded into the still wine market, but sparkling wine is Podamer's forte. His Chardonnay Brut Blanc de Blancs is one of Canada's best.

☆ Brut Blanc de Blancs

PELEE ISLAND VINEYARDS & WINERY
Kingsville

Vineyards: *40 ha (99 acres) of Chardonnay, Gewürztraminer, Johannisberg riesling and Pinot noir*
Established: *1980*

A unique property with vineyards on an island in Lake Erie, Canada's most southerly point.

☆ Riesling, Scheurebe

REIF WINERY INC
Niagara Parkway,
Niagara-on-the-Lake, L0S 1J0

Vineyards: *53 ha (130 acres)*
Established: *1983*

Entirely estate-bottled wines using only the best 25 per cent of grapes.

☆ Riesling

WILLOWBANK ESTATE WINES
15 Henegan Road, Virgil,
Niagara-on-the-Lake, L0S 1T0

Vineyards: *5 ha (12.5 acres) of Chardonnay and Johannisberg riesling*

A very modern white-wine specialist.

Other wineries

CAVE SPRING
CHARAL WINERY & VINEYARDS
CULOTTA
KONZELMANN
PAUL MASSON WINERY LTD
STONEY RIDGE CELLARS
VINELAND ESTATES

QUEBEC

LES VINS ANDRES DU QUEBEC LTEE
See Andres Wines (Ontario).

LES VINS BRIGHTS
See Brights Wines (Ontario).

Other wineries

LES ENTREPRISES VERDI
JULAC INC
LUBEC INC
LA MAISON SECRESTAT LTEE
LES VIGNOBLES CHANTECLER
LES VIGNOBLES DU QUEBEC
VIN GELOSO INC
LES VINS LA SALLE (Brights)
LES VINS CORELLI

South America

The Spanish introduced viticulture to the Americas in Mexico in 1521 and it spread through the activities of the conquistadors who opened up new areas, and the missions who followed them. Vineyards were established in Chile in 1548, Argentina in 1551 and Peru in 1566. There is little evidence to suggest that winemaking began in Uruguay before the 1870s; records mention it occurring in Brazil at about the same time.

THE BRIEF HISTORY ABOVE SHOULD NOT mislead the reader into believing that the conquistadors were concerned only with the spread of Spanish viticulture. They were essentially in South America to plunder gold for Ferdinand of Spain, and when the Indians grew bored of the coloured glass beads traded for their treasures, they took what they wanted by more direct and brutal methods. In response, the Indians poured molten gold down the throats of captured conquistadors, which no doubt quenched the Spanish thirst for the metal, but also served as a sardonic retort to the Christian missionaries who had forced them to drink wine as part of the Sacrament.

BRAZIL

Brazil is large enough to swallow up Western Europe twice, with room left over to plant the equivalent of Europe's entire vineyard area, not once, but several times. This country, which boasts ranches that are bigger than Belgium, has some 64,000 hectares (100 square miles) of vines. This is insignificant compared to Brazil's total size of 3.3 million square miles, but it is sufficient to make it the third-largest wine-growing country in South America.

By far the largest wine region is in the southernmost state of Rio Grande do Sul, bordering Uruguay. Within its Palomas district is Santana do Livramento, Brazil's newest and most promising wine area where vineyards on the Campanha Gaúcha – the vast Gaucho plainlands – are planted with more than 20 vinifera varieties,

while eight out of every ten vines in the rest of the country are labrusca. The vinifera vines include Cabernet sauvignon, Chardonnay, Johannisberg riesling, Merlot, Pinot noir, Sauvignon blanc, Sémillon, Trebbiano and Ugni blanc.

URUGUAY

Since commercial production began (rather belatedly for South America) in the 1870s, wine output has soared. The annual harvest of this country's 22,000 hectares (54,000 acres) is quoted variously as between five and 10 million cases. If the idea of Uruguayan wine is difficult to swallow for Europeans, it is not for the locals, who leave little left over for export. Uruguay's vineyards are located on rolling hills of volcanic origin spread across Montevideo, Canalones, San José, Florida, Soriano, Paysandú and along the River Plate in Maldonado. The most widespread vine is the Harriague, which is actually the Tannat of southwestern France, but acquired its name from Pascual Harriagues, one of Uruguay's nineteenth-century winegrowing pioneers. Cabernet sauvignon and an obscure variety called Vidiella are both significant varieties and others include Cabernet franc, Pinot noir, Merlot, Nebbiolo, Barbera, Sémillon, Sauvignon blanc, Grignolino, Lambrusco, Carignan, Johannisberg riesling and Pedro Ximénez.

PERU

In 1566 Francesco de Carabantes planted vines at Ica, making this one of South America's oldest winegrowing countries. Its 14,000 hectares (34,600 acres) of vines are mostly located in the provinces of Ica and Moquegua and production averages some 18,000 hectolitres (200,000 cases).

BOLIVIA

This country's 5,000 hectares (12,350 acres) of vines are grown around Sucre in the Chuquisaca region and La Paz at altitudes of between 1,600-2,400 metres (5,300-8,000 ft). The wine is mostly distilled into local Pisco brandy, with light table wines accounting for no more than 9,000 hectolitres (100,000 cases) annually. The quality is not good and exports are negligible or non-existent.

COLOMBIA

There are approximately 3,000 hectares (7,400 acres) of vines in Colombia, most of which are concentrated in three zones: Cauce Valley, Sierra Nevada de Santa Marta and Ocaña. of this total, 2,000 hectares (4,900 acres) are planted with every conceivable variety of table grape, although many wineries also utilize these for winemaking purposes. The country's most widely planted vine is Isabella, a labrusca variety that accounts for some 800 hectares (2,000 acres), and the remaining 200 hectares (500 acres) is comprised of Barbera, Müller-Thurgau, Muscat, Pinot noir, Pedro Ximénez, Johannisberg riesling and Sylvaner. These varieties are apparently on the increase, although it is almost impossible to pin down a pure Colombian-grown vinifera wine in the annual production of 198,000 hectolitres (2.2 million cases), because this production also includes "wines" made solely or in part from other fruits, plus grapes, juice and concentrate imported from

---

MAJOR WINERIES OF BRAZIL

COMPANHIA MONACO-VINHEDOS
São Paulo

Established: 1908

This is one of Brazil's oldest wineries active in the export market. Subsidiary labels are: "Alfama", "Felecien", "Fraubauen", "Kiedrich", "Renochard" and "Sommerlieder".

COMPANHIA VINICOLA RIOGRANDENSE
Caxias do Sul

Established: 1934

This company has specialized in vinifera wines since the 1930s. Wines sold under its "Granja União" label include Merlot, Saint Emilion, Moscatel Espumante and Riesling.

GEORGES AUBERT
Garibaldi

Established: 1915

A "Champagne" producer with brut, semi-sweet and rosé styles.

HEUBLEIN DO BRASIL
São Paulo

Established: 1960

One of Brazil's better wineries producing "Lejon", "Castel Chatelet", "Marjolet", "Castelet", Riesling and "Bratage" brut "Champagne".

PALOMAS
Santana do Livramento

Established: 1974

With 1,200 hectares (3,000 acres) of classic vinifera vines planted in Brazil's improving Livramento district, this lavish operation is spearheading a huge effort to set the country's wine industry on a quality footing. The range is vast, with numerous varietals produced in several styles. These are the best wines in Brazil.

VINICCIA ARMANDO PETERLONGO
São Paulo

Established: 1913

The pioneer producer of Brazilian "Champagne".

VINICOLA GARIBALDI
Garibaldi

Established: 1931

A cooperative producing Merlot, Sémillon, "Precioso", "Acquasantiera" "Machtliebewein", "Leichtwein" and "Raschiatti".

VINHOS SALTON
São Paulo

Established: 1910

A company specializing in low-alcohol wines.

MAJOR WINERIES OF COLOMBIA

Of the 112 wineries in Colombia, the following are the most important:

Bodegas Andaluzas	Grajales
Vinicola Andiña	Inverca
Bodegas Añejas	Martini & Rossi
Vinerias del Castillo	David & Eduardo Puyana
Cinzano	Rojas
Viños de la Corte	Bodegas Sevillanas
Divinos	Bodegas Venecians
Pedro Domecq Colombia	

SOUTH AMERICAN COUNTRIES: AREA UNDER VINE

Country	Hectares	(Acres)
Argentina	346,000	(855,000)
Chile	116,000	(287,000)
Brazil	64,000	(158,000)
Uruguay	22,000	(54,000)
Peru	14,000	(35,000)
Bolivia	5,000	(12,000)
Colombia	3,000	(7,000)
Paraguay	negligible	

other countries. David & Eduardo Puyana used to sell pure *vinifera* wine under its "Señorial" brand, but now uses the Isabella. Bodegas Añejas also used to use *vinifera* for its "Rioja", but no longer does. Grajales uses a blend of table and wine grapes, all of them *vinifera*, but produces no varietal wines. Around 10 per cent of the output is sparkling wine, 20 per cent is vermouth, 45 per cent is Moscatel, "Port" and "Madeira" and 25 per cent fruit-based "aperitifs".

PARAGUAY

Vines are cultivated under this country's sub-tropical climate, but the wine produced is considered less important to Paraguay's economy than palm cabbages and concentrated beef broth.

OTHER SOUTH AMERICAN WINERIES

There are no grape wines produced in Venezuela, Guyana, Surinam or French Guiana, all of which are far too close to the equator for any grape-bearing vine to survive. Grapes do not ripen under intense heat, and it is impossible to produce them on the equator, but there are always exceptions; in South America it is Ecuador, where a tiny patch of vines exists high in the mountains.

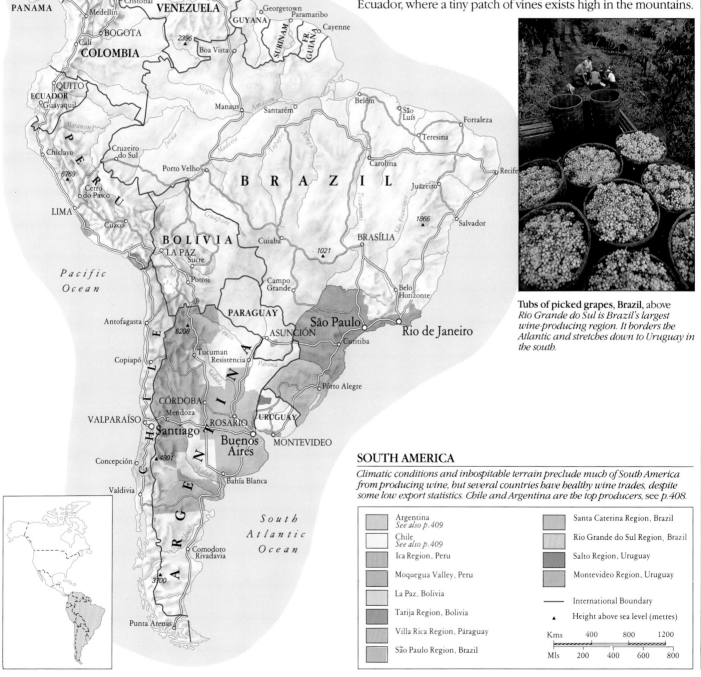

Tubs of picked grapes, Brazil, above
Rio Grande do Sul is Brazil's largest wine-producing region. It borders the Atlantic and stretches down to Uruguay in the south.

SOUTH AMERICA

Climatic conditions and inhospitable terrain preclude much of South America from producing wine, but several countries have healthy wine trades, despite some low export statistics. Chile and Argentina are the top producers, see p.408.

Argentina *See also p.409*		Santa Caterina Region, Brazil
Chile *See also p.409*		Rio Grande do Sul Region, Brazil
Ica Region, Peru		Salto Region, Uruguay
Moquegua Valley, Peru		Montevideo Region, Uruguay
La Paz, Bolivia		International Boundary
Tarija Region, Bolivia	▲	Height above sea level (metres)
Villa Rica Region, Paraguay		
São Paulo Region, Brazil		

Kms   400   800   1200

Mls   200   400   600   800

Chile and Argentina

While Chile is the showcase of South America's wine-producing countries, Argentina is its bottomless vat. Chile makes world-class Cabernet Sauvignon and a range of superior wines, and since 1989/1990 has also managed to produce world-class Chardonnay. Argentina should not be overlooked as a source of inexpensive, but well-made wines that are a joy to drink.

CHILE

THERE ARE 116,000 HECTARES (287,000 ACRES) of vines in Chile, some 60,000 of which are not irrigated. Approximately 95 per cent of Chile's production of 67 million cases comes from two major viticultural belts: the Central Valley belt (stretching from just north of Temuco to Copiapo and including the Southern, South-Central Valley, Central Valley and North-Central regions) and, between it and the Pacific Ocean, the much shorter, thinner, Secano belt (stretching from Concepcion to Valparaiso).

North-Central region

This region covers 4,125 hectares (10,190 acres) of vines within the vast provinces of Atacama and Coquimbo, where rainfall is virtually non-existent and viticulture is only possible with irrigation. The vines are found in isolated blocks, rather than in one contiguous section as is the case elsewhere, and the wines, which are high in alcohol and low in acidity, are mostly used for Pisco brandy.

Central Valley region

This is Chile's second-largest region, covering 37,150 hectares (91,800 acres) of vineyards, including those of Aconagua, the heart and soul of the country's wine industry. Rainfall varies between 30 centimetres (12 ins) in the north and 73 centimetres (29 ins) in the south. This region contains Chile's most famous viticultural area, the Maipo Valley, where very good red wines are produced. The general high quality of the region as a whole is indicated by the classic grapes that dominate its vineyards: Cabernet sauvignon, Cabernet franc, Malbec, Merlot, Petit verdot, Chardonnay, Sauvignon blanc and Riesling.

South-Central Valley region

Situated between the Southern and Central Valley regions, the South-Central Valley contains 6,650 hectares (16,500 acres) of vines. The Pais is the most commonly cultivated vine here. A native black variety, it is thought to be a derivative of the Mission grape that opened up the vineyards of California, and makes similarly ordinary, sometimes rather coarse, wine. There are small areas of Cabernet sauvignon, Sauvignon blanc and Sémillon that can, however, achieve a decent quality.

Southern region

This area is on the extreme limits of temperate cultivation and balanced wines of acceptable quality are hard to produce. There

---

HOW TO READ CHILEAN AND ARGENTINIAN WINE LABELS

Many terms seen on South American wine labels are the same as, or similar to, those found on Spanish labels. *See* How to read Spanish wine labels, p.268. This example is Chilean.

Brand name

Envasado en Origen
Estate-bottled, or bottled on the producer's premises. This is also seen as *Embotellado en Origen*.

Viñedos propios
The company has its own vineyards.

ENVASADO EN ORIGEN
Santa Carolina
VIÑEDOS PROPIOS
1981
RESERVA ESPECIAL
Cabernet Sauvignon
VALLE DEL MAIPO
VIÑEDO LOS TOROS
PRODUCIDO Y EMBOTELLADO POR VIÑA SANTA CAROLINA S.A. SANTIAGO-CHILE. GRADO ALCOHOLICO 12°G.L.
CONTENIDO NETO 0,75 L.

Contenido neto
In Chile, the volume is stated in ml (millilitres); in Argentina it is given in cubic centimetres (equivalent to millilitres).

Grado alcoholico
The alcoholic strength

Name and address of the producer
In this case it is Viña Santa Carolina SA of Santiago.

Other terms that may be on Chilean and Argentinian labels include:

Viña Vineyard

Industria Argentina Produce of Argentina

Producido y fraccionado por . . . Produced and bottled by . . .

Vino fino tinto
Literally "fine red wine". The *fino* is not controlled by law and has no official connotation. In Chile, wines may be labelled *"Gran Vino"* – "Grand" or "Great" wine; again, this means nothing in an official sense.

FACTORS AFFECTING TASTE AND QUALITY

 Location
In Chile vines are grown along 1,290 kilometres (800 miles) of Pacific coast and are most concentrated south of Santiago. In Argentina, vineyards are mostly situated in the provinces of Mendoza and St. Juan, to the east of the Andes foothills and due west of Buenos Aires.

Climate
Extremely variable conditions prevail in Chile, ranging from arid and extremely hot in the north to very wet in the south. The main wine area around Santiago is dry with 38 centimetres (15 ins) of rain per year, no spring frosts and almost continuous clear skies with bright sun. The proximity of the Andes, whose high peaks are snow-covered even in the summer, allows a massive air-drainage of cold air at night, enabling the grape acids to remain high. In the Central Valley, daytime temperatures of 30-35°C (86-95°F) are followed by night-time temperatures of 12-15°C (54-59°F).

In Argentina's intensively cultivated Mendoza district the climate is officially described as continental-semi-desertic, having even less rainfall than Chile, a mere 20-25 centimetres (eight to ten ins), although this is mercifully spread over the summer growing months, and temperatures ranging from 10°C (50°F) at night to 40°C (104°F) in the day.

 Aspect
In both countries most vines are grown on the flat coastal and valley plains extending into the foothills of the Andes. In Chile, the unirrigated hillside vineyards are found in the Central Zone, although irrigation is widely utilized in other parts of this country. In Argentina, by contrast, the hillside vineyards are usually levelled to a minimal slope to allow for more efficient use of water.

Soil
Vines are grown on a vast variety of soils in these two countries. The deeper limestone soils of some parts of Chile are one reason for the generally better quality of wines from this country. In Argentina the soils range from sandy to clay, with a predominance of deep, loose soils of alluvial and aeolian origin.

Viticulture and vinification
While Chile uses traditional methods for most of its wines and often uses Bordeaux techniques, Argentina relies more on bulk production methods. But traditional methods are also harnessed in Argentina for its increasing production of higher-grade premium varietals. Since the Chilean government's economic policy of 1974, modern equipment, stainless-steel vats and improved technology have been introduced into many of its wineries. Thanks to Miguel Torres Jnr., many of Chile's quality wine-producers are using cold-fermentation and other techniques and producing much fresher, fruitier white wines as a result.

 **Grape varieties**
Barbera, Bonarda, Cabernet franc, Cabernet sauvignon, Cereza, Chardonnay, Chenin blanc, Criolla, Ferral, Grenache, Grignolino, Johannisberg riesling, Lambrusco, Malbec, Malvasia, Merlot, Muscat, Nebbiolo, Pais, Palomino, Pedro Ximénez, Petit verdot, Pinot blanc, Pinot gris, Pinot noir, Refosco, Renano, Sangiovettoe, Sauvignon blanc, Sémillon, Sylvaner, Syrah, Tempranillo, Torrontes, Ugni blanc

Miguel Torres' vineyards, above
*These vines beside the Andes' foothills,
belong to Chile's top wine-producer.*

Bottling line, Los Roblos, below
*A winery in Curicó, an important
wine-producing province of Chile.*

are still over 8,000 hectares (20,000 acres) of vineyards, but these are generally on the decline.

Central Secano region

Some 9,000 hectares (22,000 acres) of unirrigated vineyards in the foothills of the coastal mountain range, it is parallel to the Central Valley region, which lies between it and the Andes, and has an annual rainfall in excess of 100 centimetres (40 ins). The major grape variety cultivated here is the Pais, but, unirrigated, it produces a slightly more characterful wine than it does in the South-Central Valley region, especially when grown in the Cauquenes area, which has a unique microclimate peculiarly suited to this variety.

South-Central Secano region

The southern continuation of the Secano viticultural belt, like the area to the north, comprises unirrigated hillside vineyards possessing a more than adequate annual rainfall of at least 100 centimetres (40 ins). Although geographically much smaller than the Central Secano region, it is more intensively cultivated, containing some 45,000 hectares (112,000 acres) – nearly 40 per cent of Chile's total viticultural area. Again the Pais dominates and, again, under non-irrigated conditions produces acceptable wines, but the real potential for this region lies in the cultivation of white grapes: Sauvignon blanc, Riesling and Muscat have all fared exceptionally well, albeit in relatively small quantities.

CHILE AND ARGENTINA

*South America's southernmost two large countries
are its best wine producers. Both come under the
influence of the Andes mountains; one of the factors
that has prevented the entry of phylloxera to Chile.*

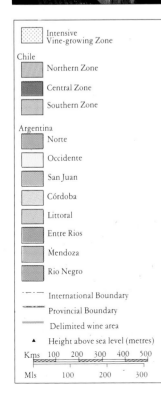

Intensive Vine-growing Zone	

Chile
- Northern Zone
- Central Zone
- Southern Zone

Argentina
- Norte
- Occidente
- San Juan
- Córdoba
- Littoral
- Entre Rios
- Mendoza
- Rio Negro

--- International Boundary
--- Provincial Boundary
--- Delimited wine area
▲ Height above sea level (metres)

Kms 100 200 300 400 500
Mls 100 200 300

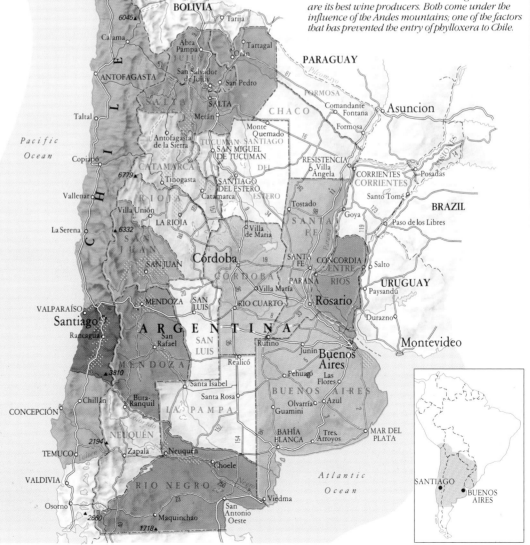

Pest-free vineyards

One of Chile's greatest viticultural assets is that its soils are phylloxera-free. This does not necessarily mean that the wines they produce are any better or, indeed, any different, but it does allow the vine to remain productive for 100 rather than 30 or 35 years. In Europe, California, Australia and elsewhere, a conscientious wine-grower has to stick rigidly to a continuous, costly and labour-intensive vineyard replanting programme. The Chilean wine-grower can thank Lady Luck and Silvestre Ochagáva for his good fortune, for, in 1851, long before phylloxera first appeared in France, he imported cuttings of Cabernet sauvignon, Merlot, Pinot noir, Sauvignon blanc, Sémillon and other classic vines of the purest stock. With no subsequent need to import vines, and with Chile's unique situation, bounded by the Pacific Ocean to the west, the Andes to the east, vast deserts to the north and the Antarctic to the south, the dreaded phylloxera has not found its way to any of this country's vineyards.

ARGENTINA

This country boasts 346,000 hectares (855,000 acres) of vines and is the fifth-largest wine country in the world. Scarce rainfall dictates that these vines depend on irrigation for survival. There is much rain and snow in the Andes, however, in the winter. The rain and melting snow is stored up in conveniently located hydraulic works and distributed by an irrigation system that is one of the most advanced of its kind in the world. In addition to this, a network of some 30,000 wells have been dug in order to tap the underground water resources.

THE WINES OF ARGENTINA

Mendoza

With 260,000 hectares (642,000 acres) of vines, this is the largest viticultural region in Argentina and accounts for more than two-thirds of its total wine production. There are more than 30,000 individual growers in this predominantly red-wine area, where Malbec is the most important variety, Cabernet sauvignon the best; others include Tempranillo, Pinot noir and Syrah. The white grapes, which cover some 40,000 hectares (99,000 acres), a minor per centage of Mendoza yet, significant in national terms, include Chardonnay, Chenin blanc, Johannisberg riesling and Muscat.

San Juan

Drier and hotter than Mendoza, this is essentially a white-grape region and much of its high-alcohol, low-acidity grapes are exported as grape concentrate.

Rio Negro

This region, which also includes Neuquén, is the most suitable for grape-growing, yet possesses less than five per cent of Argentina's vineyards. Now that this country has a more stable political climate, the Rio Negro could well attract much-needed foreign expertise, whether European, Antipodean or Californian, and prove to be the hub of Argentina's future fine-wine production.

La Rioja

Unlike its original Spanish counterpart, this is a ferociously hot region producing wines high in alcohol, low in acidity and, as often as not, oxidized in bottle.

Catamarca

A region with a very small area under vine, the grapes of which are mostly used for local brandy.

Salta

This region includes the Juyjuy province, but covers less than half of one per cent of all the vines in the country. The quality is, however, reasonable in Argentinian terms, and with an injection of foreign expertise, could prove to be a surprise fine-wine area.

Penaflor Winery at Maipu, near Mendoza, Argentina, *with the Andes providing a distant but impressive backdrop.*

Major wineries of Chile

JOSÉ CANEPA
Moneda 1040, Suite 1401, Santiago

Vineyards: *600 ha (1,500 acres) of Cabernet sauvignon, Malbec, Muscat, Sauvignon blanc and Sémillon*
Established: *1930*

A high-tech winery producing elegant wines with a perfectly clean line, great clarity of fruit and excellent finesse.

☆ "Gran Brindis" Cabernet, "Gran Brindis" Sémillon, Gran Vino Chilean Cabernet, Sauvignon Blanc

CONCHA Y TORO
Barros Errázuriz Nr. 1968, 10th Floor, Santiago

Vineyards: *1,400 ha (3,460 acres) of Cabernet sauvignon, Chardonnay, Chenin blanc, Gewürztraminer, Johannisberg riesling, Malbec, Merlot, Sauvignon blanc, Sémillon and Petit Verdot*
Established: *1883*

The largest winery in Chile and a good one too, Concha y Toro's wines are clean and correct, with ample fruit.

☆ Cabernet "Marqués de Casa Concha", (Cabernet Sauvignon/Merlot), Merlot

VIÑA COUSIÑO MACUL
Huérfanos 979, Suite 704, Santiago

Vineyards: *264 ha (652 acres) of Cabernet sauvignon, Chardonnay, Merlot, Petit verdot, Riesling, Sauvignon blanc and Sémillon*
Established: *1862*

Chile's best winery produces wines that are fine by any yardstick, especially the Cabernets: full-bodied, deep-coloured and richly flavoured.

☆ Antigua Reserva Cabernet Sauvignon, "Don Luis" Cabernet Sauvignon, Chardonnay, "Don Matias" Cabernet Sauvignon

VIÑA LINDEROS
Libertador Bernardo O'Higgins Av. 1370, Suite 502, Santiago

Vineyards: *81 ha (200 acres) of Cabernet sauvignon, Chardonnay, Riesling, Sauvignon blanc and Sémillon*
Established: *1865*

A reliable producer of some of Chile's most elegant Cabernet Sauvignon wines, this estate also produces Sémillon, Riesling and Chardonnay

☆ Cabernet Sauvignon

VIÑA SANTA RITA
Gertrudis Echeñique 49, Santiago

Vineyards: *145 ha (358 acres) of Cabernet sauvignon, Chardonnay, Sauvignon blanc, Sémillon*
Established: *1880*

The "120" brand is so-called because Bernardo O'Higgins, the liberator of Chile, and his 120 men hid in these cellars after the battle of Rancagua.

☆ Casa Real, "120" brand Cabernet 1984, Gran Vino "Casa Real" (Cabernet Sauvignon), Gran Vino "120 Medalla Real" (Cabernet Sauvignon), Gran Vino "120 Tres Medallas" (Cabernet Sauvignon), Gran Vino "120 Una Medalla" (Cabernet Sauvignon)

MIGUEL TORRES
Panamericana Sur, No. 195, Curicó

Vineyards: *150 ha (370 acres) of Cabernet sauvignon, Chardonnay, Merlot, Riesling, Sauvignon blanc and Gewürtraminer*
Established: *1979*

Spain's most innovative winemaker is producing excellent wines in Chile and has transformed perception of the potential of white wine in this country.

☆ "Santa Digna" (Cabernet Sauvignon Rosado), "Don Miguel" (Cabernet

Sauvignon/Merlot), "Bellaterra" Sauvignon Blanc Roble, Chardonnay, Riesling

UNDURRAGA
Agustinas 972, Suite 513, Santiago

Vineyards: *195 ha (482 acres) of Cabernet sauvignon, Chardonnay, Pinot noir, Riesling and Sauvignon blanc*
Established: *1885*

The first winery to export Chilean wines to the USA. I have seldom found any exciting examples.

AGRICOLA VIÑA LOS VASCOS
Isidora Goyenechea Av. 3156, Santiago

Vineyards: *170 ha (420 acres) of Cabernet sauvignon, Chardonnay, Sauvignon blanc and Sémillon*
Established: *1982*

This winery, founded by a Spanish-based Basque family, produces firm clean wines, brimming with fruit.

☆ Sauvignon/Sémillon "Chevrier", Cabernet

The best of the rest

CASONA
Agustinas 972, Suite 513, Santiago

Established: *1980*

CHAMPAGNE ALBERTO VALDIVIESO
Celia Solar 55, Santiago

Vineyards: *85 ha (210 acres) of Cabernet sauvignon, Chardonnay, Pinot blanc, Pinot noir, Sauvignon blanc and Sémillon*
Established: *1879*

CHAMPAGNE SUBERCASEAUX
Fernando Lazcano 1220, Santiago

Established: *1967*

COOPERATIVA AGRICOLA VITIVINICOLA DE CURICÓ
Balmaceda Av. 565, Curicó

Vineyards: *1,414 ha (3,494 acres) of Cabernet sauvignon, Chardonnay, Malbec, Merlot, Pinot noir, Riesling, Sauvignon blanc and Sémillon*
Established: *1939*

COOPERATIVA AGRICOLA VITIVINICOLA DE TALCA
San Miguel Av. 2631, Talca

Vineyards: *1,160 ha (2,866 acres) of Cabernet franc, Cabernet sauvignon, Malbec, Merlot, Pinot noir, Sauvignon blanc and Sémillon*
Established: *1944*

SOCIEDAD AGRICOLA SANTA ELISA
Fernando Lazcano 1220, Santiago

Vineyards: *281 ha (694 acres) of Cabernet sauvignon, Chardonnay, Malbec, Pinot noir and Sémillon*
Established: *1978*

SOCIEDAD VIÑA CARMEN
Villaseca s/n, Buin

Vineyards: *113 ha (279 acres) of Cabernet sauvignon, Malbec, Pinot noir, Riesling and Sauvignon blanc*
Established: *1850*

TARAPACÁ EX ZAVALA
Tobalaba Av. Nr. 9092, La Florida, Santiago

Vineyards: *70 ha (173 acres) of Cabernet sauvignon, Pinot noir and Sauvignon blanc*
Established: *1874*

A small winery producing entirely estate-bottled wines.

VIÑA ERRAZURIZ-PANQUEHUE
Bandera 206, Suite 601, Santiago

Vineyards: *150 ha (370 acres) of Cabernet sauvignon, Sauvignon blanc and Sémillon*
Established: *1879*

VIÑA MANQUEHUE
Vicuña Mackenna 2289, Santiago

Vineyards: *171 ha (433 acres) of Cabernet sauvignon, Chardonnay, Riesling, Sauvignon blanc and Sémillon*
Established: *1927*

VIÑA OCHAGAVIA
Til Til 2228, Santiago

Established: *1851*

VIÑA SAN PEDRO
Aysén Nr. 115, Santiago

Vineyards: *330 ha (815 acres) of Cabernet sauvignon and Sauvignon blanc*
Established: *1865*

VIÑA SANTA CAROLINA
Rodrigo de Araya 1431, Santiago

Established: *1875*

VINOS DE CHILE S.A. "VINEX"
Aysén 115, Santiago

Established: *1942*

VITIVINICOLA Y COMERCIAL MILLAHUE
Camino El Arpa s/n, Alto Jahuel Buin

Vineyards: *35 ha (86 acres) of Cabernet sauvignon, Sauvignon blanc and Sémillon*
Established: *1970*

Major wineries of Argentina

ANDEAN VINEYARDS
See Bodegas Trapiche.

BIANCHI
San Rafael, Mendoza

This winery belongs to Seagram, the giant Canadian drinks company.

☆ Cabernet Particular, Bianchi Borgogña

CAUTIVO
See José Orfila

CRILLON
Sanchez de Bustamante 54, 1173 Buenos Aires

Another subsidiary of Seagram.
Second label: "Embajador", "Monitor"

EMBAJADOR
Still-wine label belonging to Crillon. *See* Crillon.

MONITOR
See Crillon.

JOSÉ ORFILA
J. Salguero 1244, 1177 Buenos Aires

Vineyards: *275 ha (680 acres) of Cabernet sauvignon, Chardonnay*

The best wines of this winery are sold under its "Cautivo" label.

☆ Cabernet

PROVIAR
Florida 378, 5° Piso, 1351 Buenos Aires

Long-established arm of Moët & Chandon, making mostly sparkling wines, but also some still varietals.

☆ Champania "M. Chandon"

SAN TELMO
I am not very familiar with this winery, but it has a good reputation.

☆ Cabernet, Chardonnay, Malbec, Merlot, Traminer

BODEGAS TRAPICHE
Av. Juan B. Justo 5735, 1416 Buenos Aires

The largest winery in Argentina, producing a wide variety of fresh wines.
Second label: "Andean Vineyards"

☆ "Medella", Fond de Cave (Cabernet), Malbec

The best of the rest

BODEGAS ARIZU
Warnes 2280, 1427 Buenos Aires

BODEGAS ESMERALDA
Guatemala 4555, 1425 Buenos Aires

Vineyards: *Cabernet sauvignon, Malbec, Sauvignon blanc and Sylvaner*

☆ "St. Felicien" Cabernet

BODEGAS GARGANTINI
Av. San Martín 3379, 1416 Buenos Aires

BODEGAS LOPEZ
Godoy Cruz 2000, 1414 Buenos Aires

Vineyards: *1,000 ha (2,471 acres)*

☆ "Château Montchenot" ("Don Federico" on some export markets)

BODEGAS LA RURAL
Belgrano 271 – Piso 4, 1092 Buenos Aires

Vineyards: *250 ha (617 acres)*

Wine sold under the Felipe Rutini, San Felipe and Viña San Felipe labels.

☆ Riesling

HUMBERTO CANALE
Martín García 320, 1165 Buenos Aires

Vineyards: *Cabernet sauvignon, Merlot and Lambrusco*

☆ Cabernet Sauvignon

COPERCO SACIA
Emilio Civit 757, 5500 Mendoza

EST. VITIVIN. ESCORIHUELA
Av. San Martín 3499, 1416 Buenos Aires

ESTORNELL EXPORTA
Av. Centenario 1868, 1643 Beccar, Buenos Aires

ARNALDO ETCHART
Nicaragua 4994, 1414 Buenos Aires

☆ "Cafayate", "Reservo Blanc", Riesling, "Torrontes"

FINCA FLICHMAN
Cerrito 866 – Piso 10°, 1336 Buenos Aires

☆ "Caballero de la Cepa", Chardonnay

FLORIO
Av. Juan B. Justo 951, 1425 Buenos Aires

ANGEL FURLOTTI
Av. Juan B. Justo 1207, 1414 Buenos Aires

Vineyards: *1,000 ha (2,470 acres) of Cabernet sauvignon, Lambrusco and Merlot*

GOYENECHEA
Alsina 1970/74, 1090 Buenos Aires

Vineyards: *300 ha (741 acres)*

☆ "Aberdeen Angus" (Cabernet Sauvignon and Sirah)

SANTIAGO GRAFFIGNA
Warnes 2208, 1427 Buenos Aires

GRECO
Punta Arenas 1612, 1416 Buenos Aires

GERARDO IGLESIAS
C.A. López 3548, 1419 Buenos Aires

J. E. NAVARRO CORREAS
Olazábal 3710, 1430 Buenos Aires

☆ Sauvignon Blanc, Syrah, Pinot Noir

B. F. NAZAR ANCHORENA
Vélez Sarsfield 3180, 1640 Martinez, Buenos Aires

E. J. P. NORTON
Suárez 2857, 1284 Buenos Aires

Vineyards: *500 ha (1,235 acres)*

☆ "Perdriel" Cabernet, Chardonnay, Riesling

CASA PALMERO
Belgrano 634 – Piso 12°, 1092 Buenos Aires

☆ Merlot

RECOARO
Av. Argentina 5671, 1439 Buenos Aires

RESERO
Godoy Cruz 2562, 1425 Buenos Aires

EL RIVERO
Cangallo 61, 1704 Buenos Aires

SAINT REMY
Charcas 4040, 1425 Buenos Aires

SANTA ANA
San Martin 579 – Piso 1°, 1004 Buenos Aires

Vineyards: *40 ha (99 acres) of Barbera, Bonarda and Syrah*

☆ Chenin

SUTER
San Rafael, Mendoza

☆ Etiqueta Maron "Pinot Blanc", Etiqueta Blanca red

SAINTE SYLVIE
Lafayette 575, 1284 Buenos Aires

PASCUAL TOSO
Alberdi 808, 5519 San José, Mendoza

☆ Barrancas Cabernet Sauvignon

LA SUPERIORA VIÑEDOS Y BODEGA
Godoy Cruz 2200, 1414 Buenos Aires

MICHEL TORINO
Chacabuco 314 – Piso 9°, 1069 Buenos Aires

VINOS RODAS
Cangallo 2933, 1198 Buenos Aires

WEINERT
Parana 720, 1017 Buenos Aires

☆ Chardonnay

THE WINES OF
AUSTRALIA
AND
NEW ZEALAND

Australia

The first Australian vineyard was planted at Farm Cove in New South Wales in 1788, with vines originating not from France, but from Rio de Janeiro and the Cape of Good Hope. These were collected by the first governor, Captain Arthur Phillip, en route to Sydney aboard his flagship HMS Sirius.

THE RICH SOIL OF FARM COVE AND ITS HUMID CLIMATE proved fine for growing vines, but not for making wine. Phillip persevered, however, and planted another vineyard in the garden of Government House at Parramatta, just north of Sydney. The soil and climate were more suitable for vine-growing and the success of this new venture encouraged Phillip's official requests for technical assistance. England responded by sending out two French prisoners-of-war, who were offered their freedom in exchange for three years' service in New South Wales, in the belief that all Frenchmen knew something about making wine. These did not. One was so bad at the job that he was transported back to England; the other could only make cider, but mistakenly used peaches instead of apples!

THE GROWTH OF AUSTRALIA'S WINE TRADE

From these shaky beginnings an industry grew, but with no thanks due to the British. At first, Australia's wine trade was monopolized and shaped by the needs of the British Empire and of the Commonwealth. It consequently gained a reputation for producing cheap fortified wines – not because it could only make such wines, but because Britain *wanted* cheap fortified wines, so Australia supplied them. Unfortunately, Australians also acquired a taste for these wines. Although Australia made (and still makes) some of the world's finest dessert wines, most wines were heavy, very sweet and sluggish at a time when the rest of the world was drinking lighter and finer wines. Small quantities of truly fine table wine were produced, but until the 1960s, most of those that were exported were remarkably similar in style, whatever their grape variety or area of origin.

Although the Australians were late starters in the fine-wine field, today they make some of the greatest, most exciting and ridiculously good-value wines in the world.

HOW TO READ AUSTRALIAN WINE LABELS

Although crude forms of controlled appellation have reached only a minority of Australia's wine areas, this country's wine labels are among the most straightforward in the world, clearly showing the basic details of what the wine is, who made it and where, in addition to further information (often on back labels), supplying details of harvest, vinification, maturation and tasting notes. The basic information shown on virtually all Australian wine labels includes:

Show or Show Reserve
Used only on (domestic) award-winning wines. Australian wine competitions are a first-class indication of sources of superior wines. This is not simply because of the highly professional organization of these events and the relatively modest proportion of winners, but because the term can only be applied to wines that come from exactly the same vat, or even barrel, as the prize-winning wine. This prevents a producer collecting medals for a *tête de cuvée* then blending it into more wine under the same label.

Grape variety
Most of Australia's greatest wines are pure varietal wines from classic grapes, so the label will reveal names such as Cabernet Sauvignon, Chardonnay, Sémillon and Shiraz. Some more obscure grape names may be encountered, many of which are synonyms for better-known varieties (*see* p.416).
When two or more grapes are indicated on a label, they are listed in order of importance, so that a Sémillon-Chardonnay will have a greater proportion of Sémillon than a Chardonnay-Sémillon, and a Shiraz-Malbec-Cabernet will have more Shiraz than Malbec, but more Malbec than Cabernet.

Brand or company name
The Rosemount Estate name on this example is the brand name of Rosemount Estates Pty. Ltd., whose name and address are clearly indicated at the bottom of the label.

Vintage
This can be relied on, although there are no regulations controlling it unless the wine is exported to a country with its own strict laws, as in the EEC, for instance.

Wood Matured
Usually means the wine has been aged in *new* oak, although there is no legal requirement that this should be so.

District, region or state of origin
Australian winemakers are open and straightforward when it comes to indicating the origin of their wines. In this case it is the Hunter Valley. If individual regions or districts on the label are unknown to you, the name of one of the five mainland states or Tasmania will always be indicated somewhere on the bottle, which should help you to narrow down more specific areas. Indeed, many wines will only indicate a state of origin if blended from various areas – often the case with large-production wines.
On the other hand, extensive inter-state trucking of grapes makes the origin of some wines somewhat dubious. Very few Australian wine districts have certified Wine of Origin systems, and those that do lack the cohesive benefit of a national regulating body (*see* p.416).

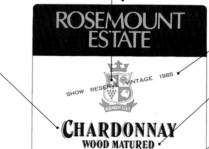

Alcoholic strength
This is expressed in per cent by volume. The information, taken for granted in many classic wine areas, can be very significant in countries that grow wines in baking heat (although not all Australian wine areas are extremely hot). In such areas, alcoholic strength gives a rough guide to the style – the higher the alcohol the bigger the wine. A high alcohol level invariably indicates a traditionally made wine, while the lower it is, the lighter the wine, with the lowest almost certainly the product of very modern vinification methods.

Produce of Australia
All wines exported carry "Produce of Australia" or "Product of Australia".

Other information that may be found on Australian wine labels:

Bin number/code, Private Bin or Reserve Bin
These terms imply a better grade of wine within a company's range, a selected *cuvée* or reserve quality, although there are no legal requirements.

Wine type
The existence of so-called "generic" wines such as Burgundy, Chablis or Champagne, is more rife in Australia than in New Zealand, although it represents less of a problem than in America. There are, however, indigenous generics, such as the luscious Liqueur Muscat that Australia has made its own.

Certified Appellation Wine
Guarantee of origin found on very few Australian wines such as those from Mudgee, New South Wales.

Auslese
Adopted from German terminology and used for late-harvested, sweet wines that may show some botrytis character.

Beerenauslese
Adopted from German terminology and used for intensely sweet, blatantly botrytis wines.

Spätlese
Adopted from German terminology and used for late-harvested, medium-sweet wines that rarely show any true botrytis character.

AUSTRALIAN WINE PRODUCTION BY REGION

The production of South Australia dwarfs that of the rest of the country. It produces 55 per cent of Australia's wine, its nearest rival being New South Wales with 27 per cent of the total production. Although the wines of Western Australia often attract international praise, they represent the smallest proportion of the country's vineyards – just 4.6 per cent – and have an ultra-low yield, underlining the region's quality (rather than quantity) potential.

REGION	AREA UNDER VINE Ha (Acres)	PRODUCTION Hl (Cases)
New South Wales	9,000 (22,240)	1,093,500 (12,150,999)
Victoria	2,500 (6,180)	526,500 (5,850,000)
South Australia	27,000 (66,700)	2,227,500 (24,750,000)
Western Australia	2,000 (4,940)	60,750 (675,000)
Others	3,350 (8,280)	141,750 (1,575,000)
National Total	43,850 (108,340)	4,050,000 (45,000,000)

South Australia vineyards and landscape, above
These vines belong to Coriole Vineyards, a small estate producing red wines in McLaren Vale. Over 60 per cent of Australia's vineyards are in South Australia.

AUSTRALIA

Wine is produced in every state, although most of the vineyards are centred on a semicircular band running from Sydney in New South Wales to Adelaide in South Australia. As yet there is no country-wide appellation system with officially delimited wine-producing areas.

New South Wales
See also p. 418

Victoria and Tasmania
See also p. 423

South Australia
See also p. 430

Western Australia
See also p. 437

● Other wine-producing areas

----- State Boundary

▲ Height above sea level (metres)

Kms   200   400   600   800

Mls   100   200   300   400   500

Lindeman's Cellars, Hunter Valley, above
Australia's largest winery with an output of nearly four million cases, Lindeman's produces wines from its own vineyards in New South Wales and South Australia.

THE RENAISSANCE OF AUSTRALIAN WINES

Over the last 20 years, the technology of Australian winemaking has soared, taking with it the quality of its wines. Better quality does not necessarily follow in the footsteps of improved technology – there must be not only an understanding of the equipment, but also a realization of the potential of grapes and soil conditions and a certain vision and passion in order to produce finer, more expressive wines. Technology can often "wash out" essential characteristics, but the Australians did not allow this to happen. Once committed to taking part in the international "fine-wine contest", they made such fast progress that Australian wine climbed to the top of the quality ladder before foreign producers realized there was any competition.

Australia is now on a par with France and can compete with it in every classic wine category. Until the French improved their *vins de pays*, Australia's cask-wines totally outshone the cheap French equivalents. For red wines, the Australians now rely less on the Shiraz grape (Syrah), and more on Cabernet sauvignon, with Cabernet franc, Merlot and Malbec increasingly used to effect a better balance in blends. Chardonnay is probably the top grape on export markets, but the position is strongly contested by Sémillon, and even by obscure varieties like Marsanne.

Cool fermentation has not been taken to extremes, and the emphasis in research has been switched to improving the quality of the raw material in the vineyard. It is quite possible to ruin good fruit with poor vinification, and hide faults with technology or chemistry, but it is impossible to make excellent wine without excellent grapes. Cooler areas have been cultivated, alcohol levels have dropped, acidity has increased, and new oak plays an integral, yet restrained, role. This has resulted in the emergence of recognizable regional characteristics: the Cabernet sauvignon grown in Victoria, for example, has a distinctive minty taste, while in Coonawarra, it has a flavour reminiscent of rich fruit cake and mulberries. Australia is such a vast country and alive with so much activity and experimentation in high-tech installations that I can hardly believe its total production, an average of 45 million cases, is simply the equivalent of three-quarters of the annual output of the huge E. & J. Gallo winery of California!

SHOULD AUSTRALIA HAVE APPELLATIONS?

Since France set up its AOC system in 1935, every winemaking country has at some time considered the question of whether or not to introduce a similar scheme. Western Australia's Margaret River and Mudgee in New South Wales were the first to introduce controlled appellations, followed by Tasmania, Victoria and, more recently, Queensland's Granite Belt and the Hunter Valley in New South Wales. However, of these, only the voluntary Mudgee and state-backed Tasmanian schemes are still working effectively.

The debate on whether or not to define and control the use of wine names persists; the success or failure of an established system merely seems to excite one side or the other. I believe that a good appellation system is vital for every serious wine country. It not only guarantees the authenticity of a product for the consumer, it also protects winemakers from unfair or fraudulent competition and helps them to establish a clear image when promoting their wines in a new market.

Does an appellation system guarantee quality?

The argument that an appellation system can guarantee origin and, perhaps, grape variety or varieties, but is unable to ensure the quality of a wine, is an enduring one. Although I have heard many a Frenchman complain about the AOC "guarantee of mediocrity", it is theoretically possible to set the standards of compulsory blind-

WORLD SALES OF AUSTRALIAN WINE BY TYPE

This table includes both domestic and export sales. The current trend is for a drop in fortified wines and an increase in light wines, this looks set to continue into the 1990s.

Wine Type	Sales	
	Cases	Proportion
Red	4,500,000	13%
Rosé	800,000	2%
Dry white	19,500,000	56%
Sweet	3,800,000	11%
Fortified	2,200,000	6%
Sparkling	3,500,000	10%
Aromatized	700,000	2%
Total	**35,000,000**	**100%**

TOP AUSTRALIAN WINE EXPORT COUNTRIES 1986-1987

Until the early 1980s, as much as 99 per cent of Australia's wine was consumed domestically. When production dramatically increased, producers looked to export markets. Exports now account for more than ten per cent of total (world) sales and continue to increase.

Country	Cases		Difference
	1986	1987	
Sweden	350,000	865,000	+147%
USA	190,000	545,000	+187%
UK	210,000	540,000	+157%
Japan	135,000	235,000	+74%
Canada	175,000	295,000	+69%
New Zealand	155,000	270,000	+74%
Other countries	585,000	930,000	+59%
Total Exports	**1,800,000**	**3,680,000**	**+104%**

tastings and analysis as high as is necessary. The quality level of these tests is entirely the decision of those responsible for establishing them. Important as it is, it is my opinion that quality is not the first priority of an appellation system. It should be set at the *minimum level* required to ensure a quality that is compatible with the reputation of the appellation in question.

The French evade the issue of quality by declaring that a wine should be "typical". But what help is it to the consumer to know that a thin, brown, acidic Pinot Noir is typical of a dreadful Burgundy vintage such as 1974 or 1975? No Burgundy should be thin, brown and acidic, just as no Sémillon from the Hunter Valley should be dark, flabby and turgid. The misfortune of bad weather should not come into play; if the wine does not reach the required quality levels, it must be refused its right of appellation.

The experience of other countries

Some people argue that an appellation works well enough in France and Germany, where the districts and the grapes appropriate to them have been defined over a thousand years or so, but it has proved very different in Italy where the 20-year-old DOC/DOCG system is unsatisfactory. In fact this is to oversimplify the examples of France and Germany. Both still have unworkable, unjust, contradictory and confusing elements, despite centuries of natural evolution. In my view, this anti-appellation argument does not carry much weight. And after so many mistakes in other countries, surely the Australians might be expected to do a better job?

The problem of regional blended wines

Some wine experts feel that to talk of origin is to imply a denigration of regional blends, not to mention the difficulties for the majority of the larger Australian wineries who make and blend wines from grapes grown in areas spread across thousands of kilometres. But to set up a system of appellations is not to deny anyone the right to make blends, it is merely to prevent them from dishonestly labelling a wine "Margaret River", for instance, when only a proportion of its grapes might be from that district.

Winery signs, Mudgee, New South Wales, above
Mudgee boasts a healthy, voluntary appellation system. This profusion of signs, some with well-known names, some less so, could almost be found in the Médoc.

The ideal solution

So far, the majority of independent regional systems have foundered. With all the transporting of grapes from state to state, it would make sense for Australia to have some form of appellation system authorized (though not necessarily run) by national government. The country is young enough to set up what could be one of the most exciting, open and forward-thinking appellation systems in the world. There is nothing to stop Australia from setting up a totally independent organization of viticultural, oenological and legal professionals that might be funded by levies on growers and wineries, and empowered by national and state legislation. The aim need not be simply to create and control appellations, but also to assist and guide every aspect of the industry's future development, from research to marketing. It would be a brave move for Australia's independently-minded states, but one well worth taking as far as its wine industry is concerned.

GUIDE TO AUSTRALIAN GRAPE VARIETY SYNONYMS

Many grape varieties in Australia are not what they might first appear to be. Although much of the confusion was cleared up as long ago as the mid-1970s, numerous confusing synonyms persist. Sometimes these are limited to isolated vineyards, but others remain widespread and some, such as Tokay, which is the Australian synonym for the Muscadelle grape, are not likely to be eradicated, particularly when they have assumed a generic status, as in the case of Australia's Liqueur Tokay, for example.

Albillo Synonym for the Chenin blanc.

Belzac *See* Mataro.

Cabernet gros Erroneous synonym for the Bastardo, used for making Australian "Port".

Carignan Erroneous synonym for the Bonvedro, a minor Portuguese variety.

Clare riesling Erroneous synonym for a minor variety called the Crouchen.

Esparte *See* Mataro.

Frontignac Synonym for the Muscat blanc à petits grains. Also known as the White Frontignan.

Fruity gordo *See* Gordo.

Gordo In various formats: Gordo blanco, Muscat gordo, Muscat gordo blanco and, on one of Berri Estates' high-volume wine-casks, Fruity gordo, this is a synonym for the Muscat d'Alexandrie that is often used in fresh, cool-fermented, semi-sweet wines made to popular tastes.

Hermitage A common synonym for the Syrah.

Hunter riesling *See* Hunter River riesling.

Hunter River riesling Erroneous synonym for the Sémillon, the use of which is now on the decline due to the rapid rise to fame of its genuine name.

Also wrongly called Hunter riesling or, simply, Riesling.

Irvine's white A Victorian synonym for the Ondenc, a minor variety from Bergerac in France that can be useful for sparkling wines, due to its high natural acidity.

Jacquez Synonym for the Black Spanish, a *teinturier* hybrid from Madeira, also called Troya and Uva de Troia. It is claimed that Jacquez and Rubired are the only hybrid varieties grown in Australia.

Lexia Synonym for the Muscat d'Alexandrie, some times seen on fine Liqueur Muscat labels.

Mataro Synonym for the Mourvèdre, along with Belzac and Esparte.

Muscat gordo *See* Gordo.

Muscat gordo blanco *See* Gordo.

Paulo A synonym for the Palomino of Jerez in Spain.

Petite sirah Erroneous synonym for the Durif, a modest French variety that can occasionally shine in New World countries.

Rhine riesling The true Riesling.

Riesling *See* Hunter River Riesling.

Sémillon Whereas the Sémillon is known as the Hunter River Riesling in New South Wales, the Chenin blanc is called Sémillon in Western Australia.

Sercial Erroneous South Australian synonym for the Ondenc, a minor variety from Bergerac in France.

Shiraz Not so much a synonym, as *the* Australian name for the Syrah grape.

Tokay Erroneous synonym for the Muscadelle grape of Bordeaux.

Touriga Erroneous synonym for the Bastardo, used for making Australian "Port".

Traminer Synonym for the Gewürztraminer.

Trebbiano Common synonym for the Ugni blanc.

Troya *See* Jacquez.

Uva de Troia *See* Jacquez.

White Frontignan *See* Frontignac.

White grenache Erroneous synonym for a minor Mediterranean variety called the Biancone.

White Hermitage Erroneous synonym for the Ugni blanc.

White Shiraz Erroneous synonym for the Ugni blanc.

New South Wales

From the hefty Hunter Valley Hermitage to the honeyed succulence of Murrumbidgee's botrytis Sémillon, the wines of Australia's one-time most famous wine state are even better and more varied than ever, despite being overtaken in the fame game by other areas. New South Wales should not be forgotten.

IN THIS DAY AND AGE OF CLEAN, VITAL and pure-tasting wines, it is hard to imagine that the Hunter Valley established its once unassailable reputation on a huge, beefy, red Shiraz wine that gave off a strong, gamey, sweat-and-leather odour and possessed an earthy, almost muddy taste that was "chewed" rather than swallowed. But the valley grew no other black grape until 1963. This peculiar aroma, which gave rise to the infamous "sweaty saddles" description, is supposed to derive from the Hunter's volcanic basalt soil, although in some areas, this Shiraz and basalt combination has yielded nothing but pure peppery-varietal Shiraz with not the slightest hint of "sweaty saddles".

I attribute this phenomenon to hot climate, bad viticultural practices and sloppy winemaking – a combination that was once just as much the norm as the high-tech, spotless facilities and excellent winemaking skills of today. And just because some of the sweatiest Shiraz have turned into "magnificent monsters" after a few decades in the bottle, it does not necessarily follow that to be great a Shiraz has to be "sweaty". The "sweaty saddles" syndrome is still talked about, but the characteristic smell to which it refers is mild and unoffensive. It *is* a distinctive wine, but not one that reeks, so do not be put off.

Sémillon has always been a classic Hunter Valley grape, but few

FACTORS AFFECTING TASTE AND QUALITY

Location
The southern part of Australia's east coast, between Victoria and Queensland.

Climate
Temperatures during the growing season are similar to those of the Languedoc. Cloud cover can temper the heat in the Hunter Valley, but the accompanying rains often promote rot. The growing season is later, and the climate sunnier in Mudgee, while it is hotter and drier in the Murrumbidgee Area.

Aspect
Vines are grown on generally low-lying, flat or undulating sites, but also on some steeper slopes such as the fringes of the Brokenback Range in the Lower Hunter Valley where vines are grown up to 500 metres (1,600 ft), and in Mudgee on the western slopes of the Great Dividing Range where some vineyards can be found at an altitude of 800 metres (2,600 ft).

Soil
Soils are varied with sandy and clay loams of varying fertility found in all areas. Various other types such as the red-brown volcanic loams are scattered about the Lower Hunter region and the fertile, but well-drained alluvial sands and silts of the flat valley floors.

Viticulture and vinification
Irrigation is practised throughout the state, particularly in the mainly bulk-wine-producing inland area of Murrumbidgee. The range of grape varieties is increasing, and the grapes are harvested earlier. Stainless-steel vats are replacing wood and concrete for cooler, temperature-controlled fermentation and new oak is used judiciously.

Grape varieties
Cabernet sauvignon, Chardonnay, Chasselas, Clairette, Colombard, Crouchen, Doradillo, Frontignan, Grenache, Marsanne, Mataro, Muscat d'Alexandrie, Palomino, Pedro Ximénez, Pinot noir, Rhine riesling, Sauvignon blanc, Sémillon, Shiraz, Muscadelle, Gewürztraminer, Trebbiano, Verdelho

NEW SOUTH WALES

North of Sydney, the Lower and Upper Hunter Valley and the Mudgee areas excel, whilst the Murrumbidgee Irrigation Area to the southwest proves that quantity can, to a certain extent, co-exist with quality.

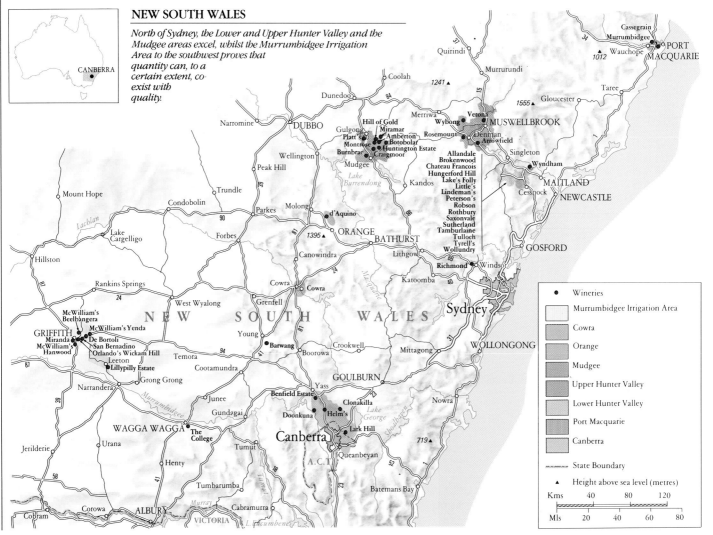

Wineries
Murrumbidgee Irrigation Area
Cowra
Orange
Mudgee
Upper Hunter Valley
Lower Hunter Valley
Port Macquarie
Canberra
State Boundary
▲ Height above sea level (metres)

people realize that there are more white grape varieties grown in this area than black and, in the Upper Hunter Valley, the Sémillon alone outnumbers the Shiraz by 40 per cent. The Sémillon, traditionally called the Hunter riesling (though further from a true Riesling it could not be), makes rich, round and honeyed wines that take a lot of oak and age extremely well. Modern winemaking tends to produce lighter, fresher, crisper wines with more delicate varietal flavours, but the richness is there and, if you analyze the wines, you will find that quite a few have a gram or two of sugar to emphasize this delicate richness. The wines still taste dry and one tends to associate the sweetness with the oak — which illustrates how expertly the residual sugar is integrated into the overall character of the wine by the winemaker.

The "new" grape varieties are led by Chardonnay, pioneered by Tyrrells' Vineyards, and Cabernet sauvignon, first planted by Max Lake at Lake's Folly in 1963. Both have now spread throughout the state and make some of Australia's finest wines, either in their pure form, or blended with other grapes. And wineries in the self-proclaimed appellation of Mudgee are fighting to establish a new reputation with mouthwatering Chardonnay, with the bouquet and flavour of lime and tropical fruit, and delicate strawberry-flavoured Pinot Noir. Rhine riesling and Gewürztraminer have surprisingly large cultivations in New South Wales, but only excel occasionally in isolated locations, while the Pinot noir has been at least as successful, despite the fact that Rhine riesling and Gewürztraminer outnumber it by fifteen to one vines.

Oak maturation, Rosemount Estate, above
One of New South Wales' leading wineries, Rosemount's winemaking expertise has few peers in Australia.

Vineyards, Mudgee, right
Perhaps atypical to the area, these vineyards occupy flat land rather than western slopes of the Great Dividing Range.

The wines of New South Wales

CANBERRA

Although often referred to as the Canberra district, this area can also be called the Yass Valley.

At the end of the last century there was a flourishing wine industry around the Yass area, but its vineyards could not compete with the warmer regions in the business of making fortified wines, the fashionable drink of the day. The last recorded winery, Ainsbury, ceased operation in 1908. Canberra was rediscovered as a viticultural area in 1971 when Dr. Edgar Riek established the Cullarin Winery (now Lake George Winery) and Dr. John Kirk planted the Clonakilla vineyard in Murrambateman. Four more sprang up within three years and, there are now 12 operational wineries in the area.

Although the area's early downfall was due to its inability to compete with warmer areas, it is a widespread misconception that Canberra is cool in viticultural terms. The summers are warm and dry, and the new generation of winegrowers is only just beginning

to accept that irrigation will be indispensable if the area is to develop.

🍷 **RED:** 1983, 1984, 1985, 1986, 1987, 1988, 1989

🍷 **WHITE:** 1982, 1983, 1985, 1986, 1987, 1988, 1989

CENTRAL NORTH-WEST

Alternative name for the Forbes-Wellington area, a minor winegrowing district west of Sydney.

CENTRAL WEST
See **Cowra.**

COROWA

Situated east of Lake Mulwala, some 56 kilometres (35 miles) west of Albury, just across the Murray River from Wahgunyah, this declining dessert wine district is New South Wales' most southerly wine area and can be

geographically viewed as an extension of the Rutherglen area in northeast Victoria. Lindeman's brought commercial winemaking to the scattered Touriga vineyards in 1872, but has since vacated the area.

COWRA

This small but growing viticultural area, sometimes referred to as the Central West district, is situated well inland from Sydney, north of Canberra. There is a winery called Cowra Wines, which owns some 40 hectares (99 acres) and this is the site of Rothbury's 90-hectare (222-acre) Lachlan vineyard. Cabernet sauvignon, Gewürztraminer and Chardonnay dominate, but Rhine riesling, Pinot noir, Shiraz, Sémillon and Sauvignon blanc are also grown.

FORBES-COWRA

A name sometimes given to vineyards within the Forbes-Cowra-Wellington triangle.

HUNTER VALLEY
See **Lower Hunter Valley and Upper Hunter Valley.**

LOWER HUNTER VALLEY

This is the "original" Hunter Valley. Its vineyards were pioneered in the 1820s by such growers as William Kelman of Kirkton and George Wyndham of Dalwood, over 130 years before the Upper Hunter was opened up. The area has long been famous for its rich Sémillons, traditionally and erroneously called Hunter Rieslings, and for its forceful Shiraz, the Syrah of Côte Rôtie and Hermitage. The famous Shiraz "sweaty saddles" smell is supposed to have originated here, due, allegedly, to the Hunter's basalt subsoil, although I doubt it very much. The true Hunter Shiraz style is a distinctive earthy character, and many beautifully clean berry-fruit renditions of this grape are now being made. More and more

Continued overleaf

emphasis is also being placed on Chardonnay and Cabernet sauvignon.

The Lower Hunter is not ideal grape country, being too hot and humid, although the nightly air-drainage from the Brokenback Range cools the vines and prevents the acidity of ripening grapes from dropping too rapidly. Unlike many of Australia's vineyards, there is no need for irrigation. Lindeman's, the country's largest winery, has all but given up this area for greener pastures at Padthaway and Coonawarra in South Australia and, although one or two new wineries (such as Allanmere) have appeared, there is no indication of a repeat of the rush witnessed in the 1960s and 1970s, when Allandale, Brokenwood, Hungerford Hill and other wineries started up.

RED: 1980, 1983, 1985, 1986, 1987, 1988, 1989

WHITE: 1982, 1983, 1985, 1986, 1987, 1988, 1989

MUDGEE

This district is best known for unilaterally establishing its own appellation in 1979. This was proposed and agreed by the growers themselves. This makes its status somewhat different from that of Western Australia's Margaret River, the first district to achieve an official Appellation of Origin system backed by state legislation.

Aside from Mudgee's laudable "go-it-alone" policy, it is one of Australia's most underrated areas. Situated 260 kilometres (160 miles) northwest of Sydney at an altitude of 450-650 metres (1,500-2,000 ft), the vineyards are cooler than in the Hunter and harvests are considerably later, stretching the growing season and thus improving the acidity-sugar ratio.

The best wines are Cabernet Sauvignon, Cabernet-Shiraz, Chardonnay, Sémillon, Sémillon-Chardonnay, and Shiraz, with some very good Pinot Noir, Traminer and Marsanne, and interesting Barbera-Nebbiolo and Pinot Noir-Shiraz blends. The Botobolar and Miramar wineries make some very good wines, but it is Craigmoor, Huntington and Montrose that consistently perform the best, producing stunning, fruity wines.

RED: 1981, 1982, 1983, 1985, 1986, 1987

WHITE: 1982, 1983, 1985, 1986, 1987

MURRUMBIDGEE IRRIGATION AREA

By flooding and pumping the Murrumbidgee River, this district, also known as Griffith-Leeton Riverina, is irrigated in much the same way as the Murray River irrigates South Australia's Riverland (see page p.432). This previously infertile land now cultivates

plenty of rice and all kinds of fruit, including enough grapes to make one-tenth of all the wine in Australia. These wines are not all cheap plonk and include such vinous miracles as De Bortoli's Sémillon Sauternes. Other wines that excel here beyond the dreams of most winegrowers who irrigate their vineyards are late-harvested Rhine Riesling and Traminer.

RED: 1980, 1982, 1984, 1986, 1987, 1988, 1989

WHITE: 1982, 1984, 1986, 1987, 1988, 1989

BOTRYTIS: 1982, 1984, 1985

ORANGE

This isolated area north of Cowra has recently spawned two new vineyards, but I have not yet tasted the wines.

PORT MACQUARIE

Hastings Valley at Port Macquarie is a minor but expanding wine area that supported several vineyards in the 1860s. Production ceased around 1930 and vines were not cultivated here again until ex-Murray Tyrrell man John Cassegrain established a vineyard in 1980.

RIVERINA

See Murrumbidgee Irrigation Area.

UPPER HUNTER VALLEY

The Upper Hunter was pioneered in the 1960s by Penfolds and put on the map internationally by the sensational performance of Rosemount Estate, easily the district's largest producer. It was Rosemount's sweet-ripe-vanilla Show Reserve Chardonnay that took export markets by storm in the early 1980s. Later, it made its mark with a super-concentrated, far richer and more complex Chardonnay from Roxburgh, a prized vineyard acquired some years before. As well as alerting the outside world to the wines of the Upper Hunter, Rosemount opened the floodgates for the rest of Australia.

Although this district is just as hot as the Lower Hunter and the growing season very similar, the climate is drier and the vineyards need irrigation. Yet, with irrigation, fertile alluvial soils and high yields – two factors that do not augur well for quality – some very fine wines are made. Chardonnay and Pinot noir are on the increase in the Upper Hunter, and Merlot is being used more and more for blending with Cabernet sauvignon.

RED: 1982, 1983, 1984, 1985, 1986, 1987, 1988, 1989

WHITE: 1982, 1983, 1984, 1985, 1986, 1987, 1988, 1989

YASS VALLEY

See Canberra.

Major wineries of New South Wales

THE ALLANDALE WINERY
Lovedale Road,
Pokolbin via Maitland, NSW 2321

Production: 7,200 cases
Vineyards: 7 ha (17 acres) of Pinot noir, Sémillon and Chardonnay
Established: 1978

Edward Jouault specializes in wines from various hand-picked vineyards. This is an exciting venture that should be copied elsewhere.

☆ Cabernet Sauvignon (Leonard Vineyard), Chardonnay (Dawson Vineyard, Trevena Vineyard), Sémillon (Leonard Vineyard), Shiraz (Leonard Vineyard)

ARROWFIELD WINES
Highway 213, Jerrys Plains, NSW 2330

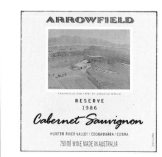

Production: 10,000 cases
Vineyards: 300 ha (741 acres) of Chardonnay, Sémillon and

Cabernet sauvignon
Established: 1969

This estate dates back to 1824 when Governor Macquarie granted the land to one George Bowman, who named the huge fields on his property after variations of his family name, hence "Arrowfield". After purchase of the land by a holding company, 460 hectares (1,137 acres) were planted between 1969 and 1974, with every single vine covered by a massive drip-irrigation system. The vineyard area has been reduced and the irrigation cut down so quality has improved.

☆ Hunter Valley Chardonnay, Hunter Valley Sémillon, Fumé Blanc

BOTOBOLAR VINEYARD
Mudgee, NSW 2850

Production: 9,000 cases
Vineyards: 23 ha (57 acres) of Syrah, Cabernet sauvignon, Mataro, Crouchen, Chardonnay, Marsanne, Rhine riesling and Gewürztraminer
Established: 1971

Interesting, good-quality, organically produced wines from the highest vineyard in the Mudgee district.

☆ Marsanne, "St. Gilbert", Shiraz

BROKENWOOD
McDonalds Road,
Pokolbin, NSW 2321

Production: 6,000 cases
Vineyards: 20 ha (49 acres) of Cabernet sauvignon, Hermitage and Chardonnay
Established: 1970

1986

BROKENWOOD

cabernet sauvignon

'graveyard vineyard'

750 ml WINE OF AUSTRALIA 12.5% ALC/VOL

Wine author (and maker) James Halliday is an ex-shareholder of this producer of atypical but medal-winning wines.

☆ Chardonnay (Graveyard vineyard), Sémillon Wood Matured, Cabernet Sauvignon, (Cabernet Sauvignon-Hermitage, Hermitage Cabernet Sauvignon, to be discontinued)

CHATEAU FRANCOIS
Broke Road,
Pokolbin, NSW 2321

Production: 900 cases
Vineyards: 2.4 ha (6 acres) of Syrah, Pinot noir, Sémillon and Chardonnay
Established: 1969

This small outfit's Sémillon and Shiraz have won medals in the past. Its best wines are Burgundian varietals.

☆ Chardonnay, Pinot Noir

CRAIGMOOR WINERY
Craigmoor Road,
Mudgee, NSW 2850

Production: 12,000 cases
Vineyards: 30 ha (74 acres) of Chardonnay, Sémillon, Gewürztraminer, Rhine riesling, Cabernet sauvignon, Syrah and Pinot noir
Established: 1858

Since the mid-1980s, these wines have displayed an increasing degree of finesse. In 1988, Craigmoor was purchased by Wyndham Estate.

☆ Chablis, Sémillon Chardonnay, Chardonnay, Cabernet Sauvignon, Cabernet Shiraz

DE BORTOLI WINES
De Bortoli Road,
Bilbul, NSW 2680

Production: *500,000 cases*
Vineyards: *60 ha (148 acres) of Muscat hamburg, Syrah, Colombard, Merlot, Muscat d'Alexandrie, Palomino, Pedro Ximénez and Sémillon*
Established: *1928*

This winery has a huge production of modest wine under numerous labels, but is also capable of producing some excellent wines in large quantities particularly in the sweet white category. The 1982 Sémillon Sauternes did taste like Sauternes, and from a top château in a great year too.

☆ Fumé Blanc, Riesling *Beerenauslese*, Sémillon Sauternes, Vittorio Spumante, Yarrinya Estate (Shiraz, Cabernet Sauvignon)

HUNGERFORD HILL VINEYARDS
Broke Road,
Pokolbin, NSW 2321

Production: *50,000 cases*
Vineyards: *143 ha (353 acres) of Chardonnay, Verdelho, Cabernet sauvignon, Rhine riesling, Merlot, Pinot, Gewürztraminer, Syrah and Sémillon*
Established: *1967*

Hungerford Hill blends some of the wines from its two vineyards, one in the Hunter Valley and the other in Coonawarra, some 1,130 kilometres (700 miles) apart – rather like blending a Rioja with a wine from the Great Hungarian plains! Happily the results are excellent.

☆ "Pokolbin Collection" (Chardonnay, Cabernet Sauvignon), "Coonawarra Collection" (Rhine Riesling, Shiraz, Cabernet Sauvignon), Chardonnay Pinot Noir Méthode Champenoise

HUNTINGTON ESTATE
Cassilis Road,
Mudgee NSW 2850

Production: *18,000 cases*
Vineyards: *42 ha (104 acres) of Cabernet sauvignon, Syrah, Merlot, Pinot noir, Sémillon, Chardonnay and Sauvignon blanc*
Established: *1969*

Bob Roberts entered the business with a law degree and learned winemaking through a British-based correspondence course. Not the strongest base for success, perhaps, but his

clean, fleshy, well-balanced, stylish wines regularly outshine wines made by highly qualified professionals.

☆ Sémillon Medium Dry, Pinot Noir Shiraz, Cabernet Sauvignon "Bin FB 13", Cabernet Merlot "Bin FB 12", Shiraz "Bin FB 16"

LAKE'S FOLLY
Broke Road,
Pokolbin, NSW 2321

Production: *4,200 cases*
Vineyards: *15 ha (37 acres) of Cabernet sauvignon and Chardonnay*
Established: *1963*

This winery is the passion of Sydney surgeon Max Lake, who pioneered Cabernet Sauvignon and Chardonnay in the (then) traditional Shiraz country of the Hunter Valley. He also introduced the use of new oak to the region and consistently produces vivid, vibrant and stylish wines.

☆ Cabernet Sauvignon, Chardonnay

LILLYPILLY ESTATE
Lillypilly Road,
Leeton, NSW 2705

Production: *6,000 cases*
Established: *1982 (Vineyard 1972)*

Lillypilly Estate produces better white wines than red. A very direct varietal appeal can be found in the improving Chardonnay and Sémillon wines, but the intense, fruity, aromatic and richly textured *Spatlese* Lexia is consistently its best wine.

☆ *Spatlese* "Lexia"

LINDEMAN'S WINES
31 Nyrang Street,
Lidcombe, NSW 2141

Production: *3.4 million cases*
Vineyards: *900 ha (2,224 acres) of Cabernet sauvignon, Chardonnay, Chasselas, Clairette, Colombard, Crouchen, Doradillo, Frontignan, Grenache, Marsanne, Mataro, Muscat d'Alexandrie, Palomino, Pedro Ximénez, Pinot noir, Rhine riesling, Sauvignon blanc, Sémillon, Shiraz, Muscadelle, Gewürztraminer, Trebbiano and Verdelho.*
Established: *1843*

This is the country's largest winery, but although Lindeman's churns out nearly four million cases of some 400 different wines, it also manages to produce many truly superb wines and its 1981 Limestone Ridge Coonawarra Shiraz Cabernet is one of the greatest Australian wines I have tasted. Among its vinous acquisitions are Rouge Homme in Coonawarra and Leo Buring

in Tanunda. Other wineries are at Pokolbin, Padthaway and Karadoc.

☆ Hunter River Sémillon "Bin 4976", Lindeman's Limestone Ridge Coonawarra Cabernet "Bin 5330", "Bin 77" South Australian Sémillon, "Bin 23" South Australian Rhine Riesling, Padthaway Chardonnay, Limestone Ridge Coonawarra Shiraz Cabernet, White Burgundy Reserve "Bin 6470", Burgundy Reserve "Bin 4000"

McWILLIAM'S WINES
100-132 Bulwara Road,
Pyrmont, NSW 2009

Production: *2.3 million cases*
Vineyards: *202 ha (498 acres) of Chardonnay, Sémillon, Hermitage, Rhine riesling, Malbec, Pinot noir, Syrah and Cabernet sauvignon*
Established: *1877*

Huge production from wineries at Beelbangera, Hanwood, Yenda, Mount Pleasant and Robinvale.

☆ Mount Pleasant Vintage Port

MIRAMAR WINES
Henry Lawson Drive,
Mudgee, NSW 2850

Production: *9,000 cases*
Vineyards: *20 ha (49 acres) of Chardonnay, Rhine riesling, Sémillon, Cabernet Syrah*
Established: *1974*

Fine-quality wines in big, rich, true Mudgee style.

☆ Sémillon, Sémillon Chardonnay, Chardonnay, Cabernet Sauvignon

MONTROSE WINES
Henry Lawson Drive,
Mudgee, NSW 2850

Production: *54,000 cases*
Vineyards: *72 ha (178 acres) of Chardonnay, Sémillon, Rhine riesling, Gewürztraminer, Pinot noir, Cabernet sauvignon, Syrah, Barbera, Nebbiolo, Sangiovese, Merlot and Sauvignon blanc*
Established: *1974*

The quality of these wines is exciting and constantly improving. Montrose and its excellent Craigmoor winery are now owned by Wyndham Estate.

☆ Wood Matured Sémillon, Stoney Creek Chardonnay, Poets Corner Chardonnay, Sauternes, Barbera Nebbiolo

THE ROBSON VINEYARD
Mount View, NSW 2325

Production: *6,000 cases*
Vineyards: *10 ha (25 acres) of Gewürztraminer, Sauvignon blanc, Merlot, Sémillon, Malbec, Hermitage, Pinot noir, Cabernet sauvignon and Black muscat*
Established: *1972*

The overall quality of this small winery is good, but the reds excel and can be truly exceptional.

☆ Traditional Sémillon, Malbec, Cabernet Sauvignon

ROSEMOUNT ESTATE
Rosemount Road,
Denman, NSW 2328

Vineyards: *480 ha (1,186 acres) of Chardonnay, Pinot noir, Sémillon, Gewürztraminer, Sauvignon blanc, Cabernet sauvignon and Syrah*
Established: *1969*

With a fastidiously high level of winemaking expertise and an aggressive export marketing policy, Rosemount has become a sort of Australian super-Mondavi.

☆ Fumé Blanc, Chardonnay (especially "Show Reserve" and "Roxburgh"), Sémillon, Sémillon Sauternes, Shiraz, "Roxburgh" Cabernet Sauvignon, Chardonnay Brut (*méthode champenoise*)

SAXONVALE WINES
Fordwich Estate,
Broke Road,
Broke, NSW 2330

Production: *50,000 cases*
Vineyards: *123.04 ha (304 acres) of Sémillon, Chardonnay, Gewürztraminer, Sauvignon blanc, Pinot noir, Syrah and Cabernet sauvignon*
Established: *1974*

High-tech winery producing a fine range of wines, but excelling in whites.

☆ Limousin Oak Chardonnay "Bin 1", Sémillon

J.Y. TULLOCH & SONS
Glen Elgin Estate,
De Beyer's Road,
Pokolbin, NSW 2321

Production: *21,000 cases*
Vineyards: *16 ha (40 acres) of Chardonnay, Verdelho, Sémillon, Syrah and Cabernet sauvignon*
Established: *1893*

The quality of these wines is generally good, with the occasional star-performer.

☆ "Glen Elgin Private Bin" Hunter River Riesling, Private Bin Dry Red Hermitage

TYRRELL'S VINEYARDS
"Ashmans", Broke Road,
Pokolbin, NSW 2321

Production: *120,000 cases*
Vineyards: *240 ha (593 acres) of Sémillon, Chardonnay, Gewürztraminer, Blanquette, Trebbiano, Sauvignon blanc, Syrah,*

Continued overleaf

Merlot, Malbec and Cabernet
Established: *1858*

This old-established winery has a huge range. Its best wines are uncompromising in their richness and complexity.

☆ "Anniversary" Hermitage, Chardonnay "Vat 47", "Long Flat Red", "Old Winery" Pinot Chardonnay, Pinot Noir *(méthode champenoise)*, "Vat 1" Riesling, "Vat 11" Hermitage

WYNDHAM ESTATE WINES
Dalwood via Branxton, NSW 2335

Production: *360,000 cases*
Vineyards: *450 ha (1,112 acres) of Chardonnay, Gewürztraminer, Sémillon, Rhine riesling, Verdelho, Sylvaner, Muscadelle, Sauvignon blanc, Muscat, Malbec, Hermitage, Cabernet sauvignon, Ruby cabernet, Pinot noir and Matara*
Established: *1971*

A large source of good-value wines; the Hunter Estate and Richmond Grove are supposed to be superior labels, but the basic Wyndham Estate label can be just as good.

☆ Wyndham Estate Cabernet Sauvignon "Bin 444", Cabernet-Merlot "Bin 888"

The best of the rest

AMBERTON WINES
Henry Lawson Drive,
Mudgee, NSW 2850

Production: *6,000 cases*
Vineyards: *30 ha (74 acres) of Chardonnay and Sauvignon blanc*
Established: *1975*
Now owned by Wyndham Estate.

☆ Traminer, Lowes Peak Sauvignon Blanc, Chardonnay, Cabernet Sauvignon, Syrah

BARWANG VINEYARDS
Barwang Road,
Young, NSW 2594

Production: *2,700 cases*
Vineyards: *10 ha (25 acres) of Sémillon, Rhine riesling, Chardonnay, Cabernet sauvignon, Syrah, Cabernet franc, Merlot, Pinot noir and Muscat*
Established: *1974*

☆ Late-Picked Sémillon

BENFIELD ESTATE
Fairy Hole Road,
Yass, NSW 2582

Production: *3,500 cases*
Vineyards: *11 ha (27 acres) of Chardonnay, Rhine riesling, Sémillon, Gewürztraminer, Cabernet sauvignon, Cabernet franc, Merlot, Malbec and Frontignan*
Established: *1980*

☆ Cabernet Sauvignon, Sémillon "Vat 1"

BURNBRAE
Hargraves Road,
Mudgee, NSW 2850

Production: *1,800 cases*
Vineyards: *10 ha (25 acres)*
Established: *1976*

☆ Cabernet Shiraz, Cabernet Sauvignon Vintage Port

CASSEGRAIN VINEYARDS
Pacific Highway,
Port Macquarie, NSW

Production: *12,000 cases*
Vineyards: *16 ha (40 acres) of Pinot noir, Merlot, Chardonnay, Cabernet sauvignon, Chamboucin, Sauvignon blanc and Gewürztraminer*
Established: *1980*

☆ Coonawarra Cabernet Sauvignon

"THE COLLEGE" WINERY
Boorooma Street,
Wagga Wagga, NSW 2650

Production: *6,000 cases*
Vineyards: *15 ha (37 acres) of Rhine riesling, Chardonnay, Pinot gris, Gewürztraminer, Cabernet sauvignon, Cabernet franc, Merlot and Touriga*
Established: *1977*

☆ Cabernet Sauvignon Merlot

DOONKUNA ESTATE
Barton Highway,
Murrumbateman, NSW 2582

Production: *900 cases*
Vineyards: *5.5 ha (14 acres) of Chardonnay, Rhine riesling, Sauvignon blanc, Sémillon, Cabernet sauvignon, Pinot noir and Syrah*
Established: *1974*

☆ Cabernet Sauvignon, Pinot Noir

HILL OF GOLD
Henry Lawson Drive,
Mudgee, NSW 2850

Production: *2,400 cases*
Vineyards: *12 ha (30 acres)*
Established: *1974*

☆ "Gold Medal" Port

LARK HILL
Gundaroo Road,
Bungendore, NSW 2621

Production: *1,300 cases*
Vineyards: *6 ha (15 acres) of Chardonnay, Rhine riesling, Sémillon, Cabernet sauvignon and Pinot noir*
Established: *1978*

☆ Carbonic Maceration Shiraz

LITTLE'S WINERY
Palmers Lane,
Pokolbin, NSW 2321

Production: *3,000 cases*
Vineyards: *14 ha (35 acres) of Chardonnay, Pinot noir, Sémillon, Gewürztraminer, Blanquette, Cabernet and Syrah*
Established: *1984*

☆ Honeytree Sémillon, Chardonnay (Oak matured)

PETERSONS WINES
Mount View Road,
Mount View, NSW 2325

Production: *6,000 cases*
Vineyards: *12 ha (30 acres) of Chardonnay, Sémillon, Hermitage, Cabernet sauvignon and Pinot noir*
Established: *1971*

☆ Chardonnay, Sauternes, Hermitage

PLATT'S
Mudgee Road,
Gulgong, NSW 2852

Production: *6,000 cases*
Vineyards: *10.2 ha (25 acres) of Chardonnay, Sauvignon blanc, Sémillon, Cabernet, Pinot noir and Gewürztraminer*
Established: *1979*

☆ Mudgee Pinot Noir

RICHMOND ESTATE
Gadds Road,
North Richmond NSW 2754

Production: *500 cases*
Vineyards: *6.5 ha (16 acres) of Malbec, Syrah and Cabernet*
Established: *1967*

A tiny vineyard producing a small quantity of good but variable-quality wine. The Shiraz is the best and the most reliable.

☆ Shiraz

THE ROTHBURY ESTATE
Broke Road,
Pokolbin, NSW 2321

Production: *100,000 cases*
Vineyards: *170 ha (420 acres) of Chardonnay, Sémillon, Sauvignon blanc, Gewürztraminer, Pinot noir, Cabernet sauvignon and Hermitage*
Established: *1968*

☆ Rothbury Estate Marsanne, "Black Label" Wood Matured Sémillon, Len Evans Sémillon Chardonnay, "Black Label" Chardonnay, "White Label" Homestead Hill Hermitage, "Black Label" I.P. Hermitage (Rothbury Vineyard)

SUTHERLAND WINES
Deasey's Road,
Pokolbin, NSW 2321

Production: *6,000 cases*
Vineyards: *22 ha (54 acres) of Chardonnay, Sémillon, Chenin blanc, Syrah, Cabernet sauvignon and Pinot noir*
Established: *1979*

☆ Sémillon, Oak Matured Sémillon Chardonnay

TAMBURLAINE
McDonalds Road,
Pokolbin, NSW 2321

Production: *3,000 cases*
Vineyards: *10 ha (25 acres) of Syrah, Cabernet sauvignon and Sémillon*
Established: *1966*

☆ Pokolbin Sémillon Oak Matured

VERONA VINEYARD
New England Highway,
Muswellbrook, NSW 2333

Production: *1,600 cases*
Vineyards: *27 ha (67 acres) of Chardonnay, Rhine riesling, Sémillon, Gewürztraminer, Sauvignon blanc, Cabernet sauvignon and Syrah*
Established: *1972*

☆ Premium Chardonnay

WOLLUNDRY WINES
(Now Calais Estate)
Palmers Lane, Pokolbin, NSW 2321

Vineyards: *24 ha (59 acres) of Chardonnay, Sémillon, Gewürztraminer, Hermitage and Cabernet sauvignon*
Established: *1971*

☆ Chardonnay

WYBONG ESTATE (Horderns')
Yarraman Road,
Wybong, NSW 2333

Production: *6,000 cases*
Vineyards: *20 ha (49 acres) of Chardonnay, Sémillon, Syrah, Gewürztraminer and Rhine riesling*
Established: *1969*

☆ Sémillon (Wood-aged)

Victoria and Tasmania

Of these two high-quality wine regions, Victoria is the older, more traditional area, Tasmania the newcomer. The wines range from the magnificent and uniquely Australian liqueur muscat and other dessert wines, through the deep-coloured, intensely *cassis*-flavoured Cabernet Sauvignons, to light, delicate and racy Rhine Rieslings, the spicy Traminers and the rich, oaky Chardonnays and Sémillons to top-quality sparkling wines.

VICTORIA

JOHN BATMAN ESTABLISHED MELBOURNE in 1834 and within four years, William Ryrie, a pastoralist, had planted the first Yarra Valley vineyard at what was to be Yering. The most important sequence of events in the viticultural history of the state began with the appointment of Swiss-born Charles La Trobe as Superintendent of Melbourne in 1839 and culminated in the arrival of 11 fellow Swiss *vignerons* from his home canton of Neuchâtel in 1846. It was this band of Swiss who formed the great foundation of Victoria's future wine industry, when they settled in the Geelong district and planted vineyards around their homes.

TASMANIA

Although this is really a new wine region, the first vines planted here were established in 1823 at Prospect Farm by Bartholomew Broughton, an extraordinary convict who was granted a pardon

FACTORS AFFECTING TASTE AND QUALITY

Location
Victoria is the smallest of Australia's mainland states, situated in the very southeastern corner of the continent. The island of Tasmania lies 160 kilometres (100 miles) due south of Victoria.

Climate
Climates are extremely varied, ranging from the hot continental conditions of the North West around Mildura, to the temperate coastal climes of the Yarra Valley and the cooler conditions of Tasmania.

Aspect
Vines are grown on all types of land from the flat or undulating low-lying valley plains, mostly producing vast quantities of basic-quality wines, to the steeper, sloping sites favoured for premium wines where vineyards are planted to an altitude of 500 metres (1,600 ft) and higher.

Soil
A wide variety of soils, ranging from the red loam of North East Victoria producing its famous fortified wines, through the sandy alluvial soils of the Murray Basin that mainly produce bulk wines, the gravelly soil mixed with quartz and shale on a clay subsoil found in the premium wine-producing Pyrenees area, the rich, poorly drained soils in Geelong, to the clay of Tasmania.

Viticulture and vinification
Victoria is the only Australian state to have been totally devastated by phylloxera and, unlike neighbouring South Australia, its vines all have to be grafted onto American rootstock. It generally utilizes high-quality wine-producing techniques. The North East is traditionally dessert wine country, but here, as elsewhere in Australia, winemakers have searched for cool-climate areas to expand the state's premium varietal industry since the 1970s. The famous *méthode champenoise* sparkling wines of Victoria's Great Western region suffered in comparison to new up-and-coming sparkling wine areas such as the French-influenced Bendigo district to the east.
Tasmania has also taken to sparkling wine and its cool climate has led to a varied cultivation of classic grape varieties. Viticulture and methods of vinification are in a constant state of flux as the tiny new wineries seek to establish a style.

Grape varieties
Cabernet franc, Cabernet sauvignon, Chardonnay, Chasselas, Chenin blanc, Cinsault, Dolcetto, Folle blanche, Frontignan, Gewürztraminer, Malbec, Marsanne, Mataro, Merlot, Müller-Thurgau, Muscat d'Alexandrie, Pinot meunier, Pinot noir, Rhine riesling, Rubired, Sauvignon blanc, Shiraz, Sémillon, Tokay, Traminer, Troia

VICTORIA AND TASMANIA

The relatively small state of Victoria lies beneath New South Wales and neighbouring South Australia. Tasmania lies due south, on the same latitude as New Zealand's South Island. This area covers a wide variety of climates, terrains and wines.

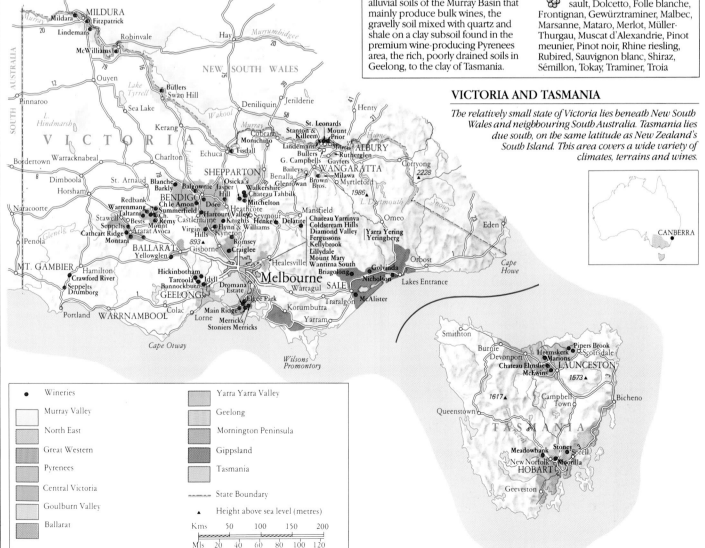

Legend

- ● Wineries
- Murray Valley
- North East
- Great Western
- Pyrenees
- Central Victoria
- Goulburn Valley
- Ballarat
- Yarra Yarra Valley
- Geelong
- Mornington Peninsula
- Gippsland
- Tasmania
- ----- State Boundary
- ▲ Height above sea level (metres)

Kms 50 100 150 200
Mls 20 40 60 80 100 120

and eventually came to own a substantial amount of property. By 1827 the quality of his wines had prompted the *Colonial Times* to contrast them with those of Gregory Blaxland, whose Parramatta River vineyard near Sydney had already produced Australia's first exported and first medal-winning wine. The paper reported that Dr. Shewin, who had tasted Blaxland's famous wine, remarked that by comparison Broughton's was "as far superior as fine Port to Blackstrap". But such was the cruelty of Britain's penal system in the colonies that it took its toll on Broughton's lifespan. His successful attempt to be pardoned suggests that he probably suffered less than most convicts at the time, but it was sufficient to cut short the luxury of his freedom. He died in 1828, aged 32.

Captain Charles Swanston purchased Broughton's property and continued with winegrowing. By 1865 there were no less than 45 different varieties of vines flourishing at various sites on the island. Yet, by the end of the same decade, virtually all the vineyards had disappeared. Swanston's successor was not interested in viticulture and a combination of personal ruin and Gold Rush fever disposed of the rest. Except for an ephemeral resurgence in the 1880s, Tasmania's wine industry was non-existent until the renaissance of the 1950s, led by a Frenchman called Jean Miguet.

Miguet was not a *vigneron* by profession; his arrival in Tasmania was due to the construction of a hydro-electric development. But his new home at La Provence, north of Launceston, reminded him of his native Haute-Savoie and, as it was protected from ocean winds by trees, he believed that grapes might ripen there. In 1956 he cleared his bramble-strewn land and planted vines that grew successfully enough to encourage another European, Claudio Alcorso, to establish a vineyard on the Derwent River in 1958. Alcorso and his Moorilla Estate are still prospering, but after fifteen years, ill-health forced Miguet to abandon his vineyard and return to France, where he sadly died from leukaemia in 1974.

After thirty years, the Tasmanian wine industry is still tiny, but the quality is high. It is an island whose destiny is to produce Australia's most fragrant and aromatic white wine and probably some of its finest *méthode champenoise* too.

Pipers Brook Vineyard, Tasmania, above
One of the pair of major wineries (the other being Heemskerk) that dominate Pipers Brook, the most successful wine-producing district of Tasmania.

Chateau Tahbilk, Goulburn Valley, left
This well-known Victorian winery's huge output consists of traditionally made wines. Its Cabernets can be very tannic, requiring at least ten years in bottle.

The wines of Victoria and Tasmania

AVOCA

This is the old name for the vineyards around Mount Avoca, Redbank and Moonambel, *See* Pyrenees.

BALLARAT

Situated within Central Victoria, some 120 kilometres (75 miles) northwest of Melbourne, this district includes vineyards growing at an altitude of 430 metres (1,400 ft) in Scarsdale, Creswick and Ballan. The climate is cooler than at Bendigo. Ballarat could become one of Australia's best sparkling wine areas.

SPARKLING: 1980, 1984, 1985

BAROOGA
See Murray River.

BENDIGO

North of Ballarat, situated about 160 kilometres (100 miles) northwest of Melbourne, this part of the Central Victoria region has a dry climate, although only some of its vines are irrigated, with the others digging deep into the water-retentive subsoil to survive. This is goldmining country, and viticulture began here at the time of the 1850s Gold Rush. The main growing areas are in Baynton, Big Hill, Bridgewater, Heathcote, Harcourt, Kingower, Maiden Gully, Mandurang and Mount Ida. Primarily known for its menthol-eucalyptus-tasting red wines, the red clay, quartz and ironstone soil is suited to producing fine Shiraz, but Cabernet sauvignon and Chardonnay can also excel and with Moët & Chandon's recent multi-million dollar interest in the area, the potential for quality sparkling wines must also exist.

RED: 1980, 1982, 1983, 1984, 1985, 1986, 1987, 1988

WHITE: 1980, 1982, 1984, 1985, 1986, 1987, 1988

BEVERFORD
See Murray River.

CENTRAL VICTORIA

This region is comprised of a loose association of viticultural areas, Bendigo, Ballarat and Macedon being the most important. *See* Ballarat, Bendigo and Macedon.

COASTAL VICTORIA

This remote region, which encompasses East Gippsland and South Gippsland and is sometimes simply called Gippsland, was revived in the 1970s when Dacre Stubbs planted the Lulgra vineyard. Apart from occasional fine Cabernet Sauvignon, Pinot Noir or Chardonnay from one or two tiny wineries, little is happening as yet in this backwater wine area.

DRUMBORG

A remote area in southwest Victoria, best known for its Seppelts Drumborg winery, which was established when the firm was searching out more grapes to supply its growing production of sparkling wines in the 1960s. The soil is volcanic and the climate so cold that some varieties did not ripen. It is surprising, therefore, that the Cabernet sauvignon should be so successful here, but it can be excellent; Rhine Riesling and Traminer are also very good. Other wineries that have now opened up within this district include Crawford River Wines, which produces superb Rhine Riesling between Condah and Hotspur, and Cherrita Wines near Branxholme.

RED: 1980, 1982, 1984, 1985, 1986, 1987, 1988

WHITE: 1981, 1984, 1985, 1986, 1987, 1988

EAST GIPPSLAND
See Coastal Victoria.

GEELONG

South of Ballarat, along the coast from the Yarra Valley, the vineyards of this district fan out through the hinterland of Corio Bay. Originally worked by Swiss immigrants in the mid-1800s, the viticultural revival arrived in 1966, somewhat earlier than in other rediscovered areas of Australia, when the Seftons planted the Idyll vineyard. A combination of cool climate and volcanic soil produces wines with fine acidity readings and strong varietal character. Idyll and Hickinbotham are the best producers.

RED: 1984, 1985, 1986, 1987, 1988

WHITE: 1980, 1982, 1984, 1985, 1986, 1987, 1988

GIPPSLAND
See Coastal Victoria.

GLENROWAN

Part of the Northeast district, this area is probably best known outside of Australia as Milawa – the use of this alternative name is preferred by Brown Brothers, who put it on their widely exported wines. Glenrowan is, however, more widely used by other winemakers.

This is a classic dessert wine area, but individual vineyards such as Koombahla and Meadow Creek produce scintillating, *cassis*-rich Cabernet Sauvignon and other premium varietals.

RED: 1980, 1982, 1983, 1984, 1985, 1986, 1987, 1988

WHITE: 1982, 1983, 1984, 1985, 1986, 1987, 1988

GOULBURN VALLEY

For years, the excellent Chateau Tahbilk was the solitary exponent of fine wines in this traditional wine area 120 kilometres (75 miles) north of Melbourne. Now many new wineries are attracting attention. Cabernet Sauvignon is the best wine produced here – a pure varietal or, more traditionally, blended with Shiraz. Chardonnay and Rhine Riesling can be terrific and Mitchelton even makes an excellent wood-matured Marsanne.

Tisdall dominates the northern Goulburn Valley; Sémillon, Merlot and fast-improving Pinot noir are found.

RED: 1980, 1982, 1983, 1984, 1985, 1986, 1987, 1988

WHITE: 1980, 1982, 1983, 1984, 1985, 1986, 1987, 1988

GREAT WESTERN

This famous old sparkling wine area of the Central Victoria vineyards has been revitalized by increasing interest from recently established ventures. The best of the new-wave wines are the deliciousiy crisp and delicate Chardonnay and zippy-spicy Rhine Riesling. Top-performing wineries are Montara, Mount Chalambar and Seppelt Great Western.

RED: 1980, 1982, 1984, 1985, 1986, 1987, 1988

WHITE: 1980, 1982, 1984, 1985, 1986, 1987, 1988

IRYMPLE
See Murray River.

KARADOC
See Murray River.

LAKE BOGA
See Murray River.

LINDSAY POINT
See Murray River.

MACEDON

A developing district within the Central Victoria region, Macedon encompasses about 90 hectares (220 acres) of vineyards in and around Mount Macedon, Sunbury, Romsey, Lancefield and Kyneton. Soil and topography vary greatly and strong winds are the only common climatic factor. Cabernet sauvignon, Chardonnay and Rhine riesling are the most successful grape varieties so far and Flynn & Williams, Craiglee Vineyards, Knight's Wines (makers of "Granite Hills") and Virgin Hills the best wineries.

RED: 1982, 1983, 1984, 1985, 1986, 1987

WHITE: 1982, 1983, 1984, 1985, 1986, 1987

MERBEIN
See Murray River.

MID-MURRAY

A sub-region in the Murray River, it includes the wine-producing districts of Swan Hill, Lake Boga and Mystic Park. *See* Murray River.

MILAWA

Essentially interchangeable with Glenrowan, although it could be argued that the Milawa area is limited to the immediate vicinity of Milawa itself and Glenrowan to the much larger area on the eastern shore of Lake Mokoan. *See* Glenrowan.

MILDURA

Not to be confused with the Mildara winery, this is an important, high-yielding irrigated region in the Murray River district. *See* Murray River.

MORNINGTON PENINSULA

After an early, but unsuccessful, start in the 1950s, a number of growers have established vineyards in this area overlooking Port Phillip Bay, south of Melbourne, although only a handful have established wineries.

Merricks Estate Shiraz is one of Australia's very best – a stupendous wine with all the magnificent, spicy-rich, clean and flavoursome varietal character this grape can, and should, give. But the Dromana Estate, Elgee Park, Main Ridge Estate and Merricks (not to be confused with Merricks Estate) are all capable of producing wines of breathtaking brilliance from various red and white grapes. Provided the vineyards are adequately protected from strong sea winds that whip up over the bay,

Mornington Peninsula's cool, often wet, climate shows great potential for first-class winemaking.

RED: 1982, 1983, 1984, 1985, 1986, 1987, 1988

WHITE: 1982, 1983, 1984, 1985, 1986, 1987, 1988

MURRAY RIVER

This region takes its name from one of Australia's great wine rivers. Further upstream is the Rutherglen area, while just downstream is Riverland, the "bottomless vat" of South Australia. The Murray River region brings together several areas of mainly irrigated vineyards dotted along the banks of the middle section of the river. Under two sub-regional groupings, they are: Sunraysia (Mildura, Robinvale, Merbein, Irymple, Karadoc) and Mid-Murray (Swan Hill, Lake Boga, Mystic Park). Most wineries are relatively new and producing a decent quality of cask-wine and mid-premium range Chardonnay and Sauvignon Blanc. With high yields, they have quickly established good profit margins and as the vineyards (most of which were planted in the 1970s) mature, the quality will rise and many of the producers are likely to diversify into limited editions of more upmarket products.

RED: 1982, 1983, 1985, 1986, 1987

WHITE: 1982, 1983, 1984, 1985, 1986, 1987

MYSTIC PARK
See Murray River.

THE NORTH EAST

The heart of Victoria's wine industry, the districts of Rutherglen and Milawa/Glenrowan encompassed by this region are most especially famous for their dessert liqueur wines. The area is in a state of flux, with many wineries "taking to the hills" to find cool climates in which to produce fine varietal wines. The great dessert wines are, however, as fabulous as ever. *See* Rutherglen and Glenrowan.

PYRENEES

Formerly known as the Avoca district, the vineyards around Mount Avoca, Redbank and Moonambel are now called Pyrenees, although no doubt the former name will stick for a while. Pyrenees, the name of a nearby mountain range, was chosen by local wine growers as an expressive marketing "hook" upon which to "hang" their wines. By whatever name, this area was originally perceived to be red wine country, making wines of a distinctive and attractive minty character. By virtue, however, of the efforts of Taltarni and Chateau Remy, the Pyrenees is rapidly gaining fame as a white wine district, most notably for Rhine Riesling, Sauvignon Blanc, sparkling wine and, more recently, Chardonnay.

RED: 1982, 1983, 1985 (not in Avoca area), 1986, 1987, 1988

WHITE: 1982, 1983, 1984, 1985, 1986, 1987, 1988

ROBINVALE
See Murray River.

RUTHERGLEN

Rutherglen, whose name is interchangeable with that of Milawa, has always been the heart of the North East region and the soul of Victoria's wine industry. It is the hub around which the entire state's viticultural activities revolve, comprised of a collection of wineries and vineyards clustered either side of the Murray Valley Highway between Lake Mulwala and Albury, on the left bank of the Murray River. The right bank is also cultivated, but is actually in New South Wales (although most people would consider the two as a pair) and this should be officially recognized if and when any appellation system is undertaken. Rutherglen has an exciting emergent light wine industry, with innovative winegrowers exploiting the district's cooler areas. Chardonnay and Sémillon are clean, fresh and vibrant, Gewürztraminer is performing well and Durif, Carignan, Shiraz and Cabernet Sauvignon all show promise of one degree or another. Rutherglen is, however, Australia's greatest dessert wine country. Its liqueur Muscats and Tokays know no peers.

RED: 1982, 1983, 1984, 1985, 1986, 1987

WHITE: 1982, 1983, 1984, 1985, 1986, 1987

SOUTH GIPPSLAND
See Coastal Victoria.

SUNRAYSIA

A sub-region in the Murray River, it includes the districts of Mildura, Robinvale, Merbein, Irymple and Karadoc. *See* Murray River.

SWAN HILL
See Murray River.

TASMANIA

Tasmania is Australia's ultimate cool-climate location. The first vines were planted at Prospect Farm near Hobart in 1823 by Bartholomew Broughton, but viticulture did not last long on what was then Van Dieman's Land. The wine industry was gradually rekindled in the 1950s. There are no big wineries here as yet, but Louis Roederer has teamed up with Heemskerk, and other sparkling-wine specialists are likely to move into the area to exploit its European-type climate. The industry is on course for a significant expansion.

The best wines produced in Tasmania so far have not been sparkling, but the intensely flavoured, vibrantly fruity Cabernet Sauvignon, Chardonnay and Rhine Riesling from top wineries such as Chateau Elmsie, Heemskerk, Marion's Vineyard (formerly sold under the Tamar Valley Vineyard label), Meadowbank, Moorilla Estate – for which see winery entries below.

On January 1, 1986, the Tasmanian government followed the lead set by

Continued overleaf

the Mudgee district in New South Wales by legislating an official appellation system. Now no wine may be labelled Tasmanian unless it is made from 100 per cent Tasmanian-grown grapes. Wineries are subject to checks and audits by officers of the Department of Agriculture and the Licensing Commission, and the wines must undergo analysis and tasting tests. Although not yet separately delimited by Tasmania's Appellation of Origin system, there are five main areas. The major one is Pipers Brook, with half the island's vineyards

(best wineries: Pipers Brook, Heemskerk). Next in importance is the Tamar Valley, with one-quarter of the area under vine (best wineries: Chateau Elmslie, Marion's Vineyard, McEwins), then comes the East Coast, accounting for ten per cent of the area, followed by the Coal River Area, with eight per cent (best winery: Stoney Vineyard), and the South Hobart-Derwent Valley Area, with five per cent (best wineries: Meadowbank, Moorilla). The remaining two per cent are located in remote areas of the island in very tiny plots.

RED: 1984, 1985, 1986, 1987, 1988
WHITE: 1984, 1986, 1987, 1988

YARRA VALLEY

The vines growing on the grey and red loam soils of the newly established vineyards in this area not only benefit from the enriching after-effect of the land's former utilization, sheep-farming, but from one of the coolest climates in Australia. The rainfall is a healthy 81 centimetres (32 ins), the growing

season advantageously long and the yields light. The combination of these factors in the hands of some of the country's most talented winemakers results in some astonishingly fine Chardonnay and Cabernet Sauvignon and lettuce-crisp Rhine Riesling. Gewürztraminer and Pinot Noir are also promising.

RED: 1983, 1984, 1986, 1987, 1988
WHITE: 1980, 1982, 1983, 1984, 1985, 1986, 1987, 1988

Major wineries of Victoria and Tasmania

BAILEYS OF GLENROWAN
Taminick Gap Road, Glenrowan, Vic. 3675

Production: *12,000 cases*
Vineyards: *104 ha (257 acres) of Muscat, Muscadelle, Cabernet sauvignon, Syrah, Rhine riesling and Chardonnay*
Established: *1870*

Rich and stunning dessert wines.

☆ Late Harvest Lexia, "Founder" Liqueur Muscat, "Winemaker's Selection", "Gold Label" and "HJT" Liqueur Muscats, Hermitage "Classic Style", Show Tokay

BALGOWNIE VINEYARD
Hermitage Road, Maiden Gully, Vic. 3551

Production: *7,000 cases*
Vineyards: *13 ha (32 acres)*
Established: *1969*

Top-quality, firm Cabernet Sauvignon and improving Burgundian varietals.

☆ Chardonnay, Pinot Noir, Cabernet Sauvignon

BEST'S WINES
Great Western, Vic. 3377

Production: *48,000 cases*
Vineyards: *50 ha (124 acres)*
Established: *1866*

Large range that includes a few interesting, fine-quality wines.

☆ Chardonnay "Bin No. 0", Hermitage "Bin No. 0", Chardonnay (*méthode champenoise*)

BROWN BROTHERS
Milawa, Vic. 3678

Production: *200,000 cases of premium bottled wine, plus,*

additional bulk production
Vineyards: *145 ha (358 acres) of Cabernet sauvignon, Chardonnay, Pinot noir, Rhine riesling and Syrah*
Established: *1889*

For many years this was the only winery trying to convince world export markets of its country's exciting potential in the quality wine sector. Brown Brothers is constantly adding new gems to its treasure chest, including the amazing 1978 Koombahla Cabernet Sauvignon.

☆ Chardonnay, Koombahla (Cabernet Sauvignon, Chardonnay, Late Harvest Rhine Riesling, Pinot Noir), Late Harvest Orange Muscat, Meadow Creek Cabernet Shiraz, Milawa Estate (Chardonnay, Noble Riesling, Shiraz-Mondeuse-Cabernet), Muscat Blanc (Late Harvest, Liqueur), Noble Riesling, Sémillon, Very Old Tokay

CAMPBELLS WINERY
Murray Valley Highway, Rutherglen, Vic. 3685

Production: *36,000 cases*
Vineyards: *70 ha (173 acres)*
Established: *1870*

Fortified wine specialist now branching out into varietal wines.

☆ "Bobbie Burns" Shiraz, Liqueur Muscats (all), Cabernets

CHATEAU LE AMON
Calder Highway, Big Hill, Bendigo, Vic. 3550

Production: *2,000 cases*
Vineyards: *4 ha (10 acres) of Rhine riesling, Sémillon, Syrah and Cabernet sauvignon*
Established: *1973*

Owned by Ian Leamon, and named after a play on his family name.

☆ "Marong" Shiraz, Cabernet Sauvignon, Hermitage-Cabernet Sauvignon

CHATEAU REMY
Vinoca Road, Avoca, Vic. 3467

Production: *20,000 cases*
Established: *1963*

Best known for its good and constantly improving *méthode champenoise*, but also the producer of a very fine Cabernet-based red wine.

☆ "Blue Pyrenees Estate", Cuvée Speciale Brut

CHATEAU TAHBILK
Tahbilk, Vic. 3607

Production: *30,000 cases*
Vineyards: *80 ha (198 acres) of Cabernet sauvignon, Syrah, Cabernet franc, Marsanne, Sauvignon blanc, Chardonnay, Sémillon, Rhine riesling, Chenin blanc and White hermitage*
Established: *1860*

The oldest winery in Victoria, making very traditional wines that always improve in bottle.

☆ Cabernet Sauvignon (especially "Private Bin"), "Gold Label" (Chardonnay, Marsanne), Shiraz

COLDSTREAM HILLS
Maddens Lane, Gruyere via Coldstream, Vic. 3770

Production: *3,600 cases*
Vineyards: *4.5 ha (11 acres)*
Established: *1985*

This young winery is the enterprise of James Halliday, the doyen of Australia's wine writers. So far, all the signs indicate that he will not give the critics a field day – although he obviously intends giving the consumers one.

☆ Cabernet Sauvignon, Chardonnay, Pinot Noir, Show Chardonnay

ELGEE PARK
Wallaces Road, Merricks North, Vic. 3926

Production: *100 cases*
Established: *1972*

The wines, once made at Ian Hickinbotham's Anakie winery, have been produced on the property since the 1980 vintage, and a new-winemaking facility was constructed in 1984.

☆ Rhine Riesling, Chardonnay, Cabernet Sauvignon, Cabernet-Merlot

THE HEATHCOTE WINERY
183-185 High Street, Heathcote, Vic. 3523

Production: *5,000 cases*
Vineyards: *16 ha (40 acres) of Chardonnay, Pinot noir, Chenin blanc and Gewürztraminer*
Established: *1978*

The soil at Heathcote is renowned for its exceptional potential for producing Shiraz, but all the wines here are very good and the Chardonnay can be a stunningly rich example of soft, ripe grapefruit flavours.

☆ Chardonnay, Shiraz

THE HEEMSKERK VINEYARD
"Heemskerk", Pipers Brook, Tas. 7254

Production: *8,000 cases*
Vineyards: *30 ha (74 acres) of Cabernet sauvignon, Chardonnay and Pinot noir*
Established: *1974*

The success of Heemskerk's cool-climate vineyards persuaded Roederer Champagne to take a share in this venture. Great things are expected from Tasmania's first *méthode champenoise*.

☆ Cabernet Sauvignon, Chardonnay, Rhine Riesling

HICKINBOTHAM WINEMAKERS
2 Ferguson Street,
Williamstown, Vic. 3016

Production: *16,000 cases*
Vineyards: *15 ha (37 acres) of Cabernet sauvignon, Cabernet franc, Riesling, Chardonnay and Merlot*
Established: *1980*

Alan Hickinbotham established the now famous oenology course at the Roseworthy Agricultural College. His son Ian, a well-known wine columnist, took over the Anakie vineyard to fulfil his ambition of making his own wine. After graduating from Bordeaux University, Ian's son Stephen was just beginning to establish a reputation as one of the country's most talented winemakers when he was killed in an air-crash. Stephen's brother Ian, who established his own vineyard on the Mornington Peninsula, now assists his father and, despite its tragic loss, the family goes from strength to strength.

☆ Anakie Chardonnay, Anakie Cabernet, Anakie Shiraz, "Ultima Thuley"

MERRICKS
Thompsons Lane,
Merricks, Vic. 3916

Production: *250 cases*
Vineyards: *5 ha (12 acres) of Cabernet sauvignon, Pinot noir and Chardonnay*
Established: *1984 (first release)*

Confusingly, there are two Merricks and both in Thompsons Lane, Merricks! This one is owned by Brian Stonier and the excellent wines are now made by Ted Dexter at Elgee Park.

☆ Cabernet Sauvignon

MERRICKS ESTATE
62 Thompsons Lane,
Merricks, Vic. 3916

Production: *300 cases*
Vineyards: *7 ha (18 acres) of Cabernet sauvignon, Chardonnay, Rhine riesling, Pinot noir and Syrah*
Established: *1978*

After a shaky start, during which the self-taught amateur George Kefford admits that he poured some of his mistakes down the drain, the quality of this tiny production has rocketed.

☆ Shiraz, Cabernet Sauvignon

MILDARA WINES
Wentworth Road,
Merbein, Vic. 3505

Production: *1,080,000 cases*
Vineyards: *254 ha (628 acres) of Cabernet franc, Cabernet sauvignon, Merlot, Malbec, Pinot noir, Chardonnay, Rhine riesling, Sauvignon blanc, Gewürztraminer and Syrah*
Established: *1888*

As this book goes to press, Mildara celebrates its centenary, and since the late-1970s, it has moved on from a reputation based almost entirely on fortified wines to develop a faithful following for its rather elegant style of varietal wines.

☆ "Bin 47" Cabernet Shiraz, Sauvignon Blanc, Hermitage, Cabernet Merlot, "J.W. Classic" Cabernet Shiraz

MITCHELTON VINTNERS
Mitchellstown,
Via Nagambie, Vic. 3608

Production: *70,000 cases*
Vineyards: *110 ha (272 acres) of Chardonnay, Marsanne, Rhine riesling, Sémillon, Ugni blanc, Cabernet sauvignon, Cabernet franc, Syrah and Merlot*
Established: *1969*

Superior selections from other areas (usually Coonawarra or Mount Barker in Western Australia) are sold under the "Winemakers Selection" label. The straight Mitchelton label is for wines from its own excellent Goulburn Valley. Mature "Classic Release" wines are always worth looking out for, and wines marketed under the "Thomas Mitchell" label can be good value.

☆ Rhine Riesling (especially "Winemakers Selection" and Botrytis-affected "Winemakers Selection"), "Classic Release" Marsanne, Sémillon Wood Matured, "Thomas Mitchell" Chablis Wood Matured

MOORILLA ESTATE
655 Main Road,
Berriedale, Tas. 7011

Production: *3,000 cases*
Vineyards: *15 ha (37 acres) of Pinot noir, Riesling, Cabernet sauvignon and Gewürztraminer*
Established: *1958*

After 30 years, this pioneering Tasmanian winery has firmly established that the island is capable of producing great wines from cool-climate grapes such as Chardonnay, Pinot noir and Riesling.

☆ Pinot Noir, Botrytis Rhine Riesling, Chardonnay

MORRIS WINES
Rutherglen, Vic. 3685

Production: *55,000 cases*
Vineyards: *80 ha (198 acres) of Syrah, Durif, Cabernet sauvignon, Muscadelle, Brown muscat, Sémillon and Blue imperial*
Established: *1859*

Old-established firm producing outstanding traditional liqueur Muscats and Tokays. Now belongs to Orlando.

☆ Sémillon, Chardonnay, "Old Premium" Tokay, "Old Premium" Muscat

PIPERS BROOK VINEYARD
Pipers Brook, Tas. 7254

Production: *4,500 cases*
Vineyards: *11 ha (27 acres) of Riesling, Chardonnay, Gewürztraminer, Cabernet sauvignon and Pinot noir*
Established: *1972*

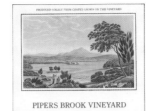

PRODUCED SOLELY FROM GRAPES GROWN ON THIS VINEYARD

PIPERS BROOK VINEYARD

1986 PINOT NOIR

Tasmania

This winery consistently produces delightful and stylish wines of the highest quality, with one of the most attractive Australian labels.

☆ Pinot Noir, Cabernet Sauvignon, Cabernet Blend, Chardonnay, Rhine Riesling

ST. HUBERTS
St. Huberts Road,
Coldstream, Vic. 3770

Production: *18,000 cases*
Vineyards: *20 ha (49 acres) of Cabernet sauvignon, Syrah, Pinot noir, Merlot, Chardonnay, Rhine riesling and Sauvignon blanc*
Established: *1966*

When this winery is on form the wines recommended can be outstanding.

☆ Cabernet Sauvignon, Chardonnay, Rhine Riesling *Beerenauslese*

ST. LEONARDS VINEYARD
Wahgunyah, Vic. 3687

Production: *12,000 cases*
Vineyards: *40 ha (99 acres) of Cabernet sauvignon, Merlot, Malbec, Syrah, Chardonnay, Chenin blanc, Sauvignon blanc, Sémillon, Gewürztraminer and Orange muscat*
Established: 1973

Brown Brothers, who own the property in conjunction with a syndicate, started to make and sell these wines under their own label in 1980.

☆ Cabernet Sauvignon, Chardonnay, Gewürztraminer, Late Bottled Port, Orange Muscat

SEVILLE ESTATE
Linwood Road,
Seville, Vic. 3139

Production: *1,200 cases*
Vineyards: *3.6 ha (9 acres) of Cabernet sauvignon, Merlot, Cabernet franc, Pinot noir, Syrah, Chardonnay and Rhine riesling*
Established: *1970*

Just occasionally the quality of these wines can slip, but virtually every wine produced is outstanding. The luxurious style can only be accomplished in small quantities. A *Trockenbeerenauslese* is

sometimes made, but I have not tasted it, nor heard any reports of it.

☆ Rhine Riesling *Beerenauslese*, Pinot Noir, Cabernet Sauvignon

TALTARNI VINEYARDS
Moonambel, Vic. 3478

Production: *42,000 cases*
Vineyards: *110 ha (272 acres) of Rhine riesling, Ugni blanc, Chenin blanc, Sauvignon blanc, Chardonnay, Cabernet sauvignon, Malbec, Syrah and Merlot*
Established: *1972*

Taltarni is Aboriginal for "red earth", the soil in this vineyard being an iron-rich siliceous clay and duly red. This site was selected on the basis of its soil and climate, and was established by the sons of André Portet, technical director of Château Lafite-Rothschild between 1955 and 1975. This blend of French and Australian influences is obviously magical. The wines have been excellent from the start and continue to improve with each and every vintage.

☆ Blanc des Pyreness Chablis Style, Brut Blanc de Blancs, Cabernet Sauvignon, French Syrah, Fumé Blanc, Rhine riesling

TISDALL WINES
19 Cornelia Creek Road,
Echuca, Vic. 3564

Production: *72,000 cases*
Vineyards: *130 ha (321 acres) of Chardonnay, Sauvignon blanc, Rhine riesling, Sémillon, Chenin blanc, Columbard, Ugni blanc, Gewürztraminer, Pinot noir, Cabernet sauvignon, Merlot, Syrah, Ruby cabernet and Malbec*
Established: *1979*

An ambitious but successful operation, Tisdall not only dominates the North Goulburn River district, it also represents one of the largest and most consistent of Victoria's quality wine producers.

☆ "Mount Helen" Chardonnay, "Selected Series" Sémillon, Tisdall Cabernet Merlot, "Mount Helen" Cabernet Sauvignon

VIRGIN HILLS VINEYARDS
Kyneton, Vic. 3444

Production: *2,000 cases*
Vineyards: *13.5 ha (33 acres) of Cabernet sauvignon, Syrah, Malbec,*

Continued overleaf

Merlot, Chardonnay, Gewürztraminer and Rhine riesling
Established: *1968*

The creation of Hungarian-born Melbourne restaurateur Tom Lazar, this "one-wine-winery" must be unique in Australia. The wine is labelled simply "Virgin Hills", with no indication of varietal or generic character; in fact it is approximately 75 per cent Cabernet sauvignon, blended with Syrah and a little Malbec. Lazar did not even learn his winemaking from a correspondence course, he simply read a book, planted a vineyard and made his wine. Since he retired, Mark Sheppard has taken over the winemaking, but continues to follow Lazar's methods and the wine remains one of the country's best. With Chardonnay, Gewürztraminer and Rhine riesling also planted, there may well be some good white wines on the way.

☆ Virgin Hills

WANTIRNA ESTATE
Bushy Park Lane,
Wantirna South, Vic. 3152

Production: *1,200 cases*
Vineyards: *4 ha (10 acres) of Cabernet sauvignon, Merlot, Pinot noir and Chardonnay*
Established: *1963*

Reg Egan, a Melbourne solicitor, produces fine wines in his spare time.

☆ Pinot Noir, Cabernet Sauvignon and Merlot

YARRA YERING
Briarty Road,
Gruyere via Coldstream, Vic. 3770

Production: *3,500 cases*
Vineyards: *12 ha (30 acres) Cabernet sauvignon, Malbec, Merlot, Pinot noir, Chardonnay, Sémillon and Syrah*
Established: *1969*

Dr. Bailey Carrodus was the first wine-maker in the Yarra Valley. His pure varietals are often an unknown quantity, although when the Pinot Noir is performing well, it is excellent. But where Dr. Carrodus really excels is in his basic blended wines: the Dry Red No. 1 is a Bordeaux-type blend of Cabernet sauvignon, Malbec and Merlot, while the No. 2 is a Rhône-type blend based on 85 per cent Syrah.

☆ Dry Red "No. 1", Dry Red "No. 2"

YARRINYA ESTATE
See De Bortoli Wines

YELLOWGLEN VINEYARDS
White's Road,
Smythesdale, Vic. 3351

Production: *12,000 cases*
Vineyards: *18 ha (44 acres) of Pinot noir, Chardonnay and Cabernet sauvignon*
Established: *1971*

This exciting little operation has recently started in the sparkling wine business. Started by Australian Ian Home and Champenois Dominique Landragin, it is now owned by Mildara. The wines would be superior if aged a little longer before disgorging, but this is a new venture. I believe that Yellowglen could become more successful than Chateau Remy in the nearby Pyrenees.

☆ Home and Landragin (Chardonnay Méthode Champenoise, Crémant Brut Extra, Blanc de Noirs)

The best of the rest

BANNOCKBURN VINEYARDS
Midland Highway,
Bannockburn, Vic. 3331

Production: *6,000 cases*
Vineyards: *16 ha (40 acres) of Pinot noir, Chardonnay, Cabernet sauvignon, Sauvignon blanc and Syrah*
Established: *1973*

☆ Shiraz

BLANCHE BARKLY WINES
Rheola Road,
Kingower, Vic. 3517

Production: *5,000 cases*
Established: *1972*

☆ Hermitage Nouveau, "Johanne" Cabernet Sauvignon

BRIAGOLONG ESTATE
Valencia-Briagolong Roads,
Briagolong, Vic. 3860

Production: *100 cases*
Vineyards: *2 ha (5 acres) of Pinot noir, Chardonnay and Sauvignon blanc*
Established: *1979*

☆ Pinot Noir

BULLERS
Three Chain Road,
Rutherglen, Vic. 3685

Production: *3,000 cases*
Established: *1955*

☆ Vintage Port

CATHCART RIDGE ESTATE
Cathcart via Ararat, Vic. 3377

Production: *2,000 cases*
Vineyards: *13.5 ha (33 acres) of Cabernet sauvignon, Merlot, Chardonnay, Rhine riesling and Syrah*
Established: *1977*

☆ Shiraz

CHATEAU ELMSLIE
McEwins Road,
Legana, Tas. 7251

Production: *55 cases*

☆ Cabernet Sauvignon

CRAIGLEE
Sunbury Road,
Sunbury, Vic. 3429

Production: *2,000 cases*
Vineyards: *Syrah, Cabernet, Chardonnay and Pinot noir*
Established: *1976*

☆ "Craiglee" (red)

CRAWFORD RIVER
Crawford,
via Condah, Vic. 3303

Production: *600 cases*
Vineyards: *7 ha (17 acres) of Rhine riesling, Cabernet sauvignon and Merlot*
Established: *1975*

☆ Riesling, Riesling *Beerenauslese*

DELATITE WINERY
Pollards Road,
Mansfield, Vic. 3722

Production: *7,500 cases*
Vineyards: *20 ha (49 acres) of Rhine riesling, Gewürztraminer, Sylvaner, Chardonnay, Sauvignon blanc, Cabernet sauvignon, Syrah, Pinot noir, Malbec and Merlot*
Established: *1969*

☆ Cabernet Sauvignon Merlot

DIAMOND VALLEY VINEYARDS
Kinglake Road,
St. Andrews, Vic. 3761

Production: *1,500 cases*
Vineyards: *2.8 ha (6 acres) of Rhine riesling, Cabernet sauvignon, Merlot, Malbec, Cabernet franc and Pinot noir*
Established: *1976*

☆ Cabernet, Pinot Noir

DROMANA ESTATE
Harrisons Road,
Dromana, Vic. 3936

Production: *550 cases*
Vineyards: *5 ha (12 acres) of Pinot noir, Cabernet sauvignon, Chardonnay, Cabernet franc and Merlot*
Established: *1981*

☆ Cabernet Sauvignon

FERGUSSON'S WINERY
Wills Road,
Yarra Glen, Vic. 3775

Production: *5,400 cases*
Vineyards: *16 ha (40 acres) of Riesling, Chardonnay, Chenin blanc, Syrah, Cabernet sauvignon and Cabernet franc*
Established: *1968*

☆ Cabernet Sauvignon

GOLVINDA WINES
Lindenow Road,
Lindenow South, Vic. 3865

Established: *1972*

☆ Cabernet Sauvignon

HARCOURT VALLEY VINEYARDS
Calder Highway,
Harcourt, Vic. 3453

Production: *1,200 cases*
Vineyards: *4 ha (10 acres) of Cabernet sauvignon, Syrah, Rhine riesling and Chardonnay*
Established: *1976*

☆ Cabernet Sauvignon

THE HENKE WINERY
Henke's Lane,
Yarck, Vic. 3719

Production: *1,200 cases*
Vineyards: *5 ha (12 acres) of Syrah,*
Cabernet sauvignon, Sémillon and Crouchen
Established: *1970*

☆ Shiraz Cabernet

IDYLL VINEYARD
265 Ballan Road,
Moorabool, Vic. 3221

Production: *6,000 cases*
Vineyards: *20 ha (49 acres) of Cabernet sauvignon, Syrah and Gewürztraminer*
Established: *1966*

☆ Gewürztraminer Wood Matured, Gewürztraminer, Cabernet Shiraz

JASPER HILL VINEYARD
Drummonds Lane,
Heathcote, Vic. 3523

Production: *1,100 cases*
Vineyards: *15 ha (37 acres) of Cabernet franc, Riesling, Sauvignon blanc and Pinot noir*
Established: *1976*

☆ "Emily's Paddock" Shiraz, "Georgia's Paddock" Shiraz

KELLYBROOK WINERY
Fulford Road,
Wonga Park, Vic. 3115

Production: *3,600 cases*
Vineyards: *13 ha (32 acres) of Chardonnay, Rhine riesling, Gewürztraminer, Pinot noir, Cabernet sauvignon and Syrah*
Established: *1960*

☆ Shiraz, Cabernet Sauvignon

KNIGHT'S WINES
R.S.D. 83,
Baynton via Kyneton, Vic. 3444

Production: *3,000 cases*
Vineyards: *8 ha (20 acres)*
Established: *1971*

☆ Rhine Riesling

LILLYDALE VINEYARDS
Davross Court,
Seville, Vic. 3139

Production: *3,000 cases*
Vineyards: *7.8 ha (19 acres) of Chardonnay, Gewürztraminer, Rhine riesling, Sauvignon blanc, Cabernet sauvignon and Merlot*
Established: *1976*

☆ Chardonnay

LONGLEAT
Old Weir Road,
Murchison, Vic. 3610

Production: *2,500 cases*
Vineyards: *30 ha (74 acres) of Cabernet sauvignon, Syrah, Pinot noir, Sémillon, Rhine riesling and Chardonnay*
Established: *1975*

☆ Cabernet Shiraz

MAIN RIDGE ESTATE
William Road,
Red Hill, Vic. 3937

Production: *800 cases*
Vineyards: *2.5 ha (6 acres) of Cabernet sauvignon, Cabernet franc, Pinot meunier, Pinot noir, Chardonnay and Gewürztraminer*
Established: *1975*

☆ Gewürztraminer, Chardonnay, Pinot Meunier, Pinot Noir

MARION'S VINEYARD
Foreshore Road,
Deviot, Tas. 7251

Production: *1,000 cases*
Vineyards: *4.5 ha (11 acres) of Müller-Thurgau, Pinot noir, Cabernet sauvignon and Chardonnay*
Established: *1980*

☆ Pinot Noir

McEWINS VINEYARD
Loop Road,
Glengarry, Tas. 7251

Production: *500 cases*

☆ Cabernet Sauvignon

MEADOWBANK VINEYARD
Glenora, Tas. 7150

Production: *600 cases*
Vineyards: *3 ha (7 acres)*
Established: *1974*

☆ Cabernet Sauvignon

MONICHINO WINES
Berry's Road,
Katunga, Vic. 3640

Production: *8,000 cases*
Vineyards: *25 ha (62 acres) of Chardonnay, Sémillon, Sauvignon blanc, Cabernet sauvignon, Syrah, Malbec, Gewürztraminer, Rhine riesling, Orange muscat and Muscat*
Established: *1962*

☆ Chardonnay

MONTARA
Chalambar Road,
Ararat, Vic. 3377

Production: *5,000 cases*
Vineyards: *17 ha (42 acres) of Pinot noir, Cabernet, Syrah, Rhine riesling, Chardonnay and Ondenc*
Established: *1970*

Also known as McRae's Montara Vineyard

☆ Ondenc, Pinot Noir

MOUNT AVOCA VINEYARD
Moates Lane, Avoca, Vic. 3467

Production: *9,000 cases*
Vineyards: *20 ha (49 acres) of Cabernet sauvignon, Syrah, Chardonnay, Sauvignon blanc, Ugni blanc and Sémillon*
Established: *1978*

☆ Sémillon, Cabernet Sauvignon

MOUNT MARY VINEYARD
Coldstream West Road,
Lilydale, Vic. 3140

Production: *2,400 cases*
Vineyards: *7.5 ha (19 acres) of Cabernet sauvignon, Cabernet franc, Merlot; Malbec, Petit verdot, Pinot noir, Chardonnay, Sauvignon blanc, Sémillon and Muscadelle*
Established: *1971*

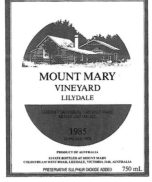

This winery makes decent whites and outstanding reds.

☆ Pinot Noir, Cabernet

MOUNT PRIOR VINEYARD
Howlong Road,
Rutherglen, Vic. 3685

Production: *12,000 cases*
Vineyards: *50 ha (124 acres) of Chardonnay, Gewürztraminer, Chenin blanc, Sauvignon blanc,*
Cabernet sauvignon, Syrah, Malbec, Durif, Cabernet franc, Grenache and Carignan
Established: *1974*

☆ Chardonnay, Gewürztraminer

NICHOLSON RIVER WINERY
Liddell's Road,
Nicholson, Vic. 3882

Production: *150 cases*
Vineyards: *8 ha (20 acres) of Cabernet, Merlot and Chardonnay*
Established: *1978*

☆ Pinot Noir

OAKRIDGE ESTATE
Aitken Road,
Seville, Vic. 3139

Production: *1,300 cases*
Vineyards: *7 ha (18 acres) of Cabernet sauvignon, Merlot, Syrah, Rhine riesling, Crouchen and Cabernet franc*
Established: *1982*

☆ Cabernet Shiraz

OSICKA'S VINEYARD
Major's Creek Vineyard,
Graytown, Vic. 3608

Production: *7,000 cases*
Established: *1955*

☆ Cabernet Sauvignon

REDBANK
Redbank, Vic. 3478

Production: *2,000 cases*
Vineyards: *16 ha (40 acres) of Cabernet sauvignon, Cabernet franc, Malbec, Merlot, Syrah and Pinot noir*
Established: *1973*

☆ "Sally's Paddock"

STANTON & KILLEEN
Murray Valley Highway,
Rutherglen, Vic. 3685

Production: *6,000 cases*
Vineyards: *22 ha (54 acres) of Cabernet sauvignon, Syrah, Durif, Touriga, Muscat and Muscadelle*
Established: *1875*

☆ "Moodemere" Shiraz, Vintage Port

STONEY VINEYARD
Campania, Tas. 7202

Production: *200 cases*
Vineyards: *0.5 ha (1.2 acres)*
Established: *1975*

☆ Cabernet Sauvignon, Zinfandel, Rhine Riesling

SUMMERFIELD WINES
Moonambel, Vic. 3478

Production: *1,500 cases*
Established: *1970*

☆ Hermitage

TARCOOLA VINEYARDS
Maude Road, Lethbridge, Vic. 3332

Production: *2,400 cases*
Vineyards: *7.2 ha (18 acres) of Cabernet sauvignon, Syrah, Rhine riesling, Chasselas and Müller-Thurgau*
Established: *1972*

☆ Shiraz

WALKERSHIRE WINES
Rushworth Road,
Bailieston, Vic. 3608

Production: *1,200 cases*
Vineyards: *2.5 ha (6 acres) of Cabernet sauvignon, Syrah and Merlot*
Established: *1976*

☆ Cabernet Shiraz, Cabernet Sauvignon

WARRAMATE
4 Maddens Lane,
Gruyere, Vic. 3770

Production: *700 cases*
Vineyards: *2 ha (5 acres) of Cabernet sauvignon, Syrah and Rhine riesling*
Established: *1970*

☆ Cabernet Sauvignon, Shiraz Cabernet

WARRENMANG VINEYARD
Mountain Creek Road,
Moonambel, Vic. 3478

Production: *2,000 cases*
Vineyards: *10.5 ha (26 acres) of Cabernet sauvignon, Syrah, Merlot, Chardonnay and Sauvignon blanc*
Established: *1974*

☆ Shiraz, Cabernet Sauvignon

YARRA BURN VINEYARDS
Settlement Road,
Yarra Junction, Vic. 3797

Production: *2,000 cases*
Vineyards: *4 ha (10 acres)*
Established: *1976*

☆ Cabernet Sauvignon, Pinot Noir, Chardonnay

YERINGBERG
Maroondale Highway,
Coldstream, Vic. 3770

Production: *1,200 cases*
Vineyards: *2 ha (5 acres) of Chardonnay, Marsanne, Roussanne, Pinot noir, Merlot, Malbec, Cabernet sauvignon and Cabernet franc*
Established: *1969*

A small production of consistently fine, sometimes exceptionally fine, wines.

☆ Pinot Noir, Marsanne

South Australia

The country's most important wine region, South Australia produces some 60 per cent of all Australian wines. These encompass all styles, ranging from cask-wine, through *macération carbonique* products, to medium- and top-quality premium varietals, also including late-harvest and botrytis wines, "Port" and "Sherry" types, and liqueur muscats.

THE BEGINNINGS OF THIS VAST MARKET-GARDEN of grapes can be traced back to a certain Barton Hack, who planted vines at Launceston in lower North Adelaide in 1837. In the following year a George Stevenson established a vineyard in North Adelaide. However, Hack's vines were removed in 1840, in order to make way for urbanization, starting an incessant trend. Virtually all of Adelaide's metropolitan vineyards have since been uprooted in the name of the city's creeping concrete progress, leaving part of just one, Penfold's historic Magill. This vineyard highlights the variety of the state's output as it originated Australia's greatest and most expensive wine, Grange Hermitage, whilst around it the cheapest and least heard-of cask-wines are made. From South Australia's seemingly bottomless vat comes also the most blatant (but legal) abuse of classic European names such as "Burgundy", "Claret" and "Chablis".

***Remuage*, Kaiser Stuhl**, above
Giant gyropalettes are indicative of the scale of the operation at their Penfolds-owned Barossa Valley cooperative.

SOUTH AUSTRALIA

The state perches over the eastern half of the Great Australian Bight, a bay whose climatic effects are felt less and less the further inland one travels.

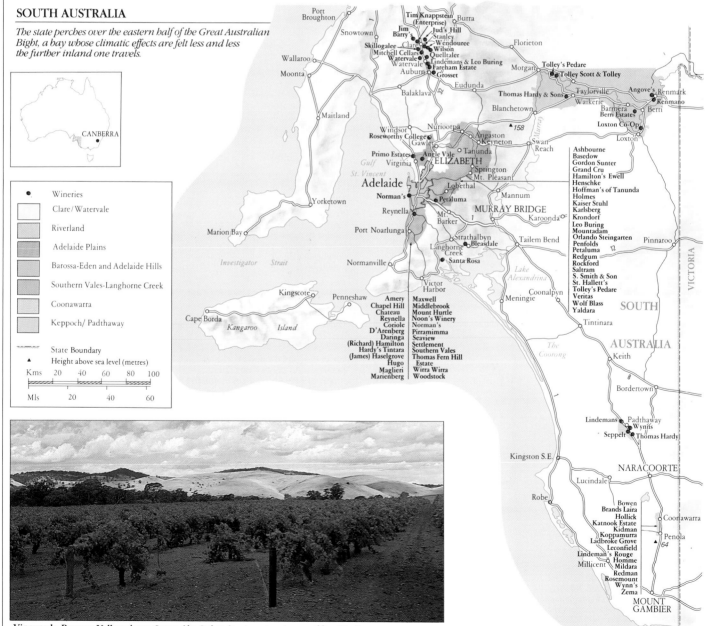

Wineries

Clare/Watervale

Riverland

Adelaide Plains

Barossa-Eden and Adelaide Hills

Southern Vales-Langhorne Creek

Coonawarra

Keppoch/Padthaway

State Boundary

Height above sea level (metres)

Vineyards, Barossa Valley, above *Owned by Orlando wines, producers of fine Rieslings.*

FACTORS AFFECTING TASTE AND QUALITY

Location
The southern central part of the country, with Australia's five other mainland states to the east, north and west, and half of the Great Australian Bight forming the coastline to the south.

Climate
The climate varies greatly, from the intensely hot continental conditions of the largely cask-wine producing Riverland area, through the less extreme but still hot and dry Barossa Valley, to the cooler but still dry Coonawarra region. Sea breezes reduce humidity in the plains around Adelaide, which receives low annual rainfall, as does the whole region.

Aspect
Vines are grown on all types of land, from the flat coastal plain around Adelaide, and flat interior Riverland district to the varied locations of the Barossa Valley, where vines are grown from the valley floor at 250 metres (820 ft), up to the slopes to a maximum of 600 metres (1,970 ft) at Pewsey Vale.

Soil
Soils are varied, ranging from sandy loam over red earth (*terra rossa*) on a limestone-marl subsoil in the Adelaide and Riverland areas (the latter having suffered for some time from excess salinity); through variable sand, loam and clay topsoils, over red-brown loam and clay subsoils in the Barossa Valley, to the thin layer of weathered limestone, stained red by organic and mineral matter, over a thick limestone subsoil in the Coonawarra area.

Viticulture and vinification
This varies enormously, from the bulk-production methods of the large modern wineries that churn-out vast quantities of clean, well-made, inexpensive wine from grapes grown in Riverland's high-yielding irrigated vineyards, to the use of new oak on restricted yields of premium quality varietals by top estate wineries in areas such as Coonawarra, the Barossa Valley and the up-and-coming Padthaway or Keppoch districts, which produce some of Australia's greatest wines.

Grape varieties
Cabernet sauvignon, Chardonnay, Crouchen, Doradillo, Frontignan, Grenache, Malbec, Mataro, Merlot, Muscat d'Alexandrie, Palomino, Pedro Ximénez, Pinot noir, Rhine riesling, Sémillon, Shiraz, Sauvignon blanc, Gewürztraminer, Ugni blanc

The harvest, Barossa Valley, right
Many of the best premium varietal producers in South Australia have some sort of interest in the Barossa Valley, the state's most important area.

The wines of South Australia

ADELAIDE HILLS

An ill-defined district in the hills overlooking Adelaide, the Adelaide Plains and McLaren Vale, this is part of the much larger Barossa-Eden & Adelaide Hills region. Adelaide Hills is one of the fastest-changing and frantically expanding new wine regions in the world, where many spirited and talented winemakers are busily trying to establish a reputation. Chardonnay, Rhine Riesling and Cabernet Sauvignon are the classics of the future, and Petaluma is producing a *méthode champenoise.*

RED: 1982, 1983, 1984, 1985, 1986, 1987, 1988

WHITE: 1982, 1983, 1984, 1986, 1987, 1988

ADELAIDE METROPOLITAN AREA

An area that has been urbanized to such an extent that very few vines are left, those that are belonging to Penfolds' legendary Magill winery. *See* also Adelaide Plains.

ADELAIDE PLAINS

The Adelaide Plains now includes the famous Magill vineyard, the one-time base for Penfolds' remarkable "Grange

Hermitage". Wines produced solely from Magill grapes are now sold as "The Magill Estate". On a lower level, but a good wine nonetheless, is the Gordon Sunter Cabernet Sauvignon.

RED: 1983, 1984, 1986, 1987, 1988

WHITE: 1982, 1983, 1984, 1986, 1987, 1988

BAROSSA VALLEY

Part of the Barossa-Eden & Adelaide Hills region, this district is the oldest and most important of South Australia's premium varietal areas. With a hot, dry climate, the vines mostly grow on flat lands at an altitude of 240 to 300 metres (800 to 1,000 ft) and produce firmly structured reds in the very best traditional Australian styles. It is strange, therefore, that more white grape vines, particularly Rhine riesling, are planted than red. The white wines range from being full-bodied to quite delicate. The vines found at altitudes as high as 550 metres (1,800 ft), where the climate is considerably cooler, can yield vital, fresh, lettuce-crisp wines.

RED: 1980, 1982, 1984, 1985, 1986, 1987, 1988

WHITE: 1980, 1982, 1984, 1985, 1986, 1987, 1988

BAROSSA-EDEN AND ADELAIDE HILLS REGION

This region encompasses the Barossa Valley, Keyneton, Springton, Eden Valley and the Adelaide Hills districts. *See* separate entries for each district.

CLARE VALLEY

Part of the Clare-Watervale region, this is the most northerly wine district in South Australia and its climate is correspondingly hotter and drier. Many of the vineyards are not irrigated, however, and the result is a low yield of very intensely flavoured, big-bodied, often strapping wines. The Rhine riesling is the valley's most important variety and botrytis-affected wines are rich, fine and mellifluous. Other good wines are Cabernet sauvignon (often blended with Malbec or Shiraz), Sémillon and Chardonnay.
The grip the bigger companies once had on wine production in the district has loosened. These wineries still produce excellent wines, but the emphasis has shifted to young, new, "boutique" wineries.

RED: 1980, 1982, 1984, 1985, 1986, 1987

WHITE: 1980, 1982, 1984, 1985, 1986, 1987

CLARE-WATERVALE

Located some 65 kilometres (40 miles) north of Barossa, this region encompasses the Clare Valley and Watervale districts. *See* separate entries for each district.

COONAWARRA

This famous district, which is the most southerly in South Australia, also gives its name to the wider Coonawarra region, an area that also encompasses the area to the north known as Padthaway or Keppoch. Coonawarra, which is Aboriginal for "wild honeysuckle", happens to be easy on Anglo-Saxon tongues and this has been useful when winemakers have marketed their wines in other English-speaking countries.
The Coonawarra's vines grow on red earth, or *terra rossa*, over a limestone subsoil with a high water table and this combination, together with its unique climate (it has the lowest heat summation in mainland Australia – 2170 or 1205 degree-days, compared to 2300°F or 1280°C in Beaune) is responsible for some of Australia's outstanding Cabernet Sauvignon wines. However, in a mistaken bid to make wines better suited to more sophisticated markets, some larger companies have tended

Continued overleaf

to pick too early and make the wines too light.

🔲 RED: 1980, 1982, 1984 (strict selection vital), 1985, 1986, 1987

🔲 WHITE: 1980, 1982, 1984, 1985, 1986, 1987

COONAWARRA REGION

This region encompasses the Coonawarra itself and the Keppoch/Padthaway districts. *See* the separate entries for Keppoch and Padthaway.

EDEN VALLEY

Part of the Barossa-Eden & Adelaide Hills region, the Eden Valley has a similar soil and climate to the Barossa Valley, and is often treated as part of that district because it lies within the Barossa Range. However, some people still place it in the Adelaide Hills. Ewell Vineyard is the best-known winery in the area.

KEPPOCH

Keppoch should have been a town some 16 kilometres (10 miles) north of Padthaway: it was surveyed and planned, but not a brick was laid! The name Padthaway is now interchangeable with that of Keppoch and the former seems to appear on more bottles. *See* Padthaway.

KEYNETON

Part of the Barossa-Eden & Adelaide Hills region, this district is generally seen as part of the Barossa Valley. *See* Barossa Valley.

LANGHORNE CREEK

A tiny, traditional area 40 kilometres (25 miles) southeast of Adelaide on the Bremer River, in the northwest hinterland of Lake Alexandrina. This district was named after Alfred Langhorne, a cattle-herder from New South Wales, who arrived in 1841. With a meagre rainfall of 35 centimetres (14 ins), the vineyards are still irrigated. The area is reputed for its beefy reds and its dessert wines.

🔲 RED: 1980, 1984, 1985 (Cabernet Sauvignon only, pure or blended with Malbec), 1986, 1987

🔲 WHITE: 1980, 1982, 1984, 1985, 1986, 1987

McLAREN VALE

The most important viticultural district in the Southern Vales-Langhorne Creek region, this name is sometimes used synonymously with Southern Vales. The rolling green hills of McLaren Vale's vineyards and orchards begin south of Adelaide and extend to south of Morphett Vale.

With a respectable 56 centimetres (22 ins) of rain and a complex range of soils, including sand, sandy loam, limestone, red clay and many different forms of rich alluvium, there is great potential for quality in a range of styles from various grapes. This is perhaps why it is the most volatile wine district, attracting a lot of new blood, but also seeing wineries close or change hands.

McLaren Vale produces big reds of excellent quality from Shiraz and Cabernet sauvignon (often blended with Merlot), with some increasingly fresh and vital white wines from Chardonnay, Sémillon, Sauvignon blanc and Rhine riesling. Fine dessert wines are also produced.

🔲 RED: 1980, 1984, 1985 (Cabernet Sauvignon only, pure or blended with Malbec), 1986, 1987

🔲 WHITE: 1980, 1984, 1985, 1986, 1987

PADTHAWAY

Part of the Coonawarra region, this district is also known as Keppoch. The development of the area has been carried out almost exclusively by the larger companies, using a considerable amount of marketing muscle. Provided the smaller businesses are not unreasonably prevented from buying land within the area, this should benefit all types of operation. The success of small ventures should be welcomed by the larger companies because it endorses the intrinsic quality-potential of the district they are promoting.

Hardy's "The Hardy Collection" and Lindeman's astonishing Padthaway Vineyard Chardonnay show that this area has an obvious affinity with Chardonnay. Sauvignon Blanc and Rhine Riesling are also excellent and Pinot Noir has shown promise, albeit with less consistency.

🔲 RED: 1981, 1982, 1984, 1985, (Cabernet Sauvignon only, pure or blended with Malbec), 1986, 1987, 1988

🔲 WHITE: 1980, 1982, 1984, 1985, 1986, 1987, 1988

POLISH HILL RIVER

An appellation used by some wineries in the Clare-Watervale region.

RIVERLAND

The wine areas that cluster around the Murray River in Victoria continue into South Australia with Riverland, South Australia's irrigated answer to Riverina in New South Wales and Mildura in Victoria. Although a lot of cheap cask-wine is made in Riverland, rarely is a bad one encountered. Cabernet Sauvignon, Cabernet Sauvignon-Malbec, Chardonnay and Rhine Riesling fare well, with some relatively inexpensive wines produced under Berri Estates' "Renmano" and "Angove's" labels.

🔲 RED: 1980, 1981, 1982, 1984, 1985 (Cabernet Sauvignon only, pure or blended with Malbec), 1986, 1987

🔲 WHITE: 1980, 1982, 1984, 1985, 1986, 1987

SOUTHERN VALES
See McLaren Vale.

SOUTHERN VALES-LANGHORNE CREEK

This region encompasses the McLaren Vale and Langhorne Creek districts. *See* separate entries for each district.

SPRINGTON

Part of the Barossa-Eden & Adelaide Hills region, just south of Eden Valley and on the edge of the Adelaide Hills. Some people would place this district within the Adelaide Hills, again underlining the need for an appellation system to define boundaries. The wine's quality is good, Shiraz being the best.

WATERVALE

The smaller, southern half of the Clare-Watervale region, this district is best known for its fine Shiraz and Cabernet Sauvignon, either pure or blended. Lindeman's and Jim Barry both sell wines under Watervale labels, and Mount Horrocks makes an excellent Watervale Rhine Riesling.

🔲 RED: 1980, 1982, 1984, 1985, 1986, 1987

🔲 WHITE: 1980, 1982, 1984, 1985, 1986, 1987

Major wineries of South Australia

ANGOVE'S
Bookmark Avenue,
Renmark, SA 5341

Established: *1886*

Angove's is best known for two wines: "Tregrehan Claret", which was named after a Cornwall estate that once belonged to an ancestor of the Angove family, and "Bookmark Riesling", which takes its title from the Aboriginal name for the original station property. These are good commercial wines, but there are better wines available in what is a vast range of rich reds and fresh, light whites.

☆ Chardonnay, Cabernet Sauvignon

JIM BARRY'S WINES
Main North Road, Clare, SA 5453

Production: *24,000 cases*
Vineyards: *45 ha (111 acres) of Chardonnay, Sauvignon blanc, Rhine riesling, Cabernet sauvigon, Malbec and Merlot*

Established: *1974*

Jim Barry describes the winemaking techniques employed by himself and his two sons, Mark and Peter, as "an exciting blend of mature wisdom and the innovative enthusiasm of youth".

☆ Lodge Hill Riesling, "Sentimental Bloke" Vintage Port

BASEDOW WINES
161-165 Murray Street,
Tanunda, SA 5352

Production: *30,000 cases*
Established: *1896*

A small property producing some fine and improving wines.

☆ Chardonnay, Cabernet Sauvignon Merlot Cabernet Franc

BERRI-RENMANO ESTATES
Sturt Highway
Glossop, SA 5344

Production: *4.5 million cases*
Vineyards: *2,100 ha (5,190 acres) of Muscadelle, Cabernet sauvignon, Mataro, Grenache, Rhine riesling, Pedro Ximénez, Chardonnay, Palomino, Doradillo, Syrah, Colombard, Crouchen and Muscat*
Established: *1922*

A huge combine of cooperatives producing surprisingly good quality for such inexpensive wines. Cabernet Sauvignon has triumphed in blind tastings against wines two and three times its price.

☆ Cabernet Sauvignon, Cabernet-Shiraz, Fine Old Tawny Port, Wine-Cask

WOLF BLASS WINES
Sturt Highway, Nuriootpa, SA 5355

Production: *330,000 cases*
Vineyards: *57 ha (141 acres) of Cabernet sauvignon, Syrah, Merlot and Rhine riesling*
Established: *1980*

This huge range of aggressively marketed wines wins more medals than any other winery in Australia.

☆ "Grey Label" *Spatlese* Rhine Riesling, "Grey Label" Cabernet Sauvignon, "Yellow Label" Hermitage, "Shareholders" Reserve Cabernet Shiraz, "Black Label" Cabernet Sauvignon Shiraz

BLEASDALE VINEYARDS
Langhorne Creek, SA 5255

Production: *42,000 cases*
Vineyards: *50 ha (124 acres) of Cabernet sauvignon, Syrah, Malbec, Merlot, Grenache, Verdelho, Palomino, Rhine riesling, Doradillo and Chardonnay*
Established: *1850*

A reliable, old-fashioned producer of good-value wines. Its "Pioneer Port" label depicts the antique red-gum press made by founder Frank Potts and its Shiraz-Cabernet Sauvignon label features HMS Buffalo, the ship on which Potts arrived in Australia.

☆ Cabernet Sauvignon, Shiraz-Cabernet Sauvignon

BOWEN ESTATE
Penola-Naracoorte Road, Coonawarra, SA 5263

Production: *4,000 cases*
Vineyards: *24 ha (60 acres) of Cabernet sauvignon, Syrah, Rhine riesling, Merlot and Chardonnay*
Established: *1975 (first vintage)*

Exceptional wines from Doug Bowen.

☆ Cabernet Sauvignon, Shiraz

BRANDS LAIRA
Main Highway, Coonawarra, SA 5263

Production: *10,500 cases*
Vineyards: *28 ha (69 acres) of Cabernet sauvignon, Syrah, Merlot, Malbec, Chardonnay, Rhine riesling and Cabernet franc*
Established: *1965*

A red-wine specialist that consistently produces classically structured products that age well.

☆ Shiraz, Cabernet Sauvignon, Original Vineyard Shiraz, Cabernet Malbec

CHATEAU REYNELLA
Reynell Road, Reynella, SA 5161

Production: *45,000 cases*
Vineyards: *54 ha (133 acres)*
Established: *1838*

This old-established firm now belongs to Thomas Hardy, and is also known as Thomas Hardy's Reynella winery. However, wines are made and kept separately and are consistently fine. Its vintage Ports are exceptional.

☆ Cabernet Sauvignon, Vintage Port, Vintage Reserve Chablis

CORIOLE
Chaffeys Road, McLaren Vale, SA 5171

Production: *9,000 cases*
Vineyards: *22 ha (54 acres) of Cabernet sauvignon, Syrah, Chenin blanc, Rhine riesling, Grenache and Pinot noir*
Established: *1967*

A small range of generally fine-quality wines with an emphasis on reds, which usually fare better than the whites.

☆ French Oak Shiraz Cabernet, "Special" Burgundy

D'ARENBERG WINES
Osborn Road, McLaren Vale, SA 5171

Production: *60,000 cases*
Vineyards: *78 ha (193 acres) of Cabernet sauvignon, Syrah, Mataro, Grenache, Palomino, Chenin blanc, Chardonnay, Sauvignon blanc, Doradillo and Rhine riesling*
Established: *1928*

A well-established and reliable winery that produces a very traditional range.

☆ Shiraz, Selected Port, White Muscat of Alexandria

RICHARD HAMILTON
Willunga Vineyards, Main South Road, Willunga, SA 5172

Production: *17,000 cases*
Vineyards: *50 ha (123 acres) of Cabernet franc, Cabernet sauvignon, Chardonnay, Rhine riesling, Sauvignon blanc and Semillon*
Established: *1837*

Dr. Richard Hamilton makes an interesting, if somewhat eclectic, range of white wines that are worth watching. The Fumé Blanc is by far the best.

☆ Fumé Blanc

HARDY'S
Thomas Hardy & Sons
Reynell Road, Reynella, SA 5161

Production: *2 million cases*
Vineyards: *440 ha (1,087 acres) of Cabernet sauvignon, Chardonnay, Gewürztraminer, Malbec, Pinot noir, Rhine riesling and Syrah*
Established: *1853*

This large company, which owns Houghton and Chateau Reynella, purchased the Stanley Wine Company in December 1987. It produces a vast range and enormous quantities, covering the entire spectrum of styles and qualities, with the notable exception of cask-wines. Its acquisition of the Stanley Wine Company, with its successful cask-wine sales, now effectively gives it a share of that market. The stylishly labelled "Hardy Collection" series fare best from the Padthaway district. Hardy's traditionally produced Nottage Hill Claret and Vintage Port are outstanding in their class.

☆ "The Hardy Collection" (Padthaway Chardonnay, Padthaway Fumé Blanc, Padthaway Rhine Riesling *Beerenauslese*), "Early Bird White", Nottage Hill Claret, "Reserve Bin" Show Port, Siegersdorf Rhine Riesling, Vintage Port

HEGGIES
See S. Smith & Son.

HENSCHKE CELLARS
Moculta Road, Keyneton, SA 5353

Production: *30,000 cases*
Vineyards: *80 ha (198 acres)*
Established: *1868*

One of Australia's older wineries, whose essentially traditional, firm, well-structured wines are generally of very high quality.

☆ Cyril Henschke Cabernet Sauvignon, Hill of Grace, Mount Edelstone, Sémillon Wood-Matured, Gewürztraminer, Rhine Riesling *Auslese*

KATNOOK ESTATE
Penola Road, Coonawarra, SA 5263

Production: *83,000 cases*
Vineyards: *560 ha (1,383 acres) of Cabernet sauvignon, Syrah, Pinot noir, Merlot, Rhine riesling, Chardonnay and Sauvignon*
Established: *1979*

Only 15,000 cases of this large estate's production are released under its Katnook Estate and Riddoch Estate labels. The very finest, those recommended below, are sold under the former. The quality of these wines is high, sometimes exceptionally so.

☆ Sauvignon Blanc, Rhine Riesling, Chardonnay, Pinot Noir, Cabernet Sauvignon

TIM KNAPPSTEIN ENTERPRISE WINES
2 Pioneer Avenue, Clare, SA 5453

Production: *20,000 cases*
Vineyards: *42 ha (104 acres) of Rhine riesling, Gewürztraminer, Sauvignon blanc, Chardonnay, Cabernet sauvignon, Cabernet franc, Merlot and Pinot noir*
Established: *1976*

Tim Knappstein, who won a Gold Medal when he passed the oenology course at Roseworthy, Australia's first and foremost wine college in 1964, was winemaker for the Stanley Wine Company when it was owned by his family. While there, he won no less than 500 awards with the Leasingham range. The quality of his Enterprise Wines is every bit as high and interesting.

☆ Cabernet Sauvignon, Cabernet Shiraz, Rhine Riesling

KRONDORF WINERY
Krondorf Road, Tanunda, SA 5352

Production: *200,000 cases*
Vineyards: *72 ha (178 acres) of Cabernet sauvignon, Chardonnay, Crouchen, Gewürztraminer, Muscat, Rhine riesling, Sauvignon blanc, Sémillon and Syrah*
Established: *1978*

A large range of extremely fine wines, the very best of which are sold under the "Burge and Wilson" label, which is named after the two brilliant founders who established the fame of this winery, before selling it in 1986.

☆ "Burge and Wilson" (Chardonnay, Eden Valley Rhine Riesling, Barossa Valley Cabernet Sauvignon), Chardonnay, Cabernet Sauvignon & Cabernet Franc

MARIENBERG WINERY
Black Road, Coromandel Valley, SA 5051

Production: *15,000 cases*
Vineyards: *18 ha (44 acres) of Cabernet sauvignon, Pinot noir, Sémillon, Rhine riesling, Sauvignon blanc, Syrah and Chenin blanc*
Established: *1966*

A distinctive range of wines made by Ursula Pridham, Australia's most prominent woman winemaker, whose picture is on all the labels. Her delight is to produce small lots of limited releases, and they are certainly her best wines.

☆ Limited Release Shiraz

NORMAN'S WINE ESTATE
Grants Gully Road,
Clarendon, SA 5157

Production: 60,000 cases
Vineyards: 60 ha (148 acres) of Pinot noir, Chardonnay, Sauvignon blanc, Cabernet sauvignon, Merlot, Rhine riesling, Chenin blanc and Syrah
Established: 1851

The Norman family produces a large range of consistently good wines from its own vineyards, the Evanston Estate in the Adelaide Plains and at Clarendon, where it recently took over the Coolawin winery, in the Adelaide Hills, and from grapes purchased on an occasional basis from various areas.

☆ Adelaide Plains Pinot Noir, Coonawarra Cabernet Sauvignon, Evanston Estate – Barossa Chardonnay, Barossa Valley Sauvignon Blanc Fumé, "Norman's Conquest" Brut

ORLANDO WINES
Barossa Valley Highway,
Rowland Flat, SA 5352

Production: 3 million cases
Vineyards: 50 ha (123 acres) of Sémillon, Syrah, Rhine riesling, Gewürztraminer and Chardonnay
Established: 1847

A gigantic operation owned by the multi-national Reckitt & Colman company. Its bulk-wine production plant at Wickham Hill, in New South Wales, churns out mostly "Coolabah" cask wine and flagon stuff, although occasionally releases limited editions of finer Sémillon and Shiraz. Orlando Rieslings come from its Steingarten vineyard in the Eastern Barossa Ranges, but most of its high-quality wines come from its Rowland Flat winery in the Barossa Valley.

☆ Steingarten Rhine Riesling, Jacobs Creek Rhine Riesling, "St. Helga" Rhine Riesling, "RF" Chardonnay, "RF" Cabernet Sauvignon, "St. Hugo" Cabernet Sauvignon

PENFOLDS WINES
Tanunda Road,
Nuriootpa, SA 5355

Production: 1.8 million cases
Vineyards: 600 ha (1,483 acres) of Syrah, Cabernet sauvignon, Chardonnay, Riesling and Gewürztraminer
Established: 1844

Penfolds' superb Grange Hermitage is considered by many to be Australia's finest wine. It certainly is its most famous, and through it Penfolds has become a living legend.
Theoretically "Grange" should mean Magill, a small vineyard on the eastern outskirts of Adelaide, but the amount of Magill Shiraz used has varied between 15 and 70 per cent, the balance of the Shiraz coming from Kalimna, Clare and Koonunga. In 1982 a large part of the Magill vineyard was sold off for urban development. The remainder is no longer used for Grange Hermitage and its produce is now sold exclusively under the Magill Estate label.
Grange Hermitage remains one of Australia's greatest wines and its theoretical Magill-based content is not important. It is historically a blend to which, in some years, even a little Cabernet Sauvignon has been added. The wine, in fact, tastes more like Cabernet Sauvignon than Shiraz. Its construction is a remarkable balancing act, providing a powerful punch of flavour, yet showing great finesse. It has size and power, but there is a certain restraint.
Interestingly, The Magill Estate is in a different style – it is as deep-coloured and intensely flavoured as one would have expected from the one-time soul of Grange Hermitage, but the style is less traditional and more accessible. Expensive though it may be for an Australian wine, Penfolds Magill must be considered a veritable bargain at just over half the price of Grange Hermitage. Penfolds' two other top of the range wines are St. Henri Claret (Cabernet-Shiraz), which I find can be a bit ungenerous, and the stunning Cabernet Sauvignon Bin 707.

☆ Bin 128 Coonawarra Shiraz, Cabernet Sauvignon Bin 707, Kalimna Shiraz Bin 28, Grange Hermitage, The Magill Estate

PETALUMA
Crafers, SA 5152

Production: 26,000 cases
Vineyards: 125 ha (309 acres) of Rhine riesling, Chardonnay, Sauvignon blanc, Sémillon, Pinot, Cabernet, Merlot, Malbec and Cabernet franc
Established: 1979

Ask the people who believe that Penfolds' Grange Hermitage is the finest Australian wine which is the best winery and the majority will say Petaluma. This is probably because, whereas Petaluma might not have a Grange Hermitage that scores 20 out of 20, every single wine it does have would rate at least 19.

☆ Croser Méthode Champenoise, Rhine Riesling, Botrytis Rhine Riesling, Chardonnay, Coonawarra

PEWSEY VALE
See S. Smith & Son.

PIRRAMIMMA
Johnston Road,
McLaren Vale, SA 5171

Production: 36,000 cases
Vineyards: 55 ha (136 acres) of Rhine riesling, Pedro Ximénez, Palomino, Cabernet sauvignon, Cabernet franc, Merlot, Syrah and Grenache
Established: 1892

An old-established, yet rapidly improving winery.

☆ Cabernet Sauvignon, Vintage Port

RENMANO WINES
Renmark Avenue,
Renmark, SA 5341

Production: 1.2 million cases
Vineyards: 900 ha (2,224 acres) of Chenin blanc, Malbec, Cabernet sauvignon, Rhine riesling, Chardonnay, Palomino, White Frontignan, Doradillo, Syrah, Colombard, Crouchen, Gordo, Sauvignon blanc, Sémillon, Ugni blanc, Merlot and Ruby Cabernet
Established: 1914

Part of the Berri Estates operation, the Renmano wines are extraordinarily good value, particularly those under the "Chairman's Selection" label and in its wine-casks.

☆ "Chairman's Selection" (Cabernet Sauvignon, Rhine Riesling), Old Tawny Port, Wine Casks

ROUGE HOMME
Coonawarra, SA 5263

Vineyards: 60 ha (148 acres) of Cabernet sauvignon, Chardonnay, Malbec, Pinot noir, Rhine riesling and Syrah
Established: 1908

Although part of the large Lindeman's combine since 1965, the integrity of these wines has been maintained. The label might look a bit old-fashioned and garish, but behind it lie some of the finest Coonawarra wines.

☆ Auslese Rhine Riesling, Coonawarra Claret, Coonawarra Cabernet Sauvignon, Coonawarra Chardonnay

SALTRAM WINERY
Angaston Road,
Angaston, SA 5353

Production: 500,000 cases
Vineyards: 28 ha (70 acres) of Cabernet Sauvignon, Chardonnay, Malbec, Merlot, Rhine riesling and Sémillon
Established: 1859

This important winery, which was founded by Englishman William Salter, was purchased by the giant Canadian-based Seagram Group in 1979.

☆ Pinnacle (Cabernet-Malbec, Coonawarra Auslese Rhine Riesling, Show Tawny Port, Old Liqueur Muscat)

SEAVIEW WINERY
Chaffeys Road,
McLaren Vale, SA 5171

Vineyards: 190 ha (470 acres) of Cabernet sauvignon, Rhine riesling, Syrah, Sémillon and Sauvignon blanc
Established: 1850

Part of the Penfolds Group of Companies

☆ Cabernet Sauvignon, "Edmond Mazure"

SEPPELT
181 Flinders Street,
Adelaide, SA 5000

Production: 2.5 million cases
Vineyards: 2,000 ha (4,492 acres) of Cabernet sauvignon, Chardonnay, Chasselas, Doradillo, Gewürztraminer, Grenache, Muscadelle, Odenc, Palomino, Pinot noir, Syrah, Sylvaner, Rhine riesling and Touriga
Established: 1851

Huge quantities of a vast number of wines, under a bewildering range of labels. Like so many of the big producers in Australia, they manage to make more than their fair share of medal-winning wines.

☆ Chardonnay, Chardonnay/Sauvignon Blanc, DP117 Show Fino Flor Sherry, DP90 Tawny Port, Auslese Rhine Riesling, Late Harvest Rhine Riesling Beerenauslese, Great Western Show Champagne

S. SMITH & SON
Yalumba Winery, Eden Valley Road,
Angaston, SA 5353

Production: 720,000 cases
Vineyards: 565 ha (1,396 acres) of Rhine riesling, Sémillon, Chardonnay, Pinot noir, Viognier, Cabernet franc, Merlot, Pinot meunier, Malbec, Syrah, Gewürztraminer, Sauvignon blanc and Cabernet sauvignon
Established: 1849

A vast range of styles and qualities under four basic categories of label: Yalumba for non-estate wines, but including some fine premium products; wines from the family estate; and Pewsey Vale and Heggies for wine grown from cool-climate grapes on high-altitude vineyards. Also owns Nautilus in New Zealand.

☆ Heggies (Rhine Riesling, Botrytis Affected Late Harvest) Pewsey Vale (Rhine Riesling) Cabernet Sauvignon LDR, Hill Smith Estate (Wood Matured Sémillon, Autumn Harvest Botrytis Affected Sémillon) Yalumba ("Angus" Brut, "Carte d'Or" Rhine Riesling, "Thoroughbred Series" Vintage Port)

SOUTHERN VALES WINERY
151 Main Road,
McLaren Vale, SA 5171

Production: 24,000 cases
Established: 1901

After the Southern Vales Cooperative Winery wound-up due to financial difficulty in 1982, it was purchased by Hong Kong millionaire George Lau. The wines are of a decent commercial quality, but nothing exceptional. The Cabernet Sauvignon and Tatachilla Fine Old Tawny Port have so far proved the most successful wines.

STANLEY WINE COMPANY
7 Dominic Street,
Clare, SA 5453

Production: 2 million cases
Vineyards: 230 ha (568 acres) of Rhine riesling, Cabernet sauvignon, Malbec, Syrah, Gewürztraminer, Sauvignon blanc, Chardonnay, Muscadelle, Crouchen and Pedro Ximénez
Established: 1893

Most wines are sold under the Leasingham label, even the wine-casks. The Leasingham range was created under the ownership of the Knappstein family and, with Tim Knappstein as winemaker, the wines won 500 awards, including 120 gold medals. The very best wines are now marketed as the Winemakers Selection. The firm was purchased by Hardy's in December 1987 and parts of its vineyard holdings have been sold off.

☆ Gewürztraminer "Winemakers Selection", Leasingham (Cabernet "Bin 49", Cabernet-Malbec "Bin 56"), Rhine Riesling "Bin 7", Watervale-Coonawarra Shiraz-Cabernet

TOLLANA WINES/ TOLLEY SCOTT & TOLLEY
Tanunda Road,
Nuriootpa, SA 5355

Production: *750,000 cases*
Vineyards: *560 ha (1,384 acres)*
Established: *1888*

Once entirely estate-produced, many of these wines now contain grapes from various other locations. The quality remains very good, though.

☆ McLaren Vale Chardonnay, *Beerenauslese*, Eden Valley Rhine Riesling

TOLLEY'S PEDARE WINES
30 Barracks Road,
Hope Valley, SA 5090

Production: *250,000 cases*
Vineyards: *177 ha (437 acres) of Cabernet sauvignon, Pinot noir, Merlot, Malbec, Gewürztraminer, Chardonnay, Sémillon, Rhine riesling, Chenin blanc, Sauvignon blanc, Muscadelle, Muscat and Sylvaner*
Established: *1893*

A large private winery that makes an elegant style of wine. It is one of many to be advised by Tony Jordan and Brian Crose.

☆ Chablis, Fumé Blanc, Pinot Noir, Late Harvest Muscat à Petit Grains

WYNNS
Memorial Drive,
Coonawarra, SA 5263

Production: *450,000 cases*
Vineyards: *600 ha (1,483 acres) of Touriga, Syrah and Rhine riesling*
Established: *1891*

Although this company still makes fine wines, its one-time superstar, the Coonawarra Cabernet Sauvignon, has not been the same since Wynns adopted a lighter, more herbaceous style in the early 1970s. Its best wines are now Hermitage and Chardonnay.

☆ Coonawarra (Cabernet Sauvignon, Chardonnay, Hermitage), High Eden (Rhine Riesling), "John Riddoch" Cabernet Sauvignon

YALUMBA
See S. Smith & Son.

The best of the rest

AMERY VINEYARDS (KAY BROS.)
Kays Road,
McLaren Vale, SA 5171

Production: *12,000 cases*
Vineyards: *7 ha (17 acres) of Gewürztraminer, Pinot noir and Sauvignon blanc*
Established: *1890*

☆ Liqueur Muscat, "Block 6" Shiraz

ASHBOURNE WINE CO.
2 Gilpin Lane,
Mitcham, SA 5062

Production: *1,500 cases*
Vineyards: *6 ha (15 acres) of Cabernet, Merlot, Chardonnay and Riesling*
Established: *1980*

☆ Coonawarra Cabernet Sauvignon, Coonawarra Rhine Riesling

CHAPEL HILL WINERY
Chapel Hill Road,
McLaren Vale, SA 5171

Production: *2,000 cases*
Vineyards: *8 ha (20 acres) of Rhine riesling, Chardonnay, Cabernet sauvignon, Syrah and Grenache*
Established: *1979*

☆ Chapel Hill Shiraz, Muscat de Fleurieu

DENNIS DARINGA CELLARS
McLaren Vale, SA 5171

Production: *6,000 cases*
Vineyards: *20 ha (49 acres) of Syrah, Cabernet Sauvignon, Sauvignon blanc, Chardonnay and Muscat*
Established: *1972*

☆ Sauvignon Blanc, Chardonnay, Cabernet Sauvignon

EAGLE HAWK
Watervale, SA 5452

Formerly Quelltaler Wines, these products have been sold under the Eagle Hawk label since 1988, one year after the firm was purchased by Wolf Blass.

FAREHAM ESTATE
Main North Road, Watervale, SA 5452

Production: *2,000 cases*
Vineyards: *8 ha (19 acres)*
Established: *1976*

☆ Sauvignon Blanc, Cabernet Sauvignon

GORDON SUNTER WINES
P.O. Box 658,
Gawler, SA 5118

Production: *2,000 cases*
Established: *1976*

☆ Cabernet Sauvignon

JEFFREY GROSSET WINES
King Street,
Auburn, SA 5451

Production: *3,500 cases*
Established: *1981*

☆ Polish Hill Rhine Riesling, Watervale Rhine Riesling, Cabernet Sauvignon/ Cabernet Franc blend

JAMES HASELGROVE WINES
Foggo Road,
McLaren Flat, SA 5171
(Wineries at Coonawarra and McLaren Flat)

Production: *7,000 cases*
Vineyards: *16 ha (40 acres) of Rhine riesling, Gewürztraminer, Chardonnay, Cabernet sauvignon, Syrah and Malbec*
Established: *1981*

☆ Rhine Riesling, Traminer Riesling, *Auslese* Rhine Riesling, Coonawarra Cabernet Sauvignon, Méthode Champenoise Brut

HOFFMANS OF TANUNDA
Para Road, North Para,
Via Tanunda, SA 5352

Production: *30,000 cases*
Vineyards: *Cabernet sauvignon, Rhine riesling, Syrah and Muscat*
Established: *1847*

☆ Sternagel *Auslese* Rhine Riesling, Old Tawny Port

HOLLICK WINES
Racecourse Road,
Coonawarra, SA 5263

Production: *6,000 cases*
Vineyards: *10 ha (25 acres) of Cabernet sauvignon, Cabernet franc, Merlot, Pinot noir, Rhine riesling and Chardonnay*
Established: *1983*

☆ Rhine Riesling, Cabernet Sauvignon

HOLMES
Main Street,
Springton, SA 5235

Production: *1,500 cases*
Vineyards: *15 ha (37 acres) of Rhine riesling, Cabernet sauvignon, Syrah and Pinot noir*
Established: *1976*

☆ Shiraz

HUGO WINERY
Elliott Road,
McLaren Flat, SA 5171

Production: *1,200 cases*
Vineyards: *15 ha (37 acres)*
Established: *1980*

☆ Muscat of Alexandria

JUD'S HILL
P.O. Box 128,
Stepney, SA 5069

Production: *12,000 cases*
Vineyards: *33 ha (82 acres) of Cabernet sauvignon, Cabernet franc, Merlot, Rhine riesling and*

Malbec
Established: *1977*

☆ Clare Rhine Riesling, Clare Cabernet Sauvignon, Clare/Keppoch Cabernet Malbec

KAISER STUHL WINES
Sturt Highway,
Nuriootpa, SA 5355

Production: *1.8 million cases*
Vineyards: *600 ha (1,482 acres) of Syrah, Rhine riesling and Cabernet sauvignon*
Established: *1912*

☆ "Green Ribbon" Rhine Riesling, "Red Ribbon" Shiraz

KARLSBURG ESTATE
Gomersal Road,
Lyndoch, SA 5351

Production: *7,000 cases*
Vineyards: *32 ha (79 acres) of Chardonnay, Sauvignon blanc, Syrah and Cabernet sauvignon*
Established: *1972*

☆ Pinot Noir

KIDMAN WINERY
Coonawarra, SA 5263

Production: *4,000 cases*
Vineyards: *52 ha (128 acres) of Cabernet sauvignon, Syrah and Rhine riesling*
Established: *1971*

☆ Rhine Riesling

KOPPAMURRA
Joanna via Naracoorte, SA 5271

Production: *2,000 cases*
Vineyards: *11 ha (27 acres)*
Established: *1974*

☆ Cabernet Merlot, Cabernet Sauvignon

Continued overleaf

LADBROKE GROVE WINES
Millicent Road,
Penola, SA 5277

Production: *1,200 cases*
Established: *1982*

☆ Rhine Riesling, Late Picked Rhine Riesling, Cabernet Sauvignon

LECONFIELD
Penola-Naracoorte Road,
Coonawarra, SA 5263

Production: *5,000 cases*
Vineyards: *30 ha (74 acres) of Cabernet sauvignon, Merlot, Riesling, Chardonnay and Cabernet franc*
Established: *1974*

☆ Cabernet Sauvignon

MAGLIERI WINES
13 Douglas Gully Road,
McLaren Flat, SA 5171

Production: *36,000 cases*
Vineyards: *36 ha (89 acres) of Cabernet sauvignon, Rhine riesling, Syrah and Grenache*
Established: *1972*

☆ Rhine Riesling

MAXWELL WINES
24 Kangarilla Road,
McLaren Vale, SA 5171

Production: *5,000 cases*
Established: *1979*

☆ Cabernet Shiraz

MIDDLEBROOK WINERY
Sand Road,
McLaren Vale, SA 5171

Production: *36,000 cases*
Established: *1880*

☆ Chardonnay, Highcrest Shiraz

MOUNT HURTLE (GEOFF MERRILL)
Cnr. Pimpala & Byards Road,
Reynella, SA 5171

Production: *18,000 cases*
Established: *1983*

☆ Sémillon, Cabernet Sauvignon

MOUNTADAM VINEYARD
High Eden Road, High Eden Ridge,
Eden Valley, SA 5235

Production: *12,000 cases*
Vineyards: *40 ha (99 acres) of Chardonnay, Cabernet, Rhine riesling and Pinot noir*
Established: *1970*

☆ Chardonnay

NOON'S WINERY
Rifle Range Road,
McLaren Vale, SA 5171

Production: *1,500 cases*
Vineyards: *3 ha (7 acres) of Grenache*
Established: *1976*

☆ Shiraz Grenache, Shiraz Cabernet, Burgundy, Claret

PRIMO ESTATE WINES
Old Port Wakefield Road,
Virginia, SA 5120

Production: *12,000 cases*
Vineyards: *21 ha (52 acres) of Cabernet sauvignon, Syrah, Rhine riesling, French colombard, Sauvignon blanc, Chardonnay and Sémillon*
Established: *1973 (vineyard)*

☆ Sauvignon Blanc Fumé Style, Chardonnay, Botrytis Riesling *Auslese*, Double Pruned Cabernet Sauvignon

THE REDGUM VINEYARD
Barossa Valley Highway,
Lyndoch, SA 5351

Production: *27,000 cases*
Vineyards: *60 ha (148 acres) of Chardonnay, Sauvignon blanc, Sémillon, Rhine riesling, Gewürztraminer, Muscadelle, Sercial, Pedro Ximénez, Cabernet sauvignon, Cabernet franc, Syrah and Grenache*
Established: *1969*

☆ Kies Lyndoch Hills Rhine Riesling *Auslese*

ROCKFORD WINES
Krondorf Road,
Tanunda, SA 5352

Production: *3,000 cases*
Vineyards: *Rhine riesling*
Established: *1984*

☆ Sauvignon Blanc, *Spätlese* White Frontignan

ROSEWORTHY COLLEGE CELLARS
Roseworthy, SA 5371

Production: *8,500 cases*
Vineyards: *8 ha (19 acres) of*
Syrah, Pedro Ximénez, Sauvignon blanc, Rhine riesling, Colombard, Chenin blanc, Chardonnay, Sultana, Ruby cabernet, Mondeuse, Cabernet sauvignon, Carignan, Grenache and Cabernet franc*
Established: *1936*

☆ Eden Valley (Rhine Riesling, Chardonnay)

SANTA ROSA WINES
Winery Road,
Currency Creek, SA 5214

Production: *15,000 cases*
Vineyards: *12.5 ha (31 acres) of Sauvignon blanc, Sémillon, Pinot noir, Riesling, Syrah, Cabernet sauvignon and Chardonnay*
Established: *1968*

☆ Wood Aged Sémillon, Sauvignon Blanc, Chardonnay Chablis, Deer Park Late Harvest Rhine Riesling

THE SETTLEMENT WINE CO.
Settlement Road,
McLaren Flat, SA 5171

Production: *6,000 cases*
Vineyards: *6 ha (15 acres)*
Established: *1971*

☆ Carbonic Maceration

SKILLOGALEE VINEYARDS
Skillogalee Valley Road,
Via Sevenhill, SA 5453

Production: *5,000 cases*
Vineyards: *22 ha (54 acres) of Rhine riesling, Syrah, Cabernet sauvignon, Cabernet franc, Malbec, Gewürztraminer and Muscat*
Established: *1976*

☆ Rhine Riesling Bin 2

ST. HALLETT'S WINES
St. Hallett's Road,
Tanunda, SA 5352

Production: *30,000 cases*
Vineyards: *Cabernet sauvignon, Grenache, Syrah, Touriga, Tinta amarella, Merlot, Chardonnay, Pedro Ximénez, Rhine riesling, Sauvignon blanc, Sémillon*
Established: *1944*

☆ Old Block Shiraz, Frangos Trophy Vintage Port

THOMAS FERN HILL ESTATE
Ingoldby Road,
McLaren Flat, SA 5171

Production: *3,500 cases*
Vineyards: *1 ha (2.5 acres) of Cabernet sauvignon*
Established: *1975*

☆ Chardonnay

VERITAS WINERY
94 Langmeil Road,
Tanunda, SA 5352

Production: *12,000 cases*

Vineyards: *Rhine riesling, Gewürztraminer, Sémillon, Chardonnay, Sauvignon blanc, Cabernet sauvignon, Cabernet franc, Syrah, Merlot and Malbec*
Established: *1951*

☆ Chri-ro Estate Late Picked Rhine Riesling

WATERVALE CELLARS
North Terrace,
Watervale, SA 5452

Production: *2,500 cases*
Vineyards: *12 ha (30 acres) of Cabernet sauvignon, Syrah, Rhine riesling, Grenache, Pedro Ximénez and Cabernet franc*
Established: *1977*

☆ Shiraz Cabernet, Cabernet Shiraz

WENDOUREE
Wendouree Road,
Clare, SA 5453

Production: *3,600 cases*
Vineyards: *10 ha (25 acres) of Syrah, Cabernet sauvignon, Malbec and Rhine riesling*
Established: *1892*

☆ Cabernet Sauvignon, Cabernet Malbec, Malbec Cabernet, Shiraz

THE WILSON VINEYARD
Polish Hill River Road,
Sevenhill, SA 5453

Production: *2,500 cases*
Vineyards: *7 ha (17 acres) of Cabernets, Merlot, Malbec, Pinot noir, Zinfandel and Rhine riesling*
Established: *1974*

☆ Cabernet Sauvignon Malbec

WIRRA WIRRA VINEYARDS
McMurtrie Road,
McLaren Vale, SA 5171

Production: *20,000 cases*
Vineyards: *51 ha (126 acres)*
Established: *1968*

☆ Sauvignon Blanc, Hand Picked Rhine Riesling, Chardonnay, Church Block Cabernet Merlot Shiraz

WOODSTOCK WINE CELLARS
Douglas Gully Road,
McLaren Flat, SA 5171

Production: *12,000 cases*
Vineyards: *6 ha (15 acres)*
Established: *1974*

☆ Noble Dessert Wine, Cabernet Sauvignon, Vintage Port

ZEMA ESTATE
Penola-Naracoorte Road,
Coonawarra, SA 5263

Production: *3,000 cases*
Vineyards: *8 ha (20 acres)*
Established: *1982*

☆ Rhine Riesling, Late Harvest Rhine Riesling, Shiraz

Western Australia

Twenty years ago the Margaret River was not readily associated with wine. Now it is probably producing not just Western Australia's, but the country's greatest wines; certainly more great wines than any other single district.

THERE ARE OTHER GOOD WINE AREAS in Western Australia, but the Margaret River must be singled out for its vineyards, planted entirely with classic grapes, its climate and soil, which produce grapes of unparalleled ripeness and balance, and its winemakers, who are fanatics who care only about quality.

THE ORIGINS OF THE REGION'S WINE INDUSTRY

As the state was founded a few years before Victoria and South Australia, the vineyards of Western Australia were established correspondingly earlier, in 1829, by either Thomas Waters or Captain John Septimus Roe. If it was Roe, he would not have made any wine; his vines bore table grapes and raisins. Waters bought eight hectares (20 acres) of what was to become Olive Farm.

Waters was a botanist who had learned his winemaking skills from the Boers in South Africa. He arrived in Australia with numerous seeds and plants, and by 1842 was making and bartering wine. In 1835, King William IV granted over 3,000 hectares (7,400 acres) of Swan Valley land to one Henry Revett Bland, who sold it to a trio of British army officers soon afterwards. These new owners, Messrs Lowis, Yule and Houghton, were stationed in India, but one, Yule, was despatched by the senior officer, Colonel Houghton, to run the property. Thus Houghton Wines, the first commercial winery in Western Australia, takes its name from a man who never set foot in the country.

The Swan Valley remained the hub of the state's wine industry and, with an influx of Europeans, notably from Dalmatia, all experienced in viticultural and winemaking techniques, the expertise of this industry grew. Gradually Mount Barker evolved as a wine area, then Frankland and last, but certainly not least, the Margaret River. For most foreign wine drinkers, it is the last of these appellations that has given the most excitement and pleasure.

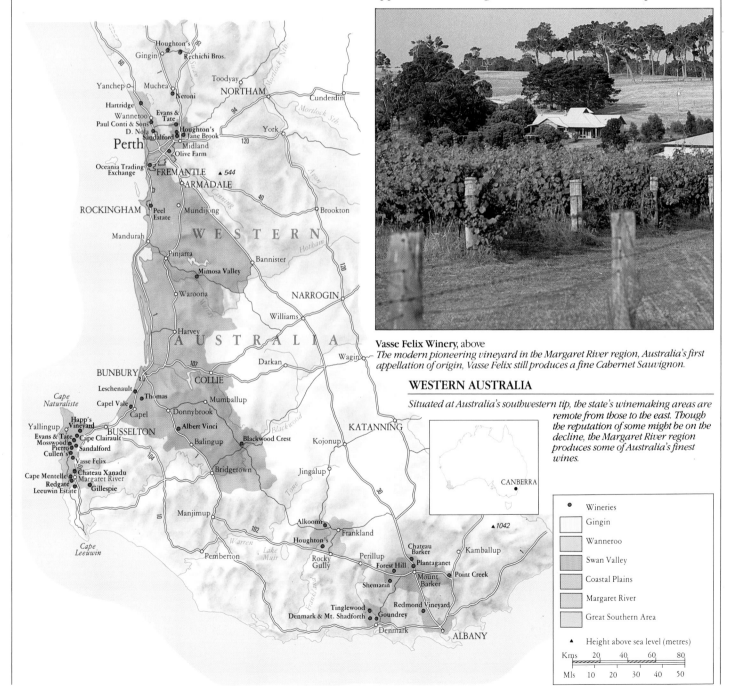

Vasse Felix Winery, above
The modern pioneering vineyard in the Margaret River region, Australia's first appellation of origin, Vasse Felix still produces a fine Cabernet Sauvignon.

WESTERN AUSTRALIA

Situated at Australia's southwestern tip, the state's winemaking areas are remote from those to the east. Though the reputation of some might be on the decline, the Margaret River region produces some of Australia's finest wines.

CANBERRA

- • Wineries
- Gingin
- Wanneroo
- Swan Valley
- Coastal Plains
- Margaret River
- Great Southern Area
- ▲ Height above sea level (metres)

Kms 20 40 60 80
Mls 10 20 30 40 50

THE APPELLATION SYSTEM

As a result of initiatives by local growers in the Margaret River and Mount Barker-Frankland River areas, the Western Australian government sponsored a pilot scheme for regional certification of its wines in 1978. Sponsorship commenced in 1978 and lasted for four years. It was not a full appellation scheme and had only limited success. Exporting wineries certainly favoured it, perhaps not least because Western Australia's remoteness from major population centres other than Perth, and its lack of a "wine identity", had apparently been a problem for all but the most successful Margaret River wineries.

FACTORS AFFECTING TASTE AND QUALITY

Location
Western Australia's vine-growing areas include the Swan Valley behind Perth, the coastal plain mainly to the south of the city, and the Margaret River Valley and Lower Great Southern areas moving south and east around the coast to Albany.

Climate
This is very variable, from the long, very hot, dry summers and short, wet winters of the Swan Valley, one of the hottest wine-growing areas of the world, through the Mediterranean-type conditions of the Margaret River, with a higher rainfall and summer heat tempered by ocean breezes, to the even cooler Lower Great Southern Area, which also has some light rainfall in summer. Ocean winds can exacerbate salinity problems and high coastal humidity helps with the development of botrytis.

Aspect
Most vines are planted on the relatively flat coastal plain and river valley basins, but also on some rather more undulating hilly areas, such as those around Denmark and Mount Barker near Albany in the south and east of the region.

Soil
Soils are fairly homogenous, being mainly deep, free-draining, alluvial and clay loams over clay subsoils. The Southwest Coastal area has a fine, white-grey topsoil called tuart sand over a base of limestone.

Viticulture and vinification
Drip irrigation is widespread because of the general lack of summer rain and the free-draining nature of the soil, though, ironically, winter water-logging due to clay sub-soils is also a problem. Wide planting, mechanized harvesting and the use of the most modern vinification techniques typify the area, which has generally concentrated on developing the cooler areas away from the Swan Valley in recent years.

Grape varieties
Cabernet franc, Cabernet sauvignon, Chardonnay, Chenin blanc, Pinot noir, Malbec, Merlot, Riesling, Sauvignon blanc, Sémillon, Shiraz, Verdelho, Zinfandel.

Swan Valley vineyards, above
This flat plain belongs to one of the hottest winegrowing regions in the world, and the first of Western Australia's wine districts to be established.

The wines of Western Australia

Note: Certain "Best recent vintages" are marked with an asterisk to denote that careful selection is needed when choosing wines from those years. This is because some wines were of excellent, even exceptional quality.

FRANKLAND

Small area on the western edge of the Great Southern Area, Frankland is primarily known for its Houghton Frankland River Winery. Good Cabernet Sauvignon, promising Rhine Riesling.

 RED: 1981, 1983*, 1984, 1985, 1986, 1987

WHITE: 1981, 1983*, 1984, 1985, 1986, 1987

GINGIN

A small area just north of Perth in the Southwest Coastal Plain district. *See* Southwest Coastal Plain.

GREAT SOUTHERN AREA

A region encompassing the Mount Barker and Frankland districts, sometimes referred to as the Mount Barker/Frankland River Area. This is the coolest of Western Australia's winegrowing areas, although it generally has the same climatic influences as the Margaret River, but with a much lower rainfall, approximately 35 centimetres (14 ins). There are about 250 hectares (617 acres) of vines, mostly Riesling, Cabernet sauvignon, Shiraz, Malbec, Pinot noir and some Chardonnay, but, despite its "Great" title, the area under vine is slowly shrinking and the number of wineries decreasing. *See* Frankland and Mount Barker

MARGARET RIVER

Situated 320 kilometres (200 miles) south of Perth, this district attracted much attention in 1978 when it established Australia's first Appellation of Origin system. Like other similar schemes, it was ill-equipped to work effectively and was unsuccessful.

Although thought of as a "new" wine region, the first vineyard was planted in the Margaret River area at Bunbury, as long ago as 1890. However, it was a vineyard planted by Dr Tom Cullity, a Perth heart specialist, at Vasse Felix in 1967, that was the first step in the Margaret River's journey to success. What made Dr Cullity take the risk, in an area that had become devoid of vines? The catalyst was a report by Dr John Gladstone, concluding that the climate of the Margaret River area held advantages for viticulture over "all other Australian vine districts". So Cullity planted his vineyard and was followed by a veritable surgery of winegrowers: Dr Bill Pannel (Moss Wood, 1969), Dr Kevin Cullen (Cullen, 1971), Dr John Lagan and Dr Eithne Sheridan (Chateau Xanadu, 1977) and Dr Michael Peterkin (Pierro, 1980). It was, in fact, Cullen's grandfather, Ephraim Clark, who planted the first vines at Bunbury in 1890. Dr Gladstone's findings were correct, as

the number of star-performing wineries in the district indicate.

Although relatively minor, problems do exist in the area, notably oidium, parrots, wind and, most serious, the dry summer. The oidium seems to be under control, the parrots eat the grapes and swear at the vineyard workers who plant sunflowers to distract them from the vines, and rye grass acts as a windbreak. A lot of vines experience water-stress, not a heat-related problem, but a dry-summer-induced one, and this is exacerbated by the wind-factor. In the 1985-86 season, for example, the Margaret River had a healthy rainfall of some 100 centimetres (40 ins), but the wind-dried evaporation in the vineyards amounted to 150 centimetres (60 ins) – leaving a deficit of 50 centimetres (20 ins). So even in the Margaret River irrigation is being considered, though growers might be advised to follow Miguel Torres' intensive cultivation system (*see* p.278).

The greatness of Margaret River

wines cannot be disputed; they are of classic stature by any standards. This is because the quality of fruit is better than elsewhere in Australia. But it is not simply a question of the district's intrinsic quality potential. Part of the Margaret River's phenomenal success can be attributed to the deliberate, if unorchestrated, policy of its many quality-conscious winemakers to grow exclusively classic varieties. They also totally ignore the wine-cask market, starting their ranges at premium varietal and working upwards towards even higher quality wines. The best grape is the Cabernet sauvignon, but there are some fabulous wines being made from Chardonnay, Sémillon, Sauvignon blanc, Syrah, Pinot noir and even Zinfandel. The top wines are produced by a galaxy of great names (plus a few lesser known ones): Cape Mentelle, Chateau Xanadu, Cape Clairault, Cullens, Happs, Pierro and Redgate. In almost the same league are Leeuwin Estate (its Chardonnay belongs in the former category) and Vasse Felix.

RED: 1982, 1985, 1986, 1987

WHITE: 1982, 1985, 1986, 1987

MOUNT BARKER

Part of the Great Southern Area, the appellation of this wine district has been certified, following in the footsteps the Margaret River. The wineries here have a reputation for Rhine Riesling and Cabernet Sauvignon.

RED: 1981, 1983*, 1984, 1985, 1986, 1989

WHITE: 1981, 1983*, 1984, 1985, 1986, 1987, 1989

MOUNT BARKER/ FRANKLAND RIVER AREA
See Great Southern Area.

SOUTHWEST COASTAL PLAIN

The common factor that joins these vineyards together is the tuart sands on which they are established. This very fine white or light grey sand covers a limestone base that has a fairly high water-table. The one exception is Capel Vale where the soil is a dark, fertile, sandy-alluvial-loam. Moderated by marine winds, the district has a frost free climate, and one in which neither rain nor hail are common hazards at harvest time. Chardonnay, Chenin blanc, Gewürztraminer, Rhine riesling, Sauvignon blanc, Sémillon and Shiraz all fare well here.

RED: 1980, 1982, 1986, 1987

WHITE: 1981, 1982, 1985, 1986, 1987

SWAN VALLEY

Located in the eastern suburbs of Perth, the Swan Valley has the distinction of being one of the hottest wine-growing regions in the world. Partly because of this and partly as a reaction to the phenomenal success of the Margaret River, several wineries have deserted the area and the vineyards are shrinking. What was once the traditional centre of Western Australia's wine industry is now a waning force. Its 86 centimetres (34 ins) of rain would usually be perfect for viticulture, but it all falls during the winter and spring. This factor, together with the deep, fertile, sandy, alluvial soil and temperatures as high as 40°C (104°F), leads to a very full and traditional style of wine. If the tidal Swan River were utilized for irrigation, it would soon create toxic levels of salinity. Although some bore-holes have been drilled to supply suitable irrigation water, most vines rely on tapping the water-table some 6 metres (20 ft) below ground, the topsoil itself being up to 12 metres (40 ft) deep and easily penetrated. Exceptions to the old, foursquare style are made by Evans & Tate and Houghton's, and, with less reliability, by Jane Brook and Sandalford. The most successful grapes are Cabernet sauvignon, Chenin blanc and Shiraz.

RED: 1980, 1982, 1984*, 1986, 1987, 1988, 1989

WHITE: 1981, 1982, 1984, 1985, 1986, 1988, 1989

WANNEROO

Small area just north of Perth in the Southwest Coastal Plain district. *See* Southwest Coastal Plain.

Major wineries of Western Australia

ALKOOMI WINES
Manjimup Road,
Frankland, WA 6396

Production: *12,000 cases*
Vineyards: *13 ha (32 acres) of Cabernet sauvignon, Rhine riesling, Syrah, Malbec and Sémillon*

Sheep farmers Mervyn and Judy Lange turned their hand to winemaking and their fresh, fruity, rich-flavoured wines are an excellent indication of the potential of the up-and-coming Frankland area.

☆ Cabernet Sauvignon, Malbec, Shiraz

CAPEL VALE WINES
Lot 5 Stirling Estate,
Capel, WA 6271

Production: *7,000 cases*
Vineyards: *9.5 ha (23 acres) of Cabernet sauvignon, Syrah, Merlot, Rhine riesling, Gewürztraminer, Chardonnay and Sauvignon blanc*
Established: *1975*

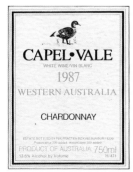

This rapidly up-and-coming winery is an example of how ignorance of viticulture and oenology can lead to great success when starting up a winery.

Dr Peter Pratten, a Bunbury radiologist, had no experience whatsoever when he began making wine on the banks of the Capel River, but his delicious, vibrantly fruity wines are some of Western Australia's finest.

☆ Shiraz, Chardonnay, Traminer, Riesling, Sémillon Sauvignon blanc, Gewürztraminer

CULLENS
Caves Road,
Cowaramup, WA 6284

Production: *9,000 cases*
Vineyards: *22 ha (54 acres) of Chardonnay, Sauvignon blanc, Sémillon, Rhine riesling, Cabernet sauvignon, Cabernet franc, Merlot and Pinot noir*
Established: *1971*

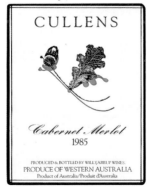

Diana Cullen produces a wide range of good, sometimes exceptional, wines from Margaret River vineyards. They show an early vivacity of fruit that can often develop into great complexity.

☆ Cabernet Merlot, Sauvignon Blanc, Sauternes Style, Sauvignon Blanc, Chardonnay

EVANS & TATE
Swan Street,
Henley Brook, WA 6055

Production: *10,000 cases*
Vineyards: *29 ha (72 acres) of Cabernet sauvignon, Sauvignon blanc, Sémillon, Syrah, Chardonnay, Merlot and Cabernet franc*
Established: *1972*

This winery owns vineyards in both the Swan Valley and Margaret River areas, and produces stunning wines that combine richness with finesse.

☆ "Redbrook" branded wines, Gnangara Shiraz, Three Vineyards Cabernet Sauvignon

HOUGHTON WINES
Dale Road,
Middle Swan, WA 6056

Production: *300,000 cases*
Vineyards: *283 ha (699 acres) of Rhine riesling, Chardonnay, Sémillon, Verdelho, Sauvignon blanc, Chenin blanc, Muscadelle, Cabernet sauvignon, Syrah, Pinot noir and Malbec*
Established: *1836*

This winery, now owned by Hardy's, also has vineyards at Frankland River. It continues to make exceptional wines even though changes, perhaps coincidental, have occurred. Its popular White Burgundy ("Houghton's Supreme" on some export markets), for example, changed style with the 1985: previous to this the wine was tangy and citrussy in a most attractive way. Now it is softer and almost Chardonnay in character, despite there being no change to the basic Chenin blanc and Muscadelle blend–a case of improving an already good product.

☆ Cabernet Sauvignon, Moondah Brook (Cabernet Sauvignon, "Estate" Verdelho, "Estate" Chenin Blanc), Houghton (Cabernet Sauvignon, Autumn Harvest Sémillon, White Burgundy)

LEEUWIN ESTATE
Gnarawary Road,
Margaret River, WA 6285

Production: *24,000 cases*
Vineyards: *92 ha (227 acres) of Rhine riesling, Cabernet sauvignon, Chardonnay, Pinot noir, Sauvignon blanc and Gewürztraminer*
Established: *1978*

This high-tech winery was established with advice from Californian Robert Mondavi. Its scintillating Chardonnay is one of Australia's finest.

☆ Chardonnay, Pinot Noir, Cabernet Sauvignon

PEEL ESTATE
Fletcher Road,
Baldivis, WA 6171

Production: *5,000 cases*

Continued overleaf

Vineyards: *15 ha (37 acres) of Chenin blanc, Sauvignon blanc, Chardonnay, Sémillon, Verdelho, Cabernet, Syrah, Zinfandel and Merlot*
Established: *1980*

The delicious, honeyed, buttery Chenin blanc proves the grape performs far better in Australia than it does in France.

☆ Chenin Blanc Wood Matured

PLANTAGENET WINES
46 Albany Highway,
Mount Barker, WA 6324

Production: *15,000 cases*
Vineyards: *28 ha (69 acres) of Rhine riesling, Chardonnay, Chenin blanc, Muscat, Syrah, Cabernet sauvignon, Pinot noir, Malbec and Merlot*
Established: *1968*

A winery named after the shire in which it is situated. Once an apple-packing shed it was the first enterprise to cultivate Mount Barker and one of the first wineries to be established in the district.

☆ "Fleur de Cabernet", Cabernet Hermitage, Cabernet Sauvignon, Frontignac (Bindoon), Wyjup Rhine Riesling, "Kings Reserve" Chardonnay

The best of the rest

CAPE CLAIRAULT
CMB Carbunup River, WA 6280

Production: *2,500 cases*
Vineyards: *7 ha (18 acres) of Cabernet sauvignon, Rhine riesling, Sémillon, Sauvignon blanc, Merlot and Cabernet franc*
Established: *1977*

☆ Cabernet Sauvignon, Cabernet Sauvignon Port

CAPE MENTELLE VINEYARDS
Walcliffe Road,
Margaret River, WA 6285

Production: *12,000 cases*
Vineyards: *17 ha (42 acres)*
Established: *1977*

☆ Cabernet Sauvignon, Hermitage, Zinfandel

CHATEAU XANADU
Off Walcliffe Road,
Margaret River, WA 6285

Production: *5,000 cases*
Vineyards: *16 ha (39 acres) of Cabernet sauvignon, Cabernet franc, Sémillon, Chardonnay and Sauvignon blanc*
Established: *1977*

☆ Sémillon (Wood Matured), Chardonnay, Cabernet Sauvignon

PAUL CONTI
529 Wanneroo Road,
Wanneroo, WA 6065

Production: *10,000 cases*
Vineyards: *9 ha (22 acres) of Syrah, Chardonnay, Sauvignon blanc and Muscat*
Established: *1948*

☆ Marginiup Hermitage, Wanneroo (Chardonnay, Chenin Blanc), *Spatlese* White Frontignac, Late Bottled White Frontignac

FOREST HILL VINEYARD
Muir Highway, Forest Hill
via Mount Barker, WA 6324

Production: *2,500 cases*
Vineyards: *24 ha (60 acres) of Rhine riesling, Gewürztraminer, Chardonnay, Sauvignon blanc and Cabernet sauvignon*
Established: *1966*

☆ Rhine Riesling, Chardonnay

GILLESPIE VINEYARDS
Davis Road,
Witchcliffe, WA 6286

Production: *3,000 cases*
Vineyards: *10 ha (25 acres) of Sémillon, Sauvignon blanc, Rhine riesling and Cabernet sauvignon*
Established: *1976*

☆ Cabernet Sauvignon

GOUNDREY WINES
11 North Street,
Denmark, WA 6333

Production: *4,500 cases*
Vineyards: *12 ha (30 acres) of Cabernet sauvignon, Rhine riesling, Chardonnay, Sauvignon blanc and Gewürztraminer*
Established: *1975*

☆ Rhine Riesling, Cabernet Sauvignon

HAPP'S VINEYARD
Commonage Road,
Yallingup, WA 6282

Production: *2,500 cases*
Vineyards: *6 ha (15 acres) of Cabernet sauvignon, Syrah, Merlot, Verdelho, Chardonnay, Touriga, Muscat, Tina Cao and Souzao*
Established: *1978*

☆ Cabernet Sauvignon, Shiraz, Vintage Port, Merlot

HARTRIDGE WINES
1964 Wanneroo Road,
Wanneroo, WA 6065

Vineyards: *Cabernet sauvignon, Chenin blanc, Chardonnay, Malbec and Pinot noir*
Established: *1970*

☆ Chenin Blanc

JANE BROOK ESTATE WINES
Toodyay Road,
Middle Swan, WA 6056

Production: *6,000 cases*
Vineyards: *12 ha (30 acres) of Chenin blanc, Sauvignon blanc, Cabernet sauvignon, Syrah, Rhine riesling, Verdelho, Muscadelle, Taminga and Merlot*
Established: *1972*

☆ Jane Brook Cabernet Sauvignon

LESCHENAULT
Minnimup Road,
Gelarup, WA 6230

Production: *3,000 cases*
Vineyards: *16 ha (39 acres) of Gewürztraminer, Chardonnay, Sémillon, Pinot noir, Syrah and Cabernet*
Established: *1973*

☆ Kempston Vintage Port

PIERRO
Caves Road,
Willyabrup, WA 6284

Production: *1,200 cases*
Vineyards: *5 ha (12 acres) of Chardonnay, Sauvignon blanc and Pinot noir*
Established: *1980*

☆ Cabernet Sauvignon, Pinot Noir, *Spatlese* Riesling

REDGATE WINES
Boodjidup Road,
Margaret River, WA 6285

Production: *4,200 cases*
Vineyards: *16 ha (39 acres) of Rhine riesling, Sémillon, Chenin blanc, Sauvignon blanc, Chardonnay, Cabernet sauvignon, Pinot noir, Merlot, Syrah, Cabernet franc*
Established: *1981*

☆ Cabernet Sauvignon, Rhine Riesling

REDMOND VINEYARD
Albany, WA 6330

Production: *1,200 cases*

Vineyards: *45 ha (11 acres) of Rhine riesling, Cabernet sauvignon, Gewürztraminer and Sauvignon blanc*
Established: *1974*

SANDALFORD WINES
West Swan Road,
Caversham, WA 6055

Production: *70,000 cases*
Vineyards: *180 ha (445 acres) of Chenin, Verdelho, Cabernet, Zinfandel, Riesling, Syrah, Sémillon and Gewürztraminer*
Established: *1840*

☆ Verdelho, "Matilde" Rosé

SHEMARIN WINES
18 Muir Street,
Mount Barker, WA 6324

Production: *4,200 cases*
Vineyards: *Chardonnay and Sauvignon blanc*
Established: *1980*

☆ Zinfandel

TINGLEWOOD WINES
Glenrowan Road,
Denmark, WA 6333

Vineyards: *4 ha (10 acres) of Syrah, Riesling, Cabernet and Gewürztraminer*
Established: *1981*

☆ Rhine Riesling

VASSE FELIX
Harmans South Road,
Cowaramup, WA 6284

Production: *6,600 cases*
Vineyards: *8.5 ha (21 acres) of Cabernet sauvignon, Riesling, Hermitage and Malbec*
Established: *1967*

☆ Cabernet Sauvignon

Queensland and Northern Territory

Though covering nearly half of Australia, Queensland and Northern Territory contain barely 15 per cent of its population. The majority of these inhabitants live in the city of Brisbane, on Queensland's eastern coast, whilst the rest of the land is sparsely populated outback. This is the hinterland of Australia's wine industry, with the only serious vine-growing area located in Queensland's Granite Belt.

QUEENSLAND

ONE OF THE LAST PLACES ON EARTH that one might expect to find a vineyard, Queensland actually has some 15 wineries and a small wine industry that dates back to the 1850s. Surprisingly, the summers are cooler than they are at Riverland in South Australia, and the Mudgee and the Hunter Valley in New South Wales, and the relatively wet weather between the *veraison* and harvest-time makes the vines prone to rot. Since the growers of the Granite Belt recently introduced their Shiraz "Balandean Nouveau", I have wondered why they do not try making it with the Gamay grape, which should perform well here. The wine is, after all, of a Beaujolais type, made by *macération carbonique*. The climate seems acceptable and granite is the only successful soil so far encountered for the Gamay.

NORTHERN TERRITORY

A less likely location for a winemaking area than Queensland is hard to imagine, but its western neighbour, Northern Territory, is such a place. Very hot and dry for the most part, the land elsewhere is crocodile-infested swamp. As testimony to this, the local tourist board advises visitors to run in a zig-zag when chased by a crocodile! Curiously it is illegal to drink alcohol in a public place within two kilometres (one mile) of a licensed bar (except, of course, *in* one). Outback machismo might be expected to

preclude wine drinking as effeminate and impractical, bearing in mind the cooling properties attributed to some of Australia's beers. Despite all this, the town of Alice Springs is home to Chateau Hornsby and its three hectares (seven acres) of vineyards.

An outback station in Alice Springs, *where the hot, dry climate means irrigation is necessary for the area's red-sand soil.*

The wines of Queensland and Northern Territory

ALICE SPRINGS

Northern Territory's only winery, Chateau Hornsby, is at Alice Springs. The vines, grown on red sand-ridges, are Cabernet sauvignon, Rhine riesling, Sémillon and Syrah. They are all drip-irrigated and the harvest is in January, although I could believe December!

BALLANDEAN

The name of a town at the epicentre of the Granite Belt district in Queensland. It has its own self-decreed appellation, to be used by the entire winemaking fraternity of the Granite Belt, for a generic Beaujolais-type wine released on the same day

each year, under a communal "Balandean Nouveau" label. *See* Granite Belt.

GRANITE BELT

The vines here are grown in an area surrounding the town of Ballandean, on an elevated granite plateau 240 kilometres (150 miles) west of Brisbane. It is the altitude of this district, between 790 and 940 metres (2,600 and 3,100 ft), that provides a sufficiently cool climate in which wine-grapes may successfully grow. The good quality varietal-wine industry of the Granite Belt was once described as Queensland's greatest secret. That changed with the masterful plan to establish the region's name in 1985. Made from the

Shiraz grape and produced by *macération carbonique*, every winery launched a Beaujolais-type wine on the same day, bearing the same vivid, purple-pink, generic "Balandean Nouveau" label (only the winery's name in small print at the bottom of the label was different). What the wines actually tasted like was not the point, nor whether the annual event actually survived (which it has), because it was a brilliant marketing ploy that introduced people to the district's other, finer wines. The most successful grape varieties are Cabernet sauvignon, Rhine riesling, and Sémillon. No winery has great consistency across the range, but those making the best wines are Old Caves, Robinsons Family and Rumbalara.

RED: 1985, 1986, 1987

WHITE: 1984, 1985, 1986, 1987

ROMA

With the possible exception of Alice Springs, this small, hot, dry and relatively unknown wine area in Queensland is as inappropriate a place as could be found to grow grapes, but there are some 25 hectares (62 acres) of vines growing on rich alluvial or sandy loam soils. Bassetts is the only winery.

RED: 1984, 1985, 1986, 1987

WHITE: 1984, 1985, 1986, 1987

Major wineries of Queensland and Northern Territory

BASSETTS ROMAVILLA WINERY
**Northern Road,
Roma, Qld. 4455**

Production: *3,000 cases*
Established: *1975*
Vineyards: *20 ha (49 acres) of Riesling, Chenin blanc, Crouchen, Syrah, Muscats, Syrian, Durif and Mataro*

An important output, in terms of Queensland, of some 20 different wines.

BUNGAWARRA
**Marshall's Crossing Road,
Ballandean, Qld. 4382**

Production: *3,500 cases*
Vineyards: *11.5 ha (28 acres)*

Originally founded in the 1920s by Angelo Barbagello, this winery was re-established in 1979 by Alan Dorr and Philip Christensen, who won a gold medal with their first wine.

☆ Light Dry Red (LDR)

CHATEAU HORNSBY
**Petrick Road,
Alice Springs, NT 5750**

Production: *1,500 cases*
Vineyards: *3 ha (7 acres) of Rhine riesling, Sémillon, Syrah and Cabernet sauvignon*
Established: *1976*

Who would believe a winery could produce anything drinkable from grapes grown at Alice Springs in the arid, hot dead-centre of Australia? The whites almost prove that it is impossible, although a bottle of the Riesling

Sémillon, with its rather nice picture of Alice Springs on the label, is certainly a curiosity. On the other hand, Chateau Hornsby's Alice Springs Shiraz-Cabernet is actually very drinkable.

☆ Alice Springs Shiraz-Cabernet

ELSINORE WINES
**Back Creek Road,
Glen Aplin, Qld. 4381**

Vineyards: *18 ha (44 acres) of Syrah, Cabernet sauvignon, Palomino, Rhine riesling and Sémillon*
Established: *1982*

One of Queensland's more successful wineries, Elsinore has won several gold medals for its light red wines. Its Vintage Port is also appreciated.

☆ Cabernet Sauvignon, Cabernet-Shiraz

FELSBERG VINEYARDS-WINERY
**Townsends Road,
Glen Aplin, Qld. 4381**

Vineyards: *4.5 ha (11 acres) of Chardonnay, Gewürztraminer, Rhine riesling, Cabernet sauvignon, Pinot noir, Syrah, Merlot and Malbec*
Established: *1983*

KÓMINOS WINES
**Accommodation Creek Road,
Lyra, Qld.**

Production: *1,500 cases*
Vineyards: *6 ha (15 acres) of Syrah, Cabernet sauvignon, Sémillon, Rhine riesling, Chenin blanc, Pinot noir and Chardonnay*
Established: *1976*

A winery whose Balandean Nouveau is well thought of by lovers of *macération carbonique*.

MOUNT MAGNUS
**Donnelly's Castle Road,
Pozieres via Stanthorpe,
Qld. 4352**

Production: *3,500 cases*
Vineyards: *12 ha (30 acres) of Syrah, Cabernet and Chardonnay*
Established: *1933*

Various wines from a relatively new owner include a surprisingly good Shiraz.

☆ Shiraz

OLD CAVES WINERY
Stanthorpe, Qld. 4380

Production: *3,000 cases*
Established: *1980*

The premium varietals are really quite good, and the Riesling is one of the best wines currently produced in Queensland. Forget the Coffee Marsala.

☆ Riesling, Shiraz

ROBINSONS FAMILY
**Lyra Church Road,
Ballandean, Qld. 4382**

Production: *5,500 cases*
Vineyards: *18 ha (45 acres)*
Established: *1969*

John Robinson got his passion for wine when living in France, close to the

Beaujolais region. He then studied wine science at Riverina College under Brian Croser, now one of the country's leading consultants. Heather Robinson's family, the Salters, founded Saltrams Wines in the Barossa Valley, one of the wineries that Croser advises. The combination of these wine interests has led to the formation of what must be Queensland's premier winery.

☆ Cabernet Sauvignon, Chardonnay

RUMBALARA VINEYARDS
**Fletcher Road,
Fletcher, Qld. 4381**

Production: *5,000 cases*
Vineyards: *20 ha (49 acres) of Sémillon, Chardonnay, Riesling, Sylvaner, Cabernet sauvignon, Syrah, Pinot noir, Merlot and Muscat*
Established: *1974*

Not as good all round as the Robinsons Family, but the Sémillon is perhaps the best single wine made in Queensland.

☆ Sémillon

OTHER WINERIES OF QUEENSLAND AND NORTHERN TERRITORY

FOSTER & COMPANY
Kalunga via Herberton, Qld. 4872

Production: *2,500 cases*
Vineyards: *25 ha (62 acres)*
Established: *1971*

SUNDOWN VALLEY VINEYARDS
**Sundown Valley Road,
Ballandean, Qld. 4380**

Production: *10,000 cases*
Vineyards: *30 ha (74 acres) of Syrah, Cabernet sauvignon, Sylvaner and Rhine riesling*
Established: *1970*

New Zealand

In what is the most exciting new wine region in the world today, Sauvignon blanc competes on equal terms with the very best that Sancerre and Pouilly Fumé have to offer. It rarely drops to the periodical dismal depths of its Loire counterparts in poor years; at the same time, it is significantly cheaper. The Chardonnay and Sémillon wines are also first-rate.

HOW QUICKLY THIS COUNTRY'S REPUTATION HAS GROWN! My first comprehensive tasting of New Zealand wines was in London in February 1982, cocooned inside the High Commissioner's penthouse suite perched on top of New Zealand House. The sun shone through its plate-glass windows and transformed a cold but cloudless British winter's day into a warm and sunny Pacific one. I was in New Zealand before the first drop of wine touched my lips! My concept of this country's wine had previously been limited to a Germanic-style off-dry or semi-sweet Müller-Thurgau and just two producers—Cooks and Montana.

THE LIEBFRAUMILCH SYNDROME

My misconception about this country was due to the clever marketing strategy of Cooks and Montana in the late 1970s. They hit the British market with the right product at the right time. While the British undoubtedly have the greatest range of the finest wines available anywhere in the world, they also drink more Liebfrau-milch than any other country. The British like the concept of dry wines, but actually prefer some sweetness. A wine may contain as much sugar as its maker likes to put in it, just as long as the word "dry" appears somewhere on the label and is, preferably, qualified by words like "fresh" and "grapey".

In the mid-1970s when the "Lieb-boom" was in full swing the sharp marketing men at Cooks and Montana quickly launched

their Müller-Thurgau wines onto Britain's Liebfraumilch-based market and explained that the grape was the same one that dominated its "favourite" wine. They also revealed to a "Lieb-sick" wine press that it was a combination of New Zealand's European-type climate and its widespread practice of "back-blending" that enabled it to produce wines of distinctly Germanic style. Back-blending, we were told, is synonymous with the addition of *süssreserve*, blending back unfermented grape juice into a finished, fully-fermented, dry wine. This adds sugar, but the sweetness is disguised by the juice's freshness and high acidity, and is more readily perceived as tanginess and grapeyness, particularly if the consumer is told this by the label. The *süssreserve* process is especially important in the production of German wines, *see* p.206.

Mission Vineyards, North Island, above
This Hawkes Bay winery, established in the mid-nineteenth century, has made a recent effort to upgrade its wines.

NEW ZEALAND

Although South Island has a younger wine trade, it boasts a slightly more favourable winegrowing climate than North Island, having a lighter rainfall.

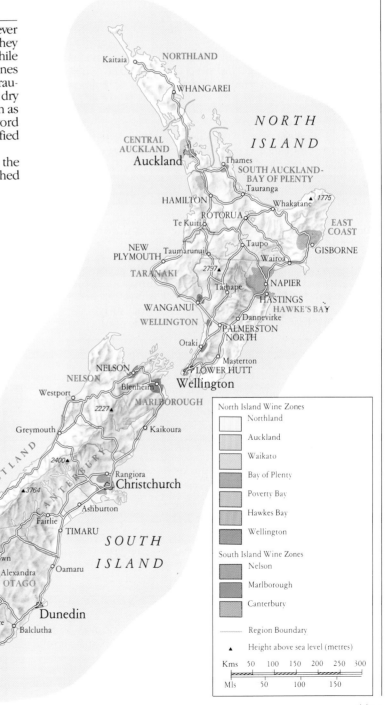

North Island Wine Zones
Northland
Auckland
Waikato
Bay of Plenty
Poverty Bay
Hawkes Bay
Wellington

South Island Wine Zones
Nelson
Marlborough
Canterbury

—— Region Boundary

▲ Height above sea level (metres)

Kms 50 100 150 200 250 300

Mls 50 100 150

MY FIRST COMPREHENSIVE TASTING

Many writers, including myself, enthusiastically endorsed the Müller-Thurgau wines. We recommended them as New Zealand's more honest alternatives to Liebfraumilch; more "honest" because they were not anonymous blends of different grapes from different areas, but individual wines from one grape grown in one area and thus varietally pure and more characterful. However, the argument I expounded left me with an over-simplistic view of New Zealand's wine industry. So I attended the New Zealand House wine tasting blissfully ignorant of the fact that I was totally fooled by my own propaganda! There were, of course, some people present at the tasting who had a far more complete picture of these wines than I had. A few had visited New Zealand fairly recently and had tasted extensively in its little roadside wineries. For most of us, however, the New Zealand House tasting was to be a turning point in our understanding of these wines.

It was a revelation! Of the 50 wines available that day, the whites included Chardonnay, Chenin Blanc, Furmint, Riesling, Sauvignon Blanc, Sémillon and Pinot Gris. There was also Gewürztraminer, both in a pure varietal form and as part of a blend with Riesling, which was rather novel at the time. The styles ranged from dry, through off-dry and medium-sweet, to late-picked. There were some wines with various degrees of oak influence from barrel-fermented to cask-aged, and there were even some artificial "ice wines" made by deep-freezing fresh grape juice. (This froze out much of the water content and concentrated sugars and acids prior to fermentation.) The red wines included Cabernet Sauvignon, Pinotage and Pinot Noir, with some new oak.

Everyone, including myself, was impressed. The standard was very high, the styles were both attractive and interesting. The Chardonnay seemed to have the best potential, but the tasting included just one Sauvignon Blanc, and we were unaware of the stunning success this variety was to have in later years. In the mid-1980s, it was predicted that New Zealand would be the only region in the world outside of Burgundy where the Pinot noir would succeed. This has not yet been realized, but it is still early days, and several winemakers remain firmly convinced that they are on the right track. As if in confirmation of our initial judgement, the quality of Chardonnays has now reached a point where it seriously challenges the superiority of Sauvignon.

Since the first New Zealand House tasting the improvement has been startling–the skill of these winemakers seems to grow by at least 100 per cent each year. Their ability to adapt to the vagaries of the country's less-than-stable climate has been well demonstrated, as has their curiosity to try out different techniques and their willingness to explore new methods and listen to criticism.

UPROOTING THE MÜLLER-THURGAU

New Zealand's wine industry has not always been a success story, however, and ironically it was the Müller-Thurgau that precipitated an over-production crisis in the mid-1980s. The commercial value of this vine became apparent in the 1960s, when its early-ripening ability and high yield were first appreciated. Per capita consumption of wine jumped from 1.74 litres (0.45 US galls) in 1960 to 3.08 litres (0.8 US galls) in 1965, domestic wineries began to worry about the supply problem and everyone began planting Müller-Thurgau in vast quantities. By 1980 the average New Zealander was consuming 11.9 litres (3 US galls) per year, mostly light table wine, and Müller-Thurgau accounted for more than half of it, yet the supply problem persisted.

At this time there were five big wineries: Cooks, Corbans, McWilliams, Montana and Penfolds. Their marketeers looked at Australia, saw that New Zealand was where her great neighbour had been almost ten years before and that its consumption had doubled in the meantime. They planned the bulk of their future production almost entirely on inexpensive Müller-Thurgau blends.

By 1985, the grapey Müller-Thurgau was no longer so popular; consumers moved on to higher-quality varietals such as Sauvignon Blanc and Chardonnay. Despite a makeshift change of plans to

VARIETAL EVOLUTION

The boom between 1970 and 1983, when New Zealand's vineyards exceeded the target set for 1986 despite impending overproduction, is self-evident. Since 1983, new vineyards of classic grapes such as Sauvignon blanc, Chardonnay, Cabernet sauvignon and Pinot noir have actually been planted, although the net effect of the government's vine extraction scheme has resulted in an overall drop in these varieties.

VARIETAL FLUCTUATION 1970-1987 (HECTARES)

Grape variety	Year of survey			Change	
	1970	1983	1987	1970-83	1983-87
Müller-Thurgau	194	1,873	1,360	+ 865%	− 27%
Cabernet sauvignon	39	414	352	+ 906%	− 15%
Chardonnay	35	402	351	+ 915%	− 13%
Chenin blanc	—	372	274		− 26%
Muscat varieties	—	331	274		− 17%
Palomino	243	408	272	+ 68%	− 33%
Chasselas	129	236	183	+ 83%	− 22%
Gewürztraminer	—	284	176		− 38%
Sauvignon blanc	—	200	170		− 15%
Gamay	—	157	141		− 10%
Pinot noir	21	139	120	+ 562%	− 14%
Pinotage	61	100	74	+ 56%	− 26%
Sémillon	—	86	73		− 15%
Hybrids	631	256	184	− 60%	− 28%
Others	115	618	411	+ 437%	− 33%
Total planted	1,468	5,876	4,415	+ 300%	− 25%

accommodate more of these better vines, New Zealand's wine industry was left with 40 per cent of its vineyards providing grapes of a variety that was falling from grace. If this was not bad enough, the five year period had witnessed an unprecedented and unpredictable accumulation of wine taxes. Little wonder, then, that per capita consumption failed to soar according to the marketeers' graphs. In fact it virtually stagnated.

In response to the overproduction situation, the government introduced a scheme to reduce these vineyards by as much as 30 per cent and offered growers an incentive of NZ$6,175 for every

Coopers Creek Winery, North Island, above
Situated in the Huapai Valley, this winery produces exceptionally stylish wines. Talented North Island winemakers use both traditional and high-tech methods.

hectare (2.47 acres) pulled up. Within four months, 1,583 hectares (3,912 acres) had been scrapped. Unlike a similar scheme that had been operated in Australia, New Zealanders were not prevented from replanting. Although much of the land was put to other uses, for growers who were in the process of upgrading their vineyards to higher-quality varietals, it was a prayer answered.

THE PRICE WAR

The "big five" wineries knew that they had expanded out of all proportion to the market's actual size and that only one, or possibly two, of them would survive in the long term. They entered into a price-cutting war to increase their market share at almost any cost. At the end of it all, Cooks had swallowed up McWilliams and in turn had been taken over by Corbans, and Montana had purchased Penfolds. As Cooks/Corbans and Montana now control 85 per cent of all New Zealand wines and a merger between them is unlikely to be allowed, the need to fight it out at the bottom end of the market has evaporated and it may be assumed that they will gradually trade up.

THE NEED FOR AN APPELLATION SYSTEM

New Zealand has an extraordinary range of areas with different climatic, geographical and geological conditions. These dictate the boundaries of general regions such as Poverty Bay and Marlborough, within which exist various districts such as Gisborne in Poverty Bay and Blenheim in Marlborough. Inside these districts, the variation of wine styles produced from the same grape, grown by identical viticultural methods and using very similar vinification techniques, proves the existence of numerous areas with specific *terroirs*.

The boundary of even a well-known region like Marlborough is debatable, but the area merits the dignity of a meaningful appellation, just as the consumer deserves a guarantee of authenticity. While many mediocre wine-producing countries have introduced systems of little consequence based on inadequate, even dubious reputation, it is ironic that New Zealand's high-performance industry with its wealth of genuine statistics has not seen fit to establish a much-needed system of its own.

Neudorf Vineyard, South Island, above
The Nelson area offers a favourable climate for fine-wine production. This vineyard produces 2,000 cases annually from its 4.5 hectares (11 acres).

FACTORS AFFECTING TASTE AND QUALITY (NORTH ISLAND)

Location
North Island, the northerly of New Zealand's two principal islands, situated 2,575 kilometres (1,600 miles) east of Melbourne.

Climate
Cool maritime type similar to that of Bordeaux in terms of average temperatures. Rainfall is, however, generally much higher, ranging from an acceptable 76 centimetres (30 ins) in Hawkes Bay to an excessive 160 centimetres (63 ins) in Northland. The crucial autumn periods are rarely dry; heavy rains and high humidity lead to problems of grape damage and rot.

Using the Californian heat summation system, *see* p.362, the most important viticultural areas in both islands are all Region I (less than 2,500 degree-days in Celsius).

Aspect
Most vines are on flattish land that is easy to work. Some north-facing slopes have been planted in Auckland and Te Kauwhata; these provide better drainage and longer hours of intensive sunlight.

Soil
Varied soils ranging from shallow clay over sandy-clay subsoil in Northland, through heavy loams on clay subsoil in Waikato and alluvial loams over sandy or volcanic subsoils in Poverty Bay, to clay loams and alluvial sand over gravelly or volcanic subsoils in Hawkes Bay. Poor drainage is a feature of most of the soils, although those of Hawkes Bay are lighter and better in this respect.

Viticulture and vinification
Harvests begin in March and April, six months ahead of wine regions in the Northern Hemisphere. Although the emphasis is very much on higher-quality varietals such as Chardonnay, Sauvignon blanc, Cabernet sauvignon and Pinot noir, Müller-Thurgau still dominates, despite much of it being pulled up between 1983 and 1986. This is traditionally made in an off-dry style by back-blending with sweet, sterilized, unfermented grape juice.

Most wineries are of the "boutique" type with very small but well equipped premises. They often have brand new oak barrels and restrict their production to limited editions of high-quality varietals. At the other end of the spectrum there are just two large wine companies accounting for some 85 per cent of all New Zealand's wines. They produce just as many medal-winning wines as the smaller "boutiques", but their widest-selling, Germanic-style, bulk-produced Müller-Thurgau, often sold in large 1.5-litre bottles or bag-in-the-box, are the most readily encountered. Between these two groups are several medium-sized wineries producing bulk and premium wines.

 Grape varieties
Albany surprise, Baco blanc, Baco noir, Cabernet sauvignon, Chardonnay, Chasselas, Chenin blanc, Gamay teinturier, Gewürztraminer Iona, Müller-Thurgau, Palomino, Pinotage, Pinot gris, Pinot meunier, Pinot noir, Sémillon, Siebels, Sauvignon blanc, Trousseau gris

FACTORS AFFECTING TASTE AND QUALITY (SOUTH ISLAND)

Location
South Island, the southerly of New Zealand's two principal islands, situated 16,900 kilometres (10,500 miles) northeast of Antarctica.

Climate
Average temperatures during the growing season are highest in the Marlborough area, which often has the country's most hours of sunshine. The mean temperature gradually drops as one moves southwards and is generally cooler than on North Island or, indeed, in Bordeaux. Rainfall is variable, but generally lighter than in the North Island, ranging from 61-76 centimetres (24-30 ins) in Marlborough and Canterbury to 99-124 centimetres (39-49 ins) in Nelson. Persistent, warm, dry, northwesterly winds cause problems of drought and damage to young leaves in the Marlborough area.

Aspect
The majority of vines are planted on flat or gently sloping land. The hills and mountains running down the spine of the island protect the vineyards on the eastern side from the heaviest autumn rains that often blight the vines in Nelson.

Soil
Very varied soils ranging from the generally clay loams of Nelson, through silty-alluvial loams over gravel subsoils in Marlborough and parts of Canterbury, to volcanic, loess, chalky, often lime-rich loam soils in other areas around Canterbury. These soils generally offer better drainage than most of those found in the North Island.

Viticulture and vinification
Harvests begin in March and April, six months ahead of wine regions in the Northern Hemisphere. The viticultural industry of the South Island has really only developed since the 1970s and so is technologically very advanced, with vines planted in wide rows to allow for mechanical cultivation and harvesting. *See* Viticulture and vinification, North Island, for wineries, methods and styles.

 Grape varieties
Cabernet sauvignon, Chardonnay, Gewürztraminer, Müller-Thurgau, Muscat, Pinotage, Pinot blanc, Pinot gris, Pinot noir, Refosco, Riesling, Sauvignon blanc, Sylvaner

The wines of New Zealand

NORTH ISLAND

The more important of the country's two islands, North Island supports some 70 per cent of the population. The 1960s New Zealand wine renaissance logically began at Auckland and Hawkes Bay, within easy reach of the largest population centres.

AUCKLAND

Vineyards: *802 ha (1,980 acres)*
Appellations: *Henderson (West Auckland), Kumeu, Huapai Valley, Waimauku, Riverhead, Ihumatao (South Auckland), Waiheke*

On the western outskirts of Auckland city, around the town of Henderson, is the oldest, largest and most traditional of Auckland's wine areas with the most operational wineries in the country. During the late-1960s and early-1970s, land prices soared; it now accounts for less than half of Auckland's vineyards, compared to 80 per cent in 1960. New areas are centred around Waimauku, where the climate is drier and cooler, and on the Ihumatao peninsula.

🍇 Cabernet sauvignon generally and, in specific areas, Pinot noir, Sauvignon blanc, Gewürztraminer and Chardonnay (in Waimauku district); Cabernet sauvignon and Pinotage generally and, in specific areas, Chardonnay, Gewürztraminer and Müller-Thurgau (in Henderson); Cabernet sauvignon and Merlot (Waiheke); Gewürztraminer, Rhine riesling (on Ihumatao)

📖 1981 and 1982 (red only), 1983, 1985, 1986, 1987 (red only), 1988

BAY OF PLENTY

Vineyards: *10 ha (2.5 acres)*
Appellations: *Bay of Plenty*

Morton's top-performing vineyard has put this area on the map and it is not likely to remain a one-estate district for long. White grapes perform best.

🍇 Chardonnay, Sauvignon blanc
📖 1983, 1985, 1986

HAWKES BAY

Vineyards: *1,870 ha (4,620 acres)*
Appellations: *Hawkes Bay, Esk Valley*

Both geographically and output-wise, Hawkes Bay's position is immediately beneath Poverty Bay, the country's top wine region. The two regions produce two-thirds of all New Zealand wines. Hawkes Bay soil is much lighter and although half of its vines are high-yielding Müller-Thurgau, late-picked versions are more in evidence and the wines are generally more serious. Cabernet sauvignon has flourished here since the mid-1960s, unlike neighbouring Poverty Bay where red wines have been very difficult to produce.

🍇 Cabernet sauvignon, Müller-Thurgau
📖 1981 and 1982 (red only), 1983, 1985, 1986, 1987 (red only), 1988

NORTHLAND

Vineyards: *14 ha (35 acres)*
Appellations: *none*

It was here that the first vines were planted by Samuel Marsden in 1819. James Busby made the first wine in 1832, but there are not many vines here and the wines, mostly sweet and fortified, are consumed locally.

🍇 None
📖 None recommended

POVERTY BAY

Vineyards: *1,782 ha (4,403 acres)*
Appellations: *Poverty Bay, Gisborne, East Cape, Tolaga Bay, Tikitiki*

This region has been dubbed "carafe country" because of the enormous yield of Müller-Thurgau from its very fertile soil, but more classic varietals are also made, and have won medals. Red wines have not been so successful.

Poverty Bay grew rapidly to be New Zealand's most important wine region by 1982, but expansion slowed to a trickle when phylloxera appeared and overproduction loomed. For complete-

ness, I include the areas of Tolaga Bay and Tikitiki within this region.

🍇 Chardonnay, Gewürztraminer, Müller-Thurgau
📖 1983, 1985, 1986

WAIKATO

Vineyards: *200 ha (494 acres)*
Appellations: *Waikato, Te Kauwhata, Mangatawhiri Valley, Waihou*

Situated inland, around the northern shore of Lake Waikere, this district is some 65 kilometres (40 miles) south-east of Auckland and encompasses the Te Kauwhata area. Yields are lower, rainfall, sunshine and mean temperatures higher. I also include the Mangatawhiri Valley and Waihou Estuary.

🍇 Cabernet sauvignon, Chenin blanc, Müller-Thurgau (Waikato) Sémillon (in the Mangatawhiri Valley), Chenin blanc (on the Waihou Estuary)
📖 1983, 1985, 1986

WELLINGTON

Vineyards: *18 ha (44 acres)*
Appellations: *Wellington, Wairarapa, Waikanae, Manawatu*

This minor region incorporates vines at Waikanae, north of Wellington, and at Martinborough in the Wairarapa.

🍇 Yet to be established
📖 None

SOUTH ISLAND

South Island has a lower population than North Island, and was cultivated at a much later date, but it shows great potential for premium varietals. Temperatures are low, but not too low, and it has a pleasingly low rainfall.

CANTERBURY

Vineyards: *40 ha (99 acres)*
Appellations: *Canterbury*

Although the summers here can be as warm as in Marlborough, the autumn is cooler and overall temperatures are lower.

🍇 Pinot noir and others show promise, but are not yet proven
📖 1983, 1985, 1986, 1987

MARLBOROUGH

Vineyards: *1,000 ha (2,470 acres)*
Appellations: *Renwick, Marlborough*

The first vines in Marlborough were planted as recently as 1973, since when it has become the fastest-growing of New Zealand's new wine areas. It is a fine white-wine area, but whether it will be New Zealand's very own "champagne" region, as some suggest, has yet to be proved.

🍇 Chardonnay, Rhine riesling, Sauvignon blanc
📖 1982 (red only), 1983, 1985, 1986, 1987 (red only), 1988, 1989

NELSON

Vineyards: *42 ha (104 acres)*
Appellations: *Nelson*

Frosty nights, long warm summers, cool autumn nights, the highest amount of sunshine in New Zealand, a unique topography that prevents widescale mechanized cultivation and a stony, well-drained soil, combine to make Nelson one of the country's best areas for small "boutique" wineries.

🍇 Cabernet sauvignon, Gewürztraminer
📖 1981 (red only), 1982 (red only), 1983, 1985, 1986, 1987 (red only)

OTHER AREAS

Experimental vineyards have been established at Timaru, halfway down the island's eastern coast, and at Otago further south. Results of wines made from these grapes at the Te Kauwhata research station are encouraging.

Major wineries of New Zealand

BABICH WINES
Babich Road,
Henderson, Auckland

Production: *42,000 cases*
Vineyards: *30 ha (74 acres) of Chardonnay, Sauvignon blanc, Cabernet sauvignon, Pinot noir, Pinotage, Merlot and Palomino*
Established: *1916*

This well-established winery is making its mark on export markets. Winemaker Joe Babich has been chairman of New Zealand's National Wine Competition and knows how to make a wine that impresses. He is one of the most successful exponents of Pinot noir and his Reserve Port is well worth trying.

☆ Chardonnay ("Irongate"), Pinot Noir, Cabernet Sauvignon, Sémillon/Chardonnay, Reserve Port

BROOKFIELDS VINEYARDS
Brookfields Road, R D 3,
Meeanee, Napier

Vineyards: *10 ha (25 acres) of Cabernet sauvignon, Sauvignon*

blanc, Chardonnay, Gewürztraminer, Pinot gris, Merlot and Cabernet franc
Established: *1937*

Since this one-time Sherry winery was purchased from founder Richard Ellis in 1977, the emphasis has been decisively and successfully switched to

light table wines, particularly the ripe, gentle and satisfying Pinot Gris.

☆ Cabernet Sauvignon, Chardonnay, Pinot Gris

CLOUDY BAY
Jacksons Road,
Blenheim

Production: *15,000 cases*
Vineyards: *25 ha (62 acres) of Sauvignon blanc, Sémillon and Chardonnay*
Established: *1985*

Owned by Western Australia's Cape Mentelle, Cloudy Bay's star-performing Sauvignon Blanc has quickly acquired a cult following, but its Chardonnay and Cabernet-Merlot are even finer.

☆ Sauvignon Blanc, Chardonnay, Cabernet-Merlot

COLLARD BROTHERS
303 Lincoln Road,
Henderson, Auckland

Vineyards: *21 ha (52 acres) of Riesling, Cabernet franc, Gewürztraminer, Cabernet sauvignon, Merlot, Chardonnay and Sauvignon blanc*
Established: *1910*

This winery was founded by English horticulturist J. W. Collard and is still in family ownership, with brothers Bruce and Geoffrey Collard sharing duties.

☆ Riesling, Gewürztraminer, Cabernet Sauvignon/Merlot, "Rothesay" Sauvignon Blanc

COOKS
Paddy's Road,
Te Kauwhata

Production: *1 million cases*
Vineyards: *110 ha (272 acres) of Cabernet sauvignon, Pinot noir, Chardonnay, Sauvignon blanc, Chenin blanc, Müller-Thurgau and Sylvaner*
Established: *1969*

The full name is Cooks McWilliams Ltd, Cooks having taken over its competitor McWilliams in 1984. In 1987 the tables were turned on Cooks, who were acquired by Corbans. At the time of writing, Corbans intend to keep Cooks' identity both separate and intact. These wines are inexpensive and consistently well made, sometimes outstandingly so.

☆ Chardonnay (especially Premium Varietal), Cabernet Sauvignon, Gewürztraminer, Chenin Blanc, Müller-Thurgau

COOPERS CREEK VINEYARDS
Main Road (Highway 16),
Huapai, Auckland

Vineyards: *4 ha (9 acres) of Cabernet sauvignon, Merlot, Sauvignon blanc, Chardonnay and Gewürztraminer*
Established: *1981*

The reputation of this winery was originally earned by Californian Randy Weaver. It makes a fine range of firm, dry wines.

☆ Gewürztraminer, Chardonnay (especially "Swamp Road"), Cabernet/Merlot, Fumé Blanc

CORBANS WINES
Great North Road,
Henderson, Auckland

Production: *480,000 cases*
Vineyards: *385 ha (951 acres) of Chardonnay, Sauvignon blanc, Rhine riesling, Gewürztraminer, Sémillon, Müller-Thurgau, Chenin blanc, Cabernet sauvignon, Merlot and Pinot noir*
Established: *1902*

Lebanon is not the first country that comes to mind when talking wine, but, forty years before Gaston Hochar established one of the seven wonders of the modern wine world, Chateau Musar, another Lebanese by the name of Assid Abraham Corban set sail for New Zealand. At the time Assid could not have contemplated that wine might be his destiny, for he was merely a humble stonemason. But, after ten years and as many jobs, Assid realized he would not carve out a living for himself plying his old trade, so in 1902 he purchased some land in the Henderson area, planted a vineyard and made wine. Corban was a natural, his business flourished and soon became one of the largest wineries in New Zealand. In 1987, Corbans acquired Cooks McWilliams Ltd.

☆ Marlborough Rhine Riesling, "Stoneleigh" (Sauvignon Blanc, Chardonnay), Private Bin (Chardonnay, Fumé Blanc), Select Dry Gewürztraminer, Gewürztraminer, Sauvignon Blanc/Sémillon

DELEGAT'S
Hepburn Road,
Henderson, Auckland

Vineyards: *Chardonnay, Sauvignon blanc, Cabernet sauvignon, Rhine riesling, Gewürztraminer, Müller-Thurgau and Sémillon*
Established: *1947*

A smoothly run operation producing a fine range of medal-winning wines.

☆ Chardonnay, Pinot Gris, Late Harvest Selected Vintage Müller-Thurgau, "Huapai" Cabernet Sauvignon, Rhine Riesling, Sauvignon Blanc

DE REDCLIFFE ESTATES
Lyons Road,
Mangatawhiri Valley

Production: *6,000 cases*
Vineyards: *16 ha (40 acres) of Chardonnay, Cabernet sauvignon, Merlot, Sémillon and Pinot noir*
Established: *1976*

This attractive riverside vineyard was planted by Chris Canning, whose apprenticeship abroad lasted 20 years and included France and Tuscany.

☆ Sémillon

GLENVALE VINEYARDS
Main State Highway 2,
Hawkes Bay

Production: *120,000 cases*
Vineyards: *75 ha (185 acres) of Chardonnay, Cabernet sauvignon, Gewürztraminer and Pinot noir*
Established: *1933*

Formerly a fortified wine specialist, this winery has very successfully crossed over into the premium varietal market. So successfully, in fact, that it was snapped up by George Fistonich, the owner of Villa Maria and Vidal.

☆ Esk Valley Sauvignon Blanc, Chardonnay, Cabernet/Merlot

GOLDWATER ESTATE
Putiki Bay,
Waiheke Island, Nr. Auckland

Vineyards: *6 ha (15 acres) of Cabernet sauvignon, Cabernet franc, Merlot and Sauvignon blanc*

This tiny island vineyard has a privileged microclimate.

☆ Cabernet/Merlot, Sauvignon Blanc

HUNTER'S WINES
Rapaura Road,
Blenheim

Production: *20,000 cases*
Vineyards: *27 ha (67 acres) of Chardonnay, Sauvignon blanc, Riesling, Müller-Thurgau, Gewürztraminer, Pinot gris and Cabernet sauvignon*
Established: *1982*

This winery achieved its initial acclaim via the skills of Almuth Lorenz, a remarkable German lady who produced medal-winning wines using improvized equipment in an old fruit factory. The late Ernie Hunter learned the ropes and made excellent wines himself, albeit with the advice of Australian consultant Tony Jordan. In complete contrast to the crude conditions Lorenz had to endure, Hunter's Wines is now one of the most modern boutique wineries on South Island and its success is assured.

☆ Chardonnay, Sauvignon Blanc, Fumé Blanc

KUMEU RIVER WINES
2 Highway 16,
Kumeu, Auckland

Vineyards: *32 ha (79 acres) of Chardonnay, Pinot noir, Cabernet sauvignon, Cabernet franc, Merlot and Sauvignon blanc*

After passing his oenology course at Roseworthy in Australia with honours, young Michael Brajkovich spent his study tour in California, Italy and France and it is the latter of these that shows through in his skilful wine-making at Kumeu River Wines, particularly in his Bordeaux-type blend.

☆ Cabernet/Merlot, Pinot Noir

LINCOLN VINEYARDS
130 Lincoln Road,
Henderson, Auckland

Vineyards: *32.5 ha (81 acres)*
Established: *1937*

Founded by Peter Fredatovich and with his son now in charge. I am not an enthusiast of imitation fortified wines, but Lincolns "Old Tawny" should be tried before judgement is passed.

☆ "Old Tawny"

MATAWHERO WINES
Riverpoint Road, R D 1,
Gisborne

Production: *15,000 cases*
Vineyards: *32 ha (79 acres) of Chardonnay, Gewürztraminer, Sauvignon blanc, Chenin blanc, Cabernet sauvignon, Merlot, Malbec and Pinot noir*
Established: *1974*

These medal-winning wines have a German bias, but are difficult to find, even in New Zealand where Matawhero devotees usually rely on mail order.

☆ Cabernet/Merlot, Chardonnay, Gewürztraminer

MATUA VALLEY WINES LIMITED
Waikoukou Valley Road,
Waimauku, Auckland

Production: *39,000 cases*
Vineyards: *23 ha (157 acres) of Cabernet sauvignon, Sauvignon blanc, Pinot noir, Müller-Thurgau, Chardonnay and Gewürztraminer*
Established: *1974*

This high-tech winery produces fine, characterful, exuberant wines that are full of fruit and enjoyment, including an excellent Pinot Noir Blanc.

☆ Chardonnay, Cabernet Sauvignon, Pinot Noir Blanc

MISSION VINEYARDS
Church Road,
Greenmeadows, Napier

Production: *26,000 cases*
Vineyards: *43 ha (106 acres) of Cabernet sauvignon, Sémillon, Sauvignon blanc, Merlot, Gewürztraminer, Müller-Thurgau, Pinot gris, Chasselas, Chardonnay, Pinot noir and Dr. Hogg Muscat*
Established: *1851*

In recent years, this historic winery has made an effort to improve its wines.

☆ Sémillon/Sauvignon Blanc

MONTANA WINES
171 Pilkington Road,
Glen Innes, Auckland

Production: *1.5 million cases*
Vineyards: *950 ha (2,347 acres) of Sauvignon blanc, Chardonnay, Pinot noir, Müller-Thurgau, Rhine riesling, Cabernet sauvignon, Pinotage, Sémillon and Gewürztraminer*
Established: *1964*

Like Cooks, often the only alternative to it on export markets, Montana manages to excite foreign palates with its delicious wines sold at inexpensive prices and this naturally leads consumers to search out more New Zealand wines. This is New Zealand's largest wine company; there are two high-tech installations, one at Blenheim, the other at Gisborne. I recommend the bubbly within the context of New Zealand sparklers, although it tastes sweeter than its sugar-acidity readings suggest; I feel the best is yet to come.

☆ Marlborough (Sauvignon Blanc, Sauvignon Blanc/Sémillon, Cabernet Sauvignon Wairau Valley, Rhine Riesling), Gisborne Chardonnay/Sémillon, Lindauer Brut

MORTON ESTATE
Kati Kati,
Bay of Plenty

Production: *27,000 cases*
Vineyards: *40.5 ha (100 acres) of Chardonnay, Sauvignon blanc, Pinot noir and Cabernet sauvignon*
Established: *1982*

White-wine specialist utilizing oak for fermentation of its best wines and maturation of most of the others. It also produces sparkling wines, but I have not tasted these.

☆ Chardonnay (especially "Black Label"), Gewürztraminer, Fumé Blanc ("Black Label")

NGATARAWA WINES
Ngatarawa Road,
Bridge Pa, Hastings

Production: *3,300 cases*
Vineyards: *11 ha (27 acres) of*

Chardonnay, Sauvignon blanc, Rhine riesling, Cabernet sauvignon and Merlot
Established: *1981*

A quality-conscious winery making its mark with distinctive wines.

☆ Hawkes Bay Chardonnay, "Stables Red"

NOBILO'S
Station Road,
Huapai, Auckland

Production: *90,000 cases*
Vineyards: *145 ha (358 acres) of Cabernet sauvignon, Pinotage, Pinot noir, Merlot and Malbec*
Established: *1943*

These rich, characterful wines occasionally lapse into a heavy-handed style due, no doubt, to an over-zealous search for quality, but a good Nobilo is a great Nobilo.

☆ Dixon Vineyard Chardonnay, Sauvignon Blanc

PENFOLDS WINES
Pilkington Road,
Glen Innes, Auckland

Established: *1963*

Originally founded by the Abel family, this was taken over by the Australian Penfolds operation and is now a subsidiary of Montana. There are no vineyards, but the firm has contracts with growers owning about 1,000 hectares (2,470 acres).

☆ Private Bin Chenin Blanc, Private Bin Chardonnay, Private Bin Gewürztraminer

SELAK WINES
Old North Road,
Kumeu, Auckland

Production: *27,000 cases*
Vineyards: *28 ha (69 acres) of Chardonnay, Sauvignon blanc, Sémillon and Pinot noir*
Established: *1934*

Like so many New Zealand families, the Selaks are of Yugoslav descent. This is a modern winery producing fine-quality, clean-cut, well-made wines.

☆ Chapelle Brut, Chardonnay (especially Founder's Reserve), Sauvignon Blanc, Sauvignon Blanc/Sémillon, Muscat Liqueur

ST. HELENA WINE ESTATE
Coutts Island, R D 4,
Christchurch

Vineyards: *24 ha (59 acres) of Rhine riesling, Gewürztraminer, Pinot blanc, Pinot gris, Müller-Thurgau, Pinot noir, Cabernet sauvignon and Chardonnay*
Established: *1978*

This is New Zealand's leading Pinot Noir exponent, making a wine that combines varietal purity with satisfying fruit – still a rare combination in this pioneering Pinot country.

☆ Pinot Noir

TE MATA ESTATE
Te Mata Road, Havelock North,
Hawkes Bay

Production: *13,000 cases*
Vineyards: *25 ha (62 acres) of Cabernet sauvignon, Merlot, Sauvignon blanc and Chardonnay*
Established: *1896*

Te Mata Estate, the oldest winery in New Zealand, was purchased by John Buck, a former member of the British wine trade, in 1978. Despite a low-key marketing approach, the intrinsic quality and exceptional character of these wines is hard to ignore.

☆ "Coleraine" Cabernet/Merlot, "Awatea" Cabernet/Merlot, "Elston" Chardonnay

TOTARA VINEYARDS
Main Road,
Totara, Thames

Vineyards: *14 ha (35 acres)*
Established: *1950*

Behind Jade Cow (Totara's Kiwi fruit and cream liqueur), one can find some delightful varietal wines from this Chinese-owned winery.

☆ Chenin Blanc, Müller-Thurgau, Chasselas

VIDAL WINERY
St. Aubyn Street,
Hastings

Production: *90,000 cases*
Vineyards: *70 ha (173 acres) of Chardonnay, Gewürztraminer, Sauvignon blanc, Cabernet sauvignon, Pinot noir, Merlot and Cabernet franc*
Established: *1905*

This winery, owned by George Fistonich of Villa Maria, consistently produces some of the most exciting wines in the Hawkes Bay area, including an excellent *méthode champenoise* and one of the country's best Pinot Noirs.

☆ Vidal Brut, Chardonnay Reserve, "Private Bin" Fumé Blanc, "Private Bin" Cabernet Sauvignon, "Private Bin" Pinot Noir

VILLA MARIA ESTATE
Mangere, Auckland

Production: *210,000 cases*
Vineyards: *180 ha (445 acres) of Chardonnay, Gewürztraminer, Sauvignon blanc, Cabernet sauvignon, Pinot noir, Müller-Thurgau, Chenin blanc, Merlot and Cabernet franc*
Established: *1961*

One of the largest wineries in New Zealand, Villa Maria wines are produced by modern techniques designed to enhance fruit and freshness. Where oak is used, the touch is light and the balance perfect.

☆ Gewürztraminer, Chardonnay (especially Reserve and Gisborne Reserve), Pinot Noir, Sauvignon Blanc

Other wineries of New Zealand

AMBERLEY ESTATE VINEYARD
Reserve Road,
Amberley

ASPENRIDGE ESTATE WINES
Waerenga Road,
Te Kauwhata

BALIC ESTATE WINES
Sturges Road,
Henderson, Auckland

CELLIER LE BRUN
Terrace Road,
Renwick, Marlborough

CHIFNEY WINES
Huangarua Road,
Martinborough

DRY RIVER
Purautanga Road,
Martinborough

HOLLY LODGE ESTATE WINERY
Papaiti Road,
Wanganui

KARAMEA WINES
Pirongia Road,
Frankton

KOREPO WINES
Korepo Road, R D 1,
Upper Moutere, Mapua

LOMBARDI WINES
Te Mata Road,
Havelock North, Hawkes Bay

MARTINBOROUGH VINEYARD
Princess Street,
Martinborough

THE MILLTON VINEYARD
Papatu Road,
Manutuke, Gisborne

NEUDORF VINEYARDS
Neudorf Road, R D 2,
Upper Moutere, Nelson

PIERRE
Elizabeth Street,
Waikanae

RANZAU WINES
Patons Road, R D 1,
Richmond

SAN MARINO VINEYARDS
2 Highway 16,
Kumeu, Auckland

SOLJANS WINES
263 Lincoln Road,
Henderson, Auckland

TE WHARE RA WINES
Anglesea Street,
Renwick, Blenheim

VICTORY GRAPE WINES
Main Road South,
Stoke, Nelson

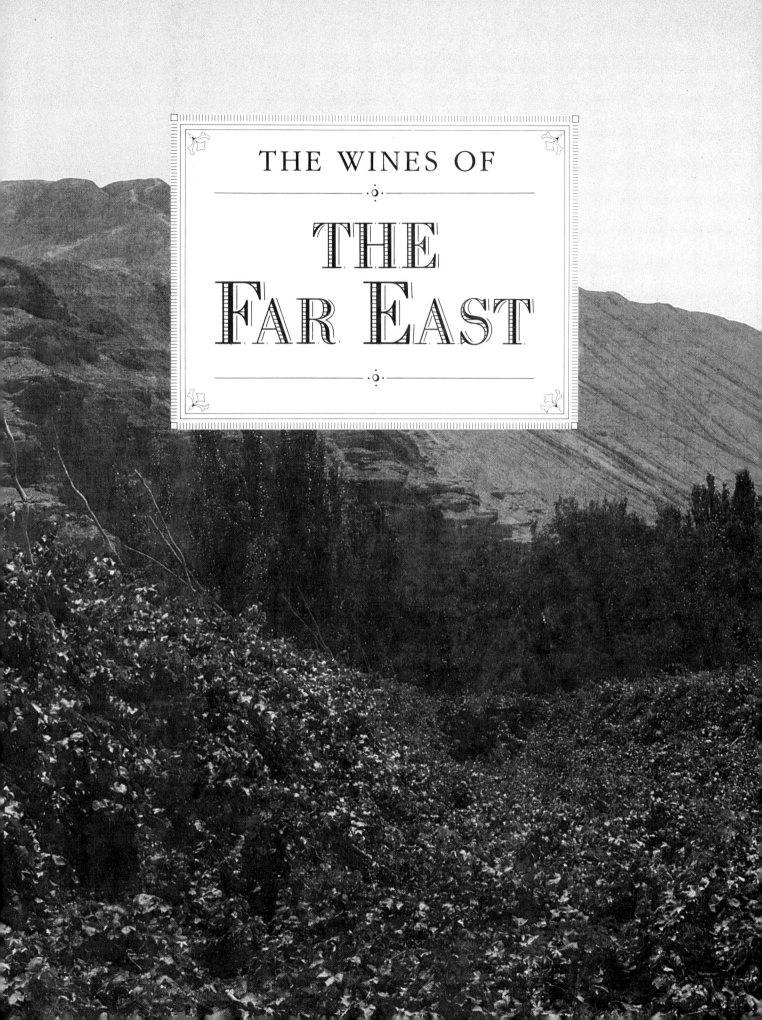

THE WINES OF

THE FAR EAST

The Far East

In viticultural terms, few parallels can be drawn between such diverse countries as India, China and Japan. However, Eastern races generally favour sweet wines, and this is reflected in the types of wines all the countries traditionally produce.

DESPITE THE TASTE FOR SWEET WINES there is one sparkling *méthode champenoise* wine made in India, called "Omar Khayyam", that has an extraordinarily European character. China, though, has been disappointing to date, despite technical assistance from France, but it is beginning to show promise under the guidance of Charles Whish, an Australian winemaker. And, although "Produce of Japan" does not mean that a wine is necessarily made from grapes grown in Japan, the quality of Japanese products is nevertheless good and one wine, Château Lumière, is exceptional.

INDIA

Wine has been made in parts of India on a sporadic basis for more than 2,000 years, but very little wine is produced there today. The country has 12,500 hectares (31,000 acres) of vineyards, but wine production is so small that there are no official statistics. Until the early-1970s, the wine produced was thick, sweet and not very pleasant. Most still is, but in 1972, an Indo-French company called Vinedale was set up and began marketing red wines under the "Shah-Eh-Shah" label. It was a

Grape drying, western China, above
Surrounded by a jungle of vines and other foliage, grapes are dried on a roof-top.

THE FAR EAST

A grouping of convenience, with little more than being part of the Asian continent in common, India, China and Japan all have wine industries of different degrees of sophistication.

▨	Vine-growing Zone	
	Grape growing province	
	International Boundary	
- - -	State/Provincial Boundary	
▲	Height above sea level (metres)	

FACTORS AFFECTING TASTE AND QUALITY

Location
A "region" of convenience encompassing the principal vine growing areas of India (Maharashtra State), China (north) and Japan.

Climate
India is hot throughout the year with no real winter and little rain in the growing season. China's vineyards have a climate that is classified as "humid micro-thermal cool", a type similar to that of Michigan, Ontario, Austria and Hungary, where continental conditions are heavily influenced by great water masses. Japan suffers extremes of climate, freezing in Siberian winter winds, with spring and autumn monsoon rains and summer typhoons. Its mean temperatures drop as one moves northwards towards Hokkaido.

Aspect
India
Maharashtra's vineyards are generally located on the east-facing slopes of the Sahyadri Mountains at an altitude of 750 metres (2,460 ft).

China
Recent plantings have been on well-drained, south-facing slopes to overcome the earlier problem of high water tables on the flatter sites.

Japan
In the most important wine area of Honshu Island, the best vineyards are planted on south-facing slopes of the valley around Kofu.

Soil
The Maharashtra vineyards of India are planted on lime-rich soils, those of China are generally alluvial, and Japan has predominantly acidic soils that are unsuitable for viticulture, except around Kofu, where it is gravelly and of volcanic origin.

Viticulture and vinification
In Maharashtra, India, vines are grown using the Lenz Moser high system (see the "High Culture" system, p.104) and *méthode champenoise* has been introduced by experts from Champagne. Recent developments in Japan have concentrated on the growing of top European varietals and experimented with botrytis-affected Riesling and Sémillon grapes. China does not have a cohesive wine industry, but no doubt one will develop as more foreign technology and expertise is brought in. With the benefit of a ready-made, sophisticated trading centre, when Hong Kong becomes Chinese in 1997, the country may become an exciting new wine centre in the twenty-first century.

Grape varieties
India
Primary
Anab-e-shahi, Arkavti, Arka Kanchan, Arka Shyam, Bangalore blue, Chardonnay, Ruby red, Ugni blanc, Pinot noir
Secondary
Cabernet sauvignon, Karachi gulabi, Pinot noir

China
Primary
Beichun, Dragon's Eye
Secondary
Cabernet sauvignon, Cabernet franc, Carignan, Cow's nipple, Cock's heart, Gamay, Gewürztraminer, Muscat à petits grains, Muscat d'Hambourg, Merlot, Pinot noir, Rkatsiteli, Saperavi, Welschriesling

Japan
Primary
Campbell's early, Delaware, Muscat Bailey, Koshu
Secondary
Cabernet sauvignon, Chardonnay, Merlot, Müller-Thurgau, Riesling, Sémillon

further 10 years before another Indo-French venture really shook up the wine world. In 1982, Bombay millionaire Sham Chougule, whose Indage Group controls a chain of hotels and is heavily involved in engineering and shipping, asked Piper-Heidsieck to provide technical assistance in a project aimed at producing fine, sparkling *méthode champenoise* Indian wines. Piper-Heidsieck despatched to India a young oenologist called Jean Brisbois, who was then attached to the firm's subsidiary company, Champagne Technologie. Brisbois chose a site at Narayangaon, in the state of Maharashtra, and constructed an ambitious, four-million-pound, high-tech winery set into the side of the Sahyadri Mountains. The vineyards are located on the lime-rich soil of the surrounding, east-facing slopes at an altitude of some 750 metres (2,460 ft). Chardonnay is used in conjunction with Ugni blanc, the latter providing acidity, and the technical level of production is as high as can be found in Champagne itself. The wine, which is sold under the "Omar Khayyam" label, is fine by any standards. It has an excellent *mousse* of small bubbles, a nicely neutral base flavour, with delicate autolytic aromas that deepen upon further aging (up to two years after purchase). It is also dry, with good acidity, and shows a degree of finesse. The vineyards are still very young, so the wine can only get better. The one criticism I have is of the price, but it is perhaps too much to expect such a miraculous wine to be a bargain as well!

CHINA

Wine districts: *Shantung (Shandong) Peninsula, Jungsu (Kiangsu), Shaanxi (Shensi), Shanxi (Shansi), Hebei, Liaoning*

Chinese grape-winemaking (as opposed to rice-winemaking) began near Peking in 100 BC, but little development occurred until French and German merchants established a rudimentary industry on the Shantung Peninsula at the turn of the century. In more recent times, the French Cognac company Rémy Martin was brought in to give technical assistance and "Dynasty" was developed. Supposed to be of international standard, it was not a good advertisement for China or French technical assistance. The other brand that is the result of the collaboration, "Tsingta", is not much more exciting. Chinese wines that are produced without foreign help, such as "Great Wall" and "Heavenly Palace" are even worse. However, there is news of an acceptable, dry, light, clean Cabernet-based red called "Cabernet d'Est", produced by a Sino-Japanese consortium in the Yantai area on the Shantung peninsula, but I haven't tasted the wine.

Wines of the Shandong province are apparently the most reliable in the country, especially those from around Qingdao (formerly Tsingtao), a town on the Yellow Sea coast. A Sino-British/Hong Kong venture has produced a good Qingdao Riesling at the Haudong Winery, under the auspices of Charles Whish, an Australian winemaker. This wine, apparently, is just the beginning of a string of varietals.

JAPAN

Wine districts of Honshu: *Yamanashi, Kofu Valley, Yamagata, Okayama, Nagano, Tokyo, Osaka*
Wine districts of Hokkaido: *Sapporo, Kushiro*
Wine districts of Kyushu: *Fukuoka*

The Japanese have been making grape wine for as long as the Chinese and have a set of inscrutable wine laws that allow foreign wines to be labelled as "Produce of Japan". The largest wine companies are Suntory, Mercian and Mann's, and their level of technology is high, as can be the quality of their wines, both when they are pure Japanese or blends from several countries. Good, genuinely Japanese wines are made at Château Lumière, which is owned by the ancient family of Toshihiko Tsukamoto. Greatly influenced by Bordeaux, the red comes from Cabernet sauvignon, Cabernet franc and Merlot vines that were supplied by Château Margaux. The white is made from botrytized Sémillon and Sauvignon blanc grapes. Both are exceptionally fine wines.

SUNTORY WINE

Koshu

PRODUCED AND BOTTLED BY
SUNTORY LIMITED
ESTABLISHED 1899
PRODUCT OF JAPAN

The harvest, above
Pickers at Suntory in Japan sport a corporate image even in the vineyard.

Storing and serving wine

The greatest preoccupation for those storing wine is temperature. The mistaken idea that there is one ideal temperature for keeping wine and that a degree above or below will be the ruination of the whole cellar has unfortunately become established.

STORAGE TEMPERATURES

While 11°C (52°F) is supposed to be the perfect storage temperature, in fact anything between 5–18°C (40–65°F) will do perfectly well, providing there is no great temperature variation over a relatively short period of time. Higher temperatures increase the rate of oxidation in a wine, thus a bottle of wine stored at 18°C (65°F) will gradually get "older" than the same wine stored at 11°C (52°F). But a constant 18°C (65°F) is far kinder to a wine than erratic temperatures that often hit 11°C (52°F), but jump 3°C (5°F) up one day and 3°C (5°F) below the next.

The effect of light

We know that it is the ultra-violet end of the light spectrum that is most harmful to wine and that both sunlight and artificial lighting should be avoided. Brown-glass bottles offer better protection than green-glass and some, if not all, of the photo-chemical effects of ultra-violet light can be reversed by cellaring the affected wine in darkness for a few months. These problems are still being studied, but it is sensible to consider darkness of almost equal importance to the storage of wine as temperature.

Physically storing bottles

Bottles should be stored horizontally and cases stacked on their sides to keep the corks moist, thus fully swollen and airtight. Storing a bottle upright will in time result in a shrunken, dried-out cork. This will expose the wine to air, causing oxidation. For long-term storage, a certain humidity is ideal as a cork can also dry from the outside, but low humidity should not present problems.

SERVING WINE: THE RIGHT TEMPERATURE

Traditionally, white wines have been served chilled and red wines at room temperature, or *"chambré"*. The odorous compounds found in all wines are more volatile at higher temperatures, so the practice of serving full-bodied red wines *chambré* has the effect of releasing more aromatics into the bouquet. One major effect of chilling wine is that more carbonic gas is retained at lower temperatures. This enhances the crispness and freshness and tends to liven the impression of fruit on the palate. It is vital to serve a sparkling wine sufficiently chilled as this keeps it bubbling longer. However the now-widespread use of refrigerators and central heating means that white wines are all too frequently served too cold, red wines too warm.

Controversy will probably always surround the subject of the temperature at which wines are served. The dangers of extreme temperatures are well known. Over-chilling wine kills its flavour and aroma as well as making the cork difficult to remove; the wax on a cork adheres to the bottle at lower temperatures. Over-warm wine, on the other hand, is bland to taste, with the alcohol volatizing in the air. So forget expressions like "iced" and "room temperature"; it is best to think in terms of wine being either "chilled" or "free from chill" and to be ready to amend general guidelines to suit your own personal taste.

Modern aberrations it is wise to avoid are wine temperature charts and wine thermometers. Frankly wine is for enjoying and a drinker unable to estimate whether a white wine is "chilled" enough, or whether a red wine is "free from chill", is not going to be able to tell whether a wine is served at 17° or 17.5°C (63° or 63.5°F). The rough guide below is more than you need to start with.

Wine type	Serving temperature
Sparkling (red, white and rosé)	4.5–7°C (40–45°F)
White	7–10°C (45–50°F)
Rosé and light-bodied reds	10–12.5°C (50–55°F)
Medium-bodied red	12.5–15.5°C (55–60°F)
Full-bodied red	15.5–18°C (60–65°F)

RAPID CHILLING AND INSTANT *CHAMBRÉ*

It is fine to chill wine in a refrigerator for a couple of hours, but try not to leave it much longer because the cork may stick. Also, the refrigeration process actually extracts moisture from a cork.

Tips for "putting a chill on" and "taking the chill off" wine in an emergency include the use of the deep-freeze and the microwave! Ten or 15 minutes in the coldest part of a deep-freeze has never done a wine any harm; this has absolutely nothing to do with the long-term, cumulative effect of large temperature variations. And 60 to 90 seconds in a 750-watt microwave oven on half-power is the kindest way of "taking the chill off". Whereas the cold in a deep-freeze seems to creep evenly into a bottle of wine, traditional methods of applying direct heat, such as standing a bottle in front of a fire or putting it under a running hot tap, tend to make some of the wine too hot, leaving the rest too cold.

SERVING WINE: DECANTING

With increasing age, many wines, especially red, throw a natural deposit of tannins and colouring pigments that collect in the base of the bottle. Both red and white wines, particularly white, can also shed a crystalline deposit due to a precipitation of tartrates. Although these deposits are harmless, their appearance is distracting; and decanting will be necessary to remove them.

Preparing the bottle and pouring the wine

Several hours prior to decanting, move the bottle to an upright position. This allows the sediment lying along the side of the bottle to fall to the bottom. Cut away the top quarter-inch or so of capsule. This could well reveal a penicillin growth or, if an older vintage, a fine black deposit, neither of which will have had contact with the wine, but to avoid any unintentional contamination when removing the cork it is wise to clean the lip of the bottle neck and the top of the cork with a clean, damp cloth. Gently insert a corkscrew and withdraw the cork. Before decanting, insert a clean finger inside the top of the bottle and carefully remove any pieces of cork or any tartrate crystals adhering to the inside of the neck. Wipe the lip of the bottle neck, but this time with a clean, dry cloth.

Slowly lift the bottle in one hand and the decanter in the other and bring them together over a source of light such as a candle or a torch, which will reveal any sediment as the wine is poured. Aim to pour the wine in a slow, steady flow so that the bottle does not jerk and wine does not "gulp for air". Such mishaps will disturb the sediment, spreading it through a greater volume of liquid that will have to be retained in the bottle as soon as it approaches the neck and threatens to cloud up the decanted wine.

FILTERING DREGS

Personally, I flout tradition by pouring cloudy dregs through a fine-grade coffee filter paper. Naturally I hedge my bets by attempting to decant the maximum volume, thereby filtering the minimum, but I have never been able to tell the difference between the pure-decanted wine and that augmented by a small volume that has been filtered. And of all my expert friends and colleagues who have doubted my assertion, not one has been able to score higher than 50 per cent when trying to identify which is which in blind tastings.

Allowing wine to breathe

Once you open a bottle of wine, it will be "breathing" – exposed to the air. Wine "feeds" on the small amount of air trapped inside the bottle between the wine and the cork, and on the oxygen naturally absorbed by the wine itself. It is during this slow oxidation that, over a period of time, various elements and compounds are formed or changed in a complex chemical process known as maturation. Thus, allowing a wine to breathe is, in effect, creating a rapid, but less sophisticated maturation.

This artificial aging may or may not be beneficial to specific still wines for many reasons, only some of which are known. About the only generalization that usually holds true is that breathing is likely to improve young, full-bodied, tannic, red wines.

Wine and food

Although there are no specific rules, there is, however, one general rule that must be treated as golden: if you are selecting a wine to accompany a dish, the more delicately flavoured the dish, the more delicately flavoured the wine should be. Fuller-flavoured foods can take fuller-flavoured wines. And when constructing a menu around specific wines, choose delicate dishes to accompany delicate wines, fuller foods for fuller wines.

THIS "GOLDEN RULE" IS VERY FLEXIBLE because it is capable of adapting to personal circumstances. We all have different thresholds of perception for various tastes and smells, therefore if one person has a blind spot for, or is especially sensitive to, a particular characteristic such as acidity, sweetness or bitterness, then their perception of the delicacy or fullness of a certain dish or wine will be somewhat different from other people's. The best approach is to start with conventional food and wine combinations, but use them as a launch-pad for experimentation.

When using the food and wine combinations below to plan a menu, always aim to ascend in quality and flavour, serving white before red, dry before sweet, light-bodied before full-bodied and young before old. The reason for this is twofold. Obviously, a step back in quality will be noticed. Equally important, if you go straight to a reasonably fine wine, without first trying a lesser wine, you are likely to miss many of the better wine's subtle qualities.

Try also to make the sequence of wines proceed in some sort of logical order or according to a theme. The most obvious one is to remain faithful to the wines of one area, region or country. There are many other themes, such as the wines of one grape variety. You could plan a dinner around the Pinot Noirs of the New World, or the Cabernet Sauvignons of Italy for example. The theme could be one wine type or style, maybe just Champagne or Sauternes, a popular ploy in those regions. It could be even more specific, such as different vintages of one specific grower's vineyard or a comparison of the "same" wine from different growers.

APERITIFS

Planning a meal, whether a one-course supper, or a full dinner menu, starts with the aperitif, which should not be an afterthought. Inevitably, the most delicate dishes in a meal arrive first and nobody will be able to appreciate them if palates have been saturated with strong spirits or highly flavoured concoctions. Choose the most suitable aperitif according to your taste; do not offer a choice.

Sherry

Fino Sherry is a traditional aperitif, but its use has been abused. If the first course is sufficiently well-flavoured, includes Sherry as an ingredient, or if Sherry is to be served with it, then it can be an admirable choice. Mostly, however, even the lightest *Fino* will have too much alcohol and flavour.

Proprietory aperitifs and spirits

Proprietory brands of aromatized aperitif such as Vermouths, inevitably also fall into the trap of being too alcoholic and too strong-tasting. All spirits, especially if they are not mixed, are too aggressive to allow the palate to appreciate most first courses.

Wines

It is customary in a few countries, notably France, to serve a sweet wine such as Sauternes as an aperitif. For most occasions, this will be inappropriate, but it can work.

Perfect all-purpose aperitifs are light-bodied, dry or off-dry, still or sparkling, white wines, although a rosé may be suitable if the first wine served with the meal is also a rosé or a light red. Excellent choices for a white wine aperitif may include Mâcon Blanc or Mâcon Villages, good Muscadet, lighter Alsace wines such as Pinot Blanc or Sylvaner, new-wave Rioja, aromatic dry whites from Northeastern Italy, many English wines, young Mosel (up to *Spätlese*) or Rhine (up to *Kabinett*), light-bodied Chardonnay, Sauvignon, Chenin or Colombard from California, Australia, New Zealand or South Africa. The list is endless. If the choice is to be a rosé, try to choose one from the same area and preferably grape, as the

first wine of the meal. The aperitif *par excellence* in every conceivable situation is Champagne, with Crémant de Bourgogne or Crémant d'Alsace making excellent alternatives.

☆ **Budget choice:** Cava Brut

STARTERS

Not too long ago, it was almost as if one had to get through the first course before it was permitted to serve the wine, but the combination of food and wine flavours at each stage of a meal is vital, whether to lead on to the next taste experience, or to follow the previous one.

Asparagus

There are two perfect accompaniments, a fine Champagne and a young Muscat d'Alsace. Medium-weight white Burgundy and Californian or Pacific-Northwest Chardonnay also work well.

☆ **Budget choice:** Raimat Chardonnay Blanc de Blanc Brut

Artichoke

If served with butter, a light but slightly assertive, dry Sauvignon Blanc from the Loire is best. The same wine might also accompany artichokes with Hollandaise sauce, although a dry rosé with a highish balance of acidity such as a Coteaux d'Ancenis Rosé from the Loire, Arbois Rosé from the Jura, or Schilcher from Austria is also suitable.

☆ **Budget choice:** Sauvignon de Haut-Poitou

Avocado

Although many wines of excellent acidity, such as Champagne or Chablis are extremely successful partners, Gewürztraminer, which is naturally low in acidity, is the best choice.

☆ **Budget choice:** Muscadet

Caviar

Champagne is the classic partner.

☆ **Budget choice:** Mineral water

Garlic butter

Choose the general style of wine recommended for the main ingredient, but opt for one with more body and a more assertive flavour or higher acidity.

Pâtés

Whether fish or fowl, pâté should be partnered according to the main ingredient or flavour. Look in the appropriate entries and choose a similar wine. *Foie gras*, which is in a totally different class, is fabulous with a fine vintage Champagne or mature Sauternes and, although diverse in character, Gewürztraminer or Tokay d'Alsace are both perfect partners.

Salads

Plain green salads normally need little more than a light, dry white such as a Muscadet, unless there is a predominance of bitter leaves, in which case something more assertive, but just as light, such as a lesser Loire Sauvignon, should be chosen. A firm Champagne is the best accompaniment to salads that include warm ingredients.

☆ **Budget choice:** Cava Brut

Snails

Modest village Burgundy from the Côte d'Or, either red or white.

☆ **Budget choice:** Côtes de Roussillon

Soups

Champagne or any fine sparkling wine is ideal with most purée, velouté, or cream soups, especially the more delicately flavoured recipes favoured by *nouvelle cuisine* and its many derivatives. It is virtually essential with a chilled soup, whether a jellied consommé or a cold purée soup such as Vichysoisse. Most sparkling wines can match the flavour of a shellfish bisque, but a pink Champagne makes a particularly picturesque partner. Rich-flavoured soups can take fuller wines, often red: a good game soup, for example, can respond well to the heftier reds of the Rhône, Bordeaux, Burgundy and Rioja.

The frothy character of Lambrusco cuts through the texture of a genuine

minestrone. The sweet cherry flavour of Lambrusco also matches the soup's rich, tomato tang.

☆ **Budget choice:** Blanquette de Limoux

Terrines

Fish, shellfish and meat terrines should be partnered according to the main ingredient or flavour (see appropriate entry). Most vegetable terrines go well with young, dry or off-dry, light-bodied, still, sparkling or aromatic white wines from the Loire, Alsace, Germany, Austria, Northeastern Italy, New Zealand and England.

☆ **Budget choice:** Crémant d'Alsace

Vinaigrette

Starters with vinaigrette are difficult to partner. Conventional wisdom suggests a *Fino* or *Manzanilla* Sherry, or Montilla, although many believe it best not to serve any wine. I have found that an Alsace Gewürztraminer is one of the few wines that can take on vinaigrette and come out on top.

☆ **Budget choice:** Supermarket Gewürztraminer

EGG, RICE AND PASTA DISHES

Champagne is the perfect foil to the bland flavour of any egg dish, the texture of which is cut by the wine's effervescence. Any suitable Champagne alternative will obviously be a suitable accompaniment to dishes such as omelettes, quiches, soufflés, eggs cooked *en cocotte,* coddled, fried, scrambled or poached. Savoury mousses or mousselines, whether hot or cold, fish or fowl, should be partnered according to the main ingredient or flavour, but one with slightly less body and at least the same acidity or effervescence (if applicable).

Good sparkling wine is equally useful for all rice and pasta dishes, particularly the more delicately flavoured ones. Richer ingredients should be matched by the wine.

☆ **Budget choice:** Saumur Brut

SEAFOOD

Most fish and shellfish go well with dry white wines, but red, rosé, sparkling and sweet styles are all possible in certain circumstances.

Fish with sauces and pan-fried fish

Whatever the fish, pan-fried, cream sauce or butter sauce dishes require wines with more acidity or effervescence than normal. If the sauce is very rich or if the fish is smoked, then consider wines with a greater intensity of flavour.

☆ **Budget choice:** Crémant de Loire

Fish stews

Although red wine and fish usually react violently in the mouth, fish dishes cooked in red wine, such as the many highly-flavoured Mediterranean fish stews, present no such problems.

Mackerel

An assertive but modest Loire Sauvignon is needed for mackerel, although a richer Sauvignon from various New World countries is preferable with smoked mackerel.

☆ **Budget choice:** Sauvignon de Touraine

River fish

Generally, most river fish go well with a fairly assertive rosé, the fish and the wine having a complementary earthiness, but an assertive white such as Sancerre is just as effective. Sancerre, white Graves and Champagne are especially good with pike. Champagne or Montrachet is classic with salmon or salmon-trout, whether baked, grilled, pan-fried, poached or smoked, but any good-quality dry sparkling wine or white Burgundy will be excellent, as will top Chardonnay wines from California, the Pacific-Northwest, New Zealand, Australia and South Africa. Riesling, Alsace or German, is almost obligatory with trout, particularly when cooked *au bleu* (rapidly, in stock with plenty of vinegar).

☆ **Budget choice:** Pink Cava Brut

Sardines

Vinho Verde is the ideal wine with sardines, especially if freshly caught and cooked on a beach in Portugal.

☆ **Budget choice:** Vinho Verde

Shellfish

Choose a top estate Muscadet, a Bourgogne Aligoté from a sunny vintage, a Loire Sauvignon, an English wine or a Mosel with most modest forms of shellfish (prawns, shrimps, mussels etc); a fine but assertive Sancerre or Pouilly Fumé with crayfish; a *Grand Cru* Chablis or a good

Champagne with crab, lobster, oysters and scallops. Choose a wine with more acidity or effervescence if the dish includes a cream sauce.

☆ **Budget choice:** Crémant de Bourgogne

White fish

White fish have the lightest flavours and it would be a pity to overwhelm their delicate nuances with a dominant wine. Grilled sole, plaice and mullet are enhanced by youthful *blanc de blancs* Champagne, top quality estate Muscadet, Savennières, Pinot Blanc from Alsace, Pinot Grigio from Northeastern Italy, and fine estate Vinho Verde with authentically tart dryness and just the barest prickle. Haddock, hake, halibut, turbot, cod and sea bream are good with all the wines mentioned above, but can take slightly richer dry white wines.

☆ **Budget choice:** Crémant d'Alsace

MEAT DISHES

Few people have not heard the old maxim "red wine with dark meat, white wine with light", but it is perfectly acceptable to reverse the rule and drink white wine with dark meat and red wine with light meat, providing that the one golden rule mentioned above is observed.

Beef

Claret is the classic accompaniment to roast beef. Choose a younger, perhaps lighter and livelier, style if the meat is served cold. A good Cabernet Sauvignon from Australia, California, Chile, Italy, New Zealand or South Africa would do just as well and would be preferable in the case of steaks that are charred on the outside and pink in the middle. For pure beef burgers, an unpretentious, youthful red Côtes-du-Rhône with an honest, chunky, peppery flavour is ideal. But, frankly, almost any drinkable red wine of medium, medium-full or full body from anywhere will accompany all beef dishes with some degree of competence, as will most full-bodied, rich-flavoured white wines.

☆ **Budget choice:** Bulgarian Cabernet Sauvignon

Casseroles, dark

Dark meat casseroles require fuller-bodied reds from Bordeaux, Burgundy, the Rhône or Rioja. Chateau Musar from Lebanon and Chateau Carras from Greece are both ideal, as are many Italian wines, from the Nebbiolo wines of Piedmont, through the fuller Sangiovese wines of Chianti, Carmignano and Montalcino, to the Montepulciano wines of Abruzzi and the Aglianico del Vulture, not to mention all the super *barrique* wines that are popping up in Tuscany and Northeastern Italy. The richer the casserole, the more robust can be the flavour and the more tannin needed.

☆ **Budget choice:** Inexpensive Zinfandel

Casseroles, light

Light meat casseroles are best with young Beaujolais, Loire reds (particularly Bourgeuil or Chinon), various medium-bodied reds from Southwest France and Coteaux du Languedoc, Pinot Noir from Alsace and soft-styled Chianti. For the white wine drinker, new-wave Rioja, Mâcon Blanc, Tokay d'Alsace and inexpensive French Colombard or Chenin Blanc from California or South Africa are all worth trying.

☆ **Budget choice:** Californian dry white jug wine

Chilli con carne

If it is a good chilli, forget wine and stick to ice-cool lager or water.

☆ **Budget choice:** Iced water

Curries

Some say Gewürztraminer stands up to curry, but in my experience this applies only to mild curries and even then I am not sure that the flavour combination works. A cold beer or iced water is best.

☆ **Budget choice:** Iced water

Duck

Roast duck is very versatile, but the best accompaniments include certain *crus* Beaujolais such as Morgan or Moulin-à-Vent, fine red and white Burgundy, especially from the Côte de Nuits and mature Médoc. With cold duck, a lighter *cru* Beaujolais like Fleurie should be considered. Duck in orange sauce shows very well with softer styles of red and white Burgundy, southern Rhône wines, especially Châteauneuf-du-Pape, red Rioja and Zinfandel.

☆ **Budget choice:** Quinta da Bacalhôa

Game

For lightly hung winged game, the wines that are suitable are the same as for poultry. If it is mid-hung, try a fullish *cru* Beaujolais; well-hung birds require a full-bodied red Bordeaux or Burgundy. Pomerol is the classic choice with well-hung pheasant. Treat lightly hung ground game in the same way as lamb, mid-hung meat in the same way as beef. Well-hung ground game can take the biggest Hermitage, Côte Rôti, Cornas, Châteauneuf-du-Pape, red Rioja, or an old vintage of Chateau Musar. White wine drinkers should opt for old vintages of Rhône or Rioja or a Tokay d'Alsace Vendange Tardive (vinified dry).

☆ **Budget choice:** Australian Shiraz

Goose

I find it hard to choose between Chinon, Bourgeuil, Anjou Rouge and (sometimes) Chianti on the red side, and Vouvray (still or sparkling), Riesling (preferably but not necessarily Alsace), and Champagne on the white. The one characteristic they all have in common is plenty of acidity, which is

needed for this fatty bird. If the goose is served in a fruity sauce, stick to the white wines; a little sweetness in the wine will do no harm.

☆ **Budget choice:** South African Chenin Blanc

Goulash

When on form, "Bull's Blood" is the obvious choice, otherwise any East European full-bodied, robustly-flavoured red wine will suffice.

☆ **Budget choice:** Bulgarian Kadarka

Ham, bacon

Ham can react in the mouth with some red wines in a similar way to white fish, particularly if it is unsmoked, but young Beaujolais, Loire Gamay and Chianti are usually safe bets. Sparkling white wine is perhaps best of all, although I have known that to react strangely at times. Champagne with bacon and eggs is an occasional luxury I indulge in on holiday.

☆ **Budget choice:** Cava Brut

Lamb

Claret is as classic with lamb as it is with beef, although Burgundy works at least as well, particularly when the meat is a little pink. It is well known in the wine trade that the flavour of lamb brings out every nuance of flavour in the finest of wines, which is why it is served more often than any other meat when a merchant is organizing a special lunch or dinner to show off something special. Rack of lamb with rosemary seems to be favourite. As with beef, it is possible to drink almost any red wine, although this should, if anything, be a little lighter.

☆ **Budget choice:** Bourgogne Rouge (Buxy)

Meat pies

For hot pies and puddings, treat as for dark- or light-meat casseroles, depending on their content. Cold pork, veal and ham, or ham and turkey pies require a light- or medium-bodied red with firm acidity, such as Chinon or Bourgeuil, while cold game pies call for something at least as rich, but softer, such as a New Zealand Cabernet Sauvignon.

☆ **Budget choice:** Saumur Brut

Moussaka

For romantic association, choose one of the better, medium-to-full bodied reds from Greece, such as Naoussa, Goumenissa or Côtes de Meliton. White wine drinkers require something of substance, that is not too full or oxidative. A few Greek wines fit ("Lac des Roches" from Boutari comes to mind), but something Spanish might be better, such as one of the "inbetweenie" white Riojas.

☆ **Budget choice:** Bulgarian Merlot

Offal

Kidneys go with full, well-flavoured, but round wines, such as a mature red or white Châteauneuf-du-Pape or a Rioja. But much depends upon what kidneys they are and how they are cooked: a ragout of lamb's kidneys, for example, requires something with the finesse of a mature *cru classé* Médoc.

The choice of wine to accompany liver varies enormously depending on the type of liver served. The finest livers, which are lamb's and calf's, go well with a Syrah that is very good, but not too heavy, such as a mature Côte Rôti or Hermitage from a top producer in a medium-good vintage. Chicken livers are quite strong and require something with a penetrating flavour such as a good Gigondas, Fitou or Zinfandel. Pig and ox livers are the coarsest in texture and flavour and require a full, robust, but not too fussy red – maybe a modest *vin de pays* from the Pyrénées Orientales.

Either red or dry-to-medium-dry white wine may be served with sweetbreads, which are rich yet delicate. Lamb's sweetbreads are the best, and take well to fine St.-Emilion or St.-Julien, if in a sauce, or a good white Burgundy if pan-fried.

☆ **Budget choice**: Crémant de Bourgogne

Pork, poultry and veal

These meats are very flexible, capable of taking a diverse range of wines from modest *méthode champenoise*, through almost every type of medium or full-bodied dry or off-dry white wine, to light reds from Beaujolais, Champagne, Alsace and Germany, literally any medium-bodied red wine, whatever its origin, and a large number of full-bodied ones too. The quality suitable can be anything from the most modest (but well-made) wine, to the greatest. For chops, cutlets or escalopes, grilled, pan-fried or in a cream sauce, it is advisable to choose something with a higher acidity balance or some effervescence. Beaujolais is perhaps the best all-round choice; it works well with roast pork, particularly served cold.

☆ **Budget choice**: Gamay de Touraine

Pot-roast

Consult the entry for the appropriate meat, and choose a similar wine. Because of the extra flavour from the added vegetables, it is possible, though by no means necessary, to serve a slightly less fine wine than with the corresponding straight roast.

☆ **Budget choice**: Côtes de Duras

Stroganoff

An authentic Stroganoff requires a full red with a good depth of flavour, but with some finer characteristics, not too robust and preferably well rounded with age. Try a modest Médoc, a good Cahors or one of the better Bergeracs.

☆ **Budget choice**: Bulgarian Cabernet Sauvignon-Merlot (Oriahovica)

DESSERTS

While a dessert wine can easily be drunk on its own, there is no reason why it has to be, although there are those who believe that the finest points of a great dessert wine are lost or overshadowed by a sweet. But this can only happen if the golden rule of partnering food and wine is not followed.

Cakes, gâteaux, puddings and pastries

Many cakes, sponges and gâteaux do not require wine, but I have found that Tokay enhances those with coffee or vanilla flavours, various Iberian Moscatels are very good when almonds or walnuts are present, and sweet sparkling Vouvray or Coteaux du Layon go well with fruit-filled, fresh cream gâteaux and fruit-flavoured cheesecakes. Iberian Moscatels are superb with Christmas or plum pudding and, on a similar theme, Asti Spumante is ideal with mince pies. Chocolate is more difficult, and although some people consider it possible to drink wines ranging from Sauternes to *brut* Champagne with chocolate fudge cake or profiteroles, I am not one of them.

☆ **Budget choice**: Iced water

Crème brulée, crème caramel

Something rich, sweet and luxurious is required to accompany crème brulée. German or Austrian wines would be too tangy, a top Sauternes or one of the richer Barsacs would be excellent, but perhaps best of all would be a Tokay d'Alsace Sélection de Grains Nobles.

Fruit

A fresh peach, plump and juicy, makes the ideal partner for a Rheingau Riesling *Auslese* or *Beerenauslese*, or a late-harvest, botrytis Riesling from California or Australia. Asti Spumante, Californian Muscat Canelli and Clairette de Die may also partner peaches, especially if served with strawberries and raspberries. These wines go well to one degree or another with virtually every other fruit, including fresh fruit salad. Lighter Sauternes and Barsacs, Coteaux du Layon or sweet sparkling Vouvrays are also good with fruit salad and are the best choice for apple, pear or peach pies, tarts and flans.

An Austrian Grüner Veltliner or Gewürztraminer *Auslese* with strawberries and fresh coarse-ground black pepper (no cream) is a revelation. A fine claret or Burgundy with fresh raspberries that have been macerated in the same wine is appreciated by some, as is a top-quality Mosel *Auslese* with strawberries and fresh raspberry purée (no cream). Apple Strudel, Dutch Apple Pie and other spicy fruit desserts need Tokay, an Iberian Moscatel or Austrian Gewürztraminer *Beerenauslese*. Pies made with darker, richer fruits require fuller Sauternes, Bonnezeaux or Quarts de Chaume.

☆ **Budget choice**: Moscato Spumante

Ice cream

When ice cream is just part of a dessert, it is the other ingredients that should be considered when choosing a wine. Ice cream on its own rarely calls for any accompaniment, but there is one perfect combination – Muscat de Beaumes de Venise with Brown Bread Ice Cream.

☆ **Budget choice**: Moscatel de Valencia

Meringue

For meringue served as part of a vacherin or pavlova, my choice would be a still or sparkling Moscato, Californian Muscat Canelli or late-harvested botrytized Riesling, a top Mosel *Beerenauslese*, a sweet Vouvray or a good Sauternes. For meringue desserts with nutty, coconutty or biscuity ingredients, then a Tokay Essencia, Tokay d'Alsace Sélection de Grains Nobles, Torcolato from Veneto or Malmsey Madeira would be equally successful. Lightly poached meringue served as floating islands or snow eggs, needs something of somewhat less intensity – a Tokay d'Alsace Vendange Tardive perhaps. An *Eiswein* is the perfect partner to lemon meringue pie – a dessert that demands luxury, acidity, and a vibrant sweetness.

☆ **Budget choice**: Iberian Moscatel

CHEESES AND CHEESE DISHES

There is a relatively recent school of thought that does not believe in the traditional concept of cheese and wine as ideal partners. I am not one of its pupils – most cheeses are flattered by many wines; only the most delicate or most powerful of cheeses or wines require careful consideration before trying to partner them.

Blue-veined cheeses

A good blue cheese is best partnered by a sweet wine – a piquant combination of flavours not dissimilar to that found in sweet and sour dishes. Many dessert wines will suffice and the choice will often depend on personal taste, but I find hard blues such as Stilton and Blue Cheshire go best with Port, while soft blues are enhanced by sweet white wines. Lighter Barsacs, Coteaux du Layon, German *Beerenauslese* or a mature Sélection de Grains Nobles from Alsace for Bleu de Bresse types, and richer Sauternes, Austrian Gewürztraminer *Trockenbeerenauslese* or Tokay are needed for more powerful-flavoured Roquefort and Gorgonzola.

☆ **Budget choice**: Moscatel de Valencia

Soft and semi-soft mild cheeses

A light Beaujolais Nouveau or an elegant Pinot Noir from Alsace (as opposed to the deep-coloured, oak-aged reds that are now being made in increasing numbers) will partner most soft and semi-soft cheeses of the mild type, although something even more delicate, such as one of the many fragrant dry white wines of North-eastern Italy or a soft *crémant* from Champagne should be considered for double and triple cream cheeses.

☆ **Budget choice**: Blanquette de Limoux

Soft and semi-soft strong cheeses

Munster demands a strong Gewürztraminer; and the most decadent way to wash down a perfectly ripe Brie de Meaux or Brie de Melun is with a 20-year-old vintage Champagne. Washed-skin cheeses (that have been bathed in water, brine or alcohol while ripening), need an assertive red Burgundy or a robust claret.

☆ **Budget choice**: Young Côtes du Rhône

Hard cheeses

Dry and off-dry English wines are ideal with Caerphilly, while sweeter styles of English wine are perfect with Wensleydale served with a slice of homemade apple pie. Mature Cheddar and other well-flavoured, hard English cheeses demand something full and red like a fine claret or, if it has a bite, Châteauneuf-du-Pape or Chateau Musar. Sangiovese-based wines bring out the sweet flavour of fresh (but mature) Parmesan. Gewürztraminer and Tokay d'Alsace are ideal with Gruyère, although something with a little more acidity, such as a Californian Sauvignon Blanc, is better with Emmental.

☆ **Budget choice**: New World Macération Carbonique

Goat cheeses

These little cheeses require an assertive, dry white wine such as Sancerre or Gewürztraminer, although a firm but light *cru* Beaujolais would also suit.

☆ **Budget choice**: Sauvignon de Haut-Poitou

Cheese fondue

It is possible to drink a wide range of red, dry white and sparkling wines with fondue, but it is fitting to serve a wine from the same area of origin as the dish; Fendant from the Valais with a Swiss fondue, for example, or Apremont or Crépy with fondue Savoyarde.

☆ **Budget choice**: Edelzwicker

Cheese soufflé

A cheese soufflé requires a good sparkling wine, preferably Champagne. If it is a very rich soufflé, such as soufflé Roquefort, then the wine must have the power to match it – a *blanc de noirs* such as Bollinger's "Vieilles Vignes" would be superb.

☆ **Budget choice**: Blanquette de Limoux

Glossary of tasting and technical terms

1 Most terms that are fully explained as entries in the **Guide to Vineyard Soils** (*see* p.14) are not covered in this Glossary.

2 Terms that are explained more comprehensively within the main body of the book are accompanied by a cross-reference to the appropriate page.

3 For ease of cross-reference, terms that appear within Glossary definitions and which have their own entry in the Glossary appear in ***bold italic*** type.

Fr. French   Ger. German   It. Italian   Port. Portuguese   Sp. Spanish
S. Afr. South African

Acetaldehyde The principal *aldehyde* in all wines, but found in much greater quantities in Sherry. In light, unfortified table wines, a small amount of acetaldehyde enhances the *bouquet,* but an excess is undesirable, unstable, halfway to complete *oxidation* and evokes a *Sherry-like* smell.

Acetic acid The most important *volatile acid* found in wine, apart from *carbonic acid*. Small amounts contribute positively to the attractive flavour of a wine, but large quantities produce a taste of vinegar.

Acetification The production of *acetic acid* in a wine.

Acetobacter The vinegar bacillus that can cause *acetification*.

Acidity Essential for the life and vitality of a wine. Too little natural fruit acidity makes a wine dull, *flat* and *short;* too much and it is *sharp* and raw. With just the right *balance,* the *fruit* is refreshing and its flavour lingers in the mouth. *See Total acidity* and *pH*.

Active acidity Acids contain positively charged hydrogen ions, the concentration of which determines the *total acidity* of a wine. The *pH* is the measure of the electrical charge of a given solution (positive acidity hydrogen buffered by negative alkalinity hydrogen ions). Thus a wine's *pH* is a measure of its active acidity.

Adega (Port.) Cellar or winery. Often used as part of a firm's title.

Aerobic In the presence of air.

Aftertaste The flavour and *aroma* left in the mouth after the wine has been swallowed.

Ages gracefully A wine that retains *finesse,* sometimes even increases in *finesse* as it ages.

Aggressive The opposite of *soft* and *smooth.* Young wines can seem aggressive, but may *round* out with a little time in bottle.

Albariza (Sp.) White-surfaced soil formed by diatomaceous deposits, found in the Sherry-producing area of Spain. *See* Southern Spain p.282.

Alcohol, alcoholic In wine terms, this is *ethyl alcohol;* a colourless flammable liquid.

Aldehyde The intermediary stage between an *alcohol* and an *acid,* formed during the *oxidation* of an alcohol. *Acetaldehyde* is the most important of common wine aldehydes.

Ampelographer An expert who studies, records and identifies grape-vines.

Anaerobic In the absence of air.

Anbaugebiet (Ger.) A wine region in Germany such as Rheinpfalz or Mosel-Saar-Ruwer that is divided into districts or *Bereich*. All *QbA* and *QmP* wines must show their Anbaugebiet of origin on the label.

Antioxidant Any chemical that prevents grapes, *must* or wine from oxidizing, ascorbic acid or *sulphur dioxide* for example.

AOC (Fr.) Commonly used abbreviation of *Appellation d'Origine Contrôlée.* The first national wine regime ever implemented, it is a guarantee of origin system with rudimentary quality controls that accounts for 20-25 per cent of French production.

Aperitif Originally used exclusively to describe a beverage prescribed for laxative purposes, aperitif now describes any drink taken before a meal to stimulate the appetite.

Aquifer A water-retaining geological formation into which rainfall from the surrounding area drains.

Aroma This should really be confined to the *fresh* and *fruity* smells reminiscent of grapes, rather than the more winey or *bottle-mature complexities* of *bouquet;* but it is not always possible to use the word in its purest form, hence aroma and *bouquet* may be read as synonymous.

Aromatic grape varieties The most aromatic classic grapes are Gewürztraminer, Muscat, Riesling and Sauvignon blanc. There are exceptions to the rule, but generally, aromatic grapes are most successful when vinified at low temperatures, under *anaerobic* conditions and drunk young and fresh.

Aromatized wine Usually *fortified,* these wines are flavoured by as few as one, or as many as fifty, aromatic substances and range from bitter-sweet *vermouth* to retsina. The various herbs, fruits, flowers and other less appetizing ingredients include: strawberries, orange peel, elderflowers, wormwood, quinine and pine-resin.

Aseptic A characteristic of a substance such as sorbic acid or *sulphur dioxide* that can kill bacteria.

Assemblage (Fr.) Blend of base wines that creates the final *cuvée.*

Atmospheres A measure of atmospheric pressure: 1 atmosphere = 15 pounds per square inch. The average internal pressure of a bottle of Champagne is six atmospheres, the equivalent of a double-decker bus tyre.

Attack A wine with good attack suggests one that is *complete* and readily presents its full range of taste characteristics to the palate. The wine is likely to be youthful rather than *mature,* and its attack augurs well for its future.

Auslese (Ger.) Category of German *QmP* wine, (above *Spätlese,* but beneath *Beerenauslese*), that is very sweet, made from late-picked grapes and may contain some botrytized grapes.

Austere A wine that lacks *fruit* and is dominated by harsh *acidity* and/or *tannin.*

Autolysis The enzymatic breakdown of yeast cells that increases the possibility of bacterial spoilage; the autolytic effect of aging a wine on its *lees* is therefore undesirable in most wines, exceptions being those bottled *sur lie* (mostly Muscadet) and sparkling wines.

Back-blend To blend fresh, unfermented grape juice into a *fully-fermented* wine, with the aim of adding a certain fresh, *grapey* sweetness commonly associated with German wines. A term often used in New Zealand when describing the production of Müller-Thurgau wines and synonymous with the German practice of adding *süssreserve.*

Backward A wine that is slow to develop (the opposite of precocious).

Baked Applies to wines of high *alcoholic* content giving a sensory perception of grapes harvested in great heat, either from a hot country, or from a classic wine area in a sweltering hot year. This characteristic can be controlled to some extent by early harvesting, night harvesting, rapid transport to the winery and modern *cool-fermentation* techniques.

Balance The harmonious relationship between *acid, alcohol, fruit, tannin* and other natural elements in wine.

Ban de vendange (Fr.) Official regional declaration setting the date for the commencement of grape-picking for the latest vintage.

Barrel-fermented White wines are still traditionally fermented in *oak* barrels – new for top-quality Bordeaux, Burgundy and premium varietal wines, old for middle-quality wines and top-quality Champagnes. New barrels impart positive *oaky* characteristics, but the older the barrels, the less *oaky,* more *oxidative* the influence. Barrel-fermented wines have more complex *aromas* than wines that have simply been *matured* in wood. *See* Stainless steel or oak? p.19.

Barrique (Fr.) Lit. barrel, refers to small wooden cask of 225-litre capacity or thereabouts, depending on area of origin, in which white wines may be *fermented* and both red and white *matured*. This is rapidly becoming an international term and its use on a label invariably denotes the use of new oak in the *fermentation* and/or *maturation* of the wine.

Baumé (Fr.) Scale of measurement used to indicate the amount of sugar in grape *must*.

Beerenauslese (Ger.) Category of German *QmP* wine that comes above *Auslese,* but beneath *Trockenbeerenauslese* and is made from *botrytized* grapes. It has more *finesse* and *elegance* than any other intensely sweet wine, with the possible exception of *Eiswein.*

Benchland The flat land between two slopes, this term describes a form of natural, rather than man-made, terrace.

Bentonite A fine clay containing a volcanic ash derivative called montromillonite, a hydrated silicate of magnesium that activates a precipitation in wine when used as a *fining* agent. *See* Fining, p.20.

Bereich (Ger.) A wine district in Germany that contains smaller *Grosslagen* and is itself part of a larger *Anbaugebiet.*

Big vintage, big year Terms usually applied to great years, because the exceptional weather conditions produce bigger *(fuller, richer)* wines than normal. May also be used to describe a year with a big crop.

Big wine A *full-bodied* wine with an exceptionally *rich* flavour.

Biscuity Desirable aspect of *bouquet* found in some quality sparkling wines, derived from a certain preponderance of *acetaldehyde* owing to age in the bottle or the method of vinification.

Bite A very positive qualification of *grip*. Usually desirable but an unpleasant "bite" is possible.

Bitterness (1) An unpleasant aspect of a poorly made wine. (2) An expected characteristic in some Italian wines. (3) The result of an as yet undeveloped concentration of flavours that should, with *maturity,* become *rich* and delicious. An *edge* of bitterness may result from raw *tannin.*

Blackstrap Derogatory term that originated when Port was an unsophisticated product, coloured by elderberries and very coarse.

Blanc de blancs (Fr.) White wine made solely from white grapes. Often seen on sparkling wines and, because it is perceived as an "upmarket" term but not regulated, it is commonly used on cheap blends of *vin de table.*

Blanc de noirs (Fr.) Theoretically a white wine made solely from black grapes, but often used synonymously with *blush wine.*

Blind tasting A tasting where the identity of wines is unknown to the taster until after notes and scores have been given. All competitive tastings are blind.

Blowzy An overblown and exaggerated *fruity aroma* and smell, often attributed to basic Californian wines. It is something that experts feel is vulgar, while many consumers find it pleasing.

Blue-fining Ferrocyanide used to fine out heavy metals such as copper and iron. Of the relatively small number of specialist fining agents, this is the most commonly used, although its use has dropped dramatically, since the widespread use of stainless steel prevents contamination by heavy metals. Most often used in Germany; banned in some countries. *See* Fining p.20.

Blush wine A pale rosé.

Bodega (Sp.) The Spanish equivalent of *Adega*; ie cellar or winery.

Body The *extract* of *fruit* and *alcoholic* strength that together give an impression of *weight* in the mouth.

Botrytis A generic term for rot, but is often used synonymously with *Botrytis cinerea*.

Botrytis cinerea The technically correct name for *noble rot*, the only rot that is welcomed by winemakers, particularly in the sweet-wine areas, as it is responsible for the world's greatest sweet wines. *See* Sauternes, p.70.

Botrytized grapes Lit. "rotten grapes", but commonly used for grapes that have been affected by *Botrytis cinerea*.

Bottle-age, bottle-maturity The length of time a wine spends in bottle before it is consumed. A wine that has good bottle-age is one that has sufficient time to *mature* properly. The development in bottle is more *reductive* than *oxidative*.

Bouquet This should really be applied to the combination of smells directly attributable to a wine's *maturity* in bottle – thus *aroma* for grape and bouquet for bottle. But it is not always possible to use these words in their purest form, hence *aroma* and bouquet may be used synonymously.

Breed The *finesse* of a wine that is due to the intrinsic quality of grape and *terroir* combined with the skill and experience of a great winemaker.

Brut (Fr.) Normally reserved for sparkling wines, it literally means "raw" or "bone-dry". The necessarily high *acidity* of sparkling wines (to carry the flavour through the bubbles on to the *palate*) demands that a brut wine be aged for at least ten years or sweetened with up to 15 grams per litre of sugar.

Burnt Synonymous with *baked*, marginally uncomplimentary.

Butt Generally synonymous with *cask*, although specific butts are of certain standard sizes.

Buttery A *rich*, *fat* and positively delicious character found in some Chardonnay wines, particularly if produced in a great vintage or warm country.

Buyer's Own Brand (BOB) A brand that belongs to the buyer (in the eyes of the producer – the seller as far as the consumer is concerned), which could be a wine merchant, supermarket or restaurant.

CO₂ Commonly used chemical formula for *carbon dioxide*. This is naturally produced in wine during *fermentation*, when the sugar is converted into almost equal parts of *alcohol* and CO_2. The CO_2 is normally allowed to escape as a gas, although a tiny amount will always be present in its dissolved form, *carbonic acid* (H_2CO_3), in any wine, even a still one, otherwise it would taste dull, *flat* and lifeless. If the gas is prevented from escaping, the wine becomes sparkling.

Cantina (It.) Winery.

Cantina sociale (It.) Growers' cooperative.

Carbon dioxide *See* CO₂.

Carbonic acid The correct term for *carbon dioxide (CO_2)* when dissolved in water (H_2O), which is the main ingredient of wine, and is expressed as H_2CO_3. It is sometimes referred to as a *volatile acid*, although the acid is held in equilibrium with the gas in its dissolved state and cannot be isolated in its pure form.

Carbonic gas Synonymous with *CO_2 (carbon dioxide)*.

Casein A milk protein sometimes used for *fining*. *See* Fining, p.20.

Cask-fermented Synonymous with *barrel-fermented*.

Cassis (Fr.) Lit. "blackcurrant". If "cassis" is used by wine-tasters in preference to "blackcurrant", it probably implies a richer, more concentrated and viscous character.

Cedarwood A purely subjective word applied to a particular *bouquet* associated with the *bottle-maturity* of a wine previously stored or fermented in wood, usually *oak*.

Centrifugal filtration Not filtration in the pure sense, but a process where unwanted matter is separated from wine or grape juice by so-called "centrifugal force". *See* Filtration, p.18.

Cep (Fr.) Vine, often used as part of a brand name.

Cépage (Fr.) A variety of vine or grape, commonly seen on labels of pure varietal wines, e.g., Cépage Sauvignon.

Ceramic filtration An ultra-fine *depth-filtration* that utilizes *perlite*.

Chaptalization The addition of sugar to fresh grape juice to raise a wine's *alcoholic* potential. Theoretically it takes 1.7 kilograms of sugar per hectolitre of wine to raise the *alcoholic* strength by one per cent, but red wines actually require 2 kilograms to allow for evaporation during the *remontage*. The term is named after Antoine Chaptal, a brilliant chemist and technocrat who served Napoleon as minister of the interior from 1800 to 1805 and instructed wine-growers on the advantages of adding sugar at pressing time.

Charm Another subjective term: a wine that charms or appeals without blatantly attracting.

Château (Fr.) Lit. "castle" or "stately home". Whereas many château-bottled wines do actually come from magnificent edifices that could truly be described as châteaux, many may be modest one-storey villas, some are no more than purpose-built *cuveries*, while a few are merely tin sheds! The legal connotation is the same as for any domain-bottled wine.

Cheesy Characteristic element in the *bouquet* of a very old Champagne, although other wines that have an extended contact with their *lees*, possibly those that have not been *racked* or *filtered*, may also possess it. It is probably caused by the production during *fermentation* of a very small amount of butyric acid that may later develop into an *ester* called ethyl butyrate.

Chewy An extreme qualification of *meaty*.

Chip-budding Method of propagating vines where a vine-bud with a tiny wedge-shape of phloem (live bark) and xylem (inner wood) is inserted into a *rootstock* with an existing root system.

Chlorosis A vine disorder caused by mineral imbalance (too much active-lime, not enough iron or magnesium), often called "green sickness".

Chocolatey, chocolate-box Subjective term often used to describe the odour and flavour of Cabernet sauvignon or Pinot noir wines. Sometimes "chocolate-box" is used to describe the *bouquet* of fairly *mature* Bordeaux. The *fruity* character of a wine can become chocolatey in wines with a *pH* above 3.6.

Cigar-box Subjective term often applied to a certain complex *bouquet* in wines that have been *matured* in oak, usually red Bordeaux, and have received good *bottle-age*.

Citrus, citrussy Subjective term for a tangy *fruit* flavour found in some white wines that is more *racy* than *lemony* and suggests a certain *finesse*. It is closely associated with the *petrol* character of a fine, mature Riesling.

Clairet (Fr.) A wine that falls somewhere between a dark rosé and a light red wine.

Claret English term for a red Bordeaux wine. Etymologically it has the same roots as the French term *clairet*.

Classic, classy Both subjective words to convey an obvious impression of quality. These terms are applied to wines that not only portray the correct characteristics for their type and origin, but possess the *finesse* and *style* indicative of top-quality wines.

Classico (It.) May only be used on wines produced in the historic, or classic area of an appellation, usually a small, hilly area at the centre of the *DOC*.

Clean Straightforward term applied to a wine devoid of any unwanted or unnatural *undertones* of *aroma* and flavour.

Climat (Fr.) Single plot of land with its own name, located within a specific vineyard.

Clone Variety of vine that has developed differently due to a process of selection, either natural, as in the case of a vine adapting to local conditions, or by man. *See* Clones and Cloning, p.24.

Clos (Fr.) Synonymous with *climat*, except this plot of land is either enclosed by walls, or was once.

Closed Refers to the *nose* or *palate* of a wine not showing very much at all and implies that some of its qualities are "hidden" and should develop with time in bottle.

Cloying Sickly and sticky character of a poor sweet wine, where the *finish* is heavy and often unclean.

Coarse A term applied to a rough and ready wine, not necessarily unpleasant, but certainly not fine.

Compact fruit Suggests a good *weight* of *fruit* with a correct *balance* of *tannin* (if red) and *acidity* that is presented on the *nose* and *palate* in a manner that is opposite to *open-knit*.

Complete Refers to a satisfaction in the mouth indicating that the wine has all the qualities of *fruit, tannin, acidity, depth, length*, etc.

Complexity Refers to many different nuances of smell or taste. Great wines in their youth may have a certain complexity, but it is only with *maturity* in bottle that a wine will eventually achieve its potential in terms of complexity.

Cooked Similar to *baked*, but may also imply the addition of grape concentrate to the wine during fermentation.

Cool-fermentation Generally used to refer to the *fermentation* of white wine at temperatures of 18°C (64°F) and below, in modern, stainless-steel vats equipped with efficient temperature control. If conducted properly, the result should be fresher, lighter and more aromatic. *See* White wines, p.22.

Corked Correctly used, the term applies to a penicillin infection inside the cork. Sadly, infected corks are turning up quite regularly these days and can be recognized by an almost *green*, musty-woody smell and flavour in the wine. Sometimes it is possible to confuse these characteristics with those of a young Cabernet franc wine.

Correct A wine with all the correct characteristics for its type and origin. Not necessarily an exciting wine, but one that cannot be faulted.

Côte, côtes (Fr.) Slope(s) or hillside(s) of one contiguous slope or hill.

Coteaux (Fr.) Slopes and hillsides in a hilly area, not contiguous.

Coulure (Fr.) A physiological disorder of the vine that occurs as a result of alternating periods of warm and cold, dry and wet conditions after the bud-break. If this culminates in a flowering during which the weather is too sunny, the sap rushes past the *embryo bunches* to the shoot-tips, causing vigorous growth of foliage, but denying the clusters an adequate supply of essential nutrients. The barely formed berries dry up and drop to the ground.

Coupage (Fr.) To blend by *cutting* one wine with another.

Creamy Subjective term used to convey the impression of a creamy flavour that may be indicative of the variety of grape or method of *vinification*. Sweet *botrytis* wines are often very creamy.

Creamy-oak A more subtle, lower-key version of the *vanilla-oak* character that is most probably derived from *wood lactones* during *maturation* in small *oak* barrels.

Crémant (Fr.) Traditionally ascribed to a Champagne with a gentler *mousse* than usual, but now applied to fully sparkling wines from other areas.

Crisp A *clean* wine, with good *acidity* showing on the *finish,* yielding a *fresh* and positive *aftertaste.*

Cross A vine that has been propagated by crossing two or more varieties within the same species (*Vitis vinifera* for example), while a *hybrid* is a cross between two or more varieties from more than one species.

Cross-flow filtration A relatively new, high-speed form of microfiltration in which the wine flows across (not through), a membrane filter, thus avoiding build-up.

Cryptogamic Refers to cryptogamic or fungus-based disease like grey rot.

Cru (Fr.) Lit. "growth", used to describe a specific vineyard, e.g. that which belongs to châteaux in Bordeaux.

Cru Bourgeois (Fr.) Non-classified growths of the Médoc.

Cru classé (Fr.) An officially classified vineyard.

Cultivar Term used mainly in South Africa for a cultivated variety of wine grape.

Cut (1) In blending, a wine of a specific character may be used to cut a wine dominated by an opposite quality. This can range from a bland wine that is cut by a small quantity of very *acidic* wine, to a white wine that is cut with a little red wine to make a rosé, as in pink Champagne. The most severe form of cutting is also called *stretching* and involves diluting wine with water, an illegal practice. (2) In matching food and wine, a wine with high *acidity* may be used to cut the *organoleptic* effect of grease from a grilled or fried dish, or an oily fish, just as the effervescence of a fine sparkling wine cuts the creamy texture of certain soups and sauces.

Cuvaison (Fr.) The *fermentation* period in red wine production during which the juice is kept in contact with its skins. *See* Fermentation, p.21.

Cuve (Fr.) Vat.

Cuve close (Fr.) Bulk-production method of making inexpensive sparkling wine through a natural second fermentation inside a sealed vat. Invented in 1907 by Eugène Charmat and also known as the Charmat method. *See* Cuve close, p.23.

Cuvée (Fr.) (1) Contents of a wine vat (2) Blend of Champagnes or a special lot of wine.

Cuverie, Cuvier (Fr.) The room or building housing the *fermenting* vats.

DO (Sp.) Commonly used abbreviation for *Denominación de Órigen,* the Spanish equivalent of the French *AOC.*

DOC (It.) Commonly used abbreviation for *Denominazione di Origine Controllata.* The Italian equivalent of the French *AOC.*

DOCG (It.) Commonly used abbreviation for *Denominazione di Origine Controllata e Garantita.* The highest classification of Italian wines.

Definition A wine with good definition is one that is *clean,* with a correct balance of *acidity, tannin* and *fruit* and a positive expression of *varietal character.*

Dégorgement (Fr.) The act of removing or disgorging the sediment created during the *second fermentation* of Champagne or a sparkling wine made by the *méthode champenoise.*

Degree-days *See Heat summation.*

Delicate Describes the quieter characteristics of quality that give a wine *charm.*

Demi-sec Lit. "half-dry"; in practice semi-sweet.

Département (Fr.) Geopolitical division of France, similar to county in the UK or State in the USA.

Depth Refers first to a wine's depth of flavour and second to its depth of interest.

Depth filtration This form of filtration uses *diatomaceous earth,* which is packed into a cake through which wine is passed. It derives its name from the fact that unwanted particles penetrate the filter medium to a certain depth before they are retained by it and clear wine is permitted to pass.

Diatomaceous earth Also known as *Kieselguhr,* a fine, powdered, silaceous earth evolved from decomposed deep-sea algae called diatoms. *See also Perlite, Ceramic filtration* and *Polishing.*

Dirty Applies to any wine with an unpleasant off-taste or off-smell, probably the result of poor *vinification* or bad bottling.

Disgorgement *See dégorgement.*

Distinctive A wine with a positive character. All *fine wines* are distinctive to one degree or another, but not all distinctive wines are necessarily fine.

Doble pasta (Sp.) Red wines macerated with double the normal proportion of grape skins to juice during *fermentation. See* How to read Spanish wine labels, p.268.

Dosage (Fr.) Sugar added to a sparkling wine after *dégorgement,* the amounts of which are controlled by the terminology used on the label – *brut, demi-sec* etc.

Doux (Fr.) Sweet, as applied to wines.

Drip irrigation Various forms exist, but at its most sophisticated, it is a computer-controlled watering system programmed with the vine's general water requirement and constantly amended by a continuous flow of data from soil sensors. The water is supplied literally drip by drip through a complex system of pipes with metered valves.

Drying up A wine that has dried up has lost some of its *freshness* and *fruit* through aging in the bottle. It may still be enjoyable, but remaining bottles should be drunk up quickly.

Dusty Akin to *peppery* in a red wine; a blurring of *varietal* definition in a white wine.

Earth filtration Synonymous with *depth filtration.*

Earthy A drying impression in the mouth. Some wines can be enjoyably earthy, but finest-quality wines should be as *clean* as a whistle.

Easy A simple, enjoyable quality in a wine that is probably *soft* and cheap.

Eau-de-vie (Fr.) Literally, "water of life"; specifically a grape-derived spirit.

Edelfaule (Ger.) *Noble rot, see Botrytis cinerea.*

Edelkeur (S. Afr.) South African term for *noble rot, see Botrytis cinerea.*

Edge Almost, but not quite, synonymous with *grip;* wine can have an edge of *bitterness* or *tannin.* Edge usually implies that a wine has the capacity to develop, while *grip* may be applied to a wine in various stages of development, including fully *mature* wine.

Edgy Synonymous with *nervous.*

EEC Commonly used abbreviation for European Economic Community.

Egg white A traditional *fining* agent that fines out negatively charged matter. *See* Fining, p.20.

Einzellage (Ger.) Single-vineyard wine area; smallest geographical unit allowed by German wine law.

Eiswein (Ger.) Originally a German concept, this rare wine resulted from the tradition of leaving grapes on the vine in the hope of attracting *Botrytis cinerea.* The grapes are frozen by frost or snow, then harvested and pressed when frozen. This is done because only the ice freezes and as this rises to the top of the vat, it can be scraped off to leave a concentrated juice that produces a wine with a unique *balance* of sweetness, *acidity* and *extract.*

Elegant, elegance Subjective term applied to wines with a certain *style* and *finesse.*

Eleveur, élevage (Fr.) Lit. "bringing up" or "raising" the wine. Both terms refer to the traditional function of a *négociant,* as it originated in France, namely to buy ready-made wines after the harvest and take care of them until they are ready to be bottled and sold. The task involves *racking* the wines and blending them into a marketable product as each house sees fit.

Embryo bunches In spring, the vine develops little clusters of miniature green berries that will form a bloom a few weeks later. If a berry successfully flowers, it is capable of developing into a grape and the embryo bunch is thus an indication of the potential size of the crop.

Encépagement (Fr.) The proportion of grape varieties in a blend.

En-primeur (Fr.) Classic wines such as Bordeaux are offered for sale en-primeur, which is to say within a year of the harvest, before the final blend and bottling has taken place. For experienced buyers given the opportunity to taste, this is a calculated risk and the price should reflect this element of chance.

Esters Sweet-smelling compounds, contributing to the *aroma* and *bouquet* of a wine, formed during *fermentation* and throughout *maturation.*

Estufagem (Port.) Process whereby Madeira is heated in ovens called estufas, then cooled. *See* Madeira, p.305.

Ethanoic acid Synonymous with *acetic acid.*

Ethanol Synonymous with *ethyl alcohol.*

Ethyl alcohol The main *alcohol* in wine is so important in quantative terms that to speak of a wine's *alcohol* is to refer purely to its ethyl alcohol content.

Everyday wines Inexpensive, easy-drinking wines.

Ex-cellars Wines offered *en-primeur* are usually purchased ex-cellars; the cost of shipping the wine to the importer's cellars is extra, on top of which any duty and taxes will be added.

Expressive A wine that is expressive is true to its grape variety and *terroir.*

Extract Sugar-free soluble solids that give *body* to a wine. The term covers everything from proteins and vitamins to *tannins,* calcium and *iron.*

Fall bright Commonly used term for any liquid that becomes limpid after cloudy matter falls as sediment to the bottom of the vessel.

Farmyard A term used by many people to describe a wine, quite often Chardonnay or Pinot, that has *matured* beyond its initial *freshness* of *fruit,* past the desired stage of *roundness* and the pleasing phase when it acquires certain *vegetal undertones.* The wine is still healthy and drinkable – for some, it is at the very *peak* of perfection.

Fat A wine full in *body* and *extract.*

Fatty acids A term sometimes used for *volatile acids.*

Feminine Subjective term used to describe a wine with a preponderance of delicately attractive qualities, rather than *weight* or strength. A wine of striking beauty, grace and *finesse* with a silky texture and exquisite style.

Fermentation The biochemical process by which enzymes secreted by *yeast* cells convert sugar molecules into almost equal parts of *alcohol* and *carbonic gas*. *See* Fermentation, p.18.

Filter, filtration There are three basic methods of filtration: *depth filtration* (also known as *earth filtration*); *pad filtration* (also known as *sheet filtration*), and *membrane filtration* (also known as *micro-porous filtration*). There is also *centrifugal filtration,* which is not filtration in the pure sense but achieves the same objective of removing unwanted particles suspended in wine or grape juice. *See* Filtration, p.18.

Fine wines Quality wines, representing only a small percentage of all wines produced, of which great wines are the very élite.

Finesse That elusive, indescribable quality that separates a *fine wine* from those of slightly lesser quality.

Fining The clarification of fresh grape juice or wine is often speeded up by the use of various fining agents that operate by an electrolytic reaction to fine out oppositely charged matter. *See* Fining, p.20.

Finish The quality and enjoyment of a wine's *aftertaste* and the length of time it continues.

Firm Refers to a certain amount of *grip*. A firm wine is a wine of good constitution, held up with *tannin* or *acidity*.

First pressing The first pressing yields the sweetest, cleanest, clearest juice.

Fixed acidity This is the *total acidity* less the *volatile acidity*.

Fixed sulphur The principal reason why SO_2 (sulphur dioxide) is added to grape juice and wine is to prevent *oxidation,* but only *free sulphur* can do this. Upon contact with wine, some SO_2 immediately combines with oxygen and other elements, such as sugars and acids, and is known as fixed or bound sulphur. What remains is *free sulphur,* capable of combining with molecules of oxygen at some future date.

Flabby The opposite of *crisp,* referring to a wine lacking in *acidity,* which is dull, weak and *short*.

Flash pasteurization A sterilization technique that should not be confused with full pasteurization. It involves subjecting the wine to a temperature of about 80°C (176°F) for between 30 seconds and one minute. *See* Heat, p.18.

Flat Sparkling wine that has lost all its *mousse*. Also used interchangeably with *flabby,* especially when referring to a lack of *acidity* on the *finish*.

Fleshy A wine with plenty of *fruit* and *extract*.

Flor The scum-like yeast growth that floats on the surface of Fino Sherry as it matures in part-filled butts. It is from a particular strain of yeast called *Saccharomyces beticus* that gives the wine its inimitable character.

Flurbereinigung (Ger.) Modern viticultural method of growing vines in rows running vertically up and down slopes rather than across, in terraces.

Fortified The fortification with pure alcohol, (usually very strong grape spirit of between 77 and 98 per cent), can take place either before fermentation (as in Ratafia de Champagne and Pineau des Charentes), during fermentation (as in Port and Muscat de Beaumes de Venise), or after fermentation (as in Sherry). *See* p.23.

Foudre (Fr.) A large wooden cask or vat.

Foxy The very distinctive, highly perfumed character of certain indigenous American grape varieties that can be sickly sweet and cloying to unconditioned European and Antipodean palates.

Free-run juice *See Vin de goutte*.

Free sulphur The active element of SO_2 in wine, free sulphur combines with intruding molecules of oxygen.

Fresh, freshness Wines that are *clean* and still vital with youth.

Frizzante (It.) Semi-sparkling.

Frizzantino (It.) Very lightly sparkling, between still and semi-sparkling (i.e. *perlant*).

Fruit Wine is made from grapes and must therefore be 100 per cent fruit, yet it will not have a fruity flavour unless the grapes used have the correct combination of *ripeness* and *acidity*.

Fruit-cakey Wine tasting or smelling of fruit cake.

Full Usually refers to *body,* e.g., full-bodied. But a wine can be light in body yet full in flavour.

Fully fermented A wine that is allowed to complete its natural course of *fermentation* and so yield a totally dry wine.

Garrigue (Fr.) A type of moorland found in Languedoc-Roussillon.

Gelatine A positively charged *fining* agent used for removing negatively charged suspended matter in wines, especially an excess of *tannin. See* Fining, p.20.

Generic Used to denote a regional appellation wine, as distinct from a more specific local appellation, usually blended.

Generous A generous wine gives its *fruit* freely on the palate; all wines should have some degree of generosity.

Genus The botanical family Ampelidaceae has ten genera, one of which, Vitis, through the sub-genus Euvites, contains the species *Vitis vinifera,* to which all the famous wine-making varieties belong.

Gobelet (Fr.) Spur-training system for growing vines. *See* Regional styles of vine training, p.15.

Good grip A healthy structure of *tannin* supporting the *fruit* in a wine.

Gout de terroir (Fr.) Lit. "taste of earth", a term for an *earthy* taste. It can denote a particular flavour imparted by certain soils, not the taste of the soil itself, in a wine.

Graft The joint between the *rootstock* and the *scion* of the *producer vine*.

Grand cru (Fr.) Lit. "great growth", in regions such as Burgundy, where its use is strictly controlled, it has real meaning (i.e. the wine should be great – relative to the quality of the year), but in other winemaking areas where there are no controls, it will mean little.

Grapey Can be applied to the *aroma* and flavour of a wine that is reminiscent of grapes rather than wine, a particular characteristic of German wines. Wines from certain grape varieties like the Muscat (as is Asti), Morio-muskat and Gewürztraminer can also produce a grapey character.

Grassy Often used to describe certain Gewürztraminer, Scheurebe and Sauvignon wines portraying a grassy type of *fruitiness*.

Green Young and *tart,* as in Vinho Verde. It can be either a derogatory term, or simply an indication of youthful wine that might well improve.

Grip A term applied to a *firm* wine with a positive *finish*. A wine showing grip on the *finish* indicates a certain *bite* of *acidity* and, if red, *tannin*.

Grosslage (Ger.) A wine area in Germany that is part of a larger district or *Bereich*.

Growth *See Cru*.

Gutsy A wine full in *body, fruit, extract* and, usually, *alcohol*. Normally applied to ordinary-quality wines.

H_2CO_3 *See Carbonic acid*.

H_2S *See Hydrogen sulphide*.

Hard Indicates a certain severity, often due to excess *tannin* and *acidity*.

Harsh A more derogatory form of *coarse*.

Heat summation System of measuring the growth potential of vines in a specific area in terms of the environmental temperature, expressed in degree-days. A vine's vegetative cycle is only activated above a temperature of 10°C (50°F). The time during which these temperatures persist equates to the vine's growing season. To calculate the number of degree-days, the proportion of the daily mean temperature significant to the vine's growth – the daily mean minus the inactive 10°C (50°F) – is multiplied by the number of days of the growing season. For example, a growing season of 200 days with a daily mean temperature of 15°C (59°F) gives a heat summation of 1,000 degree-days in Celsius: (15-10) x 200 = 1,000 (1,800 in Fahrenheit).

Herbal, herbal-oak Descriptive term applied to certain wines that are *matured* in cask, but unlike *vanilla-oak, creamy-oak, smoky-oak* and *spicy-oak,* its origin is unknown. A herbal character devoid of oak is usually derived from the *varietal* character of a grape and is common to many varieties.

High-tone A term used in this book to describe *aromas* of *bouquet* that aspire to *elegance,* but that can become too exaggerated and be slightly reminiscent of vermouth.

Hollow A wine that appears to lack any real flavour in the mouth compared with the promise shown on the *nose*.

Honest Applied to any wine, usually of a fairly basic quality, which is true in character to its type and origin and does not give any indication of being *souped-up* or blended in any unlawful way. It is more complimentary than *typical*.

Hot Synonym for *baked*.

House claret An unpretentious, and not too expensive, *everyday* drinking red Bordeaux.

Hybrid A cross between two or more grape varieties from more than one species.

Hydrogen sulphide When hydrogen combines with *sulphur dioxide,* the result is a smell of bad eggs. If this occurs prior to bottling and is dealt with immediately, it can be rectified. If allowed to progress, the hydrogen sulphide can develop into *mercaptans* and ruin the wine.

Ice Wine *See Eiswein*.

Inky Can refer to either the opacity of colour, or to an inkiness of character indicating a deep flavour with plenty of *supple tannin*.

Iron Found as a trace element in fresh grapes grown in soils where relatively substantial ferrous deposits are located. Wines from such sites may naturally contain a tiny amount of iron barely perceptible on the *palate*. If there is too much, the flavour becomes medicinal. Above 7 milligrams per litre for white, 10 milligrams per litre for red, there is a danger of the wine going cloudy. But wines of such iron levels should have been *blue-fined* prior to bottling. *See* Fining, p.20.

Isinglass A gelatinous *fining* agent obtained from the swim-bladder of freshwater fish and used to clear hazy, low-tannin wines. *See* Fining, p.20.

Jammy Commonly used to describe a *fat* and eminently drinkable red wine *rich* in *fruit,* if perhaps a bit contrived and lacking a certain *elegance*.

Jug wine California's mass-produced *vin de table*.

Kabinett The first rung of predication in Germany's *QmP* range, one below *Spätlese* and often drier than a *QbA*.

Lactic acid The acid that develops in sour milk, which is also created in wine during the *malolactic* fermentation.

Lagar (Port.) Rectangular concrete receptacle in which people tread grapes.

Laid-back A term that has come into use since the arrival of Californian wines on the international scene in the early-1980s. It usually implies a wine that is very relaxed, *easy* to drink and confident of its own quality.

Landwein German equivalent of *vin de pays*.

Leaching A term sometimes used when referring to the deliberate removal of *tannin* from new oak by steaming, or when discussing certain aspects of soil, such as *pH*, that can be affected when carbonates are leached by rainwater.

Lees Sediment left in the cask or vat during *fermentation,* consisting mostly of dead *yeast* cells. As these yeast cells undergo *autolysis,* a source of possible bacterial infection, most wines are *racked* several times prior to bottling. A wine described on the label as *sur lie* has been kept on its lees until bottling to increase its flavour, e.g. Muscadet and sparkling wines.

Lemony Many dry and medium-sweet wines have a tangy, fruity *acidity* that is suggestive of lemons.

Length, long Refers to a wine where the flavour *lingers* in the mouth a long time after swallowing.

Lie (Fr.) Lees: *sur lie* refers to a wine kept in contact with its *lees.*

Light vintage, light year A year that produces relatively light wines. Not a great vintage, but not necessarily a bad one either.

Linalool C$_{10}$H$_{18}$O found in some grapes, particularly Muscat varieties. It contributes to the peachy-flowery fragrance that is the *varietal* characteristic of wines made from Muscat grapes.

Lingering Normally applied to the *finish* of a wine – an *aftertaste* that literally lingers.

Liqueur de tirage (Fr.) The bottling liqueur: wine, *yeast* and sugar added to still Champagne to induce the *mousse.*

Liquoreux (Fr.) Lit. "liqueur-like", this term is often applied to dessert wines of an unctuous quality.

Liquorice An often-detected characteristic of Monbazillac, but it can be found in any *rich* sweet wine. It refers to concentration of flavours from heat-shrivelled, rather than *noble rot*-shrivelled, grapes. It is, for example, the difference between the power of the 1976 Sauternes and the *elegance* of the 1975 Sauternes, the former having been considerably concentrated by heat before *botrytis cinerea* attacked.

Liveliness A term that usually implies a certain youthful *freshness* of *fruit* due to good *acidity* and an above-average *carbonic gas* content.

Luscious, lusciousness Almost synonymous with voluptuous, although more often used for an unctuous, sweet white wine than a succulently rich red.

Macération (Fr.) Usually applied to the period during the *cuvaison* when the *fermenting* juice is in contact with the grape skins. This has traditionally been applied to red-winemaking, but it is on the increase for white wines, utilizing *prefermentation macération* techniques.

Macération carbonique (Fr.), **Maceration style** Generic terms that group together several similar methods of initially vinifying wine under pressure of *carbon dioxide.* These methods produce *fresh,* early-drinking wines of good colour, *soft fruit* and a *pear-drop aroma. See* Macération carbonique, p.21.

Maderized All Madeiras are maderized by the *estufagem* process of slowly heating the wines in specially constructed ovens, then cooling them. This is undesirable in all but certain Mediterranean wines that are deliberately made in the *rancio* style. An ordinary, light, table wine that is maderized will often be erroneously diagnosed as *oxidized,* but there is a significant difference in the symptoms: it will have a duller nose, will rarely hint of any *sherry-like* character and will be flat on the *palate.* All

colours and styles of wine are capable of maderizing and the likely cause is storage in bright sunlight or too much warmth.

Made wine A wine made from imported grape juice or, more commonly, concentrate. All so-called British wines are made wines, whereas English wines are natural wines made from freshly grown, local grapes.

Malic A tasting term that describes the green apple *aroma* and flavour found in some young wines, due to the presence of *malic acid,* the dominant *acid* found in apples.

Malic acid A very strong-tasting acid that diminishes during the fruit's ripening process, but still persists in ripe grapes and, although reduced by *fermentation,* in wine too. The quantity of malic acid present in a wine may be considered too much, particularly for a red wine, and the smoothing effect of replacing it with just two-thirds the quantity of the much weaker *lactic acid* is often desirable. See Malolactic Fermentation, p.18.

Malolactic The so-called malolactic fermentation is sometimes referred to as a *secondary fermentation,* but it is actually a biochemical process that converts the hard *malic acid* of unripe grapes into soft *lactic acid* and *carbonic gas. See* Malolactic fermentation, p.18.

Manta The cap of skins that rises to the top of the vat during *cuvaison.*

Manurey A very extreme form of *farmyardy.*

Marc (1) The residue of skins, pips and stalks after pressing. (2) The name given to a 4,000-kilogram (4-ton) load of grapes in Champagne. (3) A rough brandy made from the residue of skins, pips, and stalks after pressing.

Marque A brand or make.

Mature, maturity Refer to a wine's development in bottle, as opposed to *ripe,* which describes the maturity of the grape itself.

Mean An extreme qualification of *ungenerous.*

Meaty Suggests a wine so *rich* in body and *extract* that the drinker feels almost able to *chew* it. Wines with a high *tannin* content are often meaty.

Mellow Round and at its *peak* of *maturity.*

Membrane filter A thin screen of biologically inert material, perforated with micro-sized pores that occupy 80 per cent of the membrane. Anything larger than these holes is denied passage when the wine is pumped through during *filtration.*

Mercaptans Methyl and *ethyl alcohols* can react with *hydrogen sulphide* to form mercaptans, foul-smelling compounds, often impossible to remove, which can ruin a wine. Mercaptans can smell of garlic, onion, burnt rubber or stale cabbage.

Méthode Champenoise (Fr.) Process whereby an effervescence is produced through a *second fermentation* in bottle, used for Champagne and other good-quality sparkling wines.

Méthode gaillacoise (Fr.) A variant of *méthode rurale* involving *dégorgement.*

Méthode rurale (Fr.) The precursor of *méthode champenoise,* it involves no *secondary fermentation.* The wine is bottled before the first alcoholic fermentation has finished, and *carbonic gas* is produced during the continuation of *fermentation* in the bottle. There is also no *dégorgement.*

Metodo champenois (It.) *See Méthode Champenoise.*

Microclimate Due to a combination of shelter, exposure, proximity to mountains, water mass and other topographical features unique to a given area, a vineyard can enjoy (or be prone to) a specific microclimate.

Micro-porous filter Synonymous with *membrane filter.*

Millerandage (Fr.) A physiological disorder of the vine that occurs after cold or wet weather at the time of the flowering. This makes fertilization very difficult, and consequently many berries fail to develop. They remain small and seedless even when the rest of the bunch is full-sized and ripe.

Mineral Some wines can have a minerally *aftertaste* that can sometimes be unpleasant. Vinho Verde has an attractive, almost tinny, mineral *aftertaste* when made from certain grape varieties.

Mistelle (Fr.) Fresh grape juice that has been *muted* with *alcohol* before any *fermentation* can take place.

Moelleux (Fr.) Lit. "soft" or "smooth", this term usually indicates a rich, medium-sweet wine.

Mousse (Fr.) The effervescence of a sparkling wine, which is best judged in the mouth; a wine may appear to be *flat* in one glass and vigorous in another due to the different surfaces. The bubbles of a good mousse should be small and persistent, the strength of effervescence depending on the style of wine.

Mousseux (Fr.) Denotes a sparkling wine.

Must Unfermented juice extracted from grapes.

Must weight Amount of sugar in ripe grapes or *must.*

Mutage (Fr.) The addition of pure *alcohol* to a wine or fresh grape juice either before *fermentation* can take place, as in the case of a *vin de liqueur,* or during *fermentation,* as in the case of *vin doux naturel. See* Mutage, p.23.

Négociant (Fr.) Trader or merchant. The name is derived from the traditional practice of negotiating with growers (to buy wine) and wholesalers/customers (to sell it).

Négociant-éleveur (Fr.) Wine firm that buys in ready-made wines for *élevage.* The wines are then blended and bottled under the *négociant's* label.

Nervy, nervous Subjective term usually applied to a dry white wine that is *firm* and vigorous, but not quite settled down.

Neutral grape varieties Such grapes include virtually all the minor, nondescript varieties that produce bland tasting, low-quality wines, but also encompass better known varieties such as the Melon de Bourgogne, Aligoté, Pinot blanc, Pinot meunier and even classics like Chardonnay and Sémillon. The opposite of *aromatic grapes,* these varieties are ideal for *oak-maturation,* bottling *sur lie* and turning into fine sparkling wines because their characteristics are enhanced rather than hidden by these processes.

Noble rot A condition caused by the fungus *Botrytis cinerea* under certain conditions. See *Botrytis cinerea.*

Nose The smell or odour of a wine, encompassing both *aroma* and *bouquet.*

Oak, oaky, oak-aged, oak-matured Oak casks are often used for the *maturation* of wines and, less frequently, for their *fermentation.* Oak-matured wines often display a positive odour of *vanilla* from the *aldehyde vanillin* found naturally in oak. The type, degree, subtlety and *complexity* of oak on the *bouquet* and flavour of a wine is affected by many contributory factors: the type of oak (Limousin, Nevers etc.); whether it was kiln-dried or weathered (and how long it was weathered); if it was sawn or split (and how it was sawn or split); the degree to which the barrel was toasted during its manufacture; the size of the barrel; whether it was new or had been used (and, if so, how many times); if the wine was *barrel-fermented* in addition to oak-aged and the length of time the wine was kept in wood. Wines also react differently to the same barrel-fermentation and oak-aging conditions according to their levels of *acidity, tannin* and *alcohol.* It is the sum-effect of all these factors that determines not only the degree of oak encountered in a wine, but also the type of oak character detected. There are in my vocabulary five basic, oak-influenced *aromas* and flavours: *vanilla-oak, creamy-oak, smoky-oak, spicy-oak* and *herbal-oak*. A wine may be predominantly of one category or a combination of two, three, four or all five and the result can induce the use of many other subjective words, including *cedarwood, cigar-box* and, in higher *pH* wines, *chocolate-box*. *See* The choice of oak, p.19.

Oechsle level (Ger.) System of measuring the sugar content in grapes for wine categories in Germany and Austria, *see* p.204.

Oenology The scientific study of wine.

Off vintage, off year A year in which many poor wines are produced due to climatic conditions.

Oidium Fungal disease of the vine that turns leaves powdery grey and dehydrates the grapes.

Oily Subjective term meaning *fat, flat* and *flabby*.

Oloroso (Sp.) A Sherry style, naturally dry but usually sweetened for export markets.

Open-knit An open and enjoyable *nose* or *palate*, usually found in a modest wine not capable of very much development.

Opulent Suggestive of a rather luxurious *varietal aroma*, very *rich,* but not quite *blowzy*.

Organic wines A generic term covering wines that are produced using the minimum amount of *SO$_2$,* from grapes that have been grown without chemical fertilizers, pesticides or herbicides.

Organoleptic Affecting a bodily organ or sense, usually taste and smell.

Osmotic pressure When two solutions are separated by a semi-permeable membrane, water will leave the weaker solution for the other in an endeavour to equalize the differing solution strengths. In winemaking this is most usually encountered when *yeast* cells are expected to work in grape juice with an exceptionally high sugar content. Since water accounts for 65 per cent of a yeast cell, osmotic pressure causes the water to escape through its semi-permeable exterior. The cell caves in, (a phenomenon called plasmolysis), the yeast dries up and eventually dies.

Overtone A dominating element of *nose* or *palate* and usually one that is not directly attributable to the grape, e.g. *oak*.

Oxidation, oxidized These terms are ambiguous; from the moment grapes are pressed or crushed, oxidation sets in and the juice or wine is oxidized to varying extents. Oxidation is an essential and unavoidable part of *fermentation* and, combined with *reduction,* it is the process by which wine *matures* in bottle. All wine is therefore oxidized to a certain extent. What is generally meant by this term, when used derogatorily, is that the wine is in a prematurely advanced stage of oxidation. Such a wine would have a noticeable *Sherry-like* odour.

Oxidative Wine matures by an interaction of *reductive* and oxidative processes. The latter is recognized by characteristics so subtle that they merely bridge the divide between the smell of *fermentation* and the *aroma* of young wine, through various *buttery, biscuity, spicy* characteristics, that develop *richness* and *complexity* along the way.

Pad filtration Filtration system utilizing a series of cellulose, asbestos or paper sheets through which wine is passed.

Palate Flavour or taste of a wine.

Passerillage (Fr.) Grapes without *noble rot* that are left on the vine are cut off from the plant's metabolic system as its sap withdraws into its roots. The warmth of the day, followed by the cold of the night, causes the grapes to dehydrate and concentrate in a process known as passerillage. The sweet wine produced from these grapes is prized in certain areas. A passerillage wine from a hot autumn will be totally different to one from a cold autumn.

Passito (It.) The equivalent of *passerillage*. Passito grapes are semi-dried, either outside on the vine, or on mats; or inside a warm building. This concentrates the pulp and produces strong, often sweet wines.

Pasteurization A generic term for various methods of stabilization and sterilization. *See* Heat, p.18.

Peak The so-called peak in the *maturity* of a wine is a matter of individual preference. Those who prefer *fresh, crisp* wines will perceive an earlier peak in the same wine than "golden oldy" drinkers.

Pear-drop An *aroma* redolent of pear-drop sweets, often noticed in Beaujolais Nouveau and other wines that have undergone intensive *macération carbonique* techniques. The pear-drop *aroma* is due to the increased ethyl acetate content produced by *macération carbonique* and is often confused with the *varietal* character of the Gamay grape.

Peppery (1) Applied to young wines whose various components are raw and not yet in harmony, sometimes quite fierce and prickly on the *nose*. (2) The characteristic odour and flavour of southern French wines, particularly those that are Grenache-based.

Perfume Agreeable scented quality of *bouquet*.

Perlant (Fr.) Very slightly sparkling, less so than *crémant* and *pétillant*.

Perlite A fine, powdery, light and lustrous substance of volcanic origin with similar properties to *diatomaceous earth*. When perlite is used for *filtration,* it is sometimes referred to as *ceramic filtration*.

Pétillant, pétillance (Fr.) A wine with enough residual *carbonic gas* to create a light sparkle.

Petrol, petrolly With some *bottle-age,* the finest Rieslings have a *vivid* and *zesty bouquet* that some refer to as petrolly. The petrolly character has an affinity with various *zesty* and *citrussy* odours, but many *lemony, citrussy, zesty* smells are totally different from one another and the Riesling's petrolly character is both singular and unmistakable.

pH Commonly used chemical abbreviation of *potential hydrogen-ion concentration*. A measure of the *active acidity* or alkalinity of a liquid. It does not give any indication of the *total acidity* in a wine, but neither does the human palate. When we perceive the acidity in wine through taste, it is more closely associated with the *pH* than the *total acidity*.

Phylloxera Worldwide vine louse that spread from America to virtually every viticultural region in the late nineteenth century, destroying many vines. New vines had (and still have) to be *grafted* to phylloxera-resistant American *rootstocks*.

Piquant (Fr.) Usually applied to a pleasing white wine with a positive underlying *fruit* and *acidity*.

Plummy Wine that is *rich* and flavoursome, resembling plums.

Polishing The very last, ultra-fine *filtration* of a wine, usually with *Kieselguhr* or *perlite,* is so called because it leaves the wine bright; many high-quality wines are not polished because the process can wash out natural flavours.

Pourriture Noble (Fr.) *Noble rot,* caused by the fungus *Botrytis cinerea* under certain conditions, *see* Botrytis cinerea.

Prefermentation maceration A much-in-vogue practice of maceration whereby the juice of white grapes is in contact with the skins prior to fermentation. This enhances the *varietal* character, as the skins contain most of the aromatic properties of a grape. *See* White wines, p.22.

Premier cru (Fr.) Lit. a "first growth", but only of relevance in areas where the term is controlled, e.g. Burgundy, Champagne.

Press Wine *See Vin de presse*.

Prickly Wine with residual *carbonic gas,* but with

less than the light sparkle of a *pétillant*. It can be desirable in some *fresh* white and rosé wines, but it is usually taken as a sign of an unwanted *secondary fermentation* in red wines, although it is deliberately created in certain South African examples.

Producer vine Vines are usually *grafted* onto *phylloxera*-resistant *rootstock,* but the grapes produced are characteristic of the above-ground producer vine, which is normally a variety of *Vitis vinifera*.

Protein haze Protein is present in all wines. Too much protein can react with *tannin* to cause a haze, in which case *bentonite* is usually used as a *fining* agent to remove it. *See* Fining, p.20.

PVPP (Polyvinylpolypyrrolidone) *Fining* agent used to remove compounds sensitive to browning from white wines. *See* Fining, p.20.

QbA (Ger.) Commonly abbreviated form of *Qualitätswein bestimmter Anbaugebiet*. Lit. a "quality wine from a specified region", this term is used to indicate a level of quality above *Landwein,* but one beneath *Kabinett*.

QmP (Ger.) Commonly abbreviated form of *Qualitätswein mit Prädikat*. Lit. a "quality wine with predication", this term is used for any German wine above *QbA,* from *Kabinett* upwards. The predication carried by a QmP wine depends upon the level of ripeness of the grapes used in the wine.

Quaffing wine Unpretentious wine that is *easy* and enjoyable to drink.

Quinta (Port.) Wine estate.

Racking Draining a wine off its *lees* into a fresh cask or vat. *See* Racking, p.20.

Racy Often applied to wines of the Riesling grape. It accurately suggests the *liveliness,* vitality and *acidity* of this grape.

Rancio Description of a *vin doux naturel* stored in oak casks for at least two years, often with the barrels exposed to direct sunlight. This imparts a distinctive flavour that is popular in the Roussillon area of France.

Ratafia Liqueur made by combining *marc* with grape juice.

Recioto (It.) Strong, sweet wine made from *passito* grapes.

Redox The aging process of wine was originally conceived as purely *oxidative,* but it was then discovered that when one substance in wine is *oxidized* (gains oxygen), another is *reduced* (loses oxygen). This is known as a *reductive-oxidative,* or redox reaction. *Organoleptically,* however, wines either reveal *oxidative* or *reductive* characters. In the presence of air, a wine is prone to *oxidative* character, but shut off from a supply of oxygen, *reductive* characteristics begin to dominate, thus the *bouquet* of *bottle-age* is a *reductive* one and the *aroma* of a *fresh,* young wine is more *oxidative* than *reductive*.

Reductive The less exposure it has to air, the more reductive a wine will be. Different as they are in basic character, Champagne, Muscadet *sur lie* and Beaujolais Nouveau are all examples of essentially reductive, as opposed to *oxidative,* wine from the vividly *autolytic* Champagne, through Muscadet *sur lie* with its barest hint of *autolytic* character, to the *pear-drop aroma* of Beaujolais Nouveau.

Refractometer An optical device used to measure the sugar content of grapes when out in the field.

Remontage (Fr.) Pumping the wine over the cap or *manta* of skins during the *cuvaison* of red wine. *See* How wine is made, p.18.

Remuage (Fr.) Intrinsic part of *méthode champenoise;* deposits thrown off during *secondary fermentation* are eased down to the neck of the bottle and are then removed at *dégorgement*.

Reticent Suggests that the wine is holding back on

its *nose* or *palate,* perhaps through youth, and may well develop with a little more *maturity.*

Rich, richness A *balanced* wealth of *fruit* and a good *depth* on the *palate* and *finish.*

Ripasso (It.) Refermentation of wine on the *lees* of a *recioto* wine.

Ripe Wine with the *richness* that only ripe grapes can give. It applies to the ripeness of grapes, rather than the *maturity* of wine.

Ripe acid *Tartaric acid,* as opposed to *malic* or unripe *acid.*

Roast Describes the character of grapes subjected to the shrivelling or roasting of *noble rot.*

Robust A milder form of *aggressive,* often applied to a *mature* product, i.e. the wine is robust by nature, not *aggressive* through youth.

Rootstock The lower rooting part of a grafted vine, usually *phylloxera*-resistant. *See* Rootstock, p.11.

Round A wine that has rounded off all its edges of *tannin, acidity, extract,* etc. through *maturity* in bottle.

Saccharometer Laboratory device used for measuring the sugar content of grape juice, based on specific gravity.

Saignée (Fr.) The process of drawing off surplus liquid from the fermenting vat in order to produce a rosé wine from the free-run juice. In cooler wine regions, the remaining mass of grape pulp may be used to make a darker red wine than would normally be possible because of the greater ratio of solids to liquid, providing more colouring pigment.

Scion The part of the *graft* that belongs to the *fruit* and leaf-bearing *producer vine,* as opposed to the *rootstock.*

Sec (Fr.) Dry, as applied to wines, i.e. wines without any sweetness. This does not mean there is no *fruit:* wines with plenty of very ripe *fruit* can seem so *rich* they may appear to have some sweetness.

Second fermentation, secondary fermentation Strictly speaking this is the *fermentation* that occurs in bottle during the *méthode champenoise,* but is sometimes mistakenly used to refer to the *malolactic fermentation.*

Sekt (Ger.) Sparkling wine.

Selection de Grains Nobles (Fr.) In Alsace, a rare, intensely sweet, *botrytized* wine.

Sharp Applies to *acidity,* whereas *bitterness* applies to *tannin.* An immature wine might be sharp, but this term is usually a derogatory one if used by professional tasters.

Sheet filtration Synonymous with *pad filtration.*

Sherry-like Odour of a wine in an advanced state of *oxidation,* and undesirable in wine except Sherry.

Short A wine that may have a good *nose* and flavour, but which falls short on the *finish,* the taste quickly disappearing after the wine has been swallowed.

Smokiness, smoky, smoky-complexity, smoky-oak Some grapes have a smoky character (particularly Syrah and Sauvignon blanc). This can also come from well-toasted *oak* casks, but it is a characteristic that can also indicate an unfiltered wine. Some talented winemakers do not *rack* their wines and sometimes do not *filter* them. This is a passionate bid to retain maximum character and create an individual and *expressive* wine.

Smooth The opposite of *aggressive* and more extreme than *round.*

SO₂ Commonly used chemical formula for *sulphur dioxide.* An *antioxidant* with *aseptic* qualities used in the production of wine. It should not be noticeable in the finished product, but sometimes a whiff may be detected on recently bottled wine. A good swirl in the glass or a vigorous decanting should remove this and after a few months in bottle it ought to disappear altogether. The acrid odour of

sulphur in a wine should, if detected, be akin to the smell of a recently extinguished match. It it has a rotten egg *aroma,* the sulphur has been reduced to *hydrogen sulphide* and the wine may well have formed *mercaptans* that you will not be able to remove. *See* The use of Sulphur, p.20.

Soft Interchangeable with *smooth,* although it usually refers to the *fruit* on the *palate,* whereas *smooth* is more often applied to the *finish.* Soft is very desirable, but "too soft" is derogatory, implying a weak and *flabby* wine.

Solera A system of continually refreshing an established blend with a small proportion of new wine to effect a wine of consistent style and quality. *See* Sherry, p.285.

Solid Interchangeable with *firm.*

Solumological The science of the soil and, in the context of wine, the relationship between specific soil types and vine varieties.

Souped-up A wine that has been blended with something *richer* or more *robust.* Wine may well be legitimately souped-up, or it could mean that the wine has been played around with. The wine might not be *correct,* but it could still be very enjoyable.

Sous-marque (Fr.) Another *marque* under which wines, usually second-rate in quality, are offloaded.

Southern-style The obvious characteristics of a wine from the hot, sunny south of France. For reds, it may well be complimentary at an *honest* basic level, indicating a full-bodied, full-flavoured wine with a *peppery* character. For whites, it will probably be derogatory, implying a *flabby* wine with too much *alcohol* and too little *acidity* and *freshness.*

Soutirage (Fr.) *Racking.*

Sparging The introduction of *carbonic gas* into a wine prior to its bottling, often simply achieved through a valve in the pipe between the vat and the bottling line. *See* Carbonation, p.23.

Spätlese (Ger.) A *QmP* wine that is one step above *Kabinett,* but one below *Auslese.* It is fairly sweet and made from late-picked grapes.

Spicy (1) A *varietal* characteristic (e.g. Gewürztraminer, Scheurebe, etc.). (2) An aspect of a *complex bouquet* or *palate,* probably derived from *bottle-age* after time in wood.

Spicy-oak Subjective term describing complex *aromas* derived from *fermentation* or maturation in oak that can give the impression of various spices, usually "creamy" ones such as cinnamon or nutmeg, and that are enhanced by *bottle-age.*

Spritz, spritzig (Ger.) Synonymous with *pétillant.*

Spumante (It.) Fully sparkling.

Stage A period of practical experience. It has long been traditional for vineyard owners to send their sons on a stage to a great château in Bordeaux. Now the Bordelais send their sons on similar stages to California and Australia.

Stalky (1) A *varietal* characteristic of Cabernet grapes. (2) Lit. applies to wines made from grapes which were pressed with the stalks. (3) Could be indicative of a *corked* wine.

Stretch To dilute or *cut* a wine with water, which is illegal. It can also refer to wine that has been produced from vines that have been stretched to yield a high volume of attenuated *fruit.*

Stuck fermentation When fermentation stops. A stuck fermentation is always difficult to rekindle and, even when successful, the wine can taste strangely bitter. The most common causes are (1) high temperature: when the heat rises to 35°C (95°F) or above; (2) nutrient deficiency: *yeast* cells can die if denied an adequate supply of nutrients; (3) high sugar content: *yeast* cells may die from *osmotic pressure.*

Stylish Wines possessing all the subjective qualities of *charm, elegance* and *finesse.*

Subtle Suggests a wine with a significant yet understated characteristic.

Sulphur dioxide *See SO₂.*

Supple Indicates a wine that is easy to drink, not necessarily *soft,* but suggesting more ease than simply *round* does. With age (or in certain wines, eg. Californian) the *tannin* in wine becomes supple.

Supple tannin Wine *tannin* has a characteristically *hard* tactile effect in the mouth, but it may be described as *supple* in a *mature* wine in which the *tannin* has been *rounded.* There is also the *tannin* that is extracted from very ripe grapes at the earliest stages of *macération.* These hydrolysed *tannins* are the most *supple* of all. Many *tannins* extracted from new oak are hydrolysed.

Sur lie (Fr.) Refers to wines, usually Muscadets, that have been kept on the *lees* and have not been *racked* or *filtered* prior to bottling. Although this increases the possibility of bacterial infection, the risk is worth taking for wines made from *neutral grape varieties.* In the wines of Muscadet it enhances the *fruit* of its normally bland Melon de Bourgogne grape and adds a *yeasty* dimension of depth that can give the flavour of a modest white Burgundy. It also avoids aeration and retains more of the *carbonic gas* created during *fermentation* imparting a certain *liveliness* and *freshness.*

Süssreserve (Ger.) Unfermented, fresh, grape juice commonly used to sweeten German wines up to and including *Spätlese* level, and is also added to cheaper *Auslesen.* It is far superior to the traditional French sweetening method that utilizes grape concentrate because it provides a *fresh* and *grapey* character that is desirable in inexpensive medium-sweet wines.

Table wine A term that often implies a modest-, even poor-quality wine because it is the literal translation of *vin de table,* the lowest level of French wine. However, it is not necessarily a derogatory term as it may also be used to distinguish between a light and a *fortified* wine.

Tafelwein (Ger.) *Table wine* or *vin de table.*

Tannic, tannin Generic terms for various polyphenols in wine derived from the skin (the most *supple*), the pips and stalks (the harshest), sometimes added during the *fining* of a wine. They may also be picked up from new wooden casks, where the type of *oak* used will determine the relative hardness of the tannins found. Tannin may dominate a young red wine with its astringent, mouth-puckering dryness, but *softens* to an *inky* dryness and, finally, a *suppleness* with age.

Tart Refers to a noticeable *acidity,* somewhere between *sharp* and *piquant.*

Tartaric acid The *ripe acid* of grapes that increases slightly when the grapes increase in sugar during the *véraison.*

Tartrates, tartrate crystals Tartaric acid deposits that look like sugar crystals at the bottom of a bottle and are sometimes precipitated when wines have experienced low temperatures. A fine deposit of glittering crystals can be deposited on the base of a cork if it has been soaked in a sterilizing solution of metabisulphite prior to bottling. Both are harmless. *See* Cold Stabilization, p.20.

Tastevin (Fr.) A shallow, dimpled, silver cup used for tasting, primarily in Burgundy.

TbA (Ger.) Commonly abbreviated form of *Trockenbeerenauslese.* A *QmP* for wines produced from individually picked, *botrytized* grapes that have been left on the vine to shrivel. The wine is golden-amber to amber in colour, intensely sweet, viscous, very complex and as different from *Beerenauslese* as that wine is from *Kabinett.*

Teinturier Grape variety with coloured (red), as opposed to clear, juice.

Terroir (Fr.) Lit. the "earth", but in a viticultural sense it refers to the complete growing environment of soil, aspect, altitude, climate and any other factor that may affect the life of a vine.

Tête de cuvée (Fr.) The first flow of juice during the pressing, the cream of the *cuvée*. It is the easiest to extract and the highest in quality with the best *balance* of *acids,* sugars and minerals.

Thin Wine lacking in *body* and *fruit.*

Tight Firm wine of good extract and possibly significant *tannin* that seems to be tensioned like a spring waiting to be released. Its potential is far more obvious than *reticent* or *closed.*

Tobacco Subjective bouquet/tasting term often applied to *oak-matured* wines, usually Bordeaux.

Total acidity The total amount of *acidity* in a wine is usually measured in grams per litre and, because each *acid* is of a different strength, expressed either as sulphuric or *tartaric acid.*

Transvasage (Fr.) Method whereby non-*méthode champenoise* sparkling wines undergo a *second fermentation* in bottle, and are then decanted, *filtered* and re-bottled under pressure to maintain the *mousse.*

Trie (Fr.) Usually used to describe the harvesting of selected overripe or botrytized grapes by numerous sweeps or tries, through the vineyard.

Trockenbeerenauslese See *TbA.*

Typical An over-used and less than honest synonym for *honest.*

Ullage (Fr.) (1) The space between the top of the wine and the head of the bottle or cask. An old bottle of wine with an ullage beneath the shoulder of the bottle is unlikely to be any good. (2) The practice of topping up wine in a barrel to keep it full and thereby prevent excessive *oxidation.*

Undertone *Subtle,* supporting and not dominating like an *overtone.* In a fine wine the *oak*-aging character, for example, will be a relatively strong and simple *overtone* during its formative years and a delicate undertone when the wine is mature, adding to the many other nuances that give it *complexity.*

Ungenerous Wine that has little or no *fruit* and far too much *tannin* and *acidity.*

Unripe acid *Malic acid,* as opposed to *tartaric* or ripe *acid.*

Up-front Suggests an attractive, simple quality immediately recognized, which sums up the wine. Inexpensive Californian wines are often up-front and *laid-back.*

Uvaggio (It.) Wine blended from various grape varieties.

VDL Commonly used abbreviation for *Vin de liqueur.* A *fortified* wine that is normally *muted* with *alcohol* before *fermentation* can begin.

VDN Commonly used abbreviation for *Vin doux naturel.* Fortified wine, such as Muscat de Beaumes de Venise, that has been *muted* during *fermentation,* after it has achieved between 5 and 8 per cent *alcohol.*

VDQS Commonly used abbreviation for *Vin Délimité de Qualité Supérieure.* Quality control system below *AOC,* but above *Vin de table* and *Vin de pays.*

VQPRD Commonly used abbreviation for *Vin de Qualité Produit dans une Région Délimitée.*

Vanilla, vanilla-oak Often used to describe the *nose* and sometimes *palate* of an *oak-aged* wine, especially Rioja. It is the most basic and obvious of *oak*-induced characteristics. *See Oak.*

Vanillin An aromatic *aldehyde* found naturally in both *oak* and vanilla pods.

Varietal, varietal aroma, varietal character The characteristics portrayed in a wine that are directly attributable to and indicative of the variety of grape from which it is made, for example the blackcurrant aroma of Cabernet sauvignon.

Vegetal Applied to wines of a certain *maturity,* often Chardonnay or Pinot, that are well *rounded* and have taken on a *bouquet* pleasingly reminiscent of vegetation, rather than fruit.

Vendange tardive (Fr.) Late harvest.

Véraison (Fr.) The *ripening* period when the grapes do not change much in size, but gain in colour, if black, and increase in sugar and *tartaric acid,* while decreasing in unripe *malic acid.*

Vermouth An *aromatized* wine. The name originates from "wermut", the German for wormwood, its principal ingredient. Earliest examples made in Germany in the sixteenth century were for local consumption only; the first commercial vermouth being Punt-é-Mes, created by Antonio Carpano of Turin in 1786. Traditionally, Italian vermouth is red and sweet, while French is white and dry, but both countries make both styles. Very bland base wines (two or three years old, from Apulia and Sicily in Italy and Languedoc-Roussillon in France) are blended with an extract of aromatic ingredients, then sweetened with sugar and *fortified* with pure *alcohol.* Chambéry, a pale and delicately aromatic wine made in the Savoie, France, is the only vermouth with an official appellation.

Vigneron (Fr.) Vineyard worker.

Vignoble (Fr.) Vineyard.

Vin de garde (Fr.) Wine capable of significant improvement if allowed to age.

Vin de glace (Fr.) French equivalent of *Eiswein.*

Vin de goutte (Fr.) Free-run juice. In the case of white wine, this is the juice that runs free from the press before the actual pressing operation begins. With red wine, it is the fermented wine drained off from the *manta. See* p.21.

Vin Délimité de Qualité Supérieur *See VDQS.*

Vin de l'Année (Fr.) Synonymous with *vin primeur.*

Vin de liqueur *See VDL.*

Vin de paille (Fr.) Lit. "straw wine". Complex sweet wine produced by leaving late-picked grapes to dry and shrivel in the sun on straw mats. *See* the Jura, p.181.

Vin de Pays (Fr.) A rustic style of country wine that is one step above *Vin de table,* but one beneath *VDQS. See* Vin de Pays, p.197.

Vin primeur Young wine made to be drunk within the year. Beaujolais Primeur is the official designation of the most famous vin primeur, but export markets see it labelled as Beaujolais Nouveau most of the time.

Vin de presse (Fr.) Very dark, *tannic,* red wine pressed out of the *manta,* after the *vin de goutte* has been drained off. *See* p.21.

Vin de Qualité Produit dans une Région Délimitée *See VQPRD.*

Vin de table (Fr.) Lit. *table wine,* although not necessarily a direct translation of it. It is the lowest level of wine in France and is not allowed to give either the grape variety or the area of origin on the label. In practice it is likely to consist of various varieties from numerous areas that have been blended in bulk to produce a wine of consistent character, or lack of it, as the case may be.

Vin doux naturel *See VDN.*

Vin d'une nuit (Fr.) A rosé or very pale red wine that is allowed contact with the *manta* for one night only.

Vin gris (Fr.) A delicate, pale version of rosé.

Vin jaune (Fr.) The famous "yellow wine" of the Jura derives its name from the honey-gold colour that results from a deliberate *oxidation* beneath a Sherry-like *flor.* The result is similar to an aged Fino Sherry, although it is not *fortified.*

Vin nouveau (Fr.) Synonymous with *vin primeur.*

Vin ordinaire (Fr.) Lit. "an ordinary wine", this term is usually applied to a French *vin de table,* although it can be used in a derogatory way for anything up to and including an AOC wine.

Vinification The entire process of making wine, from grape-picking to bottling.

Vinimatic An enclosed, rotating *fermentation* tank with blades fixed to the inner surface, that works on the cement-mixer principle. Used initially to extract the maximum colour from the grape skins with the minimum *oxidation,* it is now being utilized for *prefermentation macération.*

Vino da tavola (It.) *Vin de table,* table wine.

Vino de Mesa (Sp.) Table wine, *vin de table.*

Vino novello (It.) Synonymous with *Vin nouveau* (as in Beaujolais Nouveau).

Vinous Winey, characteristic of wine. When used to describe a wine, it infers basic qualities only.

Vintage A vintage wine is the wine of one year's harvest only (or at least 85 per cent according to EEC regulations) and the year may be anything from poor to exceptional. It is a misnomer to use vintage to indicate a wine of special quality.

Vitis vinifera Species covering all varieties of vines providing classic wine-making grapes.

Vivid The fruit in some wines can be so *fresh, ripe,* clean-cut and *expressive* that it quickly gives a vivid impression of *complete* character in the mouth.

Volatile acids These acids, sometimes called *fatty acids,* are capable of evaporating at low temperatures. Too much volatile acidity is a sign of instability, but small amounts play a significant role in the taste and *aroma* of a wine. Formic, butyric and proprionic are all volatile acids found in wine, but *acetic* and *carbonic* are the most important.

Warmth Suggestive of a good-flavoured red wine with a high *alcoholic* content, possibly fairly *mature,* probably a *southern style* wine.

Watershed An area where water drains into a river system, lake or some other body of water.

Watery An extreme qualification of *thin.*

Weight, weighty This term usually refers to the *body* of a wine. It is possible to use weight in contrast to *body,* stating, for example, that a particular wine has "a good weight of *fruit* for such a light-bodied wine".

Weissherbst (Ger.) A single-variety rosé wine produced from black grapes only. *See* p.205.

Wine Lake *EEC* surplus of low-quality *table-wine.*

Winkler scale Synonymous with *Heat Summation* system.

Wood lactones Various *esters* that are picked up from new *oak* and that may be the source of certain *creamy-oak* characteristics.

Wood-matured Normally refers to a wine that has been aged in new *oak.*

Yeast A kind of fungus vital in all winemaking. Yeast cells excrete a number of enzymes, some 22 of which are necessary to complete the chain reaction known as *fermentation. See* Yeast, p.19.

Yeast enzymes Each enzyme acts as a catalyst for one activity and is specific for that task and no other in the *fermentation* process.

Yeasty Not a complimentary term for most wines, but a yeasty *bouquet* can be desirable in a good-quality sparkling wine, especially when young.

Zesty Lively characteristic that suggests a *zippy,* tactile impression, possibly combined with a hint of *citrussy* aroma.

Zing, zingy, zip, zippy All indicative of something refreshing, lively and vital, resulting from a high *balance* of *fruit* and *acidity* or, perhaps, from a *prickle* or *pétillance.*

Guide to good vintages

This chart provides a useful fingertip reference to the comparative performance of over 850 vintages, covering 28 different categories of wine. As with any vintage chart, the ratings should merely be seen as "betting odds". They express the likelihood of what might be reasonably expected from a wine of a given year and should not be used as a guide to buying specific wines. No blanket rating can highlight the many exceptions that exist in every vintage, although the higher the rating, the fewer the exceptions; quality and consistency do to some extent go hand in hand.

KEY TO VINTAGE RATINGS

100*	No vintage can be accurately described as perfect, but those achieving a maximum score are truly great vintages.
90-99*	Excellent to superb
80-89	Good to very good
70-79	Average to good
60-69	Disappointing
40-59	Very bad
0-39	Disastrous

Vintage	1990	1989	1988	1987	1986	1985	1984	1983	1982	1981	1980	1979	1978	1977
BORDEAUX: Médoc/Graves	90	95	88	78	90	92	75	88	98	82	78	85	90	45
BORDEAUX: St.-Emilion/Pomerol	92	95	88	75	85	92	65	85	98	82	75	85	80	45
BORDEAUX: Sauternes/Barsac	92	95	95	60	90	85	60	100	70	70	80	80	65	50
BURGUNDY: Côte d'Or – Red	95	92	98	70	78	100	70	88	80	75	60	75	85	40
BURGUNDY: Côte d'Or – White	98	95	92	80	92	90	80	88	86	85	72	80	88	50
BURGUNDY: Beaujolais – Red	90	90	85	78	85	90	70	90	72	74	55	60	90	55
CHAMPAGNE	85	90	—	—	80	90	—	90	92	90	70	90	80	—
ALSACE	90	95	90	78	88	90	75	100	80	89	60	85	40	33
LOIRE: Sweet White	90	90	90	60	85	87	65	90	85	70	65	55	75	30
LOIRE: Red	90	90	85	40	85	90	75	85	85	80	70	60	80	45
RHÔNE: Northern Rhône – Red	96	95	95	88	86	95	70	98	92	75	78	81	100	50
RHÔNE: Southern Rhône – Red	90	95	92	70	88	90	70	92	88	87	83	78	98	72
GERMANY: Mosel-Saar-Ruwer	100	98	95	75	93	95	50	100	70	75	50	85	55	50
GERMANY: Rhine	95	95	90	78	93	95	50	98	73	75	50	88	55	50
ITALY: Barolo	93	95	95	88	82	95	55	90	95	80	60	85	100	40
ITALY: Chianti	90	65	90	83	80	93	60	85	90	80	70	85	88	75
SPAIN: Rioja	78	85	80	80	80	80	75	88	100	85	80	60	80	25
PORTUGAL: Vintage Port	—	—	—	—	—	90	—	95	85	—	85	—	75	100
USA: California – Red	80	80	85	90	88	98	92	90	88	85	88	80	88	80
USA: California – White	80	82	88	85	90	84	95	86	86	88	90	80	88	85
USA: Pacific Northwest – Red	85	85	85	85	86	96	50	95	84	88	88	80	88	80
USA: Pacific Northwest – White	88	80	80	85	90	96	70	95	83	80	87	80	88	80
AUSTRALIA: Hunter Valley – Red	—	85	80	88	95	90	80	90	80	80	90	98	80	80
AUSTRALIA: Hunter Valley – White	—	90	90	90	95	90	80	90	80	85	98	90	70	70
AUSTRALIA: Barossa Valley – Red	—	85	85	80	88	95	95	70	90	85	80	92	70	80
AUSTRALIA: Barossa Valley – White	—	70	80	80	90	95	95	85	90	70	80	92	90	70
AUSTRALIA: Margaret River – Red	—	85	88	88	88	90	80	80	90	85	80	80	70	90
AUSTRALIA: Margaret River – White	—	88	85	88	88	90	80	80	90	85	90	80	45	70

Low-rated vintages should be treated with extreme caution, but should not be ignored. Although wine investors buy only great vintages of blue-chip wines, the clever wine-drinker makes a beeline for unfashionable vintages at a tasting and searches for the exceptions. This is because no matter how successful the wine, if it comes from a modest year it will be relatively inexpensive.

Close scoring wines Obviously, the smaller the gap between two scores, the less difference one might expect in the quality of the wines, but many readers may think that to discriminate by as little as one point is to split hairs. Certainly a one-point difference reveals no great divide but, on balance, it indicates which vintage has the edge.

*Remember that some wines are not particularly enjoyable, nor even superior, in so-called "great years". Such wines, normally light-bodied, aromatic whites that are best drunk while young, fresh and grapey (e.g. Musct d'Alsace, German *QbA* or *Kabinett* etc.), favour vintages with ratings of between 70 and 85, or lower.

1976	1975	1974	1973	1972	1971	1970	1969	1968	1967	1966	1965	1964	1963	Earlier great vintages
80	90	60	80	40	83	90	62	25	65	92	20	80	15	1961, 1953, 1949, 1945, 1929, 1928, 1900
80	90	60	78	40	83	87	60	25	70	90	20	87	15	1961, 1953, 1949, 1945, 1929, 1928, 1900
85	90	50	65	55	85	85	60	30	88	86	40	72	15	1962, 1959, 1955, 1949, 1947, 1945, 1937
88	20	70	65	85	90	80	98	10	75	89	10	87	20	1961, 1959, 1949, 1945, 1929, 1919, 1915
80	80	75	72	80	85	80	90	20	82	86	10	90	25	1962, 1928, 1921
90	50	55	80	70	85	75	88	45	70	80	55	75	55	1961, 1959, 1957, 1949, 1945, 1929
85	85	60	88	—	88	90	90	—	—	90	—	100	—	1959, 1947, 1945, 1928, 1921, 1914
10	92	50	85	40	90	84	90	40	70	90	30	80	35	1961, 1959, 1953, 1949, 1945, 1937, 1921
92	90	20	85	10	90	84	90	10	65	85	—	85	—	1961, 1959, 1949, 1945, 1921
90	92	85	80	10	85	85	90	10	70	88	10	85	10	1961
85	72	78	85	90	86	93	87	30	88	88	60	90	50	1961
85	68	80	86	90	85	90	87	45	95	88	60	90	35	1961
100	98	45	90	40	98	85	90	40	85	85	40	94	60	1959, 1953, 1949, 1945, 1921
98	100	40	88	40	100	85	92	40	88	85	40	94	60	1959, 1953, 1949, 1945, 1921
80	70	83	50	20	90	85	80	82	88	70	75	90	30	1958, 1947, 1931, 1922
40	85	75	70	65	98	86	85	85	60	40	30	60	30	1947, 1931, 1928, 1911
85	85	84	75	30	45	95	75	95	45	45	75	100	88	1962, 1942, 1934, 1924, 1920, 1916
—	80	—	—	78	—	98	—	—	75	85	—	—	100	1945, 1935, 1931, 1927, 1908
88	86	95	88	80	70	90	79	90	80	78	88	94	70	1951, 1946
80	88	90	88	65	85	92	78	80	90	78	89	92	72	
88	90	88	—	—	—	—	—	—	—	—	—	—	—	
88	88	88	—	—	—	—	—	—	—	—	—	—	—	
70	100	45	80	45	25	70	80	45	80	80	100	75	50	
80	70	80	88	80	20	80	80	80	92	—	—	—	—	
90	80	20	20	—	—	—	—	—	—	—	—	—	—	
90	70	20	25	—	—	—	—	—	—	—	—	—	—	
45	30	45	—	—	—	—	—	—	—	—	—	—	—	
65	30	45	—	—	—	—	—	—	—	—	—	—	—	

Index

Note: Page numbers in *italic* refer to the illustrations.

A

Aan de Doorns Koöp Wynkelder, 354
Aargau, 318
Abad, Tomás, 289
Abelé, Henri, 148
Abruzzi, 260, 262
Abstatt, 237
Abtey, Grosslage, 228
Acacia Winery, 375
Achkarren, 240
Ackermann-Laurance, 158, 163
Aconagua, 408
Adams Vineyard, 391
Adelaide Hills, 431
Adelaide Metropolitan Area, 431
Adelaide Plains, 431
Adelberg, Grosslage, 228
Adelsheim Vineyard, 391
Adgestone, 311
Adler Fels Winery, 372
Aegean, 340
Africa, 349
African Distillers (Afdis), 349
Agassac, Château d', 45, 47
Agawam grape, 403
Agenais, 197
aging, Champagne, 139
Agiorgitiko grape, 29
Agioritikos, 338
Aglianico dei Colli Lucani VT, 265
Aglianico del Vulture DOC, 265
"Agrícola de Gandesa", Cooperativa, 281
Agricola Viña los Vascos, 411
Agronavarra Cenal, 276
aguardente, 296
Agulha, 302
Ahern Winery, 388
Ahlgren Vineyard, 382
Ahr, 214-15
Ain, 197
Airén grape, 268
Ajaccio AOC, 195
Alabama, 398
Alameda, 289
Alameda County AO, 380
Alavesas, Bodegas, 275
Albalonga grape, 24
Albana di Romagna DOCG, 261
Albert-Grivault, Cuvée, 122
Alberta, 404
Albig, 229
Albillo grape, 417
Alcamo DOC, 266
Alcobaço, 307
alcohol, fortified wines, 18, 23
Alden grape, 403
Alderbrook Vineyards, 372
Aldermoor, 311
Aleatico VT, 258
Aleatico di Puglia DOC, 264
Aleatico grape, 364
Alella DO, 279
Alenquer, 307
Alentejo VR, 307
Alexander Valley AVA, 371
Alexander Valley Vineyards, 371
Alezio DOC, 265
Algarve RD, 307
Algeria, 344
Alicante DO, 291

Alicante VT, 258
Alicante bouschet grape, 29, 364
Alice Springs, 441, *441,* 442
Aligoté grape, 24, *24,* 402
Alkoomi Wines, 439
Allandale Winery, 420
Allegro Vineyards, 397
Allesverloren Estate, 351
Allied-Lyons, 287
Allobrogie, 197
Almadén Vineyards, 380
Almansa DO, 291
Almeirim, 307
Aloxe-Corton AOC, 121, 123
Aloxe-Corton Premier Cru AOC, 123
Alpes de Haute Provence, 197
Alpes-Maritimes, 197
Alphen Wines, 350
Alsace, 149-55, 238, 464-5
Alsace Grand Cru AOC, 154
Alsace Sélection de Grains Nobles AOC, 154
Alsace Vendange Tardive AOC, 154
Alsheim, 229
Alta Vineyard Cellar, 377
Altesse grape, 24
Alto Adige DOC, 250, 251-2
Alto Estate, 351
Altus AVA, 398
Altydgedacht Estate, 351
Alvarinho de Monção-Cepa Velha, 301
Alvarinho grape, 24
Amador Foothill Winery, 387
Amberley Estate Vineyard, 448
Amberton Wine, 422
American Wine Growers, 389
Amery Winery, 435
Amigne grape, 317
Amity Vineyards, 391
Amizetta Vineyards, 377
Le Amon, Chateau, 426
Ampuis, *174*
Ampurdán, Cavas del, 281
Ampurdán-Costa Brava DO, 279
Amynteon AO, 338
Anchialos AO, 340
Andalusia WO, 350
Andaluzas, Bodegas, 406
Anderson (S.) Vineyard, 377
Anderson Valley AVA, 369
Anderson Valley Vineyards, 399
André, Pierre, 110, 111
Andres Wines, 404
Andrew Wolf Wine Cellars, 404
Andron-Blanquet, Château, 51, 52
Añejas, Bodegas, 406, 407
L'Angelus, Château, 86
Angers, 163
Anghelu Ruju VT, 266
Angludet, Château, 67
Angove's, 432
Anjou AOC, 165
Anjou Coteaux de la Loire AOC, 165
Anjou Gamay AOC, 165
Anjou Mousseux AOC, 165
Anjou Pétillant AOC, 165
Anjou-Saumur, 156, 163-6
Annereaux, Château des, 98
AP code numbers, 204
aperitifs, 453
Appellation systems:
Appellation d'Origine Contrôlée, 11, 34; Australia, 416-17, 438; USA, 358-9
Aprilia DOC, 259

Apulia, 263-5
Aquilea DOC, 253
Aramon grape, 29
Arbois, 181, 182
Arbois grape, 24
Arbois Mousseux AOC, 182
Arbois Pupillin AOC, 182
Arbois Vin de Paille AOC, 182
Arbois Vin Jaune AOC, 182
Arbor Crest, 391
Arborea DOC, 266
Archambeau, Château d', 75
Archamboult, Pierre, 158
Archanes AO, 340
Arche, Château d', 77
Ardailhou, 197
Ardèche, 197
Argens, 197
Argentina, 406, 407, 408, 410, 412
Argonaut Winery, 387
Argüeso, Herederos de, 289
Argüeso, Manuel de, 289
Arinto grape, 24
Arizona, 398
Arizu, Bodegas, 412
Arkansas, 398
Arkansas Mountain AVA, 398
Armagnac, 184
Armenia, 335
Arras, Château des, 43
L'Arrosée, Château, 86
Arrowfield Wines, 420
Arroyo Seco AVA, 380
Arrabida, 307
Arruda, 307
Arsac, 63
Arsac, Château d', 47
Arterberry, 391
Artisan Wines Ltd, 377
Arvine grape, 317
Ascot, 311
Ashbourne Wine Co., 435
aspect, 13
Aspen Ridge Estate Wines, 448
aspersion, *137*
Assmannshausen, 226
Association of Charta-Estates, 225
Association of Port Wine Shippers, 295
Assyrtiko grape, 24
Asti Spumante DOC, 246
Astley, 311
Atacama, 408
Atlantic Northeast (USA), 392-7
Attilafelsen, Grosslage, 240
Aube, 136
Aubert, Georges, 406
Aubert Fils, 158
Auckland, 446
Aude, 197
Audy, 95
Auflangen, Grosslage, 228
Auggen, 240
Augusta AVA, 399
Ausbruch, 321
Auslese QmP, 213
Ausone, Château, 83, *83,* 86
Australia, 414-42, 464-5
Austria, 319-24
Auxerrois AOC, 154
Auxerrois grape, 24, 149, 403
Auxey-Duresses AOC, 123
Auxey-Duresses Premier Cru AOC, 123
Avaux, Cuvée Clos des, 122
Aveleda, Quinta de, 301
Avignon, 173
Avoca, 424
Avonwood, 311

Ayala & Co., 142
Aymaville VT, 249
Azeitão, 307
Azerbaijan, 335
Azpilicueta Martinez, Félix, 275

B

Babich Wines, 446
Baccala, William, 369
Bacchus grape, 24, 234
Bacharach, Bereich, 217
Bacheroy-Josselin, 110
Backsberg Estate, 351
Baco noir grape, 403, 404
Bad Bergzabern, 232
Bad Dürkheim, 231, 232
Bad Kreuznach, 223
Bad Münster am Stein, 223
Baden, 203, 207, 238-9
Badisches Frankenland, Bereich, 239
Badsberg Koöp Wynkelder, 354
Badstube, Grosslage, 220
Baga grape, 29, 303
Bages, *189*
Bahèzre de Lanlay, Cuvée, 122
Baileys of Glenrowan, 426
Bairrada, 293, 303-4
Baja Montana, 273
Bajo Penedés, *278*
Balaton, Lake, 329
Baldinelli Vineyards, 387
Balgownie Winegrowers, 426
Balic Estate Wines, 448
Ballandean, 442
Ballarat, 424
Ballard Canyon Winery, 384
Ballue-Mondon, Château, 106
Balmes Dauphinoises, 197
Balverne Winery & Vineyards, 372
Banat, 331
Bandiera Winery, 372
Bandol, 194, 195
Bannockburn Vineyards, 428
Banyuls AOC, 190
Banyuls Grand Cru AOC, 190
Barancourt, 142
Barbadillo, 287
Barbaresco DOCG, 246
Barbarossa di Bertinoro VT, 261
Barbé, Château, 101, 102
Barbeito, 306
Barbera d'Alba DOC, 246
Barbera d'Asti DOC, 247
Barbera del Monferrato DOC, 247
Barbera di Linero VT, 249
Barbera grape, 29, 245, 332, 364, 406
Barbier, René, 280
Bardingley, 311
Bardolino DOC, *251,* 254
Bargetto's Santa Cruz Winery, 381
Barkham Manor Vineyard, 311
Barnes Wines, 405
Barnsgate Manor Vineyards, 311
Barolo Chinato DOC, 247
Barolo DOCG, 246, 464-5
Barón, Herederos de Manuel, 289
La Baronnie, 40
Barossa-Eden and Adelaide Hills Region, 431

Barossa Valley, *430, 431,* 464-5
Barrail, Domaine du, 106
Barrique wines, 207, 256, 257
Barry, Jim, 432
Barsac, 36, 69, 70, 71, 72, 73, 77-9, 464-5
Barton & Guestier, 40, 61
Barton Manor, 311
Barwang Vineyard, 422
Bas-Médoc, 45
Basedow Wines, 432
Basel, 318
Basignani, 395
Basilicata, 264, 265
Basque country, 184
Bass Charrington, 66
Bassett's Romavilla Winery, 442
Bastardo grape, 29
Bastor-Lamontagne, Château, 80
Batailley, Château, 56
Bâtard-Montrachet AOC, 123
Baudot, Cuvée, 122
Bay Cellars, 382
Bay of Plenty, 446
Bayerischer Bodensee, Bereich, 237
Béarn AOC, 186
Beau-Séjour-Bécot, Château, 86
Beau-Site, Château, 51, 52
Beau Val Wines, 387
Beaucastel, Château de, 179
Beaujeu, Clos, 171
Beaujolais, 109, 133-5, 464-5
Beaujolais Nouveau AOC, 134
Beaujolais *Primeur* AOC, 133, 134
Beaujolais Supérieur AOC, 134
Beaujolais-Villages AOC, 134
Beaulieu (Britain), 311
Beaulieu Vineyard (California), 377
Beaumet Chaurey, 148
Beaumont, Château, 47
Beaune AOC, 123
Beaune Premier Cru AOC, 123
Beauregard, Château de (Entre-Deux-Mers), 106
Beauregard, Château (Pomerol), 95
Beauséjour, Château, 86
Bécade, Château, 47
La Bécasse, Château, 58
Bechtheim, 229
Beenleigh Manor, 311
Beerenauslese QmP, 213
Bégot, Château, 101
Beiras VR, 307
Bel-Air, Château (Entre-Deux-Mers), 106
Bel-Air, Château de (Pomerol), 98
Bel-Air, Château (St.-Emilion), 98
Bel-Air Lagrave, Château, 47
Bel-Air Marquis d'Aligre, Château, 67
Bel-Orme-Tronquoy-de-Lalande, Château, 47
Belair, Château, 86
Belair-Montaiguillon, Château, 98
Belcier, Château de, 98
Belgrave, Château, 46
Bell Mountain AVA, 399
Belle Rose, Château, 58
Bellerose Vineyard, 371
Bellet AOC, 194, 195
Bellevue, Cave Coopérative, 41
Bellevue, Château, 86

Bellingham, 350
Belvedère le Boucou, Cuvée du, 180
Belzac grape, 417
Ben Lomond Mountain AVA, 380
Bendigo, 424
Benede Oranje WO, 350
Benfield Estate, 422
Benmarl Wine Company, 396
Benoit, Chateau, 391
Benoit, Domaine, 69, 75
Bénovie, 197
Bensheim, 233
Bérange, 197
Berberana, Bodegas, 275
Bereich see individual Bereiche
Berg Schlossberg, 225
Bergat, Château, 86
Bergerac AOC, 184, 186
Bergerac Sec AOC, 186
Bergkeller, 350
Bergkloster, Grosslage, 229
Bergsig Estate, 351
Bergstrasse-Kraichgau, Bereich Badische, 240
Beringer Vineyards, 377
Berliquet, Château, 86
Bern, 318
Bernkastel, 220
Bernkasteler Doctor, 218-19, 218
Beronia, Bodegas, 275
Berri-Renmano Estates, 432
Bertin, Château de, 43
Bertinerie, Château, 43
Bertrams Wines, 350
Berwick Glebe, 311
Berzé-le-Ville AOC, 131
Besombes, Albert, 158
Bessan, 197
Besserat de Bellefon, 142
Best's Wines, 426
Bétault, Cuvée Hugues et Louis, 122
Beychevelle, Château, 61
Beyer, Leon, 152
Bèze AOC, Clos de, 117
Bianchello del Metauro DOC, 262
Bianchi, 412
Bianco Capena DOC, 259
Bianco dei Colli Maceratesi DOC, 262
Bianco del Molise VT, 262
Bianco della Val di Nievole DOC, 258
Bianco di Custoza DOC, 254
Bianco di Pitigliano DOC, 258
Bianco di Scandiano DOC, 261
Bianco Pisano di San Torpé DOC, 258
Bianco Toara VT, 254
Bianco Vergine della Valdichiana DOC, 258
Bichot, A., 110
Bickensohl, 240
Biddenden, 311
Bienvenues-Bâtard-Montrachet AOC, 123
Bierzo DO, 291
Biferno DOC, 262
Bigorre, 197
Bilbaínas, Bodegas, 275
Billardet, Cuvée, 122
Les Billaux, 81
Billecart-Salmon, 142
Biltmore Estate Winery, 399
Bingen, Bereich, 228
Bingen-Kempten, 228
Bingen-Rüdesheim, 228
Birkweiler, 232
Birot, Château, 106
Bischofskreuz, Grosslage, 232

Biston-Brillette, Château, 47
Blaauwklippen, 351
Black Malvoisie grape, 364
Black Tower, 210
Blagny AOC, 123
Blagny Premier Cru AOC, 123
Blaignan, 45
blanc de blancs Champagne, 141
Blanc de Cossan VT, 249
Blanc de la Salle VT, 249
Blanc de Morgex VT, 249
blanc de noirs Champagne, 141
Blanc Vineyards, 369
Blanche Barkly Wines, 428
La Blancherie, Château, 75
La Blancherie-Peyrat, Château, 75
Blanck, Paul, 152
Blandy Brothers, 306
Blanquefort, 44
La Blanquerie, Château, 106
Blanquette de Limoux AOC, 186
Blanquette grape, 24
Blansingen, 240
Bláquez, Hijos de Agustín, 287
Blauburger grape, 322
Blauburgunder grape, 317
Blauer Portugieser grape, 322
Blauer Wildbacher grape, 322
Blaufränkisch grape, 29, 322
Blaye, 100-1, 102
Bleasdale Vineyards, 433
blended wines, Australia, 417
blending, Champagne, 138, 138
Blenheim (New Zealand), 445
Blondeau, Cuvée, 122
Blue Nun, 210, 227
Bobadilla, 289
Boberg Region WO, 350
Boca DOC, 247
Bockenheim, 231
Bodegas see individual Bodegas
Bodenheim, 229
Bodensee, Bereich, 239, 240
Boeger Winery, 387
Bohemia, 329
Boillot, Cuvée, 122
Boirac, Marquis de, 43
Boisset, Jean-Claude, 110, 112
Boizel, 148
Bolandse Koöp Wynkelder, 354
Bolgheri DOC, 258
Bolivia, 406, 407
Bollinger, J., 142
Le Bon, Cuvée Philippe, 122
Bon Courage, 351
Le Bon Pasteur, Château, 95
Bonalgue, Château, 95
Bonfoi, 351
Le Bonheur Estate, 351
Bonnes Mares AOC, 117
Bonnet, 148
Bonnet, Château, 103, 106
Bonnet, Pierre, 158
Bonnezeaux AOC, 165
Bonny Doon Vineyard, 380
Bookers, 311
Boordy Vineyards, 395
Boplaas Estate, 351
Borba, 307
Bordeaux, 36-107, 464-5
Bordeaux AOC, 42
Bordeaux Clairet AOC, 42, 43
Bordeaux-Côtes-de-Francs AOC, 82

Bordeaux-Côtes-de-Francs Liquoreux AOC, 82
Bordeaux Haut-Benauge AOC, 105
Bordeaux mixture, 44
Bordeaux Mousseux AOC, 42, 43
Bordeaux Rosé AOC, 42, 43
Bordeaux Sec, 42
Bordeaux Supérieur AOC, 42
Bordeaux Supérieur Clairet AOC, 42
Bordeaux Supérieur Rosé AOC, 42, 43
Borie-Manoux, 40, 42
Bosch-Guell, Bodegas, 281
Boschendal Estate, 352
Bosco Eliceo VT, 261
Boskydel Vineyard, 395
Le Boscq, Château, 51, 52
Bosquet des Papes, 180
Botha Koöp Wynkelder, 354
Bothy, 311
Botobolar Vineyard, 420
botrytis cinerea, 17, 17, 71, 72, 72, 328
Bottelary Koöp Wynkelder, 354
Botticino DOC, 249
bottle fermented wine, 23
Bötzingen, 240
Bouchaine Vineyards, 377
Bouchard Aîné & Fils, 110
Bouchard Père & Fils, 110
Bouches-du-Rhône, 173, 197
Bourbonnais, 197
Bourdieu, Château (Blaye), 102
Le Bourdieu, Château (Bordeaux), 47
Bourg, 44, 100-2
Bourges, 171
La Bourgette, Château, 106
Bourgneuf-Vayron, Château, 95
Bourgogne AOC, 113
Bourgogne-Aligoté AOC, 113
Bourgogne Aligoté Bouzeron AOC, 129
Bourgogne Clairet AOC, 113
Bourgogne Clairet Hautes-Côtes de Beaune AOC, 123
Bourgogne Clairet Hautes-Côtes de Nuits AOC, 117
Bourgogne Côte Chalonnaise AOC, 129
Bourgogne Coulanges-La Vineuse AOC, 115
Bourgogne Epineuil AOC, 115
Bourgogne Grand-Ordinaire AOC, 113
Bourgogne Grand-Ordinaire Clairet AOC, 113
Bourgogne Hautes-Côtes de Beaune AOC, 124
Bourgogne Hautes-Côtes de Nuits AOC, 117
Bourgogne Irancy AOC, 115
Bourgogne Mousseux AOC, 113
Bourgogne Passetoutgrains AOC, 113
Bourgueil AOC, 164, 168
Bouscaut, Château, 73
Bousquet, Château du, 101
"boutique" wineries, 362
Bouvet Ladubay, 158
Bouvier grape, 24, 322
Bouyot, Château, 80
Bowen Estate, 433
Boyd-Cantenac, Château, 65
Boyton Vineyards, 311
Brachetto d'Acqui DOC, 247
Brachetto d'Alba VT, 247
Brachetto d'Asti VT, 247
Bramaterra DOC, 247
Branaire-Ducru, Château, 61

Branas-Grand-Poujeaux, Château, 47
Brandeston Priory, 311
Brands Laira, 433
brandy, fortification of Port, 296-7
Brane-Cantenac, Château, 65
Braren Pauli Winery, 369
Brauneberg, 220
Braunberger Bereich, 240
Brazil, 406, 407
Breaky Bottom, 311
"breathing", 452
Breërivievallei WO, 350
Breganze DOC, 254
Breisgau, Bereich, 240
Brethous, Château, 106
Briagolong Estate, 428
Bricco del Drago VT, 247
Bricco Manzoni VT, 246
Bricout & Koch, 148
La Bridane, Château, 62
Bridgehampton Winery, 396
Brights Wines, 405
Brillette, Château, 47
Brindisi DOC, 265
Brisbane, 441
British Columbia, 404
British wine, 310
Britton Cellars, 388
Broadfield, 311
Broadwater, 311
Brogsitter's Zum Dom Herrenhof, 210
Brokenwood, 420
Brookfields Vineyards, 446
Brotherhood Winery, 396
Brouilly AOC, 133, 134
Broustet, Château, 77
Brown Brothers, 426, 427
Bru, Domaine du, 43
Bruce, David, 381
Bruisyard, 311
Brulescaille, Château, 101
Brun, René, 148
Brunello di Montalcino DOCG, 257
Brunet, Cuvée, 122
Brympton d'Evercy, 311
Bual grape, 24, 306
Buehler Vineyards, 377
Buena Vista Winery, 362, 363, 371
Buffalo grape, 403
Buitenverwachting, 352
Bulgaria, 325-6
"Bull's Blood", 327
Bullers, 428
Bully Hill Vineyards, 396
Bungawarra, 442
Burdon, John William, 287
Burg, Grosslage, 235
Burg Lichteneck, Grosslage, 240
Burg Neuenfels, Grosslage, 240
Burg Rosenstein, Grosslage, 229
Burg Zähringen, Grosslage, 240
Burgeff, 210
Burgenland, 323
Burger grape, 366
Burgess Cellars, 377
Burgundy, 108-35, 464-5
Burgweg, Grosslage, 223, 225, 235
Burkheim, 240
Burnbrae, 422
Bustamante, José, 289
Buzet, 184
Buzzetto di Quiliano VT, 249
Byrd Vineyards, 395

Branas-Grand-Poujeaux, ...
Caballero, Luis, 287
La Cabane, Terroir de, 62
Cabanelas, Casa de, 302
La Cabanne, Château, 95
Cabardès VDQS, 190
Cabernet d'Anjou AOC, 165
Cabernet de Saumur AOC, 165
Cabernet franc grape, 29, 29; Anjou-Saumur, 164; Australia, 416; Austria, 322; Bordeaux, 36, 38; California, 364; Chile, 408; Libournais, 81; Touraine, 167; Uruguay, 406
Cabernet grape, 29
Cabernet gros grape, 417
Cabernet sauvignon grape, 29, 29; Argentina, 410; Australia, 416; Austria, 322; Bordeaux, 36, 38; Brazil, 406; Bulgaria, 325; California, 364; Canada, 403; Chile, 408, 410; Lebanon, 342; New South Wales, 419; New Zealand, 444; Pauillac, 54; Uruguay, 406; Victoria and Tasmania, 423; Yugoslavia, 332
Cabo Girão, 305
Cabrière Estate, Clos, 352
Cabrières AOC, 191
Cabrières, Domaine de, 180
Cacc'e mmitte di Lucera DOC, 265
Cadaujac, 69
Cadet-Bon, Château, 86
Cadet-Piola, Château, 87
Cadillac AOC, 105
Cagnina VT, 261
Cahors AOC, 184, 186
Caillou, Château, 77
Les Cailloux, Domaine, 179
Cain Cellars, 377
Cakebread Cellars, 377
Calabria, 264, 266
Calçada, Casa da, 301
Caldaro DOC, 252
Cálem, 301
Calera Wine Company, 380
California, 356, 361-88, 464-5
California Shenandoah Valley AVA, 387
Callaway Vineyard & Winery, 388
Calon, Château, 98
Calon-Ségur, Château, 52
Calona Wines Ltd, 404
Caluso Passito DOC, 247
Calvet, 40
Calvimont, Château de, 75
Cambiaso Vineyards, 372
Cambon-La-Pelouse, Château, 47
Camensac, Château, 46
Camina grape, 29
Campania, 264, 265
Campbell's early grape, 29
Campbells Winery, 426
Campidano de Terralba DOC, 266
Campillo, Bodegas, 275
Campo de Borja DO, 291
Campo Romano VT, 247
Campo Viejo, Bodegas, 275
Canada, 402-5
Canaiolo nero grape, 29
Canale, Humberto, 412
Canandaigua Wine Company, 396
Canard Duchene, 142
Canberra, 419

Candia dei Colli Apuani DOC, 258
Cane End, 311
Canepa, José, 411
Canet, Château, 106
Canneto VT, 249
Cannery Wine Cellars, 382
Cannonau di Sardegna DOC, 266
Canon, Château, 87, 98
Canon de Brem, Château, 98
Canon-Fronsac, 100
Canon-La-Gaffelière, Château, 87
Cantemerle, Château, 46
Cantenac, 63
Cantenac-Brown, Château, 65
Canterbury (New Zealand), 446
Canuet, Château, 67
Cap Corse, 194
Cap de Merle, Château, 98
Cap de Mourlin, Château, 87
Cap-Léon-Veyrin, Château, 47
Capbern Gasqueton, Château, 52
Cape Clairault, 440
Cape Mentelle Vineyards, 440
Capel Vale Wines, 439
Capitel San Rocco VT, 254
Capri DOC, 265
Capriano del Colle DOC, 249
Capton, 311
Caramino VT, 246
carbonation, sparkling wines, 23
carbonic gas, 18
Carbonnieux, Château, 72, 73
Carcassonne, 185
Carcavelos RD, 307
Cardaillan, Château de, 75
La Cardonne, Château, 45, 47
La Carelle, Château, 102
Carema DOC, 247
Carey (J.) Cellars, 384
Carignan grape, 29, 364, 406, 417
Carignano del Sulcis DOC, 266
Cariñena DO, 291
Carmel Valley AVA, 380
Carmenère grape, 30
Carmenet Vineyard, 371
Carmes-Haut-Brion, Château, 76
Carmignano DOC, 255, 257
Carnelian grape, 364
Carneros AVA, 375
Carneros Creek Winery, 375
Caronne-Ste-Gemme, Château, 47
Carr Taylor, 311
Carrousel Cellars, 382
Carso DOC, 253
Cartaxo, 307
La Carte, Château, 85, 87
Casa Larga Vineyards, 396
Casa Madero, 401
Casa Martell, 401
Casa Nuestra, 377
Casa Pedro Domecq, 401
Casabello Wines, 404
Casal Garcia, 302
Casal Mendes, 302
Casalinho, 302
Casona, 411
Cassagne-Haut-Canon, Château, 98
Cassan, 197
Cassayre-Forni Cellars, 377
Cassegrain Vineyards, 422
La Cassemichère, Château de, 161

Cassis AOC, 195
Castegens, Château, 98
Castel del Monte DOC, 265
Castel Frères, 40
Castel Mitrano VT, 265
Castell, 235
Castell del Remei, 281
De Castellane, 142-3
Castellblanch, 280
Casteller DOC, 252
Castelli Romani VT, 259
Castelo Rodrigo, 307
Castéra, Château, 48
Castets, Château de, 102
Castillo de Perelada, Cavas del, 281
Castle Cary, 311
Castle Vineyards, 311
Catalan, 197
Catalonia, 277-81
Catamarca, 410
Catawba grape, 403
Cathcart Ridge Estate, 428
Catoctin AVA, 394
Catoctin Vineyards, 395
Cauce Valley, 406
Cauquenes, 409
Caux, 197
Cava DO, 279
Cavas de San Juan (Vinos Hidalgo), 401
Cave Spring, 405
Cavendish Manor, 311
Cayd, 287
Caymus Vineyards, 375
Cayo, Bodegas Simón, 276
Cayuga Lake AVA, 394
Cecubo VT, 259
Les Cèdres, 180
Cellars de Scala Dei, 281
Cellatica DOC, 249
Celler Hisenda Miret, 281
Cellier Le Brun, 448
Central Coast AVA (California), 367
Central Delaware Valley AVA, 394
Central North-West (New South Wales), 419
Central Valley (California), 385-6
Central Victoria, 424
Central Vineyards, Loire, 156, 171-2
Centurion grape, 364
Cerasuolo di Scilla VT, 266
Cerasuolo di Vittoria DOC, 266
Cérons, 69, 70, 72, 73
Cérons, Château de, 76
Certain-Giraud, Château, 95
Certan de May, Château, 93
Certan de May de Certan, Château, 95
Certan-Giraud, Château, 93
Certinaia VT, 258
Cerveteri DOC, 259
Cesanese del Piglio DOC, 259
Cesanese di Affile DOC, 259
Cesanese di Olevano Romano DOC, 259
César grape, 30
Cessenon, 197
Cetto, L.A., 401
Chablis, 109, 114-15, 171
Chablis Grand Gru AOC, 115
Chablis Premier Cru AOC, 115
La Chablisienne, Cave Coopérative, 112
Chadds Ford Winery, 397
Chalet Debonné, 397
Chalk Hill AVA, 371
Chalk Hill Winery, 372
Chalkhill, 311
Chalone AVA, 380
Chalone Vineyard, 380

Chambave Rouge VT, 249
Chambert-Marbuzet, Château, 52
Chambertin AOC, 117
Chambertin-Clos de Bèze AOC, 117
Chambolle-Musigny AOC, 117
Chambolle-Musigny Premier Cru AOC, 117
Champagne, 136-48, 171, 464-5
Champagne Alberto Valdivieso, 411
Champagne Subercaseaux, 411
Champtoceaux, 156
Chamusca, 307
Chanctonbury, 311
Chandesais, Emile, 110
Chandon, Domaine, 375
Chanet, Château, 43
Chanson, Cuvée Paul, 122
Chanson Père & Fils, 110
Chante Cigale, 179
Chante Flûté labels, 128
Chante Perdrix, 180
Chantegrive, Château de, 76
Chanut Frères, 110
Chapel Hill Winery, 435
Chapelle-Chambertin AOC, 117
Chapelle-Madeleine, Château, 85, 87
Chappellet Vineyards, 375
Charal Winery & Vineyards, 405
Charbaut & Fils, A., 143
Charbono grape, 364
Chardonnay grape, 25, 25; Alsace, 149; Argentina, 410; Australia, 416; Austria, 322; Barrique wines, 207; Brazil, 406; California, 366; Canada, 402, 403, 404; Chablis, 114; Champagne, 136; Chile, 408; Côte de Beaune, 121; Mâconnais, 130; New South Wales, 419; New Zealand, 443, 444; Victoria and Tasmania, 423
Charentais, 197
Charlemagne AOC, 124
Charles Vineyard, 311
Charmant, Château, 67
Charmat method, 23
Charmes, Château des (Canada), 405
Charmes-Chambertin AOC, 117
Charron, Château, 102
Charta-wines, 225
Chassagne-Montrachet AOC, 124
Chassagne-Montrachet Premier Cru AOC, 124
Chasse-Spleen, Château, 48
Chasselas AOC, 154
Chasselas grape, 25, 149, 316, 317, 403, 444
Chastelet, Domaine de, 106
Chateau Boswell Winery, 377
Château-Chalon AOC, 182
Chateau Chevalier Winery, 377
Chateau Chevre Winery, 375
Chateau Elan Ltd, 398
Chateau Esperanza Winery, 396
Chateau-Gai Wines, 405
Chateau Grand Travers, 395
Chateau Montelena Winery, 375
Château system, 36; see also individual Châteaux
Chateaumeillant VDQS, 160
Châteauneuf-du-Pape, 176, 177, 179-80

Châtillon-en-Diois AOC, 175
Chaudron, Cuvée Cyrot, 122
Chauvenet, F., 110
Chauvet, A., 148
Chauvin, Château, 87
Chaves, 307
Cheilly-lès-Maranges AOC, 124
Cheilly-lès-Maranges Premier Cru AOC, 124
Chelois grape, 403
Chénas AOC, 134-5
Chêne Marchand, Clos du, 171
Chenin blanc grape, 25, 25; Anjou-Saumur, 163, 164; Argentina, 410; California, 366; Canada, 403; Loire, 156; New Zealand, 444; Touraine, 167
Cher, 197
Cheurlin, 148
Cheval Blanc, Château, 83, 87
Cheval Noir, 92
Cheval Quancard, 40
Chevalier, Domaine de, 73
Chevalier-Montrachet AOC, 124
Cheverny VDQS, 167, 168
Chianti, 242, 255-6, 464-5
Chianti DOCG, 257
Chicama Vineyards, 395
Chicane, Château, 76
Chickering, 311
Chiddingstone, 311
Chifney Wines, 448
Chilford Hundred, 312
Chilling wine, 452
Chilsdown, 312
Chiltern Valley, 312
China, 450, 451
Chinon, 164
Chinon AOC, 167, 168
Chiroubles AOC, 135
Chispa Cellars, 387
Chivite, Bodegas Julián, 276
Chorey-lès-Beaune AOC, 124, 125
Christian Brothers, 375
Chuquisaca, 406
Churchill, 301
Cie de la Vallée de la Loire, 159
Ciel, Clos de, 352
Cienega Valley AVA, 380
Cilento VT, 265
Cilurzo Vineyard & Winery, 388
Cinque Terre DOC, 249
Cinsault grape, 30, 342
Cinzano, 406
"Cirbonera", Cooperativa, 276
Ciro DOC, 266
Cissac, Château, 48
Citran, Château, 48
Clairet AOC, 154
Clairette de Bellegarde AOC, 190
Clairette de Die AOC, 175
Clairette de Die Tradition AOC, 175
Clairette du Languedoc AOC, 190
Clairette grape, 25
La Clape AOC, 191
Clare riesling grape, 417
Clare Valley, 431
Clare-Watervale, 431
claret, 36
Clarke, Château, 48
Clarksburg AVA, 385
classification: Bordeaux, 39; Burgundy, 108; Champagne, 140; French wine, 34; Graves, 70; Sherry, 285

Clastidio VT, 249
Clastidium VT, 249
Clear Lake AVA, 388
Les Clefs d'Or, 180
Clerc Milon, Château, 56
climate, 12
Climens, Château, 70, 77
Clinet, Château, 95
Clinton Vineyards, 396
Clocher, Clos du, 95
clones, grapes, 24
Clotte, Château de (Côtes de Castillon), 98
La Clotte, Château (St.-Emilion), 88
Cloudy Bay, 446
La Clusière, Château, 88
La Clyde, Château, 106
Coastal Region WO (South Africa), 349
Coastal Victoria, 424
Cockburn, 299
Codorníu, 280
Coggeshall Vineyard, 312
Colares RD, 307
cold stabilization, 20
Coldstream Hills, 426
Cole Ranch AVA, 369
Colio Wines, 405
Collard Brothers, 447
Colle del Calvario VT, 249
Colle Picchioni VT, 259
"The College" Winery, 422
Collery, 143
Colli Albani DOC, 259
Colli Altotiberini DOC, 259
Colli Berici DOC, 254
Colli Bolognese DOC, 261
Colli di Bolzano DOC, 252
Colli di Parma DOC, 261
Colli dei Trasimeno DOC, 259
Colli Euganei DOC, 254
Colli Goriziano DOC, 252
Colli Lanuvini DOC, 259
Colli Morenici Mantovani del Garda DOC, 254
Colli Orientali del Friuli DOC, 252-3
Colli Perugini DOC, 259
Colli Piacentini DOC, 261
Colli Tortonesi DOC, 247
Collignon, Cuvée Madeleine, 122
La Colline de Sarre et Chesallet VT, 249
Collines de la Moure, 197
Collines Rhodaniennes, 197
Collioure AOC, 190
Colombard grape, 25
Colombia, 406-7
Colombier-Monpelou, Château, 58
Colorado, 398
colour, of wine, 7, of grapes, 24
Columbia Valley AVA, 390
Columbia Winery, 391
La Commanderie, Château, 92
Commanderie St. John, 341
Commonwealth Winery, 395
Compagnie Française des Grands Vins, 158
Companhia Monaco-Vinhedos, 406
Companhia Vinicola Riograndense, 406
Compostela, Casa de, 301
Comté de Grignan, 197
Comté Tolosan, 197
Conca de Barberá DO, 279
Concannon Vineyard, 381
Concha y Toro, 411
Concord grape, 30, 402, 403
Condado de Huelva DO, 286

Conde de Caralt, 281
La Condesa, 289
Condrieu, 173, 174, 175
Confrérie des Chevaliers du Sacavins, 163
Confrérie des Chevaliers du Tastevin, 116
Confrérie des Vignerons de Oisly et Thesée, 159
Conghurst, 312
Congress Springs Vineyard, 380
Conilh-Libarde, Château, 101
Conn Creek Winery, 375
Connecticut, 395
La Conseillante, Château, 95
Consejo Regulador, 270
Constantia WO, 349
Constantin, Château, 69, 76
Constantin, Paul, 440
Contino, 274
Contra Costa County AO, 380
Convento de Alpendurada, 302
Cook (R. & J.) Winery, 386
Cook-Ellis Winery, 382
Cooks, 443, 444, 445, 447
cool fermentation, 103, 104
Coonawarra, 416, 431, 432
Cooperativa Agricola Vitivinicola de Curicó, 411
Cooperativa Agricola Vitivinicola de Talca, 411
coopératives: Alsace, 153; Bordeaux, 41; Burgundy, 112; Catalonia, 281; Champagne, 148; Germany, 209-10; Loire, 159; Navarra, 276; Rioja, 276; South Africa, 354
Coopers Creek Vineyards, 444, 447
Coperco Sacia, 412
Copertino DOC, 265
Coquimbo, 408
Corbans, 444, 445, 447
Corbières AOC, 190
Corbin, Château, 88
Corbin Michotte, Château, 88
Cordeillan, Château de, 58
Cordeliers, 43
Cordier, 40, 42, 53, 60, 61, 62, 171
Cordtz Brothers Cellars, 373
Cori DOC, 259
Coriole, 433
corks, Champagne, 139, 139
Cornas AOC, 174, 175
Coron, Père & Fils, 110
Corowa, 419
Corral, Bodegas, 275
Corsica, 193-6
Cortese dell'Alto Monferrato DOC, 247
Cortese di Gavi, 246
Corton-Charlemagne AOC, 124
Coruche, 307
Corvina grape, 30
Corvo VT, 266
Cos d'Estournel, Château, 51, 51, 52
Cos Labory, Château, 52
"Cosecheros Alaveses", Sociedad Cooperativa, 276
Cossart Gordon, 306
Coste, Edmund & Fils, 40
Costello Vineyards, 377
Costers del Segre DO, 279
Costières de Nîmes VDQS, 190
Côte Baleau, Château, 88
Côte Châlonnaise see Mercurey
Côte de Beaune, 109, 121-6

Côte de Beaune-Villages AOC, 125
Côte de Brouilly AOC, 135
Côte de Nuits, 109, 116-20
Côte de Nuits-Villages AOC, 118
Côte d'Or, 464-5
Côte Rôtie, 173, 174
Côte Rôtie AOC, 175
Côte de Sézanne, 136
Côte Vermeille, 197
Coteaux d'Aix-en-Provence AOC, 194, 195
Coteaux d'Aix-en-Provence-les-Baux AOC, 195
Coteaux d'Ancenis VDQS, 162
Coteaux de l'Ardèche, 198
Coteaux de l'Aubance AOC, 165
Coteaux des Baronnies, 198
Coteaux de Bessilles, 198
Coteaux de la Cabrerisse, 198
Coteaux Cévenols, 198
Coteaux de Cèze, 198
Coteaux Champenois AOC, 148
Coteaux Charitois, 198
Coteaux du Cher et de l'Arnon, 198
Coteaux de la Cité de Carcassonne, 198
Coteaux d'Enserune, 198
Coteaux des Fenouillèdes, 198
Coteaux Flaviens, 198
Coteaux de Fontcaude, 198
Coteaux du Giennois Cosne-sur-Loire VDQS, 172
Coteaux du Giennois VDQS, 172
Coteaux de Glanes, 198
Coteaux du Grésivaudan, 198
Coteaux du Langeudoc AOC, 190-1
Coteaux de Laurens, 198
Coteaux du Layon AOC, 164, 165
Coteaux du Layon-Chaume AOC, 166
Coteaux du Layon Villages AOC, 166
Coteaux de Lézignanais, 198
Coteaux du Libron, 198
Coteaux du Littoral Audois, 198
Coteaux du Loir AOC, 167, 168
Coteaux du Lyonnais AOC, 135
Coteaux de Miramont, 198
Coteaux de Murviel, 198
Coteaux de Narbonne, 198
Coteaux de Peyriac, 198
Coteaux de Pierrevert VDQS, 177
Coteaux du Pont du Gard, 198
Coteaux du Quercy, 198
Coteaux du Salagou, 198
Coteaux du Salavès, 198
Coteaux de Saumur AOC, 166
Coteaux du Termenès, 198
Coteaux et Terrasses de Montauban, 198
Coteaux du Tricastin AOC, 177
Coteaux Varois VDQS, 195-6
Coteaux du Vendômois VDQS, 167, 168
Côtes Catalanes, 198
Côtes d'Auvergne VDQS, 160
Côtes de Bergerac AOC, 186
Côtes de Bergerac Moelleux AOC, 186

Côtes des Blancs, 136, 140
Côtes de Blaye AOC, 101
Côtes-de-Bordeaux-St.-Macaire AOC, 105
Côtes de Bourg AOC, 101
Côtes du Brian, 198
Côtes du Brulhois VDQS, 186-7
Côtes de Buzet AOC, 186
Côtes-Canon-Fronsac AOC, 82
Côtes-de-Castillon AOC, 82
Côtes du Céressou, 198
Côtes du Condomois, 198
Côtes de Duras AOC, 186
Côtes de Forez, Cave Coopérative, 159
Côtes de Forez VDQS, 160
Côtes du Frontonnais AOC, 187
Côtes de Gascogne, 198
Côtes du Jura AOC, 182
Côtes du Jura Mousseux AOC, 182
Côtes du Jura Vin de Paille AOC, 182
Côtes du Jura Vin Jaune AOC, 182
Côtes de Lastours, 199
Côtes de Libac, 200
Côtes du Lubéron VDQS, 177
Côtes de la Malepère VDQS, 191
Côtes du Marmandais AOC, 187
Côtes de Montestruc, 199
Côtes de Montravel AOC, 186
Côtes de Pérignan, 199
Côtes de Prouillé, 199
Côtes de Provence AOC, 196
Côtes-du-Rhône AOC, 173, 175, 177
Côtes-du-Rhône Beaumes-de-Venise, 178
Côtes-du-Rhône Cairanne, 178
Côtes-du-Rhône Chusclan, 178
Côtes-du-Rhône Laudun, 178
Côtes-du-Rhône Pantaléon-les-Vignes, 178
Côtes-du-Rhône Rasteau, 178
Côtes-du-Rhône Roaix, 178
Côtes-du-Rhône Rochegude, 178
Côtes-du-Rhône Rousset-les-Vignes, 178
Côtes-du-Rhône Sablet, 178
Côtes-du-Rhône St.-Gervais, 178
Côtes-du-Rhône St.-Maurice-sur-Eygues, 178
Côtes-du-Rhône Séguret, 178
Côtes-du-Rhône Vacqueyras, 178
Côtes-du-Rhône Valreas, 178
Côtes-du-Rhône-Villages AOC, 177-8
Côtes-du-Rhône Vinsobres, 178
Côtes-du-Rhône Visan, 178
Côtes Roannaises VDQS, 160
Côtes du Roussillon AOC, 191
Côtes du Roussillon Villages AOC, 191
Côtes du Roussillon Villages Caramany AOC, 191
Côtes du Roussillon Villages Latour de France AOC, 191
Côtes de Saint-Mont VDQS, 186
Côtes du Tarn, 199
Côtes de Thau, 199
Côtes de Thongue, 199
Côtes de Toul VDQS, 154
Côtes du Ventoux AOC, 178

Côtes du Vidourle, 199
Côtes du Vivarais VDQS, 178
Cóto, Bodegas el, 274
Coturri & Sons Ltd, 373
Coufran, Château, 48
Couhins, Château, 74
Couhins-Lurton, Château, 74
Courlat, Château du, 98
La Couronne, Château, 58
Coursou, Château, 106
Courtey, Château, 43
La Couspaude, Château, 88
Coustolle Vincent, Château, 98
Coutet, Château, 78, 88
Le Couvent, Château, 88
Cova de Beira, 307
Covial, 276
Covides, 281
Cowra, 419
Coxley, 312
Craiglee, 428
Craigmoor Winery, 420
Cranmore, 312
Crasto, Quinta do, 302
Crawford River, 428
crémant Champagne, 141
Crémant d'Alsace AOC, 154
Crémant de Bordeaux AOC, 42
Crémant de Bourgogne AOC, 113
Crémant de Limoux AOC, 187
Crémant de Loire AOC, 159
Creme du Vien de Nus VT, 249
Crépy AOC, 182
Crescini Wines, 382
Cresta Blanca, 369
Crete, 340
Criots-Bâtard-Montrachet AOC, 125
Croatia, 333
Le Crock, Château, 52
Croffta, 312
Croft, 287, 295, 299
Croft Castle, 312
La Croix, Château, 95
La Croix de Gay, Château, 95
Croizet-Bages, Château, 56
Cronin Vineyards, 382
Croque Michotte, Château, 88
Cros, Château du, 106
Crose, Brian, 435
Crosswood Vineyards, 395
Croute-Courpon, Château, 101
Crozes-Hermitage AOC, 175
Cru Bourgeois, 38
Cru Classé, 38
Cruchen blanc grape, 25
Crusquet-de-Lagarcie, Château, 102
Cruzeau, Château du, 76
Cruzeiro, Quinta do, 302
Cucugnan, 199
La Cuesta, 289
Culbertson Winery, 388
Culemborg Wines, 350
Cullens, 439
Culotta, 405
Cumberland Valley AVA, 394
Cunhas, Casa dos, 302
Curé Bon La Madeleine, Château, 88
Curvos, Quinta de, 302
Cuvaison, 375
cuve close, 23
cuvées de prestige Champagne, 141
Cuvillo, 287
CVBG, 40
CVNE, 274
Cyclades, 340
Cygnet Cellars, 381
Cyprus, 341-2
Czechoslovakia, 327, 328, 329

D

D'Agostini Winery, 387
Dalem, Château, 98
Dalsheim, 229
Dames de la Charité, Cuvée, 122
Dames Hospitalières, Cuvée, 122
Dão, 293, 303-4
Daphnes AO, 340
D'Arenberg Wines, 433
Daringa, Dennis, Cellars, 435
D'Armailhac, Château, 56
Dassault, Château, 88
Daubhaus, Grosslage, 225-6
Daume Winery, 388
La Dauphine, Château de, 98
Dauzac, Château, 65
David & Foillard, 110
De Bortoli Wines, 421
De Chaunac grape, 404
De Loach Vineyards, 373
De Moor Winery, 377
De Muller, 281
De Redcliffe Estates, 447
De Rivoyre & Diprovin, 40
De Vite VT, 252
decanting wine, 452
Deckrot grape, 30
Deer Park Winery, 377
dégorgement, Champagne, 139
Dehlinger Winery, 371
Deidesheim, 231, 232
Deinhard, 208, 210, 219
Deiss, Domaine Marcel, 152
Delaforce, 299
Delaire Vineyards and Wines, 352
Delatite Winery, 428
Delaware, 395
Delaware grape, 25, 403
Delegat's, 447
Delgado Zuleta, 287
Delheim Wines, 352
Delicato Vineyards, 386
Delorme, André, 110
Denby's, 312
Denominación de Origen (DO), 270
Denominación de Origen Calificada (DOCa), 270
Denominazione di Origine Controllata (DOC), 242-4
Denominazione di Origine Controllata e Garantita (DOCG), 243-4
Desmirail, Château, 65
Desmoulins, A., 148
dessert wines, Australia, 414
Destieux, Château, 92
Detzem, 221
Deutelsberg, Grosslage, 226
Deutscher Qualitätsschaumwein Bestimmter Anbaugebiete (QbA), 213
Deutscher Sekt, 213
Deutscher Tafelwein, 212
Deutz and Geldermann, 143, 210
Deux-Sèvres, 199
Devil's Cauldron Vineyard, 312
Devlin Wine Cellars, 382
Deyrem-Valentin, Château, 67
Dezize-lès-Maranges AOC, 125
Dezize-lès-Maranges Côte de Beaune AOC, 125
Dezize-lès-Maranges Premier Cru AOC, 125
Diamond Creek Vineyards, 375

Diamond Valley Vineyards, 428
Die, 174
Dienheim, 229
diethylene glycol, 320
Díez-Mérito, 287
Dintrans, Château, 106
Dirmstein, 232
Distribuidora Valle Redondo, 401
Ditchling, 312
Divinos, 406
Dobrudja, 331
Doctor, 218-19, *218*
Dodecanese, 340
Doisy-Daëne, Château, 78
Doisy-Dubroca, Château, 78
Doisy-Védrines, Château, 78
Dolceacqua DOC, 249
Dolcetto VT, 247
Dolcetto d'Alba DOC, 247
Dolcetto d'Acqui DOC, 247
Dolcetto d'Asti DOC, 247
Dolcetto di Diano d'Alba DOC, 247
Dolcetto di Dogliani DOC, 247
Dolcetto delle Langhe Monregalesi DOC, 247
Dolcetto di Ovada DOC, 247
Dôle OA, 317
Dom Ferraz, 302
Domaines *see individual Domaines*
Domblick, Grosslage, 229
Domecq, Bodegas, 275
Domecq, Pedro, 287-8
Domeyne, Château, 51, 52
Domherr, Grosslage, 228
Domina grape, 30
La Dominique, Château, 88-9
Donatien Bahuaud, 158
Donauland-Carnuntum, 324
Donna Marzia VT, 265
Donnaz DOC, 249
Donnici DOC, 266
Doonkuna Estate, 422
Dopff & Irion, 152
Dopff "Au Moulin", 152
Dordogne, 199
Dorin OA, 317
Dorsheim, 223
Doudet-Naudin, Maison, 110
Douglas WO, 350
Douro, 295-302
Dourthe Frères, 40, 42
Dow's & Co., 300
Downers, 312
Drappier, André, 148
Drathen, Ewald Theodor, 210
Drôme, 200
Dromona Estate, 428
Drouhin, Cuvée Maurice, 122
Drouhin, Joseph, 110, 111
Drumborg, 424
Dry Creek Valley AVA, *370,* 371
Dry Creek Vineyard, 371
Dry River, 448
Du Barry, Château, 92
Du Bois, Clos, 371
Du Toitskloof Koöp Wynkelder, 354
Duboeuf, Georges, 110
Dubos Frères, 40, 42
Dubroca, Louis, 40
Duckhorn Vineyards, 375
Ducru-Beaucaillou, Château, 61
Duff Gordon, 288
Duhart-Milon-Rothschild, Château, 56
Dulong Frères & Fils, 40
Dummay, Cuvée Charlotte, 122
Dunavska Raunina, 326
Dunn Vineyards, 375

Durand Laplaigne, Château, 98
Durbach, 240
Durbanville WO, 349
Durfort-Vivens, Château, 65
Durieu, Domaine, 180
Durney Vineyard, 381
Dutruch-Grand-Poujeaux, Château, 48
Duttweiler, 232
Duval, Jules & Fils, 143
Duval-Leroy, 143

E

Eagle Hawk, 435
Early Burgundy grape, 365
Eberstadt, 237
Echézeaux AOC, 118
Ecuador, 407
Edelzwicker AOC, 154
Eden Valley, 432
Edenkoben, 232
Edesheim, 232
Edmeades Vineyards, 369
Edna Valley AVA, 383
Edna Valley Vineyard, 384
Eersterivier Valleise Koöp Wynkelder, 354
Efringen-Kirchen, 240
Eger, 329
Eglantine, 312
L'Eglise, Château du Domaine de, 95
L'Eglise, Clos, 93, 96
L'Eglise-Clinet, Château, 96
Egypt, 342
Ehlers Lane Winery, 377
Ehrenfelser grape, 25
Eibelstadt, 235
Eikendal Vineyards, 352
Eitelsbach, 221
El Dorado AVA, 387
El Dorado Vineyards, 387
Elba DOC, 258
Elbling grape, 25, 317
Elgee Park, 426
Elham Valley, 312
Elk Run Vineyard, 395
Elmham Park, 312
Elms Cross, 312
Elmslie, Chateau, 428
Elsinore Wines, 442
Eltville, 226
Elvira grape, 403
Embajador, 412
Emerald Riesling grape, 25, 366
Emilia-Romagna, 260, 261
L'Enclos, Château, 96
Encostas da Aire, 307
Enfer d'Arvier DOC, 249
England *see* Great Britain
English Viticultural Association (EVA), 313
English Wine Centre, 312
Les Enterprises Verdi, 405
Entre-Deux-Mers, 103-7
Entre-Deux-Mers-Haut-Benauge AOC, 105
Enz Vineyards, 382
Epirus, 339
Erbach, 226
Erbaluce di Caluso DOC, 247
Erden, 221
Erntebringer, Grosslage, 226
L'Escardre, Château, 102
Eschbach, 232
Eschenauer, Louis, 40, 42, 67, 75, 158
Escherndorf, 235
Esmeralda, Bodegas, 412
Esparte grape, 417

Essex Crown Vineyards, 312
Est! Est! Est! di Montefiascone DOC, 259
Est. Vitivin. Escorihuela, 412
Estévez, José, 289
Estornell Exporta, 412
Estrella River Winery, 384
Estremadura VR, 307-8
Etchart, Arnaldo, 412
Etna DOC, 266
L'Etoile AOC, 182
L'Etoile Mousseux AOC, 182
European Economic Community (EEC), 293
L'Evangile, Château, 93, 96
Evans & Tate, 439
Evensen Vineyards & Winery, 377
Ewig Leben, Grosslage, 235
"eye" of a wine, 7
Eyquem, Château, 101
Eyrie Vineyards, 391

F

Faber, 211
Faber grape, 25
Faget, Château, 53
Fairview Estate, 352
Faiveley, Maison, 110-11
Il Falcone DOC, 264
Falerio dei Colli Ascolani DOC, 262
Falerno VT, 259, 265
Far East, 450-1
Far Niente, 377
Fara DOC, 247
Fareham Estate, 435
Fargues, Château de, 70, *71,* 80
Farm Cove, 414
Faro DOC, 266
Faugas, Château, 43
Faugères AOC, 191
Faurie de Souchard, Château, 89
Faustino Martínez, Bodegas, 275
Favorita VT, 247
Fayau, Château, 106
Feher Szagos grape, 366
Felsberg Vineyards-Winery, 442
Felsted Vineyards, 312
Felton-Empire Vineyards, 381
Fendant OA, 317
Fenestra Winery, 381
Fenlandia Vineyards, 312
Fenn Valley Vineyards, 395
Fennville AVA, 394
Fergusson's Winery, 428
fermentation, 18-19, *19,* 21, 23; Bordeaux, 38; Champagne, 138-9, *138-9;* cool, 103, 104; malolactic, 114, 138; Port, 296-7; Sherry, 284
Fernandez (Antonio) y Cia, 401
Ferrand, Château de, 92
Ferrande, Château, 76
Ferraud, Pierre & Fils, 111
Ferreira, 300
Ferrer Mateu, José, 281
Ferret, Cavas, 281
Ferrière, Château, 65
Fetzer Vineyards, *368,* 369
Feuerberg, Grosslage, 231
Feytit-Clinet, Château, 96
Fiano di Avellino DOC, 265
Ficklin Vineyards, 386
Fiddletown AVA, 387
Fiefs Vendéens VDQS, 162
Field Stone Winery, 373
Fieuzal, Château, 74

Figeac, Château, 83, *83,* 89
Filhot, Château, 78
Filippi (J.) Vintage Co., 388
Filsinger Vineyards & Winery, 388
filtering dregs, 452
filtration, 18
Filzen, 221
Finca Flichman, 412
Fines-Roches, Château des, 180
Finger Lakes AVA, 394
Finger Lakes Wine Cellars, 396
fining, 20
Finn Valley Vineyard, 312
Firestone Vineyard, 384
Fisher Vineyards, 373
Fitou AOC, 191-5
Fitzpatrick Winery & Vineyards, 387
Five Chimneys, 312
Fixin AOC, 118
Fixin Premier Cru AOC, 118
Flein, 237
La Fleur, Château, 92
Fleur Cardinale, Château, 92
Fleur du Cap, 350
La Fleur-Milon, Château, 58
La Fleur Pétrus, Château, 93, 96
La Fleur Pourret, Château, 92
Fleurie AOC, 133, 135
Flexerne, 312
Flints, 312
flor, Sherry, 284
Flora grape, 366
Flora Springs Wine Company, 375
Florida, 398
Floridène, Clos, 76
Florio, 412
Fogarty (Thomas) Winery, 382
Folie à Deux, 375
Folle Blanche grape, 25, 366
Fombeney, Jammy, 80
Fombrauge, Château, 92
Fonbadet, Château, 58
Fonchereau, Château, 43
Fongrave, Château, 106
Fonplégade, Château, 89
Fonréaud, Château, 48
Fonroque, Château, 89
Fonseca, 300
Font du Loup, Domaine, 180
Font de Michelle, Domaine, 180
Fontanelle VT, 262
Fonthill, 312
food and wine, 453-5
Foppiano Vineyards, 373
Forbes-Cowra, 419
Forest Hill Vineyard, 440
Forman Vineyards, 377
Formex Ibarra, 401
Forneret, Cuvée, 122
Fornerot, Château, 92
Forrester, Baron Joseph, 298
Forst an der Weinstrasse, 231-2
Forta grape, 25
Fortia, Château, 179
fortified wines, 18, 23, 296-7, 414
Fortino Winery, 381
Foster & Company, 442
Fouché, Château, 43
Fouquerand, Cuvée, 122
Fourcas-Dupré, Château, 48
Fourcas-Hosten, Château, 48
Le Fournas Bernadotte, Château, 48
Fourtet, Clos, 87
Franc Bigoroux, Château, 92
Franc-Mayne, Château, 89
La Française d'Exportation, 158

France, 34-200; classification of wines, 34; *vins de pays,* 197-200; wine production, 34; *see also individual regions*
Franche Comté, 200
Franciacorta, 248
Franciscan Vineyards, 375
Franco Españolas, Bodegas, 275
Francois, Chateau, 420
Françoise-de-Salins, Cuvée, 122
Franconia VT, 253
Franken, 234-5
Frankland, 437, 438
Franschhoek Vineyard Koöp Wynkelder, 354
Franzia Winery, 386
Frascati DOC, 259
Frauenzimmern, 237
Fredericksburg AVA, 399
Freinsheim, 232
Freisa d'Asti DOC, 247
Freisa di Chieri DOC, 247
Freisamer grape, 25
Freixedas, Bodegas J., 281
Freixenet, 280
Freemark Abbey Winery, 375
French Colombard grape, 366
French Guiana, 407
Fretter Wine Cellars, 382
Frey Vineyards, 369
Fribourg, 318
Frick Winery, 382
Frithsden, 312
Fritz Cellars, 373
Friuli-Venezia Giulia, 251, 252-3
Frog's Leap Winery, 375
Fronsac AOC, 82, 100
Frontignac grape, 417
Frontonnais, 184
frost, aspersion, *137*
Frühroter Veltliner, 322
Fruity gordo grape, 417
Fryars Vineyard, 312
Fulton Valley Winery, 373
Furlotti, Angel, 412
Furmint grape, 25, 322, 332, 444
Fürsteneck, Grosslage, 240
Fürstlich Castell'sches Domänenamt, 210

G

Gabiano DOC, 247
Gaby, Château du, 98
La Gaffelière, Château, 89
Gaillac AOC, 187
Gaillac Doux AOC, 187
Gaillac Mousseux AOC, 187
Gaillac Premières Côtes AOC, 187
Gaillac Sec Perlé AOC, 187
Galestro VT, 258
Gallaire & Fils, 40
Gallo (E. & J.) Winery, 386, 416
Gamay Beaujolais grape, 365
Gamay blanc grape *see* Muscadet grape
Gamay della Valle d'Aosta VT, 249
Gamay grape, 30, *30;* Beaujolais, 133; California, 365; Canada, 402, 404; Mâconnais, 130; New Zealand, 444; Switzerland, 317; Touraine, 167
Gamay-Pinot Nero VT, 249
Gamba, 302
Gambellara DOC, 254

Gamlingay Vineyard, 312
La Garance, Château, 69
García-Delgado, Fernando, 289
Gard, 200
Le Gardera, Château, 106
La Gardine, Château de, 180
La Garence, Château, 76
Garganega bianco grape, 25
Gargantini, Bodegas, 412
Garnacha grape, 272
Garrafeira, 308
Garvey, 288
Gascony, 184
Gatão, 302
Gattinara DOC, 246-7
Gau-Bickelheim, 228
Gauvain, Cuvée, 122
Gavi DOC, 246
Le Gay, Château, 96
Gazela, 302
Gazin, Château, 96
Gebiets-Winzergenossenschaft Deutsches Weintor eG, 209
Gebiets-Winzergenossenschaft Franken eG, 209
Gebietswinzergenossen-schaft Rietburg eG, 210
Gedeonseck, Grosslage, 217
Geelong, 424-5
Geisenheim, 225
Geisweiler, 111
Gemello Winery, 381
generic wines: Bordeaux, 42-3; Burgundy, 113; Germany, 212-13; Graves, 73; Loire, 159
Geneva, 317
Génibon, Château, 101
Gentili (J.H.) Wines, 382
Gentilini, 339-40
Georgia (USA), 398
Georgia (USSR), 335
Germain, H. & Fils, 148
Germain, Vins René, 40
Germany, 202-39:
cooperatives, 209-10; generic wines, 212-13; labels, 202, 204, 205; legislation, 202; Sekt, 210-11, 213; vintages, 464-5; wine production, 204; wineries, 208-9; see also individual regions
Gerwer Winery, 387
Gevrey-Chambertin AOC, 118
Gevrey-Chambertin Premier Cru AOC, 118
Gewürztraminer AOC, 154
Gewürztraminer grape, 25, 25; Alsace, 149; Austria, 322; California, 366-7; Canada, 402, 404; Hessische Bergstrasse, 233; New South Wales, 419; New Zealand, 444; Yugoslavia, 332
Geyser Peak Winery, 371
Ghemme DOC, 247
Gibson Wine Company, 386
Gigondas AOC, 176, 178-9
Gil Luque, M., 289
Gilbeys, 350
Gilette, Château, 70, 80
Gillespie Vineyards, 440
Gingin, 438
Gipfel, Grosslage, 221
Girard, Cuvée Arthur, 122
Girard Winery, 377
Giraud, Robert, 40
Giraud-Bélivier, 92
Girò di Cagliari DOC, 266
Gironde, 39, 44, 200
Gisborne, 445
Giscours, Château, 64, 65
Giumarra Vineyards, 386

Givry AOC, 129
Glana, Château du, 62
glasses, for tasting wine, 9
Glen Ellen Winery, 373
Glen Oak Hills Winery, 388
Glenora Wine Cellars, 396
Glenrowan, 425
Glenvale Vineyards, 447
Gloria, Château, 62
Gloria grape, 26
glossary, 456-63
Godramstein, 232
Goede Hoop Estate, 352
Golan Heights, 341
Gold Seal Vineyards, 396
Goldbäumchen, Grosslage, 220
Goldburger, 322
Goldental, 223
Goldwater Estate, 447
Golvinda Winery, 428
González Byass, 288
Gorce, Château de, 106
Gordo grape, 417
Gordon, Luis G., 289
Gordon Sunter Wines, 435
Gorges et Côtes de Millau, 200
Gorges de l'Hérault, 200
Goron OA, 317
Gosset, 143
Gotteshilfe, Grosslage, 229
Gottesthal, Grosslage, 226
Goudichaud, Château, 106
Goulburn Valley, 425
Gould Campbell, 301
Goulet, Georges, 143
Goumenissa AO, 338
Goumin, Château, 106
Goundrey Wines, 440
Goureau, Cuvée, 122
Goyeneghea, 412
Graach, 220
Graciano grape, 30, 272
Gradignan, 69
Grafenstück, Grosslage, 231
Graffigna, Santiago, 412
Gräflich von Kageneck'sche Sektkellerei, 211
Grafschaft, Grosslage, 220
Graham, W. & J. & Co., 300
Graiselound, 312
Grajales, 406, 407
Grand-Baril, Château, 98
Grand Barrail, Domaine du, 102
Grand Barrail Lamarzelle-Figeac, Château, 89
Grand Champs, Château, 92
Le Grand Chemarin, 171
Grand Corbin, Château, 89
Grand-Corbin-Despagne, Château, 89
Grand Cru, 38
Grand Cru Classé, 38
Grand Cru Vineyards, 371
Grand Enclos du Château de Cérons, 76
Grand-Launay, Château, 101
Grand Listrac, Cave Coopérative, 41
Grand Mayne, Château, 90
Grand Monteil, Château, 106
Grand Pierre, Château du, 102
Grand-Pontet, Château, 90
Grand Pré Wines, 404
Grand-Puy-Ducasse, Château, 56
Grand-Puy-Lacoste, Château, 56
Grand River Valley AVA, 394
Grand River Winery, 397
Grand Roussillon AOC, 192
Grand Vin, 38
Grandes Murailles, Château, 89
Grands Echézeaux AOC, 118

Grange Hermitage, 430, 434
Granite Belt (Queensland), 416, 441, 442
Granite Springs Winery & Vineyards, 387
grapes, 10-11; Ahr, 214, 215; Argentina, 410; Australia, 417; Bordeaux, 36, 38; California, 364-7; Canada, 402-3, 404; Chile, 408; Germany, 207; growing, 12-17; New South Wales, 418-19; North America, 356; Port, 296; Rioja, 272; Sherry, 282; Switzerland, 317; varieties, 24-32
Gratien, Alfred, 143
Gratien, Meyer & Seydoux, 158
Grattamacco VT, 258
Graubünden, 318
Grauer Burgunder grape, 207
La Grave, Château de, 101
La Grave, Domaine de, 69, 76
Grave del Friuli DOC, 253
La Grave Figeac, Château, 92
La Grave Trigant de Boisset, Château, 93, 96
Gravelines, Château, 106
Graves, 38, 69-80, 464-5
Graves de Vayres AOC, 105
Graves Supérieur AOC, 70, 73
Gravina DOC, 265
Gray Monk Cellars, 404
Gray Riesling grape, 367
Great Britain, 310-15
Great Plain (Hungary), 329
Great Shoesmiths Farm, 312
Great Southern Area (Western Australia), 438
Great Western (Australia), 425
Great Western Winery (USA), 396
Grechetto VT, 259
Greco (Argentina), 412
Greco VT (Italy), 247
Greco di Bianco DOC, 266
Greco di Tufo DOC, 265
Greece, 336-40
Green & Red Vineyard, 377
Green Hungarian grape, 367
Greenstone Winery, 387
Greenwood Ridge Vineyards, 369
Grenache blanc grape, 26
Grenache grape, 30, 31, 173, 176, 365
Grenouileau, Aurelien, 40
Gressier-Grand-Poujeaux, Château, 48-9
Grgich Hills Cellar, 375
Grignolino d'Asti DOC, 247
Grignolino del Monferrato Casalese DOC, 248
Grignolino grape, 365, 406
Grillet, Château, 174, 174, 175
Grinalda, 302
Griottes-Chambertin AOC, 119
Grisons, 318
Grolleau grape, 30, 163, 167
Groot Constantia Estate, 352
Groppello VT, 249
Gros Plant VDQS, 162
Gros Plant Nantais VDQS, 162
Gross Highland Winery, 396
Grosset Wines, 435
Grosskarlbach, 231
Grosslage see individual Grosslagen
Grosslagenfrei, 235
Grosslagereuschberg, 235
Groth Vineyards & Winery, 375

Groupement de Producteurs de Lugny-St.-Gengoux-de-Scissé, 112
Grover Gulch Winery, 382
growing grapes, 12-17
Gruaud-Larose, Château, 60, 61
Grüner veltliner grape, 26, 319, 322, 332
Grünstadt, 231
Gua, Château du, 106
Guadet St.-Julien, Château, 90
Guenoc Valley AVA, 388
Guenoc Winery, 388
Guerry, Château, 101
Guglielmo (E.) Winery, 381
Güglingen, 237
Guigal, 174
Guigone de Salins, Cuvée, 122
Guild Wineries, 386
Guionne, Château, 101
Guiraud, Château, 43, 70, 78
Güldenmorgen, Grosslage, 228
Guldental, 223
Gundelsheim, 237
Gundlach-Bundschu Winery, 371
Guntersblum, 229
Guntrum (Louis) Weinkellerei, 208
La Gurgue, Château, 67
Gurpegui, Bodegas, 275
Gutenborner grape, 26
Gutes Domtal, Grosslage, 229
Guttenberg, Grosslage, 232
Gutturnio dei Colli Piacentini DOC, 261
Guyana, 407

H

Hacienda Winery, 371
Haight Vineyards, 395
Hallgarten, 226
Hallgarten, Arthur, 208
Hambledon Vineyard, 312
Hamilton, Richard, 433
Hamilton Russell Vineyards, 352
Hamlet Hill Vineyards, 395
Hammelburg, 235
Hammerstein, Grosslage Burg, 217
Hamstead, 312
Handley Cellars, 369
Hanteillan, Château, 49
Hanzell Vineyards, 371
Happ's Vineyard, 440
Haraszthy de Mokesa, Agoston, 361-2
Harbledown & Chaucer, 312
Harbor Winery, 386
Harbourne, 312
Harcourt Valley Vineyards, 428
Harden Farm, 312
Hardy's, 433
Harriague grape, 406
Hárslevelü grape, 26
Hart Winery, 388
Hartenberg Vineyards, 352
Hartridge Wines, 440
harvesting, 15, 17, 283-4
Harveys, 288, 306
Haselgrove (James) Wines, 435
Hattenheim, 226
Haura, Château, 76
Haut-Bages-Avérous, Château, 58
Haut-Bages-Libéral, Château, 56

Haut-Bailly, Château, 74
Haut-Batailley, Château, 56
Haut-Bommes, Château, 80
Haut-Brignon, Château, 107
Haut-Brion, Château, 69, 74
Haut Brisson, Château, 92
Haut-Chaigneau, Château, 98
Haut-Chatain, Château, 98
Haut-Comtat VDQS, 179
Haut-Corbin, Château, 90
Haute Garonne, 200
Haut-Guiraud, Château, 101
Haut-Macô, Château, 102
Haut-Marbuzet, Château, 53
Haut-Médoc, 44, 46
Haut-Montravel AOC, 187
Haut-Peyraguey, Château Clos, 77
Haut Plantey, Château, 92
Haut-Poitou AOC, 160
Haut-Poitou, Cave Coopérative du, 159
Haut-Pontet, Château, 92
Haut-Quercus, 92
Haut-Rousset, Château, 102
Haut-Sarpe, Château, 90
Haut Sociondo, Château de, 102
Haut-Tuquet, Château, 98
Haute-Vallée de l'Aude, 200
Haute-Vallée de l'Orb, 200
Hauterive en Pays d'Aude, 200
Hautes-Côtes de Beaune, 109, 121-2
Hautes Côtes de Beaune et Nuits, Cave Coopérative des, 112
Hautes-Côtes de Nuits, 109, 116
Hauts de Badens, 200
Les Hauts-Conseillants, Château, 98
Hautvillers, 136
Hawaii, 398
Hawkes Bay, 443, 446
La Haye, Château, 51, 53
Haywood Winery, 373
heat treatment, vinification, 18
Heathcote Winery, 426
Hecker Pass Winery, 382
Heemskerk Vineyard, 426
Heidsieck, Charles, 143-4
Heidsieck & Co. Monopole, 144
Heilbronn, 237
Heiligenstock, Grosslage, 226
Heiligenthal, Grosslage, 235
Heimersheim, 215
Heissen Stein, Grosslage vom, 220
Heitz Wine Cellars, 375
Helderberg Koöp Wynkelder, 354
Hendred Vineyard, 313
Henke Winery, 428
Henkell, 211
Henriot, 144
Henschke Cellars, 433
Heppenheim, 233
Hérault, 200
Hermann AVA, 399
Hermannhof Winery, 399
Hermanus, 348
Hermitage, 171, 174, 175
Hermitage Blanc, 317
Hermitage grape, 417
Hermitage Vin de Paille AOC, 175
Heroldrebe grape, 30
Heron Hill Vineyards, 396
Herrenberg, Grosslage, 217, 235
Herres, Peter, 211
Herrlich, Grosslage, 232

Herzegovina, 333
Hessische Bergstrasse, 233
Heublein do Brasil, 406
Heuchelberg, Grosslage, 237
Heywood, 313
Hickinbotham Winemakers, 427
Hidalgo, Emilio M., 289
Hidalgo, Vinícola, 289-90
High Tor Vineyards, 396
"high-culture" system, 103, 104
Highfield, 313
Hill, Cavas, 281
Hill of Gold, 422
Hill (William) Winery, 377
Hillebrand Estates Wines, 405
Hillgrove, 313
Himrod grape, 403
"hippy" wineries, 362
Hiram Walker, 111
Hochheim, 204, 226
Hochheim, Haus, 211
Hochmess, Grosslage, 231
Hochstadt, 232
Hock, 204
Hoffmans of Tanunda, 435
Hofrat, Grosslage, 235
Hofstück, Grosslage, 231
Hogue Cellars, 391
Hohenberg, Grosslage, 239
Hohenneuffen, Grosslage, 237
Höllenpfad, Grosslage, 231
Hollick Wines, 435
Holly Lodge Estate Winery, 448
Hollybush, 313
Holmes, 435
The Holt, 313
Homburg, 235
Honigberg, Grosslage, 226, 235
Honigsäckel, Grosslage, 231
Hooksway, 313
Hop Kiln Winery, 373
Hopkins Vineyards, 395
Hornsby, Chateau, 442
Hörstein, 235
Hortevie, Château, 62
Horton Vineyard, 313
Hospices de Beaune, 122
Houghton Wines, 437, 439
Houissant, Château, 53
Howell Mountain AVA, 375
HRH Vineyard, 313
Hudson River Region AVA, 394
Huesgen, Adolph, 208
Hugel, 149, 152
Hugo Winery, 435
Hultgren & Samperton, 373
Humagne, 317
Humblot, Cuvée Jehan, 122
Hungary, 327-9
Hungerford Hill Vineyards, 421
Hunter riesling grape, 417, 419
Hunter Valley, 416, 418-19, 464-5
Hunter's Wines, 447
Huntington Estate, 421
Husch Vineyards, 369
Huxelrebe grape, 26

I

Ica, 406
Idaho, 390, 391
IDV France, 40, 42
Idyll Vineyard, 428
Ightham, 314
Iglesias, Gerardo, 412

Ihringen, 240
Ile de Beauté, 194, 200
Illats, 69, 70
Illinois, 398
India, 450-1
Indiana, 398
Indre, 200
Indre-et-Loire, 200
Infantes de Orleans Borbon, Bodegas, 289
Ingelheim, 228
Inglenook Vineyards, 376
Inniskillin Wines, 403, 405
Institut National de la Récherche Agronomique (INRA), 74
Internacionales, Bodegas, 287
Inverca, 406
Ionian Islands, 339-40
Iowa, 398
Iphofen, 235
Irache, Bodegas, 276
Irancy, 114
Iron Horse Vineyards, 371
Irouléguy AOC, 184, 187
Irroy, 144
Irvine's white grape, 417
Isabella grape, 406
Ischia DOC, 265
Isle of Ely, 314
Isle St. George AVA, 394
Isonzo DOC, 253
Israel, 342
Issan, Château d', 65
Italy, 242-66, 464-5

J

Jaboulet, 174
Jaboulet-Vercherre, 111
Jacobins, Château Clos des, 87
Jacobins, Couvent des, 88
Jacobsdal Estate, 352
Jacquère grape, 26
Jacquesson & Fils, 144
Jacquez grape, 417
Jadot, Louis, 111
Jaffelin, 111
Jane Brook Estate Wines, 440
Japan, 450, 451
Jardin de la France, 200
Jasmin, 174
Jasnières AOC, 167, 168-9
Jasper Hill Vineyard, 428
Jean, Clos, 107
Jean Faure, Château, 90
Jeandeman, Château, 99
Jekel Vineyards, 358, 379, 380-1
Jerez de la Frontera, 282-3
Jim Barry's Wines, 432
Joanne, Roger, 40, 42, 78
Johannisberg, 224, 226, 317
Johannisberg, Bereich, 225
Johannisberg riesling grape, 26, 402, 403, 404, 406, 410
John Daniel Society, 375
Johnson Turnbull Vineyards, 377
Johnson's Alexander Valley Wines, 373
Johnston, Nathaniel, 40
Jolinaka na Struma, 326
Jordan, 342
Jordan & Ste.-Michelle Cellars, 405
Jordan Vineyard & Winery, 372
Joyous Garde Vineyard, 314
Jublinäumsrebe, 322
Jud's Hill Estates, 435
Juge, Château du, 107
Jugenheimer, 228

Julac Inc, 405
Julien, Chateau, 382
Juliénas AOC, 135
Jumilla DO, 291
Jumilla Monastrell DO, 291
Junayme, Château, 98
Jura, 181-3
Jurançon AOC, 184, 187
Jurançon Sec AOC, 187
Les Justices, Château, 80
Juvé & Camps, 281
Jujuy, 410

K

Kabinett QmP, 212
Kadarka grape, 30, 332
Kaiser Stuhl Wines, 430, 435
Kaiserpfalz, Grosslage, 228
Kaiserstuhl-Tuniberg, Bereich, 240
Kaiserstühler Winzergenossenschaft Ihringen eG, 209
Kalin Cellars, 388
Kallstadt, 231
Kamtal-Donauland, 324
Kanawha River Valley AVA, 394
Kanonkop Estate, 352
Kantza AO, 339
Kanzem, 221
Kanzler grape, 26
Kapellenberg, Grosslage, 235
Karamea Wines, 448
Karlsburg Estate, 435
Karlstadt, 235
Karly Wines, 387
Kärnten, 324
Kasel, 221
Katnook Estate, 433
Kazakhstan, 335
Keenan (Robert) Winery, 377
Kellybrook Winery, 428
Kendall-Jackson Vineyards and Winery, 388
Kendermann, Hermann, 208
Kennedy (Kathryn) Winery, 382
Kents Green, 314
Kentucky, 398
Kenwood Vineyards, 372
Kenworthy Vineyards, 387
Kenya, 349
Keppoch, 432
Kerner grape, 26, 206, 223, 234
Kessler, 211
Kidman Winery, 435
Kiedrich, 226
Kientzler, André, 152
Kings Green, 314
Kingsland, 314
Kintzingen, 235
Kinver, 314
Kirchberg, Grosslage, 235
Kirchenweinberg, Grosslage, 237
Kirchheim, 232
Kirigin Cellars, 382
Kirwan, Château, 66
Kistler Vineyards, 373
Klein Constantia Estate, 352
Kleinbottwar, 237
Klevener de Heiligenstein AOC, 155
Klevner, 317
Klipfel, Domaine, 152
Kloss Foerster, 211
Kloster Liebfrauenberg, Grosslage, 232
Klosterberg, Grosslage, 215
Knappstein (Tim) Enterprise Wines, 433

Knights Valley AVA, 371
Knight's Wines, 428
Knudsen Erath Winery, 391
Kobnert, Grosslage, 231
Kobrand, 111
Kocher-Jagst-Tauber, Bereich, 237
Kocherberg, Grosslage, 237
Kolbenhofer VT, 252
Kolor grape, 30
Kominos Wines, 442
Königsbach, 232
Königsberg, Grosslage, 221
Königsgarten, Grosslage, 232
Konocti Winery, 388
Konzelmann, 405
Kopf, Grosslage, 237
Kopke, C.N. & Co., 295
Koppamurra, 435
Korbel Champagne Cellars, 372
Korepo Wines, 448
Kornell (Hanns) Champagne Cellars, 376
Kosovo, 333
Kressmann, 40-1, 42, 75
Kreuznach, Bereich, 223
Kreydenweiss, Marc, 152
Krondorf Winery, 433
Kronenberg, Grosslage, 223
Krötenbrunnen, Grosslage, 229
Krug, Charles, 376
Krug & Co., 144
Kruse (Thomas) Winery, 382
Kuentz-Bas, 152
Kumeu River Wines, 447
Kupferberg, 211
Kurfürstenstück, Grosslage, 228
Kurfürstlay, Grosslage, 220
KWV, 350-1

L

Lan, Bodegas, 276
La Paz, 406
La Vina Winery, 399
Labarde, 63
Labarde, Clos, 92
Labastida, Cooperativa Vinícola de, 276
Labatut, Château, 107
Labégorce, Château, 68
Labégorce-Zédé, Château, 68
labels: Alsace, 149; America, 360; Argentina, 408; Australia, 414; Austria, 321; Bordeaux, 38; Bulgaria, 326; Burgundy, 108; Champagne, 141; Chante Flûté, 128; Chile, 408; Czechoslovakia, 329; France, 34; Germany, 204, 205; Greece, 337; Hospices de Beaune, 122; Hungary, 329; Mexico, 400; Portugal, 294; Romania, 331; South Africa, 346; Spain, 268; Switzerland, 317; *Tastevinage*, 116; USSR, 335
Labouré-Roi, 111
labrusca vines, 356, 403, 406
Lacombe-Cadiot, Château, 43
Lacoufourque, Château de, 62
Lacrima di Morro DOC, 262
Ladbroke Grove Wines, 436
Ladoix AOC, 125
Ladoix Premier Cru AOC, 125
Lafaurie-Peyraguey, Château, 78
Lafite, Château, 94, 107
Lafite-Rothschild, Château, 44, 57

Lafleur, Château, 96
Lafleur-Gazin, Château, 96
Lafon-Rochet, Château, 52
Lafue, Château, 107
Lagos, B.M., 290
Lagosta, 302
Lagrange, Château, Pomerol 96
Lagrange, Château, St.-Julien 61
Lagrange-les-Tours, Château, 43
La Lagune, Château, 44, 46
Lagunilla, Bodegas, 276
Lahntal, Grosslage, 217
Lake County, 388
Lake Erie AVA, 394
Lake Michigan Shore AVA, 394
Lake's Folly, 419, 421
Lakeside Vineyard, 395
Lakespring Winery, 377
Lalande-Borie, Château, 62
Lalande-de-Pomerol AOC, 82
La Lalnade Saint-Jean, Château, 43
Lamanceau, Château, 102
Lamarque, Château, 49
Lamberhurst, 314
Lambert Bridge, 373
Lamblin & Fils, 111
Lambrays AOC, Clos des, 117
Lambrusco VT, 260, 261
Lambrusco di Sorbara DOC, 261
Lambrusco grape, 30, 406
Lambrusco Grasparossa di Castelvetro DOC, 261
Lambrusco Mantovano VT, 249
Lambrusco Reggiano DOC, 261
Lambrusco Salamino di Santa Croce DOC, 261
Lamezia DOC, 266
Lamont Winery, 386
Lamothe, Château, 78, 107
Lamothe-Guignard, Château, 78
Lancaster Valley AVA, 394
Landeiro, Casa do, 302
Landes, 200
Landmark Vineyards, 373
Landskroon Estate, 352
Landwein, 212
Lanessan, Château, 49
Lang-Biémont, 148
Langenbach, 208, 211
Langenlonsheim, 223
Langguth Erben, 208
Langham Vineyard, 314
Langhorne Creek, 432
Langoa-Barton, Château, 61
Languedoc-Roussillon, 189-92
Laniote, Château, 90
Lanson Père & Fils, 144
Lapelletrie, Château, 92
Lapeyère, Château, 43
Larcis Ducasse, Château, 90
Lark Hill, 422
Larmande, Château, 90
Laroque, Château, 92
Larose-Trintaudon, Château, 49
Laroze, Château, 90
Larrivet-Haut-Brion, Château, 76
Lascombes, Château, 66
Lascombes, Rosé de, 43
Latisana DOC, 253
Latium, 256, 259
Latour, Château, 43, 57, 59, 94, 106, 107
Latour, Maison Louis, 111
Latour à Pomerol, Château, 93, 96
Latricières-Chambertin AOC, 119

Lauffen, 237
Laugel, Maison Michel, 152
Laumersheim, 232
Launay, Château, 106
Laurel Glen Vineyard, 372
Laurent-Perrier, 144
Laurets, Château des, 99
Laurette, Château, 107
Laurier, Domaine, 373
Laville, Château, 43
Laville-Haut-Brion, Château, 69, 74
Lavilotte, Château, 51, 53
Layteron, 43
Lazar, Tom, 428
Lazy Creek Vineyard, 369
Le Brun, Albert, 148
Le Roux, J.C., 351
Leacock, 306
Lebanon, 342
Lebelin, Cuvée, 122
Leconfield Coonawarra, 436
Leeds Castle, 314
Leeford Vineyards, 314
Leelanau Peninsula AVA, 394
Leelanau Wine Cellars, 395
Leeuwin Estate, 439
Leeward Winery, 388
Légnan, 69
Legras, R. & I., 148
Leinsweiler, 232
Leiwen, 221
Lemberg Estate, 352
Lemberger grape, 207
Lemnos AO, 340
Lemon Creek Winery, 395
Len de l'Elh grape, 26
Lenz Möser system, 104
Lenz, Patricia & Peter, 396
León, Jean, 280
Leonetti Cellar, 391
Léoville-Barton, Château, 40, 61
Léoville-Las Cases, Château, 61
Léoville-Poyferré, Château, 62
Lepitre, Abel, 145
Leroy, 111
Lesbos, 340
Leschenault, 440
Lescure, Château, 43
Lesparre, 45
Lessini Durello DOC, 254
Lessona DOC, 248
Lestage-Darquier-Grand-Poujeaux, Château, 49
Lettere VT, 265
Levant, 341-2
Leverano DOC, 265
Lexham Hall, 314
Lexia grape, 417
Leyneton, 432
Libertas, Chateau, 350
Libournais, 81-99
Libourne, 81
Lichine, Alexis & Co., 41, 67
Lidonne, Château, 102
Lieberstein, 348
Liebfrauenmorgen, Grosslage, 229
Liebfraumilch, 206, 227, 230, 443
Lievland, 352
light, storing wine, 452
Liguria, 245-6, 249
Lillydale Vineyards, 429
Lillypilly Estate, 421
Lime Kiln Valley AVA, 380
Limoux AOC, 187
Lincoln Vineyards, 447
Lindauer Seegarten, Grosslage, 237
Lindelberg, Grosslage, 237
Lindemans Wines, 421
Linganore AVA, 394
Liot, Château, 80

liqueur d'expédition, 139
liqueur de tirage, 138
Liquor Boards, Canada, 402, 403
Lirac AOC, 179
Lison-Pramaggiore DOC, 253
Listrac AOC, 44, 46
Little Karoo WO, 350
Little's Winery, 422
Livermore Valley AVA, 380
Livermore Valley Cellars, 382
Liversan, Château, 49
Livração, Quinta da, 302
Llano Estacado Winery, 399
Llopart, Cava, 281
Locorotondo DOC, 265
Loddiswell, 314
Lodge Farm, 314
Lodi AVA, 385
Lohr (J.) Winery, 381
Loir-et-Cher, 200
Loire, Les Caves de la, 159
Loire-Atlantique, 200
Loire Valley, 156-72, 464-5
Loiret, 200
Lombardi Wines, 448
Lombardy, 245, 248-9
Lomelino, 306
London Winery, 405
Long-Depaquit, Louis, 115
Long Island Vineyard, 396-7
Long Vineyards, 376
Longleat, 429
Lopez, Bodegas, 412
Loppin, Cuvée, 122
Loramie Creek AVA, 394
Loreleyfelsen, Grosslage, 217
Lorentz, Gustave, 152
Lorettoberg, Grosslage, 240
Loron & Fils, 111
Lorraine, 149, 154-5
Los Angeles, 290
Los Carneros AVA, 371
Loubens, Château, 107
Loudenne, Château, 45, 49
Loudenne, Gilbey de, 40
Louisiana, 398
Loupiac AOC, 105
Loupiac-Gaudiet, Château, 107
Lousteau-Vieil, Château, 107
La Louvière, Château, 76
Lower Hunter Valley, 419-20
Lower Lake Winery, 388
Lubec Inc, 405
Ludon, 44
Ludwigshöhe, Grosslage Schloss, 232
Lugagnac, Château de, 43
Lugana DOC, 249
Lugugnac, Château de, 107
Lumassina VT, 249
Lumière, Château, 450, 451
Lupé-Cholet, 111
Lurton, André, 41, 74, 76, 106
Lurton, Lucien, 50, 65, 68, 73, 74
Lussac, Château de, 81, 99
Lussac-St.-Emilion AOC, 82
Lustau, 288
De Luze, 41
Lyeth Vineyard Winery, 372
Lymington, 314
Lyminster, 314
Lynch-Bages, Château, 57
Lynch Moussas, Château, 57
Lyonnat, Château du, 99
Lytton Springs Winery, 372

M

Macabéo grape, 26
McDowell Valley AVA, 369
McDowell Valley Vineyards, 369

Macedon, 425
Macedonia, 333, 338
macération carbonique, 21
McEwins, 429
McGregor Vineyards, 397
McHenry Vineyard, 382
Machorre, Château, 107
McLaren Vale, 432
Mâcon AOC, 131, 173
Mâcon-Aze AOC, 131
Mâcon-Bissy-la-Mâconnaise AOC, 131
Mâcon-Burgy AOC, 131
Mâcon-Busières AOC, 131
Mâcon-Chaintre AOC, 131
Mâcon-Chânes AOC, 131
Mâcon-La Chapelle-de-Guinchay AOC, 131
Mâcon-Chardonnay AOC, 131
Mâcon-Charnay-lès-Mâcon AOC, 131
Mâcon-Chasselas AOC, 131
Mâcon-Chevagny-lès-Chevrières AOC, 131
Mâcon-Clessé AOC, 131
Mâcon-Crèches-sur-Saône AOC, 131
Mâcon-Cruzille AOC, 131
Mâcon-Davaye AOC, 131
Mâcon-Fuissé AOC, 131
Mâcon-Grévilly AOC, 131
Mâcon-Hurigny AOC, 131
Mâcon-Igé AOC, 131
Mâcon-Leynes AOC, 131
Mâcon-Loché AOC, 131
Mâcon-Lugny AOC, 131
Mâcon-Milly-Lamartine AOC, 131
Mâcon-Montbellet AOC, 131
Mâcon-Péronne AOC, 131
Mâcon-Pierreclos AOC, 131
Mâcon-Prissé AOC, 131
Mâcon-Pruzilly AOC, 131
Mâcon-La Roche Vineuse AOC, 131
Mâcon-Romanèche-Thorins AOC, 132
Mâcon-St.-Amour-Bellevue AOC, 132
Mâcon-St.-Gengoux-de-Scissé AOC, 132
Mâcon-St.-Symphorien-d'Ancelles AOC, 132
Mâcon-St.-Vérand AOC, 132
Mâcon-Sologny AOC, 132
Mâcon-Solutré AOC, 132
Mâcon Supérieur AOC, 132
Mâcon-Uchizy AOC, 132
Mâcon-Vergisson AOC, 132
Mâcon-Verzé AOC, 132
Mâcon-Villages AOC, 131
Mâcon-Vinzelles AOC, 132
Mâcon-Viré AOC, 132
Mâconnais, 109, 130-2
McWilliams, 421, 444, 445
Madeira, 293, 305-6
Madeleine Angevine grape, 26
La Madeleine, Clos, 87
Madera AVA, 385
Madiran AOC, 184, 188
Madrona Vineyards, 387
Magdelaine, Château, 90
Magence, Château, 76
Maglieri Wines, 436
Magnan la Gaffelière, Château, 92
Mahler-Besse, 41, 66
Mahler-Besse, 41, 66
Maikammer, 232
Mailles, Château des, 107
Main Ridge Estate, 429
Maindreieck, Bereich, 235
Maine-et-Loire, 200
Mainviereck, Bereich, 235
Maipo Valley, 408
Maison Blanche, Château, 99
La Maison Secrestat Ltee, 405

Málaga DO, 286
Malartic-Lagravière, Château, 74
Malbec grape, 30, 38, 365, 408, 410, 416
Malescot St.-Exupéray, Château, 66
Malet-Roquefort, Comte Léo de, 89, 92
Malineau, Domaine de, 43
Malle, Château de, 78
Malleret, Château, 49
Malmsey grape, 306
malolactic fermentation, 18-19, 114, 138
Malvasia bianca grape, 367
Malvasia delle Lipari DOC, 266
Malvasia di Bosa DOC, 266
Malvasia di Cagliari DOC, 266
Malvasia di Casorzo d'Asti DOC, 248
Malvasia di Castelnuovo Don Bosco DOC, 248
Malvasia di Planargia VT, 266
Malvasia grape, 272
Malvoisie OA, 317
Malvoisie de Cossan VT, 249
Malvoisie de Nus VT, 249
La Mancha DO, 291
Mandelhöhe, Grosslage, 232
Mandrolisai DOC, 266
Mannaberg, Grosslage, 239
Manseng grape, 26
Mantinia AO, 339
Manzanilla, 286, 287-90
Maquin-St.-Georges, Château, 99
Marbuzet, Château de, 53
Marches (Italy), 260, 262
Marches de Bretagne, 200
Marcilly (P. de) Frères, 111
Marcoux, Domaine de, 180
Maréchal Foch grape, 404
Maremma VT, 258
Margaret River, 416, 437, 438-9, 464-5
Margaux, 38, 44, 45, 46, 63-8
Margaux, Château, 63, 63, 64, 66, 94
Marienberg Winery, 433
Mariengarten, Grosslage, 231-2
Mariensteiner grape, 26
Marienthal, 215
Marin County, 388
Marinier, Château, 102
Marino DOC, 259
Marion's Vineyard, 429
Mark West Vineyards, 372
Markgraf Babenberg, Grosslage, 235
Markgräflerland, Bereich, 240
Markham Vineyards, 377
Markko Vineyard, 397
Marksburg, Grosslage, 217
Marlborough (New Zealand), 445, 446
Marmandais, 184
Marne & Champagne, 88, 145
Marqués de Aguayo, 401
Marquis d'Alesme-Becker, Château, 66
Marqués de Cáceres, 274
Marqués de Monistrol, 280
Marqués de Murrieta, 275
Marqués del Puerto, Bodegas, 276
Marqués de Riscal, 276
Le Marquis de Saint-Estèphe, 53
Marquis-de-Terme, Château, 66
Marsac-Séguineau, Château, 68
Marsala DOC, 266
Marsannay AOC, 119

Marsanne grape, 26, 416
Martha's Vineyard AVA, 394
Martillac, 69
Martin Winery, 388
Martinborough Vineyard, 448
Martinens, Château, 68
Martinet, Château, 92
Martínez Bujanda, Bodegas, 274
Martínez Lacuesta, Bodegas, 276
Martini, Louis M., 376
Martini DOC, 265
Martini & Rossi, 406
Maryland, 395
Mas Rabassa, 280
Mascaró, 281
Masía Bach, 280
Masia Vallformosa, 281
Masianco VT, 254
Massachusetts, 395
Massé, 145
Massol, Cuvée Jehan de, 122
Masson (Paul) Vineyards, 381
Masson (Paul) Winery, 362, 405
Mastantuono, 384
Matanzas Creek Winery, 372
Mataro grape, 365, 417
Matawhero Wines, 447
"Mateus", 293
Mathews (Joseph) Winery, 377
Matino DOC, 265
Matras, Château, 90
Matschoss, 215
Matua Valley Wines, 447
maturation, 38-9, 452
Mau, Yvon, 41
La Maubastit, Château, 107
Maucaillou, Château, 49
Maufoux, Prosper, 111
Maulbronn, 237
Maures, 200
Maurizio Zanella VT, 248
Maury AOC, 192
Mausse, Château, 99
Mauvezin, Château, 90
Mauzac grape, 26
Mavrodaphne of Cephalonia AO, 340
Mavrodaphne of Patras AO, 339
Mavroud grape, 30
Maximin Grünhaus, 221
Maxwell Wines, 436
Mayacamas Vineyards, 376
Mayne, Château du, 80
Mayne-Binet, Château, 76
Mayne-Vieil, Château, 99
Mazarin, Château, 107
Mazeris, Château, 99
Mazeyres, Château, 96
Mazis-Chambertin AOC, 119
Mazoyères-Chambertin AOC, 119
Mazuelo grape, 30, 272
Mazza Vineyards, 397
Meadowbank Vineyards, 429
Meddersheim, 223
Medina, José, 290
Medio Penedés, 278
Médoc, 44-68, 83, 464-5
Médot & Cie, 148
Meerendal Estate, 352-3
Meerlust Estate, 353
Meerspinne, Grosslage, 232
Mehrhölzchen, Grosslage, 226
Meireles, 302
La Méjanelle AOC, 191
Melissa DOC, 266
Meliton AO, Côtes de, 338
Melmsheim, 237
Melon de Bourgogne grape, 26
Menaudat, Château, 102

Mendoce, Château, 102
Mendocino County, 368-9
Mendoza, 410
Menetou-Salon AOC, 171, 172
Ménota, Château de, 80
Méntrida DO, 291
Menuts, Clos des, 92
Meon Valley Vineyard, 314
Meranese di Collina DOC, 252
merchants, 108
Mercier, 145
Mercurey, 109, 128-9
Mercurey Premier Cru AOC, 129
Meredyth Vineyards, 397
De Merie, 148
Mérignac, 69
Merlot blanc grape, 26
Merlot grape, 31, *31*; Australia, 416; Austria, 322; Bordeaux, 36, 38; Brazil, 406; California, 365; Canada, 403; Chile, 408, 410; Libournais, 81; Pomerol, 94; Switzerland, 317; Uruguay, 406; Yugoslavia, 332
Merricks, 427
Merricks Estate, 427
Merritt Island AVA, 385
The Merry Vintners, 372
Mertes, Peter, 208
Merxheim, 223
Mesenich, 220
Mesilla Valley AVA, 399
Mestres, 280
Mestrezat, 41
méthode champenoise, 23, 137, 269
méthode rurale, 23
Metsovo AO, 339
Meursault AOC, 125
Meursault-Côte de Beaune AOC, 125
Meursault Premier Cru AOC, 125
Meurthe-et-Moselle, 149
Meuse, 200
Mexico, 400-1
Meyer, Jos, 152
Meyney, Château, 51, 53
Le Meynieu, Château, 49
La Michelerie, Château, 43
Michelfeld, 239
Michelsberg, Grosslage, 220
Michigan, 395-6
Mid-Murray, 425
Middelvlei Estate, 353
Middle Rio Grande Valley AVA, 399
Middlebrook Winery, 436
Midi, 176, 189
Mihaly (Louis K.) Vineyard, 378
Milano Winery, 369
Milawa, 425
Mildara Wines, 427
Mildura, 425
Mill Creek Vineyards, 372
Millet, Château, 76-7
Milon, Château, 99
Milton Vineyard, 448
Mimbres Valley AVA, 399
minerals, 13
Minervois AOC, 192
Minho, 295, 298-302
Minnesota, 398
Miogo, Quinta do, 302
Miramar Wines, 421
Mirassou Vineyards, 381
Mirita, 302
Mission grape, 365
La Mission-Haut-Brion, Château, 74
Mission Hill Vineyards, 404
Mission Vineyards, *443, 447*
Mississippi, 398-9

Mississippi Delta AVA, 399
Missouri, 399
Mitchelton, 427
Mittelburgenland, 323
Mittelhaardt-Deutsche Weinstrasse, Bereich, 231
Mittelrhein, 216-17
Moët & Chandon, 145, 363
Moillard, 111
Les Moines, Château, 102
Moines-Martin, Château, 43
Moldavia, 331, 335
Molise, 260, 262
"Mollet de Perelada", Cooperativa de, 281
Mommessin, 111
Monarch Wine Company, 397
Monastrell grape, 30
Monbazillac AOC, 184, 188
Monbousquet, Château, 92
Monbrison, Château, 68
Moncets, Château, 99
Mondavi (Robert) Winery, 376
Mondeuse grape, 31
La Mongie, Château, 43
Monica de Cagliari DOC, 266
Monica di Sardegna DOC, 266
Monichino Wines, 429
Monis Wineries, 349
Monmousseau, 158
Mont Baudile, 200
Mont Blois Estate, 353
Mont Bouquet, 200
Mont Caume, 200
Mont Marcal, 280
Mont-Olivet, Clos du, 179
Mont-Redon, Domaine de, 180
Mont St. John Cellars, 378
Montagne, 81
Montagne de Reims, 136, 140
Montagne-St.-Emilion AOC, 82
Montagny AOC, 129
Montagny Premier Cru AOC, 129
Montana Wines, 443, 444, 445, 448
Montara, 429
Montaudon, 148
Montbray Wine Cellars, 395
Montbrun, Château, 68
Monte Antico VT, 258
Montebello, 145
Montecarlo DOC, 258
Montecillo, Bodegas, 276
Montecompatri-Colonna DOC, 259
Montefaro, 302
Montello e Colli Asolani DOC, 254
Montenegro, 333
Montepulciano d'Abruzzo DOC, 262
Montepulciano di Basilicata VT, 265
Montepulciano Cerasuolo del Molise VT, 262
Montepulciano delle Marche VT, 262
Montepulciano del Molise VT, 262
Monterey AVA, 380
Monterey County AO, 380
Monterey Peninsula Winery, 381
Monterey Vineyard, 381
Montescudaio DOC, 258
Monteviña, 387
Monthélie AOC, 125
Monthélie Premier Cru AOC, 125
Monticello AVA, 394
Monticello Cellars, 378
Montilla-Moriles DO, 286

Montlouis AOC, 167, 169
Montlouis Mousseux AOC, 169
Montlouis Pétillant AOC, 169
Montpeyroux AOC, 191
Montrachet AOC, 126
Montravel AOC, 188
Montravin Cellars, 405
Montrose, Château, 52
Montrose Winery, 421
Les Monts Damnés, 171
Monts de la Grage, 200
Monzingen, 223
Moorilla Estate, 424, 427
Moquegua, 406
Moravia, 329
Moreau, J. & Fils, 111
Morellino di Scansano DOC, 258
Morey-St.-Denis AOC, 119
Morey-St.-Denis Premier Cru AOC, 119
Morgan, 301
Morgan Winery, 382
Morgon AOC, 135
Morillon, Château, 43
Morio-Muskat grape, 26
Morlan-Tuilière, Château, 107
Mornington Peninsula, 425
Morocco, 345
Morris (J.W.) Winery, 372
Morris Wines, 427
Morton Estate, 448
Morton Manor Vineyard, 314
Moscadello di Montalcino DOC, 258
Moscatel de Sétubal RD, 308
Moscato d'Asti DOC, 247
Moscato di Chambave VT, 249
Moscato di Noto DOC, 266
Moscato di Pantelleria DOC, 266
Moscato di Scanzo VT, 248
Moscato di Siracusa DOC, 266
Moscato di Sorso-Sennori DOC, 266
Moscato di Strevi VT, 247
Moscato di Trani DOC, 265
Moscato del Vulture VT, 265
Moscato grape, 245
Moscato Naturale d'Asti DOC, 247
Mosel, 204, *206, 207*
Mosel-Saar-Ruwer, 218-21, 464-5
Moselle, 149
Moseltor, Bereich, 221
Mouchac, Château, *103*
Moueix, Armand & Fils, 41, 42
Moueix, Jean-Pierre, 41
Moulin-à-Vent, Château, 49
Moulin-à-Vent AOC, *109,* 135
Moulin du Cadet, Château, 90
Moulin de Launay, Château, 106
Moulin de Romage, Château, 107
Moulin-de-la-Rose, Château, 62
Moulin Haut-Laroque, Château, 99
Moulin Neuf, Château, 99
Moulin Rouge, Château, 99
Moulinet, Château, 96
Moulis AOC, 44, 46
Moulis-en-Médoc AOC, 46
Mount Avoca Vineyard, 429
Mount Barker, 437, 438, 439
Mount Eden Vineyards, 381
Mount Hurtle, 436
Mount Magnus, 442
Mount Mary Vineyard, 429
Mount Palomar Winery, 388
Mt. Pleasant Vineyards, 399

Mount Prior Vineyard, 429
Mount Veeder Winery, 378
Mountadam Vineyard, 436
Mountain House Winery, 369
Mountain View Winery, 382
Moura Basto, 302
Mourvèdre grape, 31, 176
Mouton, Château, 94
Mouton-Rothschild, Château, 36, 57
Mudgee, 416, 419, 420
Muerza, Bodegas, 276
Muga, Bodegas, 274
Müller, Matheus, 211
Müller, Rudolf, 209, 211
Müller Thurgau di Ziano VT, 261
Müller-Thurgau grape, 26; Austria, 322; Colombia, 406; Franken, 234; Hessische Bergstrasse, 233; Liebfraumilch, 206; Nahe, 223; New Zealand, 443, 444; Rheinhessen, 227; Switzerland, 317
Multaner grape, 26
Mumm, G.H. & Co., 145
Mundelsheim, 237
Münster, 223
Münzlay, Grosslage, 220
Muré, 152
Murray River, 425
Murrumbidgee Irrigation Area, 420
Murúa, Bodegas, 276
Musar, Château, 341, 342
Muscadelle grape, 26
Muscadet, 162, 511
Muscadet des Coteaux de la Loire AOC, 162
Muscadet de Sèvre-et-Maine AOC, 162
Muscadet grape, 161
Muscat AOC, 155
Muscat à petits grains grape, 26, *26*
Muscat blanc à petits grains grape, 149
Muscat blanc grape, 367
Muscat d'Alexandrie grape, 27
Muscat de Beaumes-de-Venise AOC, 176, 179
Muscat of Cephalonia AO, 340
Muscat de Frontignan AOC, 192
Muscat de Lunel AOC, 192
Muscat de Mireval AOC, 192
Muscat of Patras AO, 339
Muscat de Rivesaltes AOC, 192
Muscat de St.-Jean-de-Minervois AOC, 192
Muscat of Lemnos AO, 340
Muscat of Rhodes AO, 340
Muscat of Samos AO, 340
Muscat gordo grape, 417
Muscat grape, 26, 282, 317, 406, 409, 410, 444
Muscat Hamburg grape, 365
Muscat Ottonel grape, 27, 149
Muscat Rion of Patras AO, 339
Muscat rosé à petits grains grape, 149
Musigny AOC, 119
Muskat-Ottonel, 322
Muskateller, 322
Mussbach, 232
mutage, 23
Muteau, Cuvée, 122
Mutenia, 331
Myrat, Château de, 72

N

Nacktarsch, Grosslage, 221
Nadal, Cavas, 281
Nahe, *202,* 206, 207, 222-3
Nairac, Château, 70, 72, 78
Nalys, Domaine de, 180
Nantais, Pays, 161-2
Nantes, 156, 161
Naoussa AO, 339
Napa County, 374-8
Napa Creek Winery, 378
Napa Valley, *361,* 374, 375
Napoleon, 145
Narbusto VT, 248
Nardo DOC, 265
Nasco di Cagliari DOC, 266
Navarra, 271, 273, 274, 276
Navarro Correas, J.E., 412
Navarro Vineyards, 369
Naylor Wine Cellars, 397
Nazar Anchorena, B.F., 412
Néac AOC, 82
Nebbiolo d'Alba DOC, 247
Nebbiolo del Piemonte VT, 248
Nebbiolo grape, 31, *31,* 245, *246,* 406
Nederburg Wines, 351
Neef, 220
Neethlingshof Estate, 353
négociants, 36, 108, 128
Neil Ellis Vineyard Selection, 351
Neippperg, 237
Nelson, 446
Nemea AO, 339
Nenin, Château, 97
La Nerte, Château, 180
Neuburger, 322
Neuchâtel, 317
Neudorf Vineyards, *445,* 448
Neuenahr, 215
Neuquén, 410
Neusiedler See, 323
Neustadt-Diedesfeld, 232
Neustadt-Gimmeldingen, 232
De Neuville, 158
Neuweier, 240
Nevards, 314
New Hall Vineyards, 314
New Jersey, 396
New Mexico, 399
New South Wales, 415, 416, 418-22
New York, *358,* 396-7
New York muscat grape, 403
New Zealand, 443-8
Newton Vineyards, 378
Ngatarawa Wines, 448
Niagara, *402, 403,* 404
Niagara grape, 402, 403
Nicholson River Winery, 429
Niebaum-Coppola Estate, 376
Niederflörsheim, 229
Niederösterreich, 323-4
Nierstein, 227, *227,* 228, 229
Nierstein, Bereich, 228
Nièvre, 200
Nissley Vineyards, 397
Nobel Vineyards, 386
Nobilo's, 448
noble rot, 17, *17,* 36, 71, 72, *72,* 328
Noblessa grape, 27
Nobling grape, 27
non-dosage Champagne, 141
non-vintage Champagne, 141
Noon's Winery, 436
Nordale Koöp Wynkelder, 354
Nordheim, 235
Norheim, 223
Norman's Wine Estates, 434
North Africa, 344-5

North America, 356-401
North Carolina, 399
North-Central Coast (California), 379-82
North Coast AVA (California), 367
North East (Victoria), 425
North Fork of Long Island AVA, 394
North Fork of Roanoke AVA, 395
North Yuba AVA, 385
Northern Neck George Washington Birthplace AVA, 394
Northern Sonoma AVA, 371
Northern Territory (Australia), 441-2
Northland, 446
Norton, E.J.P., 412
Nortons Farm, 314
"nose", 7
Nostrano, 317
Nova Scotia, 404
Noval, 300
Nozet, Château de, *157*
"Nuestra Señor del Romero", Sociedad Cooperativa, 276
Nuits-St.-Georges AOC, 119
Nuits-St.-Georges Premier Cru AOC, 119-20
Nuñez, Antonio, 290
Nuragus di Cagliari DOC, 266
Nussdorf, 232
Nutbourne Manor, 314
Nuy Koöp Wynkelder, 354

O

oak casks, 19, 39
Oak Knoll Winery, 391
oak maturation, *Barrique* wines, 207
Oak Ridge Vineyards, 386
Oakridge Estate, 429
Oasis Vineyard, 397
Oberbergen, 240
Oberer Neckar, 237
Obermoschel, 223
Obermosel, Bereich, 221
Oberösterreich, 324
Oberrotweil, 240
Obester Winery, 381
Oc, 200
Ocaña, 406
Ochagavá, Silvestre, 410
Ochoa, Bodegas, 276
Ockfen, 221
Oeil de Perdrix, 317
Oelspiel, Grosslage, 235
Oestrich, 226
Offley Forrester, 301
Ohio, 397
Ohio River Valley, 395
Oklahoma, 399
Olarra, Bodegas, 274
Old Caves Winery, 442
Old Mission Peninsula AVA, 395
Olifants River WO, 350
Olivier, Château, 74-5
Olson Vineyards, 369
Oltenia, 331
Oltrepò Pavese DOC, 248
"Omar Khayyam", 450, 451
Ondenc grape, 27
Ontario, 402-3, 404-5
Oporto, 295
Oporto Wine Company, 295
Oppenheim, 228-9
Optima grape, 27
Orange, 420
Orange River WO, 350
L'Oratoire, Clos de, 87

L'Oratoire des Papes, Clos de, 180
Ordensgut, Grosslage, 232
Oregon, 390, 391
Orfila, José, 412
Orlando Wines, 434
Orléans, 171
L'Ormarins Estate, 353
Les Ormes de Pez, Château, 53
Les Ormes-Sorbet, Château, 45, 50
Orta Vova DOC, 265
Ortega grape, 27
Ortenau, Bereich, 239
Ortenberg, 240
Orvieto DOC, 259
Osborne, 288
Osicka's Vineyard, 429
Ostertag, Domaine, 152-3
Osthofen, 229
Ostuni DOC, 265
Ostuni Ottavianello DOC, 265
Otaolaurruchi, Carlos de, 290
Oude Libertas Wines, 351
Oude Meester Group, 351
Oudinot, 146
Outeiro de Baixo, Quinta do, 302
Overberg WO, 350
Overgaauw Estate, 353
oxidation, 452
Ozark Highlands AVA, 399
Ozark Mountain AVA, 398
Ozeki San Benito, 382

P

Paarl WO, 348, 349
Pacheco Pass AVA, 380
Pacheco Ranch Winery, 388
Pacherenc du Vic-Bilh AOC, 188
Pacific Northwest (USA), 389-91, 464, 465
Paço d'Anha, 302
Paço de Teixeiró, 301
Padouën, Château, 80
Padthaway, 432
Páez, Luis, 290
Pagadebit VT, 261
Page Mill Winery, 382
Paicines AVA, 380
Païen, 317
Paillard, Bruno, 146
Pais grape, 408, 409
Palacio, Bodegas, 276
Palácio da Brejoeira, 301
"palate", 7
Palette AOC, 194, 196
Palmer, Château, 63, 66
Palmero, Casa, 412
Palomas, 406
Palomino & Vergara, 288
Palomino grape, 27, 282, 367, 444
Pamid grape, 31
Papagni Vineyards, 386
Pape-Clément, Château, 75
Papes, Clos des, 180
La Papeterie, Château, 99
Paradiesgarten, Grosslage, 223
Paradis, Clos du, 171
Paraguay, 407
Pardaillan, Château, 102
Parducci Wine Cellars, 369
La Paroisse, Cave Coopérative, 41
Paros AO, 340
Parramatta, 414
Parramatta River, 424

Parrina DOC, 258
Parro Guerrero, Antonio, 290
Parsac, 81
Parsac-St.-Emilion AOC, 82
Parsons Creek Winery, 369
Parxet, 281
Paso Robles AVA, 383
Pasquier-Desvignes, 111
Passito di Chambave VT, 249
pasteurization, 18
Patache-d'Aux, Château, 45, 50
Paternina, Federico, 276
Patriarche Père & Fils, 111
Patrimonio AOC, 196
Patris, Château, 92
Patras AO, 339
Paulliac, 44, 45, 46, 54-8, *55*
Paulo grape, 417
Paulsen (Pat) Vineyards, 373
Paveil-de-Luze, Château, 68
Pavie, Château, 91
Pavie Décesse, Château, 91
Pavie Macquin, Château, 91
Pavillon-Cadet, Château, 91
Pavillon Figeac, Château, 92
Pays Nantais, 161-2
Pécharmant AOC, 188
Pecota (Robert) Winery, 376
Pécs, 329
Pédesclaux, Château, 58
Pedrizzetti Winery, 382
Pedro Domecq Colombia, 406
Pedro Ximénez grape, 282, 367, 406
Pedroncelli Winery, 373
Peel Winery, 439-40
Peju Province Winery, 378
Pelee Island Vineyards & Winery, 405
Peligon, Clos de, 43
Peloponnese, 339
Pemartín, José, 290
Penaflor Winery, *410*
Penbeth Valley Vineyard, 314
Pendleton Winery, 381
Penedés, 277, 278, 279
Penedés, Compañía Vinícola del, 281
Penedés Superior, 278
Penela, Casa de, 302
Penfolds, 434, 444, 445, 448
Pennsylvania, 397
Penshurst, 314
Pentro di Isernia DOC, 262
Pepi (Robert) Winery, 378
Pérez Megía, 290
Perico, Jean, 281
Pérignon, Dom, 136-7
Perl, 221
Perlan OA, 317
Perle grape, 27
Pernand-Vergelesses AOC, 126
Pernand-Vergelesses Premier Cru AOC, 126
Pernaud, Château, 80
Perrier-Jouët, 146
Peru, 406, 407
Pesenti Winery, 384
Pessac, 69
Pessac-Léognan AOC, 73
Peste, Cuvée Docteur, 122
Petaluma, 434
Petersberg, Grosslage, 217, 229
Petersons Wines, 422
Petit Chablis AOC, 115
Petit-Faurie-de-Soutard, Château, 91
Petit-Figeac, Château, 92
Petit-Gravet, Château, 92
Petit-Pey, Château, 107
Petit Rouge VT, 249
Petit Val, Château, 92

Petit verdot grape, 31, 38, 408
Petit Village, Château, 93, 97
Petite Arvine, 317
Petite Crau, 200
Petite sirah grape, 365, 403, 417
Les Petits Arnauds, Château, 102
Pétrus, Château, 36, 93, 94, 97, 363
Peverella grape, 367
Peychaud, Château, 102
Peynaud, Professor, 38, 61, 65, 67, 86
Peyreau, Château, 92
Peyrebon, Château, 106
Peyredoulle, Château, 102
Peyrere, Château, 102
Peyrines, Château, 107
Pez, Château de, 51, 53
Peza AO, 340
Pézenas, 200
Pfaffengrund, Grosslage, 232
Pfaffenheim-Gueberschwihr, Cave Vinicole de, 153
Pfarrgarten, Grosslage, 223
Pheasant Ridge Winery, 399
Phélan-Ségur, Château, 53
Phelps (Joseph) Vineyards, *361,* 376
Philipponnat, 146
Philips, 349
phylloxera, 11, 171, 410
Piat Père et Fils, 111
Piave DOC, 254
Pic-St.-Loup AOC, 191
Piccone VT, 248
Pichon-Bellevue, Château, 107
Pichon-Lalande, Château, *54, 55*
Pichon-Longueville-Baron, Château, 57
Pichon-Longueville-Comtesse-de-Lalande, Château, 57
Picketberg WO, 350
Picol Ross VT, 261
Piconi Winery, 388
Picque-Caillou, Château, 69
Piedmont, 245, 246-7
Piedmont Vineyards & Winery, 397
Pierre, 448
Pierro, 440
Piesport, 220
Pignan, Clos, 180
Pilgerpfad, Grosslage, 229
Pilton Manor, 314
Le Pin, Château, 93, 97
Pindar Vineyards, 397
Pindefleurs, Château, 92
Pine Ridge Winery, 378
Pineau d'Aunis grape, 31, 163, 167
Pinet AOC, 191
Pinot Blanc AOC, 155
Pinot blanc grape, 27, 149, 322, 367, 403
Pinot gris grape, 27, *27,* 149, 322, 403, 444
Pinot meunier grape, 31, 136, 236
Pinot Noir AOC, 155
Pinot noir grape, 31, *31;* Alsace, 149; Argentina, 410; Austria, 323; Brazil, 406; California, 365; Canada, 402, 404; Central Vineyards, 171; Champagne, 136; Chile, 410; Colombia, 406; Côte de Nuits, 116; Mâconnais, 130; New South Wales, 419; New Zealand, 444; Uruguay, 406; *see also* Spätburgunder grape
Pinot St. George grape, 365

Pinotage grape, 31, 444
Pinson Hnos, 401
Piper-Heidsieck, 146, 451
Piper Sonoma, 372
Piper-Sonoma Winery, 363
Pipers Brook Vineyard, *424, 427*
Pirramimma, 434
"Pisse Vieille", 133
Plagnac, Château, 50
Plam Vineyards, 378
Plane's Cayuga Vineyard, 397
Plantagenet Wines, 440
Platina grape, 332
Platt's, 422
Plavać mali grape, 332
Plince, Château, 97
Ployez-Jacquemart, 148
Poças, 301
Podbalkanski Raion, 326
Podensac, 69, 70
Point Loma Winery, 388
La Pointe, Château, 97
Pointe de Lima, 302
Pol Roger & Co., 146
Polish Hill River, 432
Pollino DOC, 266
Polmassick, 314
Pomerol, 38, 81, 82, 93-9, 464-5
Pomina DOC, 258
Pommard AOC, 126
Pommard Premier Cru AOC, 126
Pommeraie Vineyards, 373
Pommery & Greno, 146-7
Pomys, Château, 53
Ponnelle, Maison Pierre, 112
Pont de Guestres, Château du, 99
Pontac-Lynch, Château, 68
Pontet-Canet, Château, 58
Pontette-Bellegrave, Château, 107
Ponzi Vineyards, 391
Port, 293, 295-6; fermentation and fortification, 296-7; grapes, 296; houses, 299-301; maturation and blending, 297; styles, 299; vintages, 298, 464-5
Port Macquarie, 420
Portalto, 290
Portela, Quinta da, 302
Portet, 69
Portgal, 293-308, 464-5
Portugieser grape, 31, 214, 215
Portulano VT, 265
Potensac, Château, 45, 50
Potter Valley AVA, 369
Pouchaud-Larquey, Château, 43
Pouget, Château, 66
Pouilly-Fuissé AOC, 132
Pouilly Fumé AOC, 38, 172
Pouilly-Loché AOC, 132
Pouilly-sur-Loire AOC, 172
Pouilly-Vinzelles AOC, 132
Poujeaux, Château, 50
Poulsard grape, 27
La Poussie, Clos de, 171
Poverty Bay, 445, 446
Power, Drury & Co., 306
Les Pradines, Château, 53
Prager Winery and Port Works, 378
Prato de Canzio DOC, 253
Preiss-Zimmer, Jean, 153
Premier Cru, 38
Premier Grand Cru, 38
Premier Grand Cru Classé, 38
Premières Côtes de Blaye AOC, 101
Premières-Côtes-de-Bordeaux AOC, 105

President grape, 403
presses, Champagne, 138, *138*
"Le Prestige Bordeaux", 43
Preston Vineyards, 372
Preston Wine Cellars, 391
Le Prieuré, Château, 91
Prieuré-Lichine, Château, 67
Primitivo di Manduria DOC, 265
Primitivo grape, 31
Primo Estate Wines, 436
Prince Michael Vineyards, 397
Principauté d'Orange, 200
Priorato DO, 279
Probstberg, Grosslage, 221
Productos de Uva, 401
Prohibition, 356
Prosecco di Conegliano-Valdobbiadene DOC, 254
Prosecco grape, 27
Prospect Vineyard, 314
Protheau, F. & Fils, 111
Provence, 176, 193-6
Proviar, 412
Provincial Liquor Boards, Canada, 402, 403
Prudence Island Vineyards, 397
Puisseguin, 81
Puisseguin-St.-Emilion AOC, 82
Pulham, 314
Puligny-Montrachet AOC, 126
Puligny-Montrachet Premier Cru AOC, 126
Puy, Château du, 99
Puy-de-Dôme, 200
Puy Razac, Château, 92
Puycarpin, Château, 99
Puyfromage, Château, 43
Puygueraud, Château, 99
Pyrénées (Victoria), 425
Pyrénées-Atlantiques, 200
Pyrénées-Orientales, 200

Quady Winery, 386
Quail Ridge, 378
Qualitätswein Bestimmter Anbaugebiete (QbA), 212
Qualitätswein mit Prädikat (QmP), 212
quality control, Germany, 202
Quancard, Marcel, 40
Quarles Harris, 295, 301
Quarts-de-Chaume AOC, 166
Quatourze AOC, 191
Quebec, 405
Queen Court, 314
Queensland, 416, 441-2
Quincy AOC, 171, 172
Quinsac, Cave de, 43
Quinta classification, Douro, 297
Quinta do Côtto, 301
Quintão, Quinta da, 302

Rabaner grape, 27
Rabaud-Promis, Château, 78-9
Rabigato grape, 27
Raboso DOC, 254
racking, 20
Rafanelli, A., 373
Rahoul, Château, 69, 77
Raimat, 280

Rainera Pérez Marín "La Guita", Hijos de, 288
Ramage-la-Batisse, Château, 50
La Rame, Château, 107
Rameau-Lamarosse, Cuvée, 122
Ramitello VT, 262
Ramón Bilbao, Bodegas, 276
Ramos-Pinto, 301
Ranchita Oaks Winery, 384
Rancho de Philo, 388
Randersacker, 235
Ranzau Wines, 448
Rapsani AO, 340
Rasteau AOC, 179
Rasteau "Rancio" AOC, 179
Rauenthal, 226
Rausan-Ségla, Château, 67
Räuschling, 317
Rauzan-Gassies, Château, 67
Ravello VT, 265
Ravensburg, Grosslage, 235
Ravenswood, 372
Ray, Martin, 382
Rayas, Château, 180
Raymond-Lafon, Château, 80
Raymond Vineyard and Cellar, 376
Rayne-Vigneau, Château, 79
Rayón, Bodegas, 289
Real Tesoro, 288
Rebstöckel, Grosslage, 232
Recioto Bianco di Campociesa VT, 254
Recioto della Valpolicella DOC, 254
Recioto di Soave DOC, 254
Recioto di Soave dei Capitelli DOC, 253
Recoaro, 412
red wine: colour, 7; German, 204; serving, 452; tasting, 9; vinification, 21
Redbank, 429
Redgate Wines, 440
Redgum Vineyard, 436
Redmond Vineyard, 440
Refosco grape, 332
Regaleali VT, 266
Regner grape, 27
Reh, Franz & Sohn KG, 209
Reh (Günther) Group, 209
Rehbach, Grosslage, 229
Reichensteiner grape, 27
Reichenstein, Grosslage Schloss, 217
Reif Winery Inc., 405
Reig, Rafael, 290
Reignac, 59
La Reine Pédauque, Caves de, 111
Remélluri, 275
Remoissenet Père & Fils, 111
Remshalden-Grunbach, 237
Remstal-Stuttgart, Bereich, 237
remuage, Champagne, 139, *139*
Remy, Chateau, 426
Remy-Pannier, 158
Renault Winery, 396
Rendufe, Casa de, 302
René, Clos, 97
Renmano Wines, 434
Renon, Château, 43
Resero, 412
Respide-Médeville, Château, 77
Retsina, 338, 339
Retz, 200
Retzbach, 235
Reuilly AOC, 171, 172
Rex Hill Vineyards, 391
Reynella, Chateau, 433
Reynon, Château, 43
Reynon-Peyrat, Château, 107

Rèze, 317
Rheinberg Kellerei, 209
Rheinblick, Grosslage, 229
Rheinburgengau, Bereich, 217
Rheinfels, Grosslage Burg, 217
Rheingarten, Schloss, 211
Rheingau, 206, 207, 224-6
Rheingrafenstein, Grosslage, 228
Rheinhessen, 206, 207, 227-9
Rheinpfalz, 206, 230-2
Rhine, 204, 464-5
Rhine riesling grape, 417, 419, 423
Rhine Terrace, 227
Rhode Island, 397
Rhodes AO, 340
Rhoditis grape, 27
Rhône valley, 173-80, 464-5
Rias Baixas DO, 291
Ribatejo VR, 308
Ribeiro DO, 291
Ribera Alta, 273
Ribera Baja, 273
Ribera del Duero, 269
Ribera del Duero DO, 291-2
Ricaud, Château, 107
Richebourg AOC, 120
Richmond Estate, 422
Ridge Vineyards, 381
Rieslaner grape, 27, 234
Riesling AOC, 155
Riesling grape, 27, *27*; Ahr, 215; Alsace, 149; Australia, 417; Austria, 319, 323; *Barrique* wines, 207; Chile, 408, 409; Hessische Bergstrasse, 233; Liebfraumilch, 206; Mittelrhein, 216; Mosel-Saar-Ruwer, 218; Nahe, 223; New Zealand, 444; Rheingau, 224; Württemberg, 236
Riesling-Sylvaner OA, 317
Rietvallei Estate, 353
Rieussec, Château, 70, 79
Rio Grande do Sul, 406, *407*
Rio Negro, 410
La Rioja (Argentina), 410
Rioja (Spain), 269, *270*, 271-2, 274-6, 464-5
Rioja Alavesa, 272
Rioja Alta, 272, 275
Rioja Baja, 272
Rioja Santiago, Bodegas, 276
Riojanas, Bodegas, 274
Ripeau, Château, 91
Riquewihr, *150*
Ritterhof, 211
Rittersberg, Grosslage, 239
La Riva, 288
River Oaks Vineyards Wines, 373
River Run Vintners, 382
Riverland, 432
El Rivero, 412
Rivesaltes AOC, 192
Riviera, 194
Riviera del Garda Bresciano DOC, 249
Riviera Ligure di Ponente DOC, 249
La Rivière, Château, 99
Rkatsiteli grape, 27
Robert, Bodegas, 281
Robertson WO, 350
Robertson Brothers, 301
Robertson Koöp Wynkelder, 354
Robin, Château, 99
Robinsons Family, 442
Robola of Cephalonia AO, 340
Robola grape, 27
Robson Vineyard, 421

Roc Blanquant, 92
Roc de Cayla, Château, 43, 107
La Roche AOC, Clos de, 117
Rocher-Bellevue, Château, 99
Rochioli (J.) Vineyards, 373
Rochmorin, Château de, 77
Rock Lodge, 314
Rockford Wines, 436
Rocky Knob AVA, 395
Rodeck, Grosslage Schloss, 240
Rödelsee, 235
Rodet, Antonin, 111
Roding Valley Red, 314
Roederer, Louis, 147
Roederer USA, 369
Roero DOC, 248
Rojas, 406
Rolin, Cuvée Nicolas, 122
Rolland, Château de, 80
Rolland-Maillet, Château, 92
Rolly Gassmann, 153
Roma, 442
La Romanée AOC, 120
Romanée-Conti AOC, 93, 120
Romanée-St.-Vivant AOC, 120
Romania, 330-1
Romansrivier Koöp Wynkelder, 354
Romate, 290
Rombauer Vineyards, 378
Romer, Château, 79
Romer-du-Hayot, Château, 79
Römerlay, Grosslage, 221
Romorantin, 171
Romorantin grape, 27, 167
Romero, Pedro, 290
Ronco Casone VT, 261
Ronco dei Ciliegi VT, 261
Ronco delle Acacie VT, 253
Ronco delle Ginestre VT, 261
Ronco di Mompiano VT, 249
Le Rondailh, Château, 107
Rondinella grape, 31
Roodezandt Koöp Wynkelder, 354
Rooiberg Koöp Wynkelder, 354
rootstocks, 11
Ropiteau Frères, 112
Roquetaillade-La-Grange, Château de, 77
Rosa del Golfo VT, 264
Rosa di Albenga VT, 249
Rosato del Molise VT, 262
Rosato del Molise-Fiore VT, 262
Rosato della Lega CT, 258
Rosato delle Marche VT, 262
Rosato di Montanello VT, 262
Rosé VR, 308
rosé Champagne, 141
Le Rosé de Clarke, 43
Rosé de Loire AOC, 159
Rosé des Riceys AOC, 148
La Rose Pauillac, 58
La Rose Pauillac, Cave Coopérative, 41
rosé wines: colour, 7; Provence, 193; vinification, 22
Rosemount Estate, *419, 421*
Rosenblum Cellars, 381
Rosenbühl, Grosslage, 232
Rosengarten, Grosslage, 223
Rosenhang, Grosslage, 220
Rosette AOC, 188
Roseworthy College Cellars, 436
Ross (Don Charles) Winery, 378
Rossese di Dolceacqua DOC, 249
Rosso Armentano VT, 261

Rosso Barletta DOC, 265
Rosso Canosa DOC, 265
Rosso Cònero DOC, 262
Rosso della Bissera VT, 261
Rosso di Cerignola DOC, 265
Rosso delle Colline Lucchesi DOC, 258
Rosso di Corinaldo VT, 262
Rosso della Lega VT, 258
Rosso del Molise VT, 262
Rosso di Montalcino DOC, 257
Rosso di Sava VT, 265
Rosso Piceno DOC, 262
Rosstal, Grosslage, 235
Rotberger grape, 31
Roter Veltliner, 323
Rotgipfler, 323
The Rothbury Estate, 422
Rothschild, Domaine, 79
Rott, Grosslage, 233
Roudier, Château, 99
Roudon-Smith Vineyards, 381-2
Rouge Homme, 434
Rouget, Château, 97
Roumieu, Château, 80
Roumieu-Lacoste, Château, 80
Round Hill Cellars, 378
Roussanne grape, 27
Rousseau-Deslandes, Cuvée, 122
Rousset, Château, 102
Roussette du Bugey VDQS, 183
Roussette de Savoie AOC, 183
Rowney, 314
Roxheim, 223
Royal Kedem Winery, 397
Royal Oporto, 301
Royalty grape, 365
Rubino di Cantavenna DOC, 248
Rubino VT, 262
Rubired grape, 365
Ruby cabernet grape, 31, 365
Ruchottes-Chambertin AOC, 120
Rüdesheim, 223, 225
Rueda DO, 292
Ruinart Père & Fils, 147
Rully AOC, *128*, 129
Rully Premier Cru AOC, 129
Rumbalara Vineyards, 442
Ruppertsberg, 231
Ruppertsberger Winzerverein "Hoheburg" eG, 210
La Rural, Bodegas, 412
Russia, 335
Russian River Valley AVA, 371
Rust-en-Vrede Estate, 353
Rustenberg, 353
Rutherford & Miles, 306
Rutherford Hill Winery, 378
Rutherford Vintners, 376
Rutherglen, 425

Saaleck, 235
Saar-Ruwer, Bereich, 221
Saarburg, 221
Sables, 81
Sables du Golfe du Lion, 200
La Sablière-Fongrave, Château de, 107
Sacy grape, 28
Saint-Amande, Château, 80
St.-Amour AOC, 135
Saint Anne's, 314
St.-Aubin AOC, 126

St.-Aubin Premier Cru AOC, 126
St-Bonnet, Château, 50
Ste. Chapelle, 391
St.-Chinian AOC, 192
St.-Christol AOC, 191
St.-Christophe, 81
St. Clare, 404
St. Clement Vineyards, 378
Ste.-Croix-du-Mont, 105
St.-Denis AOC, Clos, 118
St.-Drézéry AOC, 191
St.-Emilion, 38, 44, 81, 82, 83-92, 83, 464-5
Saint-Emilion grape, 28, 367
St.-Estèphe, 44, 45, 46, 51-3
Ste.-Foy-Bordeaux, 105
Saint-Gallen, 318
St.-Georges, 81
St.-Georges, Château (Côte Pavie), 91
Sto.-Georges, Château (St.-Emilion), 99
Saint-Georges, Clos, 77
St.-Georges-d'Orques, 191
St.-Georges-St.-Emilion AOC, 82
Saint George's Waldron, 314
St. Hallett's Wines, 436
St. Helena Wine Estate, 448
St. Huberts, 427
St.-Jean, Cave Coopérative, 41
St. Jean, Chateau, 371
St.-Joseph AOC, 175
St. Julian Wine Company, 396
St.-Julien, 44, 45, 46, 59-62
St.-Lambert, 59
St.-Landelin, Clos, 152
St. Laurent, 323
St. Leonards Vineyard, 427
St. Macaire grape, 365
De Saint-Marceaux, 147
St.-Martin, Clos, 87
St. Michael, Grosslage, 221
Ste. Michelle, Chateau, 391
Saint Nicholas of Ash, 314
St.-Nicolas-de-Bourgeuil AOC, 169
St.-Péray AOC, 174, 175
St.-Peray Mousseux AOC, 175
St.-Pierre, Château, 62
Saint-Pourçain VDQS, 160
Saint Remy, 412
St-Roch, Caves, 41
St.-Romain AOC, 126-7
Saint-Sardos, 200
St.-Saturnin AOC, 191
St.-Seurin-de-Cadourne, 45
Sainte Sylvie, 412
St. Ursula Weingut, 209
St.-Véran AOC, 132
St.-Yzans, 45
Saint-Yzans, Cave Coopérative de, 41
Saintsbury, 378
Sakonnet Vineyards, 397
Sales, Château de, 97
Salice Salentino DOC, 265
Salon, 147
Salta, 410
Saltram Winery, 434
Salvador grape, 365
Salvagnin OA, 317
Salzberg, Grosslage, 237
Sampigny-lès-Maranges AOC, 126
Sampigny-lès-Maranges Premier Cru AOC, 126
Samsons, Cellier des, 112
San Benito AVA, 380
San Benito County AO, 380
San Benito Vineyards, 382
San Colombano al Lambro DOC, 249
San Colombano DOC, 249
San Juan, 410

San Lucas, 380
San Luis Obispo AO, 383
San Marino Vineyards, 448
San Martin Winery, 382
San Mateo County AO, 380
San Pasqual AVA, 387-8
San Pasqual Vineyards, 388
San Severo DOC, 265
San Telmo, 412
Sancerre, 38, 171, 172
Sanchez Creek Vineyards, 399
Sandalford Wines, 440
Sandeman, 288, 300
Sanford & Benedict Vineyards, 384
Sang des Salasses VT, 249
Sangiovese dei Colli Pesaresi DOC, 262
Sangiovese delle Marche VT, 262
Sangiovese di Romagna DOC, 261
Sangiovese grape, 32, 32, 255
Sankt Alban, Grosslage, 229
Sankt Rochuskapelle, Grosslage, 228
sans-chêne red wine, 272
Sansonnet, Château, 91
Santa Ana, 412
Santa Barbara AO, 383
Santa Barbara Winery, 384
Santa Clara County AO, 380
Santa Clara Valley AVA, 380
Santa Cruz Mountain Vineyard, 382
Santa Cruz Mountains AVA, 380
Santa Leocádia, Casa de, 302
Santa Maddalena DOC, 252
Santa Maria Valley AVA, 383-4
Santa Mavra, 340
Santa Rosa Wines, 436
Santa Ynez Valley AVA, 384
Santa Ynez Valley Winery, 384
Santana do Livramento, 406
Sant'Anna di Isola Capo Rizzuto DOC, 266
Santenay AOC, 126
Santenay Premier Cru AOC, 126
Santino Winery, 387
Santo Claudio, Quinta de, 302
Santo Tomás, Bodegas de, 401
Santorini AO, 340
Sarah's Vineyard, 382
Sardinia, 264, 266
Sarrail-la-Guillamerie, Château, 43
Sarrau, 112
Sarthe, 200
Sattui (V.) Winery, 378
Sauman, Château, 102
Saumur, 163, 164, 166
Saumur-Champigny, 163, 164, 166
Saumur Mousseux AOC, 166
Saumur Pétillant AOC, 166
Sausal Winery, 373
Saussignac AOC, 188
Sautejeau, Marcel, 158
Sauternes, 36, 69, 70, 71-2, 73, 77-9, 464-5
Sauvignon blanc grape: Austria, 323; Bordeaux, 36, 38; Brazil, 406; California, 367; Central Vineyards, 171; Chile, 408, 410; New Zealand, 443, 444; Touraine, 167; Uruguay, 406
Sauvignon de St.-Bris, 114, 115
Sauvignon vert grape, 367
Sauvion & Fils, 158
Savagnin grape, 28
Savatiano grape, 28

Savennières AOC, 166
Savigny-lès-Beaune AOC, 126
Savigny-lès-Beaune Premier Cru AOC, 126
Savoie, 181-3
Savory & James, 290
Savuto DOC, 266
Saxonvale Wines, 421
Schaffhausen, 316, 318
Schalkstein, Grosslage, 237
Schapiro's Winery, 397
Scharffenberger Cellars, 369
Scharzberg, Grosslage, 221
Scheurebe grape, 28, 223, 323
Schild, Grosslage, 235
Schillerwein, 236
Schillerwein AOC, 155
Schioppettino VT, 253
Schloss Böckelheim, Bereich, 223
Schlossberg, Grosslage, 233, 235
Schlossböckelheim, 223
Schlosskapelle, Grosslage, 223
Schlosskellerei Affaltrach, 211
Schlossstück, Grosslage, 235
Schlumberger, Domaines, 153
Schmitt, G.A., 209
Schnaufer, 211
Schnepfenflug an der Weinstrasse, 232
Schnepfenflug vom Zellertal, Grosslage, 232
Scholl & Hillebrand, 209
Schönberger grape, 28
Schönborn, Schloss, 211
Schönburg, Grosslage Schloss, 217
Schozachtal, Grosslage, 237
Schramsberg Vineyards, 376
Schröder & Schyler, 41, 66
Schug Cellars, 376
Schutter-Lindenberg, Grosslage, 240
Schwarze Katz, Grosslage, 220
Schwarzerde, Grosslage, 232
Schwarzlay, Grosslage, 221
Schwarzriesling grape, 236
Schweigen-Rechtenbach, 232
Scorza Amara VT, 261
SDVF, 41
Sea Ridge Winery, 373
Seaview Winery, 434
Sebastiani Vineyards, 372
Secano, 409
sediment, decanting wine, 452
Sedlescombe, 314
Segonzac, Château, 102
Segura Viudas, 280
Sehndorf, 221
Seizim, Casa de, 301
Sekt, 207, 210-11, 213
Selak Wines, 448
Sellards Winery, 373
Sémillon grape, 28, 28; Australia, 416, 417; Bordeaux, 36, 38; Brazil, 406; California, 367; Chile, 408, 410; New South Wales, 419; New Zealand, 443, 444; Uruguay, 406; Victoria and Tasmania, 423; Yugoslavia, 332
Señorio de Sarría, 276
Seppelt, 434
Septimer grape, 28
Sequoia Grove Vineyards, 378
Serbia, 333
Sercial grape, 28, 306, 417
La Serre, Château, 91
Serre du Coiran, 200

Serres, Bodegas Carlos, 275
Serrig, 221
serving wine, 452
Settlement Wine Co., 436
Setúbal, 293, 308
Sevillanas, Bodegas, 406
Seville Estate, 427
Sèvre-et-Maine, 161
Seymours, 314
Seyssel AOC, 183
Seyssel Mousseux AOC, 183
Seyval blanc grape, 28, 403, 404
Seyve villard grape, 403, 404
Shafer Vineyards, 378
Shaw, Charles F., 376
Shemarin Wines, 440
Shenandoah Valley AVA, 395
Shenandoah Vineyards, 387
Sherrill Cellars, 382
Sherry, 269, 282-90, 296, 453
Sherston Earl, 314
Shiraz grape, 416, 417, 418, 419, 441
Shown & Sons, 378
Siaurac, Château, 99
Sichel, H. Söhne, 209
Sicily, 264, 266
Siebengebirge, Bereich, 217
Siegerrebe grape, 28
Sierra Foothills, 387
Sierra Nevada de Santa Marta, 406
Sigalas-Rabaud, Château, 79
sight, tasting wine, 7, 8-9
Silva & Cosens, 300
Silvaner grape, 206, 223, 227, 233, 234, 323
Silver Mountain Vineyards, 382
Silver Oak Cellars, 376
Silverado Vineyards, 378
Simi Winery, 363, 370, 372
Simon, Château, 80
Simonnet-Febvre, 112
Simonsig Estate, 353
Simonsvlei Koöp Wynkelder, 354
Sipp, Louis, 153
Siran, Château, 68
Sitia AO, 340
Sittmann, Carl, 209
Sizzano DOC, 248
Skillogalee Vineyards, 436
Slanghoek Koöp Wynkelder, 354
Slovakia, 329
Slovenia, 333
smell, tasting wine, 7, 8-9
Smith, S. & Son, 434
Smith-Haut-Lafitte, Château, 75
Smith-Madrone, 376
Smith Woodhouse, 301
Snipe, 314
Soave DOC, 242, 253
Soave Classico Capitel Foscarino, 253-4
Soave Classico Monteforte, 254
Sociando-Mallet, Château, 50
Sociedad Agricola Santa Elisa, 411
Sociedad Viña Carmen, 411
Société Civile J. Janoueix, 95
Söhnlein Rheingold, 211
Sokol Blosser Winery, 391
Solano County, 388
Solano County Green Valley AVA, 388
Solar das Bouças, 302
Solar de Ribeiro, 302
Solera blending system, Sherry, 285
Solicchiato Bianco di Villa Fontane VT, 266

Soljans Wines, 448
Solopaca DOC, 265
Solutré, 130
Sommerach, 235
Sommerhausen, 235
Somontano DO, 292
Sonnenborn, Grosslage, 223
Sonnenbühl, Grosslage, 237
Sonnenufer, Grosslage, 240
Sonoita AVA, 398
Sonoma Coast AVA, 371
Sonoma County, 370-3
Sonoma County Green Valley AVA, 371
Sonoma-Cutrer Vineyards, 372
Sonoma Mountain AVA, 371
Sonoma Valley AVA, 371
Sopron, 329
sorbic acid, 18
Sorni DOC, 252
Soto, José de, 290
Sotoyome Winery, 373
Soussans, 63
Soutard, Château, 91
South Africa, 346-9, 350-4
South America, 406-12
South Australia, 415, 430-6
South Carolina, 399
South-Central Coast (California), 383-4
South Coast AVA (California), 367
South Coast Cellar, 388
South Island (New Zealand), 446
Southeastern New England AVA, 395
Southern Vales-Langhorne Creek, 432
Southern Vales Winery, 434
Southwest Coastal Plain, 439
Southwest France, 184-92
Souto Vedro, 302
Souverain Winery, 372
Sovicop Producta, 41
Spain, 268-92, 464-5
Spanna VT, 247
sparkling wine: Anjou-Saumur, 163; German, 207; Lombardy, 248; Piedmont, 247; Sekt, 210-11, 213; Spain, 279; tasting, 9; Trentino-Alto Adige, 252; Tuscany, 257; vinification, 23
Sparr, Pierre, 153
Spätburgunder grape, 207, 214, 215; see also Pinot noir grape
Spätlese QmP, 212-13
Spiegelberg, Grosslage, 229
Spier Estate, 353
Spinello VT, 262
Spottswoode Vineyard & Winery, 376
Spring Barn Vineyard, 314
Spring Farm, 314
Spring Mountain Vineyards, 378
Springton, 432
Spruitdrift Koöp Wynkelder, 354
Squinzano DOC, 265
Stag's Leap District AVA, 375
Stag's Leap Wine Cellars, 376
Stahleck, Grosslage Schloss, 217
stainless-steel vats, 19
Stanlake Park, 314-15
Stanley Wine Company, 434-5
Stanton & Killeen, 429
Staple, 315
Staplecombe, 315
Starkenburg, Bereich, 233
Stauffenberg, Grosslage, 237
Steen grape, 28
Steigerwald, Bereich, 235

Steil, Grosslage, 226
Steinmächer, Grosslage, 226
Stellenbosch WO, 348, 349
Stellenbosch Farmers'
  Winery (SFW), 348, 351
Stellenryck Collection, 351
Stemmler (Robert) Winery,
  373
Steri VT, 266
Sterling Vineyards, 376
Stetten, 237
Stevenot Winery, 387
Steyning Vineyards, 315
Stiftsberg, Grosslage, 239
Stitchcombe, 315
Stockheim, 237
Stocks Vineyard, 315
Stonegate Winery, 378
Stoneridge, 387
Stoney Ridge Cellars, 405
Stoney Vineyard, 429
Stony Hill Vineyard, 376
storing wine, 452
Story Vineyard, 387
Storybook Mountain
  Vineyards, 378
Stromberg, Grosslage, 237
Strong (Rodney) Vineyards,
  373
Styria, 324
Suau, Château, 79
Subileau, Antoine, 158
Sucre, 406
Süd-Oststeiermark, 324
Südburgenland, 323
Südliche Weinstrasse,
  Bereich, 232
Südsteiermark, 324
Suduiraut, Château, 70, 79
Suisun Valley AVA, 388
Sullivan Vineyards, 378
sulphur dioxide, 18, 20
Sulzfeld, 235, 239
Sumac Ridge Estate Winery,
  404
Summerfield, 429
Summerhill Vineyards, 382
Sundown Valley Vineyards,
  442
Sunraysia, 425
Sunrise Winery, 382
sunshine, 12, 13
La Superiora Viñedos y
  Bodega, 412
Surinam, 407
Susiné Cellars, 388
süssreserve, 206, 443
Suter, 412
Sutherland Wines, 422
Sutter Home Winery, 378
Swan (Joseph) Vineyards, 373
Swan Valley, 437, 438, 439
Swartland WO, 349
sweetness, German wines,
  202-3
Swellendam WO, 350
Swiftsden, 315
Switzerland, 316-18
Sybillenstein, Grosslage, 229
Sycamore Creek Vineyards,
  382
Sylvaner AOC, 155
Sylvaner grape, 28, 28, 149,
  367, 406
Syndale Valley, 315
Syrah grape, 32, 32, 173, 174,
  342, 365, 410, 416
Syria, 342

T

Tabor Hill Bronte Wines, 396
Tabor Hill Vineyards, 396
Tacelenghe VT, 253

La Tâche AOC, 120
Tafelwein, 212
Tahbilk, Chateau, 424, 426
Tailhas, Château du, 97
Le Taillan, 44
Taillefer, Château, 97
Taittinger, 147
Takara Sake USA, 382
Talbot, Château, 60, 62
Talbott (Robert) Vineyards,
  382
Talence, 69
Taltarni Vineyards, 427
Tamariz, Quinta do, 302
Tamburlaine, 422
Tâmega, 302
Tanesse, Château, 107
tank method, sparkling
  wines, 23
Tannat grape, 32
Tapada, Casa da, 302
Tapestry, 315
Tarapacá Ex Zavala, 411
Tarcoola Vineyards, 429
Tarn-et-Garonne, 200
Tarragona DO, 279
Tarreyo, Château, 99
Tart AOC, Clos de, 118
Tastes, Château des, 107
Tastevinage label, 116
tasting wine, 7-9; glossary,
  456-63
Tauberberg, Grosslage, 237
Tauberklinge, Grosslage, 239
Taurasi DOC, 265
Taveau, 165
Tavel AOC, 179
Tayac, Château, 68
Taylor California Cellars, 381
Taylor, Fladgate & Yeatman,
  300
Taylor Wine Company, 397
Taylor's, 295
Te Mata Estate, 448
Te Whare Ra Wines, 448
technical terms, glossary,
  456-63
Tedeschi Vineyard and
  Winery, 398
Telmont, J. de, 148
Temecula AVA, 388
temperature: growing
  grapes, 13; serving wine,
  452; storing wine, 452
Templeton, 384
Tempranillo grape, 32, 272,
  410
Tennessee, 399
Tenterden, 315
Tequila, 400
Terfort, Château, 107
Terlano DOC, 252
Teroldego Rotaliano DOC,
  252
Terra Alta DO, 279
Terre Rosse Chardonnay VT,
  261
Terrey-Gros-Caillou,
  Château, 62
terroir, 60
Terroirs Landais, 200
Terry, 289
Terry, Carlos y Javier de, 290
Tertre, Château du, 67
Tertre Daugay, Château, 92
Teufelstor, Grosslage, 235
Tewksbury Wine Cellars, 396
Texas, 399
Teynac, Château, 62
Thermenregion, 324
Thessaly, 340
Thibaud-Bellevue, Château,
  99
Thieuley, Château, 43, 106
Thomas Fern Hill Estate, 436
Thorin S.A., 112

Thornbury Castle Vineyard,
  315
Thrace, 338
Thrakiiska Nizina, 326
Three Choirs, 315
Three Corners, 315
Thüngersheim, 235
Thurgau, 318
Ticino, 318
Tierra Estella, 273
Tignanello, 256
Tijsseling, 369
Timberlay, Château, 43
Tingle-Wood Wines, 440
Tinta amarela grape, 296
Tinta barroca grape, 32, 296
Tinta cão grape, 32, 296
Tinta Madeira grape, 366
Tinta roriz grape, 296
Tintern Parva, 315
Tirol, 324
Tisdall Winery, 427
TKC Vineyards, 387
Tocai di San Martino della
  Battaglia DOC, 249
Tokay, 327, 328, 329
Tokay d'Alsace AOC, 155
Tokay grape, 417
Tokay-Pinot Gris AOC, 155
Tollana Wines, 435
Tolley's Pedare Wines, 435
Tolly Scott & Tolley, 435
Topolos Russian River
  Vineyards, 373
Torbato di Alghero VT, 266
Torcolato VT, 254
Torello, Cavas, 281
Torgan, 200
Torgiano DOC, 259
Torino, Michel, 412
Tormes, 302
Toro DO, 292
Torre Alemanna VT, 265
Torre Quarto VT, 265
Torres, 280-1
Torres, Miguel, 411
Torres Vineyards, 372
Torrette VT, 249
Toso, Pascual, 412
Totara Vineyards, 448
Toumalin, Château, 99
La Tour de Bessan, Château,
  68
La Tour Blanche, Château, 79
La Tour-de-By, Château, 45,
  50
La Tour-Carnet, Château, 46
Tour-de-l'Esperance,
  Château, 43
La Tour Figeac, Château, 92
La Tour-Haut-Brion, Château,
  75
Tour-du-Haut-Moulin,
  Château, 50
La Tour-Martillac, Château,
  75
La Tour de Mons, Château, 68
Tour-du-Pas-St.-Georges,
  Château, 99
Tour Petit Puch, Château, 43
La Tour de Pez, Château, 53
La Tour-Pibran, Château, 58
La Tour du Pin Figeac,
  Château, 92
La Tour Saint-Bonnet,
  Château, 45, 50
Tour St.-Christophe,
  Château, 92
Tour-de-Tourteau, Château,
  102
Touraine, 156, 164, 167-70
Touraine-Amboise AOC, 169
Touraine Azay-le-Rideau
  AOC, 169-70
Touraine-Mesland AOC, 170
Touraine Mousseux AOC, 170
Touraine Pétillant AOC, 170

Tourelles, Château des, 99
Touriga Francesca grape, 32,
  296
Touriga nacional grape, 32,
  32, 296, 417
Tournefeuille, Château, 99
Tours, 167, 171
Tours, Château des, 99
Toutigeac, Château de, 107
Toyon Winery & Vineyards,
  373
Traminer grape, 417, 423
Transylvania, 331
Trapiche, Bodegas, 412
Trappenberg, Grosslage, 232
Trás-os-Montes VR, 308
Trebbiano d'Abruzzo DOC,
  262
Trebbiano di Romagna DOC,
  261
Trebbiano grape, 406, 417
Trefethen Vineyards, 376
Trentadue Winery, 372
Trentino DOC, 252
Trentino-Alto Adige, 250,
  251-2
Las 3 Candidas, 290
Tres Marias, 302
Trimbach, F.E., 153
Trimoulet, Château, 92
Tristo di Montesecco VT, 262
Trittenheim, 220
Trocken wines, 225
Trockenbeerenauslese QmP,
  213
Trois-Chardons, Château des,
  68
Trois-Moulins, Château, 92
Trollinger, 323
Trollinger grape, 32, 236
Tronquoy-Lalande, Château,
  53
Troplong Mondot, Château,
  92
Trotanoy, Château, 93, 97
Trottevieille, Château, 92
Trousseau gris grape, 28
Troya grape, 417
Tschernomorski Raion, 326
Tualatin Vineyards, 391
Tudal Winery, 378
Tulbagh WO, 349
Tulloch, J.Y. & Sons, 421
Tulocay Winery, 376
Tunisia, 345
Turckheim, Cave Vinicole de,
  153
Turkey, 341, 342
Tursan VDQS, 188
Tuscany, 255-6, 257-8
Twanner, 317
Twee Jongegezellen Estate,
  353
Tyland Vineyards, 369
Tyrrell's Vineyards, 419,
  421-2
Tytherley, 315

U

Uerzig, 221
Ugni blanc grape, 28, 406
Uitkyk Estate, 353
Ukraine, 335
Umbria, 256, 258-9
Umpqua Valley AVA, 390
Umstadt, Bereich, 233
Undurraga, 411
Ungstein, 231
Uni-Médoc, 41
Union de Producteurs
  (St.-Emilion), 41, 83
Union de Vignerons (Loire),
  159

Union des Coopératives
  Vinicoles de Bourgogne
  de Saône-et-Loire, 112
Union Vinicole du Val de
  Loire, 159
Union Wine Group, 351
United States of America,
  356, 358-99; appellation
  system, 358-9; labels, 360;
  vintages, 464-5
Univitis, 41
Unlacke Estate Wines, 404
Upper Hunter Valley, 420
Urfe, 200
Uruguay, 406, 407
USSR, 334-5
Utiel-Requena DO, 292
Uva de Troia grape, 417
Uzège, 200

V

Val, Clos du, 375
Val d'Arbia DOC, 258
Val-de-Cesse, 200
Val-de-Dagne, 200
Val de Montferrand, 200
Val d'Orbieu, 200
Val Peligna VT, 262
La Valade, Château, 99
Valais, 318
Valcalepio DOC, 249
Valdadige DOC, 252
Valdeorras DO, 292
Valdepeñas DO, 292
Valdepenas grape, 366
Valdespino, 289
Valdizarbe, 273
Valeig, 220
Valençay VDQS, 170
Valencia DO, 292
Valeyrac, 45
Valle-d'Aosta, 246, 249
Valle Isarco DOC, 252
Vallée de la Marne, 136, 140
Vallée du Paradis, 200
Valley of the Moon, 373
Valley Wines, 351
Valpantena DOC, 254
Valpolicella DOC, 254
"Valpolicella" Ripasso VT, 254
Valrose, Domaine de, 193
Vals d'Agly, 200
Valtellina DOC, 249
Valtellina Superiore DOC,
  248
Van Buren grape, 403
Var, 200
Vasse Felix Winery, 437, 440
Vaucluse, 200
Vaud, 318
Vaunage, 200
Vee blanc grape, 403
Veeport grape, 403
Vega Sicilia, 269
Vega Vineyards Winery, 384
Velletri DOC, 259
Vendée, 200
Venecians, Bodegas, 406
Veneto, 250-1, 253-4
Venezuela, 407
Ventana Vineyards Winery,
  382
Ventura grape, 403, 404
Vérargues AOC, 191
Verdea, 340
Verdelet grape, 403
Verdelho grape, 28, 306
Verdicchio dei Castelli di Jesi
  DOC, 262
Verdicchio di Matelica DOC,
  262
Verdicchio grape, 29
Verdier, Claude, 159

Verdignan, Château, 50
Vergara, Juan Vicente, 290
Vergenoegd Estate, 353
Veritas Winery, 436
Vermentino di Gallura DOC, 266
Vermouth, 23
Vernaccia di Oristano DOC, 266
Vernaccia di San Gimignano DOC, 258
Vernaccia di Serrapetrona DOC, 262
Vernaccia grape, *256*
Verona Vineyard, 422
Verrenberg, 237
Vesuvio DOC, 265
Veuve Amiot, 159
Veuve Clicquot-Ponsardin, 147
Vichon Winery, 378
Vicomté d'Aumelas, 200
Victoria, 415, 416, 423-9
Victory Grape Wines, 448
Vidal blanc grape, 403, 404
Vidal Winery, 448
Vidiella grape, 406
La Vieille Cure, Château, 99
Vienna, 324
Vienne, 173, 200
Viénot, Charles, 112
Vieux Château Certan, 93, *93*, 98
Le Vieux Donjon, Domaine, 180
Vieux Moulin, Château, 43
Vieux-St.-André, 99
Vieux Télégraphe, Domaine de, 179
Vignerons de Buxy, Cave des, 112
Vignerons de la Noëlle Cana, 159
Vignerons de Saumur à Saint Cyr en Bourg, Cave des, 159
Les Vignobles Chantecler, 405
Les Vignobles du Quebec, 405
Vila Boa, Casa de, 302
Vila Nova, Casa de, 302
Vila Nova de Gaia, 296, 297
Vilacetinho, Casa de, 302
Vilaverde, Casa de, 302
Villa Helena Winery, 378
Villa Maria Estate, 448
Villa Mt. Eden Winery, 376
Villa Paradiso Vineyards, 382
Villafranca de Navarra, Bodegas, 276
Villamont, Henri de, 112
Villard blanc grape, 29
Villard noir grape, 403, 404
Villars, Château, 99
Villegorge, Château, 50
Villemaurine, Château, 92
Villenave d'Ornan, 69
Villiera Estate, 353
Vin de Blanquette AOC, 188
Vin de Corse AOC, 196
Vin de Corse Calvi AOC, 196
Vin de Corse Coteaux du Cap Corse AOC, 196
Vin de Corse Figari AOC, 196
Vin de Corse Porto Vecchio AOC, 196
Vin de Corse Sartène AOC, 196
vin de goutte, 21
Vin de Moselle VDQS, 155
Vin de Pays, 34
vin de presse, 21, 38-9
Vin de Savoie AOC, 183
Vin de Savoie Ayze Mousseux AOC, 183
Vin de Savoie Ayze Pétillant AOC, 183

Vin de Savoie Mousseux AOC, 183
Vin de Savoie Pétillant AOC, 183
Vin de Table, 34
Vin Délimité de Qualité Supérieure (VDQS), 34
Vin d'Estaing VDQS, 188
Vin du Bugey VDQS, 183
Vin du Bugey Cerdon Pétillant VDQS, 183
Vin du Bugey Mousseux VDQS, 183
Vin du Bugey Pétillant VDQS, 183
Vin Geloso Inc, 405
Vin Santo VT, 258, 259
Viña Cousino Macul, 411
Viña Errazuriz-Panquehue, 411
Viña Linderos, 411
Viña Manquehue, 411
Viña Ochagavia, 411
Viña San Pedro, 411
Viña Santa Carolina, 411
Viña Santa Rita, 411
Viña Tondonia, 275
Vina Vista, 373
Viñas SA, 290
Vineland Estates, 405
Vinerias del Castillo, 406
Vinet, André, 159
vineyards, growing grapes, 12-17
Vinho Verde, 293, 298, 299, 301-2
Vinhos Salton, 406
Viniccia Armando Peterlongo, 406
Vinicola Andiña, 406
Vinicola de Aguascalientes, 401
Vinicola del Vergel, 401
Vinicola Garibaldi, 406
Vinícola Navarra, 276
La Vinicole de Touraine, 159
vinifera vines *see vitis vinifera*
Vinifera Wine Cellars, 397
vinification, 18-23
Vino della Signora VT, 258
Vino Nobile di Montepulciano DOCG, 257
Vino Novello di Erbusco VT, 249
Vinos de Chile S.A. "Vinex", 411
Viños de la Corte, 406
Vinos Rodas, 412
Les Vins Corelli, 405
Vins de Lavilledieu VDQS, 188
Vins de liqueurs, 23
Vins de l'Orléanais VDQS, 172
Vins de Marcillac AOC, 188
vins de paille, 181
vins de pays, 193, 197-200
Vins d'Entraygues et du Fel VDQS, 188
Vins d'Estaing VDQS, 188
Vins du Thouarsais VDQS, 166
Vin Sec de Bordeaux AOC, 42
vins jaunes, 181
Les Vins la Salle (Brights), 405
Les Vins Touchais, 158
Vintage Tunina VT, 253
vintages, 18, 464-5; Champagne, 141; Port, 298
Viognier grape, 29, *29*
La Violette, Château, 98
Viré, Cave de, 112
Virgin Hills, 428
Virginia, 397
Visp, 173
Vistrenque, 200
Viti OA, 317

viticulture, 15
vitis labrusca, 356
vitis vinifera, 10, 11, *11,* 356, 392-3, 403, 406
Vitivinicola y Comercial Millahue, 411
Viura grape, 272
Vlottenburg Koop Wynkelder, 354
Vogelsgarten, Grosslage, 229
Vogtei Röttelm, Grosslage, 240
Vojvodina, 333
Volkach, 235
Volnay AOC, 126
Volnay Premier Cru AOC, 126
Volnay-Santenots AOC, 126
Von Loveren, 353
Vorarlberg, 324
Vosne-Romanée AOC, 120
Vosne-Romanée Premier Cru AOC, 120
Vougeot AOC, 120
Vougeot AOC, Clos de, 108, *116,* 118
Vougeot Premier Cru AOC, 120
Vouvray AOC, *156,* 167, 170
Vouvray Mousseux AOC, 170
Vouvray Pétillant AOC, 170
Vrai-Canon-Boyer, Château, 99
Vray Croix de Gay, Château, 98
Vredenburg, 351
Vredendal Koöperatiewe Wynkelder, 354
Vriesenhof, 353
Vulkanfelsen, Grosslage, 240

W

Waboomsrivier Koöp Wynkelder, 354
Wachau, 323
Wachenheim, 232
Wachenheim, Schloss, 211
Wagner Vineyards, 397
Waikato, 446
Wales, 310
Walker Bay, 348
Walker Valley Vineyards, 397
Walker Wines, 382
Walkershire Wines, 429
Walla Walla Valley AVA, 390
Wallhausen, 223
Wallis, 318
Walloporzheim, 215
Walporzheim-Ahrtal, Bereich, 215
Walsheim, 232
Wanneroo, 439
Wantirna Estate, 428
Warner Vineyards, 396
Warramate, 429
Warre & Co., 295, 300
Warren Hills AVA, 395
Warrenmang Vineyard, 429
Wartbühl, Grosslage, 237
Washington, 390, 391
Watervale, 432
Watervale Cellars, 436
Wawern, 221
Wehlen, 220
Weikersheim, 237
Weimer (Hermann J.) Vineyard, 397
Weinbach, Domaine, 153
Weinert, 412
Weingut Schwarzer Adler, 207

Weinhex, Grosslage, 220
Weinsberg, 237
Weinsteige, Grosslage, 237
Weisenheim, 231
Weisser Burgunder grape, 207
Weissherbst, 238
Weiviertel, 324
Welgemeend Estate, 354
Wellington, 446
Wellow, 315
Welmoed Koöp Wynkelder, 354
Welschriesling grape, 29, 323
Wendouree, 436
Wente Bros., 381
West Virginia, 397
West-Whitehill Winery, 397
Westbury Vineyard, 315
Western Australia, 415, 416, 437-40
Western Connecticut Highlands, 395
Weststeiermark, 324
De Wetshof Estate, 354
Whaler Vineyards, 369
Whatley, 315
Wheeler (William) Winery, 372
White Frontignan grape, 417
White Grenache grape, 417
White Hermitage grape, 417
White Riesling grape, 367
White Shiraz grape, 417
white wine: colour, 7; serving, 452; vinification, 22
Whitehall Lane Winery, 378
Whitmoor House, 315
Whitstone, 315
Wickenden, 315
Wickham Vineyards, 397
Wiederkehr Wine Cellars, 398
Wild Horse Valley AVA, 384
Willamette Valley AVA, 390
Williams & Humbert, 289
Willow Creek AVA, 388
Willow Grange, 315
Willowbank Estate Wines, 405
Wilson Vineyard, 436
Wiltingen, 221
Windesheim, 223
Windsor Vineyards, 397
Wine of Origin, South Africa, 346
winemaking, 18-23
Winkel, 226
Winzergenossenschaft Friedelsheim eG, 209
Winzergenossenschaft Mayschoss-Altenahr, 209
Winzergenossenschaft Thüngersheim eG, 210
Winzergenossenschaft Vier Jahreszeiten-Kloster Limburg, 210
Winzergenossenschaft Wachtenburg-Luginsland eG, 210
Winzergenossenschaft & Weinkellerei Rheingrafenberg eG, 210
Winzerkeller Südliche Bergstrasse/Kraichgau eG. 210
Winzersekt, 211
Wirra Wirra, 436
Wisconsin, 399
Wisdom & Warter, 290
Wolf Blass, 432
Wolfberger-Cave Vinicole Eguisheim, 153
Wolfsmagen, Grosslage, 233
Wollersheim Winery, 399
Wollundry Wines, 422
Wonnegau, Bereich, 229
Woodbury Vineyards, 397

Woodside Vineyards, 382
Woodstock Wine Cellars, 436
Wootton, 315
Worcester WO, 350
Wraxall, 315
Wunnenstein, Grosslage, 237
Württemberg, 207, 236-7
Württembergisch Bodensee, Bereich, 237
Württembergisch Unterland, Bereich, 237
Würzburg, 235
Würzburger, 234
Würzer grape, 29
Wybong Estate, 422
Wyndham Estate Wines, 422
Wynns, 435

X

Xanadu, Chateau, 440
Xarello grape, 29
Xynomavro grape, 32

Y

Yakima Valley AVA, 390
Yarra Burn Vineyards, 429
Yarra Valley, 423, 426
Yarra Yering, 428
Yarrinya Estate, 428
Yass Valley, 419
Yearlstone, 315
yeasts, 19, 139
Yecla DO, 292
Yellowglen Vineyards, 428
Yerba Buena Winery, 382
Yering, 423
Yeringberg, 429
Yon-Figeac, Château, 92
Yonne, 114, 200
York Mountain AVA, 384
York Mountain Winery, 384
Yquem, Château, 70, *70,* 71, 72, 79, 94
Yugoslavia, 332-3

Z

Zaca Mesa Winery, 384
Zagarolo DOC, 259
Zandvliet Estate, 354
ZD Wines, 376
Zell, 220, 232, 240
Zell, Bereich, 220
Zellerbach (Stephen) Vineyard, 373
Zeltingen, 220
Zema Estate, 436
Zentralkellerei Badischer Winzergenossenschaft eG, 210
Zentralkellerei Mosel-Saar-Ruwer eG, 210
Zentralkellerei Rheinischer Winzergenossenschaft, 210
Zevenwacht, 354
Zierfandler, 323
Zilavka grape, 332
Zimbabwe, 349
Zimmermann-Graef, 209
Zind Humbrecht, Domaine, 153
Zinfandel grape, 32, *32,* 366, 403
Zitsa AO, 339
Zonnebloem Wines, 351
Zurich, 318

Acknowledgments

Author's Acknowledgments

To name everyone to whom I am indebted in the wine trade would take up more room than the index, but I would like to say a general "thank you" to the many producers throughout the world who have extended their hospitality to me during the preparation of this book. I hope that the recommendation of some of their wines or the appearance of one of their labels may be a small recompense for the omission of their name from a list that would frankly be so long that nobody would read it. My special thanks go to those who have magnanimously brought to my attention the lesser-known but greatly talented winemakers in their midst and to those who have been instrumental in securing detailed information about some of the more obscure wine-making countries in which they happen to be more active than the inept government agenices.

In the sphere of research, there is no-one to whom I am more indebted than my great friend Michael Schmidt. It took me a solid two weeks and no less than 20,000 words merely to outline what I wanted on each and every map in the book, so it was no surprise to me that it took Michael almost a year to complete his studies. The fact that some maps, such as those of the Médoc and Graves, to name just two, are totally different in shape to those we are used to, does not astound me. It is obvious that many publications have reproduced other people's original mistakes, but the maps in this book have been researched back to source. They represent the largest collection of the most accurate wine maps in the world. No researcher, cartographer or printer is perfect, however, but if we do have mistakes, at least they are our own.

I must thank editors Vicky Davenport, Caroline Ollard, James Allen and Elizabeth Eyres, for keeping me on the straight and narrow. It is all too common for authors to defend any criticisms, yet to unquestioningly accept all forms of praise, however irrational. When criticism cannot be defended, an author is more than likely to blame poor editing, but whereas this can exist, the truth is that more books are saved than ruined by editors. In a book of this size and complexity, the disciplined mind of a good editor is essential.

Last, but not least, I have to thank the designer, Derek Coombes. The fact that the encyclopedia has such a tasteful appearance is primarily due to Derek, although Dinah Lone, the initial designer, also played a part.

Picture research by Lesley Davy

Production
Judy Sandeman and Jeanette Graham

Original photography pages 8/9 by Ian O'Leary
Illustrations by Sandra Fernandez (Glossary of grape varieties); all others by Kuo Kang Chen
All maps produced by Lovell Johns Ltd, except pages 137 and 140 by Thames Cartographic Services Ltd, and pages 11 and 218 by Kuo Kang Chen

Dorling Kindersley would like to thank: Hilary Bird; Deirdre Clark; Caves de la Madeleine; Elizabeth Eyres; Catherine Francou at Scope; Ben Hill, Steve Ramsay, Dave Windle and all at Lovell Johns; Stuart Jackman; Margaret Little; Peter Luff; Deirdre McGarry; Norman Miles, Peter Bates and all at Modern Text; Janet Price; Radius; Michael Schmidt; Jimmy Tsao and Josephine How at Colourscan, Singapore; Lucinda Whatley at Yapp Brothers.

Photographic credits

2 John Sims; 11 Sonia Halliday/F.H.C. Birch; 12 Cephas/Mick Rock; 13 Left, Zefa/W.H. Mueller; right, Patrick Eagar; 16 top left, Harry Baker; top right and bottom left, Scope/Michel Guillard; bottom right, Champagne Bureau; 17 top left, Champagne Bureau; top right, Scope/Jean-Daniel Sudres; bottom left, Scope/Michel Guillard; centre right, Denis Hughes-Gilbey; bottom right, Food and Wine from France; 18 Scope/Jacques Guillard; 19 top, Scope/Michel Guillard; bottom, Cephas/Mick Rock; 21 top, Janet Price; bottom, Scope/Michel Guillard; 22 left, Scope/Michel Guillard; right, Zefa/F. Damm; 23 Cephas/Mick Rock; 33 Scope/Jacques Guillard; 36 top, Scope/Michel Guillard; centre, Jerrican/Ivaldi; bottom, Scope/Michel Guillard; 44 Visionbank/Colin Maher; 45 Tom Stevenson; 51 Scope/Michel Guillard; 54 Scope/Michel Guillard; 55 top left and right, Scope/Michel Guillard; bottom, Visionbank/Colin Maher; 59 Scope/Michel Guillard; 60 left and right, Scope/Michel Guillard; 63 Michael Busselle; 64 top, centre and bottom left, Scope/Michel Guillard; bottom right, Janet Price; 69 top, Scope/Michel Guillard; bottom, Château Haut-Brion; 70, top, Scope/Michel Guillard; bottom left and bottom right, Tom Stevenson; 71 left, Scope/Michel Guillard; right, Tom Stevenson; 72 left, Visionbank/Colin Maher; right, Janet Price; 81 Visionbank/Colin Maher; 83 top left, Scope/Michel Guillard; top right, Visionbank/Colin Maher; bottom, Janet Price; 93 Anthony Blake; 94 top and bottom right, Scope/Michel Guillard; bottom left, Anthony Blake; 103 top, Janet Price; bottom, Patrick Eagar; 104 top, Patrick Eagar; bottom, Scope/Michel Guillard; 109 Scope/Jean-Luc Barde; 114 Scope/Jacques Guillard; 116 Janet Price; 121 top, Janet Price; bottom, Claude Bouchard (Bouchard Père et Fils); 128 Scope/Jean-Luc Barde; 130 Michael Busselle; 133 Scope/Jean-Luc Barde; 136 top, CIVC Epernay; bottom, Champagne Bureau; 137 Champagne Pommery; 138 from top to bottom, Laurent Perrier; Laurent Perrier; CIVC Epernay; Krug; bottom left, Champagne Deutz; bottom right, Champagne Bureau; 139 from top to bottom, Louis Roederer; Louis Roederer, Champagne Bureau; 140 top, Champagne Bureau; bottom, Visionbank/Colin Maher; 149 top, Scope/Jacques Guillard; bottom, Tom Stevenson; 150 left, Janet Price; right, Michael Busselle; 151 Scope/Jacques Guillard; 156 left, Picture Index/Guy Gravett; right, Patrick Eagar; 157 top left and bottom left, Patrick Eagar; bottom right, Landscape Only/Charlie Waite; 161 top, Scope/Jacques Guillard; bottom, Anthony Blake; 163 Food and Wine from France; 164 top, Anthony Blake; bottom left, Scope/Jacques Guillard; bottom right, Denis Hughes-Gilbey; 167 Scope/Jean-Daniel Sudres; 174 top, Janet Price; bottom, Yapp Brothers; 181 French Government Tourist Office; 185 top, Zefa/Dr Baer; middle and bottom, Scope/Jean-Luc Barde; 189 Scope/Jacques Sierpinski; 193 left, Janet Price; right Scope/Michel Guillard; 201 Bildagentur Mauritius/Vidler; 202 Zefa/F. Damm; 206 Bildagentur Mauritius/Rossenbach; 207 Bildagentur Mauritius/E. Gebhardt; 214, Zefa/Til; 215 Zefa/ W. Rötzel; 217 Zefa/K. Oster; 224 Bildagentur Mauritius/Rossenbach; 225 Anthony Blake; 227 Jon Wyand; 228 Bildagentur Mauritius/Koch; 230 Bildagentur Mauritius/Vidler; 238 Bildagentur Mauritius/Grimm; 239 Zefa/Eigen; 241 Janet Price; 242 Cephas/Mick Rock; 246 Jon Wyand; 251 Cephas/Mick Rock; 256 left and right, Landscape Only/Charlie Waite; 263 Cephas/Mick Rock; 267 Jon Wyand; 270 top, Cephas/Mick Rock; bottom left, Michael Busselle; bottom right, Anthony Blake/G. Buntrock; 273 Cephas/Mick Rock; 278 top and bottom Cephas/Mick Rock; 282 Michael Busselle; 293 Cephas/Mick Rock; 294 Anthony Blake; 295 Cephas/Mick Rock; 298 Bruce Coleman/Herbert Kranwetter; 303 top and bottom, Cephas/Mick Rock; 304 left and right, Cephas/Mick Rock; 305 left, Susan Griggs Agency/John Kegan; right, Stephanie Colasanti; 306 Stephanie Colasanti; 309 Susan Griggs Agency/Adam Woolfitt; 310 Janet Price; 316 Zefa/Justitz; 317 Bruce Coleman/Mark Boulton; 320 Susan Griggs Agency/Adam Woolfitt; 321 Zefa/Harlicek; 326 Bulgarian Wine Company; 328 John Lipitch Associates; 330 Zefa/Fotostudio; 331 Zefa/Fotostudio; 335 Tass Agency; 337 Zefa/Conrad Helbig; 338 Sonia Halliday/F.H.C. Birch; 342 Sonia Halliday; 343 Bruce Coleman/Gerald Cubitt; 344 Zefa/Haro Schumacher; 345 Bruce Coleman/Sandro Prato; 348 Bruce Coleman/Gerald Cubitt; 355 Click Chicago/Peter Fronk; 356 Click Chicago/Peter Fronk; 358 left, Click Chicago/John Lawlor; right, Jon Wyand; 361 top, Click Chicago/Chuck O'Rear; bottom, Visionbank/Michael Freeman; 368 top, Jon Wyand; bottom, Visionbank/Michael Freeman; 370 Jon Wyand; 374 Zefa/Armstrong; 379 Jon Wyand; 385 Jon Wyand; 390 Click Chicago/ Peter Fronk; 392 Ohio Wine Institute; 393 Click Chicago/Peter Fronk; 400 left and right, Pedro Domecq; 401 Pedro Domecq; 403 top, Image Bank/Gary Cralle; bottom, Tom Stevenson; 407 Image Bank/S. Barbosa; 409 top and bottom, Janet Price; 413 Janet Price; 415 Janet Price; 416 Janet Price; 417 Janet Price; 419 left, Rosemount Estate; right, Janet Price; 424 left, Janet Price; right, Pipers Brook Vineyard; 430 top and bottom, Janet Price; 431 Horizon/Milton Wordley; 437 Patrick Eagar; 438 Tony Stone; 441 Tony Stone/Fritz Prenzl; 443 Margaret Harvey; 444 Impact/Pamla Toler; 445 Impact/Pamla Toler; 448 Robert Harding/G.P. Corrigan; 450 Robert Harding; 451 Suntory Limited/Keiichi Kimura